WileyPLUS Learning Space

An easy way to help your students learn, collaborate, and grow.

Personalized Experience

Students create their own study guide while they interact with course content and work on learning activities.

Flexible Course Design

Educators can quickly organize learning activities, manage student collaboration, and customize their course—giving them full control over content as well as the amount of interactivity between students.

Clear Path to Action

With visual reports, it's easy for both students and educators to gauge problem areas and act on what's most important.

Instructor Benefits

- Assign activities and add your own materials
- Guide students through what's important in the interactive e-textbook by easily assigning specific content
- Set up and monitor collaborative learning groups
- Assess learner engagement
- Gain immediate insights to help inform teaching

Student Benefits

- Instantly know what you need to work on
- Create a personal study plan
- Assess progress along the way
- Participate in class discussions
- Remember what you have learned because you have made deeper connections to the content

We are dedicated to supporting you from idea to outcome.

WILEY

SECOND CANADIAN EDITION

PSYCHOLOGY AROUND US

RONALD COMER
Princeton University

NANCY OGDEN
Mount Royal University

MICHAEL BOYES
University of Calgary

ELIZABETH GOULD
Princeton University

WILEY

Production Credits
VP & Director of Market Solutions: Veronica Visentin
Senior Marketing Manager: Patty Maher
Editorial Manager: Karen Staudinger
Production and Media Specialist: Meaghan MacDonald
Developmental Editor: Gail Brown
Media Editor: Luisa Begani
Editorial Assistant: Maureen Lau
Cover and Interior Design: Joanna Vieira
Typesetting: Laser Words (Spi-Global)
Printing and Binding: Manufactured in the United States by RR Donnelley
Front cover photo, © Patrik Giardino/Corbis; back cover photo, © nico_blue/iStockphoto.com; abstract background, © marigold_88/iStockphoto.com; Before You Go On photos: ©iStockphoto.com/PeopleImages, © iStockphoto.com/ Ljupco, © iStockphoto.com/Yuri, © iStockphoto.com/RyanKing999.

Printed and bound in the United States of America
1 2 3 4 5 RRD 19 18 17 16 15

John Wiley & Sons Canada, Ltd.
90 Eglinton Ave. E., Suite 300
Toronto, Ontario, M4P 2Y3
Visit our website at: www.wiley.ca

TO OUR CHILDREN:

Jon and Jami

Greg and Emily

R.C.

Michael, Daniel, Danielle, David, Emily, and Kathryn

N.O.

Michael, Daniel, Danielle, David, Emily, and Kathryn

M.B.

Lindsey, Sean, and William

E.G.

About the Authors

RONALD COMER has taught in Princeton University's Department of Psychology for the past 35 years and has served as Director of Clinical Psychology Studies for most of that time. He has received the President's Award for Distinguished Teaching at the university. Comer also is the author of the textbooks *Abnormal Psychology*, now in its seventh edition, and *Fundamentals of Abnormal Psychology*, now in its sixth edition, and the coauthor of *Case Studies in Abnormal Psychology*. He is the producer of various educational videos, including The Introduction to Psychology Video Library Series. In addition, he has published journal articles in clinical psychology, personality, social psychology, and family medicine.

NANCY OGDEN is a professor at Mount Royal University in the Department of Psychology where she has taught for the past 23 years. She is also currently serving as a Co-Director for the Centre for Child Well-Being at Mount Royal University. She has previously published another Canadian introductory psychology textbook that went to three editions. Ogden has twice received the Teaching Excellence Award at Mount Royal University. She works and publishes in the areas of social and emotional development in children and adolescents and their families, homeless youth, physical literacy in early childhood, and in data management for nonprofit agencies serving children, youth, and families. She also does research in areas pertaining to the development of study strategy information in undergraduates.

MICHAEL BOYES has taught at the University of Calgary in the Department of Psychology for 25 years. He has previously published another Canadian introductory psychology textbook. Boyes received the University of Calgary Student Union Teaching Award. He works and publishes in the areas of cognitive and social development in children and adolescents, as well as in programs aimed at eliminating family violence. He assists with the development and telling the stories (evaluation) of programs by and for urban Aboriginal children, youth, and families. He has also served as an expert witness in cases related to matters of adolescent consent.

ELIZABETH GOULD has taught in Princeton University's Department of Psychology for the past 12 years. A leading researcher in the study of adult neurogenesis, she has published numerous journal articles on the production of new neurons in the adult mammalian brain. Gould has been honoured for her breakthrough work with a number of awards, including the 2006 NARSAD Distinguished Investigator Award and the 2009 Royal Society of the Arts Benjamin Franklin Medal. She serves on the editorial boards of *The Journal of Neuroscience*, *Neurobiology of Learning and Memory*, *Biological Psychology*, and *Cell Stem Cell*.

Brief Contents

Contents

To the Instructor

Psychology is all around us. If ever there was subject matter that permeates our everyday lives, it is psychology. Behaviour occurs everywhere, and mental processes affect all that we do; therefore the study of individual behaviour and mental processes can help shed light on a wide range of events and issues.

Psychology Around Us, **Second Canadian Edition**, helps open students' minds to the notion that psychology is indeed around them every day and that its principles are immediately applicable to a whole host of life's questions. It also features classroom-proven pedagogy to keep students engaged and help them master the material.

Among the four authors of this text, we have taught a wide variety of psychology courses for over 100 years combined. Throughout those years, we have always been struck by how differently students react to various areas within psychology. For example, students are fascinated by failures in thought (schizophrenia), communication (autism), or coping (posttraumatic stress disorder), yet almost nonchalant about the fact that people mostly attend, think, communicate, and cope quite well.

We are committed to demonstrating for students the relevance and interconnectedness of all areas of psychology. The textbook aims to encourage students to examine not only what they know about human behaviour but how they know it, and seeks to open students up to an appreciation of how psychology pervades the world around them.

About the Text

As instructors and researchers, we (the authors) are passionate about the study of psychology and genuinely fascinated by behaviour, thought, and emotion and the way they interact. When we teach a course, we consider ourselves successful if we have engaged our students in the rigorous study of psychology while simultaneously transferring our passion for the subject. These same criteria of success should be applied to a textbook in psychology: It should broaden the reader's knowledge about the field and, at the same time, move, excite, and motivate the student. To achieve this goal, our textbook includes a range of features—some traditional, others innovative.

Our textbook is unique in that while each topic is still covered in its own separate part, the integrated nature of psychology permeates every page. How can students get a full appreciation of memory without discussing the vital role of the hippocampus, or how memory develops, or Alzheimer's disease? *Psychology Around Us*, **Second Canadian Edition** is the first book available that is truly integrated—that actually brings all of these elements together into one, complete discussion of any given topic of psychology.

This integration is accomplished by offering a thorough presentation of the nature, explanations, applications, and research (including key Canadian research) of each topic, but also includes sections on neuroscience, development, dysfunctions, and individual differences that illustrate how each of these key areas is tied to other areas of psychology. These sections present psychology as a united and integrated discipline, therefore allowing students to see "the big picture."

New to this Edition

Writing a textbook is an iterative process. Our goal for the second Canadian edition of *Psychology Around Us* was to continue to make it as engaging as possible for students and as supportive as possible for instructors. To this end we used an extensive review process, involving many instructors as an editorial peer advisory panel in preparing this edition. We asked reviewers to provide us with constructive input in terms of the strong science base of the book, their own concerns regarding key topics for inclusion, and what their students found engaging about the material—what they wanted to know, what questions they asked, and what seemed to most pique their interest. We have incorporated many of the suggestions made by reviewers.

Currency

To incorporate developments across a wide range of fields, numerous new references have been added to the text, with the majority of these references reflecting research completed in the past three years. Many of the additional references emphasize Canadian research. As well, a number of changes were made throughout the text to reflect the changes in the assessment, diagnosis, and treatment of disorders due to revisions made in the 5th edition of the *Diagnostic and Statistical Manual of Mental Disorders* (*DSM-5*) (American Psychiatric Association, 2013).

Content Changes

Information about biology and psychopathology continues to be integrated throughout the text but in a more understated and clear manner, with the bulk of information moved to Parts 3 Neuroscience, 15 Psychological Disorders, and 16 Treatment of Psychological Disorders. Parts 3 and 4 from the first edition were switched, so that Part 3 is now Neuroscience and Part 4 is now Human Development. As well, individual parts on motivation and emotion have been combined to form Part 11 Motivation and Emotion. In merging this material we have streamlined the content covered, yet maintained the vibrancy and focus of the original content.

Wholesale changes were made to update content in a number of parts, including:

- Part 3 Neuroscience: The information was completely reorganized, updated, and modified, with a particular focus on areas of the brain, to increase readability and understanding.

- Part 4 Human Development: Information regarding age categories and cutoffs was reorganized and modified to avoid repetition and to increase readability and understanding.

- Part 13 Social Psychology: Information on the emerging field of positive psychology was added.

- Part 15 Psychological Disorders: Modifications as they related to the *DSM-5* were made throughout.

- Part 16 Treatment of Psychological Disorders: Modifications as they related to the *DSM-5* were made throughout and a significantly expanded modification was made to the section on drug therapy.

Canadian Content

One aim of this edition was to more obviously highlight Canadian researchers in meaningful ways. Examples of trailblazing Canadian work highlighted include fMRI research on creativity from Melissa Ellamil and her colleagues at the University of British Columbia (Part 3); the work of Lili-Naz Hazrati and her colleagues at the University of Toronto on chronic traumatic encephalopathy (Part 3); Kevin Englehart and colleagues at the University of New Brunswick's work on neural machine interface for control of artificial limbs (Part 3); the work of E. David Klonsky and his colleagues at the University of British Columbia on the mechanisms of self-harm (Part 7); research on memory and aging by Fergus Craik and colleagues at the Rotman Research Institute in Toronto (Part 8), research on prejudice by Bertram Gawronski and his colleagues at Western University and by Kerry Kawakami and others at York University (Part 13); research by Jitender Sareen and colleagues at the University of Manitoba on socio-economic class and psychopathology (Part 15); and the work of Paul Whitehead and colleagues at Western University on the effects of deinstitutionalization (Part 16).

Special Pedagogical Tools

Tying It Together

To achieve our goal of showing students how psychology is indeed all around us, and to bring our textbook in line with the course curricula of most professors, we have structured each of the parts in our textbook in a very particular way—with a cross-sectional presentation. Using a **Tying It Together** approach, every part on a substantive area of psychology includes icons highlighting the integration of the four subfields of psychology—*development, brain function, individual differences,* and *dysfunctions.* These icons, entitled **How We Develop, What Happens in the Brain?, How We Differ,** and **Facing Adversity**, enable students to readily integrate the material into what they already know.

Your Brain and Behaviour

Many introductory psychology students consider the study of neuroscience to be difficult and at times irrelevant to the study of human behaviour. In recent years, however, neuroscience has been tied to virtually every subfield of psychology. Remarkable brain imaging studies, in conjunction with animal studies, have helped us to identify the neural mechanisms of everyday experience. Accordingly, *Psychology Around Us*, **Second Canadian Edition**, incorporates neuroscience information into coverage where it has traditionally been absent, such as social psychology and consciousness.

In addition, the text offers a key teaching feature that helps bring neuroscience directly into the lives of readers: Exciting and accessible two-page layouts appear throughout the book illustrating the link between the brain and behaviour when people are performing such common activities as eating pizza, learning to play a video game, acquiring a second language, giving a speech in public, or running a marathon. These layouts, which include neuroimages and findings from both human studies and relevant animal experiments, draw students into the brain and provide them with up-to-date information about the neural mechanisms at work during their everyday experiences. And to make sure they have a firm understanding of the concepts, each feature includes questions that allow students to test their knowledge (answers are available on the book companion site or *WileyPLUS Learning Space*). Regardless of their background in neuroscience, students come away intrigued by material that has traditionally been considered difficult.

Additional Features

Part Opener Outline

Every part begins with an outline of the modules covered, with the accompanying learning objective. Each part also starts with a description about a person or situation to introduce concepts and excite students about the upcoming content. This introductory material helps to give readers a big picture overview of the modules and helps to prepare them for the material they will need to learn.

Guided Learning

A **Learning Objective** for each module identifies the most important material for students to understand while reading that section. These learning objectives also serve as the driving principle in *WileyPLUS Learning Space*.

Following each section is a **Before You Go On** feature with questions that help students check their mastery of the important items covered. Answers to the Before You Go On questions are available online, through *WileyPLUS Learning Space* or the textbook's companion website. **What Do You Know?** questions prompt students to stop and review the key concepts just presented. **What Do You Think?** questions encourage students to think critically on key questions in the modules.

Special Topics on Psychology Around Us

The text highlights interesting news stories, current controversies in psychology, and relevant research findings that demonstrate psychology around us. The number of these features has been reduced from the previous edition and they have been streamlined to ensure they are topical, relevant, and engaging.

- The **Psychology Around Us** boxes highlight how psychology affects us in our everyday lives, in every way, with examples from Canada and around the world.
- The **Practically Speaking** box emphasizes the practical application of everyday psychology.

Thorough Coverage

Psychology Around Us, **Second Canadian Edition,** contains 16 parts that cover all the topics of psychology in depth. Instead of combining material on stress and emotion, or psychological disorders and their treatment, each topic is given full coverage in its own, separate part. This gives you ultimate flexibility in determining how much time you want your students to devote to each topic. If you want to cover neuroscience briefly, then simply assign the relevant modules from that part; but if you want to cover neuroscience in depth, you have material at your disposal that presents detailed and integrated coverage of the topic.

Helpful Study Tools

- **Key Terms** are listed at the end of each module with page references.
- **Marginal Definitions** define the key terms discussed in the text.
- **Marginal Notes** present interesting facts and quotes throughout the text.

Module Summary

The end-of-module summary reviews the main concepts presented with reference to the specific module Learning Objective. New to this edition, end-of-module Self-Study Questions have been added, with answers provided, to help students do a quick check of key concepts covered.

Resources

Psychology Around Us, **Second Canadian Edition,** is accompanied by a host of instructor and student resources and ancillaries designed to facilitate a mastery of psychology.

Resources can be found within the ***Psychology Around Us***, Second Canadian Edition, *WileyPLUS Learning Space* course and on the text's companion website, www.wiley.com/go/comercanada.

WileyPLUS Learning Space

The factors that contribute to success—both in university and college, and in life—aren't composed of intellectual capabilities alone. In fact, there are other traits, strategies, and even daily habits that contribute to the overall picture of success. Studies show that people who can delay instant gratification, work through tasks even if they are not immediately rewarding, and follow through with a plan have the skills that are not only valuable in the classroom, but also in the workplace and their personal lives. A place where students can define their strengths and nurture these skills, *WileyPLUS Learning Space* transforms course content into an online learning community. *WileyPLUS Learning Space* invites students to experience learning activities, work through self-assessment, ask questions, and share insights. As they interact with the course content, peers, and their instructor, *WileyPLUS Learning Space* creates a personalized study guide for each student.

WileyPLUS Learning Space

As research shows, when students collaborate with each other, they make deeper connections to the content. When students work together, they also feel part of a community so that they can grow in areas beyond topics in the course. With *WileyPLUS Learning Space*, students are invested in their learning experience and can use their time efficiently as they develop skills like critical thinking and teamwork.

Through a flexible course design, you can quickly organize learning activities, manage student collaboration, and customize your course—having full control over content as well as the amount of interactivity between students.

WileyPLUS Learning Space lets you:

- Assign activities and add your own materials
- Guide your students through what's important in the interactive e-textbook by easily assigning specific content
- Set up and monitor group learning
- Assess student engagement
- Gain immediate insights to help inform teaching

Defining a clear path to action, the visual reports in *WileyPLUS Learning Space* help both you and your students gauge problem areas and act on what's most important.

With the visual reports, you can:

- See exactly where your students are struggling for early intervention
- Help students see exactly what they don't know to better prepare for exams
- Give students insight into their strengths and weaknesses so that they can succeed in your course

Videos

The *Psychology Around Us* series of psychology and concept (or "lecture-launcher") videos help bring lectures to life and, most important, engage students. They help demonstrate that psychology is all around us and that thought and behaviour, from the everyday to the abnormal, is truly fascinating. Averaging about five minutes in length, this collection of videos covers a range of relevant topics. Each video is a high-quality excerpt from various agencies or independent video libraries chosen from a televised news report, documentary, lab study, or the like, and illustrates a particular lecture point, bringing the topic to life in exciting ways.

The large selection of clips in this package focus on topics ranging from the split-brain phenomenon to conformity and obedience, emotions of fear or disgust, sensations of taste and smell, infant facial recognition, gender orientation, and brain development.

The video program is readily accessible and easily integrated into any introductory psychology course through the *Psychology Around Us*, **Second Canadian Edition**, *WileyPLUS Learning Space* course. If instructors choose not to use any or all of the videos in the classroom they have the option of assigning videos to students for viewing outside of class. Instructors can also use the prepared quizzes that test understanding of the video's content and relevance.

Psychology Around Us Video Lab Activities

Psychology Around Us, **Second Canadian Edition**, offers a series of active learning video projects that students can conduct on their own. Traditionally, such exercises have been presented in book form, with *written* exercises guiding students through paper-and-pencil tasks. Today, students can *interact* with computerized exercises, become more engaged by video and animated material, and receive immediate feedback about the effects and accuracy of their choices.

These lab activities use extensive video material to drive student learning. The combination of video footage and digital interactive technology brings the lab exercises to life for students, actively engaging the students and helping them to better process the lesson at hand. The kinds of video material included in the *Video Lab Activities* range from laboratory footage about the brain to videos of everyday events to psychology documentary excerpts.

For example, one video lab exercise on *Memory Manufacturing and Eyewitness Testimony* unfolds as a cluster of video-digital lab exercises on memory. They guide the student to also explore (1) pre-event and post-event memory interference, (2) childhood memory limits, (3) snapshot memories, and (4) the creation of false memories.

As with the videos, the Video Labs are accessible through the **Psychology Around Us**, **Second Canadian Edition**, *WileyPLUS Learning Space* course. Should instructors so choose, they have the option of assigning the Video Labs to students for completion outside of class; the student's work is then viewable by the instructor in the Gradebook section.

Instructor's Manual

Prepared by Evelyn Field, *Mount Royal University*
This Instructor's Manual is designed to help instructors maximize student learning and encourage critical thinking. It presents teaching suggestions using the book's objectives as well as including ideas for lecture classroom discussions, demonstrations, and videos. This manual will also share activity-based applications to everyday life.

PowerPoint Presentations

Prepared by Evelyn Field, *Mount Royal University*
PowerPoint Presentations feature a combination of key concepts, figures and tables, and problems and examples from the textbook. The instructor's version also includes notes for additional discussion points or activities you can use during your lecture.

In addition, each PowerPoint contains links to videos and animation tutorials available for that content. Using these presentations in your class means that the rich array of videos discussed above are simply a mouse-click away.

Test Bank

Prepared by Cheryl Techentin, *Mount Royal University*
The Test Bank contains over 200 questions per part with a variety of question types—multiple choice, true/false, short answer, and essay. The Test Bank is available in a Word® document format, as well as a Computerized Test Bank, which allows you to upload the test bank into your learning management system. The questions are available to instructors to create and print multiple versions of the same test by scrambling the order of all questions found in the Word version of the test bank. This allows users to customize exams by altering or adding new problems.

Practice Quizzes

Prepared by Wendy Tarrel, *Nova Scotia Community College*

This resource offers 20 questions per part that students can use to test their knowledge of the content.

Clicker Questions

Prepared by Wendy Tarrel, *Nova Scotia Community College*

This resource offers 10 to 15 questions per part that can be used with a variety of personal response (or "clicker") systems.

Wiley Psychology Weekly Updates Site

This site (**http://wileypsychologyupdates.ca**) features articles and videos to help keep learners up to date on the field of psychology and illustrates the real-world significance of psychology in everyday life. Discussion questions are provided to help guide an understanding of the article or video and to encourage class participation.

Online Study Tools

Psychology Around Us, **Second Canadian Edition**, provides students with a website containing resources to help them enhance their understanding of the concepts, such as answers to Before You Go On questions and web resources. The website can be accessed at **www.wiley.com/go/comercanada**.

Acknowledgements

The writing of this text has been a group effort involving the input and support of many individuals. We owe an enormous debt of gratitude to the people at Wiley for their encouragement, support, and assistance in guiding and developing the production of this text. We thank those whom we worked with most closely, in particular VP & Director of Market Solutions, Veronica Visentin and Gail Brown, Developmental Editor, who was clear, thoughtful and, when necessary, supportive about timelines. Gail's insights and suggestions have made this text infinitely stronger.

We are extremely thankful to the entire editorial, production, and sales and marketing teams, for their expertise and support of this book, including: Patty Maher, Senior Marketing Manager; Karen Staudinger, Editorial Manager; Kyle Fisher, Director of Sales; Luisa Begani, Media Editor; Sara Tinteri, Custom Project Editor; Meaghan MacDonald, Production and Media Specialist; Maureen Lau, Editorial Assistant; Joanna Vieira, Multimedia Designer; and Deanna Durnford, Supplements Coordinator. We are truly grateful for the efforts and expertise of Janice Dyer, copyeditor and Laurel Hyatt, proofreader, as well as photo and permissions researchers Julie Pratt and Mary Rose MacLachlan, and indexer Belle Wong.

We thank George Alder for his past contributions to Part 2 and for the single-handed creation of Appendix B, which introduces students to statistics and their importance in psychology research. George explains theories and concepts about research and statistics in ways that are uniquely comprehensible to students, and we know that the book is stronger because of this. As well, Evelyn Field developed and wrote the section on Evolutionary Psychology in Part 3, and we thank her for sharing her expertise and for her cogent writing. Like George, Evelyn is skilled at drawing students into material that is typically viewed as "dry" or "uninteresting," and we are confident that her work will engage students, thereby aiding their understanding. We also thank Genevieve Thurlow for her content expertise on neuroscience in Part 3. Gen reviewed the extensive revisions to Part 3, and her careful and thorough review and editing has allowed for a detailed, yet engaging and user-friendly coverage.

We thank also research assistants Alison Flett and Erika Gomez for their contributions to the text. Alison searched for and acquired hundreds of citation sources and worked tirelessly on the manuscript. Erika's assistance in finding key references, photo options, and Canadian data were essential contributions to the work. We would also like to acknowledge the past work of Daniel Cryderman who created answers for the Before You Go On questions and to Keegan Patterson who made insightful contributions to some of the content.

On a personal note, we thank our families, friends, and colleagues for their encouragement and support.

Finally, a very special thank you goes out to the faculty members who have contributed to the development of this text (both the previous and current editions), its digital resources, and its powerful supplemental program. We would particularly like to thank Evelyn Field, Wendy Tarrel, and Cheryl Techentin for their extraordinary and creative work. To the reviewers and editorial advisory board members who gave their time and constructive criticism (both to the development of the previous edition and this current edition), we offer our heartfelt thanks. We are deeply indebted to the following individuals and trust they will recognize their significant contributions throughout the text.

To the Student

How to Use This Book

This book includes features that are intended to promote your reading comprehension, reflection, problem-solving skills, and critical-thinking skills. These skills are key to success in the course and in your life beyond. In addition, interspersed with the text material at just the right points on each page are elements such as relevant and exciting boxes, current controversies in psychology, relevant research, and perfectly selected photos, all from Canada and around the world.

Let's walk through the pedagogical features that will help you learn the material in this book.

Part Opener

Every part begins with an outline of the modules covered, with the accompanying learning objective. This helps to give readers a big picture overview and helps to prepare them for the material they will need to learn.

Guided Learning

Learning Objectives summarize what you should be able to do once you have studied each module. You can use the learning goals in following way. First, study them before reading to get an overall picture of how the concepts in the part are related to each other and what you will be learning. Then, after reading, use the learning objectives to review what you have learned, either individually or in peer study groups. You can improve learning and retention without significantly increasing study time.

Helpful Study Tools

Following each section is a **Before You Go On** feature that helps you check your mastery of the important items covered. Answers to the Before You Go On questions are available online, through *WileyPLUS Learning Space* or the textbook's companion website. **What Do You Know?** questions ask you to stop and review the key concepts just presented. **What Do You Think?** questions encourage you to think critically about key questions in the module.

PART 7

LEARNING

PART OUTLINE

Module 35: What Is Learning?
LEARNING OBJECTIVE 35 Define learning and distinguish between associative and non-associative learning.

Module 36: Classical Conditioning
LEARNING OBJECTIVE 36 Describe the basic processes of classical conditioning and explain how classical conditioning is relevant to learning.

Module 37: Operant Conditioning
LEARNING OBJECTIVE 37 Describe the basic processes of operant conditioning and explain how shaping can be used to teach new behaviours.

Module 38: Observational Learning
LEARNING OBJECTIVE 38 Define observational learning and summarize concerns about observational learning from the media.

Module 39: Learning and Cognition
LEARNING OBJECTIVE 39 Define spatial navigation learning, implicit and latent learning, and insight learning.

Module 40: Factors that Facilitate Learning
LEARNING OBJECTIVE 40 Define massed and spaced practice and tell what conditions are best for learning semantic material, such as facts in your classes.

Module 41: Prenatal and Postnatal Learning
LEARNING OBJECTIVE 41 Summarize the types of learning that occur before we are born and during early postnatal life.

Module 42: Specific Learning Disorder
LEARNING OBJECTIVE 42 Define specific learning disorder and describe three major types of learning disorders.

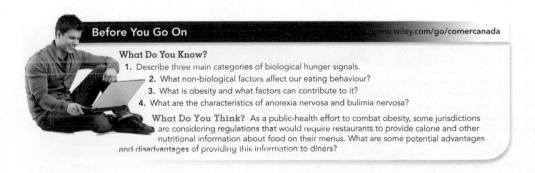

Before You Go On

www.wiley.com/go/comercanada

What Do You Know?
1. Describe three main categories of biological hunger signals.
2. What non-biological factors affect our eating behaviour?
3. What is obesity and what factors can contribute to it?
4. What are the characteristics of anorexia nervosa and bulimia nervosa?

What Do You Think? As a public-health effort to combat obesity, some jurisdictions are considering regulations that would require restaurants to provide calorie and other nutritional information about food on their menus. What are some potential advantages and disadvantages of providing this information to diners?

Margin Notes present interesting facts and quotes throughout the text.

while others would be skeptical (Duesbury, 2011). Dream content varies widely as can be seen in **Table 31-1**, which shows the percentage of people who recall dreaming about particular events or experiences. It is easy to see why we might assume there is life-relevant meaning in the content of our dreams. In this section we will examine ways in which different theorists and researchers have come to understand dreams (Cartwright, 2010; Moorcroft, 2003).

Research suggests that actions in dreams run in real time—that is, it takes you as long to accomplish something in the dream as it would if you were performing the action while you were awake.

31.5.1 Information-Processing Theory

Information-processing theory offers a cognitive view of dreaming. According to this view, dreams are the mind's attempt to sort out and organize the day's experiences and to fix them in memory. Consistent with this perspective, studies have revealed that interrupting REM sleep—and so interrupting dreams—impedes a person's ability to remember material learned just before going to sleep (Empson, 2002). Also, in support of this view, researchers have found that periods of REM sleep (during which we dream) tend to

information-processing theory hypothesis that dreams are the mind's attempt to sort out and organize the day's experiences and to fix them in memory.

Key Terms are listed at the end of each module with page references.

Margin Definitions define the key terms discussed in the text.

Each part includes feature box discussions, entitled **Psychology Around Us** and **Practically Speaking**, that demonstrate the real-world relevance of psychology to students' lives.

Psychology Around Us Goalie Psychology

The Yerkes-Dodson law has obvious applications to sports. Athletes who fail to get sufficiently "psyched up" or aroused may never even get into the game. On the other hand, getting too "revved up" or over-aroused might lead to "choking." Ryan Gelinas and Krista Munroe-Chandler at the University of Windsor have examined how this and other psychological issues in motivation can impact the performance of hockey goaltenders (Gelinas & Munroe-Chandler, 2006; Hallman & Munroe-Chandler, 2009). They point out that each goalie (and each athlete in general) has an optimal level of arousal at which

they perform their best. Some goalies need to get "psyched up" or excited to reach that optimal level, while others need to calm down so as not to become over-aroused. High levels of arousal, especially when associated with anxiety, lead to muscle tension that can slow a goalie down. It can also narrow the goalie's visual attentional field, making it less likely that the individual will take in all the information needed to properly position him or herself in the net. The aim for goaltenders is to keep them in the "zone" of optimal arousal so that they can consistently perform at their best throughout the game.

Practically Speaking Getting a Good Start Sometimes Means Getting a Head Start

The school dropout rate for Canadian Aboriginal and Métis youth is three times that of the general population (25 percent versus 8 percent) (Bushnick, 2003; Gingras, 2002). In an effort to address this issue, the government of Canada has provided funds for the development of Aboriginal Head Start (AHS) preschool programs in urban and northern communities across Canada. These programs provide a half-day preschool experience for 3- to 5-year-old Aboriginal and Métis children. Parents are encouraged to participate as well, to become optimal supporters of and advocates for their children's academic and social development. In addition, the program provides support for development of Aboriginal

culture and language, education, and school readiness programming, along with health promotion, nutrition, and social support (Mashford-Pringle, 2012; Public Health Agency of Canada (PHAC), 2011).

Early evaluation data gathered at Alberta Aboriginal Head Start sites (dela Cruz, 2010) showed that AHS participants perform at or above the averages for children their age in the general Canadian population as they enter the school system. This indicates that the AHS program is meeting its immediate goals. Next researchers need to follow these children through school to see if the AHS program also helps to reduce Canadian Aboriginal and Métis youth school dropout rates.

Seeing the "Big Picture" in Psychology

Tying It Together

Psychology is an integrated discipline. Everything is connected to everything else—your ability to react with fear or excitement is tied to neuroscience and your past development, for example. Every part on a substantive area of psychology in this text not only offers a thorough presentation of the nature, explanations, and applications of that area, but also includes sections on the development, brain function, individual differences, and dysfunctions that occur in that realm of mental life. Your success in this course will depend on how well you can integrate this information meaningfully. The more often you review your prior knowledge and connect it with new knowledge, the more automatic and refined learned knowledge and skills become.

26.1 Tactile Senses and the Brain

Our brains use a variety of related processes to help us perceive general information about a range of non-painful touch sensations, including pressure, temperature, and general touch. Pain perception is also an important function.

WHAT HAPPENS *in the* **BRAIN?**

26.1.1 The Touching Brain

When we touch something, or something touches us, our free nerve endings send tactile information into the spinal cord. The signals travel up the spinal cord to the brain, as shown in **Figure 26-2**. In the brain, touch information is first received in the thalamus, and then routed from there to the somatosensory cortex (located in the parietal lobe). Information about pressure and vibration is generally transmitted to the brain in a similar way, after being converted to neural impulses by the specialized receptors described above.

Our brain processes tactile information *contralaterally*, or on the opposite side of the brain from the side of the body where the touch occurred. So, if you touch something with your left hand, the information is processed by the somatosensory cortex on the right side of your brain.

As we discussed in Part 3, the somatosensory cortex does not have an equal representation of all parts of the body (Kakigi et al., 2000). For example, tactile inputs from the hands take up proportionately more space in the somatosensory cortex than those from the back. This seems reasonable, given the fact that our hands are specialized for object manipulation, and we need to process information from them in great detail. Information about pressure and vibration is generally transmitted to the brain in a similar way

26.3 Tactile Senses: Individual Differences

HOW WE DIFFER

Humans differ greatly in their ability to detect physical stimuli on the skin. In addition, they differ in the degree to which they find certain tactile stimulation pleasurable or aversive. For example, some people enjoy an intense back massage, while others do not. Of all the somatosensory experiences, the one that has received the most research attention is that of pain. Pain management for surgical procedures and other medical conditions is a critical part of patient care. There are dramatic differences in both the threshold to detect pain and the degree to which pain causes emotional suffering.

Although learning plays some role, people also differ in the actual sensation and perception of pain as a result of physical differences in their sensory systems. Studies have shown, for example, that women have a lower threshold for detecting pain than do men. They report greater pain intensity than men in response to the same stimulus (Garcia et al., 2007). One interpretation of this sex difference is that women are just less able to cope psychologically with painful stimuli since they haven't been "toughened up." In fact, research suggests that women may have about twice as many pain receptors in their facial skin than men (Minerd, 2005). This suggests a physical cause for at least some of the differences in pain sensitivity.

Neuroimaging studies show that people's brains react differently depending on their sensitivity to pain (Dubé et al., 2009).

75.1 Attitudes

HOW WE DEVELOP

Early in life, parents play a major role in shaping children's beliefs and opinions about things and people (Simpkins et al., 2012; Day et al., 2006). As we observed in Part 4, children are socialized when they acquire beliefs and behaviours considered desirable or appropriate by the family to which they belong. You are reading this textbook right now because you have been socialized in a number of ways—perhaps to believe in the value of a post-secondary education or the need for hard work to achieve your goals. This socialization may have occurred by direct transmission (your parents lecturing you about these values) or in subtler ways (Egan et al., 2007). Perhaps your mother or father praised you for your grades or punished you for not doing your homework. Over time, you might generalize these individual experiences into an overall attitude about the value of what you are doing.

As children mature, their peers, their teachers, and the media also begin to significantly influence their attitudes (Prislin & Crano, 2012; Prislin & Wood, 2005). Recall that in vicarious learning, children observe their classmates and take note of the rewards and punishments those students experience based on their behaviour. If a child sees a

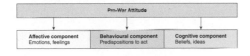

Pro-War Attitude		
Affective component Emotions, feelings	**Behavioural component** Predispositions to act	**Cognitive component** Beliefs, ideas

61.5 Hunger and Eating Disorders

FACING ADVERSITY

We have seen that our motivation to eat is very complex, affected not only by intricate biological processes, but also by psychological, social, and cultural influences. As with any complex system, we face the potential for problems in our eating behaviour. Two of the most common problems include obesity, often related to too much eating, and eating disorders, which often involve eating too little.

obesity overweight characterized as a body mass index of over 30.

body mass index (BMI) weight-to-height ratio.

61.5.1 Obesity

Obesity, a condition of extreme overweight, is determined on the basis of a weight-to-height ratio, called the **body mass index (BMI)**. Adults with a BMI of 30 or higher are considered obese, and those with BMIs between 25 and 30 are categorized as *overweight* (Health Canada, 2003). Obesity is a major health problem in North America. Twenty-five percent of the adult Canadian population is obese (Navaneelan & Janz, 2014). Being overweight or obese is associated with a variety of health problems, most notably diabetes and heart disease (Poirier et al., 2006; Huang, 2005). In addition to the physical risks they face, obese people are also more likely than those of normal weight to suffer from mood disorders, such as depression and anxiety (Friedlander et al., 2003).

Obese people are also often the victims of discrimination. A study found that people describe obese individuals as less attractive than thinner people, and ascribe a number of other unfavourable characteristics to people who are obese (Puhl & Heuer, 2010). Although overweight people are often considered as "friendly" and "happy," they are also judged more often as "lazy," "stupid," and "incompetent" than are people of normal weight (Puhl et al., 2008; Friedman et al., 2005). Obese individuals are more often turned down for jobs (NAAFA, 2009). This discrimination can even affect normal-weight individuals associated with obese people. One study looked at the hiring rate of normal-weight job applicants who happened to be sitting next to an obese person just before their interview

Your Brain and Behaviour

It's our hope that you will come to see the fascination of psychology and develop a passion for this field of study. One example of how we demonstrate this to you is a regular feature throughout the textbook—a two-page spread called Tying It Together: Your Brain and Behaviour. Centring on a common everyday activity, these lively spreads clarify the remarkable brain events that help give life to the activity and serve as awe-inspiring reminders that psychology is everywhere.

Tying It Together: **Your Brain and Behaviour**

Eating Pizza

Is this the best pizza you have ever had or does it fall short? When you dig into a slice of pizza, several neural circuits are activated to give you the overall experience. The appearance of your food can play an important role in its enjoyment. Photoreceptors in the eye transmit this information to the brain via the optic nerve, which passes through the brainstem, followed by the thalamus, and finally the visual cortex. Taste receptor cells, as well as sensory cells that respond to touch and temperature, are activated on your tongue. These nerves carry impulses into the brain where they pass through the brainstem, thalamus, and sensory cortex (gustatory cortex and somatosensory cortex). Taste is combined with smell information to produce flavour. Olfactory receptor neurons transduce pizza odorants and send this information on to the olfactory bulb and then to the olfactory cortex (smell is the only sensory modality that bypasses the thalamus on its way to the cortex).

Information about taste, smell, texture, temperature, and appearance is integrated in various association regions of the neocortex. These circuits, together with those that store memories related to your previous pizza experiences, work to produce your perception of this particular slice.

Questions

1 Explain how multiple senses (vision, smell, taste, touch) are involved in our experience of eating.

2 Explain how the taste of food may be enhanced if we close our eyes.

3 Which areas of the brain are responsible for integrating information about various components of eating (e.g., taste, smell, texture)?

Stockbroker/Age Fotostock

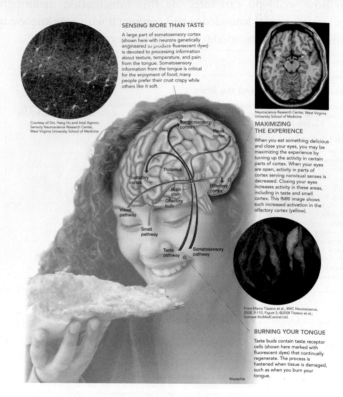

SENSING MORE THAN TASTE
A large part of somatosensory cortex (shown here with neurons genetically engineered to produce fluorescent dyes) is devoted to processing information about texture, temperature, and pain from the tongue. Somatosensory information from the tongue is critical for the enjoyment of food; many people prefer their crust crispy while others like it soft.

Courtesy of Drs. Hang Hu and Ariel Agmon, Sensory Neuroscience Research Center, West Virginia University School of Medicine

Neuroscience Research Center, West Virginia University School of Medicine

MAXIMIZING THE EXPERIENCE
When you eat something delicious and close your eyes, you may be maximizing the experience by turning up the activity in certain parts of cortex. When your eyes are open, activity in parts of cortex serving nonvisual senses is decreased. Closing your eyes increases activity in these areas, including in taste and smell cortex. This fMRI image shows such increased activation in the olfactory cortex (yellow).

From Marco Tizzano et al., BMC Neuroscience, 2008, 9:110, Figure 5; ©2008 Tizzano et al.; licensee BioMedCentral Ltd.

BURNING YOUR TONGUE
Taste buds contain taste receptor cells (shown here marked with fluorescent dyes) that continually regenerate. The process is hastened when tissue is damaged, such as when you burn your tongue.

Masterfile

(brain diagram labels: Somatosensory cortex, Visual cortex, Thalamus, Olfactory cortex, Brain stem, Olfactory bulb, Gustatory cortex, Visual pathway, Smell pathway, Taste pathway, Somatosensory pathway)

Review Main Concepts

Module Summary

Each module ends with a summary and list of key terms aimed at representing the scope and emphasis of a relatively large amount of material in an efficient and concise form. The summary reviews the concept presented in the module with reference to the specific Learning Objective. You can write your own summary first, as a review strategy, and then check your work against the text summary to self-evaluate your understanding of the big picture in each module. As well, new end-of-module Self-Study Questions will help you to do a quick check of key concepts covered. Answers to the questions are provided in the appendix at the end of the book.

Summary

Module 8: How Do Psychologists Conduct Research?

LEARNING OBJECTIVE 8 List steps in the research process and key characteristics of descriptive and experimental psychological research methods.

- Psychological research is rooted in first generating a hypothesis, or prediction, about the relationship between two or more variables based on observations.
- Psychologists conduct research with a sample, a small group meant to represent the larger population of interest. The best means of selecting a sample is random selection, a procedure in which everyone in the population has an equal chance of being selected to be in the sample.
- Descriptive research methods include case studies, naturalistic observations, and surveys.
- Case studies are in-depth observations of a single individual.
- Naturalistic observation involves observing people in settings outside of laboratories where their behaviour occurs naturally.
- Surveys may be conducted in interviews or with questionnaires.
- Only experiments allow researchers to draw conclusions about cause-and-effect relationships.
- All research methods have advantages for particular uses and all are subject to various drawbacks. Researchers must plan carefully to avoid subject bias, researcher bias, and demand characteristics.

Key Terms

case study 54	double-blind procedure 58	independent variable 52	sample 53
control group 56	experiment 56	naturalistic observation 55	survey 56
dependent variable 52	experimental group 56	operationalize 52	variable 52
descriptive research methods 54	Hawthorne effect 55	random selection 53	

Study Questions

Multiple Choice

1. A researcher observed the eating patterns of laboratory rats while manipulating the amount of sleep they received during a week-long study. In this example, what type of variable is "sleep"?
   a) observable
   b) dependent
   c) independent
   d) extraneous

2. Which of the following is not a descriptive research method?
   a) case study
   b) experiment
   c) naturalistic observation
   d) survey

Fill-In-the-Blank

1. A subset of a population is known as a(n) _____

2. The research methodology that asks participants to answer a series of questions is called a(n) _____

PART 1

PSYCHOLOGY: YESTERDAY AND TODAY

How many friends do you have on Facebook? Are they your friends or are they "friends?" Are Facebook friends the same as "real" friends? Are there consequences to the way people share information on Facebook that could actually be changing how we think about friendship and other important human relationships?

Psychologists have studied friendship for many years, but additional research may be needed to better understand how Facebook friendships are similar to and different from more traditional friendship. Ninety-eight percent of Canadian 16- to 24-year-olds were on the Internet in 2009, placing them among the most connected in the world. Most (96 percent) use a home computer, and even more have access to computers through their schools or libraries (Statistics Canada, 2010). Moreover, 67 percent of Canadian teens who log on to the Internet say that they participate in online social networking (Statistics Canada, 2010). This social phenomenon is providing many opportunities for fascinating psychological research.

A study by Amy Muise, Emily Christofides, and Serge Desmariais (2009) at the University of Guelph suggested that more Facebook use leads to more jealousy in close relationships. They found that people in relationships who reported spending more time looking at each other's Facebook pages also reported experiencing more feelings of jealousy based on what they were seeing on their partner's Facebook page.

Social networks like Facebook are also changing other aspects of our relationships. For example, do online contact opportunities help us get started in new relationships? A study by Robert Stephure and Susan Boon at the University of Calgary and Stacey MacKinnon at UPEI (2009) showed that those who use online contacts to start a relationship process (dating, etc.) are more likely to be older (middle aged and beyond). Younger Canadians also make use of social media within their relationships, but they seem to move more easily back and forth between their real and virtual lives. Think about your own experiences. What are some of the ways in which you use social media in and around your friendships and other relationships?

American anthropologist Ilana Gershon, in her book *The Breakup 2.0: Disconnecting over New Media* (2010), demonstrated that university students see clear roles for social media in their "real world" relationships. For example, students reported that Facebook might best be seen as a place for initiating *casual* relationships, while texting moves relationships up to another level of seriousness. Texting, in turn, may lead to cell phone calls, and ultimately to a face-to-face date. In addition, Gershon's students indicated that they would sometimes fake information on their own Facebook page by exaggerating some claims and minimizing others to make themselves look better. However, despite this they also said they tended to trust what others had posted on their own Facebook pages.

While psychology can help us try to understand new behaviour, like having hundreds of Facebook "friends," it also helps us to understand far more common things that we all do. Why do people use Facebook in the first place, for example? As you read this book, you'll see that all the topics we examine contribute not only to our understanding of unusual or problematic behaviours, but also to things that happen all around us, every day.

We'll discuss human development, examining how we mature and what shapes us as we age. Maybe the ease of online communication helps some otherwise shy children gain early confidence and establish more and better social relationships. We'll look at motivation and emotion, getting some ideas about why people do things and how we experience our feelings. What drives people to spend hours every day on the Internet, for example? We'll look at theories of intelligence, including one that suggests that the kind of intelligence needed to hack into websites and steal social insurance numbers is different from the kind of intelligence needed to empathize with people such

CJG – Technology/Alamy

Online friendships. Psychologists study all kinds of mental processes and behaviours, including using social media.

practically Speaking | Myths and Misconceptions

Have you ever heard anyone refer to "psycho-babble?" We have. This is usually a term applied to a speaker when the listener feels that the speaker is using psychological jargon to create an illusion of credibility about the issue at hand. Generally the assumption is that the speaker, an "arm chair psychologist" (Kelly, 1955), is using concepts they are unqualified to use and that they do not understand. We hope that by the time you finish reading this book you will have a good idea of how to tell pseudoscience from real science. Why does this matter? In their book, *50 Great Myths of Popular Psychology: Shattering Widespread Misconceptions about Human Nature*, Lilienfeld, Lynn, Ruscio, and Beyerstein (2010) say that it is important to know about myths for three reasons: (1) they can be harmful; (2) myths can create indirect damage; and (3) accepting myths in one area impedes thinking in other areas. We will present research data throughout the book to counter common myths, but first let's examine a few common myths and misperceptions and also identify data that refute these beliefs.

- *People use only 10 percent of their brains.* Electrical brain stimulations have not identified *any* inactive areas in the brain (Beyerstein, 1999).
- *It is better to express anger than to bottle it up.* When people behave in an angry way their levels of aggression go up, not down (Bushman, Baumeister, & Stack, 1999).
- *Some people are primarily right brained whereas others are primarily left brained.* The typical brain works in an integrated fashion (Corballis, 2007).
- *You can recall forgotten information under hypnosis.* Forensic psychologists believe that hypnosis either has no effect on memory or that it distorts recall (Erdelyi, 1994; Lynn, Neuschatz, Fite, & Rhue, 2001).
- *People with schizophrenia have two personalities.* People with schizophrenia have only one personality; people with a form of dissociative identity disorder may have more than one personality, although even this idea is controversial (Lilienfeld & Lynn, 2003).
- *Opposites attract.* People are far more likely to choose romantic partners and friends who share similar personality traits (Lewak, Wakefield, & Briggs, 1985; Nangle, Erdley, Zeff, Stanchfield, & Gold, 2004).
- *Some look like their purebred dogs.* True (Roy & Christenfeld, 2004).

Vedros & Associates/Getty Images

as parents who have lost a child. Along the way, our goal is to help you gain insight not only into the attention-grabbing and sometimes bizarre things that can go wrong, but also into the often-overlooked but miraculous things that often go right.

Every journey begins with a first step, and in this part, the first step is to learn what psychology is and how it developed into the discipline we have now. After that, we'll discuss where psychology originated and how it developed. Finally, we'll learn more about psychology today, including what psychologists do, where they do it, and what's new and changing in what they do.

Module 1: What Is Psychology?

psychology the study of mental processes and behaviours.

mental processes activities of our brain when engaged in thinking, observing the environment, and using language.

behaviour observable activities of an organism, often in response to environmental cues.

From our earliest beginnings, people have been curious about the inner workings of the mind and have attempted to explain and predict the thoughts and emotions of themselves and of others. Today, the science of studying *mental processes* and *behaviour* is known as **psychology**. Psychology as a discipline is concerned with empirically examining the mind and behaviour and determining how each is influenced by the psychobiology of the organism as well as the effects of the external environment.

Mental processes describe the activity of our brains when we are engaged in thinking, processing information, and using language. Mental processes include complex experiences such as thinking, imagining, and remembering. During psychology's early history, the primary method for exploring internal mental processes was to observe outward **behaviour**, our observable actions, and make inferences, or guesses, about what was happening in the mind. Since psychology became an experimental science in the nineteenth century, however, psychological researchers have sought more direct ways to examine mental processes. In fact, the advent of brain imaging and other forms of technology have enabled scientists to uncover fascinating connections between behaviour and mental processes and to move toward a more comprehensive view of how mental processes occur in various individuals and situations.

When psychologists study mental processes and behaviour, they generally have one of four goals in mind:

- *Description.* Psychologists seek to *describe* very specifically the things that they observe. As you read this book, you'll see that psychologists have described phenomena ranging from how babies learn to talk to how we fall in love, how a human being is affected by early experience to how we make decisions, and more.
- *Explanation.* Telling what, where, when, and how is sometimes not enough. A key goal for many psychologists is to answer the question of "Why?" As we'll see, psychologists have developed hypotheses and theories to *explain* a huge variety of events, from why people develop addictions to substances to why we get hungry.
- *Prediction.* Psychologists also seek to *predict* the circumstances under which a variety of behaviours and mental process are likely to occur. You'll learn later in this book, for example, about research that predicts the conditions under which we are most likely to offer help to a stranger in need.
- *Control.* We often encounter situations in which we want to either limit or increase certain behaviours or mental processes—whether our own or those of others. Psychology can give students advice on controlling their own behaviours that ranges from how to limit unhealthy stress to how to increase what you remember from a class.

To describe, explain, predict, or control mental processes and behaviours, we need to recognize the many influences on them. All our thoughts and actions, down to the simplest tasks, involve complex activation and coordination of a number of levels—the levels of the *brain*, the *individual*, and the *group*. As you will see throughout this textbook, no psychological process occurs solely at one of these levels. Analyzing how the brain, the individual, and the group influence each other reveals much about how we function—insights that might be overlooked if we were to focus on only one of these levels alone (see **Table 1-1**).

At the *level of the brain*, psychologists consider the neuronal (brain cell) activity that occurs during the transmission and storage of information. They also focus on the structure of the brain and the genes that guide its formation. As we'll see later in this part, technological advances in the fields of molecular biology and brain imaging have made it possible to study how brain structure and activity differ from person to person and

> **"** Man is the only animal for whom his own existence is a problem which he has to solve. **"**
>
> —*Erich Fromm, psychologist and philosopher*

TABLE 1-1 The Levels of Analysis in Psychology

Level	What Is Analyzed	Example: Using Social Media
The brain	How brain structure and brain cell activity differ from person to person and situation to situation	What are the patterns of brain activation as people interact with "friends" online?
The person	How the content of the individual's mental processes form and influence behaviour	Are there personality factors that influence how much people use different types of social media? Can online social support or crisis resources improve people's decision-making and quality of life?
The group	How behaviour is shaped by the social and cultural environments	What features of social networking sites, such as relative anonymity, ease of access, and lack of face-to-face contact, increase or decrease users' feelings of belonging and connectedness?

Source: Adapted from Gardner, 1993.

situation to situation. For example, a psychologist studying the brain can now look at what parts of the brain are activated by the administration of a drug, or the brain changes that accompany anxiety and depression (Damsa et al., 2009).

At the *level of the person*, psychologists analyze how the *content* of mental processes—including emotions, thoughts, and ideas—form and influence behaviour. To use a computer analogy, this level relates to the software rather than the mechanical functioning, or hardware, of the brain. The level of the person includes ideas such as consciousness, intelligence, personality, and motivation. Although internal biological structures of the brain allow such person-level processes to occur, we cannot understand the processes unique to each individual, such as personality or motivation, without also studying this level.

culture a set of shared beliefs and practices that are transmitted across generations.

Psychologists must also look beyond the individual to the *level of the group*. This perspective recognizes that humans are shaped by their social environment and that this environment changes over time. A *group* can be made up of friends, family members, or a large population. Often a large group shares a **culture**, a set of common beliefs, practices, values, and history that are transmitted across generations. The groups to which people belong or perceive themselves to belong can influence their thoughts and behaviours in fundamental ways (Prinstein & Dodge, 2008). Canadian culture is rooted in the history of the First Nations as well as of the early settlers and of immigrants, resulting in a diverse population of mixed ethnic groups and cultures.

> "Everything that irritates us about others can lead us to an understanding of ourselves."
>
> —*Carl Jung, psychiatrist and philosopher*

When they conduct research, psychologists may focus on a single level of analysis. It is important to recognize, however, that activity does not take place only at one level or another. During even our most everyday activities, we are operating at all three levels at once. The levels also interact. Brain activity is affected by other levels, even by our broad cultural contexts. Similarly, changes in the biology of our brains can cause significant changes in our general state of being.

Let's go back for a moment to our earlier discussion of virtual relationships on Facebook. If psychologists set out to understand behaviour involved in virtual relationships, they could examine it at various levels. Operating at the level of the brain, they could explore patterns of brain activation in

©iStockphoto.com/Photawa

Diversity of Canadian culture. Canadian culture is often characterized as multicultural, encompassing influences from a wide range of nationalities as well as from its own indigenous culture.

Facebook users to see what brain changes occur when they go online or seek to link to or interact with others. At the level of the person, psychologists could explore questions of intelligence and personality to see whether there are certain characteristics related to the type and extent of Facebook use. Finally, at the level of the group, psychologists might examine how anonymity buffers Facebook groups if they bend general standards of polite behaviour, or how users' participation on Facebook strengthens bonds to other users and decreases (or perhaps increases) their broader sense of connection to the population at large. As you'll see throughout this book, the notion of multiple levels of analysis has played an important role in the development of psychological theories (Fodor, 2007, 2006, 1968).

Having examined what psychologists study and how they do it, let's next consider how psychology got its start, how historical and societal factors affected the way psychologists studied the mind and behaviour, and how perspectives and approaches vacillated over the discipline's rich and varied history. We'll examine how psychologists shifted their focus among the different goals and levels of analysis throughout psychology's history. You cannot truly appreciate psychology as it is now without a brief review of the growth and development of the field as it was shaped to become the discipline we have today.

Before You Go On

www.wiley.com/go/comercanada

What Do You Know?

1. How is behaviour different from mental processes? How are they the same?
2. What are the three levels of analysis in psychology?

What Do You Think?
What would be the focus of each of the four goals of psychology when studying the use of Facebook and other social media? How would the questions and actions of a psychologist who seeks to describe social media use differ from those of someone who wants to limit children's and adolescents' use levels, for example?

Summary

Module 1: What Is Psychology?

LEARNING OBJECTIVE 1 Define *psychology* and describe the goals and levels of analysis psychologists use.

- Psychology is the study of mental processes and behaviour.
- The goals of psychology are to *describe, explain, predict,* and *control* behaviour and mental processes. Psychologists vary in the degree to which they focus on some of these goals more than others.
- The study of psychology must occur at multiple levels, including the level of the *brain* (the biological activity associated with mental processes and behaviour), the level of the *person* (the content of mental processes), and the level of the *group* (social influences on behaviour).

Key Terms

behaviour 4

culture 5

mental processes 4

psychology 4

Study Questions

Multiple Choice

1. Psychology is defined as:
   a) the science of behaviour.
   b) the study of mental processes.
   c) the study of mental disorders and their treatment.
   d) the science of behaviour and mental processes.

2. Which of the following statements is true regarding the levels of analysis in psychology?
   a) Each thought or behaviour occurs at one of the following levels: the level of the brain, the level of the person, or the level of the group.
   b) The level of the brain is the most important level of analysis in psychology.

   c) Thoughts and behaviours are analyzed at the group level by sociologists and anthropologists, not by psychologists.
   d) All thoughts and behaviours occur at all three levels simultaneously.

Fill-in-the-Blank

1. During psychology's early history, the primary method for exploring internal mental processes was to observe outward _____.

2. Psychology's goal of _____ is associated with the desire to limit or increase behaviour.

Module 2: Psychology's Roots in Philosophy

LEARNING OBJECTIVE 2
Describe the influences of
early myths and ancient Greek
philosophies on psychology.

Historically, humans have attempted to explain inexplicable events in their natural environments through *myths*. Myths are stories of forgotten origin that seek to explain or rationalize the fundamental mysteries of life and are universal, that is, common to all cultures. Myths seek to explain topics such as the reason for earthquakes, why crops are poor or plentiful, how humans came to be, and so on. A number of ceremonies and rituals based on these beliefs were then devised. Some theorists today believe that myths developed into some systems of religion, and that myths reflect an innate human need to understand and make sense of people and the natural world. In fact, according to these theorists, science is somewhat similar to mythology in that science represents our attempt to describe, explain, predict, and control our reality (Waterfield, 2000).

Although they focused on supernatural, life-giving forces, early belief systems as well as the cosmogonies (studies of the origin of the universe) of the Near East contributed to the intellectual curiosity and quest for knowledge that characterized the early Greek philosophers in the fourth and fifth centuries B.C.E. Although they did not consistently rely on empirical methods to examine questions, the great thinkers of ancient Greece moved beyond supernatural explanations. Instead, they tried to find ways to determine the nature of reality and the limitations of human awareness. To accomplish these difficult goals, they engaged in open, critical discussions of each other's ideas.

The intellectual history of psychology (like much of Western thought) starts with the history of Greek philosophy because unlike other important world philosophies, the Greeks had a recorded language (Boeree, 2006). *Philosophy* is defined as the study of knowledge, reality, and the nature and meaning of life. Among many other questions, the ancient philosophers such as Socrates, Plato, and Aristotle queried how the human mind worked, how the human body related to the mind, and whether knowledge was inborn or had to be learned from experience (Hothersall, 1995). In addition, the Greek philosophers developed a method of introducing problems and then questioning proposed solutions that is at the core of modern scientific methods; methods we will discuss in greater detail in Part 2. Greek philosophers also emphasized that theories, ideas about the way things work, are never final, but rather are always capable of improvement. Psychologists still take this view.

Chuck Stoody/The Canadian Press

Rituals. Many ceremonies and celebrations developed as a way to understand the natural and human world. The Coast Salish peoples of British Columbia passed down their oral history, including customs and beliefs, through stories, songs, and dances.

The Granger Collection

Hippocrates' psychological theory. This medieval manuscript illustrates the psychological effects of the humors proposed by the Greek physician. The illustration on the left demonstrates the melancholia produced by black bile, while the one on the right depicts the joyous, musical, and passionate personality produced by blood.

Hippocrates (ca. 460–377 B.C.E.), a Greek physician, believed that disease had a physical and rational explanation and that it was not caused by evil spirits or as a punishment from the gods. He erroneously suggested that an individual's physical and psychological health is influenced by an excess or a lack of bodily *humors*. He believed that these four bodily fluids (blood, phlegm, yellow bile, and black bile) collectively determined a person's personality and character, and predicted the individual's well-being and responses to environmental events. Although Hippocrates' medical theory of *humorism* was wrong, he was the first to recognize the importance of good food, fresh air, and rest, and he accurately diagnosed the symptoms for pneumonia and epilepsy. He also correctly identified the brain as the organ of mental life, and argued that thoughts, ideas, and feelings originated in the brain and not in the heart—as was commonly believed at the time. Hippocrates tested his theories with direct observation and some dissections. Because of such early efforts, academic study became rooted firmly in detailed scientific methods of study.

Other Greek philosophers, such as Socrates (ca. 469–399 B.C.E.) and Plato (ca. 427–347 B.C.E.), considered whether the mind and the body were one thing or whether each functioned separately. They concluded that the mind and body are distinct and that the mind continues after the body dies. They believed that "truth" lies in the mind and that this knowledge was innate—that is, inborn or existing within a person from birth—and is highly dependent upon our perceived, or subjective, states. Socrates therefore looked for concepts that were the "essence" of human nature and searched for elements that various concepts had in common. He tried, for example, to identify *why* something was beautiful, and what essential factors an object must possess in order to be beautiful. His student, Plato, believed that certain ideas and concepts were pure and signified an ultimate reality. Plato believed that we could use reasoning to uncover the core ideas deeply imbedded in every human soul. The ideas of these two philosophers represented early studies of mental states and processes.

©iStockphoto.com/Hans Laubel ©iStockphoto.com/thegreekphotoholic ©iStockphoto.com/PanosKarapanagiotis

Greek philosophers. Socrates mentored Plato who, in turn, mentored, Aristotle.

Similarly, Aristotle (ca. 384–322 B.C.E.), a student of Plato's, and one of the most famous thinkers of the Greek period, made key contributions to the foundations of psychology. His writings represent some of the first important theories about many of the topics discussed throughout this book, such as sensations, dreams, sleep, and learning (Lorusso, 2010). Aristotle was one of the first to promote empirical, or testable, investigations of the natural world. He looked inward at sensory experiences and also scrutinized his environment carefully, searching for the basic purpose of all objects and creatures. In his studies, he formed ideas about how living things are hierarchically categorized, concluding—centuries before Charles Darwin—that humans are closely related to animals.

2.1 Psychology's Roots in Physiology and Psychophysics

As Europe emerged from the Dark Ages, the philosophies of the ancient Greek scientists and philosophers were rediscovered approximately 2,000 years after they lived and re-emerged to influence European thinkers throughout the Renaissance. Although mysticism declined as a form of explanation for human nature, there remained great confusion and disagreement regarding human motives and origins.

In the centuries both during and after the Renaissance through to Associationism, European society underwent a scientific revolution. A spiritual worldview, which had dominated for several centuries, was increasingly replaced by a view of the world based on mathematics and mechanics. By the 1600s, modern science began to thrive and over time both the universe and human beings were viewed as machines subject to fixed natural laws. The dominant view was that the brain controlled the body by moving fluids from one area to another. The roles of magic and mysticism in science essentially disappeared (Leahey, 2000).

©iStockphoto.com/ilbusca

René Descartes. First of the modern philosophers.

During this time, Francis Bacon (1561–1626), an English philosopher, scientist, and statesman who was fascinated by the human mind, became a prominent figure in scientific methodology and natural philosophy. He is widely regarded as the creator of *empiricism*: the view that all knowledge originates in experience. He established and popularized the scientific method, gathering data, analyzing data, and performing experiments.

Like Socrates and Plato, René Descartes (1596–1650), the first of the modern philosophers and an early scientist, viewed all truths as ultimately linked and believed that the meaning of the natural world could be understood through science and mathematics. Descartes contemplated the nature of existence and dualism of the mind and body, believing the mind to be distinct from the body. He identified the point of contact between the two as the pineal gland, and he believed that the mind (which he viewed as synonymous with the soul) would survive the death of the body and was therefore the "province of God" (Pickren & Rutherford, 2010, p. 5).

The theories of both Bacon and Descartes influenced the work of British philosopher John Locke (1632–1704), who believed that we learn by our experiences. He notably argued that the mind at birth is a *tabula rasa*—a blank slate—"a white paper, void of all characters, without any ideas" (Locke, 1689), waiting for experience to imprint knowledge. That is, Locke thought that at birth the human mind has no innate ideas but instead acquires all knowledge through experience.

While philosophers debated about the nature of the human experience, other researchers believed that important insights about the brain and body could be understood by combining empirically established facts with philosophical thinking. The area of psychophysics, pioneered by prominent physiologist Johannes Müller (1801–1858), maintained that researchers needed to study the relationship between physical stimuli and their psychological effects, that is, the sensations and perceptions they affect. Psychophysics examined questions such as how much sound or light needs to be present to be detected, and how much sound or light must be added to an initial signal before we notice the change. Herman von Helmholtz (1821–1894), a student of Müller's, was the first to measure the speed of a nerve impulse and determined that nerve impulses occur over time rather than instantaneously. This finding led to the understanding that thought and movement are linked, but are not the same thing. The work of von Helmholtz contributed to the foundation of modern physiological psychology and neuroscience (Benjamin, 2007).

Gustav Fechner (1801–1887) was a German philosopher and physicist who is considered to be one of the founders of experimental psychology. He published a book summarizing this work in 1860, called *Elements of Psychophysics*. In the book, Fechner (1860) lays out many of the methods and study techniques that would come to be used in the emerging field of psychology. His evidence of the relationship between physical and mental events demonstrated that psychology had the potential to become a quantified science. While Fechner completed his manuscript, a physiologist, Wilhelm Wundt (1832–1920), came to work in the laboratory with Helmholtz. As we will see, these two events contributed to the foundation of psychology as a discipline.

Before You Go On

www.wiley.com/go/comercanada

What Do You Know?

1. What do the earliest myths have in common with today's scientific studies?
2. Greek philosophers who believed reasoning would uncover ideals or core ideas were focused on which aspect of psychology?
3. How did the Greek philosopher Hippocrates explain mental processes and behaviour? How did Hippocrates's research methods influence today's study of psychology?

What Do You Think? What advantages do you think a scientific approach has for explaining behaviour and mental processes compared to a supernatural approach?

Summary

Module 2: Psychology's Roots in Philosophy

LEARNING OBJECTIVE 2 Describe the influences of early myths and ancient Greek philosophies on psychology.

- Early explanations of human behaviour were rooted in superstition and magic.
- Later, philosophers, beginning with the ancient Greeks, tried to develop more objective theories of human consciousness and reality.
- The work of such early philosophers as Hippocrates, Socrates, Plato, and Aristotle contributed to the later formation of psychology as a natural science.

Study Questions

Multiple Choice

1. Whereas the Greek philosopher _____ correctly identified the brain as the organ of mental life, _____ believed that the brain was of minor importance.
    a) Aristotle; Hippocrates
    b) Plato; Aristotle
    c) Hippocrates; Aristotle
    d) Hippocrates; Socrates

2. With respect to the way that we acquire knowledge, _____ emphasized the role of the mind and reasoning, whereas _____ pointed to the role of sensory experience.

    a) Hippocrates; Socrates
    b) Aristotle; Hippocrates
    c) Plato; Aristotle
    d) Aristotle; Plato

Fill-in-the-Blank

1. In describing a natural disaster, when ancient peoples said that "the earth spirits were angry," they were explaining their environment through the use of _____.

Module 3: The Early Days of Psychology

LEARNING OBJECTIVE 3 Name important early psychologists and describe their major theories and research methods.

Bob Thomas/Popperfoto/Getty Images

Charles Darwin (1809–1882). The theories by the English naturalist about human evolution shifted scientific attention toward human origins and behaviour.

In the latter part of the nineteenth century, Charles Darwin (1809–1882), in his book *The Origin of Species* (1859, 1872), proposed the theory of evolution, making the radical suggestion that all life on Earth was related and that human beings were just one outcome of many variations from a common ancestral point. Darwin also suggested natural selection as the mechanism through which some variations survive over the years while other variations fall out of existence. *Natural selection* proposes that chance variations are passed down from parent to offspring, and that some of these variations are *adaptive*— better suited to an organism's environment. These adaptive variations help the organism to survive and reproduce in their specific environment. On the other hand, less-adaptive variations reduce the ability of an organism to survive.

3.1 The Founding of Psychology

In this atmosphere of heightened interest in the mind–body duality debate and the nature–nurture debate among philosophers, physicians, and scientists, psychology emerged as a distinct scientific field of investigation. As we have observed, prior to the late nineteenth century, psychology was virtually indistinguishable from the study of philosophy. In 1879, however, the physiologist Wilhelm Wundt (1832–1920) opened a laboratory in Leipzig, Germany, dedicated exclusively to the study of psychology. As a natural scientist, Wundt believed that the study of mind and behaviour ought to be conducted using the experimental methods of other sciences such as chemistry and physics, so he established a program that trained students to perform empirically-driven experiments in psychology. Psychology's emphasis on rigorous, scientific experimentation continues to this day, as we'll see in Part 2.

Archives of the History of American Psychology, The Center for the History of Psychology, The University of Akron

The father of experimental psychology Wilhelm Wundt (far right) works with colleagues in his laboratory at the University of Leipzig, one of the first laboratories devoted exclusively to psychological research.

Wundt exposed research participants to simple, standardized, repeatable situations and then asked them to make observations, an approach similar to the one used in the study of physiology. One of Wundt's most famous experiments involved a clock and pendulum. Wundt found that when determining the exact location of the pendulum at a specific time, his observations were always off by 1/10 of a second. He believed that he had found evidence that humans have a limited attention capacity and that it requires 1/10 of a second to shift focus from one object to another (Wundt, 1883).

Wundt studied the content and processes of **consciousness**, the awareness of immediate behaviours and mental processes. Wundt hoped to emulate the experimental methods observed in the natural sciences and believed that consciousness could be broken into basic elements, "atoms" of the mind, much as chemistry had identified chemical elements according to their atomic numbers, electron configuration, and so on. In his laboratory, he was particularly interested in studying the idea of *will* and how it influences what individuals choose to attend to in their environments. He believed that the will organized the mind's content into higher-level, more complex, thought processes. He further believed that much of behaviour is motivated and that attention is focused for an explicit purpose. For example, he believed that behaviours could be altered to adjust for changing circumstance. To distinguish between automatic and controlled actions and perceptions, Wundt developed a psychological paradigm he called **voluntarism**. Voluntarism refers to voluntary and willful acts of decision in human behaviour. Later, Wundt also went on to form theories about emotion and the importance of historical and social forces in human behaviour. His ideas about cultural psychology are in fact appreciated today for their early recognition that an individual's social context must also be taken into account to fully explain his mental processes and behaviour (Benjamin, 2007, 1997).

Beyond his own direct contributions to the new field of psychology, Wundt also served as teacher and mentor to many students who went on to shape the future of psychology. G. Stanley Hall was one of the first Americans to visit Wundt's lab. Hall would go on to found one of the first American experimental psychology laboratories at Johns Hopkins University in 1883. He also launched America's first psychology journal (in 1887), and was the driving force behind, and first president of, the American Psychological Association. James McKeen Cattell was the first American to earn his doctorate with Wundt, and would go on to establish psychology labs at the University of Pennsylvania and Columbia University. Princeton graduate, James Mark Baldwin, trained for a year in Germany where he became enamoured of the "new psychology" based on the ideas of Wundt and Fechner. He later moved to Canada and there established the first laboratory of experimental psychology at the University of Toronto. Directly and indirectly, Wundt did much to shape the emerging science of psychology.

3.2 Structuralism: Looking for the Components of Consciousness

Edward Titchener (1867–1927), an Englishman, emigrated to the United States in 1892 and expanded upon Wundt's approach, forming a theoretical paradigm called **structuralism** at Cornell University. Titchener's goal was to uncover the structure, or basic elements, of the conscious mind, much like looking at the parts that make up a car engine or bicycle or the individual bricks in a Lego sculpture, and to then determine how these elements were related. Titchener and other researchers attempted to break mental processes down into their most basic fundamental components, such as sensations or feelings. Structuralists then endeavoured to identify the laws governing the relationships between these elements and to ascertain how these elements interacted with the mind and body.

To study the conscious mind, the structuralists relied heavily on a method originated by Wundt, called **introspection**, which literally means "looking inward." Introspection involved the careful reflective and systematic observation of the details of mental processes and how they expand simple thoughts into complex ideas. It required the self-observation

consciousness personal awareness of ongoing mental processes, behaviours, and environmental events.

voluntarism a theory in which will is regarded as the ultimate agency in human behaviour; belief that much of behaviour is motivated and that attention is focused for an explicit purpose.

University of Toronto Archives

James Mark Baldwin (1861–1934). Shown here 1890 while at University of Toronto, Baldwin established the first psychology lab in the British Empire in Toronto in 1890 (Pantalony, 1997).

structuralism a philosophical approach that studies the structure of conscious experience.

introspection a method of psychological study involving careful evaluation of mental processes and how simple thoughts expand into complex ideas.

Psychology Around Us — Introspection of a Harsher Kind

Shashi Deshpande (1988) said that when we try to introspect, "the real picture, the real you never emerges.... Ten different mirrors show you ten different faces."

How could such an elusive process further the cause of science, as it did for Edward Titchener and other structuralists early in the twentieth century? Well, they were using a different kind of introspection—one that was more concrete and exacting. For example, psychologists Duane Schultz and Sydney Schultz (2012) described one of the techniques of introspection used in Titchener's lab: "Graduate students [in his lab] were made to swallow a stomach tube in the morning and keep it in place throughout the day. Apparently, many of them vomited at first…, before they gradually got used to it. In between their lectures and other activities they would report to the lab where hot water would be poured down the tube, and the subjects would introspect on the sensations they were experiencing. The process would be repeated with iced water" (1987, p. 91). And you thought some of your courses were difficult!

---

and self-reflection of individuals' own experiences. If shown a house made of Lego, for example, an introspecting structuralist would describe the smooth, shiny texture of each brick, the colour of the brick, the tiny gap between it and the adjoining bricks, and so forth.

Introspection proved unreliable (Benjafield et al., 2010) because regardless of how systematic an observation was, structuralists were not always able to agree. In these instances there was no real way to resolve differences. Moreover, it was argued that reflection on a feeling or experience changes the feeling or experience, so critics claimed that no real act of introspection could occur.

Toward the end of the 1800s, arguments began to emerge against the use of introspection as an experimental technique. Skeptics pointed out that scientists using introspection often arrived at diverse findings, depending on who was using the technique and what they were trying to find. The school of structuralism also came under attack for its failure to incorporate the study of animals and to examine issues of abnormal behaviour.

The major concern many psychologists had with structuralism, however, was its emphasis on gathering knowledge for its own sake without any further agendas such as a desire to apply our knowledge of the mind in practical ways. Recall the four goals of psychology discussed earlier. The goal of the structuralists was to use introspection to *describe* observable mental processes rather than to *explain* the mechanisms underlying consciousness or to try to *control* such mechanisms. They believed that speculation about unobservable events had no place in the scientific study of psychology. Ultimately, even Titchener himself acknowledged the need to understand the purpose of human thought and behaviour rather than to merely describe it.

Although many of structuralism's principles did not survive, its propositions that psychologists should focus largely on observable events and that scientific study should focus on simple elements as building blocks of complex experience have lived on in certain modern schools of thought.

3.3 Functionalism: Toward the Practical Application of Psychology

William James (1842–1910), brother to well-known author Henry James and a student of Helmholtz, was a philosopher, physician, and psychologist. James wrote one of the first important psychology texts, *Principles of Psychology* (1890). He was instrumental in shifting attention away from the structure of mental content to the purposes and functions of our mental processes. James admired the work of Darwin and argued that human thoughts, perceptions, and emotions have helped humans to adapt and therefore to survive, and that it was therefore important to understand how consciousness functions. He reasoned that consciousness had to serve an important biological function because it

Library of Congress/Getty Images

William James (1842–1910). The influential psychologist and philosopher investigated the purposes and functions of our mental processes. His book, *Principles of Psychology*, took 12 years to write and was 1,200 pages in length.

was a trait in humans that had been naturally selected, and he argued that psychologists needed to determine what those functions were (Hoffman & Thelen, 2010). Thus, James's approach was called **functionalism**. Functionalism was based on the belief that scientists should examine the function or purpose of consciousness, rather than simply focusing on its structure. To use our earlier analogy, functionalists were less interested in describing the parts of a car engine or bicycle, and more interested in what the engine or bicycle could do under a variety of conditions.

James viewed consciousness as an ever-changing stream of mental events rather than the more or less static set of components that the structuralists were seeking. For this reason, James and his colleagues were also interested in understanding how the mind adapted and functioned in a changing environment.

Functionalism did not rely primarily on a single research method, such as introspection. Instead, it used a variety of empirical methods that focused on the causes and consequences of behaviour. The functional approach also highlighted differences among individuals rather than identifying only those characteristics that they shared. And unlike structuralism, functionalism emphasized the need for research to include animals, children, and persons with mental disorders in order to understand both normal and abnormal psychological functioning (Richardson, 2006; Keller, 1973).

An example of research demonstrating the shift from structuralism to functionalism was apparent in an early experiment on how humans locate sound. Participants in the experiment were asked to point to the location of a sound (Angell, 1903). A structuralist would have asked each participant to provide an introspective report of her conscious experience of the sound. Functionalists, however, were more concerned with issues like how accurately participants could point in the direction in which the sound was physically located.

Although it never really became a formal school of psychology, functionalism helped to focus psychologists' attention on what the mind can and does accomplish. Spurred by the emphasis of functionalists on providing applicable and concrete information, psychology began to tackle socially relevant topics. Researchers William Lowe Bryan and Noble Harter (1897), for example, performed a famous investigation regarding how quickly telegraph operators could learn necessary typing skills. Their findings were used to improve training for railroad telegraphers, and the study is now widely regarded as one of the first to have a significant social and commercial impact. Functionalism also marked the beginning of exploration into socially important issues, such as learning and education, and indeed, *educational psychology* remains a significant area of research in the field today.

> **functionalism** a philosophical approach that considers how mental processes function to adapt to changing environments.

3.4 Gestalt Psychology: More than Putting Together the Building Blocks

While opponents of structuralism in North America were raising concerns that structuralism did not examine the uses of consciousness, Max Wertheimer (1880–1943) and other psychologists in Germany were questioning the structuralist idea that consciousness can be reduced to pieces or to basic mental elements. **Gestalt psychology** is based on the idea that we have inborn tendencies to impose structure on what we see, and these tendencies cause us to perceive things as broad "perceptual units" rather than as individual sensations. Indeed, the word *Gestalt* is of German origin, meaning "whole" or "form." The Gestalt school rejected the molecularism of the structuralists and instead subscribed to the idea that "the whole is greater than the sum of its parts." Researchers using this approach studied illusions and errors in perception, memory, and judgment to identify why subjective experience differed from objective reality.

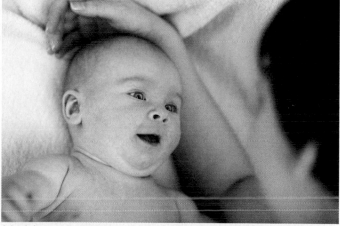

©iStockphoto.com/Marina_Di

Facial recognition. Even babies younger than 3 months of age can piece together the component parts of a face and recognize it as a whole object. In particular, they can recognize the familiar face of their mother.

> **Gestalt psychology** the field of psychology arguing that we have inborn tendencies to structure what we see in particular ways and to structure our perceptions into broad perceptual units.

FIGURE 3-1 Kanzia illusion. This visual illusion causes the visual system to create a floating square that does not actually exist (to prove this to yourself, cover all four circles and you will see the square disappear).

For example, when you look at a computer screen you see complete pictures, when in fact each picture is made up of thousands of small dots, called *pixels*. If you get close enough to the screen, you can see the picture break down, but our brains still favour integrating those dots into a cohesive picture or whole. Wertheimer and colleagues believed that the mind imposed organization on perceptions and that this organization of a holistic perception prevented people from seeing what they were being shown by the experimenter. This phenomenon can be observed in **Figure 3-1**, where a visual illusion is created when the visual system tries to make sense of what it sees. The brain assumes that the missing pieces of the circle are caused because a square shape is lying on top of the circles and occluding pieces of them. So, rather than experiencing four incomplete circles, we experience a floating square. Similar findings have been gathered regarding our tendency to group eyes, noses, and mouths into recognizable human faces. Children 3 months of age or younger show a preference for human faces, but only when the component parts of faces are arranged correctly in a facial orientation (Turati et al., 2010; Morton & Johnson, 1991).

Gestaltists developed over 100 perceptual principles to describe how the brain and sensory systems perceive environmental stimuli. Some of the Gestalt laws will be discussed in Part 5. Gestaltists also viewed learning as tied to perception—the recognition and identification of stimuli that come through our senses. They believed that problem solving occurs when a person develops a sudden and complete insight into a solution—indeed, they believed that problems remain in an unsolved state until such points of insight occur.

Together with the functionalists, the Gestalt school helped guide psychology away from the study of individual elements and toward a broader view of the human mind and functioning. Many of its concepts and the importance of the study of perception are still present in modern psychology.

Before You Go On

www.wiley.com/go/comercanada

What Do You Know?

1. What is introspection, and which early school of psychologists relied most heavily upon it?
2. What is the main difference in approach between functionalism and structuralism?
3. What did the Gestalt psychologists study?

What Do You Think? Which early school of psychology most closely resembles the way you view the human mind? Why?

Summary

Module 3: The Early Days of Psychology

LEARNING OBJECTIVE 3 Name important early psychologists and describe their major theories and research methods.

- The development of psychology has been strongly influenced by shifts in the social environment and development of new technology.
- The first psychology laboratory was founded in Leipzig, Germany, by physiologist Wilhelm Wundt. Wundt was interested in human consciousness and will, which he studied through small, structured activities that could be easily watched and replicated.
- Structuralism, a school of thought developed by one of Wundt's students, relied upon the use of introspection, the careful observation of human perception. The goal of the structuralists was to find the smallest building blocks of consciousness.
- William James helped shift the field's focus to the functions of mental events and behaviours, forming a school of thought known as functionalism.
- Gestalt psychologists studied human tendencies to perceive pattern rather than dividing consciousness into its smallest parts. They focused on putting together the "parts," or individual sensations, to create a "whole" or perception that went beyond the sum of the parts.

Key Terms

consciousness 13

functionalism 15

Gestalt psychology 15

introspection 13

structuralism 13

voluntarism 13

Study Questions

Multiple Choice

1. In which of the goals of psychology were the structuralists most interested?
   a) description
   b) prediction
   c) explanation
   d) control

2. Which American psychologist is credited with developing the functionalist approach?
   a) Freud
   b) Pavlov
   c) James
   d) Watson

Fill-in-the-Blank

1. The Gestalt psychologists made their most lasting contributions to the psychology of _____.

2. The _____ were the first psychologists to examine socially relevant topics.

Module 4: Twentieth-Century Approaches

LEARNING OBJECTIVE 4
Summarize the major principles of the psychoanalytical, behaviourist, humanistic, cognitive, and neuroscience approaches to psychology.

From the late 1800s into the twentieth century, psychology continued to grow as a science. In the years leading up to World War I and through World War II, there was tremendous growth in the field of psychology. The number of psychologists rapidly expanded, and popular interest in psychology grew.

As more people became interested in the field, perspectives toward behaviour and mental processes continued to emerge. Several twentieth-century schools of thought had major influence on the field, including the psychodynamic approach, the behaviourist approach, the humanistic approach, the cognitive approach, and the sociobiological approach. Next we'll explore the defining features of each of these approaches.

4.1 Psychoanalysis: Psychology of the Unconscious

Wundt, Titchener, and the structuralists, James and the functionalists, and the Gestaltists held very different views about how the mind is structured and how it should be studied. But they were all alike in one way: they all focused on consciousness, behaviours, and mental processes of which we are aware. And, as you will see in Part 6, their early endeavours into the conscious experience remain an area of considerable study in psychology today. Other theorists, however, focused on mental processes of which we are unaware, those that happen in the **unconscious** mind.

unconscious hypothesized repository of thoughts, feelings, and sensations outside human awareness, thought in some theories to have a strong bearing on human behaviour.

Sigmund Freud (1856–1939), a Viennese neurologist, suggested that many of our thoughts and feelings exist beyond the realm of awareness, in the unconscious. Freud described the conscious mind as being only the tip of the intellectual and perceptual iceberg; he believed the unconscious mind existed well below the surface of conscious awareness, but nevertheless exerted enormous influence on behaviour. Freud did not conduct experimental studies of laboratory participants; instead he built his theory on information from patients he saw in his medical practice who were coping with irrational fears, obsession, and anxieties. Freud was particularly interested in patients who had a condition that was then known as *hysteria*. These patients, who were most often women, suffered a transient loss of perceptual, cognitive, or motor function without any known physical cause, causing blindness, paralysis, amnesia, or other catastrophic losses. Freud believed that in most cases, the patients' symptoms could be traced to toxic events from their childhoods. He was persuaded that the impact of these "lost" memories indicated the presence of an unconscious mind.

psychoanalytic theory psychological theory that human mental processes are influenced by the competition between unconscious forces to come into awareness.

Based on his detailed observations of these people's cases, Freud became convinced that the root cause for many of his patient's maladies was mental and not physical. He came to believe that the mind is a complex interaction of the thoughts and memories that exist at different levels of awareness, some conscious and some unconscious. He viewed psychological conflict as largely due to disturbances existing at an unconscious level and then reaching awareness. We will discuss these levels of awareness and consciousness further in Part 12. Freud's theory was developed over decades and is called **psychoanalytic theory**.

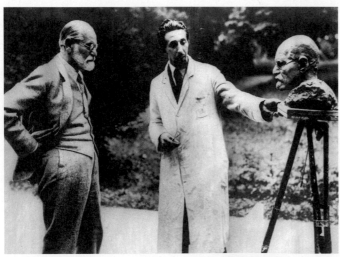

Wide World Photos/AP

Eye to eye. Sigmund Freud, founder of psychoanalytic theory, examines a sculptured bust of himself at his village home in 1931.

Freud further believed that childhood experiences help set the stage for later psychological functioning by contributing to effective or ineffective interactions among conscious and unconscious forces. According to Freud, certain developmental milestones must be achieved successfully in order for a person to achieve emotional adjustment. He also was interested in how children unconsciously adopt social and moral norms from their parents and, in turn, develop a conscious awareness of what constitutes acceptable and unacceptable expressions of their internal desires. Freud suggested that these conscious standards lead to unavoidable tensions between our unconscious primal needs and our conscious social or moral restraints. According to Freud, the back-and-forth tension within and between the conscious and unconscious mind is what shapes personality, helps produce abnormal behaviours in some cases, and governs virtually all behaviour (Bushman, 2002). In fact, Freud and his followers saw the conscious mind as a thin mask over a deep unconscious mental world, a world that contains impulses and urges that cannot be expressed freely given the constraints of a person's social environment.

As we will see later in the textbook, psychoanalytic notions typically have not held up well when subjected to rigorous scientific study. For evidence, Freud relied on anecdotes and case histories of remarkable changes in his patients. Researchers have not been able to find much support for his claims when they test them with larger groups of people (Nicholls, 2010; Wallerstein, 2006). The lack of research support, as well as philosophical differences, prevented many of his contemporaries from accepting Freud's theories. William James, the functionalist, for example, rejected the psychoanalytic notion of the unconscious. To him, conscious ideas were not a product of underlying machinery (i.e., the unconscious); what was observed in the conscious mind was the complete experience.

Nevertheless, to this day, psychoanalysis remains an influential theory of mental functioning and personality in the field of psychology (Barratt, 2013). Clearly, Freud's theory increased the applications of psychology to many aspects of everyday life. It stirred interest in motivation, sexuality, child development, dreams, and abnormal behaviour—all topics we will discuss later in this book. Freud's use of "the talking cure" as a therapeutic technique helped lead to the creation of psychiatry and clinical psychology as influential therapeutic methods, and these methods continue to thrive.

Although many of Freud's ideas have been challenged, they certainly marked a turning point in the understanding of human nature. Psychoanalytic theory was among the first psychological theories to provide a comprehensive view of human nature, and it helped make psychology relevant to more people (Chessick, 2010).

4.2 Behaviourism: Psychology of Adaptation

In addition to theories about the conscious and the unconscious mind, a third area of psychology, called **behaviourism**, emerged in the early part of the twentieth century. This school of thought was founded on the belief that psychology should study only behaviours that are directly observable rather than abstract mental processes.

Early behaviourists tended to focus on the relationships between **stimuli**—things that trigger changes in our internal or external states—and **responses**—the ways we react to stimuli. As you'll read in more detail in Part 7 on Learning, the behaviourists developed a number of influential ideas about how responses produce consequences and how those consequences in turn affect an organism's future responses to stimuli.

Behaviourism originated in North America and Russia. In North America, animal research was growing in popularity, while in Russia, Ivan Pavlov's (1849–1936) discovery of a phenomenon that came to be called *conditioning* linked various animal behaviours to events in the animals' environments (Bitterman, 2006; Bauer, 1952). Pavlov, a physiologist, observed that dogs salivated when his lab assistants brought them food. Later, he noticed that the dogs also salivated when the lab assistants appeared—even when they brought no food. The dogs had been *conditioned*—that is, they had learned—to associate

behaviourism a branch of psychological thought arguing that psychology should study only directly observable behaviours rather than abstract mental processes.

stimuli elements of the environment that trigger changes in our internal or external states.

response the way we react to stimuli.

one stimulus (food) with another (lab assistants) and to respond in the same way to both. You will read more about Pavlov's work in Part 7. Such successful studies of non-human behaviour called into question the methods being used to investigate human behaviour. Even though animals could not engage in introspection, scientists were learning a great deal by observing their behaviour.

Edward Thorndike (1874–1949), who was technically a functionalist, helped transition the field of psychology toward behaviourism by proposing that animal findings could help explain human behaviour. As behaviourism proved increasingly fruitful and popular, tensions grew between investigators who used introspection and those who relied on observation.

John Watson (1878–1958) is generally credited with pioneering the school of behaviourism. He agreed with Thorndike that animals could be useful in guiding our understanding of human psychology, and he sharply disagreed with psychoanalysis and with

John Lehmann/The Globe and Mail/The Canadian Press

Olympic gold! Do team players train for love of the game, to win medals, for the camaraderie, or for endorsement contracts? It probably varies by person, but something reinforces each of these players.

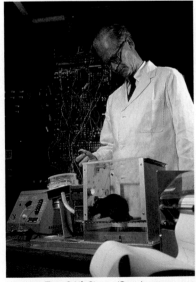

Nina Leen/Time & Life Pictures/Getty Images

The box! B.F. Skinner developed the "Skinner box" to help him investigate how consequences reinforce behaviour. Here he uses the box to train a rat to press a lever for a food reward.

the notion of unobservable mental processes as appropriate approaches to studying the mind and behaviour. As we'll discuss in Part 7, he was able to extend Pavlov's animal work to young children, and he essentially launched modern psychological theory by demonstrating that children could be conditioned by researchers to fear various objects and situations.

B.F. Skinner (1904–1990), who emerged as the leading behaviourist after World War II, helped expand behaviourism's perspective by acknowledging that internal, mental processes may indeed be at work in some situations, such as when an animal runs to get food. But even here, Skinner argued, empirical—observable—information should be gathered first, and then theories about causation could be formulated from that. That is, even when behaviourists acknowledged that internal mental processes were probably at work, they held that their primary job was to describe empirical phenomena, not to explain them (Schultz & Schultz, 2012). For example, when observing the behaviour of a monkey who is attempting to obtain food, a behaviourist might describe how the animal distinguishes a particular food from other stimuli, how it approaches the food, and what steps it takes to obtain it—observations meant to reveal how particular responses come to be associated with the food stimulus.

An idea central to behaviourism is that the consequence resulting from a particular behaviour serves to either increase or decrease the likelihood that an organism will perform that same behaviour again in the future. If the consequence of a given behaviour is rewarding, the consequence is regarded as a **reinforcement**, and the organism will be more likely to repeat the behaviour in the future. A behaviour is *positively* reinforced when it brings about a desired outcome (such as food or money), and *negatively* reinforced when it helps an organism avoid an undesirable outcome (such as an electrical shock or loud noise). For example, procrastination may be negatively reinforcing to the extent that it helps people avoid the pain of actually sitting down to study. Remember, if a particular behaviour is reinforced, either positively or negatively, we are more likely to repeat the behaviour later.

> **reinforcement** a learning process that increases the likelihood a given response will be repeated.

The term *negative reinforcement* is sometimes confused with **punishment**, but the latter is really a very different factor in behaviour. Unlike negative reinforcements, *punishments* render behaviours less likely to be repeated. Denying a child his dessert for not eating his broccoli is a punishment. However, if the parent was nagging the child to eat broccoli and then stops when the child eats it, the child has been negatively reinforced, that is, the unpleasant nagging has stopped; therefore the child has been negatively reinforced in this situation and will eat the food the parent insists in order to avoid the unpleasant nagging.

> **punishment** an experience that produces a decrease in a particular behaviour.

The principles of behaviourism became widely used in advertising and in helping businesses address personnel problems. As behaviourism grew in popularity, its principles were applied to numerous industries as well as to courts, schools, and even the military. During this period, researchers also placed great emphasis on the development of controlled scientific methods that might establish psychology once and for all as a true science. Given the appeal of its objective and controlled methods of investigation, behaviourism reached considerable prominence in the academic field, dominating the field from the 1930s for over twenty years. Behaviourism continues to have a strong influence on psychology today. Indeed, most of today's experimental studies continue to adhere to rigorous research standards similar to those devised by behaviourists.

Markus Botzek/zefa/Corbis

Behaviourism was not embraced by all, however. Some psychologists criticized John Watson and other prominent behaviourists for popularizing and, in their view, cheapening psychology. In 1929, for example, psychologist Joseph Jastrow wrote that behaviourism's portrayal in popular magazines and newspapers undermined psychology's role as a valid science (1929). Many other psychologists also raised questions about the merits of behaviourism; some of their concerns are raised below.

The real teachers. These young Bonobo chimpanzees, along with other animals, learn behaviours in their natural environments where their parents and other important figures inadvertently apply reinforcements and punishments.

Moreover, the behaviourists themselves began to disagree with each other and to divide into competing schools of thought. In the 1960s, for example, the Mundare, Alberta-born psychologist Albert Bandura (1925–) demonstrated that children often seem to learn not by conditioning or clear rewards and punishments, but by *social observation*, or *modelling*. Bandura and other psychologists also showed that people could learn without any apparent change in their overt behaviour, a phenomenon that suggested individual changes might reflect some kind of internal representations and mental processes after all. With these and related developments, pure behaviourism (that is, behaviourism with no attention to mental processes, such as beliefs or thoughts) began to lose some of its influence. In fact, a new field, *cognitive behaviourism*, gained ground; this new approach combined conditioning and cognition to better explain behaviour (Zentall, 2002).

humanistic psychology theory of psychology that sought to give greater prominence to special and unique features of human functioning.

© Roger Ressmeyer/Corbis

Humanistic pioneer. Carl Rogers was the founder of client-centred therapy, which promotes an equal relationship between therapists and clients and helps clients to achieve their full potential.

4.3 Humanistic Psychology: A New Direction

By the 1950s and 1960s, psychoanalytic and behaviourist theories were at opposite ends of the psychology spectrum, one focusing exclusively on mental processes and the other exclusively on behaviour. The 1960s were a particularly troubled time socially and economically in North America. It was also a time when heated debates took place regarding the relationship between people and authority figures and when questions were raised about essential human rights. In this atmosphere, **humanistic psychology** emerged as an alternative theory that took an optimistic view of human nature and sought to give greater prominence to the special and unique features of human functioning rather than to the mechanistic principles that they believed characterized psychoanalysis and behaviourism. Humanists emphasized the unique qualities of humans and acknowledged their rationality as well as their central human drive for freedom and personal, positive growth.

Founding humanistic theorists Carl Rogers (1902–1987) and Abraham Maslow (1908–1970) rejected the approach of behaviourists. They felt that behaviourists looked at humans just as they looked at animals—that is, as machines that could be predicted and controlled—but giving little or no weight to consciousness and other distinctly human characteristics. Humanism, in contrast, focused on the potential of individuals and highlighted each person's subjectivity, consciousness, free will, and other special human qualities. According to humanistic psychologists, all people have the potential for creativity, positive outlook, and the pursuit of higher values. They claimed that if we can fulfill our full potential, we will inevitably lead a positive life of psychological growth (Wertz, 1998).

Maslow, in fact, proposed that each of us has a basic, broad motive to fulfill our special potential as human beings, which he called the drive for *self-actualization*. He suggested that anyone who achieved this broad motive would indeed lead a positive and fulfilling life. Maslow's hierarchy of human needs is examined further in Part 11.

The humanists developed innovative treatments for psychological adjustment issues and disorders, many of which are frequently used today. Carl Rogers developed a humanistic alternative to the psychoanalytic approach to psychotherapy, which he called **client-centred therapy**. According to Rogers, therapists should respect their clients as equals. He argued that the therapist should establish a trusting and warm relationship with the client by "mirroring" feelings and conveying unconditional support and positive regard for the client. This very human approach to therapy played an important role in the establishment of the fields of clinical and counselling psychology after World War II. We will discuss therapy in greater detail in Part 16.

© Bettmann/Corbis

Abraham Maslow. Maslow prioritized our numerous needs and believed that we must satisfy basic physiological and safety needs first. Only then can we progress up the hierarchy to satisfy other needs and achieve self-actualization.

client-centred therapy an approach to therapy founded by Carl Rogers, based on the notion that the client is an equal and positive gains are made by mirroring clients' thoughts and feelings in an atmosphere of unconditional positive regard.

The humanists believed that behaviourism was too limited in their focus on the objective realm, and that psychoanalysis failed to acknowledge the free will and autonomy of individuals. The goal of humanists, in contrast, was to jolt people from a psychological rut and to help them realize their innate potential for growth. Although humanism did not ultimately have as great an impact on psychology as the schools of behaviourism and psychoanalysis, it sparked a greater appreciation of human consciousness and helped to establish a balance between the prevailing views of psychology. Perhaps most importantly, the movement triggered an increased interest in mental processes.

Maslow believed that only around 2 percent of all people achieve full self-actualization. Such people might be rich or poor, famous or unknown, and from just about any walk of life. To help clarify the notion of self-actualization, however, he listed famous individuals whom he believed were self-actualizers. His list included Albert Einstein, Eleanor Roosevelt (American first lady), Frederick Douglass (American social reformer), Abraham Lincoln, Thomas Jefferson, Jane Addams (first American woman to receive the Nobel Peace Prize), William James, Albert Schweitzer (physician and humanitarian), Walt Whitman (American poet and essayist), Mohandas Ghandi (Indian spiritual and political activist and leader), Martin Luther King, Jr., and George Washington. Why might Maslow have considered these people to be fully self-actualized? What well-known people in today's world might be considered fully self-actualized?

4.4 Cognitive Psychology: Revitalization of Study of the Mind

In the years after World War II, a new school of psychology emerged whose goal was to effectively measure mental processes. The famous psychologist George A. Miller (1920–2012) has recalled that period as a time when "cognition [mental process] was a dirty word because cognitive psychologists were seen as fuzzy, hand-waving, imprecise people who really never did anything that was testable" (Baars, 1986, p. 254). While serving as president of the American Psychological Association in 1960, the Canadian psychologist Donald Hebb (1904–1985) urged the psychological community to apply the rigorous experimental standards seen in behavioural studies—that is, controlled and objective methods—to the study of human thought.

In 1967, Ulric Neisser (1928–2012), a student of Miller's, published the influential text *Cognitive Psychology* in which he described *cognition* as "all the processes by which....sensory input is transformed, reduced, elaborated, stored, recovered, and used" (Neisser, 1967, pg. 4). Neisser went on to define **cognitive psychology** as the study of **information processing**, the means by which information is stored and operates internally. Despite its unpopular beginning, the cognitive perspective is currently the prevailing perspective in psychology.

Cognition is defined as the mental processes involved in knowing, perceiving, and remembering and includes research in areas such as decision-making, problem solving, and understanding language. Many cognitive psychologists compare the human mind to a computer, likening mental processes to the mind's *software* and the human nervous system to the system's *hardware*. Early cognitive psychologists reasoned that if modifying software can control the "behaviour" of computers, identifying and modifying specific mental processes ought to control *human* behaviour. Cognitive psychology has become the dominant model of the mind.

Not surprisingly given their focus, cognitive psychologists focused their attention on the *functioning* of cognitive mechanisms rather than on their content. Cognitive researchers were able to observe the "inputs" and "outputs" of the mental system through carefully controlled experimentation, and then to theorize about the internal mechanisms that must underlie such mental functioning.

Cognitive psychology continues to influence contemporary theory and research into memory, perception, and consciousness, among other areas that we will discuss throughout the text. The rigorous experimental standards established by cognitive scientists continue to define current methods for studying how information is stored and

cognitive psychology the field of psychology studying mental processes as forms of information processing, or the ways in which information is stored and operated in our minds.

information processing the means by which information is stored and operates internally.

cultural psychology the study of how cultural practices shape psychological and behavioural tendencies and influence human behaviour.

cross-cultural psychology the study of what is generally or universally true about human beings regardless of culture.

manipulated by the brain across different situations. Moreover, at the core of a relatively new field called **cultural psychology** is an interest in how cognitive processing may vary across different populations due to the influences of their distinct socio-cultural environments. While cultural psychology looks to see how human thought and action might vary across cultures, **cross-cultural psychology** uses cognitive experimental methods to help distinguish mental processes that are *universal* or common to all humans from those that are shaped by particular variables in the social and physical environment (Jensen, 2011).

4.5 Psychobiology/Neuroscience: Exploring the Origins of the Mind

Interest in the biological basis of psychological phenomena can be traced through the work of Hippocrates, Aristotle, and Pavlov, as well as myriad other researchers, including Freud. Thus, it is not surprising that eventually a distinct area of psychology, called *psychobiology*, emerged. Psychobiology attempts to explain psychological functions by looking primarily at their biological foundations (Gariepy & Blair, 2008; Hergenhahn, 2005). In particular, psychobiology explores brain structure and brain activity and the ways they might be related to individual behaviours and group dynamics. The term *psychobiology* has fallen into disuse, although this subfield of psychology has grown exponentially. It is now referred to as **neuroscience**.

neuroscience the study of psychological functions by looking at biological foundations of those functions.

Early psychobiology gained momentum with the advancement of scientific and medical techniques. Karl Lashley (1890–1958), one of the most influential psychobiologists working in the area of learning and memory, based his work on the study of animal neurological functioning. He used surgical techniques to destroy certain areas in the brains of animals and then observed the effects of such destruction on memory, learning, and other cognitive processes. Lashley found that the tissues within certain areas of the brain were often linked to particular cognitive functions. His ultimate goal was to pinpoint all areas of the brain responsible for memory, learning, and other higher functions. He was never able to fully accomplish this goal, and it continues to be of primary interest in contemporary research.

Canadian neuropsychologist Donald Hebb (1904–1985) developed the concept of the *cell assembly* to describe a network of neurons that develop strengthened internal synaptic connections with repeated stimulation; this assembly activates together during particular mental processes. He strongly opposed radical behaviourism and is often credited for rejuvenating interest in physiological psychology at a time when behaviourism was dominating the field (Klein, 1999).

While working with Donald Hebb and Peter Milner at McGill University, James Olds (1922–1976) discovered the "reward centre" in the brain by demonstrating that electrical stimulation in the brain could evoke emotional responses in animals (Olds & Milner, 1954). They discovered that rats would press a lever for electrical stimulation in a brain area known as the septal region at the same rate as animals working for natural rewards such as food and water (1956, 1958), indicating that the electrical stimulation was rewarding and served as a reinforcer for the lever press.

Roger Sperry (1913–1994), a researcher who was influenced greatly by Lashley, pioneered *split-brain* research on animals. In 1981, Sperry won the Nobel Prize in Physiology and Medicine for his split-brain work (he shared the prize that year with two other Nobel laureates, David Hubel from Canada and Torsten Wiesel from Sweden, for their work on the structure and function of visual cortex). Sperry and his colleagues severed the connections responsible for relaying information between the left and right hemispheres, or halves, of the brain. They found that even after the brain is split surgically, the two hemispheres of animals can often function and learn independently. Later investigators found similar results when they studied human beings who had undergone a similar split-brain surgery to stop severe seizures from spreading from one side of the brain to the other

Chris F. Payne/McGill University Archives, PR000387

Donald Hebb. The Canadian Psychological Association awards the *Donald O. Hebb Award for Distinguished Contributions to Science* to a Canadian psychologist who has made a significant and sustained contribution to the science of psychology.

(Gazzaniga, 2010, 2005). Split-brain research on both animals and humans made it possible to study the separate functioning of the brain's hemispheres, which, as we'll see in Part 3, remains a popular topic in contemporary psychology.

A number of psychological subfields have been influenced by the field of neuroscience, as well as by Darwin's early work on evolution. **Behavioural genetics**, for example, studies the influence of genes on cognition and behaviour. This is not a completely new field. Early in the twentieth century, and even during the rise of behaviourism, a number of animal researchers used evolutionary principles to help explain human behaviour.

Although it can be difficult and at times misleading to identify evolutionary roots for today's behaviours, the study of genetic inheritance continues to play an important role in psychology. Indeed, many investigations conducted over the past two decades have established the importance of genetic influences on human development. Few of today's psychologists question the contribution of genetic factors to mental functioning and behaviour.

Karen Kasmauski/Corbis

Studying the human brain. Neuroscientists examine brain structure and brain activity to determine how they are related to behaviour. Here a researcher dissects the brain of a former patient with dementia as part of a study to learn more about memory and memory disorders.

Similarly, **sociobiologists**, as they were initially called, theorized that humans have an innate concept of how social behaviour should be organized. In 1975, the father of sociobiology, Harvard neurobiologist and naturalist Edward O. Wilson (1929–), a world renowned specialist on ants, brought great attention to this view with his book *Sociobiology: The New Synthesis*. Wilson used sociobiological and evolutionary principles to argue that animal behaviour is governed by epigenetic rules. Epigenetics is the study of how environmental influences affect gene expression and change behaviour (we will discuss epigenetics in greater detail in Part 4). This claim began a heated debate about whether this "biological basis for behaviour" applies to humans. Wilson and other sociobiologists argued that the concept of *tabula rasa* is incorrect because humans are genetically more predisposed than other organisms to learn language, create culture, protect territory, and acquire specific societal rules and regulations. Sociobiologists did not claim that genetic influences are necessarily more important than environmental factors, such as parenting or the mass media. Rather, they proposed that our social behaviour is the result of biological *and* cultural influences. However, they note that the environment is limited by genetics in terms of the influence environmental factors can exert in altering human behaviour.

The subfield of sociobiology is now part of a still broader subfield called **evolutionary psychology**. Evolutionary psychologists maintain that the body and brain are largely products of evolution and that genetic inheritance plays an important role in shaping thought and behaviour (see **Table 4-1**). The laws of evolutionary psychology are thought to apply to all organisms and to a diverse range of mental functions and behaviours (not only social ones), just as the laws of physics apply to matter and energy.

Evolutionary psychology has become a popular topic in contemporary psychology (Confer et al., 2010; Buss, 2009, 2005, 1999). Evolutionary psychologists suggest that some behaviours and mental processes are more effective than others at solving problems of living—namely, those that help people to survive and reproduce. These successful strategies are naturally selected and passed on to future generations. We'll look at evolutionary psychology in greater detail in Part 3.

One goal of evolutionary psychologists is to identify **cultural universality**, human behaviours and practices that occur across all cultures. Just as behaviourists study animal behaviour to identify simple actions that form the basis of more complex human behaviours, evolutionary psychologists believe that uncovering universal human behaviours will help identify inborn functions common to all humans. Theoretically, such knowledge will answer important questions about the relative impact of biological factors and life experiences on our development.

behavioural genetics a subfield of psychology looking at the influence of genes on human behaviour.

sociobiologists theorists who believe humans have a genetically innate concept of how social behaviour should be organized.

evolutionary psychology a field of study believing that the body and brain are products of evolution and that genetic inheritance plays an important role in shaping the complete range of thoughts and behaviours.

cultural universality behaviours and practices that occur across all cultures.

TABLE 4-1 The Major Perspectives in Psychology Today	
Perspectives	**Major Emphases**
Psychoanalytic	Interactions between the conscious and unconscious mind govern virtually all behaviour; childhood experiences set the stage for later psychological functioning.
Behaviourist	Only observable behaviour can be studied scientifically. Perspective focuses on stimulus–response relationships and the consequences for behaviour.
Humanist	People can be helped to realize their full and grand potential, which will inevitably lead to their positive psychological growth.
Cognitive	Mental processes are studied using an information processing model (inputs/outputs).
Neuroscience/ Psychobiological	Psychobiological functions are explained primarily in terms of their biological foundations.
Evolutionary	Behaviour and mental processes are explained in terms of evolution, inheritance, and adaptation.

Thefinalmiracle/Dreamstime/GetStock

Cultural universality. Psychologists are interested in what stays the same and what varies across cultures within human families.

Throughout this book, we'll be observing a number of common practices displayed by people across cultures, such as using specific facial expressions to express emotions, displaying a fear of death, telling stories, and giving gifts (Chomsky, 2005; Brown, 1991). But are such commonalities the direct result of evolutionary forces? Have these behaviours and reactions been passed on from generation to generation largely because they remain highly adaptive? In fact, two evolutionary biologists, Stephen Jay Gould and Richard Lewontin (1979), did not think so. They argued that some of the traits and behaviours seen across cultures are no longer evolutionarily advantageous and instead may be *by-products* of behaviours that served adaptive functions a long time ago. Initially, for example, the human smile may have represented a submissive baring of teeth often seen in animals, designed to ward off attacks by enemies. Over many, many years, however, it has come to be used in human social environments to signal the presence of a friend, or to signal humour.

©iStockphoto.com/azmendoza   ©iStockphoto.com/ruizluquepaz   ©iStockphoto.com/hadynyah   ©iStockphoto.com/hadynyah

That certain look. Facial expressions of sadness (left two photos) and happiness (right two photos) are universal across all cultures. Are these commonalities related to our evolutionary history?

Before You Go On

What Do You Know?

1. Which theorist is most closely associated with psychoanalytic theory—the theory that unconscious conflicts, rooted in childhood, affect much of our behaviour?
2. According to behaviourist theorists, what are the various reinforcement principles, and what impact does each have on behaviour?
3. What did humanist theorist Abraham Maslow suggest is the ultimate goal of human beings?
4. What are cognitions?
5. What is the main idea of evolutionary psychology?

What Do You Think? Which of the theories presented here depend largely on biological principles? Which of the theories seem to be based more on environmental explanations? And which appear to rely on an interaction of factors? Do you find one theory to be more plausible than the others? Why?

Summary

Module 4: Twentieth-Century Approaches

LEARNING OBJECTIVE 4 Summarize the major principles of the psychoanalytical, behaviourist, humanistic, cognitive, and neuroscience approaches to psychology.

- Over the years, different fields of psychology emerged, with different ideas about what was the appropriate area of study for human psychology. Some of the most influential fields were the psychoanalytic, behaviourist, humanistic, cognitive, and neuroscience schools of thought.
- Sigmund Freud's psychoanalytical theory focused on the importance of unconscious mental processes.
- Behaviourists believed strongly that psychology should restrict its focus to the careful study of observable behaviours.
- Humanistic psychologists reacted against the mechanical portrayals of people by the behaviourists, and emphasized individuals' potential for growth and self-actualization.
- Cognitive psychologists reignited interest in the study of mental processes, comparing the workings of the mind to the workings of computers.
- Biological science, including interest in the workings of the brain and in our genetic inheritance, was the major influence on neuroscience approaches.

Key Terms

behavioural genetics 25
behaviourism 19
client-centred therapy 22
cognitive psychology 23
cross-cultural psychology 24

cultural psychology 24
cultural universality 25
evolutionary psychology 25
humanistic psychology 22
information processing 23

neuroscience 24
psychoanalytic theory 18
punishment 21
reinforcement 21
response 19

sociobiologists 25
stimuli 19
unconscious 18

Study Questions

Multiple Choice

1. Which statement best captures Freud's view of the relationship between the conscious and the unconscious minds?
   a) The conscious and unconscious minds operate in isolation from one another.
   b) The conscious and unconscious minds cooperate harmoniously.
   c) The conscious and unconscious minds are often in conflict.
   d) The conscious and unconscious minds are essentially the same.

2. Which twentieth-century perspective in psychology is correctly matched with its emphasis?
   a) psychoanalytic perspective—emphasizes people's motivation to grow and develop and gain control over their destinies
   b) humanistic perspective—emphasizes how people process information
   c) behavioural perspective—emphasizes observable behaviour and objectivity
   d) cognitive psychology—emphasizes the unconscious influences on thought and behaviour

Fill-in-the-Blank

1. Theoretically speaking, undesirable behaviours are less likely to be repeated if the technique of _____ is used.

2. Maslow proposed that we have a basic motive to fulfill our full potential as human beings, which he described as _____.

3. Behavioural genetics and sociobiology can be seen as subfields of _____.

Module 5: Psychology Today

In the contemporary field of psychology, we can recognize the influence of various schools of thought that date back to the days of Greek philosophers. The psychological orientations we have discussed in this part, such as neuroscience, behaviourism, and cognitive science, have not disappeared, but rather continue to develop and interact with one another. Indeed, today there is broad recognition that psychology must be as diverse as the humans whose behaviour it attempts to explain (Sternberg & Grigorenko, 2001).

More detailed information is available now than ever before about how the brain functions, and this information in fact emphasizes the importance of analyzing human thought and behaviour at a variety of levels. Brain-imaging studies have, for example, been used to test behavioural principles, identifying which areas of the brain are activated when a behaviour is performed or when an outcome is better (or worse) than expected (Aguirre, 2010). Similarly, cognitive psychologists and biologists have examined psychoanalytic notions, such as the proposal that our unconscious minds hold memories that might be too anxiety-provoking for our conscious minds. Recent investigations have linked real memories to one pattern of brain activity and false memories to another (Garoff-Eaton, Slotnick, & Schacter, 2006).

As the diversity of the field has increased, so too has the need for there to be communication among its various voices. Indeed, Canada's nearly 19,000 psychologists (Statistics Canada, 2006a) are represented in various professional organizations, including the Canadian Psychological Association (5400 members), the Canadian Society for Brain, Behaviour and Cognitive Science (500 members), and the American Society for Neuroscience (38,000 members), which collectively address the interests and needs of more than 50 different specialties in psychology. **Figure 5-1** shows the variety of fields of study in psychology today.

5.1 Branches of Psychology

The three current key branches of psychology are: *academic psychology*, *clinical and counselling psychology* (including clinical, counselling, and clinical neuropsychology), and *applied psychology* (the rest, including school, rehabilitation, industrial/organizational, health, and forensic psychology). **Figure 5-2** shows the popularity of these three branches of psychology, as well as the subfields within them. Psychologists from all three branches share an interest in mental processes and behaviour. They differ in the amount of emphasis they each place on the psychology of individuals, the discovery of general principles of psychology, and the

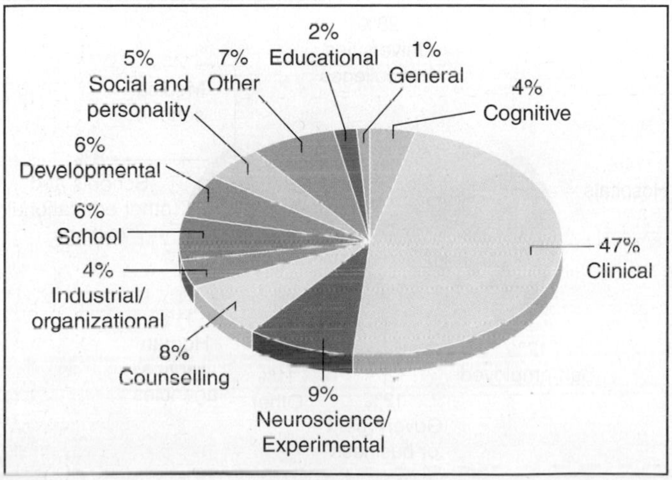

> **LEARNING OBJECTIVE 5**
> Describe the three major branches of psychology and summarize key trends in psychology.

FIGURE 5-1 **Percentage of recent doctorates awarded in each subfield of psychology.** Psychologists today have a wide variety of areas to pursue. Source: Ciccarelli, Saundra K.; White, J. Noland, *Psychology*, 2nd Edition, © 2009, p. 18. Reprinted by permission of Pearson Education, Inc., Upper Saddle River, NJ.

FIGURE 5-2 **The branches of psychology.** Percentage of psychologists in each branch of psychology (based on data from the College of Ontario Psychologists, 2010).

Source: Based on College of Ontario Psychologists, 2010

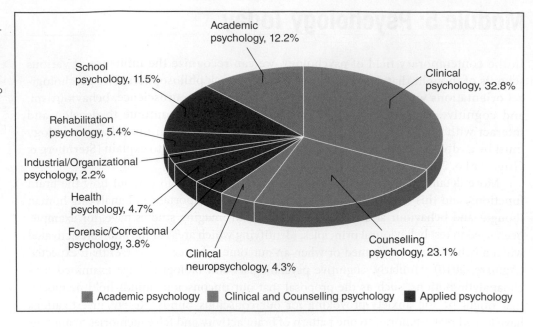

academic psychology a branch of psychology focusing on research and instruction in the various areas or fields of study in psychology.

application of psychological knowledge to groups of people. **Figure 5-3** summarizes the range of settings in which academic, applied, and clinical and counselling psychologists work.

5.1.1 Academic Psychology

When Wilhelm Wundt founded psychology as a discipline distinct from philosophy in 1879, his goal was to examine "pure" academic knowledge and human nature (Hergenhahn, 2005). He did not focus on questions of how psychology could be applied or used outside the laboratory. Today, the branch of psychology known as **academic psychology** involves research and instruction on a wide variety of psychological topics.

Academic psychologists typically work at colleges and universities, where they often divide their time between teaching and conducting research in their particular fields of interest. A *developmental psychologist*, for example, may teach courses on child development while also researching how children think and behave. The efforts of academic researchers have resulted in a large body of psychological knowledge, and, for the most part, the parts throughout this textbook reflect their considerable work and findings.

FIGURE 5-3 **Where psychologists work.** The primary work settings for recent Ph.D. graduates in psychology are post-secondary institutions, hospitals, the government, businesses, and human-service agencies. Source: Ciccarelli, Saundra K.; White, J. Noland, *Psychology*, 2nd Edition, © 2009, p. 18. Reprinted by permission of Pearson Education, Inc., Upper Saddle River, NJ.

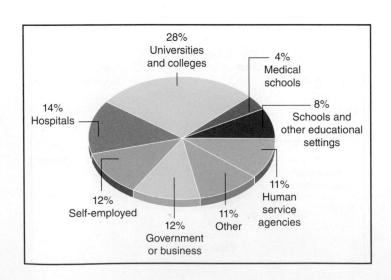

Psychology is the study of behaviour and mental life. Students who major in psychology gain a broad understanding of what makes people "tick" from a wide range of perspectives, including developmental, social, clinical, and biological. They also acquire a body of knowledge and set of skills that help qualify them for a broad range of career choices.

Individuals who want to become psychologists will find that an undergraduate degree in psychology prepares them to pursue graduate degrees in any number of psychology subfields, including clinical, health, cognitive, social, neuroscience, organizational, educational, and sports psychology. Alternatively, being an undergraduate major in psychology can help open the door to graduate study in many other fields, such as law, business management, economics, and medicine.

Even if graduate study is not for you, an undergraduate degree in psychology can lead to interesting jobs and careers. Psychology majors are typically viewed by prospective employers as well-qualified to work in fields that require people skills, as well as having strong analytical, research, and writing abilities. "But," you might say, "just about every job deals with people." Yes, that's the point.

An undergraduate degree in psychology particularly qualifies individuals for entry-level jobs in people-oriented careers such as communications, marketing, human resources, sales, and business. Beyond people skills, the analytic, research, and writing skills of psychology majors enhance their eligibility for human-service, legal, and law-enforcement jobs, including positions as paralegals and corrections officers. Furthermore, the same skills may make individuals good candidates for

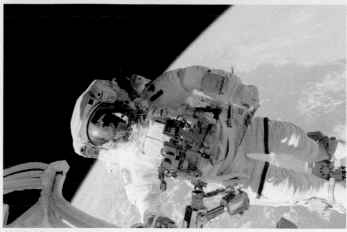
Canadian Space Agency/NASA

Psychology's wide influence. Astronaut Chris Hadfield on a mission STS-100 spacewalk. The Canadian Space Agency has two directorates (the Canadian Astronaut Office and Space Sciences) that focus on applied psychological and neuroscience research to maximize astronauts' performance.

careers in general business, marketing research, management consulting, computer game design, and investment banking.

In short, psychology is related to so much in our world that a degree in this discipline can lead to work and careers in more areas and fields than you might imagine. Keep in mind, for example, that psychologists Daniel Kahneman (2002) and Herbert Simon (1978) are Nobel Laureates in *economics*, while the neuroscientists Eric Kandel (2000), Rita Levi-Montalcini (1986), and Roger Sperry (1981) won their Nobel Prizes in *medicine* and *physiology*.

5.1.2 Applied Psychology

Today, the branch of psychology called **applied psychology** involves the application of psychological principles to help solve practical problems in education, marketing, and other fields (Davey, 2011). Lawyers may consult with psychologists to help determine who to select for a jury or how best to defend a client. Advertisers may consult with psychologists to conduct research to determine how best to market products to teenagers. Throughout this book, we will examine a wide range of research developments, both those with immediate practical applications and those that serve to further our insights about the human mind and behaviour. There are also a number of specialized programs of study within applied psychology. *Sports psychologists*, for example, may provide guidance to athletes or teams, helping them overcome feelings of anxiety or frustration or teaching them to focus their energy more effectively.

applied psychology the branch of psychology applying psychological principles to practical problems in other fields, such as education, marketing, or industry.

5.1.3 Clinical and Counselling Psychology

Clinical and counselling psychology help individuals to cope more effectively or to overcome abnormal functioning. Actually, there are several different types of mental-health practitioners.

clinical and counselling psychology the study of abnormal psychological behaviour and interventions designed to change that behaviour.

Clemens Bilan/AFP/Getty Images

The couch. Sigmund Freud's signature therapy procedure was to have patients lie on a couch and say whatever came to mind while he took notes behind them. This wax recreation of the neurologist and his office is on display at a museum in Berlin, Germany.

- *Clinical psychologists* generally provide *psychotherapy*, which involves helping people to modify thoughts, feelings, and behaviours that are causing them distress or inhibiting their functioning. They also may administer and interpret psychological tests to provide further information relevant to treatment. Many clinical psychologists earn a Ph.D. degree awarded by a university graduate program, which typically requires training in therapeutic practices and in the conduct and interpretation of research. Some clinical psychologists earn a Psy.D. (doctorate of psychology) degree. This degree is awarded by graduate programs that place less emphasis on research and greater emphasis on psychotherapy and psychological testing. As well, clinical psychologists who wish to practise psychotherapy in Canada must be registered with their provincial College of Psychologists, which establishes and oversees practice guidelines and the ethics of clinical practice.

- Counselling psychologists and psychiatric social workers also provide psychotherapy for people with psychological problems. These professionals may also help individuals and families deal with issues tied to relationships, careers, child-rearing, and other important areas of functioning. In addition, some social workers provide aid to families through social service systems that are available in the community. Counselling psychologists earn a Ph.D. or Psy.D. in their field, while social workers earn either an M.S.W. (masters of social work) or D.S.W. (doctorate of social work) degree from a school of social work.

- Canadian psychologists are not able to prescribe drugs for their clients. In the United States, only New Mexico and Louisiana currently grant prescription privileges to psychologists who receive special pharmacological training. The U.S. territory of Guam also grants such privileges to psychologists.

- Psychiatrists, who may also provide guidance and therapy to individuals, are professionals who attend medical school and earn an M.D. (doctorate of medicine). Psychiatrists generally have less training in psychological research and testing than clinical psychologists, but they have medical knowledge and the ability to prescribe medications for abnormal emotional states or behaviour problems.

5.2 Shared Values

Although the three branches of psychology—academic, applied, and clinical and counselling—have different goals and ways of meeting those goals, they do share important values that guide their work. Many of those values will shape our discussions throughout this textbook, so let's take a look at them here.

- *Psychology is theory-driven.* If you're going to explain human behaviour, you have to have a theory. We will describe the elements of a good theory in Part 2. Psychologists have developed theories, or potential answers, for many key questions: Do mental processes exist? What are the relative roles of biological inheritance and environmental influence in shaping human psychology? How do we explain deviant behaviour, such as bullying? Each school of psychology provides ideas to help answer such questions. And every branch of psychology uses its potential answers to guide research or improve psychological interventions.

- *Psychology is empirical.* From the beginning, psychology differed from other human disciplines, such as philosophy, because of its emphasis on controlled observations and experimentation. Psychology finds more use and value in ideas that receive strong empirical, or research, support than in ideas, even seemingly compelling ones that cannot be supported with evidence from systematic testing.

- *Psychology is multi-level.* As we discussed at the beginning of this part, to understand the complete picture of human mental processes and behaviour, psychologists must account for what is happening at the levels of the brain, the person, and the group. Although certain theories place more emphasis on one level than another, all of the levels are indeed operating to influence whatever mental process or behaviour we may be observing. Thus, in parts throughout this textbook, we will be presenting evidence about what happens at each of these three levels.
- *Psychology is contextual.* At one time the thought of Internet social networks—actually, even the thought of the Internet—was unimaginable to most people. As the history of psychology shows, however, technological advances have had a strong influence on the development, rise, and fall of particular theories. Without the computer, for example, the field of cognitive psychology would have been described very differently. In fact, technological and other societal changes force us to look at human behaviour from new perspectives that broaden our awareness. All of this means that some of the theories you're studying today may eventually go the way of structuralism—influential but dramatically changed in nature. This is the way that science progresses.

5.3 Current Trends in Psychology

The values of psychology—theory-driven, empirical, multi-level, and contextual—work together to drive constant progress and change in the field. Today, those values, as well as larger social developments, are shaping several trends in psychology. In particular, the field is growing more diverse, continuing to profit from technological advances, and continuing to give birth to new schools of thought.

5.3.1 Growing Diversity

Early in the history of psychology, few women or members of racial minority groups were able to obtain the advanced education and professional status necessary to contribute to the field. As psychology itself has grown more diverse, however, so have psychologists. As well, psychology now has more women earning graduate degrees than does any other science. Indeed, 70.5 percent of psychologists in Canada are women (Statistics Canada, 2006). In addition, 16 percent of newly earned Ph.D.s are awarded to minority group members, compared to 7 percent 30 years ago (APA, 2009).

collectivist a culture whose members focus more on the needs of the group and less on individual desires.

individualistic a culture that places the wants or desires of the person over the needs of the group.

Growing diversity among psychologists has overlapped with an increased interest in the diversity of the people they study, treat, and influence. *Cultural psychology* has, for example, become an important area of investigation. As we observed earlier, this field of study seeks to uncover mental processes that exist across all cultures, as well as important cultural differences.

©iStockphoto.com/Wavebreak

Cultural psychologists often focus on differences between **collectivist** cultures and **individualistic** cultures. Members of *collectivist* cultures emphasize the needs of the group and subsume individual desires to those of the family or peer group. In contrast, *individualistic* cultures stress the needs of persons over those of the group. One study of differences between these two types of cultures examined positive emotions, such as happiness. Individuals from Eastern cultures, which tend to be more collectivist, and Western cultures, which tend to be more individualistic, appear to hold different beliefs about the sources of happiness. When asked to talk about events that make them feel happy, Chinese research participants focused on interpersonal interactions and evaluations from others, while Western participants pointed to personal achievement and self-evaluation (Lu & Shih, 1997).

Growth of women Ph.D.s in psychology. Over a 30-year period, the increase in the percentage of women earning Ph.D.s has been dramatic, especially in the clinical, developmental, and counselling fields (Gathercoal et al., 2010; Cynkar, 2007).

Psychology Around Us — Notable Women in Psychology

As you have already no doubt observed, the early history of psychology largely recognizes the work of men, as is typical of most fields. Nevertheless, from early on women were very much involved in shaping psychology. A small number of these women's contributions are noted below. Today the majority of our undergraduate and graduate students in psychology are women. Here are but a few of the field's female pioneers (Keates & Stam, 2009).

- The work of Mary Whilton Calkins (1863–1930) was noteworthy for her emphasis on the self, consciousness, emotions, and dreams, which stood in stark contrast to John Watson's behaviourist movement at the time. Calkins was the first woman president of the American Psychological Association (APA).
- Leta Hollingsworth (1886–1939) was best known for her studies of "mentally deficient" and "mentally gifted" individuals, and for her views on gender differences in mental functioning. She was one of the first theorists of her time to challenge the notion that women were biologically inferior, arguing instead that women were victims of a male-dominated social order.
- Magda Arnold (1903–2002) is generally thought of as the "mother of modern emotion theory" (Keates & Stam, 2009). She received her Ph.D. at the University of Toronto in 1942. Her book *Emotion and Personality* (1960) consolidated her position as a leader in emotion research.
- Mary Salter Ainsworth (1913–1999) was also a University of Toronto graduate, obtaining her Ph.D. in 1939. She is internationally known for her work on mother–infant attachment and for the development of the Strange Situation method of assessing attachment in toddlers.
- Mary Wright (1915–2014) is best known for her work on the history of Canadian psychology. She also wrote of the history of the development of the Canadian Psychological Association. She was elected the first woman president of the CPA in 1968.
- Brenda Milner (1918–) has been a pioneer in the study of memory and other cognitive functions in humans. She was the first to investigate how damage to the brain's hippocampus affects memory through her study of a famous amnesia patient known as H.M. in the research literature.
- For further information, Alexandra Rutherford at York University maintains a website for the American Psychological Society: Society for the Psychology of Women Heritage at www.psych.yorku.ca/femhop.

Research has also indicated that even within a broad culture, subcultures may differ with regard to happiness. Studies have shown, for example, that positive emotions—such as strong self-acceptance—are, on average, a bit lower among individuals from southern parts of the United States than among those from the West or Midwest. Some researchers have hypothesized that these lower levels of well-being and self-acceptance may reflect a subculture that is relatively more concerned with showing hospitality and respecting tradition than with fostering positive self-concepts and promoting personal growth (Markus et al., 2004).

5.3.2 Advances in Technology

As we observed earlier, technological shifts also contribute to shifts in psychological theory. The development of computers in the 1950s and 1960s contributed to the cognitive psychology revolution. Technology has continued to change the face of science and psychology in more recent years. Innovations such as brain imaging and effective pharmacological, or drug, treatments for mental disorders have revealed a great deal about human mental processes and behaviour. As you'll see in Part 3, for example, the development of brain-imaging technology has made it possible for researchers to directly observe activity in the brain.

In fact, in recent years a new area of psychological study and theory has emerged: **cognitive neuroscience** focuses not only on mental processes, but also on how mental processes interact with the biological functions of the brain. That is, what happens in the brain when we are remembering something, making a decision, or paying attention to something? One goal of cognitive neuroscientists is to link specific mental processes to particular brain activities. Similarly, a field called **social neuroscience** has emerged,

cognitive neuroscience the study of mental processes and how they relate to the biological functions of the brain.

social neuroscience the study of social functioning and how it is tied to brain activity.

which seeks to link social functioning to particular brain activities. Recent studies have, for example, found that there is a network of nerve cells in the brain that is activated when we show empathy, our ability to understand the intentions of others.

Cognitive and social neuroscience are currently among psychology's more active areas of theory and research. We have indicated sections relevant to neuroscience research throughout the book with the icon "What Happens in the Brain?" In these sections, you'll learn about the neuroscience of memory, emotions, social behaviour, and the like. You'll discover, for example, what happens in the brain when you are learning new material before an important test, and then again when you get together with friends to celebrate the completion of that test.

The development of imaging tools, computer technology, and a number of biological techniques has also helped enhance our understanding and treatment of mental dysfunction in recent years. These tools have enabled researchers to look directly at the brains of disturbed persons while they are feeling sad or anxious, hearing voices, or recalling repressed memories. Such studies have helped reveal that depression, for example, is related not only to traumatic childhood experiences, significant losses in life, and feelings of helplessness, but also to abnormal activity of key chemicals in the brain. Given such wide-ranging insights, we have indicated relevant sections throughout the book with the icon "Facing Adversity." In these sections, we discuss what happens when typical psychological processes, such as memory, emotional coping, social engagement, and so on develop in a different way.

At first glance, psychology's intensified focus on the brain may make it appear that technology and biology are dominating contemporary psychology. However, it is unlikely that psychology will ever be overtaken by biology. Indeed, recent findings in cognitive neuroscience and other areas suggest that our insights about mental functions (and dysfunctions) and about behaviour are most complete when the different branches of the field intersect and cooperate. In clinical psychology, for example, it is now clear that many mental disorders are best understood and treated when explanations and techniques from different schools of thought are combined.

One important area of psychology that has intersected with other areas of the field for many years is developmental psychology, the study of how we change over the course of our lives. Developmental psychology has both incorporated and contributed to research in areas such as our use of language, our emotions, our personalities, and the structure of our brains. We indicate the cross-fertilization of development with other areas throughout the book with the icon "How We Develop."

5.3.3 New Schools of Thought

As we saw earlier, historical schools of thought in psychology sow the seeds for related but new ideas. We can see, for example, influences of the functionalists, who were interested in applying psychological research, and the humanists, who were interested in helping people achieve their highest potential, when we look at a relatively new movement in the field called *positive psychology*. Positive psychology studies human strengths, fulfillment, and creativity (Compton & Hoffman, 2013; Synder, Lopez, & Pedrotti, 2011). Positive psychologists point out that psychology is too focused on psychopathology, psychological damage, and ways to heal suffering. They argue that psychology ought to also consider the factors that make life worthwhile, including

Ian Berry/Magnum Photos

Accentuating the positive. Residents of a small Spanish village cry out in joy as they are drenched with 30 tonnes of water during a water festival. Positive psychologists study the impact that happiness and positive emotions have on human functioning.

happiness, meaning in life, and character strengths, as well as increased attention to how those features of positive living might be more readily developed (Baumgardner & Crothers, 2009; Seligman & Csikszentmihalyi, 2000; Seligman, 2002). In fact, an estimated 150 psychology departments in the United States now offer courses in positive psychology (Senior, 2006).

A growing body of research does indeed suggest that positive emotions can have a profound impact on development and behaviour. As you'll see in a later part, when we discuss stress, coping, and health, a number of studies have found that having a positive outlook promotes *resilience*, the ability to bounce back in the face of adversity (Garbarino, 2011). Similarly, studies indicate that positive emotions may boost the functioning of our immune systems. Research even suggests that our emotions help influence how well we resist common colds (Cohen et al., 2008, 2003)!

In Part 16, we'll see that some psychologists have even developed a new form of therapy, called *positive psychotherapy*. This type of therapy does not target specific symptoms of mental dysfunction, but rather focuses on increasing the positive emotions and sense of engagement and meaning experienced by clients (Seligman et al., 2006). According to proponents of positive psychology, certain techniques and behaviours can be of particular help to people in their efforts to achieve happiness or return to happiness after unpleasant events.

5.3.4 What Changes and What Remains Constant?

Since the early years of Greek philosophy, theorists have attempted to determine how the human mind operates and whether there are universal laws that govern mental processes and behaviours. Those questions remain at the forefront of contemporary psychology as today's neuroscientists, cultural theorists, and other psychologists try to determine how the mind and body are related, whether there are knowable universal truths about mental processes and human behaviours, and whether such truths are best understood through the perspective of the brain, the individual, or the group, or a particular combination of the three. It is not likely that psychology can ever provide complete answers to these complex questions. However, striving to uncover even partial answers has already uncovered a wealth of information about how human beings function and has produced a range of compelling theories and research findings.

As you read about these theories and findings throughout this textbook, you will do well to keep asking yourself a question raised by Carl Jung (1875–1961), one of the field's most famous clinical theorists: "How much truth [is] captured by this [particular] viewpoint?" Ideas move in and out of vogue, and what is accepted today as a useful or accurate outlook might not be seen the same way tomorrow.

Both historical and social forces determine the focus of scientific energy. Psychology, perhaps more than any other field, struggles constantly to achieve a proper balance between popular trends and interests, societal influences, and scientific objectivity (Leahey, 2000). Although fads and fashions will likely continue to exert some influence on the development of psychology in the coming years, it is important to recognize that such fads hardly comprise the substance of the field. Moreover, we must always keep in mind the limitations of psychology (or of any discipline) in answering the basic questions of human existence. As we noted at the beginning of this part, scientific knowledge serves as a *means* for exploring such questions rather than an end.

What Do You Know?
1. What are the three major branches of psychology?
2. What is cultural universality, and what kinds of psychologists are interested in it?
3. What is the focus of positive psychology?

What Do You Think? Which branch of psychology most appeals to you as a potential profession? Why? What kinds of things do you think would be important for positive psychologists to study?

Summary

Module 5: Psychology Today

LEARNING OBJECTIVE 5 Describe the three major branches of psychology and summarize key trends in psychology.

- The theoretical and cultural diversity of the field of psychology has increased dramatically over recent years.
- There are three key branches of psychology: academic, applied, and clinical/counselling.
- Across the three branches and many specialty areas in psychology, psychologists are united by their shared values. Psychologists generally agree that psychology is *theory-driven*, *empirical*, *multi-level*, and *contextual*.
- Currently, psychology appears to be developing as a science in response to a growing diversity throughout the field, advances in *technology* (such as brain scanning), and the development of *new schools* such as positive psychology.

Key Terms

academic psychology 30

applied psychology 31

clinical and counselling psychology 31

cognitive neuroscience 34

collectivist 33

individualistic 33

social neuroscience 34

Study Questions

Multiple Choice

1. The advent of computer technology in the 1950s and 1960s spurred growth in the field of _____. More recently, advances in imaging have sparked growth in the field of _____.
   a) cognitive psychology; neuroscience
   b) neuroscience; cognitive psychology
   c) experimental psychology; neuroscience
   d) developmental psychology; neuroscience

2. A cultural psychologist would describe American culture as _____ and would describe Chinese culture as _____.
   a) individualistic; collectivist
   b) individualistic; communal
   c) collectivist; collectivist as well
   d) individualistic; individualistic as well

Fill-in-the-Blank

1. A _____ psychologist would likely help individuals cope more effectively or overcome abnormal functioning.

2. A new school of thought that focuses on the more upbeat features of human functioning like happiness and the meaning of life is referred to as _____.

PART 2

PSYCHOLOGY AS A SCIENCE

Here is a simple question: Does watching a violent program on television or playing a violent video game cause people to become more aggressive or violent? Should we be especially concerned about the sorts of programs and images that children are watching on television or the sorts of games children and adolescents are playing online? What do you think?

From children's cartoons, to dramatic programs, to televised hockey (*Hockey Night in Canada*), to games like *Grand Theft Auto* and *Call of Duty* (which are supposed to be restricted to older adolescent use but rarely actually are), there are many opportunities to see acts of aggression and violence on television and to virtually engage in such acts while gaming. But does watching or gaming acts of aggression and violence make children more aggressive and violent? It may be the case that watching violence or playing violent games provides children with ideas for behaviours that would not otherwise have occurred to them. It also may be that exposure to video violence suggests that violence is an acceptable way to solve disputes. On the other hand, it may be that children who are already prone to violent behaviour as a result of their genes, temperaments, and the ways they have been raised seek out more violent television programs and prefer to play more violent games. In that case, their viewing and gaming patterns are just symptoms of other violence-causing factors.

Many people have strong opinions about this issue, but what we really need to answer the question is some good scientific research. How would you design a study to examine whether watching violent programming or playing violent video games makes children behave more violently? The design process is complicated by the fact that virtually every household in Canada already has at least one television in it, and most Canadian children have access to some sort of gaming system (Gorman, 1996). So children who have not watched violent television programming or played violent games might be hard to find and might not be representative of the "typical" Canadian child.

So is there a straightforward answer to the question of whether watching violence on television or playing violent video games makes children more violent? The question is so complex that one study will certainly not provide a clear answer. In terms of television violence, Jonathan Freedman, a social psychologist at the University of Toronto, in his book *Media Violence and its Effects on Aggression* (2002), concludes that "the scientific evidence simply does not show that watching violence either produces violence in people, or desensitizes them to it." In terms of gaming violence, the case seems to be a bit clearer, with exposure

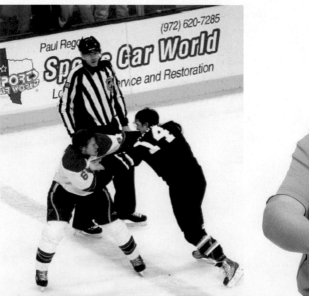

Dreamstime/GetStock   ©iStockphoto.com/karelnoppe

Viewing violence and gaming violence. It may be that watching or engaging in virtual acts of aggression and violence models that behaviour for children or suggests that it is an appropriate way to behave.

to violent video games being linked to increases in violent behaviour, aggressive thoughts, and feelings, and decreases in levels of helping behaviour (Anderson, 2004).

It is evident that even seemingly simple questions do not have simple answers. Welcome to the challenge of designing and conducting good research into human behaviour.

In this part, you'll find out exactly what the scientific research methods of psychologists are and how psychologists use them. We'll begin the part by defining what science is. Then we'll consider just how well psychology fits with the definition of a science, particularly in comparison to other fields. Next, we'll examine in some detail the methods that psychologists use to conduct research, including, by way of example, research into the nature and impact of television viewing habits. Finally, we'll look at the statistics that help researchers interpret their results and the ethical rules that guide them when working with humans or animals.

Module 6: What Is a Science?

LEARNING OBJECTIVE 6 List two core beliefs of science, and describe the steps in the scientific method.

Before we look at psychology in particular, take a moment to try to answer the general question, what is a science? You might answer by listing types of sciences, such as chemistry, biology, or physics. You might envision a white-coated person in a lab, mixing strangely bubbling chemicals or lecturing students about where to start an incision on the frog in the tray in front of them. Such things are only *sometimes* associated with science. Two characteristics that all sciences share, however, are similar principles, or beliefs, about how best to understand the world, and reliance on the *scientific method* as a way to discovering and sharpening knowledge.

6.1 Scientific Principles

Joe Raedle/Getty Images

Law seeking. This meteorologist relies on physical laws to describe and predict the force and path of hurricanes. Similarly, psychologists seek out laws that describe and predict mental processes and behaviour.

Science is built on a foundation of core beliefs about the world. Two essential beliefs are as follows:

- *The universe operates according to certain natural laws.* Scientists believe that things happen in and around us in some kind of orderly fashion that can be described using rules or laws. The natural law of cause and effect, for example, suggests that when something is set in motion, it has an effect on other things. Psychologists look for the laws that describe mental processes and behaviour.
- *Such laws are discoverable and testable.* By carefully observing what happens in the natural world, we can figure out the laws governing those events. In turn, we can use these laws to make predictions about what might happen, and we can then experiment to see whether those predictions come true.

As a natural science, psychology operates according to these two core beliefs. Psychology also shares with other sciences a similar logical approach to discovering and testing laws about how things happen: the scientific method (Lalasz, 2011).

6.2 The Scientific Method

deductive reasoning reasoning proceeding from broad basic principles applied to specific situations.

The scientific method relies on processes of logical reasoning derived from philosophy. One way to apply our knowledge of the world is to start with big, general ideas (broad basic principles), and then apply those ideas to specific situations. This approach is called **deductive reasoning**. If you have ever bet (with friends for no money, of course) that a particular team will win a playoff game because it is the home team and you believe the home team has an advantage, then you have used deductive reasoning (home teams win more often than visitors, so I will bet that the home team wins). Can you think of any problems with this approach to reasoning?

biases distorted beliefs based on a person's subjective sense of reality.

Sir Francis Bacon, a British philosopher and statesman in the early 1600s, was one of the first to question the deductive reasoning approach (O'Hara, 2010). Bacon felt deductive reasoning was too susceptible to the thinker's **biases**—personal beliefs or conventional wisdom that a particular thinker mistakenly accepts as broad, basic truths. We all want our own home team to win, so maybe that hope affects our ability to make objective predictions as to who will win an important playoff game. We'll see throughout this book that psychological research has shown many times that widely accepted conventional wisdom can be incomplete, biased, or just plain wrong. For example, people typically consider themselves to be free and independent thinkers who will always stand up for what they believe to be right. As we'll discuss in Part 13, however, scientists have been able to demonstrate that, when confronted by an authority figure or even just a small group of people with opposite views, many people go along with the higher authority or the crowd rather than follow their own beliefs.

How might we avoid this sort of bias? Well we could start small and focused and build up to a big understanding. What if we made careful observations of how a number of teams do at home and away over the course of several seasons, and then use the total of home and away wins to decide if there is a *home arena effect*? Bacon argued that this type of approach, which proceeds in the opposite direction—from specific facts or observations to general ideas—would avoid bias. Such processes are called **inductive reasoning**. Here, thinkers use controlled direct observations to generate broad conclusions, and over time such conclusions are combined to achieve non-biased truths about the laws of the universe.

Psychologists using inductive reasoning would begin the search for natural laws by making **empirical**, or objectively testable, observations of mental processes and behaviours (e.g., things people actually do or think). Their cumulative observations would in turn lead them to develop **theories**, or big ideas about the laws that govern those processes and behaviours.

Today, inductive reasoning is still seen to be a key part of much scientific research. There are so many factors governing human behaviour, however, that if psychologists were to rely entirely on induction, or observation, they could never discover and specify all of the potential factors affecting human behaviour—the factors needed to generate accurate broad theories. Thus, to build on the best of both deductive and inductive reasoning approaches, psychologists today typically employ a blended model known as **hypothetico-deductive reasoning** (Sprenger, 2011; Locke, 2007). They begin with a deductive process: identifying a hypothesis.

According to the famous philosopher Karl Popper (1902–1994), a sound scientific theory must establish, in advance, the observations that would refute it (Popper, 1963, 1959). In other words, a sound, properly organized theory runs the risk of being proven false. To test the soundness of their theories, researchers create **hypotheses**, specific statements that are objectively falsifiable (that is, they can be disproved). A physicist, for example, might generate a hypothesis based on a theory of weight and gravity, which states that objects of different weights will fall at different rates. If researchers (such as Galileo) were then to discover that cannon balls of different weights, when dropped at the same time from the same height, hit the ground at the same time, the hypothesis would be disproved and scientists would have to reconsider their theory of the relationship between weight and gravity (involving a standard rate of acceleration for all falling objects when air resistance is controlled).

Similarly, in the hypothetico-deductive approach, psychologists set out to create controlled observations that will prove or disprove their hypotheses. In many cases, research results do indeed disprove their hypotheses. Psychologists may then reject or modify their theories and generate new hypotheses for further testing. Through repetition of this process, theories evolve over time to become more and more accurate explanations of human thought and behaviour. **Figure 6-1** outlines this approach.

inductive reasoning reasoning process proceeding from small specific situations to more general truths.

empirical able to be tested in objective ways.

theories ideas about laws that govern phenomena.

hypothetico-deductive reasoning process of modern science where scientists begin with an educated guess, perhaps based on previous research, about how the world works, and then set about designing small controlled observations to support or invalidate that hypothesis.

hypothesis a general statement about the way variables relate that is objectively falsifiable.

DEDUCTIVE REASONING	INDUCTIVE REASONING	HYPOTHETICO-DEDUCTIVE REASONING
Theory	Observation/experiment	Hypothesis
Predictions	Predictions	Observation/experiment
Observation/experiment	Theory	Hypothesis supported or not supported: theory built

FIGURE 6-1 **Reasoning and the scientific method.** Several different kinds of reasoning may be used as scientists carry out their work. Most psychological researchers use the hypothetico-deductive approach.

As we discussed at the beginning of the part, many people have ideas about whether watching violence on television causes people to exhibit more violent behaviour. To produce a scientific theory about the effects of televised aggression and violence, people would need to step outside their personal beliefs to avoid bias. A scientific approach would involve the steps described below:

- *Make observations.* We might first examine what teenagers do after playing a video game containing virtual violence. For example, do they exhibit aggressive behaviour in social situations after playing *Call of Duty* for two hours? That is, do they engage in behaviours that suggest increased levels of aggression and violence?

- *Develop hypotheses.* After making such observations, we would generate hypotheses about what led to the behaviour we observed. If the gamers acted more aggressively, for example, did the game's aggressive play cause players to think of their fellow human beings in a more negative light? Or were the players simply modelling themselves after the game characters? Whatever our explanation, we would generate a falsifiable hypothesis to test. One hypothesis, for example, might be that players increase their levels of aggressiveness in social interaction in response to spending two hours virtually interacting with violent game characters.

- *Test hypotheses.* As we'll see in this part, there are several kinds of research studies we could conduct to see if this hypothesis can be disproved.

- *Build a theory.* If the hypothesis is, indeed, disproved, we might modify or even throw it out and develop and test a new hypothesis. If our hypothesis that people who play *Call of Duty* change their behaviour to be more like the players in the game is not disproved, we might test it further. We might, for example, decide to study the players of a variety of video games (e.g., *Grand Theft Auto, Minecraft*, or *Diablo III*). If the results continue to support our hypothesis, the hypothesis can become a theory. A theory, in turn, can become a framework to generate additional hypotheses

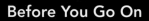

Before You Go On

www.wiley.com/go/comercanada

What Do You Know?

1. What are the two core beliefs of a science?
2. What is the difference between inductive and deductive reasoning?
3. What is the difference between a hypothesis and a theory?
4. What is the hypothetico-deductive method?

What Do You Think? Based on what you know about the scientific method, do you think psychology is a science in the same way chemistry, biology, and physics are sciences?

Summary

Module 6: What Is a Science?

LEARNING OBJECTIVE 6 List two core beliefs of science, and describe the steps in the scientific method.

- Science is an approach to knowing the world built on the core principles that (1) the universe operates according to certain natural laws, and (2) these laws are discoverable and testable.
- Science is founded upon the scientific method, a process that moves from making controlled, direct observations to generating progressively broader conclusions and tests and attempting to disprove hypotheses.

Key Terms

biases 42

deductive reasoning 42

empirical 43

hypothesis 43

hypothetico-deductive
reasoning 43

inductive reasoning 43

theories 43

Study Questions

Multiple Choice

1. A given field of study is defined as a science by virtue of its
   a) scientific methods.
   b) equipment.
   c) subject matter
   d) findings.

2. Most psychologists today use a type of reasoning termed _____ reasoning.
   a) theoretico-inductive
   b) theoretico-deductive
   c) hypothetico-inductive
   d) hypothetico-deductive

3. Which approach to psychology advocated focus on observable behaviours only?
   a) hypothetico-deductive
   b) inductive reasoning
   c) pseudopsychology
   d) behaviourism

Fill-in-the-Blank

1. The natural law of _____ suggests that when something is set in motion, it has an effect on other things.

2. Ideas that psychologists develop about the laws that govern processes and behaviour are called _____.

Module 7: Is Psychology a Science?

As we saw in Part 1, prior to the nineteenth century, psychology was a field based largely on philosophy, religion, and even mysticism. With a rise in the popularity of animal research in the nineteenth century, however, scientists began to develop an increased interest in physiology and how human actions are tied to innate biological functions. Charles Darwin's theories on evolution, along with advances in the field of biology, raised questions about the interactions between humans and our environments. Given such roots, many credit the influence of biological science for shifting psychology from a philosophy toward becoming a science (Hergenhahn, 2005).

Although psychology is now defined as a natural science that uses experimental methods to study mental processes and behaviour, it does differ from the physical sciences, such as biology, in key ways, including how it pursues scientific goals and its role in influencing personal and social values.

7.1 Goals of Psychology

As we saw in Part 1, all sciences share the goals of describing, explaining, predicting, and controlling the phenomena they study. However, the emphasis each field places on these goals may vary. One key difference between psychology and the physical sciences, for example, is in the area of description. A core goal of many physical sciences is to isolate and describe the smallest elements that contribute to a larger whole. Biologists look at how a cell contributes to the overall functioning of an organism, for example. Chemists and physicists examine how atoms and subatomic particles make up the structure of, well, everything. Although psychology also attempts to isolate fundamental elements of behaviour and mental processes, psychologists face an additional task because behaviour is determined by many such factors simultaneously.

The basic factors that affect behaviour can be temporary or permanent fixtures in a person's life. The atomic structure of gold, for example, is the same in all gold all over the world, but a complex behaviour, such as reading this textbook, cannot be broken down into a standard set of elements that work the same for every person. The reading behaviour of a student might be influenced by a temporary factor, such as anticipation of an upcoming exam, which does not affect the reading behaviour of non-students. The idea behind psychological research is both to *isolate* the relative contribution of such factors and to think about how these factors *come together* across different situations to influence human behaviour.

© ARISTIDE ECONOMOPOULOS/Star Ledger/Corbis

Multiple influences. Behaviour is complex and is determined by many factors operating simultaneously. What different factors—temporary, permanent, or both—might be influencing each of these people to take part in a Polar Bear Club swim?

Psychologists face an additional challenge because much of what they study does not have a clear and observable physical reality like the basic units of study in other scientific fields. With the help of special tools, scientists in those fields can observe even the tiniest bits of matter, including atoms and DNA. Of course, this is also true of psychology *to some degree*. Behaviours, sensations, or physiological responses, for example, can be directly observed, measured, and explained. In his review of science, the great German philosopher Immanuel Kant suggested that when studying phenomena such as these, psychology is indeed empirical and very close to a "real" science (Kant, 2003). Other psychologists, such as the behaviourist B. F. Skinner, also advocated this view of psychology. In fact, as we saw in Part 1, many behaviourists have stated that, as scientists, psychologists should study *only* what is directly observable.

©iStockphoto.com/fotostorm

©iStockphoto.com/nyul

Thoughts versus behaviours. Thoughts cannot be observed directly, but behaviours can. Thus psychologists can be more certain about the romantic feelings of the woman on the right than those of the woman on the left.

On the other hand, as Kant himself observed, many of the processes that form the basis of psychology cannot be observed or described directly. We have no microscopes or tests that will allow us to see a thought or an emotion, for example, with the same clarity as a cell. Granted, good scientific work and sound experimental study have enabled us to look at many of the ways thoughts and feelings can influence behaviours, and psychologists are always seeking out new ways of objectively defining these and other elusive features of mental functioning. But direct observation continues to be a difficult task in the field of psychology.

7.2 Values and the Application of Psychology

Psychology is also distinct from other scientific fields since it deals in major ways with issues associated with values, morality, and personal preference—issues that historically were addressed exclusively by spiritual and political leaders. Like all scientists, psychologists try to provide society with useful information that has practical applications. But people are particularly inclined to use psychological information to decide issues that overlap with philosophy, religion, the law, and other such realms of life. For example, on its website (www.cpa.ca), the Canadian Psychological Association offers policy statements based on psychological research on topics ranging from the death penalty (studies show it does not reduce homicide rates), bullying (research shows solutions require relationship changes), and physical punishment of children (findings indicate it is an ineffectual way of controlling a child's behaviour and it models aggressive behaviour for the child).

Of course, other sciences also influence the values and ethics of human beings to various degrees. The field of genetic research, for example, was pioneered by biological scientists who were looking for better farming practices. However, some early geneticists soon came to believe that selective breeding could be applied to humans to increase the likelihood of desired offspring. Their research contributed to a field eventually known as *eugenics,* a social movement that advocates improving the human race by encouraging reproduction by people with desirable genetic traits and discouraging (sometimes through forced sterilization) the reproduction of people with undesirable traits (Osborn, 1937). Eugenics influenced not only many people's personal childbearing decisions, but also contributed to policies of governments and social agencies in some locations that required forced sterilization surgery for people deemed unfit to reproduce (Whitaker, 2002).

China Foto Press/Getty Images

Happy birthday! Yangyang, a female goat cloned by Chinese scientists in 2000, wears a wreath at her sixth birthday party. Advances in genetic research and genetic engineering hold much promise, but it is important to consider the ethical implications.

Angus McLaren (1990), of the University of Victoria history department, points out that Alberta established a eugenics board in 1927 to rule on involuntary sterilizations; it was not disbanded until 1972. Indeed, eugenics has often been associated with racism and homophobia.

Today, the field of genetic research sparks concerns and debate about food practices, stem cell research, human cloning, and other such issues. Every scientific field must wrestle with questions of how to ethically apply the knowledge it discovers about the world, but few more so than the field of psychology. In addition, few sciences are as plagued as psychology is with popular imitations and misrepresentations of their work.

7.3 Misrepresentation of Psychology

It is natural for people to seek guidance periodically on how to live their lives. And psychologists certainly do not shy away from helping people with their problems, as evidenced by the thriving areas of clinical and counselling psychology and other applied disciplines described in Part 1. Ultimately, however, science—even psychology—cannot answer fundamental and subjective questions about human nature, such as what are people basically like.

People who claim to do so are misrepresenting the science of psychology with *pseudopsychology* (Leahey, 2005). Pseudopsychology, or *pop psychology*, is not based on the scientific method, yet it takes on the appearance of science. Pseudopsychologists often have hidden goals, such as promoting certain moral or religious values (Hergenhan, 2005). A fundamental difference between pseudopsychology and psychology is that psychology does not claim to address all human issues, whereas pseudoscientists argue that psychological principles can provide the answers to all of life's major questions (Leahey, 2005).

Clearly, psychologists must maintain a difficult balance. On the one hand, it is important to encourage the human drive to seek guidance and derive meaning about how to live effectively. On the other hand, psychology must distance itself from pseudoscience to maintain its status as a natural, empirically-based science. As one researcher wrote, "Mainstream psychologists have a problem differentiating themselves from what they regard as a pseudoscience without seeming dogmatically intolerant" or narrow minded (Hergenhahn, 2005, p. 532). It is essential that we think critically and scientifically about all claims being made about human behaviour and the factors that direct human actions.

> "Do you believe in UFOs, astral projections, mental telepathy, ESP, [and] clairvoyance...? Uh, if there's a steady paycheck in it, I'll believe anything you say."
>
> —*Dialogue from the 1984 movie* Ghostbusters

Psychology Around Us   Psychology...Not!

Astrology is a good example of pseudopsychology. It uses Zodiac "signs" to predict a person's future and give advice about an individual's relationships and decisions. Astrology's guiding principle is that all human beings have particular personality traits that are based on the alignment of planets on their dates of birth. Moreover, astrologers believe that those celestial-based traits determine how people will react to events and interact with others. While many people claim to see some validity in their daily horoscope, it is likely that they would continue to do so even if we cut all the horoscopes out of the paper, removed the astrological signs associated with each, picked one at random, and gave it to people telling them it was theirs. The predictions, connections, and claims of astrology have no such scientific foundation. Most of them cannot, by definition, be tested and falsified, while others have consistently failed to receive any support. Yet the methods and tests used in astrology bear some resemblance to psychological personality tests. Thus, astrologers often adopt the terminology and topics of psychology, confusing many individuals—including many astrologers themselves—into believing that their field is scientifically based.

Courtesy of Dr. Stanley Coren

Stan Coren

Within many scientific disciplines, charismatic researchers and practitioners are able to describe their complex topics so that almost anyone can understand the concepts. These individuals present facts about science in ways that engage the public's imagination. As a result, some of them become well-known figures in the popular media, such as in mass-market books, magazines, television, and radio. Psychology has its share of such individuals.

Fraser Mustard (1927–2011) was a Canadian physician who, during a long career at McMaster University, was involved in establishing its unique problem-focused approach to medical training. After retiring, he became internationally known for his work on the *Early Years Study* and as an advocate for the critical importance of the first six years of life in establishing children's intellectual potential and future achievements (McCain & Mustard, 1999). His work led to the expansion of many early education programs, improving developmental outcomes for Canadian children.

Another well-known researcher is psychologist Brenda Milner, Ph.D., who trained under another well-known Canadian cognitive psychologist, Donald Hebb. Milner specializes in brain functioning (frontal lobes and lateralization). As well, she has pioneered work into spatial memory and language using recently-developed brain imaging techniques. Milner has been recognized for her work by being made a member of the Royal Society of Canada and the National Academy of Science (in the United States), as well as winning the Swiss international Balzan Prize for Cognitive Neurosciences.

And then, of course, there are the celebrity practitioners—professionals who are very well known to the public as book authors or from work on radio and television. Some of these practitioners are well trained and have appropriate professional credentials. Stan Coren, a cognitive psychologist at the University of British Columbia, has written one of the most used textbooks on sensation and perception (Coren, Ward, & Enns, 2004). As well, he has written widely-read books on handedness (1993), the effects of sleep deprivation on everyday life (1996), and many books on the intelligence, behaviour, and role of dogs (1997, 1998, 2003, 2006a, 2006b, 2008a, 2008b, 2010a, 2010b), in addition to hosting a Life Channel show on dog behaviour called *Good Dog!*.

But a critical thinking tip! For each Coren, who is well qualified, there are many more celebrity practitioners who do not have proper training or appropriate credentials in their supposed areas of expertise, including some of the media's most popular TV and radio advisors. Before listening too closely, it is always best to check the qualifications of a psychologist or other professional who is dispensing advice on radio, television, or the Web, or take some time and look into whether they actually have *scientific* research support for their claims.

Before You Go On

www.wiley.com/go/comercanada

What Do You Know?
1. What are the four goals of psychology?
2. What is the main difference between psychology and pseudopsychology?

What Do You Think?
Why do you think that pseudopsychology appeals to so many people even though it is not based on science and does not reflect the truth?

Summary

Module 7: Is Psychology a Science?

LEARNING OBJECTIVE 7 Compare and contrast psychology with other natural sciences, such as biology, chemistry, and physics, and with pseudosciences, such as astrology.

- Psychology shares with every science the primary goals of describing, explaining, predicting, and controlling the objects of study. The goals of psychology differ from those of other sciences because the search for elements of mental processes and behaviour is complicated by constantly shifting human factors.
- Psychology also shares more similarity with the fields of religion and philosophy than many sciences do because psychological findings are more often associated with values, morality, and personal preference.
- Psychology is different from pseudopsychology. Although the latter also attempts to answer fundamental questions about human nature and behaviour, it has no basis in the scientific method.

Study Questions

Multiple Choice

1. Which of the following is an example of pseudopsychology?
   a) astronomy
   b) astrology
   c) Gestalt
   d) Maharishi

Fill-in-the-Blank

1. The field of _____ is often credited with shifting psychology from a philosophy to a science.
2. Forced sterilization and controlled breeding are two consequences of _____.

Module 8: How Do Psychologists Conduct Research?

Let's go back to the controversy over violent video gaming and aggressiveness. Suppose that you frequently play *Call of Duty* or another combat-based game. Let's say that after a long gaming session, you notice that you drive a bit more aggressively. You wonder whether all people who play that game become more aggressive than those people who do not. How would you, as a psychological researcher, study this question?

As we described earlier, the scientific method begins with observation. So, after noting your own reaction, you may decide to observe other gamers. Maybe you get together with some friends, rather than meeting online for a gaming session, and you watch how everyone interacts with each other during and after the game play—though you will have to be aware of influences other than the game if, for example, everyone is drinking!

LEARNING OBJECTIVE 8 List steps in the research process and key characteristics of descriptive and experimental psychological research methods.

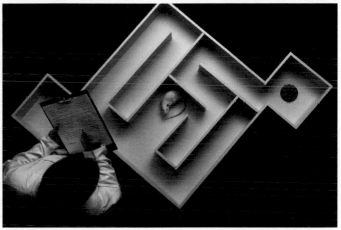

David M. Dennis/Maxx Images

Observation. Watching rats run through mazes is only a very small part of how psychologists conduct research.

8.1 State a Hypothesis

After you've made such observations, you need to generate a prediction; this is your research hypothesis (see **Figure 8-1**). As we have noted, a hypothesis defines what you think will happen and states your prediction in a way that can be tested and found to be either true or false. Your hypothesis might be: playing a violent video game typically increases players' aggressive behaviour.

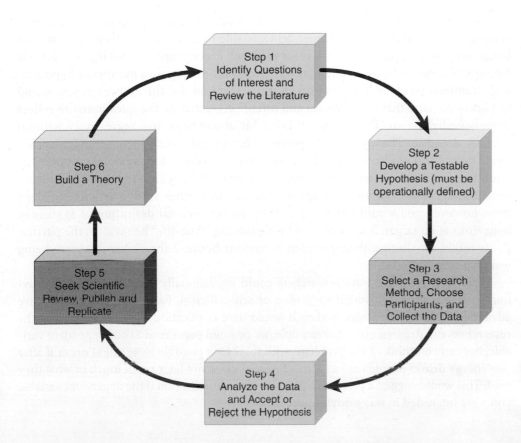

FIGURE 8-1 How do psychologists conduct research? Psychologists follow certain steps and confront a number of choice points as they study questions about mental processes and behaviours.

variable condition, event, or situation that is studied in an experiment.

independent variable condition or event that is thought to be a factor in changing another condition or event.

dependent variable condition or event that you expect to change as a result of variations in the independent variable.

operationalize to develop a working definition of a variable that allows you to test it.

Notice in your hypothesis that you are saying that one thing results in another thing. The two things are called *variables*. A **variable** is a condition or event or situation—it can really be many things. A condition or event that is thought to be a factor in changing another condition or event is known as an **independent variable**. We call it the independent variable because it is the one the researcher sets loose to see what changes it will cause. In this study, playing or not playing a violent video game such as *Call of Duty* is an independent variable. A researcher could change this variable to see how it affects aggressive behaviour. Aggressive behaviour (we could look at physical aggression or verbal aggressiveness) would be a **dependent variable**, the condition or event you expect to change as a result of varying the independent variable. It is the dependent variable because if our hypothesis is correct, then people's scores on this variable will "depend" on their exposure to the independent variable.

How about another example? If you wanted to see if drinking an energy drink would help you read more pages of your textbook in an hour of studying, you could read for an hour without any energy drink, drink one energy drink and read for an hour, then drink a second energy drink and read for another hour. You could count the number of pages you read in each of the three hours. So in this study, what is the independent variable? (It is the amount of energy drink consumed). What is the dependent variable? (If you thought "pages read," you are right). Of course, just counting pages read tells you nothing about how well you have read them or what you will recall later from what you have read as you write the exam. We turn to this sort of issue next.

In addition to defining these variables, you also have to **operationalize** the variables—develop very precise definitions of the independent and dependent variables that allow you to measure and test them (McGrath, 2011). In this case, you might define the independent variable as the length of time players spend playing the game. As a researcher, you may require the participants in your study to play for an hour or for three hours or even play several different games over a period of time. In our other example above, we operationalized stimulant drink use as zero, one, or two cans, but we could have operationalized it as zero, half, one, one-and-a-half, or two cans (note that you are not supposed to drink more than two cans of energy drink).

While it may be relatively easy to create an operational definition of watching, it is harder to operationalize the dependent variable in this study, aggressive or violent behaviour. You might have participants fill out a questionnaire asking about their feelings of anger or hostility and their intentions for managing a number of hypothetical situations (such as being cut off in traffic). If you did this, however, you would not know for sure that the attitudes and intentions stated on the questionnaire reflect aggressive behaviour. People may think a lot about behaving aggressively without actually doing so. Thus, you might prefer to have participants in your study demonstrate some kind of actual aggressive behaviour. You could, for example, set up a situation in which each participant spends 30 minutes playing an online game involving potential aggression or violence against one or more other study participants. Even here, however, you would not be sure that your operational definition of aggressive behaviour is on target. You might not be measuring "true-life" behaviour; the participants might be altering their research behaviour because they know they are being watched or monitored.

There are yet other ways researchers could operationally define aggressive behaviour—perhaps involving verbal aggression or self-criticism. Each definition would have advantages and disadvantages, and each would have implications for the conclusions the researchers can draw. In our other example, we counted pages read as our dependent variable, but can you think of any problems with that? One possible issue might occur if after two energy drinks people read a lot more pages but do not later recall much of what they read. This would suggest a problem with your operationalization if the dependent variable you were interested in was studying success.

8.2 Choose Participants

Once you have identified your variables, you need to select the people who will participate in your study. It generally isn't feasible for researchers to go out into the world and study the entire population of people whose behaviour interests them. Indeed, a population of interest could sometimes include everybody in the whole world. Even when psychologists are not interested in the entire human population, their populations of interest may be very large groups, such as all Canadians, adults, teenagers, children, men, or women. In your gaming violence study, the population of interest includes everyone who plays violent video games and everyone who doesn't play them at all or who plays them to a lesser degree.

Because they cannot usually study an entire population, researchers must obtain a subset, or **sample**, from their population of interest (McGrath, 2011). This subset stands in for the population as a whole. Population sampling of this kind is used very frequently. Political pollsters, for example, interview samples of the voting population to predict which candidate will win a national, provincial, or civic election.

In most instances, researchers prefer to obtain their samples through **random selection**. Random selection is simply a fancy term for choosing your participants in such a way that everybody in the population of interest has an equal chance of becoming part of the sample. That way, you can minimize *sampling biases*—that is, you will not inadvertently select a group that is especially likely to confirm your hypothesis (such as people who game for 8 to 12 hours a day or not at all). If you include only your gaming friends in your sample, the study probably will yield very different results than if you include only people opposed to the sale of violent video games. Indeed, neither sample would be fully representative of the population at large.

Truly random selection can be elusive. The members of your population who do not play video games include, for example, 3-year-olds, who probably are not interested in gaming (yet!) and probably are not capable of making the same kinds of choices about

©iStockphoto.com/AbdolhamidEbrahimi

Proper sampling. Which of the people in this photo should be included in a study? All of them and others too, if a researcher wants to draw conclusions about the entire population. Only some of them, if the researcher seeks to understand just a certain age group, just women, or other subgroups.

sample the group of people studied in an experiment, used to stand in for an entire group of people.

random selection identifying a sample in such a way that everyone in the population of interest has an equal chance of being involved in the study.

Psychology Around Us | Wrong Sample, Wrong Conclusion

Although this is an example based on American history, it is a good example. In 1936, in the midst of the Depression, President Franklin Delano Roosevelt ran for re-election against Kansas governor Alfred Landon. Landon ran on a platform of cutting government spending, and he seemed to be a heavy favourite.

Back in those days, the *Literary Digest* was America's most popular magazine. It predicted that Landon would win, based on the largest number of people to ever reply to a poll: 2.4 million! In fact, the *Digest* had correctly called the winner in every presidential election since 1916.

But as you may know, Landon did not win the 1936 election. The *Digest's* prestige suffered and, partly because of this, it went bankrupt a few years later. The magazine had predicted that Roosevelt would get only 44 percent of the vote, when in fact he wound up winning with a total of 62 percent of the vote!

What went wrong? Simple. The *Literary Digest* picked its sample incorrectly. The magazine mailed 10 million questionnaires using addresses from the phone book and club membership lists. By doing so, it tended to miss poor voters who did not have phones and did not join clubs (only one household in four had a phone at that time). Poor people were overwhelmingly in favour of Roosevelt, but few of their voices were represented in the *Digest* poll. As a result, "sampling bias" created a sample that was non-representative.

A new polling organization run by George Gallup used "random" methods of selection in that same election and predicted that Roosevelt would win with 56 percent of the vote—close enough to help launch the famous and still-going-strong Gallup Polling (Squire, 1988).

aggressive behaviour that 18- or 25-year-old persons might make. Thus, you may decide to narrow your sample to include adolescents or young adults only. Of course, such a choice would mean that your findings will be relevant to adolescents or young adults only, rather than to the entire human population. Researchers in psychology often try to choose samples that make their results relevant to the broadest possible segments of their populations of interest.

8.3 Pick a Research Method

Researchers have several options when designing studies to test their hypotheses (McGrath, 2011). Research methods differ in their goals, samples, and the ability of researchers to generalize their results (suggest that they might apply) to a population. Most of the methods we describe next, including case studies, naturalistic observation, and surveys, are known as **descriptive research methods**. They allow researchers to pursue the goal of description: to determine the existence (and sometimes the strength) of a relationship between the variables of interest. In addition to such descriptive methods, we will also describe *experiments*, which allow researchers to explain the *causes* of behaviour (see **Figure 8-2**). Understanding the differences between descriptive, also called correlational, studies and experimental studies, and particularly understanding what each can or cannot say about the causes of the behaviour each observes, is critical to properly understanding psychological research.

8.3.1 Case Studies

A **case study** focuses on a single person. Medical and psychological practitioners who treat people with problems often conduct case studies to help determine whether therapeutic interventions affect their client's symptoms (Lee, Mishna, & Brennenstuhl, 2010). A case study can be a good resource for developing early ideas about phenomena. One disadvantage of a case study, however, is that it can be affected greatly by *researcher bias*, which occurs when researchers see only what they expect to see in their studies. Some clinician/researchers may, for example, note only the healthy behaviours of persons after they have provided treatment to those individuals. Another disadvantage of case studies is that researchers cannot confidently generalize to other situations from the study of a single person (Lee et al., 2010). Suppose, for example, that you conduct a case study to test your hypothesis that playing violent video games increases aggressive

descriptive research methods studies that allow researchers to demonstrate a relationship between the variables of interest, without specifying a causal relationship.

case study study focusing on a single person.

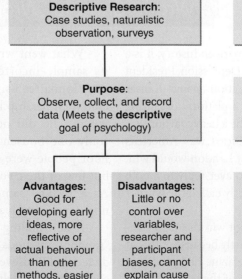
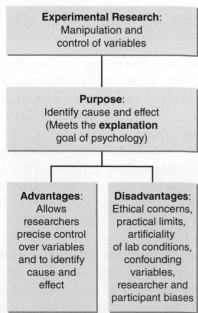

FIGURE 8-2 **Descriptive versus experimental research.** Because descriptive methods and experimental methods each serve particular purposes and have different advantages and disadvantages, psychological research includes both kinds of approaches. Adapted with permission of John Wiley & Sons, Inc., from Carpenter, S., & Huffman, K. (2008). *Visualizing Psychology*. Hoboken, NJ: Wiley, p. 15.

behaviour: you closely observe one fellow student who plays such a game, and you find that he later reports himself to be non-violent and gentle, even when frustrated by the behaviour of other drivers while driving. Your case study observation might indicate that your hypothesis is worthy of further research, but without a larger number of comparison participants, it is impossible to say much about other players of the game. You would not know whether this person's behaviour after playing the game is the norm or an exception.

8.3.2 Naturalistic Observation

In **naturalistic observations**, researchers watch as unobtrusively as possible while people behave as they normally do, similarly to how Jane Goodall observed troops of chimpanzees living in the wild or how Dian Fossey studied Mountain gorillas. Researchers often make naturalistic observations of children in schools or daycare centres. As a researcher, perhaps you could go into participants' homes over multiple weeks and see whether they watch hockey games at all. You could then observe whether those people who watch games engage in more aggressive behaviour and whether those who don't watch behave less aggressively. Naturalistic observations have the advantage of being more reflective of actual human behaviour than most other research designs.

naturalistic observation a study in which researchers directly observe people in a study behaving as they normally do.

A disadvantage of this type of research, however, is that naturalistic observations can be subject once again to researcher bias—observers may notice only what they expect to see, and there is often no one else observing at the same time so that observations can be compared (Goodwin, 2011; Connor-Greene, 2007).

Another potential problem with naturalistic observation is that the mere presence of a researcher or even a video camera in an otherwise natural environment can change the behaviour of the participants. The next time you are walking past an elementary school at recess, look for the "duty teacher" on the playground and then look to see if the children in front of the teacher are behaving differently than those behind and out of the teacher's line of sight. Many people become nicer or more considerate when they are aware that they are being watched, for example. This problem was

Jeff Greenberg/PhotoEdit

A first-hand look. Unlike case studies or surveys, naturalistic observations enable researchers to directly observe people in their natural settings. Here, for example, a psychologist observes a preschool classroom through a one-way mirror.

first identified in the psychological literature by Landsberger (1958) in his study of the productivity of factory workers. In his studies, he found that the workers' productivity increased whenever changes to the workplace were implemented, regardless of what type of change was imposed. For example, lowering or brightening the lights in the factory both resulted in productivity increases. Landsberger suggested that this increase in productivity occurred because the workers were motivated to perform better because they knew that they were being observed. This phenomenon has since been termed the **Hawthorne effect** (Goodwin, 2011) because the study was conducted at the Hawthorne plant of Western Electric near Chicago.

Many of the potential problems with naturalistic observation can actually be effectively addressed. Multiple observers can be used to control for individual observer bias by comparing observations across several observers. Observers can be used who are not informed about the specific hypothesis under investigation, thus limiting opportunities

Hawthorne effect people who are being observed in studies or at their workplace improve or change some of their behaviour simply because they are being watched or studied, not in response to an experimental manipulation.

for bias to affect their observations. Observers can spend a lot of time in the setting they wish to observe so that they become an accepted part of the setting and their presence does not disrupt usual behaviour. As we will see in later parts, some of psychology's most important studies were descriptive studies involving naturalistic observation.

8.3.3 Surveys

survey study in which researchers give participants a questionnaire or interview them.

A third descriptive approach, frequently used in psychological research, is the **survey**. In a survey, researchers ask people a series of questions. Researchers can conduct surveys using in-person, telephone, or email interviews, or they may ask the questions via a written questionnaire. To test your aggressive behaviour hypothesis, for example, you might design a questionnaire that asks people about their *gaming* habits and about their aggressive attitudes, and use their answers to determine whether or not a relationship exists between the two variables.

The advantage of a survey approach is that surveys allow researchers to obtain information that they might not be able to gather using case studies or naturalistic observations. It might be hard, for example, to tell whether a person in a case study is avoiding aggressive behaviour because he wishes to do the right thing, or whether the individual is avoiding aggressive behaviour to get some kind of reward. A survey can help pin down such issues. Another reason surveys are sometimes favoured by psychologists is that they can also provide data that enable researchers to measure how strong the relationship is between two variables of interest.

Surveys do suffer some disadvantages, however (McGrath, 2011). Their data can be unreliable because people frequently answer in ways that are socially acceptable rather than in ways that are reflective of their true attitudes, a problem known as *participant bias*. Thus, people in your gaming study may describe themselves on a survey as less aggressive than they actually are because they know that being aggressive is considered a socially inappropriate trait. Similarly, participants in a survey study may be unaware of just how aggressive they are. Also, we cannot be certain that all participants understand all the survey questions the same way. For example, some people might interpret a question about whether other drivers frustrate them as applying only if another driver makes then really angry, while others might assume we mean any small annoyance is frustrating. Although subject bias obviously is a common concern for survey researchers, it can occur in experiments and other types of research as well, as we shall soon see.

Another problem is that survey data cannot tell us the *direction* of the relationship between variables. Do people who play a lot of violent video games become more aggressive, or are highly aggressive people drawn to play a lot of violent video games? A survey cannot help you answer this question. Despite these concerns, a great deal of very informative descriptive research is conducted in psychology.

8.3.4 Experiments

experiment controlled observation in which researchers manipulate the presence or amount of the independent variable to see what effect it has on the dependent variable.

experimental group group that is exposed to the independent variable.

control group group that has not been or will not be exposed to the independent variable.

If you want to know what *causes* what, you have to design an experiment (McGrath, 2011). An **experiment** is a controlled observation in which researchers manipulate levels of one variable—the independent variable—and then observe any changes in another variable—the dependent variable—that result from their manipulation.

One way of experimentally testing your violent gaming hypothesis in this kind of study would be to divide your sample into two groups: an **experimental group** and a **control group**. An experimental group is the one exposed to the independent variable. In our example, the experimental group would consist of people who are instructed to play several hours of a violent video game. A control group, in contrast, consists of people who are similar to those in the experimental group but who are not exposed to the independent variable—for example, people not instructed to play a game at all. By comparing the aggressive behaviour of the two groups after one group plays a violent game and the other does not, you might conclude with some degree of confidence that differences in aggressive behaviour are caused by playing the violent video game. You could also create a more complex experiment, in which multiple experimental groups game for varying amounts of time, or where some play games that involve high levels of violence while others play less violent or completely non-violent games. You could then compare them with the non-playing control group participants to determine whether the amount of gaming or the type of games being played affects levels of aggressive behaviour.

Many psychology experiments involve different levels of the independent variable of interest, as such higher levels of design complexity better match the real world reality we are trying to study. For example, we could set up our study so that the experimental groups either played a little or a lot of more or less violent games. This sort of design allows us to look for *interaction effects*. It may be that playing a small amount of a violent game has no effect on aggressive behaviour, while playing a lot of it does increase aggressive behaviour. This sort of interaction effect could be observed and reported using this more complex experimental design.

The composition of experimental and control groups needs careful attention. In our example, no one in the control group games at all (see **Figure 8-3**), and none will be instructed to do so for the study. But what about the experimental group? Should you include people who have played the game previously or regularly? Or should you begin with a group of participants who—like the control group—have never played the game, and then expose the experimental group to a marathon of gaming? Either approach is acceptable, but the two approaches may lead to different conclusions.

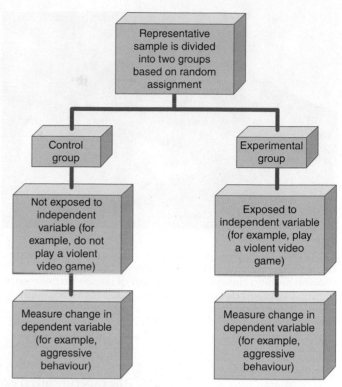

FIGURE 8-3 **The experimental design.** Key features of experimental designs are independent and dependent variables and random assignment of experimental and control groups.

Other kinds of differences—past or present—between the experimental and control groups may also influence the results of an experiment. What if more people with gaming experience or with emotional control issues (bad tempers) ended up in the control group than in the experimental group? That could affect the results of your study. You could carefully ensure that the groups are equally balanced on all variables you can think of that might affect the results, but you can never think of them all. Researchers deal with this problem by using *random assignment* to make sure that everyone in their sample has an equal chance of being in either the control or experimental group and that the groups are equally balanced in terms of *any* factor or variable that could influence results other than the independent variable (Remler & Van Ryzin, 2011). Ideally, random assignment controls for all such factors so that you can say with more confidence that any differences you find are likely due to your manipulation of the independent variable. Even so, however, researchers still run the risk that the groups will differ in some important ways. Suppose that you randomly assign gaming participants to each of your groups, but nevertheless wind up with more males in one group and more females in the other group. Such an unintended group difference may affect the participants' subsequent aggressive behaviours and so may lead you to draw incorrect conclusions. Some researchers pre-interview or give questionnaires to participants in both the experimental and control groups to make sure that the groups are comparable to one another, especially in terms of variables the researcher is concerned could make a big difference in the results. Their goal is to help guarantee that whatever effects emerge in the study are caused by the experimental manipulation of the independent variable and are not attributable to other,

Picture Partners/Alamy

Experimental answer. Do complex visual images stimulate babies? To answer this causal question, experimenters showed swirling designs to one group of babies (experimental group) and bland designs to another group (control group). Babies in the experimental group typically attended to their designs longer than did those in the control group, suggesting that complex images do indeed attract the attention of babies.

double-blind procedure study in which neither the participant nor the researcher knows what treatment or procedure the participant is receiving.

pre-existing variables, such as income level. If the groups are fairly large, random assignment will largely take care of these group membership concerns.

In addition, experimenters must be careful when deciding what tasks will be performed by participants in the control group. Researchers often have the participants in a control group engage in an activity of some kind, just to make sure that the changes seen in the experimental participants are indeed due to the impact of the independent variable and not the result of the experimental participants being particularly active during the study. You might, for example, have your control group participants play another game that is engaging but less violent, such as a basketball video game. If afterwards the experimental participants still demonstrate more aggressive behaviour than the control participants, you can be more certain that the violent video game is in fact responsible.

Finally, experimenters must be careful to avoid bias in their studies. Once again, they must avoid subject bias and researcher bias—sources of bias that we discussed earlier. In addition, they must set up their studies so that they do not unintentionally convey to participants the outcome that they (the experimenters) expect to see, an undesired effect known as a *demand characteristic*. If a researcher were to tell participants in the experimental group of the video gaming study that their answers to an assertiveness and aggressiveness questionnaire will indicate how much violent video games contribute to problematic real-life behaviour, the researcher might be creating a demand characteristic that encourages those participants to understate their aggressive inclinations. For this reason, while it is sometimes hard to do, many studies, particularly pharmaceutical ones, are designed so that the persons who administer the study or who evaluate the behaviour of participants are unaware of the hypotheses of the study (Remler & Van Ryzin, 2011). Indeed, many studies use a specialized method known as a **double-blind procedure**, in which neither the participant nor the researcher knows which group—experimental or control—the participant is in. In drug studies, some participants get real medication while others get pills designed to look like the real medication but which actually do not contain any of the active drugs being assessed. This information about who gets which drug is sealed and only revealed after the data for the study have been collected (Wender et al., 2011). Double-blind studies help keep researchers from observing or creating what they want to observe and participants from intentionally acting in ways that confirm a researcher's hypothesis.

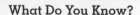

Before You Go On

wiley.com/go/comercanada

What Do You Know?

1. Which variable is controlled or manipulated by an experimenter?
2. What are three descriptive research methods used in psychology?
3. Which research method allows researchers to say that one variable causes another?

What Do You Think? What would you conclude if people's aggressive behaviour increased after an hour of violent video game playing? How would that conclusion be different if aggressive behaviour only increased after a marathon of violent video game playing?

Summary

Module 8: How Do Psychologists Conduct Research?

LEARNING OBJECTIVE 8 List steps in the research process and key characteristics of descriptive and experimental psychological research methods.

- Psychological research is rooted in first generating a hypothesis, or prediction, about the relationship between two or more variables based on observations.
- Psychologists conduct research with a sample, a small group meant to represent the larger population of interest. The best means of selecting a sample is random selection, a procedure in which everyone in the population has an equal chance of being selected to be in the sample.
- Descriptive research methods include case studies, naturalistic observations, and surveys.
- Case studies are in-depth observations of a single individual.
- Naturalistic observation involves observing people in settings outside of laboratories where their behaviour occurs naturally.
- Surveys may be conducted in interviews or with questionnaires.
- Only experiments allow researchers to draw conclusions about cause-and-effect relationships.
- All research methods have advantages for particular uses and all are subject to various drawbacks. Researchers must plan carefully to avoid subject bias, researcher bias, and demand characteristics.

Key Terms

case study 54	double-blind procedure 58	independent variable 52	sample 53
control group 56	experiment 56	naturalistic observation 55	survey 56
dependent variable 52	experimental group 56	operationalize 52	variable 52
descriptive research methods 54	Hawthorne effect 55	random selection 53	

Study Questions

Multiple Choice

1. A researcher observed the eating patterns of laboratory rats while manipulating the amount of sleep they received during a week-long study. In this example, what type of variable is "sleep"?
   a) observable
   b) dependent
   c) independent
   d) extraneous

2. Which of the following is not a descriptive research method?
   a) case study
   b) experiment

   c) naturalistic observation
   d) survey

Fill-in-the-Blank

1. A subset of a population is known as a(n) _____.

2. The research methodology that asks participants to answer a series of questions is called a(n) _____.

Module 9: How Do Psychologists Make Sense of Research Results?

Once researchers obtain results from an experiment or descriptive study, what do they do with them? Can they simply eyeball their findings and say that there's a relationship between this and that variable, or that the two groups under study are different? No, scientists cannot depend just on impressions or logic. If they tried, they would have no way of knowing whether a relationship found between variables or a difference between groups actually matters.

Psychologists use *statistics* to describe and measure relationships between variables. Scientists use many statistical analyses to look at the differences and similarities between groups (Goodwin, 2011). We won't go into a lot of depth about statistics here (for more details see Appendix B at the end of this text). We will, however, give you a few tips to help you understand the research findings you'll be reading about in this book and elsewhere. We will discuss correlations, which describe the relationships between variables, and then go on to discuss the statistical tests researchers use to determine how likely it is that their results are occurring simply by chance. Then, we will examine how researchers use the statistical results to decide whether or not their hypothesis has been supported and to guide the next steps in the research process.

9.1 Correlations: Measures of Relationships

correlation predictable relationship between two or more variables.

correlation coefficient statistic expressing the strength and nature of a relationship between two variables.

positive correlation relationship in which, on average, scores on two variables increase together.

negative correlation relationship in which, on average, scores on one variable increase as scores on another variable decrease.

perfect correlation one in which two variables are exactly related, such that low, medium, and high scores on both variables are always exactly related.

A predictable relationship between two or more variables is called a **correlation** (for more detailed information on correlation, see Appendix B). To describe correlations, especially in descriptive studies, psychologists use a statistic called a **correlation coefficient**.

A correlation coefficient can range from −1.00 to +1.00. The number itself and the positive or negative sign in the correlation coefficient each convey different information.

The positive or negative sign tells you the direction of the relationship. When scores on both variables get bigger together, the relationship is known as a **positive correlation**. In our example, we predicted a positive correlation between violent video gaming and aggressive behaviour: as playing increases, so will aggressive behaviour. If we had suggested that aggressive behaviour does not increase, but actually drops, as people game more and more (perhaps because violent gaming could serve to release and thus reduce aggressive urges), then we would be predicting a **negative correlation**. When the variables are negatively correlated, higher scores on one variable are related to lower scores on another variable. **Figure 9-1** shows various types of relationships.

In addition to looking at the positive or negative sign, we must consider the value of the number in the correlation coefficient. The number tells the size, or strength, of the relationship between variables—that is, how well we can predict one variable if we know the other. The larger the number, the stronger the relationship and the tighter packed the data cloud in the graph appears to be. Thus, a correlation coefficient of 0 means that there is no linear relationship between the two variables and if you look at the graph of the zero correlation data you can easily see that there appears to be no clear relationship at all between the graphed variables. Knowing a person's score on one variable tells you nothing about the person's score on the other. The farther a correlation coefficient gets from 0 in either the positive or negative direction, the stronger the relationship between the two variables. A high positive correlation coefficient means that scores on the two variables under examination typically rise and fall together (and produce a rather tight data cloud when graphed), and a high negative correlation coefficient means that a rise in one of the variables usually is accompanied by a fall in the other. A correlation of −1.00 or +1.00 is known as a **perfect correlation**, one in which the variables' scores are always perfectly related. One score always rises or falls in direct proportion to the changes in the other

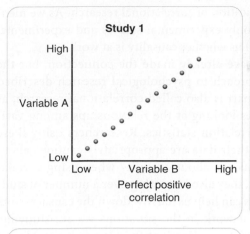

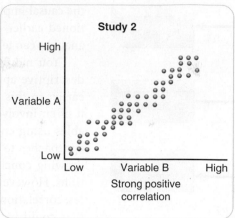

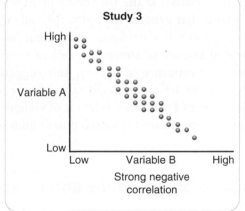

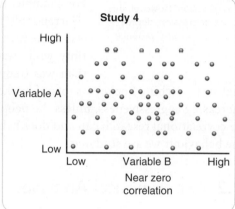

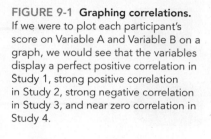

FIGURE 9-1 **Graphing correlations.** If we were to plot each participant's score on Variable A and Variable B on a graph, we would see that the variables display a perfect positive correlation in Study 1, strong positive correlation in Study 2, strong negative correlation in Study 3, and near zero correlation in Study 4.

variable. We do not see this sort of relationship very often in psychology as things are often much more complicated in our studies.

Again, it is important to keep in mind that in correlation coefficients, the positive and negative sign and the number itself provide two different pieces of information. A correlation with a negative coefficient is not weaker than one with a positive coefficient. In fact, the relationship may be stronger if, for example, the negative correlation is −0.7 and the positive correlation is +0.2. A negative correlation of −0.7 would mean that the two variables are quite strongly related in such a way that low scores on one variable very often are associated with high scores on the other (see **Figure 9-2**).

In psychology, really exciting relationships are often reflected by a correlation coefficient of 0.3 and above. This is far from a perfect correlation, largely because relationships between behaviours, thoughts, and emotions can be so complex and because so many other variables may also be at work in such relationships. Nevertheless, 0.3 or above typically means that the two variables in question do indeed have some kind of predictable relationship.

Correlations offer lots of useful information, particularly when we are interested in the scientific goal of prediction (Girden & Kabacoff, 2011). The correlation coefficient tells us just how well we can use one piece of information about someone, such as how much the person plays violent video games, to predict her behaviour in another realm, in this case aggressive behaviour. One key piece of information correlations do *not* tell us, however, is *causality* (Remler & Van Ryzin, 2011). That is, they do not shed light on whether or not a change in one variable actually causes the change in the other (see **Figure 9-3**). We will get positive correlations if violent gaming causes aggressive behaviour, but we will also get positive correlations if aggressive people prefer to play violent video games. So we must be careful when talking about

+1.00	Perfect positive relationship
+.88	Very strong positive relationship
+.62	Strong positive relationship
+.38	Moderate positive relationship
+.12	Weak positive relationship
0.00	No relationship
−.12	Weak negative relationship
−.38	Moderate negative relationship
−.62	Strong negative relationship
−.88	Very strong negative relationship
−1.00	Perfect negative relationship

FIGURE 9-2 **How to read a correlation coefficient.** The sign of the coefficient tells us the direction and the number tells us the magnitude, or strength, of the relationship between two variables.

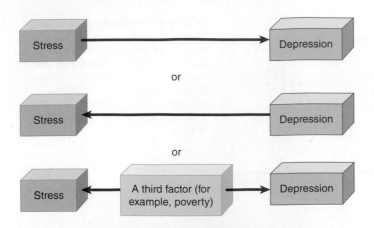

FIGURE 9-3 Correlation versus causation. Research has found a strong correlation between stress and clinical depression. However, this correlation does not tell us whether stress causes depression, depression causes stressful events, or other factors, such as poverty, produce both stress and depression.

the causal implication of correlational research. As we mentioned earlier, only experimental studies and experimental analyses can tell us whether causality is at work.

You may have already made the connection, but the descriptive approach to psychological research described earlier in this part is also called correlational research, as it often involves looking at the relationships among variables using correlation statistics. Researchers using these approaches to their data are appropriately cautious about drawing conclusions about causality when using correlations. However, they also know that over a number of studies, correlations can help us narrow down the causal factors that could be at work in the situations we are studying. For example, Andrew Harrell at the University of Alberta (Harrell, 1981) found that general tolerance for violence was more strongly positively correlated with verbal hostility while watching hockey (a somewhat violent sport) than was frequency of exposure to hockey. This suggests that just watching hockey or lots of hockey may not be a significant causal factor in increasing aggressiveness, unless the people involved are already tolerant of violence. So correlational research can and does help us narrow down the causal possibilities in the behaviour we are studying.

9.2 Experimental Analyses: Establishing Cause and Effect

If you want to examine differences between groups and determine the cause of such differences, you have to do a particular kind of statistical analyses. Collectively, these are called *experimental analyses* because they are associated with experiments. Researchers sometimes divide experimental analyses into two categories: *descriptive statistics*, which describe or summarize the data gathered from a study, and *inferential statistics*, which tell researchers what they can conclude, or infer, more broadly from their results (for more information, see Appendix B).

In order to describe differences between the scores of experimental groups and control groups, researchers calculate the *mean* and *standard deviation* of each group. The **mean** is the arithmetic average of the scores of all participants in a

mean arithmetic average of a set of scores.

©iStockphoto.com/stefanoborsani

©iStockphoto.com/slobo

Correlation versus causality. The repeated co-occurrence of two events (correlation) does not necessarily mean that one is causing the other. Children who eat ice cream, for example, tend to have bike accidents. It may be that eating ice cream while riding causes young bikers to have more accidents. Or, it may be that parents typically treat their children to ice cream whenever they have accidents. Or, perhaps hot summer days lead to increases in both ice cream eating and bike riding.

group. This is the same average you've been calculating since Grade 4 math class. Big differences between the mean—the average score—of an experimental group and the mean of a control group may indeed suggest big differences between the participants in the groups.

To be certain of this, however, researchers also look at the **standard deviation**, an index of how much the participants' scores *vary* from one another within each group (basically it is the square root of the average of the squared differences between each score and the group average... think about it, it makes sense). Suppose, for example, you have ten control-group participants who play a video soccer game and then obtain scores of 4, 5, 4, 6, 5, 4, 4, 7, 5, and 6 on an aggressiveness scale, and ten experimental-group participants who play a first person shooter combat video game, then obtain scores of 1, 2, 12, 11, 5, 9, 4, 1, 3, and 2. Each group would have a mean score of 5 aggressiveness points. Unless you also examine the standard deviations for both groups (1.05 for the control group and 4.20 for the experimental group), you might not realize that there are more extreme reactions in the first person shooter game group than in the other group (see **Figure 9-4**).

After determining the mean and standard deviation of each group, researchers can compare the two groups. Psychologists typically compare means using statistical procedures known as *t-tests* (for two groups) or *analyses of variance* (for two or more groups). These procedures look both at the mean differences and at the variance within the groups, as well as at the size of the groups, and essentially ask whether the two groups in the sample being studied are different given their average scores and the variability of their scores as reflected by their standard deviations. The statistical procedures are known as significance tests because they measure whether the differences found between groups are *statistically significant*.

In statistics, the word *significant* has a slightly different meaning from most people's everyday use of the same word. A test of statistical significance tells us how likely it is that the differences found between groups (drawn from a larger populations) are due to experimental manipulations rather than due to chance. Such tests indicate this likelihood by calculating a *probability statistic*. If a test of statistical significance yields a probability statistic of $p = .05$, it means that if researchers were to conduct the same study 100 times, they would, by chance alone, get the same result found in the current study less than 5 percent of the time, if there really were no difference between

standard deviation statistical index of how much scores vary within a group.

Aggressiveness	
Soccer game	*First person shooter game*
4	1
5	2
4	12
6	11
5	5
4	9
4	4
7	1
5	3
6	2
5 ⟵ Mean ⟶ 5	
1.05 ⟵ Standard deviation ⟶ 4.20	

FIGURE 9-4A Variability and the standard deviation. Although these two sets of data have the same mean, or average, score of aggressiveness in our fictitious study, players of a first person shooter game are much more varied in their aggressiveness scores (high standard deviation) than are players of soccer (low standard deviation).

	Violent First Person Shooter		Less Violent (Questing) First Person Shooter	
	Soccer	Game	Football	Game
	4	5	2	3
	5	7	5	6
	4	9	4	9
	6	9	6	9
	5	7	5	7
	4	9	4	9
	4	5	1	4
	7	7	10	7
	5	5	5	6
	6	8	8	10
Means	5	7	5	7
Standard Deviations	1.1	1.7	2.6	2.3
	Significant		**Not Significant**	

FIGURE 9-4B Statistical significance. In these two studies, the aggressiveness differences between soccer game players and the violent first person shooter game players is real or statistically significant because the means are different and variability in each group is low while the same differences between the football group and a less violent (questing) first person shooter game group are not significant because there are higher standard deviations or greater variability in those two groups.

Thinkstock/Getty Images

Analyzing the results. A big part of conducting good research is knowing how to properly handle the numbers gathered and the findings they represent.

the populations from which the samples were obtained. In other words, there's an extremely low probability that the result found in the current study occurred simply as a random act of chance. Most likely, it occurred because of a real difference between the two groups of subjects in the study. By convention, when a test of statistical analysis yields a probability of less than .05 ($p < .05$), psychological researchers conclude that the difference they have found between groups in their study is statistically significant—there is likely to be a real difference that is due to the manipulations carried out in the study.

Keep in mind that the numerical difference between group means and the probability statistic says nothing about the size of the effect you're seeing in your study. Let's say that participants who play a first person shooter game later display a higher mean aggressiveness score than do those who play soccer, and that the probability statistic is less than 0.01 ($p < .01$). This does not necessarily mean that the first person shooter gamers have become *much* more aggressive than the soccer players. It just means that there's less than 1 chance in 100 that you obtained that result by chance. If you want to know how big the effect of violent gaming is, you need to calculate yet another statistic, known as *effect size*, which describes the strength of the relationship between two variables. If you were to find a large effect size in your study, it would suggest that violent gaming strongly increases aggressive behaviour (for more information, see Appendix B).

9.3 Using Statistics to Evaluate and Plan Research

replication repeated testing of a hypothesis to ensure that the results you achieve in one experiment are not due to chance.

If you get a result like this—a difference between groups that is very unlikely to have occurred by chance—does it mean you have fully supported your hypothesis and should sit back and toast your success? Well, not yet. Scientists need to be sure. They need to go back and test their hypotheses some more. It is only through **replication**, taking the data from one observation and expanding on it to see if it holds up under multiple conditions and in multiple samples that we can determine whether what we hypothesize is correct. Over time, replication enables hypotheses to become theories and theories to become laws.

Another important part of science is to use different research methods to explore the same research question (McGrath, 2011). If researchers use several approaches, including surveys, experimentation, and independent observations, and obtain the same results, they can be more certain that their hypotheses are accurate and have confidence about incorporating those hypotheses into theories.

As we described earlier in our discussion of the scientific method, a theory is also a framework to generate additional hypotheses. If your hypothesis about violent video gaming proves correct, and people on average report themselves to be more aggressive and exhibit more aggressive behaviours on experimental tasks after playing a first person shooter game, you have reason to continue your line of research. You can conduct the same experiment with other games, and see whether the hypothesis continues to hold up for all kinds of aggressive or violent games. You may also decide to look at other forms of social behaviour besides aggressiveness, such as empathy or sense of fair play. If you continue to replicate these results with other games and other social behaviours, you are effectively supporting the theory that violent gaming in fact contributes to increased aggressive behaviour within Canadian culture. A Nobel Prize (or perhaps the Order of Canada) is inevitable.

practically Speaking | Tips on Reading a Scientific Journal Article

As a psychology student, particularly if you major in psychology, you will most likely read journal articles for some of your required classes. Initially, this task may seem overwhelming. The authors of journal articles tend to use unfamiliar language, condense complex concepts into a small space, and make assumptions about the reader's knowledge of their topic. However, you can turn this task into something interesting and worthwhile by following a few simple steps.

When you read a research paper, try to understand the scientific contributions the authors are making. You should read the paper critically and not assume that the authors are always correct.

You do not need to read the paper sequentially to get the gist of it. First, you might read the abstract, the introduction, and the conclusions. Next, look through the references to determine whose work is at the root of the current research. After this first read-through, try to summarize the article in one or two sentences.

Then, go back and read the entire paper from beginning to end. Study the figures, re-read parts that are difficult to understand, and look up unfamiliar words. Make notes in the margins or on separate sheets of paper. And answer the following questions as you work:

- **Title:** What does this tell you about the problem?
- **Abstract:** What does this general overview tell you about the current paper?
- **Introduction:** What are the authors' assumptions, important ideas, and hypotheses?

©iStockphoto.com/Alejandro Rivera

- **Methods:** Do the methods seem to effectively test the authors' hypotheses?
- **Related work:** How does the current work relate to past work? What is new or different about the current study?
- **Conclusions:** What were the study's results, and do they make sense? What were the study's limitations? What do the authors propose for future research? How does the study contribute to a better understanding of the problem?

You also may choose to outline, summarize, or keep more detailed notes, especially if you are using the article for a term paper.

Before You Go On

www.wiley.com/go/comercanada

What Do You Know?

1. What two pieces of information does a correlation coefficient give about the relationship between variables?
2. What do the mean and standard deviation tell you about scores of a group?
3. What do t-tests tell experimenters?

What Do You Think? What are some examples of positive and negative correlations that you have observed in everyday life?

Summary

Module 9: How Do Psychologists Make Sense of Research Results?

LEARNING OBJECTIVE 9 Describe what information is conveyed by statistics, including correlation coefficients, means, and standard deviations, and explain how psychologists draw conclusions about cause and effect.

- Correlations allow us to describe and measure relationships between two or more variables. A correlation coefficient tells the direction and size of a correlation.
- Researchers use the mean and standard deviation to describe and summarize their results.
- Researchers use probability statistics to determine the statistical significance of results. Effect size tells how strong the relationship is between variables.
- Replication of experiments and repeated study of the same predictions using different methods help hypotheses become theories.

Key Terms

correlation 60	mean 62	perfect correlation 60	replication 64
correlation coefficient 60	negative correlation 60	positive correlation 60	standard deviation 63

Study Questions

Multiple Choice

1. What method do psychologists use to analyze study data?
   a) logic
   b) induction
   c) statistics
   d) deduction

2. Which of the following statistical procedures can be used to determine to what degree participants' scores within a group vary?
   a) standard deviation
   b) mean

   c) t-test
   d) analysis of variance

Fill-in-the-Blank

1. Analyzing data through the use of _____ allows researchers to describe and measure relationships between variables.

2. Researchers are able to conclude more broadly from their results through the use of _____ statistics.

Module 10: What Ethical Research Guidelines Do Psychologists Follow?

LEARNING OBJECTIVE 10
Describe what ethical steps psychologists take to protect the rights of human research participants.

Today, psychological research must be designed with the goal of protecting the participants (human or animal) involved with the study. Psychology researchers are bound by the same broad ethical principles that govern doctors and other clinicians. The Code of Ethics of the Canadian Psychological Association (CPA) states it clearly: "psychologists have a higher duty of care to members of society than the general duty of care that all members of society have to each other" (CPA, 2000).

Research ethics in Canada are guided by a joint statement on the ethics of research involving human participants created by the three main research grant agencies: the Canadian Institutes of Health Research (CIHR), the Natural Science and Engineering Research Council of Canada (NSERC), and the Social Sciences and Humanities Research Council of Canada (SSHRC). To ensure that researchers follow proper ethical practices, **research ethics boards (REBs)** provide oversight in academic and other research settings across the world. Any institution (university, private corporation, government agency, or medical school) conducting research involving human participants is expected to appoint an REB, which consists of a mixture of researchers from inside and outside the field. REBs examine research proposals and rule on the potential risks and benefits of each study's procedures (CIHR, NSERC, SSHRC, 2010). If the risk or discomfort associated with a proposed study is deemed to outweigh the potential scientific benefit from the study, then the undertaking is rejected. REBs generally require that psychologists studying human participants take the following steps to protect human participants:

research ethics board (REB) research oversight group that evaluates research to protect the rights of participants in the study.

- *Obtain informed consent.* **Informed consent** from participants requires that researchers give as much information as possible about the purpose, procedures, risks, and benefits of a study, so participants can make informed decisions about whether they want to be involved in the study (Nagy, 2011). If participants include children, researchers must obtain informed consent from both the parents or caregivers and the child.

informed consent requirement that researchers give as much information as possible about the purpose, procedures, risks, and benefits of the study so that a participant can make an informed decision about whether or not to participate.

- *Protect participants from harm and discomfort.* In addition to medical or physical risks, such as those faced by the patients in Cameron's experiments, researchers must avoid putting participants in situations that could cause them undue emotional stress, for example.
- *Protect confidentiality.* Researchers must have in place, and explain to participants, careful plans to protect information about the identities of participants and the confidentiality of their research responses.
- *Make participation voluntary.* Researchers must make it clear that participants have the right to decide not to participate in the study and that their decision will in no way affect their treatment or involvement in a related class or any other activity. Further, participants have the right to end their participation at any point or to decline to answer any particular questions during the study.
- *Do not use deception or incomplete disclosure.* Researchers must be completely open about the methods and purpose of their research so that participant consent is fully informed. Deception, such as providing participants with false feedback on a test to manipulate their moods, is rarely permitted, and then only when no alternative methods are available. Steps

©iStockphoto.com/skynesher

Consent has its limits. To protect children who participate in studies, researchers must also obtain informed consent from their parents or caregivers.

Psychology Around Us A Notorious Project

Between 1957 and 1964, a psychiatrist named Donald Cameron working at Allen Memorial Institute at McGill University worked under a contract with the American Central Intelligence Agency (CIA) as part of a larger project called MKULTRA (Collins, 2002; Klein, 2007). As part of that project, Cameron administered LSD (a drug that influences brain neurochemistry and produces hallucinations) and electroconvulsive therapy (ECT, a shock delivered to the brain that induces epileptic seizures) to patients who had entered the institute with relatively minor mental health issues, such as postpartum depression or anxiety disorders.

Linda Macdonald was one of those participants. In 1963 she checked into a Canadian institution to be treated for fatigue and depression. Six months later, she couldn't read, write, cook a meal, or make a bed. She did not remember her husband, her five children, or any of the first 26 years of her life. During her stay, Ms. Macdonald was given massive doses of various drugs, put into a drug-induced sleep for 86 days, given more than 100 electroconvulsive treatments, and exposed to "psychic driving," a technique in which repetitive taped messages were played for her 16 hours a day. The purpose was not to treat this woman's depression, but to gather information about the causes and effects of brainwashing (Davis, 1992; Powis, 1990).

During this project, the drug and ECT were administered without the patients' consent and were not primarily intended to treat their conditions. Instead, they were used to examine the drug's and ECT's potential effectiveness as interrogation or mind control techniques. The patients sustained permanent damage as a result of their treatments, including loss of identity or loss of speech, and loss of memory. When this work was made public by the TV show *the fifth estate* in 1985, it was discovered that the Canadian government was aware of the research. The patients were unable to sue the CIA for their treatment, but they did eventually receive a $100,000 payment from the Canadian government.

These sorts of horror stories illustrate the potential for serious harm in some psychological studies. Participants need to be clearly informed about just what they are getting into, and that they have the right to refuse or discontinue involvement in research at any point. It also shows the need for a set of strict guidelines regarding the ethical treatment of research participants and the ethical design and conduct of psychological experiments.

---

must be clearly taken to ensure the long-term effects of such deception are negligible. In addition, supports must be immediately available for negatively-affected participants.

- *Provide complete debriefing.* In some cases, if participants were to have full knowledge about the purposes and goals of a study before it began, their responses during the study might be influenced by that knowledge. Researchers often try to balance giving participants enough information before a study to protect their rights, yet withholding information that may affect participants' responses. Thus, at the end of a study, researchers are required to offer a **debriefing** to participants—an information session during which they reveal any information that was withheld earlier.

debriefing supplying full information to participants at the end of their participation in a research study.

In addition to ruling on the costs and benefits of the study, research ethics boards also assess other issues. They look, for example, at the compensation individuals receive for their participation (to make sure that participants are not tempted to participate in potentially dangerous studies by high levels of compensation), and they determine whether particular groups (such as men, women, or members of minority ethnic groups) are singled out unnecessarily.

As a result of these ethical guidelines, several of the older "classic" psychological studies we will discuss later in this book would not be approved by a university REB. See if you can identify which studies these are, and why, when we discuss them.

The ethical research guidelines we have discussed so far cover research with human beings. However, as you may already know, a lot of research in psychology involves the use of animals as participants. Animal rights advocates point out that animals are especially vulnerable research participants since they cannot give their consent to be part of a study. They also argue that animals may be exposed to more extreme risks than humans, for sometimes unclear benefits.

Psychologists take their ethical obligations toward animal research participants very seriously. The Canadian Council on Animal Care (CCAC, 1989) has crafted a set of ethical guidelines for research involving animals and works to ensure that the guidelines are followed. Its code includes the following points:

- "The use of animals in research, teaching, and testing is acceptable ONLY if it promises to contribute to understanding of fundamental biological principles, or to the development of knowledge that can reasonably be expected to benefit humans or animals."
- Animals should be used only if the researcher's best efforts to find an alternative have failed.
- Those using animals should employ the most humane methods on the smallest number of appropriate animals required to obtain valid information.
- Other parts of the code seek to limit pain or distress, ensure proper recovery periods, and ensure general humane treatment of animal participants.
- All such guidelines—for both animal and human research undertakings—help ensure not only more ethical procedures, but better science as well.

Psychology Around Us Facts and Figures on Animal Research

As will be clear as we move through this book, research in psychology is conducted with both human and animal participants. Research involving animals has been the focus of scrutiny and debate in recent years. The importance of animal research to our psychological understanding means that we need to clarify some important facts and figures about animal research (CCAC, 2012, 2011).

1. The welfare of animal subjects is of great interest and concern not only to animal activists, but also to animal researchers, government agencies, scientific organizations, and the public.

2. Around 8 percent of psychological research involves the use of animals; 90 percent of the animals used are rodents and birds (mostly rats and mice); only 5 percent are monkeys and other primates.

3. Every regulated institution that conducts animal research must be certified by the CCAC, which carefully reviews and oversees all such studies at their institution. The CCAC ensures that each study follows all ethical, legal, and humane guidelines, and the council pays close attention to such issues as the prevention or alleviation of animal pain, alternatives to the use of animals, and the clinical and scientific importance of the study.

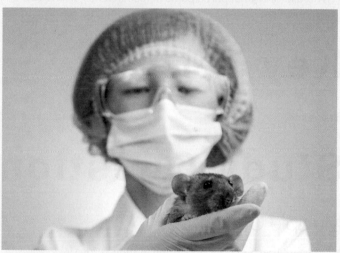
©iStockphoto.com/Remains

4. In surveys (Hagelin, Carlsson, & Hau, 2003), 75 percent of the public say that they can accept animal research as long as it is for scientific purposes—though this level of agreement varies from 29 percent to 100 percent depending on the study. Most respondents even approve of experiments that bring some pain to animals when those investigations are seeking a cure for childhood leukemia, AIDS, or other significant problems.

What Do You Know?
1. What does a research ethics board do?
2. What is informed consent and how does it relate to debriefing?

What Do You Think? Are ethical standards different for psychology than those for other sciences? Should they be?

Summary

Module 10: What Ethical Research Guidelines Do Psychologists Follow?

LEARNING OBJECTIVE 10 Describe what ethical steps psychologists take to protect the rights of human research participants.

- Today, oversight boards called research ethics boards (REBs) help to protect human rights.
- Psychological researchers must obtain informed consent from human participants, protect them from harm and discomfort, protect their confidentiality, and completely debrief them at the end of their participation.
- The use of animal participants in research has also raised ethical concerns. An oversight council called the Canadian Council on Animal Care (CCAC) works to protect animals' needs and comfort in experiments.

Key Terms

debriefing 68   informed consent 67   research ethics board (REB) 67

Study Questions

Multiple Choice

1. Researchers may use deception in their study designs
   a) only when no alternative method is available
   b) only if they inform their participants before they begin the study
   c) under no circumstances
   d) only if they obtain permission from their college or university counselling centre.

2. Which of the following sequences best reflects the order of events in a typical experimental session?
   a) informed consent → debriefing → experiment
   b) informed consent → experiment → debriefing

   c) debriefing → informed consent → experiment
   d) debriefing → experiment informed → consent

Fill-in-the-Blank

1. Before a researcher can test his hypotheses by collecting data, a(n) _____ must provide ethical oversight.

2. Protecting the identity and information collected from individual respondents in a research study refers to maintaining _____.

PART 3

NEUROSCIENCE

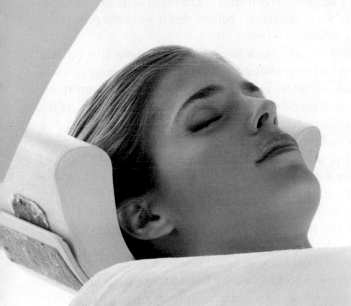

neuroscience the study of the brain and the nervous system.

Some people believe that once scientists figure out the human brain and nervous system, all of our experiences—our thoughts, our feelings, our plans and strategies, our ups and downs—will be explained by our understanding of the actions and interactions of the neurons (cells of the brain) in our brain and nervous system. How does that sound to you? Will we ever be able to potentially control or adjust any facet of our experience? Do you think it would be a good thing if we could? There are some astonishing theories arising out of **neuroscience** research. Some are even claiming that discoveries in this area will eventually lead to immortality!

Is this possible? Human lifespans have quadrupled in the last 300 years. Will this trend continue? One area of research has focused on telomeres—a part of the chromosome that prevents genes from degrading or recombining with our genetic material (e.g., DNA). Telomeres get smaller and smaller with each cell replication, until eventually they are gone and the cell stops replicating and dies. When large numbers of cells stop replicating we age (Waterstrat et al., 2008). Some researchers believe that if we could protect the telomeres our cells could replicate indefinitely (Fossel, 2010).

In his book, *The Dream of Eternal Life*, Mark Benecke (2002) states that cellular life and death determine the aging and time of death of human beings. Benecke (2002) examines why we age and die and speculates about alternative routes to immortality, including cloning, brain and head transplants, and cryonically freezing humans for regeneration in the future. Are these techniques something arising from science fiction or could they become a reality? Brain and head transplants involve removing the brain or the entire head of one organism and transferring it to the body of another. This work has been attempted with animals with nominal degrees of success but it has never been attempted with humans (Canavero, 2013; White, 1999; 1975). Similarly, cloning has been successfully carried out with many species but to date efforts at human cloning have been restricted to creating embryonic stem cells for research (Tachibana et al., 2013).

But what about preserving your dead body in liquid nitrogen to wait for the day that future technology will restore you to full health? Perhaps you have heard that Walt Disney, who died of lung cancer following a three-pack-a-day smoking habit, was cryopreserved and is currently in storage under the *Pirates of the Caribbean* attraction in *Disneyland*? Not so. Approximately 200 people worldwide are currently in cryonic suspension but Walt Disney is not one of them. He was cremated (Mikkelson & Mikkelson, 2014).

Life and death are tied to the development of the body and of the brain. For many of the hypothesized routes to immortality we are not yet sufficiently technologically advanced to even consider the ethical, legal, and social impacts of implementing such methods. But even if these were viable techniques would you choose to use them? Think as you read this part about what makes you the person you are. After being cryonically preserved for two or three hundred years in a vat of liquid nitrogen would you be the same when revived? Would you become the same person you are today if your DNA were cloned and you began again as an infant? What if your brain was in the body of another person? Would you still be the same person you are now?

In this part we examine many established findings about the biological underpinnings of psychology. However, you will also see that, although considerable progress has been made in understanding the organization and function of the brain, there remain large gaps in our knowledge about how the actions of the tens of millions of microscopic cells in the brain produce complex behaviours such as thought and personality. For example, researchers have been unable to build a machine able to exhibit the conscious awareness experienced by humans (Reggia, 2013). That is, a machine (or computer/robot) can identify a rose but it is unable to consciously experience the colour red or the smell of the rose; nor can a machine understand language, feel emotion, or think about itself (Gennaro, 2012).

Why do you think that is the case? As you read about the physical structure of the brain and of the nervous systems consider what in this extraordinarily complex system makes you "*you*."

We will see in this part that, although considerable progress has been made in understanding the organization and function of the brain, there remain large gaps in our knowledge about how the actions of the millions of microscopic cells in the brain produce complex behaviours, such as thought.

Module 11: How Do Scientists Study the Nervous System?

In the past, researchers of psychological issues in humans often avoided analyzing the brain, mainly because of limits in our study methods and technologies. Until recently it was difficult, if not impossible, to study what goes on in the human brain without causing damage to brain tissue (Chudler, 2011). Several decades ago, human neuroscience relied largely on one of the following methods:

- *Examining autopsy tissue.* This method allows neuroscientists to see what our brains look like, but has the obvious drawback of telling them little about how these systems worked when the person was alive and using them (Love, 2004).
- *Testing the behaviour of patients with damage to certain parts of the brain.* Scientists called *neuropsychologists* have learned a great deal about the brain from studying patients with brain damage. Patients with localized brain damage often have loss of some particular function. The type of loss of function then suggests what the brain region did before it was damaged. Therefore this approach relies on inference. That is, the neurophysiological approach involves researchers making assumptions based on information about the normally functioning brain from the damaged brain (Morgensen, 2011). In other words researchers are unable to compare the undamaged brain of a given individual to the same person's damaged brain and so cannot make statements about cause and effect. As well, even patients with localized brain damage may have smaller undetectable abnormalities in other areas of the brain. Or, it could be that a pathway carrying information to or from the area related to the lost function has been damaged, rather than a specific area itself. Also, the damaged brain may undergo reorganization over time so abnormalities in behaviour may not reflect what goes on in the intact brain (Benton, 2000).
- *Recording electrical brain activity through multiple electrodes attached to the surface of the scalp.* Scientists have used *electroencephalograms*, or EEGs, as a non-invasive way to measure or learn about the activity of our brains during certain states (awake and asleep) and during certain behavioural tasks (Lomas et al, 2014; Niedermeyer & da Silva, 2004), as well as to make predictions about the functional effect of brain injuries and identify types of seizure disorders (Breedlove & Watson, 2013). The drawback of this type of analysis is that surface recordings only provide a summary of surface activity over a large expanse of the scalp—pinpointing the location of activity using this method can only be done in a general sense. However, researchers have refined the electroencephalographic technique through the analysis of *event related potentials* (ERP) to timelock EEG activity. Here a computer notes when a sensory, cognitive, or motor event takes place and the experimenter then focuses on the wave patterns in place at the time of, and following, the stimulus presentation. For example, ERP methodology is a useful approach for examining central nervous processing activities, such as audition in nonverbal infants (Hoehl & Wahl, 2012). In such cases, the infant's brain reactions to sound stimuli are measured in order to assess the infant's ability to process the stimuli. This technique allows researchers to know exactly *when* events take place, but is not ideal for identifying *where* in the brain the activity occurred because the skull attenuates (or dilutes) the electrical signals.
- *Animal studies.* Studies on animal nervous systems have made it possible to look closely at parts of functioning brains. Animal studies include microscopically examining specific brain regions, electrically recording from specific brain areas

or specific neurons, temporarily activating or deactivating parts of the brain and observing the outcome, or targeting specific brain areas for destruction and observing the effects on behaviour—a process called *lesioning* (Hilton et al., 2013; Howland et al., 2008). Although human brains can be examined microscopically after death, clearly, we cannot lesion live human participants, but a technique that temporarily impairs brain function in humans has been developed. *Transcranial magnetic stimulation* (TMS) delivers an electromagnetic pulse to a targeted brain area, disrupting localized brain activity in a conscious person (Horvath et al., 2013). If following an electromagnetic pulse (i.e., the "temporary lesion") to a specific brain area a person shows impaired task performance, the assumption is that the affected brain area must be involved in that particular task.

Taken together, these and other approaches have provided us with a great deal of information about the brain and the nervous system in general, but they all share a drawback: they tell us little about activity in specific regions of healthy, living, human brains.

Aaron MCcoy/Photolibrary/Getty Images

Electroencephalography (EEG). Electroencephalography is a noninvasive technique used to detect and localize electrical activity in the brain.

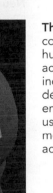

Courtesy Leigh Nystrom & Jonathan Cohen, Princeton University

The brain at work. This 3D computer-generated image of a human brain shows areas of brain activation (coloured areas) in an individual undergoing a moral decision-making task. This study employed fMRI technology that uses changes in blood flow as a measure of changes in the neural activity.

Psychology Around Us Creativity

Positron emission tomography (PET) scans and functional magnetic resonance imaging (fMRI) enable researchers to see which brain areas are particularly active during certain tasks (Forbes et al., 2004). For example, researcher Melissa Ellamil, at the University of British Columbia, and her colleagues used fMRI to locate specific neural networks and brain areas activated during the generation and evaluation components of the creative process. The participants in this study were undergraduates from the Emily Carr University of Art and Design. All participants were monitored while designing book cover illustrations using a custom made fMRI-compatible drawing tablet (Ellamil et al., 2012). Participants alternated between generating novel ideas (drawing) and evaluating those ideas (writing). The results indicated that areas of the brain not typically networked for other problem-solving tasks are co-activated for creative tasks, combining both rational and emotional thinking as well as measured and spontaneous forms of thought. Similar types of co-activation have also been reported when participants' minds wander (Christoff et al., 2009) or when they watch films (Golland et al., 2007).

Over the past few decades, however, new structural **neuroimaging** techniques have been developed to study brain activity. These methods include computerized (or computed) axial tomography (CAT or CT), magnetic resonance imaging (MRI), and diffusion tensor imaging (DTI).

Computed tomographic scans (CT scans) produce clear, detailed, two-dimensional X-ray images of the brain or other organs. Computer combination of many X-ray images taken from multiple angles results in a three dimensional brain image that can be virtually "sliced" and examined from any angle. CT images provide greater detail than traditional X-rays.

neuroimaging techniques that allow for studying brain activity and structure by obtaining visual images in awake humans.

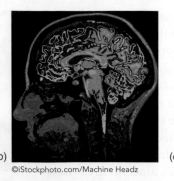
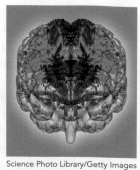

(a) ©iStockphoto.com/stockdevil   (b) ©iStockphoto.com/Machine Headz   (c) Science Photo Library/Getty Images

Neuroimaging. (a) Computed axial tomography (CAT) scan, (b) magnetic resonance imaging (MRI), and (c) diffusion tensor imaging (DTI).

Instead of X-rays, *magnetic resonance imaging* (MRI) uses a strong magnetic field to produce images of the anatomy and physiology. The computer creates a three-dimensional image of the brain or the body. MRI scans produce much clearer images than CT scans and do not use radiation.

So if the MRI has lower risks associated with it and it produces a better image, why use a CT scan at all? There are several reasons: CT scans are better at detecting problems, such as brain diseases or blood vessel abnormalities, in certain parts of the body such as the brain. As well, CT scans are the preferred method for identifying many forms of cancer, whereas MRIs are better at detecting soft tissue injuries in tendons and ligaments, as well as injuries to the spinal cord or brain. CT scans are also faster to administer and so are useful in emergencies, and they cost less. As well, an MRI cannot always be used; for example, people who have pacemakers, shrapnel, or other metal in the body or those with certain types of injuries cannot be examined using a powerful magnet. In accidents involving metal, such as car accidents or work-related accidents, the magnet can rip the object free, causing further injury or death.

Diffusion tensor imaging (DTI) is the newest structural imaging technique. It measures the orientation and integrity of white matter (described later in the part) to assess damage in the brain and produces a DTI colour map. Research indicates that white matter damage is involved in a number of brain disorders (Shenton et al., 2012). For example, mild traumatic brain injury (mTBI), also called concussion, is difficult to diagnose as the brain often appears normal on CT or MRI scans because these more conventional techniques do not assess white matter injury (Little, 2010).

Structural images are very helpful but they do not enable researchers to identify brain regions that become active under specific conditions. Functional neuroimaging tells us about activity in particular brain areas during specific behaviours. As discussed above, the EEG is a technique that examines brain function but allows us to visualize and localize it only very crudely. Activity detection methods include positron emission tomography and functional magnetic resonance imaging.

In *positron emission tomography* (PET), a harmless radioactive substance is injected into a person's blood. Radiation detectors are then used to scan the person's brain. Active brain areas have more blood flow and thus display a higher amount of radioactivity (Phelps, 2006). *Functional magnetic resonance imaging* (fMRI) likewise allows for the detection of changes in blood flow, a presumed indicator of changes in the activity of neurons (Mason et al., 2009; Devlin, 2007; Ogawa et al., 1992). More specifically, fMRI detects the amount of oxygenated hemoglobin (the blood molecules responsible for carrying oxygen) after a person is exposed to magnetic pulses. If the technology is available, fMRI is preferable to PET because it does not require radiation and is also able to very quickly detect changes in brain activity.

The availability of these neuroimaging technologies has produced an explosion of research. While the results have confirmed many previously held claims about brain function and structure, they have also raised additional questions. As a result of rapid improvements in neuroimaging, methods are becoming more and more sensitive.

Psychology Around Us | "Mild" Brain Injury

Jonathan Daniel/Getty Images

Sidney Crosby. Pittsburgh Penguins' Sidney Crosby hits the ice after a collision during an exhibition game in 2013.

Repeated mild traumatic brain injuries (mTBI), particularly when associated with loss of consciousness, can lead to a concussive- or subconcussive-related degenerative brain disease called Chronic Traumatic Encephalopathy (CTE) (Levin & Smith, 2013). Repeated traumas may cause the death of neurons and may lead to the progressive buildup of abnormal proteins called tau proteins within months to decades following the injury. CTE is associated with a constellation of neurocognitive symptoms, including personality change, memory loss, progressive dementia, mood swings, confusion, tremors, speech and gait abnormalities, depression, and suicidal ideation and completion. The presence of CTE has been confirmed through autopsy in the brains of professional and amateur athletes, members of the military exposed to blasts in combat, and others who have experienced repetitive mild head injuries (McKee et al., 2013, 2009).

The development of CTE following even repeated and severe concussion is not inevitable. Researchers at the University of Toronto report that some athletes who have experienced multiple concussions never develop CTE and therefore argue that the causes for this neurocognitive degenerative disease are as yet unclear (Hazrati et al., 2013). Since CTE can only be definitively diagnosed after death, athletes and others at risk have no way of knowing if slips of memory or bouts of depression are early signs of CTE or may have a less ominous explanation, such as stress or fatigue.

Gary Small and colleagues at the Semel Institute for Neuroscience and Human Behavior at UCLA have therefore developed what they hope will become a noninvasive means of diagnosing (or eliminating) the presence of abnormal tau proteins in living individuals with suspected CTE (Small et al., 2013). In this procedure, a radioactive isotope called FDDNP is injected into the bloodstream where it binds to abnormal tau proteins; a PET scan is then used to identify where these abnormal tau proteins have accumulated in the brain. Small and colleagues report identifying higher levels of FDDNP in regions of the brains of athletes with suspected CTE similar to patterns previously observed at autopsy in affected athlete's brains. The tau binding patterns in the affected athlete's scans involved areas of the brain associated with learning, memory, and emotion. The hope of Small and other researchers is that this non-invasive approach will be used for early detection, which will in turn lead to treatment and prevention.

But others, including many professional athletes, are arguing that traumatic brain injury, particularly in sports, is completely preventable. They are therefore calling for changes to rules in their respective leagues to reduce or eliminate the risks of repeated concussions to players. Players such as Pittsburgh Penguins' Sidney Crosby, who famously suffered from recurrent post-concussion symptoms for well over a year following two consecutive blows to the head, are at considerable risk for severe neurological injury. In fact, it turns out that for many, these repeated "mild" brain injuries are deadly.

Before You Go On

www.wiley.com/go/comercanada

What Do You Know?

1. Describe how studies of people with brain damage and EEGs have contributed to our knowledge of the brain and nervous system.
2. What are the main advantages of neuroimaging methods over earlier neuroscience research methods?

What Do You Think? Do you think it will eventually be possible to use neuroimaging techniques to determine what a person is thinking? What would be the ethical implications of using this technology?

Summary

Module 11: How Do Scientists Study the Nervous System?

LEARNING OBJECTIVE 11 Understand the key methods that scientists use to learn about brain anatomy and functioning.

- Neuroscientists examine autopsy tissue and patients with localized brain damage to learn about brain anatomy and brain function.
- EEGs and neuroimaging, such as PET scans and fMRI, allow scientists to study brain function in the living brain.

Key Terms

neuroimaging 75

Study Questions

Multiple Choice

1. What can neuropsychologists learn about the brain from studying patients with brain damage?
   a) They can identify the cause of the brain damage.
   b) They can see the connections between brain regions.
   c) They can hypothesize what the brain region does when undamaged.
   d) They can detect changes in blood flow within the brain.

2. Neuroimaging techniques such as PET scans and fMRI enable researchers to:
   a) examine brain cells microscopically.
   b) see what parts of the brain are active during certain tasks.
   c) summarize activity over a large expanse of tissue.
   d) record brain waves from the surface of the scalp.

Module 12: How Does the Nervous System Work?

The **neuron**, or nerve cell, is the fundamental building block of the nervous system (Jones, 2007). Communication among neurons is necessary for normal functioning of the brain and spinal cord. The peripheral nervous system that runs throughout the rest of our bodies, outside the brain and spinal cord, is also made up of neurons.

The structure and function of individual neurons, as well as the ways in which these cells work together in groups (called *networks*) have been the subject of considerable scientific inquiry for over a century (Jones, 2007). Neuroscientists have discovered that neurons have specialized structures that enable them to communicate with other neurons using both electrical and chemical signals. As we will see later, our emerging understanding of how these signals work is leading toward the development of treatments for adjusting our neurochemistry when things go wrong.

But neurons are not the only cells in the nervous system. Neuroscientists have increased their attention to *glia*, the other type of cell found in our nervous systems.

LEARNING OBJECTIVE 12
Describe the two major types of cells in the nervous system and describe the primary functions of each.

neuron a nerve cell.

12.1 Neurons and Glia

The human brain contains about 86 billion neurons (Azevedo et al., 2009; Herculano-Houzel, 2014, 2009). **Figure 12-1** shows the basic structure of a neuron. Like most of our other cells, neurons have a cell body filled with cytoplasm that contains a nucleus (the residence of chromosomes that contain the genetic material). In addition, neurons contain organelles that enable the neuron to make proteins and other molecules, produce energy, and permit the breakdown and elimination of toxic substances. Just as our own organs make it possible for our bodies to live and function, so too do organelles make it possible for our neurons to live and function (López-Muñoz et al., 2006).

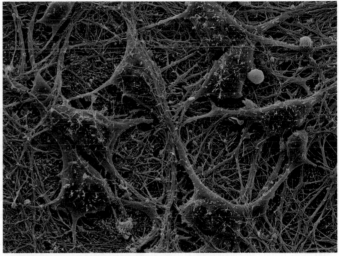
David Scharf/Science Source/Photo Researchers

Neurons. Human cortical neurons (brain cells), showing an extensive network of interconnecting dendrites.

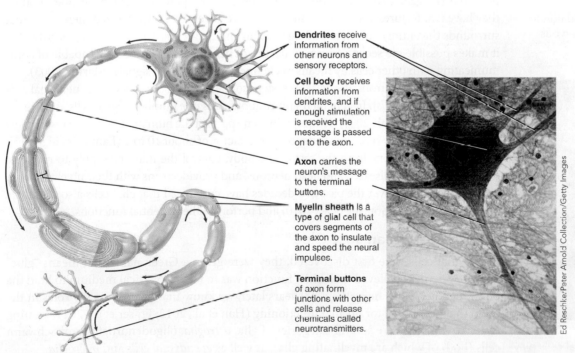

Dendrites receive information from other neurons and sensory receptors.

Cell body receives information from dendrites, and if enough stimulation is received the message is passed on to the axon.

Axon carries the neuron's message to the terminal buttons.

Myelin sheath is a type of glial cell that covers segments of the axon to insulate and speed the neural impulses.

Terminal buttons of axon form junctions with other cells and release chemicals called neurotransmitters.

Ed Reschke/Peter Arnold Collection/Getty Images

FIGURE 12-1 The neuron. The major structures of the neuron include the cell body, the axon, and the dendrites. Dendrites typically receive information from other neurons, while axons send information away from the cell body to communicate with other neurons. Arrows indicate the direction of information flow. Reprinted with permission of John Wiley & Sons, Inc., from Tortora, G., & Derrickson, B. H. (2009). *Principles of Anatomy and Physiology* (12e). Hoboken, NJ: Wiley, Figure 12.2, p. 418.

dendrites the parts of neurons that receive input from other neurons.

axon the part of the neuron that carries information away from the cell body toward other neurons.

axon terminal the end of a neuron's axon, from which neurotransmitters are released.

However, as Figure 12-1 shows, neurons are different from other cells. They have specialized structures called *dendrites* and *axons* that are important for communication with other neurons.

Dendrites extend like branches from the cell body to collect inputs from other neurons. Neurons can have many dendrites and, indeed, some have very extensive dendritic "trees" that allow a single neuron to receive more than 200,000 inputs from other neurons.

An **axon** also extends from the cell body. Unlike dendrites, however, axons typically function to carry information away from the cell body toward other neurons. A two-molecule-thick neuron membrane completely covers the cell body, dendrites, and axon. Axons have a specialized region at the end, called the **axon terminal**. At the end of each axon (a region known as the axon terminal) are many specialized structures (synapses) where information is passed from one neuron to another across a very small fluid-filled space. When an electrical impulse (an *action potential*) reaches the axon terminal, it causes fluid-filled sacs called *vesicles* (filled with chemicals called *neurotransmitters*) to migrate to, and fuse with, the neuronal membrane and to then release neurotransmitters into the synapse. We will discuss this process in greater detail shortly. Unlike dendrites, neurons have only one axon leaving the cell body. Axons, however, can be highly branched; these branches, or *collaterals*, greatly increase the number of neurons that the axon contacts. Axons can also be very long. For example, if you stub your toe, the neuron axon that carries pain information from your toe runs from the end of your toe all the way to your spinal cord. In addition, some axons (but not all) are covered with a fatty covering called a *myelin sheath* (which we describe in greater detail later in the part).

There are many different kinds of neurons (e.g., sensory neurons with specialized sensory endings in the skin that respond to pressure, temperature, and pain, or in the muscles or ligaments that respond to changes in muscle length or tension; motor neurons that stimulate our many muscle cells into action; and interneurons that communicate with both sensory and motor neurons and with other interneurons). Some are large (such as the primary sensory neurons, which can be as large as 1.5 metres), while others are very small (such as many of the neurons found in the brain) (**Figure 12-2**). Some have very elaborate dendritic trees (brain neurons), while others possess a single unbranched dendrite (some sensory neurons) (Hogan, 2010). Although these cells all look quite different from one another, they have two features in common: all neurons are covered by a specialized membrane that surrounds the entire neuron, including its axon and dendrites. This membrane is critical as it makes possible the second common feature of neurons: All neurons are capable of communicating with other cells by means of chemical and electrical signals (Martin, 2003).

glia the cells that, in addition to neurons, make up the nervous system.

In addition to neurons, the nervous system contains a large number of non-neuronal cells called **glia** (or *glial cells*). In general there are about the same number of glial cells as there are neurons (Azevedo et al., 2009). However, in some parts of the human brain, some researchers contend that glia may outnumber neurons by a factor of about 10 to 1 (Laming et al., 2011). Glia buffer the neurons from the rest of the body, control the nutrient supply to neurons, destroy and remove diseased and dead neurons, and provide axons with their myelin sheath. As well, discoveries over the past two decades have confirmed that glial cells also modulate neurotransmission (Gourine et al., 2010) and perform other essential functions.

12.1.1 More than Just Glue

When glial cells were first discovered, they were given a Greek name that means "glue" because scientists believed their chief function was to form a physical medium to hold the brain together. Now, more than 100 years later, we know that glia play many roles in the brain that are critical for normal functioning (Han et al., 2012; Fraser et al., 2011; Laming et al., 2011). There are several categories of glia: *astroglia*, oligodendroglia, and Schwann cells (both of which are myelinating glia), as well as *ependymal cells* and *microglia*.

Astroglia are so-named because most are shaped like stars (see photo). This glial type is important for creating what is referred to as the blood–brain barrier, a system that regulates the passage of molecules from the blood to the brain. Astroglia regulate

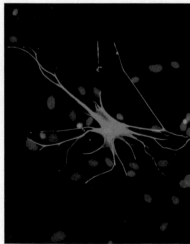

Riccardo Cassiani-Ingoni/Photo Researchers

Astroglial cell. Astroglial cells play a critical role in the creation of the blood–brain barrier. However, all types of glial cells are essential for brain function.

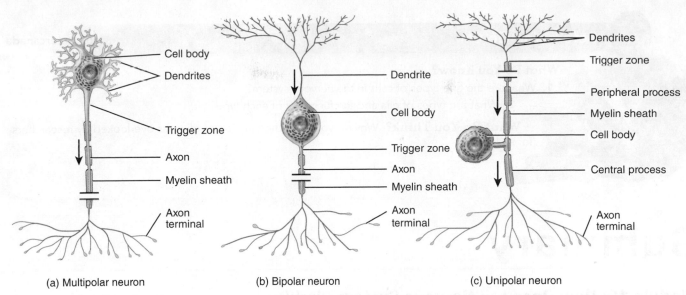

FIGURE 12-2 **Various shapes.** These examples illustrate the diversity in the shape of neurons. Source: Reprinted with permission of John Wiley & Sons, Inc., from Tortora, G., & Nielsen, M. (2014). *Principles of Human Anatomy*, 13th edition. Hoboken, NJ: Wiley, p. 550.

the flow of blood into different brain regions as those regions increase or decrease in neuronal activity, thus providing more or less nutrition support or oxygenation as required (Iadecola & Nedergaard, 2007). Astroglia also function to absorb or clean up chemicals released by neighbouring neurons and to provide important growth-promoting molecules to neurons. Astroglia migrate to the site of brain injury, where they enlarge and multiply to form a glial scar (Fitch & Silver, 2008). In addition, astroglia also serve to communicate with neurons, influencing their electrical activity by absorbing excess potassium ions (Haydon et al., 2009). Another type of astroglia serves as a stem cell in the adult brain. These cells are capable of dividing and producing new cells, including new neurons (Chaudhuri & Bhattacharya, 2013; Doetsch, 2003).

The *oligodendroglia* (central nervous system, including the brain and spinal cord) and Schwann cells (peripheral nervous system, the nervous system outside of the brain and spinal cord) are important for providing a protective fatty sheath, or coating, called *myelin* that insulates the axons of neurons from nearby neuronal activity (Baumann & Pham-Dinh, 2001). This protective function is particularly important in the brain and spinal cord, where neurons are very closely packed and axons are often organized into bundles. Importantly, myelin also speeds up the passage of electrical signals down the axon (Jessen & Mirsky, 2005). Multiple sclerosis is a progressive disease that involves demyelination, or loss of myelin, on the axons of neurons. Demyelination occurs when the affected person's immune system attacks the myelin sheath. Loss of myelin leads to inefficient transmission of electrical information among neurons, causing a range of symptoms including vision loss, pain, and muscle weakness (depending on where the demyelination has occurred). Research on multiple sclerosis has focused on finding ways to stimulate remyelination (Franklin & French-Constant, 2008).

Ependymal cells are specialized neuroglial cells that line the walls of the ventricles, fluid-filled spaces within the brain. They create and secrete cerebrospinal fluid (CSF) that fills the ventricles and surrounds the brain and spinal cord, and are thought to make up the blood–cerebrospinal fluid barrier (Del Bigio, 1995; Johansson et al., 1999). Finally, *microglia*, so-named because they are very small, are important for cleaning up the debris of degenerating or dead neurons and glia so that brain regions can continue with their normal functioning. This cleaning function makes microglia an important brain defence against infection and illness (Gehrmann, 1996; Streita, 2006).

Summary

Module 12: How Does the Nervous System Work?

LEARNING OBJECTIVE 12 Describe the two major types of cells in the nervous system and describe the primary functions of each.

- The two major types of brain cells are neurons and glia.
- Neurons communicate with other cells by producing and sending electrochemical signals.
- Glia are involved in various functions, such as forming the blood–brain barrier, producing myelin, and clearing the brain of debris.

Key Terms

axon 80

axon terminal 80

dendrites 80

glia 80

neuron 79

Study Questions

Multiple Choice

1. The central nervous system consists of
   a) all nerve cells in the body.
   b) the brain and spinal cord.
   c) the somatic and autonomic nervous system.
   d) the sympathetic and parasympathetic nervous system.

Fill-in-the-Blank

1. The nervous system is made up of neurons and _____ cells.

2. Neurons receive messages from other neurons via the _____.

3. The type of glial cells that produce new cells in the adult brain are called _____.

Module 13: How Do Neurons Work?

As the basic cells in the central nervous system (CNS), neurons process all of the motor, sensory, and cognitive information that enters, leaves, or is in the CNS. So everything we smell or taste or see or dream or plan or think or remember or do or feel is handled by neurons. Processing this sheer amount of exceptionally diverse information means that we not only need many types of neurons, but we also need a *lot* of them. In fact fairly recent research suggests that we have about 200 specific types of neurons, conservatively totalling about 86 billion neurons in the brain (Azevedo et al., 2009; Herculano-Houzel, 2014, 2009), each communicating with somewhere between 5,000 to 200,000 other neurons. This means that the number of synapses or points of neuron-to-neuron communication in the brain is in the neighbourhood of quadrillions (a quadrillion is a thousand trillions, 10^{15}; see www.kokogiak.com/megapenny/seventeen.asp for a visual depiction of what a quadrillion looks like).

In order to process information, neurons have to communicate with other neurons. Neurons send messages to one another via complex electrochemical interactions, meaning that chemicals cause an electrical signal to be generated within a neuron. A sudden change in the electrical charge of a neuron's axon causes it to release a chemical (neurotransmitter) that can be received by other neurons, which then can react in several ways. One typical reaction to the receiving of a neurotransmitter is a change in the electrical charge of the receiving neuron. In this way, an electrical signal can be passed along one neuron and, via a neurotransmitter, created in another. Let's take a closer look at this process.

LEARNING OBJECTIVE 13
Describe what happens when a neuron "fires" and how neurons send messages to one another.

13.1 The Action Potential

Ions are atoms and molecules that have a relative imbalance of protons and electrons, and are thus either positively or negatively charged. The ratio of negative to positive ions in the cytoplasm (*intracellular fluid*) is different from the ratio in the *extracellular fluid* that surrounds the neuron. Therefore, the overall charge inside a neuron differs from the overall charge outside, creating a difference in charge across the neuron membrane, known as the membrane potential. It is important to note that even when a neuron is at rest, or inactive, the inside of the neuron is negatively charged in comparison to the outside. We say that the neuron in this state is *polarized*.

In the 1950s, neurophysiologists Alan Hodgkin and Andrew Huxley carried out a series of experiments aimed at identifying the ionic mechanisms that underlie the difference in potential across the neuron membrane and, more important, how changes in that difference in charge allow neurons to communicate with one another (Hodgkins & Huxley, 1952). They received the 1963 *Nobel Prize in Physiology or Medicine* for this work (Nobel Prize, 2013), sharing the prize with Sir John Carrow Eccles. Hodgkin and Huxley discovered that an inactive polarized neuron has a stable negative resting charge, the **resting potential**, which is typically around −70 millivolts (mV), although values range from about −50 mV to −80 mV, relative to outside of the cell (Pinel, 2009). The resting membrane potential is negative because, by convention, the charge inside of the neuron is always compared to the charge outside, and the inside of a resting neuron is roughly 70 mV more negative than the outside. **Figure 13-1** illustrates how a membrane potential can be recorded in a manner similar to the remarkable work of Hodgkin and Huxley.

Have you wondered about the negative charge associated with the resting potential? That is, why is there a difference in electrical charge across the membrane at all? Under certain circumstances, ions can move back and forth across the neuron membrane—it

> The brains of adults are approximately 60% water—two-thirds of this water is intracellular and one-third is extracellular.
>
> —*Faller & Schuenke, 2004*

resting potential the electrical charge of a neuron when it is at rest.

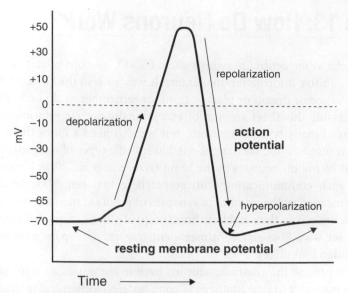

FIGURE 13-1 Resting membrane potential and action potential. One way to measure a membrane potential is to compare the charge at the tip of a microelectrode inserted into the intracellular space (inside the neuron) with the charge recorded outside the neuron. An oscilloscope can analyze and amplify the millivolt (mV) electrical differences and visually display them. The membrane potential of an inactive neuron is maintained at about −70 mV more negative inside the neuron than outside; this difference in charge across the membrane is known as the *resting membrane potential* (blue line). When a neuron is stimulated, a very rapid reversal of the membrane potential occurs as the potential changes from about −70 mV to about +50 mV and back again. This change in voltage (sometimes called a *spike* or a *neuron impulse*) is the *action potential* (red line). Source: Courtesy Genevieve Thurlow. Reprinted by permission.

concentration gradient the difference in concentration of sodium ions inside and outside of the neuron.

is permeable. With a permeable membrane between the intracellular and extracellular fluids, we would expect the charge on either side of the membrane to be the same. Since the ions are in constant random motion, we would expect that diffusion would distribute ions evenly over time thus eliminating their **concentration gradient**. In other words, since movement down the concentration gradient involves net movement from areas of high concentration to areas of low concentration, we would assume that ions would eventually achieve a state of even distribution. Additionally, we would expect the force of *electrostatic pressure* to also promote a state of even distribution. Electrostatic pressure exists because ions with opposite charges attract one another and ions with the same charge repel one another. Thus the negative and positive ions on either side of the membrane ought to be attracting and repelling one another to maintain equilibrium or balance. So, given that these two forces are at work, why is the charge on the inside of the neuron not equal to the charge on the outside (Wickens, 2005)?

Before we answer this question, let's take a closer look at the four main types of ions that contribute to the resting potential: the positively charged sodium (Na+) and potassium (K+) ions and the negatively charged chloride (Cl−) ions, as well as various negatively charged protein ions called anions (A−). When the neuron is at rest, Na+ ions (and Cl− ions) are higher in concentration outside of the cell than inside, and K+ ions and anions (A+) are higher in concentration inside than outside the cell. Despite the balancing effect of the two forces of diffusion and electrostatic pressure, no one class of ions is distributed equally over the two sides of the membrane (Pinel, 2009).

ion channels pores in the cell membrane that can open and close to allow certain ions into and out of the cell.

The unequal distribution of charges occurs for two reasons. First, the neuron's membrane exhibits *selective permeability* to ions—that is, the membrane is not equally permeable to all ions. Embedded in the membrane are specialized **ion channels**, or pores, that only allow the passage of certain ions into and out of the cell. In the resting neuron,

K+ and Cl− easily pass through the membrane, Na+ passes through the membrane with greater difficulty and therefore to a much lesser degree, and the large anions, most of which are negatively charged, are trapped inside the neuron and cannot pass through at all (Bear et al., 2007).

Diffusion, electrostatic force, and a selectively permeable membrane can't fully explain the resting membrane potential; it still needs some fine tuning. This is accomplished through the actions of **sodium-potassium pumps**, complex molecules in the neuron membrane that use energy to hold the resting potential at −70 mV by continuously pumping Na+ out of the axon, and K+ in. How does exchanging one positive ion for another positive ion maintain a negative charge? Sodium-potassium pumps are not even-handed; the pumps push out three sodium ions for every two potassium ions pumped in (Breedlove & Watson, 2013).

Think of a neuron at the resting membrane potential like a battery. Positive and negative poles are kept separate when the battery is just sitting around. But when a switch is turned on and the poles are connected, current is allowed to flow, and work can be done. The work of neurons is communication. When a neuron receives input directing it to communicate with another neuron, the electrical charge across the membrane fundamentally changes. For a very brief instant the membrane potential reverses polarity. So, for about a millisecond, the inside of the neuron becomes positive relative to the outside. This rapid reversal in voltage across axon membranes is caused by the movement of ions across the membrane and is called an **action potential**. The action potential, also called a "spike" or a "neuron impulse" or "firing," is a brief reversal of the membrane potential that causes an electrical signal to be propagated at high speed down the axon. An action potential occurs when the effects of excitatory input from other neurons outweighs the effects of inhibitory input, and the membrane potential shifts from the resting membrane potential and reaches the **threshold of excitation**.

Where do excitatory and inhibitory signals come from? Recall from our discussion about the structure of neurons that when a neuron fires it releases neurotransmitters that diffuse across the synapse and interact with receptors on other neurons. A given neuron is constantly influenced by neurotransmitters from other neurons. These neurotransmitters have one of two effects: they either **depolarize** the resting membrane potential of the receiving neuron (moving it closer to zero), or they **hyperpolarize** the membrane potential (moving it further away from zero). Postsynaptic depolarizations increase the chance the neuron will fire and so are called *excitatory postsynaptic potentials* (EPSPs). *Inhibitory postsynaptic potentials* (IPSPs) hyperpolarize the membrane and thereby decrease the likelihood that the cell will fire. A given neuron may receive input from hundreds or thousands of other neurons, and whether or not it fires depends on the net effect of the excitatory and inhibitory signals (this is a process known as *summation*).

When the membrane potential depolarizes, moving from −70 mV to around −55 to −40 mV, an action potential is generated, and the neuron is said to "fire" (Wickens, 2005). The action potential (shown in **Figure 13-2**) is created at the point where the axon leaves the neuron cell body. To initiate an action potential, ion channels that allow the passage of sodium (Na+) through the membrane rapidly open and then close. The opening of the Na+ channels enables Na+, which is present in higher concentrations outside of the axon, to rush through the Na+ channels into the axon. The sudden influx of positive Na+ ions depolarizes the axon membrane. So much positively charged Na+ rushes in that, just for an instant, the inside of the axon membrane is about +50 mV (50 mV more positive inside than out). As depolarization occurs, the increase in membrane potential causes neighbouring Na+ channels to open, more Na+ to enter, and further depolarization to occur as the action potential sweeps down the axon of the neuron (Pinel, 2009). As the membrane potential reverses and the inside of

sodium-potassium pump protein molecules in the membrane of cells that push out sodium ions and push in potassium ions.

action potential a sudden positive change in the electrical charge of a neuron's axon, also known as a spike or firing; action potentials are rapidly transmitted down the axon.

threshold of excitation the point at which the relative influence of other neurons succeeds in causing a neuron to initiate an action potential.

depolarization the inside of the neuron membrane becomes *less* negative relative to the outside.

hyperpolarization the inside of the neuron membrane becomes *more* negative relative to the outside.

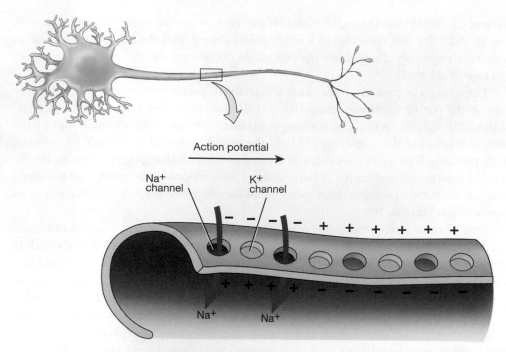

Action potential →

Na+ channel

K+ channel

− − − − + + + + + +

+ + + − − − − − − −

Na+   Na+

(a) When stimulated by a sufficiently strong signal, an "at rest" (polarized) axon become depolarized, creating an action potential. The affected section of the axon opens sodium channels embedded in the axon membrane and positively charged sodium ions (Na+) rush into the axon, changing the previously negative charge inside the axon to a positive charge.

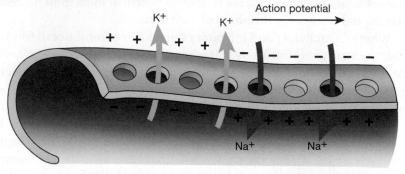

Action potential →

K+   K+

+ + + + − − − − − −

− − − − + + + + + +

Na+   Na+

(b) The depolarization produces an imbalance of ions in the adjacent axon membrane, causing the action potential to move down the axon (in a manner similar to people doing "the wave" at a football game). As the action potential moves down the membrane the initially depolarized section closes the sodium channels and opens potassium (K+) channels allowing K+ ions to flow out. This allows the first section to repolarize, restoring the resting potential.

FIGURE 13-2 **The action potential.**

the membrane becomes relatively positive, potassium channels open and electrostatic force moves K+ ions out of the axon. So many positively charged K+ ions move out of the axon that the membrane briefly becomes hyperpolarized (the refractory period; see Figure 13-2) (Brodal, 2010; Siegel et al., 2006).

As Figure 13-2 shows, the action potential, once created, travels down the axon, away from the cell body toward the axon terminal. As the action potential occurs, it recreates itself, rapidly moving along the axon in a wave of Na+ channel (depolarization) followed by K+ channel (repolarization) activation (see **Figure 13-2**). Following the passage of the action potential, during the refractory period, the sodium-potassium pumps (which operate continuously) re-establish the resting membrane potential (Siegel et al., 2006).

Action potentials are not graded—that is, there cannot be weaker or stronger action potentials. Instead, action potentials follow the *all-or-none* principle. Since action potentials are all-or-none, either initiated or not, they don't convey a lot of specific information. If the excitatory input to a neuron exceeds a certain threshold, it fires; otherwise, it does not. Think of the firing of a gun: if you squeeze the trigger, the gun either fires or it doesn't. Once fired, regardless of how hard you squeezed the trigger, the bullet has only one velocity. So, how does a neuron pass on information indicating that one stimulus is more intense than another? Stronger stimuli cause more neurons to fire and to fire more often; thus, higher frequencies send information about more intense stimuli (Stein et al., 2005). The pattern of action potentials, whether they occur in rapid succession or at a slow pace, whether they are regular or more sporadic, can therefore provide a specific neural code.

To facilitate the movement of the action potential down the axon, the axons of many neurons are surrounded and insulated by **myelin**, a white fatty layered coating produced by specialized glial cells. At regularly spaced gaps (*nodes of Ranvier*) in the myelin, the neuronal membrane is exposed to the extracellular fluid. As **Figure 13-3** shows, action potentials travel very quickly down myelinated axons by jumping from node to node in a process known as *saltatory conduction*.

After each action potential, during the *refractory period*, a neuron is unlikely to fire again, thus limiting its firing frequency. Immediately following an action potential, during the **absolute refractory period**, the axon is completely unable to fire no matter how strong the stimulus to the neuron. Following this, during the **relative refractory period**, the stimulus required to create an action potential must be greater than if the membrane potential were at the resting level (Siegel et al., 2006).

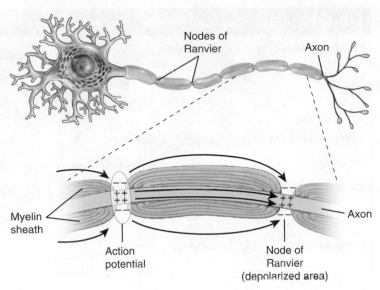

FIGURE 13-3 **Nodes of Ranvier.** The nodes of Ranvier are the regions of exposed axon between areas wrapped in myelin. Action potentials travel down the axon by jumping from node to node.

myelin a fatty, white substance formed from glial cells that insulates the axons of many neurons.

absolute refractory period a very brief period of time after an action potential during which a neuron is completely unable to fire again.

relative refractory period a brief period just after the absolute refractory period during which a neuron can only fire if it receives a stimulus stronger than its usual threshold level.

13.2 Communication Across the Synapse

Once the positive charge of an action potential reaches the axon terminal, it initiates actions that enable the passage of information to other neurons. Neurons are not physically connected to one another; they are separated by small gaps. These gaps, called **synapses**, are tiny spaces (about 20 nm or 0.00002 mm wide) usually between the axon terminal of one cell and the dendrite of another cell. As already mentioned, communication across these spaces involves specialized chemicals called **neurotransmitters**. Neurotransmitter molecules are usually contained within small **synaptic vesicles** in the axon terminal, also known as the *presynaptic* terminal, of the neuron sending information.

> **"**You are your synapses. They are who you are.**"**
>
> —*Joseph LeDoux, 2003 (in* Synaptic Self*)*

synapses tiny spaces between the axon terminal of one neuron and the neuron through which chemical communication occurs.

neurotransmitters specialized chemicals that travel across synapses to allow communication between neurons.

synaptic vesicles membrane-bound spheres in the axon terminals of neurons in which neurotransmitters are stored before their release.

13.2.1 Role of Neurotransmitters

There are a number of different neurotransmitters, and some are associated with specific brain functions—though the relationships are far from simple. Many drugs that alter psychological functioning are designed to interfere with or enhance neurotransmitter functions. For example, the neurotransmitter **serotonin** has been implicated in a number of important functions, such as activity levels and mood regulation (Lowry et al., 2008).

serotonin neurotransmitter involved in activity levels and mood regulation.

TABLE 13-1 Common Neurotransmitters and Drugs Associated with Each

Neurotransmitter	Function	Associated Drugs
Glutamate	Learning, movement	Ketamine
GABA	Learning, anxiety regulation	Valium (diazepam, used to relieve anxiety, muscle spasms); Ambien (Zolpidem, used to treat insomnia)
Acetylcholine (ACh)	Learning, attention	Nicotine
Dopamine	Movement, reward learning	Cocaine; heroin; methamphetamine
Serotonin	Mood regulation	Ecstasy (MDMA); LSD (hallucinogens); monoamine oxidase inhibitors (MAOIs), selective serotonin reuptake inhibitors (SSRIs; antidepressants)
Norepinephrine	Attention, arousal	Adderall (a stimulant made up of dextroamphetamine and amphetamine)

Several popular drugs used to treat depression and anxiety increase the action of serotonin, thereby improving mood. **Table 13-1** lists some major neurotransmitters, their associated functions, and some drugs that can be used to manipulate these neurotransmitter systems. Later in the part, you will see that certain neurotransmitters are also associated with specific brain regions.

When an action potential reaches the presynaptic axon terminal, it causes the release of neurotransmitter molecules into the synapse. As **Figure 13-4** shows, the neurotransmitter then diffuses across the synapse and binds to neurotransmitter receptors on the dendrite of the receiving, or *postsynaptic*, neuron. **Neurotransmitter receptors** are proteins in the cell membrane that recognize specific molecules. They operate in a lock and key fashion such that receptors can only receive the specific neurotransmitter that "fits" to them (Deutch & Roth, 2008). There are perhaps 100 or more different neurotransmitters, including dopamine, serotonin, and norepinephrine, and many of these neurotransmitters "fit" and activate several different receptor subtypes (Zorumski & Rubin, 2011). We will discuss neurotransmitters in greater detail below.

neurotransmitter receptors proteins in the membranes of neurons that bind to neurotransmitters.

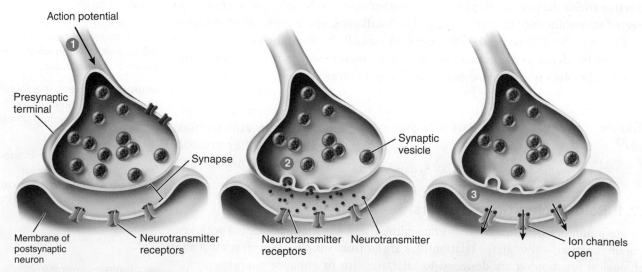

FIGURE 13-4 Communication across the synapse. (1) An action potential reaches the end of the axon; (2) the membrane depolarization stimulates release of neurotransmitters from membrane-bound vesicles into the synapse; (3) neurotransmitters bind to receptors on the postsynaptic neuron membrane; specific ion channels open or close and electrical membrane potential in the postsynaptic neuron changes.

As we saw above, when a neurotransmitter binds to a receptor, the combination stimulates an electrical event in the postsynaptic membrane. These electrical events, called **postsynaptic potentials**, can be *excitatory* or *inhibitory*. The electrical response of the postsynaptic cell is determined by the receptor. If the receptor has an excitatory action, then the postsynaptic cell will be depolarized; the membrane potential will become less negative. Depolarizations that arise from inputs of a single neuron may not be great enough to trigger an action potential in the postsynaptic neuron, but they can be summed together with other depolarizations. In this way, the threshold will be reached and the neuron will fire, sending the information on to the next neuron in the chain. Alternatively, if the receptor has an inhibitory action, then the postsynaptic cell will be hyperpolarized: its membrane potential will become more negative. Hyperpolarization makes it less likely that the postsynaptic neuron will fire an action potential.

Repeated release of neurotransmitters into the synapse can result in long-lasting changes at the synapse in both presynaptic and postsynaptic neurons. Postsynaptic effects can include changes in neurotransmitter receptors. According to Costa-Mattioli and his colleagues at McGill University (2009), such effects may play a role in memory consolidation. We will discuss consolidation further in Part 8.

Once a neurotransmitter has bound with the postsynaptic receptor, one of two processes terminates the activity of the neurotransmitter and halts the communication. This process of termination is essential or the postsynaptic receptor could be blocked from receiving further input, or neurotransmitter molecules could accumulate in the synapse, obscuring future discrete chemical signals. The first process is *enzymatic degradation* and involves the breaking down of the neurotransmitter by enzymes. Often the products of the breakdown are reabsorbed by the cell and are used to synthesize additional neurotransmitter molecules. An example of a neurotransmitter inactivated by a special enzyme is acetylcholine (broken down by an enzyme called *acetylcholinesterase*). The second, more common, process is known as *reuptake*; in this process, neurotransmitters are drawn back into the presynaptic neuron and recycled for future use. Examples of neurotransmitters terminated mostly by reuptake are norepinephrine, dopamine, and serotonin (Bear et al., 2007). Drugs such as the selective serotonin reuptake inhibitors (SSRIs) commonly used to treat depression (e.g., fluoxetine, trade name Prozac) inhibit (as its name would suggest) the reuptake of serotonin, thereby increasing the total amount of serotonin available in the synapse (Cowen & Lucki, 2011).

postsynaptic potentials electrical events in postsynaptic neurons that occur when a neurotransmitter binds to one of its receptors.

13.2.2 Neurotransmitters and Their Functions

Now that you have a basic understanding of the crucial role that neurotransmitters play in human behaviour and functioning, let's examine a few specific neurotransmitters in greater detail. First, although something of an oversimplification, neurotransmitters can be identified by function, that is, as excitatory (causing action potentials to be generated) or inhibitory (preventing action potentials from being generated). However, some neurotransmitters can be either excitatory or inhibitory depending on the type of receptor that is present. Second, neurotransmitters can be classified by type (e.g., location, type of receptor it binds to, etc.). Although it is important to understand that systems of classification exist, we will just discuss a few of the better understood neurotransmitters below and will not concern ourselves with further classification. Before we begin, however, you need to be aware that identifying specific behavioural or physical outcomes from a single neurotransmitter is complicated. Neurotransmitters play multiple complex roles, their functions often overlap or interact, and their effects can differ considerably depending where they are released in the nervous system.

Acetylcholine German biologist Otto Loewi isolated acetylcholine (ACh) in 1921. ACh is important for stimulating muscles and plays a key role in communicating between motor and sensory neurons. It is also important for attention, arousal, and memory, and plays a part in REM (dream) sleep. The venom from some snakes and spiders prevents the release of ACh into the synapse or blocks ACh receptors, disrupting or slowing motor control, often with fatal consequences (Lewis & Gutmann, 2004). Widespread loss of ACh is evident in Alzheimer's disease (Craig et al., 2011). As well, the poison botulin prevents the axons from releasing ACh, causing paralysis and death. Given in very small doses, Botox, a derivative of the poison botulin, temporarily reduces wrinkles by preventing nerve cells from signalling to the muscles to contract.

Dopamine   This neurotransmitter is associated with mood, control of voluntary movement, and reward mechanisms in the brain (Koob, 2013). A number of drugs increase dopamine levels including heroin, alcohol, opium, and nicotine. An excessive amount of dopamine in the frontal lobes is associated with schizophrenia (Kendler & Schaffner, 2011); drugs that block dopamine help to control the symptoms of schizophrenia. On the other hand, too little dopamine in the motor areas of the brain is implicated in Parkinson's disease (Torrente et al., 2012). Parkinson's disease is a neurological condition that involves the death of dopaminergic neurons—those that produce the neurotransmitter dopamine—in the substantia nigra (Jankovic & Aguilar, 2008). A precursor drug to dopamine (L-dopa) helps alleviate some of the symptoms of Parkinson's disease.

> "All the most acute, most powerful, and most deadly diseases, and those which are most difficult to be understood by the inexperienced, fall upon the brain."
>
> —*Hippocrates, fourth-century B.C.E.*
> *Greek philosopher*

Norepinephrine   This excitatory neurotransmitter is also known as noradrenaline and is involved in stimulating the sympathetic nervous system, affecting arousal, vigilance, and mood (Berridge & Waterhouse, 2003). Strong emotions such as fear or anger cause an increase in heart rate and muscle strength, as well as increases in blood carbohydrate metabolism and respiration (Zimmerman et al., 2012). Norepinephrine constricts blood vessels, raises blood pressure, and dilates the bronchi. Norepinephrine also plays a role in learning, memory, sleep, and emotion. People with depressive disorders may have low levels of norepinephrine, whereas excessive levels have been linked to anxiety.

Robin Marchant/Getty Images

Parkinson's disease. In 1991, at only 30 years of age, Canadian Michael J. Fox was diagnosed with Parkinson's disease. He went public with his diagnosis in 1998. He founded the Michael J. Fox Foundation for Parkinson's Research to support research and Parkinson's patient care, which has granted more than $450 million in research to date.

Serotonin   This inhibitory neurotransmitter is involved in the regulation of mood, appetite, and sleep (Cappadocia et al., 2009; Häuser, 2013; Young & Leyton, 2002) as well as in the perception of pain (Hamel, 2007). Serotonin also plays a role in activity level (Lowry et al., 2008) and cognitive functions such as learning and memory (Kuhn et al., 2014). As already discussed, many antidepressant medications block the reuptake of serotonin, increasing the amount available to receptors in the synapse, and resulting in elevation of mood.

GABA (gamma-amino butyric acid)   GABA, the most common inhibitory neurotransmitter in the brain, reduces the activity of the neurons it binds to. GABA has been implicated in sleep (Chong, 2014) and associated with reduction of arousal of the nervous system. Abnormal levels have been implicated in eating disorders (Dennis & Pryor, 2014) as well as in epilepsy (Maru & Ura, 2014). As shown in Table 13-1, benzodiazepines such as Valium mimic GABA by binding to, and activating, GABA receptors and reducing neural activity.

Glutamate   This neurotransmitter is believed to be the most important transmitter for normal brain function (Brannon et al., 2008). It is released by up to half of the brain's neurons and is therefore the most common excitatory transmitter in the brain (Meldrum, 2000). At normal concentrations, glutamate is involved in a wide range of behaviours and plays a central role in learning and in the formation of new memories (Peng et al., 2011). A drug targeting glutamate receptors used since the mid-1960s as a surgical anesthetic for procedural sedation (Strayer et al., 2008) is now demonstrating promise for treating fears and phobias (Bloch et al., 2012; Davis et al., 2006) as well as depression (Bloch et al., 2012; Mathews et al., 2012). However, glutamate has also been implicated in neurodegenerative disorders such as Huntington's disease. Current research suggests that Huntington's may be related to excessive glutamate activation (excitotoxicity) causing particular neurons to die (Padowski et al., 2014). Huntington's disease is an inherited condition that results in the death of neurons in a part of the brain called the striatum. People suffering from this disease exhibit awkward movements and often show symptoms of psychosis (Paulsen, 2009). Like ALS and Parkinson's disease, Huntington's disease is progressive and, as yet, there is no cure.

stem cells undifferentiated cells that can divide to create new cells that have the potential to become any other cell type, including neurons.

Psychology Around Us — Transplanting Stem Cells to Treat Neurological Disorders

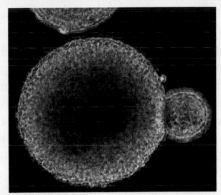

Riccardo Cassiani-Ingoni/Science Source

Neural stem cells. Shown in this microscopic image, neural stem cells have been a focus of research into restoration of function to damaged or diseased nervous systems. These cells can divide and produce different types of neurons depending on their environment.

Medical and neuroscience researchers have not yet developed significantly effective treatments for many of the devastating neurological diseases discussed in this part. Some neuroscientists have therefore turned their attention to the possibility of repairing damaged brain regions by transplanting new tissue into the brain.

Early work ruled out the possibility of transplanting fully differentiated brain tissue into a damaged region. In most cases, these transplants did not survive or integrate properly into the existing circuitry. Subsequent attempts to transplant fetal brain tissue into brains of adults suffering from Alzheimer's or Parkinson's disease also met with little success (Isacson & Kordower, 2008; Freed, 2000).

Thus, transplantation research has focused primarily on the possibility of restoring damaged circuits by transplanting stem cells. **Stem cells** were first identified by Ernest McCulloch and James Till working at the University of Toronto in 1960. Stem cells are undifferentiated cells that have the potential to grow into any cell type if given the appropriate environmental cues. The most versatile stem cells come from embryonic tissue (Srivastava et al., 2008). Researchers have obtained stem cells from embryos created as part of *in vitro* fertilization, a procedure sometimes used to help infertile couples have babies. Eggs are fertilized with sperm in the laboratory, and some of the resulting embryos are implanted into a woman's uterus. Remaining, or extra, embryos, at very early stages of development, can provide a source for stem cells that can then be cultured and reproduced. Embryos are destroyed in the process of obtaining these stem cells, so this procedure is controversial. Researchers are now working to find other sources of stem cells, including reproducing them from adult tissue (Temple, 2001).

Thus far, stem-cell transplantation studies in animals have been moderately successful, particularly in animal models of Parkinson's disease (Takahashi et al., 2009; Hovakimyan et al., 2008). The effectiveness of stem-cell treatment may depend on what kind of brain cell is damaged and where the damaged cells are located. For instance, Parkinson's disease arises predominantly from the death of dopaminergic neurons in the *substantia nigra*, a movement-related part of the brain. Creating dopamine-producing cells from stem cells and grafting them into the striatum may help reduce the symptoms of Parkinson's; results thus far, while promising, have been mixed. Other neurological diseases that cause more widespread damage might not respond as well to stem-cell treatment. For example, patients with Alzheimer's disease (which we discuss in some detail in Part 8) lose neurons throughout their brains. The disease also causes the formation of abnormal clusters of non-degradable protein that interfere with neuronal function (Rafii & Aisen, 2009). Therefore, replacing only certain types of dead neurons may not be sufficient to overcome the widespread devastation characteristic of that disease.

13.3 Neural Networks

In the brain, neurons do not work alone or even in very small groups. A single neuron cannot effect change of any kind on its own in a complex nervous system like ours. Instead, millions of neurons work in unison developing patterns of neural activity, firing together or in temporal sequence or pattern to influence behaviour (Song et al., 2005). Collections of neurons that communicate with one another in a sequential fashion are referred to as *neural circuits* or *neural networks*. In his influential book, *The Organization of Behavior* (2002, 1949), Donald Hebb, perhaps one of Canada's most famous psychologists, inferred the existence of what he called *cell assemblies*, networks of neurons underlying complex cognitive behaviours. Hebb's description of cell assemblies was instrumental in shaping the current approach to the study of neural networks. Cell assemblies are networks of neurons that begin with essentially random connections, but become organized to work together as an interconnected entity. As particular mental processes are repeated, synaptic connections are strengthened, building units for memory and cognitive functioning. The notion that effective synapses thrive at the expense of inefficient synapses was a precursor to more recent work on *synaptic pruning* (Tapia & Lichtman, 2008), and research examining the long-term changes that occur at the synapse in response to input. In Hebb's honour, synapses that change as a result of input or experience are known as *Hebbian synapses* (Pinel, 2009). Both past and current neuroscientists have focused attention on the Hebbian synapse and individual neural systems to better grasp the complex functioning of neural circuits as they relate to learning, memory, and behaviour (Schultz et al., 1997; Paulsen & Sejnowski, 2000; Del Giudice, 2009).

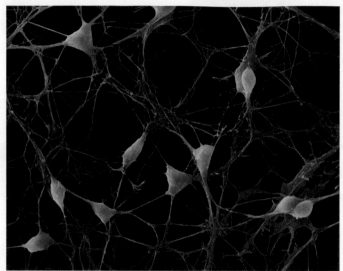

Dennis Kunkel/Phototake

Neural network. Neurons form circuits or networks that expand the communication among different brain regions. This image shows axons and dendrites (red) extending from the neuronal cell bodies (shown in blue).

13.4 Neuroplasticity

We now know that behaviour and experience can physically alter the brain. For example, children raised in homes where they learn both French and English have brains that are different (in terms of certain structures) from the brains of children raised in homes where they were exposed to only one language (Huttenlocher, 2009). The same is the case for children raised in homes where they were subject to neglect or abuse versus children raised in homes with nurturing and appropriately responsive parents (Cicchetti, 2012). The capacity of neurons and neural connections in the brain to reorganize in response to experiences or changes in the environment or to injury is generally referred to as **neuroplasticity** or neural plasticity (Morris et al., 2014; Morgensen, 2011). Plasticity refers to the brain's ability to form new neural connections or to repurpose neurons to take up functions lost through the loss of other neurons (Doidge, 2007). There is evidence that some areas of the brain, including the hippocampus (Cowansage et al., 2010) and the olfactory bulb (Rakic, 2002), as well as the cerebellum (Ponti et al., 2008) and prefrontal cortex (McEwen & Morrison, 2013) can generate new brain cells to replace lost cells, even into older adulthood. Plasticity at the synapse, such as the changes that occur from repeated release of neurotransmitters, is called *synaptic plasticity*. Neuroscientists have extensively studied synaptic plasticity because evidence suggests that it may explain some types of learning, as we will describe further in Part 7.

neuroplasticity the brain's ability to create new neural pathways as a result of experience or following an injury.

What Do You Know?

1. How do neurons work?
2. What happens in the axon of a neuron during an action potential?
3. When an action potential reaches the axon terminal, what happens?
4. How does a postsynaptic neuron receive and respond to messages from other neurons?

What Do You Think? Long axons are vulnerable to damage. What do you think some advantages might be of having a neuron with a very long axon (for example, one with a cell body in the spinal cord and axon terminal in the toe or finger)?

Summary

Module 13: How Do Neurons Work?

LEARNING OBJECTIVE 13 Describe what happens when a neuron "fires" and how neurons send messages to one another.

- Communication within a neuron occurs electrically by means of the action potential, whereas communication between neurons occurs at the synapse via chemical signals called neurotransmitters.
- Neurotransmitters are released by the presynaptic neuron, diffuse across the synapse, and bind to receptors on the postsynaptic site.
- The response of a receiving neuron to a neurotransmitter is determined by the receptor on the postsynaptic, or receiving, neuron's membrane. Depending on the type of receptor, the postsynaptic neurons will fire or not.

Key Terms

absolute refractory period 87
action potential 85
concentration gradient 84
depolarization 85
hyperpolarization 85

ion channels 84
myelin 87
neuroplasticity 92
neurotransmitter receptors 88
neurotransmitters 87

postsynaptic potentials 89
relative refractory period 87
resting potential 83
serotonin 87
sodium-potassium pump 85

stem cells 91
synapses 87
synaptic vesicles 87
threshold of excitation 85

Study Questions

Multiple Choice

1. Selective permeability and sodium-potassium pumps are responsible for:
   a) the unequal distribution of charges across the cell membrane.
   b) the equal distribution of charges across the cell membrane.
   c) graded action potentials.
   d) non-graded action potentials.

Fill-in-the-Blank

1. The _____ principle maintains that action potentials are not graded, that is, they cannot be weak or strong.
2. _____ is the process through which stem cells develop characteristics specific to a certain type of cell.
3. The poison botulin prevents axons from releasing the neurotransmitter _____, resulting in paralysis and death.

Module 14: How Is the Nervous System Organized?

afferent neurons neurons that carry sensory information from the body to the CNS.

efferent neurons neurons that carry information out from the CNS to the muscles and glands.

interneurons neurons that typically have a short axon and serve as a relay between different classes of neurons; in the spinal cord, interneurons communicate with both sensory and motor neurons.

somatic nervous system all the peripheral nerves that transmit information about body sensation and movement to and from the central nervous system.

autonomic nervous system portion of the peripheral nervous system that comprises the sympathetic and parasympathetic nervous systems.

sympathetic nervous system the part of the autonomic nervous system that is activated under conditions of stress.

parasympathetic nervous system the part of the autonomic nervous system that is active during restful times.

As shown in **Figure 14-1**, the human nervous system can be divided into two main components: the central nervous system (CNS) and the peripheral nervous system (PNS). The *central nervous system* consists of the brain and spinal cord. The *peripheral nervous system* is made up of the many nerves throughout our bodies that deliver information back and forth between the periphery and the central nervous system. Neurons that carry signals from the PNS to the CNS are called **afferent neurons**. Neurons that carry signals from the CNS to the PNS are called **efferent neurons**. **Interneurons** are neurons that connect two or more neurons. For example, a signal produced by an afferent sensory neuron in the skin near your ankle would be communicated via one or more interneurons before it reached a neuron in a sensory area of the brain.

14.1 The Peripheral Nervous System (PNS)

The peripheral nervous system consists of the somatic nervous system and the autonomic nervous system. The **somatic nervous system** is made up of all of the nerves that gather sensory information (typically about touch and pain) from all over the body, neck, and head and deliver it to the spinal cord and brain, as well as the nerves that send information about movement from the CNS to the muscles of the body, neck, and head. As we will see shortly, the somatic nervous system doesn't serve any function without the integrating capacity of the CNS. The main function of the PNS is to send information to and receive information from the CNS. Even very simple reflexes require the CNS.

By contrast, parts of the **autonomic nervous system** operate mostly without help from the CNS. The autonomic nervous system can be subdivided into two parts: the *sympathetic nervous system* and the *parasympathetic nervous system*. Both components of the autonomic nervous system are made up of collections of nerve cells distributed throughout the body. However, they serve opposing functions. The sympathetic nervous system is activated under conditions of stress, whereas the parasympathetic nervous system is inhibited during those times, but is active during more restful times.

The **sympathetic nervous system** is responsible for the "fight-or-flight" reaction, the physiological response that enables us to respond to potentially life-threatening situations. Imagine that you are hiking on what you know to be a safe path in the woods and you hear rustling behind you. You turn to look, but cannot see anything. You chide yourself for being imaginative and continue walking, but then you hear the rustling again; this time it is closer. Your sympathetic system activates at this point: Your pupils dilate to maximize the amount of light entering your eyes, your heart rate and respiration increase so you can get more oxygen to your muscles, glucose is released into your system to provide energy to your muscles, and your blood pressure increases and blood flow is diverted to your brain and muscles. Nonessential functions, that is, those activities not devoted to helping you survive (such as digestion and elimination) are slowed down or stopped entirely. At this point you see a bear and drop your bag, sprinting to the nearest tree, quickly climbing it. Once the emergency has passed, the **parasympathetic nervous system** takes over and helps reverse the effects of the sympathetic system to return the body to its normal resting state. Once the bear has opened your pack, eaten your lunch, and ambled away your heart rate slows and your breathing normalizes and eventually you feel safe enough to climb down from the tree. Since the parasympathetic system returns the system to its resting state it is sometimes called the "rest and digest" system (Lang & Bradley, 2013).

Sometimes the sympathetic nervous system is activated when humans are not necessarily at risk of bodily harm, but are in social situations where the major fear is one of

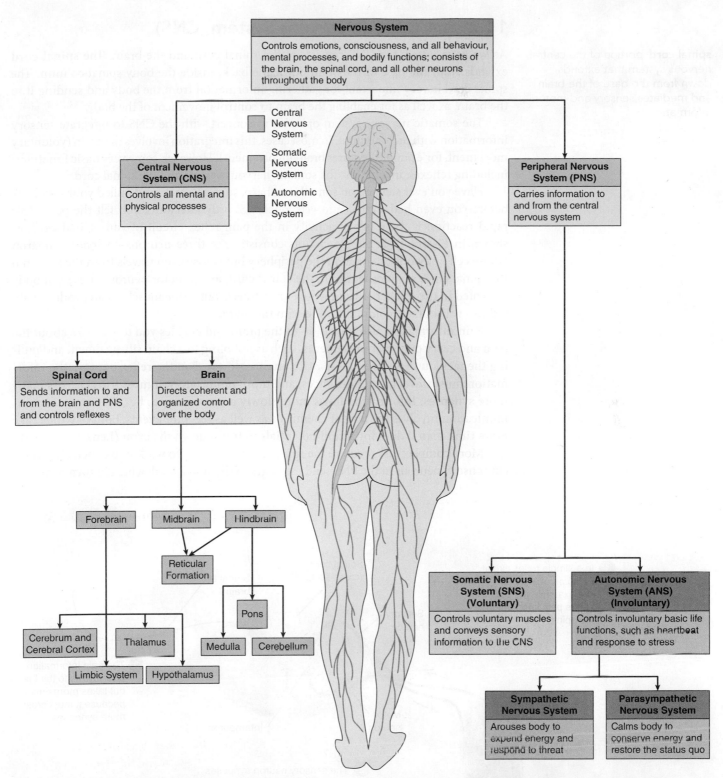

FIGURE 14-1 Organization of the nervous system. The nervous system is divided into the central nervous system (consisting of the brain and spinal cord) and the peripheral nervous system (consisting of the somatic nervous system and the autonomic nervous system). The autonomic nervous system is further subdivided into the sympathetic and parasympathetic nervous systems. Source: Reprinted with permission of John Wiley & Sons, Inc., from Huffman, K. (2010). *Psychology in Action*, 9th edition. Hoboken, NJ: Wiley, Figure 2.4, p. 60.

embarrassment and humiliation, such as presenting in front of a class or giving a speech at a friend's wedding (Rash & Prkachin, 2013). Have you ever given a speech in front of a group of people? Many people experience a strong stress response to such situations. They develop a rapid heart rate, increased respiration, and a dry mouth, signs that the sympathetic nervous system has activated and a clear example of stress activating physiological systems.

14.2 The Central Nervous System (CNS)

spinal cord portion of the central nervous system that extends down from the base of the brain and mediates sensory and motor information.

As we have noted, the CNS consists of the spinal cord and the brain. The **spinal cord** extends from the base of the brain down the back, inside the bony spinal column. The spinal cord is very important for gathering information from the body and sending it to the brain, as well as for enabling the brain to control movement of the body.

The somatic nervous system operates in concert with the CNS to integrate sensory information with motor output. In most cases, this integration involves the brain (voluntary movement, for example, requires brain involvement). However, some very basic functions, including reflexes, involve just the somatic nervous system and the spinal cord.

Have you ever stepped on something sharp, such as a tack, and pulled your foot back before you even had a chance to yell "ouch"? Shortly afterward, you felt the pain. This rapid reaction is the result of activity in the pain reflex circuit of your spinal cord, as shown in **Figure 14-2**. Simple circuits consisting of three neurons—a sensory neuron whose cell body is located out in the periphery but whose axon travels from the skin into the spinal cord, an interneuron in the spinal cord, and a motor neuron whose cell body is located in the spinal cord and whose axon travels out to the muscle—can produce pain reflexes without any communication with the brain.

Pain information also travels up to the brain and enables you to vocalize about the pain and carry out other movements, such as hobbling to a chair, sitting down, and pulling the tack out. However, these reactions are slower than the reflex because the information must travel greater distances, and more importantly, it must travel across many more synapses. Information flows more slowly across synapses because synaptic communication involves the flow of chemicals as well as receptor events, both of which take more time than it does for action potentials to travel down the axon (Lenz et al., 2010).

More complex tasks require the spinal cord and brain to work in partnership. Afferent sensory neurons in the PNS send messages to the spinal cord, which in turn relays the

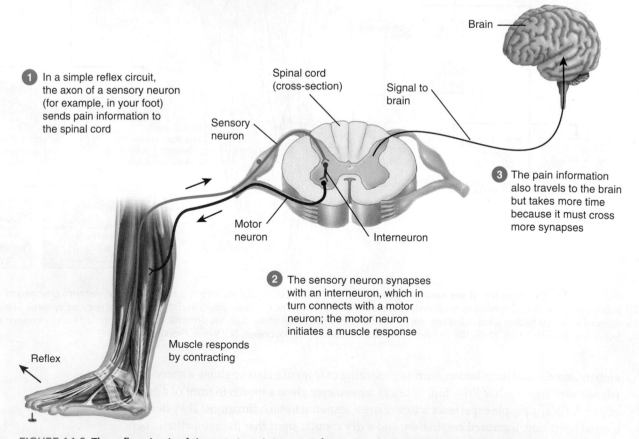

1. In a simple reflex circuit, the axon of a sensory neuron (for example, in your foot) sends pain information to the spinal cord

Spinal cord (cross-section)

Sensory neuron

Brain

Signal to brain

3. The pain information also travels to the brain but takes more time because it must cross more synapses

Motor neuron

Interneuron

2. The sensory neuron synapses with an interneuron, which in turn connects with a motor neuron; the motor neuron initiates a muscle response

Reflex

Muscle responds by contracting

FIGURE 14-2 The reflex circuit of the spinal cord. Sensory information travels into the spinal cord along sensory neurons that synapse on interneurons. Interneurons send information to the motor neurons in the spinal cord, which then send impulses back out to the periphery to contract the muscle and induce movement.

message to the brain. The brain sends commands through efferent neurons to the spinal cord motor neurons, which in turn relay the message to the skeletal muscles, signalling them to contract. Damage to the spinal cord disconnects the brain from the sensory and motor neurons essential for sensory and motor function.

14.3 Spinal Cord Injuries

A neck "break" refers to broken bones (vertebrae) in the neck. A spinal cord injury occurs when the nerves that make up the spinal cord itself are damaged. As such, it is possible to break your neck and not have a spinal cord injury, though the two often occur together. In addition to controlling simple reflexes, the spinal cord is very important for carrying sensory information up to the brain and motor information back out to the body. When the spinal cord is damaged such that the flow of information to and from the brain is disrupted, individuals become paralyzed, as well as incapable of perceiving touch or pain sensations on the body. The higher up the spinal cord the damage occurs (the closer it occurs to the brain), the larger the proportion of the body that is afflicted. Thus, when individuals break their necks and permanently damage the spinal cord close to the brain, they lose touch and pain sensation everywhere but their heads and faces and they become *quadriplegic*, paralyzed everywhere but the head and neck. If the damage occurs farther down the back, then they may retain sensation and usage of the upper limbs and torso, but not of the lower limbs.

Rick Hansen, a well-known Canadian with a spinal cord injury, began to raise awareness and money for spinal cord research with his Man in Motion world tour in 1985. Since then he has established the Rick Hansen Institute, which encourages and supports spinal cord research. Spinal cord damage is devastating and afflicts a large number of people; currently affecting about 86,000 Canadians who are living with some form of spinal injury (Farry & Baxter, 2010). Scientists are looking at ways to enhance regeneration of severed axons in the spinal cord, as well as examining the potential for replacing motor neurons destroyed by injury (Liu, 2013; Barnabé-Heider et al., 2008).

Although some progress has been made in the treatment of spinal cord injury, there is much work to be done. Freda Miller, working at The Hospital for Sick Children in Toronto together with colleagues in Toronto and British Columbia, contributed to progress in this area in 2007 (Miller & Gauthier, 2007). Miller discovered that stem cells produced from a person's own skin are similar to neural stem cells and are capable of producing Schwann cells. This is promising because Schwann cells seem to create an environment in which injured nerve fibres can regenerate, something that normally does not occur after CNS damage. (Neuron axons in the PNS, myelinated by Schwann cells, do regenerate under certain conditions, and Schwann cells are necessary for that regeneration to occur.) While this work is still in the experimental phase, it holds out the possibility that one day in the not too distant future we may be able to repair damaged spinal cords.

FACING
ADVERSITY

Derek Leung/Getty Images

Rick Hansen. In 1973, at the age of 15, Rick Hansen was involved in an accident that left him paralyzed from the waist down. In 1985 he embarked on his Man in Motion Tour to wheel over 40,000 km across 34 countries around the world. After the tour, he established the Rick Hansen Foundation to fund research into spinal cord injuries.

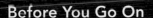

Before You Go On

www.wiley.com/go/comercanada

What Do You Know?

1. What are the two parts of the central nervous system?
2. What happens when the sympathetic nervous system is operating? How does that compare to the operation of the parasympathetic nervous system?
3. How do the brain and spinal cord work together?
4. What neuron types are important for simple reflexes?
5. What determines how much disability will result from a spinal cord injury?

What Do You Think? Describe an occasion when you have experienced the workings of the sympathetic nervous system. Have you ever been able to control your sympathetic or parasympathetic reactions? If so, how?

Summary

Module 14: How Is the Nervous System Organized?

LEARNING OBJECTIVE 14 Name and describe the functions and subdivisions of the two major parts of the nervous system.

- The two major divisions of the nervous system are the central nervous system, which consists of the brain and spinal cord, and the peripheral nervous system, which consists of nerves that extend throughout the body outside the central nervous system.
- The peripheral nervous system has two divisions: the somatic nervous system, which sends information about the senses and movement, and the autonomic nervous system, which controls involuntary functions and responses to stress.
- The autonomic nervous system is divided into the sympathetic "fight-or-flight" nervous system, which responds to stress by activating the autonomic system.
- The parasympathetic "rest and digest" nervous system is responsible for returning the autonomic system to baseline.

Key Terms

afferent neurons 94

autonomic nervous system 94

efferent neurons 94

interneurons 94

parasympathetic nervous system 94

somatic nervous system 94

spinal cord 96

sympathetic nervous system 94

Study Questions

Multiple Choice

1. Which nervous system is responsible for activating the body's reaction to a stressful situation?
   a) central
   b) parasympathetic
   c) somatic
   d) sympathetic

Fill-in-the-Blank

1. The _____ subdivision of the peripheral nervous system controls voluntary motor activity.

Module 15: Structures of the Brain

The human brain weighs about 1,400 grams (about 3 pounds) and is roughly the size of your two fists put together. Except for a few structures, the brain is almost entirely bilaterally symmetrical (i.e., the two sides appear the same). If it were laid flat, it would be too large, much too large, to fit in the skull (unfolded, the area of the cerebral cortex, the wrinkled outer layer of the brain, covers 2,000 cm²—roughly the size of a pillowcase). To be compact enough to fit inside the skull the brain had to fold upon itself as it developed, forming a number of convolutions or folds known as *gyri* or *sulci*. To think about this, imagine for a minute that you are trying to put a piece of tissue into a small box. A 20 cm × 25 cm piece of tissue won't fit into a 5 cm square box. How do you solve this problem? Easy. You scrunch up the tissue and then it fits easily into the box. In this same way, greater brain surface can be accommodated without having to give up function and power. **Figure 15-1** shows the major structures of the brain.

> **LEARNING OBJECTIVE 15**
> List key structures of the brain and describe their relationships to our behaviour.

> Your brain uses 20 percent of your body's energy, but it makes up only 2 percent of your body's weight.

15.1 The Hindbrain

The part of the brain closest to the spinal cord is called the **hindbrain**. The hindbrain consists of the medulla, the pons, and the cerebellum. The reticular formation inside begins in the hindbrain and extends to the midbrain.

hindbrain the part of the brain closest to the spinal cord that consists of the medulla, the pons, and the cerebellum; the reticular formation begins here and extends to the midbrain.

15.1.1 The Medulla

The **medulla** extends up from the spinal cord and is important for basic bodily functions, including respiration and heart rate regulation, as well as for regulating reflexes such as sneezing and coughing. Although most of the actions of the brainstem occur without our conscious knowledge or control, this part of the brain is critical for survival and normal functioning. Damage to the medulla, as a result of stroke or trauma, is often fatal (Eggers et al., 2009). High levels of alcohol can also suppress medulla activity and cause heart or respiratory failure (Figueredo & Purushottam, 2013; Blessing, 1997).

medulla part of the brain that controls basic bodily processes and regulates certain reflexes.

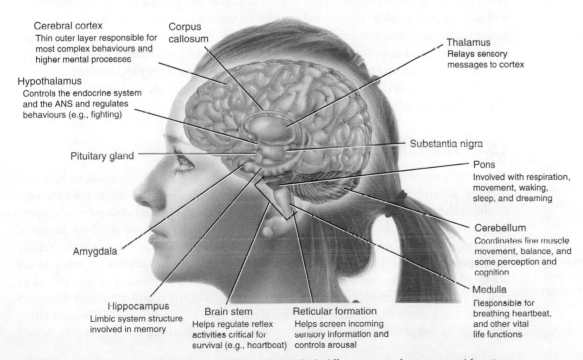

Cerebral cortex
Thin outer layer responsible for most complex behaviours and higher mental processes

Corpus callosum

Thalamus
Relays sensory messages to cortex

Hypothalamus
Controls the endocrine system and the ANS and regulates behaviours (e.g., fighting)

Pituitary gland

Substantia nigra

Pons
Involved with respiration, movement, waking, sleep, and dreaming

Amygdala

Cerebellum
Coordinates fine muscle movement, balance, and some perception and cognition

Hippocampus
Limbic system structure involved in memory

Brain stem
Helps regulate reflex activities critical for survival (e.g., heartbeat)

Reticular formation
Helps screen incoming sensory information and controls arousal

Medulla
Responsible for breathing heartbeat, and other vital life functions

FIGURE 15-1 The brain is subdivided into many regions which differ in terms of structure and function.

pons uppermost or anterior (front) part of the brainstem that includes the locus coeruleus.

norepinephrine a neurotransmitter that is important for arousal and attention.

cerebellum part of the brain, near the base of the back of the head, important for motor coordination.

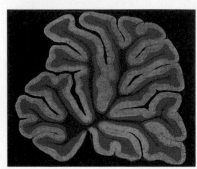

Courtesy Thomas Deerinck, NCMIR, University of California, San Diego

A convoluted brain region. The cerebellum is a highly folded structure, as shown here in this fluorescent image of a slice through this part of the brain.

reticular formation a complex neural network extending from the hindbrain into the midbrain that plays a central role in regulating consciousness and arousal.

dopamine neurotransmitter produced by neurons in the brain stem and involved in movement and reward mechanisms.

15.1.2 The Pons

Above the medulla is a region called the **pons**, named for the Latin word for "bridge." The pons acts as a bridge (hence its name) between the medulla and other brain areas. The pons is involved in sleep, dreaming, breathing, swallowing, eye movements, and facial sensation and expression. This part of the brain contains the *locus coeruleus*. Neurons of the locus coeruleus have long axons that project throughout the brain and spinal cord and are thus able to influence much of the CNS. These neurons use the neurotransmitter **norepinephrine** and are important for arousal and attention. It may be, for example, that under-functioning of the neurons in this area plays a role in attention deficit disorder (Viggiano et al., 2004).

15.1.3 The Cerebellum

Sitting at the back of the brain on top of, and connected to, the brainstem at the pons is the **cerebellum**. This part of the brain is important for motor coordination. People with cerebellar damage often have an awkward gait and have difficulty reaching for objects without trembling (Spencer et al., 2003). In addition to its role in motor coordination, the cerebellum is important for certain types of learning involving movement. For example, when you learn to tie your shoelaces or to play the piano, your cerebellum is at work. Also, if you are asked to participate in a field sobriety test to see if you are impaired, you could be asked to walk heel to toe along a line or close your eyes and touch your nose with your finger (Rubenzer, 2008). Both of these tasks require the sort of smooth movements that the cerebellum makes possible (unless you are drunk!). Other parts of the brain participate in controlling motor behaviours as well, particularly in cases where the task involves paying attention to a complicated series of instructions (for example, when learning how to execute a gymnastics move where you have to learn to backward jump with a quarter turn and a side flip). Once it's completely learned, the cerebellum then stores the learned motor information, ready to be recalled automatically when needed (Barlow, 2002).

15.1.4 The Reticular Formation

A complex network of nuclei (clusters of neurons that work together) extends from the hindbrain to the midbrain and together form an area known as the **reticular formation**. The reticular formation regulates the sleep-wake cycle and plays a role in wakefulness as well as level of arousal. Many general anesthetics work by reducing activity in the reticular formation and thus rendering the patient unconscious (Antognini et al., 2003). Some nuclei are engaged in other types of functioning, including attention, movement, maintaining muscle tone, and other cardiac, circulatory, and respiratory functions (Breedlove & Watson, 2013). Several groups of neurons in the reticular formation are a primary brain source of the neurotransmitter serotonin (Lowry et al., 2008).

15.2 The Midbrain

Above the pons sits the *midbrain*. The midbrain, which is relatively small in humans, contains a number of different nuclei, among them the *substantia nigra*. Like the cerebellum, the substantia nigra is important for movement, but this area serves different movement-related functions from those of the cerebellum. Like neurons in some other regions of the brain, neurons in the substantia nigra produce the neurotransmitter **dopamine**. These particular dopamine producers communicate with other brain regions located in the forebrain; the pathways are critical for fluidity of movement as well as inhibition of movement. The substantia nigra is the major structure damaged in *Parkinson's disease* (Meyer et al., 2010; Cenci, 2007), a neurological disorder characterized by progressive degeneration of dopamine-containing cells. Cell loss in this structure is slow and occurs over a period of time, but the symptoms only appear after extensive cell death has taken place (Coelho & Ferreira, 2012).

15.3 The Forebrain

The largest subdivision of the human brain is the forebrain, which controls complex cognitive, emotional, sensory, and motor functions. The forebrain is divided into two cerebral hemispheres connected by a band of white matter called the *corpus callosum* (which is described in more detail later in this part). Each side of the brain controls the opposite (*contralateral*) side of the body. The outermost layer of each hemisphere is composed of grey matter (largely neuron and glia cell bodies) called the *cerebral cortex*. Beneath the cortex are the subcortical (below the cortex) structures.

The subcortical lie buried inside the forebrain and include the thalamus, hypothalamus, pituitary gland, limbic system, basal ganglia, and substantia nigra.

15.3.1 The Thalamus

The **thalamus** is a large collection of nuclei located anterior to, or in front of, the substantia nigra. It sits in the centre of the brain between the midbrain and higher areas of the forebrain. Some of the thalamic nuclei serve as relay stations for incoming sensory information. In fact, all of our sensory systems, with the exception of the sense of smell, have a major pathway that synapses in the thalamus (Buck, 1996). Two structures of note in the thalamus are the *lateral geniculate nucleus* (LGN) and the *medial geniculate nucleus* (MGN). The LGN is important for relaying visual information to the visual area of the cortex, and the MGN is important for relaying auditory information to the auditory area of the cortex (Carlson, 2009).

thalamus an area of the brain that serves, in part, as a relay station for incoming sensory information.

15.3.2 The Hypothalamus

The **hypothalamus** is aptly named because this collection of nuclei sits beneath the thalamus (the prefix *hypo* comes from ancient Greek for below or under). Regions of the hypothalamus are important for a number of motivated behaviours necessary for our survival as a species, including eating, drinking, sex, and maternal behaviour. Damage to discrete parts of the hypothalamus can dramatically alter these basic behaviours. The hypothalamus is also critical for the control of the **endocrine**, or hormonal, **system** (Saper, 2010).

hypothalamus brain structure important for motivation and control of the endocrine system.

endocrine system the system that controls levels of hormones throughout the body.

15.3.3 The Pituitary Gland

The hypothalamus is connected to the **pituitary gland**, a small structure at the under surface of the forebrain immediately under the hypothalamus. The pituitary works with the hypothalamus to control a particular class of chemical messengers in the body—hormones—that are important for growth, reproduction, metabolism, and stress reactions. The pituitary produces releasing factors that control endocrine glands, such as the ovaries, the testes, the thyroid, and the adrenal glands.

pituitary gland brain structure that plays a central role in controlling the endocrine system.

15.3.4 The Limbic System

The hippocampus, the amygdala, the hypothalamus, parts of the thalamus, and several other areas are sometimes referred to as the **limbic system**. While its anatomical boundaries are somewhat unclear, the limbic system structures are involved in the regulation of motivation, emotion, and learning and memory. Its name means "edge" in Latin, which refers to the way that the limbic system connects many other brain areas (MacLean, 1954). There is some debate about whether the limbic system designation should be abandoned and whether it is still useful, as many researchers believe that the individual cortical and subcortical nuclei and structures cannot really be described as a "system" (Ledoux, 2003).

limbic system a group of interconnected brain structures that are associated with learning, memory, basic emotions, and drives.

amygdala brain area involved in processing information about emotions, particularly fear.

The **amygdala** is located deep within the brain, in a region referred to as the temporal lobe. Like the thalamus and hypothalamus, the amygdala is not a homogeneous structure. Instead, it is a collection of nuclei that serve different functions. The amygdala is involved in recognizing, learning about, and responding to stimuli that induce fear (LeDoux, 2007). This brain region has been the focus of considerable attention by neuroscientists because it is involved in the development of phobias, or abnormal fears (Åhs et al., 2007). In addition, the amygdala has been implicated in processing information related to more positive emotions (Hamann, Ely, Hoffman, & Kilts, 2002).

hippocampus brain region important for certain types of learning and memory.

The amygdala communicates with the **hippocampus**, a brain region important for certain types of learning and memory. Neuroscientists have extensively studied individuals with damage to the hippocampus and found that they are incapable of forming new *episodic* memories, or memories about events (Bindschaedler, et al., 2011). Research suggests that the hippocampus only temporarily stores information about events, after which the memories are stored elsewhere (Squire et al., 2004). In addition to its role in the formation and transient storage of episodic memories, the hippocampus is important for learning about one's spatial environment. Learning how to navigate around a new campus, for instance, requires the hippocampus.

The hippocampus has been extensively studied as a region of neuroplasticity. In fact, it is a region known to produce entirely new neurons in adulthood (Gould, 2007; Cameron & McKay, 2001). The function of these new neurons remains unclear, but their presence suggests that the adult brain is capable of regenerative processes, leading to the hope that the production of new neurons, or *neurogenesis*, may be harnessed for brain repair.

Thomas Northcut/Getty Images

The amygdala in action. The amygdala processes the stimuli that elicit fear, such as occurs when you are out alone on a dark night.

15.3.5 The Basal Ganglia

The basal ganglia are a group of nuclei that work as a cohesive functional unit and include the caudate nucleus and the putamen (which together form the striatum), as well as the globus pallidus, substantia nigra, and nucleus accumbens. These nuclei are strongly interconnected with many brain areas, including the cerebral cortex, thalamus, and hindbrain structures. As a group, the basal ganglia are believed to play a role in aspects of cognition (Stocco et al., 2010) and in regulating and coordinating voluntary movement control by exerting an inhibitory effect on various motor systems (Chakravarthy et al., 2010).

nucleus accumbens a brain area important for motivation and reward.

One area of the basal ganglia, the **nucleus accumbens**, is important for motivation and reward learning (Goto & Grace, 2008). It receives important projections from neurons in the midbrain that use dopamine as a neurotransmitter. Dopamine release in the nucleus accumbens has been associated with reward learning and has been implicated in drug abuse (Nestler, 2004).

15.3.6 The Substantia Nigra

substantia nigra a brain region important in fluidity of movement and inhibiting movements.

The **substantia nigra** is one of the brain regions involved in control of eye movements as well as fluid body movements, such as those needed to hit a tennis ball or to skate gracefully, and is important for coordination. Damage to this brain region produces a collection of debilitating motor symptoms (Schnabel, 2010) and deterioration of neurons in this area of the brain is associated with Parkinson's disease (Kwon et al., 2012).

15.3.7 Cerebral Cortex

cerebral cortex the largest portion of the brain, responsible for complex behaviours including language and thought.

The **cerebral cortex**, the folded outer covering of the cerebral hemispheres, is highly developed in humans and is responsible for many of our most complex functions, including consciousness, language, and thought (Willimzig et al., 2012). The cerebral cortex is said to be the only structure that can think about itself. Although some of the functions of specific cortical regions are not well understood, there is consensus among neuroscientists that, within the cortex, there is localization of function. This means that specific parts of the cortex are important for specific behaviours or abilities (Breedlove & Watson, 2014).

Based on functional and anatomical differences, neuroscientists have subdivided the cortex into four major cortical regions or *lobes*, as shown in **Figure 15-2**: occipital, temporal, parietal, and frontal. Each of the lobes has quite distinct functions. However, in undamaged brains, the four lobes are in constant communication and thereby perform many high-level functions collaboratively. The cerebral cortex can also be subdivided according to function into two broad categories:

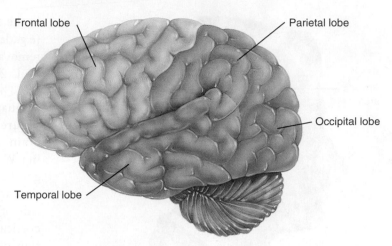

FIGURE 15-2 **The lobes of the cortex.** The cortex can be subdivided into four lobes: frontal, parietal, occipital, and temporal.

1. *Primary sensory and/or motor areas.* These areas are responsible for processing basic sensory information as well as directions for voluntary movement. As we will see, the primary sensory and motor parts of the cortex process information related to the opposite, or *contralateral*, side of the body.
2. *Association cortex.* **Association cortex** is responsible for many complex functions, including higher-order sensory processing, integrating information from different senses (how you know that an object that looks like a violin is producing the music you hear), thinking, planning, and other complex functions.

association cortex areas of the cortex responsible for complex functions, including higher-order sensory processing, thinking, and planning—all of cortex that is neither purely sensory nor motor.

The Occipital Lobe

The **occipital lobe**, at the back of the cerebral cortex, contains the *primary visual cortex*, an area important for processing information about visual stimuli. Visual information is processed contralaterally. That is, information received from each side of the visual world (each visual field) is passed to the opposite side of the brain. As a result, your right primary visual cortex processes information from the left visual field and vice versa (Bear, Connors, & Paradiso, 2007). Information about colour, complex patterns, and motion, is communicated along separate subcortical pathways from the eyes, and is not integrated until it reaches visual cortex (Collignon et al., 2011; Braddick et al., 2001).

occipital lobe lobe of the cortex at the back of the skull, important for processing visual information.

The occipital lobe is very well developed in humans. However, it is important to realize that visual information is also processed in other parts of the brain. In fact, some estimates suggest that 50 percent of the human brain is devoted to some sort of vision related task (Goldstein, 2010)! Connections to other parts of the cortex (association cortex) enable us to link visual information to information from other sensory modalities, as well as with our memory stores. This *cross-modal* integration allows us, for example, to hear a bird's song and imagine a visual image of the bird.

temporal lobe part of the cortex important in processing sound, in speech comprehension, and in recognizing complex visual stimuli, such as faces.

The Temporal Lobe

The **temporal lobe** is located on the side of the brain and wraps around the hippocampus and amygdala. The temporal lobe includes areas important for processing information about auditory stimuli and language. The *primary auditory cortex* in the temporal lobe processes sound frequency (Recanzone & Sutter, 2008), and other areas in the temporal lobe create meaning from the sound. Some people who have epileptic seizures centred in this region report "hearing" very loud music during seizures (Engmann & Reuter, 2009). Neurosurgery to remove neurons that appear to be generating seizures is particularly dangerous

Chad Slatterly/Getty Images

Parallel processing. Air traffic controllers must react to an array of sensory stimuli and make quick decisions. Communication within and between the lobes of the brain allows us to perform such complex functions simultaneously.

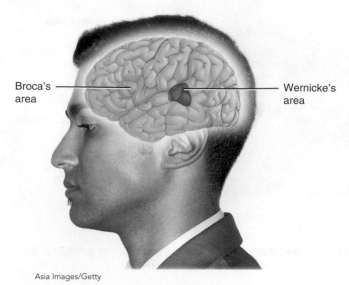

Broca's area

Wernicke's area

Asia Images/Getty

FIGURE 15-3 Major brain regions important for speech production and language comprehension. Broca's area, located in the frontal lobe, is critical for speaking; Wernicke's area, located in the temporal lobe, is critical for understanding language.

Wernicke's area an area of the temporal cortex important in helping us understand language.

parietal lobe lobe of the cortex involved in processing information related to touch and complex visual information, particularly about locations.

somatosensory strip an area of the parietal cortex that processes tactile information coming from our body parts.

frontal lobe lobe of the cortex involved in many functions, including movement and speech production.

in the temporal lobe since there are so many critical functions (e.g., language and memory) that may be disrupted during the removal of neighbouring neurons (Hrazdil, et al., 2013; Kaido et al., 2010; Foldvary et al., 2000).

The temporal lobe also contains regions important for language comprehension (Damasio et al., 2004). Shown in **Figure 15-3**, **Wernicke's area** is located on the left side of the brain in the vast majority of humans (over 90 percent). (Finding Wernicke's area in the left hemisphere of the brain is a good example of a phenomenon called *lateralization of function*, which means that a particular ability is localized to one side of the brain.) Wernicke's area communicates with other cortical areas, including a region important for the recognition of appropriate syntax (language rules) and a language area important for the production of speech, called *Broca's area*, located in the frontal lobe.

In addition to the temporal lobe involvement in hearing and language comprehension, this lobe also plays important roles in learning and memory as well as in recognition of objects via visual cues. Regions of the temporal cortex respond to complex visual stimuli, such as faces (Gross, 2005). Neuroimaging studies have shown that parts of this brain region are activated when people view photos of faces, particularly familiar faces. These findings are strengthened by the fact that recording electrodes placed into these same brain regions show changes in neuronal activity, or firing rate, when the same complex visual stimuli are presented (Trautner et al., 2004).

The Parietal Lobe The **parietal lobe**, located on the top middle region of the brain, contains the primary sensory area responsible for the somatosensory system. This region is known as the **somatosensory strip** and is a band of cortex that processes tactile (e.g., touch, pressure, vibration, and pain) information from different body parts. As **Figure 15-4** shows, this area of the brain forms a systematic body map, but one in which some parts of the body are represented to a greater degree than others. For instance, somatosensory information about the lips (which are particularly sensitive) is processed by a greater amount of cortex than is somatosensory information about the elbow. Also, remember that the somatosensory cortex (and motor cortex, which we will discuss shortly) in each hemisphere communicates only with the opposite side of the body.

In addition, the parietal lobe plays an important role in the higher-order processing of visual stimuli. As we will see in Part 5 on sensation and perception, processing visual stimuli involves localizing visual cues in space. The parietal lobe is included in a system known as the "where pathway" that enables us to see and respond to visual information in a spatially appropriate way. People with damage to the "where pathway" can find it impossible to pour water from a pitcher into a glass. This deficiency is not due to a motor disturbance, but rather to an inability to properly determine where the glass is located relative to the pitcher.

The Frontal Lobe Located at the front of the brain (behind the forehead) is the **frontal lobe**. The frontal lobe is a relatively large cortical region and is proportionately larger in humans compared to less complex animals. Like the other cortical lobes, the frontal lobe is not just one homogeneous area, but a large collection of regions that serve numerous functions. Broadly speaking, the frontal lobe is important for planning and movement. The *primary motor strip*, shown in Figure 15-4, is involved in the control of voluntary (non-reflexive) movement. For a long time it has been known that stimulation of different parts of the primary motor strip invokes

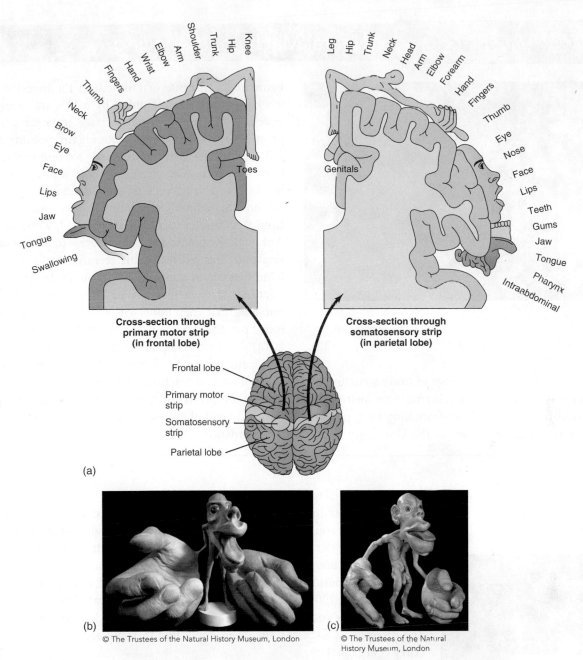

Cross-section through
primary motor strip
(in frontal lobe)

Cross-section through
somatosensory strip
(in parietal lobe)

Frontal lobe

Primary motor
strip

Somatosensory
strip

Parietal lobe

(a)

(b)

(c)

FIGURE 15-4 Motor and sensory cortices are organized according to body parts. Adjacent neurons in motor cortex send information to adjacent muscle groups, and adjacent neurons in somatosensory cortex receive tactile information from adjacent skin regions; thus activity in these cortical regions can be said to form maps representing the skin and body musculature. Some regions are overrepresented, including the mouth and hands. (a) A motor *homunculus*, and (b) a sensory *homunculus*. Homunculus is Latin for "little man."

movement in specific groups of muscles (Fulton, 1938). Recent research suggests that parts of motor cortex also coordinate the use of these muscles in complex movements (Graziano, 2006).

In addition to its role in controlling movement, the left (in most people) frontal lobe contains a region called **Broca's area**, which is critical for speech production and for providing grammatical structure to language. Individuals with damage to this region, or to the connections between Wernicke's and Broca's areas, suffer speech impairment despite having normal language comprehension (Code et al., 1999).

The part of the frontal lobe closest to the front of the head is referred to as the **prefrontal lobe** and is important for a large number of functions including short-term memory or working memory (Soto et al., 2008). When you look up a phone number and

Broca's area a brain region located in the frontal lobe that is important for speech production.

prefrontal lobe portion of the frontal cortex involved in higher-order thinking, such as memory, moral reasoning, and planning.

Psychology Around Us | Neural Machine Interfacing

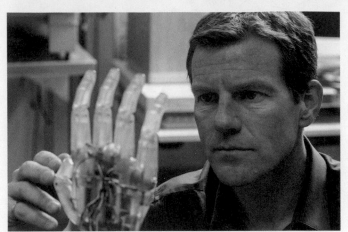

Brian Atkinson/The Globe and Mail

Kevin Englehart, a researcher at the University of New Brunswick's Institute of Biomedical Engineering, works on an artificial hand.

With more sophisticated knowledge of brain structure and function, neuroscientists are developing new methods for treating loss of function resulting from long-term paralysis or amputation. Kevin Englehart, at the University of New Brunswick's Institute of Biomedical Engineering, has been working with a team funded by a U.S. defence agency to develop a neural machine interface to control upper limb prostheses so that amputees can regain mobility and motor function. Nerves are redirected to reinnervate muscles (a process to restore nerve supply to a place from which it was lost) and electronics are embedded into the body so that the prosthetic limb can reliably receive and encode signals from the muscles (Scheme, et al., 2014; Zhou et al., 2007). Although the bionic arm project drew to a close in 2009, Dr. Englehart has redirected his research to focus on a bionic hand that can be controlled by thought. In similar research, scientists at the University of Pittsburgh are testing brain implants that they hope will enable paralyzed patients to move prosthetic arms with their thoughts (Collinger et al., 2012). Electrodes implanted in the motor cortex will interpret patients' brain signals and send signals about hand orientation and reaching to a computer, which will in turn control the precise and specific movements of a prosthetic arm and hand, thereby allowing individuals to recover their independence.

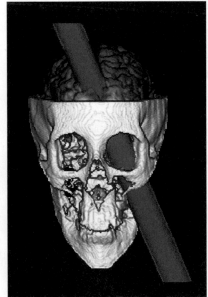

From H. Damasio, T. Grabowski, R. Frank, A.M. Galaburda, A.R. Damasio (1994). The return of Phineas Gage: Clues about the brain from a famous patient. *Science*, 264:1102–1105. Dornsife Neuroscience Imaging Center and Brain and Creativity Institute, University of Southern California.

FIGURE 15-5 After the accident. This reconstruction shows how the spike likely entered Gage's head, damaging the prefrontal cortex.

"hold" that number in your mind while you dial, you are using your prefrontal cortex. In addition, when you execute complex plans, such as figuring out how to fit in studying around your work schedule, or determining which public transport systems to take to get to a friend's house, you are using your prefrontal cortex.

Moral reasoning has also been localized, at least in part, to an area in the prefrontal cortex (Greene, 2003). People with damage to the prefrontal cortex can have difficulty understanding ethical principles despite having a normal IQ (Anderson et al., 1999). The prefrontal cortex has also been implicated in some aspects of mood regulation (Urry et al., 2004).

One of the earliest documented examples of localization of function involved an individual with damage to the prefrontal cortex. In 1848, a 25-year-old construction foreman named Phineas Gage was tamping blasting powder into a hole in a rock while helping to build a railroad in Vermont. Unbeknownst to him, there was flint in the rock and the flint generated a spark when struck by the tamping rod, causing the charge to explode prematurely. As shown in **Figure 15-5**, the force of the explosion drove the rod (3 cm thick and 90 cm long) through Gage's left cheek and out the top of his head, passing through the prefrontal lobes of his brain (Damasio et al., 1994). Almost immediately following the accident, Gage was able to talk and walk back to the wagon with the help of his men. He miraculously recovered physically, but those who knew him before the accident reported that his personality had changed. Once a responsible, likeable, mild-mannered individual, Gage became irreverent, impatient, and impulsive, and was so unreliable that he lost his job and was never able to hold a responsible position again (Harlow, 1848; Macmillan, 2008).

Gage's accident and the consequences of the accident were of particular importance because, at the time, physiologists were debating whether specific parts of cortex carried out different functions. The case of Phineas Gage provided clear support for the localization of function hypothesis.

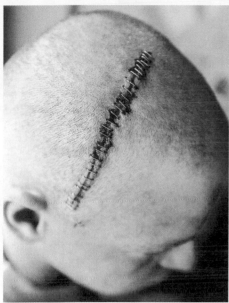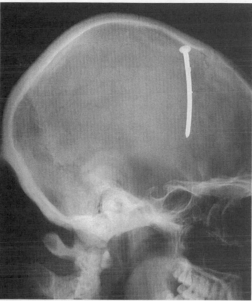

Jeff Thompson/AP Photo/Eau Claire Leader-Telegram (left and right)

Brain injury and nail guns. Although nail gun accidents can and do occur, they rarely cause brain injury as the nail generally fails to penetrate the skull. However, in 1998, construction worker Travis Bogumill was accidentally shot with a nail gun near the rear of his right frontal lobe. Bogumill experienced only an impaired ability to perform complex mathematical problems, consistent with experimental research showing that the frontal lobes are responsible for mathematical calculations.

Additional data supporting localization of function was collected in the 1930s when two neuroscientists, Klüver and Bucy (1939), discovered that bilateral removal of the temporal lobes in monkeys led to significant reductions in aggression and fear. The animals displayed difficulties with visual recognition, as well as a tendency to fixate on oral stimulation and a marked increased interest in sex. Following discoveries that brain lesions alter emotional responding, clinicians began to devise surgical means of treating serious behavioural disorders in people. A procedure called a prefrontal lobotomy was used in the 1940s and 1950s to treat thousands of individuals with problems ranging from severe mental illness to non-conformity and rebellion (Heller et al., 2006). Although reports indicated that such surgery had a calming effect on chimpanzees (Jacobson et al., 1935), in humans it was associated with apathy, blunted emotional responding, changes in personality, irresponsibility, and seizures. Today, more limited destruction of the prefrontal cortex is used for a small number of patients suffering from severe depression or other forms of mental illness who do not respond to drug therapy (Riestra, et al., 2011; Abosch & Cosgrove, 2008).

Before You Go On

www.wiley.com/go/comercanada

What Do You Know?

1. Which part of the brain is essential to basic functioning, such as breathing?
2. Describe the role of the brain in regulating hormones throughout the body.
3. Which part of the brain has been linked with our fear responses?
4. What function is most closely linked to the hippocampus?
5. Which of our senses is linked primarily with the occipital cortex? With the temporal cortex? With the parietal cortex?
6. What are the primary functions of Broca's and Wernicke's areas, and where are they located?
7. What mental functions are associated with the frontal cortex?
8. What structure is important in allowing the two hemispheres of the brain to communicate?

What Do You Think? What are the potential pitfalls in making inferences about brain function from studying a single brain area?

Summary

Module 15: Structures of the Brain

LEARNING OBJECTIVE 15 List key structures of the brain and describe their relationships to our behaviour.

- The brain can be subdivided into many regions, each of which serves one or more specialized functions.
- The brainstem participates in movement and sensation of the head and neck as well as in basic bodily functions, such as respiration and heart rate.
- The midbrain includes the substantia nigra, an area important for movement.
- The hypothalamus controls basic drives (food, drink, sex) and hormones, while the thalamus serves as a relay station for sensory information on its way to the cerebral cortex.
- Many brain regions participate in different types of learning—the hippocampus is important for spatial navigation learning and learning about life's events; the amygdala is important for fear learning; the cerebellum and striatum are important for motor learning; and the nucleus accumbens is important for reward learning.
- A large part of the brain consists of the cerebral cortex. The cerebral cortex can be subdivided into frontal, parietal, temporal, and occipital lobes. The cortex controls movement, integrates sensory information, and serves numerous cognitive functions.

Key Terms

amygdala 102
association cortex 103
Broca's area 105
cerebellum 100
cerebral cortex 102
dopamine 100
endocrine system 101

frontal lobe 104
hindbrain 99
hippocampus 102
hypothalamus 101
limbic system 101
medulla 99
norepinephrine 100

nucleus accumbens 102
occipital lobe 103
parietal lobe 104
pituitary gland 101
pons 100
prefrontal lobe 105
reticular formation 100

somatosensory strip 104
substantia nigra 102
temporal lobe 103
thalamus 101
Wernicke's area 104

Study Questions

Multiple Choice

1. Dopamine is the neurotransmitter primarily implicated in
   a) Huntington's disease.
   b) Alzheimer's disease.
   c) Parkinson's disease.
   d) Multiple sclerosis.
2. The brain region most directly related to the processing of fear-relevant information is the
   a) amygdala.
   b) brain stem.
   c) nucleus accumbens.
   d) striatum.

Fill-in-the-Blank

1. The temporal cortex is important for processing _____ sensory stimuli.
2. The _____ is important for basic bodily functions, including respiration and heart rate regulation, as well as for regulating reflexes such as sneezing and coughing.

Module 16: Brain Side and Brain Size

You may have heard popular theories about "left-brained" or "right-brained" types of people, or jokes about the female brain versus the male brain. Neuroscience tells us that, although the importance of such generalizations may be exaggerated in the public mind, there are, indeed, some differences among the brains of different groups of individuals. Much of the research in the area of hemispheric specialization has come from the study of *split-brain patients*.

16.1 Differences in Brain Lateralization

Communication from one side of the cortex to the other occurs via a dense bundle of neural fibres (axons) that make up a large structure called the **corpus callosum**, shown in **Figure 16-1**. The corpus callosum connects the two **hemispheres**. As previously noted, each hemisphere controls the movement of, and receives information from, the opposite side of the body.

In most people, cortical areas specialized for language exist only on one side of the brain. Wernicke's and Broca's areas, related to speech and language, for example, are on the left side of most people's brains—but not everybody's. The exceptions occur most often in left-handed individuals. Some left-handers (about 18 percent, Springer & Deutsch, 1993) have language areas located on the right side of their brains, or on both sides.

In 1981, Roger Sperry won the *Nobel Prize in Physiology and Medicine* (shared with David Hubel and Torsten Wiesel) for his work on brain lateralization. He and his colleague Michael Gazzaniga (Sperry, Gazzaniga, & Bogen, 1969) designed a number of study techniques that allowed them to examine the functioning of the hemispheres of *split-brain patients*. Split-brain patients are individuals who have undergone a surgical procedure to treat severe epilepsy. In this surgery, the corpus callosum is severed to stop the spread of seizures from one side of the brain to the other. Following the surgery, these patients lack the ability to integrate information from the two hemispheres (Gazzaniga, 2005, 2009). Studies on these patients highlight the fact that the two hemispheres need the corpus callosum to communicate. Although split-brain patients are largely unaffected by the surgery in their day-to-day lives, the results of split-brain studies clearly show the hemispheric localization of a number of perceptual and cognitive functions.

For example, as illustrated in **Figure 16-2**, suppose a split-brain patient is given a pencil to hold in his left hand under a table where he cannot see it; a divider is placed beneath the table so that he cannot pass the pencil to his right hand. (Remember that tactile and visual information cross from one side of the body to the opposite side of the brain for processing, so that information gathered by touch on the left side of the body or visually from the left visual field is sent first to the right hemisphere of the brain for processing.) If a person's corpus callosum is intact, then information from either side of the body is almost immediately shared with both hemispheres. But in split-brained patients this is not the case; information received by only one side of the body goes only to the opposite hemisphere of the brain.

If we asked this patient what he had held in his left hand, do you think he could tell us in words? If you remembered that the language production area (Broca's area) is located in the left hemisphere of the brain, you would have answered this question correctly—no, he could not verbally tell us what had been in his hand because his left hemisphere did not receive the tactile pencil information. If shown a set of pictures, however, he could

HOW WE
DIFFER

corpus callosum bundle of axons that allows communication from one side of cortex to the other.

hemispheres two sides of the brain.

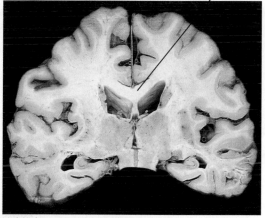

Mark Nielsen

FIGURE 16-1 The corpus callosum. This cross-section of the human brain shows the large bundle of axons that allows communication between the two hemispheres.

Courtesy of Zazzle Inc

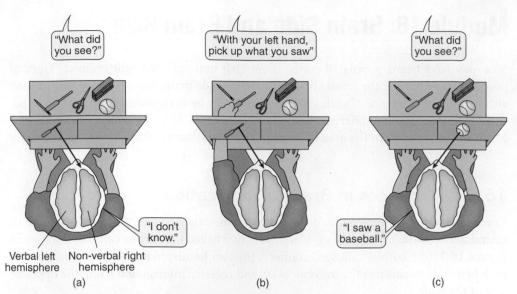

FIGURE 16-2 **Split-brain research.** (a) When a picture of a screwdriver is flashed to a split-brain patient's left visual field, the information goes to his non-verbal right hemisphere and he cannot name the object. (b) When instructed to use his left hand (controlled by his right hemisphere) to feel behind a screen among a variety of objects and select the one that matches the picture just seen, the patient correctly selects the screwdriver. (c) When a picture of a baseball is flashed to the patient's right visual field, he easily names it.

> **"Can the brain understand the brain?"**
>
> —*David Hubel, neuroscientist and Nobel laureate in medicine*

use his left hand to point to a picture of a pencil. He could do this because his left hand is controlled by his right hemisphere; therefore, tactile information about the pencil would go to his right hemisphere and he would then be able to use his left hand to identify the object. That is, he (or at least his right hemisphere!) knows what the object is, but cannot say it.

Although split-brained patients show processing problems under very artificial laboratory conditions, they show very few problems overall. This is because in their real world interactions, both sides of the brain receive almost exactly the same information (Kozlovskiy et al., 2012).

In addition to these rather clear-cut functional and anatomical asymmetries, many people believe that more general thought processes are lateralized, such that people who think a certain way use proportionately more of one side of their brain than the other side. For example, the right hemisphere of the brain is thought by some to be dominant in artists and engineers. By contrast, the left hemisphere of the brain is thought to be dominant in individuals with strong analytical and verbal skills.

What then is the scientific evidence for "right-brain" dominant and "left-brain" dominant thinking? Certainly the work with split-brained patients shows that there is, indeed, some localization of function in one or the other of our hemispheres. However, the possibility that one side of our brain is in charge and dominates the functioning of the other side of our brain is not supported by neuroscientific research. Since the corpus callosum allows for virtually instant communication from one side of the brain to the other, it means that, in everything we do, both sides of the brain are involved (Nielsen et al., 2013).

Overall, the research shows that, aside from the language areas noted above, the two hemispheres are more similar than they are different. Indeed, even when right–left differences are detected in function, these differences are usually relative. For example, the left brain can accomplish what the right brain can accomplish, it's just less efficient at some tasks and more efficient at others.

> **"What it comes down to is that modern society discriminates against the right hemisphere."**
>
> —*Roger Sperry, neuroscientist and Nobel laureate in medicine*

practically Speaking   How Can You Prevent Decline in Brain Function?

©iStockphoto.com/Get4Net

Preventing cognitive decline. There is no guaranteed way to prevent cognitive decline as you age; however, aerobic exercise increases blood flow to the brain and improves performance on cognitive tasks.

The short answer is that you can't. In spite of the many "brain games" promising to improve cognitive health (Millington, 2012) there is no *guaranteed* way to prevent cognitive decline as you age (Naqvi et al., 2013). However, following the common adage of "Use it or lose it" probably gives you the best protection you can have.

One type of experience that typically makes a difference in cognitive performance is physical exercise. In humans, aerobic exercise increases blood flow to the brain, improves performance on cognitive tasks, and elevates mood (Pereira et al., 2007). Nadar Fallah and colleagues (2009) at the University of British Columbia investigated ways in which exercise is associated with cognitive change and mortality in the elderly. Their results indicate that exercise is strongly associated with cognitive improvement and stabilization in men and with increased survival rates in women. It is important to note that the relationship between exercise and improved cognitive functioning in adulthood is not limited to the elderly, but is relevant for people of all ages (Ratey & Loehr, 2011). As well, studies in experimental animals have shown that physical exercise increases neurogenesis (generation of new neurons) in the hippocampus, as well as stimulating the health of neurons in general throughout other brain structures that support cognitive functioning (Stranahan et al., 2007, 2006).

So there's good scientific evidence to get up and get moving, and to keep moving!

practically Speaking   Are Men Smarter Than Women?

On average, the brains of women are smaller than those of men. Does this mean men are smarter than women? It does not. The overall size of the brain appears to be more closely related to the size of the body than to function. Historically, researchers have claimed that a relationship between brain size and intelligence doesn't exist (Tramo et al., 1998), except at the two ends of the spectrum; people with abnormally small or abnormally large brains are both more likely to exhibit mental deficiencies than those with brains whose size falls in the normal range. However, more recent data suggest that there is a small positive correlation between brain size and intelligence (Kievit et al., 2012; Johnson et al., 2012), as well as a relationship between human intellectual ability and cerebral cortex thickness (Menary et al., 2013) and brain volume (Brouwer et al., 2014). However, these modest relationships do not vary by gender (Burgaleta et al., 2012).

In addition to the overall size difference, researchers have reported some differences in the size of particular brain regions in humans. For example, part of the corpus callosum, connecting the two hemispheres of the brain, has been shown to be larger in women (Luders et al., 2014). This finding has contributed to the much-overstated suggestion that women are more likely to use both sides of their brains than men are. Research by the late Doreen Kimura conducted at University of Western Ontario and at Simon Fraser University carefully examined how the brains of males and females process information. Kimura's research shows that on some tasks, such as defining words, men use only their left hemisphere, while women tend to use both hemispheres (Kimura, 2002, 2000).

It is important to note that even in cases where differences have been reported in the size of brain regions, the overall differences between men and women are very small, so much so that they really don't tell us much about individuals of either gender.

16.2 The Integrated Brain

It's important to remember that many of the above-mentioned brain areas, including the cortical regions, can be subdivided into multiple areas or nuclei, each of which is involved in different functions. However, no brain region works alone. To process information, integrate it with previous information, and then formulate and execute a reaction requires neural circuitry undoubtedly not contained within a single brain region. Understanding how a brain region works requires sophisticated knowledge about information that flows into and out of the area, and of course, the important computations that occur within the neurons of that given brain region.

Before You Go On

www.wiley.com/go/comercanada

What Do You Know?

1. What does research show about "right-brained" thinking versus "left-brained" thinking?
2. On which side of the brain do most people have their language-related areas? What about left-handed people?
3. Does overall brain size matter in how well brains function?

What Do You Think? What are some of the ethical problems associated with searching for structural differences in the brains of different groups of people?

Summary

Module 16: Brain Side and Brain Size

LEARNING OBJECTIVE 16 Explain the neuroscience evidence regarding brain lateralization, as well as research on the significance of brain size.

- Research shows that the two hemispheres are more similar than different and that any differences are usually relative.
- Brain size appears to be related to overall body size and not to brain function.

Key Terms

corpus callosum 109

hemispheres 109

Study Questions

Multiple Choice

1. Which brain structure tends to be larger in women than in men?
   a) cerebellum
   b) corpus callosum
   c) hippocampus
   d) prefrontal cortex

Fill-in-the-Blank

1. _____ exercise has been shown to improve cognitive function and elevate mood.
2. In nearly all right-handed people, brain areas responsible for language are located in the _____ hemisphere of the brain.

Module 17: Evolutionary Psychology

As we have seen, the brain is a complex organ. But how did it develop this way? Back in Part 1 we briefly introduced you to the subfield of **evolutionary psychology**. In this module, we will explore the theory of evolution in more detail and how it has shaped the development of both our brain and behaviour.

LEARNING OBJECTIVE 17
Describe the basic theory of evolution and explain how it has influenced our understanding of the human brain and behaviour.

17.1 The Theory of Evolution

The theory of evolution proposes that all life on Earth is interrelated and derives from one common ancestor, also referred to as LUCA (last universal common ancestor). We can trace the **phylogeny**, or evolutionary history, of all life on the planet from this original common ancestor. As time progressed, those animals that survived and reproduced passed on their traits via their genetic material to their offspring; those that did not pass on their genetic material did not contribute their unique physiology and behaviour to future generations.

Fossil evidence of multicellular organisms (of which we are one) suggests that they evolved about 1.8 billion years ago. It isn't until somewhere between 600–500 million years ago (mya), however, that we see a sudden increase in the variety of plants and animals living on Earth (Zimmer, 2001). Over millions of years, the process of evolution shaped the development of *chordates* (about 450 mya), which had large nerves that ran just below the surface of their backs (also called the dorsal surface), then *vertebrates* (about 425 mya), which had a boney structure protecting the dorsal nerve cords. *Amphibians* (about 400 mya) were the first creatures to move onto land because of the emergence of structures such as air-breathing lungs and legs to move around on. *Reptiles* (about 300 mya) had new adaptive traits that allowed them to move even farther away from the water, such as thick skin that prevented dehydration and the ability to lay shell-covered eggs that could survive out of water. About 180 mya, *mammals* evolved from an offshoot of reptiles. Mammals are differentiated by the ability of females to keep their eggs inside their bodies and gestate their young internally, and also the ability to nurse their young with milk produced by mammary glands (hence the name *mammals*).

At present all life forms, current or extinct, are classified into one of three super kingdoms: Eucharia, Archea, or Bacteria (Woese, Kandler, & Wheelis, 1990). Each super kingdom is further broken down into smaller kingdoms of living things; for instance, human beings fit into the kingdom Animalia, which is part of the super kingdom Eucharia (**Figure 17-1**). The Animalia kingdom is unique because it is the only division of life on Earth that contains organisms with nervous systems. While it may seem that plants and animals are the most prevalent life forms on Earth, there are a huge number of life forms that you can't see, such as bacteria. The reality is that plants and animals represent only a small fraction of the types and numbers of individual organisms that live on the planet.

Characteristics that are similar between species and that can be traced back to a common ancestor are referred to as *homologous*; the traits that have evolved independently in different species are called *analogous*. The way to determine if a physical adaptation or behavioural trait is homologous or analogous is to do a comparative analysis between species and to ascertain whether animals that have the same traits can be linked

evolutionary psychology field of study that examines how the process of evolution has shaped the body and brain via the interaction of our genes and the environment to produce our thoughts and behaviours.

phylogeny the development of unique species over time.

Courtesy of the University of Chicago

The missing link. For many years, one of the criticisms of evolutionary theory was the lack of fossil evidence of a transitionary animal; that is, how did fins, which aren't very well suited for moving around on land, evolve into arms or legs? In 2005–2006, Neil Shubin discovered the missing link—a fish in the Canadian Arctic (dated around 375 million years ago (mya)) that had a primitive wrist with finger-like bones. The Nunavut Council of Elders were consulted as to what to call this species, and it was named *Tiktaalik*, an Inuit word meaning freshwater fish (Shubin, 2008).

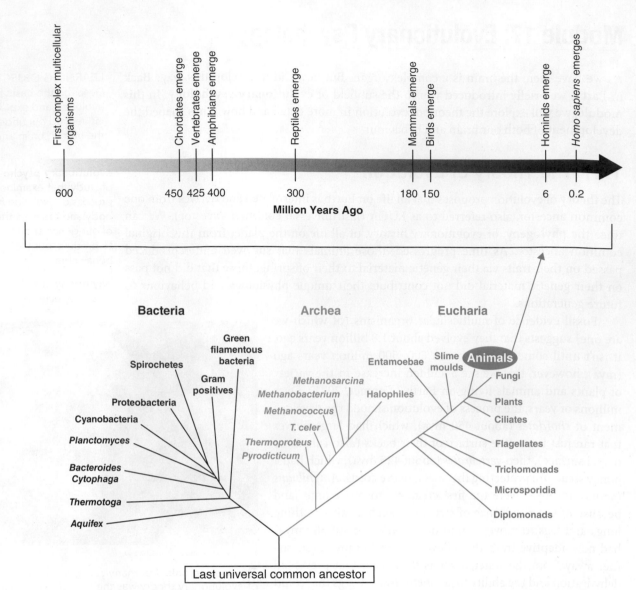

FIGURE 17-1 The universal tree of life and a timeline of evolution. This figure shows the overall relationship of the three domains to the kingdoms in which life is organized. The timeline shows the evolutionary history of animals; *Homo sapiens* come from the Hominid line and have only been in existence for a short period of time (approximately 200,000 years).

convergent evolution the development of similar physical characteristics or behaviours in different species that do not share a common ancestor; occurs because of exposure to similar environmental conditions for different species.

to a common ancestor. The process of analogous evolution leading to similar adaptations is called **convergent evolution**. For example, birds and bees both have wings, but when you trace their ancestral tree they do not have a common ancestor that had wings. Thus, the evolution of wings has happened at least twice in two different species, making it an example of an analogous process leading to similar adaptations in distinct species.

People have been working on and thinking about the idea of evolution for centuries, but the theory of evolution as we know it today is relatively new (Mayr, 2001). Charles Darwin's famous book *On the Origin of Species* (1859), which shifted scientific attention toward human origins, was only published about 155 years ago. For many years, however, biologists had been studying fossilized remains and noticing differences among the same species over time. In addition, many of Darwin's scientific contemporaries, specifically Arthur Wallace, were also putting together the fundamentals of the theory of evolution. What set Darwin apart was the enormous amount of work he conducted describing differences between species and how changes in the environment could influence which individuals within a species would survive and reproduce. Much of this work came from the five-year trip Darwin took on the HMS Beagle (1831–36), which sailed from England to South America, Australia, and South Africa. Darwin, who was hired as the ship's botanist at the last minute, made critical observations supported by copious notes and dozens of animal specimens that he brought back from the five-year journey (Hergenhahn, 2009).

Darwin almost lost the job as the HMS Beagle's botanist because the captain didn't like the shape of his nose. During the early 1800s, it was thought that you could determine the characteristics of a person's personality by assessing the bumps on their skull (phrenology) and from the shape of their face (physiognomy), claims that have been proven incorrect over the years.

From the specimens he gathered, Darwin began to realize that the process of change in a specific species over generations was likely due to how well a particular animal adapted to the environment it lived in. The animals with physical and behavioural attributes that were well suited to their environment were more likely to survive, reproduce, and pass on their traits to their offspring. He called this process **evolution by natural selection**, which is influenced by an individual's **fitness**, or ability to survive and reproduce in a given environment. Genetic inheritance is something many people take advantage of today by breeding specific animals to enhance the development of specific traits. For example, dog breeders will breed specific dogs to end up with offspring that are bigger, faster, meaner, or cuter than the parents.

Darwin made four critical observations to explain the diversity of life on the planet:

1. As more and more fossil evidence became available, Darwin realized that there were subtle changes in the form of animals that were fossilized. That is, animals were changing over time.
2. Aspects of species that seem different on the surface, such as a human hand, a bat's wing, and a cat's paw, had structural similarities underneath. For all three of these animals, the number and arrangement of the bones under the skin, while different sizes, are the same (**Figure 17-2**).
3. Selective breeding of captive animals leads to changes in the appearance of the animal in question.
4. Not all animals that are born will survive to maturity and reproduce.

In addition to these four observations, Darwin also made a fundamental inference from his observations: animals of a given species that will survive and reproduce are those that can adapt and therefore survive best in their current environment. These individuals are considered to be the fittest members of their species. (Note that the phrase "survival of the fittest," which was coined by sociologist Herbert Spencer, is not completely accurate because it implies some level of perfection in an individual that is able to survive and reproduce. "Survival of the fit enough" would be a more accurate phrase.) Thus, as the environment changes, the organisms that successfully live in that environment will also change, and these changes will be passed on to their offspring. Therefore, over generations, shifts in the physical and behavioural aspects of a species will occur.

Canadian researcher Bill Cade, who is currently at the University of Lethbridge, is studying aspects of this evolutionary process in *Teleogryllus oceanicus* crickets (Logue et al., 2010). The male of this species sings to attract mates, but their song also attracts parasitic flies that lay their eggs on the cricket. After the eggs of the fly hatch, the young flies use the cricket as their food source. Over generations, the crickets that are quieter have preferentially survived, and now this is a species with a significant proportion of silent male crickets. The implications of the loss of song on the long-term survival of this cricket species are still unknown, but research to answer this question is underway (Tinghitella & Zuk 2009).

Bob Thomas/Popperfoto/Getty Images

Charles Darwin, the father of evolution. Darwin's extensive cataloguing of various life forms he encountered during his voyage on the HMS Beagle led to his famous book, *On the Origin of Species*, and to scientific acceptance of the theory of evolution.

evolution by natural selection the differential likelihood between members of a species in their ability to survive and reproduce.

fitness the ability of an individual to successfully grow to maturity and have offspring that perpetuate the existence of the species that the individual belongs to.

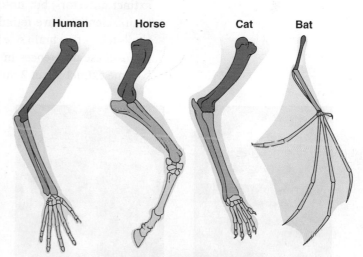

FIGURE 17-2 **Comparative anatomy.** Similarities among organisms demonstrate how they are related. These similarities among four vertebrate limbs illustrate that, while proportions of bones have changed in relation to each organism's way of life, the forelimbs have the same basic bone structure. Notice that the number of "fingers" on the human hand, cat paw, and bat wing are the same on all three.

Darwin did not know about the underlying genetic processes that led to the inheritance of traits between generations. Although he speculated about the existence of genes (which he called *gemmules*), he had no evidence for them. It wasn't until many decades later that Darwin's theory of evolution was integrated with Gregor Mendel's discovery of genetic processes. The initial integration of our knowledge of genetics and evolution occurred in the early 1920s and is now known as the *modern synthesis* (Mayr, 2001).

It is important to remember that the process of evolution never stops. All living things continue to evolve today in response to changes in the environment (a present-day example is antibiotic-resistant bacteria). There are no perfect animals, only animals that can survive and reproduce in the environment they currently live in. This is true of *all* animals, including humans. If our environment changed drastically tomorrow, say an asteroid hits the Earth or there is an explosion of a super volcano, we might not have the tools or resources to survive the dramatic change in the environment. Remember, as *Homo sapiens* we have only been around for a blink of the geological eye, and there is no guarantee that we will be around for much longer from the perspective of geological time.

17.2 The Evolution of the Brain

Scientists today do not see humans as the pinnacle of life on Earth, but rather as one species out of many that has adapted to fit a particular (and admittedly very broad) niche. However, the evolution of our species has led to some noticeable differences between us and other species on Earth—most notably in the development of our nervous system, of which our brain is a part.

One way to understand how the human brain has evolved differently from that of other animals is to compare the difference in the size of our brain relative to the brain size of other organisms. Clearly we're not referring to simple volume and weight comparisons—by these measurements the brain of an elephant will beat out a human brain every time. To compare the overall size of the brain between species, it is more appropriate to discuss the ratio of brain weight to body weight for the animal in question. What specifically sets apart the brains of primates relative to other species is the size of the cortex. For most primates it is the largest part of the brain, taking up about 50 percent of the brain. For modern humans this number is even larger, with about 80 percent of our brain consisting of the cortex (Dunbar, Barrett, & Lycett, 2007).

It would be wonderful to actually be able to study and dissect the brains of our extinct ancestors, but unfortunately tissue doesn't fossilize well (the earliest preserved brain scientists have found to date is only a couple thousand years old). But fossilized skulls tell us that brain size has increased significantly in Hominids. To give you an example of these differences in skull size, compare the skull of an Australopithecus (which became extinct about 2 million years ago) to that of a *Homo sapiens* in **Figure 17-3**. The first major difference you can see is that the overall size of the Australopithecus skull is much smaller. Scientists estimate that the Australopithecus brain was about the size of a current chimpanzee brain (Larry, Young Owl, & Kersting, 2005), which is about one-third the size of a *Homo sapiens* brain. (That being said, the Australopithecus were quite successful as a species and existed for about 2 million years before going extinct.)

Finally, look at the shape of the skull as well as its size. The area at the front of the skull has expanded in modern *Homo sapiens*, which implies that the area underneath, presumably the frontal cortex, has expanded as well. This expansion of the cortex in modern humans has been essential to the development of many of the social and technological advancements we have made as a species. While we cannot easily go back and

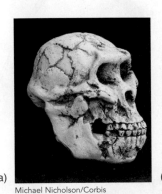
(a)
Michael Nicholson/Corbis

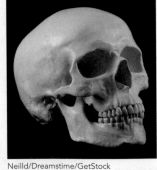
(b)
Neilld/Dreamstime/GetStock

FIGURE 17-3 Skull size. The Australopithecus skull (a) is not only smaller in size than the present-day human skull (b), but it has a much smaller frontal area, which leads to the assumption that the frontal cortex in the Australopithecus was also smaller.

look at the environmental events that have shaped the development of the modern human brain, specifically the expansion of the cortex, many theories have been proposed, including the development of complex societies (Dunbar, 2009; Dunbar & Schultz, 2007), tool use, and language development (Stout & Chaminade, 2012).

17.3 The Evolution of Behaviour

Psychologists are not only interested in the evolution of the brain itself, but also in the evolution of the *behaviours* that result from the brain or nervous system each species is equipped with. This is the heart of evolutionary psychology, where we combine knowledge of biology, genetic relatedness between species, the study of the organization of life on the planet, and the study of behaviour. All behaviour is interesting to psychologists, but for the purposes of the following discussion we will focus on the evolution of two behaviours that influence the likelihood of reproductive success and thus survival: mate selection and the parenting of offspring.

17.3.1 Mate Choice

All species need to reproduce to survive. The majority of animal species have certain qualities that they find desirable in a mate; quite simply, members of a species that display those qualities have a better chance of mating and reproducing. This is true for humans, too. Even if you can't fathom the thought of being a parent right now, for many of you, chances are good that at some point you will want to have children. Whether you realize it or not, the person you choose to have children with has been or will be selected based in part on your perception of his or her fitness to reproduce.

Peacocks provide an excellent example of how evolution has led to desirable qualities for mating. Female peahens prefer mates with elaborate tails—the more elaborate the better! Over time, this preference has led to a male phenotype (observarable characteristic) with an elaborate tail; that is, males with elaborate tails are more frequently chosen as mates by females, and therefore the genes necessary for the production of more elaborate tails have been passed on. What females prefer about a male peacock's tail feathers is still being studied, but Canadian researchers Roslyn Dakin and Robert Montgomerie (2011) have shown that one factor that seems to matter to peahens is the absolute number of "eyes" the tail has. Their data indicate that if a peacock has only 120 to 130 eyespots on his tail, his chances of mating are low; but having more than 138 eyespots makes a male a definite contender as a future mate. Thus, the peacock's tail is thought to have evolved the elaborate fan that it currently sports because of females choosing males with bigger and more elaborately designed tails.

Shawnhemp/Dreamstime/GetStock

Evolution at work. A peacock's elaborate tail is a consequence of evolution in action. Peahens prefer mating with peacocks that have many eyes on their tails, which has led to the large, ornate fan you see here.

Humans don't have elaborate tails, but clearly there are many physical differences between men and women. Think about what you would like in a potential partner. If a male reproductive partner is what you are looking for, chances are you would prefer broad shoulders and narrower hips. If you are looking for a female reproductive partner, a small waist and curvy hips is likely your preference (Smith et al., 2009). Scientists have determined that females prefer males with a hip to waist ratio of 0.9, and males prefer females with a hip to waist ratio of 0.7–0.8 (Singh, 1995, 1994), and these preferences are not culturally specific. Hip to waist ratio is only one example of the physical qualities that we rate as attractive—facial symmetry (Fink et al., 2006), the perceived masculinity and femininity of a face (Glassenberg et al., 2010), symmetry in movement (Brown et al., 2005), voice pitch (Apicella et al., 2007; Feinberg et al., 2006), and body odour (Gangestad & Thornhill, 1998) have also been shown to play a role in what we perceive as attractive in a potential mate.

Why have these preferences evolved? We don't know for sure, but what has been hypothesized is that these differences give us clues about the physiological and reproductive health of a potential mate. For instance, some argue that these traits tell us about an individual's development (Shackelford & Larsen, 1997), current hormonal status (Miller et al., 2007), or immune system function (Roberts et al., 2005). Ultimately it will take further scientific research to determine why these preferences have evolved. For now, what we can say is that, just like peacocks, humans have preferences for certain physical and/or behavioural traits in potential mates.

We partly choose mates based on physiology and behaviour, but we also choose based on the resources that the individual might be able to contribute to caring for our offspring. Resources are essential due to the length of time that it takes to get a human child to reproductive maturity. Beginning in the 1990s, David Buss established that across cultures, males prefer younger women who have a greater likelihood of being able to become pregnant and carry to term viable offspring. Females, in contrast, prefer males with resources—in the case of humans, the idea of "resources" often equates to money (Botwin, Buss, & Shackelford, 1997; Buss, 2009). Reproductive females put a great deal of their biological resources into carrying a child to term and then caring for it after birth. Males, by contrast, can fertilize and "run." Thus, for males, physical resources in potential female mates may not be as important as physiological characteristics such as age. Ultimately, however, both males and females want to put their resources into raising children that are their own.

17.3.2 Parental Investment

Compared to many other animals, humans spend an enormous amount of time—often decades—caring for their offspring. In contrast, Pacific coast salmon provide no parental care for their offspring. Once the eggs have been laid by the female and fertilized by the males, both parents die. Canada geese care for their young for the first year of life, and grizzly bears care for their young for up to two years. In part, the increased need for parental investment in humans is due to the decades that it takes for the human brain to mature. In order for us to increase the likelihood of the survival and eventual reproduction of our offspring, we need to take care of our young until they can survive independently. This takes us back to mate selection—selecting a genetically strong reproductive partner that will provide some level of parental care increases the likelihood that the offspring will reach the age of reproduction.

For females, maternity is generally a certainty—a woman knows that the offspring she is carrying is her own (surrogates are an obvious exception to this). For males, however, paternity is not a certainty; it is possible that a female is carrying a child that she says has been fathered by one individual when in fact another has fathered it. When it comes to parental investment of resources, most males want to support infants that carry their genes. To test this idea in humans, Canadian researchers Daly and Wilson (1988) examined perpetrators of child murders. They speculated that stepfathers would be more likely to murder stepchildren than fathers would be to murder their biological children. Mercifully such events do not happen often, but the data in both Canada and the United States indicate that men are more likely to kill children they are not genetically related to than those they are genetically related to (Weekes-Shackelford & Shackelford, 2004). Not all scientists agree with these findings, however. Temrin and colleagues (2000) conducted a similar study in Sweden and did not find that child homicide rates were higher in families with a male step-parent. Thus, further research into social and cultural influences on child homicide, in addition to potential explanations from an evolutionary perspective, still need to be conducted.

Ultimately, we still have a great deal to learn when it comes to understanding how our evolutionary history has shaped behaviours such as mate choice and parental involvement. And these are not the only two behaviours that are influenced by our evolutionary past. Behaviours such as childhood play, aggression, and social networking are also areas of study for evolutionary psychologists. While the field of evolutionary psychology is still in its infancy, there are likely to be many exciting new findings in the decades to come describing how our evolutionary past has influenced the development of our nervous systems and behaviours.

Before You Go On

www.wiley.com/go/comercanada

What Do You Know?

1. What are Darwin's four observations and one inference, and how are they important for our understanding of how to breed domestic animals, such as cats, dogs, and dairy cows, for specific traits?

2. Describe how mate selection in humans has been influenced by our evolutionary history.

What Do You Think? Given the information you now have on the process of evolution and its role in shaping our behaviour, what other areas of human behaviour do you think should/could be studied from an evolutionary perspective? How could this be accomplished?

Summary

Module 17: Evolutionary Psychology

LEARNING OBJECTIVE 17 Describe the basic theory of evolution and explain how it has influenced our understanding of the human brain and behaviour.

- All life on Earth is interrelated and derives from one common ancestor through a process known as evolution.
- An organism's ability to survive and reproduce (thereby transferring their traits to their offspring) is referred to as the individual's *fitness*.
- The brains of modern-day humans are much larger than any other animal species or of Hominid species that have gone extinct.
- Many of our behaviours are shaped by our evolutionary past, including mate choice and parental investment.

Key Terms

convergent evolution 114

evolutionary psychology 113

evolution by natural selection 115

fitness 115

phylogeny 113

Study Questions

Multiple Choice

1. The evolutionary concept of _____ maintains that those with adaptive genetic traits survive to transmit their genes to their offspring.

a) a matter of brain size
b) modern synthesis
c) parental investment
d) fitness

Lane Oatey/Getty Images

PART 4

HUMAN DEVELOPMENT

What is your earliest memory? According to Carole Peterson and her colleagues at Memorial University in St. John's, Newfoundland (2005), most people's earliest memory is typically something that happened when they were about 3 years old and tends to focus on a family event. Beyond a significant event or two, however, we recall little of our earliest years. Not only that, but the younger we are when asked to recall the memory, the less reliably we recall our earliest memory—changing our story from one time to the next (Peterson et al., 2011)! Given that we can remember basically none of our first years, how important can our early experiences actually be for our development as individuals? How important is it to have at least one responsive parent looking after us, ensuring that our physical, social, and emotional needs are being met? Although psychologists are certain that parents *are* important, we cannot examine this question experimentally. Not ethically.

However, what if there were infants and children who, for varying amounts of time—from weeks to months to years—were living in conditions where there was only one person caring for up to 18 children at a time? Where each child spent 18 to 20 hours a day in a crib without any human contact whatsoever, even being fed by bottles propped on pillows? How do you think children raised in such deprived circumstances would turn out as they grew up? Elinor Ames, Professor Emeritus at Simon Fraser University, and colleagues discovered a natural opportunity to study just such an occurrence. In the early 1990s, as a result of social policies, a great many infants in Romania were given to state-run orphanages. The infants lived in the impoverished conditions described above. Once word of their situation got out internationally, many people, including many Canadians, tried to adopt Romanian orphans to help them escape the isolation and deprivation that characterized their lives. A number of Romanian orphans joined families in Canada. In 1991, Ames established the Romanian Adoption Project to study the progress of adopted Romanian children in British Columbia (Chisholm et al., 1995; Morison et al., 1995; Fisher et al., 1997).

Romano Cagnoni/Getty Images

Romanian orphans. In the 1990s, children in state-run Romanian orphanages were often left in cribs by themselves all day, without any human contact. What effects do you think this would have on a child's development?

How did things work out? For about one-third of the children, things turned out well. These children were more likely to have been adopted before 4 months of age, as compared to the two-thirds of children who did not fare as well. All of the children were somewhat developmentally delayed (behind other infants their age) when they first arrived, but many (two-thirds) made up their relative developmental delays within the first six months. The developmental problems encountered included a refusal to eat solid food, while other children did not seem to know when to stop eating as they had never been given more than they could eat at a single meal before. Many took longer than usual to develop basic social skills, and about one-third continued to have trouble with peers into grade school. Children in this group also tended to show indiscriminately friendly behaviour toward strangers (Ames & Chisholm, 2001). And unfortunately, some of the orphans continue to struggle today.

developmental psychology the study of changes in behaviour and mental processes over time and the factors that influence the course of those constancies and changes.

If you were charting the development of vulnerable infants, what would you focus on? Unlike other fields in psychology that often focus on what a person is like at a specific moment in life, **developmental psychology** is interested in how behaviour and mental processes change over time and how various factors influence the characteristics that change and those that remain relatively stable. In addition to noticing similarities between groups of people, developmental psychologists are also interested in differences between individuals.

TABLE P4-1 Developmental Stages over the Lifespan

Stage	Approximate Age
Prenatal	Conception to birth
Infancy and toddlerhood	Birth to 2 years
Early childhood	2–6 years
Middle childhood	6–12 years
Adolescence	12–20 years
Emerging adulthood	20–25 years
Young adulthood	25–45 years
Middle adulthood	45–60 years
Later adulthood	60 years to death

Thinking about the development of Romanian orphans is interesting, but so is considering our own origins. What happened to make you into the person that you have become? Was it genes? Parents? Teachers? Do changes occur because of biological factors or because of our experiences? When are we fully developed? Are we ever? In fact, developmental psychology researchers acknowledge that developmental changes do not stop when we leave childhood (see **Table P4-1**).

In fact, lifespan developmental psychology involves the study of the entire course of human life, from conception to death. For instance, in the Lifespan Development program at the University of Victoria, researchers study how individual, genetic, social, and historical forces influence the entire course of development. As we will see later in this part, a trend toward a longer human lifespan and a growing interest in the lifespan developmental perspective has also given rise to fields of study such as gerontology and the psychology of aging (Jensen, 2011; Overton & Lerner, 2010).

"We worry about what a child will become tomorrow, yet we forget that he is someone today."

—*Stacia Tauscher, author*

Module 18: How Is Developmental Psychology Studied?

LEARNING OBJECTIVE 18
Describe and discuss the
advantages and disadvantages of
cross-sectional and longitudinal
designs for researching
development.

cross-sectional design a research
approach that compares groups
of different-aged people to one
another.

As we've noted, developmental psychologists are interested in learning about changes that happen as we age. But how do they go about measuring those changes?

Working with people who are growing and developing over time requires researchers to devise a research design that will allow them to assess how individuals change (or remain the same) over time, regardless of what they hope to assess. One approach is to use the **cross-sectional design**. In this approach, researchers compare groups of different-aged people to one another at a single point in time (Memmert, 2011). For example, they might compare a group of 60-year-olds to a group of 30-year-olds on a memory task to see how memory changes over time. The benefit of the cross-sectional approach is that it's easy and straightforward, as well as convenient, for both researchers and participants.

The big problem with the cross-sectional approach is that it assumes that any changes found in a study are the result of age. Researchers must remember to also consider other factors that might influence their results. Let's say that the task used to measure memory differences between the two age groups mentioned above is computer-based. If the 30-year-olds perform better on the memory task, the researchers might conclude that the results are due to age-related changes in memory. But the findings could be related more to the fact that 30-year-olds are more familiar with and less intimidated by computer technology than some 60-year-olds are.

These sorts of historical differences are called *cohort effects*. A *cohort* is any group of people born at about the same time. As a result of when they were born, the development of people in a particular cohort will be affected by the cultural and historical changes to which they were exposed. Wars, recessions, natural disasters, famines, and anything else that provides particular cohorts with unique experiences or challenges can influence development. If the two groups in your cross-sectional study come from different cohorts, then you cannot be sure whether the differences you see are due to development or cohort differences. For example, several years ago the provincial government in Alberta cut educational funding by reducing the number of hours of kindergarten education for children. If we were comparing the development of Alberta children in Grades 1 and 3, we might miss the fact that the better school performance of the Grade 3 children is at least partially a cohort effect of their longer kindergarten experience, and not entirely due to developmental differences (Hughes et al., 1996).

Another drawback of cross-sectional research is that it does not provide much explanation of how or when age-related changes may have occurred. For example, if in the memory study researchers find that older participants demonstrate memory declines, the researchers wouldn't know whether the declines occurred suddenly or accumulated gradually over the past 30 years.

Because of the many drawbacks associated with cross-sectional research, many developmental researchers prefer to use a **longitudinal design** (see **Figure 18-1**). This design allows researchers to follow the same group of people over a period of time, administering the same tasks or questionnaires to them at different points in their lives to see how their responses change. We will discuss one of the most famous of these longitudinal studies in Part 10 when we talk about an extended longitudinal study of extremely intelligent people (Feldhusen, 2003; Jolly et al., 2011).

The main benefit of longitudinal research is that researchers can be reasonably confident that the observed changes are a function of time and developmental experiences. Unfortunately, longitudinal studies require considerable time and money. Moreover, many participants in longitudinal studies drop out of the studies over the course of their lives because they move away, lose interest, become ill, or even die (see **Table 18-1**). And,

longitudinal design a research
approach that follows the same
people over a period of time by
administering the same tasks or
questionnaires and seeing how
their responses change.

CROSS-SECTIONAL RESEARCH

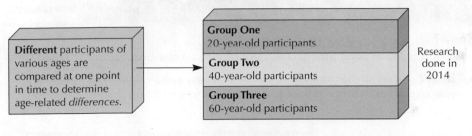

LONGITUDINAL RESEARCH

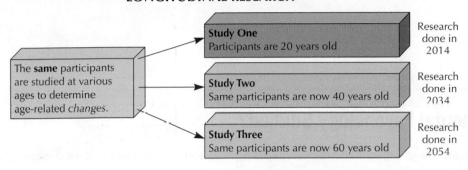

FIGURE 18-1 **Cross-sectional versus longitudinal research design.** Cross-sectional research studies different participants of various ages at one point in time to examine age-related differences. Longitudinal research studies the same participants over a longer period of time to determine age-related changes. Adapted with permission of John Wiley & Sons, Inc., from Carpenter, S., & Huffman, K. (2013). Visualizing psychology, 3rd edition. Hoboken, NJ: Wiley, p. 232.

finally, the cohort effect poses a problem for the longitudinal design as well. Individuals being followed belong to a single cohort; so, although age effects can be observed in the cohort group under study, there is no way to know whether the observations can be generalized to other cohort groups.

Seeking to address the cohort effect, some developmental researchers use a design that combines both the cross-sectional and the longitudinal methods. A **cohort-sequential design** comprises two or more longitudinal studies, each covering the same spans of time but conducted with different age groups (de Haan, Prinzie, & Deković, 2010). For example, to compare patterns in alcohol use, one study followed children from three age groups for four years (Duncan, Duncan, & Strycker, 2006). One group was followed from ages 9 to 12, another from ages 11 to 14, and another from ages 13 to 16. By using this design, the researchers could measure any differences between the groups that persisted over time, but in different cohort groups. However, because of the age overlap among groups over time, they could also look at differences that might result from age.

cohort-sequential design blended cross-sectional and longitudinal research, designed to look at how individuals from different age groups compare to one another and to follow them over time.

	Cross-sectional Design	Longitudinal Design
Advantages	• Quick, easy, and straightforward • Convenient for both researchers and participants • Yields information about age differences	• Gives reasonably reliable information about age changes • Gives information about the stability or instability of traits • Gives information about the effects of early experiences
Disadvantages	• Cohort effects are difficult to separate from age effects • Does not explain how or when changes may have occurred—measures behaviours at only a single point in time	• Requires considerable time and money • Many participants drop out over the course of study • Cohort effects are not controlled as all participants come from the same cohort

TABLE 18-1 Comparison of Cross-sectional and Longitudinal Research Designs

What Do You Know?

1. What is the main advantage of using a longitudinal design instead of a cross-sectional design?

What Do You Think? If a researcher today finds differences between a group of 20-year-olds and a group of 70-year-olds, what historical, social, and cultural factors might have contributed to those differences?

Summary

Module 18: How Is Developmental Psychology Studied?

LEARNING OBJECTIVE 18 Describe and discuss the advantages and disadvantages of cross-sectional and longitudinal designs for researching development.

- Two major research approaches in developmental psychology are cross-sectional (comparing different age groups to assess change) and longitudinal (studying the same group to see how responses change over time).
- The cohort-sequential research design combines elements of the cross-sectional and longitudinal approaches.

Key Terms

cohort-sequential design 125   cross-sectional design 124   longitudinal design 124

Study Questions

Multiple Choice

1. Which of the following is an advantage of cross-sectional research?
   a) Gives reliable information about age changes.
   b) Cohort effects are easy to separate.
   c) Explains how and when changes might have occurred.
   d) Easy and straightforward.

Fill-in-the-Blank

1. A _____ research design studies the same people over a significant period of time.

Module 19: Understanding How We Develop

Before we discuss what happens in development, it's useful to consider some of the key issues that concern developmental psychologists. These issues are often foundations for theory, research, and clinical work, but they are not always directly tested. As you read through the rest of the part, you may want to think about how the theories we discuss fit with these big ideas about human development.

LEARNING OBJECTIVE 19
Understand the key debates underlying research and theory in child development.

19.1 What Drives Change? Nature and Nurture

A key historic debate in human development is how much of our growth, personality, and behaviour is influenced by *nature*, our genetic inheritance, and how much is influenced by *nurture*, a term that encompasses the environment around us as well as our experiences as we grow.

Scientists who take a strong view of the influence of genetics or biology on development look at development as biologically programmed to happen sequentially, a process known as **maturation**. Other scientists believe that our experiences have a greater influence on how we develop.

What do you see as the main influence accounting for the difficulties some of the Romanian orphans, which were discussed earlier, experienced? Clearly, while nature may play a role, there is a lot of nurture involved in the difficulties the orphans experienced as well, both in Romania and in Canada.

It is not as easy, however, to attribute the characteristics of people in general to either nature or nurture exclusively. Our traits and behaviours are almost always influenced by an interaction between genes and environment. It is better to think of development as an inevitable and ongoing interaction between nature *and* nurture. In fact, we know that experiences cause **epigenetic** changes to genes that can be passed down from parent to child (Riddihough & Zahn, 2010). Nevertheless, in spite of the clear evidence that nature and nurture work together, some researchers continue to debate whether nature or nurture is more important. You will see that the so-called nature–nurture issue applies not only to specific questions about development, but also to ideas about intelligence (Part 10), social behaviour (Part 13), and psychological disorders (Part 15).

Monkeybusinessimages/Dreamstime/GetStock

Nature versus nurture. How much of our growth, personality, and development is attributed to our genetic inheritance or the environment we grow up in is still a key debate in human development.

maturation the unfolding of development in a particular sequence and time frame.

epigenetic changes in gene expression that are independent of the DNA sequence of the gene.

19.2 Qualitative versus Quantitative Shifts in Development

Throughout this part, whether we are referring to physical development, social development, or cognitive development, you will notice that we often talk about stages. A stage is a developmental point or phase within which children, adolescents, or adults think, experience emotions, or behave in particular ways. Stages usually involve *discontinuous* development with clear qualitative differences in thinking or behaviour between one stage and another.

It is important to understand what is meant by quantitative and qualitative change. *Quantitative change* involves gradual increases in some element, such as height or weight. In contrast, when we talk of *qualitative change*, it is not just that we are bigger, faster, or more coordinated, but that we are *different* in some way. For example, a caterpillar can grow little by little into a bigger caterpillar—a quantitative change—but when the caterpillar becomes a butterfly, there has been a qualitative change. We will talk about Piaget's theory of cognitive development shortly; as you will see, Piaget argued that children think differently at different stages of development. He therefore viewed this type of thinking behaviour, called cognition, as a qualitative change that occurs over the lifespan.

stage a distinct developmental phase in which organisms behave, think, or respond in a particular way that is qualitatively different from the way they responded before.

Although stages are typically associated with *qualitative* change, some developmental researchers argue that stages represent instead *quantitative* shifts in the growth of individuals (see **Figure 19-1**). According to these theorists, development is the result of an ongoing acquisition of new information and new experiences. What may seem like a sudden developmental change may instead actually represent the result of a gradual accumulation of many small changes, often so small that they are hard to notice, reaching a detectable threshold after the accumulation of many quantitative changes. For example, some theorists and researchers believe that walking comes as a result of a series of small developmental changes, including the steady growth of our muscles until they can hold our body weight and the development of our brains until they can control physical coordination (Lloyd et al., 2010).

Quantitative theorists have an easier time than qualitative theorists accounting for individual differences in the timing of milestones, but a harder time explaining why most people go through similar sequences of development during similar times of life, despite considerable variations in their experiences. As we will see, human development involves both qualitative and quantitative processes.

19.3 Do Early Experiences Matter? Critical Periods and Sensitive Periods

critical periods points in development when an organism is extremely sensitive to environmental input, making it easier for the organism to acquire certain brain functions and behaviours.

Related to the question of stage theories versus continuous theories of development is the question of whether there are **critical periods** in human development. A *critical period* is a point in development when the organism is extremely sensitive to a particular environmental input that can either encourage or discourage the development of certain brain functions (Anderson et al., 2011). So, if environmental input does not occur at a specific point in time, or if a noxious substance or experience is encountered, development will be thrown off track (hence, the term *critical*). For example, ethologist Konrad Lorenz (1970, 1971, 2002) found that goslings will forever connect with whatever goose-sized moving stimuli they see most often during the first 36 hours of their lives. In Lorenz's work, he was able to get certain goslings to think of him (or more specifically, his boots) as their mother. He used the term *imprinting* to describe the development of this attachment—the goslings imprinted upon Lorenz. The results are clear in the photo on the next page.

Psychologists have long been curious about whether critical periods operate in the lives of human beings. Of course, it would be unethical for researchers to deprive

FIGURE 19-1 **Do stages represent qualitative or quantitative shifts in development?** (a) Some theorists believe that individuals make qualitative, discontinuous jumps in development as they move from stage to stage. (b) Others think that development is a steady continuous process.

(a) Qualitative development

(b) Quantitative development

Infancy   Adulthood

Infancy   Adulthood

Nina Leen/Time & Life Pictures/Getty Images

The followers. Ethology pioneer Konrad Lorenz led these baby geese into viewing him as their mother by being sure he (or more specifically, his boots) was the first approximately goose-size being they saw when they hatched. For geese, the first 36 hours after birth is a critical learning period during which they become imprinted to their mother—or in this case, a mother substitute.

human beings of their usual early experiences to see what would happen. However, cases of human deprivation—extreme poverty or chronic abuse at the hands of parents, for example—do sometimes tragically occur without artificial intervention. By studying the histories of children in these adverse situations, researchers have learned that serious psychological disabilities may result from early deprivation (Pollak et al., 2010; Rutter et al., 2010). At the same time, however, other studies have found that subsequent changes in environmental input (for example, removing deprived children from their early negative environments and placing them in more positive ones) can help the children recover partially or, in some cases, completely (Sheridan et al., 2012).

Because individuals can recover at least partially even after deprivation during key time periods in their lives, most of today's psychologists and biologists believe that critical periods are better defined as *sensitive periods*, times when individuals are especially receptive to environmental input, but not rigidly so (Baird, 2010; Michel & Tyler, 2005). Terri Lewis and Daphne Maurer at McMaster University (2005) have studied infants and young children with cataracts and have shown that critical and sensitive periods in early life are particularly influential in the development of the visual system. They found that timing for specific aspects of vision varied, with the sensitive period for motion detection being much shorter than those for acuity and peripheral vision. For more complex cognitive and social development, however, theorists today are less inclined to believe that particular environmental experiences are essential during a critical period; instead, they view sensitive periods as largely *experience-driven*, flexible, and with less well-defined boundaries than a critical period (Armstrong et al., 2006).

Robert van der Hilst/Corbis

All is not lost. Early deprivation, such as that experienced by these young children at a Vietnamese orphanage, can result in severe psychological disabilities. Moving the children to more positive and stimulating settings, however, can help many of them to recover at least partially.

What Do You Know?

1. How do quantitative theories of development differ from qualitative theories of development?
2. What is the difference between a critical period and a sensitive period?

What Do You Think? Do you see biological or environmental factors as playing more of a major role in your own development?

Summary

Module 19: Understanding How We Develop

LEARNING OBJECTIVE 19 Understand the key debates underlying research and theory in child development.

- Developmental psychology is the study of changes in our behaviour and mental processes over time and the various factors that influence the course of those changes.
- Key philosophical issues in the study of developmental psychology are what drives change (biological or environmental factors); what is the nature of the change (qualitative or quantitative); and the role of early experiences in shaping later development.

Key Terms

epigenetic 127	maturation 127	critical periods 128	stage 127

Study Questions

Multiple Choice

1. What is the difference between a critical period and a sensitive period?
   a) Critical periods are more rigid than sensitive periods.
   b) Sensitive periods are more rigid than critical periods.
   c) Animals have sensitive periods, while humans have critical periods.
   d) Critical periods and sensitive periods are the same thing.
2. A non-genetic, or environmental, influence on gene expression is called a(n) _____ effect.
   a) proximodistal growth
   b) epigenetic
   c) nature
   d) synaptogenesis

Fill-in-the-Blank

1. A developmental jump, as opposed to slow and steady development, is called a _____ shift.

Module 20: Heredity and Prenatal Development

The **prenatal period** encompasses the nine months or so from conception to birth. At conception, each biological parent contributes half of the genetic material required to create a new person. Thus, at the moment of conception the baby's genes and sex are set. Growth following conception occurs at an exponential (rapid) rate.

LEARNING OBJECTIVE 20
Discuss patterns of genetic inheritance and describe stages and potential problems during prenatal development.

20.1 In the Beginning: Genetics

Genes are the most basic building blocks of our biological inheritance (Kagan, 2010). Each gene is composed of a specific sequence of **deoxyribonucleic acid**, or **DNA**, molecules. DNA and genes are arranged in strands called **chromosomes**, found in each cell of our bodies. In most cases each sperm and each egg (ovum) have 23 chromosomes. When the sperm fertilizes the ovum, a single-celled organism, usually with 46 chromosomes, is created. Although the majority of conceptions containing errors in the number of chromosomes end in miscarriage (American College of Obstetricians and Gynecologists (ACOG), 2005), about 1/150 children are born with a chromosomal abnormality, where they have too few or too many chromososmes (ACOG, 2001; Carey, 2003).

Twenty-three chromosomes are contributed by each of our biological parents, and the resulting combination is called our **genotype**, which broadly refers to a person's genetic inheritance. A person's **phenotype** is the observable manifestation of that genotype, the physical and psychological characteristics that are on display in each individual.

It is difficult to determine a person's genotype solely on the basis of his phenotype—appearance or behaviour. Consider the appearance of freckles. Freckles are genetically determined; either you are born with them or not (Bastiaens et al., 2001). If you have freckles, you display a freckles phenotype. Without further information, however, we cannot say exactly what your genotype is. Variations of the same gene, such as the gene for freckles, are called **alleles**. If both parents contribute the same allele, then the person is **homozygous** for the trait—that is, she has two matching alleles of the same gene. If you have freckles, you *may* be homozygous for the freckles gene.

It turns out, however, that people have freckles if they inherit a freckles allele from one of their parents and a non-freckles allele from the other. In such instances, individuals have the observable phenotype of freckles, but their genotype is **heterozygous**, a combination of two different alleles. Thus, if you have freckles, you are displaying a freckles phenotype, and this phenotype may reflect either a homozygous or a heterozygous genotype (see **Figure 20-1**).

Depending on the trait in question, any of three different phenotypes can result when a person has a heterozygous combination of different alleles (adapted from Truett et al., 1994):

- One possibility is that the trait either will be expressed in its entirety or will not be expressed at all. This is the case with freckles. If you have one "freckles" allele and one "non-freckles" allele, you will

prenatal period the period of development from conception to birth.

genes basic building blocks of our biological inheritance.

deoxyribonucleic acid (DNA) molecules in which genetic information is enclosed.

chromosomes strands of DNA; each human being has 46 chromosomes, distributed in pairs.

genotype a person's genetic inheritance.

phenotype the observable manifestation of a person's genetic inheritance.

allele variation of a gene.

homozygous both parents contribute the same genetic material for a particular trait.

heterozygous parents contribute two different alleles to offspring.

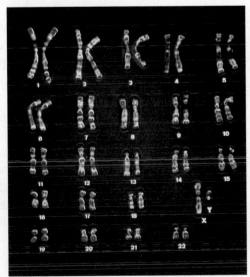

CNRI/Photo Researchers

Magical pairs. A person's entire genetic inheritance is contained in 23 pairs of chromosomes, with each parent contributing one chromosome to each pair. Here we see an individual's chromosomes stained with dyes and photographed under a microscope.

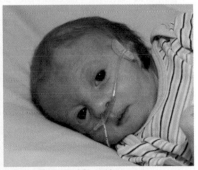

Courtesy of Matt and Ginny Mooney

Genetic defects. Eliot Mooney was born with Trisomy 18, a chromosomal abnormality due to an error in cell division resulting in three #18 chromosomes instead of two. Most children born with this condition do not live to their first birthdays. Eliot lived 99 days, each day celebrated and recorded by his parents, Matt and Ginny Mooney. In 2007 they established www.99balloons.org to help disabled children and their families. A video of Eliot's life can be found on this website http://mattandginny.blogspot.ca/.

FIGURE 20-1 **Genotype versus phenotype.** Individuals with freckles may have either a homozygous or a heterozygous genotype for freckles. In contrast, people who do not have freckles must have a homozygous genotype for freckles.

Genotype:	Homozygous		Heterozygous		Homozygous	
Parent Contributions:	Mother: freckles allele	Father: freckles allele	Mother: freckles allele	Father: non-freckles allele	Mother: non-freckles allele	Father: non-freckles allele
Phenotype:	Freckles trait will be expressed		Freckles trait will be expressed		Freckles trait will not be expressed	

David Roth/Getty Images

Freckles and genes. Freckles are small, concentrated spots of a skin pigment called melanin, controlled primarily by the MC1R gene. Freckles show a dominant inheritance pattern: parents who have freckles tend to have children with freckles. Variations, also called alleles, of MC1R control freckle number. Other genes and the environment influence freckle size, colour, and pattern. For example, sun exposure can temporarily cause more freckles to appear.

dominant trait a trait that is expressed in a phenotype, no matter whether the genotype is homozygous or heterozygous for the trait.

recessive trait a trait that is only expressed if a person carries the same two genetic alleles (e.g., is homozygous for the trait).

codominance in a heterozygous combination of alleles, both traits are expressed in the offspring.

discrete trait a trait that results as the product of a single gene pairing.

polygenic trait a trait that manifests as the result of the contributions of multiple genes.

zygote a single cell resulting from successful fertilization of the egg by sperm.

have freckles. Having freckles is a **dominant trait**, a trait that is expressed in your phenotype regardless of whether your genotype is homozygous or heterozygous for the trait. A **recessive trait**, on the other hand, is one that is expressed in your phenotype only when you are homozygous for that trait. Not having freckles is recessive. You must have two matching "non-freckles" alleles to be prevented from having freckles.

- For some traits, a person with a heterozygous pair of alleles may show a *mixture* of genetic coding. For example, children of couples who have different racial backgrounds can have features associated with the backgrounds of both parents, such as blended skin colour or eye shape.

- For yet other traits, persons with a heterozygous pair of alleles may express *both* of the parents' genes in their phenotype. This outcome is called **codominance**. An example of codominance is found in blood type. If one parent has blood Type A and the other parent has Type B, the child can express both in the form blood Type AB.

The thing that makes the study of genetics particularly challenging is that only a few of our traits are **discrete traits**, the product of a single gene pair. Instead, most human traits are **polygenic traits**, traits like height, weight, intelligence, or skin colour, which involve the combined impact of multiple genes. It is especially likely that traits affecting our behaviour are polygenic. There is evidence, for example, to suggest that schizophrenia (Purcell et al., 2014) and depression (Holmes et al., 2012) may be polygenic.

However, it is important to remember that very few genetic influences occur without environmental modification. Our environment plays a very strong role in determining our developmental outcome. DNA provides a blueprint, but at critical points in development experience creates a genetic memory—via trace chemicals—that change how the instructions on the DNA are carried out. These epigenetic changes to the DNA can be temporary or reversible, but many times these changes are permanent and possibly heritable (Alberta Family Wellness Initiative (AFWI), 2013).

20.2 Prenatal Development

Prenatal development begins with *conception* when a sperm fertilizes an egg, resulting in the creation of a single cell, called a **zygote**. The first two weeks after conception is known as the *germinal stage*. During the first 36 hours of this stage, the single cell zygote divides and becomes two cells. These two cells then divide to become four, those four divide and become eight, and so on. As its cells keep multiplying, the zygote moves through the mother's Fallopian tube (where it was first fertilized) to her uterus. After the fourth day following conception, the zygote is now referred to as the *blastocyst*. About a week after fertilization, the blastocyst implants itself to the side of the uterus. The other major transition that occurs during the germinal stage is the formation of a nutrient-rich structure called the **placenta**, which attaches to the wall of the uterus. The placenta allows the circulatory system of the mother to interact with the circulatory system of the embryo to exchange oxygen and nutrients through the umbilical cord.

Implantation signals the second stage of the prenatal period, called the *embryonic stage* (2 to 8 weeks). Most of the major systems of the body, such as the nervous and circulatory systems, as well as the basic structure of the body, begin to take shape during this stage. It is during this stage that the new organism is most vulnerable to environmental influence. By the eighth week, most of the basic organ systems are complete and the third stage of development, or *fetal stage*, begins (see **Figure 20-2**). The fetal stage lasts from the

placenta a nutrient-rich structure that serves to feed the developing fetus.

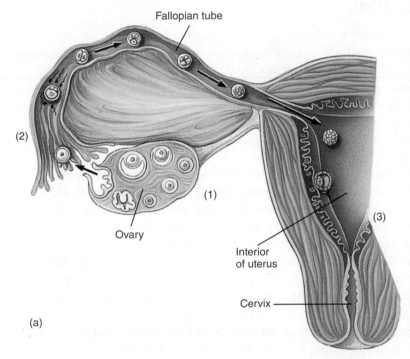

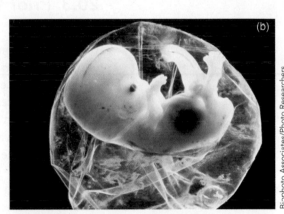

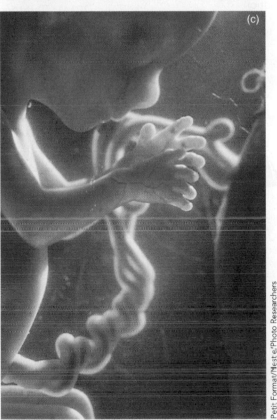

FIGURE 20-2 **Prenatal development.**
(a) *Germinal period: From ovulation to implantation:* After the egg leaves the ovary (1), it travels to the opening of the Fallopian tube (2) where it is fertilized and becomes a zygote. About a week later, the zygote reaches the uterus, implants itself in the wall of the uterus (3), and triggers the formation of the nutrient-rich placenta. (b) *Embryonic stage:* The zygote grows rapidly once it is implanted. By 8 weeks, many external body structures and internal organs have been formed. Notice that the head grows faster than the rest of the body. At this stage, the embryo is vulnerable to miscarriage. (c) *Fetal stage:* From 8 weeks to birth, the fetus continues to enlarge rapidly and the basic structures undergo substantial change.

end of the embryonic stage until the birth of the baby (9 to 40 weeks). Although most of the basic organ systems are already formed by the end of the embryonic stage, these early body systems are neither fully developed nor functional and therefore cannot sustain life on their own. During the fetal stage, these immature organ systems and structures continue to grow and develop. Especially during the last three months, the fetus' brain begins to grow at a remarkable pace (Dobbing & Sands, 1973).

miscarriage discharge of the fetus from the uterus before it is able to function on its own.

Abnormalities may arise during prenatal development and may lead to a **miscarriage** (or spontaneous abortion). A miscarriage occurs when the pregnancy is naturally and spontaneously expelled from the uterus before the embryo or fetus is able to function on its own (prior to about the 20th week of pregnancy). Miscarriages are fairly common; in fact, the Canadian Federation for Sexual Health estimates that one in every four conceptions ends in a miscarriage. In addition, Healthlink BC states that one in six women who know they are pregnant will experience a miscarriage (Healthwise, 2005). The *age of viability* refers to the point at which the baby can survive on its own (Moore & Persaud, 2008).

20.3 Prior to Birth

The fetus is vulnerable to any number of influences immediately following conception. As you will see throughout the book, many disorders are inherited from the parents. Some of these disorders, such as sickle-cell anemia, cystic fibrosis, or phenylketonuria (PKU), are linked to recessive genes, whereas others, such as Marfan syndrome or Huntington disease, are caused by dominant genes. Still other disorders are linked to chromosomal problems. In Part 10, for example, when we talk about intelligence, we will also talk about *Down syndrome*, a pattern caused by the presence of an extra chromosome in the twenty-first chromosome pair.

teratogens any environmental agent that causes damage during gestation.

In addition to genetic and chromosomal problems, a number of environmental agents, called **teratogens,** can cause damage during the prenatal period. The word "teratogen" stems from the Greek word terato-, meaning "marvel" or "monster" (Harper, 2014). Teratogens can negatively disrupt development during the prenatal period. A great number of agents (diseases, toxins, drugs, hormones, etc.) can interfere with typical prenatal development. The nature and extent of their impact upon the developing fetus vary depending on a number of factors, including the dose of the teratogen, the timing and extent of exposure, and the age of the organism (zygote, embryo, or fetus). It is important to note that not all teratogenic effects result in immediate physical impairment; instead, some health effects are delayed and may not appear until later in childhood or even until adulthood. Below we list just a few teratogens, along with their potential effects:

- Over half of the infants exposed to rubella (also known as three-day measles) during the embryonic period suffer from serious defects, such as deafness, intellectual disability, and a number of internal system defects (Duszak, 2009; Eberhart-Phillips, Frederick, & Baron, 1993). Infants exposed in the fetal period show fewer physical defects, but are at increased risk of mental illness in adulthood, particularly schizophrenia (A. S. Brown, 2006; Brown & Susser, 2002), as well as diabetes, cardiovascular disease, anxiety, and thyroid and immune function problems (Bale, 2009; Cunningham et al., 2010).
- Some other diseases that exert a teratogenic effect are syphilis, genital herpes, and AIDS (Devi et al., 2009; Shepard & Lemire, 2004).
- Research carried out by Peter Fried at Carleton University suggests that prenatal exposure to marijuana may be linked to disturbances in executive functioning (Fried et al., 2005; Porath & Fried, 2005). Such a cognitive disturbance would cause difficulties with impulsiveness, overactivity, inattention, and problem-solving.

Health Canada. Licensed under Health Canada copyright.

Smoking and prenatal development. Some effects of smoking during prenatal development include premature birth, low birth weight, and sudden infant death syndrome.

Prenatal marijuana exposure is also linked to increased risk for depression and anger and aggression (Jutras-Aswad et al., 2009).

- Smoking tobacco at any point in the pregnancy increases the likelihood of a miscarriage, the baby being born with low birth weight, increased risk for cleft lip and palate, or premature birth. Smoking tobacco in pregnancy is also related to other postnatal risks, such as sudden infant death syndrome, asthma, and the development of cancer in later childhood (Eichenwald & Stark, 2008; Jaakkola & Gissler, 2004; Knopik, 2009; Mossey et al., 2009).

- Exposure to alcohol affects prenatal development at any point in pregnancy, but especially when brain growth is most rapid early in gestation. Prenatal exposure to alcohol interferes with the production of neurons and prevents neurons from migrating to where they are needed to form neural networks in the brain. As well, the oxygen required to metabolize alcohol uses oxygen required for cell growth. Therefore, drinking alcohol during pregnancy is inadvisable; it can result in fetal alcohol spectrum disorder (FASD), a preventable lifelong disability involving a range of physical, mental, and behavioural outcomes. Although there are currently no accurate statistics on FASD rates in Canada, it has been estimated that 3,000–4,000 FASD-affected infants are born each year in Canada (Fuchs et al., 2010).

- There are three primary diagnoses associated with FASD: Fetal Alcohol Syndrome (FAS); Partial Fetal Alcohol Syndrome (p-FAS), and Alcohol Related Neurodevelopmental Disorder (ARND). FAS is generally associated with heavy maternal drinking throughout the pregnancy, and includes slow physical growth, facial abnormalities, and brain injury (Caley et al., 2008). Children diagnosed with p-FAS have the characteristics associated with FAS, but fewer of them. This diagnosis is associated with mothers who drank less during the pregnancy and/or may be associated with paternal alcohol use at the time of conception (Ouko et al., 2009). ARND is associated with maternal alcohol use in pregnancy. It is not associated with facial or physical abnormalities of any type; however, it impacts three areas of mental functioning (see Chudley et al., 2005 for Canadian guidelines for diagnoses).

- The latest edition of The Diagnostic and Statistical Manual of Mental Disorders (DSM-5, 2013) classifies all forms of FASD as "Neurodevelopmental Disorder associated with Prenatal Alcohol Exposure (ND-PAE)."

- Heroin use in pregnancy causes babies to be born with low birth weight and addicted to heroin; they must go through withdrawal after birth (Steinhausen, Blattman, & Pfund, 2007).

David H. Wells/Corbis

Fetal alcohol syndrome. Caused by early prenatal exposure to alcohol, FAS presents several characteristic facial features (as shown by this boy), including short eyelid opening, a thin upper lip, and a smooth philtrum, the groove between the bottom of the nose and the crease of the upper lip.

Before You Go On

What Do You Know?
1. What are the possible phenotypic outcomes from a heterozygous genotype?
2. What are teratogens and what do their effects depend upon?
3. What are the three stages of prenatal development, and what happens at each stage?

What Do You Think? Given that teratogens are considered to be any environmental agent that can cause damage to the developing organism, what other factors, other than those identified above, could be considered teratogenic? (Hint: physical injury to the mother that affects the developing zygote, embryo, or fetus.)

Summary

Module 20: Heredity and Prenatal Development

LEARNING OBJECTIVE 20 Discuss patterns of genetic inheritance and describe stages and potential problems during prenatal development.

- Our genetic inheritance comes from both parents, who each contribute half our chromosomes. Genes can combine in various ways to make up our phenotype, or observable traits.
- Genetics can influence the manifestation of both physical traits and psychological traits, including temperament, although environment also plays a role.
- Prenatal development begins with conception and is divided into three stages: germinal, embryonic, and fetal, each characterized by specific patterns of development.
- Individuals are susceptible to multiple influences by biological and environmental forces before they are even born, during the prenatal period.

Key Terms

allele 131
chromosomes 131
codominance 132
deoxyribonucleic acid
   (DNA) 131

discrete trait 132
dominant trait 132
genes 131
genotype 131
heterozygous 131

homozygous 131
miscarriage 134
phenotype 131
placenta 133
polygenic trait 132

prenatal period 131
recessive trait 132
teratogens 134
zygote 132

Study Questions

Multiple Choice

1. A person's genetic code or inheritance is that person's
   a) phenotype.
   b) genotype.
   c) gene.
   d) chromosome.

Fill-in-the-Blank

1. A _____ trait occurs when both parents contribute the same alleles for a gene.

Module 21: Infancy and Childhood

One of the most extraordinary things about development is how rapidly humans change and grow and develop over the life span. Neonates become infants, infants become children, children become adolescents, and adolescents become adults. As outlined in Table P4-1 earlier in this part, all stages of development are important, but the foundation of brain architecture is established early in life, and therefore the early years are of paramount importance. In 2011, Canadians Hon. Margaret McCain (former lieutenant governor of New Brunswick), the late Fraser Mustard (a founding member of McMaster University's medical school), and Kerry McCuaig (Fellow in Early Childhood Policy at the Atkinson Centre at OISE) published a report called *Early Years Study 3: Making Decisions and Taking Action*, documenting the vital importance of investing in early learning opportunities for Canadian children. They presented impressive evidence to support their argument that experiences from conception onward shape the architecture and function of the brain. Further, they argued that what happens in the early years has lifelong consequences for both the individual and the society in which the individual lives. Let's examine some of the evidence for why the early years are so crucial to long-term outcomes.

21.1 Physical Development

Two patterns are apparent in babies' growth and development, both pre- and postnatal. First, growth follows a **proximodistal pattern**. That is, parts closer to the centre of the body grow and develop sooner than parts at the outer edges (the extremities) (Logsdon, 2011). In this way, our most vital organs and body parts form first. For example, brain and body developments such as myelinization primarily follow a proximodistal pattern, in which parts closer to the centre (that is, the spine) develop sooner than parts at the outer edges (the extremities). Second, growth follows a **cephalocaudal pattern**, from head to foot. You have probably noticed, for example, that the heads of infants are much larger in proportion to their bodies than the heads of toddlers or adolescents (see **Figure 21-1**).

Compared to some other species, human infants are still relatively "unfinished" at birth and remain dependent on their caregivers for longer than virtually all other species on our planet. Our key senses develop fully during our first months and we learn to walk after about a year or so, but our brains—although they also show amazing development during infancy (see **Figure 21-2**)—are not fully developed until we are teenagers or young adults.

Perhaps you have heard claims that most of our brain development happens before age 3. Is this claim correct? As with many questions in psychology, the answer here is not definitive. Infancy is, however, a time of remarkable change in the brain.

Two key processes are responsible for the amazing growth of the brain in the earliest years of life. The first is a sheer increase in connections among *neurons*, the brain's nerve cells. As we described in Part 3, information is passed from neuron to neuron at transmission points called **synapses**. Born with 100 billion neurons, the child acquires synaptic connections at a staggering rate, expanding from 2,500 such connections per neuron at birth to around 15,000 per neuron by age 2 or 3 years (Bock, 2005; Di Pietro, 2000).

As babies, we actually develop far greater numbers of synapses than we will eventually need. As we grow older, two-thirds of our early synaptic connections disappear (Bock, 2005; Di Pietro, 2000; Zelazo & Lee, 2010). Our experiences help to stimulate and strengthen some of the connections, while synapses that are not used weaken and disappear. This process of reducing unnecessary connections is called **synaptic pruning** because of its similarity to pruning, or cutting away, the dead branches of a tree or bush to help the healthy, live branches flourish (Edin et al., 2007).

LEARNING OBJECTIVE 21
Summarize the major physical, cognitive, and emotional developments that take place during infancy and during childhood.

©iStockphoto.com/Jani Bryson

proximodistal pattern a pattern in which growth and development proceed from the centre to the extremities.

cephalocaudal pattern a pattern in which growth and development proceed from top to bottom.

 **WHAT HAPPENS** *in the* **BRAIN?**

synapses transmission points between neurons.

synaptic pruning developmental reduction of neuronal connections, allowing stronger connections to flourish.

FIGURE 21-1 Cephalocaudal pattern. The proportion of the head to the rest of the body changes as we develop. Two months following conception the fetal head is almost half the size of the fetal body. In infancy the head is about one fourth the size of the body. By the time we reach adulthood the head is one-eighth the size of the body.

©iStockphoto.com/Aynur_sib

FIGURE 21-2 Brain growth in the first two years. This illustration shows the increases in the complexity of neurons that occur over the course of infancy.

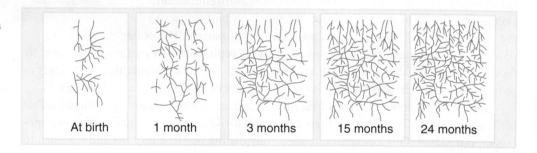

myelination development of fatty deposits on neurons that allow electric impulses to pass through neurons more efficiently.

Another neural process that accounts for increased brain growth is **myelination**. Recall from Part 3 that myelin is a fatty white deposit that forms around and insulates portions of many neurons, helping electric impulses pass through a neuron more. During infancy, a great deal of myelination occurs in the spinal cord and in areas of the brain primarily associated with movement, reflexes, sensory responses, and certain low-level learning processes.

21.1.1 Senses

The senses of taste, smell, and touch are all highly developed at birth. A baby can distinguish the scent of his mother's milk from another woman's milk (Porter & Winberg, 1999) and can make fine distinctions between various tastes after only a few days out of the womb (Tatzer, Schubert, Timischl, & Simbruner, 1985).

Other senses are less developed. Immediately following birth, hearing is somewhat immature and affected by amniotic fluid that continues to fill space in the newborn's ears. These limitations change quickly, however. Within a few days the baby can distinguish familiar speech from new sounds and words that they have not heard before. However, because hearing is so crucial to social development, it is important to identify infants with hearing difficulty as quickly as possible. Work by Martyn Hyde (2005) at the University of Toronto indicates that special efforts taken to screen young infants for hearing issues allows for timely and appropriate interventions to ensure that hearing losses have a minimal effect on development. Indeed, Fitzpatrick et al. (2014) analyzed 20 years of data gathered from the Children's Hospital of Eastern Ontario both before and after implementation of a newborn hearing program. Prior to screening, the median age for the identification of hearing loss was 5 years of age; following program implementation, the median age for identification was 0.8 years.

Vision is a baby's least developed sense (Bedinghaus, 2010; Kellman & Arterberry, 1998; Maurer & Lewis, 2014). Newborns cannot clearly see objects much more than 20 or 25 centimetres away. Similarly, their ability to scan objects is limited and they have poor colour discrimination until they are 3 months of age (Kellman & Arterberry, 2006). At first, these visual limitations do not have serious consequences; after all, babies do not travel very far, and they can see far enough to make eye contact with their mothers while nursing. Research by Daphne Maurer and Terri Lewis (2014; 2001) at McMaster University tells us much about the rate at which infants' visual skill develops. At birth, an infant's vision is about 20/400 or 20/800; that is, the level of detail that an adult can see at 400–800 feet (122–244 m) a baby can only see at 20 feet (6 m). Interestingly, their vision improves steadily, and by the time infants are about a year old their vision is almost adult-like (Skoczenski & Norcia, 2002), although it doesn't reach 20/20 until about 4 years of age (Slater et al., 2010).

21.1.2 Reflexes

In addition to our senses, we are also born with certain **reflexes**, programmed reactions to certain cues that do not require any conscious thought to perform. For example, babies pucker their lips and begin to suck whenever something brushes their cheeks or is put in their mouths, a response called the *rooting reflex*. Other common reflexes are listed in **Table 21-1**. Being automatic, reflexes do not tell us much about infants' current ability levels. However, reflexes do allow us to see whether the nervous system is appropriately wired and working the way it is supposed to be working (Kimmel & Ratliff-Schaub, 2007).

For this reason, checking reflexes is an important part of early infant developmental assessments.

©iStockphoto.com/mikanaka

Babinski reflex. When the sole of an infant's foot is stroked, the toes spread apart. This characteristic response is a sign of neurological health until a child is about 2 years of age. However, if present in children older than 2 years of age, it may indicate an injury or disease to the brain or spinal cord.

reflexes programmed physical reactions to certain cues that do not require any conscious thought to perform.

TABLE 21-1 Common Newborn Reflexes			
Reflex	**Stimulation**	**Response**	**Function**
Rooting	Touch the corner of the infant's cheek	Infant turns toward the stimulation and begins to suck	Helps infant begin feeding
Grasping	Press finger against infant's palm	Infant grasps finger and holds on	Allows infant to hold onto caregiver for safety
Moro	When infant is lying flat on a blanket, slap the blanket sharply on either side of the head to startle the infant	Infant flings arms outward and then inward in a hugging motion	May help infant to hold on to caregiver when support is lost
Babinski	Stroke sole of infant's foot	Toes spread apart	Unknown (but its presence indicates the integration of the nervous system)

TABLE 21-2 Milestones in Motor Development		
Motor Milestone	Average Age Achieved	Age Range
When prone, lifts chin up	2 months	3 weeks–4 months
Rolls over	2 months	3 weeks–5 months
Sits alone	7 months	5–9 months
Crawls	7 months	5–11 months
Stands holding furniture	8 months	5–12 months
Stands alone	11 months	9–16 months
Walks alone	11 months, 3 weeks	9–17 months
Walks up steps	17 months	12–23 months

Based on Laura E. Berk, *Infants, Children, and Adolescents*, 6e (Boston: Allyn & Bacon, 2008) Table 5.2, p. 188.

21.1.3 Movement

motor skills the ability to control bodily movements.

By the end of their first year, most babies are up and moving. **Motor skills**, the ability to control bodily movements, include achievements such as grasping objects, crawling, and eventually walking. **Table 21-2** shows the typical ages at which children in Canada and the United States reach particular motor-development milestones. As we noted earlier in the part, most babies acquire motor skills in roughly the same order, which suggests that there may be a maturational explanation for the way in which they unfold.

At the same time, and as Table 21-2 also shows, there is considerable variability regarding when a child reaches a particular milestone. In addition to genetic variation, the timing of motor development can be influenced by a number of environmental factors.

Negative influences, such as abuse, neglect, or poor nutrition, can slow a child's motor development. Cultural practices that either encourage or discourage early motor development can also influence the timetable. For example, the Kipsigis people in Kenya begin encouraging babies shortly after birth to sit up, stand, and walk (Super, 1976). As a result, Kipsigis children achieve these milestones about a month before children raised in North America. On the other hand, the Ache parents in Paraguay worry about their children moving more than a few feet away, and they actively discourage independent motor development in their children. As a result, Ache children do not walk until an average of one year later than children in North America (Kaplan & Dove, 1987). There are no indications that these differences translate into significant differences later in life. Esther Thelen and others (Adolph & Berger, 2006; Thelen, 1989; Thelen & Smith, 2006) have shown that motor development does not occur in isolation, but rather occurs as a number of complex systems blend to work synergistically. This *dynamic systems approach* is due to a number of factors coming together, including the environmental support provided for the skill.

21.1.4 How Does the Body Grow During Childhood?

Growth during early childhood, which lasts from about the ages of 2 to 6 years, and middle childhood, which lasts from about age 6 until 12, is not as dramatic as it is from conception through to the second year. During early childhood, we grow only about 5 to 7 centimetres a year. We do however master a good deal of motor and physical control

practically Speaking   Getting a Good Start Sometimes Means Getting a Head Start

The school dropout rate for Canadian Aboriginal and Métis youth is three times that of the general population (25 percent versus 8 percent) (Bushnick, 2003; Gingras, 2002). In an effort to address this issue, the government of Canada has provided funds for the development of Aboriginal Head Start (AHS) preschool programs in urban and northern communities across Canada. These programs provide a half-day preschool experience for 3- to 5-year-old Aboriginal and Métis children. Parents are encouraged to participate as well, to become optimal supporters of and advocates for their children's academic and social development. In addition, the program provides support for development of Aboriginal culture and language, education, and school readiness programming, along with health promotion, nutrition, and social support (Mashford-Pringle, 2012; Public Health Agency of Canada (PHAC), 2011).

Early evaluation data gathered at Alberta Aboriginal Head Start sites (dela Cruz, 2010) showed that AHS participants perform at or above the averages for children their age in the general Canadian population as they enter the school system. This indicates that the AHS program is meeting its immediate goals. Next researchers need to follow these children through school to see if the AHS program also helps to reduce Canadian Aboriginal and Métis youth school dropout rates.

during this period. Younger children develop basic control over bodily functions, and they solidify a preference for their right or left hand for most tasks.

As children move from early into middle childhood, around age 6, there is a jump in coordination and skill. Children's motor abilities improve dramatically as they gain coordination, agility, and strength (Drummond, 2011). At the same time, the first major physical distinctions between boys and girls begin to appear. Girls experience a growth spurt in height and weight during their tenth or eleventh year, while boys have to wait a couple of years more for their growth spurt. On the other hand, boys develop somewhat more muscle mass, meaning they can throw and jump a little farther and run a little faster. Girls tend to be a bit more agile on average. As we will see later in the part, these average differences in childhood become much more pronounced as children move into adolescence.

Throughout early and middle childhood, the brain becomes more efficient due to a continued combination of the myelination and synaptic pruning that began in infancy. During childhood, myelination is concentrated in the brain areas known as the *association regions*. These areas of the brain coordinate the activity and operation of other regions of the brain, such as putting together sensory information so that we connect what things look like with what they sound like, feel like, or taste like (Bartzokis et al., 2010; Paus et al., 1999). As they become myelinated, the increased efficiency of the association regions leads to more sophisticated planning and problem-solving abilities.

WHAT HAPPENS *in the* **BRAIN?**

As we discussed earlier, synaptic pruning helps solidify the neural connections that are most beneficial to the child. As childhood draws to a close, pruning trails off. The numbers of synaptic connections between particular neurons and the overall electric activity in the brain both begin to stabilize.

21.2 Cognitive Development

In just two short years, humans proceed from reflexive, speechless babies who are completely dependent on others to active, talking, problem-solvers. What happens during this period of time that triggers such rapid skill development? We will talk about how we learn language in Part 9. Here, we discuss the important changes in thinking ability that happen during those first two years.

21.2.1 Piaget's Theory

cognitive development changes in thinking that occur over the course of time.

One of the world's most influential developmental psychologists, Jean Piaget, focused on **cognitive development**, how thinking and reasoning changes through the active manipulation and exploration of the environment (Piaget, 1985, 2000, 2003; Piaget et al., 2009). Piaget's theory began with naturalistic observations of children, particularly his own, in real life situations (Mayer, 2005). On the basis of his observations, Piaget hypothesized that young children's thinking processes might differ from those of adults. He then proceeded to test his hypotheses by making small changes in the children's situations and watching to see how they responded to those changes (Phillips, 1975; Piaget, 1981). Based on the results of these tests, Piaget developed a theory of how children acquire knowledge and the abilities to use it.

scheme Piaget's proposed mental structures or frameworks for understanding or thinking about the world.

According to Piaget, all people have mental frameworks or structures for understanding and thinking about the world. He called these frameworks **schemes**, and he believed that people acquire and continuously build their schemes through their experiences in the world. For example, children may acquire a scheme about birthday parties, based on their experiences. When they go to another birthday party, they can predict that there will be presents, some food, a cake, activities, and possibly a treat bag to take home at the end of the party.

assimilation one of two ways of acquiring knowledge, defined by Piaget as the inclusion of new information or experiences into pre-existing schemes.

Piaget believed that when children gain new knowledge, their schemes change. This change in schemes can happen in two ways. The first, **assimilation**, was defined by Piaget as the inclusion of new information or experiences into pre-existing schemes. For example, when one of our daughters was 3 years old, she visited a farm for the first time. When taken out to see the animals, she was initially terrified by the HUGE dog they had penned up. In fact the huge dog was a cow, but our city-raised daughter had *assimilated* the cow to her existing scheme for larger four-legged furry things (dogs); calling all four-legged creatures "dogs" is assimilation.

accommodation one of two ways of acquiring knowledge, defined by Piaget as the alteration of pre-existing mental frameworks to take in new information.

On the other hand, sometimes we come across new information so different from what we already know that we cannot simply add it to our old schemes. We must alter a pre-existing schema significantly to fit in new information or experiences or create an entirely new scheme, an adjustment Piaget called **accommodation**. With expanding experience, children can *accommodate* and expand or add to their schemes. So, our 3-year-old created a new four-legged scheme of "cow" to go alongside her existing scheme of "dog."

equilibrium balance in a mental framework.

According to Piaget, engaging in assimilation and accommodation helps us to reach a mental balance, or **equilibrium**. When things are in balance, children (and adults too for that matter) are comfortable and able to assimilate new information. When things are not in balance, children experience disequilibration and are in a state of cognitive discomfort. They experience discomfort because they realize that their current schemes will not suffice and are therefore forced to modify their existing schemes to fit new information. Once they are cognitively comfortable, they move back toward equilibrium and are able to assimilate once again. To see a very helpful animation of assimilation and accommodation by Daurice Grossniklaus and Bob Rodes, go to www.simplypsychology.org/piaget.html (McLeod, 2009).

Piaget's theory is a stage theory. He believed that there were important differences between the thinking of children and the thinking of adults. He suggested that we move through several stages of cognitive development over the lifespan, progressing from having only reflexes as babies to being able to perform complicated mental feats of logic as teenagers and adults. Piaget believed strongly that, as we move from stage to stage, *qualitative* shifts occur in our thinking. Children in one stage not only know more, but actually become different kinds of thinkers than they were at earlier stages. **Table 21-3** shows the four developmental stages and age ranges proposed by Piaget (1981). He proposed that, during infancy, we are in the earliest, or sensorimotor, stage.

TABLE 21-3 Piaget's Four Stages of Cognitive Development

Stage	Age	Description	
Sensorimotor	Birth to age 2	Infant or toddler uses senses and motor skills; initially has no thought beyond immediate experience but eventually develops object permanence. Example: Babies enjoy games like peekaboo once they realize that people and objects continue to exist even if they can't see them.	© Digital Vision/Getty Images
Preoperational	Age 2–7	Although children cannot yet perform "operations" they are able to hold representations or ideas of objects in imagination. They are unable to consider another's point of view when it is different than their own (egocentric) or to understand that not all things are living (animistic). Example: Children may believe that a doll experiences hunger.	©iStockphoto.com/ssj414
Concrete operational	Age 7–11	Child can now operate on concrete objects and so they can think logically about complex relationships (cause and effect, categorization) and understand conservation. They are unable to think abstractly or hypothetically. Example: Children in this stage begin to question concepts like Santa Claus or the tooth fairy.	Hill Street Studios/Blend Images/Getty Images
Formal operational	Age 11 on	Adolescent can think abstractly and hypothetically. Example: Adolescent can now engage in scientific experiments.	©iStockphoto.com/Pamela Moore

Piaget's Sensorimotor Stage Piaget named the first stage the sensorimotor stage because he thought that, early on, babies can think only about the world in terms of what they can sense directly or do with it using simple motor actions. For example, a ball, a favourite toy, or a person is present only insofar as the baby can sense it directly or engage with it in some way—for infants, objects are primarily graspable or suckable. If they lose sensory contact with an object, they cannot hold the idea of the object in their mind. For example, if the baby is playing with a ball and it rolls under the couch, once the ball rolls under the couch, it's gone; out of sight is out of mind.

> **"**...[A]ssessing the impact of Piaget on developmental psychology is like assessing the impact of Shakespeare on English literature or Aristotle on philosophy—impossible. The impact is too monumental to embrace and at the same time too omnipresent to detect.**"**
>
> —*Harry Beilin (1992), psychologist*

Piaget thought that much of our early learning happens as a result of our reflexes. He observed that even though reflexes are "hardwired" into infants, they are susceptible to change. Thus, as babies engage in reflexive behaviours, they get feedback about how those responses affect them and the surrounding world. For example, the rooting reflex often brings food to a hungry infant, while the grasping reflex allows for basic manipulation of objects. In this way, babies acquire knowledge that contributes to the formation of early schemes.

object permanence an infant's realization that objects continue to exist even when they are outside of immediate sensory awareness.

Piaget believed that a major cognitive milestone of the sensorimotor stage is the development of **object permanence**, developing at around 8 months of age (although he did not believe that infants obtained full object permanence until much later). Object permanence is the realization that objects continue to exist even when they are out of a baby's immediate sensory awareness. At a particular point in development, a child may cry when a toy rolls under the couch because the child knows it still exists but it is now frustratingly out of reach, for example. When children begin to demonstrate awareness of things out of their immediate sensory awareness, it suggests that they are beginning to hold concepts in mind. That is, they have developed mental schemes of those objects—they can form mental representations of objects they cannot currently see or touch.

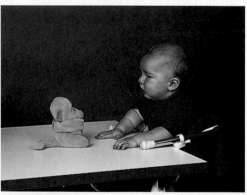 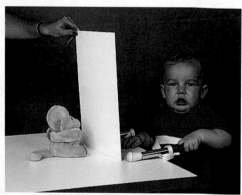

Doug Goodman/Photo Researchers   Doug Goodman/Photo Researchers

Out of sight, out of mind. Prior to 8 months of age, babies have no recognition of object permanence. For example, here a young infant stares fixedly at a stuffed animal, but displays no awareness that the toy continues to exist after an experimenter hides it from sight.

Eventually, babies become able not only to hold objects in their minds, but also to manipulate and make predictions about those objects and how they interact with other objects. A baby may try to lift a cloth to look under it for a hidden toy, for example, or play peek-a-boo with a mother hiding behind her hands. By the end of the sensorimotor stage, Piaget believed that the young child's schemes have changed from needing a direct experience of the world to one in which ideas and concepts stand in for those objects.

Piaget's Preoperational Stage According to Piaget, as children move into the **preoperational stage**, which lasts between the ages of 2 through 7, they become able to hold memories, or representations, of objects in their imaginations and to work with them as ideas (Bialystok & Craik, 2010; Müller & Racine, 2010). This way of thinking represents a dramatic shift from the earlier sensorimotor stage in which they were able only to manipulate actual objects. The thinking of children at this stage still shows some limitations compared to adult thinking, however.

One major limitation is what Piaget called *irreversibility*. Although children in this stage can work with symbols and concepts (representations) that stand in for real-world objects, children at the preoperational stage still think in rather simplistic ways about the relationships between those concepts and objects. For them, changes in relationships happen in one direction only. One researcher offers the following example of a 4-year-old boy who was asked about his family:

> "Do you have a brother?"
>
> "Yes."
>
> "What's his name?"
>
> "Jim."
>
> "Does Jim have a brother?"
>
> "No."
>
> (Phillips, 1975)

The boy is able to hold the idea of his brother Jim in his head, even though Jim is not there, indicating he has developed object permanence. At the same time, he has adopted this concept in one direction only: Jim is *my* brother. The boy is unable to think about the reverse relationship—that he is Jim's brother also.

The reason this child cannot think of himself as Jim's brother, according to Piaget, is because he cannot take Jim's point of view, an inability Piaget referred to as **egocentrism** (Kesselring & Müller, 2010). Piaget did not use the term *egocentrism* to mean the boy is arrogant or self-centred; his use of the term refers strictly to children's flaws in logical reasoning. This boy cannot yet realize that he, himself, is also a brother. Piaget believed that this type of *perspective-taking skill*, the ability to take another person's point of view, is not mastered until the next, concrete operational, stage.

Irreversibility is also related to a lack of **conservation**, the ability to understand that something can stay the same even though its appearance changes. Piaget used a now-famous task to demonstrate young children's problems with conservation. He gave a child two identical beakers with equal amounts of water in each and asked which of the beakers held more water. Children over 2 years of age were usually able to say that both beakers held the same amount. Piaget would then ask the child to pour the water into two new beakers that were shaped differently, one shallow and wide and the other tall and narrow. After the children poured the water, Piaget again asked which held more water. Children between the ages of 2 and 7—even after they themselves had poured the water into the new beakers—were more likely to say the tall, narrow beaker held more water. Piaget believed this indicated that the children could not mentally reverse the pouring of the water to imagine that the two amounts of water would once again match if both were returned to their original containers. In addition, Piaget believed the children could not see that, logically, it was still the same water just in a different container, or that the new container was taller but also narrower than the previous container.

Children's lack of conservation also may be related to difficulty in making distinctions between *appearance* and *reality*. In one classic example of this confusion, researcher

preoperational stage according to Piaget, a developmental stage during which children begin to develop ideas of objects in the external world and the ability to work with them in their mind.

©iStockphoto.com/vitapix

Egocentrism and perspective-taking. A child in the preoperational stage may acknowledge that he has a brother, but not yet realize that this means that he himself is also a brother.

egocentrism flaws in children's reasoning based on their inability to take another person's perspective.

conservation the understanding that certain properties of an object (such as volume and number) remain the same despite changes in the object's outward appearance.

©Spencer Grant/PhotoEdit   ©Spencer Grant/PhotoEdit

Shapes can be misleading. In the classic test for conservation, a child is shown two identical short thick glasses, each filled with liquid. The child then watches as the liquid from one glass is poured into a tall thin glass and is asked to indicate which glass now has more liquid. Most children between 2 and 7 years incorrectly pick the tall thin glass.

©iStockphoto.com/dmbaker/©iStockphoto.com/KrissiLundgren

Appearance versus reality. Younger children have a harder time looking beyond the dog mask to understand that the cat is still a cat.

concrete operational stage Piagetian stage during which children are able to talk about complex relationships, such as categorization and cause and effect, but are still limited to understanding ideas in terms of real-world relationships.

operations Piagetian description of children's ability to hold an idea in their mind and mentally manipulate it.

Rheta DeVries (1969) allowed children to play with her cat, Maynard. After a while, DeVries and her assistants hid Maynard's front half from view while they strapped a dog mask onto the cat's face. (We have no idea how she got a cat to tolerate wearing a dog mask.) DeVries then asked the toddlers what kind of animal Maynard was. Even though Maynard was never completely out of view, the majority of the 3-year-old participants, and a good number of 4- and 5-year-olds, thought the cat had magically become a dog. By the age of 6, when they were nearing the concrete operational stage, none of the children made this mistake. The younger children could not look past the surface appearance of the masked cat to see that in reality it was still a cat and not a dog. For these preschool children, appearances were the only reality they could conceive of.

Piaget's Concrete Operational Stage During the **concrete operational stage**, lasting from age 7 through 11 or 12, children demonstrate the ability to think about ideas. School entry coincides with the development of the logical cognitive skills that Piaget called **operations**, the ability to hold an idea in mind and manipulate it mentally. Piaget considered this to be a significant change in thinking, because children in this stage show that they are capable of applying simple logic to their thinking. They start to talk with confidence about complex relationships between variables, such as cause and effect and categorization. They can take others' perspectives and reverse (mentally undo) operations or actions, as in conservation tasks. By now, they consider the notion that a cat can mysteriously become a dog ridiculous. They know dogs and cats fit into certain hard and fast categories, and they can now extend those categories to other organisms that share the same features.

Children at this stage show a mastery of real-world relationships. This mastery is limited to physical objects, actual people, places, or things children have observed. This is why Piaget referred to this stage as the *concrete* operational stage. Children in this stage have difficulty with abstract relationships between objects that do not exist in the real world, such as abstract mathematical relationships or logical questions, such as how many unique combinations can be made from four different things. They also find it difficult to think about hypothetical, alternate possibilities and have trouble speculating on questions such as, "What ways can this situation play out?" A mastery of those kinds of relationships is left for the next stage of development, the formal operational stage.

Piaget's Formal Operational Stage Piaget suggested that at around the age of 11 or 12 years, we cross over into mature adult thinking processes, a final stage known as the **formal operational stage**. Piaget believed that the hallmark achievement of this stage is the ability to think about ideas conceptually without needing concrete referents from the real world. They can now reason based on hypothetical concepts, engaging in hypothetico-deductive reasoning. In this type of thinking, individuals begin with a hypothesis, or prediction, and then deduce logical, testable interpretations arising from the hypothesis. They then systematically test variables in isolation or in combination to see which of their theories are correct.

formal operational stage Piaget's final stage of cognitive development when children achieve hypothetical deductive reasoning and the ability to think abstractly.

The successful transition to the formal operational stage means that older children and adolescents are no longer bound by the concrete realities of their world. They can conceive of other worlds and other possible realities, even ones that exist outside their own imaginations, engaging in propositional thought—that is, evaluating the logic of statements (propositions) without considering reality. For example, consider the logic of the following statements. If you assume the first statement is correct, is the second statement also correct?

1. *All dogs can fly.*
2. *Your dog Rex can fly.*

What is the correct answer? Although flying dogs are contrary to reality, a formal operational thinker treats the problem abstractly and is therefore able to correctly answer, *"Yes, my dog Rex can fly."* A concrete thinker would experience difficulty with the problem because it violates what they know to be factually true in the real world.

By adjusting their approaches to focus more on children's capacities rather than on their ability to manipulate objects or events, information-processing researchers have found that cognitive development may involve fewer qualitative shifts (and more quantitative growth) than Piaget believed. Nevertheless, Piaget's ideas remain influential. In addition, Piaget's theory continues to encourage developmental psychologists to generate research that seeks both to support the theory and to rebut it. If nothing else, the intense research activity ignited by Piaget's ideas has helped us think about how to best study children's thought processes. Perhaps most importantly, Piaget encouraged psychologists to stop thinking of children as organisms programmed by biology or by early experiences, and instead to think of them as active interpreters of their world.

Evaluating Piaget: Information Processing Views of Cognitive Development

Piaget has often been criticized for looking at what children could not do and then using their mistakes to determine their cognitive abilities. Today, however, psychologists who adhere to the **information-processing theory** study how children learn, remember, organize, and use information—they look to see what children *can* do, as opposed to what they cannot do. Such theorists have found that Piaget probably underestimated children's competencies in the various developmental stages (Li, 2010; Lourenç & Machado, 1996).

information-processing theory a developmental theory focusing on how children learn, remember, organize, and use information from their environment.

To see whether a baby developed object permanence, for example, Piaget would hide an object under a cloth and see whether the baby looked for it. Searching for the object, by pulling the cloth off the object, suggests that the baby still had the object in her mind. As we have noted, however, it takes some time for babies to master control over their bodies enough to move purposefully and conduct a search. To accomplish the task of retrieving the desired object, you have to carry out two sequential behaviours: you have to pull the obstacle away from the object and then you have to grasp the hidden object. To address this confound, other researchers such as Renée Baillargeon, from Quebec, have suggested that a better indicator of object permanence is to observe how babies respond when their expectations have been violated (Baillargeon, 1987; Charles & Rivera, 2009).

violation-of-expectation an experimental approach capitalizing on infants' and toddlers' heightened reactions to an unexpected event.

To carry out a **violation-of-expectation** approach to test object permanence, Baillargeon and colleagues habituated babies to a particular event. When babies **habituate**, they stop responding over time to the same stimulus if it is presented again and again—they get

habituation the process of habituating, in which individuals pay less attention to a stimulus after it is presented to them over and over again.

bored with it. In the violation-of-expectation method, babies are generally habituated to an expected, or possible, event (one that obeys a physical law or scientific generalization). After the babies show a decline in looking at the expected event, they are shown an unexpected event. When the babies indicate surprise or increase their looking time, the assumption is made that they had a representation of the object. After all, to be surprised, babies had to have had an expectation that was challenged in some way. Such surprise implies that the babies had a mental representation of the situation and that their representations were shown to be wrong. For example, in one violation-of-expectation experiment, Baillargeon and colleagues habituated babies to an expected, possible event, a short or a tall carrot going behind a tall screen and coming out the opposite side. They then violated the babies' expectation with an impossible event; they had the tall carrot go behind the cut-out screen and then had it appear on the opposite side—without being seen through the cut-out screen as it made the crossing from one side to the other. Using expressions of surprise as the evidence that the babies recognized that the object (in this case a carrot) had continued to exist (when it was unseen behind the screen), Baillargeon and colleagues argued that babies as young as 3 months display some form of object permanence (Baillargeon, 2004).

Using this *violation-of-expectation* approach, another group of researchers were able to show that babies understand rudimentary mathematics. As amazing as it may sound, infants may actually be capable of mathematical equations using small numbers! As you can see in **Figure 21-3**, psychologist Karen Wynn conducted a series of studies in which she showed 5-month-old babies a sequence of events where one doll is put in a case behind a screen followed by another doll (McCrink & Wynn, 2004; Newman & Nave, 2010; Wynn, 1992, 2002). She found that when the screen was dropped, the babies expressed surprise and looked longer if only one doll was in the case than if both dolls were present. The babies seemed to know that the case should hold two dolls. This result has been replicated with even larger numbers (five to ten dolls) in 9-month-old children!

Many critics have challenged Piaget's belief that children in the preoperational and concrete operational stages have problems taking others' point of view. In fact, some researchers have become very interested in young children's awareness of their own minds

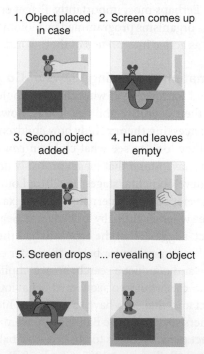

1. Object placed in case   2. Screen comes up

3. Second object added   4. Hand leaves empty

5. Screen drops ... revealing 1 object

FIGURE 21-3 Baby math. To see whether 5-month-old infants have an appreciation of addition and subtraction, Karen Wynn showed them the sequence of events illustrated above. If the infants express surprise when the screen drops and they see only one object, it suggests that they understand that 1 + 1 = 2. Based on Weiten, W. (2007). *Psychology: Themes and variations* (7th ed.). Belmont, CA: Thomson Higher Education. Adapted by permission from Macmillan Publishers Ltd: Nature, K. Wynn, Addition and subtraction by human infants, vol. 358, pp. 749–750, © 1992.

FIGURE 21-4 Theory of mind. Young research participants are told a story in which a child first sees his mother place chocolate in an upper cupboard, then he leaves while she makes a chocolate cake. In his absence, the mother places the leftover chocolate in a lower cupboard, and the child then returns looking for leftover chocolate. Participants with a theory of mind recognize that the child in the story will look for the leftover chocolate in the original upper cupboard, because the child is not aware of the mother's switch of locations.

and the minds of others, a field of research called **theory of mind** (Carpendale & Lewis, 2010; Mar, Tackett, & Moore, 2010).

Theory of mind was first studied in an experiment with children between 3 and 9 years of age. Each child participant was told a story about a boy named Maxi who tries to sneak some chocolate from his mother (Wimmer & Perner, 1983). According to the story, Maxi's mother brings home some chocolate to make a cake, and while Maxi is watching, she puts the chocolate in a blue cupboard (see **Figure 21-4**). Maxi then goes out to play. While he is outside, his mother makes the cake and puts the remaining chocolate in a green cupboard. Next, Maxi comes back in, wanting some chocolate. The researchers then asked the children in the study where Maxi would look for the chocolate.

This deceptively simple task actually requires a high level of thought. Children have to not only remember where the chocolate has travelled, but also take the viewpoint of Maxi and realize that Maxi has no way of knowing that his mother moved the chocolate. Three- to 4-year-olds regularly fail such tests, suggesting this task is too complicated for them, while most 4- to 5-year-olds passed the task, and 6-year-olds regularly succeeded. Experiments such as these support Piaget's notion that young children are egocentric or focused on their own knowledge or perspective, but also suggest that children are able to take other people's thoughts and feelings into account much sooner than Piaget had predicted—at around age 4 as opposed to age 6 or 7 years.

Another way that researchers assess theory of mind is to assess children's understandings of *false-beliefs*. False beliefs are based on a premise that is not true; the ability to understand false beliefs usually develops by the age of 5 years (Wellman, Cross, & Watson, 2001). Canadian researchers Alison Gopnik and Janet Astington (1988) devised the well-known *Smarties* task to test a young child's understanding of false beliefs. They asked children to guess what was in a *Smarties* box. The children confidently guessed candy, but were then shown that the box was in fact full of small pencils. After the researcher closed the box, they asked the children to guess what they thought a peer who had not yet seen the actual contents of the box would say when asked what was in it. Many 4-year-olds and most 5-year-olds were able to guess "*Smarties*," but some 4-year-olds and most 3-year-olds incorrectly guessed, "pencils." When the children who failed the task were asked why they thought their peer would not guess *Smarties*, they said, "Because it *isn't Smarties*, it's pencils."

In part, Piaget's approach may have been limited by a failure to listen to his own theory. Piaget believed that thought preceded language—that our thinking develops faster than our ability to use words. Yet, his tests of his theories rested on observations

theory of mind an awareness of one's own mental states and the mental states of others.

of children's performances on language-based tasks, such as the question about Jim's brother. Other researchers, by focusing on non-verbal responses or by making their questions more age-appropriate or child-friendly, have found evidence that children develop certain cognitive competencies sooner; for example, pictures accompanied the story of Maxi. More recent research has linked theory of mind to general language development (Astington & Baird, 2005).

Still other critics, such as Jeremy Carpendale from Simon Fraser University, have charged that Piaget's theory fails to account fully for *social* factors, the influences that other people may have on a child's cognitive development (Carpendale & Lewis, 2010; Freund & Lamb, 2010; Symons, 2004). Instead, Piaget's theory focuses on how children guide their own development through experimentation and reflection. Later in his life, Piaget himself also wondered whether his theory said enough about the role of social experiences in development (Inhelder & Piaget, 1979; Piaget, 1972), and indeed his theory underestimated the role of culture in reasoning. As we will see next, a contemporary of Piaget's, Lev Vygotsky, had more to say about social influences on cognitive development.

21.2.2 Vygotsky and the Role of Socio-cultural Theory

While Piaget was focusing on how children's private experiments and reflections shape their thinking, a Russian psychologist named Lev Vygotsky was becoming increasingly interested in how social interactions with more mature members of their culture shaped the development of children. Unlike Piaget, who viewed a child's development as a process of individual achievement, Vygotsky (1978, 1991, 2004) believed that constructive interactions with parents, older children, teachers, and siblings helped the child develop ways of thinking about and functioning in the world. In Vygotsky's view, an older mentor, such as a parent, helps the child by initially taking responsibility for the basic skills and capabilities the child is developing. Over time, the mentor takes less and less responsibility. Jerome Bruner (1983, 1986), a Vygotskian researcher, referred to the mentor's step-by-step assistance as **scaffolding**, while Barbara Rogoff (1990) referred to this process as an *apprenticeship in thinking*. Vygotsky labelled the gap between what children can accomplish by themselves and what they can accomplish with the help of others as the **zone of proximal development**.

Because Vygotsky believed that other individuals are critical to helping children develop, he also believed that there is a great deal more variability in how children develop. He believed that each culture has its own specific challenges, and that those challenges change over the course of life, meaning that development has to meet those challenges.

Because of his death at the young age of 37 and the chilly political climate between the former Soviet Union and the West, Vygotsky's ideas have only become more widely studied in North America in recent years. However, developmental psychologists have found numerous ways to apply Vygotsky's ideas (Trawick-Smith & Dziurgot, 2011). He has become one of today's most influential developmental theorists (Eun, 2010; Feldman, 2003). Indeed, the ideas of scaffolding and zones of proximal development are now an important part of educational systems throughout North America (Holzman, 2009). When helping children learn to read, for example, many teachers begin by reading books to them, and then gradually turn over responsibility for various reading skills. The children may first follow along with the pictures as the teacher reads the words, then point to letters. Eventually, they learn to read single words, then sentences, and finally entire books on their own, as the teacher provides less and less scaffolding and the children's zone of proximal development becomes smaller.

21.3 Social and Emotional Development in Infancy and Childhood

While we tend to think of young infants as completely helpless, they actually bring a number of behavioural tendencies to their early interactions with their parents.

scaffolding developmental adjustments that adults make to give children the help that they need, but not so much that they fail to move forward.

zone of proximal development the gap between what a child could accomplish alone and what the child can accomplish with help from others.

As we noted in Part 1, many psychological researchers are interested in trying to determine how much of the way we think and act is influenced by our genetic inheritance, a field of study called *behavioural genetics*. Developmental psychologists are often in a position to examine the influence of genetics. One of the key areas of focus of both behavioural genetics and developmental psychology, for example, is **temperament**, defined as a biologically-based tendency to respond to certain situations in similar ways throughout a person's lifetime (Bates, 1989; Bates, Schermerhorn, & Goodnight, 2010; Henderson & Wachs, 2007; van den Akker et al., 2010). Although temperament and personality are related, they are not the same thing. Many personality characteristics are learned or acquired, whereas temperamental traits are considered genetic (Rothbart & Bates, 2006). In a longitudinal study that began in the 1950s, the *New York Longitudinal Study*, researchers Stella Chess and Alexander Thomas (1996; Thomas & Chess, 1977) collected data suggesting that, as infants, people tend to fall into one of four temperament categories:

- *Easy.* (40 percent) Babies with easy temperaments are described as cheerful, regular in routines, such as eating and sleeping, and open to novelty.
- *Difficult.* (10 percent) Babies with difficult temperaments tend to be irritable and are likely to have intensely negative reactions to changes or new situations.
- *Slow-to-warm-up.* (15 percent) Babies in this category are less active and less responsive than babies in the other two categories. In general, they tend to withdraw in the face of change, but their withdrawal is not as sharply negative as those with difficult temperaments.
- *Unique.* (35 percent) Babies in this category show unique blends of characteristics from the other categories. For example, a child might be cautious in new situations but have regular routines and be relatively cheerful.

Following Chess and Thomas's (1996; Thomas & Chess, 1977) studies, many other researchers have also examined how temperament relates to later personality characteristics. Psychologist Jerome Kagan (2001, 2008, 2010, 2011) conducted a longitudinal study examining the relationship between babies' levels of *behavioural inhibition*, the tendency to withdraw from new or different situations, and levels of shyness later in life. He found that children who were highly inhibited at 21 months of age were more likely than uninhibited toddlers to be shy when they were 12 to 14 years old.

Kagan's research illustrates two key aspects of temperament:

1. *Temperament is inborn.* Kagan argues that individual differences in arousal of the amygdala are involved in this aspect of temperament (Kagan & Fox, 2006). The amygdala is involved in avoidance reactions; thus, in inhibited children the amygdala is excited by minimal stimulation, whereas in uninhibited children the amygdala requires a great deal more stimulation to become excited. Other physiological correlates, such as higher heart rates (Schmidt et al., 2007), higher concentrations of the stress hormone cortisol (Zimmerman & Stansbury, 2004), greater pupil dilation, higher blood pressure (Kagan & Fox, 2006), as well as EEG activity in the right frontal lobe (Kagan & Fox, 2006) also indicate higher emotional arousal in inhibited infants and children.

2. *Temperament is stable across situations and time.* The participants in Kagan's study who were most inhibited temperamentally were the ones who were most inhibited at many different times and in different situations. Researchers have also established that other aspects of a person's temperament are stable over time and place (Bates et al., 2010; Henderson & Wachs, 2007; Majdandžić & van den Boom, 2007). This is not to say, however, that there is no variability at all from time to time and situation to situation. In fact, investigators have found greater stability of temperament when measuring behaviour across similar situations, such as in various family situations, than when comparing temperamental influences on children's behaviour across different situations, such as school versus home (Rothbart, Derryberry, & Hershey, 2000).

temperament a biologically-based tendency to respond to certain situations in similar ways throughout a person's lifetime.

©iStockphoto.com/arekmalang

Toddler temperaments. Infant and toddler temperaments can be observed in the typical behaviours they display.

WHAT HAPPENS *in the* **BRAIN?**

Despite the biological factors implied above, it is important to recognize that our environments also play important roles in how we behave. Kagan's studies (Kagan & Snidman, 2004) revealed, for example, that not all of the babies who were inhibited at birth later developed into shy teenagers, suggesting that environmental factors are also important in shaping personality. There is also ample evidence to suggest that both genetics and environment interact to influence behaviour. For example, difficult children with sensitive parents regulate emotion better over time than difficult children with insensitive or inconsistent parents (Coplan et al., 2003; Paulussen-Hoogeboom et al., 2007; Raikes et al., 2007).

So, both infants and parents bring their temperaments and personalities to their early interactions, and the characteristics of each influences the relationship. We now turn our attention to how those early interactions contribute to relationships as the infant and caregivers begin to form the important attachment relationship.

21.3.1 Attachment

attachment a significant emotional connection to another person, such as a baby to a primary caregiver.

Attachment theorists argue that the relationship between a caregiver and an infant is crucial to the child's long-term social and emotional development (Allen, 2011; Nelson & Bennett, 2008). Researchers have therefore long been interested in determining what fosters attachment. Attachment is defined as a significant and enduring emotional connection that serves as an essential foundation for future relationships.

Freud argued that the infant's emotional tie to the mother formed the foundation for all other relationships, and further argued that feeding was the basis for building this emotional connection. To test Freud's assertion that feeding was at the basis of all mother–infant relationships, Harry Harlow and Robert Zimmerman (Harlow & Zimmerman, 1959) carried out a now famous experiment in the 1950s. Baby rhesus monkeys were removed from their mothers at birth and were reared in isolation for six months with two "surrogate mothers." One "mother" was fashioned of soft terry cloth, whereas the other "mother" was made of wire-mesh. The wire-mesh "mother" held the bottle. Baby monkeys spent almost all of their time clinging to the soft "mother"—only leaving her to go to the wire "mother" when driven to eat. Harlow concluded from the results that the crucial element in forming attachments is contact comfort.

Nina Leen/Time & Life Pictures/Getty Images

Contact comfort. Infant rhesus monkeys showed clear preference for the soft "mother" over the wire "mother."

Another well-known psychodynamic theorist, Erik Erikson (1959, 1984, 1985), developed a psychosocial stage theory of development to describe the impact of social development across the lifespan. Erikson believed that individuals had to develop a particular social competency—or *psychosocial strength*—at each of eight stages in the lifespan. Erikson argued that, because they are completely dependent and vulnerable, infants in the first year of life need to develop trust. He viewed trust as the foundation of human development. He argued that viewing others as safe and dependable leads to the enduring belief that the world is a secure place. Erikson believed that appropriately responsive and sensitive parenting contributed to the development of trust. On the other hand, infants that experience rejection or harsh or inconsistent parenting come to develop a sense of mistrust. We will look further at Erikson's theory later in the part.

The ethological perspective of British psychiatrist John Bowlby asserts that human beings are born with a drive to form an attachment, to become emotionally close to one particular caregiver, usually their mother. He suggested that early positive experiences with that caregiver are critical to health and well-being, and they shape how well the individual will function emotionally, socially, and even cognitively later in life (Bowlby, 1969, 1999).

Bowlby also argued that the behaviours of infants are aimed at bringing them closer to their mothers. He believed, for example, that reflexes such as rooting or reaching out help babies build relationships with their mothers (Bowlby, 1958). To Bowlby, the presence of these reflexes provided evidence that attachment processes are inborn and crucial to the survival and well-being of babies. Bowlby also thought that children with strong attachments to their mothers would actually feel safer than children who were more independent and less attached to their mothers. Indeed, he suggested that appropriate, consistent responsiveness to a baby's needs is actually the best way for a mother to eventually bring about an independent and well-functioning child. Initially, the scientific community reacted negatively to this assertion (Holmes, 1993). The psychological wisdom of Bowlby's day held that parents who respond to children's needs in this way would only succeed in promoting neediness and dependence.

Mary Ainsworth, a colleague of John Bowlby, was one of the first women to earn a Ph.D. in Psychology at the University of Toronto and to take up a faculty position there in 1939. She went on to work with Bowlby and conducted naturalistic observations in Uganda that supported Bowlby's ideas that mother–child attachment occurs around the world (Ainsworth, 1967, 1985, 1993, 2010). Like Bowlby, Ainsworth argued that babies attach to their mothers because that is how their needs get met (Bretherton, 1992; Hughes, 2009). Ainsworth further noticed that some mothers, whom she labelled "highly sensitive," seem to form attachments that are more successful in fostering their children's independence.

Ainsworth developed a way to test the attachment between babies and their mothers in a laboratory setting. In Ainsworth's procedure, called the *Strange Situation* (see **Figure 21-5**), a baby plays in a laboratory room with the mother nearby. After a time, a stranger enters the room, speaks with the mother, and attempts to interact with the baby. Then the mother leaves the room. The baby, left alone with the stranger, generally is in some distress. The researchers are most interested in how the baby reacts to the mother when she returns, as well as how willing the baby is to explore when the mother is present.

Based on her experimental findings, Ainsworth identified three basic attachment styles:

- *Secure attachment* (60 percent): The infant uses the mother as a secure base from which to explore and as a support in time of trouble. The infant is moderately distressed when the mother leaves the room and happy when she returns.
- *Anxious/avoidant attachment* (15 percent): The infant is unresponsive with the mother and is usually indifferent when she leaves the room and when she returns.
- *Anxious/ambivalent/resistant attachment* (10 percent): The infant reacts strongly when the mother leaves the room. When she returns, the infant shows mixed emotions, seeking close contact and then squirming away angrily.

Later, psychologist Mary Main noted that some children fail to show any reliable way of coping with separations and reunions, exhibiting features of all three of the other styles

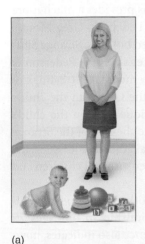    

(a)   (b)   (c)   (d)   (e)

FIGURE 21-5 Abbreviated Strange Situation procedure. (a) The baby plays while the mother is nearby. (b) A stranger enters the room, speaks to the mother, and approaches the child. (c) The mother leaves and the stranger stays in the room with an unhappy baby. (d) The mother returns and the stranger leaves. (e) The baby is reunited with the mother.

FIGURE 21-6 **Styles of attachment.** Ainsworth and Main identified four styles of attachment.

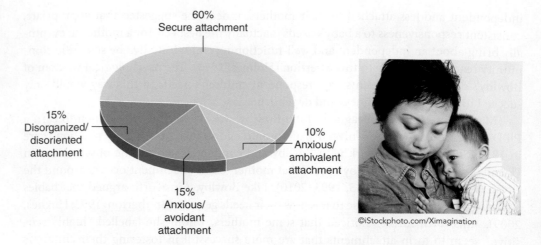

60%
Secure attachment

15%
Disorganized/ disoriented attachment

10%
Anxious/ ambivalent attachment

15%
Anxious/ avoidant attachment

(Main, Hesse, & Kaplan, 2005; Main & Solomon, 1990). Ainsworth and Main therefore added a fourth category to describe this pattern:

- *Disorganized/disoriented attachment* (15 percent): The infant displays confused and contradictory behaviour when the mother returns. For example, the infant may ignore the mother while being held, appear flat and depressed, look dazed, cry out, and/or show a rigid posture.

Figure 21-6 shows the incidence of all four styles.

In 1969, Bowlby suggested that early attachment experiences help people create an *internal working model* of the world, themselves, and the others with whom they form early attachment relationships. If children come to think of themselves as worthy of love and affection, view other people as supportive and responsive, and view relationships as positive experiences as a result of having sensitive mothers, Bowlby suggested that this positive model will influence their later relationships in a healthy way. In contrast, children who develop a working model that they are not worthy of love and affection, view their relationship partner as insensitive, and view their early relationships as negative, may be at risk for poor adjustment or difficult relationships with other people later in their lives.

One of the drawbacks to Ainsworth's work is that she suggests that children are either securely attached or not. This categorical approach does not make it easy to talk about degrees of security or degrees of anxiousness in children's attachment patterns. An alternative approach, called the *Q-sort approach*, involves observers of parent–child interactions placing descriptions of various attachment behaviours into nine piles, with frequent behaviours at one end and infrequent behaviours at the other. This provides a much more fluid estimate of the child's general attachment patterns. David Pederson, Greg Moran, and Sandi Bento from the University of Western Ontario compared both the Strange Situation and the Q-sort attachment assessment methods (Pederson et al., 1999; Pederson & Moran, 1996). The researchers found that there was much agreement in the ratings of security found using the Strange Situation in a lab setting and the Q-sort in the child's home setting. They also found, however, that the Q-sort technique used in the child's home was more sensitive to child ambivalence (finding it at twice the rate of the Strange Situation method). Given that ambivalence can predict later social adjustment issues, the Q-sort might be the better assessment to use if you are looking to ensure that children and families in need of support are identified.

The vast majority of attachment research has focused on mothers, and indeed, cultural practice bears out the importance of the mother–child relationship; in almost every society, mothers do the majority of childcare (Parke, 1995). Evidence also indicates, however, that fathers are capable of responding in highly sensitive ways, and that highly sensitive fathers have babies that generally turn out to be securely attached (Grossmann et al., 2002; Howes, 1999; Verissimo et al., 2011).

practically speaking

Childcare in Canada: How Are We Doing?

Many families have help in caring for their children (see **Figure 21-7**) (Bushnick 2006). Although 70 percent of infants are cared for by their mothers in the first year in Canada (Côté et al., 2008), over 60 percent of single-parent Canadian families and over 50 percent of two-parent families use some form of non-parental care for their children after the first year (Statistics Canada, 2006b). Figure 21-7 shows the different types of care arrangements used. What quality of care are Canadian children receiving? Canada recently placed 21st out of 29 countries for general child well-being in childcare (Keon, 2009; Leitch, 2007). As well, the United Nations Children's Fund found that Canada had only managed to achieve one of the ten benchmarks of quality in childcare and early learning (Hertzman, 2009). Unlike Sweden, which provides universal childcare from birth into the school years, Canada currently has no national childcare policy.

Some provinces are starting to overcome these disadvantages. Quebec has a broad childcare policy and program where many parents can obtain childcare for $7 a day (Bushnik, 2006). The wages of Quebec childcare workers have nearly doubled from where they were several years ago—on par with those of parking lot attendants. This means that

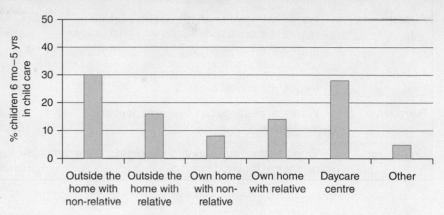

FIGURE 21-7 Childcare in Canada. Distribution of children aged 6 months to 5 years by type of main non-parental care arrangement, 2002–2003.

Source: Statistics Canada, Child Care in Canada: Children and Youth Research Paper Series, Bushnick, Tracey (2006) Catalogue no. 89-599-MIE2006003, April 2006, Figure 6, 2002–2003, page 14.

more people are prepared to make daycare their career and obtain higher levels of training and experience (Hertzman, 2009). Saskatchewan and Prince Edward Island have moved responsibility for daycare into their education ministries (Beach & Bertrand, 2009). Most other provinces are implementing programs aimed at improving early childhood education with the belief that additional costs will be offset down the road by the benefits of a healthier, better educated population.

21.4 Parenting Styles

Once attachment theory gave psychologists a way of *operationalizing* (or defining in a measurable way) the relationship between parents and children, other researchers began applying those insights to understanding how parent behaviours might contribute to development. For example, Diana Baumrind, a psychologist at the University of California-Berkeley, conducted interviews and observations of primarily white, middle-class preschool children and their parents and found that two characteristics of parental behaviour seem particularly important: how many demands the parent puts on the child, and how responsive the parent is to the child (Baumrind, 1991; Baumrind et al., 2010). Combining those two dimensions, Baumrind identified four parenting styles and the child outcomes associated with them, as depicted in **Table 21-4**.

A key question about Baumrind's theory has been how well it applies outside largely white, individualistic cultures. *Individualistic cultures* are those in which people are expected to be self-reliant and self-achieving, while *collectivist cultures* expect people to be focused primarily on the needs of the group. Cross-cultural research on parenting has found that parents in a variety of cultures can be classified into the same four styles. It is not clear, however, that the outcomes of the four parenting styles are the same across different cultures. Research by Xinyin Chen at the University of Western Ontario (Chen et al., 1999) suggests, for example, that in Asian cultures, the high-demand, low-responsiveness, authoritarian parenting style does not necessarily lead to negative child

TABLE 21-4 Parenting Styles

Parental Style	Parental Behaviour	Associated Outcome in Children
Authoritative	Warm, sensitive to child's needs, nurturing; makes reasonable demands and encourages appropriate autonomy	High self-esteem, cooperativeness, self-control, social maturity
Authoritarian	Cold, rejecting; makes coercive demands; frequently critical of child	Low self-esteem, anxious, unhappy, often angry and aggressive
Permissive	Warm, accepting, but overindulgent and inattentive	Impulsive, disobedient, overly dependent on adults, low initiative
Uninvolved	Emotionally detached and depressed; little time or energy for child rearing	Anxious, poor communication skills, antisocial behaviour

Psychology Around Us

What Do Fathers Have to Do with Development? A Lot!

Jessica Ball, at the University of Victoria (Ball & Moselle, 2007), reviewed the Canadian and relevant international research on fathers' contributions to children's well-being. The Public Health Agency of Canada included Dr. Ball's review in a general initiative looking at father involvement for healthy child outcomes (PHAC, 2007). The following findings indicate that fathers today play a direct and active role in their children's development:

- Fathers play a direct role in ensuring that their children have access to quality early childhood education, schooling, and supportive media.
- Fathers' ability to generate income for their families provides stability in housing, nutrition, and leisure activities, among other areas, which in turn reduces the risk of negative health outcomes associated with poor nutrition, obesity, and injuries.
- Youth who are close to their fathers are less likely to engage in substance use.
- When fathers are more actively involved in their children's school, the children do better academically.
- Fathers' involvement in their children's development is self-sustaining, meaning that the more involved fathers become, the more satisfaction they receive and the more skill they develop.

So, given that father involvement is so good, shouldn't we find ways to encourage more fathers to play a more active role in their children's lives? That is precisely what members of the fathers' Involvement Research Alliance under the guidance of Kerry Daly from the University of Guelph are trying to do (Allen & Daly, 2007). This group consists of researchers,

©iStockphoto.com/Kali Nine LLC

community agencies, and fathers, and is committed to exploring and enhancing fatherhood among seven Canadian populations, including indigenous fathers, new fathers, young fathers, immigrant and refugee fathers, gay fathers, divorced fathers, and fathers of children with special needs.

Karen Benzies at the University of Calgary, along with her colleagues there and at the University Alberta (Benzies et al., 2008), have shown that a simple program (two home visits with the father and infant), designed to encourage first-time fathers to become more actively involved in their new child's development, successfully increased father commitment and involvement.

outcomes as it often does in Canada. In fact, the authoritarian style can benefit children's academic performances during adolescence.

Another important question researchers have examined is how children's behaviours affect parenting styles, a transaction known as **reciprocal socialization**. Highly boisterous children are, for example, more likely to evoke authoritarian control behaviours in their parents (Caspi, 1998; Chan, 2010). Most of today's research on reciprocal socialization emphasizes the transaction between the parent and the child and holds that a *good fit* between a parent and child's behavioural styles is more important than some objectively right or wrong style (Talwar, Nitz, & Lerner, 1991).

At the beginning of this module, we noted that the *Early Years Study 3: Making Decisions and Taking Action* (2011) report emphasized the importance of early experience. We now know that sustained early exposure to serious ongoing stress can disrupt the wiring of the brain, leading to changes in brain anatomy and altered gene expression. For illustration of the specific effects of early deprivation, let's return to our earlier discussion of Romanian orphans. There is a large body of data identifying the detrimental and injurious effects of early deprivation in this group of children. Specifically, data from diverse research laboratories indicates that as a group, children reared in Romanian institutions received inadequate stimulation to scaffold normal brain development (Nelson et al., 2012). As a result, these children experienced significantly reduced brain matter (Sheridan et al., 2012), significantly impaired head growth (Rutter et al., 2012), and the risk for socio-emotional and behavioural problems due to the role of critical periods (Julian, 2013). It is important to note that sustained early exposure to any type of extreme stress places a child at risk. Infants and children do not need to be institutionalized to experience changes in brain anatomy and gene expression in the brain and the increased risks over the lifetime accompanying these changes, including increased risk for behavioural issues, mental health problems, and addictions (AFWI, 2013).

reciprocal socialization the transactional relationship between parent and child.

practically Speaking — Building Better Futures by Building Better Brains

Scientists now know that early experience—both good and bad—alter the development of the brain's architecture. We also know that gene expression can be changed by environmental factors. Scientists also know that brains are built from the bottom up. That is, complex circuits and skills are built on more basic circuits and skills, creating either a strong or a weak foundation for future learning. Finally, scientists also know that brain plasticity decreases over time; once circuits are stabilized, they are difficult to modify (Shonkoff & Bales, 2011). There is therefore no doubt that the quality of the early environment is crucially important in the early years. Infants and children exposed to extreme, ongoing levels of intolerable stress experience changes in brain anatomy that place them at risk for increased susceptibility to physical and mental illness. So, how does this important message get to the public?

In Alberta, a dedicated group of researchers, the Alberta Family Wellness Initiative (AFWI), is asking just that question. Influenced by Harvard's National Scientific Council on the Developing Child and the Frameworks Institute (www.frameworksinstitute.org), they have developed a "core story" about development. This story uses language that is easily accessible to anyone—regardless of whether they have a background in science or not. For example, the story talks about bidirectional communication between a parent and infant as "serve and return," likens executive functioning to "air traffic control in the child's mental airspace," and refers to intolerable stress as "toxic." To watch two short but powerful videos designed to convey the important message about the role of early experience in brain development, go to www.albertafamilywellness.org/resources/video/how-brains-are-built-core-story-brain-development to see How Brains are Built: The Core Story of Brain Development (AFWI), and www.albertafamilywellness.org/resources/video/brain-hero to see Brain Hero (Harvard Center on the Developing Child, www.developingchild.harvard.edu).

What Do You Know?

1. What is the role of myelination in the development of the brain?
2. What is the Strange Situation?
3. What are the major parenting styles, and what are the primary child outcomes associated with each style?
4. In what areas of the brain is myelination concentrated during childhood, and how does myelination of these areas affect the child's cognitive functioning?
5. What are the crucial differences between Piaget's view of cognitive development and Vygotsky's view of cognitive development?
6. How are the ideas of scaffolding and zone of proximal development reflected in contemporary educational practices?

What Do You Think? How do you think the various attachment styles correlate with Baumrind's parenting styles? Do you think there is one optimal form of parenting?

Do you think that men and women reason differently about morality? If the outcome is the same in our moral choices, does the reasoning we used to achieve that outcome matter?

Summary

Module 21: Infancy and Childhood

LEARNING OBJECTIVE 21 Summarize the major physical, cognitive, and emotional developments that take place during infancy and during childhood.

- Infants make dramatic gains in both physical and psychological capabilities. Our brains grow during this period, preparing us to learn and encode the information that will organize those changes.
- One of the most important developmental theorists, Jean Piaget, proposed a theory of cognitive development that suggested that through learning and self-experimentation, we help our thinking to grow progressively more complex.
- Piaget believed we pass through multiple stages on the way to formal adult reasoning and that each transition is accompanied by the acquisition of a new cognitive capability. During the sensorimotor stage in infancy, we become able to hold memories of objects in our minds.
- Information-processing researchers have suggested that babies may develop mental capacities at earlier ages than Piaget believed they did.
- Attachment theory suggests that babies are biologically predisposed to bond and form a relationship with a key caregiver, thus ensuring that their needs are met. The security of the attachment relationship will have later implications for how secure individuals feel in their emotional and social capabilities.
- Baumrind found evidence that different parenting styles can also affect the overall well-being of the child, although subsequent research suggested that outcomes might vary depending on other environmental and cultural influences.
- Physical growth continues at a generally slower pace in childhood than in infancy. Myelination and synaptic pruning continue to shape the brain.
- Piaget believed that children pass through the stages of preoperational and concrete operational thinking, learning to manipulate their mental schema. Other researchers have suggested children's thinking may not be as limited during these stages as Piaget thought it was.
- Theories of moral development often focus on moral reasoning (the reasons why a child would do one thing or another) rather than values. Generally, research supports the movement from morality rooted in submitting to authority to morality rooted in more autonomous decisions about right and wrong.
- Some researchers suggest that moral reasoning may vary across gender and culture. Other researchers question whether morality theories would be better served by measuring behaviour instead of expressed reasoning or attitudes.

Key Terms

accommodation 142

assimilation 142

attachment 152

cephalocaudal pattern 137

cognitive development 142

concrete operational stage 146

conservation 145

egocentrism 145

equilibrium 142

formal operational stage 147

habituation 147

information-processing theory 147

motor skills 140

myelination 138

object permanence 144

operations 146

preoperational stage 145

proximodistal pattern 137

reciprocal socialization 157

reflexes 139

scaffolding 150

scheme 142

synapses 137

synaptic pruning 137

temperament 151

theory of mind 149

violation-of-expectation 147

zone of proximal development 150

Study Questions

Multiple Choice

1. The purpose of myelin is to
   a) increase the number of synaptic connections.
   b) eliminate excess synaptic connections.
   c) help electrical impulses pass more efficiently.
   d) allow colour vision to develop.

2. According to Ainsworth and Main's research into attachment styles, the majority of infants' attachment is
   a) anxious/ambivalent.
   b) secure.
   c) anxious/avoidant.
   d) emotionally close.

3. What area of research focuses on young children's beliefs about how their minds and the minds of others work?
   a) theory of mind
   b) metacognition
   c) egocentrism
   d) scaffolding

4. The gap between what children can accomplish by themselves and what they can accomplish with the help of others is called _____, according to Vygotsky.
   a) scaffolding
   b) zone of proximal development
   c) reciprocal determinism
   d) conservation

Fill-in-the-Blank

1. The process that removes some of our early neural connections is called synaptic _____.

2. _____ refers to a child's understanding that things continue to exist even when out of sight.

3. In Piaget's theory of cognitive development, children aged 7 to 12 years are in the _____ stage.

Module 22: Adolescence

LEARNING OBJECTIVE 22
Summarize the major physical, cognitive, and emotional changes that take place during adolescence.

With the possible exception of the first couple years of life, the rapid changes associated with adolescence rivals that of any other developmental passage. Most crucially, puberty begins. In the cognitive sphere, adolescents display features of both children and adults, and they begin to learn how to function independently. In this module, we will describe the key biological, cognitive, and social transitions that characterize this dramatic period.

22.1 Physical Development

puberty development of full sexual maturity during adolescence.

primary sex characteristics changes in body structure that occur during puberty that have to do specifically with the reproductive system, including the growth of the testes and the ovaries.

secondary sex characteristics changes that occur during puberty and that differ according to gender, but aren't directly related to sex.

Puberty refers to the physical development of primary and secondary sex characteristics (Herdt, 2010). **Primary sex characteristics** are the body structures that have to do specifically with the reproductive system, including growth of the testes and the ovaries. **Secondary sex characteristics** refer to non-reproductive body events that differ according to gender, such as the deepening of the male voice or the increase in female breast size (see **Figure 22-1**).

The onset and course of puberty is influenced largely by the *pituitary gland*, which coordinates the activities of the rest of the endocrine system (Blakemore, Burnett, & Dahl, 2010). As you will see in Part 3, the endocrine system includes the *adrenal glands*, *testes*, and *ovaries*. During adolescence, events throughout this system stimulate the growth of body hair and muscle tissue and trigger the onset of the female menstrual cycle, among other changes. One of the most important changes is a *growth spurt* triggered by the thyroid gland that, as we observed earlier, actually begins for girls in middle childhood and for boys during early adolescence (Drummond, 2011) (see **Figure 22-2**). The growth spurt occurs about two years before the primary sex characteristics develop and is not only a harbinger of those later changes, but also helps prepare the body for them (Rekers, 1992).

The changes of puberty stabilize after a couple years. In the meantime, however, many of those changes can be very disruptive to adolescents (Drummond, 2011). For both boys and girls, variations from age norms for puberty can be upsetting; girls who mature early and boys who mature late report more problems making the transitions through adolescence than those who enter puberty "on time" (Blakemore et al., 2010; Hayatbakhsh et al., 2009).

WHAT HAPPENS *in the* **BRAIN?**

The brain also goes through significant changes during adolescence (Ernst & Hardin, 2010; Roberson-Nay & Brown, 2011). Myelination continues to increase and synaptic connections continue to decrease as a result of synaptic pruning (Giedd et al., 1999, 2006; Toga et al., 2006). Many of these brain changes appear to be localized; they now focus on the *prefrontal cortex*, the brain area that helps coordinate brain functions and is instrumental in making sound judgments. Development of the prefrontal cortex is incomplete until individuals reach their early to mid-twenties (Gogtay, 2004). Many psychologists point to immaturity in the prefrontal cortex as one reason teenagers often display poor judgment in their daily functioning (Compas, 2004). Immature brain areas, however, are not the whole story (Steinberg, 2008). For example, adolescents are also strongly affected by their peers (Rubin et al., 2010).

22.2 Cognitive Development

As we mentioned above, adolescent thinking has features of both child cognition and adult cognition. Teenagers show increased capacity for reasoning about abstract things, but also have deficits in their abilities to see outside of the moment or to take others' points of view. These strengths and limitations both come into play in their social and emotional growth as adolescents attempt to define themselves as persons. The shift into the formal operational stage opens the door to higher-level moral thinking (Kohlberg, 1963, 1994, 2008). Adolescents may recognize, for example, that rules serve a societal purpose, not just a personal one. With this growth in cognitive and moral thought, adolescents begin looking at the validity of rules very closely. They realize, for example, that an 11:00 p.m. bedtime is, in many respects,

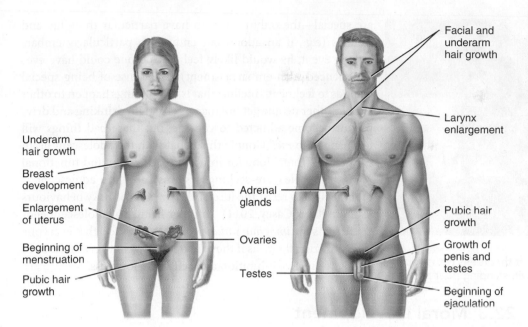

FIGURE 22-1 **Primary and secondary sex characteristics.** The complex changes in puberty primarily result when hormones are released from the pituitary gland, adrenal gland, and ovaries and testes.

an arbitrary rule that can be challenged and perhaps changed. Similarly, they become aware that adults often behave in ways that contradict what they say. According to pioneering developmental psychologist David Elkind, these realizations may cause adolescents to feel angry and upset and may produce a desire to rebel (Elkind, 1978, 2007; Oda, 2007). This is a reason why conflict between parents (and other adults) increases in adolescence.

Elkind notes that adolescents' mastery of formal operational thinking enables them not only to tune in to the flaws of other people, but also to recognize their own flaws. They become very sensitive to what other people may be thinking about them. Correspondingly, they display a psychological phenomenon called *adolescent egocentrism*, the mistaken belief that, like they themselves are doing, everyone else is also focusing largely on them and their behaviour.

One feature of adolescent egocentrism is the *personal fable, the adolescent belief that they are unique and invincible.* Over the course of searching for a sense of identity and spending time deeply focused on their own thoughts and feelings, adolescents may become convinced that they

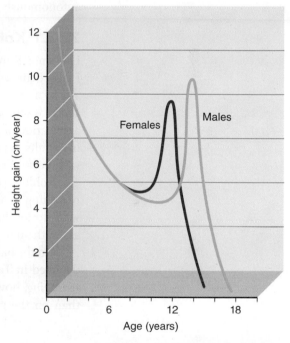

FIGURE 22-2 **Adolescent growth spurt.** The growth spurt of girls occurs, on average, two years before that of boys. Thus, between the ages of 10 and 14 years, the average girl is taller than most boys. Adapted by permission from BMJ Publishing Group Limited. Archives of Disease in Childhood, J.M. Tanner, R.N. Whitehouse, and M. Takaislu, vol. 41, pp. 451–471, 1966.

©iStockphoto.com/monkeybusinessimages

Adolescent behaviour. Immature brain areas and peer pressure contribute to adolescent's poor judgment in their daily functioning.

©iStockphoto.com/David Pereiras Villagrá

Not the boss of me! Studies suggest that teens who argue with their mothers may be better at withstanding peer pressure (Allen et al., 2012).

are special—the only person to have particular thoughts and feelings (e.g., if an adolescent endured a particularly embarrassing event, he would likely feel that no one could have ever experienced such embarrassment). This sense of being special extends to feeling invincible; that is, "Bad things happen to other people, other people get pregnant, get caught drinking and driving, or become addicted to cocaine; but these bad things will not happen to *me*." Couple this belief with the adolescent brain (immature frontal lobe for inhibiting behaviour and functional reward and pleasure-seeking systems) and the adolescent is often unable to resist the lure of the rewards of risky behaviours (Somerville & Casey, 2011). Another feature of adolescent egocentrism is the *imaginary audience*. Teenagers feel that everyone is scrutinizing them, as if they are on stage, a notion that leads to strong feelings of inhibition and self-consciousness.

22.3 Moral Development

Moral development focuses on cognitive *moral* understanding, how children and adolescents acquire an appreciation of right and wrong that is necessary if they are to function autonomously and safely in a complex society.

22.3.1 Kohlberg's Theory of Moral Development

Lawrence Kohlberg was particularly interested in Piaget's ideas on moral development. Piaget believed that, as with general logical reasoning, children learn how to reason morally by applying their emerging logical thinking to the issue of different perspectives and social wants and interactions—seen in children's games and their understanding and application of game rules. He proposed that children's morality is based initially on obeying adults. As they get older, the basis of their moral reasoning shifts toward cooperation with peers (Piaget, 1965).

Kohlberg expanded upon Piaget's ideas and developed a method to evaluate the moral reasoning processes of children. He presented children, adolescents, and young adults with stories that included moral dilemmas, such as the story of Heinz in **Figure 22-3**, and asked them to say what the main characters in the stories should do and why.

On the basis of his studies, Kohlberg developed a stage theory of moral development, depicted in **Table 22-1** (Kohlberg, 1963, 1994, 2008). The focus of this theory is *moral reasoning*, how children come to their decisions about what is right and wrong, rather than on the particular decisions that they make. Kohlberg argued that in the earliest

FIGURE 22-3 Kohlberg's moral dilemma story. Paragraph excerpted from Scott Lilienfeld, Steven Lynn, Laura Namy, and Nancy Wolf, *Psychology: From Inquiry to Understanding* (2008; Boston: Pearson: Allyn & Bacon.)

Heinz and the Drug

In Europe, a woman was near death from a special kind of cancer. There was one drug that the doctors thought might save her. It was a form of radium that a druggist in the same town had recently discovered. The drug was expensive to make, but the druggist was charging ten times what the drug cost him to make. He paid $400 for the radium and charged $4,000 for a small dose of the drug. The sick woman's husband, Heinz, went to everyone he knew to borrow the money and tried every legal means, but he could only get together about $2,000, which is half of what it cost. He told the druggist that his wife was dying, and asked him to sell it cheaper or let him pay later. But the druggist said, "No, I discovered the drug and I'm going to make money from it." So, having tried every legal means, Heinz gets desperate and considers breaking into the man's store to steal the drug.

Question: Should Heinz steal the drug? Why or why not?

TABLE 22-1 Kohlberg's Stage Theory of Moral Development		
Stage	**Reason to Steal Drug**	**Reason Not to Steal Drug**
Preconventional: Morality centres on what you can get away with	If he saves his wife she will continue to take care of his children.	He will be caught and go to jail.
Conventional: Morality centres on avoiding others' disapproval and obeying society's rules	If he doesn't steal the drug people will think he is a bad husband.	If he steals people will think he is a criminal; it's against the law.
Postconventional: Morality is determined by abstract ethical principles.	The right to life is universal and takes precedence over the right to property.	Laws are necessary to maintain order in society; individuals cannot break laws just because they disagree with them or we will lose all social order.

stages, individuals' moral decisions are based on external rewards and punishments. Then individuals move to a stage where they internalize the standards of others. Finally, individuals develop an internalized, personal moral code.

Although Kohlberg believed that moral reasoning often is correlated with other areas of development, such as cognition or intelligence, he held that it develops independently. Larry Walker (1980), at the University of British Columbia, demonstrated that children's cognitive development makes it possible for them to take up more mature understandings of the nature of others' perspectives, which in turn make it possible for them to develop higher (Kohlberian) stages of moral reasoning. To reach the highest stages of moral reasoning, Kohlberg believed, individuals must be exposed to complex social situations.

Like Piaget's theory of general cognitive development, Kohlberg's (1981) theory suggests that each stage of moral development is not just a shift in complexity, but instead represents a new framework, or way of thinking, for making moral decisions. Each such stage forms a foundation for the next stage, and children must travel through the stages of moral development in sequence. A child may be delayed or perhaps even fail to reach some of the higher stages, but he must go through each earlier stage to reach the next one.

Finally, Kohlberg believed that the process of moral development is universal and happens the same way in every culture. Kohlberg's original research included boys only, but he later studied girls and conducted moral dilemma interviews in villages in Mexico, Taiwan, and Turkey (Nisan & Kohlberg, 1982).

22.3.2 Gilligan's Theory of Moral Development

One of Kohlberg's collaborators, Carol Gilligan (1993), eventually questioned some of his findings and ideas, partly because his studies initially focused on boys alone, and also because his later studies that did include girls seemed to suggest that girls were morally less developed than boys. Kohlberg believed that girls did not have as many complex social opportunities as boys and, as a result, were excessively concerned with the standards of others and therefore often failed to achieve higher stages of moral reasoning.

Gilligan (1993) interpreted the boy–girl findings differently. She argued that the moral reasoning used by girls is indeed different from that of boys, but not inferior. She argued that boys tend to base their decisions about moral dilemmas on abstract moral values, such as justice and fairness. Many girls look at the situations differently. Instead of the abstract values involved, they focus more on care—on the value of relationships between the principal players. A boy's answer to the Heinz dilemma might centre on the importance of property value for the druggist, for example, while a girl's answer might stress that Heinz will not be able to help his wife if he is jailed for stealing the drug (Gilligan, 1993). Gilligan argued that the reasoning of boys and girls is equally sophisticated, but the moral orientation with which they approach dilemmas may differ. Gilligan found that both males and females were capable of both justice- and care-based moral thinking, and which one they used varied depending on the circumstances in which they were asked.

Other studies have not always supported Gilligan's theory that women and men differ in their moral orientation, nor have they always supported Kohlberg's notions of moral superiority among males (Turiel, 2010; Walker, 2006). However, Gilligan's ideas have had a broad influence on psychology, anthropology, and other social sciences. As a result of her arguments, many researchers now include more females in their studies. In addition, most of today's researchers think of differences among participants as individual variations rather than positive or negative characteristics (Jensen, 2011).

Finally, a number of moral development researchers, including Dennis Krebs at Simon Fraser University, have investigated whether the moral attitudes of people is reflective of their actual decision making (Krebs & Denton, 2006). As we will see in our discussion of attitudes in Part 13, people do not always actually do what they say they will do in moral situations (an experience you've perhaps had once or twice in your own life). Because the vast majority of research into moral reasoning has relied on Kohlberg's moral dilemma interviews, many researchers argue that we may be able to say a fair amount about people's moral *philosophies* but little about their moral *behaviours*. However, Krebs also argues that because morality serves an evolutionarily adaptive function by allowing individuals to foster their own self-interest while befitting others, moral thought is often reflected in behaviour (Krebs, 2008).

22.4 Social and Emotional Development

Although identity formation is a lifelong task, adolescents spend a lot of time trying to figure out who they are and how they fit into the world. The adolescent has the cognitive ability to integrate previous and current identities into a coherent whole. Erik Erikson viewed identity development as the task of adolescence (Clark, 2010; Erikson, 1959, 1984, 1985).

As **Table 22-2** shows, Erikson believed that each stage of development is associated with a potentially positive outcome versus a potentially negative outcome.

The key developmental task faced by adolescents is to resolve the conflict between *identity* and *role confusion*. During adolescence, teenagers start making decisions that affect their future roles, such as where they want to go to college or university or what they want to do with their lives, as well as decisions about abstract aspects of their identities, such as political or religious beliefs.

According to Erikson, if we do not reach a successful resolution of the conflict confronted at a particular stage, we may find it harder to meet the challenges of subsequent stages. Teenagers who do not effectively resolve the conflicts of their earlier psychosocial stages may enter adolescence with heightened feelings of mistrust and shame. These lingering feelings may render the teens particularly confused about which roles and beliefs truly reflect their own values and which ones reflect autocratic peer and family influences. Peer relationships are extremely important to all teenagers, and Erikson believed that vulnerable teens are particularly likely to be confused about where their own beliefs start and the wishes of others end.

Other issues can make it difficult to establish a strong sense of personal identity. For members of visible minority groups, such as Canada's Aboriginal youth, identity development is made more difficult both by a sense of difficulty in fitting into mainstream cultural identity options and opportunities, as well as difficulty in finding positive, healthy images of personal and cultural history and ideals to lean on for support.

One large-scale study conducted in British Columbia shows the central roles of culture and community in positive adolescent developmental outcomes. Michael Chandler at UBC and Chris Lalonde at the University of Victoria (2008; Chandler, Lalonde, Sokol, & Hallett, 2003) examined the rates of youth suicide in many of the First Nations bands across the province. Rather than focusing on individual suicides, they examined instead what they called cultural continuity factors, markers of personal, cultural, and community efforts to take charge of and advance culture and heritage. Specifically, they looked to see whether individual bands had taken or were taking steps toward self-government, including control of the education of their children; control of their health services; contr ol of police and fire services;

Darryl Dyck/The Canadian Press

Canadian Aboriginal youth. An Aboriginal youth participates in the Squamish Nation Youth Pow Wow in North Vancouver, B.C. About 140 dancers gathered to compete in the 27th annual event to compete for prizes and showcase their culture.

practically speaking | Bullying: A Continuing Problem

©iStockphoto.com/Christopher Futcher

According to the Canadian Public Health Association, *bullying* is the intentional use of power by one person over another and can be seen in physical, social, verbal, and electronic forms (Lemstra et al., 2012). A report examining the many school shootings that have occurred across Canada and the United States over the past decade found that bullying was a factor in most of them (Crisp, 2001; Gonzalez, 2010). Sometimes the shooters had been bullies; more often, they had been the *victims* of bullying. One survey asked children aged 8 to 15 years what issues in school troubled them most, and the children pointed to teasing and bullying as "big problems" that ranked even higher than racial discrimination, AIDS, and/or peer pressures (Cukan, 2001). Overall, over one-quarter of students report being bullied frequently, and more than 70 percent reported having been victimized at least once, leading in many cases to feelings of humiliation or anxiety (Jacobs, 2008; Nishina et al., 2005; Smith, 2010). In addition, our online world has broadened the ways in which children and adolescents can be bullied, and today cyberbullying—bullying by email, text-messaging, or the like—is increasing (Jacobs, 2008). Qing Li (2005), of the University of Calgary, found that 25 percent of Grade 7 students had experienced cyberbullying. Shaheen Shariff of McGill University describes cyberbullying as verbal and written assaults carried out by way of websites, chat rooms, cell phones, social networking sites, and email (Shariff, 2005).

In response to these alarming trends, many schools—elementary through high school—have started programs that teach students how to deal more effectively with bullies, work to change the thinking of bullies, train teachers, conduct parent discussion groups, and apply classroom prevention measures (Frey et al., 2005; Jacobs, 2008; Twemlow et al., 2003). Furthermore, public health campaigns try to educate the public about antibullying programs. For information about bullying, see the following organizations and programs: Canadian Children's Rights Council, www.canadiancrc.com/Bullying_Canada-Public_Safety_Canada.aspx; Canadian Safe School Network, www.canadiansafeschools.com; and the Government of Canada (Public Safety Canada) Bullying Prevention in Schools Program, www.publicsafety.gc.ca/cnt/rsrcs/pblctns/bllng-prvntn-schls.

Although recognizing the negative—and potentially tragic—impact of bullying, some experts worry that the sheer prevalence of bullying may make it a very difficult problem to overcome. It is hard, for example, for educators and clinicians to identify which bullies or bullied children will turn violent, given that a full 70 percent of children have experienced bullying. Can we really rid our schools and communities of a problem as common as this? One observer has even argued, "Short of raising kids in isolation chambers...bullying behaviours can never be eliminated entirely from the sustained hazing ritual known as growing up" (Angier, 2001).

whether the band had initiated land claims; and finally whether there was a structure on their land specifically dedicated to the recognition and promotion of their culture and heritage. **Figure 22-4** indicates that the more engaged in taking or re-taking cultural control a First Nations community is and the more they assert their cultural authority over aspects of self-determination, the lower their rate of adolescent suicide—approaching zero when all six markers of community control of culture and heritage are present. When the cultural or social side of the individual/community interaction that defines identity formation is strong, youth can develop strong identities and can see clear, culturally- and community-defined and supported pathways for them to walk as they move forward into adulthood.

Tying It Together: **Your Brain and Behaviour**

Growing from Infancy to Adolescence

Although all brain regions have already started to form before a baby is born, we can tell by their limited abilities and dependence on others that they still have a long way to go. The production of new nerve cells or neurons continues to occur in several brain regions, including those important for learning and memory, throughout infancy, childhood, and beyond.

Somewhat surprisingly, many of the neurons and connections that formed during early development are lost during the postnatal period. Neurons that fail to make appropriate connections die and connections that are not strong enough are eliminated. The death of neurons and elimination of connections play an important role in sculpting the circuitry that develops into a fully-functioningW mature brain. And last but not least, the insulation of nerve fibres by the myelin sheath, produced by non-neuronal cells called glia, continues throughout childhood and into young adulthood. This process enables brain regions to send information more quickly and efficiently—its completion during young adulthood coincides with more mature cognitive abilities.

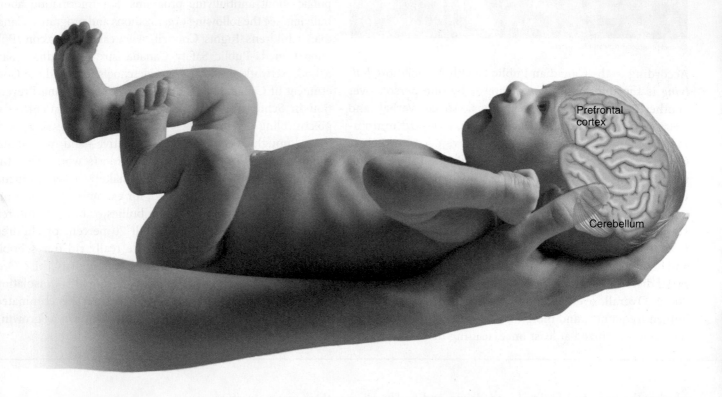

Prefrontal cortex

Cerebellum

Masterfile

Questions

1 How do changes in the prefrontal cortex help explain infants' enjoyment of hide-and-seek games?

2 Improvement in which skills is most directly related to the development of the cerebellum during childhood?

3 Explain how the sequence of brain development contributes to the finding that adolescents tend to make more impulsive decisions than adults do.

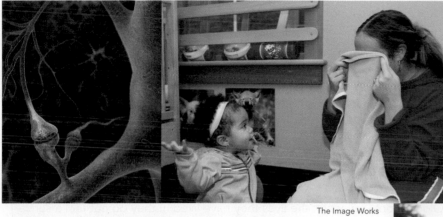

The Image Works

PLAYING PEEK-A-BOO

Around 9 months, synapses (shown in this image) in the pre-frontal cortex are eliminated. The prefrontal cortex is a brain region that is important for cognitive processes like short-term memory. This reduction in the number of synapses seems to coincide with the ability to hold a memory of an object while it is out of sight. Around this time, babies seem to delight in playing peek-a-boo.

WALKING, RUNNING, KICKING

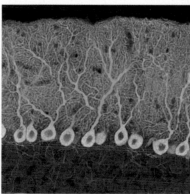

Postnatal neurogenesis occurs in the cerebellum (as shown in this image), a brain region important for coordination of movement and certain types of learning. The continual addition of new neurons to this brain region after birth and into childhood may participate in the emergence of motor skills such as walking, running, and kicking a ball.

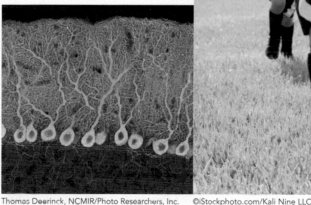

Thomas Deerinck, NCMIR/Photo Researchers, Inc.   ©iStockphoto.com/Kali Nine LLC

MAKING BETTER DECISIONS

During adolescence, more myelin (shown here in red) forms in the prefrontal cortex. Myelin levels develop earlier in other brain regions, making the prefrontal cortex the latest brain region to reach maturity. The prefrontal cortex is important for moral reasoning, decision making, and planning. The late development of this brain region may explain why teenagers often seem to lack the ability to make good decisions about the future!

Thomas Deerinck, NCMIR/Photo Researchers, Inc.

©iStockphoto.com/fotostorm

TABLE 22-2 Erikson's Stages of Psychosocial Development

Stage 1 Trust versus mistrust (birth–age 1) Infants develop a basic trust in others. If their needs are not met by their caregivers, mistrust develops.

Stage 2 Autonomy versus shame and doubt (ages 1–3) Children exercise their new motor and mental skills. If caregivers are encouraging, children develop a sense of autonomy versus shame and doubt.

Stage 3 Initiative versus guilt (ages 3–6) Children enjoy initiating activities and mastering new tasks. Supportive caregivers promote feelings of power and self-confidence versus guilt.

Stage 4 Industry versus inferiority (ages 6–12) Children learn productive skills and develop the capacity to work with others; if not, they feel inferior.

Stage 5 Identity versus role confusion (ages 12–20) Adolescents seek to develop a satisfying identity and a sense of their role in society. Failure may lead to a lack of stable identity and confusion about their adult roles.

Stage 6 Intimacy versus isolation (ages 20–30) Young adults work to establish intimate relationships with others; if they cannot, they face isolation.

Stage 7 Generativity versus self-absorption (ages 30–65) Middle aged-adults seek ways to influence the welfare of the next generation. If they fail, they may become self-absorbed.

Stage 8 Integrity versus despair (ages 65+) Older people reflect on the lives they have lived. If they do not feel a sense of accomplishment and satisfaction with their lives, they live in fear of death.

Jessica Ball of the University of Victoria states that the culture within the individual (2004, 2008, 2010; Ball & Simpkins, 2004) is an important determinant of healthy development. Successful identity development is an integral part of a successful transition to adulthood, and one that for Aboriginal youth can involve community as well as individual development (Kirmayer, Tait, & Simpson, 2009).

FIGURE 22-4 Aboriginal youth suicide rate by number of cultural factors present in the community. This figure shows that the more a First Nations band community does to take active control of their culture, the lower is the rate of youth suicide in that community.

Source: Based on Chandler, M. J. & Lalonde, C. E. (2008). Cultural continuity as a moderator of suicide risk among Canada's first nations. In L. J. Kirmayer & G. G. Valaskakis (Eds), *Healing traditions: The mental health of aboriginal peoples in Canada.*

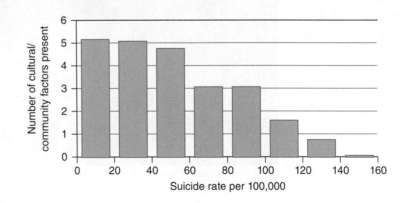

Before You Go On

www.wiley.com/go/comercanada

What Do You Know?

1. If a child arrives at puberty significantly earlier or later than her peer group, how might that affect her adjustment?
2. Define the formal operational stage.
3. Describe what Erikson believed was the major dilemma and risk for adolescence.
4. How do contemporary theories of moral reasoning differ from Piaget, Kohlberg, and Gilligan?
5. What are some differences between first-borns and later-borns?

What Do You Think? How might Erikson explain extremely altruistic or aggressive adolescents?

Summary

Module 22: Adolescence

LEARNING OBJECTIVE 22 Summarize the major physical, cognitive, and emotional changes that take place during adolescence.

- Adolescence is generally associated with many substantial changes, including the onset of full sexual and physical maturity, as well as reasoning capabilities that approach adult levels. However, teenagers have certain limitations that influence their ability to make sound judgments and avoid risky situations.

- Erikson proposed a theory of development that stretches across the lifespan and incorporates various dilemmas that need to be successfully reconciled for development to stay on track.

Key Terms

primary sex characteristics 160   puberty 160   secondary sex characteristics 160

Study Questions

Multiple Choice

1. Students about to graduate from high school sometimes have difficulty deciding whether to go to college or university or go directly into the workforce. Which of Erikson's stages is relevant to this issue?
   a) intimacy versus isolation
   b) identity versus role confusion
   c) industry versus inferiority
   d) generativity versus self-absorption

Fill-in-the-Blank

1. According to Carol Gilligan, Kohlberg's assumption that the moral reasoning of girls is less well developed than that of boys is faulty because the moral reasoning of girls is oriented toward _____ rather than abstract principles.

2. The _____ gland controls the onset of puberty.

3. The biggest concern reported by school children of all ages is _____.

Module 23: Adulthood

LEARNING OBJECTIVE 23
Describe the key physical, social, and emotional changes that take place throughout adulthood.

Traditionally, developmental psychology viewed adulthood as an outcome rather than a period of time worthy of study. As we will see, however, adulthood is in fact a time of continuing change—and by change, we do not necessarily mean decline.

The journeys through each stage of adulthood correspond to many of the rites of passage associated with adulthood, including marriage, parenting, retirement, and death—events that we will be discussing further throughout the book. It is worth noting that, in many societies, the timing and form of such milestones of adulthood are now more variable than they were in earlier days. In the past, for example, the length of time a couple would spend married before having their first child was relatively short; that time has extended greatly in recent decades. Moreover, the number of couples who choose to remain childless has doubled since 1960 (Demo et al., 2000; Rubino, 2011). It has also become more acceptable in some societies for people who are not married to raise children (Weinraub et al., 2002).

©iStockphoto.com/monkeybusinessimages

Similarly, the average human lifespan continues to increase, lengthening the time that older adults remain part of the workforce, as well as part of the retired population, before dying (Elrod, 2010; Volz, 2000). Such cultural shifts have opened new areas of study for psychologists, who are seeking to understand how these shifts may affect adult development.

Although the foundations for development are laid down in childhood and adolescence we spend most of the lifespan in adulthood. Adulthood moves us through a number of stages and transitions and changes. Let's take a look at some of them.

23.1 Physical and Cognitive Development

With the end of adolescence comes full maturity. Nevertheless, the body continues to go through changes during adulthood. And, so does the brain.

23.1.1 What Happens in the Body During Adulthood?

Generally, physical attributes, such as strength, reaction time, and overall body function, are at their peak during our 20s (Schneider & Davidson, 2003). As we move into our 30s, the body begins to decline slowly. Our metabolism slows, for example, and it is harder to keep fit.

During our 30s and 40s, we begin to show the first significant signs of aging. Due to loss of collagen and fat, skin begins to lose some of its tautness and hair begins to grey and thin. Declines in vision and hearing are experienced after the age of 40 years of age (Drummond, 2011). Individuals become more farsighted, finding it hard to read or see small objects close to them, and have difficulty seeing in the dark or recovering from sudden glares of light (Scialfa & Kline, 2007). At this same time, individuals, especially men, become less sensitive to high-frequency sounds (Fowler & Leigh-Paffenroth, 2007).

Women go through a major change called **menopause**, typically in their 50s (Nosek et al., 2010). *Menopause* involves a series of changes in hormonal function that eventually lead to the end of the menstrual cycle and reproductive capabilities. The early phase of menopause is often associated with a variety of physical experiences, such as hot flashes, headaches, and sudden shifts in mood due to sudden changes in levels of hormones.

As adults move into late adulthood during their 60s and 70s, they may become a bit shorter and thinner due to changes in skeletal structure and metabolism (Bord-Hoffman &

LookatSciences/Phototake

Downward slide. In this computer illustration, the green-glowing proteins at the end of the chromosomes are telomeres, tiny structures that help cells to reproduce. The structures appear to grow shorter and shorter with repeated use, leading eventually to reduced cell reproduction and poor self-repair by the body. Then, when the telomeres are gone, the cell stops duplicating.

menopause series of changes in hormonal function occurring in women during their 50s, which lead to the end of the menstrual cycle and reproductive capabilities.

Suddenly, I'm the Adult?

When does adulthood first strike? For columnist Richard Cohen, it was on a summer night in Cape Cod:

"Several years ago, [my parents and my family were eating at a restaurant]. That's when it happened. My father did not reach for the check.

"In fact, my father did nothing. Conversation continued. Finally, it dawned on me. Me! I was supposed to pick up the check. After all these years, after hundreds of restaurant meals with my parents, after a lifetime of thinking of my father as the one with the bucks, it had all changed. I reached for the check and whipped out my American Express card. My view of myself was suddenly altered. With a stroke of a pen, I was suddenly an adult....

"One day you go to your friends' weddings. One day you celebrate the birth of their kids. One day you see one of their kids driving, and one day those kids have kids of their own. One day you meet at parties and then at weddings and then at funerals....

"One day I made a good toast. One day I handled a headwaiter. One day I bought a house. One day—what a day!—I became a father, and not too long after that I picked up the check for my own. I thought then and there it was a rite of passage for me. Not until I got older did I realize that it was one for him, too." (Cohen, 1987)

Donius, 2005; Drummond, 2011). The immune system also begins to decline in function, leaving them at higher risk for illness. Vision and hearing continue to decline, joined by the sense of taste. The pupils shrink, so that less light reaches the retina, making it harder to see in low light (Scialfa & Kline, 2007).

The story is not as simple as a long, slow, inevitable decline, however. Environmental factors, such as exercise, stress, diet, and life experience, can have a dramatic influence on the course and impact of these changes (Brach et al., 2003; Drummond, 2011; Larson et al., 2006). Although declines are common, many of the changes can be subtle and have minimal impact on how well older adults function in the world.

23.1.2 Cognitive Changes in Adulthood

 **WHAT HAPPENS** *in the* **BRAIN?**

Until recently, neuroscientists believed that our brains begin to shrink during adulthood, both in terms of volume and weight, and that much of this loss is attributable to the shrinkage and loss of active brain cells (Miller & O'Callaghan, 2005). Research over the past decade, however, has revealed that no significant loss of neurons occurs in adulthood, except in cases of brain pathology (Miller & O'Callaghan, 2005); that new neurons keep being formed in certain parts of the brain throughout life, including during adulthood (Gould, 2007; Leuner & Gould, 2010); and that such neurons may be the result of new learning, may play a role in further learning, or both (Leuner, Glasper, & Gould, 2010; Leuner, Gould, & Shors, 2006). Given the stability and even addition of neurons during adulthood, it is not surprising that most of our broad intellectual capabilities remain intact throughout our lives. We're able to solve problems and process information in our adult years about as quickly as we could in our 20s (Park & Gutchess, 2006; Park et al., 2002).

Once adults move into their 40s and 50s, recovering information from long-term memory starts to take a little longer, and it takes somewhat longer to learn new material. During their 60s and 70s, memories decline, as does adults' confidence in their ability to remember and to solve problems (Freedman et al., 2001; Ornstein & Light, 2010).

Some declines are more serious, however. In *dementia*, severe memory problems combine with losses in at least one other cognitive function, such as abstract thinking or language (Travers et al., 2010). The occurrence of dementia is strongly related to age. Around 1 to 2 percent of people 65 years of age have dementia, compared with some 50 percent of people over 85 (Apostolova & Cummings, 2008). We will discuss dementia in depth in Part 8.

©iStockphoto.com/AvailableLight

Dementia. Dementia is a symptom of brain disease or injury and is associated with memory loss, impaired reasoning, and personality change.

cellular clock theory theory suggesting that we age because our cells have built-in limits on their ability to reproduce.

wear-and-tear theory theory suggesting we age because use of our body wears it out.

free-radical theory theory suggesting we age because special negatively-charged oxygen molecules become more prevalent in our body as we get older, destabilizing cellular structures and causing the effects of aging.

23.1.3 Why Do We Age?

Although scientists have offered many theories about why we age, no single explanation is widely accepted (Pierpaoli, 2005). One important theory of aging, the **cellular clock theory**, suggests that aging is built into our cells. Tiny structures on the ends of DNA strands, called *telomeres*, aid in cell reproduction but grow shorter each time they are used. Eventually they become too short, and cells can no longer reproduce themselves. As a result, the body is less able to repair itself. The various changes of aging—saggy skin and decreases in vision and memory, for example—are the direct result of those events (Davoli et al., 2010).

Two other theories of aging are more rooted in our experiences and the impact that life events can have on us. The *wear-and-tear* and *free-radical* theories suggest that years of use help wear out our bodies. The **wear-and-tear theory** boils down to this: the more mileage we put on our bodies through living (augmented by factors such as stress, poor diet, and exposure to environmental teratogens), the sooner we wear out (Hawkley et al., 2005). The **free-radical theory** provides a chemistry-oriented explanation (Boldyrev & Johnson, 2007; Perluigi et al., 2010). Free radicals are oxygen molecules that are negatively charged. A negative charge on a molecule can attract small particles of matter called *electrons* from other molecules. According to the free-radical theory of aging, free radicals become more prevalent in our system as we get older, increasingly destabilizing cell structures and doing progressively more damage to our bodies—resulting in the aging effects described above.

23.2 Social and Emotional Development

Although the social and emotional changes that occur in adulthood are more gradual than those that characterize childhood, adults do in fact experience multiple transitions throughout the adult stage of the lifespan (Aldwin, Yancura, & Boeninger, 2010; Freund & Lamb, 2010; Holcomb, 2010; Palkovitz et al., 2001; Roberts et al., 2002, 2006). As you saw in Table 22-2, Erikson proposed that individuals confront important psychosocial conflicts as they travel from early adulthood to old age. A number of other theorists have made similar claims.

23.2.1 Social and Emotional Features of Early and Middle Adulthood

According to Erikson, during early adulthood (20 to 30 years of age), people form intimate relationships and sexual unions that call for self-sacrifice and compromise. In fact, he believed that the primary goal of this period is to attain love. As well, the ethical convictions developed in adolescence and the sense of moral obligation formed in childhood contribute to ethical strength in young adulthood. These early acquisitions are important, he believed, because a sense of morality is required for the truly loving relationships of adulthood. Erikson further believed that people who are unable to successfully meet the challenges of young adulthood tend to become isolated and may actually avoid the contacts that create and sustain intimacy. Thus, he concluded that young adulthood is dominated by a conflict between *intimacy* and *isolation*.

Erikson proposed that during middle adulthood (30 to 65 years of age), people are inclined to turn their attention to younger people. Their focus is to help create, or at least contribute to, the next generation. Erikson used the term *generativity* to describe this focus. Caring for younger people, whether through parenthood or by mentoring junior colleagues at work, is a major concern. This process enriches individuals who engage in it. Erikson believed that people who fail to develop such activities may experience stagnation and boredom. Middle adulthood, then, is dominated by a conflict between *generativity* and *stagnation*.

Several theorists have extended Erikson's work on early and middle adulthood. One particularly broad investigation of these life stages was conducted by psychologist Daniel Levinson (1977, 1984, 1986; Levinson & Levinson, 1996). According to Levinson's findings, the stage of *early adulthood* (which he defined as 22 to 40 years of age) is characterized simultaneously by high energy and abundance and by contradiction and stress. The aspirations of individuals in this age range tend to be youthful. They establish a niche in society, they may raise a family, and ultimately they reach a relatively "senior" position in the adult world.

For many, this period brings great satisfaction and creativity. But early adulthood can also be a period of enormous stress. The burden of becoming a parent, undertaking an occupation, incurring financial obligations, and making other critical decisions about marriage, family, work, and lifestyle often fills people with anxiety and tension.

©iStockphoto.com/Goldmund Lukic

Erikson's stage of generativity. In middle age individuals turn their attention to younger generations, including in many cases to their children and their grandchildren.

Levinson described *middle adulthood* (30 to 65 years of age) as a stage in which biological functioning, although less than optimal, is still sufficient for an "energetic, personally satisfying and socially valuable life." During this stage, people usually become "senior members" of their particular world. They take responsibility for their own work, that of others, and the development of younger adults. This, too, can become a period of self-satisfaction and peace of mind. At the same time, growing biological problems, numerous responsibilities, and anticipation of upcoming old age may also produce considerable stress and tension.

Although the stages of early and middle adulthood may themselves be sources of stress, Levinson believed that the periods of *transition* that people must pass through as they move from one stage to another can be even more pressure-filled. During such transitional periods, people confront particularly difficult career, marital, and family issues and reflect on and adjust their dreams.

The *early adult transition*, often called "emerging adulthood," bridges adolescence and early adulthood. During this period, which lasts from approximately 17 to 22 years of age, people may go through a very unsettled time. They take steps toward individuation and modify their relationships with family, friends, and social institutions, but they may feel insecure in these efforts and, correspondingly, may experience anxiety and

practically speaking Emerging Adulthood

Generally, when we think of 20-somethings, we think of young people making their initial journey into independence. But increasingly, and around the world, young adults are returning home after college or university, or never leaving in the first place. In some countries, the trend is so strong that it has inspired name-calling. In Germany, young adults who live with their parents are called *Nesthockerin*, or birds that stay too long in the nest. In Italy, they're *bamboccioni*, or overgrown babies. In the United Kingdom, they're *kippers*, or "kids in parents' pockets, eroding retirement savings."

This group has received the most negative attention in Japan, where sociologist Masahiro Yamada coined the term parasite singles to describe them. Parasite singles are often accused of being unwilling to take on the responsibilities of adulthood, spending their money on nights out and personal luxuries. Many of these young adults point out that entry-level jobs are hard to come by, and those that are available do not pay enough. The average rent in Japan constitutes two-thirds of the average young adult's salary.

Some researchers have begun to study this widespread phenomenon and argue that a new stage of development might be emerging, much as adolescence developed initially in response to social changes that outlawed child labour and made education more widely available.

confusion. Indeed, in today's world, more and more individuals seem to be having difficulty completing this early adult transition.

Even more stressful for some people, according to Levinson, is *middle life transition*, a period lasting from ages 40 to 45 that bridges early and middle adulthood. During this period, individuals experience significant changes in the character of their lives. On the positive side, they may become more compassionate, reflective, and judicious; less conflicted; and more accepting and loving of themselves and others during these years. On the negative side, however, some individuals feel overwhelmed as they increasingly recognize that they are no longer young and vibrant, that time is passing, that life's heaviest responsibilities are falling on them, that they must prepare for the future, and that some of their dreams may not be met. These individuals may question their accomplishments in life and conclude that they have achieved and will continue to achieve too little. In certain cases, they may even try to deny the passage of time and to recapture their youth, a phenomenon popularly labelled the *midlife crisis*.

23.2.2 Social and Emotional Features of Old Age

"Old age" is typically defined in our society as people who are 65 years old and above. Psychologists further distinguish between the young-old, people between 65 and 74; the old-old, those between 75 and 84; and the oldest-old, individuals 85 and above. Many experts believe that rather than focusing on chronological age, functional age should be used to distinguish between groups of elderly people. In any case, using the current system, the old-old are the fastest growing age group in Canada. The over 85 year group tripled from 1981 to 2000, and it is estimated that by the year 2051 there will be over two million people in Canada in this age group (Health Canada, 2003a). The majority of these people will be women.

Old age brings special pressures, unique upsets, and, as we saw earlier, profound biological changes. People become more prone to illness and injury as they age. They also are likely to experience the stress of loss—the loss of spouses, friends, and adult children, as well as the loss of former activities and roles (Etaugh, 2008). Some lose their sense of purpose after they retire.

Nevertheless, elderly people do not necessarily become depressed or feel overwhelmed (Edelstein et al., 2008). Indeed, Erikson believed that, for many, old age is characterized by accumulated knowledge and understanding and by mature judgment. The goal of old age, he proposed, is to attain wisdom, a detached yet active concern with life in the face of death. Wisdom is achieved through the integration of insights gained from the past and the present regarding a person's place in the stream of life. Erikson believed that those who do not effectively meet the challenges of this stage may experience an extreme fear of death or despair, show bitterness and disgust, and feel that time is too short. He therefore categorized old age as a conflict between *integrity* and *despair*.

Research indicates that many older persons do indeed use the changes that come with aging as opportunities for learning and growth. One case in point: the number of elderly—often physically limited—people who use the Internet to connect with people of similar ages and interests doubled between 2000 and 2004, doubled again between 2004 and 2007, and doubled yet again by 2011. Individuals such as these Web searchers seem likely to remain involved and active right up to the end of their lives, health permitting.

It is also worth noting that, despite the common themes of old age, the population of elderly adults is actually quite heterogeneous. That is, older adults are more *unlike* than similar to one another. Elderly people have very different life experiences,

Dave Pratt/PA Wire/Associated Press

Active in old age. For many old age is time to relax and focus on the things you enjoy. George Moyse, a 97-year-old man from Dorset, England, skydives strapped to an instructor after jumping from a plane flying at 10,000 feet.

adapt to change in uniquely personal ways, and age at different rates. Thus, psychologists make a point of distinguishing between chronological age and functional age. *Chronological age*, or the number of years a person has lived since birth, is regarded as little more than a "short-hand variable" because it is not a true indicator of an elderly person's functional capacities. *Functional age*, however, reflects the individual's capacity to adapt his behaviour to the changing environment. This aspect of aging is influenced by a person's coping skills, social pursuits, emotions, motivation, and self-esteem, among other factors.

Before You Go On

www.wiley.com/go/comercanada

What Do You Know?

1. What is the difference between the wear-and-tear theory of aging and the free-radical theory of aging?

2. Describe and define Erikson's major crises of adult development.

What Do You Think? Do you think that life experiences may actually increase adults' cognitive, or mental, abilities? Why might this be so?

Summary

Module 23: Adulthood

LEARNING OBJECTIVE 23 Describe the key physical, social, and emotional changes that take place throughout adulthood.

- Adult physical and psychological development is often characterized by some degree of decline. However, most basic faculties remain intact across the lifespan.

- According to Erikson, the challenge of early adulthood is to resolve the conflict between intimacy and isolation; of middle adulthood, to resolve the conflict between generativity and stagnation; and of old age, to resolve the conflict between integrity and despair. Levinson pointed out that transitions from one stage to the next can also cause conflicts.

- The ages at which adults are expected to reach major social and emotional milestones, such as marriage and parenting, are more flexible now in many societies than they were in the past.

Key Terms

cellular clock theory 172
free-radical theory 172

menopause 170
wear-and-tear theory 172

Study Questions

Multiple Choice

1. Which theory of aging provides a chemical-oriented explanation?
   a) wear-and-tear
   b) free radical
   c) cellular clock
   d) use-it-or-lose-it

Fill-in-the-Blank

1. Our metabolism begins to slow when we are in our _____ .

PART 5

SENSATION AND PERCEPTION

When you hear the word "river" do you feel angry or disgusted? Can you see a noise or taste a word? Some people experience involuntary and consistent links, or intermixing, between their sensory systems. This condition is called *synesthesia*. The name *synesthesia* comes from two Greek words: *syn*, meaning together, and *aesthesis*, meaning perception, and therefore refers to *"joined perception."* People who have synesthesia experience a stimulus that typically would be perceived by one sense in most people in two or more sensory modalities.

How many people have some form of synesthesia? This is a difficult question to answer because many people with synesthesia assume that the sensations they experience are also experienced by others and so the phenomenon often goes unreported. However, prevalence estimates range from as low as 1 in 2,000 to as high as 1 in 23 people (Ramach-andran & Hubbard, 2001).

The most common form of synesthesia is called *grapheme-colour synesthesia*. A person who has this form of synesthesia always sees a colour in response to a specific letter or number (e.g., the number "9" is always perceived as turquoise, or the letter "J" is always perceived as orange). There are also synesthetes who smell particular odours in response to touch, or who hear noises in response to smell, or who feel a tactile stimulus in response to sight, whereas others experience unpleasant emotions elicited by specific sounds (Cytowic & Eagleman, 2009). There are even some individuals who possess synesthesia involving three or more senses, but this type of synesthesia is very rare.

Neuroimaging studies have shown that sensory areas normally not affected by particular stimuli are activated in a synesthetic experience (Nunn el al., 2002). For example, the auditory cortex and visual cortex of sight-sound synesthetes activate in response to particular visual stimuli. Thus the brain of a person who can hear a picture or colour responds as though the visual stimulus were also producing sound waves, as well as reflecting light waves. Other research suggests that the phenomenon may not be strictly sensory for at least some forms of synesthesia, but may also be semantic (that is, based on perception) (Nikolić, 2009). For example, in one study grapheme-colour synthesetes were shown two identical stimuli but were told in one case that they were looking at the number "5" and in another case that they were looking at the letter "S." The person's sensation of colour changed based on whether they perceived the stimulus to be a number or a letter (Dixon, 2006).

Although the majority of individuals do not have synesthesia, we all take physical energy from the environment and change it to a neural code to be used in the brain to perceive the world. Why does the world appear stationary as you walk through it? Why does food taste different when you have a cold? Why does something appear red when the light is on and appear to have no colour when the room is dim? Why can some people walk across red hot coals in their bare feet without seeming to experience pain? We will examine these types of questions as we move through this part and discuss how the various sensory systems engage in two processes called *sensation* and *perception*.

We are surrounded by energy in our environments at all times, including electro-magnetic energy such as radiant heat and ultraviolet and infrared light, and mechanical energy such as pressure or sound waves of varying intensity. Our sensory systems are able to detect only some of this energy. However, all that we experience is dependent on the electrical signals generated by the nervous system. That is, everything that we experience, every taste, every smell, every sight, every sound, and every feeling, is based on the energy absorbed by the sensory receptors and converted to neural impulses that are transmitted to the brain (Goldstein, 2014). As a consequence, much of what happens in the world goes unrecognized by our perceptual systems.

Two closely related processes are involved in sensory perception. One process is **sensation**, the act of using our sensory receptors to detect a stimulus present in the environment and to then transmit a signal to the brain with information about this

sensation the act of using our sensory systems to detect environmental stimuli.

environmental stimulus. Transformation of physical energy from the environment into electrical signals for the brain occurs in a process called transduction. Once acquired, this sensory information must be interpreted in the context of past and present sensory stimuli. This process, which also involves recognition and identification, is broadly defined as **perception**.

Sensation *and* perception are both critical for our interpretation of, and interaction with, the environment. Accurate functioning of our sensory systems is critical for survival. For example, imagine how greatly diminished your chances of survival would be if you could not see a fire, feel its heat, hear others crying "fire," smell the smoke, or interpret any of these sensations and perceptions appropriately as signalling danger.

perception the conscious recognition and identification of a sensory stimulus.

Module 24: Common Features of Sensation and Perception

sensory receptor cells specialized
cells that convert a specific form of
environmental stimuli into neural
impulses.

sensory transduction the process
of converting a specific form of
environmental stimuli into neural
impulses.

absolute threshold the minimal
stimulus necessary for detection
by an individual.

Each of our sensory systems is set up to convert a narrow window of the physical stimuli we receive from the world we perceive outside our bodies into electrical neural signals that can be used by the brain. Sensation and perception occur differently in each of our sensory modalities, but our senses also share some common processes. Each of the senses has a set of specialized cells called **sensory receptor cells** that convert a specific form of environmental stimuli into neural impulses, the form of communication used in our brains and nervous systems (see **Figure 24-1**). This conversion is called **sensory transduction**. **Table 24-1** lists the different physical stimuli for each sensory system that are converted to brain activity through sensory transduction.

24.1 The Limits of the Senses: Thresholds

Our sensory receptors can be activated by very weak stimuli. A stimulus must, however, reach a certain level of intensity before we can detect it, because the conversion of physical stimuli into neural impulses only occurs when the stimuli reach this level or threshold. The minimal stimulus necessary for detection by an individual is called the **absolute threshold** (**Table 24-2**). Although the absolute threshold varies from person to person, in most cases it is surprisingly small. For instance, many normal humans are capable of

FIGURE 24-1 Sensory receptor cells.
Each sensory system contains specialized cells that are activated by particular physical stimuli.

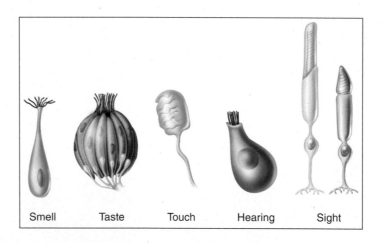

Smell   Taste   Touch   Hearing   Sight

TABLE 24-1 Sensory Transduction Converts Environmental Stimuli into Neural Activity

Sensory System	Physical Stimuli
Olfactory (smell)	Odorants (airborne chemicals)
Somatosensory (touch, heat, pain)	Pressure or damage to the skin
Gustatory (taste)	Chemicals (typically in food)
Auditory (hearing)	Sound waves
Visual (sight)	Light (photons)

TABLE 24-2 Absolute Thresholds for Various Senses

Sense	Absolute Threshold
Smell	A drop of perfume diffused throughout a six-room apartment
Taste	5 millilitres of sugar in 9 litres of water
Touch	An insect's wing falling on your cheek from a height of about a centimetre
Hearing	The tick of a watch at 6 metres in a quiet room
Sight	A candle flame 50 kilometres away on a clear, dark night

detecting a candle flame up to 50 kilometres away on a clear pitch black night (Galanter, 1962). Anything that falls below the sensory threshold goes unnoticed. Researchers have also worked to determine the smallest difference that we can detect between two stimuli, called the **difference threshold** or **just noticeable difference**. If you are listening to your iPod, how much do you have to turn up the volume before you notice that the music is louder? This amount, or just noticeable difference, depends on how loud the music was in the first place. When sensory systems are working optimally, the difference threshold is also remarkably small.

Thresholds may limit our abilities in some ways, but they are also very useful to us. For example, imagine how distracting it would be if you noticed every little change in wind pattern or each individual fibre in your clothing. You probably wouldn't be very comfortable if you noticed all these small details, nor would you be able to focus on what was important.

difference threshold or **just noticeable difference** the minimal difference between two stimuli necessary for detection of a difference between the two.

24.2 Surrounded by Stimuli: Sensory Adaptation

Our senses are generally organized to detect change. This makes adaptive sense since a great deal of the stimuli we are exposed to are not important enough to warrant our attention. Imagine how difficult it would be to concentrate on reading this part if sensory information about the odours in your environment, the taste of your mouth, the sound of the clock ticking, the sensations of blinking and breathing, and the touch of your clothing were all competing with your ability to read! To combat the possibility of being unable to focus on the salient or important cues, our sensory systems respond to the continual presence of the same stimulus or to a repetitive stimulus with a decreased response to that stimulus, a process called **sensory adaptation**. What happens is this: when some stimulus in our surroundings stays the same for a period of time, such as the pressure of our clothing on our skin, our sensory cells respond to it less and less. This response keeps the brain from being overloaded with redundant information. After a time, in some cases we no longer notice the stimulus at all. All of our sensory systems exhibit some form of adaptation, but the sense of smell is particularly sensitive to adaptational effects (Dalton, 2000).

sensory adaptation the process whereby repeated stimulation of a sensory cell leads to a reduced response.

Olfactory adaptation occurs when a change in sensitivity to a particular odour reaches a point where the odour cannot be distinguished after a prolonged exposure to it. That is, our ability to detect specific odours gradually fades when we are in their presence for a prolonged period. Sensory adaptation can be overcome by providing a much stronger stimulus. Something like this may have happened to you when you were at *Starbucks* or *Tim Hortons*. When you first entered the shop you probably smelled a strong odour of coffee. After a time you no longer noticed this odour. However, when the barista brings you your own cup of coffee, you are once again able to savour the smell of coffee. Now that the source of the smell is more concentrated in your vicinity, your ability to smell the odour is renewed. Although the sense of smell is perhaps most prone to this response, all of our sensory systems exhibit some form of adaptation (Goldstein, 2014).

24.3 Processing Sensory Information

bottom-up processing perception that proceeds by transducing environmental stimuli into neural impulses that move into successively more complex brain regions.

top-down processing perception processes led by cognitive processes, such as memory or expectations.

perceptual set readiness to interpret a certain stimulus in a certain way.

Sensation and perception almost always happen together. Researchers, however, have studied each process separately to determine how the two work together. Perception can occur through **bottom-up processing**, which begins with the physical stimuli from the environment, and proceeds through transduction of those stimuli into neural impulses. The signals are passed along to successively more complex brain regions, and ultimately result in the recognition of a visual stimulus. For example, when you look at the face of your best friend, your eyes convert light energy into neural impulses, which travel into the brain to visual regions. This information forms the basis for sensing the visual stimulus and ultimately its perception. Equally important to perception, however, is **top-down processing**, which involves previously acquired knowledge. As a result, when you look at your best friend's face, brain regions that store information about what faces look like, particularly those that are familiar to you, can help you to perceive and recognize the specific visual stimulus.

The power of top-down processing goes far beyond just using our memories to recognize our best friend's face. Knowledge about how things typically appear, our perceptual expectations, or **perceptual sets**, can actually prepare us to perceive certain things in particular ways. For example, a photo showing a fuzzy UFO will look very different to you depending on whether you believe there is such a thing as UFOs. And perceptual sets do not relate only to vision. Consider, for example, whether a dish would taste exactly the same to you if you thought it was chicken or if you thought it was rattlesnake. Many elements—our experiences, our cultures, the contexts in which we find ourselves—affect our perceptual sets.

Perceptual sets may come into play when we are faced with *ambiguous stimuli*—stimuli that could be interpreted in different ways. A well-known visual example is presented in **Figure 24-2**. Looked at one way, the drawing shows a young woman looking over her shoulder—you can see her jawline, her ear, and a bit of her nose. Looked at another way, it shows an old woman with her chin to her chest. If someone pointed out this drawing to you by saying, "Look at this picture of an old woman with a big nose," that's most likely what you would see—because that's what you would expect to see.

Typically, perception involves both bottom-up and top-down processing occurring at the same time. The combination lets us rapidly recognize familiar faces and other stimuli. Bottom-up and top-down processing are involved in sensation and perception of all sensory modalities. For example, recognizing familiar songs involves not only information carried from the ear to the brain, but also the matching of that information with previously stored information about the music. We also combine bottom-up and top-down processes to help us recognize the smell or taste of a familiar food, and to put a name to a face, and so on.

24.4 The Senses

Sensory systems are a part of the nervous system consisting of sensory receptors that receive stimulus information and conduct information to parts of the brain responsible for processing sensory information. Each system consists of sensory receptors, neural pathways, and areas of the brain involved in sensory perception.

FIGURE 24-2 Old or young? What you see when you look at this drawing depends in part on what you expect to see.

In general it is agreed that there are five senses: smell, taste, touch, sound, and sight. However, beyond these five senses we can also consider our kinesthetic sense, which gives us information about the body's movement, posture, and position. As well, the vestibular sense gives us information about the head's position and movement in space, stabilizing gaze as well as maintaining balance and posture. Together, these two senses, as well as other senses (particularly the visual system), combine to provide proprioceptive feedback, sometimes considered the body's sixth sense. Proprioceptive feedback is the unconscious awareness of the self and spatial orientation arising from stimulation within the body. Although we will discuss each of these major sensory systems separately in this part, in most of our day-to-day experiences, we actually use these sensory systems or modalities in combination to experience the world.

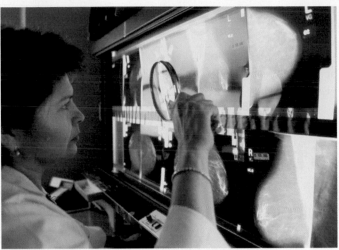

ER Productions/Corbis

A critical difference. A radiologist carefully examines a mammogram, looking for the slightest indication of a tumour. An individual's ability to detect a difference between two visual stimuli (such as normal versus abnormal tissue) can be increased by special training, practice, and instruments, but it is still limited to some degree by sensory difference thresholds.

Before You Go On

www.wiley.com/go/comercanada

What Do You Know?

1. What is sensory transduction?
2. What are absolute and difference thresholds?
3. Compare and contrast bottom-up and top-down processing.

What Do You Think? Describe examples of sensory adaptation that you have experienced in two or more of your sensory modalities.

Summary

Module 24: Common Features of Sensation and Perception

LEARNING OBJECTIVE 24 Describe characteristics shared by all the senses, including receptor cells, transduction, and thresholds, and differentiate between top-down and bottom-up processes of perception.

- Our sensory systems convert physical stimuli into neural information with specialized cells called sensory receptor cells that convert a specific form of environmental stimuli into neural impulses by a process called sensory transduction.
- The conversion of physical stimuli into neural impulses only occurs when the stimuli reach a certain level, or threshold. The absolute threshold is the minimum level of a stimulus we can detect. The difference threshold is the smallest difference we can detect between two similar stimuli.
- Our sensory systems are set up to detect change. With continuous exposure to a stimulus, adaptation occurs.
- Bottom-up processing begins with the physical stimuli from the environment and proceeds through to perception. In top-down processing, prior knowledge is used to interpret perceptual information.

Key Terms

absolute threshold 180

bottom-up
    processing 182

difference threshold or just
    noticeable difference 181

perceptual set 182

sensory adaptation 181

sensory receptor
    cells 180

sensory transduction 180

top-down
    processing 182

Study Questions

Multiple Choice

1. If a light bulb does not produce a light that can be detected by a person, what threshold has not been surpassed?
   a) difference
   b) absolute
   c) stimulus
   d) transduction

2. Which of the following statements most accurately expresses the relationship between top-down and bottom-up processing?
   a) Some stimuli are processed in a bottom-up fashion, while others are processed in top-down manner.
   b) Bottom-up processing precedes top-down processing during the perception of most stimuli.
   c) Top-down processes only contribute to perception when stimuli are highly novel, unexpected, or ambiguous.
   d) Top-down and bottom-up processes occur simultaneously during the perception of many, if not all, stimuli.

Fill-in-the-Blank

1. The sensory system that responds to pressure or damage to the skin is the _____ system.

2. The conversion of environmental stimuli into neural impulses is called _____.

Module 25: The Chemical Senses: Smell and Taste

Smell and taste are separate senses but are usually together called the *chemical senses* because they involve responses to particular chemicals. Smell, our **olfactory sense**, and taste, our **gustatory sense**, emerged early in our evolutionary history (Doty, 1986). The sense of smell, in particular, is more sensitive and of greater significance to less complex animals, who use it for social communication as well as finding food and avoiding predators (Yahr, 1977; Mech & Boitani, 2003). This is less so for humans who rely more heavily on vision. However, the contributions of both smell and taste to the safety, social communication, and overall quality of life in humans are often underestimated. The ability to detect dangerous odours, such as smoke or a gas leak, or dangerous flavours, such as tainted food or poison, can be critical to our survival. In addition, some of our greatest pleasures in life come from the ability to smell and taste—to smell a rose or, as we all know, to enjoy a good meal.

In this module, we will explore the environmental stimuli that create aromas and flavours, the organs we use to sense those stimuli, and how we transform environmental stimuli into brain signals that eventually help us perceive different smells and tastes. We will also discuss the development of these abilities, some very interesting differences among people in their ability to taste and smell things, and some problems that can occur in the olfactory and gustatory systems.

> **LEARNING OBJECTIVE 25**
> Summarize the biological changes that underlie smell and taste.

olfactory sense our sense of smell.

gustatory sense our sense of taste.

25.1 Smell and Taste: How They Work

25.1.1 Smells Around Us

Sensation in the smell or olfactory system begins when chemicals called **odorants** enter the nose, as shown later in the part in the feature "Tying it Together: Your Brain and Behaviour." Odorants are converted to neural signals at sensory receptors located in our nasal mucosa. These sensory receptors are located on the *cilia*, or hairlike structures, of **olfactory receptor neurons** (McEwen et al., 2008).

When odorants enter the nose, these chemicals bind to specific receptors located on the olfactory receptor neurons in a lock-and-key fashion. Only certain airborne chemicals bind to specific receptors (Pernollet et al., 2006; Buck, 1996). When enough odorant molecules have bound to receptors, the combination sets off an action potential in the olfactory receptor neuron. As we described in Part 3, the action potential or *firing* of a neuron sends a message to other neurons. The firing of olfactory receptor neurons is transmitted to the brain, as we will see next.

Continuous binding of certain odorants will result in fatigue of the olfactory receptor neurons to which they bind. In other words, the cell will stop responding to the odorant unless it's given a chance to recover so it can fire again (Dalton, 2000). If you were to step outside a restaurant to make a phone call, for example, you would probably notice the food smells again when you stepped back into the restaurant because your olfactory receptor neurons would have gotten a break from constant exposure to the food odorants. When a stimulus is continuously present, however, such as when you remain sitting in the restaurant, the only way the olfactory receptor neurons will respond to the odorant would be if the stimulus increases in magnitude, such as when the food is brought directly to your table. Many more odorant molecules are now available to your nose and its olfactory receptor neurons.

odorants airborne chemicals that are detected as odours.

olfactory receptor neurons sensory receptor cells that convert chemical signals from odorants into neural impulses that travel to the brain.

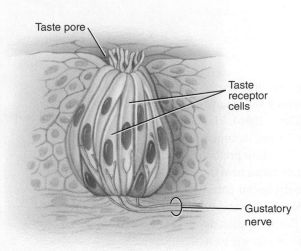

FIGURE 25-1 One of 9,000 taste buds in the human system. The receptor cells for taste are clustered within the taste buds found in the bumps, or papillae, covering your tongue.

papillae bumps on the tongue that contain clumps of taste buds.

taste buds clusters of sensory receptor cells that convert chemical signals from food into neural impulses that travel to the brain.

25.1.2 Types of Tastes

In humans, the sense of smell is very closely tied to the sense of taste. In fact, what we normally call *taste* is really *flavour*, which is a combination of smell and taste. However, taste, the gustatory sense, is itself independent of smell. The top of the tongue, the major organ of taste, is covered with bumps, called **papillae**. As shown in **Figure 25-1**, papillae contain clumps of **taste buds**, each of which contains 60 to 100 sensory receptor cells for taste.

Taste receptor cells have cilia that contain the actual receptors. These cilia extend through the pores of the taste receptor and are exposed to the contents of your mouth.

There are five major kinds of taste receptors. Each responds to a specific taste in our food: sweet, sour, bitter, and salty (Sugita, 2006). The fifth type of taste receptor is called *umami*. Umami is the taste of monosodium glutamate (MSG), a chemical additive used in cooking some Asian food and Western fast food (DuBois, 2010; Kinnamon, 2009). Each of these five types of taste receptors uses a slightly different mechanism for transduction of the chemicals in food to neural impulses in the gustatory system. For example, salt activates its taste receptors by sending sodium ions into the channels on the taste receptor cell. Since sodium ions are positively charged, the electrical charge of the taste receptor then becomes more positive. Taste buds are not evenly distributed across the tongue, but most tastes can be recognized to a greater or lesser degree on most parts of the top of the tongue.

25.1.3 Eating: It's More Than Smell and Taste

The overall sensations we experience when we eat food are not just the result of combined interactions between olfactory and gustatory senses. Much of the information we get about food is delivered to us through one of the touch or *tactile* senses. The consistency of a particular food is not relayed to the brain via the taste receptors, but rather by inputs from touch receptors located on the tongue. The role of food consistency in determining preference is much greater than you might imagine. Many adult humans reject certain foods, such as raw oysters or cooked okra, specifically because those foods have a "slimy" texture.

In addition, the sensation we experience when we eat a spicy meal is related to a component of the tactile system that communicates information about pain. A chemical called *capsaicin*, from chili peppers, activates pain receptors located in the tongue (Numazaki & Tominaga, 2004). These pain impulses, in conjunction with tactile information about the food texture, as well as the flavours (smell and taste) associated with the food, can combine to produce a sensation that is pleasurable to many people.

Psychology Around Us   Starve a Cold

Have you ever noticed how food doesn't taste as good when you have a bad cold? Often you can't taste much of anything at all for a few days. This effect is due, in large part, to mucous blocking the olfactory receptors located on the cilia in your nose. Air can't get to these receptors, and so the odorants that travel in the air can't get there either. A cold doesn't affect your taste buds, so the actual taste of the food remains the same. It's the flavour that suffers—and that's because flavour results from taste and smell working together.

Suppose a food is hot because it just came out of the oven. We have all had the experience of burning our mouths, which can damage the taste receptors on the tongue. The sensory receptors of taste are unusual because they regenerate when this happens.

25.2 How the Brain Processes Smell and Taste

Signals from our olfactory receptor neurons travel to the brain via the olfactory nerve. As **Figure 25-2** shows, information carried along the olfactory nerves travels first to a structure called the **olfactory bulb**, located at the base of the front of the brain, beneath the frontal lobes. Olfactory information is then sent to regions of the cerebral cortex that are important for recognizing and discriminating among odours, including the piriform cortex (Wilson, 2001).

The ability of our cortex to recognize patterns of inputs from a variety of olfactory receptors is most likely responsible for our detection of certain odours. Studies have shown that the piriform cortex is *plastic* or changeable in adulthood (Li et al., 2008). That is, the parts of piriform cortex that normally recognize specific odorants can change with experience, actually remapping this brain region. The chemical structures of some pairs of molecules are so similar that untrained humans can't discriminate between them (the two odours are usually below the just noticeable difference). However, if exposure to one of the chemicals is paired with a painful shock to the leg, humans can be taught to discriminate between the odours (Li et al., 2008). This is a remarkable example of top-down processing. Learning about associations between odours and other experiences (such as a shock) can influence our ability to perceive sensory information in the future.

The olfactory bulb also sends information to the amygdala, an area important for emotions and fear, as well as indirectly to the hippocampus, an area important for learning and memory. Many people report that certain smells evoke past memories (Lehrer, 2007). For example, the smell of baking might remind you of visiting your uncle the baker as a young child, the smell of school paste and old lunches might remind you of your elementary school, and so on. The ability of smells to retrieve memories is probably related in part to olfactory connections to the hippocampus and amygdala.

Taste receptor cells do not have axons, but instead connect with sensory neurons in the tongue to send information to our brains. Taste information is sent to the *thalamus*, and eventually, the cerebral cortex. We will see throughout this part that the thalamus is a relay station for incoming sensory information of many kinds; all of our sensory systems except olfaction have a main pathway through the thalamus.

Taste information is integrated with reward circuits in the brain (Norgren et al., 2006), and rewarding tastes seem to be processed separately from aversive tastes. Tastes that are considered to be rewarding, such as salty and sweet, activate overlapping areas in the taste cortex.

By contrast, tastes generally considered to be less pleasurable, such as bitter and sour, activate regions that overlap less with rewarding tastes and more with one another in the taste cortex (Accolla et al., 2007). Taste and smell information is processed through separate pathways, but there is convergence in the associated parts of neocortex, namely in the prefrontal cortex.

In addition to integrating information about taste in general, part of the cortex that receives taste information, called the *insula*, is associated with the emotion of disgust. Neuroimaging studies have shown that this brain region becomes activated not only when we smell or taste something revolting, but also when we view repulsive visual images (Calder et al., 2007; Schienle et al., 2008).

WHAT HAPPENS *in the* **BRAIN?**

olfactory bulb the first region where olfactory information reaches the brain on its way from the nose.

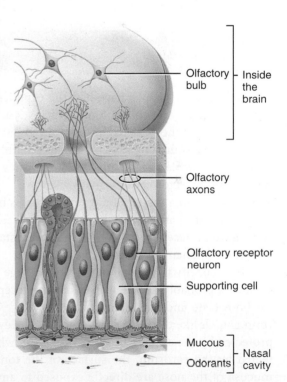

Olfactory bulb — Inside the brain

Olfactory axons

Olfactory receptor neuron

Supporting cell

Mucous — Nasal cavity
Odorants

FIGURE 25-2 The smell route. Olfactory receptor neurons (shown here in blue) transduce information from odorant molecules that enter the nose. This information is carried by the olfactory nerve into the brain where it synapses in the olfactory bulb.

25.3 The Development of Smell and Taste

HOW WE DEVELOP

©iStockphoto.com/KarynaChe

Sheer joy. The obvious pleasure on this woman's face after she bites into the dessert serves as a vivid reminder that taste information is integrated with the reward circuits in the brain.

The sense of smell is relatively well-developed at birth. Research suggests that, within hours of birth, newborn babies are capable of telling their own mother from another woman using only the sense of smell. In fact, olfactory functioning seems to be in place even before birth. Newborn infants show a learned preference to the odours of their mother's amniotic fluid. After birth, infants quickly learn to recognize the smell of their own mother's milk. Exposure to odours of their mother's milk has a calming effect on infants when they are experiencing a brief, minor painful stimulus, such as a needle stick in the heel (Nishitani et al., 2009). This effect doesn't appear to be as specific to the milk as it is to the mother—exposure to other odours that the baby has associated with the mother, such as vanillin, has the same calming effect as mother's milk odour (Goubet et al., 2007).

The ability to taste is also well-formed in humans at birth. Newborn humans show an innate preference for sugar and aversion to bitter or sour tastes. Babies move their faces toward a sweet substance and make sucking movements with their mouths, but turn away and grimace when presented with a sour or bitter substance (Rosenstein & Oster, 1988).

Researchers have shown that by about 7 years of age, children develop a preference for sour tastes (Liem & Mennella, 2003). This may explain the popularity of candies such as Sour Patch Kids. However, the aversion to bitter tastes typically lasts until young adulthood when bitter foods, such as blue cheese and dark chocolate, start to emerge as favourites.

Many of these developmental changes are the result of learning. As children grow, they become accustomed to different tastes. However, there is some evidence to suggest that the gustatory system itself changes from infancy to adulthood. We form taste buds before we are even born, and as newborns, have higher concentrations of them on our

Practically Speaking   Regeneration in the Taste and Smell Systems

If you, like most people, have had the experience of burning your tongue on too-hot food or drink, you've probably noticed that by the next day or so, your ability to taste has returned and your tongue is no longer painful. This is due to the remarkable regenerative characteristics of the taste buds. Taste receptor cells normally turn over—they die and are replaced—in a matter of days. The process happens even faster when they are damaged. Under normal circumstances, our olfactory receptor neurons are also constantly turning over (Bermingham-McDonogh & Reh, 2011).

The capacity to regenerate on such a large scale and so rapidly is probably necessary because the receptor neurons for both taste and smell are exposed to the external environment. Unlike the sensory receptors of the eye, which are protected by the eyeball, or those of the ear, which are protected by the eardrum, the surface of the tongue and the mucosa of the nose are directly exposed to any number of noxious chemical molecules that may enter our mouths or noses. Because destruction of receptors is likely under such circumstances, we need to constantly regenerate receptor cells just to continue normal functioning of our smell and taste systems.

Neurobiologists are studying the regenerative capabilities of the taste buds and olfactory receptor neurons in hopes

©iStockphoto.com/coloroftime

of understanding exactly how these cells are constantly rejuvenating. Scientists and medical professionals hope that understanding these mechanisms may one day enable replacement of other types of cells, ones that currently don't seem capable of repair when they are damaged.

tongues than we will as adults. Children also have taste buds on their palates, inside the cheeks, and at the back of their mouths. Although these regions continue to contain taste buds in adults, their numbers decline with time (Nilsson, 1979).

The high number of taste buds in children may explain why they are often picky eaters. The tastes of certain foods may seem too strong to children because their larger number of taste buds produce more neural impulses than adults would generate from the same food. Some researchers suggest that this developmental phenomenon might actually be adaptive in helping us survive. If young children enjoyed ingesting substances with strong or bitter tastes, they might be at higher risk of poisoning.

25.4 Individual Differences in Smell and Taste

Have you ever felt a bit faint when you were closed in an elevator with someone wearing perfume, while others in the elevator seemed not to notice? Humans vary greatly in their ability to detect certain odours. Some people seem relatively insensitive to even very strong smells, while others seem very sensitive. Some of these individual differences are related to learning. Exposure to particular odours during childhood lessens the reaction to those odours in adulthood.

In addition to these learned differences, research suggests that females are generally more sensitive to smell than males are, and that this sensitivity varies with the stage of the menstrual cycle (Derntl et al., 2013). Around the time of ovulation, women are more sensitive to odours than during other stages of the cycle. Women's ability to detect different odours also diminishes after menopause (Hughes et al., 2002). The exact biological mechanisms that underlie these differences are not known, but it is possible that reproductive hormones, such as estrogen, alter the excitability, or the likelihood, of firing of olfactory neurons (Hoyk et al, 2014).

There is also considerable individual variability in the ability to taste. Researchers group people into three different categories with respect to taste sensitivity: non-tasters (25 percent of people), medium tasters (50 percent), and supertasters (25 percent). These groups are distinguished based on their ability to detect and respond negatively to a specific bitter substance (Bartoshuk et al., 1996). Supertasters are repulsed by the bitter chemical. Non-tasters do not even notice the bitter taste, although they are capable of detecting other tastes. Medium tasters notice it, but do not find the taste particularly offensive. These functional differences are the result of variations in the concentration of taste buds on the tongue.

Women make up a higher proportion of supertasters than do men (Pickering et al., 2013). This heightened sensitivity of both chemical sensory systems, smell and taste, is likely to have had adaptive significance for women. Since the chemicals in women's diets are passed along to their children when women are pregnant or nursing, the ability to detect and avoid potentially harmful odours and tastes may have contributed to survival of the species by protecting infants from toxic substances.

Finally, the number of taste buds starts to decline at about 50 years of age, and the sense of smell may decline starting at age 60. A consequence of these two declines may be a gradual loss of interest in food, which can be counteracted by adding taste to food by way of spices and food choices (Mojet, Christ Hazelhof, & Heidema, 2001).

25.5 Smell and Taste Disorders

True taste disorders are rare. In fact, most people who seek medical assistance complaining that they cannot taste are actually suffering from problems with their olfactory, as opposed to gustatory, systems. People with a condition called **anosmia** have lost the ability to smell.

©iStockphoto.com/Bronwyn8

Infants and odours. Exposure to odours that an infant associates with her mother can have a calming effect.

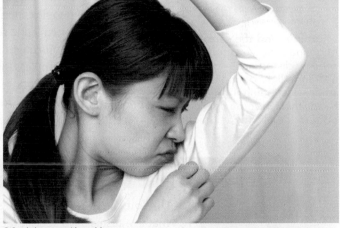

©iStockphoto.com/deeepblue

A special gift? People who are highly sensitive to odours such as underarm odour, often find employment that puts their special ability to use, for example as scent testers (or "noses") who determine whether a new deodorant produces a pleasant result.

anosmia inability to smell.

They can often still taste sweet, salty, sour, bitter, and umami, but they can no longer detect other flavours, since those require the additional information provided by food odorants.

In some rare cases—typically as a result of head trauma or problems during oral surgery—humans lose the ability to taste itself, a condition called **ageusia**. They can often still taste sweet, salty, sour, bitter, and umami, but they can no longer detect other flavours that require the information from the odorants of food.

ageusia inability to taste.

Head trauma is also a leading cause of anosmia (Haxel et al., 2008). Sometimes the nerves that carry olfactory information from the olfactory receptor neurons to the olfactory bulb can be sheared, cutting off the pathway by which information about smell reaches the brain. People with Alzheimer's disease also suffer from a diminished sense of smell that is probably due to a combined degeneration of olfactory receptor neurons and neurons located in olfactory brain regions (Djordjevic et al., 2008).

Although humans can certainly survive without the ability to smell, their quality of life is considerably diminished. Many people with anosmia report feelings of depression. In addition, there are safety and social issues to consider. Since we use our sense of smell to detect dangers, such as smoke or spoiled food, anosmia increases the risk of injury. Moreover, socially acceptable cultural practices of hygiene may become difficult to follow with anosmia, since humans often use olfactory cues to make decisions about bathing, washing clothes, and brushing teeth. People with anosmia can learn to cope effectively with their condition by using other sensory systems to detect danger. They might, for example, use sound cues, such as a blaring smoke detector to notice smoke, or visual cues, such as appearance and freshness dates, to detect spoiled food.

25.6 Migraines, Epilepsy, and the Sensory Systems

The chemical senses are also involved in the symptoms of some people with migraine headaches or epilepsy. For instance, a specific odour can initiate the onset of a migraine (Kelman, 2007). Likewise, patients with a certain form of epilepsy, called *reflex epilepsy*, will experience a seizure only after exposure to a specific odour (Ilik & Pazarli, 2014). Although the reasons for this remain unknown, these individuals find it necessary to avoid specific intense odorants. In other patients suffering from migraines or epilepsy, stimuli from the other sensory systems, such as touch, sound, and sight, can initiate the headaches or seizures.

Some people experience hallucinations called *auras* either before or during migraine headaches or epileptic seizures. Auras can involve any of the sensory systems. People with these conditions might have touch, sound, or sight hallucinations, and some experience strong, often unpleasant, smells or tastes. The involvement of different senses indicates which brain circuits are compromised in these conditions. For example, if a person's seizure is preceded by strong olfactory hallucinations, it's likely that the olfactory pathways are initiating the seizure, or at least participating in its generation.

©iStockphoto.com/alvarez

Migraines and the senses.
Migraine sufferers often experience sensory distortions—for example, a strange light or unpleasant smell—just before or during their headaches. In some cases, specific odours actually trigger migraines.

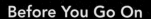

Before You Go On

www.wiley.com/go/comercanada

What Do You Know?
1. What five tastes have specific receptors?
2. Which parts of the brain are involved in sensing and perceiving odours?
3. What are supertasters?
4. How are smell and taste involved with migraines and epileptic seizures?

What Do You Think? This module listed some ways for people with anosmia to compensate for their lack of smell, such as using smoke detectors. What other ways can you suggest that people with anosmia might use to replace the safety and pleasures that a sense of smell provides?

Summary

Module 25: The Chemical Senses: Smell and Taste

LEARNING OBJECTIVE 25 Summarize the biological changes that underlie smell and taste.

- Smell, our olfactory sense, converts chemical odorants into neural signals that the brain can use. Taste, our gustatory sense, is closely intertwined with smell. Most flavours are a combination of scents with the five basic tastes we can discern: sweet, salty, sour, bitter, and umami.
- Taste buds in papillae on the tongue convert chemicals in our food to neural signals the brain can use. Taste receptors and smell receptors are routinely replaced, since they are more vulnerable to damage than other sensory receptors.
- Information about smell goes directly from the olfactory bulb to the olfactory cortex. Areas of the brain that process smells and tastes are plastic, or changeable. Processing of smells also sometimes overlaps with emotions and memories.
- Our preferred tastes change as we mature from childhood to adulthood, probably from a combination of learning and physical changes in the mouth.
- True disorders of taste are rare; people more frequently lose part or all of their sense of smell. Anosmia can present safety risks and diminish pleasure in life.

Key Terms

ageusia 190

anosmia 189

gustatory sense 185

odorants 185

olfactory
 bulb 187

olfactory receptor
 neurons 185

olfactory sense 185

papillae 186

taste buds 186

Study Questions

Multiple Choice

1. Which of the following statements most accurately describes the responsiveness of an individual olfactory receptor?
   a) A given olfactory receptor responds only to a specific airborne chemical.
   b) A given olfactory receptor responds to a wide range of odorants.
   c) A given olfactory receptor responds to one of four or five basic classes of odorants.
   d) A given olfactory receptor responds to virtually any airborne chemical.

2. Which of the basic tastes are considered rewarding? Which are considered aversive?
   a) Salty and sweet are considered rewarding. Sour and bitter are considered aversive.
   b) Sweet is considered rewarding. Salty, sour, and bitter are considered aversive.

   c) Sweet and sour are considered rewarding. Salty and bitter are considered aversive.
   d) Sweet, sour, and salty are considered rewarding. Bitter is considered aversive.

Fill-in-the-Blank

1. The human tongue is covered with bumps called _____.

2. The olfactory bulb sends information to the _____, a brain area important for learning and memory.

Module 26: The Tactile or Cutaneous Senses: Touch, Pressure, Pain, Vibration

LEARNING OBJECTIVE 26
Describe how the different senses
of touch work and what can
happen when things go wrong.

"Your skin keeps people from seeing the inside of your body, which is repulsive, and it prevents your organs from falling onto the ground, where careless pedestrians might step on them.**"**

—*Dave Barry, 1985, page 2*

free nerve endings sensory receptors that convert physical stimuli into touch, pressure, or pain impulses.

Meissner's corpuscles sensory receptors that convert physical stimuli about sensory touch on the fingertips, lips, and palms.

Merkel's discs sensory receptors that convert information about light to moderate pressure on the skin.

Ruffini's end-organs sensory receptors that respond to heavy pressure and joint movement.

Pacinian corpuscles sensory receptors that respond to vibrations and heavy pressure.

Tactile, as we mentioned earlier, means "touch." As with the chemical senses, there are rewarding and aversive types of tactile stimuli. The pleasure associated with a relaxing back massage or stroking a baby's cheek stands in stark contrast to the discomfort of getting a scrape or burn. The tactile or somatosensory system is actually a complex sense. As shown in **Figure 26-1**, our skin contains a variety of sensory receptors to register different types of physical stimuli (Schiff & Foulke, 2010).

- **Free nerve endings** are located mostly near the surface of the skin and function to detect touch, pressure, pain, and temperature.
- **Meissner's corpuscles** transduce information about sensitive touch and are found in the hairless regions of the body, such as the fingertips, lips, and palms.
- **Merkel's discs** transduce information about light to moderate pressure on the skin.
- **Ruffini's end-organs** are located deep in the skin. They register heavy pressure and movement of the joints.
- **Pacinian corpuscles** are also buried deep in the skin and respond to vibrations and heavy pressure.

Pressure on the skin activates free nerve endings that give us the sense of being touched. As you may have noticed, your skin is not equally sensitive to tactile stimuli over your whole body. Certain parts of your body, for example, the skin on your elbow, are much less sensitive to touch than other areas, such as your face and hands. These differences likely arise as a result of different densities of free nerve endings. Areas that are more sensitive have more free nerve endings.

We can also experience sensory adaptation, resulting in reduced tactile sensation from depression of the skin that continues for a period of time. This happens to you every

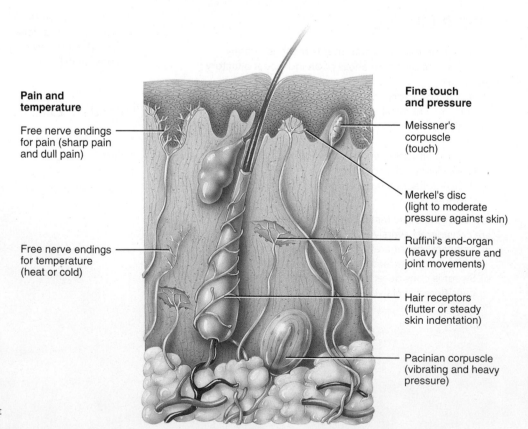

Pain and temperature

Free nerve endings for pain (sharp pain and dull pain)

Free nerve endings for temperature (heat or cold)

Fine touch and pressure

Meissner's corpuscle (touch)

Merkel's disc (light to moderate pressure against skin)

Ruffini's end-organ (heavy pressure and joint movements)

Hair receptors (flutter or steady skin indentation)

Pacinian corpuscle (vibrating and heavy pressure)

FIGURE 26-1 Sensory receptors in the skin. The tactile senses rely on a variety of receptors located in different parts of the skin.

day when you put on your clothing; shortly after getting dressed, you are no longer aware of the tactile stimulus your clothing provides (unless, of course, it is too tight).

26.1 Tactile Senses and the Brain

Our brains use a variety of related processes to help us perceive general information about a range of non-painful touch sensations, including pressure, temperature, and general touch. Pain perception is also an important function.

WHAT HAPPENS *in the* **BRAIN?**

26.1.1 The Touching Brain

When we touch something, or something touches us, our free nerve endings send tactile information into the spinal cord. The signals travel up the spinal cord to the brain, as shown in **Figure 26-2**. In the brain, touch information is first received in the thalamus, and then routed from there to the somatosensory cortex (located in the parietal lobe). Information about pressure and vibration is generally transmitted to the brain in a similar way, after being converted to neural impulses by the specialized receptors described above.

Our brain processes tactile information *contralaterally*, or on the opposite side of the brain from the side of the body where the touch occurred. So, if you touch something with your left hand, the information is processed by the somatosensory cortex on the right side of your brain.

As we discussed in Part 3, the somatosensory cortex does not have an equal representation of all parts of the body (Kakigi et al., 2000). For example, tactile inputs from the hands take up proportionately more space in the somatosensory cortex than those from the back. This seems reasonable, given the fact that our hands are specialized for object manipulation, and we need to process information from them in great detail. Information about pressure and vibration is generally transmitted to the brain in a similar way after being converted to neural impulses by the specialized receptors described above.

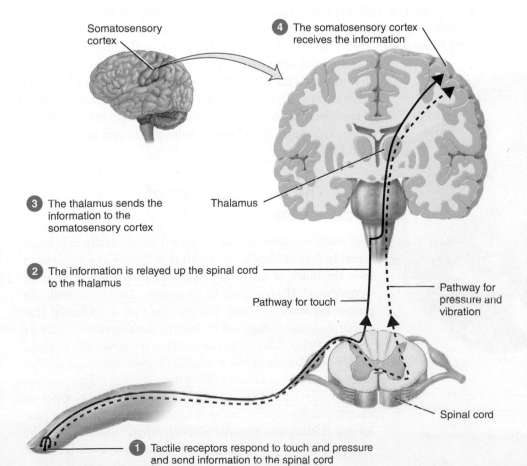

Somatosensory cortex

4 The somatosensory cortex receives the information

FIGURE 26-2 **Somatosensory pathways in the central nervous system.**

3 The thalamus sends the information to the somatosensory cortex

Thalamus

2 The information is relayed up the spinal cord to the thalamus

Pathway for touch

Pathway for pressure and vibration

Spinal cord

1 Tactile receptors respond to touch and pressure and send information to the spinal cord

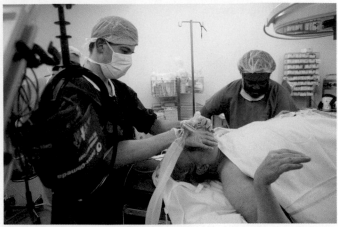

Owen Franken/Corbis

Using the brain to counteract pain. Anesthesia is a procedure that helps block pain sensations, enabling patients to undergo surgery. Drug-induced anesthetic approaches that act through the brain are general anesthesia (seen here) and sedation.

HOW WE
DEVELOP

Dreamstime/GetStock

Somatosensory input Tickling activates somatosensory pathways.

Beyond these sorts of sensory reactions, we can extend our senses mechanically. The Canadian Space Agency, which developed the Canadarm used to manipulate cargo on the space shuttle, has been working with NASA on the development of virtual environment generating headgear called the Canadian Space Vision System. This technology will allow operators to "see" what the next generation of remote manipulator arms can see. Using this equipment will allow astronauts to literally "walk" the manipulators hand over hand along the outside of the space ship, and then perform manipulation tasks that the operator can see and control despite being safely back inside the ship (Guenther et al., 2012; Paquet, 2000).

26.1.2 Pain and the Brain

Like general touch information, painful sensations are also transmitted to the brain via free nerve endings. Pain information travels to the brain via two different types of pain fibres. One system, called the *fast pathway*, uses myelinated axons that, as we discussed in Part 3, carry signals faster than unmyelinated axons. Messages about sharp, localized pain travel along the fast pathway directly up the spinal cord to the thalamus and to areas of the somatosensory cortex. Pain information received via the fast pathway helps us to respond quickly with a withdrawal reflex, such as pulling a hand away after touching a hot stove. The slower pain pathway uses more unmyelinated axons— these inputs communicate with brain regions involved in processing emotions. Pain we perceive via the slow pathway is more often burning pain than sharp pain (Prescott et al., 2014).

Like all other sensory systems we have discussed so far, the pain system shows evidence of sensory adaptation. A common example of this can be experienced when eating a spicy meal. Recall that the sensation of eating chili peppers is mostly due to the activation of pain fibres located on the tongue. Oftentimes, when a very spicy food is first ingested, the pain response seems great. However, as the meal progresses, the response diminishes and we are less likely to experience discomfort. This is due to adaptation of the pain fibres and a subsequent decrease in their activity. However, when pain is associated with actual tissue damage or an abnormality in the pain system, as discussed below, pain can be persistent and debilitating.

26.2 The Development of Tactile Senses

Like smell and taste, the tactile senses are generally in place at birth. In fact, studies have shown that fetuses can respond to even the touch of a hair at a relatively early stage in prenatal development (Lagercrantz & Changeux, 2009). As well, the pioneering work of Harry Harlow (see Part 4) indicated that physical contact is required for healthy development in infancy (Harlow, 1958). After birth, the ability to recognize and respond to different somatosensory stimuli is dependent on further brain development as well as learning.

For some children, one of the more enjoyable types of somatosensory input is being tickled. Although rough or prolonged tickling can become abusive, when tickled under the right circumstances, children often explode with laughter.

The reaction children have to tickling is a result of activation of somatosensory pathways in an uneven, uncontrollable, and unexpected manner. Not only are our sensory systems organized to detect change, but they are most-tuned to stimuli that are unexpected and surprising. When you move your body and produce tactile sensations, these stimuli are less noticeable to you than are sensations produced by another individual. The sensations of your own legs touching one another when you cross your legs, for example, is generally less noticeable than a similar touch on your leg would be if someone sitting next to you brushed their leg against yours.

Likewise, your reaction to your cat jumping onto your lap is likely to be much greater if you have eyes closed when it happens. This differential response to surprising tactile stimuli appears to be a defence mechanism that has adaptive significance. It is probably also the reason why being tickled by someone else is more effective at producing an emotional reaction than trying to tickle yourself. Our enjoyment of being tickled generally diminishes as we age. This is likely due to the fact that adults are better at anticipating stimuli, and hence are more difficult to surprise, than are children. It may also reflect a change in tactile thresholds (becoming less sensitive to touch) with age.

gate control theory of pain theory that certain patterns of neural activity can close a "gate" to keep pain information from travelling to parts of the brain where it is perceived.

26.3 Tactile Senses: Individual Differences

HOW WE
DIFFER

Humans differ greatly in their ability to detect physical stimuli on the skin. In addition, they differ in the degree to which they find certain tactile stimulation pleasurable or aversive. For example, some people enjoy an intense back massage, while others do not. Of all the somatosensory experiences, the one that has received the most research attention is that of pain. Pain management for surgical procedures and other medical conditions is a critical part of patient care. There are dramatic differences in both the threshold to detect pain and the degree to which pain causes emotional suffering.

Although learning plays some role, people also differ in the actual sensation and perception of pain as a result of physical differences in their sensory systems. Studies have shown, for example, that women have a lower threshold for detecting pain than do men. They report greater pain intensity than men in response to the same stimulus (Garcia et al., 2007). One interpretation of this sex difference is that women are just less able to cope psychologically with painful stimuli since they haven't been "toughened up." In fact, research suggests that women may have about twice as many pain receptors in their facial skin than men (Minerd, 2005). This suggests a physical cause for at least some of the differences in pain sensitivity.

Neuroimaging studies show that people's brains react differently depending on their sensitivity to pain (Dubé et al., 2009). People exposed to a high temperature stimulus in one study exhibited varied responses, for example. Those who reported feeling pain showed changes in activity in their thalamus, somatosensory cortex, and cingulate cortex areas. Those who did not report feeling pain showed similar activity in the thalamus, but no changes in the cortical regions. Although there may be differences in the two groups' sensory receptors in their skin, these findings suggest that differences in activation of brain circuitry may also underlie varied responses to painful stimuli.

One classic theory, the **gate control theory of pain** by Canadians Ronald Melzack and Patrick Wall (1982), attempts to explain the relationship of brain activity to pain by suggesting that some patterns of neural activity can actually create a "gate"

Robbie Jack/Corbis

High pain threshold. This performer lifts concrete blocks and other heavy objects with a chain attached to his pierced tongue—an act that is unbearable for most people to even watch. Although hours of practice and conditioning and certain tricks of the trade each play a role in this behaviour, a high pain threshold is certainly a prerequisite.

that prevents messages from reaching parts of the brain where they are perceived as pain. So for example, we can rub a shin we have knocked into something and dull the pain (Melzack, 1999).

Early versions of this theory hypothesized that pain signals were blocked in the spinal cord, but later research has focused on neurochemicals or patterns of activity in the brain itself. Individual differences in gating mechanisms may result in the wide range of pain sensitivity across people (Romanelli & Esposito, 2004).

26.4 Disorders of the Tactile Senses

As we have seen, sensing and perceiving pain are normal, and important, functions of our tactile senses. Some people, however, experience either too much pain or too little. Sometimes people even feel pain and other sensations in limbs or other body parts that have actually been removed.

26.4.1 Chronic Pain

The most common abnormality associated with the somatosensory system is that of chronic pain, or pain that lasts longer than three months. A relatively large percentage of North Americans, with estimates ranging from one in six to one in three, report suffering from chronic pain (Moulin et al., 2002; Institute of Medicine, 2011). There are multiple causes of chronic pain, although in some cases the cause cannot be identified. In all cases, however, pain management is a critical issue, since prolonged pain sensations can interfere with daily functioning and may lead to depression or even suicide. One study indicated that 50 percent of Canadians living with chronic pain have severe levels of depression, with 34.6 percent reporting that they were thinking about suicide (Choiniere et al., 2010).

endorphins and enkephalins belong to a naturally occurring class of opiates that reduce pain in the nervous system.

Researchers have identified two groups of chemicals naturally produced by our nervous systems that have pain-relieving properties: **endorphins** and **enkephalins**. Endorphins and enkephalins belong to a class of molecules called *opiates*. As we will see in Part 6, this class of chemicals also includes pain-killing drugs, such as morphine, heroin, and oxycodone. When opiates are naturally present in the nervous system, they are referred to as *endogenous opiates*. These molecules are released by neurons after intense physical exercise, stress, and sexual experience. They are also thought to be responsible for the ability of some people to perform heroic physical actions under extreme duress (Boecker et al., 2008).

Medical practitioners use opiate drugs that mimic or stimulate the endogenous opiate system for pain relief. However, people easily become addicted to opiate drugs. Opiate drugs are not only addictive when they are abused illegally, such as with heroin, but they are also addictive when they are prescribed medically, as happens with morphine, and more recently, oxycodone (OxyContin). Repeated use of these drugs to treat chronic pain can produce a physiological dependence that is very difficult to overcome. In addition, these drugs become less effective with continual use, so higher and higher doses are needed to achieve pain relief. The need for high doses can be lethal, however, as opiates suppress breathing. Eventually, people with chronic pain can reach a point where the dose of medicine needed to reduce their pain would be enough to stop their breathing and kill them, but lower doses do not provide them with pain relief.

26.4.2 Acute Pain

Medical practitioners are constantly seeking ways to provide relief to patients in chronic, or continuing, pain. But what about acute pain, such as the short-term pain you feel when you burn yourself or you bump your leg on a table?

Gate control theory suggests that touch sensations, which frequently travel along fast fibres, can help prevent some pain sensations travelling on the slow pathways from reaching areas of the brain where they are perceived. According to this theory, the brain only processes so much input, so touch can help to set up a "gate" that stops pain

(Wall, 2000). This explains why we have a tendency to rub the skin of areas of our body that have been injured. For example, if you walk into a piece of furniture, you might rub your leg to dampen the pain. Focusing on your breathing may also help. We often tend to gasp and then hold our breath when we injure ourselves. Formal methods of pain control, such as the Lamaze method for childbirth, work in part by altering this natural tendency by teaching people to breathe in short, panting gasps (Leventhal et al., 1989). Distraction can also help (and distraction may actually be why focusing on your breathing helps), whereas anxiously focusing on pain can make it worse (Armel & Ramachandran, 2003).

26.4.3 No Pain

Some people are incapable of detecting painful stimuli. While the idea of feeling no pain may sound appealing at first, the fact is that our ability to recognize and respond to discomfort is critical for preventing physical damage to the body. Consider how often you shift position in your chair when you are studying or sitting in a lecture. If you were unable to receive signals of discomfort from your body, you would not move to relieve pressure on your skin. The parts of your skin under continuous pressure would develop sores or bruises. Since many everyday experiences would be damaging to our bodies if we were not able to detect discomfort, a lack of ability to detect pain can be very dangerous.

Some people are born unable to feel pain. A rare genetic condition called *familial dysautonomia* is associated with an inability to detect pain or temperature (Axelrod, 2004). Children with this disorder are at grave risk of life-threatening injuries and must be monitored very carefully. Loss of pain sensation can also be acquired later in life. Some medical conditions, including diabetes, can cause *neuropathies*, or nerve dysfunctions, that block pain sensations arising from the person's extremities. People with such neuropathies may not notice if they sustain an injury in an affected area, such as a toe. Sometimes tissue can get so damaged that it must be amputated.

26.4.4 Phantom Limb Sensations

Many individuals with amputated limbs report tactile hallucinations or *phantom* sensations of touch, pressure, vibration, pins and needles, hot, cold, and pain in the body part that no longer exists. Some people even feel the sensation of a ring on the finger or a watch on the wrist of an amputated arm. Others report feeling as if their phantom limb is tightly curled up and very painful. Similar phantom experiences have been reported in women who have undergone a mastectomy for the treatment of breast cancer (Björkman et al., 2008).

Researchers believe that such phantom sensations are the result of abnormal activity in the somatosensory cortex of the brain. When a body part is removed, the part of somatosensory cortex that previously received its input does not become inactive (Melzack & Katz, 2004). Instead, somatosensory inputs from intact body parts expand to occupy those regions of the cortex (Ramachandran, 2005). Since information from the face is represented in an area of the somatosensory cortex located near that of the arm and hand, a person whose arm was amputated is likely to experience an expansion of the somatosensory inputs from her face into the arm and hand regions of cortex.

Although researchers do not fully understand how reorganization of the somatosensory cortex produces phantom sensations, there is clearly a memory component to the phenomenon.

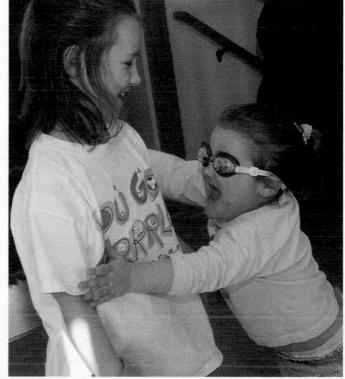

Jim Mone/AP

She feels no pain. The child on the right looks like any other 3-year-old welcoming her big sister home from school, except for the goggles she is wearing. The child, who suffers from a severe case of familial dysautonomia, cannot detect any pain to her body and must wear goggles to protect her eyes from excessive rubbing and scratching. By age 3 she has lost one eye, damaged the other, and inadvertently chewed apart portions of her tongue and mouth and therefore had to have all of her teeth removed.

People are more likely to experience phantom sensations that they actually felt previously, as opposed to random sensations. For example, someone who previously wore a ring or a watch is more likely to have the sense of wearing one after an amputation than is a person who didn't wear a watch or ring. Similarly, people who previously experienced considerable pain in their now-missing body part are much more likely to feel phantom pain. There are some amazing case studies involving phantom body parts. For example, a woman born with only stumps of arms can still sense her "hands" and reports gesturing with them when she talks. Children who have lost a hand say they still use their missing "fingers" to help them with counting (Gawande, 2008).

Vilayanor Ramachandran developed "mirror box" therapy for amputees experiencing pain in a missing limb. The mirror box, as its name suggests, involves placing mirrors around the individual on the same side as their missing arm. To the participant it looks like their missing arm is back, though it is only the reflection of their remaining arm. Moving their intact limb creates the sensation of movement in their missing limb and, over time, can lessen the pain in the missing or phantom limb (Ramachandran & Rogers-Ramachandran, 1996; Chan et al., 2007).

Before You Go On

www.wiley.com/go/comercanada

What Do You Know?

1. List the different types of tactile receptors in the skin and the primary functions of each.
2. Compare and contrast slow and fast pain pathways.
3. Why do children so often enjoy getting tickled?
4. What are some possible explanations for individual differences in pain sensitivity?

What Do You Think? Have you experienced an occasion when your senses have worked together to either enhance or diminish pain or another touch sense? For example, did certain sights or sounds make pain better or worse?

Summary

Module 26: The Tactile or Cutaneous Senses: Touch, Pressure, Pain, Vibration

LEARNING OBJECTIVE 26 Describe how the different senses of touch work and what can happen when things go wrong.

- A variety of sensory receptors throughout our bodies convert touch, pressure, or temperature stimuli into neural impulses that our brains can perceive.
- The sensory cortex of the brain maps touch sensations. Especially sensitive or important body parts receive disproportionately large representation in the cortex.
- Pain travels to the brain via both a fast pathway and a slow pathway.
- The gate control theory of pain suggests that certain patterns of neural activity can close a "gate" so that pain information does not reach parts of the brain where it is perceived.
- Medical professionals continue to search for ways to relieve people's chronic pain. Opiate drugs that simulate natural pain-killing endorphins or enkephalins are addictive. Sometimes practitioners resort to neurosurgery, which stops a patient from receiving all touch signals.
- People who have lost body parts surgically or through accidents often feel phantom sensations in the missing body part. These may be related to reorganization of the somatosensory cortex after an amputation.

Key Terms

endorphins and
  enkephalins 196

free nerve
  endings 192

gate control theory
  of pain 195

Meissner's
  corpuscles 192

Merkel's
  discs 192

Pacinian
  corpuscles 192

Ruffini's
  end-organs 192

Study Questions

Multiple Choice

1. Which of the following tactile sensory receptors is *correctly* matched with a function?
   a) Merkel's disc—responds to vibrations and heavy pressure
   b) Ruffini's end-organ—registers light to moderate pressure
   c) Meissner's corpuscle—transduces information about sensitive touch
   d) Pacinian corpuscle—registers heavy pressure and movement of the joints

2. With respect to the development of the tactile senses, which of the following statements is *true*?
   a) Although the tactile senses are highly developed at birth, there is still substantial development in these senses for many years following birth.
   b) The tactile senses are almost fully developed at birth; there is only minimal development in these senses following birth.

   c) Although the tactile senses are poorly developed at birth, the development of these senses is virtually complete by the age of 2.
   d) The tactile senses are poorly developed at birth. The development of these senses continues for many years following birth.

Fill-in-the-Blank

1. Relative to the location of the stimulation, tactile information is processed on the _____ side of the brain; that is, it is processed _____.

2. The pain-relieving chemicals naturally produced by the nervous system belong to a class of substances called _____.

Module 27: The Auditory Sense: Hearing

As we will see, vision is the major sense, with more of the cortex devoted to vision than any other sense (Schwartz, 2010). However, the auditory sense plays a crucial role in social communication, as well as in our ability to detect danger. In addition to these clearly adaptive roles, the ability to hear enriches our lives through music and other pleasurable sounds.

27.1 From Sound Waves to Sounds

The auditory system is designed to convert sound waves, vibrations of the air, into neural impulses. **Sound waves** have two major qualities that produce our perceptions of different sounds:

- *Frequency.* The *frequency* of a sound wave refers to the number of cycles the wave completes in a certain amount of time. Frequency of a sound wave is measured in units called *Hertz* (Hz), which represent cycles per second. The frequency of a sound wave is responsible for producing the *pitch* of a sound. The crying of a baby is a high-frequency sound wave that produces a high-pitched sound. Although the range of human hearing is quite large, we hear sounds best within the range of 2,000–5,000 Hz, which encompasses the frequencies of most sounds that humans actually make, such as babies crying and people talking.
- *Amplitude.* The *amplitude* of a sound wave refers to the strength of a given cycle. Waves with higher peaks and lower bottoms are of higher amplitude than those that do not reach such extremes. The amplitude of a sound wave is responsible for our detection of *loudness*. Waves with high amplitudes produce loud sounds, while those with low amplitudes sound soft. Loudness is measured in units called *decibels* (dB).

Our detection of sound begins, of course, in the ear. Sound waves are converted to neural impulses in the ear through several steps (Hackney, 2010), as shown in **Figure 27-1**.

1. First, sound waves enter the outer ear and at its deepest part, deflect the ear drum or **tympanic membrane**.
2. Vibrations of the tympanic membrane set in motion a series of three tiny bones or **ossicles**, called the maleus (*hammer*), incus (*anvil*), and stapes (*stirrup*). The stapes, which is the last bone in the chain, hits the **oval window**, a membrane separating the ossicles and the inner ear.
3. Deflection of the oval window causes a wave to form in the fluid-filled **cochlea** of the inner ear. When fluid moves in the cochlea, it deflects the **basilar membrane** that runs down the middle of the cochlea. The basilar membrane is covered with rows of hair cells, the auditory sensory receptors. Movement of the basilar membrane bends the **hair cells** that transduce the "fluid sound wave" into electrical activity (Hackett & Kaas, 2009).
4. The hair cells communicate with nerves in the cochlea that, in turn, send the neural impulses to the brain.
5. After auditory information is transduced from sound waves by the hair cells in the basilar membrane of the cochlea, it travels as signals from nerves in the cochlea to the brainstem, the thalamus, and then the auditory cortex, which is located in the temporal lobe.

Part of the primary auditory cortex is organized in a **tonotopic map**. That is, information transmitted from different parts of the cochlea (sound waves of different frequency, and therefore sounds of different pitch) is projected to specific parts of the auditory cortex, so that our cortex maps the different pitches of sounds we hear. Auditory information from one ear is sent to the auditory cortex areas on both sides of the brain. This enables us to integrate auditory information from both sides of the head and helps us to locate the sources of sounds.

sound waves vibrations of the air in the frequency of hearing.

tympanic membrane the ear drum.

ossicles tiny bones in the ear called the maleus (*hammer*), incus (*anvil*), and stapes (*stirrup*).

oval window a membrane separating the ossicles and the inner ear, deflection of which causes a wave to form in the cochlea.

cochlea fluid-filled structure in the inner ear; contains the hair cells.

basilar membrane structure in the cochlea where the hair cells are located.

hair cells sensory receptors that convert sound waves into neural impulses.

tonotopic map representation in the auditory cortex of different sound frequencies.

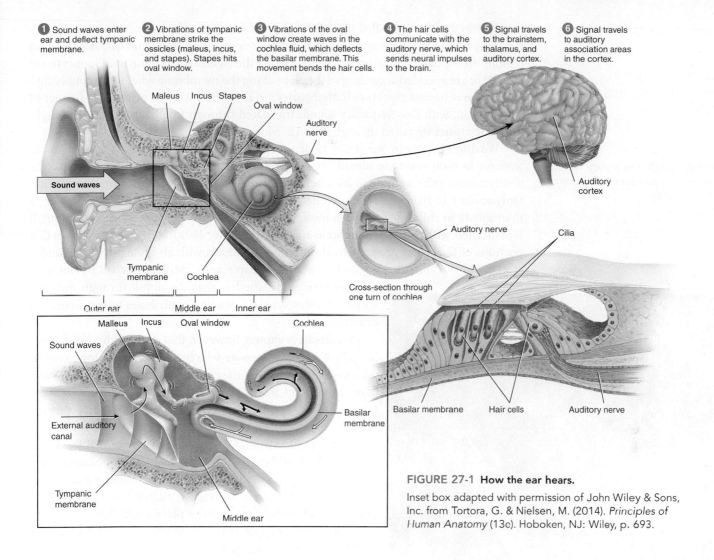

① Sound waves enter ear and deflect tympanic membrane.

② Vibrations of tympanic membrane strike the ossicles (maleus, incus, and stapes). Stapes hits oval window.

③ Vibrations of the oval window create waves in the cochlea fluid, which deflects the basilar membrane. This movement bends the hair cells.

④ The hair cells communicate with the auditory nerve, which sends neural impulses to the brain.

⑤ Signal travels to the brainstem, thalamus, and auditory cortex.

⑥ Signal travels to auditory association areas in the cortex.

FIGURE 27-1 How the ear hears.

Inset box adapted with permission of John Wiley & Sons, Inc. from Tortora, G. & Nielsen, M. (2014). *Principles of Human Anatomy* (13e). Hoboken, NJ: Wiley, p. 693.

6. From the primary auditory cortex, auditory information moves on to the auditory *association areas* in the cortex. As we described in Part 3, association areas of the brain's cortex are involved in higher-order mental processes. For example, association areas help to link the sounds we hear with parts of the brain involved in language comprehension.

Association areas also integrate or coordinate auditory information with signals from other sensory modalities. Have you ever noticed how distracting it is to watch a movie that has the audio slightly out of synchrony with the video image? This is because the brain is set up to integrate information from multiple sensory systems. Over time, we learn to have expectations about the coincidence of certain visual stimuli with specific sounds. When the sounds in a movie do not match the visual images the way they would in real life, our expectations are violated and our attention is drawn to this discrepancy from the norm.

27.2 Identifying Frequency and Pitch

There are two major theories about how the auditory system converts sound waves into all the various sounds we can perceive. The first, called *frequency theory*, suggests that different sound frequencies are converted into different rates of action potentials or firing in our auditory nerves. According to this theory, high frequency sounds produce a more rapid firing than do low-frequency sounds. Although there may be some truth to frequency theory—different firing rates contribute to sound perception of low tones—researchers agree that this theory cannot fully explain sound perception.

The second theory, called *place theory*, seems to account for a greater degree of auditory perception. Place theory holds that differences in sound frequency activate different regions on the basilar membrane. Regions along the basilar membrane send inputs to the brain that are encoded according to the place along the membrane where the inputs originated. It may be that aspects of both theories are actually at work in processing frequency information, with low-frequency sounds translated through frequency coding and high-frequency tones signalled through pitch (B. Moore, 2010; Yost, 2010).

absolute pitch the ability to recognize or produce any note on a musical scale.

We differ greatly in our ability to detect specific sounds. People show particular differences in their ability to identify certain notes in a scale. **Absolute pitch** refers to the ability to recognize an individual note in isolation. This is very difficult for most people. Only about 1 in 10,000 people in Western countries has absolute pitch. This ability seems to originate in childhood between the ages of 3 and 6 years, through musical training. It is associated with differences in brain anatomy (Zatorre, 2003). Research has shown that portions of the cortex are actually thinner in individuals with absolute pitch (Bermudez et al., 2009). Although it's not clear whether people with absolute pitch start out with a thinner cortex or whether they develop it through training, it's possible that synaptic pruning contributes to this structural difference.

WireImage/Getty Images

Absolute pitch. Singer Mariah Carey was born with absolute or perfect pitch—the ability to recognize or produce any note on a musical scale.

Studies have shown, however, that people who speak tonal languages, or languages in which differences in tone convey meaning, such as Vietnamese and Mandarin Chinese, are more likely to develop absolute pitch than those speaking Western languages. This again suggests the possibility that early learning of auditory information related to tones can have a permanent effect on the functioning of this sensory system (Liu, Xu, & Larson, 2009). Robert Zatorre at the Montreal Neurological Institute argues against this cultural conclusion, pointing out that tonal languages rely on relative pitch rather than absolute pitch. Instead, he believes genetics plays a role (Zatorre, 2003).

Just as some people exhibit absolute pitch, others are tone deaf, or unable to discern differences in pitch. Although tone deafness or *amusia* is sometimes the result of damage to the auditory system, it can be present from birth, and researchers believe it may be related to genetics (Peretz et al., 2007). Tone deafness affects up to 4 percent of the population and

Psychology Around Us — Going, Going, Gone!

Have you ever left a loud concert or club or party with a ringing in your ears? You may have had a great evening, but you have probably done irreparable damage to your hearing. In fact, hearing loss among young people in North America is on the rise, particularly in males (Zogby, 2006). Research by Robert Harrison at Toronto's Hospital for Sick Children indicates that Canadian teens listen to music that is dangerously loud (Harrison, 2008). According to a recent study, about one in five U.S. teens also has some hearing loss—an increase of about 30 percent over the past 20 years or so (Shargorodsky et al., 2010). Frequent exposure to loud music—whether live or through earphones—is largely responsible for this loss of hearing. Portable listening devices such as iPods can deliver music as loud as 100 decibels through headphones. And this is bad—very bad. Research by Jos Eggermont at the University of Calgary has shown that chronic exposure to sounds 85 decibels and above can be hazardous to your long-term auditory health (Eggermont, 2010). Although there is ample evidence suggesting that young people do not take their auditory health very seriously (Vogel et al., 2007), you need to be an exception. If you want to continue to enjoy music as you get older, you would do well to protect your hearing today. Noise-induced hearing loss is irreversible.

mostly results in a diminished appreciation for music. Although music appreciation is an important enriching ability, people with tone deafness are able to enjoy all other aspects of life. This condition only presents serious social problems when it occurs in cultures where the language is tonal.

27.3 Drowning Out the Noise

As with the other sensory systems we have discussed, adaptation also occurs in the auditory system when we are continuously exposed to sounds. We can adapt to sounds in several ways. First, our ears respond to very loud sounds by contracting muscles around the ear's opening so that less of the sound wave can enter the ear. This also happens when we talk, so that the sound of our own voice, which is so close to our ear, is not deafening.

©iStockphoto.com/Slonov

Second, the hair cells of the ear also become less sensitive to continuous noises. Unfortunately, if the noise is loud enough, it can actually damage the hair cells (Petrescu, 2008). Unlike receptors for the chemical senses, our sensory receptors in the ear are not readily replaced, so damage to the hair cells makes the ear permanently less sensitive.

Finally, the brain can filter out many sounds that are not important, even if they are relatively loud. This ability enables you to carry on a conversation with your friends at a noisy party. This phenomenon, often referred to as the *cocktail party effect*, is another example of top-down processing. The brain is able to attend to, and pick up on, relevant sounds, even in a very noisy environment. These relevant sounds, such as your name or the names of people who interest you, grab your attention and focus your auditory perception because you have previously learned their importance. So background noise, even if it's also the sounds of people talking, interferes minimally with hearing a conversation, as long as the conversation is of interest to you.

What television? This teen seems oblivious to the loud sounds coming from the television. He is concentrating on his studying while filtering out the irrelevant TV noise.

27.4 Sounds in Space

To determine the importance of a particular sound, it's necessary to localize it in space, to figure out where it is coming from. For example, if you're driving in a car and you hear the sound of an ambulance siren, you need to determine whether the ambulance is far away or close up so you can decide whether or not to pull over to the side of the road to let the ambulance pass. You also need to determine from which direction the sound is approaching. The auditory system uses several cues to help localize sound:

- *General loudness* We learn from many early experiences that loud sounds are usually closer to us than are quiet sounds, so that eventually we automatically use the loudness of a sound to assess the distance between ourselves and the source of the sound.
- *Loudness in each ear* Because of the distance between our ears and the presence of the head between our ears, there are slight differences between each ear in the loudness of the same sound wave. The ear closer to the sound hears a louder noise than the ear farther from the sound. This difference is particularly useful in detecting the location of high-frequency sounds.

George Steinmetz/Corbis

Digitized music not perfect (yet). M.I.T. professor Neil Gershenfeld and a graduate student work on project Digital Stradivarius, an attempt to build a digital model that can match the sound of the great violins of Stradivarius. When digital-produced and instrument-produced sound waves are each converted into neural impulses in the brains of musical experts, the experts can detect a difference. The instrument remains the champ.

- *Timing* Another cue used to localize sound is differences in the time at which sound waves hit each ear. Sound waves will reach the ear closer to the source of the sound before they reach the ear farther away. Since the ears are separated in space, a sound wave will also hit each ear at a slightly different part of its wave cycle, creating a phase difference. This cue is particularly useful to us in localizing sounds with low frequencies.

We also adjust our heads and bodies to assess the location of sounds. These movements allow us to hear how the sound changes while we're in different positions and to use those changes to help make a reasonable approximation of its location. Finally, the use of other sensory systems, such as vision, may come into play. For instance, you might confirm the location of the ambulance when you look into your rearview mirror and see it approaching.

27.5 Development of Hearing

Our ears are formed and are capable of transducing sound waves before we are even born. In fact, human fetuses have been shown to respond to noises long before birth. Research has shown that fetuses respond to loud noises with a startle reflex, and that after birth, they are capable of recognizing some sounds they heard while in utero. Sound conduction is inefficient at birth, but the ability to recognize and respond appropriately to a wide variety of sound stimuli is acquired in the first few months (Saffran et al., 2006). Infants prefer speech sounds to non-speech sounds (Vouloumanos, 2010) and prefer their mother's voice to other voices. We describe language development in more detail in Part 9.

Sensitive periods exist for the development of both language and music learning (Knudson, 2004). As we described in Part 4, we acquire certain abilities during sensitive periods of development much more easily than we do after the sensitive period has ended. The tonotopic map in the primary auditory cortex of the brain is organized during such a sensitive period of development (de Villers-Sidani et al., 2007). Experiments with animals have shown that exposing animals to pure tones during a certain time in development leads to a larger representation of those sounds in the auditory cortex. The same exposure after the sensitive period in development is over has no such effect. If a sound is made important to the animal, however, by pairing it either with a reward, such as water, or a punishment, such as an electric shock, the primary auditory cortex can be reorganized so that more of it responds to the relevant tone (Bakin et al., 1996). Such top-down processing of tones indicates that this region of the brain still shows plasticity after the sensitive period is over. However, it is not as easy to remap the brain after a sensitive period as it is during one. The stimuli needed to produce changes in older animals must be very strong and important compared to those needed for younger animals (Kuboshima & Sawaguchi, 2007).

Gareth Brown/Corbis

A bit too early. A pregnant woman tries to introduce music to her fetus by positioning headphones on her stomach. Although fetuses do indeed respond to loud noises and can detect certain sounds, the acquisition of musical skills cannot take place until sensitive periods unfold during the preschool years.

27.6 Hearing Loss

FACING ADVERSITY

Based on the above discussion of the auditory system, you might be able to predict the two major causes of deafness. One, called *conduction deafness*, occurs when there is some sort of occlusion or break in the various processes by which sound is transmitted through the inner ear. Wax buildup, infection, ear drum damage, or water in the ear can cause temporary or permanent deafness. *Nerve deafness* results from damage or malformations of the auditory nerve in the brain. All congenital (from birth) incidents of deafness are of this second type.

There are many conditions that lead to abnormalities in the auditory system. Some cause either partial or total **deafness**, the loss of hearing. Some deafness occurs after a period of hearing, while some who are deaf have never heard sound. Deafness has a variety of causes. It can be genetic or caused by infection, physical trauma, or exposure to toxins, including overdose of common medications such as aspirin. Abnormalities in the auditory system can also add unwanted auditory perceptions.

deafness loss or lack of hearing.

Since speech is an important mode of communication for humans, deafness can have dramatic consequences for socialization. This is a particular concern for children, because young children need auditory stimulation to develop normal spoken language skills. For this reason, physicians try to identify auditory deficits at an early life stage. Auditory deficits range from those with limited hearing to those who are profoundly deaf. Many deaf individuals learn to use sign language. There are hundreds of sign languages worldwide. *American Sign Language (ASL)* is the predominant sign language used in the United States and in English-speaking Canada, whereas French Canadians use *Quebec Sign Language* or *Langue des signes québécoise (LSQ)*. Sign languages have their own vocabulary, phonology, and grammatical structure.

Research has also made progress in the construction of cochlear implants that help individuals with deafness to hear sounds (Sharma et al., 2009). Although this work is developing at a rapid pace, there remain many deaf people who are not helped by cochlear implants, particularly adults who never learned to process sound as children (Battmer et al., 2009). This is one reason why many individuals and families choose to avoid them. As well, some in the deaf community also believe that hearing is not necessary to lead a productive and fulfilling life. For them, the potential benefits of implants may not outweigh the potential risks of surgery required to place them in the cochlea (Hyde & Power, 2006).

Landov

A world of new possibilities. After undergoing successful cochlear implant surgery, this 4-year-old child practises the violin under the instruction of his music teacher at the Memphis Oral School for the Deaf.

Some individuals are troubled by annoying sounds rather than hearing loss. About 1 of every 200 people is affected by *tinnitus*, or ringing in the ear. Tinnitus has multiple causes, some of which are related to abnormalities in the ear itself (Lanting et al., 2009). Some people are able to cope with the noise, but some find it too loud and distracting to ignore. Patients with epilepsy in the temporal cortex have reported the perception of hearing complex auditory stimuli, such as a musical tune (Wieser, 2003). This symptom, which can be completely distracting and disturbing to the patient, is the result of abnormal electrical activity in brain circuits that store complex auditory memories.

> "I have unwittingly helped to invent and refine a type of music that makes its principal exponents deaf. Hearing loss is a terrible thing because it cannot be repaired."
>
> —*Pete Townshend, rock musician of the band The Who*

Before You Go On

www.wiley.com/go/comercanada

What Do You Know?
1. What happens in the ear to transduce sound waves into neural signals?
2. What is a tonotopic map?
3. What are sensitive periods and how are they important for hearing?
4. What is tinnitus?

What Do You Think? How might researchers develop an effective program that would get adolescents and young people to be more aware of and cautious about chronic exposure to loud music?

Summary

Module 27: The Auditory Sense: Hearing

LEARNING OBJECTIVE 27 Summarize what happens when we hear.

- The frequency and amplitude of sound waves produce our perceptions of pitch and loudness of sounds.
- When sounds enter the ear, they move the ear drum, which sets in motion the ossicles. The last of these, the stirrup, vibrates the oval window, setting into motion fluid in the cochlea. Hair cells on the basilar membrane in the cochlea transduce movements along the basilar membrane into neural signals the brain can interpret.
- Frequency theory suggests that patterns in the firing rates of the neurons are perceived as different sounds. Place theory suggests that information from different locations along the basilar membrane is related to different qualities of sound.
- Top-down processing lets us use the general loudness of sounds, as well as differences in the signals received from each ear, to determine location of a sound.
- Different pitches are represented in a tonotopic map in the auditory cortex of the brain. Association areas of the cortex help us recognize familiar sounds, including speech.
- The brain integrates information from multiple sensory systems to enable the appropriate recognition and response to stimuli. Some people experience an overlap of sensory systems, known as synesthesia.
- As young children, we experience a sensitive period during which it is especially easy for us to learn auditory information, including language and music. Some people, particularly those exposed to pure tones during this sensitive period, develop absolute pitch.
- Common hearing problems include hearing loss and deafness, as well as hearing unwanted sounds, such as tinnitus.

Key Terms

absolute pitch 202	hair cells 200	tonotopic map 200
basilar membrane 200	ossicles 200	tympanic membrane 200
cochlea 200	oval window 200	
deafness 205	sound waves 200	

Study Questions

Multiple Choice

1. Which theory of audition states that different frequencies are converted into different rates of action potentials in our auditory nerves?
   a) Tonotopic
   b) Place
   c) Frequency
   d) Association

2. What cues are used to localize sound?
   a) loudness in each ear
   b) timing
   c) adjusting our heads
   d) all of the above

Fill-in-the-Blank

1. When we describe the "loudness" of a sound, we are referring to its _____.

Module 28: The Visual Sense: Sight

The ability to see and make sense of the visual world around us plays a very important role in human life. We use vision in virtually all of our activities. Vision is especially important for non-verbal communication, where facial expressions and body language are used to convey information that is often lost in spoken language alone. Have you ever experienced a misunderstanding over text or email because, without non-verbal facial and body cues accompanying your message, the receiver misunderstood what you were trying to say? No doubt related to its importance to us, the visual sense is particularly well-developed in humans. Some estimates suggest that about half of the cerebral cortex of our brains is devoted to processing some type of visual stimuli (Grady, 1993).

As we have seen, each sensory system is most receptive to some form of physical energy. Taste and smell respond to chemical stimuli, touch to changes in temperature or pressure, and hearing to vibrating air molecules (sound waves). The stimulus for vision is electromagnetic radiation, which produces light. Light is made up of particles called *photons*. The light that we can see is part of the electromagnetic spectrum of energy that also includes many forms we cannot see, such as X-rays and radio waves. Like sound, light travels in waves. The visible spectrum of light ranges from about 400 to 700 nanometres in wavelength (a nanometre is a billionth of a metre). As shown in **Figure 28-1**, different wavelengths within our visible spectrum appear to us as different colours. Objects in the world absorb and reflect light in varying levels and patterns—those that reflect more light are perceived as brighter.

LEARNING OBJECTIVE 28
Describe key processes in visual sensation and perception.

28.1 Seeing the Lights

Vision begins when light enters the eye, as shown in **Figure 28-2**. Muscles in the iris—the coloured part of the eye—adjust the size of our pupils to let in more or less of the light reflected from objects around us. Muscles also adjust the shape of the lens, enabling it to bring both near and far objects into focus. The lens therefore serves to focus the light that enters the eye onto a specialized multi-layered sheet of nerve cells in the back of the eye, called the **retina**. If the lens of the eye cannot quite manage the task of focusing light, it can be assisted by glasses or contact lenses, or it can sometimes be reshaped by laser surgery so that it can do its job of focusing light onto the retina. The retina is an extension of the brain and is where light produces chemical changes that in turn produce a neural signal.

retina a specialized sheet of nerve cells in the back of the eye containing the sensory receptors for vision.

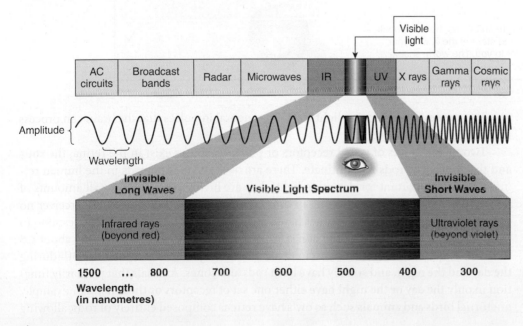

FIGURE 28-1 **Visible light and the electromagnetic spectrum.** The part of the electromagnetic spectrum that our visual receptors can detect is restricted to a narrow range. Source: Reprinted with permission of John Wiley & Sons, Inc. from Huffman, K. (2009). *Psychology in Action* (9e). Hoboken, NJ. Wiley, Figure 4.4, p. 138.

FIGURE 28-2 **How the eye sees.**

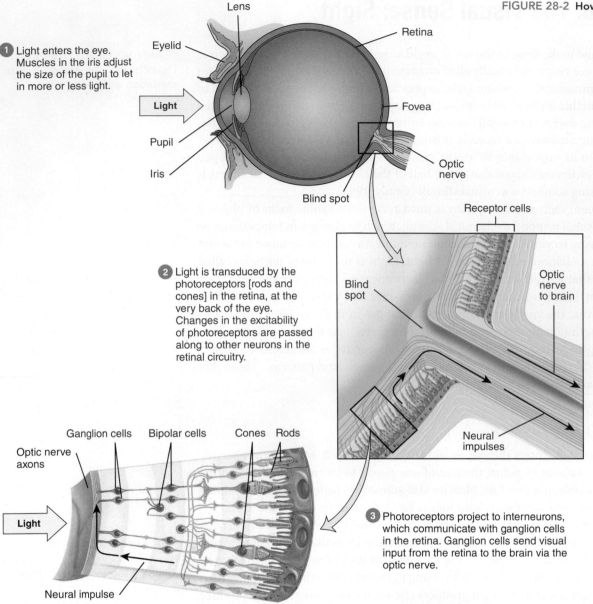

1 Light enters the eye. Muscles in the iris adjust the size of the pupil to let in more or less light.

2 Light is transduced by the photoreceptors [rods and cones] in the retina, at the very back of the eye. Changes in the excitability of photoreceptors are passed along to other neurons in the retinal circuitry.

3 Photoreceptors project to interneurons, which communicate with ganglion cells in the retina. Ganglion cells send visual input from the retina to the brain via the optic nerve.

Find your blind spot

The blind spot is not normally noticeable. To find yours, hold this book about a foot away, close your right eye, and stare at the X with your left eye. Very slowly, bring the book closer to you. The worm should disappear and the apple become whole.

transduction process that involves converting stimulus energy into neural impulses that can be interpreted by the brain.

photoreceptors the sensory receptor cells for vision, located in the retina.

rods photoreceptors most responsive to levels of light and dark.

cones photoreceptors responsive to colours.

This process of converting light waves into neural impulses that the brain can process is known as **transduction**.

Two major classes of visual receptors or **photoreceptors** exist in the retina, the **rods** and the **cones**. The rods predominate. There are over 100 million rods in the human retina. Rods are important for detecting light; they are highly sensitive to small amounts of light and are critical for functioning in dim light or at night. Rods give the perceiver no colour sensation. Cones, on the other hand, are colour receptors because they respond to light of different wavelengths. The cones are much fewer in number, with only about 4.5 to 6 million per human retina (Curcio et al., 1990). People have to function both during the day and the night, and so they have both rods and cones. Animals that primarily function in only the day or the night have either one set of receptors or the other. For example, nocturnal birds and animals such as owls have retinas composed entirely of rods, allowing them to survive in very low light conditions. Conversely, diurnal birds and animals such as the pigeon or chipmunk have only cones in the retina, allowing them to function effectively in a richly-coloured environment under optimal light conditions (Dossenbach & Dossenbach, 1998).

When light reaches the photoreceptors, a series of chemical reactions take place. The rods and cones stimulate the bipolar cells that, in turn, cause ganglion cells to then fire. The axons of almost one million ganglion cells are bundled together to form the **optic nerve**. Signals from the ganglion cells travel along the optic nerve out of the eye and into the brain. The location where the optic nerve leaves the retina is therefore completely lacking in rods and cones and is called the *blind spot*, or *optic disc*. This means that when light strikes that area of the retina, there are no visual receptor cells to respond to it. Although there are no receptor cells in this area, you do not experience a "hole" in the visual field because the brain fills in the incomplete image. Also, the blind spot in each eye is offset, so that missing information from one eye is replaced by the other. With some manipulation of the visual input shown in Figure 28-2, however, you can identify your blind spot.

Rods and cones are not evenly distributed throughout the retina. Cones are concentrated more in the centre than the periphery of the retina. The **fovea**, the region of the retina where our vision is at its sharpest, is entirely made up of cones. Rods are distributed throughout the rest of the retina and, unlike cones, are concentrated at the peripheral edges of the retina. Have you ever noticed that your peripheral vision is not particularly acute? It mostly enables you to detect movement, but not necessarily details. This is due to that fact that rods dominate the peripheral parts of the retina.

Like the other sensory systems we previously discussed, the visual system also undergoes sensory adaptation. Dilation and constriction of the pupil, the opening in the centre of the iris, is one way that the visual system adapts to light. When you go from inside your home to outside on a bright, sunny day, you may immediately feel the need to squint and shade your eyes. Your eyes quickly adapt to the brighter light, however, in part by constriction of the pupil that decreases the amount of light entering the eye. Conversely, to allow vision to occur in dark places, such as when you first enter a dark movie theatre, the pupil will open further to let in more light.

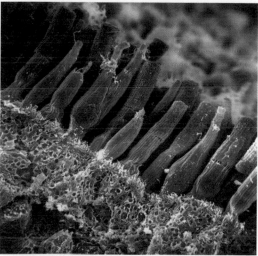

Omikron/Photo Researchers

The photoreceptors. This colourized scanning electron micrograph shows the retina's photoreceptors—the rods and cones—which help pass visual signals through the optic nerve to the brain. Rods (pink) are the photoreceptors that detect light. Cones (olive) are photoreceptors that detect wavelength, creating the perception of colour.

optic nerve the bundle of axons of ganglion cells that carries visual information from the eye to the brain.

fovea centre of the retina, containing only cones, where vision is most clear.

28.2 Seeing in Colour

As we noted earlier, cones enable us to see colour. In fact, colour exists only in the brain. An object reflects a particular wavelength, which is then detected by the cones, creating chemical changes that in turn generate a neural signal. This signal is processed by the brain, giving rise to the sensation of colour. How does the brain experience so many colours? The experience of colour can be described along three dimensions: hue, saturation, and brightness. The variety of colours we can perceive is related to the different combinations of these three characteristics. In fact, using these three dimensions it has been estimated that humans can detect about seven million different colours (Geldard, 1972). Not surprisingly, people can only name a small subset of these colours!

- *Hue* refers to the experience of colour based on the wavelength of light that the visual stimulus emits or reflects. This is the most basic aspect of colour, whether the stimulus is perceived as red, green, orange, blue, yellow, or some other colour.
- *Saturation* refers to the purity of a colour; that is, how bright or vivid the colour appears. If a colour is desaturated, it has white or grey mixed into it. For example, a pure red would be saturated, pink would be more desaturated, and grey would be completely desaturated (i.e., zero saturation).
- *Brightness* of a colour refers to how much light emanates or is reflected from the visual stimulus (light intensity). White is considered to be the brightest colour and black the least bright.

28.2.1 Theories of Colour Perception

No single theory yet entirely explains how we perceive colour. Two theories of colour vision in combination help to explain a good deal, however. One theory, first hypothesized in the nineteenth century, is the *Young-Helmholtz trichromatic theory* of colour vision. This theory maintains that there are three different receptors for colour and that each type of receptor responds to a different range of wavelengths of light (Balaraman, 1962). This theory is largely correct, in that people with normal colour vision have three receptor types (cones), each maximally sensitive to a particular wavelength (colour). One receptor type responds to yellowish-red wavelengths, another to green wavelengths, and the third to bluish-purple wavelengths. Why is it that we can see more than three colours if we only have three receptor types? Typically, at least two cone types will respond to a certain wavelength of visible light, but in varying increments. The combination of the signals produced by cones is what enables the brain to respond to such a multitude of colours.

Steven Senne/AP

Changing one's view. These two people at the Sensorium museum exhibit at M.I.T. wear wireless head gear that causes each of them to view the world from the visual perspective of the other. You eventually adjust to this visual manipulation, but for a while it interferes with many aspects of visual functioning, including shape, light, and colour perceptions; activity in visual regions of the brain; depth perception; and perceptual constancies.

Another nineteenth century theorist, Hering, proposed an alternative theory about colour vision called *opponent process theory* (Buchsbaum & Gottschalk, 1983). Opponent process theory maintains that colour pairs work to inhibit one another in the perception of colour. In the retinal ganglion cells, as well as the thalamus and visual cortex, colour information is analyzed in terms of antagonistic opponent colour pairs: red–green, yellow–blue, and black–white. The hypothesis of antagonistic colour-pairings is supported by the observation that we cannot mix certain combinations of colours. For example, we cannot see reddish green or bluish yellow, but we can see greenish yellow or bluish red. Opponent processing is the result of activity in a region of the thalamus that receives visual information, called the *lateral geniculate nucleus*. Inputs to this nucleus from one colour of an opposing pair inhibit those from the other colour in the pair. For example, some neurons here are turned on (excited) by red and off for green (inhibited). Other neurons are turned off by red and on for green, and so on for the other opponent pairs (DeValois & DeValois, 1975).

You can observe opponent processing at work by staring at the white dot in the middle of the green and black flag in **Figure 28-3**. After about 30 seconds, stare at a white sheet of paper. You will see a negative *afterimage* that is red and white.

The term "negative" is used to acknowledge that the afterimage is the opposite colour of the original image. This also works with other colours in the opponent pairs. A white-on-black image will produce a black-on-white afterimage, and a yellow image will produce a blue afterimage. Afterimages happen when one colour in an opponent pair inhibits the other. When we release this inhibition by looking away from the first colour, the previously inhibited colour overcompensates and creates an image in the opponent colour.

About 1 in 12 men and 1 in 200 women have some form of colour blindness. Most people (99 percent) who have what is called *colour blindness* are unable to distinguish certain colours (more accurately called *colour vision deficiency* or *CVD*). These individuals are not really blind to colour, but instead fail to see the same range of colours as individuals with normal vision. Only 1 in about 33,000 people, those who are *monochromatic*, are actually unable to see any colours at all and instead see a black and white and grey view of the world (Wong, 2011). The most common form of colour deficiency is red–green colour blindness, which is tested with images, such as the one shown in

FIGURE 28-3 The negative afterimage effect. Afterimages occur because one colour in an opponent pair is fatigued when it is viewed for a sustained period of time. When you look away from the first colour, the previously inhibited colour is activated. To see opponent processing in action, stare at the white dot in the centre of the leaf for about 30 seconds, then look away at a white sheet of paper. Reprinted with permission of John Wiley & Sons Canada, Ltd., from Huffman, 2013. *Visualizing Psychology* (2nd Canadian ed.). Toronto: Wiley, p. 119.

Figure 28-4. Studies suggest that people with this problem have a shortage of cones that respond to either the greenish or reddish wavelengths and therefore have what is more accurately called a *colour weakness*. In these cases people mix up all colours that have some red or green as part of the colour. For example, a person with red–green colour blindness might mix up a shade of blue with a shade of purple because they would have difficulty "seeing" the red in the purple colour (Carlson, 2007). Colour blindness is typically inherited but can also be acquired through diseases, medication, or aging (Tovee, 2008).

In sum, trichromacy theory and opponent process theory are not in conflict and can be used together to create a successive physiological two-stage model of colour vision. In stage one, the cones in the retina respond to three primary wavelengths and send signals to the visual cortex. Along the way, in stage two, the signal is processed by opponent process cells. The result? Colour.

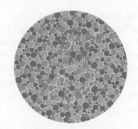

FIGURE 28-4 **Colour blindness.** People with red–green colour blindness would see only a random pattern of dots in this figure.

28.3 The Brain and Sight

Visual information leaving the retina travels via the optic nerve to neurons in the *superior colliculus*, and then communicates with the thalamus. From the thalamus, visual input travels to the primary visual cortex, located in the occipital lobe.

Basic visual information is transmitted throughout the brain via a partially-crossed set of axons (**Figure 28-5**). Visual information from the middle part of your visual field, closest to your nose, is sent, via axons that cross to the other side of your brain, to the opposite side of your visual cortex. Visual information from the lateral part of your visual field, closest to your temples, travels to the same side of the visual cortex.

WHAT HAPPENS
in the BRAIN?

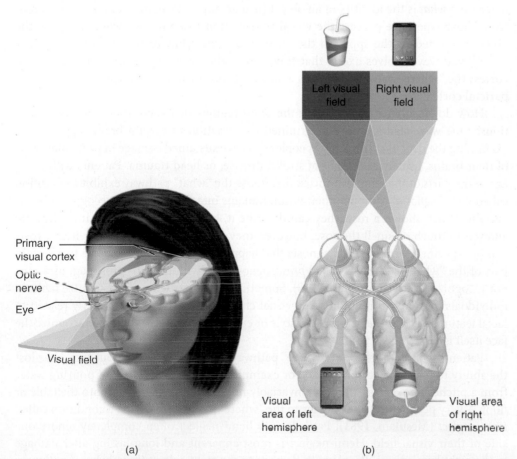

FIGURE 28-5 **The crossed visual pathway.** Before entering the brain, the optic nerves partially cross. Visual information from the middle part of your visual field travels to opposite sides of your visual cortex, while information from the lateral part of the field (closest to your temples) travels to the same side of the visual cortex.

Primary visual cortex

Optic nerve

Eye

Visual field

Left visual field

Right visual field

Visual area of left hemisphere

Visual area of right hemisphere

(a)

(b)

FIGURE 28-6. **The "what" and "where" pathways.** The "what" pathway of the brain processes information that helps us identify an object, while the "where" pathway helps us identify its location in space. Communication between the two pathways allows us to integrate complex visual stimuli.

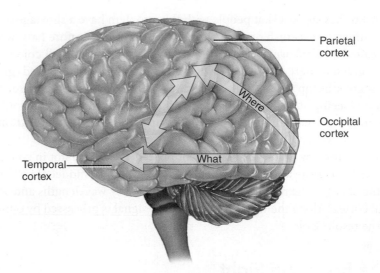

Prosopagnosia. People with prosopagnosia would see others like this and would need to recognize their friends by features other than their face—like their hat or hair, perhaps.

Once visual information reaches the primary visual cortex, it is processed to enable the detection of very simple features, such as lines and edges (Hubel & Wiesel, 1959). However, we don't see the world as a collection of lines and edges. Instead, we see a rich set of complex visual stimuli that change as we and the world around us move. Detection of complex visual stimuli occurs as a result of circuitry that involves association areas of visual cortex. Recall from our discussion of hearing that association areas are involved with higher-order processes of perception: thinking and memory.

The pathways that process information about complex visual stimuli can be roughly divided into the "*what*" and the "*where*" pathways, as shown in **Figure 28-6** (Ungerleider & Haxby, 1994). That is, the regions that process visual information to help us determine *what* is the identity of an object (is it an apple, a car, or a house) are different from those where we process the visual information to figure out *where* in space the object is located (is the apple on the table, under the table, or behind the table). The "what" pathway involves axons that travel from the occipital cortex to the temporal cortex; the "where" pathway involves axons that travel from the occipital cortex to the parietal cortex.

How do researchers know about the brain regions that serve these complex functions? One way scientists have determined the function of certain brain regions is by examining the deficits displayed by people who have sustained damage in particular areas of their brains, usually as a result of stroke, disease, or head trauma. Patients with damage to the parts of the temporal cortex that house the "what" pathway exhibit a condition called *visual agnosia*. Although their vision remains intact, they cannot recognize objects visually. When shown a rose, they can describe it, but they cannot name it. If they are allowed to touch or smell the rose, however, they can immediately identify it as a rose. A more specified form of visual agnosia that happens to people with damage to a certain part of the "what" pathway is called *prosopagnosia*. Individuals with prosopagnosia cannot recognize faces (Farah et al., 1995). Sometimes these patients can recognize familiar individuals by concentrating on some visual characteristic that is not directly related to facial features, such as the person's hairstyle or eyeglasses, but their ability to recognize the face itself is lost (Sacks, 1985).

Patients with damage to the "where" pathway have normal vision, but they have lost the ability to locate objects in space. For example, when given the task of pouring water from a pitcher into a glass, they will invariably miss and pour the water onto the table or floor. A very peculiar form of damage to the "where" pathway results in a condition called *hemi-neglect* (Mesulam, 1981). Patients with hemi-neglect often completely ignore one side of their visual field. Hemi-neglect is most apparent and long-lasting after damage to the right hemisphere. People with damage to the right side of their "where" pathways neglect the left side of their visual field. For example, when asked to copy a drawing, people with hemi-neglect will leave out one half of it (**Figure 28-7**). People with this condition have been known to apply makeup to only one side of their face, to shave only one side of their face, and to eat food on only one side of their plate (Corbetta et al., 2005; Corbetta & Shulman, 2002).

In addition to the information researchers have gained from studying patients with brain damage, neuroimaging studies of people without brain damage have confirmed the presence of the "what" and "where" pathways. Indeed, these types of studies have shown that brain activity changes in specific parts of the "what" pathways when the participants are viewing objects (Reddy & Kanwisher, 2006).

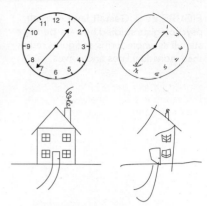

FIGURE 28-7 **Seeing only half the picture.** When asked to copy a drawing of a clock and a house, a patient with hemi-neglect copies only the right side of each image. She ignores the left side of her visual field.

28.4 Visual Perceptual Organization: From the Top Down

So far we have discussed vision from a bottom-up perspective. Light comes in through the eye and the neural impulses generated are passed to successively more complex brain regions that ultimately result in the perception of a visual stimulus. Equally important to visual perception, however, is *top-down processing*, which involves previously acquired knowledge. Like perception involving the other sensory systems, visual perception involves both bottom-up and top-down processing occurring at the same time. Brain regions that store information about what objects look like can help us to perceive visual stimuli that are partially hidden or of a different size from when we originally encountered them.

28.4.1 Putting Together the Parts: Gestalt Principles

We don't see images as a series of small patches of colour or a series of simple features. Instead, our visual system assembles this information into coherent objects and scenes. Even when we see a small part of an object or scene partially obscured by another object, we are able to perceive it as a whole, given limited visual information. Our brains are organized to fill in the missing parts so that we perceive and recognize meaningful stimuli. As we described earlier, part of our ability to perceive images comes from our use of cognitive processes, such as memory and learning, to help us recall images from prior experience that match the stimuli we are sensing.

The area of study focused on understanding principles by which we perceive and recognize visual stimuli in their entirety despite limited information is called *Gestalt* psychology. As mentioned in Part 1, Gestalt psychologists believe that perception helps us to add meaning to visual information by attempting to organize information into groups, so that the whole is more than the sum of its parts. As Kurt Koffka pointed out, though, "*It is more correct to say that the whole is something else than the sum of its parts, because summing up is a meaningless procedure, whereas the whole-part relationship is meaningful*" (Koffka, 1935, p. 176). Gestalt psychologists have identified several laws by which visual information is organized into coherent images; a few of these laws are listed below (see also **Figure 28-8**):

- *Figure Ground* perception is used to identify whether something in the visual field is the main object or the background. Illusions, or unstable perception, can be created when the figure and the background are interchangeable. The figure is generally perceived to be closer than the background.
- *Proximity* The law of proximity indicates that visual stimuli near to one another tend to be grouped together. For example, AA AA AA is seen as three groups, while AAA AAA is seen as two groups, despite the fact that each set has six As.
- *Continuity* The law of continuity indicates that stimuli falling along the same plane tend to be grouped together. $_{AAA}$ ^{AAA} would be organized into two perceptual groups because they are not on the same line.
- *Closure* The law of closure indicates that we tend to fill in small gaps in objects so that they are still perceived as whole objects.
- *Similarity* The law of similarity indicates that stimuli resembling one another tend to be grouped together. So AAaa is viewed as two groups because of the dissimilar appearance of upper and lowercase letters.

FIGURE 28-8 **Gestalt laws.** Gestalt psychologists studied how we perceive stimuli as whole forms or figures rather than individual lines and curves.

Figure Ground:
The tendency to perceive one aspect as the figure and the other as the background. You see a vase or two faces, but not both at the same time.

Proximity:
Objects that are physically close together are grouped together. (In this figure, we see 3 groups of 6 hearts, not 18 separate hearts.)

Continuity:
Objects that continue a pattern are grouped together.

When we see this,

we normally see this

plus this.

Not this.

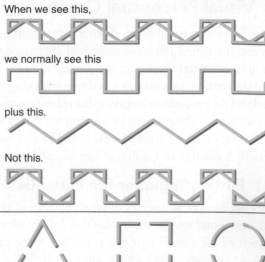

Closure:
The tendency to see a finished unit (triangle, square, or circle) from an incomplete stimulus.

Similarity:
Similar objects are grouped together (the green coloured dots are grouped together and perceived as the number 5).

These laws of visual organization put together all the "pieces" of visual stimuli to complete a "puzzle" to build meaningful information from everything we see when we look at something. Sometimes, however, the fact that our brain tends to create order among the things we are seeing can lead us to perceive sights that are illusions, such as the one shown in **Figure 28-9**. If you look closely, you can see that the drawing depicts a situation that is simply physically impossible. Although parts of the drawing are reasonable, they cannot be combined to create a meaningful holistic figure (Macpherson, 2010).

28.4.2 Getting in Deep: Binocular and Monocular Cues

When you look at the items on the table in a restaurant, how do you know which items are closer to you and which are farther away? We use a number of methods for depth perception, determining the distance of objects away from us and in relation to one another.

Because our eyes are set a slight distance apart, we do not see exactly the same thing with each eye. This **retinal disparity**, the slightly different stimuli recorded by the retina of each eye, provides us with a *binocular* cue of depth (**Figure 28-10**). Our brains use the discrepancies between the visual information received from our two eyes to help us judge the distance of objects from us. You can observe your own retinal disparity by holding up a finger at arm's length away from your face. Close first one eye, then the other, and note how the position of your finger seems to change relative to objects in the background beyond the finger.

retinal disparity the slight difference in images processed by the retinas of each eye.

FIGURE 28-9 **Impossible figure.** The brain is organized to perceive meaningful images; with impossible figures such as this, the brain tries but cannot form a stable perception. How many legs does this elephant have?

(a)

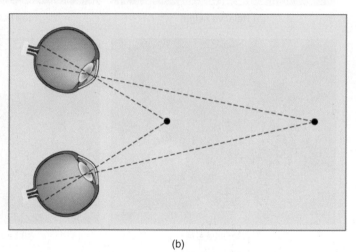

(b)

FIGURE 28-10 **Retinal disparity.** (a) Stare at your two index fingers a few centimetres in front of your eyes, holding the tips about half a centimetre apart. Do you see the "floating finger"? Move your fingers farther away and the finger will shrink. Move them closer and it will enlarge. (b) Because of retinal disparity, objects at different distances project their images on different parts of the retina. Far objects project on the retinal area near the nose, whereas near objects project farther out, closer to the ears.

Another binocular cue to depth is actually tactile. We feel the changes in the muscles around our eyes as we shift them to look at objects at various distances. Closer objects require more convergence, turning our eyes inward toward our noses. Use your finger again to demonstrate **convergence**. Start with the finger at arm's length from you and watch it as you bring it closer and closer to your face. Note the sensations you feel as you do so.

convergence inward movement of the eyes to view objects close to oneself.

In addition to these binocular cues, we also use a number of other cues to determine depth (Schiller et al., 2011). The following are sometimes called **monocular cues**, because, if needed, they can help us judge depth based on information from only one eye. Examples of each of the monocular cues described below can be viewed in **Figure 28-11**.

monocular cues visual clues about depth and distance that can be perceived using information from only one eye.

- *Interposition* When one object blocks part of another from our view, we see the blocked object as farther away.
- *Relative height (elevation)* We see objects that are higher in our visual plane as farther away than those that are lower in the visual plane.
- *Texture gradient* We see more details of textured surfaces, such as the veins in leaves, when the object is closer to us. Thus the finer (less detailed or distinct) the view of the textured object, the farther away we assume it to be.
- *Linear perspective* Parallel lines seem to get closer together (or converge) as they recede, creating the illusion of depth or distance. That is, we know that the lines remain parallel and therefore perceive the appearance of convergence as a cue to distance.

FIGURE 28-11 **Monocular cues.**

(a) Relative height

(b) Texture gradient

(c) Relative size

(d) Linear perspective

- *Light and shadow* We use light as a cue to distance. Objects that are bright are perceived as closer, whereas objects that are dark, or shaded, appear farther away. As well, we are accustomed to light, such as sunlight, coming from above us. We therefore use differences in shading to judge size and distance of objects.
- *Clarity or aerial perspective* We tend to see closer objects with more clarity than objects that are farther away. This is also sometimes referred to as a fog or smog effect.
- *Familiar size* Once we have learned the sizes of objects, such as people or buildings or trees, we assume that they stay the same size, so objects that look smaller than usual must be farther away than usual.
- *Relative size* When we look at two objects we know are about the same size, if one seems smaller than the other, we see the smaller object as farther away.
- *Motion parallax* This monocular depth cue requires that the observer be moving. Here the relative movement of objects that are stationary against their background gives us an idea about their relative distance. For example, if we look out the side window of a moving vehicle, objects that are closer to us appear to move past us more quickly than do objects that are farther away (and very distant objects, like mountains, sometimes do not appear to move at all).

Wasserman & Partners Advertising

Pavement Patty. Would seeing this on the road ahead slow you down? The British Columbia Automobile Association (BCAA) Traffic Safety Foundation and West Vancouver District had an artist design a decal that when applied flat on the road creates a three-dimensional image of what appears to be a child on the road. The image of "Pavement Patty," which plays with our two-dimensional depth cues, really made drivers slow down during its week on the road.

Although some studies show that we can perceive depth at very early ages, and may even be born with some depth perception abilities, top-down processing also plays a part in depth processing (Banks & Salapatek, 1983). We use our memories of the sizes of objects around us, for example, to help judge depth.

Artists use monocular depth cues to help us "see" depth in their two-dimensional representations. In essence, they create an illusion of depth. Because visual perception happens nearly automatically, we are quite susceptible to such visual illusions. For example, people from cultures that have a lot of architecture and structures featuring straight edges, such as Canada and the U.S., are easily fooled by the Ponzo illusion and Müller-Lyer illusion, shown in **Figure 28-12**, which both take advantage of our tendency to use linear perspective to judge distance (Masuda, 2010; Berry, 1992).

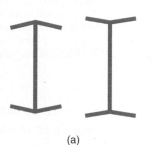
©iStockphoto.com/WendellandCarolyn

(a)   (b)

FIGURE 28-12 Perceptual illusions. (a) The Müller-Lyer illusion: The line on the right appears longer, but both lines are the same length.

(b) The Ponzo illusion: The converging lines make the upper bar seem larger, but both bars are identical in length.

28.4.3 Seeing What We Expect to See: Perceptual Constancies

Top-down processing also contributes to **perceptual constancies**, our tendency to view objects as unchanging in some ways, even though the actual visual sensations we receive are constantly shifting (Goldstein, 2010). We tend to see the food on our plate as the same colours, for example, even when a restaurant owner dims the lights for the evening and the actual light waves we are receiving change in intensity, a phenomenon known as *colour constancy* (Schiffman, 1996).

perceptual constancies our top-down tendency to view objects as unchanging, despite shifts in the environmental stimuli we receive.

Another constancy, *size constancy*, helps us in depth perception, as noted above. Once we have learned the size of an object, we expect it to stay the same. Top-down processing, based on our memory of the object's size, leads us to assume that if it looks smaller than usual, it is probably far away, instead of thinking that the object has somehow shrunk. As with our other perceptual processes, perceptual constancies, while usually very useful in helping us understand the world, can sometimes lead us to "see" illusions. A common size illusion, for example, is the moon illusion. The moon stays the same size all the time, but when we view it close to a horizon, it appears much bigger than when we see it farther from the horizon; the landscapes and objects we are viewing the moon through strip away some of the size constancy effect and we see the moon as larger (Kaufman & Rock, 1989).

©iStockphoto.com/stephaniki2

The moon illusion. The moon is the same size all the time, but it appears larger near the horizon than higher in the sky, partly because no depth cues exist in space.

Department of Tourism & Parks, New Brunswick, Canada

Sometimes what we expect is not what we get. Magnetic Hill near Moncton, New Brunswick, creates an odd impression. Which way would you expect this car to roll if it is placed in neutral and its brakes released? It looks like it should roll away from the camera, but in fact it would roll back toward the camera. The explanation has nothing to do with magnetism, but is rather an optical illusion created by the landscape suggesting that the hill runs the opposite of the way it is actually sloped. See a video version here: www.youtube.com/watch?v=F3jDOFelogg&feature=related.

Once we have formed expectations about the shape of an object, we also experience *shape constancy* (Gazzaniga, 1995a). We may get visual input of only the edge of a plate as our server carries it toward us, for example, but we perceive the plate as a round disk. A famous illusion based on both shape and size constancy involves the Ames room, shown in **Figure 28-13**. The person on the right-hand side looks huge compared with the one on the left. Why? First, we expect the room to be square, but it actually is irregularly shaped. Second, because we think the room is square, we believe that both people are the same distance from us, leading us to perceive one as much larger than the other. You may notice that even when you know how this illusion works, the people's respective sizes don't look right—indicating how strongly our expectations affect our perception. A number of Ames room sets were built for the *Lord of the Rings* movies to help make the hobbits appear smaller than Gandalf or Aragorn.

28.5 How Sight Develops

HOW WE DEVELOP

Newborn infants are capable of seeing, but their visual acuity is much less than it will be after a few months. For a short time after birth, human babies focus mostly on contrasts. For example, babies will stare at the hairline of their caregiver instead of the face.

By the time babies are about 2 months old, visual acuity has improved and infants seem to focus intently on faces. Their focal range is limited, though. They see objects best that are within a foot (about 30 cm) away. Perhaps not coincidentally, this is about the distance people tend to place their faces when interacting with babies. Over the next several months, babies' visual acuity improves so that by the end of the eighth month, their vision is quite similar to that of normal adults. These early life changes in vision are due to the postnatal development of the visual nervous system. As we will see next, proper development of the visual system requires visual experience during a specific part of early life.

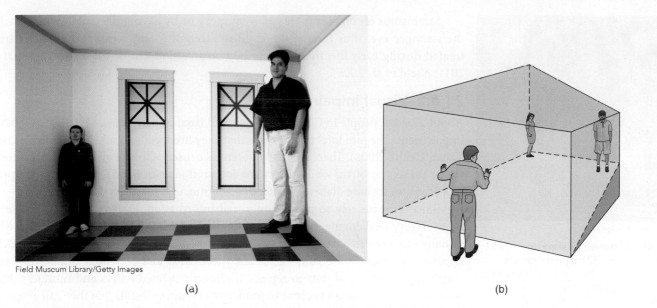

Field Museum Library/Getty Images

(a)   (b)

FIGURE 28-13 The Ames room. This specially constructed room is trapezoidal in shape, with sloping floors and ceilings. An observer can see inside only through a peephole, using one eye, so that the room appears normal. Because the observer assumes both people in the room are the same distance from him, he "sees" the people as being very different in size.

28.6 Visual Loss

Today, many common vision problems can be corrected. Increasingly common laser surgeries or the lenses in glasses or contacts can help people cope with nearsightedness, or difficulty seeing things clearly far away, and farsightedness, problems seeing near objects clearly, for example. Eye-care practitioners help with a variety of other problems as well. Sometimes, however, there is no treatment available, or treatment is begun too late to prevent people from losing vision in one or both eyes.

28.6.1 Strabismus

Typically both eyes coordinate and look in the same direction at the same object at the same time, sending a focused image to the brain. However, in 2 to 4 percent of cases, the eyes are misaligned. This misalignment is called *strabismus*. A child may be born with strabismus or the condition may be acquired later as a result of an accident or other health-related issue. Regardless of the cause, two different images are being sent to the brain—one from each eye—and if this situation is not resolved early it can result in visual loss as the child's brain will ignore the images from the weaker eye (Goldstein, 2014).

28.6.2 Amblyopia

Amblyopia is a partial or complete loss of vision due to abnormal development of the brain's visual cortex in infancy. Amblyopia is caused by one eye focusing better than the other due to a number of causes, including an extreme refractive error in one eye (due to farsightedness, nearsightedness, or astigmatism) or to a cataract (cloudy lens) on one eye. However, the most common cause of amblyopia is strabismus (Tychsen, 2012). If the ocular misalignment associated with strabismus remains uncorrected past about 6 years of age, it will eventually lead to a loss of visual abilities in the weaker eye. Occasionally amblyopia causes strabismus. For example, a child might have a cataract on one eye causing abnormal development in the visual cortex, which in turn causes ocular misalignment (Tychsen, 2012). In this case, the cataract would be treated and then the strabismus would be treated.

Billy Hustace/Getty Images

A life of accomplishment. Braille, devised in 1821 by Frenchman Louis Braille, has greatly improved the level of accomplishment and quality of life of people who are sightless. Here a computer developer reads Braille at his workstation.

© Rune Hellestad/Corbis

Movement as art. Highly skilled acts of contortion and gymnastics, as displayed by these Cirque du Soleil performers, relies on both the kinesthetic and vestibular system.

Strabismus is commonly treated by surgery or by having the child wear a patch over the stronger eye, thus forcing the child to strengthen the weaker one. If children are treated during early life, their normal binocular vision can be preserved (Stewart et al., 2011; Nield et al., 2008).

28.6.3 Visual Impairment

About 278,000 people in Canada suffer from visual impairments. Of them, 108,000 have impairments that are total or so severe that they are legally blind (National Coalition for Visual Health, 2008). There are many potential causes of loss of vision. Some are congenital, or present at birth, while others are acquired later in life. Diseases that can produce loss of vision include diabetes, glaucoma, and macular degeneration.

Since humans rely so heavily on visual information, living without adequate visual input is very challenging. A number of devices have been created to help those who are visually impaired live independently. Braille, a system of reading that involves touch, has significantly improved quality of life for those with loss of vision. Braille uses various combinations of raised dots to replace traditional printed letters and numbers. Visually impaired individuals can become so proficient at reading Braille that they can actually read faster than people with normal vision typically read printed material. Researchers have found that individuals with vision loss who become experts at reading Braille are actually using parts of their "visual" brain to process the sophisticated tactile information. Neuroimaging studies have shown that parts of the occipital and temporal cortices that normally process visual information are activated in individuals with vision loss while they read Braille. It is also noteworthy that the individuals with congenital vision loss use more of their visual brains to read Braille than do those who lose their vision later in life. This may be another example of a critical period at work.

The acquisition of Braille reading skills as a child may allow for the reorganization of the visual system to serve some new function. Learning Braille later in life may lead to less dramatic reorganization because those parts of the visual brain have already become "hard-wired," or less plastic and open to change (Amedi et al., 2005). It also seems to be the case that many individuals with vision loss are able to purpose some of their visual system neural wiring to assist them in processing speech. Some people with vision loss are able to turn up the speed of the devices that play them audio books to such a rate that they can get though three books in the time it takes a sighted person to read just one (Dietrich et al., 2010; Hertrich et al., 2009). This is another example of neural plasticity, or the brain's ability to adapt to new ways of interacting with the world.

28.7 The Other Senses: Vestibular and Kinesthetic Senses

How do you know when you are moving if your eyes are closed? As you wake up and before you open your eyes, how can you tell if you are lying flat on your bed or are propped up on a bunch of pillows? Why is it that many spinning carnival rides, some movie scenes, and some boat trips make some people throw up? The answers to all of these questions involve your kinesthetic and vestibular systems. Receptor cells in your muscles respond if they are squeezed and their shape is changed by movement, thus they tell us when our muscles are moving; other cells respond when stretched and tell us that our muscles are working hard. This information tells us whether we are still or moving in a particular direction without having to look—this is our *kinesthetic sense* (Schmukler, 1995).

Our *vestibular sense* is located in the semicircular canals of our inner ear where the fluid the canals contain shifts as we move in space—standing up, lying down, or swaying from side to side. The movement of the fluid is detected by hair cells embedded in a gelatinous substance that gets shifted around when our inner ear fluid moves and provides special information about our body position. Most of the time our vestibular system provides us with body movement and location information that matches the visual information provided by our eyes. However, when we are on a rolling boat, our visual and vestibular information do not match up well and we can start to feel quite ill. Ride-related illness may be partially due to a similar phenomenon, but is also likely due to our inner ear's vestibular reporting functions being overwhelmed by spinning and sudden jerky motions. If you start to feel sick at the carnival or on a boat, look into the far (and stable) distance and that may calm your inner ear. If not, try closing your eyes and taking a nap, or try chewing gum; both work to calm the inner ear (Gahlinger, 2000).

Tying It Together: **Your Brain and Behaviour**

Eating Pizza

Is this the best pizza you have ever had or does it fall short? When you dig into a slice of pizza, several neural circuits are activated to give you the overall experience. The appearance of your food can play an important role in its enjoyment. Photoreceptors in the eye transmit this information to the brain via the optic nerve, which passes through the brainstem, followed by the thalamus, and finally the visual cortex. Taste receptor cells, as well as sensory cells that respond to touch and temperature, are activated on your tongue. These nerves carry impulses into the brain where they pass through the brainstem, thalamus, and sensory cortex (gustatory cortex and somatosensory cortex). Taste is combined with smell information to produce flavour. Olfactory receptor neurons transduce pizza odorants and send this information on to the olfactory bulb and then to the olfactory cortex (smell is the only sensory modality that bypasses the thalamus on its way to the cortex).

Information about taste, smell, texture, temperature, and appearance is integrated in various association regions of the neocortex. These circuits, together with those that store memories related to your previous pizza experiences, work to produce your perception of this particular slice.

Questions

1 Explain how multiple senses (vision, smell, taste, touch) are involved in our experience of eating.

2 Explain how the taste of food may be enhanced if we close our eyes.

3 Which areas of the brain are responsible for integrating information about various components of eating (e.g., taste, smell, texture)?

Stockbroker/Age Fotostock

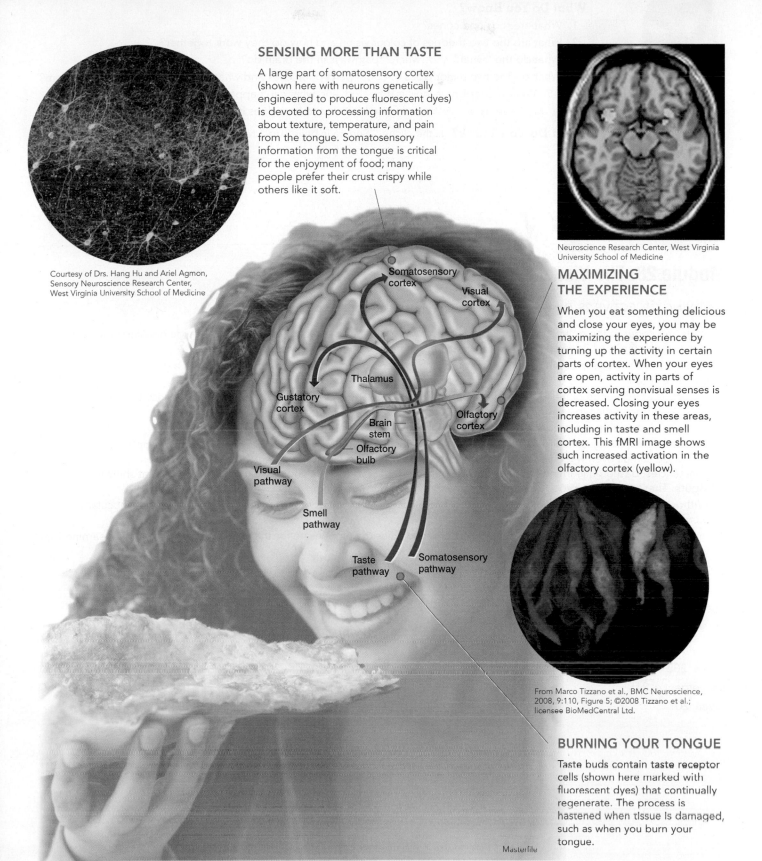

SENSING MORE THAN TASTE

A large part of somatosensory cortex (shown here with neurons genetically engineered to produce fluorescent dyes) is devoted to processing information about texture, temperature, and pain from the tongue. Somatosensory information from the tongue is critical for the enjoyment of food; many people prefer their crust crispy while others like it soft.

Courtesy of Drs. Hang Hu and Ariel Agmon, Sensory Neuroscience Research Center, West Virginia University School of Medicine

Neuroscience Research Center, West Virginia University School of Medicine

MAXIMIZING THE EXPERIENCE

When you eat something delicious and close your eyes, you may be maximizing the experience by turning up the activity in certain parts of cortex. When your eyes are open, activity in parts of cortex serving nonvisual senses is decreased. Closing your eyes increases activity in these areas, including in taste and smell cortex. This fMRI image shows such increased activation in the olfactory cortex (yellow).

Somatosensory cortex

Visual cortex

Thalamus

Gustatory cortex

Brain stem

Olfactory bulb

Olfactory cortex

Visual pathway

Smell pathway

Taste pathway

Somatosensory pathway

From Marco Tizzano et al., BMC Neuroscience, 2008, 9:110, Figure 5; ©2008 Tizzano et al.; licensee BioMedCentral Ltd.

BURNING YOUR TONGUE

Taste buds contain taste receptor cells (shown here marked with fluorescent dyes) that continually regenerate. The process is hastened when tissue is damaged, such as when you burn your tongue.

Masterfile

What Do You Know?

1. What are rods and cones?
2. What are the two theories of colour vision and how do they work together?
3. What do the "what" and "where" pathways in the brain do?
4. What are the two major types of depth perception cues and what is the difference between them?
5. What is strabismus, how is it treated, and what can happen if it is not treated promptly?
6. Where is our vestibular sense located and how does it work?

What Do You Think? Is the cliché, "Seeing is believing," really true? Why or why not?

Summary

Module 28: The Visual Sense: Sight

LEARNING OBJECTIVE 28 Describe key processes in visual sensation and perception.

- Rods and cones in the retina at the back of the eye change light into neural impulses. Cones provide detailed vision and help us perceive colour, while rods provide information about intensity of light.
- Two different theories in combination—trichromatic theory and opponent process theory—explain a good deal of how we perceive colour.
- The fovea at the centre of the retina contains only cones and provides our sharpest vision. We have a blind spot where the optic nerve leaves the retina to carry information to the brain.
- Damage to the brain can produce deficits in sensation, as well as abnormal sensory experiences.
- Top-down processing is involved in much visual perception. Gestalt theorists have identified several principles by which we recognize stimuli even when visual inputs are limited. We use binocular and monocular cues for depth perception. Perceptual constancies, based on learning from previous experiences, help us to see things as stable despite constant shifts in our visual inputs. These top-down processes can be "fooled" by visual illusions.
- Without adequate visual stimulation through both eyes during a critical period of life, we may not develop binocular vision, a condition known as amblyopia.
- Individuals with loss of vision can use other sensory modalities to compensate for the loss of visual information. Learning Braille with touch involves the use of brain areas normally used for vision.

Key Terms

cones 208
convergence 215
fovea 209

monocular cues 215
optic nerve 209
perceptual constancies 217

photoreceptors 208
retina 207
retinal disparity 214

rods 208
transduction 208

Study Questions

Multiple Choice

1. In what region of the retina is vision the sharpest due to the largest concentration of cones?
   a) fovea
   b) optic nerve
   c) saturation
   d) where the optic nerve leaves the eye

2. Which of the following Gestalt laws is *correctly* defined?
   a) Similarity—we tend to fill in small gaps in objects
   b) Continuity—stimuli falling along the same plane tend to be grouped together

   c) Proximity—stimuli near to one another tend to be grouped together
   d) Closure—stimuli resembling one another tend to be grouped together

Fill-in-the-Blank

1. Dilation and constriction of the _____ is one way that the visual system adapts to light.

2. The "what" visual pathway terminates in the _____ lobe; the "where" visual pathway terminates in the _____ lobe.

PART 6
CONSCIOUSNESS

Have you met Eugene Goostman? Probably not face to face, but you might have had a chat session with him. Eugene is a 13-year-old Ukrainian boy. Eugene likes hamburgers and candy and his father works as a gynecologist. He will chat with you about any topic you choose (www.princetonai.com/bot). Eugene comes across as a normal, conscious, young boy. What is most interesting about Eugene, however, is that he passed the Turing Test—and that he is not a real conscious human. He is actually a computer program. The Turing Test was developed by Alan Turing in 1950 (Turing, 1950) as a means for determining when an artificial intelligence program had reached the point where it appeared to have human-like consciousness. The test is simple: real humans interact via teletype (chat these days) either with a real human or a program (they are not told which). After 5 minutes, they have to say whether they have been interacting with a human or a machine. Turing said that if a machine could fool 30 percent of the people who interact with it into thinking it was human and conscious, then it passed the test and we would deem it to be a genuine artificial intelligence form.

Eugene fooled just over 30 percent of the humans who chatted with him in a controlled series of tests at the University of Reading in England in June 2014. In this part we will not consider the question of how Eugene's program "fakes" consciousness, or whether the actual version of the Turing Test he passed was valid (Mann, 2014; Masnick, 2014). Instead, the key psychological question we *will* consider here is just what is human consciousness? How does it work and what does it involve? Within the field of psychology, interest in the nature and complexity of human consciousness goes back to the early work of William James over 100 years ago, though human reflection on the nature of consciousness goes back much longer than that.

consciousness our immediate awareness of our internal and external states.

Consciousness is often defined as our immediate awareness of our internal and external states. But how aware is "aware"? Sometimes we are keenly aware of something, and other times only dimly so. In addition, sometimes we do not seem to be paying much attention to complex stimuli, yet we wind up recalling information about them later. Consciousness is one of the most intriguing—as well as one of the most mysterious—things that psychologists study.

Reflections on the nature of consciousness have been part of many spiritual traditions, such as Buddhism, going back many centuries (Harvey, 2012). The systematic study of consciousness is more recent and has undergone many historical shifts. As you may recall from Part 1, early psychologists defined psychology entirely as the study of consciousness. The influential American psychologist William James, for example, noted that our conscious awareness continually shifts based on what we're paying attention to and how intensely we are attending (Schooler, 2011; Singer, 2003).

At the same time, we feel continuity from moment to moment. Many things we do, like driving, require little or none of our conscious awareness. Yet if that changes while we are driving, we are able to turn more of our attention to the new situation and respond in a safe and appropriate manner. James coined the term "stream of consciousness" to signify how we experience our conscious life because consciousness, like a running stream, keeps moving yet seems to be the same.

Partly in response to the difficulties of conducting research on elusive concepts, such as the inner working of the conscious mind, many researchers during the first half of the twentieth century—especially those in North America—shifted their interest from consciousness to observable behaviour. As you read in Part 1, they equated psychology with behaviourism (J. Moore, 2010; Baars, 2003). Theorists and researchers in Europe, however, continued to pay significant attention to consciousness, and even unconsciousness.

Lisa F.Young/Shutterstock

Heightened awareness. Navigating an automobile requires full concentration for new drivers such as this individual. This is not the case, however, for people who have been at it for years, many of whom are barely conscious of the driving-related tasks they are performing.

During the latter part of the twentieth century, with important developments in neuroscience and computer technology, consciousness reemerged as a topic of major interest in psychology (Frith, 2003). With the help of neuroimaging techniques, investigators have been able to meaningfully explore the relationship between brain activity and various states of consciousness (Baars & Gage, 2010). Indeed, a considerable body of research is now directed at the study of conscious, less conscious, and non-conscious states (Revonsuo, 2010).

Module 29: When We Are Awake: Conscious Awareness

LEARNING OBJECTIVE 29 Define different levels of conscious awareness and describe key brain structures and functions associated with those levels.

©iStockphoto.com/robcocquyt

No room for error. As we interact with our environment, we constantly monitor both ourselves and the situations at hand to help ensure that we attend to key features of the interactions. When performing a dangerous task, such as climbing a mountain, careful monitoring can take on life-and-death importance.

Attention is a key part of our conscious awareness. The relationship between attention and consciousness is the topic of lively debate in psychology. One possibility is that attention is a prerequisite for consciousness. Psychiatric researcher John Ratey (2001) has pointed out that "Before we can be conscious of something…we have to pay attention to it." At the same time, attention does not equal consciousness; we need something more. To be fully conscious of something, we must be *aware* that we are attending to it (Lewis, 2010). Inattention blindness, for example, refers to the consistent research finding that people who are not paying attention to a picture, video, or scene are unable to report on the details of what those visual stimuli contain (Mack & Rock, 1998). But things may not be that straightforward. It may be that some of our consciousness is not tied to our attention. If participants are shown a picture for a very brief interval (30 ms) they are not able to report any of the details in that picture (no attention), however they are able to report the *gist* (general or overall impression) of what was in the picture. So if it was an animal or nature scene as opposed to an abstract art image of a city scene, participants will be able say something general about it (e.g., it's a nature picture). This finding suggests that participants could actually be somewhat conscious of something they have not been able to focus attention on (Koch & Tsuchiya, 2007).

Conscious awareness of ourselves, our needs, and how to satisfy them has directly helped us in survival, contributing mightily to our evolutionary progress. To be conscious of our thirst, for example, is to understand that water is necessary to quench it, and to know that we may need to plan to get or have water even before we are thirsty. Clearly, conscious awareness involves elements beyond attention (Sewards & Sewards, 2000).

Psychology Around Us — A Different Kind of Thoughtlessness

Human beings have a remarkable ability to multi-task—to keep whole sets of complicated tasks and ideas in mind while still managing to engage in the basic activities of living. On the other hand, consciousness sometimes has "blind spots"— episodes in which conscious behaviours and intentions seem to break down.

Dr. Baba Shiv, a marketing professor, conducted a study with undergraduates at the University of Iowa (Ferraro, Shiv, & Bettman, 2005). He asked students to memorize a number that was either two digits long or seven digits long. After the memorization task, the students were asked to go down a hall to another room where they were to be tested on their recollections. On the way down the hall, however, a stranger (actually a confederate of Shiv's) stopped them and offered them a snack, either a nutritious, healthy fruit salad, or a decadent, tempting chocolate cake.

Shiv found something interesting—people who were required to hold a seven-digit number in mind chose the chocolate cake twice as often as the people who were holding on to only a two-digit number. Shiv believed that this happened because the cognitive processes of people holding seven-digit numbers in mind were too overloaded to have the conversations we usually have with ourselves when we are offered chocolate cake. That is, their minds were too overloaded to consider notions such as "Chocolate cake is just too fattening" or "I don't want my teeth to get all chocolaty." Shiv also believed that this is the kind of thing that happens to our cognitive processing whenever we get stressed or overloaded in life.

Something to think about the next time you reach for the cookie dough ice cream when you're studying for an exam or fighting with a girlfriend or boyfriend.

29.1 When We Are Awake

Brian Kolb and Ian Whishaw, working at the University of Lethbridge, are two respected Canadian neuroscientists. They argue that multiple brain processes and structures must be operating simultaneously for us to be conscious of our world or ourselves (Kolb & Whishaw, 2009). In fact, research has shown that when we are awake, most if not all of the neurons in our brains are constantly active. Despite popular claims made in movies like *Lucy* with Scarlett Johansson, we do not typically only make use of 10 percent of our brain—we use all of it. Of course, certain neurons become especially active when an individual is stimulated by particular objects or events, but even in the absence of such stimulation, neurons are still active at a steady, low level and are communicating with other neurons (Hopkin, 2010; Llinás & Ribary, 2001).

WHAT HAPPENS
in the BRAIN?

Recall from Part 3 that neurons tend to work together in groups, or *networks*, and those networks become more and more efficient with repeated use (Jones, 2007). For us to experience conscious awareness of something, such as a thought or a pedestrian about to run out into the road in front of us, many of these networks must become particularly active at once. While one set of networks is enabling us to pay attention to the stimulus, other biological events must also be at work, enabling us to be aware and recognize that we are attending. Still others are allowing us to monitor, remember, and control.

Researchers have not yet pinpointed all of the brain areas and events that are responsible for such *complex processing*, but research has suggested that two areas of great importance to consciousness are the *cerebral cortex*, the brain's outer covering of cells, and the *thalamus*, the brain structure that often relays sensory information from various parts of the brain to the cerebral cortex (Haber, 2003).

The work of Ronald Resnick (2000; Resnick, O'Regan, & Clark, 1997) at the University of British Columbia shows that unless you pay attention to the appropriate aspects of a scene, you can miss even the most conspicuous events around you (like a gorilla walking through a video you are watching). If you go to Resnick's website, you can download several short videos containing examples of inattentional blindness, which is basically our failure to notice things around us to which we are not paying attention (http://viscoglab. psych.ubc.ca/research/robust-inattentional-blindness/).

29.1.1 The Cerebral Cortex

Evidence has accumulated that some areas of the brain are responsible for attention, while other areas—particularly ones in the cerebral cortex—are in charge of one's awareness of that attention. Investigations by Lawrence Weiskrantz (2009, 2002, 2000; Sahraie et al., 2010) on *blindsight* illustrate how this works in the visual realm.

Weiskrantz studied people whose visual areas in the cerebral cortex (**Figure 29-1**) had been destroyed, leaving them blind, so far as they were aware. When Weiskrantz presented such people with a spot of light on a screen and asked them to point to it, the individuals were totally unaware of the light and could not fulfill the request. Yet, when he told the same individuals to "just point anywhere," they typically pointed in the direction of the light. Similarly, these individuals could generally avoid chairs, tables, and other objects as they walked through a room, denying all the while that they were seeing anything at all. In short, the patients in Weiskrantz's studies could and did readily attend to visual objects, yet because the visual areas in their cerebral cortex had been destroyed, they were unaware of those objects. Weiskrantz and others have concluded that the areas of the brain that help us *attend* to visual stimuli are different from the visual areas in the cerebral cortex that help us to be *aware* that we are attending to such stimuli.

Recall the work by Sperry and Gazzaniga (Gazzaniga, 2010, 2005; Colvin & Gazzaniga, 2007; Sperry, 1998, 1982) discussed in Part 3 where patients who had their corpus collosum severed were briefly presented with an object or a word in their left or right visual fields (Thompson, 2000). The investigators found that when they showed a word

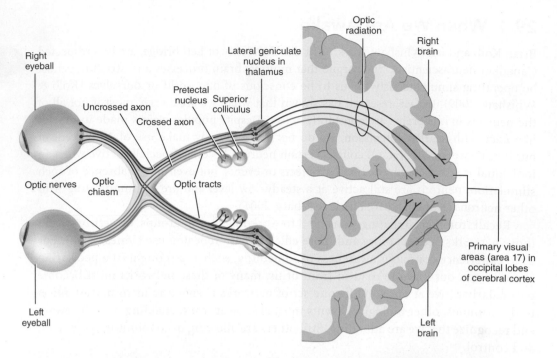

FIGURE 29-1 **Visual areas in the cerebral cortex.** We typically think of blindness as involving damage to, or malformation of, the retinas but they are really only part of the visual perceptual process. Weisenkrantz's work on blindsight involves people with intact retinas but with damage to their primary visual cortex or, in more rare cases, their superior colliculus. While they claim not to be able to see anything they can often provide correct responses to simple questions when asked to guess.

Source: Reprinted with permission of John Wiley & Sons, Inc. from Tortora, 2014. *Principles of Human Anatomy* (13e). Hoboken, NJ: Wiley, p. 685.

to a patient's left hemisphere, the individual was readily able to say and write the word. When a word was flashed to the right hemisphere, however, the individual could *not* name or write it. Apparently, the left cerebral cortex is responsible for verbal awareness.

In contrast, the right cerebral cortex seems to be responsible for non-verbal forms of conscious awareness. In one study, for example, the experimenters flashed a picture of a screwdriver to the patient's right hemisphere. The individuals were then instructed to feel a variety of real objects with their left hand from behind a screen, including a real screwdriver, and on the basis of touch to select the object that matched the picture they had just seen; all correctly selected a screwdriver. This suggests that the right cerebral cortex can produce tactile awareness, and perhaps other kinds of non-verbal awareness as well, but not verbal awareness. Of course, for most of us, our two hemispheres are connected, and these various kinds of awareness occur simultaneously, helping to produce a broad and complete sense of conscious awareness.

29.1.2 The Thalamus

We might think of the networks of neurons in the brain as similar to the different train lines in a complicated subway system, like that of London, England. For trains to get from place to place on schedule without collision, a train conductor or a system manager (or even a whole group of them) must oversee the process. Researchers have nominated several brain areas as potential conductors, involved in routing messages along the proper neural network "subway lines" of our brains. Two of the most

©iStockphoto.com/Plus

Hello there. Does this baby know he is looking at himself in the mirror? We can test this by secretly putting red makeup on his nose and then watching how he reacts in front of the mirror. When babies look into a mirror and then touch their own nose because it is red, they show us that they are aware of themselves as separate beings from others.

practically speaking — Our Brains and Consciousness

So how does the brain produce consciousness? When attempting to answer this question, researchers have typically pointed to the neural complexity of the human brain and its complex memory and language functions as possible contributors to human consciousness, as we discussed earlier. But just how that works is not clear. One radical alternative theory is that consciousness may actually emerge from finer processes within brain neurons (Penrose & Hameroff, 2011). Specially, tiny support structures within neurons called microtubules have been shown to produce quantum (small atomic components) vibrations. These neurons may actually drive the general EEG patterns within the brain and may provide a level of computational complexity up to the task of accounting for consciousness. Such quantum vibrations have been linked to photosynthesis in plant cells (Engel et al., 2007). More

directly, general anesthetics, used in surgery and which act by temporarily removing our consciousness while not affecting all non-conscious brain activities, have been demonstrated to act by affecting the microtubules in our brain neurons (Emerson et al., 2013). For example, the belief is that quantum supercomputers—once actually built and working—will represent a "quantum leap" forward in computing power by using the virtually unlimited number of possible states of subatomic particles (or quanta) rather than the basic on or off of binary transistors. Similarly, the controversial theory states that we will better understand the computational power of consciousness by understanding the role that quantum components of neural tubules might play in the functioning of consciousness. This will certainly be a theory to watch over the next decade.

prominent candidates are the *intralaminar nuclei* and *midline nuclei* of the *thalamus* (Benarroch, 2011, 2008; Van der Werf et al., 2003; 2002). Research indicates that the intralaminar and midline nuclei receive and project long axons to neurons throughout the cerebral cortex, including areas that are involved in conscious awareness (Ratey, 2001).

Consistent with this theory, investigators have observed that people actually lose all consciousness and enter a deep coma if their intralaminar and midline nuclei are broadly damaged. If, however, the damage to the nuclei occurs in only one hemisphere, individuals lose awareness of only half of their bodies. They become unaware of all events that occur on one side of their visual field, for example, or unaware of all objects that touch one side of their body (Van der Werf, Witter, & Groenewegen, 2002). In short, the intralaminar and midline nuclei seem to play an important role in conscious awareness.

29.2 Alert Consciousness

Researchers have made a number of attempts to identify consciousness in infants. As we saw in Part 4, there is evidence that even babies can direct their attention, hold concepts in mind, and engage in planned or intentional behaviours—the component skills of consciousness. Because babies are not yet able to talk very well, however, it's difficult to determine how aware they are that their experiences are things happening to them, or even whether they are fully aware of themselves as separate beings from others, a concept known as *sense of self*.

HOW WE DEVELOP

Researchers have developed some ingenious ways to try to determine when babies first experience a conscious sense of self. In one test, called the Rouge test, experimenters secretly dabbed red makeup on babies' noses while pretending to wipe them. Then they placed the babies in front of a mirror. The researchers reasoned that babies who had developed a sense or conscious awareness of self would see the makeup and touch their own noses, while those who did not understand they were looking themselves in the mirror would try to touch the makeup on the baby in the mirror. Based on such tests, it seems that most children develop a stable concept of the self by around 18 months of age (Lewis, 2010; Amsterdam, 1972; Gallup, 1970; Lewis & Brooks-Gunn, 1979).

234 Part 6 Consciousness

Some researchers suggest that the early cognitive development we discussed in Part 4 and the development of consciousness contribute to one another. That is, if infants demonstrate the ability to develop concepts and to think through their behaviours if they cannot express such thinking, they should be viewed as having a rudimentary sense of self-consciousness. Without this rudimentary sense of consciousness, babies would not be able to develop any concepts at all (Lewis, 2010; Mandler, 2004).

Other theorists suggest that consciousness itself is rooted in language and representation. Because babies do not have language—the ability to let words represent events and experiences—they cannot reflect on their thoughts and behaviours and do not have full consciousness yet (Neuman & Nave, 2010; Zelazo, 2004). These theorists suggest that a shift happens at around 22 months of age (about the time they start to recognize themselves in the mirror on the Rouge test), when babies show the ability to reason inductively and to name and categorize concepts, which in turn enables them to represent concepts in a richer and deeper way.

Thus, describing how consciousness develops during awake states remains both a philosophical and empirical question, influenced in large part by how we define consciousness. The matter is further complicated by the question we asked at the beginning of this part: Just how aware is "aware"? We'll see next that there may be levels of alert consciousness at which we are not fully aware of all our thoughts.

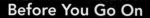

Before You Go On

www.wiley.com/go/comercanada

What Do You Know?

1. List the core cognitive processes of consciousness.
2. What is blindsight?

What Do You Think? What characteristics do you believe are essential to define alert consciousness?

Summary

Module 29: When We Are Awake: Conscious Awareness

LEARNING OBJECTIVE 29 Define different levels of conscious awareness and describe key brain structures and functions associated with those levels.

- Attention is one of the key aspects of conscious awareness. Other key cognitive activities underlying cognitive awareness include monitoring (our implicit decisions about what to attend to), memory, and planning.
- Most biological investigators believe that consciousness results from a combination of brain activities in several brain regions. Two key brain structures appear to be the cerebral cortex, which helps regulate our awareness of attentional processes, and the thalamus, which relays sensory information from various parts of the brain to the cerebral cortex for processing.

Study Questions

Multiple Choice

1. Which of the following statements best expresses the relationship between attention and consciousness?
   a) Attention is a product of consciousness.
   b) Attention is necessary for consciousness.
   c) Attention is sufficient for consciousness.
   d) Attention is the same as consciousness.

2. Which subcortical structure in the brain is especially important for consciousness?
   a) amygdala
   b) hippocampus
   c) hypothalamus
   d) thalamus

Fill-in-the-Blank

1. Patients studied by Weiskrantz demonstrated a phenomenon called _____ that led them to navigate around objects in a room but claim to see nothing.

Module 30: Preconscious and Unconscious States

LEARNING OBJECTIVE 30
Summarize the ideas of preconscious and unconscious states, including Freud's thinking on the unconscious.

preconsciousness level of awareness in which information can become readily available to consciousness if necessary.

Theorists often talk about different "levels of consciousness" or "degrees of consciousness." Some also believe that consciousness should be distinguished from two alternative states, *preconsciousness* and *unconsciousness*.

Preconsciousness is a level of awareness in which information can become readily available to consciousness if necessary. Bringing to mind what you had for lunch last Tuesday might take a bit of work, but you should be able to pull the information out of your preconscious mind. When (or if) you finally do remember that bowl of soup, the memory has reached consciousness.

Many of our most familiar behaviours occur during preconsciousness. Take a second—can you remember exactly what your morning ritual was this morning? What song was playing when you woke up? Did you count every tooth as you brushed it? Can you recall the details of every kilometre of your drive or ride to college or university today? For many morning activities, you probably do things in the same order, but you do not necessarily need to plan all the steps or think about what you're doing as you move through your ritual. Preconscious behaviours of this kind are sometimes called *automatic behaviours.* As we saw at the beginning of the part, driving can involve automatic behaviours.

An **unconscious state** is one in which information is not easily accessible to conscious awareness. Perhaps you cannot remember the name of someone you saw from a distance, despite being sure you know them. Or you cannot call up the name of someone who bullied you in school when you saw a stranger who reminded you of that person. Unexpectedly, minutes or days later the name of the person or the song you could not recover earlier jumps right out of your memory. Psychoanalytic theorists, influenced by the ideas of Sigmund Freud, would suggest that something triggered the release of the appropriate memory.

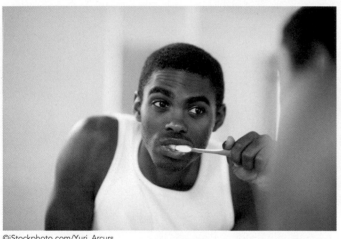

©iStockphoto.com/Yuri_Arcurs

Automatic behaviours. Do you remember the details of every time you brushed your teeth in the past week?

unconscious state state in which information is not easily accessible to conscious awareness.

30.1 Cognitive Views of the Unconscious

Throughout much of the twentieth century, scientists paid little, if any, attention to the unconscious. Rejecting Freud's psychoanalytic ideas (discussed a bit later), they also rejected the notion that people's behaviours, thoughts, and feelings may be influenced by mental forces of which they are totally unaware. This dismissal of the unconscious has shifted dramatically in recent decades. Today, most psychologists believe that unconscious functioning does occur and a number of explanations—particularly cognitive explanations—have been proposed.

Perhaps the most prominent cognitive explanation for unconscious processing points to the concept of *implicit memory* (Manelis, Hanson, & Hanson 2011; Kihlstrom et al., 2007, 2000). As we shall observe more closely in Part 8, cognitive theorists distinguish between two basic kinds of memory: *explicit memory* and *implicit memory*. Explicit memories involve pieces of knowledge that we are fully aware of. Explicit memory is the conscious, intentional recovery of a memory. Knowing the date of your birth is an explicit memory. Implicit memories refer to knowledge that we are not typically aware of—information that we cannot recall at will, but that we use in the performance of various tasks in life.

Implicit memory is usually on display in the *skills* we acquire, such as reading, playing an instrument, driving a car, or speaking a second language. Our performance of such skills improves as we gain more and more of the knowledge, motor behaviours, and perceptual information required for the skills. These gains—that is, these implicit memories—are

Psychology Around Us | Snap Decisions

Many psychologists have begun to look at the benefits of "unconscious" decision making—quick, intuitive judgments. Psychologist Gary Klein, for example, has examined decision making in firefighters. Klein had expected that, given the huge stakes involved in fighting fires, fire chiefs typically must consider a range of scenarios and carefully weigh the pros and cons before acting. What he found instead was that when fighting fires, fire chiefs typically identify one possible decision immediately, run the scenario in their head, and if it doesn't have any glaring errors, they go with it. Basically, the fire chiefs let their experience automatically generate a solution (Klein, 2004).

In contrast, neuroscientist Antonio Damasio (2010) has worked extensively with patients who have suffered damage to certain parts of their prefrontal cortex. Damasio found that these perfectly intelligent individuals are only able to make "deliberate" decisions; they can only make decisions in which they have time to systematically weigh options and arrive at a clearly advantageous course of action. If they are required to make a quick choice, like when to schedule an appointment

©iStockphoto.com/RachelDonahue

or where to go for dinner, they become paralyzed and simply can't decide. Damasio argues that intuition and unconscious decision making allow us to operate effectively in situations of uncertainty, and that most of life's decisions, even the big ones, involve a lot of uncertainty.

---

usually revealed to us indirectly by our improved performances, not by consciously recalling the acquired information and experiences that led to the improvements. Shortly after learning to drive, you may realize one day that you are able to drive and talk to a passenger at the same time, for example, but not recall the exact moment that you learned how to control the wheel and pedals well enough to add the additional activity of carrying on a conversation.

Implicit memory may also involve factual information. When we vote for a particular candidate on election day, a wealth of past experiences and information may be at the root of that behaviour, including childhood discussions with our parents about political parties, websites we have seen, articles we have read, political science classes we have taken, interviews or news stories we have read or heard, and more. As we mark an X on our ballot, however, we typically are not aware of all these past experiences or pieces of information.

Cognitive and cognitive neuroscience theorists see implicit memories as a part of everyday functioning, rather than as a way to keep unpleasant information from reaching our awareness (Czigler & Winkler, 2010; Kihlstrom et al., 2007, 2000). They have discovered research methods to test our unconscious—implicit—memories and have gathered evidence that explicit and implicit memories are stored in different pathways in the brain (Sheldon & Moscovitch, 2010).

Ideas about the nature of consciousness were around long before cognitive psychology started to study them. Freud developed an interesting historical perspective on consciousness. While little data has been found that support his particular view, you can see that he was quite successful in getting us to think about the possibility that there is a LOT going on in our minds to which we do not have easy or simple access.

30.2 Freud's Views of the Unconscious

Although there are many current views about the unconscious, most have some relationship to the historic (not scientific) explanation advanced by Sigmund Freud (Gödde, 2010). As we discussed in Part 1, Freud believed that the vast majority of our personal knowledge

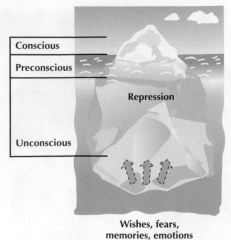

Conscious

Preconscious

Repression

Unconscious

Wishes, fears,
memories, emotions

FIGURE 30-1 Freud's view of the
unconscious. According to Freud,
material that is relegated to the
unconscious, such as repressed material, enters preconscious awareness or
conscious awareness only accidentally
or indirectly.

is located in our unconsciousness, and thus is not readily accessible (see **Figure 30-1**). According to him, one of the key functions of the unconsciousness is to house thoughts and memories too painful or disturbing for consciousness (Wilson, 2010). Indeed, Freud maintained that at some level, we may *repress* such thoughts and memories (of bullies we have known, for example), pushing them into our unconscious and prevent-ing them from entering our conscious experience.

Freud also suggested that, although it is typically inaccessible, unconscious material can enter conscious awareness (Johnson, 2011). Have you ever meant to say one thing, but something very different comes out, often to your embarrassment? Freud identified this slip of the tongue (called a *Freudian slip*) as a moment when the mind inadvertently allows a repressed idea into consciousness. Let's say that you do not enjoy your job but you're not sure why. One day you arrive at work 15 minutes late and your boss is waiting for you. Whereas you intend to say, "I'm sorry I'm late, boss," instead you say, "I'm sorry I hate boss." Suddenly you—and your boss—are well aware of why you don't like your job!

Freud also believed that our unconscious can work against us and that people who store too many emotionally-charged memories and needs in their unconscious may eventu-ally develop psychological disorders (as we will discuss in further detail in Parts 12 and 15). His theory suggests that the knowledge and memories stored in the unconscious maintain their ability to influence how we think, feel, and relate to others. If we repress too much, we may experience distortions in how we feel or relate to others, and, at the same time, we may feel helpless to change. Based on this part of Freud's theory, psychoanalytic psychotherapy attempts to bring patients' unconscious material into their conscious awareness.

Freud's ideas about unconsciousness can be quite compelling. His ideas have been drawn into aspects of popular culture so that we often wonder what our motive is for not being able to remember something. The problem is that there is really no research data supporting most of Freud's views of the unconscious (Holmes, 1990). This does not mean that all of our mental processes are conscious. Rather, it just means that the actual nature of unconscious processing is more complex than Freud envisioned (Westen, 2002).

Before You Go On

www.wiley.com/go/comercanada

What Do You Know?
1. What is the difference between preconscious and unconscious states?
2. What is the importance of implicit memory in terms of the notion of the unconscious?

What Do You Think? Do you think there are unconscious forces driving people's behaviours? If not, is it all conscious choice, or do you believe there are other explanations?

Summary

Module 30: Preconscious and Unconscious States

LEARNING OBJECTIVE 30 Summarize the ideas of preconscious and unconscious states, including Freud's thinking on the unconscious.

- In addition to our conscious level of awareness, many psychologists believe there are other levels or degrees of consciousness, and distinguish conscious awareness from two other states—unconsciousness and preconsciousness.

- Cognitive psychologists have demonstrated the existence of implicit memory; that is, memory that we do not consciously reflect upon but which, nevertheless, influences our behaviour.
- Preconsciousness is a level of awareness in which information can become readily available to consciousness if necessary.
- Unconsciousness is a state in which information is not easily accessible to conscious awareness.
- Freud viewed the human unconscious as an important storehouse for knowledge and experience, which although not directly accessible to our conscious awareness, still influences our behaviour.
- Although Freud's ideas fell into disfavour for several years, in recent years scientists have begun to re-examine the unconscious from different points of view. For example, implicit memory describes knowledge that we have and are able to apply to various tasks, without being able to recall it at will.

Key Terms

preconsciousness 236

unconscious state 236

Study Questions

Multiple Choice

1. Information of which you are currently unaware but which you can bring to mind quite easily is said to be in the _____.
   a) preconscious
   b) protoconscious
   c) subconscious
   d) unconscious

2. Freud suggested that most of one's personal knowledge is contained in the _____.
   a) conscious mind
   b) preconscious

   c) subconscious
   d) unconscious

Fill-in-the-Blank

1. The memory system that gets strengthened mainly by repeated practice, rather than through conscious attention, is called _____ memory.

Module 31: When We Are Asleep

LEARNING OBJECTIVE 31
Describe what happens when people sleep, key theories of why we sleep and dream, and problems with sleep and how they affect functioning.

We could add a third item to Benjamin Franklin's famous comment that the only sure things in life are death and taxes: sooner or later we must—absolutely must—fall and stay asleep. Sleep is so central to our lives—indeed, most people spend 25 years of their lives asleep—that we first need to ask, what important purpose does it serve?

31.1 Why Do We Sleep?

Interestingly, despite considerable research into the matter, no consensus exists about why people need to sleep (Thakkar & Datta, 2010). After all, as we shall see, the brain does not rest when we are sleeping, nor, on the surface, does sleep offer the body much more rest than it would get by sitting down and relaxing for a while. Yet all animals, including we humans, sleep (though in different amounts) (see **Figure 31-1**), and would, in fact, die if deprived of sleep for too long.

One theory, the **adaptive theory of sleep**, suggests that sleep is the evolutionary outcome of self-preservation (Worthman, 2011; Rial et al., 2010). Proponents of this view suggest that organisms sleep to keep themselves away from predators that are more active at night when our visual system, which is adapted for optimal use in daylight, does not provide us with much protection (Siegel, 2009). Our ancestors, for example, tucked themselves away in safe places to keep from being eaten by nocturnal animals on the prowl. Animals that need to graze, and so have less chance of hiding from predators, tend to sleep less. A giraffe, for example, sleeps only two hours, whereas a bat sleeps around 20 hours (Siegel, 2005). This evolutionary argument certainly could account for why we sleep at night when it is dark, though one could easily argue it might actually be safer to stay awake if there are possible predators about. What it does not do is account for why people who are sleep deprived will sleep when given a chance regardless of whether it is day or night, and why people working night shifts seem to function well as long as they get enough sleep, regardless of whether they sleep at night or in the daytime. So perhaps there are other reasons for sleep, or for needing sleep.

Several biological theories of sleep have also been proposed. One suggests that sleep plays a role in the growth process, a notion consistent with the finding that the *pituitary gland* releases growth hormones during sleep (Garcia-Garcia et al., 2011; Gais et al., 2006). In fact, as we age, we release fewer of these hormones, grow less, and sleep less.

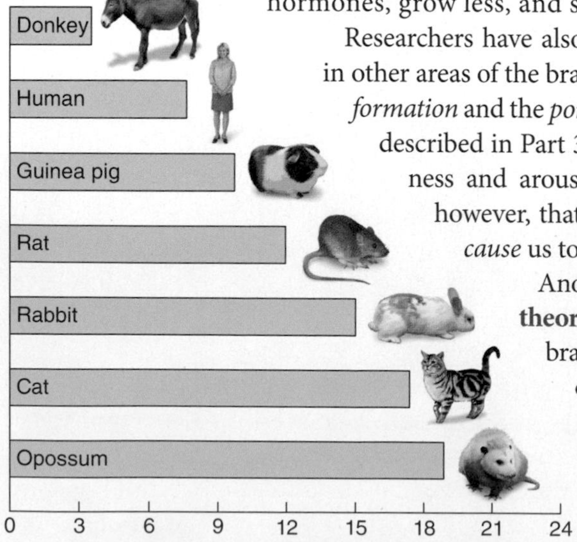

Researchers have also observed changes in neuron activity in other areas of the brain during sleep, including the *reticular formation* and the *pons*, as well as the *forebrain region*. As we described in Part 3, these regions are important in alertness and arousal. Researchers have not established, however, that changes in the activity of these areas *cause* us to sleep.

Another biological theory, the **restorative theory of sleep**, suggests that sleep allows the brain and body to restore certain depleted chemical resources, while eliminating chemical wastes that have accumulated during the waking day (Dworak et al., 2010; Irwin, 2001). There is some evidence that supports this theory. Burns on rats take

©iStockphoto.com/Dr-Strangelove

"Everyone needs to sleep." This bee takes time out from its busy agenda to sleep in a comfortable flower.

adaptive theory of sleep theory that organisms sleep for the purpose of self-preservation, to keep away from predators that are more active at night.

restorative theory of sleep theory that we sleep to allow the brain and body to restore certain depleted chemical resources and eliminate chemical wastes that have accumulated during the waking day.

FIGURE 31-1 **Sleep needs of various animals.** Animals vary greatly in how much sleep they need each day. Their sleep needs are related in part to how much awake time is needed to obtain food and protect themselves from predators (Siegel, 2005).

longer to heal if they are sleep deprived (Gumustekin et al., 2004). Sleep deprivation also reduces the functioning of the immune system (Zager et al., 2007). As well, growth hormone production increases during sleep in adults, a process that would also promote restoration of body tissues and structures (Van Cauter, Leproult, & Plat, 2000).

While we may not yet know exactly what causes sleep, we do know that sleep occurs in regular patterns, or *rhythms*, and that these rhythms reflect changes in the body's chemistry (Moorcroft, 2003).

31.2 Rhythms of Sleep

Human beings' basic pattern is called the **circadian rhythm** (see **Figure 31-2**). Within each 24-hour cycle, we experience a sustained period of wakefulness that gives way to a period of sleep. Although we tend to be awake during the day and to sleep at night, our circadian rhythms are not fully dependent on the cycles of daylight (Cartwright, 2010; Thompson, 2000).

During the circadian cycle, we also experience other, more subtle patterns of biochemical activity. As morning nears, for example, our temperature rises and continues to rise until it peaks at midday. Then it dips and we feel fatigued. Many people around the world take naps during this early afternoon lull. Later in the afternoon, body temperature rises once more, only to drop again as we approach our full evening sleep (Danovi, 2010; Johnson et al., 2004). It seems that, on average, we are most alert during the late morning peak in the circadian rhythm. This "rule," however, varies with age. Younger people tend to peak later in the day, while older people peak earlier (Yoon et al., 2003).

Along with shifts in body temperature, we also experience changes throughout the 24-hour period in blood pressure, the secretion of hormones, and sensitivity to pain. As we have discussed, for example, the release of growth hormones tends to occur during periods of sleep (Benloucif et al., 2005).

The circadian rhythm has been called our *biological clock* because the pattern repeats itself from one 24-hour period to the next. Certain events, however, can make this clock go haywire (Cartwright, 2010; Waterhouse & DeCoursey, 2004). For example, the clock can be disrupted by long-distance airplane flights when we are awake at times that we should be sleeping—a problem compounded by crossing time zones. The result: jet lag. Similarly, people who work nightshifts, particularly those who keep irregular schedules of dayshifts and nightshifts, may experience sleep disorders and, in some instances, develop problems such as depression or health difficulties (Drake et al., 2004). People with a pattern called *circadian rhythm sleep disorder* experience excessive sleepiness or insomnia as a result of a mismatch between their own sleep–wake pattern and the sleep–wake schedule of most other people in their environment (Ivanenko & Johnson, 2010; Lack & Bootzin, 2003).

31.3 "Owls" and "Larks"

Do you get up at the crack of dawn, head to the gym, and complete all of your class assignments before noon? Then you are probably a morning person (a "lark"). Or do you have trouble getting up before noon and can't really concentrate on your work until much later in the day? If so, you are likely an evening person (an "owl").

Most people have no preference for the time of day when they are most alert and active; they may shift their sleep–wake rhythms two hours earlier or later than normal with no adverse effects on their alertness or activity level (Sack et al., 2007). But for some, there is a strong preference for either earlier or later in the day.

Researchers now believe that genetics plays an important role in determining these variations in sleep–wake rhythms, and that age, ethnicity, gender, and socio-economic factors have almost no influence (Hellman et al., 2010; Paine, Gander, & Travier, 2006).

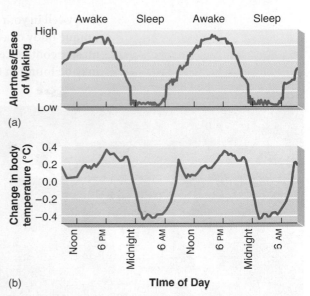

(a)

(b)

Time of Day

FIGURE 31-2 **Circadian rhythms.** Two prime examples of circadian rhythms are our cycles of alertness and shifts in body temperature.

circadian rhythm pattern of sleep–wake cycles that in human beings roughly corresponds to periods of daylight and night.

HOW WE
DIFFER

Every cell in your body has its own internal clock, and scientists are able to measure your unique body clock at the cellular level (Cuninkova & Brown, 2008). As we shall see, the master control centre for your body's internal clock and your own sleep–wake rhythm may be found in the brain area known as the *suprachiasmatic nucleus*.

©iStockphoto.com/Nullplus

©iStockphoto.com/STEEX

Sleep–wake rhythms. Researchers believe that genetics, rather than socio-economic factors—such as age, ethnicity, or gender—play a key role in determining variations in sleep–wake rhythms.

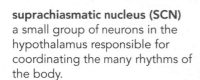
WHAT HAPPENS *in the* BRAIN?

31.4 When We Sleep

Research has uncovered what happens in our brains to control the circadian rhythms of when we wake and sleep, as well as what happens in the brain while we sleep.

31.4.1 Controlling the Clock

suprachiasmatic nucleus (SCN) a small group of neurons in the hypothalamus responsible for coordinating the many rhythms of the body.

The **suprachiasmatic nucleus (SCN)**, a small group of neurons in the *hypothalamus*, is ultimately responsible for coordinating the many rhythms of the body (Danovi, 2010; Kalsbeek et al., 2010) (**Figure 31-3**). As daylight fades into night, the SCN "notices" the change and directs the *pineal gland* to secrete the hormone *melatonin*. Increased quantities of melatonin, travelling through the blood to various organs, trigger sleepiness. Melatonin production peaks between 1:00 and 3:00 A.M. As dawn approaches, this production decreases and sleepers soon awaken. There is increasing evidence (Petrie et al., 1989; Herxheimer & Petrie, 2002) that melatonin taken in pill form after long-haul flights reduces the severity of jet lag, likely by resetting the circadian clock.

During the day, photoreceptors in the retina of the eye communicate the presence of sunlight to the SCN and melatonin secretions remain low (Berson, 2003). Photoreceptors are also sensitive to artificial light. In fact, the invention of the light bulb just over a hundred years ago has disturbed the human experience of the circadian rhythm by increasing the number of hours of light people are exposed to in a given day. This may be one reason why many people today sleep much less than our forebears.

What happens if a person is entirely deprived of access to environmental shifts in sunlight and darkness? In a number of sleep studies, participants have been placed in special settings where they are totally deprived of natural light and have no way to measure

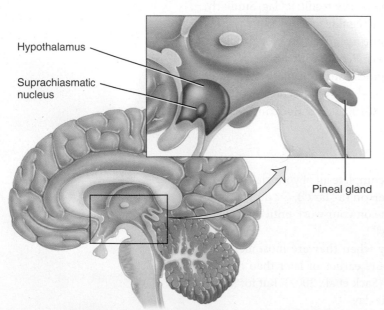

Hypothalamus

Suprachiasmatic nucleus

Pineal gland

FIGURE 31-3 The suprachiasmatic nucleus (SCN). The SCN directs the *pineal gland* to secrete the hormone *melatonin*, which causes sleepiness. Synthetic versions of melatonin are sometimes taken to reduce the effects of jet lag.

time. In such settings, the SCN extends the body's "day" by as much as an hour, to about 25 hours (Lavie, 2001). When we are deprived of light, the various circadian rhythms also become out of synch with each other. The normal cycles of body temperature and melatonin production, for example, no longer coordinate with one another (Lavie, 2001).

If we speak of a biological clock, we should also be able to speak of *setting*, or *resetting*, the clock (Waterhouse & DeCoursey, 2004). In fact, when a person who has been kept in an environment without sunlight is returned to normal living conditions, the usual 24-hour circadian rhythm is quickly restored.

31.4.2 Patterns of Sleep

Every 90 to 100 minutes over the first half of the night while we sleep, we pass through a sleep cycle that consists of five different stages (Fedotchev, 2011; Lavie, 2001). Over the latter part of the night, we tend to spend most time in the first two of these five stages and in rapid eye movement or REM sleep. Researchers have identified these stages by examining people's brainwave patterns while they sleep, using a device called an *electroencephalograph* (*EEG*). EEG readings indicate that each stage of sleep is characterized by a different brainwave pattern, as shown in **Figure 31-4**.

When we first go to bed and, still awake, begin to relax, EEG readings show that we experience what are called *alpha waves*. As we settle into this drowsy pre-sleep period, called the **hypnagogic state**, we sometimes experience strange sensations. We may feel that we are falling or floating in space, we may "hear" our name called out, or we may hear a loud crash. All of these sensations seem very real, but none actually has happened. Such sensory phenomena are called *hypnagogic hallucinations* (Jones et al., 2010). Also common during this pre-sleep stage is a *myoclonic jerk*, a sharp muscular spasm that generally accompanies the hypnagogic hallucination of falling.

When we finally doze off, EEG readings show that our brain waves become smaller and irregular, signalling that we have entered *Stage 1 sleep*. Alpha-wave patterns are replaced by slower waves, called *theta waves*. This first stage of sleep actually represents a bridge between wakefulness and sleep; it lasts only a few minutes. Our conscious awareness of street noises or the hum of an air conditioner fades. If we are roused from this stage, we might recall having just had ideas that seem nonsensical.

Eric Vandeville/Gamma-Rapho/GettyImages

Studying circadian rhythms. Maurizio Montalbini spent months living in a cavern, with no external light or means of telling the time, to study the circadian rhythms free of external or artificial influences.

hypnagogic state a pre-sleep period often characterized by vivid sensory phenomena.

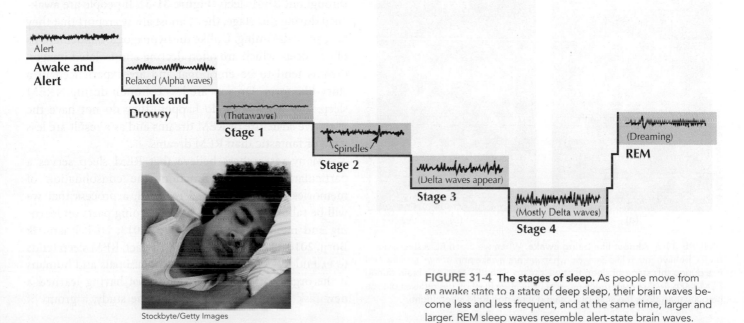
Stockbyte/Getty Images

FIGURE 31-4 **The stages of sleep.** As people move from an awake state to a state of deep sleep, their brain waves become less and less frequent, and at the same time, larger and larger. REM sleep waves resemble alert-state brain waves.

Falling deeper into sleep, we next pass into *Stage 2 sleep*. A still further slowing of brainwave activity occurs during this stage, although we may also exhibit **sleep spindles**—bursts of brain activity that last a second or two. During Stage 2, our breathing becomes steadily rhythmic. Occasionally the body twitches, although generally our muscle tension relaxes. During this stage, which lasts 15 to 20 minutes, we can still be awakened fairly easily. Toward the end of Stage 2 sleep, our brain waves slow even further and *delta waves* start to appear in addition to the theta waves. Delta waves indicate *delta sleep*, or deep sleep.

The next two stages of sleep, *Stage 3* and *Stage 4*, are characterized by very deep sleep. In Stage 3, between 20 and 50 percent of our EEG waves are delta waves. During Stage 4, the percentage of delta waves increases to more than 50 percent (Giedd, 2009; Bertini et al., 2007). During Stage 4, heart rate, blood pressure, and breathing rates all drop to their lowest levels, and the sleeper seems cut off from the world. Interestingly, although our muscles are most relaxed during this deepest phase of sleep, this is also the time when people are prone to sleepwalking. Similarly, children who wet their beds tend to do so during this stage.

Passing through all of the first four stages takes a little more than an hour of each of our first two 90-to-100-minute sleep cycles. After that, we experience the most interesting stage of sleep, **rapid eye movement,** or **REM, sleep.** In fact, all the preceding stages (Stages 1–4) are collectively called **non-REM sleep,** or **NREM.** During REM sleep, we experience rapid and jagged brainwave patterns, in contrast to the slow waves of NREM sleep. REM sleep has been called *paradoxical sleep* because, even though the body remains deeply relaxed on the surface—almost paralyzed—we experience considerable activity internally (Thakkar & Datta, 2010; Wickwire et al., 2008). The rapid brainwave pattern of REM sleep is accompanied by increased heart rate and rapid and irregular breathing, for example. Moreover, every 30 seconds or so, our eyes dart around rapidly behind our closed eyelids. Perhaps most interesting, during REM sleep people's brains behave just as they do when they are awake and active (Ratey, 2001).

Along with this brain activity, the genitals become aroused during REM sleep. Indeed, except during nightmares, men usually experience erections and women vaginal lubrication and clitoral engorgement during REM sleep, even if the content of the dream is not sexual (Andersen et al., 2010; Solms, 2007b). Men often retain their erections beyond the REM stage, explaining the occurrence of morning erections.

As we will discuss shortly, dreams usually occur throughout REM sleep (**Figure 31-5**). If people are awakened during this stage, they almost always report that they have been dreaming. Unlike the hypnagogic hallucinations of pre-sleep, which are often fleeting and isolated images, dreams tend to be emotional and are experienced in a story-like form. Dreams are less common during NREM sleep, and when they do happen, they do not have the narrative structure of REM dreams and as a result are less vivid or fantastic than REM dreams.

Many researchers believe that REM sleep serves a particularly important function—the consolidation of memories of newly learned material, a process that we will be talking about more in the coming parts on learning and memory (Rasch & Born, 2013; Diekelmann & Born, 2010a; Legault et al., 2010). In fact, REM sleep tends to extend longer than usual in both animals and humans if the organisms go to sleep after just having learned a new task (Smith, 2006, 1996). In one study, a group of

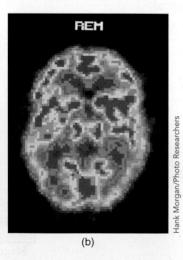

FIGURE 31-5 **Almost like being awake.** When we are in REM sleep, our brains behave much like they do when we are awake and active, and indeed it is during this stage of sleep that we dream. The PET scan of a brain during REM sleep (left) reveals much more activity (indicated by the red and orange colours) than does the scan of a brain during non-REM sleep (right).

volunteers were trained on a perceptual task just before going to sleep (Karni et al., 1994). Half of the sleepers were awakened during REM sleep, while the other half were awakened later, during the next cycle of NREM sleep. The next day, those who had been awakened during REM sleep performed more poorly on the perceptual task than those who had been awakened during the later NREM phases. Presumably, the REM-awakened volunteers had not yet had the opportunity to fully consolidate their memories of the newly learned task. (See the module "When We Sleep" for more information.)

However, this memory consolidation theory has been challenged by some studies showing that when animals are administered antidepressant drugs, which typically disrupt REM sleep, they nevertheless continue to learn and remember quite well (Vertes & Eastman, 2003). Research also finds that people with lesions to the *pons* portion of the brain, which may contribute to REM sleep, learn, remember, and function quite normally despite the disruption to the functioning of the pons.

It is worth noting that every kind of mammal whose sleep patterns have been studied, including birds, experience both NREM and REM sleep. Thus, many theorists believe that animals also dream. Of course, this comes as no surprise to dog owners who have, no doubt, observed their pets twitch their paws in a regular rhythm during REM sleep, as if running in a dream (Thompson, 2000). If you conduct a YouTube search for "BizKit the sleep walking dog" you will see an example of a dog that actually does much more than just twitch.

31.5 Dreams

Dreams—emotional, story-like sensory experiences that usually occur during REM sleep—have proven to be endlessly fascinating to scientists, clinicians, philosophers, artists, and laypeople, probably because of their vividness and mysteriousness. A woman dreams of being punched in the stomach and doubling over in pain. In thinking about the dream the next day, she notices that she feels very vulnerable. She also recalls that earlier on the day of the dream, she had learned about a poor midterm mark and about an increase in the entrance GPA to a program she had planned to enter, and she remembers having felt vulnerable because her planned major is in jeopardy. Could the dream and the poor midterm grade be related? Some psychologists would say yes, while others would be skeptical (Duesbury, 2011). Dream content varies widely as can be seen in **Table 31-1**, which shows the percentage of people who recall dreaming about particular events or experiences. It is easy to see why we might assume there is life-relevant meaning in the content of our dreams. In this module we will examine ways in which different theorists and researchers have come to understand dreams (Cartwright, 2010; Moorcroft, 2003).

> Research suggests that actions in dreams run in real time—that is, it takes you as long to accomplish something in the dream as it would if you were performing the action while you were awake.

31.5.1 Information-Processing Theory

Information-processing theory offers a cognitive view of dreaming. According to this view, dreams are the mind's attempt to sort out and organize the day's experiences and to fix them in memory. Consistent with this perspective, studies have revealed that interrupting REM sleep—and so interrupting dreams—impedes a person's ability to remember material learned just before going to sleep (Empson, 2002). Also, in support of this view, researchers have found that periods of REM sleep (during which we dream) tend to extend longer when people's days have been filled with multiple stressful events or marked by extensive learning experiences (Fogel et al., 2011; Palumbo, 1978). Thus, according to an information-processing perspective, the student who dreamed of being punched may simply have been attempting to process and give order to the stressful academic challenges that she had experienced earlier in the day.

information-processing theory hypothesis that dreams are the mind's attempt to sort out and organize the day's experiences and to fix them in memory.

TABLE 31-1 Dream Themes

Item	Total	Women	Men
School, teachers, studying	89.2	89.4	88.2
Being chased or pursued	88.7	89.1	86.8
Sexual experiences	86.7	85.6	92.7
Falling	74.3	74.2	75.0
Arriving too late	68.5	70.0	60.3
A person now alive being dead	68.0	70.7	52.9
Flying or soaring through the air	63.5	63.0	66.2
Failing an examination	60.8	63.8	44.1
Being on the verge of falling	56.5	57.7	50.0
Being frozen with fright	56.3	56.7	54.4
A person now dead being alive	45.0	46.3	38.2
Being physically attacked	44.8	44.7	45.6
Being nude	43.0	43.1	42.7
Eating delicious food	42.1	43.6	33.8
Swimming	38.7	38.0	42.7
Being locked up	38.7	37.2	47.1
Insects or spiders	37.2	37.0	38.2
Being killed	36.3	34.8	44.1
Your teeth falling out/losing your teeth	35.6	35.6	35.3
Being tied, unable to move	34.7	33.5	41.2
Being inappropriately dressed	33.1	33.2	32.3
Being a child again	32.7	32.7	32.4
Trying again and again to do something	30.4	29.5	35.3
Being unable to find, or embarrassed about using a toilet	30.0	31.1	23.5
Discovering a new room at home	29.1	29.0	29.4
Having superior knowledge or mental ability	27.0	24.5	41.2
Losing control of a vehicle	26.8	28.7	16.2
Fire	26.6	26.1	29.4
Wild, violent beasts	26.4	26.9	23.5

It response to the question "Have you ever dreamed of...." with a list of commonly reported dream themes, this table shows the percentages of men and women who reported having had a dream of each of the types listed.

Adapted from Schredl, Michael, Ciric, Petra, Gotz, Simon, and Wittmann, Lutz (2004) Typical dreams: Stability and gender differences, *The Journal of Psychology*, *138*(6), 485-494.

31.5.2 Activation-Synthesis Hypothesis

Researchers J. Allan Hobson and Robert McCarley have proposed a more biological hypothesis about dreaming, the **activation-synthesis model** (Hobson, 2009; 2005; Hobson & McCarley, 1977) (see **Figure 31-6**). They argue that as people sleep, their brains activate all kinds of signals. In particular, when dreams occur, neurons in the *brainstem* are activated. These, in turn, activate neurons in the *cerebral cortex* to produce visual and auditory signals. Also aroused are the emotion centres of the brain, including the *cingulate cortex*, *amygdala*, and *hippocampus*. Neuroimaging scans of people who are experiencing REM sleep confirm heightened activity and neuron communication in each of these brain regions.

Hobson and McCarley suggest that the activated brain combines—or *synthesizes*—these internally generated signals and tries to give them meaning. Each person organizes and synthesizes this random collection of images, feelings, memories, and thoughts in his own personal way—in the form of a particular dream story (Hobson et al., 2011, 2003, 1998). Someone who dreams of being punched in the stomach might be trying to synthesize activation in brain areas that normally receive signals from the muscles of the stomach with signals from areas of the brain that process emotions, for example.

What remains unclear in this model is why different people synthesize their onslaught of brain signals in different ways. Freud, of course, might suggest that each person's particular synthesis is influenced by her unfulfilled needs and unresolved conflicts.

FIGURE 31-6 Activation-synthesis. According to the activation-synthesis theory of dreaming, neurons in the brainstem activate neurons in other areas throughout the brain. The brain combines these various signals into a story, or dream.

Cerebral cortex

Cingulate cortex

Brain stem

activation-synthesis model theory that dreams result from the brain's attempts to synthesize or organize random internally generated signals and give them meaning.

31.5.3 Freudian Dream Theory

Sigmund Freud argued that dreams represent the expression of unconscious wishes or desires. He believed that dreams allow us to discharge internal energy associated with unacceptable feelings (Freud, 1900). Freud suggested that *dream interpretation*, in which a psychoanalytic therapist facilitates insight into the possible meaning behind a dream, may help clients appreciate their underlying needs and conflicts with the goal of being less constrained by them during waking life. For example, if a lonely and morally upstanding young man is sexually attracted to his brother's wife but is not consciously aware of this desire, he might have a dream in which he goes swimming in a private pool that is marked "No Trespassing." His therapist might help the man arrive at the conclusion that the dream about swimming in an off-limits pool symbolizes his wish to be with his sister-in-law. Such an insight eventually might help the man to overcome inhibitions he feels about finding a suitable partner for himself.

Freud called the dream images that people are able to recall the *manifest content of the dream*. The unconscious elements of dreams are called the *latent content*. In our example, the young man's desire for his sister-in-law (latent content)—a scandalous idea that he would never allow himself to have—is symbolized in the dream by a swim in the pool (manifest content). His dream of a happy swim in forbidden territory is his mind's solution to a problem that he could not work out consciously.

Many of today's theorists, including a number of psychoanalytic ones, criticize Freud's theory both in terms of its focus and its lack of verifiability through research. For example, *object-relations theorists*, psychoanalytic theorists who place greater emphasis on the role of relationships in development, focus more on relationship issues when interpreting dream material (Wolman, 1979). Regarding the earlier dream in which a student gets punched, an object-relations therapist might be inclined to help the patient explore her feelings of vulnerability in various parts of her life, rather than her educational fears.

©iStockphoto.com/Decisiveimages

Dream stories. People often experience similar dream stories. For example, 80 percent of all people have had repeated dreams of running toward or away from something.

31.6 Nightmares, Lucid Dreams, and Daydreams

Dreams evoke many different feelings. Dreams filled with intense anxiety are called *night-mares*. The feeling of terror can be so great that the dreamer awakens from the dream, often crying out. Nightmares generally evoke feelings of helplessness or powerlessness, usually in situations of great danger. They tend to be more common among people who are under stress. People who experience frequent nightmares and become very distressed by their nightmares are considered to have a *nightmare disorder*.

It appears that nightmares are more common among children than adults, although there is some dispute on this issue (Schredl, Blomeyer, & Gorlinger, 2000). When children have a nightmare, simple reassurances that they are safe and that the dream does not reflect real danger are usually helpful. It is important to help the child appreciate the difference between inner and outer reality, a concept they struggle with up to and into their early school years (Gonzalez, 2010; Halliday, 2004).

In contrast to dreams and nightmares, during which dreamers feel they are caught in a real situation, **lucid dreams** are dreams in which people fully recognize that they are dreaming (Blagrove, Bell, & Wilkinson, 2010; Baars et al., 2003). Some lucid dreamers can even willfully guide the outcome of their dreams (Erlacher & Shredl, 2010; Voss et al, 2013). In a lucid dream, the woman who dreamed of being punched might tell herself—while still asleep—that she is only dreaming and is actually fine; she even might try to guide the outcome of the dream so that she prevails over her attacker. Although not necessarily subscribing to psychoanalytic theory, people who attempt to engage in lucid dreaming often believe that it is a way to open up another phase of human consciousness and perhaps help us to understand the relationships among frontal lobe function, rationality, and psychosis (Mota-Rolim & Araujo, 2013).

A third dream-related phenomenon is actually associated with waking states of consciousness—the daydream. Fantasies that occur while one is awake and mindful of external reality, but not fully conscious, are called *daydreams* (Delaney et al., 2010; Schon, 2003; Singer, 2003). Sometimes a daydream can become so strong that we lose track of external reality for a brief while. Although we may be embarrassed when caught daydreaming, such experiences may also afford us opportunities for creativity; we are, after all, less constrained during the fantasies than we would be if attending strictly to the outside world.

lucid dreams dreams in which sleepers fully recognize that they are dreaming, and occasionally actively guide the outcome of the dream.

31.7 Sleep Pattern Changes Over Development

Parents or older siblings know all too well that young babies do not sleep quite like older children or adults. Through the first four months of life, babies sleep between 14 and 17 hours each day. The amount of time that they spend sleeping declines steadily as they get older (Blumberg & Seelke, 2010; Sadeh et al., 2009). Although babies spend a lot of time asleep overall, the lengths of their sleep periods can last anywhere from minutes to hours before they are awake and crying out for attention. For parents, the good news is that sleep tends to become more structured at around 6 months of age (McLaughlin & Williams, 2009).

Babies appear to spend a great deal more time than adults in REM sleep—around eight hours per day for infants, compared with two hours for adults (Sankupellay et al., 2011; Siegel, 2005). The size of this difference has led theorists to suspect that infant sleep patterns are crucial to development in various ways. Several have speculated, for example, that REM sleep aids in the development of the central nervous system by facilitating synaptic pruning and preventing the formation of unnecessary connections, although research has not yet confirmed this belief (Krippner, 1990). Also, by slowing body activity, the extended REM sleep of babies may help to regulate the temperature

HOW WE DEVELOP

©iStockphoto.com/jfairone

of their developing brains. REM sleep tends to decrease to adult levels somewhere between the ages of 2 and 6 years (El-Sheikh, 2011; Curzi-Dascalova & Challamel, 2000).

By early childhood, an individual's total daily sleep requirement also decreases significantly (see **Figure 31-7**). Most children sleep around nine hours each day, although pediatricians recommend between 12 and 15 hours of sleep for anyone between 2 and 5 years of age. Teenagers average around seven hours of daily sleep, although pediatricians recommend at least eight hours for them (Crisp, 2010; Acebo et al., 2005). As adults, our sleep patterns continue to change. As we age, we spend less and less time in deep sleep and REM sleep, our sleep is more readily interrupted, and we take longer to get back to sleep when awakened (Bliwise, 2010; Garcia-Rill et al., 2008).

A graduate student in physiology, Eugene Aserinsky, discovered REM sleep when he attached electronic leads to his 8-year-old son's head and eyelids to monitor his sleep and waking brainwaves. He found unexpected brainwave activity, suggesting his son "had woken up even though he hadn't" (Aserinsky, 1996).

As discussed earlier, our sleep–awake cycle is tied to our body's circadian rhythms. These biological clocks are also affected by environmental demands and expectations (Worthman, 2011). Studies have, for example, contrasted parenting practices in North America with those in the Kipsigis tribe (you may remember them from Part 4). Many Western parents structure their babies' sleep by putting them down at designated times and not responding to their cries. In contrast, Kipsigis mothers keep their babies with them constantly. As a result, Kipsigis babies sleep for much shorter periods of time later into infancy than do American babies; in many cases, they do not sleep for long stretches even as adults (Super & Harkness, 2002, 1972). The body clocks of teenagers also seem to be compromised by the increased social and academic pressures that they encounter (El-Sheikh, 2011; Crowley, Acebo, & Carskadon, 2007). Many adolescents, for example, stay up late largely because that's what it takes for them to finish their homework or to keep up with their friends.

31.8 Sleep Deprivation and Sleep Disorders

How much sleep a person needs varies, depending on factors such as age, lifestyle, and genetic disposition. The amount of sleep people actually get may also be different from how much they need. Lifestyle deprives many people of sleep, and sleep disorders may also make it impossible to sleep properly.

FACING
ADVERSITY

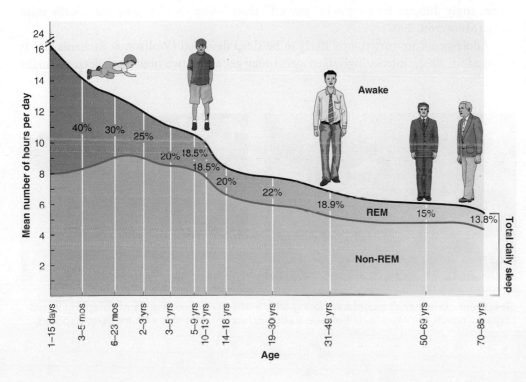

FIGURE 31-7 The effects of aging on the sleep cycle. As we get older, our total daily sleep and our REM sleep decrease. The largest shifts occur during our first three years of life.

Psychology Around Us | "Give Me Five More Minutes!"

Sylvio woke up exhausted... yet again. Personally, he blamed getting up early the day before to go to his part-time job, then getting home late from soccer practice, having a paper due, and preparing for three mid-terms coming up for his tiredness. But he might not also blame his Facebook time or his chatting with his friends or the noise of message notifications on his cell phone on his bedside table as he slept. Since Sylvio certainly wasn't ready to give up those activities, he splashed water in his face and tried to wake up and get to his first class.

Like most other first-year students studied by Nancy Galambos and her colleagues at the Unversity of Alberta (Galambos, Dalton, & Maggs, 2009), Sylvio runs on at least some level of chronic sleep deprivation. However, in addition to getting less sleep than he should, the quality of Sylvio's sleep is less than optimal. Galambos research involved having first-year students keep detailed logs of their daytime activities and their night time sleep-related behaviour over a two-week period. When they compared sleep activities to measures of general functioning, they found that getting less sleep led to more negative affect, spending less time on school work, and more socializing. Better quality of sleep led to less negative affect, more stress, and less time spent on school work (perhaps because the time spent studying was more efficient when the students were better rested). This research suggests there is significant value in terms of student quality of life to be gained by paying attention to both the quantity and quality of sleep you are getting during the school term.

31.8.1 Sleep Deprivation

Left unhindered, most people would sleep for nine or ten hours a day to awaken alert and refreshed. However, we've all had the opposite experience—that of not getting enough sleep. When lack of sleep happens, we become generally sleepy and maybe a little cranky. After a while, we may yearn for sleep.

Researchers have found that without enough sleep, people also experience a general depressed state (Orzel-Gryglewska, 2010). They display lower productivity and are more apt to make mistakes (Gunzelmann et al., 2011). Stan Coren, a researcher at the University of British Columbia, has shown that accidents and deaths are more likely to occur when drivers and pilots do not get enough sleep (Coren, 1997). He suggests that we all should watch our sleep deficit if we want to function coherently and safely. While it is possible to make up for the lost sleep of one night by sleeping a little longer the next night, it becomes increasingly difficult for people to "pay off" their "sleep debt" if they chronically miss sleep (Moorcroft, 2003).

Adolescents are particularly likely to be sleep deprived (Wolfson & Richards, 2011; Carskadon, 2002). Interestingly, teenagers today get about two hours less sleep per night

©iStockphoto.com/© CJP

©iStockphoto.com/mMediaphotos

Sleep wins. Whether it's a gardener dozing off in a wheelbarrow or a guitarist collapsing in mid-play on a couch, the need to drift off eventually catches up with those who are sleep deprived.

than teens did 80 years ago. In fact, the distinguished sleep researcher William Dement has asserted that 80 percent of students at his institution, Stanford University, are "dangerously sleep deprived" (Dement & Vaughan, 1999).

Ironically, students who pull all-nighters to complete their work actually wind up working less efficiently and effectively than they would if they were to sleep the eight or nine hours that they need. Despite such problems among young people, researchers have not conducted much research on how sleep deprivation specifically affects physical, cognitive, and emotional development (Kopasz et al., 2010; Loessl et al., 2008).

Sleep researchers used to spend most of their time examining the impact of lost sleep on simple or monotonous tasks. Today's researchers, however, often look at the impact of sleep deprivation on more complex activities (Anderson & Platten, 2011; Moorcroft, 2003; Harrison & Horne, 2000), or as Frank Wimmer at Carleton University has done, at the effects of sleep deprivation on creativity and attention management (Wimmer et al., 1992). Studies suggest that, on one hand, sleep deprivation does *not* necessarily lower one's performance on complex logical tasks. Sleep-deprived participants in such tasks often are able to avoid poor performances by being highly interested in the complex tasks at hand. Many sleep-deprived college and university students, for example, seem able to conduct research or write papers, particularly if those works interest them a lot.

Problems arise, on the other hand, when a sleep-deprived person faces unexpected turns of events, distractions, or innovations while working on a complex task, or needs to revise the task. If, for example, someone turns on the television while you're studying in a sleep-deprived state, your learning is likely to suffer considerably.

In an important set of findings, researchers have also learned that sleep loss can lower the effectiveness of people's immune systems (Bollinger et al., 2010; Dement & Vaughan, 1999). Sleep-deprived people apparently have a more difficult time fighting off viral infections and cancer, for example. Thus, it may not be surprising that people who average at least eight hours of sleep a night tend to outlive those who get less sleep (Dement & Vaughn, 1999).

31.8.2 Sleep Disorders

Sleep disorders occur when normal sleep patterns are disturbed, causing impaired daytime functioning and feelings of distress (Ivanenko & Johnson, 2010; Espie, 2002; APA, 2000). Almost everyone suffers from some kind of sleep disorder at one time or another in their lives. The sleep disorder may be part of a larger problem, such as life stress, a medical condition, or substance misuse, or it may be a *primary* sleep disorder in which sleep difficulties are the central problem. Primary sleep disorders typically arise from abnormalities in people's circadian rhythms and sleep–wake mechanisms.

People who suffer from **insomnia**, the most common sleep disorder, regularly cannot fall asleep or stay asleep (Bastien, 2011; Horne, 2010). According to a large study by Charles Morin and his colleagues at Laval University, 20 percent of Canadians are dissatisfied with the quality of their sleep (Morin et al., 2011). The telephone survey further found that 40 percent of Canadian adults experience symptoms of insomnia at least three nights each week.

insomnia sleep disorder characterized by a regular inability to fall asleep or stay asleep.

As you might expect, many cases of insomnia are triggered by day-to-day stressors. In particular, job or school pressures, troubled relationships, and financial problems have been implicated. For many people, a subtle additional stress is worrying about not getting enough sleep while trying to fall asleep. This vicious cycle can further intensify anxiety and make sleep all the more elusive (Jansson-Frojmark et al., 2011).

Insomnia is more common among older people than younger ones (Jaussent et al., 2011). Elderly individuals are particularly prone to this problem because so many of them have medical ailments, experience pain, take medications, or grapple with depression and anxiety—each a known contributor to insomnia (Taylor and Weiss, 2008). In addition, some of the normal age-related sleep changes we described earlier may heighten the chances of insomnia among elderly people. As individuals age, for example, they naturally spend less time in deep sleep and their sleep is more readily interrupted (Bliwise, 2010; Edelstein et al., 2008).

Sleepwalking most often takes place during the first three hours of sleep (Dogu & Pressman, 2011; Wickwire et al., 2008). Sleepwalkers will often sit up, get out of bed, and walk around. They usually avoid obstacles, climb stairs, and perform complex activities. Accidents do happen, however: tripping, bumping into furniture, and even falling out of windows have all been reported. People who are awakened while sleepwalking are confused for several moments. If allowed to continue sleepwalking, they eventually return to bed. The disorder appears to be inherited (Hublin et al., 2001). Up to 5 percent of children experience this disorder for a period of time, and up to 17 percent have at least one episode (Wickwire et al., 2008).

Night terrors are related to sleepwalking. Individuals who suffer from this pattern awaken suddenly, sit up in bed, scream in extreme fear and agitation, and experience heightened heart and breathing rates. They appear to be in a state of panic and are often incoherent. Usually people suffering from night terrors do not remember the episodes the next morning. Night terror disorder is not the same thing as a *nightmare disorder*, discussed earlier in the part, in which sufferers experience frequent nightmares. Sleepwalking and night terrors are more common among children than among adolescents or adults. They tend to occur during Stages 3 and 4, the deepest stages of NREM sleep (Hublin et al., 1999). Because night terrors typically stop after childhood, we do not treat them as sleep disorders but rather as developmental issues (Mindell & Owens, 2003).

Psychology Around Us **Do People Who Are Sleepwalking Know What They're Doing?**

The answer is likely no, sleepwalkers are not aware of what they are doing. While most sleepwalkers just sit up or wander around the house, some engage in more complex behaviours such as cooking meals, climbing out of windows, or even driving cars.

Sleepwalking typically occurs in deep Stage 3 to Stage 4 sleep with little or no dreaming. If you awaken a sleepwalker loudly or suddenly, it may startle or frighten them and being frightened might cause them to react defensively. Mainly they will be confused and disoriented. If possible, it is best just to speak softly to them and lead them back to bed. They will most likely have no memory of their late-night stroll when they get up in the morning (Boyd, 2004).

As an extreme example, consider the case of Ken Parks who lived in Pickering, Ontario. One night Ken fell asleep on the couch, arose in the middle of the night, drove across town, entered the home of his parents-in-law, and, using a tire iron and knife, killed his mother-in-law and nearly killed his father-in-law. He drove himself to a police station and turned himself in, saying, in a confused state, he thought he had killed someone. At trial, Ken's lawyer argued he was sleepwalking (actually, that he was in a state of non-insane automatism, or that he was not acting voluntarily) and therefore should not be held accountable for his actions. The jury agreed and acquitted him of murder. The Supreme Court of Canada upheld the acquittal. Others have tried to use this defence and been found guilty. There is currently much debate in legal, medical, and psychological circles as to whether sleepwalking ought to be considered a legitimate defence (Horn, 2005).

Fifty-four percent of married Canadians say their partners snore while sleeping. Of those, 63 percent say their partner's snoring keeps them awake at night and adds to their own fatigue (Nutravite, 2006). It is likely that many of these serious snorers suffer from **sleep apnea**, the second most common sleep disorder. People with this condition repeatedly stop breathing during the night, depriving the brain of oxygen and leading to frequent awakenings. Sleep apnea can result when the brain fails to send a "breathe signal" to the diaphragm and other breathing muscles, or when muscles at the top of the throat become too relaxed, allowing the windpipe to partially close. Sufferers stop breathing for up to 30 seconds or more as they sleep. Hundreds of episodes may occur each night. Often the individual will not remember any of them, but will feel sleepy the next day. The biggest concern with sleep apnea is that the repeated episodes of breathing cessation stress the heart and can eventually lead to cardiac arrest. As well, people with sleep apnea are not getting sufficient rest and are at increased risk for fatigue-related problems while driving or working (Shah, 2007). Sleep apnea can usually be stopped completely by using a positive flow ventilator that keeps throat tissue open and stops the snoring and the breathing interruptions associated with this issue.

sleep apnea sleep disorder characterized by repeatedly ceasing to breathe during the night, depriving the brain of oxygen and leading to frequent awakenings.

Getty Images for Reebok

Sleep apnea. NBA legend Shaquille O'Neal, who participated in a Harvard Medical School sleep study, has been diagnosed with sleep apnea (Harvard Medical School, 2013).

Narcolepsy, marked by an uncontrollable urge to fall asleep, is diagnosed in an estimated 24,000 people (based on U.S. population data, as there is no official data for Canada); almost as many people (18,000) may not be diagnosed but still have the disorder (U.S. Census Bureau, 2004; NINDS, 2006). People with this disorder may suddenly fall into REM sleep in the midst of an argument or during an exciting football game. When they wake, they feel refreshed. The narcoleptic episode is experienced as a loss of consciousness that can last up to 15 minutes. This disorder can obviously have serious consequences for people driving cars, operating tools, or performing highly precise work. Its cause is not fully known. Narcolepsy seems to run in families, and some studies have linked the disorder to a specific gene or combination of genes (Quinnell et al., 2007). Recent work by Maan Lee and his colleagues at the Montreal Neurological Institute has helped to identify orexin or hypocretin receptors in the hypothalamus and their potential role in narcolepsy. When these receptors under-function, narcolepsy results (Lee, Hassani, & Jones, 2005). This sort of finding could eventually lead to a treatment for narcolepsy.

narcolepsy sleep disorder marked by uncontrollable urge to fall asleep.

©iStockphoto.com/BrianAJackson

©iStockphoto.com/imagine632

Studying narcolepsy. Some people with narcolepsy, a sleep disorder marked by uncontrollable urges to fall asleep, further experience sudden loss of muscle tone during their narcoleptic episodes. Dogs may also struggle with narcolepsy. You can see what happens when Skeeter, a narcoleptic dog, gets excited at this YouTube link: www.youtube.com/watch?v=X0h2nleWTwI.

Tying It Together: **Your Brain and Behaviour**

Getting a Good Night's Sleep

If you're like most people, you fall asleep when you are tired and need to rest. After an uninterrupted night's sleep or nap, you probably feel refreshed and better able to face life's challenges. Given how rested you feel after sleeping, it may surprise you to hear that while you sleep, your brain is incredibly active—it's not resting at all, or at least it is certainly not inactive! Each stage of sleep is characterized by a different pattern of brain activity.

During REM sleep, a time of active dreaming, signals in the brain shut down the system that controls movement. Preventing movement probably saves us from potentially dangerous actions we could take if we acted out our dreams.

During slow-wave sleep, studies have shown that many circuits in the brain replay patterns of activity that work to strengthen new memories. That may be why being deprived of sleep, a common occurrence for college or university students, is associated with problems remembering facts over the long term. Scientists don't fully understand why we sleep, but they all agree that the brain doesn't function optimally without it.

©iStockphoto.com/101dalmatians

Questions

1 What is the physiological explanation for why people typically do not act out their dreams?

2 Inadequate sleep seems to disrupt neuron formation in which region of the brain?

3 Explain the relationship between sleep, hunger, and weight.

IMPROVING COGNITION

Sleep allows for neuronal growth in the brain. Sleep deprivation prevents the addition of new neurons to the hippocampus, a brain region important for cognition and anxiety regulation. This may be one reason sleep deprivation weakens our ability to learn and increases the likelihood of mood disturbances.

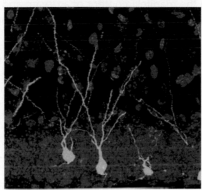

Image adapted from Neuron 54, 2007 (by Kurt Sailor, Guo-li Ming, and Hongjun Song at Johns Hopkins School of Medicine

IMPROVING METABOLISM

Sleep helps the brain to regulate metabolism. Sleep deprivation increases the peptide ghrelin and decreases the peptide leptin.

Changes in the levels of these chemicals both work on neurons of the hypothalamus, shown here as green-stained neurons, to stimulate hunger—this may be one reason why sleep-deprived people are more likely to gain weight.

Courtesy of Sebastien G. Bouret

LOCKING IN MEMORIES

During slow-wave sleep, patterns of activity that result from learning are replayed multiple times in the neurons of the hippocampus, a brain region shown here stained with fluorescent dyes. This replaying serves to strengthen connections and consolidate memories.

Livet, J.R. Sanes, J.W. Lichtman, Center for Brain Science—Harvard University

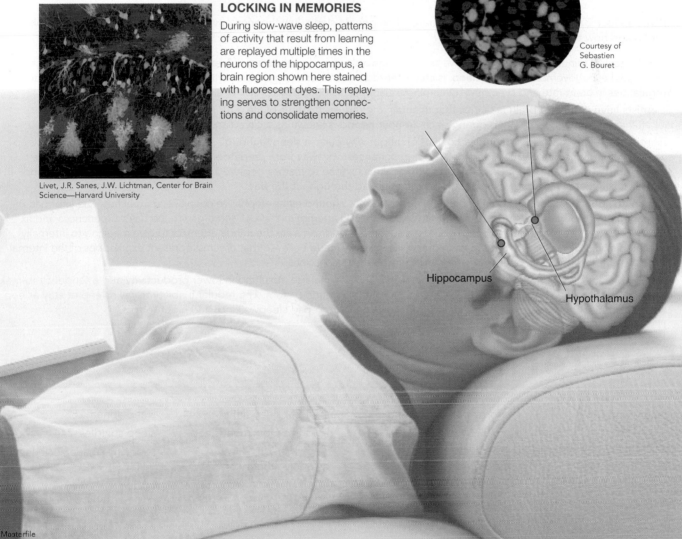

Hippocampus

Hypothalamus

Masterfile

What Do You Know?
1. What are the major theories of why people sleep?
2. What is the difference between the manifest content of a dream and its latent content?
3. What is the role of the suprachiasmatic nucleus in human consciousness?
4. What is the difference between a nightmare and a night terror?

What Do You Think? Which of the theories of dreams described in this module is closest to your own theory of dreams (before you read this module and found out about the science in this area)? Are there other studies we should do to better understand dreaming?

Summary

Module 31: When We Are Asleep

LEARNING OBJECTIVE 31 Describe what happens when people sleep, key theories of why we sleep and dream, and problems with sleep and how they affect functioning.

- Every 90 to 100 minutes when we sleep, we pass through a sleep cycle consisting of five different stages. The fifth stage of sleep, rapid eye movement, or REM sleep, is characterized by rapid and jagged brainwave patterns and eye movements and irregularities in heart rate and breathing. Dreaming usually occurs during this phase of sleep.
- Scientists have identified brain activities that maintain the regular rhythms of life. Our move from a sustained period of wakefulness into a period of sleep during each 24-hour period is known as a *circadian rhythm*.
- Scientists have not reached a definitive conclusion about why people sleep, although some scientists have suggested sleep serves an evolutionarily adaptive function, keeping our ancestors away from predators that hunted at night. Others have suggested that sleep might play a role in growth, or allow us time to restore depleted chemical resources in the brain and body and eliminate chemical wastes that have accumulated throughout the day.
- We also do not understand why people dream. Recent theories about dreams emphasize cognitive approaches. The information-processing theory of dreams suggests that dreams are the mind's attempt to sort out and organize the day's experiences and fix them in memory. The attention-synthesis hypothesis suggests that dreams are the mind's attempts to give meaning to internally generated signals firing throughout the brain during deep sleep. Freud believed that dreams represent expressions of the internal desires and wishes that have been repressed and stored in the unconscious.
- Sleep deprivation can lead to feelings of fatigue, irritability, and malaise, resulting in lower productivity and a tendency to make mistakes. Loss of sleep can also affect the functioning of the immune system. The regular inability to fall asleep or stay asleep is called insomnia. Other sleep disorders include sleep apnea, narcolepsy, sleepwalking, and night terrors.

Key Terms

activation-synthesis model 247

adaptive theory of sleep 240

circadian rhythm 241

hypnagogic state 243

information-processing theory 245

insomnia 251

lucid dreams 248

narcolepsy 253

non-REM sleep (NREM) 244

rapid eye movement sleep (REM) 244

restorative theory of sleep 240

sleep apnea 253

sleep spindles 244

suprachiasmatic nucleus (SCN) 242

Study Questions

Multiple Choice

1. The structure in the hypothalamus that coordinates the function of the pineal gland producing melatonin is the _____.
   a) pons
   b) prefrontal cortex
   c) reticular formation
   d) suprachiasmatic nucleus

2. REM sleep is sometimes called "paradoxical sleep" because:
   a) both the brain and the body are inactive.
   b) the brain is active, but the major skeletal muscles are paralyzed.
   c) the brain is less active than it is during other sleep stages.
   d) the skeletal muscles remain active, but the brain is inactive.

Fill-in-the-Blank

1. According to Freud, the portion of our dreams that we can recall upon waking (and that is often symbolic of the hidden, unconscious portion) is called the _____ content.

2. Biological processes occurring on a cycle of approximately 24 hours are termed _____ rhythms.

3. Two of the sleep disorders that tend to occur during Stages 3 and 4 of NREM sleep are _____ and night terror disorder.

Module 32: Hypnosis

hypnosis a seemingly altered state
of consciousness during which
individuals can be directed to act
or experience the world in unusual
ways.

In movie and cartoon portrayals of hypnosis, a creepy guy dressed in black tells an unsuspecting person to stare at a swinging pocket watch and says, "Follow the watch…You are getting sleepy, sleeeeepy, sleeeeepy." Soon, the person is completely under the power of the hypnotist, who often makes him or her do something completely out of character or, in more sinister films, illegal and dangerous. As you might expect, this portrayal is exaggerated and distorted.

The idea that **hypnosis** produces an altered state of consciousness or a trance-like state is only one explanation offered by psychologists (Lynn, Rhue, & Kirsch, 2010; Kihlstrom, 2007). During hypnosis, people can be directed to act in unusual ways, experience unusual sensations, remember forgotten events, or forget remembered events. An alternative explanation for these behaviours was developed by Nick Spanos working at Carleton University (Spanos et al., 1995). Spanos argued that hypnosis subjects are actually role-playing—acting as they believe hypnotized people should act. We will look at these two explanations for hypnosis in more detail.

People typically are guided into this suggestible state by a trained hypnotist or hypnotherapist. The process involves their willing relinquishment of control over certain behaviours and their acceptance of distortions of reality. For hypnosis to work, individuals must be open and responsive to suggestions made by the hypnotist.

Some people are more open to a hypnotist's suggestions than others, a quality that often runs in families (Barnier & Council, 2010; Gfeller & Gorassini, 2010). Approximately 15 percent of adults are very susceptible to hypnosis, while 10 percent are not at all hypnotizable. Most adults fall somewhere in between (Hilgard, 1991, 1982). People who are especially suggestible are also more likely to do what other people tell them to do even when they are not hypnotized, a finding that supports Spanos' view of hypnosis as role-playing (Braffman & Kirsch, 2001). Perhaps not surprisingly, therefore, children tend to be particularly suggestible (Olness & Kohen, 2010). There are big differences between the scientific study of hypnosis and the stage shows put on by hypnotists.

32.1 Hypnotic Procedures and Effects

Hypnotists use various methods to induce the hypnotic state (Gibbons & Lynne, 2010). Sometimes—in a much tamer version than the movie portrayals—a person is asked to relax while concentrating on a single small target, such as a watch or an item in a painting on the wall. At other times, the hypnotist induces a *hyperalert* hypnotic trance that actually guides the individual to heightened tension and awareness. In either case, the hypnotist delivers "suggestions" to the subject, not the authoritarian commands on display in the movies.

One area of functioning that can be readily influenced by hypnotists is motor control. If the hypnotist suggests that a person's hand is being drawn like a magnet to a nearby stapler, the individual's hand will soon move to the stapler, as if propelled by an external force.

In some cases, people can be directed to respond *after* being roused from the hypnotic trance. A predetermined signal prompts such *posthypnotic responses*. A posthypnotic response is a behaviour that was suggested while the person was hypnotized, but which is engaged in later when a specified sign is observed (Spiegel & Spiegel, 2004). During hypnosis, the hypnotist may suggest, for example, that the person will later stand up whenever the hypnotist touches a desk. After being roused, and with no understanding of why, the person will in fact stand when the hypnotist touches the desk.

©iStockphoto.com/PaulaConnelly

The power of suggestion. People can be directed to experience unusual sensations and act in unusual ways when in a hypnotic state—a trance-like altered state of consciousness marked by extreme suggestibility. Here, a female hypnotist works with a male patient. The therapist is testing for suggestibility using the light hand, heavy hand test.

Related to posthypnotic responses is the phenomenon of *posthypnotic amnesia*, in which the hypnotist directs the person to later forget information learned during hypnosis. Once again, after being roused from the hypnotic trance, the person does not remember the learned material until the hypnotist provides a predetermined signal to remember (Spiegel & Spiegel, 2004). The degree to which the earlier information is forgotten varies. Some people will not remember any of the learned material, while others will remember quite a bit.

Hypnosis can also induce *hallucinations*, mental perceptions that do not match the physical stimulations coming from the world around us. Researchers have distinguished between two kinds of *hypnotic hallucinations*: positive and negative. Positive hallucinations are those in which people under hypnosis are guided to see objects or hear sounds that are not present. Negative hallucinations are those in which hypnotized people fail to see or hear stimuli that are present. Negative hallucinations are often used to control pain. The hypnotized person is directed to ignore—basically, to simply not perceive—pain. The hallucination may result in a total or partial reduction of pain (Jensen, 2010; Patterson, 2010). Some practitioners have even applied hypnosis to help control pain during dental and other forms of surgery (Auld, 2007). Although only some people are able to undergo surgery while anesthetized by hypnosis alone, combining hypnosis with chemical forms of anesthesia apparently helps many individuals (Hammond, 2008; Fredericks, 2001). Beyond its use in the control of pain, hypnosis has been used successfully to help treat a variety of problems, such as anxiety, skin diseases, asthma, insomnia, stuttering, high blood pressure, warts, and other forms of infection (Covino & Pinnell, 2010; Mellinger, 2010).

Many people also turn to hypnosis to help break bad habits, such as smoking, nail biting, and overeating. Does hypnosis help? Research has shown that hypnosis does indeed help some people to quit smoking (Green, 2010). It also helps many people to better control their eating and lose weight, particularly if hypnosis is paired with cognitive treatments, interventions that help people change their conscious ways of thinking (Ginandes, 2006; Lynn & Kirsch, 2006).

32.2 Why Does Hypnosis Work?

There are various theories about why hypnosis works (Lynn et al., 2010; Kallio & Revonsuo, 2003). One views hypnosis as a state of *divided consciousness* (Sadler & Woody, 2010; Hilgard, 1992). Another theory suggested by Canadian Nick Spanos (Spanos et al., 1995), who worked at Carleton University (prior to his death in 1994), sees hypnosis as an implementation of *common social and cognitive processes* or role-playing (see **Figure 32-1**).

Ernest Hilgard demonstrated that people hypnotized and instructed that they could "not hear" loud noises can indicate, by raising a finger or other behavioural response, that "some part" of them could still hear noise (Hilgard, 1992). From this result, Hilgard concluded that consciousness splits into two parts and that both act at once during hypnosis, an experience called **dissociation** (Sadler & Woody, 2010; Hilgard, 1992). One part of

dissociation a splitting of consciousness into two dimensions.

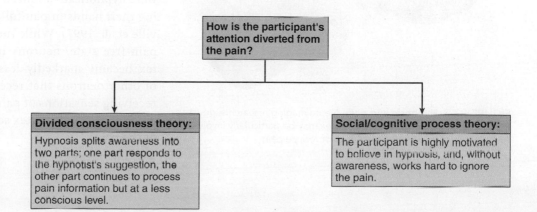

FIGURE 32-1 **Explaining hypnosis.**
Two possible theories explaining how a hypnotized individual is able to ignore pain.

How is the participant's attention diverted from the pain?

Divided consciousness theory:
Hypnosis splits awareness into two parts; one part responds to the hypnotist's suggestion, the other part continues to process pain information but at a less conscious level.

Social/cognitive process theory:
The participant is highly motivated to believe in hypnosis, and, without awareness, works hard to ignore the pain.

our consciousness becomes fully tuned into and responsive to the hypnotist's suggestions. The second part, which Hilgard called the *hidden observer*, operates at a subtler, less conscious level, continuing to process information that is seemingly unavailable to the hypnotized person. According to Hilgard, the hidden observer was the part of the student's mind that was still able to hear while hypnotized.

In direct opposition to Hilgard, Nick Spanos developed a different theory of hypnosis, which held that hypnosis is not an altered state of consciousness. Spanos' theory is that, instead of resulting from a divided consciousness, hypnotic phenomena consist simply of highly motivated people performing tasks, being extra attentive, and enacting roles that are asked of them—that is, they are playing a part in a social interaction between themselves, the "hypnotist," and the audience. Because of their strong beliefs in hypnosis, the people fail to recognize or ignore their own active contributions to the process (Dienes et al., 2009; Spanos et al., 1995). In a similar manner, people who are hypnotized and regressed to an earlier age will often be able to describe their sixth birthday in great detail, suggesting that hypnosis has greatly enhanced their memory abilities. Typically, however, audiences at hypnosis shows do not check the details of those hypnosis-assisted memories. Martin Orne (1951), in a classic study, did check the accounts of early life events told by hypnotically regressed people (by talking to their parents); he found that their vivid accounts of early birthdays and other life events were largely made up. These data better support Spanos' view than Hilgard's.

32.3 What Happens in the Brain during Hypnosis

When people are hypnotized, they are usually first guided into a state of *mental relaxation*. Studies have found that during this state, neural activity in key areas of the cerebral cortex and thalamus—brain regions that, as we noted earlier, are implicated in conscious awareness—slows down significantly (Rainville et al., 2002). Hypnotized individuals are next guided into a state of *mental absorption*, during which they focus carefully on the hypnotist's voice and instructions and actively block out other sources of stimulation, both internal and environmental. In fact, mental absorption has often been described as a state of *total focus*. During this state, cerebral blood flow and neural activity actually speed back up in key areas of the cerebral cortex, thalamus, and other parts of the brain's attention and conscious awareness systems (Naish, 2010; Oakley & Halligan, 2010; Rainville et al., 2002).

Neuroimaging research suggests that one part of the brain's cerebral cortex, the *anterior cingulate cortex*, may be particularly involved when hypnosis is used to anesthetize or reduce pain (**Figure 32-2**). This region has been implicated both in general awareness and in the unpleasantness we feel during pain. In one study, participants were hypnotically induced to ignore their pain while placing their hands in painfully hot (47 degrees) water (Rainville et al., 1997). While the individuals were in a hypnotic pain-free state, neurons in their anterior cingulate cortex became markedly less active. Although the activity of other neurons that receive pain mestthey were indeed receiving sensations of pain—the decreased activity in the anterior cingulate cortex seemed to reduce their *awareness* of the pain.

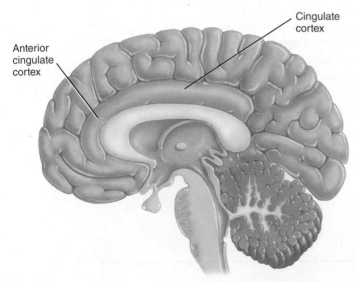

FIGURE 32-2 Hypnosis and pain. Neuroimaging research suggests that the brain's *anterior cingulate cortex* may be particularly involved when hypnosis is used to anesthetize or reduce pain.

What Do You Know?

1. What are hypnotic hallucinations and how might they be useful?
2. How does Hilgard use the idea of a divided consciousness to explain hypnosis?

What Do You Think? What are the ethical implications of using hypnosis to control behaviour?

Summary

Module 32: Hypnosis

LEARNING OBJECTIVE 32 Discuss theories and evidence about what hypnosis is, how it works, and how it can be used.

- Hypnosis is a suggestible state during which people can be directed to act in unusual ways, experience unusual sensations, remember forgotten events, or forget remembered events.
- Ernest Hilgard's theory suggests that hypnosis divides consciousness into two parts: one focused on the suggestions of the hypnotist, and the other a hidden observer. Other theorists suggest that motivated role-playing is at work in hypnosis.
- Hypnosis has been used to successfully help control pain, as well as treat anxiety, skin diseases, asthma, insomnia, stuttering, high blood pressure, warts, and other forms of infection.

Key Terms

dissociation 259

hypnosis 258

Study Questions

Multiple Choice

1. Mental perceptions that do not match the stimulation coming from the environment are called _____.
   a) delusions
   b) distortions
   c) hallucinations
   d) illusions

Fill-in-the-Blank

1. Psychologists often use hypnosis to reduce an individual's awareness of pain; this procedure attempts to induce _____ hallucinations.

Module 33: Meditation

meditation technique designed to
turn one's consciousness away from
the outer world toward one's inner
cues and awareness.

©iStockphoto.com/AnanthaVardhan

Meditation and mental well-being. Various types of meditation
go back long before it became of interest to psychologists and
the focus of research.

Meditation is a technique designed to turn one's consciousness away from the outer
world, toward inner cues and awareness, ignoring all stressors (Butler, 2011; Fontana,
2007). The technique typically involves going to a quiet place, assuming either a specific
body position or simply a comfortable position, controlling one's breathing, limiting one's
outward attention, and forming internal images. The result of such efforts is an altered
state of consciousness, accompanied by deeply relaxing and pleasant feelings.

Meditation is an ancient practice that can be traced through the history of all the
world's major religions. Pictorial evidence of what appears to be people in meditative
postures have been found on ancient walls dating back to between 5,000 and 3,500 years
BCE (Possehl, 2003). Perhaps the best-known practices derive from the *yoga* traditions
of the Hindu religion and from the Zen traditions of Buddhism. Psychologists have
become quite interested in the features of various meditative
techniques. These techniques all seem to include versions of
self-regulation practices that involve training attention and
awareness to bring our mental processes under greater voluntary control (Bond et al, 2009). When practised, they seem to
be able to positively influence mental well-being and/or impact
specific capacities such as calm, clarity, and concentration
(Walsh & Shapiro, 2006).

Two major meditation techniques seem to use opposite
approaches. In *opening-up* approaches, meditators seek to clear
their mind to receive new experiences. One opening-up technique is to imagine oneself as another person; a related opening-up technique involves the performance of a common task
in a slightly different way, designed to call better attention to
one's daily routine. In the other kind of meditation approach,
concentrative meditation, people actively concentrate on an
object, word, phrase, or idea, called a *mantra*. Concentrating
upon or repeating a mantra serves to calm and focus the mind
and, perhaps, clear your mind completely.

One of meditation's greatest secular appeals is that it can
help people relax (Brown et al., 2010). In fact, studies have
shown that people in meditative states experience increases in
the same brain waves that are associated with the relaxation
phase individuals experience just prior to falling sleep (Aftanas & Golosheikin, 2003).
More recent work by Christina Lavalee at Laurentian University suggests that this sleeplike type of relaxation effect may be most pronounced in novice meditators, and that
experienced meditators may not show the same pattern but rather seem to relax without
becoming sleepy while meditating (Lavallee, Koren, & Persinger, 2009).

Research has found that meditation also can lower respiration, heart rate, blood
pressure, and muscle tension. Because of its positive impact on physical functioning,
it has been used to help treat pain, asthma, high blood pressure, heart problems, skin
disorders, diabetes, and viral infections (Gregoski et al., 2011; Wootton, 2008). One
form of meditation that has been applied in particular to patients suffering from severe
pain is *mindfulness meditation* (Labbé, 2011; Kabat-Zinn, 2005). Here, meditators pay
attention to the feelings, thoughts, and sensations that are flowing through their minds
during meditation, but they do so with detachment and without judgment. By being
mindful but not judgmental of their feelings and thoughts, including feelings of pain,
the individuals are less inclined to label or fixate on them and, in turn, are less likely to
react negatively to them. Being mindful or being in the moment can help us look past

Psychology Around Us | Inhale...Exhale...

Reyna was worried. She was trying to study for her organic chemistry midterm, but she couldn't get past her fight with Lisa. And Lisa wasn't responding to her texts. Reyna's anxiety continued to climb about both the exam and the fight. She just couldn't find her focus. She certainly couldn't study.

Reyna finally decided to try one of the techniques she had learned in her meditation and yoga class. She sat cross-legged on the floor and closed her eyes. She noticed her breathing coming in from her nose and down into her chest. She decided to shift her breathing to take in deeper breaths through her mouth and down into her diaphragm. She began to count. Inhale one. Exhale two.

Some thoughts of organic chemistry and of the nasty things that Lisa had said still came to Reyna's mind, but now she was able to just let the thoughts drift away. And she kept pulling her focus back to her breathing. Inhale 51. Exhale 52. Reyna noticed a tingling relaxation in her hands and her back—it was a little weird, but not uncomfortable. Inhale 85. Exhale 86.

When Reyna reached 100, she let her consciousness shift away from her breathing and onto her body instead. She then opened her eyes to look around the room. She took one more quick, wistful look at her cell phone, and then returned to her desk to give studying another shot.

distractors and focus on the tasks immediately at hand. For example, a group of people who were asked to take a brief course in Zen meditation had their driving performance assessed before and after they completed the meditation course. Overall driving performance scores increased following the meditation course (Berger, 1988), suggesting that being in the moment is a good thing when you are driving!

Before You Go On

www.wiley.com/go/comercanada

What Do You Know?
1. What are the physical effects of meditation?
2. What are the main benefits of altering consciousness through meditation?

What Do You Think? Which approach to meditation appeals more to you, opening-up meditation or concentrative meditation? Why?

Summary

Module 33: Meditation

LEARNING OBJECTIVE 33 Describe the techniques and effects of meditation.

- Meditation is designed to help turn one's consciousness away from the outer world toward inner cues and awareness, and to ignore all stressors.
- Like hypnosis, meditation has been suggested to have numerous positive benefits, including successfully treating many of the same illnesses, and helping people to relax.

Key Terms

meditation 262

Study Questions

Multiple Choice

1. During concentrative meditation, a person actively concentrates on an object, word, or idea called a(n) _____.
   a) dissociation
   b) koan
   c) mantra
   d) suggestion

Fill-in-the-Blank

1. _____ meditation has been shown to relieve pain by encouraging people to pay attention to their feelings, sensations, and experiences without judging or getting too involved with them.

Module 34: Psychoactive Drugs

What is one of the first things you do every day? For millions of people, the answer is to have a cup of coffee (maybe more than one). Why do so many people do this? For most, it is to give themselves a bit of a jolt and get the day going. Similarly, people often use other substances to help improve, or at least change, how they feel or function. Many people smoke cigarettes to feel more alert, less anxious, or both. Others may have a glass of wine or beer in the evening to wind down from a hectic day.

These substances—coffee, cigarettes, and alcohol—along with many others, alter our state of consciousness and influence our moods and behaviours. Collectively, they are examples of **psychoactive drugs**, chemicals that affect awareness, behaviour, sensation, perception, or mood. Some such drugs are illegal chemicals (heroin, ecstasy, cocaine), others are common and legal, while the status of yet others (e.g., marijuana) are under review in some jurisdictions. **Table 34-1** shows the three broad categories of drugs and lists examples of specific drugs that fall within those categories.

Some of the changes brought about by psychoactive drugs are temporary, lasting only as long as the chemicals remain in the brain and body. But certain psychoactive drugs can also bring about long-term changes and problems. People who regularly ingest them may develop maladaptive patterns of behaviour and changes in their body's physical responses, a pattern commonly called **addiction**.

Those addicted to a drug feel psychologically and physically compelled to keep taking it. They rely on the drug excessively and chronically, and may damage their family and social relationships, function poorly at work, or put themselves and others in danger. Addicted individuals may also acquire a physical dependence on the drug. They may develop a **tolerance** for the drug, meaning they need larger and larger doses to keep feeling its desired effect. And, if they try to stop taking or cut back on the drug, they may experience unpleasant and even dangerous **withdrawal symptoms**, such as nausea, cramps, sweating, or anxiety. People in withdrawal may also *crave* the drug that they had been taking regularly. Even if they want to quit taking it, the knowledge that they can quickly

LEARNING OBJECTIVE 34
List and describe common depressant, stimulant, and hallucinogenic psychoactive drugs and their effects.

psychoactive drugs chemicals that affect awareness, behaviour, sensation, perception, or mood.

addiction psychological or physical compulsion to take a drug, resulting from regular ingestion and leading to maladaptive patterns of behaviour and changes in physical response.

tolerance mark of physical dependence on a drug, in which the person is required to take incrementally larger doses of the drug to achieve the same effect.

withdrawal symptoms unpleasant and sometimes dangerous side effects of reducing intake of a drug after a person has become addicted.

TABLE 34-1 Psychoactive Drugs and Their Effects			
Drug Class	**Action in the Brain**		**Effects**
Depressants		Depress activity of central nervous system	Excessive use or overdose effects
Alcohol ©iStockphoto.com/Lauri Patterson	Influences the neurochemical GABA	Slows down brain areas that control judgment, inhibition, behaviour (speech, motor functioning, emotional expression)	Anxiety, nausea, vomiting, constipation, disorientation, impaired reflexes and motor functioning, amnesia, loss of consciousness, shallow respiration, convulsions, coma, death
Sedative-hypnotics (benzodiazepines)	Influences the neurochemical GABA in calming neural activity	Produces relaxation and drowsiness, relieves anxiety	
Opioids (opium heroin, morphine, codeine, methadone)	Activates the opioid receptors in the brain, providing their analgesic effect and their related high	Reduces pain and emotional tension, produces pleasurable and calming feelings	

(continued)

TABLE 34-1 Psychoactive Drugs and Their Effects (*continued*)

Drug Class	Action in the Brain	Effects	
Stimulants		**Increase activity of central nervous system**	**Excessive use or overdose effects**
Caffeine	Blocks access to adenosine receptors, which produce sensations of drowsiness when stimulated	Increases alertness	Insomnia, restlessness, increased pulse rate, mild delirium, ringing in the ears, rapid heartbeat, irritability, stomach pains, vomiting, dizziness, cancer, heart disease, emphysema, anxiety, paranoia, hallucinations, psychosis, elevated blood pressure and body temperature, convulsions, death
Nicotine	Influences dopamine and acetocholene	Increases alertness, reduces stress	
Cocaine ©iStockphoto.com/ Andrew Bedinger	Blocks re-uptake of dopamine, norepinephrine, and serotonin	Increases energy and alertness, produces euphoric feelings of well-being and confidence	
Amphetamines	Increase release of dopamine and norepinephrine	Increases energy and alertness, reduces appetite, produces euphoric feelings	
Hallucinogens		**Enhance normal perceptions**	Panic, nausea, headaches, longer and more extreme delusions, hallucinations, perceptual distortions ("bad trips"), psychosis, perceptual and sensory distortions, fatigue, lack of motivation, impaired memory
LSD	Stimulates dopamine and serotonin receptors	Dramatically strengthens visual perceptions (including illusions and hallucinations) along with profound psychological and physical changes	
Cannabis (marijuana, THC) ©iStockphoto.com/ MmeEmil	Encourages release of endorphins and dopamine	Produces a mixture of hallucinogenic, depressant, and stimulant effects	
MDMA (Ecstasy)	Causes a "dump" of serotonin stores	Enhances sensory perceptions, increases energy and alertness, produces feelings of empathy and emotional well-being	

eliminate the unpleasant withdrawal symptoms by simply ingesting the drug makes it difficult for many users to persevere through the withdrawal period (Verster et al., 2011). In any given year, 2 percent of all teens and adults Canada, around 600,000 people, use cocaine, ecstasy, or hallucinogens, and 194,000 Canadians (0.8 percent) are dependent on illicit drugs (Statistics Canada, 2004).

34.1 Depressants

depressants class of drugs that slow the activity of the central nervous system.

Psychoactive drugs that slow down the central nervous system are called **depressants**. They reduce tension and inhibitions and may interfere with a person's judgment, motor activity, and concentration. The two most widely used groups of depressants are *alcohol* and *sedative-hypnotic drugs*.

practically speaking — Addictions: Living out of Control

Many people struggle with addiction problems. According to some clinical theorists, addictions are not only about alcohol and substance abuse; they may also cover dependencies such as food, the Internet, gambling, caffeine, shopping, sex, and exercise, to name a few (Page & Brewster, 2009; Stein, 2008). Addictive patterns do not suddenly appear; they are usually long-standing and may be rooted in various psychological problems. Whereas it takes time for individuals to lose control of their life to a dependency, it also takes time, motivation, commitment, discipline, and often the help of a professional treatment program to regain control and recover from an addiction. There are no quick fixes for recovery.

How do you know whether you or someone close to you is experiencing an addiction? This is a complex issue that typically requires careful clinical assessment for a definitive answer. Nevertheless, there are some straightforward questions that you can use to determine whether professional attention is in order. For example, is the person unable to meet responsibilities at home, school, or the office? Has the person tried to stop the repeated behaviour but cannot, and continues to engage in it despite the apparent dangers?

Although most clinicians agree that there is no substitute for careful clinical assessment and treatment of addictions, some have developed basic detection devices that can help get the ball rolling. For example, a brief tool to detect alcohol addiction is known as the CAGE questionnaire. It asks these questions: (1) Has the person ever felt that he or she should CUT DOWN on the drinking? (2) Has the person ever been ANNOYED by people criticizing the drinking?

Darryl Dyck/The Canadian Press

Reducing harm. Vancouver's Coastal Health Service opened a safe injection site near Vancouver's Downtown Eastside in 2003. It offers clean needles and supervision of injections by heroin users, as well as support and referrals for treatment.

(3) Has the person ever expressed remorse or GUILT about drinking? (4) Has the person ever started to drink in the morning as an EYE-OPENER to start the day or get rid of a hangover? A "yes" answer to at least two of these questions may indicate a problem with alcohol addiction and a corresponding need for professional assessment and treatment. More than a quarter century after the CAGE questionnaire was first developed, it has been validated in many studies as an effective, quick indicator of the need for help (O'Brien, 2008).

34.1.1 Alcohol

Alcohol, a depressant that is taken in liquid form, is one of the most commonly used psychoactive drugs. More than three-quarters of the people in Canada drink beverages that contain alcohol, at least from time to time (Statistics Canada, 2004). Nearly 35 percent of Canadians over age 15 engage in heavy drinking (five or more drinks) at least once a year, and nearly half of those (48 percent) do so at least once a month. Among heavy drinkers, males outnumber females by more than two to one, around 8 percent to 4 percent (Statistics Canada, 2004).

All alcoholic beverages contain *ethyl alcohol*, a chemical that is quickly absorbed into the blood through the lining of the stomach and the intestine. The ethyl alcohol immediately begins to take effect as it is carried in the bloodstream to the central nervous system (the brain and spinal cord). There, it acts to slow functioning by binding to various neurons, particularly those that normally receive a neurotransmitter called *gamma aminobutyric acid*, or *GABA*, and reduces the influence of GABA in causing neurons to fire.

At first, ethyl alcohol slows down the brain areas that control judgment and inhibition; people become looser and more talkative, relaxed, and happy. When more alcohol is absorbed, it slows down additional areas in the central nervous system, causing the drinkers to make poorer judgments, become careless, and remember less well. Many people become highly emotional, and some become loud and aggressive.

Charles Bowman/Getty Images

Cultural endorsement? Five men and hundreds of others around them celebrate at Oktoberfest, Germany's annual 16-day festival, marked by eating, special events, and perhaps most prominently, drinking. Almost 7 million litres of beer are served to thousands of revellers at each year's festival, an excessiveness that many believe contributes to binge drinking and alcoholism.

alcoholism long-term pattern of alcohol addiction.

As drinking continues, the motor responses of individuals decline and their reaction times slow. They may be unsteady when they stand or walk, for example. Their vision becomes blurred, and they may misjudge distances. They can also have trouble hearing. As a result, people who have drunk too much alcohol may have enormous difficulty driving or solving simple problems.

As summarized in **Table 34-2**, the *concentration*, or proportion, of ethyl alcohol in the blood determines how much it will affect a person (Ksir et al., 2008). When the alcohol concentration reaches 0.06 percent of the blood volume, a person usually feels relaxed and comfortable. By the time it reaches 0.09 percent, the drinker crosses the line into *intoxication*. If the level goes as high as 0.55 percent, death will probably result. Most people, however, lose consciousness before they can drink enough to reach this level. The effects of alcohol subside only when the alcohol concentration in the blood falls.

Though legal, alcohol is actually one of society's most dangerous drugs, and its risks extend to all age groups. In fact, 10 percent of Canadian elementary school students admit to some alcohol use, and nearly 45 percent of 15- to 19-year-olds reported at least one episode of heavy drinking over a year, with about half of those doing so at least monthly (Statistics Canada, 2004). Surveys indicate that over a one-year period, 6.6 percent of all adults in the world fall into a long-term pattern of alcohol addiction, known as **alcoholism** (Somers et al., 2004). More than 13 percent of adults experience the pattern at some time in their lives, with men outnumbering women by at least two to one (Kessler et al., 2005).

Binge drinking—the consumption of five or more drinks in a row—is a major problem in many settings, not the least of which are college and university campuses

TABLE 34-2 Alcohol's Effects on the Body and Behaviour

Number of Drinks[a] in Two Hours	Blood Alcohol Content (%)[b]	Effect
(2)	0.06	Relaxed state; increased sociability
(3)	0.09	Everyday stress lessened
(4)	0.10	Movements and speech become clumsy
(7)	0.20	Very drunk; loud and difficult to understand; emotions unstable
(12)	0.40	Difficult to wake up; incapable of voluntary action
(15)	0.55	Coma and/or death

[a] A drink refers to one 12-ounce beer, a 4-ounce glass of wine, or a 1.25-ounce shot of hard liquor.
[b] In Canada, the legal blood alcohol level for "drunk driving" varies from 0.05 to 0.08.

Source: Adapted with permission of John Wiley & Sons, Inc., from Carpenter. S., & Huffman, K. (2008). *Visualizing psychology.* Hoboken, NJ: Wiley, p. 129.

(NSDUH, 2008; Read et al., 2008). According to research, 60 percent of college- and university-aged students binge drink at least once each year, many of them at least monthly (Statistics Canada, 2004). These are higher rates than those among similar-aged individuals who do not attend college or university (Ksir et al., 2008). On many campuses, alcohol use often is an accepted part of life. Thirty-two percent of Canadian undergraduates report engaging in hazardous or harmful patterns of drinking, with the percentage being higher (43 percent) for those living in residence. Happy hours and other promotions at campus bars are seen to be part of the problem (Centre for Addiction and Mental Health, 2004).

Efforts to reduce college/university binge drinking have begun to make a difference. Some universities, for example, now provide substance-free dorms (Wechsler et al., 2002). The implications are clear: college/university drinking, including binge drinking, is more common and harmful than previously believed. And most experts agree that the time has come to attack this enormous problem head on.

According to work by Deborah Chansonneuve of the Aboriginal Healing Society in Ottawa, 75 percent of Aboriginal Canadians say they have a problem with alcohol in their community, 33 percent say it is a problem in their household, and 25 percent say they have a personal problem with alcohol (Chansonneuve, 2007). Generally, Asians in North America have lower rates of alcoholism than do people from other cultures. As many as one-half of Asians have a deficiency of *alcohol dehydrogenase*, a chemical responsible for breaking down and eliminating alcohol from the body, so they react very negatively to even a small intake of alcohol. Such extreme reactions help prevent heavy use (Wall et al., 2001; APA, 2000).

People who abuse alcohol drink large amounts regularly and rely on it to help them to do things that would otherwise make them nervous. Eventually the drinking disrupts their social behaviour and their ability to think clearly and work effectively. Many build up a tolerance for alcohol, and they need to drink greater and greater amounts to feel its effects. They also experience withdrawal when they stop drinking. Within hours, for example, their hands and eyelids begin to shake, they feel weak, they sweat heavily, their heart beats rapidly, and their blood pressure rises (APA, 2000).

Alcoholism can wreak havoc on an individual's family, social, and occupational life (Murphy et al., 2005). Medical treatment, lost productivity, and losses due to death from alcoholism cost society many billions of dollars each year. The disorder also has been implicated in more than one-third of all suicides, homicides, assaults, rapes, and accidental deaths (Ksir et al., 2008). A total of 34 percent of all fatal automobile accidents in Canada (in 2000) involved alcohol use (Mayhew, Brown, & Simpson, 2002). Children whose parents have alcoholism are also severely affected by this disorder. The home life of these children often features much conflict and, in some cases, sexual or other forms of abuse. The children themselves have elevated rates of psychological problems and substance-related disorders over the course of their lives (Hall & Webster, 2002). Many display low self-esteem, weak communication skills, poor sociability, and marital problems compared to general averages (Watt, 2002; Lewis-Harter, 2000).

Long-term excessive drinking can also cause severe damage to one's physical health (Myrick & Wright, 2008). It so overworks the liver—the body organ that breaks down alcohol—that people may develop an irreversible condition called *cirrhosis*, in which the liver becomes scarred and dysfunctional (CDC, 2008). Alcohol abuse may also damage the heart and lower the immune system's ability to fight off infections and cancer and to resist the onset of AIDS after infection.

Catherine Karnow/Corbis

Spreading the word. Perhaps the most successful public effort to reduce drunk driving fatalities has been undertaken by Mothers Against Drunk Driving (MADD). Raising public awareness through ads, campaigns, and lobbying efforts, this organization has helped reduce the number of alcohol-related automobile deaths by 47 percent since it was formed in 1980.

Finally, women who drink during pregnancy place their fetuses at risk (Finnegan & Kandall, 2008). Heavy drinking early in pregnancy often leads to a miscarriage. Excessive alcohol use during pregnancy may also cause a baby to be born with *fetal alcohol syndrome (FAS)* or *fetal alcohol effects (FAE)*, a pattern that can include intellectual disability, hyperactivity, head and face deformities, heart defects, and slow growth. It has been estimated that in the overall population, approximately 1 to 3 of every 1,000 babies are born with FAS, and 30 of every 1,000 babies are born with FAE (Health Canada, 2005a).

34.1.2 Sedative-Hypnotic Drugs

sedative-hypnotic drugs class of drugs that produces feelings of relaxation and drowsiness.

At low dosages, **sedative-hypnotic drugs** produce feelings of relaxation and drowsiness. At higher dosages, they are sleep inducers, or hypnotics. *Benzodiazepines*, anti-anxiety drugs developed in the 1950s, are the most popular sedative-hypnotic drugs available today. More than 100 million prescriptions are written each year for this group of chemical compounds (Bisaga, 2008). Xanax®, Ativan®, and Valium® are three of the benzodiazepines in wide clinical use.

This group of drugs reduces anxiety without making people as overly drowsy as alcohol or other depressant substances. Nevertheless, in high enough doses, benzodiazepines can cause intoxication and lead to addiction (Dupont & Dupont, 2005). Research by Scott Patten from the University of Calgary shows that as many as 2 percent of adults in North America become addicted to these drugs at some point in their lives (Kassam & Patten, 2006).

34.2 Opioids

opioids class of drugs derived from the sap of the opium poppy.

The term **opioids** refers to *opium* and drugs derived from it, including *heroin, morphine, codeine, and OxyContin*. Opium, a substance taken from the sap of the opium poppy, has been used for thousands of years. In the past, it was used widely in the treatment of medical disorders because of its ability to reduce both physical pain and emotional distress. Physicians eventually discovered, however, that the drug was addictive. Morphine and heroin, each of which was later derived from opium for use as a safer painkiller, also proved to be highly addictive. In fact, heroin is even more addictive than the other opioids. OxyContin is now illegal and was replaced by a less addictive version of the drug.

Additional drugs have been derived from opium, and several synthetic (laboratory-blended) opioids such as *methadone* have also been developed. Each of these various drugs has a different strength, speed of action, and tolerance level. Today, morphine and codeine are used as medical opioids, usually prescribed to relieve pain. Heroin is illegal in Canada under all circumstances.

Outside of medical settings, opioids are smoked, inhaled, snorted (inhaled through the nose), injected by needle just beneath the skin ("skin popped"), or injected directly into the blood stream ("mainlined"). An injection quickly produces a *rush*—a spasm of warmth and joy that is sometimes compared with an orgasm. The brief spasm is followed by several hours of a pleasant feeling and shift in consciousness called a *high* or *nod*. During a high, the opioid user feels very relaxed and happy and is unconcerned about food or other bodily needs.

Opioids depress the central nervous system, particularly the brain areas that control emotion. The drugs attach to brain receptors that ordinarily receive endorphins, called neurotransmitters (discussed in the previous part), that help reduce pain and emotional tension (Hart et al., 2010). When neurons receive opioids at these receptors, the opioids produce the same kinds of pleasant and relaxing feelings that endorphins would produce.

The most direct danger of heroin use is an overdose, which shuts down the respiratory centre in the brain, almost paralyzing breathing, and in many cases causing death. Death is particularly likely during sleep, when individuals cannot fight the respiratory effects by consciously working at breathing. Each year, 2 percent of those addicted to heroin and other opioids are killed by the drugs, usually from an overdose (Theodorou & Haber, 2005; APA, 2000).

34.3 Stimulants

Psychoactive drugs that speed up the central nervous system are called **stimulants**. They produce increases in blood pressure, heart rate, alertness, thinking, and behaviour. Among the most problematic stimulants are *caffeine*, *nicotine*, *cocaine*, and *amphetamines*.

stimulants substances that increase the activity of the central nervous system.

34.3.1 Caffeine

Caffeine, a mild (and legal) stimulant, is the world's most widely used stimulant. It is found in coffee, tea, chocolate, cola, and so-called *energy drinks*. Worldwide, 80 percent of all people consume caffeine in one form or another every day (Rogers, 2005). Like many other psychoactive drugs, caffeine is addictive, although this addiction does not cause the significant social problems associated with substances such as alcohol, heroin, and cocaine (Paton & Beer, 2001; Silverman et al., 1992). Still, quitting caffeine can cause unpleasant withdrawal symptoms for chronic users, including lethargy, sleepiness, anxiety, irritability, depression, constipation, and headaches. Withdrawal symptoms can start only a few hours after the individual's last consumption of caffeine.

Energy drinks are a relatively new way in which people are getting caffeine. Energy drinks contain very large amounts of caffeine and if not taken in moderation, can result in caffeine intoxication (Red Bull cans have a label saying not to drink more than two). Caffeine intoxication can involve restlessness, fidgetiness, nervousness, excitement, euphoria, insomnia, flushing of the face, increased urination, gastrointestinal disturbance, muscle twitching, a rambling flow of thought and speech, irritability, irregular or rapid heartbeat, and psychomotor agitation (Reissig, Strain, & Griffiths, 2009). If you notice any of these symptoms, check the amount of caffeine in the things you are drinking (remember cola beverages also have caffeine in them), and pace yourself a bit more carefully.

©iStockphoto.com/Barisonal

Nicotine. Nicotine is one of the most highly addictive substances. Regular smokers develop a tolerance for nicotine and must smoke more and more to achieve the same results.

34.3.2 Nicotine

Although legal, *nicotine* is one of the most highly addictive substances (Hart et al., 2010). Most commonly, it is taken into the body by smoking tobacco. Nicotine is then absorbed through the respiratory tract, the mucous membranes of the nasal area, and the gastrointestinal tract. The drug proceeds to activate nicotine receptors located throughout the brain and body. Inhaling a puff of cigarette smoke delivers a dose of nicotine to the brain faster than it could be delivered by injection into the blood stream.

Regular smokers develop a tolerance for nicotine and must smoke more and more to achieve the same results (Hymowitz, 2005). When they try to stop smoking, they experience withdrawal symptoms such as irritability, increased appetite, sleep disturbances, and a powerful desire to smoke (Dodgen, 2005; APA, 2000).

Almost one-fifth of all individuals over the age of 14 in Canada regularly smoke tobacco. Surveys also find that nearly 15 percent of all high school students smoke (Health Canada, 2008). All of this smoking eventually takes a heavy toll: 37,000 people in Canada die each year as a result of smoking. Chronic smoking is directly tied to lung disease, high blood pressure, coronary heart disease, cancer, stroke, and other fatal medical problems (Health Canada, 2008). Moreover, pregnant women who smoke are much more likely than non-smokers to deliver premature and underweight babies (NSDUH, 2008).

34.3.3 Cocaine

Cocaine, the key active ingredient of South America's coca plant, is the most powerful natural stimulant currently known. The drug was first separated from the plant in 1865. For many centuries, however, native people have chewed the leaves of the plant to raise their energy and increase their alertness.

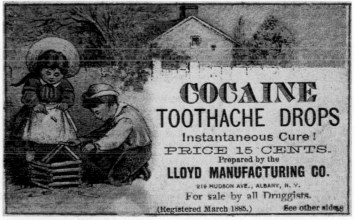

The Granger Collection

The early days. In the early twentieth century, cocaine was an ingredient in such products as Cocaine Toothache Drops and Coca-Cola soft drinks.

Processed cocaine—a white, fluffy powder—is snorted and absorbed through the mucous membrane of the nose. Some users, however, prefer the more powerful effects of injecting cocaine intravenously or smoking it in a pipe or cigarette. Around 311,000 Canadians over 14 years of age used cocaine in 2008 (Health Canada, 2009).

Cocaine brings on a rush of euphoria and well-being—an orgasmic-like reaction if the dose is high enough. Initially, cocaine stimulates the higher centres of the central nervous system, shifting users' levels of awareness and making them excited, energetic, and talkative. As more cocaine is taken, it stimulates additional areas of the central nervous system, resulting in increases in heart rate, blood pressure, breathing, arousal, and wakefulness. Cocaine apparently produces these effects largely by increasing activity of the neurotransmitter *dopamine* at key neurons throughout the brain (Haney, 2008). As the stimulating effects of cocaine subside, the user experiences a depression-like letdown, popularly called *crashing* (Doweiko, 2006).

Regular use of cocaine may lead to a pattern of addiction. Tolerance to the drug may develop, and suddenly withdrawing from it results in depression, fatigue, sleep problems, anxiety, and irritability (Hart et al., 2010). Today, almost 1 out of every 100 people over the age of 12 in the United States is addicted to cocaine (NSDUH, 2008).

Cocaine also poses serious physical dangers (Kosten et al., 2008). Use of the drug in powerful, smokable forms, known as *freebasing* and *crack*, are the major contributors to the annual number of cocaine-related overdoses (SAMHSA, 2008). In addition, cocaine use has been linked to as many as 20 percent of all suicides among people under 61 years of age (Garlow, 2002). The greatest danger of cocaine use is an overdose, which may impair breathing, produce major—even fatal—heart irregularities, or cause brain seizures (Doweiko, 2006).

> **"Drugs are a bet with your mind."**
>
> —*Jim Morrison, singer, The Doors. Died of suspected overdose in 1971.*

34.3.4 Amphetamines

Amphetamines are manufactured in the laboratory. These stimulants are most often taken in pill or capsule form, although some individuals inject the drugs intravenously or smoke them for a quicker and more powerful effect. Like cocaine, amphetamines increase energy and alertness and lower appetite in small doses, produce intoxication and psychosis in higher doses, and cause an emotional letdown when they leave the body. Also like cocaine, these drugs produce such effects by increasing the activity of the neurotransmitter *dopamine* (Haney, 2008).

Tolerance to amphetamines builds very rapidly, thus increasing the chances of users becoming addicted (Acosta, Haller, & Schnoll, 2005). People who start using the drug to help reduce their appetite, for example, may soon find they are as hungry as ever and increase their dose in response. Athletes who use amphetamines to increase their energy may also soon find that they need increasing amounts of the drug. When people who are addicted to the drug stop taking it, they fall into a pattern of deep depression and extended sleep identical to the withdrawal from cocaine. Around 0.1 percent of the Canadian population uses amphetamines (Health Canada, 2009).

One powerful kind of amphetamine, *methamphetamine* (nicknamed *crank* in one impure form or *crystal meth* in a more pure form), currently is experiencing a major surge in popularity. Over 6 percent of all people over the age of 15 in Canada have now used a form of this stimulant at least once (Department of Justice, 2007). It is available in the form of crystals (known as *ice* or *crystal meth*), which users smoke.

Most of the non-medical methamphetamine is made in small, illegal "stovetop laboratories," which typically operate for a few days and then move on to a new location (Hart et al., 2010). Although such laboratories have been around since the 1960s, they have increased eightfold over the past decade. A major health concern is that the secret laboratories produce dangerous fumes and residue (Burgess, 2001).

Around 60 percent of current methamphetamine users are men (NSDUH, 2008). The drug is particularly popular among biker gangs, in rural areas, and in urban gay communities, and has gained wide use as a "club drug," the term for drugs of choice at all-night dance parties, or "raves" (Ksir et al., 2008).

Like other kinds of amphetamines, methamphetamine increases activity of the neurotransmitter dopamine, producing increased arousal, attention, and related effects. This particular drug also may damage nerve endings, a *neurotoxicity* that is compounded by the drug's tendency to remain in the brain and body for a long time—more than six hours (Rawson & Ling, 2008). But, among users, such dangers are less important than methamphetamine's immediate positive impact, including perceptions by many that it makes them feel hypersexual and uninhibited (Jefferson, 2005). All of this has contributed to major public health problems. For example, one-third of all men who tested positive for HIV in Los Angeles in 2004 reported having used this drug (Jefferson, 2005). Similarly, according to surveys, a growing number of domestic-violence incidents, assaults, and robberies have been tied to the use of methamphetamine (Jefferson, 2005). A likely explanation for these findings links back to the effects of methamphetamine, where increased arousal leads to increased sexual activity and/or violence (Hirshfiled et al., 2004).

Methylenedioxymethamphetamine, or MDMA (better known as ecstasy), is another "club drug" form of methamphetamine often found at raves. Ecstasy produces its effects by causing a dump of the serotonin neurotransmitter substance stored in neurons in the mood regulation centre of the brain. The result is a sense of euphoria, reduced anxiety, and increased social intimacy lasting for two to four hours. The complete dump of serotonin initiated by the ecstasy means that if one takes more of the drug when the effects of the initial dose wear off, there is no additional effect. Short-term issues can include dehydration, difficulty concentrating, lack of appetite, and dry mouth. Longer-term negative effects can include depression, anxiety, paranoia, and irritability (Verheyden, Henry, & Curran, 2003; Verheyden, Maidment, & Curran, 2003).

34.4 Hallucinogens

Hallucinogens, or *psychedelic drugs*, are substances that dramatically change one's state of awareness by causing powerful changes in sensory perception, such as enhancing a person's normal perceptions and producing illusions and hallucinations. The substance-induced sensory changes are sometimes called "trips," and these trips may be exciting or frightening, depending on how a person's mind reacts to the drugs. Many hallucinogens come from plants or animals; others are laboratory-produced.

hallucinogens substances that dramatically change one's state of awareness, causing powerful changes in sensory perception.

34.4.1 LSD

Lysergic acid diethylamide, or *LSD*, is a very powerful hallucinogen that was derived by the Swiss chemist Albert Hoffman in 1938 from a group of naturally occurring substances. During the 1960s, a period of rebellion and experimentation, millions of users turned to the drug in an effort to raise their consciousness and expand their experiences. Within two hours of being swallowed, LSD brings on *hallucinosis*, a state marked by a strengthening of visual perceptions and profound psychological and physical changes. People may focus on small details—each hair on the skin, for example. Colours may seem brighter or take on a shade of purple. Users often experience illusions in which objects seem distorted and seem to move, breathe, or change shape. LSD can also produce strong emotions, from joy to anxiety or depression. Past thoughts and feelings may return. All these effects take place while the user is fully alert, and wear off in about six hours. Scientists believe that LSD produces these

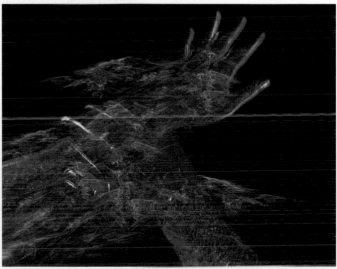

Carol and Mike Werner/Phototake

Bad trip. Ingesting LSD brings on hallucinosis, a state of sensory and perceptual distortions. Sometimes this state can be very frightening and disorienting, as captured in this photo illustration of a hallucination of hands and arms burning.

effects primarily by binding to many of the neurons that normally receive the neurotransmitter *serotonin*, changing the neurotransmitter's activity at those sites (Julien, 2008).

Just under 1 percent of all people in Canada have used LSD or another hallucinogen over the past year (Health Canada, 2009). A key problem is that LSD is so powerful that any dose, no matter how small, is likely to produce very strong reactions. Sometimes the reactions are quite unpleasant, an experience called a "bad trip." In addition, some LSD users have **flashbacks**, recurrences of the sensory and emotional changes even after the LSD has left the body (Doweiko, 2006).

flashbacks recurrence of the sensory and emotional changes after the LSD has left the body.

34.4.2 Cannabis

The hemp plant *Cannabis sativa* grows in warm climates. Collectively, the drugs produced from varieties of hemp are called *cannabis*. The most powerful of them is *hashish*; the weaker ones include the best-known form of cannabis, *marijuana*, a mixture derived from the buds, crushed leaves, and flowering tops of hemp plants.

Although there are several hundred active chemicals in cannabis, *tetrahydrocannabinol* (*THC*) is the one most responsible for its effects. The greater the THC content, the more powerful the cannabis. Due to changes in growing patterns, today's marijuana is at least four times higher in THC content than was the marijuana of the early 1970s (Doweiko, 2006; APA, 2000).

When smoked, cannabis changes one's conscious experiences by producing a mixture of hallucinogenic, depressant, and stimulant effects. At low doses, the smoker typically has feelings of happiness and relaxation, although some smokers become anxious or irritated, especially if they have been in a bad mood. Many smokers have sharpened perceptions and become fascinated with the intensified sounds and sights that they are experiencing. Time seems to slow down, and distances and sizes become greater. This overall reaction is often called getting "high." In strong doses, cannabis produces particularly unusual visual experiences, changes in body image, and even hallucinations (Mathew et al., 1993). Most of the drug's effects last two to six hours.

Because marijuana can interfere with complex sensorimotor tasks and cognitive functioning, it has been tied to many automobile accidents (Kauert & Iwersen-Bergmann, 2004). In addition, many people on a marijuana high fail to remember information, especially recently learned material; thus, heavy marijuana smokers may function poorly at school or work (Lundqvist, 2005). Some research also suggests that regular marijuana smoking may contribute to long-term medical problems, including lung disease (Ksir et al., 2008; NIDA, 2011), lower sperm counts in men, and abnormal ovulation in women (Schuel et al., 2002).

Peter Fried in the Department of Psychology at Carleton University has been running longitudinal studies into the effects of prenatal exposure to marijuana and cigarette smoke (as part of the Ottawa Prenatal Prospective Study) and the effects of marijuana use in the teenage years on IQ scores in the young adult years. Fried's work suggests that prenatal expose to marijuana shows negative impacts on response inhibition or behavioural self-control (Smith, Fried, Hogan, & Cameron, 2004) and on working memory (Smith, Fried, Hogan, & Cameron, 2006) in adolescence, even when the effects of marijuana use by the participating teenagers themselves was controlled for. In terms of IQ, Fried compared IQ scores at 9 to 12 years of age with those at 17 to 20 years of age for teenagers who were heavy users (five joints per week), light users, former users, or non-users of marijuana. The results were dose-related with heavy users showing on average about a 4-point drop in IQ scores, while others showed increases in IQ scores ranging from 3 to about 6 IQ points over the same period (Fried, Watkinson, James, & Gray, 2002).

Because of the higher THC content in marijuana grown today, many people, including 5 percent of high school seniors, are now caught in a pattern of heavy and regular use, getting high on marijuana daily, although it is not clear whether such use represents a true addiction or a strong habit (Johnston et al., 2007). Either way, a number of these users do indeed find their social, occupational, or academic lives greatly affected. Around 10 percent of people in Canada have used marijuana in the past year; just over 40 percent have used it at some point in their lives (Health Canada, 2009).

Psychology Around Us | Marijuana as Medicine

Movies such as *Your Highness, Pineapple Express,* and *Hot-tub Time Machine*—so-called "stoner films"—have helped to popularize the image of a marijuana user as a mellow hippie trying to avoid the wrath of inept authority figures (Meltzer, 2007). In fact, the many millions of individuals who have tried marijuana come in all sizes, shapes, and personalities (Earleywine, 2007). Indeed, tens of thousands of them use marijuana for a very serious purpose—as medicine.

Common medicinal uses of marijuana, or cannabis, include treatment of chronic pain, nausea associated with chemotherapy, glaucoma, and disease-related anorexia (Okie, 2005). It is not clear just what it is about cannabis that seems to help, as it contains at least 300 substances (Grotenhermen, 2002). In Canada, the use of marijuana for medicinal purposes is legal and regulated by Health Canada. For those who qualify, Health Canada provides dried marijuana from Prairie Plant Systems Inc., which has been contracted to grow it for Health Canada, and does so in an old cold war nuclear attack bunker built in Flin Flon, Manitoba, during the Diefenbaker years. Alternatively, patients can apply for seeds to grow their own.

With the help of their doctors, Canadians can apply for medical marijuana if they suffer from multiple sclerosis, spinal cord injury or disease, cancer, AIDS or HIV, severe arthritis, or epilepsy, or as part of end-of-life care. As well, doctors have the discretion to recommend medical marijuana for patients with other conditions if the doctor believes it to be appropriate.

The differences in the Canadian and American legal positions on marijuana have created a number of issues. Marc Emery, a Canadian cannabis policy reform advocate, was extradited to the United States to face charges for selling marijuana seeds to Americans as part of a mail-order business out of Vancouver. In September 2010, Emery was sentenced to five years in prison in the United States. Emery's case remains a rallying point for people on both sides of the border wishing to loosen marijuana laws. The American states of Washington, Alaska, Oregon, and Colorado have either begun or completed

Jonathan Hayward/CP

An uncommon medicine. A man suffering from chronic arthritis smokes marijuana at a protest rally, calling on the government to implement a medical marijuana program.

the processes to legalize the non-medical use of marijuana, while many more jurisdictions have legalized the medical use of marijuana. Health Canada permits the medical prescription of marijuana in limited circumstances, such as end-of-life care or debilitating conditions (Health Canada, 2005b). The federal government passed the Marijuana for Medical Purposes Regulation Act in 2013 (Minister of Justice, 2014). Under this new legislation patients can obtain a prescription for medical marijuana from their doctor whereas previously they had to apply to Health Canada for permission to obtain and use medical marijuana. As well, under the new law, only licensed commercial producers can legally grow marijuana and sell it directly to patients with prescriptions. Previously patients were permitted to grow their own marijuana for medical use. This change may make it difficult for some patients to get the strain of marijuana they have found to be most beneficial to them and their condition(s) (Carter & Belle-Isle 2013).

34.5 The Effect of Psychoactive Drugs on the Brain

As you have seen, an ingested drug increases the activity of certain neurotransmitters in the brain—chemicals whose normal purpose is to reduce pain, calm us, lift our mood, or increase our alertness—and these neurotransmitters, in turn, help produce the particular effects of the drug. Alcohol, for example, heightens activity of the neurotransmitter *GABA*; opioids raise *endorphin* activity; and cocaine and amphetamines increase *dopamine* activity. Similarly, researchers have identified a neurotransmitter called *anandamide* (from the Sanskrit word for "bliss") that operates much like THC (Hitti, 2004).

It used to be thought that each drug, along with its corresponding neurotransmitters, sets in motion a unique set of brain reactions. However, recent brain-imaging studies suggest that while each drug has its own starting point in the brain, most (perhaps all)

WHAT HAPPENS
in the BRAIN?

reward learning pathway brain circuitry that is important for learning about rewarding stimuli.

of them eventually activate a single **reward learning pathway**, or "pleasure pathway," in the brain (Haney, 2008; Koob & LeMoal, 2008) (see **Figure 34-1**). The reward learning pathway is activated by pleasurable stimuli or events and comes to anticipate (and thus motivate action toward) the arrival of desirable food, sexual experiences, or other pleasurable or rewarding experiences (Arias-Carrión & Pöppel, 2007). This brain reward learning pathway apparently extends from the midbrain to the nucleus accumbens and on to the frontal cortex (see Part 3).

The key neurotransmitter in this pathway appears to be *dopamine*. When dopamine is activated there, a person wants—at times, even craves—pleasurable rewards, such as music, a hug, or, for some people, a drug (Higgins & George, 2007; Higgins et al., 2004).

Certain drugs apparently stimulate the reward learning pathway directly. You will recall that cocaine and amphetamines directly increase dopamine activity. Other drugs seem to stimulate it in roundabout ways. The biochemical reactions triggered by alcohol and opioids each set in motion a series of chemical events that eventually lead to increased dopamine activity in the reward learning pathway.

reward-deficiency syndrome theory that people might abuse drugs because their reward centre is not readily activated by usual life events.

Research also suggests that people prone to abuse drugs may suffer from a **reward-deficiency syndrome**—their reward learning pathway is not activated readily by the events in their lives (Blum et al., 2000; Nash, 1997)—so they are more inclined than other people to turn to drugs to keep their pathway stimulated. Abnormal genes have been pointed to as a possible cause of this syndrome (Finckh, 2001; Lawford et al., 1997).

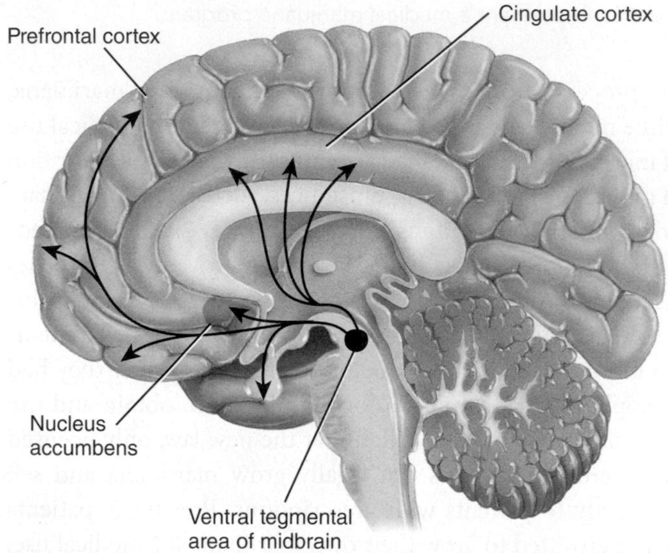

But how might people become ensnared in a broad pattern of addiction, marked by tolerance and withdrawal effects? According to one explanation, when a person takes a particular drug chronically, the brain eventually makes an adjustment and reduces its own production of the neurotransmitter whose activity is being increased by the ingested drug (Kleber & Galanter, 2008; Kosten, George, & Kleber, 2005). That is, because the drug is increasing neurotransmitter activity, natural release of the neurotransmitter by the brain is less necessary. As drug intake increases, the body's production of the neurotransmitter continues to decrease, and the person needs to take more and more of the drug to feel its positive effects. In short, drug takers are building tolerance for a drug, becoming more and more dependent on it, rather than on their own biological processes to feel comfortable or alert. In addition, if they suddenly stop taking the drug, their supply of neurotransmitters will be low for a time, producing symptoms of withdrawal that will continue until the brain resumes its normal production of the necessary neurotransmitters.

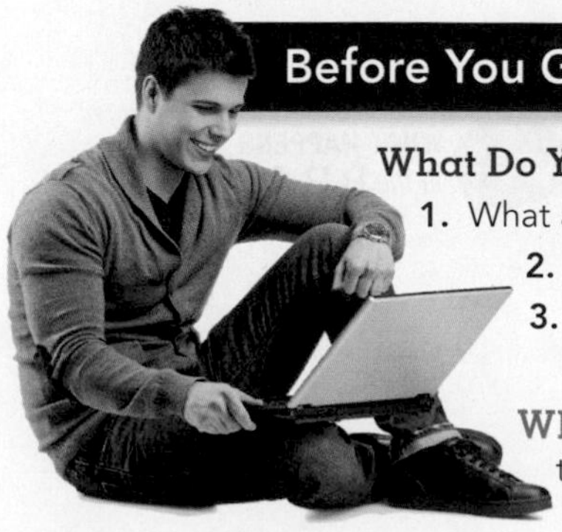

Prefrontal cortex

Cingulate cortex

Nucleus accumbens

Ventral tegmental area of midbrain

FIGURE 34-1 Reward learning pathway. The brain's reward learning pathway, or "pleasure pathway," extends from an area in the midbrain called the ventral tegmental area to the nucleus accumbens, as well as to the prefrontal cortex.

Before You Go On

www.wiley.com/go/comercanada

What Do You Know?

1. What are the major drug categories and the characteristics of each category?
2. What is addiction, and what are two key features of addiction to a drug?
3. Why is alcoholism relatively less common among Asians than in individuals of other ethnic groups?

What Do You Think? Why do you think alcohol is more acceptable culturally than some of the other drugs we are discussing here?

Summary

Module 34: Psychoactive Drugs

LEARNING OBJECTIVE 34 List and describe common depressant, stimulant, and hallucinogenic psychoactive drugs and their effects.

- The main classes of psychoactive drugs are depressants (substances that slow down brain activity), stimulants (substances that excite brain activity), opioids (substances that attach to brain receptors that ordinarily receive endorphins), and psychedelic or hallucinogenic drugs (substances that distort sensory perceptions).
- Regular ingestion of some drugs can lead to maladaptive changes in a person's behaviour patterns and physical responses, a pattern known as *addiction*. Signs of addiction can include increased tolerance, the need for larger and larger doses of a substance to get the desired effect, and symptoms of withdrawal when one discontinues the drug.
- Review the list of drugs and their effects in Table 34-1.

Key Terms

addiction 265
alcoholism 268
depressants 266
flashbacks 274

hallucinogens 273
opioids 270
psychoactive
   drugs 265

reward-deficiency
   syndrome 276
reward learning
   pathway 276

sedative-hypnotic drugs 270
stimulants 271
tolerance 265
withdrawal symptoms 265

Study Questions

Multiple Choice

1. Ethyl alcohol exerts its effects by influencing which of the following neurotransmitters?
   a) acetylcholine
   b) endorphins
   c) GABA
   d) serotonin

2. The reward learning pathway in the brain can be activated by:
   a) cocaine only.
   b) hypnosis and meditation only.
   c) psychoactive drugs only.
   d) any activity or substance the individual finds to be pleasurable.

Fill-in-the-Blank

1. Continued use of psychoactive drugs can lead an individual to need more and more of the drug to get the expected effect, a tendency known as _____.

2. Most psychoactive drugs affect the brain by activating a common pathway, whose key neurotransmitter is _____

3. In those addicted to amphetamines, abruptly stopping the drug causes a painful withdrawal process that is very similar to withdrawal from _____.

©iStockphoto.com/andresrimaging

PART 7

LEARNING

PART OUTLINE

Module 35: What Is Learning?

LEARNING OBJECTIVE 35 Define learning and distinguish between associative and non-associative learning.

Module 36: Classical Conditioning

LEARNING OBJECTIVE 36 Describe the basic processes of classical conditioning and explain how classical conditioning is relevant to learning.

Module 37: Operant Conditioning

LEARNING OBJECTIVE 37 Describe the basic processes of operant conditioning and explain how shaping can be used to teach new behaviours.

Module 38: Observational Learning

LEARNING OBJECTIVE 38 Define observational learning and summarize concerns about observational learning from the media.

Module 39: Learning and Cognition

LEARNING OBJECTIVE 39 Define spatial navigation learning, implicit and latent learning, and insight learning.

Module 40: Factors that Facilitate Learning

LEARNING OBJECTIVE 40 Define massed and spaced practice and tell what conditions are best for learning semantic material, such as facts in your classes.

Module 41: Prenatal and Postnatal Learning

LEARNING OBJECTIVE 41 Summarize the types of learning that occur before we are born and during early postnatal life.

Module 42: Specific Learning Disorder

LEARNING OBJECTIVE 42 Define specific learning disorder and describe three major types of learning disorders.

Jagat, in his first month of his first semester of university in a new city, is feeling stressed. He misses his friends and family, he is finding juggling five courses to be very difficult, and for some reason he cannot stop thinking about his grandfather, who has been dead for five years. When he first moved into the dorm all the noises kept him from sleeping, but now they no longer bother him; he worries that this may mean that he is not as alert as he should be to his new surroundings. The weather in this new city is unpredictable and the thunder and lightning storms that blow in without much warning cause him to feel unaccountably anxious. During the first week of the semester Jagat was caught outside in one of these sudden storms and was concerned then that he might be struck by lightning; now he is apprehensive that he might get caught outside during a storm again and so he has begun staying inside his room at the dorm as much as he can. One of his roommates, Nash, has noticed that Jagat is becoming increasingly withdrawn and is concerned about him. Nash, in his third term, a successful student with high grades, offers to help Jagat with his courses if he will come out with Nash and his friends to play basketball and to watch hockey. Jagat, desperate for help, agrees to leave his room and to venture outside of the dorm.

As we will see in this part, learning situations are influenced by many variables, including how difficult the learning task is, how much attention the learner is paying to the task, what sorts and levels of emotions are involved, and whether any required biological precursors to learning are in place—to name a few. The study of each will come up later in this part, and we will find out what learning theory has to say about Jagat as he faces the new learning situations described above. You will see that learning is complex and multidimensional.

Module 35: What Is Learning?

Learning is defined as a lasting change caused by experience. Learning has to be inferred from behaviour—it cannot be directly observed. For example, you may have recently memorized a complex speech, but until you give the speech there is no outward sign of this new learning. Therefore, in order to study learning, scientists measure change in behavioural responses.

It may seem strange to separate a discussion about learning from a closely related subject, memory, which is covered in the next part. Although learning and memory are indeed interrelated and many of the biological mechanisms (and brain regions) that underlie learning are also critical for memory, the study of these topics has diverged in the laboratory. Traditionally, animals (dogs, monkeys, rats, and mice) were the focus of studies on learning, whereas humans were the predominant focus of studies on memory. With the advent of neuroimaging technology and a greater public concern for understanding about learning and learning disabilities, more research on learning is focused on humans as well (Ormrod, 2011). Throughout this part, we will discuss how information that scientists have gained from animal experimentation can be applied to questions of human learning.

In general, learning can be divided into two major categories: *associative* and *non-associative* learning. **Associative learning** is a change that occurs as the result of experiences that lead us to link two or more stimuli together. An example of associative learning would be cringing at the whine of a dental drill because you associate the sound with the pain the drill has caused you in the past. **Non-associative learning** does not require the linking or association of stimuli.

For example, the first time you sleep in a new apartment you may find yourself awakened a number of times by the unfamiliar sounds in the apartment (the furnace coming on) or sounds in the neighbourhood (buses, trains, or trucks going by). However, after a few nights you find you are able to ignore these now familiar sounds and are able to sleep without interruption. You have learned not to associate those sounds with anything of meaning.

LEARNING OBJECTIVE 35
Define learning and distinguish between associative and non-associative learning.

learning a lasting change caused by experience.

associative learning learning that involves forming associations between stimuli.

non-associative learning learning that does not involve forming associations between stimuli.

35.1 Non-associative Learning

Non-associative learning is the simpler of the two types of learning. Non-associative learning refers to learning following repeated exposure to a single stimulus or event. This exposure causes a relatively permanent change in the strength of response. That is, non-associative learning does not require learning about an association between multiple stimuli. For this reason, non-associative learning is considered to be the simplest, most basic, form of learning. There are two major types of non-associative learning, *habituation* and *sensitization*.

35.2 Habituation

As you learned in Part 5, we experience *sensory adaptation* when our senses begin to respond less strongly to repeated presentations of the same sensory cue (Webster, 2012). A smell, such as baking cookies, might be a very welcome and noticeable aroma as you first walk into your house, but after a while you may barely notice the enticing odour. Even though the baking cookies continue to smell as wonderful after you have been home for a while as they did when you first walked in the door, you are no longer aware of the delicious smell—you have become adapted. Your olfactory sense responds less and less strongly, though the same stimulus continues to stimulate the sensory receptors in your olfactory system.

Tetra Images/Corbis

Studying learning. Learning occurs in both humans and animals in similar ways. Therefore, animal research has contributed enormously to our understanding of the principles of learning in both humans and animals.

Habituation is different than fatigue of neurons in the sensory receptors (i.e., sensory adaptation). It is easy to confuse habituation with sensory adaptation but the two are not the same. When we use the term **habituation** we are talking about a form of learning where organisms decrease response to a stimulus after repeated stimulus presentation. Behaviour is especially important in habituation; in habituation the animal or person has learned to ignore something that is unimportant (Thompson, 2009). That is, if something does not pose a threat or is no other way essential to our survival, the animal or person gets used to it, freeing cognitive resources for more important activities. For example, a bird guarding a nest near your front door will initially fly at you each time you walk down the sidewalk to your front entrance. However, over time this guarding behaviour will decrease and may eventually stop entirely as the bird habituates to your presence. The bird continues to detect your presence but has come to learn that you pose no danger to the nest. However, let's say that following the bird's habituation to your non-threatening presence, a friend brings his children to visit you and while outside playing one of the children pokes at the nest with a stick. Under this renewed threat the bird will dishabituate and will once more fly out to guard the nest. **Dishabituation** involves a full-strength recovery of the habituated response in the presence of a novel (new) stimulus. Thus the habituation/dishabituation response has clear adaptive value because it allows organisms to ignore stimuli that do not convey information of biological significance but to respond to stimuli that are important. Jagat, therefore, is needlessly concerned that he no longer reacts to the noises in the dorm. He has simply habituated to the sounds that were at first unfamiliar, indicating that he will, in fact, be even more alert to anything unusual in his new home, as he now knows what is usual for this place.

As you probably recall from Part 4, given preverbal children's limited response options, habituation is used as a tool for familiarizing them with stimuli and then testing for recognition and discrimination. Infants and toddlers direct their gaze to stimuli they are interested in. Therefore, once a baby stops looking at an object of interest, we know that the baby has habituated to it. Then if researchers show the baby a new stimulus and the baby shows renewed interest in the stimulus (i.e., the baby dishabituates), we know that these two stimuli look different to the baby (Columbo & Mitchell, 2009). Using this technique across the different sensory systems, researchers are able to test visual acuity (for example, whether babies can discriminate between facial expressions), auditory acuity (for example, whether babies can discriminate speech sounds), and so on. Learning theorists also study habituation by examining changes in patterns of neuronal activation in various regions of cortex (Nakano et al., 2006; 2009). For example, Nakano and colleagues (2009) demonstrated that neural activation pattern changes when the infant responds to a novel sound following habituation.

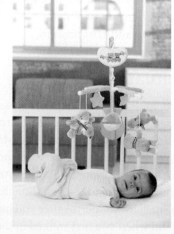

Nyul/Dreamstime/GetStock

Habituation in action. When this infant was first presented with the stimuli (the mobile), she was interested in it and stared at it and reached for it. However, over time she habituates to the stimuli and stops looking at it.

You're at the movies and the situation on the screen has become very intense. The lead female actor is the last one alive. Alone and terrified, she is creeping slowly through the dark woods. Where is the homicidal killer? She knows he's looking for her. He may be behind that tree, or that big rock. Will he jump down from somewhere? Waiting nervously for the inevitable attack, you don't notice that your partner is about to lay a hand on your shoulder until you feel a touch. Startled, you gasp out loud, and some of the people sitting around you also gasp in response as they too are sensitized.

As this example shows, horror movies manipulate our sensitization response. Have you ever noticed that after watching a frightening movie on television, you are easily startled by noises in the house, like a floor creaking, a door opening, or the wind blowing outside—noises that you normally don't even notice? You have become temporarily sensitized to these stimuli.

35.3 Sensitization

Sensitization is another form of non-associative learning that involves an altered response following the presentation of a single sensory cue. Unlike habituation, sensitization involves an increase, as opposed to a decrease, in response with learning. Imagine you are home alone at night reading quietly. Without any warning, your cat knocks over a lamp, startling you. You may jump or even shout out in fear before realizing what has happened. And, for some time after you calm down, you are likely to startle again in response to normal auditory stimuli, such as the ring tone from your cell phone. Your enhanced response to this typical stimulus may reflect the fact that sensitization has occurred. As in the case of habituation, sensitization makes good adaptive sense. An unexpected stimulus may signal danger, so an immediate magnified response to stimuli that follow may be helpful for survival.

sensitization a form of non-associative learning whereby a strong stimulus results in an exaggerated response to the subsequent presentation of weaker stimuli.

35.4 Associative Learning

Non-associative learning does not account for the majority of learning; the majority of learning is considered to be associative. Associative learning occurs when we link two events that occur close together in time, such as when we stop at a red light or when a dog becomes excited at the sight of its leash. Such learning involves making connections—or *associations*—between two or more stimuli. Most of the learning you engage in as a student is highly associative. Course material involves connecting numerous concepts and facts to produce an overall picture of a certain subject. Learning people's names or learning how to please or influence a parent involves forming associations. Animals also engage in associative learning. For example, when a dog barks at the mail carrier and the mail carrier leaves, the dog learns (in this case erroneously) that its actions have particular consequences.

Two major types of associative learning are classical conditioning and operant, or instrumental, conditioning. In classical conditioning, as we will see next, we come to associate two stimuli, eventually responding the same way to both. In operant conditioning, which we will examine after classical conditioning, we come to associate stimuli with the consequences that follow. It is important to note that many situations involve both classical and operant conditioning. We will discuss each type of conditioning separately, and then examine how they co-occur in some situations.

Jonathan Hayward/The Canadian Press

Associative learning. Dogs associate their barking as the cause of the retreat of the mail carrier, indicating that not all associations are necessarily accurate reflections of reality. That is, the mail carrier would have moved on whether the dog was barking or not; however, the dog associates the mail carrier leaving with its own behaviour (barking).

Before You Go On

www.wiley.com/go/comercanada

What Do You Know?

1. What is learning?
2. What happens during habituation? What happens during sensitization?

What Do You Think? Give an example from your own life of a time when you experienced non-associative learning.

Summary

Module 35: What Is Learning?

LEARNING OBJECTIVE 35 Define learning and distinguish between associative and non-associative learning.

- Learning is a lasting change in the brain caused by experience.
- Non-associative learning is a lasting change that happens as a result of experience with a single cue. Types of non-associative learning include habituation, in which we display decreased responses to familiar stimuli, and sensitization, in which we display increased responses to stimuli of normal strength after being exposed to an unusually strong stimulus.
- Associative learning is a lasting change that happens as a result of associating two or more stimuli. Types of associative learning include classical and operant conditioning.

Key Terms

associative learning 281

dishabituation 282

habituation 282

learning 281

non-associative learning 281

sensitization 283

Study Questions

Multiple Choice

1. How does associative learning differ from non-associative learning?
   a) Associative learning is studied experimentally. Non-associative learning is studied using non-experimental methods.
   b) Associative learning applies to humans. Non-associative learning applies to other animals.
   c) Associative learning is based on connecting two or more stimuli. Non-associative learning is not based on such connections.
   d) Non-associative learning involves memory. Associative learning does not require memory.

Fill-in-the-Blank

1. Psychologists use the term _____ to refer to a lasting change in behaviour resulting from experience.

Module 36: Classical Conditioning

Does your cat dash into the kitchen when you open a can of tomato sauce? Do you cringe when you see lightning? Do you think of someone special when you hear a particular song? Do you run out of the room when you see a mouse? It is very likely that you have experienced one of these scenarios or something very like them. This is because we all experience a type of learning known as **conditioning**. Conditioning involves the association of events in the environment. Therefore, your cat has associated the sound of the can opener with getting fed; you have come to associate the crash of thunder with the sight of lightning; a particular piece of music has become associated with a romantic interlude; and you associate mice with a fear response.

This particular type of learning, called **classical conditioning**, describes how these associations are formed. In classical conditioning a response normally evoked by a neutral stimulus also comes to be elicited by a different stimulus. For example, when you first experienced an electrical storm, you initially cringed only to the loud booming of the thunder. However, after experiencing the multiple pairings of thunder with lightning, you now also cringe at the sight of lightning because you have come to *associate* the *sight* of lightning with the *sound* of thunder.

Classical conditioning was serendipitously discovered around the turn of the nineteenth century by a Russian physiologist named Ivan Petrovich Pavlov. His discovery of conditioned reflexes made it possible to study psychic activity objectively and led the way to a systematic investigation of associative learning in the laboratory. His original research methods are still used in psychology laboratories today (for examples see Dijksterhuis, 2004; Halladay et al., 2012; Rau & Fanselow, 2009). We refer to this form of learning as "classical conditioning" because it was the first systematic study of the basic laws of learning (or conditioning).

Pavlov did not start out to study the mechanisms involved in learning. At 33 years of age, he had earned a medical degree and from there spent roughly the next two decades studying the digestive system; he was particularly interested in understanding the role of the salivary reflex on the action of the stomach during digestion. This work on the digestive system won him a Nobel Prize in 1904 (Windholz, 1997).

What does this have to do with learning, you ask? Before we can answer that question we need to have a basic idea of what Pavlov's experiment was about. First though, we need to identify the term **natural reflex**. Natural reflexes are generally present at birth and do not have to be learned, and as such are considered "hard-wired" into a species. For example, your pupil contracts—shrinks—in response to bright light; you did not have to be taught this response. Pavlov was interested in another such reflex, the salivary reflex. Many animals (including humans) experience reflexive salivation—mouthwatering—at the sight or sound or thought of food. Pavlov conducted his research on the salivary reflex with dogs, giving hungry dogs food under controlled conditions and measuring salivary output. His laboratory apparatus and method are shown in **Figure 36-1**. As time progressed, Pavlov noticed that his dogs were salivating even when food wasn't present. Instead, they began to salivate when the lab assistants first arrived or when they heard noises such as footsteps that signalled the arrival of the assistants. Although Pavlov initially viewed this premature salivation as a nuisance, he quickly came to realize that these "psychic secretions" were evidence that the dogs had learned to associate the appearance of a lab assistant with getting food. Thus, the dogs were experiencing a behavioural response (salivation) in *anticipation* of getting food (that is, the dogs learned that the assistant was a cue that the food was about to be served). Pavlov realized that the dogs' responses indicated that they were experiencing not only a physiological response, but also a psychological response—a type of learning that originated in the cerebral cortex (Babkin, 1949). He therefore began to study this type of learning in greater detail, eventually systematizing this basic form of associative learning into what is now called *Pavlovian* or *classical conditioning* (Windholz, 1987).

conditioning the association of events in the environment.

classical conditioning a form of associative learning between two previously unrelated stimuli that results in a learned response.

natural reflex an automatic involuntary response that typically occurs without learning.

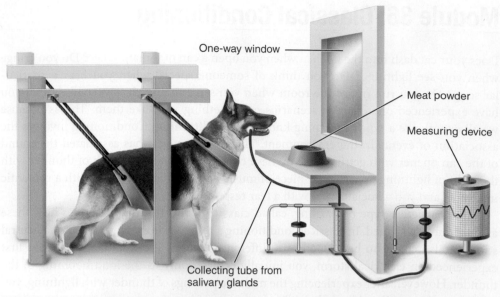

Labels in figure:
- One-way window
- Meat powder
- Measuring device
- Collecting tube from salivary glands

FIGURE 36-1 Pavlov's experiment for collecting and measuring salivation in dogs. The hungry dog is placed in a harness and given a bowl of meat powder. A tube from the salivary gland collects the saliva, which is measured and recorded.

36.1 How Does Classical Conditioning Work?

Pavlov's classical conditioning model has only four basic components. But before we begin to describe the process of classical conditioning, note that students are often intimidated at first by the unfriendly and technical jargon that Pavlov used to describe the process of classical conditioning. However, the process of classical conditioning is actually very straightforward and so we suggest that you try to guard against getting overwhelmed by the terminology and just think about the steps first—then learn the terms. Let's start.

To classically condition an organism, a few steps need to be followed. First, a stimulus has to be present that can automatically trigger a response that does not have to be learned. The stimulus that causes this reflexive response is called the **unconditioned stimulus (US)**. Because the response doesn't have to be learned, it is called the **unconditioned response (UR)**. To begin conditioning, the neutral stimulus is presented together with the unconditioned stimulus. After repeated pairings of the neutral stimulus with the unconditioned stimulus (US), the neutral stimulus alone eventually elicits the unconditioned response. After that happens, the neutral stimulus is no longer considered neutral. It is now called the **conditioned stimulus (CS)**, and the physiological response it elicits is called the **conditioned response (CR)**.

Let's now apply these newly introduced terms to Pavlov's original experiment. For Pavlov's dogs, the unconditioned stimulus was meat powder. The dogs' unconditioned response was to salivate. So, for the dogs, without any learning, the unconditioned stimulus (meat powder: US) elicited an unconditioned response (salivation: UR). The arrival of a lab assistant was, originally, a neutral stimulus to the dogs. The response is called "neutral" because it initially caused no salivation response from the dog. However, after repeated pairings of the lab assistant with the meat powder, over time, the assistant's arrival alone became a conditioned stimulus. Thus the unconditioned stimulus (the meat powder: US) became paired with the conditioned stimulus (the arrival of the lab assistant: CS). The dog then learned the association between the arrival of the lab assistant and the presentation of the meat powder. Eventually the dog responded to the conditioned stimulus (the arrival of the lab assistant) by salivating. Thus, the conditioned stimulus elicited the conditioned response (salivation: CR). Since this new response is learned (or conditioned), it is now called the conditioned response (CR) and the formerly neutral stimulus has become the conditioned stimulus (CS). The dogs' salivation, once an unconditioned response to the food, is now a conditioned response to the assistant.

This process is summarized in **Figure 36-2**.

unconditioned stimulus (US)
a stimulus that on its own elicits a response.

unconditioned response (UR)
a physical response elicited by an unconditioned stimulus; it does not need to be learned.

conditioned stimulus (CS)
a neutral stimulus that eventually elicits the same response as an unconditioned stimulus with which it has been paired.

conditioned response (CR)
a physical response elicited by a conditioned stimulus; it is acquired through experience and is usually the same as the unconditioned response.

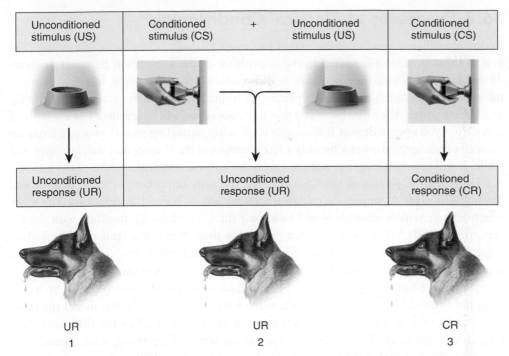

Unconditioned stimulus (US)	Conditioned stimulus (CS) + Unconditioned stimulus (US)	Conditioned stimulus (CS)
Unconditioned response (UR)	Unconditioned response (UR)	Conditioned response (CR)
UR 1	UR 2	CR 3

FIGURE 36-2 Classical conditioning. The sequence of classical conditioning is shown here, from left to right. (1) The US (meat powder) produces the UR (salivation). (2) During conditioning, the US is paired with a CS, a neutral or conditioned stimulus (a sound such as a doorknob being turned by the research assistant). (3) After conditioning, the CS alone produces the conditioned (learned) response (CR) of salivation.

Classical conditioning is not just for dogs. People can also be classically conditioned. For example, suppose that you come home from school in an unusually bad mood, but as you enter your apartment you hear your roommate playing a particular song and you feel unaccountably happy. On reflection you realize that you have come to associate this particular song with your roommate being in a really good mood and his good mood always makes you happy. Let's break this down using the classical conditioning terms we just reviewed. When your roommate is in a really good mood (US), you are happy (UR). You don't dislike this song, but you have no real attachment to it. However, your roommate repeatedly plays this song (CS) when he is in a really good mood (US). Eventually the song alone causes you to feel happy (CR). You have been classically conditioned. Even babies and young children can be classically conditioned. One of our sons, responding to the romantic music in a movie, turned to his grandmother and said, "Uh oh Gwammie, der's gonna be kissin."

There are many, many examples of classical conditioning in our day-to-day lives. Do you feel anxious when you see a police car, even when you know that you are doing nothing wrong? Do you feel even more anxious when you see a police car with its lights flashing? When you are sick, do you feel better after just one sip of ginger ale (a drink your mom always gave you when you were sick as a child)? Do you think of an old boyfriend or girlfriend whenever you smell a particular type of cologne or perfume? Do you feel relaxed the minute you step into your apartment? In the morning do you feel more awake after only one sip of coffee or tea? Have you heard of combat veterans who are frightened when they smell diesel fuel, or of a sexually abused child who is fearful whenever she sees a male with a beard? These are all examples of classical conditioning. It turns out that Jagat couldn't stop thinking about his grandfather because Nash, Jagat's roommate, used a shoe polish that Jagat's grandfather used to put on his boots. Without Jagat being consciously aware of it, the smell of the shoe polish was causing him to think of his grandfather.

The Granger Collection

A classic moment in history. In this famous image, Ivan Pavlov (centre, with beard) stands with his assistants and students prior to demonstrating his classical conditioning experiment on a dog.

36.2 Processes of Classical Conditioning

Pavlov identified a number of important processes related to classical conditioning. The first of these processes is related to the acquisition of the association between the conditioned stimulus and the unconditioned stimulus. Not surprisingly, learning is more robust when the number of CS–US pairings is high. That is, the more times that the CS and US are paired, the more likely it is that the association will be learned. For example, if every time you open a drawer it makes an unpleasant squealing sound, you will tense up prior to opening the drawer after only a few attempts. If the drawer only catches once in a while, it will take you longer to acquire an uneasy response in anticipation of the sound.

However, the pairing of the CS–US is not the only important factor in acquisition. Timing also plays an important role in the formation of learned associations. The most effective presentation schedule would be to pair the US and the CS together, with the CS occurring slightly before the US, so that the CS has predictive value. How much is slightly before? For most species, the optimal delay—that is, the delay that produces the most rapid acquisition followed by the strongest response—is a half a second delay. Why? Let's imagine that you have a fish bowl in your dining room. Each morning you feed your fish by sprinkling the fish food (US) onto the surface of the water. As soon as the fish detect the food, they swim to the surface (UR). Now let's say that just before you feed the fish you always turn on the light by the fish bowl so that you can see what you are doing. After a number of instances, you realize that the fish are swimming to the surface (CR) as soon as you turn on the light (CS). The fish have acquired a response to the learned association between the conditioned stimulus (the light) and the unconditioned stimulus (the food). Now imagine that you only turn on the light when you enter the dining room to sit down and eat your breakfast. You feed the fish only after you are finished eating. The fish are much less likely to learn the association between the light and the food with this long delay between the two events.

Why aren't people who are afraid of snakes afraid of only one type of snake? Why did Pavlov's dogs respond by salivating to *every* research assistant and not only to the single individual who consistently fed them? The answer to these questions is **stimulus generalization**. Stimulus generalization occurs when stimuli similar to the original conditioned stimulus trigger the same conditioned response. So the person or animal responds to stimuli that are similar but not identical to the conditioned stimulus. Therefore any reptile resembling a snake elicits a fear response and any assistant in a lab coat elicits a salivatory response. The more ways in which the generalized stimuli resemble the conditioned stimulus, the stronger the conditioned response will be. So, for example, an unfamiliar child in a lab coat might not create as strong a response in the dog as an unfamiliar adult in a lab coat. Stimulus generalization is important because if we rely on past learning to help us decide how to respond to somewhat familiar stimuli and events, we eliminate the need to have to learn how to respond to every single new stimulus we encounter. This frees up mental energy for more important learning.

However, at times it is important for organisms to be able to discriminate between stimuli. For instance, some plants are nutritious and others are poisonous; in order to survive, we must know how to distinguish one plant from another. **Stimulus discrimination** occurs when an organism learns to discriminate between the conditioned stimulus and other similar stimuli. Take for example, a rat that has been conditioned to expect a shock (US) when it hears a tone (CS). Following the acquisition of this response, the rat can then be taught to discriminate between different tones. If a shock follows only a high tone, the rat can learn to distinguish the tone paired with the unconditioned stimulus (shock) from the other lower tones (no shock). Similarly, at home your cat may be able to discriminate between the sound of a particular

stimulus generalization what occurs when stimuli similar to the original conditioned stimulus trigger the same conditioned response.

stimulus discrimination what occurs when an organism learns to emit a specific behaviour in the presence of a conditioned stimulus, but not in the presence of stimuli similar to the conditioned stimulus.

"I don't care if she is a tape dispenser. I love her."

©Sam Gross/The New Yorker

Stimulus generalization. Stimulus generalization occurs when stimuli similar to the original conditioned stimulus trigger the same conditioned response.

kitchen drawer opening—the one containing her treats—and the sound of any other kitchen drawer being opened.

Consider Pavlov's dogs for a moment. As you now know, each dog was conditioned to salivate to the arrival of the lab assistant. Following the acquisition of the learned association between the lab assistant (CS) and the meat powder (US), let's say that bell on the door becomes paired with the arrival of the lab assistant. Even though the bell has never been paired with the meat powder, the dog begins to salivate at the sound of the bell. This occurs because the bell (CS2) has become paired with the arrival of the lab assistant (CS). In this case the original conditioned stimulus (the lab assistant) is functioning as if it were an unconditioned stimulus. This phenomenon is known as **higher order conditioning**. Evidence of higher order conditioning is often observed in advertising. Advertisers often pair their products (CS) with sexual imagery (US); this type of advertising relies on classical conditioning. However, when a celebrity is paired with a product, advertisers are relying on higher order conditioning. The celebrity (CS) has become associated with sexual imagery (US), and the celebrity, in turn, becomes associated with the product (CS2).

Pavlov also showed that a learned response could be eliminated by presenting the conditioned stimulus repeatedly, without the unconditioned stimulus. For example, the lab assistant could come to the lab many times without offering any food to the dogs, or you could move the cat treats to another room. In time, the dog no longer associates food with the lab assistant and your cat stops running to the kitchen when she hears the former "treat" drawer being opened. This phenomenon, called **extinction**, does not represent "unlearning" or forgetting, but is instead a process by which the previously learned CR is actively inhibited (Quirk, 2006). That is, we don't forget responses that have been conditioned; we simply see a reduction in the strength of the conditioned response (CR). Therefore, a child who associates a parent with pain/fear does not forget the association even though she may no longer cower when the parent is present. For the conditioned response to be permanently removed it would have to be completely extinguished.

Evidence that the information about the previous CS–US pairing still exists after extinction training can be observed by allowing time to pass with no training after extinction has occurred. In this case, the CR will often re-emerge at a later date, at up to half the intensity of its original conditioned level, a phenomenon called **spontaneous recovery** (**Figure 36-3**). For example, if the assistant hasn't brought food for several visits and the dogs' salivation response has been inhibited by extinction, the dogs might still salivate a week after extinction when the assistant arrives, indicating that the response was not "unlearned." For this reason, a parent who has not engaged in abusive behaviour for some time may continue to elicit a fear response from a child. It is therefore obvious that the

Jodi Cobb/National Geographic Stock

Higher order conditioning in advertising. Evidence of higher order conditioning is often observed in advertising, where advertisers often pair their products with sexual imagery.

higher order conditioning what occurs when a previously conditioned stimulus functions as if it were an unconditioned stimulus for further conditioning.

extinction reduction of a conditioned response after repeated presentations of the conditioned stimulus alone.

spontaneous recovery re-emergence of a conditioned response sometime after extinction has occurred.

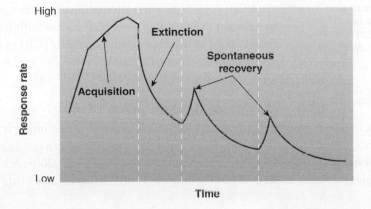

FIGURE 36-3 Acquisition, extinction, and spontaneous recovery. Acquisition occurs as the US and CS are repeatedly paired. When the CS is presented repeatedly without the US, the individual's learned response gradually decreases until extinction occurs. But the information about the previous CS–US pairing is not lost, and the extinguished response spontaneously reappears.

previously learned information has not been lost or forgotten, because it can be spontaneously recovered without any further pairing of the US–CS.

36.3 Classical Conditioning and Drug Dependency

WHAT HAPPENS
in the B R A I N ?

The research of Shepard Siegel and his colleagues at McMaster University has focused on the role of classical conditioning in drug dependency. Drug *use* begins when an individual experiences the effects of a drug as pleasurable. Drug *dependency* involves the psychological and physiological experiences that occur as the individual continues to use the drug; the body adapts to the presence of the drug and the individual experiences withdrawal if the drug is reduced or stopped. Withdrawal is the psychological and physical discomfort and distress experienced when the body is deprived of an addictive substance it has become metabolically adapted to.

Siegel has studied the role that classical conditioning plays in both the physiological and psychological tolerance that builds up within addicts who regularly inject heroin (Siegel, 2005; McDonald & Siegel, 2004). *Tolerance* develops in drug users and abusers as they require increasingly larger doses of the drug to obtain the same intensity of effect initially obtained by a smaller dose. Tolerance involves a number of factors, including possible changes at the cellular level in response to the drug (Koch & Höllt, 2008).

Deaths among addicts due to overdoses of heroin were initially thought to be accounted for by unexpected jumps in the purity or strength of the heroin being injected. However, Siegel and his colleagues (Siegel, 2005; McDonald & Siegel, 2004) argue that a learned compensatory response (US) can trigger drug tolerance (UR) and may be involved in some drug overdoses. They argue that the body seeks to compensate for the effects of a drug by initiating a compensatory response (for example, lowering body temperature in anticipation of a rise in temperature caused by heroin injection) when there are environmental cues that the drug is on its way. The greater the compensatory response, the larger the dose required to offset it.

Siegel and his colleagues further argue that the physiologic counter reaction to heroin becomes classically conditioned over time to the process of self-injection and to the location in which the injection is administered (CS). This means that the nervous system, due to classical conditioning, anticipates the arrival of the heroin based simply on external environmental cues (called *extroceptive cues*) provided by the location (e.g., the room, drug paraphernalia, or other characteristic sights and sounds) in which the addict shoots up. When the addict injects in a new environment without the familiar environmental cues, the body's anticipatory response is absent; without these counterbalancing effects, the addict's system may become overwhelmed by the usual dose of heroin, suppressing respiration and killing the individual. The work of McDonald and Siegel (2004) also explains why addicts experience cravings when attempting to quit drugs. Exposure to external drug-related cues (CS) causes withdrawal symptoms caused by a compensatory response (CR) in the absence of the drug (US), causing cravings that can lead to relapse.

Janine Wiedel Photolibrary/Alamy

Compensatory responses. The environmental context in which heroin addicts inject themselves becomes associated with their body's compensatory response to the heroin. As a result, if they inject themselves in a novel location their body's compensatory response may not be sufficient to counter the effects of the heroin, resulting in an overdose.

36.4 Classical Conditioning and Fears

As the work of Siegel and his colleagues demonstrates, classical conditioning is involved in drug tolerance. Other research has shown that classical conditioning also plays a role in other forms of physiological responding, including immune response (Ader, 2003; Ader & Cohen, 1984), allergic reactions (Teufel et al., 2007), and fear conditioning (Maren et al., 2013).

In this well-known quote, John Broadus Watson, often viewed as the founder of behaviourism, expressed his belief in the all-important role the environment played in shaping individuals. He rejected the role of introspection and the study of the mental worlds of the conscious and unconscious mind as unverifiable and instead argued that behaviourism was the experimental approach that ought to be used in psychology as behaviour was observable and therefore could be studied with complete objectivity. Fear conditioning was first studied by Watson and his student (who, incidentally, later became his wife) Rosalie Rayner (1920). Their most well-known study was the classical conditioning of an 11-month-old baby Watson and Rayner called Albert B, who subsequently became well known as "Little Albert." In the study, Watson exposed baby Albert to an initially neutral stimulus, a white rat. Initially Albert had no fear of the rat, but as he reached forward to touch it, Watson used a hammer to strike a steel bar just behind Albert's head. This loud sound frightened Albert so much that he burst into tears. Seven pairings of the white rat (CS) with the loud noise (US) made Albert cry and avoid the rat (CR).

Watson also examined the effects of stimulus generalization on creating fear. After conditioning sessions, Watson claimed that Albert, for example, came to fear not only the white rat, but also other furry stimuli, including a rabbit, a dog, a sealskin coat, and Watson in a Santa Claus beard (Karies, 1986). Albert moved away before Watson could attempt to extinguish his conditioned fear and psychologists speculated for some time about what happened to this little boy, wondering whether he grew up with a strange fear of rats, rabbits, coats, and Santa, or whether he was able to overcome his conditioning. Recently, Hall Beck and colleagues (Beck, Levinson, & Irons, 2009; Beck, 2011) tracked down Little Albert's identity as well as his fate. Albert was identified as Douglas Merritte, a boy who suffered from congenital hydrocephalus (abnormal buildup of cerebral spinal fluid in the brain); the researchers discovered that Douglas died at six years of age.

There are serious ethical and moral issues associated with Watson's research with Little Albert. This study would be considered unethical under current Canadian Psychological Association guidelines. Albert's mother was never informed of Albert's participation in the study and the study was carried out without regard for the suffering caused to Albert or for the possibility that there would be lasting harmful effects on Albert's emotional state (Field & Nightingale, 2009). Moreover, Fridlund et al. (2012) report that Watson misrepresented "Little Albert" as "healthy" and "normal" in spite of the fact that he, Watson, knew that was not the case. Further, there are clear suggestions that Watson overstated his results, as several other researchers have failed to replicate his findings (Samelson, 1980).

Nevertheless, subsequent laboratory studies with animals show that fears are very easily learned. Fear conditioning of laboratory rodents involves training them to associate a neutral cue (usually a tone) with a painful unconditioned stimulus, usually an electric shock to the feet. Naïve rodents will respond to foot shock by adopting a characteristic posture of immobilization, or "freezing." This response probably reflects adaptive behaviour that small mammals engage in when confronted with a predator and have no way to escape; they minimize movement to escape detection. Typically just a few pairings of a tone with foot shock lead to a lasting CS–US association, causing the rat to freeze to the CS tone alone (LeDoux, 2000, 2003).

> "Give me a dozen healthy infants, well-formed, and my own specified world to bring them up in and I'll guarantee to take any one at random and train him to become any type of specialist I might select—doctor, lawyer, artist, merchant-chief, and, yes, even beggar-man and thief, regardless of his talents, penchants, tendencies, abilities, vocations, and race of his ancestors."
>
> — *John B. Watson*

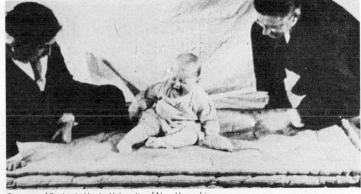

Courtesy of Benjamin Harris, University of New Hampshire

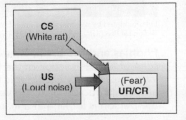

Teaching a child to fear. In an ethically-questionable study, John Watson and his colleague Rosalie Rayner used classical conditioning principles to condition 11-month-old "Little Albert" to fear white rats (shown next to Little Albert's left hand).

phobia a persistent, irrational, or obsessive fear of a specific object or situation that may arise as a result of fear conditioning.

systematic desensitization a process used to condition extinction of phobias through gradual exposure to the feared object or situation.

36.4.1 Phobias

Some scientists believe fear conditioning is the basis of the development of a category of anxiety disorders called phobias (LeDoux, 1998; Morgan, Romanski, & LeDoux, 1993). **Phobias** are extreme, irrational, persistent fears of specific objects or situations, many of which pose little real danger. People who suffer from phobias are believed to have learned an association between neutral (CS) and dangerous (US) stimuli, thus being conditioned to fear a relatively harmless cue (i.e., the CS). For example, take a case where an adult has acquired a fear (CR) of all breeds of dogs (CS) due to being injured/frightened (UR) as a small child when knocked to the ground by an over-exuberant Labrador retriever (US). Due to the generalized association of fear (CR) to all dogs (CS), this person now refuses to go outside if he sees a dog, big or small. Such learned associations are one way that people become conditioned to fear specific objects or situations (we will discuss phobias in more detail in Part 15). Any neutral stimulus can become associated with a dangerous stimulus and become the focus for a phobia. Some phobias are common, such as fear of heights, enclosed spaces, spiders, and thunder and lightning; but other phobias are less common, such as fear of forests, marriage, bald men, knees, and clowns. People can truly develop a fear of *anything*.

In fact, phobias can be very debilitating (for example, Jagat's fear of thunderstorms kept him in his room, afraid to venture outdoors), and can have detrimental effects on an individual's ability to live normally. Therefore, therapies are important to help individuals cope with phobias. The theory that phobias arise from fear conditioning has led to the development of therapies that are also based on classical conditioning. In one common process, known as **systematic desensitization**, people who suffer from phobias undergo a series of extinction trials—repeated exposure to the feared object or situation in the absence of pairing with a US (systematic desensitization will be discussed in greater detail in Part 16).

Neuroimaging studies suggest that phobias involve abnormal activity in the amygdala, a part of the brain that is active when we experience emotions, including fear (Ledoux, 2003). People with phobias show rapid activation of this brain region when exposed to the stimuli they fear most. Extinction training, by contrast, is known to activate part of the prefrontal cortex as phobias diminish (Quirk, et al., 2006; Herry et al., 2010). Recall from Part 3 that our prefrontal cortex can help us inhibit emotional impulses. Thus, phobias that have been desensitized still exist. As a result, they are prone to spontaneous recovery, similar to other classically-conditioned behaviours.

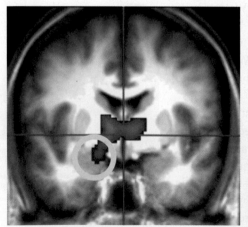 

Left: Reprinted by permission of Elsevier from L. Goossen, et al., Amygdala Hyperfunction in Phobic Fear Normalizes After Exposure, *Biological Psychiatry, 62*(10), 1119–1125, Figure 1; right: ©iStockphoto.com/espencer1

Phobias and the brain. This coloured brain scan of a cross-section of the brain reveals increased activity in a phobic individual's amygdala (region circled in yellow) while the person is looking at a feared object.

Arachnophobia. An extreme fear of spiders is one of the most common of all phobias. Around half of all women and 10 percent of all men have at least a mild fear of spiders.

36.5 Classical Conditioning and Taste Aversions

Another type of classical conditioning that has been studied in the laboratory has relevance to human learning. **Conditioned taste aversion** involves learning an association between a particular food and a subsequent stomach illness (Garcia et al., 1985). Many of us have had the following experience. You eat a certain type of food and a short time later, you are afflicted with nausea, vomiting, and diarrhea. It is possible that you have food poisoning. However, it can also happen that you eat a certain type of food and then become ill due to something unrelated to the food. For example, you might have had too much alcohol to drink and so now have a hangover, or you may have developed the stomach flu. Either way, whether or not the symptoms are directly related to the food you ate before becoming ill, you will probably develop an aversion to that particular food for some time afterwards. In this case, the US is whatever agent actually made you nauseous, whether bacterial, viral, or chemical. The food you develop an aversion to is the CS. The unconditioned physiological response (UR) is the nausea or other unpleasant gastrointestinal response. Following this initial experience, you will feel ill (experience nausea) simply when exposed to the food. Imagine that you eat salsa and tortilla chips one afternoon while at the beach. Later, you suffer flu-like symptoms due to heat exhaustion. Even though you know you were ill due to heat exhaustion you cannot bear to even look at, or think about, salsa. So, the US (heat stroke) caused you to be ill (UR); however, the salsa (CS) became paired with the heat exhaustion so that now the sight of salsa causes you to feel ill (CR). Conditioned taste aversions happen very quickly. Laboratory research has shown that a single pairing of food and nausea is frequently all that is necessary for a conditioned taste aversion to be formed (Garcia et al., 1985; Garcia & Koellig, 1971).

Not only did you develop this aversion from a single experience, but this aversion to salsa is also particularly impressive given the length of time that intervened between your exposure to the CS (salsa) and your illness. In fact, research shows that the taste of a specific food or drink can be associated with illness up to 12 hours after its ingestion (Cowan et al., 2000). Forming an association after such a long delay between the CS and US is quite remarkable; recall that we said earlier that a delay of more than 30 seconds between a CS and a US often makes it difficult to establish a relationship between two stimuli. Separation of a tone from a shock by several hours would make it very difficult, if not impossible, to produce fear conditioning, and yet conditioned taste aversions develop even when the US follows the CS after a significant period of time.

Some people are especially vulnerable to conditioned taste aversions. Pregnant women with severe morning sickness may develop intense aversions to foods that are followed by nausea. Similarly, classic research by Gary Challis and Hank Stam at the University of Calgary shows that people undergoing chemotherapy for cancer treatment can develop aversions to foods they ingest right before a chemotherapy session, due to the nausea occurring as a side effect of the drug (Challis & Stam, 1992). As a result of this research, people undergoing chemotherapy are now advised not to eat favourite foods prior to treatment to avoid developing aversions to foods they love.

36.5.1 Producing a Taste Aversion

In pioneering work, researcher John Garcia and his colleagues used classical conditioning to condition taste aversions in laboratory animals by giving them specific foods to eat or

conditioned taste aversion
a form of classical conditioning whereby a previously neutral stimulus (often an odour or taste) elicits an aversive reaction after it's paired with illness (nausea).

WHAT HAPPENS *in the* **BRAIN?**

iStockphoto.com/Lynn_Bystrom

Producing a taste aversion. Conditioned taste aversions have been used in British Columbia to keep black bears from eating human food (Homstol, 2011).

drink and then inducing nausea through injection or radiation, causing radiation sickness (Garcia & Koelling, 1971). The rats rapidly learned the association between taste and nausea. Such conditioned taste aversions, often referred to as the Garcia effect, have been used in Alberta to protect livestock from wolves, in Saskatchewan to protect cows and sheep from coyotes, and in Whistler, British Columbia to keep black bears from eating human food (Homstol, 2011). How is this accomplished? Meat (lamb or beef carcasses) or human food is treated with a substance that will cause the coyote or the bear to become ill. The animal then associates illness with the food just eaten and avoids the livestock or human food (see Gustavson et al., 1974, 1976).

Not only do taste aversions form quickly, but they are also very specific. For example, why do we form an association between the taste of food and illness? Why don't we form an aversion instead to the friends who were with us on the beach or to going to the beach or to the ocean? The answer is that we are biologically prepared to form associations between tastes and illness. Garcia and other scientists suggest that we have a biological readiness to learn certain associations due to their survival value (Gaston, 1978). This biological readiness is adaptive and probably rooted in our evolutionary history. The ability to associate potentially tainted food with a subsequent illness leads to increased survival and reproduction. Those who could not learn to avoid that which made them ill were more likely to be poisoned and to die. In this way, abilities with survival value, such as avoiding potentially tainted food and water, are passed down to future generations and therefore over time, most people in the population form conditioned taste aversions.

Biological preparedness also may help explain why taste aversions are particularly easy to learn for animals that use odour and taste for food detection (e.g., mice, rats, wolves). In these same animals, it is difficult to form an association between a visual or auditory cue and nausea. However, in animals such as birds, who select their food using visual cues, conditioned aversions to flavours or odours are difficult to produce. For example, birds can be more readily conditioned to avoid visual cues (such as a certain coloured bead) when those cues have been paired with stomach illness (Werner, Kimball, & Provenza, 2008). Birds often search for prey using vision and conversely also ignore potential prey based on visual cues alone. For example, predatory birds avoid prey with aposematic colouring (conspicuous colouring that serves as a warning; for example, on a skunk or a butterfly). It is therefore more natural for birds to associate a visual cue, rather than a gustatory or olfactory one, with a subsequent stomach illness.

iStockphoto.com/wd

Conditioned aversions and visual cues. Birds use visual cues to develop conditioned taste aversions, such as aposematic colouring to identify butterflies that produce an illness when eaten.

Before You Go On

www.wiley.com/go/comercanada

What Do You Know?

1. You take your dog in the car when going to the veterinarian. After several visits, your dog cowers and whimpers whenever he sees the car. Identify the US, UR, CS, and CR in this example of conditioned fear.

2. What is conditioned taste aversion? How does it happen?

What Do You Think? How might the principles of classical conditioning be used to keep chemotherapy patients from forming taste aversions to foods they enjoy?

Summary

Module 36: Classical Conditioning

LEARNING OBJECTIVE 36 Describe the basic processes of classical conditioning and explain how classical conditioning is relevant to learning.

- As a result of classical conditioning, a previously neutral stimulus comes to elicit a response by being paired with an unconditioned stimulus (US) that already generates the response, known as an unconditioned response (UR). The neutral stimulus becomes a conditioned stimulus (CS) when it elicits the same response as the US. The response to the CS is known as a conditioned response (CR).
- Repeated presentation of the CS without the US can lead to extinction, or suppression of the CR. Extinction does not mean we forget the CS–US association, however. The CR can be spontaneously recovered.
- Phobias and conditioned taste aversions can result from classical conditioning. Systematic desensitization uses classical conditioning to extinguish phobia responses. Conditioned taste aversions suggest that we are biologically prepared to quickly learn responses important to our survival.

Key Terms

classical conditioning 285
conditioned response (CR) 286
conditioned stimulus (CS) 286
conditioned taste aversion 293
conditioning 285

extinction 289
higher order conditioning 289
natural reflex 285
phobia 292
spontaneous recovery 289

stimulus discrimination 288
stimulus generalization 288
systematic desensitization 292
unconditioned response (UR) 286
unconditioned stimulus (US) 286

Study Questions

Multiple Choice

1. In Pavlov's study, the US was _____; the neutral stimulus was _____; and, finally, the CS was _____.
   a) meat powder; the assistant; meat powder
   b) meat powder; the assistant; the assistant
   c) the assistant; meat powder; meat powder
   d) meat powder; meat powder; the assistant

2. _____ occurs when a previously conditioned response decreases in frequency when the CS is presented in the absence of the US.
   a) Extinction
   b) Habituation
   c) Adaptation
   d) Deconditioning

Fill-in-the-Blank

1. In classical conditioning, a previously _____ stimulus is associated with an unconditioned stimulus that naturally elicits some response.

Module 37: Operant Conditioning

LEARNING OBJECTIVE 37
Describe the basic processes of
operant conditioning and explain
how shaping can be used to
teach new behaviours.

operant or **instrumental
conditioning** a form of associative
learning whereby behaviour
is modified depending on its
consequences.

law of effect behaviours leading
to rewards are more likely to occur
again, while behaviours producing
unpleasantness are less likely to
occur again.

Classical conditioning does not account for the vast majority of learning by complex organisms. Classical conditioning is a passive form of learning that does not involve the active participation of the learner. In fact, most forms of classical conditioning occur without awareness that the association is being formed. The learner has very little control over the stimuli being associated. For example, a light flashes and a shock follows. The animal or person learns to make the association between the two stimuli, but the learning is involuntary and, importantly, precedes the response. That is, the appearance of the light causes an anticipatory fear response.

In everyday life, however, the majority of our learning is active. Most of us are not passive participants in the environment. Instead, we respond to our environment and modify our behaviour according to the consequences that follow our initial response. For example, if you are only a few minutes late for work but your boss docks you an hour's pay, you can alter your behaviour the following day to increase your chances of being on time. Or, if a parent praises a child for treating a younger sibling with kindness, the older child will more likely be kind to the sibling in future encounters. Psychologists use the terms **operant** or **instrumental conditioning** to describe associative learning that is voluntary (rather than reflexive) and that acts on the environment to produce specific outcomes. The term *operant* refers to the fact that organisms are learning by *operating* on the environment. Organisms associate their behaviour with specific consequences as they attempt to receive rewards and avoid punishment.

For some of the earliest laboratory studies of operant conditioning, psychologist Edward Thorndike created a contraption called a "puzzle box." This was a cage, into which Thorndike placed a hungry cat. As shown in **Figure 37-1**, the animal could escape from the box by pressing a pedal that pulled a string. Thorndike measured the amount of time that it took the cat to free itself. Escape from the box led to a food reward. The first escape from the box occurred through the random actions of the experimental animal. In moving about, pawing at the door, floor, and walls, the cat would accidentally step on the pedal and thus receive temporary freedom and a food reward. Each time Thorndike put the cat back in the box, the cat began to more quickly engage in the same behaviour (pressing the pedal) that helped it to escape the box and obtain the food. Eventually, the cat would immediately step on the pedal when placed into the puzzle box. This work led Thorndike to develop a theory known as the **law of effect** (Thorndike, 1933), which suggests that behaviours are selected by their consequences: behaviours leading to success or to rewards are more likely to occur again, and behaviours producing unsuccessful or unpleasant outcomes are less likely to occur again. Thorndike proposed that the law of effect applied not

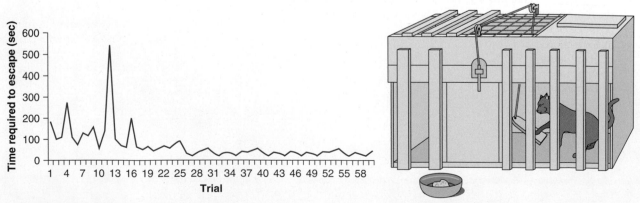

FIGURE 37-1 Thorndike's puzzle box. Edward Thorndike used a puzzle box to study operant conditioning in cats. When the cat accidentally stepped on a pedal that pulled a string, the cat escaped from the box and received a fish reward. Once the cat had done this, it performed the action more quickly when it was put back into the box, until eventually it stepped on the pedal immediately each time it was put in the box.

only to other animals, but also to humans. He called this type of learning *instrumental conditioning* because the response (stepping on the pedal) was essential (instrumental) to receiving the reward (escape and food).

37.1 How Does Operant Conditioning Work?

Thorndike's ideas about instrumental conditioning became highly influential. For several decades of the twentieth century, the dominant school of thought in psychology was **behaviourism**, the systematic study of observable behaviour (Gantt, 1980). Behaviourists believed that, unlike internal events such as thoughts or emotions, behaviour could be objectively studied and measured. Further, they believed that all behaviour could be learned through stimulus–response associations via either classical or operant conditioning. Many researchers, such as leading behaviourist B. F. Skinner, conducted learning research with laboratory animals such as rats and pigeons to understand the principles of instrumental, or operant, conditioning. Skinner believed that organisms didn't simply respond to the environment; instead they exerted influence (or "operated") on the environment, so he called this form of learning *operant conditioning*.

B. F. Skinner's work expanded on Thorndike's law of effect. Skinner developed behavioural principles based on the fact that *behaviours that are followed by favourable consequences will likely be repeated*. Using these principles, birds and animals have been taught a variety of behaviours: cockatoos have been taught to play the piano or dunk a basketball, rats have been taught to hoist flags, pigeons to bowl, and whales to wave. A great deal of human behaviour is also influenced by reinforcement, such as taking medicine for a headache, giving a child an allowance to clean her room, or obeying speed limits. Let's look at some of the key concepts associated with operant conditioning.

37.1.1 Reinforcement

In typical experiments, stimuli are provided in response to the animal's behaviour. These stimuli make it either more or less likely that the animal will engage in the behaviour again. For example, if a laboratory rat presses a lever and receives a food pellet reward, the food works as a **reinforcer**, a consequence that increases the likelihood that the rat will repeat the behaviour or press the lever again. Reinforcers are therefore typically rewarding. However, what is reinforcing for one person may not be rewarding for another; the power of reinforcers varies across individuals and cultures. For example, most people work for a paycheque, but volunteers work for the satisfaction of helping others; a trip to an exotic locale would be reinforcing to some, but anxiety-producing for others; additional income is reinforcing to some people, whereas additional time off is reinforcing to others; and so on. In some cultures money and achievement are valued above most other reinforcers, whereas in others the approval and respect of other members of the group is most reinforcing. Therefore it is important to note that reinforcers and rewards are not necessarily the same thing.

There are two kinds of reinforcement: **positive reinforcement** and **negative reinforcement**. In this instance the terms positive and negative do not mean "good" and "bad." Instead the terms are used in a manner similar to the way they are used in medical terminology. The term "positive" here means that something is present or has been added. For example, if you test positive for a sexually transmitted infection (STI), then an STI is present. On the other hand, a "negative" result would mean that there is no infection; in this case, negative means that something is absent.

Therefore, a positive reinforcer presents (or adds) something to increase the likelihood of a response: if your dog sits when you ask her to, you give her a treat; if a child says please, he gets a piece of candy; or if an adult works extra hours, she is given a raise in pay. Referring back to our case of Jagat, if Jagat goes out with Nash and his friends, Nash will help Jagat with his course work. In every instance, the animal or person is likely to repeat the behaviour because they have been given something desirable for their initial response. They have all been positively reinforced.

behaviourism the systematic study and manipulation of observable behaviour.

reinforcer an experience that produces an increase in a certain behaviour.

positive reinforcement presentation of a pleasant consequence following a behaviour to increase the probability that the behaviour will reoccur.

negative reinforcement removal of an unpleasant stimulus after a response to increase the probability that the behaviour will reoccur.

Negative reinforcement is less intuitive than positive reinforcement. To help this concept make sense to you it is important to remember that reinforcement *always* increases the likelihood that a specific behaviour will be repeated. Positive reinforcement increases the probability that a particular behaviour will occur by adding a pleasant stimulus. Negative reinforcement, on the other hand, increases a specific behaviour by *removing* an *unpleasant* stimulus. For instance, when you have a headache, you take a pain reliever. The pain reliever *takes away* your headache, thereby *increasing* the chances that next time you have a headache you will take a pain reliever. Similarly, say that you normally leave your house for school mid-morning, but in so doing you are consistently stuck in heavy traffic. One day you leave earlier and are pleasantly surprised to see that there is virtually no traffic. You start leaving for school earlier. In this case you *avoid* the heavy traffic (that is, you *take away* the heavy traffic) by increasing your behaviour of leaving home early.

Negative reinforcement is an important consideration in the behaviour of drug addicts. Addicts escape the cravings and other symptoms of withdrawal by taking a drug, thereby increasing the chances that they will take the drug again as soon as they begin to experience the symptoms of withdrawal on another occasion (Baker et al., 2006). Negative reinforcement also plays an important role in the maintenance of phobias. As already discussed, a phobia is acquired through classical conditioning. However, once the association between the US and CS has been formed, the phobia is maintained as the individual *escapes* anxiety by avoiding the feared object. For example, consider our example of the woman who is afraid of dogs. She is invited to a friend's house for tea, but to get there she has to walk by a house with a barking dog in the yard. The woman will feel anxious at the thought of going outside and encountering the dog. As her anxiety increases, she decides to stay at home and therefore her anxiety drops. She has escaped unpleasant anxiety by avoiding the feared object (the dog), and is therefore likely to resort to avoiding the feared object the next time she is anxious.

37.1.2 Punishment

punishment an experience that produces a decrease in a particular behaviour.

positive punishment presentation of an unpleasant consequence following a specific behaviour to decrease the probability of the behaviour being repeated.

negative punishment removal of a pleasant stimulus as a consequence of a behaviour to decrease the probability of the behaviour being repeated.

Punishment *decreases* the likelihood a response will reoccur, weakening the tendency to make the same response. As there is with reinforcement, there are two kinds of punishment: **positive punishment** and **negative punishment** (**Table 37-1**). Students often ask how punishment can be good. It can't. Positive punishment means that something aversive has been *presented* (added) to *weaken* a response. A child is rude to his grandmother and his mother scolds him; a young woman is texting while driving to work and drives her car into the car in front of her; a man is not watching carefully as he slices a loaf of bread and cuts his hand; or, you decide to try a new restaurant and the food is awful. In every instance, an undesirable consequence was *presented* following each person's actions, thereby reducing the probability that they will repeat the initial behaviour. They have been positively punished.

Negative punishment involves *taking away* a pleasant stimulus to *weaken* a response. An adolescent is late for his curfew and so his parents say that he cannot use the family car the following weekend; a child spits food at her sister during dinner and is therefore not allowed to have dessert; a preschooler hits another child at daycare and is put into the time out corner (without toys and away from the other children). In each situation, a pleasant stimulus was removed, thereby decreasing the probability that the behaviour would be repeated.

Let's review by taking the case of a lever-pressing rat in four different possible experiments. Positive reinforcement would provide a food reward each time the rat pressed the lever; negative reinforcement would turn off an electric shock each time the rat pressed the lever. In both cases, the rat's rate

Sarah M. Golonka/Getty Images

Positive punishment. When a young woman is texting while driving to work and drives her car into the car in front of her, she is unlikely to text while driving again. This positive punishment (crashing her car) weakens the tendency to make the same response (texting while driving).

TABLE 37-1 Types of Punishment and Reinforcement		
	Increase Behaviour	**Decrease Behaviour**
Add Something	**Positive Reinforcement**	**Positive Punishment**
	Example: Jake is sitting with friends and tells a funny story and his friends laugh. Jake tells more stories.	*Example: Meria twists her ankle while wearing her high heels on ice. Meria uses lower heels outside.*
Remove something	**Negative Reinforcement**	**Negative Punishment**
	Example: Satinder has sunburn that is very painful. She rubs on an anesthetic cream that immediately reduces the painful burn. Next time Satinder has a burn she uses the same cream.	*Example: Ansel is rude to his father and is therefore not allowed to go to a concert with his friends the following weekend. Ansel is more polite (i.e., less rude) to his father.*

of lever pressing would increase. Positive punishment would provide an electric shock each time the rat pressed the lever, and negative punishment would remove food each time the rat pressed the lever. In these instances, the rate of lever pressing would go down.

37.1.3 Types of Reinforcers and Punishers

Types of Reinforcers   Most reinforcers have survival value for organisms and include food, water, mates, or the ability to terminate pain. These types of reinforcers are called **primary reinforcers** because they satisfy biological needs and are therefore intrinsically pleasurable; that is, they are rewarding by their very nature. However, not all reinforcers satisfy physiological needs. For example, many people work for money or for grades rather than for food or for water. Some reinforcers become associated with primary reinforcers and become *conditioned* (i.e., learned) reinforcers because of this association. We call this type of reinforcer a **secondary reinforcer**. Since secondary reinforcers are learned, they vary from one species to another and from one culture to another. Common secondary reinforcers for human beings include money, grades, praise, approval, acceptance, and so on. Animals will respond to secondary reinforcers such as attention, praise, touch, toys, opportunities to engage in physical play (e.g., a walk), and so on.

Types of Punishers   Punishers can also be distinguished by whether or not they are naturally aversive or whether they are learned. A **primary punisher** is a stimulus that is naturally aversive to an organism. As such, primary punishers are usually associated with pain or discomfort. Primary punishers include stimuli such as slapping or hitting, shock, uncomfortably loud or high-pitched sounds, exposure to extreme temperature, and so on. **Secondary punishers** are neutral stimuli that take on punishing qualities due to their association with a primary punisher. Like secondary reinforcers, secondary punishers are learned and are consequently also both species and culture bound. For humans, secondary punishers include disapproval, indifference, a verbal "no," criticism, bad grades, demerits, and so on. For animals, secondary punishers include isolation, verbal rebuke, sounds (e.g., clickers or rattling objects), and so on.

In general, positive reinforcement is more effective than punishment. Punishment tells an organism what not to do by suppressing immediate behaviour, but doesn't show them what they should do instead. Reinforcement is effective at establishing new and more appropriate behaviours. For example, if a child puts himself in immediate danger by running in front of a car, a harsh scolding might be effective at stopping the immediate behaviour. However, positive reinforcement (e.g., praise) for holding a parent's hand or for remaining on the sidewalk instead of chasing a ball will teach the child what to do in future situations, rather than simply what *not* to do in the current situation. Skinner argued that what people really learn about punishment is only how to avoid it. Consequently, if we want to *change* behaviour, we have to use reinforcement.

primary reinforcer a stimulus that has survival value and is therefore intrinsically rewarding.

secondary reinforcer a neutral stimulus that becomes rewarding when associated with a primary reinforcer.

primary punisher a stimulus that is naturally aversive to an organism.

secondary punisher a stimulus that becomes aversive when associated with a primary punisher.

Positive punishment, especially physical punishment, also has a number of alarming ethical implications. Joan Grusec at the University of Toronto has reported that children who experience physical aggression are more aggressive to others (Grusec & Ungerer, 2003; Grusec et al., 2000; Grusec et al., 2013). Similarly, Elizabeth Gershoff (2002) concluded from meta analyses that physical punishment is associated with a number of long-term problems, including low self-esteem, poor self-concept, and lack of interpersonal skills, as well as delinquency, criminal behaviour, child abuse, and mental health issues. Her findings have been replicated by other researchers (Lynch et al., 2006; Marshall, 2002; Mulvany & Mebert, 2007). In spite of these findings, researchers in Quebec presented data showing that approximately 40 percent of parents in their study reported slapping or spanking their children (Clément & Chamberland, 2007). And of greater concern, parents who use physical punishment are backed by the Supreme Court of Canada, which, when challenged, upheld a ruling of Section 43 of the Criminal Code of Canada allowing parents and teachers to use "reasonable corrective force" to discipline children between the ages of 2 and 12. Canada now lags behind most European countries, which have banned physical punishment of children in schools and childcare settings, and 11 countries that have also outlawed parental physical punishment of children (Ending Legalised Violence Against Children, 2013).

Another problem with physical punishment is that children not only learn to associate fear with the unwanted behaviour, but with the punisher as well. For example, using spanking to punish a child in order to decrease unwanted behaviour is a form of operant conditioning. However, if a parent regularly spanks a child, the child will also form a classically conditioned association between the parent and pain/fear. The two types of learning are therefore related and become two aspects of a single learning experience (Allan, 1998), and contribute both to a child learning to fear a punisher and to emulate the punisher's behaviour.

Negative punishment is generally considered to be less ethically problematic than positive punishment (Kazdin & Benjet, 2003), but may still fail to change behaviour in some circumstances. Many parents and preschool teachers use a negative punishment technique called "time out" as a consequence for unwanted behaviour. This method involves removing a child from her surroundings, generally by putting her in a separate location in the classroom or home. The child has thus had a pleasurable stimulus (access to playthings and classmates) removed. Time out also removes the child from the environment that may have contributed to the bad behaviour and allows quiet time to think about the situation. The effectiveness of time out depends on the specific circumstances motivating the individual. For example, if the child was acting out to gain attention, then intervening with a negative punishment may not effectively eliminate the behaviour, as the child is receiving the attention she wanted. Also, removal from a certain environment, such as the classroom or the dinner table, may not be sufficiently unpleasant to alter the offensive behaviour. For example, removing a child who is bored sitting at the dinner table to his bedroom might be counterproductive, as being in his room might be more interesting than remaining at the table.

©iStockphoto.com/Blend Images

The house always wins. Slot machines are a good example of a variable ratio schedule reinforcement strategy. The big payout will come eventually, but you don't know when!

37.1.4 Schedules of Reinforcement

In real-life situations, we are not usually reinforced or punished every time we perform a particular behaviour. You may, for example, hold the door open many times a day for the person who walks in behind you, but only receive a pleasant "thank you" once or twice a day. Researchers have studied the effects of different schedules of reinforcement on behaviour (Skinner, 1958; Skinner & Morse, 1958). When a behaviour is reinforced every single time it occurs, reinforcement is said to be **continuous**. Continuous reinforcement results in rapid learning, but can be easily extinguished. In contrast, **intermittent** or **partial reinforcement**, when the behaviour is only sometimes reinforced, is more slowly acquired, but is difficult to extinguish. Recall Jagat's fear of thunderstorms. Since the storms occur at unpredictable times, Jagat cannot anticipate when to stay in the dorm so he stays in the dorm all of the time. There are several possible schedules of intermittent or partial reinforcement. The most common types of intermittent reinforcement schedules are described in **Table 37-2**.

In a *ratio schedule*, reinforcement is based on the *number* of behavioural responses. In a **fixed ratio schedule**, a person or animal is rewarded every time they make a pre-determined number of responses. The "frequent drinker" card at your local coffee shop may offer you a free cup of coffee after you pay for a dozen other cups, for example. In a **variable ratio schedule**, reinforcement occurs for a predetermined average number of responses. Slot machines or VLTs (video lottery terminals), if they are legally regulated, have a set variable ratio payout schedule. Depending on the local laws, VLTs pay back 80 to 95 percent of the money entered into them, but on a randomly assigned schedule.

continuous reinforcement what occurs when behaviour is reinforced every time it occurs.

intermittent or **partial reinforcement** a schedule of reinforcement where the behaviour is followed by reinforcement only some of the time.

fixed ratio schedule a schedule of reinforcement that occurs after a specific number of responses.

variable ratio schedule a schedule of reinforcement that occurs when the number of responses required for reinforcement is unpredictable.

TABLE 37-2 Intermittent Reinforcement Schedules

Schedules Based on Number of Responses

	Definition	Response Rate	Example
Fixed ratio	Reinforcement occurs after a predetermined number of responses	High, with pauses after reinforcement	A rat is reinforced for every tenth bar press
Variable ratio	Reinforcement occurs after an average number of responses	High, regular rate of response	A slot machine pays out after an average of 20 tries, but the payout intervals are unpredictable

Schedules Based on Time Intervals

	Definition	Response Rate	Example
Fixed interval	Reinforcement occurs after a fixed period of time	Low, with increases as time for reinforcement approaches	A worker receives a paycheque every week
Variable interval	Reinforcement occurs after varying lengths of time	Low, as reinforcement is tied to time rather than to output	Work breaks occur at unpredictable intervals, such as 60 minutes, 72 minutes, and 54 minutes

practically Speaking Using Punishment to Teach Children

In spite of the greater efficacy of reinforcement (van Duijven-voorde et al., 2008), there are situations where punishment is deemed necessary. Research suggests the following guidelines for using punishment effectively to promote learning:

- Positive punishment is most effective when it occurs immediately after the incorrect behaviour (Abramowitz & O'Leary, 1990).
- Negative punishment (such as a "time-out") is generally more effective than positive punishment (Kazdin & Benjet, 2003).

- Punishment is most effective when it is consistent. If behaviour warrants punishment once, the behaviour needs to be punished each time it occurs (Parke & Deur, 1972; Rudy & Grusec, 2001).
- Punishment is effective only when it is clear that the punishment is a consequence of a specific behaviour, rather than, say, a result of the teacher or caregiver's bad mood or general dislike for the child.
- Punishment should be combined with an explanation for the punishment as well as suggested alternative behaviours.

fixed interval schedule
a schedule of reinforcement that occurs every time a specific time period has elapsed.

variable interval schedule
a schedule of reinforcement that occurs after varying amounts of time.

In an *interval schedule*, reinforcement is based on elapsed *time*, rather than on the number of behavioural responses. In a **fixed interval schedule**, such as occurs with a weekly salaried paycheque, you are reinforced every time a certain period of time passes. Like a variable ratio schedule, a **variable interval schedule** provides random reinforcement, giving a predetermined number of reinforcements over time. For example, imagine a teacher who wants to reward a student for remaining on task. The teacher will arrange for a bell to ring six times over the hour and will give the child a reinforcer (for example, a piece of candy or a token to trade for a privilege) if the child is on task when the bell rings. Rather than having the bell ring every 10 minutes, the bell will ring after a random period of time has passed, but will ring six times over the hour.

Intermittent or partial reinforcement schedules take longer to train but are more effective than continuous reinforcement at maintaining behaviour. With continuous reinforcement, the behaviour is always paired with the reward. If reinforcement stops, the elimination signals a major change in the association between stimulus and response. By contrast, with intermittent reinforcement, the behaviour is followed by reinforcement only some of the time. When a response occurs but is not reinforced, it's not readily apparent whether or not the reward has stopped altogether. Continuing to engage in the behaviour makes sense in case a reward might happen. Thus, behaviours that are acquired through partial reinforcement are harder to extinguish than behaviours that are acquired through continuous reinforcement.

37.2 Using Operant Conditioning to Teach New Behaviours

Until now, we have described how operant conditioning can lead people and animals to increase or decrease behaviours that they already display at least some of the time. Thorndike's cats, for example, learned to press the pedal in the puzzle box more often than they would have by chance, but they already pressed the pedal at least once in a trial and error fashion before learning the association. However, operant conditioning can also be used to teach people and animals entirely new complex behaviours.

shaping introducing new behaviour by reinforcing close approximations of the desired behaviour.

A method, called **shaping**, rewards actions that are increasingly closer to a desired final behaviour. Shaping is a more realistic way to train a new behaviour, rather than waiting for the exact behaviour to happen by chance before providing reinforcement. Animal trainers begin by giving food rewards in response to minor movements in the direction of the desired behaviour. As the animal masters that component of the task, trainers make the food reward dependent on the animal completing more of the task. Consider training a dog to roll over. First you might provide a treat if the animal lies down on its stomach. Eventually, you would require the dog to perform something closer to rolling over in order to get the same reward; for example, you might offer a treat only when the dog lies down and turns a bit to the side. You carry on in this way, rewarding *successive approximations* to the desired behaviour until the complete behavioural sequence emerges.

Biology plays a role in determining how easy or difficult a particular learning task will be for a certain species. Although some trainers appear to be quite capable of teaching animals to engage in a wide range of unnatural behaviours, it turns out that there are, of course, limits, or *biological constraints*, to what animals of a specific species are able to master. For example, two former students of Skinner, Keller Breland and Marion Breland (1961), reported that through shaping techniques they were able to train raccoons to pick up a single coin and place it in a piggy bank. However, they were never able to train the raccoons to take more than one coin to the bank at a time. As you may know, raccoons have a natural tendency to wash food before eating it. It turns out that if the raccoons were given more than one coin at a

Kaku Kurita/Gamma-Rapho via Getty Images

A natural? No. This water-skiing monkey underwent many learning trials and received rewards for many successive approximations of this behaviour before it became skilled at water-skiing.

Psychology Around Us   Deadly Tricks

SeaWorld has long used shaping methods to train killer whales or orcas. These mammals are captured as calves from their natural environments and taken from their family pods to perform impressive tricks, including doing midair flips, carrying trainers both in and out of the water, clapping their fins, and sliding out of the water onto the side of the pool to "wave" at audiences on command. Shows feature marine mammals that appear to enjoy performing tasks that are unnatural to their species. Despite the fact that these animals are intelligent enough to be shaped to perform complex tricks, some disastrous incidents highlight the difficulty in using very large and powerful predatory animals for entertainment purposes.

In 2010, Tilikum, a 22-foot, 12,300 pound (6.7-m, 5500-kg) killer whale at SeaWorld aggressively drowned his trainer, Dawn Brancheau, by grabbing her arm and pulling her under the water and thrashing her until she died of drowning and blunt force trauma to her head, neck, and torso. Oceangoing orcas are carnivores that hunt live fish and animals, such as herrings, sea lions, seals, and walruses, and have no natural predators in their natural environment. When orcas in captivity revert to normal animal (in this case, whale) behaviour, this is called *instinctive drift* and highlights the dangers of

© Gary Crabbe/Alamy

using captive animals, which have a natural instinct to kill, for entertainment purposes.

Over the many years of his captivity, Tilikum has been responsible for two other human deaths, another female trainer and a male who surreptitiously entered his tank after park closure. These events underscore the fact that although shaping can profoundly modify behaviour in animals, the underlying instinctual responses remain.

---

time, their natural tendency to wash objects interfered with the shaping techniques, and instead of putting the coins into the bank, they become distracted, incessantly rubbing the coins together, "washing" them, instead of completing the task of putting them in the piggy bank.

Shaping is highly effective in modifying the behaviour of animals and can be used to teach people, too. Humans regularly learn behaviour through shaping as successive approximations to an identified skill are reinforced. Teachers use shaping in school to teach children how to print; coaches use it to teach skills in gymnastics or baseball; and parents use it to teach skills to their children. For example, language production involves shaping. When first learning to talk you may have referred to water as "wawa" then later as "wat a" and then now (we hope!) as "water."

A process called **behaviour modification** is frequently employed to shape the behaviour of people. The behaviour of individuals can be shaped to teach them new academic or athletic skills or to modify behaviours that are undesirable. For example, imagine a child who is disruptive in a classroom. The child's teacher wants him to sit quietly in his desk. So, the teacher systematically begins to shape the child's behaviour toward the outcome the teacher desires. The teacher has determined that playing video games is rewarding to the child. So the teacher gives the child a sticker whenever he is quiet (even if he is out of his desk). After the child gets a particular number of stickers (say seven), he is allowed to play a video game for 10 minutes. Eventually the child is only rewarded for standing quietly near his desk, then for sitting at his desk talking quietly, and so on. In this way the child's behaviour is shaped toward the desirable outcome.

behaviour modification
a systematic approach to change behaviour using principles of operant conditioning.

practically Speaking

How Does Learning Theory Explain Why Some People Deliberately Hurt Themselves?

Sometimes a person, usually an adolescent but not always, is either overwhelmed by feelings of intense, painful emotions or instead may feel numb and empty. Most people can cope with these emotional states, but some cannot and may instead engage in self-harm or self-injury as a way to provide relief from unbearable pain. *Self-harm* occurs when people try to deliberately hurt themselves without any intention to commit suicide. Individuals who engage in self-harm may cut their skin with a piece of glass, or a razor blade or a knife (this is often referred to as *cutting* and is the most common form of self-harm), or they may burn themselves, pull out chunks of their hair, pick at their skin, or insert objects under the skin or into the body. The Canadian Mental Health Association (2014a) recently reported that 13 percent of Canadian youth report harming themselves. This number is probably low as the majority of people who engage in self-harm go to great lengths to keep their behaviour a closely guarded secret. In fact, Mary Nixon and her colleagues at the University of Victoria report that only half of the 16.9 percent of British Columbian youth in their sample who reported harming themselves reported seeking help (Nixon, Cloutier & Jansson, 2008).

Why would a person intentionally harm themselves? Doesn't Thorndike's law of effect argue that only those behaviours followed by a desirable consequence will be repeated? What is desirable about physical pain? For most of us there is nothing reinforcing about physical pain. However, remember what we said earlier … reinforcers *always* increase the frequency of an associated behaviour. Therefore if a person engages in self-harm and this behaviour is repeated (i.e., strengthened), then something about the self-harm is reinforcing to the person.

In fact, youth who engage in self-harm and who report feeling numb or empty report that the self-harm causes

iStockphoto.com/grummanaa5

them to feel *something*, anything. By contrast, those youth who report feeling overwhelmed by emotional pain say that the self-harm alleviates their inner pain by turning it into physical pain. E. David Klonsky at the University of British Columbia and his colleagues report that this reduction in unpleasant emotions causes the affected person to feel a sense of "calm" and "relief," and that this sense of relief ultimately rewards the injurious behaviour (Klonsky, 2007; Klonsky & Muehlenkamp, 2007; Klonsky et al., 2011). Thus the escape from intolerable emotion becomes *negatively reinforcing*. But that is not all. When the body is injured it releases endorphins, a naturally occurring opiate. Endorphin release is often associated with a feeling of euphoria, a state of happiness and well-being. The euphoric feeling following the injury may also *positively reinforce* the self-injurious behaviour. Learning theory would therefore predict the outcome, that is, that self-harm behaviour would be strengthened.

FACING ADVERSITY

learned helplessness a situation in which repeated exposure to inescapable punishment eventually produces a failure to make escape attempts.

Sometimes our prior learning experiences can cause problems with later learning situations. One problem that can arise as the result of operant conditioning is a phenomenon known as **learned helplessness**, in which prior experiences with inescapable punishment condition people or animals to accept punishing consequences in later situations when they could actually avoid them (Seligman et al., 1980). For instance, research with rats has found that, after repeated inescapable shocks to the tail, if rats are given the option of escaping a foot shock by moving to a different area in the testing cage, many of them fail to do so (Weiss & Glazer, 1975). The rats that could not escape the tail shocks initially failed later to learn how to stop a shock to the foot. Learned helplessness occurs when organisms are exposed to conditions over which they have no control. Since there is no association between their behaviour and the consequences of their behaviour, they learn to stop trying, even when they get into situations where their behaviour could make a difference.

Learned helplessness is viewed by some researchers as an animal model of depression (Porsolt, 2000). Humans with depression are often unmotivated to act on the stimuli they receive from their environments, and some theorists suggest that these people have learned this pattern of inaction from earlier, perhaps unrelated, experiences in which they were unable to make the changes they wanted. Some researchers have claimed that learned helplessness may also partially explain some of the characteristics of battered spouse syndrome (Ali & Naylor, 2013; Clements & Sawhney, 2000). Repeated, inescapable abuse may cause learned helplessness. The victim can become withdrawn and unable to respond in an adaptive way, even if there is an option to escape an abusive situation. It is important to note, however, that some victims may not feel that they have a viable means of escape, and that learned helplessness cannot therefore account for all cases of battered spouses remaining in dangerous situations.

iStockphoto.com/John Gomez

Why do they stay? Spousal abuse occurs in at least 6 percent of Canadian homes (Statistics Canada, 2011).

Before You Go On

www.wiley.com/go/comercanada

What Do You Know?

1. What are positive reinforcement and negative reinforcement? What are the effects of each on behaviour?

2. What are schedules of reinforcement? Which schedule results in the fastest learning? Which schedule should be used if you want a behaviour to be resistant to extinction?

3. What is learned helplessness?

What Do You Think?
How could you use operant conditioning principles to get a roommate or child to regularly hang up her coat instead of throwing it on the floor?

Summary

Module 37: Operant Conditioning

LEARNING OBJECTIVE 37 Describe the basic processes of operant conditioning and explain how shaping can be used to teach new behaviours.

- Operant conditioning is a learned association between stimuli in the environment and our own behaviour. The law of effect states that we learn to repeat behaviours that will increase our rewards and help us avoid punishment.
- Reinforcers are rewarding stimuli from the environment. Positive reinforcement provides a desired stimulus; negative reinforcement takes away an unpleasant stimulus. Both increase the chance a behaviour will be repeated. Primary reinforcers are reinforcing in and of themselves. Secondary reinforcers become reinforcing because of their association with primary reinforcers.
- Positive punishment provides an unpleasant stimulus; negative punishment takes away a rewarding one. Both types lower the chances that a behaviour will be repeated.
- Schedules of intermittent reinforcement provide reinforcements after either fixed or variable intervals of time or numbers of responses. Any intermittent reinforcement modifies behaviour more effectively than continuous reinforcement.
- Shaping, or rewarding successive approximations of a behaviour, uses operant conditioning principles to teach new behaviours. People and animals are limited in the behaviours they can learn, however, by their biological endowments.
- Learned helplessness occurs when previous learning that punishment is inescapable interferes with the later ability to learn how to avoid escapable punishment. It may be related to depression or be one way to account for the behaviour of abuse victims.

Key Terms

behaviour modification 303

behaviourism 297

continuous reinforcement 301

fixed interval schedule 302

fixed ratio schedule 301

intermittent or partial
reinforcement 301

law of effect 296

learned helplessness 304

negative punishment 298

negative reinforcement 297

operant or instrumental
conditioning 296

positive punishment 298

positive reinforcement 297

primary punisher 299

primary reinforcer 299

punishment 298

reinforcer 297

secondary punisher 299

secondary reinforcer 299

shaping 302

variable interval schedule 302

variable ratio schedule 301

Study Questions

Multiple Choice

1. Paycheques and grades are delivered on a _____
   schedule of reinforcement.
   a) fixed ratio
   b) fixed interval
   c) variable ratio
   d) variable interval

Fill-in-the-Blank

1. Reinforcers that satisfy a biological need are _____
   reinforcers.

2. The process of teaching complex behaviour by reinforcing ever closer approximations of the desired behaviour is
   called _____.

Module 38: Observational Learning

Studies of animal behaviour in natural habitats have shown that members of certain species learn tasks by watching each other. A good example of this type of learning can be seen by studying a troupe of Japanese macaques. This troupe of monkeys routinely washes sweet potatoes before eating them. This washing behaviour is not innate; that is, it is not practised by macaques all over the world. Instead, it began with one creative monkey who first started washing sweet potatoes after the potatoes were introduced to the macaques by researchers. After observing this behaviour, other members of the group started to wash their own sweet potatoes—similar behaviour has now been observed in the troupe with other foods as well (Nakamichi et al., 1998). Other studies have reported that **observational learning**, or **social learning**—learning from watching the behaviour of others—led to the use of novel tools by dolphins and certain primate and bird species (Krüetzen et al., 2005). Through observational learning, animals can culturally transmit learned behaviours across generations. That is, parents or older members of a group engage in behaviour that the young observe. Observation leads to imitation, or **modelling**, which is considered evidence that learning has occurred.

observational learning or **social learning** learning that occurs without overt training in response to watching the behaviour of others, called models.

modelling what occurs when an observer learns from the behaviour of another.

In addition to contributing to learning through imitation, observation can affect other types of behaviour that indirectly signal learning has occurred. A good example of this can be seen with reward studies in capuchin monkeys (Brosnan & de Waal, 2003). Capuchins can be rather easily trained to perform a task for a food reward, such as a cucumber slice, which they like. If, however, the trained monkey observes another monkey receiving a more desirable reward (for example, a grape) for performing the same task, the monkey will respond by refusing to carry out the task again unless the reward is a grape (and may even express displeasure by throwing the cucumber at the researcher). This suggests not only that capuchin monkeys have an internal concept of fairness, but also that they have used the experience of observing the consequences of another monkey's behaviour to modify their own (see Brosnan & de Waal, 2012 for review).

There are many other examples of animals and birds learning through observation. For example, in a documentary, Jacques Cousteau (Cousteau & Diole, 1973), the well-known filmmaker and oceanographer, showed an octopus learning to open a jar through observation. He gave a hungry octopus a sealed jar with a crayfish inside. The octopus tried to break the jar by exerting pressure on it. Next, while the octopus watched, the researchers took the jar and unscrewed the lid. They then gave the octopus a second jar with a crayfish inside. The octopus immediately opened the jar by unscrewing the lid.

© Photograph by Frans de Waal from *The Ape and the Sushi Master*

Imitating Imo. A Japanese macaque washes its sweet potatoes in ocean water. This behaviour is displayed only by members of the monkey's particular troupe. Apparently they learned it by imitating the innovative behaviour of a young monkey named Imo.

Bennet Galef and his students and colleagues working at McMaster University have shown that social learning plays an important role in shaping behaviours of many animal species. For example, rats fed bad-tasting food or food that tastes like food that has made them ill in the past will watch other rats make food selections and then make the same selection for themselves, even if it is the food that made them ill (Galef, Dudley, & Whiskin, 2008). In another area, female Japanese quail will show a clear mating preference for males they have observed mating successfully with other female quails, essentially copying the other quails' mate selections (Galef & Laland, 2005).

Further, Joshua Klein (2011) has had success training crows to use a vending machine. Klein was inspired by reports of crows in a particular Japanese city devising an ingenious method for cracking nuts. Crows there enjoyed a particular type of nut but could not shell them to eat. Eventually some crows discovered that if they dropped nuts on the road, cars would run over them, opening them for the crows to eat. Unfortunately, this solution produced another problem for the crows; it was very hazardous to stand in the middle of the road to eat the nuts once they were opened. Over time, one crow apparently learned that if he dropped the nuts into city crosswalks, allowing cars to crush the nuts, but then waited for the "walk signal" before retrieving the prize, it was much safer to fly down and eat. Over time, the other crows learned how to crack nuts as well, simply through observation. Now many crows in this Japanese city eat nuts using this method. Based on his knowledge of this situation, Klein designed a vending machine that produced peanuts when coins were dropped into a large slot. He started by laying peanuts and coins around on the machine. Once crows had eaten all the available peanuts, they started sweeping coins around with their beaks looking for more peanuts. When a coin happened to fall into the slot, a peanut appeared. Over time, the crows figured out how the vending machine worked, and started picking up coins lying around on the ground and dropping them into the machine to obtain more peanuts. Again, like the Japanese crows, it was not long before more crows learned how to "buy" peanuts by watching other crows. (To see Klein's crow vending machine go here: www.ted.com/index.php/talks/joshua_klein_on_the_intelligence_of_crows.html.)

Although controversial, many biologists have argued that observation and modelling behaviours constitute a type of animal culture. Regardless of whether such behaviours are evidence of "culture," it is clear that many species of animals engage in a learning process that is socially transmitted (Laland & Galef, 2009).

Similar examples of socially transmitted behaviours are evident in human behaviour. Humans also learn through observation, using others as role models and, sometimes, modifying our own behaviour in new ways to accommodate new information. Suppose a classmate is warmly rewarded with praise for asking a question in a lecture. You now have information that the instructor welcomes questions. As a consequence of observing your classmate's rewarding experience, in the future you may be more likely to ask a question of your own. That is, you have learned to imitate your classmate's behaviour.

It is important to note that observational learning is not the same thing as imitation. When an animal or person imitates the behaviour of a model, they mimic or copy the behaviour of the model. However, when observational learning occurs, the behaviour observed is not necessarily repeated. Imagine instead that the scenario described above ended with the instructor humiliating your classmate for asking a question (*"If you had read the assigned readings you would not have to ask such a moronic question"*). You would learn *not* to ask questions, thereby learning not to repeat your classmate's behaviour; that is, you have learned not to imitate.

38.1 Observational Learning and Aggression

Some of the most famous experiments of observational learning in children were carried out by psychologist Albert Bandura (born in Mundare, Alberta). Bandura was interested in whether children learned aggressive behavioural responses by observing aggression. He showed children a movie of a woman beating up an inflatable clown punching bag, called a Bobo doll (see **Figure 38-1**) (Bandura, Ross, & Ross, 1961). After the movie, the children were allowed to play in a room full of toys, including a Bobo doll. Those who had previously watched the Bobo video were twice as likely as those who did not watch it to display aggressive behaviour toward the doll.

Bandura and his colleagues further investigated whether observational learning would be influenced by information about reward and punishment. Indeed, they found such a relationship. The children who saw a video in which beating up the Bobo doll led to rewards to the model, such as candy and praise, were more likely to act aggressively toward the doll than those who observed the model being punished for beating up Bobo (Bandura, Ross, & Ross, 1963). This type of learning is called **vicarious learning** because an individual acquires knowledge by observing (i.e., through the process of observational

© Dr. Albert Bandura, Stanford University

FIGURE 38-1 Aggressive modelling. Bandura found that children learned to abuse an inflatable clown doll by observing an adult model hit the doll.

vicarious learning learning that occurs when an individual observes the consequences to another's actions and then chooses to duplicate the behaviour or refrain from doing so.

learning) what happens to a model. The individual then modifies his own behaviour based on this knowledge, choosing to imitate the model or deliberately choosing not to behave like the model (to avoid the same punishment). For example, Jagat might manage his time better and get better grades by observing and then imitating Nash's effective study strategies.

Bandura's studies, and a great deal of research that followed, raised concerns about the role that violence on television, in movies, and in video games plays in promoting aggressive behaviour among viewers, especially children (Bandura, 1978). Some studies have demonstrated a convincing link between excessive television watching and physical and relational aggressive behaviour in children (Johnson et al., 2002; Huesmann et al., 2003; Ostrov et al., 2013). The number of violent acts in a short stretch of children's programming can be disturbingly high. One study reported 18 violent acts per hour in children's Saturday morning programs (Gerbner et al., 1994). Further, the number of such violent acts is typically highest in cartoons where there are no real consequences for violent behaviour. In fact, cartoon characters seem to have many lives, often returning unscathed after experiencing what would be horribly damaging events in reality.

Neuroscientists believe that the neural basis for imitation and observational learning is **mirror neurons** (Rizzolatti & Sinigaglia, 2008; Rizzolatti et al., 2002). These neurons were discovered by accident by researchers at the University of Parma in Italy who noted the neuronal response of a monkey at rest when it observed a researcher carrying out a similar action to the experimental task it had been carrying out earlier. These mirror neurons not only fired when the monkey reached for an object or grasped or held an object but also fired when the monkey watched another monkey or human carry out the same task. fMRI scans and PET scans show that analogous mirror neurons also exist in humans (Keysers & Gazzola, 2010) and are important for social learning, language, and the development of empathy (Singer et al., 2004; Iacoboni, 2009).

mirror neurons neurons fired when an animal or human performs an action or when they see another animal perform the same action.

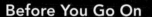

Before You Go On

www.wiley.com/go/comercanada

What Do You Know?

1. What is observational learning and what does it demonstrate when it happens?
2. What has research shown about media violence and aggressive behaviour in child viewers?
3. What is spatial navigation learning and why is it difficult to explain using operant conditioning?

What Do You Think? How might the media be used to get children—or adults—to mimic positive social behaviours?

Summary

Module 38: Observational Learning

LEARNING OBJECTIVE 38 Define observational learning and summarize concerns about observational learning from the media.

- Observational learning is learning by watching the behaviour of others. We are more likely to model, or imitate, others' behaviour that we see rewarded.
- Many people are concerned that high levels of violence in the media encourage viewers to model such aggression. Studies about the causal nature of media encouraging violence have been inconclusive.

Key Terms

mirror neurons 309
modelling 307

observational learning or social learning 307
vicarious learning 308

Study Questions

Multiple Choice

1. Which of the following statements best captures the relationship between observational learning and modelling?
   a) Observational learning and modelling refer to unrelated learning processes.
   b) Observational learning and modelling refer to the same process.
   c) Observational learning is evidence that modelling has occurred.
   d) Modelling is evidence that observational learning has occurred.

Fill-in-the-Blank

1. Bandura's "Bobo doll" experiments were intended to demonstrate _____.

Module 39: Learning and Cognition

Despite the fact that during the twentieth century some prominent behaviourists argued that everything we do comes about as a result of either classical or operant conditioning, some research has shown that learning can occur without any obvious reinforcement. Learning that occurs without awareness is referred to as **implicit learning**. Although the topic of implicit learning is somewhat controversial, proponents argue that there are many examples of implicit learning (Frensch & Runger, 2003).

39.1 Spatial Navigation Learning

One good example of learning without reinforcement arose from laboratory studies designed to assess the ability of reinforcement to train rats to learn information about spatial navigation. Laboratory rodents can be trained to navigate through a maze by providing them with reinforcement as they move through the maze. This approach is called **spatial navigation learning** (which is a form of shaping), and it involves the presentation of food rewards as rats move in the correct direction. Rats learn mazes very quickly when reinforced.

However, in the absence of reinforcers, rats typically explore a maze, but may not be motivated to find the quickest route from start to finish. Tolman (1948) and Tolman and Honzik (1930a; 1930b) carried out what are now considered by many to be classic research studies in this area. They had groups of rats run a maze over a number of trials. The first group of rats was given a reward each time they completed the maze. This group of rats progressively improved in the time it took to complete the maze over time. A second group of rats was never given any rewards and their performances were roughly the same in all trials of the experiment. The final group of rats was not reinforced in the trials in the first half of the experiment but was reinforced in the trials in the second half of the experiment. This final group of rats showed a dramatic improvement in the time it took to complete the maze once they began to receive reinforcement for completing the maze. Tolman and Honzik argued that this dramatic increase in performance demonstrated that the rats had learned and retained information about the layout of the maze, forming a *cognitive map* of the maze, as they explored it without reinforcement and were able to run the maze quickly once given incentives. They argued that when reinforcement was introduced, the rats demonstrated their previous latent learning. **Latent learning** occurs without any obvious reinforcement and is often used as evidence that learning and performance are not the same things. Tolman's work is often used to challenge the behaviourist claim that all behaviour and learning is due to reinforcements and punishments because their work, they claimed, proved that reinforcements were not necessary for learning to occur (Tolman & Gleitman, 1949).

Other researchers argue that there are alternative explanations for latent learning, other than cognitive maps, that can be used to explain the results from Tolman's experiments. They argue that Tolman's results do not prove that reinforcement did not play a role in learning prior to the incentive of food and argue that other plausible explanations

Courtesy of the American Philosophical Society

LEARNING OBJECTIVE 39
Define spatial navigation learning, implicit and latent learning, and insight learning.

implicit learning the acquisition of information without awareness.

spatial navigation learning learning that involves forming associations among stimuli relevant to navigating in space.

"Ah-hah." During the 1920s, psychologist Wolfgang Kohler conducted pioneering studies on insight learning. Here, one of Kohler's chimpanzees piles three crates on top of each other to reach a banana that had been placed out of its reach. When first confronted with this complex task, the chimp sat and contemplated the situation; then, in an apparent flash of insight, it stacked and climbed up the crates.

latent learning a form of learning that is not expressed until there is a reward or incentive.

can be employed to explain Tolman's data (Jenson, 2006). Although the scope of this discussion goes beyond this part, it is important to know that this debate is unresolved.

39.2 Insight Learning

insight learning a sudden realization of a solution to a problem or leap in understanding new concepts.

In addition to spatial navigation learning, there are other types of learning that are also often explained in terms of more cognitive (involving conscious intellectual activity) approaches to learning. One example of this type of learning is **insight learning**. Most of us have had experience with insight learning. When faced with a difficult problem, we may puzzle and struggle over it, unsure how to find a solution. Then, later—perhaps while we are not even working on the problem—we may have an "ah-ha!" or "eureka" moment when the solution suddenly pops into our mind. Some individuals even report solving problems in their dreams (Wagner et al., 2004). The Nobel laureate Otto Loewi, the discoverer of the actions of neurotransmitter chemicals, claims to have come up with his definitive study while sleeping, after pondering the question over and over while awake (Loewi, 1957). Although finding the solutions to our problems in our dreams is fairly rare, insight learning is widespread and is another type of learning that doesn't involve any obvious reinforcement.

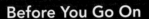

Before You Go On

www.wiley.com/go/comercanada

What Do You Know?

1. When rats who have been allowed to wander around a maze without food rewards are provided with food rewards at the end of the maze, how does their wandering behaviour affect their learning and running of the maze?

2. Describe the difference between learning something by trial and error and learning it through insight learning.

What Do You Think? Does it make sense to argue that all learning involves some form of reward or punishment?

Summary

Module 39: Learning and Cognition

LEARNING OBJECTIVE 39 Define spatial navigation learning, implicit and latent learning, and insight learning.

- Learning that occurs without awareness is referred to as implicit learning.
- Insight learning and spatial navigation learning seem to take place in the absence of any obvious reinforcement.

Key Terms

Module 40: Factors that Facilitate Learning

It's clear that we can learn in a variety of ways: through simple habituation and sensitization, by linking stimuli in classical conditioning, by associating our behaviour to its consequences through operant conditioning, or by using our observations of the consequences of another's behaviours as a model for our own. We also know that several factors can affect how well each of these learning methods works. Timing, as we have seen, is crucial in classical conditioning. It can also affect other types of learning. The amount of attention we pay when trying to learn is another factor that can facilitate, or alternatively, impede our learning, depending on the type of learning.

LEARNING OBJECTIVE 40
Define massed and spaced practice and tell what conditions are best for learning semantic material, such as facts in your classes.

40.1 Timing

You have probably noticed that you learn more information when you study for an exam over an extended period of time, as opposed to cramming for the test by pulling an "all-nighter." Why is this?

Much of the learning that you, as a student, undertake on a daily basis involves acquiring information about facts. Psychologists distinguish between this type of learning, called *semantic learning*, and *episodic learning*, which is learning about events in our own lives. We will return to the distinction between episodic and semantic learning in the next part dealing with memory, but we can offer some advice now about how to improve your learning of semantic material.

Most importantly, repetition helps. Semantic learning is facilitated by multiple exposures to the same material, such as reading the textbook, then listening carefully in class, and then reviewing your notes and textbook. Multiple exposures make it more likely that learning will occur, compared to a single exposure, such as just reading the book or just going to class.

Your learning will also be facilitated by having time intervals between these exposures. When learning trials occur close together, as they do when you try to cram reading the book and reviewing all into the night before a big test, they are referred to as *massed*. When they are separated in time, they are referred to as *spaced*. The difference in efficiency between massed and spaced trials for learning has been demonstrated not only in the laboratory, but also in real life (Healy, Kosslyn, & Shiffrin, 1992). Massed studying, or cramming, is ineffective for two reasons. First, it does not allow enough time between learning trials to maximize learning, and second, it leads to sleep deprivation, which affects the consolidation of learning.

David H. Wells/Corbis

Oh, those all-nighters! Cramming for a test the night before an exam leads to the acquisition of less information than studying for the test over an extended period of time and results in loss of sleep as well.

40.2 Context

Psychologists have long recognized that context plays an important role in learning and remembering. For example, if you take a test in the same location in which you learned the material, you are more likely to do your best. If you want the information to stick with you beyond the end of the semester, however, you may want to move to different locations during your study periods. Studies have shown that studying in several different locations increases the likelihood that you will form strong memories about the information. This phenomenon relates to the *context effect*—if you learn information in only one context (for example, in the classroom) you may be less likely to recall it when you are in a different location (at a job interview or while taking a standardized test for graduate or professional school). If you learn the information in multiple locations, then that knowledge may be less tied to the place in which it was acquired, and it may be more readily recalled later (Smith, 1984).

40.3 Awareness and Attention

Learning can occur without awareness. In most instances, however, awareness and attention enhance learning. Many forms of associative learning, including semantic and episodic learning, require awareness and are greatly enhanced by attentional processes. Because attention is so important to learning, it is worth considering an important question: how does attention work? Scientists have found that the answer to this question depends on the circumstances. Some attentional processes are automatic and occur when a particular stimulus is very different from those that surround it. Psychologist Anne Treisman, while working at the University of British Columbia, studied attention to visual stimuli and showed that in the case of a simple scene, if one stimulus differs considerably from others, it will immediately grab our attention, a phenomenon referred to as "*pop-out*" (see **Figure 40-1**). In order for pop-out to work, the stimulus must be singularly different from the surroundings (Treisman & Kanwisher, 1998). As scenes get more and more complicated, pop-out is less likely to help in guiding attentional processes. Instead, we must rely on an active searching method, where we examine material in search of the most relevant stimuli. Anyone who has enjoyed children's books such as "Where's Waldo" or "I Spy," where a relevant stimulus is buried in a complex visual scene, has engaged an *active searching* attentional process. Recall from Part 5 the distinction between bottom-up and top-down processing. Pop-out, because of its simplicity and speed, employs bottom-up processing; active searching, because of the need to draw on cognitive processes and memory, uses top-down processing.

Sometimes attentional processes can get in the way if information is inherently contradictory; for example, attending to one stimulus can block our ability to attend to another stimulus. A good example of this is the *Stroop Effect*, a psychological test that involves presenting a list of words printed in different colours. Each of the words is a colour word (for example green, red, black, blue). In one task the colour of the word and the colour of the ink the word is presented in match (for example the word "red" is presented in red ink); but in the other task, the colour word is printed in a colour that differs from that of the word (for example, the word "red" is presented in blue ink). Participants are asked to name the colour the word was printed in regardless of the name of the word (that is, if the colour "red" is in blue ink, the participant should say "blue"), thus ignoring the word. This task is difficult because it is easier for us to more quickly and automatically read words than it is to name colours, and that automatic process interferes with the more effortless task of naming the word (Herd et al., 2006).

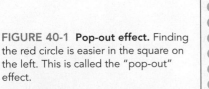

The Stroop Effect. The Stroop Effect illustrates how when information is inherently contradictory (the word "red" presented in blue ink), attending to one stimulus (the word "red") can block our ability to attend to the relevant task (naming the colour "blue").

What can we do then to maximize our attention to relevant information while trying to learn? First, it's a good idea to identify relevant information and focus on it throughout

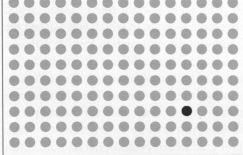

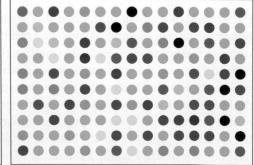

FIGURE 40-1 **Pop-out effect.** Finding the red circle is easier in the square on the left. This is called the "pop-out" effect.

Source: Dr. Gijsbert Stoet, www.psytoolkit.org/lessons/visualsearch.html

©Dr. Gijsbert Stoet, University of Glasgow

your reading. If your professor mentions topics repeatedly in class, you might use an active searching method to find additional similar material in your readings. Second, avoid dividing your attention. Our attentional processes are generally at their best when they are focused on one task. Performing other behaviours, such as answering text messages or watching TV while trying to study, usually interferes with our ability to attend to relevant material. In fact, a recent study showed that people who engage in a high degree of "multi-tasking" are less likely to perform well overall (Ophira et al., 2009).

40.4 Social Networking and Multitasking

According to reports, students who use Facebook while they study and attend lectures get lower grades than those who don't (Kirschner & Karpinski, 2010; Junco, 2012; Junco & Cotten, 2012). Specifically, research has shown that students who had Facebook or other forms of social media running while they studied—even if it was simply running in the background—tended to have lower grade point averages and fewer study hours than students who were not similarly distracted. Moreover, recent research from Farina Sana from McMaster University and her colleagues, Tina Weston and Nicholas Cepeda from York University, also indicate that students who use social media in class not only harm their own learning but negatively affect the learning of their peers. Their data indicate that comprehension is impaired for peers in view of classmates who are multitasking on a computer during a lecture (Sana et al., 2013). It is also worth noting that students themselves don't seem to be aware of this problem. More than three-quarters of Facebook users said they didn't think the practice of multitasking has any negative effects on their studying.

One interpretation of these results is that Facebook and other social media are so distracting that they prevent the focused attention necessary for effective studying; however, it is also possible that students who use Facebook while studying are weaker students with poorer study habits to begin with. It is additionally possible that distraction (divided attention) may not be the entire explanation for grade differences; instead some data suggest that heavy use of the Internet, including Facebook, may lead to changes in how people actually process and remember information (Small & Vorgan, 2008; Frein et al., 2013). That is, it may be that the very nature of surfing the Internet alters the way we learn. We are largely left to speculate as causal explanations of these data are difficult to obtain and it is extremely challenging to carry out experimental research on this topic because it is almost impossible to identify a control group that has never used social media, including Facebook (Frein et al., 2013).

40.5 Sleep

Studies have shown that sleep is important for learning and memory (this was discussed also in Part 6). Sleep deprivation impairs our ability to pay attention and learn. In addition, sleep deprivation can prevent learned information from moving into more permanent long-term memory storage. Studies in experimental animals have confirmed that sleep deprivation interferes with learning and memory (Rauchs et al., 2005; Saxvig et al., 2007). (As you will see in Part 8, memories are thought to leave physical traces in the brain—called *memory traces*.) So while staying up late to study may be unavoidable, try to get a decent amount of sleep so that you don't forget what you are staying up late to learn and ensure that you will be alert enough to learn even more new information the next day.

iStockphoto.com/Yuri_Arcurs

Sleep deprivation, attention, and learning. Sleep deprivation makes it difficult to pay attention, thus impairing our ability to learn. In addition, sleep deprivation after learning reduces our ability to retain newly-learned material.

practically speaking — To Sleep, Perchance to Learn?

Reports from two leading sleep researchers suggest that sleeping plays an important role in learning and memory. As you recall from Part 6, sleep is an episodic state of rest in which the nervous system is relatively inactive and consciousness is partially suspended. Sleep occupies approximately one-third of our lives and is present in most if not all species that have been studied (it is important to note that the universality of sleep has been debated—see Cirelli & Tononi, 2008; Siegel, 2008). But *why* do we sleep?

Giulio Tononi and Chiara Cirelli (2014) suggest that sleep decreases cortical synaptic strength, preventing the brain from becoming overloaded with an overabundance of synaptic connections. That is, sleep serves to "quiet" the brain while preserving new learning. Learning, they argue, requires energy as synapses are strengthened and this increase in energy could become unsustainable if there were no mechanisms in place to "down-regulate" or reduce these energy levels. Sleep is therefore necessary to re-establish synaptic homeostasis. Sleep gives the brain an opportunity to reset and permits newly learned material to integrate with existing memories (a process called consolidation—see Part 8). Thus the more energy expended, the greater the need for deep sleep. The take home message: you are more likely to retain what you learn when you get adequate sleep. Your mother is right!

Before You Go On

www.wiley.com/go/comercanada

What Do You Know?
1. Which would be better for helping you learn psychology facts: massed or spaced practice? Why?
2. What kinds of learning benefit from focused attention?

What Do You Think? How could you modify your own schedule or study habits to allow for spaced practice of your material or to take advantage of your most alert and attentive times of day?

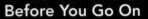

Summary

Module 40: Factors that Facilitate Learning

LEARNING OBJECTIVE 40 Define massed and spaced practice and tell what conditions are best for learning semantic material, such as facts in your classes.

- Massed practice occurs when learning episodes are closely spaced (e.g., "cramming"); this approach impedes learning.
- Repeated, spaced practice aids learning of semantic material, such as classroom information.
- According to the *context effect*, if you learn information in only one context, or location, you may be less likely to recall it when you are in a different context.
- We can learn without paying attention, but focused attention aids semantic learning.
- Sleep deprivation impairs our abilities to pay attention and to learn.

Study Questions

Multiple Choice

1. The Stroop Effect:
   a) illustrates the "pop-out" effect.
   b) demonstrates how easy it is for us to divide attention between stimuli.
   c) contradicts the notion that bottom-up attentional processing interferes with the ability to focus.
   d) demonstrates how attentional processes can block access to relevant information.

2. For which of the following types of learning are attention and awareness probably most important?
   a) semantic learning
   b) procedural learning
   c) non associative learning
   d) classical conditioning

Fill-in-the-Blank

1. Learning about events in our own lives is called _____ learning. Learning about facts is called _____ learning.

2. Heavy use of the Internet, including Facebook, may lead to changes in how people actually _____ and _____ information.

3. Giulio Tononi and Chiara Cirelli (2014) suggest that sleep gives the brain an opportunity to _____ and to allow newly learned material to _____ with previously learned material.

Module 41: Prenatal and Postnatal Learning

LEARNING OBJECTIVE 41
Summarize the types of learning that occur before we are born and during early postnatal life.

Several studies suggest that non-associative learning can occur before infants are even born. Fetuses show habituation and sensitization to smells and other sensory stimuli (Faas et al., 2000). In one set of studies, for example, infants who had been prenatally exposed to garlic—through their mothers' digestion—showed evidence, after they were born, of recognizing the garlic odour. They did not try to avoid the smell, as babies new to garlic typically do (Mennella, Johnson, & Beauchamp, 1995).

Humans are also capable of basic associative learning before birth. One team of researchers reported classical conditioning of human fetuses. These researchers paired specific music (initially a neutral stimulus) with relaxation exercises done by the mother. The maternal relaxation exercises served as an unconditioned stimulus, often leading to a slowing of fetal physical activity (an unconditioned response). After enough pairings of the music and the relaxation, the music became a conditioned stimulus, leading directly to a decrease in fetal movement (CR), with or without the relaxation exercises (see Chelli & Chanoufi, 2008 for review).

Further, in a groundbreaking study Andrew Meltzoff and M. Keith Moore (1977) demonstrated that within hours of birth, infants were able to imitate facial expressions, clearly demonstrating the ability to mirror the behaviour of another person without learning. This task has been replicated in other primates as well. Other research has shown that young children learn language best from face-to-face interactions rather than from video or television, emphasizing the role of social learning in cognitive growth and development (Kuhl, 2010).

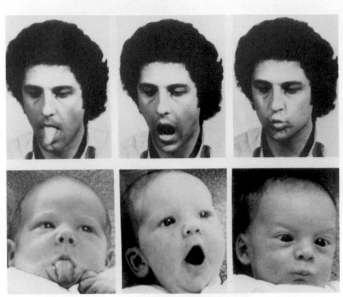

A.N. Meltzoff & M.K. Moore, "Imitation of facial and manual gestures by human neonates." Science, 1977, 198, 75–78

Infant imitation. In a series of classic studies, Meltzoff and Moore (1977) found that newborns could imitate facial movements, such as tongue protrusion, mouth opening, and lip pursing.

Psychology Around Us — Cat in the Hat

A classic study revealed that infants not only hear their mother's speech in the womb, but also pay attention to what they're hearing and remember it (DeCasper & Spence, 1986). The researchers had pregnant women read aloud the classic Dr. Seuss book *The Cat in the Hat* each day during the last several weeks of pregnancy. Soon after the babies were born, they were taught that if they sucked on a specially wired soother more rapidly than usual, a voice recording would be turned on for them to listen to. Babies sucked harder longer to hear their mothers' voices than the voices of others—and they sucked harder longest to hear their mothers read *The Cat in the Hat*.

Before You Go On

www.wiley.com/go/comercanada

What Do You Know?
1. What kinds of learning can happen before we are born?

What Do You Think? What are the advantages and disadvantages of having only very simple forms of learning intact during fetal life? What consequences would arise if we possessed intact learning about events before birth?

Summary

Module 41: Prenatal and Postnatal Learning

LEARNING OBJECTIVE 41 Summarize the types of learning that occur before we are born and during early postnatal life.

- We are capable of non-associative learning, both habituation and sensitization, before birth, as well as basic associative learning, such as classical conditioning.
- We become capable of increasingly complex forms of learning as relevant areas of our brains mature after we are born.

Study Questions

Multiple Choice

1. When does non-associative learning develop?
   a) prenatally
   b) in the first days of life
   c) in the first several months of life
   d) in the second year of life

Fill-in-the-Blank

1. Developmental _____ in children tend to occur during specific time windows.

LEARNING OBJECTIVE 42
Define specific learning disorder and describe three major types of learning disorders.

Module 42: Specific Learning Disorder

Many children with diagnosed learning disorders are high achievers and go on as adults to have successful lives and careers. However, many are prevented from realizing their full potential and therefore fail to reach this level of achievement. Reasonably current estimates suggest that each person in Canada with a diagnosed learning disability costs individuals, their families, and society $450,000 a person from birth to 65 years of age in direct costs (e.g., medical or educational) as well as through reduced earnings (Crawford, 2002).

In 2007 the Learning Disabilities Association of Canada requested access to Statistics Canada data surveys. They analyzed 10 different data sets and then released a federally funded report, "Putting a Canadian Face on Learning Disabilities (PACFOLD)." The data show that 5 percent of Canadian children between the ages of 6 and 15 have a learning disability, with slightly over 28 percent of those with learning disabilities aged 22 to 29 years of age reporting less than a high school diploma (as compared to about 11 percent in the general population for the same age group). Learning problems were typically undetected until children were in grade 5 and the problems compounded with age and affected every aspect of development. As adults, this group was likely to have lower levels of literacy, less likely to be employed, and more likely to suffer from mental health issues. The authors of the study indicated the blame cannot be placed solely on the education system, and they called for a more system solution involving a broader public policy approach, including mandatory screening of children 4 to 8 years old, public funding for education and support, and increased awareness for educators and employers. The entire report can be accessed at www.pacfold.ca.

The term *learning disability* is not included in the Diagnostic and Statistical Manual of Mental Disorders-5 (DSM-5) but most health professionals use it to group together three sets of disorders that do appear in the DSM-5: learning disorders, communication disorders, and motor skills disorders (Davison et al., 2014). A **specific learning disorder** is described in the DSM-5 as a disorder in one or more of the basic psychological processes involved in spoken or written language. It manifests as difficulty in specific aspects of learning and using academic skills, such as listening, thinking, speaking, reading, writing, spelling, or carrying out mathematical calculations. These symptoms must persist for six months or more despite interventions targeting those difficulties, and exclude learning problems that are primarily due to visual or auditory problems, intellectual impairment, and emotional disturbance, or of environmental, cultural, or economic disadvantage. The DSM-5 also specifies that those with specific learning disorders must have at least average abilities essential for thinking or reasoning. Therefore, specific learning disorders are distinct from intellectual developmental disorders (American Psychiatric Association, 2013).

The previous DSM, the DSM-IV-TR, divided learning disorders into three categories: reading disorders, mathematics disorder, and disorder of written expression. Although the DSM-5 does not use this system of categorization, it might be useful to briefly examine each of these specific disorders to give you a feel for the types of disorders that can

specific learning disorder
a disorder that interferes with the acquisition and use of one or more of the basic psychological processes involved in the development of academic skills: oral language, reading, written language, and mathematics.

occur under the more general heading of specific learning disorder. It is important to note that these disorders can occur independently or in combination and that other learning difficulties also exist. As well, note that there is no single type of disability, even within categories; symptoms vary from one individual to the next.

The most common form of learning disorder is a **reading disorder**, known in international diagnostic classifications as *dyslexia*, a deficiency in learning to read. A reading disorder involves deficits in reading comprehension, written spelling, and word recognition. There is some evidence that the same people with dyslexia have visual processing deficits that may produce perceptual problems, which in turn contribute to their difficulty in recognizing written words. Neuroimaging studies comparing children with dyslexia to those without the disability have shown that some children with dyslexia have reduced blood flow in brain regions associated with acquisition of reading skills, such as the left parietal and temporal cortex (Hoeft et al., 2006). Most people with dyslexia overcome their difficulties in learning to read with the help of extensive tutoring and specific educational programs.

A somewhat less prevalent learning disorder is a condition known as **mathematics disorder**, known in international diagnostic classifications as *dyscalculia*. Individuals with this specific learning disorder experience difficulty performing simple mathematical equations, recalling math symbols, counting numbers accurately, and quickly recalling mathematical facts or solving word problems, as well as difficulty understanding graphs and other problems related to numeracy. Some evidence suggests that parts of the left parietal and frontal cortex of the brain are less active in individuals with dyscalculia (Price et al., 2007). As with dyslexia, intensive tutoring and specific educational programs can help students with dyscalculia learn mathematical information (Butterworth, 2010; Butterworth, Varma, & Laurillard, 2011).

Disorder of written expression is the least understood of the specific learning disorders. This disorder is known in international diagnostic classifications as *dysgraphia* and is experienced as impairment in the ability to create the written word. Individuals with this specific learning disorder experience difficulty communicating in writing, exhibit poor handwriting, struggle with spelling and grammar, and have difficulty organizing and expressing thoughts and ideas in written composition. It is unclear whether disorder of written expression occurs independently of reading disorder or communication (language) disorders (Davison et al., 2014). The causes of the disorder is largely unknown. It may be that different forms of the disorder have specific underlying explanations. For example, children experiencing difficulty with forming letters may experience delays in hand–eye coordination, whereas those individuals unable to organize their thoughts in writing may experience cognitive processing problems (Sadock & Sadock, 2000).

Olivier Voisin/Photo Researchers

Studying reading disorder. A range of factors have been proposed to explain dyslexia, a deficiency in the ability to read, including deficits in visual processing, speech skills, auditory processing, and object or letter identification. Here a child diagnosed with the disorder undergoes a reading test with prism glasses.

reading disorder a deficit in reading comprehension, written spelling, and word recognition.

mathematics disorder a deficit in mathematical ability, including the ability to do calculations, as well as the ability to understand mathematical word problems and mathematical concepts.

disorder of written expression a disorder experienced as impairment in the ability to create the written word.

Tying It Together: **Your Brain and Behaviour**

Learning to Play a Video Game

You need to find that key, but watch out for those obstacles!

How do we learn to navigate through virtual reality, avoiding dangers that prevent us from moving through the game to mastery? What parts of the brain enable us to learn the rules of the game and respond to changes in the electronic world as we play?

When we learn a new video game that involves spatial navigation through a virtual three-dimensional space, trying to avoid punishments and obtain rewards all along the way, we are engaging a number of neural circuits throughout the brain. First, spatial navigation learning requires inputs from the visual cortex to the hippocampus and temporal lobe. Second, learning about rewards involves dopamine projections extending from the ventral tegmental area to the nucleus accumbens and prefrontal cortex. And third, integration and long-term storage of the information from these systems involves other cortical regions, including the parietal and temporal cortex. These changes in the brain take place as you learn the game—as your skilled movements become more automatic, brain activity shifts to the corpus striatum (basal ganglia). Will you make it to the next level?

Questions

1 How do brain activation patterns differ when one is using a 3D versus a landmark strategy for navigation?

2 Which brain region creates new neurons as we develop spatial navigation skills?

3 Which neurotransmitter is affected by our learning about rewards, such as those received during video game play?

Masterfile

PICKING A STRATEGY

People use different strategies to solve tasks that involve navigating in space. Some people use a 3D strategy, using their position relative to the environment to find their way. Others use landmarks and numbering strategies (for example, enter the second door on your right). The different strategies engage different neural systems, shown on these fMRI images. Spatial 3D strategies activate the hippocampus (top, yellow) while landmark strategies activate the basal ganglia (bottom, yellow) (Iaria et al., 2003).

Michael Petrides, J. Neurosci. 2003 Jul 2; 23 (13):5945–5952

Courtesy of Elizabeth Gould

STRENGTHENING YOUR SYNAPSES

When you learn a task that involves spatial navigation and reward, synapses in a number of brain regions, including the hippocampus and nucleus accumbens, likely undergo long-term potentiation (LTP), a form of synapse strengthening. Most postsynaptic sites that undergo synapse strengthening are located on small extensions off of dendrites, called dendritic spines (shown here labelled with a green fluorescent tracer).

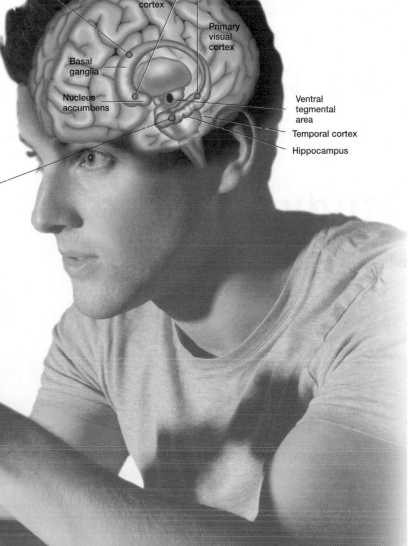

Courtesy of Elizabeth Gould

LEARNING ABOUT SPACE

Spatial navigation learning leads to an increase in the number of new neurons in the hippocampus, shown here stained with fluorescent dyes (red). Engaging the hippocampus in this way prevents newly born neurons from dying.

Masterfile

What Do You Know?

1. What are dyslexia and dyscalculia?

What Do You Think? What, in your opinion, is the purpose in collapsing all three categories of learning disorders into one category in the new DSM-5?

Summary

Module 42: Specific Learning Disorder

LEARNING OBJECTIVE 42 Define specific learning disorder and describe three major types of learning disorders.

- A specific learning disorder is a specific deficiency in one or more areas of learning, while learning in other areas takes place normally. Although the DSM-5 does not consider the three categories of learning disability referred to in the DSM-IV-TR, there was discussion of three types of specific learning disorder: reading disorder, mathematical disorder, and disorder of written expression.

Key Terms

disorder of written expression 321
mathematics disorder 321

reading disorder 320
specific learning disorder 320

Study Questions

Multiple Choice

1. Which type of learning is correctly paired with its basis in the nervous system?
   a) classical conditioning of fear–changes in sensory neurons, interneurons, and motor neurons
   b) habituation–hippocampus
   c) spatial learning–amygdala
   d) reward learning–midbrain dopamine system

2. Which of the following in not true regarding specific learning disorder as described in the DSM-5?
   a) A specific learning disorder is present for six months or more despite interventions targeting those difficulties.
   b) A specific learning disorder is divided into three categories: reading disorders, mathematics disorder, and disorder of written expression.

   c) Those with specific learning disorders must have at least average abilities essential for thinking or reasoning.
   d) A specific learning disorder is a disorder in one or more of the basic psychological processes involved in spoken or written language.

Fill-in-the-Blank

1. Synaptic plasticity, or change, illustrates _____ potentiation.

PART 8

MEMORY

©iStockphoto.com/Petardj

Now a cult classic, the 2000 film *Memento* fascinated viewers with a series of harrowing situations that confronted the main character, Leonard. In the movie, Leonard is looking for the person or people who attacked him and brutally murdered his wife. His search is particularly difficult and frightening, however, because the attack left Leonard unable to form new memories. To cope with this problem, Leonard takes Polaroid instant pictures and makes notes on them as he acquires information. He also tattoos facts on his body to help him put the puzzle together. Despite these efforts, however, scenes in the movie frequently open with Leonard being attacked by people he does not know or being chased for reasons he cannot explain until he is able to piece the information together.

At the same time, Leonard finds himself confronted with other characters who may—or may not—have his best interests at heart as they try to "help" him along his way. On top of everything, Leonard has doubts. Given his own memory loss, how can he be sure that he didn't kill his wife and then somehow cause his own memory loss to protect himself from his guilt?

Similarly, in the 2004 movie *50 First Dates*, the character Lucy, suffering from a fictitious disorder called Goldfield Syndrome (Segen's Medical Dictionary, 2011), wakes up each day believing it is the same day she has the accident that gives her the injury from which she suffers. Like Leonard, she cannot convert her new memories into longer lasting memories because of her brain injury, and so is in an eternally looping day. A second character, Henry, meets her and goes on to have a series of repeated dates with her, none of which she can recall.

The idea of the endless day has been repeated in other movies as well, such as *Groundhog Day* (1993) and *Edge of Tomorrow* (2014). In these movies, however, the main characters are aware that they are repeating the same experiences again and again.

Consider everything that memory lets you do. Obviously there are the everyday tasks, such as passing tests, turning in a paper on time, or remembering a friend's birthday. But go deeper: think of the things memory lets you do that you take for granted. Because of memory, you can have favourite foods, favourite musicians, favourite movies, and favourite TV shows. Not only can you remember friends' birthdays, you can also remember their typical behaviours and their preferences, and then predict what they might want for their birthday.

You can go deeper still. If you did not somehow encode events and people in your mind, you would not know about anything that you were not directly sensing at that moment. You would only know what was in your line of sight and would have no idea how the things that you were seeing connected to you or had any significance or meaning. Without memory, you would, like Leonard or Lucy, be a stranger to yourself, unable to form the identity, or sense of self, that comes from linking one's present to one's past and using this information to make decisions about the future (Roediger & Craik, 2014; Kihlstrom, Beer, & Klein, 2003). By keeping a record of our past, our memory takes us out of an infinite present.

Module 43: What Is Memory?

Simply put, **memory** is the faculty for recalling past events and past learning. This definition is perhaps the only thing about memory that is simple. Although psychologists often differ in their ideas about memory, they generally agree that it involves three basic activities:

- **Encoding**—Getting information into memory in the first place
- **Storage**—Retaining memories for future use
- **Retrieval**—Recapturing memories when we need them

For example, when you attend a concert, you may transform the sights and sounds produced by the performing band into a kind of memory code and record them in your brain (encoding). This information then remains stored in the brain until you retrieve it at later times—such as when you see photos of the band online, watch their music videos, or decide which of the band's songs to download. At times of retrieval, the original concert event, including the feelings of exhilaration and joy that you experienced at the concert, may come rushing back.

How do we manage to encode, store, and retrieve information? Psychologists have developed a number of models of explanation, including the *information-processing model* and the *parallel distributed-processing model*, or *connectionist model*.

The **information-processing model** of memory has its roots back in early computer science (Atkinson & Shiffrin, 1968) and was intended to chart the ways that, like computers, humans process information from their senses into memory. The information-processing model of memory holds that information must pass through three stages, or systems, of mental functioning to become a firmly implanted memory—sensory memory, working memory, and long-term memory (see **Figure 43-1**) (Estes, 2014; Kandel et al., 2014; Dudai, 2011; Nee et al., 2008).

When we first confront a stimulus, our brain retains a sensory image—or *sensory memory*—of it for less than a second. Sensory memories help us to keep items that we have experienced briefly alive a bit longer. As a result, in a sense we can then decide whether to pay further attention to them. Sensory memories are basically copies of the sensory data we have just received. For example, visual sensory memory is also called *iconic memory*, meaning it is like a small copy of the visual event we have just

memory the faculty for recalling past events and past learning.

encoding a basic activity of memory, involving the recording of information in our brain.

storage a basic activity of memory, involving retention of information for later use.

retrieval a basic activity of memory, involving recovery of information when we need it later.

information-processing model view of memory suggesting that information moves among three memory stores during encoding, storage, and retrieval.

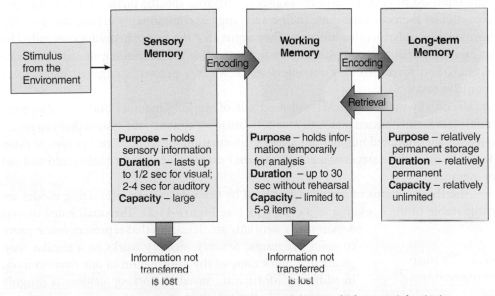

FIGURE 43-1 **The three-stage memory model.** This model is a useful framework for thinking about the three basic memory stages. Each stage differs in purpose, duration, and capacity.

encountered, just as a computer icon is a small visually descriptive representation of the program or file it represents (Dick, 1974). It is hard to know how to describe the capacity of sensory memory, but given that it can contain a complete copy of a sensory input, we assume that it has a large capacity. If, for example, we look up a person's email address, our sensory memory records the address and quickly passes it on to our *short-term memory*. We can help retain the new address in working memory by concentrating on this information or by repeating it over and over as we address an email or type it into our computer's address book. But working memory itself can hold only so many pieces of information at a time. The capacity of working memory is often claimed to be five to nine elements of information (i.e., 7 ± 2) (Miller, 1956). More recent estimates put the capacity of working memory closer to three or four elements (Farrington, 2011).

Experimental cognitive psychologists have further divided short-term memory into two related processes: *working memory*, which consists of the things we are thinking of and working with consciously (Allen et al., 2006), and the stores or places where we can put information we need to have nearby. Baddeley and Hitch identified two of these sorts of memory stores, one called the *phonological loop* (likened to a "little voice" that keeps repeating what we want to remember to keep it active in memory) and another called a *visuospatial sketchpad*, where we can temporarily store images and spatial locations we are working with (Baddeley & Hitch 1974; Allen et al., 2006; Baddeley, 2007; Jarrold et al., 2010).

The exact role of attention in short memory is unclear, but there is a relationship between the two (Fougnie, 2009). Attention involves the ability to selectively process, or enhance, specific information for further processing, while simultaneously ignoring, or inhibiting, other information. That is, attention allows us to "tune in" to some information (such as listening to a lecture or focusing on material to be studied) and to "tune out" other information (such as ignoring Facebook posts or classmates whispering). Although the topic of attention will be explored further in Part 9, we do know that the role of attention is important during encoding and manipulation of information in working memory (Fougnie, 2009).

It is important to note that attentional control is referred to as *working memory* by experimental psychologists and as *executive function* by neuropsychologists. Although executive function refers more directly to processing information as it relates to goal-directed behaviour, there is clear overlap between the two functions (Banich, 2009). Data reported by McCabe and colleagues (2010) link specific physiological structures to particular memory functions. Their results suggest commonality of function in working memory and executive function. They argue that the two systems are controlled by an *executive attention* component that is responsible for overseeing the maintenance of goals and for controlling for interference while a person is engaged in complex cognitive tasks.

Eventually the information will drop out of working memory and will disappear, unless it is further passed on to our *long-term memory* system—the system that can retain a seemingly unlimited number of pieces of information for an indefinite period of time. Together these three stages of memory explain how we process information into and out of memory.

The three systems of memory proposed by the information-processing model are comparable to the operation of a computer (see **Figure 43-2**). The small icons on our desktop are essentially small images that represent much more complex programs. *Sensory memory* works in a similar way, giving us a quick copy of the information in our environment. In addition, information saved to *working memory* is roughly equivalent to the information that a computer retains for as long as a document or website is open, but which disappears if

> **❝**Memory isn't like reading a book; it's more like writing a book from fragmentary notes.**❞**
>
> —*John Kihlström, psychologist*

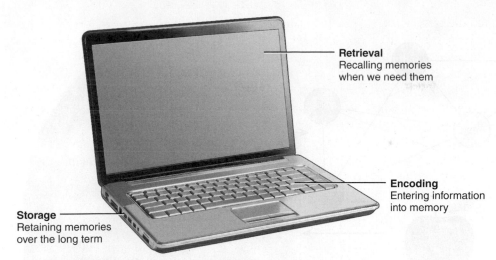

Retrieval
Recalling memories
when we need them

Encoding
Entering information
into memory

Storage
Retaining memories
over the long term

FIGURE 43-2 **Memory as a computer.** In the information-processing model of memory, the basic memory stages are analogous to a computer: encoding allows us to enter information into our brain; storage allows us to retain the information over the long term; and retrieval enables us to call up the information as we need it.

you do not save it. And the final memory system, *long-term memory*, is the equivalent of the computer hard drive, storing information until something causes disruption or loss of the memory. These three systems are sometimes referred to as *memory stores*. The information-processing model has generated a great deal of research that we will explore further in the modules that focus on encoding, storage, retrieval, and forgetting. Consider for a moment what happens when you study. In order to eliminate competing stimuli (you set your phone to vibrate, close Facebook, and tell friends you need some quiet time), you sit in an area free of distraction and focus on your work. This behaviour allows sensory memory to eliminate non-specific stimuli so that working memory can process the information for the task at hand. As you process material, the information is gradually moved to long-term storage. We will discuss ways this can be done most effectively throughout the part.

Although the information-processing model suggests that sensory memory, working memory, and long-term memory correspond roughly to computer memory structures, we need to be clear that this is just a metaphor. If you break open a computer, you can find the dedicated modules where the various forms of memory are in operation. When we look at the human brain, however, there are no equivalent dedicated structures where short-term memory and long-term memory exist.

Unlike the information-processing model, which suggests that information is stored and retrieved piece by piece, an alternative model of memory, the **parallel distributed-processing model (PDP)** (or **connectionist model**), holds that newly encountered pieces of information immediately join with other, previously-encountered pieces of relevant information to help form and grow networks of information (McClelland, 2011). Baddeley and Hitch used their working memory model to provide examples of parallel processing. They asked people to complete two tasks at once—one of the tasks was visual (using the visuospatial sketchpad watching for a visual target), and the other was sound-based (listening for a particular sound). They found that as long as the tasks were different (one visual and one auditory), people did about as well on each task as they did when they only did one of the tasks; they were able to do two things at once. However, when the tasks were the same (both visual or both auditory), people's performance suffered when they tried to do them together (Conrad & Hull, 1964; Baddeley, 1966).

These networks of information result in sophisticated memories, broad knowledge, and the ability to make better decisions and plans in life. Look, for example, at

parallel distributed-processing (PDP) (or **connectionist**) **model** theory of memory suggesting that information is represented in the brain as a pattern of activation across entire neural networks.

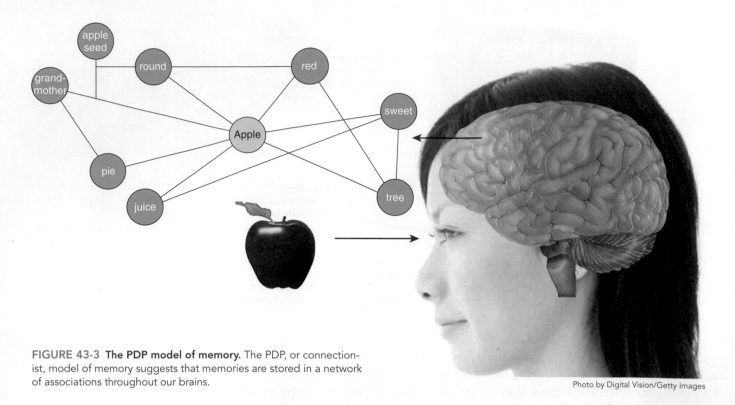

FIGURE 43-3 **The PDP model of memory.** The PDP, or connection-ist, model of memory suggests that memories are stored in a network of associations throughout our brains.

Photo by Digital Vision/Getty Images

Figure 43-3. When the person in the figure sees an apple, connections to information involving things that are round, the colour red, or possibly grandma (because of the apple tree in her backyard) are all activated, while other, less relevant connections are inhibited. These connections are all part of the network of information related to apples that this person has stored.

When one part of the "apple" network is activated, related neurons throughout the brain also become active and richer memories spring forth. The PDP model of memory has gained many proponents, largely because its principles fit well with the field's grow-ing recognition that neurons throughout our brains form networks of association as we respond to repeated learning experiences and events in life.

Before You Go On

www.wiley.com/go/comercanada

What Do You Know?

1. What are encoding, storage, and retrieval?
2. What are the three memory stores suggested by the information-processing model of memory?

What Do You Think? Judging from your own experiences, do you think memory works more like a computer, with different memory stores, or more in a connectionist fashion? Could the two ideas both be useful in explaining some of your experiences?

Summary

Module 43: What Is Memory?

LEARNING OBJECTIVE 43 Define the basic activities of memory and describe two major models of memory.

- Memory is our faculty for holding on to past events and past learning. It involves three basic activities: encoding, storage, and retrieval.
- Researchers typically take an information-processing approach to memory, talking about different memory stores that work together in a similar way to parts of a computer, each serving particular functions and holding information for varying lengths of time.
- PDP or connectionist models of memory suggest that information is stored not in a particular neuron or location in the brain, but instead across a network of connections.

Key Terms

encoding 327

information-processing
   model 327

memory 327

parallel distributed-processing (PDP)
   (or connectionist) model 329

retrieval 327

storage 327

Study Questions

Multiple Choice

1. Which of the following sequences best reflects the order of stages in the three-stage memory model, from first to last?
   a) sensory memory → long-term memory → working memory
   b) sensory memory → working memory → long-term memory
   c) working memory → long-term memory → sensory memory
   d) working memory → sensory memory → long-term memory

2. An experimenter is reading a series of digits aloud for a respondent to recite back from memory in the order they were read. The experimenter is testing the capacity of _____ memory, and the longest string the respondent is likely to be able to repeat correctly is _____ digits.
   a) sensory; 3
   b) sensory; 7
   c) working; 3
   d) working; 7

Fill-in-the-Blank

1. According to the information-processing model of memory, _____ is the first stage in which an image is retained by the brain for less than 1 second.

2. The _____ model of memory emphasizes how memories are formed and stored in a network of connections throughout the brain.

Module 44: How Do We Encode Information into Memory?

LEARNING OBJECTIVE 44
Describe how information is encoded and transferred among different memory stores and what we can do to enhance encoding.

How many steps are there from the front door of your building to your room? Can't remember? How about an easier question: what was the first word you said yesterday morning? Most of us probably cannot recall an answer to either of these questions.

Your lack of recall may be because the information was never *encoded*, or entered into your memory. Because we fail to encode many pieces of information that we come across in life, we do not actually remember most of the things that we experience. Encoding requires *attention*—that is, we need to focus on or notice the information in the first place. We can encode only what we attend to (Eysenck et al., 2010).

44.1 Using Automatic and Effortful Processing to Encode

We are not always aware that we are attending to things in our environment. Sometimes we attend to information—particularly information about *time, space,* or *frequency*—without much conscious awareness, and indeed with little or no effort. Even though you might not know how many steps there are from the front door of your building to the door of your room, you do not get lost along the way and you did not need to practise the route to figure out how to get to your room. The encoding process that allowed you to learn this basic route is called **automatic processing** (Hassin, 2005).

automatic processing encoding of information with little conscious awareness or effort.

effortful processing encoding of information through careful attention and conscious effort.

Although we use automatic processing to encode many kinds of information, the encoding of other information requires that we make conscious efforts and pay very close attention (Gilchrist & Cowan, 2010). This is the type of processing you are engaging in right now as you read this part, whether you are preparing for tomorrow's class or studying for a test. As you read through the material, you are trying to find ways to intentionally and consciously pay attention in order to process and understand this new information so it can be stored and maintained for later retrieval. This kind of encoding—which is typically needed when a person learns new information, such as new facts, names, or tasks—is called **effortful processing** (Hassin, 2005).

Keep in mind that whether you are encoding information through automatic or effortful processing, you must be paying attention. Your attention might be less apparent in automatic processing, but if you do not attend sufficiently to information, in one way or another, you will simply not be able to encode it.

There are key differences between these two kinds of processing. First, the encoding of information by effortful processing tends to be disrupted when a person is forced to perform other tasks or to attend to other information while trying to encode the information at hand. You probably would not do very well on an intense video game if you tried to play it while carrying on a lively phone conversation, for example. In contrast, automatic processing, being so effortless, is disrupted only slightly by the performance of other tasks. For example, you would not likely spill coffee or tea if you were pouring it into your cup while talking on the phone because practice has made pouring an automatic processing task.

Second, as the name might suggest, putting extra effort into effortful processing makes it more effective. Automatic processing is not significantly enhanced by a person's extra efforts to attend and encode. You could rehearse the path from your front door to your room and count the steps, but it's unlikely that you'll know

Effortful processing requires effort. Effortful processing, such as acquiring new information from a textbook, is easily disrupted when one also attends to other tasks during the encoding process.

any more about the route than you knew this morning. In contrast, extra efforts can make an enormous difference in effortful processing. Merging your class notes with the information you read in this textbook will considerably affect your ability to recall the information later on a test.

44.2 Encoding Information into Working Memory: Transferring from Sensory Memory into Working Memory

As we observed earlier, when we first confront a stimulus, our brains retain a very brief sensory image of it—an image called a **sensory memory**. If, for example, we are shown a photograph for just a moment, we retain a detailed image of all the shapes and items in the photograph for a few hundred milliseconds (in an iconic store). Studies by researcher George Sperling in the late 1950s and early 1960s provided psychologists with important insights about how sensory memories operate (Sperling, 1960).

Sperling wanted to demonstrate the presence of a brief visual storehouse—equivalent to the buffer memory of a computer—that would hold a picture of our environment for a very brief period of time. He also wanted to measure how long this buffer would last. To do so, he exposed participants to three rows of four random letters, similar to what you might see on an eye chart (although all letters were the same size; **Figure 44-1**). He presented those letters for less than a second and found that, generally speaking, participants did a pretty good job reporting the letters, most of the time remembering about half if asked to do so right away. In a second condition of the study, Sperling displayed the grid of letters for less than a second, and when the letters disappeared he played a tone that was either a low, medium, or high note. Participants only had to report the line of letters corresponding to the tone they heard, with the low note indicating the bottom row and the high note indicating the top row. If the tone sounded within about a half second of the grid disappearing, participants could usually report all the letters in the indicated row—it was as if they just had to read them off their sensory or iconic store. If there was a delay of more than half a second between the visual list of letters and the tone sounding, people's recollection of the row of letters started to fall off, as they could no longer use their sensory memory. The longer Sperling waited to play the tone after showing the letters, the more performance declined.

If we do not focus our attention on our sensory memories, as is usually the case, they will disappear forever. Those that are attended to, however, may enter the **working memory**, the second system of memory. Working memory serves several important functions in our day-to-day lives (Hofmann et al., 2011). One of the most important is that of enabling us to hold on to information—such as a phone number—that we need for short periods. Much of the time we use working memory in this way. Whenever we read, for example, our working memory enables us to keep the beginning of a sentence in mind while we are reading the last part of the sentence, so that the whole phrase will make sense to us (Just & Carpenter, 2002). It also enables us to relate new sentences, such as this one, to previous sentences we have just read. Similarly, in a conversation, working memory helps us link new comments to previous ones so that we can follow what we are hearing.

One way of helping to make sure that information is encoded into working memory is **rehearsal**, consciously repeating the information. As far back as 400 B.C.E., the ancient Greek philosophers recognized the value of rehearsal in memory. They advised students to repeat whatever they heard, on the assumption that hearing and saying the same things would transfer new information into memory (Turkington & Harris, 2009, 2001). We are rehearsing when we keep repeating a phone number we

sensory memory memory involving a detailed, brief sensory image or sound retained for a brief period of time.

> "The true art of memory is the art of attention."
>
> —*Samuel Johnson, writer*

working memory a short-term memory store that can hold five to nine items at once.

rehearsal conscious repetition of information in an attempt to make sure the information is encoded.

K	Z	R	A
Q	B	T	P
S	G	N	Y

FIGURE 44-1 **Test of sensory memory.** In his study of the duration of sensory memory, George Sperling flashed a chart of letters, similar to this one, for 1/20 of a second. He found that participants could recall almost all the letters in a particular row if asked to do so immediately, but half a second later, their performance declined.

have just heard until we can call it or add it to our phone's contact list. Such rehearsal increases the likelihood that the information will indeed enter our working memory and be available to us as we enter in the phone number. As we will see later in this part, although effective for short-term use, this form of *rote* rehearsal is less effective than more meaningful, or *elaborative*, forms of rehearsal (Craik et al., 1983).

44.3 Encoding Information into Long-Term Memory: Transferring Working Memory into Long-Term Memory

Although concentrated efforts, such as rehearsal, can lengthen the availability of information in working memory, eventually that information is either passed on to the long-term memory system or lost (Jonides et al., 2008, 2003). It is in **long-term memory** that we hold all of the information we have gathered, available for use—often at a moment's notice—in a new situation or task. When we remember past events, previously-gathered information, people we once met, past feelings, or acquired skills, we are using our long-term memory system.

long-term memory the memory system in which we hold all of the information we have previously gathered, available for retrieval and use in a new situation or task.

Just as rehearsal can help move information from the sensory memory system to the working memory system, it can also help move short-term, working memories into the long-term memory system (Nishiyama & Ukita, 2013; Neuschatz et al., 2005). Most of us rehearse information from a course's textbook and lectures, for example, when we are studying for an examination. Information is more likely to pass into long-term memory when our rehearsal sessions are spread out over a period of time, rather than attempting to take in a great deal of information all at once. As we observed in Part 7 this phenomenon is known as the **spaced practice effect**. Thus, *distributed practice*, such as studying material weekly, followed by reviews closer to the time of an exam, is usually more profitable than *massed practice*, such as studying in one "cram" session just before the exam.

spaced practice effect facilitated encoding of material through rehearsal situations spread out over time.

As we also saw in Part 7, sleep can help or hurt rehearsal. Information acquired in the hours before falling asleep tends to be encoded into long-term memory, as long as we have time to process it before sleep sets in (Backhaus et al., 2008; Stickgold, 2011). Information learned just as sleep is approaching is rarely retained, however, partly because we fall asleep before we can rehearse it. Furthermore, information that comes to us during sleep—a language tape, for example—does not typically enter our memories at all.

44.4 In What Form Is Information Encoded?

We must use some kind of code or representation to encode information into memory. Different codes are available to us (Martin, 2009). When encoding information into working memory—for example, trying to keep an address in mind before entering it into our GPS system—we can use a *phonological code*, repeating the sounds of the numbers again and again, or we can employ a *visual code*, holding an image of how the digits would look if written down. Research suggests that people tend to favour phonological codes (as if they were spoken) when recording verbal information, such as numbers, letters, and words. We rely more on visual codes for non-verbal information, such as a person's face or a speeding car (Miles & Minda, 2011).

Although adequate for most purposes, the phonological or visual codes that people use to record information in their working memory tend to be flawed. For example, we sometimes confuse words or other items that sound or look similar to the items we are trying to hold in working memory (Saeki et al., 2013). Some people, however, produce visual images with extraordinary detail and near-perfect accuracy. Although recalling an object or scene that they have just witnessed, these people behave as if they are recalling items while looking at a photograph. Thus their detailed images are called *eidetic memories*, or photographic memories. Eidetic memories usually occur among children: as many as 5 percent of children encode images with this level of detail. The eidetic images can last for several minutes (Jaensch & Jaensch, 2013; Hochman, 2010, 2001).

Thinkstock/Getty Images

Putting working memory to good use. If you are trying to decide which cereal provides the best nutritional value, you need to keep a lot of information from the cereal boxes in mind as you decide which to buy.

When we encode *non-verbal information* into long-term memory, we once again tend to use phonological or visual codes (though other codes for things like smell are also likely at play). Long after a concert, for example, audience members may remember its intensity by visualizing images of the stage and the lighting effects, re-experiencing the smells of the arena and the crowd, and calling to mind the sounds of the musical instruments, the performers' voices, and the crowd's cheers.

In contrast, to encode *verbal information* into long-term memory, we tend to use **semantic codes**, representations based on the meaning of information. This means that we link the new things we learn to the things we have already memorized based on shared meaning. Hearing that a friend of yours was seen out with someone other than her boyfriend gets linked to existing thoughts we might have had about the friend's previous commitment to the relationship, or to knowledge we might have about her tendency to hang out with a sibling fitting the description of the person she was with.

semantic code cognitive representation of information or an event based on the meaning of the information.

Because we often rely on the meaning of information when transferring items into long-term memory, our later recall of events may be flawed to some degree. If you are listening carefully to a lecture focusing on a particularly difficult concept, you may not be able to say much later on about the facial expression or the tone of voice of the lecturer, as those bits of information are not stored semantically.

It is worth noting that the various codes may operate simultaneously when information is being encoded (Morey et al., 2013; Kessels & Postma, 2002). One of these codes—semantic, phonological, or visual—may be used more actively than the others in particular instances, but when we use multiple codes, the combined impact of these codes increases the likelihood and strength of the memory.

44.4.1 Meaning and Encoding

Inasmuch as meaning often plays a key role in long-term memory, we should not be surprised that the more meaningful information is, the more readily it is encoded and later remembered. In one study, for example, people were asked to memorize 200 words of poetry, 200 nonsense syllables, and a 200-word prose passage. The poetry took 10 minutes to learn and the prose less than 20 minutes, but the nonsense syllables took an hour and a half!

Similarly, the more meaningful a personal event, the more readily it is encoded and later remembered. The day your grandfather went to the hospital was recognized by everyone in the family as a significant point in the family's life. Thus, you as well as all of your relatives clearly remember the day of his trip to the hospital with a possible heart attack. A lesser event, such as a day at the circus or a trip to the mall, might not be encoded as readily.

People can help ensure that less meaningful information proceeds into long-term memory by artificially *adding* meaning to it (Ceci et al., 2003) or by elaborating on the meaning of the information. Such efforts are known as **mnemonic devices**, which are cognitive techniques that impose additional or intensified meaning on various pieces of information (Cavallini et al., 2003). Many new music students, for example, come to appreciate that the five lines of printed music of the treble clef are called *E-G-B-D-F* by first tying those letters to the sentence "*Every Good Boy Does Fine.*" The first letter of each word in the sentence is the same as one of the lines of printed music. By giving more meaning to the musical language, the sentence helps students to encode the information into their long-term memory.

Kevin Lam photographer, www.kevinlamphoto.com, courtesy Patty Ho.

The subway? Really? Because people tend to use semantic codes (codes based on meaning) for long-term memory, people viewing this couple's wedding pictures might wonder why they went to a subway station for a photo. However, for the couple themselves, a stop at the subway station where they first met was a necessary and meaningful event.

mnemonic devices techniques used to enhance the meaningfulness of information as a way of making them more memorable.

Throughout this part, we include relevant examples that we hope will make the information more applicable and more relevant and, in turn, make your memories more available when you need to retrieve this information. We will also provide you with tips for

Psychology Around Us "There's No Stop Button"

What would it be like to remember *everything*? Jill Price (born 1965) is one of about 20 people in the world with a condition known as hyperthymesia (or hyperthymestic syndrome). She has perfect episodic memory; in other words, she has automatic, continuously looping, episodic memories. She can retrieve the details of every day of her life starting when she was 14 years of age and many from before—re-experiencing the emotions she felt originally with each recall. She automatically and uncontrollably experiences a constant bombardment of fragmented memories; a process she says is "exhausting" (Price, 2008). If you tell her a date in her life, she can tell you, in detail, what she did that day and what happened in the world that day.

In 2000, she sought out the leading memory expert in the United States, James McGaugh, the founder of the Center for the Neurobiology of Learning and Memory at the University of California, Irvine. McGaugh and his colleagues thoroughly studied Mrs. Price, exposing her to comprehensive neuropsychological tests and batteries of exams. The researchers concluded that her episodic memory was virtually perfect. Of interest, they discovered that she performs poorly on other types of memory tests, unable to recall a series of numbers or to memorize poems. As well, her ability to remember information unrelated to her day-to-day life is only average. Since publishing some of the results from their case study of Mrs. Price, referring to her as "AJ" (Parker, Cahill, & McGaugh, 2006), McGaugh and his team have been approached by others with this condition, and they now have a group of five

Chris Carlson/AP Photo

James McGaugh, left, and Larry Cahill, right

people with what they have termed highly superior autobiographical memory (HSAM).

What would it be like to never forget? Depending on your point of view, this could be both a blessing and a curse. Of course it would be good to be able to remember all the positive things that had happened to you, but imagine not being able to forget every slight, every insult, and every negative or distasteful event. Imagine that every new event brought forward a flood of recollections of every similar event you have ever experienced. Sometimes forgetting is a good thing.

---

remembering. For example, one of the best ways to elaborate is by making the target information personally meaningful. For example, if you want to remember the difference between the spelling of the words dessert (a treat that follows a meal) and desert (a dry, hot, arid place), you might remember that dessert is "something extra" following a meal and that "dessert" has an extra "s."

44.4.2 Organization and Encoding

Another important variable that can enhance the encoding of information into long-term memory is *organization*. Actually, when we add to or elaborate on the meaning of certain pieces of information or events, we are organizing them. That is, we are giving the information a structure that is more familiar and available to us. As such, we are making it easier to encode into long-term memory. Typically, we do this intuitively. If we asked you to memorize a list of words (and order of retrieval was unimportant) that included FOX, BEAR, ITALY, ENGLAND, RABBIT, SPAIN, and MOUSE, you might naturally sort the words into rough categories of "Animals" and "European Countries."

Organization by categories can be particularly useful in helping us to encode complicated situations. Cognitive psychologists have identified structures called **schemas**, knowledge bases that we develop based on prior exposure to similar experiences or other knowledge bases. Schemas can be helpful in allowing us to attend to and encode a lot of

schemas knowledge bases that we develop based on prior exposure to similar experiences or other knowledge bases.

information in a hurry. Think about the first time you walked into your university. Did it feel awkward or strange because you weren't sure of where to go or who to see? If you had previously visited other universities, the schemas you developed during your experiences there probably helped you know what to do at your university.

practically Speaking — Organizing Your Memories

Tetra Images/Getty Images

As you know by now, organizing information is necessary for the proper storage and retrieval of memories. *Chunking* is one way of organizing information to help enhance memory. Let's imagine that you are coming home from a ski trip and just as you pull into the driveway you remember that your parents are away overnight *and* that they have a new house alarm. The battery on your phone is almost dead. You call your parents and they give you the number: 19919395. Before you can program this into your phone, it dies. You stay at your grandmother's house that night. However, had you known about chunking, you could have more easily remembered 1991 93 95, and you might have been able to sleep in your own bed. (Even better, make your chunks *meaningful*—for example, you might have noticed that your parents chose a code that embedded both your birthdate and the birthdates of your two siblings.)

Another organizational technique—*organizing a list* of unrelated words into a story—has also been shown to be very successful. In a classic study, participants who used this approach were able to recall, on average, over 90 percent of the words presented to them from 12 lists, compared to only 10 percent recalled by participants who did not use this approach (Bower & Clark, 1969).

A third way to organize new material is to create a *hierarchy* of the information, separating it into sections and subsections, much like the part of a textbook. For example, if you need to memorize the names of all the muscles of the body for an anatomy class, you might group them according to their locations or by their actions.

One very useful study technique for helping readers—such as yourself—to learn and remember textbook information is, once again, based on the principle of organization (West et al., 2008). The *PQRST* method is an abbreviation named for its five steps, each of which are to be undertaken in order.

- *Preview* Skim the entire section you are required to learn. Look for the basic themes and try to get a rough idea of the information you will have to process when reading the section in more detail.
- *Question* Examine the organization of the section and turn each subsection into a question that you want to answer over the course of your reading.
- *Read* Read the section with the goal of finding the answers to your questions.
- *Self-Recitation* Ask yourself and answer aloud a set of questions that arose from the reading material. Work by Colin MacLeod at the University of Waterloo has shown that saying things out loud seems to increase their distinctiveness and make it more likely that they will be remembered later (MacLeod, 2010).
- *Test* Test yourself by trying to recall as much of the learned information as you can.

By organizing your reading in this way—by asking yourself questions about the information at hand before, during, and after reading—you stand a better chance of retaining the information than if you were to spend your time simply reading through the section several times.

In need of a schema. This young patron seems confused about how things work at Round House Restaurant in Brno, Czech Republic. His previous restaurant schemas simply have not prepared him for the Round House's unusual use of a model train to deliver food and drinks to its customers.

Tomas Hajek/isifa/Getty Images

Before You Go On

www.wiley.com/go/comercanada

What Do You Know?

1. How does increased attention affect automatic and effortful processing?
2. Why is it more effective to study all term long, rather than in one massive session right before a final exam?
3. Which type of coding would most people use to remember someone's face? Which type would most people use to remember a person's name?

What Do You Think?
As we noted earlier in the part, the author Samuel Johnson wrote, "The true art of memory is the art of attention." Can you think of experiences from your own or others' lives that bring this statement to life?

Summary

Module 44: How Do We Encode Information into Memory?

LEARNING OBJECTIVE 44 Describe how information is encoded and transferred among different memory stores and what we can do to enhance encoding.

- Encoding refers to taking information in and putting it into memory.
- Encoding can happen either automatically or through effortful processing. Either way, however, a person must attend to something to put it into memory.
- One of the most common means of effortful processing is rehearsal of material.
- Encoding takes place in the form of phonological, sound, or visual codes.

Key Terms

automatic processing 332
effortful processing 332
long-term memory 334

mnemonic
    devices 335
rehearsal 333

schemas 336
semantic code 335
sensory memory 333

spaced practice effect 334
working memory 333

Study Questions

Multiple Choice

1. For encoding to occur, individuals need to focus on environmental stimuli. This "focus" refers to what cognitive process?
   a) attention
   b) invigoration
   c) retrieval
   d) storage

Fill-in-the-Blank

1. _____, or consciously repeating information, increases the likelihood of information being encoded into working memory.

Module 45: How Do We Store Memories?

As you have seen, after entering the working memory system, information remains there for only a short period of time, usually no more than 20 to 30 seconds, unless we repeat or rehearse the information (Oberauer & Kliegl, 2006). In contrast, when information moves on to the long-term memory system, it can remain there for hours or a lifetime. The retention of information—whether brief or long—in either of these memory systems is called storage.

45.1 Storage in Working Memory

Information may enter working memory from two major sources. Sensory information is briefly stored and then lost or sent on to working memory. In addition, we can bring system information that previously has been encoded in the long-term memory system back into the working memory for use in a current situation or task.

Research suggests that memory and related cognitive functions peak at approximately age 25 (McGaugh, 2003, 1999).

During the time that information from either of these sources is residing in the working memory system, it can serve many important functions in our daily lives, from enabling us to read or carry on conversations, to helping us solve current problems (Hofmann et al., 2011). The information stored in working memory also helps us do mental computations, such as mathematical problems (Maybery & Do, 2003). We could not, for example, add together the numbers 12 plus 13 if our working memory were not reminding us that we are computing those particular numbers, that addition is the task at hand, and that 3 plus 2 equals 5 and 10 plus 10 equals 20. In fact, because working memory helps us do mental computations, it is often characterized as a *temporary scratchpad* that briefly retains intermediate information while we think and solve larger problems.

©iStockphoto.com/STEEX

Mental math and working memory. Working memory helps us to do mental computations.

45.1.1 The Storage Limits of Working Memory

Once information enters working memory, it can be stored for just a limited period of time (Cowan, 2009). Concentrated efforts, such as rehearsal, can lengthen the availability of information in working memory, but eventually it is either passed on to long-term memory system or lost (Jonides et al., 2008, 2003).

Just as striking as the limited *duration* of working memory is its limited *capacity* (Hofmann et al., 2011). On average, only five to nine items can be stored there at a given moment. This number was first uncovered back in 1885 by German researcher Hermann Ebbinghaus (1850–1909) who pioneered memory research by studying his own memory. Ebbinghaus's findings were confirmed over 70 years later by psychologist George Miller (1956).

In a typical study of this phenomenon, researchers present people with a sequence of unrelated digits, letters, or words, and then ask them to restate the items in the correct order. Because the items are unrelated and presented rapidly, it is likely that this procedure is tapping into the storage capacity of working memory only, not into some related information that has been stored in long-term memory. In study after study, almost every adult can recall sequences that consist of five items, but very few can recall lists consisting of more than nine items. Each individual displays his own **memory span**—the maximum number of items that can be recalled in the correct order—but no memory span strays very far from seven. Because research shows that almost everyone has a working memory capacity in this range, Miller described it as the "magical number seven, plus or minus two."

memory span maximum number of items that can be recalled in the correct order.

45.1.2 Enhancing Working Memory

Actually, the storage capacity of working memory is not quite as limited as it may seem from the Ebbinghaus and Miller studies. Each of the seven or so items that working memory holds can consist of more than a single digit, letter, or word. An item can consist of a "chunk" of information. **Chunking** pieces of information together into larger units enables us to encode more information in our working memory system, and it also enables our working memory to store more information at a given moment.

chunking grouping bits of information together to enhance ability to hold that information in working memory.

Say you are presented with a string of 23 letters, *o-u-t-l-a-s-t-d-r-i-v-i-n-g-n-i-g-h-t-w-a-s-i*. Because your working memory capacity is only 7 ± 2 items, you would, on the face of it, be unable to store this entire sequence of items. Assuming letter order is not important, you might recognize that these letters can be chunked into words—"out," "last," "driving," "night," "was," and "I"—and now your task changes. Instead, you need to store only six items (that is, six words) in working memory, rather than 23, and the task becomes manageable. In fact, these words can be re-ordered and then further chunked into one item: the sentence "Last night I was out driving." If you store the information in this way, you still have room in your working memory for several other items. Similarly, without realizing it, we may be taking advantage of chunking when we first try to master a song's lyrics. Rather than learn the song letter by letter or word by word, we may hold on to seven new lines at a time, repeating the lines again and again until we have them solidly memorized.

Our ability to chunk actually comes from our long-term memory system (Cowan & Chen, 2009). Recall that information may enter working memory as either new information arriving from sensory memory or through retrieval from long-term memory. In chunking, we use our stored, long-term knowledge that certain letters spell certain words, or that words can be organized to form sentences, to guide us in chunking new information.

45.2 Storage in Long-Term Memory

Whereas the sensory memory and working memory systems deal only with a limited number of short-term memories, our long-term memory system retains a seemingly unlimited number of pieces of information for an indefinite period of time, extending from minutes to a lifetime (Voss, 2009). Indeed, memory researcher Elizabeth Loftus estimates that our long-term memory system may hold as many as one quadrillion (one million billion) separate pieces of information (Loftus & Loftus, 1980). This expansive capacity and duration is critical to our functioning, for it is in this vast memory store that we hold—ready for use—all of the information that we have ever gathered. When we remember previously-gathered knowledge, past events and people, or acquired skills, we are using our long-term memory system.

Several factors influence whether particular events are stored in long-term memory. As observed, we must first attend to new information in order to have any chance of it eventually winding up in this memory system. Furthermore, items that are attended to must be encoded and briefly stored in working memory, and then encoded into long-term memory, before they can be stored in this memory system (Ceci et al., 2003). Any shortcomings in these attention and encoding activities may prevent the information from being stored in the long-term system (McGaugh, 2003). Moreover, even after information is successfully stored in long-term memory, some of it may become inaccessible (Loftus & Loftus, 1980). That is, some of the information that we have previously acquired cannot be *retrieved* from long-term memory.

The capacity for long-term memory storage, while enormous for most of us, varies greatly among people. The differences from person to person may be due to factors such as attention and the ability to move information from working memory to long-term memory.

© Lucas Jackson/Reuters/Corbis

Explicit versus implicit memories. Explicit memories include facts, but also include memories about the experiences we have had in our past. In contrast, the learned motor behaviours and perceptual information that enable Olympic freestyle gold medallist Alex Bilodeau to excel in his sport are implicit memories.

explicit memory memory that a person can consciously bring to mind, such as your middle name.

implicit memory memory that a person is not consciously aware of, such as learned motor behaviours, skills, and habits.

semantic memory a person's memory of general knowledge of the world.

episodic memory a person's memory of personal events or episodes from his life.

 **WHAT HAPPENS** *in the* BRAIN?

45.2.1 What Types of Memories Do We Store in Long-Term Memory?

Various kinds of information are stored in long-term memory, as shown in **Figure 45-1**. We will describe many of them here and a few more in later parts of this part (in the submodule on priming, for example). It is possible that different types of memory have evolved over time as different ways of specializing our memory function to optimize survival (Sherry & Schacter, 1987). Similarly, some species, like dogs, have a better memory for smell and others for sound as part of their adaptation to their particular living environments.

Explicit memories consist of the types of memories that you can consciously bring to mind, such as your mother's birthday, or the movie you watched last weekend, or the capital of Canada. But there are other types of memories that we are not consciously aware of, such as learned motor behaviours and perceptual information that help us to develop various skills and habits. These **implicit memories** are carried out without intentionality and involve something you cannot bring to conscious awareness. Examples might include typing on your computer's keyboard, tying your shoes, playing the piano, or remembering how to walk on stilts even though you have not tried this since you were a very young child.

Neuroimaging studies of patients with brain damage suggest that these two kinds of information are stored in different brain regions (Mecklinger, Brunnemann, & Kipp, 2011; Squire & Schacter, 2002). Explicit memories are converted into long-term memories in the hippocampus and then are stored permanently in various areas of the neocortex. In a sense, the hippocampus serves as a temporary storage site within the long-term explicit memory system (Yoon, Okada, Jung, & Kim 2008). In contrast, the striatum, the region located toward the midline in the brain, plays a key role in the storage of implicit memories (Rovee-Collier, Hayne, & Colombo, 2001). As we observed in Parts 3 and 7, when people need to call upon implicit memories to help them carry out various skills and habits, their striatum and its related structures become particularly active. In fact, an individual whose striatum is damaged by injury or disease may have enormous difficulty performing longtime skills and habits such as driving, yet retain most of her explicit memories.

To make things even more complicated, there are two types of explicit memories. Endel Tulving, a well-known Canadian psychologist from the University of Toronto, first distinguished between semantic and episodic memory (Tulving, 1972). **Semantic memories** include our general knowledge of such facts as 2 plus 3 equals 5. **Episodic memories** are the knowledge of personal episodes from your own life, such as when you first learned to swim or ride a bike, or when a good friend moved away. Some studies further hint that these two subgroups of explicit memories may, themselves, be stored in different ways from one another (Heisz et al., 2014; Christman & Propper, 2010; Markowitsch, Welzer, & Emmans, 2010).

45.2.2 How Are Our Long-Term Memories Organized?

How does the long-term memory system organize the many pieces of information that are stored there? Is it set up like a bookstore in which the various items are organized first by broad categories, such as fiction and non-fiction, then by subcategories (in the case

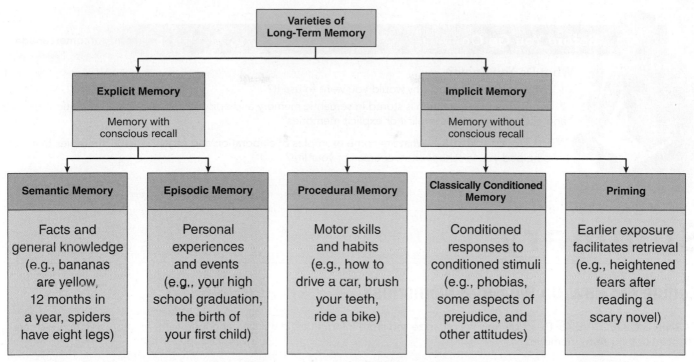

FIGURE 45-1 **The long-term memories we store.** Our long-term memories are of two main types, with various subdivisions within each.

of non-fiction, for example, "art," "health," "nature," "science," or "travel"), and finally by sub-subcategories (for example, art books whose authors' names begin with *A, B,* and so on)? Despite years of study, we do not fully understand how pieces of information are organized when stored in long-term memory.

At the same time, psychologists do now know that, regardless of their precise organization, the pieces of information stored in long-term memory are linked to each other, forming a network of interwoven associations. This web of associations enables us to travel rapidly through our long-term memory to retrieve much of the information we need for a current situation or task. As we saw earlier, the PDP, or connectionist, model of memory helps explain such networks by suggesting that our neurons also are activated in networks.

There are other quite different ways to think about memory. One such alternative is Canadian researchers Fergus Craik and Robert Lockhart's (1972) *Levels of Processing* model. This model suggests that rather than passing information through distinct types of memory (short- versus long-term), we process information to shallow or deeper depths.

©IStockphoto.com/stevecoleimages

Semantic versus episodic memories. Semantic memories include general knowledge and facts, whereas episodic memories include personal episodes from our life, such as when we learned to ride a bicycle.

Information can be superficially processed, such as the superficial attractiveness of a political candidate, or processed to greater depth, such as the stance the politician is taking on particular issues, or even further in terms of its symbolic significance, such as whether you see the politician as standing for "justice" or "equality" and so on. Information processed to greater depth is more likely to be recalled later. This means that when you are studying, you should read for understanding and for depth of understanding as this will ensure better recall of material on exams.

www.wiley.com/go/comercanada

Before You Go On

What Do You Know?

1. What is chunking, and why would you want to use it?

2. What kind of information is stored in semantic memory and episodic memory? Are semantic and episodic memories implicit or explicit memories?

What Do You Think? What are some examples of elaboration and organizational strategies that have helped you in school or other areas of your life?

Summary

Module 45: How Do We Store Memories?

LEARNING OBJECTIVE 45 Describe how we organize and store information in working and long-term memory and how we can enhance our long-term memories.

- The retention of information in memory is known as storage. Information can be stored in memory for anywhere from fractions of a second to a lifetime.
- Sensory memory is the equivalent of the small buffer on your computer, holding a very brief visual or auditory copy of information so you can decide whether or not to encode it into working or long-term memory. Sensory memory may also help maintain the continuity of your sensory input.
- Working memory is a short-term store of slightly more information that allows us to conduct simple calculations, such as memorizing a phone number so we can dial it immediately, or remembering the beginning of a sentence as we come to the end of the sentence.
- It appears that, without rehearsal, we can hold 7 ± 2 pieces of information in working memory, although we can expand that capacity through techniques, such as chunking.
- Long-term memory appears to be both infinite in capacity and storage time.
- Information taken from working memory into long-term memory appears to be organized according to its meaningfulness and relation to other concepts in long-term storage.
- Information in long-term memory may be stored in the form of explicit memories of facts or in implicit memories, knowledge about how to do something. A person cannot always articulate implicit knowledge.

Key Terms

chunking 341

episodic memory 342

explicit memory 342

implicit memory 342

memory span 340

semantic memory 342

Study Questions

Fill-in-the-Blank

1. Remembering a fact based on general knowledge requires _____ memory.

Module 46: How Do We Retrieve Memories?

LEARNING OBJECTIVE 46
Describe how we retrieve
information from memory and
how retrieval cues, priming,
context, and emotion can affect
retrieval.

As we have noted, when information is successfully encoded from working memory into long-term memory, it is not only stored there, but is available for retrieval later. When we retrieve information from our long-term memory, it becomes available once again for use in our working memory system. Upon its return to working memory, the retrieved information may be used to help clarify current issues, solve new problems, or simply re-experience past events (Baddeley, 2010; Kane et al., 2007; Hambrick & Engle, 2003). Retrieved memories of past NHL hockey games and current knowledge about player performance may, for example, help us to pick teams in a playoff hockey pool. Similarly, retrieved memories of learned math timetables help us calculate new mathematical problems, and retrieved memories of how to manoeuvre our car help us when parking in a tight space. The kind or amount of information stored in long-term memory would mean little if we were unable to retrieve it. Like a library or the Internet, the information in long-term memory must be navigated efficiently and accurately to produce needed information.

The serial position effect demonstrates two basic retrieval effects (Ebbinghaus, 1913). To demonstrate the components of the effect, read a list of 12 words to a group of people. When you get to the end of the list, ask each person to write down as many words as they can recall. As you can see in **Figure 46-1** there are two types of serial position effect. First, participants remember more of the words from the top third of the list. This is called the primacy effect, and it reflects the fact that as they were listening to the words being read, participants were able to do more working memory work (e.g., repeating the words over and over) on the words at the top of the list before other words came along and replaced them in short-term memory. Because of this, those words were more likely to be transferred to long-term memory and were better recalled by all participants. Participants also remember more of the words from the last third of the list. This is called the recency effect, and this effect reflects the fact that items at the end of the list are still in working memory and that there was less interference for the words at the end of the list.

Now redo the experiment with a different list and this time have half of the group immediately write down as many of the words as they can freely recall, while at the same time have the other half of the group count backwards from 1,000 by threes. After 30 to 40 seconds, allow the counting half of the group to stop counting and ask them to write down as many words as they can remember. Again, all participants will demonstrate a primacy effect. However, this time there will be a difference between the two groups in terms of the recency effect. Those who got to recall words immediately will likely recall more of the words in the bottom third of the list than will those people who had to count backwards for a time following the end of the word list. The non-counters will do better because the words from the bottom of the list are still in short-term memory when the reading ends. Consequently they can, and usually do, write those words down right away, sensing that they might forget them if they wait. The counting group will recall fewer of the last words on the list as they had their working memory engaged in the counting task. By the time they got to start writing down words, the ones from the end of the list were not processed into long-term memory, had faded from short-term memory, and were no longer available for recall (Ebbinghaus, 1913).

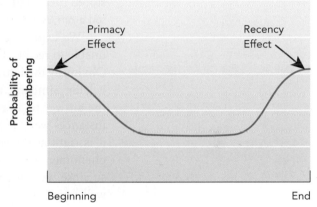

Position of the item in the list

FIGURE 46-1 **Serial position effect.** The results of a recall task plotted in the form of a curve yield this classic pattern. That is, the position of a word on a list influences how likely it is that the word will be remembered. Those words in the top third of the list (primacy effect) and the last third of the list (recency effect) are most likely to be recalled.

Source: Reprinted with permission of John Wiley & Sons, Inc., from Huffman, K. (2015). *Psychology in Action*, 11th edition. Hoboken, NJ: Wiley, p. 229.

©iStockphoto.com/Rich Legg

Recalling the past. Looking at old family photos with grandparents is a good way for her to retrieve information about family events from previous generations. The photos can serve as retrieval cues for accessing particular episodic memories.

Just as researchers do not fully understand how information is organized when stored in long-term memory, they also do not know for sure how retrieval is carried out. Some theorists propose that it is a kind of "search" process (Raaijmakers & Shiffrin, 2002, 1992). In other words, the person focuses on a specific question and scans her memory for the specific answer to that question. Other theorists believe that retrieval is more like an "activation" process in which the questions people pose to themselves activate relevant pieces of information that have been stored in long-term memory, after which this activation then spreads *simultaneously* to every other associated piece of information. The difference between these two operations is akin to the difference between the results you get to a specific question on a Wikipedia search versus the hundreds of sometimes quite diverse results you get from a Google search. Other researchers suggest that attention plays not only an important role in encoding, but is also important for retrieval (Dudukovic et al., 2009).

If we fail to locate a particular book in a library or bookstore, it can mean either that the book is not there or that we are looking for it in the wrong section. Similarly, our failure to locate a piece of information in our long-term memory may mean that it is not stored there (indicating either encoding failure or storage loss), or that we have committed a *retrieval failure* of some kind.

We experience many retrieval failures in our daily lives. Often we find ourselves unable to recall a face, an event, or a scheduled appointment, yet it comes to mind later. Obviously the information was available in our memory all along, or we would not recall it later. Similarly, all of us have experienced the frustration of being unable to recall the answer to an exam question, only to remember it soon after the test. And in some instances we may become particularly frustrated when a piece of information feels like it is right at the edge of our consciousness, an experience called the *tip-of-the-tongue* phenomenon. In this situation, we feel like the information—the memory—we need is so close we can almost taste it. For example, when attempting to recall the name of a well-known Canadian actor, we might recall that he was one of three parade marshals for the 2014 Calgary Stampede, that he was in the television program *Boston Legal*, that he hosted a reality-based television series called *Rescue 911*, that he was born in Montreal, and that he was Captain James T. Kirk in the original *Star Trek* series. We might even remember that his last name starts with an "S," but we cannot think of his *name* (William Shatner)! Whether recall of the information we need is blocked by other information or was not originally learned quite as well as we might have wanted, we can often recover the information if we back up and think a bit about the context of the memory. For example, we often give up trying to remember and just as we begin to Google the answer, it comes to us. So, in an exam setting, think of the part, module, or lecture the information comes from, and then relax—that is often enough to get past the tip-of-the-tongue problem; sometimes the harder you try, the more the information you want eludes you (Brown, 1991).

retrieval cues words, sights, or other stimuli that remind us of the information we need to retrieve from our memory.

The retrieval of information from memory is facilitated by **retrieval cues**—words, sights, or other stimuli that remind us of the information we need (what it related to or where we learned it originally, for example). Essentially, when we come across a retrieval cue, we enter our long-term memory system and activate a relevant piece of information. Because the pieces of information in this memory system are linked to each other in a network of associations, the activation of the first piece of information will trigger the activation of related pieces until a complete memory emerges (Reas, 2014).

46.1 Priming and Retrieval

priming activation of one piece of information, which in turns leads to activation of another piece, and ultimately to the retrieval of a specific memory.

If the pieces of information stored in long-term memory are indeed linked together in a network of associations, then the key to retrieving a specific memory is to locate one piece of information and follow associated pieces until arriving at the memory. This activation of one piece of information, which then triggers the activation of other pieces and leads to the retrieval of a specific memory, is called **priming** (Was, 2010; Ramponi et al., 2007).

Sometimes we consciously try to prime a memory. If, for example, we are having trouble remembering the name of an acquaintance whom we met last week, we may bring the letter *M* to mind, recalling vaguely that her name began with that letter and hoping that the *M* sound will lead to her name. Or we may try to recall our previous conversation with her, hoping that this recollection will eventually lead us back to her name.

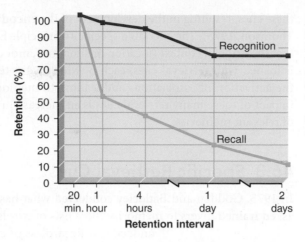

FIGURE 46-2 **Recognition versus recall.** In one study of retrieval, participants were tested for either recognition or recall of nonsense syllables over the course of two days. Retrieval on the recognition test was far superior than on the recall test.

(Source: Schwanenflugel et al., 1992; Luh, 1922)

Priming may also take place without our conscious awareness. Say you are in a store and you vaguely notice the k.d. lang version of Leonard Cohen's song "Hallelujah" is playing on the store's sound system. If you were to walk out of the store and a friend were to ask you what song had just been playing on the store's speaker, you might not be able to recall it. However, if a short while later, in an unlikely turn of events, you find yourself in the *Cash Cab* (a TV show set in a real Toronto cab where the driver asks you questions and you can win money on your way to your destination; *Taxi Payant* in Quebec), and were asked to name three classic Canadian hit songs for $500, research suggests that you would be particularly likely to include "Hallelujah" in your answer. Although you had no choice in the matter and were not even aware that it was happening—and even if you dislike k.d. lang's voice or Leonard Cohen's music and were trying to ignore the song while in the store—it would have served as a retrieval cue and primed you to recall "Hallelujah" when later quizzed about classic Canadian hits.

Given the operation of priming, we should not be surprised that the more retrieval cues we encounter, or the more informative they are, the better our retrieval of memory. This is why people perform better on **recognition tasks**, ones in which they must report whether or not they have seen a particular item before, than on **recall tasks**, those in which they are forced to produce memories using no or few retrieval cues (**Figure 46-2**) (Wixted & Squire, 2010; Tulving, 1974).

recognition tasks memory tasks in which people are asked to identify whether or not they have seen a particular item before.

recall tasks memory tasks in which people are asked to produce information using no or few retrieval cues.

context the original location where you first learned a concept or idea, rich with retrieval cues that will make it more likely you will be able to recall that information later if you are in that same location or context.

46.2 Context and Retrieval

It is often easier to retrieve particular information when we return to the setting or situation in which we first encoded it. Most of us have had personal experiences that attest to this. Upon returning to an old home or school, for example, we may find ourselves almost swamped by memories of events that we have not thought about for years. Similarly, a return to the scene of an argument or romantic encounter may evoke detailed memories of the original event. Not surprisingly, some educators believe that people perform best on exams when the exams are administered in the same rooms where the material was taught (Postle, 2003).

Clearly, returning to or duplicating the **context** in which information was learned may help us to retrieve it (Postle, 2003). Why? Once again, the answer appears to be retrieval cues. Classic research by Canadian Endel Tulving provided evidence of

John Berry/Getty Images

"Oh, yes, I remember them well." If asked to name several members of the Canadian men's 2014 Olympic hockey team (a recall task), even ardent hockey fans might have some difficulty. If, however, fans were shown this team photo (a recognition task), many fans would readily come up with such names as Sidney Crosby, P.K. Subban, Carey Price, Jonathan Toews, and Chris Kunitz.

encoding specificity principle
a theoretical framework that asserts that memory retrieval is more efficient when the information available at retrieval is similar to the information available at the time of encoding.

these cues, resulting in the development of the **encoding specificity principle** (Tulving & Thomson, 1973). The encoding specificity principle is a theoretical framework that argues that the original context (location or situation), mood, or state in which we learn material is loaded with retrieval cues, each of which activates a piece of information, triggering the activation of associations and leading to memories of the original event. The likely impact of these many retrieval cues is an increase in the number, intensity, and accuracy of relevant memories.

46.3 Specific Retrieval Cues

In 1975, Godden and Baddeley conducted what has become a classic experiment. They asked trained divers to memorize three lists of words on land or 20 feet (about 6 metres) underwater. Regardless of context for learning of the lists, participants then wrote down a list of 15 digits and then waited for four minutes before being asked to retrieve the words they could recall. Twenty-four hours later, the participants were asked to once again recall the words—either in the same context they learned them or in a different context. The results indicated that lists learned underwater were best recalled underwater, and that lists learned on land were best retrieved on land. These results clearly demonstrate the role of context in learning: this is often referred to as the *context-effect*. You may have experienced something like this. You go downstairs to get an item, but once you get there you forget what you went to get. Frustrated, you go back upstairs—only to recall the item as soon as you are back in the familiar context.

It is not always possible to return to the original site of our learning. In such cases, we can mentally revisit the context. If, in an exam, you are unable to remember something you learned in a class, try imagining the classroom to hear in your mind the professor's voice teaching you the information.

state-dependent memory memory retrieval facilitated by being in the same state of mind in which you encoded the memory in the first place.

It has also been demonstrated that retrieving memories is most effective when in the same state of consciousness as when the memory was formed (Roediger & Craik, 2014). Alcohol-related **state-dependent memory** has been empirically shown to exist in humans. Anecdotally, it has been observed that alcoholics may hide money or bottles while drinking, but cannot recall the hiding place while sober. However, once intoxicated they easily recall where they hid the objects. Such anecdotal evidence has now been empirically demonstrated in the laboratory using lists. Here individuals are better able to recall words in the same state (that is, sober or intoxicated) as they learned them (Eich, 2014). This suggests that if you are drinking coffee while studying, you should ensure that you have an equal amount of caffeine in your system when writing the exam.

©iStockphoto.com/PeopleImages

State-dependent memory.
Research indicates that individuals have better recall of information in the same state (that is, sober or intoxicated) they were in when they learned them. This suggests, for example, that if you are drinking coffee while studying, you should ensure that you have the same amount of caffeine in your system when writing the exam, so that you would be better able to recall the information you studied while drinking coffee.

Mood is also a powerful retrieval cue. In one study, participants learned a list of words while they were in a hypnotically-induced happy state of mind. Participants were found to remember the words better if they were tested later when in a happy mood rather than if they were in a sad mood (Bower, 2008, 1981; Forgas, 2008). Similarly, those who learned the words when in a sad mood recalled words better if they were tested later while sad, rather than if they were happy. Leffler and colleagues (2013) assessed mood-congruent memory and arousal levels in daily life and reported that low levels of arousal enhanced the recall of words associated with positive recall, whereas high levels of arousal enhanced the recall of words associated with negative recall.

Other theorists further believe that a person's emotions may be more than just another retrieval cue (McGaugh, 2006). As we shall see in the following submodules, they suggest that strong emotions may enhance memories by leading to increased *rehearsal, elaboration*, and *organization* of a particular event, or that intense emotions may trigger a *special memory mechanism*, producing emotional memories.

©iStockphoto.com/Aldo Murillo

Research has shown that humorous material is easier to retrieve than non-humourous material (Purzycki, 2010). Hideo Suzuki and Linda Heath (2014) have shown that the effect of humour also facilitates learning in the classroom. Their results indicated that the use of humorous video in conjunction with lectures enhanced recognition performance. However, this effect was only significant if the content in the video was relevant. There was no effect of humour on recall performance and no effect of humour if the material shown was irrelevant to the lecture material. The authors did not measure for retention of information; that is, although an immediate effect of humour on recognition was noted, it is not known whether this effect would help with subsequent retrieval. However, other research has indicated that humorous material is recalled more easily as many as six weeks after encoding (Kaplan & Pascoe, 1977). So, if your professor isn't making you laugh—think of some humorous examples of your own to help you remember and recall the material.

46.3.1 Emotional Memory: Rehearsal, Elaboration, and Organization

Research clearly shows that we remember emotionally arousing events better than neutral events (Christianson, 2014). If an event makes us particularly happy or distressed, we are better able to retrieve that information (Dolan, 2002). However, the mechanisms by which emotions influence memory are not well understood. Deborah Talmi and her colleagues at the University of Toronto (2013, 2012, 2007) argue that it is important to distinguish between the direct and deferred effects of emotion on memory. According to the *modulation hypothesis*, long-lasting emotional effects on memory can be attributed to the activation of the amygdala during the encoding of emotional events. However, this consolidation effect takes time, so it cannot account for the immediate effects of emotion on memory (Packard et al., 2013). Talmi and her colleagues suggest that the immediate effects of emotion on memory can be accounted for through the processes of attention, organization, and distinctiveness (2013; 2012; 2007).

As well, over time, emotionally-laden events are more likely to be rehearsed (McGaugh, 2006, 2003). That is, we are likely to talk about highly emotional events with friends and relatives, perhaps write about them in a personal journal, or we may even try to revisit the scene or recreate the context of the event. Such behaviours are displayed by people who have achieved a special personal accomplishment, observers of exciting sporting events, or victims of accidents, hurricanes, or other catastrophes. Together, responses of this kind amount to repeated rehearsal, elaboration, and organization of the emotionally-charged events. Think back to your grandfather's trip to the hospital with chest pain. Talking about the anxiety and fear experienced that day with relatives not only helped you to recall the event, but probably also helped you to link it to other important events in the family. We have seen already

©iStockphoto.com/Wavebreak

Emotional memory. We are likely to talk about a highly emotional event with friends or relatives. This response is a kind of repeated rehearsal, elaboration, and organization of the emotionally-charged event, and helps to improve the encoding, storage, and retrieval of the memory of the event.

that rehearsal, elaboration, and organization all are ways to improve the encoding and storage of memories; thus, we should not be surprised that exciting or upsetting events tend to be retrieved more readily than ordinary ones.

46.3.2 Special Emotional Memory Mechanisms: Flashbulb Memories

If we were asked where we were at 9:00 a.m. on Tuesday, May 2, 2006, what we were doing, and who we were talking to, few of us would be able to answer off the top of our heads. Yet, if people were asked the same questions about their whereabouts on Tuesday, September 11, 2001, at 9:00 a.m., the fateful hour when planes crashed into and brought down the twin towers of the World Trade Center (and part of the Pentagon), many people could state with apparent accuracy and remarkable confidence these and other details (Denver, Lane, & Cherry, 2010). Such detailed and powerful memories of emotionally significant events, or of the circumstances surrounding our learning of the events, are called **flashbulb memories**. Beyond widely-shared events, such as the 9/11 attacks, people also have flashbulb memories of emotional events that have more personal significance, such as the birth or death of a loved one.

flashbulb memories detailed and near-permanent memories of an emotionally-significant event, or of the circumstances surrounding the moment we learned about the event.

The kinds of details retained in flashbulb memories seem unavailable to us in our memories of other events (Edery-Halpern & Nachson, 2004). What is it about these special events that enable us to retrieve such details? According to some theorists, it is the extraordinary level of emotionality that we experience during the event. Specifically, our intense emotions may help trigger a special memory mechanism—a mechanism above and beyond the usual memory processes—that produces a near-permanent record and more likely retrieval of nearly everything we encountered during the event (McGaugh, 2006, 2003).

This proposed memory mechanism has yet to be fully identified, but certain studies do support the notion that emotionally-charged memories involve mechanisms beyond those operating for more neutral memories (LeDoux & Doyère, 2011; Kensinger & Corkin, 2003). In one study, for example, some participants were given a tranquilizer drug while hearing an emotional story about a boy who received emergency surgery, whereas other participants were given a placebo drug during the same story (Cahill et al., 1994). One week later, the participants who had been tranquilized—and due to the tranquilizer had experienced little emotionality during the intense story—remembered less about the story than did the placebo participants, whose emotions had been allowed to rise during the story. In contrast, when the study's participants were asked to recall a more neutral story, participants from both groups showed equal accuracy in their later recollections (**Figure 46-3**).

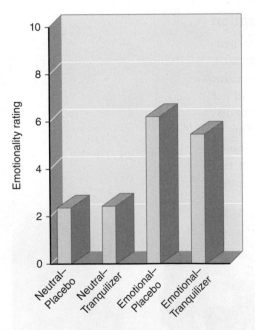

FIGURE 46-3 **Emotional arousal and memory.** In Cahill's study of emotion's role in memory, participants heard either an emotional or neutral story. Those given a tranquilizer while hearing the emotional story recalled less about the emotional story than those given the placebo. However, both groups recalled the same amount of information for the neutral story.

Source: Adapted from Cahill, L., Prins, B., Weber, M., & McGaugh, J. L. (1994). Beta-adrenergic activation and memory for emotional events. *Nature*, 371(6499), 702–704, (Fig. 2).

On the other hand, some recent research has called into question whether flashbulb memories are, in fact, as highly accurate as they have been purported to be (Marsh, 2007). One study, for example, compared undergraduates' memories of the 9/11 attacks with their memories of everyday events (Talarico & Rubin, 2009, 2007, 2003). Although the participants in the study reported a high level of confidence in the accuracy of their 9/11 memories, the data indicated that, in fact, such memories were no more accurate than those of more neutral events. For example, their recollection of who they were with when they learned of the 9/11 events as compared to when they experienced an everyday event were equally accurate, even though the participants themselves believed their memories of 9/11 were more vivid.

Sometimes we might wish we could forget dramatic events because they cause us too much pain. Some exciting work by Karim Nader at McGill University suggests that this might be possible. In the past, we have assumed that our long-term memories are consolidated and thus hard to forget. Nader's work suggests that by recalling and speaking about a traumatic event, we may actually

Psychology Around Us | Messing with Memory

Some students experience severe test anxiety. They may prepare fully for an examination, retain all of the necessary information, and score high on practice tests. Yet, on the day of the examination, they experience feelings of anxiety that grow from butterflies in their stomach due to a consuming fear that they will "not do well on the exam . . . not pass the course . . . perhaps not even complete university." Their anxiety grows so out of control as the test sits in front of them that they are unable to retrieve many of the answers that had been so available to them during practice tests the evening before. Many counsellors who work with such individuals suggest that the negative thoughts accompanying their anxiety (for example, "I will not pass this course") interfere with the retrieval of memories and cause the students to forget (Hambree, 1988). Research by Daeun Park, Gerardo Ramirez, and Sian Beilock (2014) suggests that writing meaningfully about your anxieties just prior to the exam will improve performance on the exam. Their results indicated that highly anxious math students improved test performance through just this type of expressive writing task.

Chip Somodevilla/Getty Images

Jeff Hutchens/Getty Images

Can you spell "anxiety"? Two children await their turn at the annual Scripps National Spelling Bee. Both are fully prepared, but their emotional states are another story. Who is likely to perform better?

reactivate the memory storage process and must reconsolidate the memory to re-store it. Working with mice, Nader has found that an injection with a protein synthesis inhibiter can actually remove the memory (Nader et al., 2013; Schwabe et al., 2013; Nader, 2003; Debiec et al., 2002).

Before You Go On

www.wiley.com/go/comercanada

What Do You Know?

1. If researchers show people several pictures of small rodents, then find that a lot of people include hamsters and mice when asked to name animals that make good pets, what has happened? Why did it happen?

2. Why do many educators believe it is helpful to take an exam in the same room where you learned the material?

3. How do strong emotions affect our memory processes?

What Do You Think? Have you experienced flashbulb memories or state-dependent memory? If so, when?

Summary

Module 46: How Do We Retrieve Memories?

LEARNING OBJECTIVE 46 Describe how we retrieve information from memory and how retrieval cues, priming, context, and emotion can affect retrieval.

- The access of information from memory is known as retrieval. Retrieval can be facilitated by retrieval cues that make memories easier to access.
- Retrieval cues can include priming, context, and enhancing meaningfulness of the memory by making them more personally or emotionally relevant.

Key Terms

context 347	flashbulb memories 350	recall tasks 347	retrieval cues 346
encoding specificity principle 348	priming 346	recognition tasks 347	state-dependent memory 348

Study Questions

Multiple Choice

1. Multiple choice test is to essay test as _____ is to _____.
   a) cueing; priming
   b) explicit memory; implicit memory
   c) recall; recognition
   d) recognition; recall

Fill-in-the-Blank

1. A stimulus reminding us of the information we need to retrieve from memory is termed a retrieval _____.

Module 47: Why Do We Forget and Misremember?

Throughout most of this part, we have considered which variables help us to accurately remember events and information. But people do not always remember things as well as they would like (Tsukiura et al., 2011). The elusive name, the missed meeting, and the overlooked birthday of a friend or relative are all instances of **forgetting**—the inability to recall information that was previously encoded. Sometimes we not only forget information, we distort or manufacture memories. We recall events differently from the way in which they occurred, or we remember things that never occurred at all.

47.1 Theories of Forgetting

As we have observed, some apparent losses of memory are not really instances of forgetting at all, but rather are failures of attention. If our mind is elsewhere when we are putting down a set of keys or a remote control, we simply cannot encode such acts. Correspondingly, the location of such items will not be stored in memory and available for later retrieval. At the other end of the spectrum, some material is indeed stored and available, but has weak or few retrieval cues attached to it, making it difficult for people to activate—or prime—the relevant memories in order to retrieve them from storage.

Beyond these common causes of forgetting, theorists have uncovered a number of variables that may actively interfere with memory and, in turn, produce forgetting (Macleod et al., 2010; Wixted, 2010, 2004). Each of today's leading explanations of forgetting has received some research support, but as you will see, each also has key limitations and raises significant questions.

47.1.1 Decay

German researcher Herman Ebbinghaus pioneered the study of forgetting over a century ago by systematically testing his own memory of lists of nonsense syllables (for example, *lin, wek, sul*). After rehearsing and mastering a particular list, Ebbinghaus would measure how well he had retained the syllables after various intervals of time: 20 minutes, two days, a month, and so on. He found that there was a huge drop in his retention of a list soon after learning it. However, the amount that he forgot eventually levelled off; in fact, most of the information that had been retained 10 hours after first memorizing a list remained in his memory three weeks later. Known as the *forgetting curve* (see **Figure 47-1**), this pattern of rapid memory loss followed by a stable retention of the remaining information has been supported again and again by research (Erdelyi, 2010).

Many theorists explain patterns of forgetting, such as that observed by Ebbinghaus, by pointing to *decay*. According to the **decay theory**, memories often fade away on their own simply because they are neglected or not used for a long period of time (Wixted, 2010, 2004; McGaugh, 2006, 2003). This theory is built on the notion that memories leave a physical trace in the brain—a so-called *memory trace*—when they are acquired. Theoretically, these traces fade away over time if the person does not use them.

Decay theory is a somewhat controversial theory of forgetting, although it still has proponents (Hardt et al., 2013). It cannot account for the repeated finding that people learn seemingly forgotten information or skills much more rapidly the second time around than the first time. In other words, *relearning* is faster than initial learning. If forgotten information has, in fact, eroded because of disuse—that is, if memory traces have been lost—relearning should be occurring from scratch, and it should take just as long as the initial learning did (Stone, Hunkin, & Hornby, 2001).

LEARNING OBJECTIVE 47
Summarize key theories of why we forget information and sometimes distort or manufacture memories.

forgetting the inability to recall information that was previously encoded into memory.

decay theory theory of forgetting, suggesting that memories fade over time due to neglect or failure to access over a long period of time.

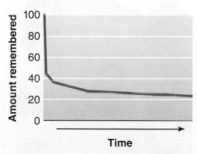

FIGURE 47-1 The forgetting curve. We forget a great deal very rapidly, but the forgetting levels off and the amount of information we retain stabilizes.

Source: Reprinted from Bahrick, Bahrick, and Wittlinger. (1974). "Those unforgettable high school days." *Psychology Today.*

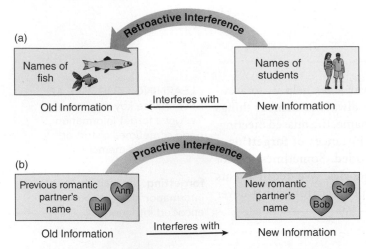

FIGURE 47-2 Retroactive and proactive interference. Forgetting is affected by interference from other information. (a) Retroactive (backward-acting) interference occurs when new information interferes with old information. For example, an ichthyology professor (fish specialist) may refuse to learn his students' names: "Every time I learn a student's name, I forget the name of a fish!" (b) Proactive (forward-acting) interference occurs when old information interferes with new information. For example, using an old romantic partner's name to refer to your new romantic partner.

Source: Reprinted with permission of John Wiley & Sons, Inc., from Huffman, K. (2015). *Psychology in Action*, 11th edition. Hoboken, NJ: Wiley, p. 228.

interference theory theory that forgetting is influenced by what happens to people before or after they take information in.

proactive interference competing information that is learned before the forgotten material, preventing its subsequent recall.

retroactive interference learning of new information that disrupts access to previously recalled information.

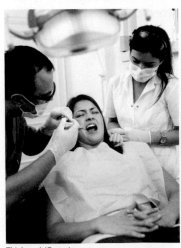

Thinkstock/Getty Images

Motivated forgetting. It does not take a lot of thought to figure out why people sometimes unconsciously forget their dental appointments.

47.1.2 Interference

According to the **interference theory**, forgetting is affected primarily by what happens to people before or after they learn information. This theory holds that information will be retained in memory as long as competing, similar information does not interfere with it (Tillman et al., 2011; Wixted, 2010, 2004). Suppose your brother's long-term relationship ends and he starts a new relationship. Even though you like the new partner very much, you constantly find yourself referring to the new partner by the old partner's name. According to the interference theory, you forgot the new partner's name because competing information—the old partner's name—interfered with the retrieval of the new partner's name.

When the competing information that prevents recall has been learned *before* the forgotten item, as in the case of the forgotten name, the process is called **proactive interference**. Alternatively, **retroactive interference** occurs when new information disrupts the retrieval of previously learned information (see **Figure 47-2**). Suppose, for example, that you need to set up a new password for computer access at work. However, shortly after setting up the new password you need to access old files from the server and the IT person asks you for your old password. You can't remember it. In this scenario, you forgot the old password because competing information—your new password—interfered with the retrieval of the old password.

We should keep in mind that old information does not always interfere with the learning or remembering of new information. Sometimes it can even help us learn and retain new information. For example, people who know how to roller skate often pick up ice skating faster than other people. Speakers of French may have an easier time learning to speak Spanish given their similar verb structures. Interference occurs only when old and new information conflict with one another.

We have observed how emotions—both positive and negative—often enhance memory by providing powerful retrieval cues, setting up additional rounds of rehearsal, or triggering special memory mechanisms. At the same time, most of us have had experiences in which negative emotions, such as anxiety, actually interfere with memory and cause us to forget (Hawley, Grissom, & Dohanich, 2011; Eysenck et al., 2010; McGaugh, 2006, 2003).

47.1.3 Motivated Forgetting

Sometimes we forget information that is unpleasant, embarrassing, or painful (Erdelyi, 2010; Mather, 2009; Kennedy, Mather, & Carstensen, 2004). Suppose, for example, that during your first year at college or university, you completely bungle a conversation with a classmate on whom you have a crush. Humiliated, you give up all hopes of pursuing the relationship, and by the end of the semester, the two of you are hardly acknowledging each other. Fast-forward three years. By now, you have become much more suave, and, as it turns out, you and your former crush meet again at a graduation party. As the two of you laugh together, talk comfortably, and discover shared values, you wonder aloud how it is that you never got together during your four years at school. Taken aback by your comment, your new friend recalls for you the first-year bungling incident. You are shocked by this revelation. On reflection, you recall vaguely that a discussion took place three years ago, but for the life of you, you have no recollection of the stammering, falling, and other embarrassing moves you made. In fact, you do not even recall having been all that interested in this person in the first place.

Clearly, you have forgotten an incident and related information that was unpleasant. But why? One possibility is that because the event was so painful, you actively worked to forget it. You avoided opportunities for rehearsal, such as sharing the humiliating experience with friends or relatives or writing about it in your personal journal. You may have even avoided retrieval cues, such as the walkway where the embarrassing interaction occurred. In short, you avoided rehearsing, elaborating, or organizing the information, making it less available for later retrieval from memory. We also sometimes forget upcoming events that we find distasteful. For example, many people forget dental appointments (Skaret et al., 2000). Why do you think that might be?

Of course, anyone who has *actively* tried to forget an upsetting event knows that this is not so easy to do. Even if we do not share the event with others, we often find ourselves thinking about it (that is, privately rehearsing the event) again and again. Moreover, like a flashbulb memory, the emotional component of such an event often increases, rather than decreases, the likelihood of our remembering it.

Why then do we seem to forget certain unpleasant events or information? Sigmund Freud explained motivated forgetting through his theory of **repression**. Freud held that all people employ repression on occasion, a process in which we unconsciously prevent some traumatic events from entering our awareness so that we do not have to experience anxiety or blows to our self-concept that the memories would bring. According to Freud, the repressed material is not lost, but rather *hidden* from consciousness. He believed that our experiences, especially childhood experiences, are too powerful to slip away altogether. In fact, the hidden material may influence later decisions or interpretations of events, although we are not aware of its impact in such cases. It is important to recognize that research has failed to demonstrate consistently that people repress unpleasant events (Erdelyi, 2010; Kihlström, 2006). In fact, as we address below, Elizabeth Loftus and others have argued that forgetting has nothing to do with repression (Garry & Hayne, 2013; George, 2013).

repression process in which we unconsciously prevent some traumatic events from entering our awareness so that we do not have to experience the anxiety or blows to our self-concept that the memories would bring.

47.2 Distorted or Manufactured Memories

Our memories can be subject to distortions. In large part, this is because, as we observed earlier, we tend to rely on semantic codes when we encode information into long-term memory. That is, we encode the *meaning* of an event, rather than its specific words or images. In turn, when we later retrieve the memory, we have to *reconstruct* it. We must fill in details from our earlier recollection. Thus, when five persons later try to remember the same event—for example, when several family members recall your grandfather being taken to hospital with chest pain at a family gathering—each person may recall the details of the event quite differently.

A number of factors may contribute to faulty reconstructions of memory—that is, to the distortion or manufacture of memories. Three of the most common are *source misattributions, exposure to misinformation*, and the *effects of imagination* (see **Table 47-1**).

Chuck Burton/AP

A terrible error. A woman talks to the man whom she had previously identified as her rapist. Her memory was eventually proved wrong by DNA evidence—after he had served 11 years of a life sentence in prison! Mistaken eyewitness memories and testimony are responsible for most wrongful convictions.

TABLE 47-1 Common Reasons Why We Distort or Manufacture Memories	
Source misattributions	We often fail to record where the information came from when we encode and store the information in long-term memory
Exposure to misinformation	New information that is inaccurate or misleading can distort our recall or lead us to manufacture new memories
Effects of imagination	Our own imagination can lead us to recall events that never took place

47.2.1 Source Misattributions

When we encode and store information in long-term memory, we often fail to record where it came from originally. In a similar manner, we often forget or are confused about where we have gathered information that is now stored in our long-term memory system. Such **source misattributions** can render our memories of certain events distorted, or in some cases, manufactured (Baym & Gonsalves, 2010; Loftus, 2005; Lindsay et al., 2004). Is your detailed recollection of getting lost at the mall when you were 4 years old a direct memory of that event? Or, are you actually remembering your parents' many stories about the event? Or are you confusing your own life with that of a cousin whose similar experience was often discussed in your family? We may have supreme confidence in our memory of the event and even "remember" vivid details about it, yet the memory may be inaccurate or even entirely false. We are remembering something, but it may not be the event itself (Ceci et al., 1994).

source misattribution remembering information, but not the source it came from; can lead to remembering information from unreliable sources as true.

47.2.2 Exposure to Misinformation

Earlier we noted that retroactive interference often causes us to forget something when we are later exposed to new competing information. Similarly, such exposure to new information, particularly misinformation, can also lead to the distortion or the manufacture of false memories (Morgan et al., 2013; Wixted, 2010, 2004).

Confident eyewitnesses are just as likely to be wrong as less-confident eyewitnesses (Gruneberg & Sykes, 1993).

Consider a situation in which a man witnesses a mugging. If a week later the eyewitness is asked, "Could you please describe the mugger," he is being called upon to rely exclusively on his memory for a description. If, however, the eyewitness is told in passing, as part of the questioning process, "We've had a number of similar muggings lately, involving a heavy, blond-haired guy with a beard," this new information may greatly influence the witness's recall of the mugger and the mugging incident. Such exposures to new information—often misinformation—are of great concern in police cases. Many a defendant has been accused or even convicted of a crime based on testimony from witnesses whose memories were unintentionally distorted or manufactured (Devenport et al., 2009; Wells & Loftus, 2003). (See "Tying It Together: Your Brain and Behaviour" at the end of the part for more information.)

The impact of misinformation on memory has received considerable study in psychology laboratories. How do researchers "plant" misinformation in memory studies? A clever investigation by psychologist Elizabeth Loftus and her colleagues (1978) illustrates how this is done. Participants in her study observed a film of a traffic accident and were then asked to remember certain details of the accident. One group of subjects was asked, "How fast were the cars going when they *smashed* into each other?" A second group was asked, "How fast were the cars going when they *hit* each other?" The experimenter's use of the word *smash* implies a very severe accident, whereas the word *hit* implies a milder accident. Not surprisingly, people who heard *smash* remembered the cars going at a faster speed than did those who heard *hit*. The researchers also asked, "Did you see any broken glass?" Those who heard *smash* were much more likely to say yes than those who heard *hit*. In fact, there was no broken glass in the film.

Mistaken eyewitness testimony is the primary cause of the conviction of innocent people (Wells et al., 1998).

Study after study has demonstrated the distorting effects of misinformation on memory. In each, participants first observe an event and later receive new, misleading information about the event from researchers (Zhu et al., 2010; Loftus, 2005). A short while after observing an uneventful interaction between two spouses, for example, participants in a study may be told, in passing, that one of the spouses is a rather hostile person, or amorous, or devious. Sure enough, in their later recollections of the observed interaction, many participants "remember" hostile, amorous, or devious acts by the spouse in question. Similarly, people have been induced, by subsequent exposures to misinformation, to "remember" objects—glasses, paintings, revolvers—that were not actually present in an observed event.

A particularly powerful way of being exposed to misinformation is through *hypnosis*. As we first saw in Part 6, people who are hypnotized enter a sleeplike state in which they become very suggestible. While in this state, they can be led to behave, perceive, and think in ways that would ordinarily seem impossible. They may, for example, become temporarily blind, deaf, or insensitive to pain. Hypnosis can also help people remember events that occurred and were forgotten years ago, a capability used by many psychotherapists. On the other hand, in recent years, it has come to the attention of researchers that hypnosis can also make people forget, distort, or manufacture memories by supplying misinformation (Erdelyi, 2010; Mazzoni, Heap, & Scoboria, 2010; Barnier et al., 2004). Witnesses who are hypnotized to help them remember an observed crime are, in fact, likely to remember details offered or implied by the hypnotist. These details, such as the time of the crime, the clothes worn by the perpetrator, or the presence of a weapon, may be inconsistent with their actual observations. For this reason, police hypnotists must be extraordinarily careful when questioning witnesses. Other research suggests that some hypnotic techniques, such as focused mediation with eye-closure technique, continue to be useful in investigative interviewing (Wagstaff et al., 2011). Even so, in 2001, the Supreme Court of Canada ruled that eyewitness recollections that were gathered under hypnosis could no longer be admitted as evidence due their lack of reliability and the risk of wrongful convictions (as cited by Roach, 2012).

47.2.3 The Effect of Imagination

It turns out that our memories can be distorted not only by misinformation supplied by others, but also by false information that comes from within, from our imaginations. Researchers have found repeatedly that when people are instructed to imagine the occurrence of certain events, many come to believe that they have in fact experienced the events (Richardson, 2011; Thomas et al., 2007).

In one study, a team of researchers asked the parents of university students to list events that had, in fact, occurred during the students' childhoods (Hyman & Kleinknecht, 1999). In later interviews, the students themselves were instructed to recall those real events, along with another event that had not actually occurred according to the parents' reports. The students were not told that this event was false. A student might, for example, be instructed to recall the false event of accidentally knocking over a table at a wedding, as well as a number of events that actually had occurred. When interviewed some days later, about one-fourth of the students fully believed that the false events had occurred during their childhood, and, in fact, they could "remember" many details of the unfortunate experiences. Clearly, misinformation from others or from our own imaginations, or from a combination of the two, can greatly influence our recollections, leading at times to forgetting, distortions, or even the manufacture of memories.

Oscar Sosa/AP

Hypnosis and memory. A police hypnotist uses the procedure to help a woman remember details of a crime that she witnessed. In fact, hypnosis often causes people to distort or manufacture memories, rather than rediscover them.

Before You Go On

What Do You Know?

1. How does the decay theory explain forgetting?
2. What is repression?
3. A late night TV show host suggests that supporters of one political party have more meaningful lives than members of the others. Although this person is obviously unqualified to know, your friends have started to tell you it's proven that members of this party make a difference, so they're thinking of switching parties. What might be happening to your friends' memories?
4. The saying, "Elementary, my dear Watson," did not appear in any of the writings of Sir Arthur Conan Doyle, the author of the Sherlock Holmes series, yet millions of fans vividly remember reading these words. What processes can explain this manufactured memory?

What Do You Think? What examples of proactive and retroactive interference or memory distortions have you experienced in your own life?

Summary

Module 47: Why Do We Forget and Misremember?

LEARNING OBJECTIVE 47 Summarize key theories of why we forget information and sometimes distort or manufacture memories.

- Forgetting is the inability to recall information that has previously been encoded.
- Initially, researchers believed that failure to access information regularly led to its loss from awareness, a theory known as decay theory. This theory is less popular now, and researchers instead emphasize other problems with remembering.
- Interference theory suggests that information gets in the way of proper encoding of information, preventing it from being remembered later. Retroactive interference comes from new information that interferes with previous memories. Proactive interference comes from earlier memories that interfere with new ones.
- Motivated forgetting hypothesizes that we try to purposely forget information that is unpleasant, embarrassing, or painful.
- In addition to being forgotten, memories can also be distorted or manufactured. We can make source misattributions, where we forget where information came from. We can also be exposed to new information that distorts previous information (as described in interference theory). Also, our own imaginations can play a role in distorting how our memories play out.

Key Terms

decay theory 353
forgetting 353

interference theory 354
proactive interference 354

repression 355
retroactive interference 354

source misattribution 356

Study Questions

Multiple Choice

1. What does the forgetting curve discovered by Ebbinghaus tell us about the way we forget material over time?
   a) At first, we forget very little of what we have learned, but as time passes, the rate of forgetting accelerates.
   b) Most forgetting happens immediately after we learn material; the rate of forgetting slows down as time goes by.
   c) We forget information at a constant rate as time passes.
   d) We forget information at a variable and unpredictable rate as time passes.

2. The need to reconstruct rather than simply retrieve memories stems from the _____ code used in long-term memory.

a) orthographic
b) phonological
c) semantic
d) visual

Fill-in-the-Blank

1. In _____ interference, information learned earlier disrupts the recall of information learned more recently; in _____ interference, recently learned information disrupts the recall of information learned earlier.

Module 48: Memory and the Brain

Much of what we know about the biology of memory has come from studies of people who have suffered injuries to specific locations of the brain (Alessio et al., 2006, 2004). Important information has also been gained through experiments in which researchers surgically or chemically change the brains of animals and then observe the effects on old memories and new learning (Schwarting, 2003). In addition, over the past decade, studies using brain scans have enabled investigators to observe brain activity and structure at the very moment that people are thinking and remembering. Finally, molecular biology studies have shed light on specific changes that may occur in our brain cells as memories form (Sweatt, 2010).

48.1 What Is the Anatomy of Memory?

Memories are difficult to locate. In the 1920s, neurological researcher Karl Lashley (1948) undertook a series of experiments with rats, in search of the specific places in the brain where memories are stored. He trained a group of rats to run through a maze, then cut out a different section of each rat's brain tissue and, following surgical recovery, set the rats loose in the maze again, checking to see whether they still remembered how to navigate through the maze. He found that all rats retained at least some memory of the maze, no matter what part of the brain he removed.

WHAT HAPPENS *in the* **BRAIN?**

Based on studies such as this, researchers have concluded that there is no specific place—no storehouse—in the brain where memories reside (Dudai, 2011), and that information in the brain is encoded across various neurons throughout the brain. As we have seen, for example, connectionist theorists see memory as a *process* rather than a place, an activity that involves changes in networks of multiple neurons throughout the brain. This conclusion that there is no single place in the brain where memories reside is similar to the Part 7 conclusion that a single learning centre in the brain does not exist. Indeed, because memory and learning go hand in hand, you'll see that several of the brain structures and activities discussed in Part 7 to account for learning are also involved here as we examine the neuroscience of memory.

Although today's theorists believe that networks of neurons located throughout the brain are involved in memory, research has clarified that some brain areas are particularly important in the formation and retrieval of memories. Among the most important structures in working memory, for example, is the **prefrontal cortex**, a key structure within the neocortex (Öztekin et al., 2009; Wang, 2005). When animals or humans acquire new information, the prefrontal cortex becomes more active (Chein, Moore, & Conway, 2011; Lian et al., 2002), holding information temporarily and working with the information as long as it is needed. To refer back to our analogy between the brain and a computer, the neurons in the prefrontal cortex seem to operate like a computer's random access memory (RAM), drawing information from various parts of the brain and holding it temporarily for use in a task, yet able to switch whenever necessary to other information and tasks.

prefrontal cortex important brain structure located just behind the forehead and implicated in working memory.

Among the most important structures in long-term memory are the *hippocampus* (see **Figure 48-1**) and other parts of the neocortex (Tsukiura et al., 2011). In our earlier discussion of explicit memories, we noted that the hippocampus converts such memories into long-term status, stores the memories temporarily, and then sends them on to various areas of the neocortex for genuine long-term storage. Destruction of the hippocampus in adulthood does not wipe out long-term memories, only those that occurred just prior to the brain damage (Jeneson et al., 2010; Wixted & Squire, 2010). In contrast, destruction of certain parts of the neocortex results in the loss of older memories. These findings suggest that the hippocampus is indeed an important temporary storage site for long-term memories and a key player in the transfer of such memories into genuine long-term status in the neocortex. However, recent research from Morris Moscovitch, at the Rotman Research Institute at the University of Toronto,

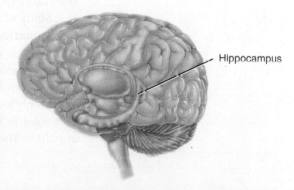

Hippocampus

FIGURE 48-1 A key to memory. The hippocampus is a crucial structure for memory. It is activated when people recall information about facts and events.

suggests that the hippocampus may also play an important role in retaining and retrieving autobiographical memories, as well as information about spatial layout (Moscovitch, 2014; Rosenbaum et al., 2014).

48.2 What Is the Biochemistry of Memory?

As we discussed earlier in this part, the PDP, or connectionist, model of memory describes the storage of information in long-term memory as a *network* of associations (McClelland, 2011). When we activate one piece of information, related ones spring into action, enabling us to travel rapidly through our long-term memory system and retrieve particular memories. But how, in fact, does the brain manage to link such pieces of information to each other? Research increasingly points to biochemical and electrical changes in certain neurons, particularly those neurons located in the key brain regions that we have just noted.

48.2.1 Neural Circuits

As we observed in Part 3, communication throughout the brain proceeds from neuron to neuron in a particular way. A given message arrives at a neuron as an impulse, travels down the axon of the neuron, and is then carried by a chemical—a *neurotransmitter*—across the synaptic space to another neuron. The next neuron is then triggered and, like the preceding neuron, passes along a message to yet another neuron, and so on. When we talk about certain pieces of information being closely linked to other pieces of information in the long-term memory system, we are really saying that certain neurons in the brain become predisposed to trigger other neurons.

The question for memory researchers is how such neural circuits form (Changeux, 2011). How is it that some neurons become predisposed to trigger other neurons, enabling us to retrieve a given memory? It appears that the repeated stimulation of certain neurons greatly increases the likelihood that these neurons will respond to future stimulation of the same kind, a phenomenon called **long-term potentiation (LTP)** (Nicholl & Roche, 2013; Wixted, 2004). LTP affects not just single neurons, but also the networks of neurons that make up neural circuits. The effects of LTP can last quite a long time (hence the name *long-term* potentiation), long enough to be a key factor in the formation and retrieval of memories (Ballard et al., 2009). Think of many sleds ridden one after another down a snowy slope, creating a groove that later sledders can easily find. LTP seems to create a kind of pattern that helps memories form, so a person can more easily retrieve a memory later by following the well-worn path.

Researchers have gathered considerable evidence that LTP also plays a role in long-term memory (Nicholl & Roche, 2013). If experimental animals are given substances known to block the development of LTP, they have difficulty transferring information from their working memory into their long-term memory (Glaser et al., 2010; Sanberg et al., 2006; Lynch et al., 1991). Conversely, drugs that enhance the development of LTP seem to improve the acquisition of long-term memories. In one study, for example, rats that were given an LTP-enhancing drug learned and remembered a water maze better than rats that were not administered the drug (Vallejo et al., 2014).

Many of the neurons and neural circuits that use *glutamate* as their neurotransmitter are particularly likely to exhibit LTP. This is not surprising because, as you may recall from Part 3, glutamate is a very common neurotransmitter, present in about 90 percent of all excitatory synapses (Brannon et al., 2008; Meldrum, 2000). Glutamate is also a key neurotransmitter in the formation of memories. Moreover, neurons that exhibit LTP are commonly located in the hippocampus and neocortex, brain regions that play such important roles in the formation of long-term memories, as we have just observed (Glaser et al., 2010; Thompson, 2000). In one study, researchers administered cocaine to rats and

long-term potentiation (LTP) a phenomenon where repeated stimulation of certain nerve cells in the brain greatly increases the likelihood that the cells will respond strongly to future stimulation.

reported long-lasting LTP under circumstances that generally result in early forms of LTP, indicating that learning and memory processes could be modulated through environmental manipulation (Fole et al., 2013).

For some time, researchers have also been aware of the important role of *acetylcholine* in learning and memory (Blockland, 1995; Winkler et al., 1995). Several important cholinergic (system related to acetylcholine) functions have been identified. First, acetylcholine probably plays a role in separating the encoding of new memories and the retrieval of existing memories so that each set of memories can be clearly segmented without interference (Hasselmo & Wyble, 1997). Second, acetylcholine is important for controlling the sleep/wake cycle, which in turn is important for the consolidation of long-term memories (Hasselmo, 1999), particularly declarative memories (facts and knowledge that can be consciously recalled) (Micheau & Marighetto, 2011; Power, 2004).

Before You Go On

www.wiley.com/go/comercanada

What Do You Know?

1. Which parts of the brain are most active in memory? How are these parts related to neurotransmitters involved in memory?

2. What is a neural network and how might long-term potentiation contribute to its formation?

What Do You Think? What side effects might occur if drugs were taken that could manipulate memory-related neurotransmitters and proteins? Should such drugs be legally available to anyone who wants them?

Summary

Module 48: Memory and the Brain

LEARNING OBJECTIVE 48 Describe how the brain is involved in memory.

- Because scientists have not been able to pinpoint the place where memories are stored in the brain, they have concluded that there is no single storehouse. Instead, memory appears to be a process, resulting from activation patterns throughout the brain.
- However, structures like the prefrontal cortex are extremely important in helping people hold information in working memory and to work with it as long as it is needed. Also, the hippocampus and other parts of the neocortex appear to be important in the transfer of memories into long-term memory.
- Memory itself appears to be a neural circuit, a network of neurons predisposed to trigger one another whenever one is activated. Through a phenomenon called long-term potentiation, repeated stimulation of certain nerve cells increases the likelihood that the neurons will respond strongly whenever stimulated.

Key Terms

long-term potentiation (LTP) 360

prefrontal cortex 359

Study Questions

Multiple Choice

1. How do the results of Lashley's research on maze memory among rats inform an evaluation of connectionist models of memory?
   a) They cast serious doubt on connectionist models of memory.
   b) They offer strong support for connectionist models of memory.
   c) They pose a challenge for connectionist models of memory.
   d) They say little with respect to connectionist models of memory.

2. Which statement best describes the role of the hippocampus in memory?
   a) The hippocampus helps encode procedural memories, but not semantic ones.
   b) The hippocampus is a "staging area" for the encoding of material into long-term memory and may store some autobiographical memories.
   c) The hippocampus is the final repository for long-term episodic and semantic memories.
   d) The hippocampus serves to transfer material from sensory to working memory in a process researchers call consolidation.

Fill-in-the-Blank

1. Adults with damage to the _____ typically find that their long-term memories are intact with the exception of memories formed just prior to the brain damage.

Module 49: Memories in the Young and Old

Young babies can remember what certain objects look like (even if they don't know what they are), and can discriminate between a new object and a familiar one. Researchers assess this type of memory by measuring the amount of time a baby spends looking at an object. Babies prefer to look at, and so focus longer on, objects that they haven't seen before. This task, called preferential looking, is a useful way to study memory in babies who are too young to speak or to perform complex motor tasks that might otherwise reveal what they remember. Based on such research, we now know that the ability to remember novel objects increases from several minutes in very young infants to several days in toddlers.

As babies gain control over their movements, they become able to learn new skills—skills that also require memory, although a different kind of memory. Memories of skills form during the first year of life as well. For example, 1-year-olds can remember how to stack blocks or to successfully play with toys that require specific movements, such as winding a crank handle to get the jack in the box to pop up. Once learned—even in very early life—this type of procedural knowledge is rarely forgotten. That is why, barring an accident, you will never forget how to tie your shoelaces or how to walk.

In short, babies and toddlers demonstrate memories—from memories of faces, places, and objects, to memories of skills and procedures. On the other hand, their specific memories of the *events* that occur in their lives are not very impressive. Prior to the age of 4 years, children do not hold onto memories of life events for very long. Correspondingly, most adults do not have any recollections of the events that occurred during their first 3½ to 4 years of life. This inability to remember events from the early years of life are often referred to as *infantile amnesia* (White & Pillemer, 2014).

Why is it that young children can remember factual information, like the names of animals, from one day to the next, and remember how to play games and perform often complex motor skills, but they cannot form a permanent memory of life events? The answer to this question is that brain regions holding different types of memories do not develop at the same rate. That is, the brain circuits responsible for storing memories of events seem to develop more slowly than the brain regions responsible for storing information about language, motor skills, and simple associations (Callahan & Richardson, 2014; Josselyn & Frankland, 2012).

As you learned in the previous module, in adults, memories about life events, often called *episodic memories*, are initially stored in the hippocampus (Chadwick et al., 2010). Only after temporary storage in the hippocampus is that information then distributed more widely throughout neocortical regions for long-term storage. We know that the hippocampus is a late-developing brain structure, and this late development might contribute to the inability to form episodic memories early on. Alternatively, it may not be a late-maturing hippocampus that is responsible for infantile amnesia, but rather the brain's early inability to transfer information out of the hippocampus to other locations in the neocortex (Rugg & Villberg, 2013).

Of course, if you spend any time with talkative 2-year-olds, you will notice they have a lot to say about what has been happening in their lives. They may tell you what a friend said at nursery school, that a sibling took their toy, or that they are expecting their mom to come home from work later in the day. This shows that young children are in fact *forming* memories of life events, but that the information is not being stored permanently. If you ask those same 2-year-olds a few months later about the same life events, unless the events have been repeated over and over, the children will not recall them.

Think back to your earliest memory of a childhood event. If the memory is accurate (and not a manufactured one), it probably has an emotional component. The emotionally-charged event that you remember may be positive, such as receiving a special birthday present, going on an exciting vacation, or experiencing the arrival of your younger brother or sister. Or the remembered event may be negative, such as travelling to the emergency

LEARNING OBJECTIVE 49
Describe the kinds of memories and memory changes that characterize early life and later life.

HOW WE DEVELOP

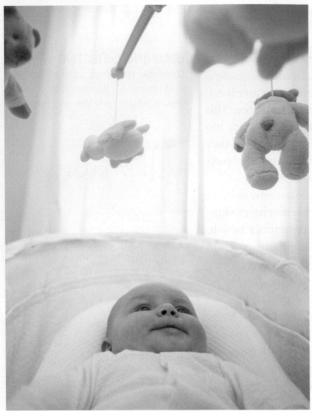

Aurelie and Morgan Da/Maxx Image

"Hey, what's that furry thing?" After being placed in his crib, this baby immediately stares at (and continues staring at) the mobile above him. Why? It has been newly added to his stimulating environment—the only object he has never seen before. An infant's interest in something novel (new) in his or her environment is known as "preferential looking."

©iStockphoto.com/toos

Emotions and early life memories. Most early life memories are emotion and may be positive or negative, such as the arrival of a new sibling.

prospective memory ability to remember content in the future.

retrospective memory ability to remember content from the past.

room after a fall off a scooter, being the victim of bullying in a pre-school class, or experiencing the arrival of your younger sibling (note this event can be experienced positively or negatively). It is unlikely that the earliest event you remember is a neutral one, particularly if it occurred before the age of 4 years. The fact that most early life memories are emotional suggests that the episodic memory system is helped along at early stages by brain regions that process emotional information, particularly the amygdala (LeDoux & Doyère, 2011).

Having looked at memory during the earliest years of life, let's take a look at memory during the later years. As we travel through middle adulthood and old age, we become more susceptible to forgetting, distortions, and misremembering (Klaasen et al., 2012). Studies suggest that in the normal course of aging, elderly people are likely to experience declines in their working memories, their ability to encode new memories, their episodic memories, certain types of short-term memory, and the sources of information that they remember (Berry et al., 2010; Hedden & Gabrieli, 2004; Nillson, 2003). Researchers also have found that older adults tend to remember positive information while ignoring the negative (Park & Reuter-Lorenz, 2009; Jacoby et al., 2005). On the other hand, the implicit (procedural) memories of aging people show little decline, several types of short-term memory remain strong throughout aging, and the semantic memories (general knowledge) of older people may actually improve (Backman & Nyberg, 2010; Fleischman et al., 2004; Verhaeghen, 2003).

An area of memory decline that is particularly upsetting for many aging people is in the operation of their **prospective memory**. A prospective memory involves remembering to perform a future intended action, as opposed to a **retrospective memory**, which involves the recall of past actions, events, or knowledge (Brandimonte et al., 2014; Baddeley et al., 2009). Prospective memories, or remembering to remember, help us to carry out our plans and effectively move through the day. They include, for example, remembering to pick up clothing at the cleaners, to call a family member, to send a birthday card, to take a prescribed medication at the right time, or to share a piece of information with a friend. Studies find that older people perform more poorly on prospective memory tasks than do younger adults, especially when the tasks become more demanding, distracting, or complex (Einstein & McDaniel, 2010, 2005, 1990). Declines in prospective memory can often be worked around by using strategies such as to-do lists.

Although the age-related changes in the way our memory functions are gradual, they actually begin in our twenties (Park & Reuter-Lorenz, 2009). Certain parts of the brain, such as the hippocampus, begin to shrink. A study of the brains of elderly individuals found that the hippocampus was about 20 percent larger in those with excellent memories than those suffering from Alzheimer's disease, a finding that also may have implications for the memory losses that accompany normal aging (Winningham, 2010; Erten-Lyons et al., 2009).

As the elderly population continues to grow, an increasing amount of research is focusing on how to improve memory and prevent, or at the very least, lessen the impairments mentioned above. Fergus Craik, another very well-known Canadian researcher, now an emeritus professor at the Rotman Research Institute in Toronto, has shown that procedural and perceptual memory is not particularly affected by aging, while working memory and episodic memory decline substantially in the course of normal aging (Craik & Salthouse, 2011; Luo & Craik, 2008). Brain fitness approaches—using computer exercises and various mental games to keep the mind "in shape"—have become very popular and are often recommended to elderly patients by health-care professionals. Although this approach has received support in a few studies (Hughes et al., 2014; Basak et al., 2008), many of today's researchers remain skeptical about whether brain puzzles and the like can in fact prevent memory decline. On the other hand, research has demonstrated repeatedly that *physical* exercise does indeed help to prevent or slow down deficiencies and impairments of memory and other forms of cognitive functioning (Snigdha et al., 2014; Hoveida et al., 2011; Smith et al., 2011).

Christiana Koci Hernandez/Corbis

Brain fitness. A growing number of cognitive fitness centres are now being developed, where elderly people work on computer tasks designed to help improve their memories and cognitive functioning. However, research has not yet clarified that brain exercises prevent cognitive decline.

Before You Go On

www.wiley.com/go/comercanada

What Do You Know?

1. Why are toddlers able to effectively remember faces, places, objects, and certain skills, but are not able to remember the events of their lives very well?

2. Why do the memories of elderly people tend to decline and what techniques seem to help prevent or slow down memory problems?

What Do You Think?
Think of three of your earliest memories in life. Did the remembered events share certain characteristics, such as the arousal of great emotion or your age at the time?

Summary

Module 49: Memories in the Young and Old

LEARNING OBJECTIVE 49 Describe the kinds of memories and memory changes that characterize early life and later life.

- Babies and toddlers display many memories—from memories of faces, places, and objects, to memories of skills and procedures. But they do not retain memories of life events for very long.
- The slow development of the hippocampus may be responsible for the slow development of life event memories.
- Physical exercise seems to help prevent or slow down memory decline more than cognitive exercise does.

Key Terms

prospective memory 364

retrospective memory 364

Study Questions

Multiple Choice

1. In terms of helping to slow or prevent memory loss in older adults, which strategy has received the most research support?
   a) completing puzzles
   b) engaging in physical exercise
   c) playing computer games
   d) taking vitamins

Fill-in-the-Blank

1. Our inability to remember events prior to age 3 or 4 is called _____ amnesia.

2. Older adults tend to have more trouble than younger adults with _____ memory, which can make it difficult for them to remember future planned events such as shopping for particular items at the grocery store.

Module 50: Disorders of Memory

At times, each of us has been inconvenienced by imperfect memories or by outright forgetting. When our memories fail to operate as we would like, we may experience dismay, frustration, or embarrassment. Imagine how upsetting and confusing life would be if memory failure were the rule rather than the exception, as it became for Leonard or Lucy, the fictional characters in the movies *Memento* and *50 First Dates*. Is this the experience of people who have memory disorders? To a large degree, the answer to that question is "yes" (McGaugh, 2003).

There are two basic groups of memory disorders: *organic memory disorders*, in which physical causes of memory impairment can be identified, and *dissociative disorders*, in which the disruptions in memory lack a clear physical cause. We will discuss dissociative disorders in Part 15.

LEARNING OBJECTIVE 50
Describe physical and psychological disorders that disrupt memory.

50.1 Organic Memory Disorders

Some changes in memory have clear organic causes, such as brain injuries or medical conditions. These injuries or conditions damage one or more of the brain regions or brain chemicals that are important in the formation, storage, or retrieval of memories (Matthews, 2011). The most common kinds of organic memory disorders are *amnestic disorders*, which primarily affect memory, and *dementias*, which affect both memory and other cognitive functions.

50.1.1 Amnestic Disorders

People with **amnestic disorders**, organic disorders in which memory loss is the primary symptom, experience retrograde amnesia, anterograde amnesia, or both (**Figure 50-1**). **Retrograde amnesia** is an inability to remember things that occurred before the organic disorder or event that triggered amnesia. **Anterograde amnesia** is an ongoing inability to form new memories after the onset of the disorder or event. Anterograde amnesia observed in amnestic disorders is often the result of damage to the brain's *temporal lobes* or *mammillary bodies*, areas that play a role in transferring information from working memory into long-term memory.

In severe forms of anterograde amnesia, such as that suffered by Leonard and Lucy, the main characters in the films *Memento* and *50 First Dates*, new acquaintances are forgotten almost immediately and problems solved one day must be tackled again the next. The person may not remember anything that has happened since the physical problem first occurred. A middle-aged patient who suffered a physical trauma more than 30 years ago, for example, may still believe that Brian Mulroney is the Prime Minister of Canada.

Head injuries are a common cause of amnestic disorders. Although *mild* head injuries—for example, a mild concussion—rarely cause much memory loss, almost half of all *severe* head injuries do cause some permanent learning and memory problems (Sadock & Sadock, 2007). Brain surgery can also cause amnestic disorders. The most famous case of memory loss as a result of brain surgery is that of Henry Molaison (known for many years by his initials H.M.), a man whose identity was protected for decades until his death in 2008 (Kensinger et al., 2001; Corkin, 1984). Mr. Molaison suffered from severe epilepsy, a disorder that produced seizures in his temporal lobes. To reduce his

amnestic disorders organic disorders in which memory loss is the primary symptom.

retrograde amnesia inability to remember things that occurred before an organic event.

anterograde amnesia ongoing inability to form new memories after an amnesia-inducing event.

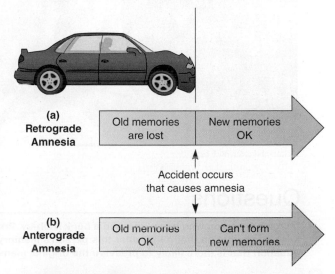

FIGURE 50-1 Two types of amnesia. An organic event can lead to two types of inability to remember. In retrograde amnesia, the individual loses memories of things that occurred before the event. In anterograde amnesia, the individual can recall the past but cannot form new memories.

Tying It Together: **Your Brain and Behaviour**

Giving Eyewitness Testimony

Imagine you have witnessed a car accident where someone was injured. You called 911 and stayed at the scene to tell the police officer what happened. A few months later, you were called to testify as an eyewitness at the trial. How accurate do you think your memory would be?

When people give eyewitness testimony, many regions of their brains are involved, including the hippocampus, amygdala, prefrontal cortex, visual cortex, thalamus, and mammillary bodies, among others. Let's see how several of these regions are involved in such eyewitness testimony.

PNC/Getty Images

©iStockphoto.com/Rich Legg

Questions

1 Imagine a person who has witnessed a bank robbery. Provide an example of a leading question that might alter this person's memory and a non-leading question that is more likely to preserve the original memory.

2 Explain how the visual cortex is activated differently when a person is remembering a witnessed event accurately versus inaccurately.

3 Discuss the role of the prefrontal cortex and the hippocampus in the storage and recall of eyewitness memory.

Image Source/Getty Images

DISTORTING THE MEMORY

Memories are often susceptible to distortions when they are recalled. Wrong information can be incorporated into an eyewitness's memory if leading questions are asked or if circumstances surrounding the inquiry are particularly frightening.

RECALLING THE EVENT

Eyewitness retrieval and recall of the observed event depends largely on neuron activity in the cerebral cortex, shown here in this image of a fluorescent pyramidal neuron. In addition, protein synthesis in the pyramidal neurons of the prefrontal cortex enables memories to be stored again after they have been used. (Nakatomi et al., 2002)

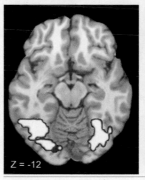

Courtesy Elizabeth Gould

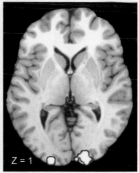

Z = -12   Z = 1

Roberto Cabeza, Duke University. From Cabeza, Cerebral Cortex, 2007, Figure 4. Reproduced with permission of Oxford University Press.

RETRIEVING AN INCORRECT MEMORY

Different parts of the visual cortex are activated when participant "eyewitnesses" accurately remember an observed event versus when they remember it inaccurately. Association parts of the visual cortex are at work in both true and false memories (orange areas on the left brain scan), whereas only true memories were active early in the visual stream (orange areas on the right). This suggests elaborative perceptual processing may be more involved in the formation of false memories than basic perceptual processing (Kim & Cabeza, 2007).

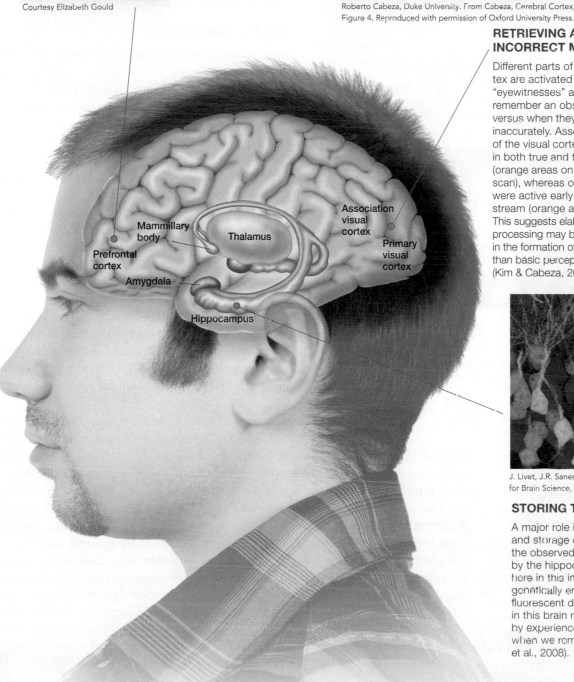

Prefrontal cortex

Mammillary body

Thalamus

Amygdala

Hippocampus

Association visual cortex

Primary visual cortex

J. Livet, J.R. Sanes, J.W. Lichtman, Center for Brain Science, Harvard University

STORING THE MEMORY

A major role in the formation and storage of memories about the observed event is played by the hippocampus, shown here in this image of neurons genetically engineered to make fluorescent dyes. The synapses in this brain region are changed by experience and are activated when we remember (Lichtman et al., 2008).

Masterfile

Elsa/Getty Images

Part of the sport? As discussed in Part 3, hard hits to the head are common in boxing, football, and hockey, leading, in many cases, to concussions/mild traumatic brain injuries (mTBI). These may lead to chronic traumatic encephalopathy (CTE), a progressive, degenerative disease of the brain in individuals with a history of multiple brain injuries. As many as 350,000 athletes endure consciousness-losing injuries each year (Gioia, 2007).

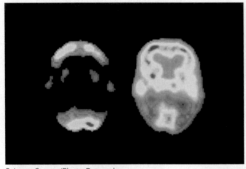

Science Source/Photo Researchers

Scans tell the story. PET scans of the brains of a person with Alzheimer's disease (left) and a person without the disease (right), taken while the two individuals were performing the same task, reveal how much less brain activity occurs in the Alzheimer's patient. Red and yellow colours on PET scans indicate areas of high brain activity.

dementia severe memory problems combined with losses in at least one other cognitive function, such as abstract thinking or language.

Alzheimer's disease most common form of dementia, usually beginning with mild memory problems, lapses of attention, and problems in language, and progressing to difficulty with even simple tasks and recall of long-held memories.

symptoms, doctors performed bilateral (both sides) surgery in 1953 that removed parts of his temporal lobes, the amygdala, and the hippocampus. At that time, the role of these brain areas in the formation of memories was not known. (Today, temporal lobe surgery is usually done on only the right or left side of the brain.) Brenda Milner, one of Canada's best-known neuroscientists, spent many years studying the effects of the surgery on Mr. Molaison's memory. Mr. Molaison experienced severe anterograde amnesia from the time of his surgery until his death, though his procedural memory remained intact (Milner et al., 1968; Scott & Milner, 1957). He continually failed to recognize anyone he met after the operation.

50.1.2 Dementias

In **dementia**, severe memory problems combine with losses in at least one other cognitive function, such as abstract thinking or language (APA, 2000). As you have seen in this part, forgetfulness is quite normal. In fact, as people move through middle age, memory difficulties, lapses of attention, and related cognitive difficulties increase and may occur with some regularity by the age of 60 or 70. Sometimes, however, people experience memory and other cognitive changes that are far more extensive; they may be victims of dementia.

Between 3 and 9 percent of the world's adult population suffer from some form of dementia (Berr et al., 2005). Its occurrence is closely related to age. Among people 65 years of age, the prevalence of dementia is around 1 to 2 percent, increasing to as much as 50 percent of those over the age of 85 (Apostolova & Cummings, 2008). Current estimates suggest that there are 747,000 Canadians living with cognitive impairment in Canada (Alzheimer's Society, Ontario, 2012) with over 60,000 new cases of dementia in Canada every year (Canadian Study of Health and Aging Working Group, 2000). More than 70 forms of dementia have been identified. Although some forms of dementia result from metabolic, nutritional, or other problems that can be corrected, most forms are caused by neurological problems, which are currently irreversible.

Alzheimer's disease, named after Alois Alzheimer, the German physician who first identified it in 1907, is the most common form of dementia, accounting for as many as two-thirds of all cases (Brookmeyer, Johnson, Ziegler-Graham, & Arrighi, 2007). This gradually progressive disease rarely appears in middle age, but most often occurs after the age of 65. The disease usually begins with mild memory problems, lapses of attention, and difficulties in language and communication. As symptoms worsen over the years, the person has trouble completing complicated tasks or remembering important appointments. Eventually patients also have difficulty with simple tasks, distant memories are forgotten, and changes in personality often become very noticeable. They may withdraw from others, become more confused about time and place, wander, and show very poor judgment. Patients may lose almost all knowledge of the past and fail to recognize the faces of even close relatives (Zahodne et al., 2013).

People with Alzheimer's disease form far more numbers of *neurofibrillary tangles* and *senile plaques* than do those without the disease (Selkoe, 2002, 2000, 1991).

Neurofibrillary tangles are twisted protein fibres found within the cells of the hippocampus and several other brain areas. **Senile plaques** are sphere-shaped deposits of a protein known as *beta-amyloid protein* that form in the spaces between cells in the hippocampus, cerebral cortex, and several other brain regions, as well as in some nearby blood vessels. Although these brain changes are normal features of aging up to a point, the presence of so many tangles and plaques indicates that enormously destructive processes are taking place in the brains of Alzheimer victims (Meyer-Luehmann et al., 2008; O'Connor et al., 2008).

Yet another line of research points to reduced activity of neurotransmitters that are typically related to memory. Many studies have found, for example, that acetylcholine and glutamate are in low supply in the brains of people with Alzheimer's disease (Chin et al., 2007; Bissette et al., 1996). This decrease is probably related to the death of neurons by plaque and tangle formations.

Alzheimer's disease can usually be diagnosed with certainty only after death, when structural changes in the person's brain can be fully identified in autopsy (Julien et al., 2008). However, researchers are working to identify other diagnostic approaches using various biomarker combinations (Struyfs et al., 2014; Landenson et al., 2013).

50.1.3 Gender and Dementia

Depending on whether you are a male or a female, you may be susceptible to different risk factors for dementia and Alzheimer's disease. Older women are more likely to develop dementia than men. Although this may be because women tend to live longer, natural age-related declines in estrogen (which is known to have a protective effect in the brain) could also be a factor (Sun, 2007).

As we age, certain conditions in men and women may increase the likelihood of developing dementia. A study of adults with mild cognitive impairment showed that stroke in men and depression in women increase the risk for dementia (Artero et al., 2008). In addition to risk factors, Alzheimer's disease also may "look" different in men and women. The brains of women with the disease, for example, typically have many more neurofibrillary tangles than do those of men (Barnes et al., 2005). Also, men with Alzheimer's disease tend to be more aggressive, while women are more likely to become depressed (Lovheim et al., 2009).

neurofibrillary tangles twisted protein fibres found within the cells of the hippocampus and certain other brain areas.

senile plaques sphere-shaped deposits of a protein known as beta-amyloid that form in the spaces between cells in the hippocampus, cerebral cortex, and certain other brain regions, as well as in some nearby blood vessels.

Trappe/Alamy/GetStock

Progressive deterioration. A staff member at a special residential facility helps a man with Alzheimer's disease shave. As memory deficits and other features of the disease worsen over the years, patients have trouble performing even simple tasks.

HOW WE
DIFFER

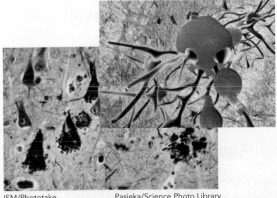
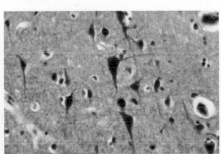

ISM/Phototake   Pasieka/Science Photo Library   Carolina Biological Supply Company/Phototake

Alzheimer's disease. Both senile plaques (protein fragments that accumulate between neurons) and neurofibrillary tangles (insoluble fibres that twist together) are thought to damage neurons in the brains of Alzheimer's patients (both shown on the left). Plaques and tangles are absent in the healthy brain (right).

What Do You Know?

1. Compare and contrast retrograde and anterograde amnesia. What are the likely causes of both?
2. What changes happen in the brains of people with Alzheimer's disease?
3. How do dissociative disorders differ from organic memory disorders?

What Do You Think? Do you think that media portrayals of amnesia and dissociative disorders have actually influenced psychotherapists and members of the public to increase the number of diagnoses of these conditions? What other reasons might explain increased diagnoses?

Summary

Module 50: Disorders of Memory

LEARNING OBJECTIVE 50 Describe physical and psychological disorders that disrupt memory.

- Disorders of memory can come about through aging, brain trauma, or the experience of traumatic events. Organic memory disorders, involving physical causes, include disorders such as amnesia and dementia. Major losses of memory without a clear physical cause are known as dissociative disorders.
- Amnesia refers to the inability to remember things before (retrograde) or after (anterograde) an organic event, such as a head injury or brain surgery.
- The other major class of organic memory disorders is dementia, characterized by severe memory problems combined with losses in at least one other cognitive function, such as abstract thinking or language.
- The most common form of dementia is Alzheimer's disease, a severe progressive form of dementia that accounts for at least half of all dementia cases.
- The brains of people with Alzheimer's disease have an extraordinarily high number of neurofibrillary tangles and senile plaques. The disease may stem from malfunctions of certain proteins or neurotransmitters involved in the normal formation of memories. A tendency toward developing these biochemical problems may be genetically inherited.

Key Terms

Alzheimer's disease 370

amnestic disorders 367

anterograde amnesia 367

dementia 370

neurofibrillary tangles 371

retrograde amnesia 367

senile plaques 371

Study Questions

Multiple Choice

1. Symptoms accompanying progressive neurodegerative diseases characterized by memory loss are called
   a) dementia.
   b) Alzheimer's disease.
   c) Parkinson's disease.
   d) dopaminergic losses.

Fill-in-the-Blank

1. Women have higher rates of dementia than men, partly because they live longer, and partly due to declines in the hormone _____ that occur with aging.

PART 9

LANGUAGE AND THOUGHT

PART OUTLINE

Module 51: Language

LEARNING OBJECTIVE 51 Define language, describe how we learn languages, describe parts of the brain that are involved in language, and discuss differences and problems that can affect people's language skills.

Module 52: The Relationship between Language and Thought

LEARNING OBJECTIVE 52 Describe how thought and language are related and summarize the linguistic relativity hypothesis.

Module 53: Thought

LEARNING OBJECTIVE 53 Describe and summarize research on thinking processes, including problem solving, decision making, and metacognition.

©iStockphoto.com/brebca

If you are like the vast majority of university and college students who responded to a survey (Elliot, 2007), you own and use a cell phone. In fact, you probably use it a lot. In June 2010 alone, Canadians sent 4.6 billion peer-to-peer text messages. People in the traditional university and college age group, 18 to 24 years old, send an average of nearly 1,400 text messages per person every month, averaging more text messages than phone calls. Thirteen- to 17-year-old females send over 4,000 texts per month, while males send over 2,500 (Canadian Wireless and Telecommunications Association, 2010; Keane, 2008). As you are well aware, cell phones have amazing capabilities, but they can sometimes even save lives. News reports often tell stories of lost hikers or others who were saved after calling for help from their cell phones, or when rescuers tracked them using the automatic global-positioning (GPS) information generated by their phones. But are we becoming too reliant on technology, and how are new technologies influencing our thought processes?

For example, passing the navigation of your car over to a GPS system can sometimes have negative consequences. In March 2011, Albert and Rita Chretien were driving from Penticton, B.C. to a trade show in Las Vegas. They compared their paper map and their GPS map and decided to take a shortcut suggested by the GPS unit. Unfortunately, the GPS unit did not also suggest they consider the time of year. The GPS route led them down a logging road that quickly became impassable; their van left the road and became mired in mud and melting snow. Cell phone reception was spotty and they could not hold a call long enough for their location to be determined. They spent three days in their van, and then Albert decided to take the GPS and walk out to get help. Rita stayed with the car, eating a small amount of candy and drinking muddy water she found near the van. She was found six weeks later, near death, by several hunters on ATVs who got her to hospital and saved her life. Albert's body was not found until six months later.

Using your cell phone and GPS requires language skills as well as some key thinking skills. You have to make several key decisions and likely solve some problems when using technologies like cell phones. The need to plan is true of GPS systems as well. For example, it is good to find out how to turn off the "use unpaved roads" setting on your GPS before letting it guide you around in Canada (especially in winter).

Language and thought are characteristics that distinguish humans from other creatures. Language enables us to communicate in a precise and often creative way. We also use language to tell stories or jokes. Language has allowed us, as a species, to learn from past generations, originally by oral storytelling and then by written language. Language is a critical component of human behaviour because it greatly facilitates progressive social interactions. Consider the difficulty involved in organizing a large group of people to build a city. Such a feat would be nearly impossible without the use of language.

Although language is communicative, sometimes we use language only in our own heads. We often think using words, but many of our thoughts are not shared. Some people write extensively but only for themselves, never intending or wanting others to read their written words. Although the processes of language and thought overlap, a clear difference exists between them. In general, psychologists study these processes separately.

cognition mental processes of thinking and knowing.

Human thought is highly complex, varies from individual to individual, and takes on many different forms. The study of thought is a major component of cognitive psychology. As we saw in Part 1, the word **cognition** refers to a variety of mental processes that contribute to thinking and knowing. Cognition is involved in learning and memory, as well as in thinking. In this part, we will discuss a number of different types of thinking, which can involve accumulating knowledge, solving problems, making decisions, and even thinking about thinking.

Module 51: Language

51.1 What Is Language?

Language, whether spoken, signed, or written, is a set of symbols used to communicate. We use symbols, mainly words, to convey our thoughts and desires to others who share an understanding of those symbols. Language can be divided into two main components: language production and language comprehension. **Language production** occurs when we generate thought through words. **Speech** involves the expression of language through sounds. Human language production is *generative* or creative; we make new sentences whenever we speak, rather than just restating old ones. In fact, humans have a remarkable capacity for producing new sentences, and we rarely repeat previously-heard sentences word-for-word. The ability to produce new sentences spontaneously and creatively is an important feature of human communication. We know that many other species communicate with sounds, but the vocalizations uttered by most species are inborn and do not change. A lion does not need to learn how to roar, for example, and it does not phrase its roar differently every time.

Very few species other than humans can learn new *vocalizations*, sounds produced in an effort to communicate (Pinker & Jackendoff, 2005). Vocal learning occurs in some species of songbirds (canaries, zebra finches), bats, aquatic mammals (whales and dolphins), and humans. It may come as a surprise that no primates other than humans learn language naturally, although monkeys and apes have an extensive repertoire of species-specific vocalizations and baboons are able to learn to recognize words (Grainger et al., 2012). However, apes that have learned some vocalizations are not capable of the complexities that characterize human language. Despite years of training in the laboratory, for example, no ape has ever learned to speak, as they lack the vocal apparatus that humans evolved over many thousands of years. Gorillas are able to use a range of signs to communicate. For example, the gorilla Koko has learned over 1,000 American Sign Language-based signs (Patterson & Matevia, 2001). See if you can understand Koko's signs here: www.pbs.org/wnet/nature/fun/game_flash.html. Alternatively, follow Sean Senechal's approach to teaching your dog some basic signs—using K9Sign (Senechal, 2009).

Humans are also endowed with an impressive capacity for **language comprehension**, the ability to understand communicative vocalizations or gestures. We can generally comprehend fragments of sentences or words that are mispronounced. We can understand people who speak with accents, people with speech impediments, such as lisps or stutters, as well as immature speech, such as the speech of toddlers. Our ability to understand speech that is incomplete or unclear is related to the fact that much of language

Define language, describe how we learn languages, describe parts of the brain that are involved in language, and discuss differences and problems that can affect people's language skills.

language a set of symbols used to communicate.

language production the structured and conventional expression of thoughts through words.

speech the expression of language through sounds.

©iStockphoto.com/TungBooWat

Language?...not. These canaries may appear to be discussing how beautiful a day it is or how well their offspring fly. However, although the word-like sounds they emit involve communication (that is, the sharing of information), they do not amount to language.

language comprehension the process of understanding spoken, written, or signed language.

Ron Cohn/The Gorilla Foundation, koko.org

Sign language. Koko is able to use over 1,000 recognizable gestures from American Sign Language.

comprehension is automatic. Typically we understand spoken language without concentrating, which is the reason we are able to carry on a conversation with limited pauses before responding.

51.2 Language Structure

The study of speech can be divided into four general areas: *phonology, semantics, syntax,* and *pragmatics.* **Figure 51-1** shows the building blocks of language. The smallest units of sound in any language are called **phonemes**, and the study of how sounds are put together to form words is called **phonology**. For example, the word *tip* has three phonemes—*t, i,* and *p.* The number of phonemes differs from language to language (Halle, 1990). The English language has about 40 phonemes (give or take a few depending on the dialect). At one end of the spectrum is the language Pirahã, an indigenous language of Brazilian people living in the Amazon, which has only 10 phonemes. At the other end of the spectrum is the Taa language (also known as !Xóõ), a language of indigenous people of Botswana and Namibia, which has 141 phonemes.

Janet Werker at the University of British Columbia has demonstrated that speakers of one language often cannot distinguish sounds of other languages if their own language does not include the phoneme (Dietrich, Swingley, & Werker, 2007; Yeung, Chen, & Werker, 2013). For example, French does not include the *h* sound at the beginning of words. French speakers would say, "'Ave you 'eard about 'arry?" When learning English, French speakers will often overcompensate by voicing the *h* sounds in words where English speakers largely omit them, such as "hour" or "honour." Such errors are particularly noticeable in older speakers learning a new language (in this case English). Later in this part we discuss how it is much easier to learn languages during an early stage of life.

While phonemes are sounds, **morphemes** are the smallest units of language that convey *meaning* or *function* (Miller, 1978). For example, the word *jumped* has two morphemes. One is *jump* and the other is *ed* (the *ed* morpheme changes the meaning, indicating that the jumping has already taken place). Therefore, words can contain more than one morpheme, but each morpheme is not necessarily a word (that is, *ed* cannot stand alone and convey meaning). The study of the meaning of words is referred to as **semantics**. For example, if we say that it is "raining cats and dogs," you do not look outside and expect to see animals falling from the sky. Instead, you know that this expression means that it is raining very heavily. The dictionary meaning of a word is referred to as its **lexical meaning**. Lexical meaning changes over time. Consider the word *awful*; it used to mean "full of awe," but now means that something is extremely bad or unpleasant.

Knowing the meaning of individual words is important, but a word's meaning is often communicated through the position of the word in a sentence. For example, if you say that Joe kissed Kelly, then your listener knows that Joe was the giver of the kiss and that Kelly was the receiver. If, however, you say that Kelly kissed Joe, then the listener knows that Kelly was the giver of the kiss and that Joe was the receiver. As well, one word can mean two things; for example, the word *blue* can mean a colour or a depressed emotional state. When heard alone, it's impossible to tell the intended meaning. However, when we hear *blue* in the context of a particular sentence, such as, "She wore a beautiful blue dress," or, "He's feeling blue today," the distinction becomes instantly clear. The way in which words are constructed into sentences is referred to as **syntax**.

phoneme the smallest unit of sound in a language; an individual sound such as ba, da, or ta.

phonology the study of how individual sounds or phonemes are used to produce language.

morpheme the smallest units of a language that convey meaning.

semantics the study of how meaning in language is constructed of individual words and sentences.

lexical meaning dictionary meaning of a word.

syntax the system for using words (semantics) and word order to convey meaning (grammar).

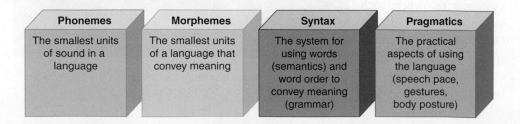

FIGURE 51-1 **The building blocks of language.**

Phonology, semantics, and syntax bring us to the point where we have sounds, words, and sentences. Communication also requires adhering to social norms, such as speed of speech, responding at appropriate intervals, making eye contact, and using acceptable body language. These aspects of communication are called **pragmatics**, because they refer to the practical use of language.

pragmatics the practical aspects of language usage, including speech pace, gesturing, and body language.

One aspect of pragmatics is our use of body language, or **non-verbal communication.** The way we move our hands, bodies, and faces can change the connotations of our speech. Suppose your instructor said, "I would like to meet with you after class." If this statement was delivered with one raised eyebrow, a sneer, and arms folded across the chest, you would

non-verbal communication body language.

likely interpret it differently than if the instructor said the sentence with a warm smile, while leaning forward with hands on a desk. Some people are not aware of the body language they are using and unwittingly send the wrong message when they attempt to communicate. An employee may believe, for example, that a boss is making inappropriate advances because the boss is unaware of the message he or she sends by standing close and touching the worker's arm while talking.

Paul Chiasson/The Canadian Press

Non-verbal communication seems to be acquired automatically, often by observing the actions of others. Non-verbal communication is related to, but not identical to, gesturing, which refers to communicative movements of the arms and hands. Gesturing facilitates speech production. While the ancient Greeks provided orators with explicit lessons in gesturing to enhance their speeches, studies have shown that gesturing appears to be innate (Tomasello, 2009). For example, people blind from birth, who have not had the chance to learn gestures by watching others, nevertheless use gestures when they speak. Gesturing is often difficult to inhibit; blind people will gesture even when they are talking to another blind person (Goldin-Meadow, 1999).

Getting her message across. The facial expression, body posture, and other non-verbal cues of former Governor General Michaëlle Jean as she interacts with local children while visiting her childhood city of Jacmel, Haiti, after its earthquake, help communicate her feelings of support and hope.

Research has shown that blind students can be helped to grasp mathematical concepts more quickly if they get information about their instructors' gestures by having the instructor wear a haptic glove interface (a glove that records information about hand movements and touch) (Oliveira, et al. 2012).

51.3 How Language Develops

You were probably too young at the time you started to speak your native language to remember learning it. Your parents may have proudly kept a record of your first words. If they did, they probably abandoned the list pretty quickly, as it became too long very quickly. Within just a few years, almost every human baby goes from being incapable of speaking or understanding language to having an extensive vocabulary.

- *Prevocal learning* Between 2 and 4 months of age, babies are capable of perceiving the phonemes of every language, including those that are not needed for the language(s) they will ultimately learn (Aslin, Jusczyk, & Pisoni, 2000). During this time, babies have a remarkable ability to distinguish among these sounds. Researchers investigated babies' abilities to distinguish among different phonemes by training the babies to turn their heads toward an interesting visual reward when they hear a change in speech sounds. Results of studies by UBC's Janet Werker and others using this type of training

©iStockphoto.com/Marina DI

Baby talk. Infants' productive vocabulary goes from zero to 50 words in 18 months and over the same time frame their comprehension vocabulary increases to three times their production level.

HOW WE DEVELOP

(which is a form of operant or instrumental conditioning, as described in Part 7) suggest that young babies can discern a much wider range of phonemes than older children or adults can (Werker, 1989). This ability declines, however, as babies begin to learn their native language (Eimas et al., 1971). With practice in only the phonemes of our native language, we lose the ability to distinguish among sounds that are only heard in other languages (Eimas, 1975; Kuhl, 2010). This pruning of phoneme processing happens without specific training, and clearly suggests that infants arrive ready to notice, tune into, and acquire the language(s) being spoken around them.

- *Cooing* By about 2 months of age, babies begin to make a non-crying vocalization that consists largely of vowel-like sounds (e.g., o-o-o-o-u-u-u). Infants may also produce brief consonant-like sounds that sound somewhat like a *k* or *g*. Although infants occasionally produce these sounds when alone, they largely appear when the infant is interacting with someone else (Hulit & Howard, 1997).

babbling babies' production of meaningless sounds.

- *Babbling* By about 6 months, babies start to babble (Sachs, 2009). **Babbling** refers to the production of meaningless speech sounds either repetitively (e.g., da-da-da-da-da) or in a more mixed manner (e.g., pa-da-ca-ca-mi-den-bo). These vocalizations do not work as communication, but they do enable the infant to experiment with vocalizations in a way that gradually approaches their soon-to-be-acquired native language. All babies babble, including those who are deaf (Wallace, Menn, & Yoshinaga-Itano, 1999; Blamey, & Sarant, 2013).

- *First words* By about 1 year, speaking begins, typically in the form of very simple words, such as *mama*, *dada*, or *hi* (Ingram, 1986). At this early stage, the baby's ability to comprehend is much greater than the ability to speak (see **Figure 51-2**). At about 1 year of age, the average baby can understand approximately 50 words, but he will not be able to speak that many words until about six months later (Fenson et al., 1994). One-year-olds can often follow commands, such as, "Get the ball and bring it to mommy," even though their spoken vocabulary may only include *ball* and *mama*.

telegraphic speech speech that consists of minimalistic sentences; characterizes early toddlerhood and is the first evidence of sentence formation.

- *Telegraphic speech* By age 2, toddlers in most language communities speak in very short (typically two-word) sentences. This is called **telegraphic speech** because, as in old-fashioned telegraph messages (for which senders were charged by the word), all but the essential words are omitted. Instead of saying, "I want a cookie," a 2-year-old is more likely to simply say, "Want cookie." The order of the words used varies by linguistic group. (For example, "Give cookie" in English and "Cookie give" in Japanese; Bloom 1970). The dropped words

FIGURE 51-2 Babies' comprehension of words. Babies can comprehend more words than they can speak. One-year-old babies understand about 50 words, but will not be able to speak them until about six months later. Adapted with permission from Fenson, Dale, Reznick, et al. (1994). Variability in early communicative development. Monographs of the Society for Research in Child Development, 59(5, Serial No. 173), Blackwell Publishers; based on Lilienfeld, S., Lynn, S., Namy, L., & Wolf, N. (2009). *Psychology: From inquiry to understanding.* Boston: Pearson/Allyn & Bacon, Figure 8-3, p. 325.

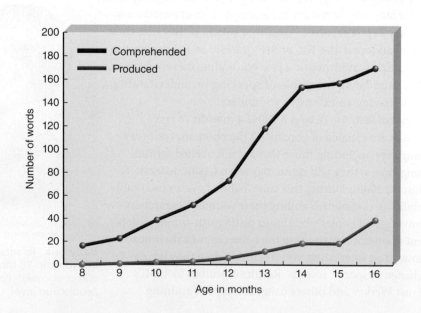

are called grammatical morphemes and they are only dropped when they are not necessary to determine the meaning of the spoken phrase in their language community (Slobin, 1986).

- *Pragmatics* By 3 years of age, the average toddler has naturally acquired some practical information about language use, including the need to pause between sentences and the knowledge that certain sentences are statements, whereas others are requests (Garvey, 1974). The average English-speaking 3-year-old vocabulary typically includes about 1,000 words (Huttenlocher et al., 1991).

- *Grammar* By age 4, children have automatically absorbed many of the rules of grammar, even though they have received no formal education about the grammar of their native languages (Tager-Flusberg, 2001). As discussed below, some of the early stages of reading often emerge around this time when children are exposed to written words at home or preschool. By age 6, the average child uses almost 3,000 words and likely understands a great many more, about 14,000 words (depending on the amount of language they were previously exposed to— see the feature, Practically Speaking: Poverty and Language Development). By age 9, practical aspects of language emerge, such as inferring meaning of obscure language, interpreting metaphors, and understanding sophisticated humour (Wellman & Hickling, 1994).

Even though the majority of language learning occurs relatively early in life, vocabulary and its usage can continue to increase in size and sophistication for decades to come. In studying for the Graduate Record Exam (part of the application process for many graduate programs, including psychology) or other university- or college-admission exams, many young adults find themselves learning words they haven't used before. Vocabulary can increase throughout adulthood, and seems to be one type of memory that is not adversely affected by the normal aging process. Elderly people with slowed reaction times and impaired memory for events in their own lives often score as high, if not higher, than young adults on vocabulary tests (Park et al., 2002).

51.3.1 Theories of Language Development

Think about experiences you have had building your vocabulary, perhaps to take exams or as part of an English course. You may also have had experience learning a second or third language later in your education, perhaps starting in late elementary school or even in high school. In either situation, whether expanding your vocabulary in your first language or adding an entirely new language, you probably experienced a much slower learning rate than you did when you learned your first language as a very young child. Language-related learning later in life probably also required concentrated attention to your studies; it most likely did not occur automatically.

The ease with which language is acquired by human infants has led many researchers to speculate that language has a biological basis. The linguist Noam Chomsky was among the first to suggest that language learning is built into our brains (Chomsky, 1964). The brain does appear to be set up to understand and communicate using language. As we have noted, the ability to detect all phonemes used in any human language exists in all human babies (as long as their hearing is intact). Other studies have also shown that the very young brain is wired to acquire language rapidly and automatically, because it is in a highly plastic, or changeable, state, ready to absorb new information about language. As humans grow and reach adulthood, the brain maintains the ability to change, but that ability diminishes (Johnson & Newport, 1989; Dong & Ren, 2013)—language learning becomes much slower and requires more effort.

Chomsky described our early capacity for language learning as working as if we had a sort of *language acquisition device* built in to our brains. As we have seen, the influence of this theoretic "device" may fade as we age and become more cognitively aware

> **"Language is a process of free creation."**
>
> —*Noam Chomsky, American linguist*

practically speaking Poverty and Language Development

Children from socio-economically disadvantaged backgrounds often struggle in academic settings. In fact, several studies suggest that poor children have deficient vocabularies when they first enter elementary school, and that these differences often get exaggerated as the years pass because vocabulary builds on itself (Lareau, 2003; Fernald, Marchman, & Weisleder, 2012).

Research has shown that the initial language deficits of poor children are due to environmental differences. On average, as infants, toddlers, and young children, students from lower socio-economic status (SES) households are exposed to fewer words than are students from households with higher socio-economic status. As shown in the table, one study found that, in any given hour, children in poor homes heard fewer than half the number of words than children in high SES homes did (Fernald, Marchman, & Weisleder, 2012). In addition, much more of the speech to which poor children were exposed was prohibitive; for example, when a parent says, "Stop it!" or "Don't touch that."

The exact reasons why poor parents communicate less, as well as less positively, with their children remain unknown. The stress of poverty and the potential lack of suitable role models for parents (parenting skills are largely acquired through one's own upbringing) are two likely causes. Work by Monique Sénéchal and Jo-Anne LeFevre (2002, 2014) at Carleton University highlights the good news that the problem of reduced vocabularies in lower SES children can be prevented by preschool intervention that includes educating parents about the benefits of talking and reading to children in the home.

©iStockphoto.com/PhotoEuphoria

Research in this area also highlights one of the key challenges with human research: we are a lot better at carefully observing human behaviour (the *whats*, as in *what is going on?*) than we are at understanding the reasons for observed behaviour (the *whys*). Finding out the underlying causes of human behaviour is understandably harder as we are ethically unable to experiment on many aspects of human condition. So, we can *see* that there appear to be SES differences in parent–child communication, but at the same time we are not really clear on *why* those observed differences exist. It is especially important that we identify what the causes are in situations like this, as we may be able to design intervention programs to lessen or remove conditions of disadvantage.

Socio-economic status	Words per hour	Affirmations	Prohibitions
Low SES	176	5	11
Mid SES	251	12	7
High SES	487	32	5

critical period a window of time in development during which certain influences are *necessary* for appropriate formation of the brain.

sensitive period a point in development during which the brain is more *susceptible* to influences.

of our learning processes. Psychologists often refer to the childhood years before age 13 as an especially important period for language acquisition (Newport, Bavelier, & Neville, 2001). Some debate exists as to whether language systems have a critical or a sensitive period (Kuhl, 2010). Recall from Part 4 that a **critical period** refers to a window of time during which certain influences are *necessary* for appropriate formation of the brain. After the critical period, these influences are no longer capable of having as profound an impact on the brain. A **sensitive period** refers to a developmental time during which the brain is more *susceptible* to influences. After the sensitive period, change can still occur, but it doesn't happen as readily (Cheung, Chudek, & Heine, 2011).

As we have seen, we can still expand our vocabularies or learn new languages later in life, suggesting that, in normal cases, we go through more of a sensitive period than a critical period for language learning. Some evidence, however, such as from the sad case of Genie described in the next module, suggests that there is a critical period during which we must have *some* language input or we do not acquire normal fluency with speech and, in fact, may miss out on the opportunity to develop a working understanding of the underlying syntactic features of language.

David Young-Wolff/PhotoEdit

Baby sign. This mother is using child-directed speech to communicate with her toddler, including special intonations in her voice and a modified form of sign language. In turn, the child's responses include a form of sign language sometimes called "baby sign."

It's clear that our brains have a biological propensity to help us acquire at least one language, but the process of language learning is not exclusively innate. Much evidence suggests that the environment plays a critical role as well. Early behaviourists, including B. F. Skinner (1957), suggested that language is acquired as a result of instrumental conditioning. They argued that toddlers are rewarded with praise for producing appropriate speech, and ignored or scolded for failure to do so. As you may have noticed, however, parents, caregivers, and other older people do not usually systematically reward toddlers for correct speech. The 2-year-old who says, "Want cookie," is just as likely to get one as another child who can ask, "Please, may I have a cookie?" Conditioning alone, therefore, cannot explain language acquisition.

Interactive theories suggest that experience interacts with biological development to enhance and guide language learning (Goldberg, 2008). As we have described, for instance, if a baby isn't exposed to certain phonemes, her capacity to distinguish among these sounds diminishes over time.

The social environments of most babies and young children also typically offer a high degree of very interactive speech. Most adults in most cultures talk to babies with a special intonation in their voices; a high-pitched and sometimes exaggerated speech that is spoken directly to an infant or child is called **child-directed speech** (Weisleder & Fernald, 2013). Child-directed speech may help babies learn words by keeping them interested in the stimulus generating them. The patterns of child-directed speech are often rich in emotions, which may have the added benefit of fostering a close emotional relationship between caregiver and child, thus enhancing the quality and quantity of communication.

child-directed speech speech characterized by exaggerated emotional responses and a slower pace that is cross-culturally common among caregivers communicating with babies and young children.

Child-directed speech is also observed when parents use sign language to communicate with babies. Whether the adult, child, or both are deaf, the use of sign language during the learning phase naturally takes the form of child-directed speech—slower in the formation of the hand signs, with longer pauses in between signs and exaggeration of facial expressions of emotions (Masataka, 1998; Lieberman, Hatrak, & Mayberry, 2014). Child-directed speech arises naturally; people adopt it without any formal instruction, suggesting that humans seem to have a biological predisposition to teach effective communication to the very young (Vouloumanos & Gelfand, 2013; Bornstein et al., 1992).

The development of syntax, or grammatical rules, also suggests an interaction of biology and environment. Even in children with hearing loss who are not formally trained in sign language but have instead developed their own form of signing, there is evidence of a grammatical structure. These findings suggest that the brain is predisposed to create a set of rules by which language will be used. Grammar rules differ from language to language, but within a given language, they remain the same and are followed fairly consistently by speakers of the language (Tomasello, 2009).

Even with such a strong biological basis, however, grammar is still affected by environment. We can see the effects of environment when children begin formal education. Children typically acquire a large vocabulary and the ability to form grammatically-correct sentences by about age 4, generally before they receive formal training in grammar (Tager-Flusberg, 2001). Once grammatical rules are consciously learned, however, children become more prone to errors. For example, once children learn that the suffix *-ed* refers to the past tense, they apply *-ed* to verbs that are irregular. A child who previously used the past tense of "*think*" correctly as "*thought*," may begin to say "*thinked*." Such mistakes are referred to as **overregularization** (Maratsos, 2000). They provide evidence that, while the tendency to readily pick up syntax exists in the very young, some aspects of grammar are learned. At the very least, there are two systems for language acquisition: one that is automatic and the other that requires conscious attention and can be learned explicitly. Overregularization is an example of how the conscious learning system can interfere with—and actually, temporarily do a worse job than—the unconscious system of language acquisition.

overregularization the process by which elementary school children over-apply newly learned grammatical rules to improperly "correct" an irregular part of speech, such as a verb (e.g., "goed" instead of "went").

© Bettmann/Corbis

Portrait of Genie. This photo shows Genie after authorities took control of her care.

51.3.2 Critical Period for Language Learning? The Case of Genie

In 1970, an adolescent girl and her blind mother were delivered to a welfare office in California (Rymer, 1994). At the hands of her sadistic father, the girl, named Genie, had spent her entire life in isolation chained to a potty chair. She was rarely spoken to except in a punitive way ("stop it"). Her father communicated with her mostly by grunting and barking. At age 13, when her mother finally left the father, Genie had been exposed to almost no speech and appeared to be nearly mute. Her vocabulary consisted of about 20 words.

Age 13 is after the time at which most researchers had assumed that the critical period for language acquisition is over. This assumption is based on the fact that after this age, people learn new languages with greater difficulty and typically speak their second languages with accents. Because Genie was 13 years old at the time when she was rescued, she was a tragic test case of whether a critical period for language exists.

During the years that followed her rescue, Genie received extensive, interactive language training. Although she did initially show progress in expanding her vocabulary, it was always limited and didn't include the acquisition of grammatical rules. Unfortunately, Genie's vocabulary regressed even further when she was under stress. Genie's experiences tended to provide support for the theory that a sensitive period for language learning does exist.

Although the case of Genie seems to support the language critical period theory, it's important to keep in mind that Genie was not only deprived of language, but also subjected to extreme physical and emotional abuse that may have contributed significantly to her inability to learn (Kyle, 1980). It has also been suggested that she may have been mildly intellectually disabled at birth, a factor that could partially limit the critical period theory (Jones, 1995). Regardless, however, it is clear that early experiences are important in first language acquisition (Steinberg, Nagata, & Aline, 2013).

51.3.3 Learning to Read

In Western cultures, most children begin formal education and start learning to read at around the ages of 5 or 6. Reading is a complicated behaviour that emerges considerably after the foundations of language production and comprehension have been laid down.

Carleton University researchers Monique Sénéchal and Jo-Anne LeFevre have shown that children typically begin the process of learning to read by telling stories from looking at pictures in a book and attempting to recognize a few simple words (Sénéchal & LeFevre, 2014; 2001). In schools in North America, reading and writing are usually a main focus of Grade 1 and Grade 2. By the end of Grade 2 (around age 8), reading becomes much less laborious for most children, as it transitions to an automatic process that requires little or no conscious thought (Ely, 2000). At this same point, parents usually start to notice their children excitedly pointing out letters and words they recognize on signs and billboards. Reading becomes challenging and fun as children begin to acquire the basic skills.

Once reading becomes automatic, most people become very proficient at it. Just as we are capable of understanding spoken fragments of sentences or words spoken in foreign accents, we can understand written abbreviations with ease. Consider the abbreviated writing of the text message: U R L8. It's very easy to determine that this means, "You are late," because the phonemes are identical to those that are used to correctly spell out these words. More complicated and non-phonetic written messages require explicit learning. Consider the abbreviated writing of the text message: 1 ctn 1 g2g il ttyl. Without prior knowledge of the acronyms *ctn*, *g2g*, and *ttyl*, the message, "I can't talk now, I've got to go, I'll talk to you later" would remain a mystery.

51.4 Language and the Brain

In most people, language production and comprehension centres are located in the left hemisphere of the brain. In a small percentage of people (about 5 percent), the language centres are lateralized to the right hemisphere of the brain. In some cases, language involves both hemispheres (Taylor & Taylor, 1990). As discussed in Part 3, one area of the left hemisphere of the brain, Broca's area, is important for our ability to speak, while another area, Wernicke's area, is important in language comprehension. In a typical conversation, both areas are active at once, along with other parts of the brain.

51.4.1 Broca's Area

Broca's area is located in the frontal lobe in what is technically the motor association cortex (Damasio & Geschwind, 1984) (see **Figure 51-3**). This area was named after the neurologist who first described patients with damage to this region. People who suffer damage in or near Broca's area develop a set of symptoms called **Broca's aphasia**. The term *aphasia* refers to an inability either in language production or in language comprehension. In Broca's aphasia, the problem is with production; people have great difficulty speaking; they speak unusually slowly and have trouble with pronunciations (Mohr et al., 1978; Lazar, & Mohr, 2011).

> **Broca's area** a brain region located in the frontal lobe that is important for speech production.
>
> **Broca's aphasia** a neurological condition arising from damage to Broca's area where the patient is unable to produce coherent speech.

Because Broca's area is located in the motor association cortex, many researchers believe that the difficulty in speaking that characterizes Broca's aphasia is caused by difficulties in making the necessary movements. Speaking requires a complex set of movements of the lips, tongue, and larynx, and movements are largely controlled by the primary motor cortex in the brain. The content of patients' speech supports the theory that difficulties in movement, rather than in thinking, are the major problems when Broca's area is damaged. Although difficult to follow, the speech of most people with Broca's aphasia makes sense. They have clear thoughts to communicate, but they have great difficulty getting them out (Broca, 1861; Denes & Pizzaliglio, 1999).

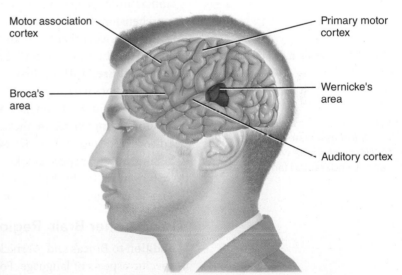

FIGURE 51-3 **Language and the brain.**

Damage to Broca's area can also produce an inability to speak with proper grammar, a condition referred to as **agrammatism**. This deficit suggests that our ability to use grammar is stored close to or within the same neural tissue that is responsible for speech production (Kean, 1977; Hillert, 2014). This close neuroanatomical relationship probably explains how grammar is automatic once it is learned. When we speak, we don't need to carefully construct grammatically correct sentences.

The agrammatism suffered by people with Broca's aphasia also tends to be linked to mild impairments in language comprehension (Schwartz, Saffran, & Marin, 1980). Individuals affected with this form of aphasia can produce some connected speech, but their speech is missing all of the required grammatical words (such as "the," "is," "and," "ing," "ed,"

> **agrammatism** a neurological condition arising from damage to a brain region just anterior to Broca's area, where the patient is incapable of using words in grammatical sequence.

Dr. Bill Vicars

Canadian Sign. Deaf Canadians communicate using either a version of American Sign Language (ASL) or Langue des signes Québécoise (LSQ). The sign above is not found in ASL but is used by Canadian signers to say "Canada." The fist is used to tap the chest, as if you were grabbing the shirt. A mnemonic for remembering this sign is the phrase "The Mounties always get their man" (even if they don't actually grab him by the shirt).

Wernicke's area a brain region located in the temporal lobe that is important for language comprehension.

Wernicke's aphasia a neurological condition associated with damage to Wernicke's area where a person cannot understand language.

or "s"). So, instead of saying, "She is going," the person with agrammatism might say, "She go." In research, people with Broca's aphasia who were asked to point to the correct picture that illustrated a phrase such as "the cat ate the food" could do so. If researchers asked these people to point to a nonsense picture illustrating the phrase "the cow was on the car," however, they were almost as likely to choose a picture of a car on a cow as to choose the correct one. The researchers concluded that people with Broca's aphasia were not able to use clues such as grammar and word order to determine the meaning of a sentence that was not obvious from its individual words (Schwartz, Saffran, & Marin, 1980).

Neuroimaging studies of people without brain damage have confirmed much of what neurologists and neuropsychologists have discovered from studying the behaviour of people with Broca's aphasia (Gernsbacher & Kaschak, 2003). Broca's area itself is active during speaking, and an area just in front of Broca's area becomes active when we try to comprehend sentences with complicated grammar.

Sign language uses brain areas similar to those important in spoken language. Neuroimaging studies show that, in people with intact brains, Broca's area and Wernicke's area are activated during signing (Braun, Guillemin, Hosey, & Varga, 2001). Since producing sign language does not require actual speech production, it does not involve as much activation of Broca's area. However, because sign language does involve use of grammar to construct meaningful sentences, using sign language activates the same motor cortex areas of neural tissue near Broca's area involved in the use of grammar when speaking. Deaf people with brain damage around Broca's area can experience deficits in grammar use with signing (Corina, 1998).

51.4.2 Wernicke's Area

Although the tissue near Broca's area seems to contribute to the comprehension of grammar in language, other parts of the brain are even more important for language comprehension. Because, for most people, speech comprehension begins when we hear, it is not surprising that the brain regions most important for understanding speech are located near the auditory cortex in the upper part of the left temporal lobe. **Wernicke's area** (see **Figure 51-4**) was first identified by a neurologist named Wernicke, who studied patients with brain damage in this area of the temporal cortex. People who suffer destruction to this part of the brain have **Wernicke's aphasia**. These individuals have impairment in auditory comprehension; they cannot understand speech and therefore produce fluent but disordered speech. In other words, patients with Wernicke's aphasia are fully capable of talking, but their speech makes no sense. For example, in response to being asked, "Are there flowers on the bush?" a patient might answer something like this, "Yes. I can eat and listen and walking and talking for this now you."

51.4.3 Other Brain Regions

In addition to Broca's and Wernicke's areas, other brain regions have important functions in specific aspects of language. For instance, the amygdala, a brain region important for fear and aggression, appears to be involved in the use of profanity (Jay, 1999).

Most people also typically use regions in the right hemisphere to understand figurative language, such as metaphors. In figurative language, the meaning of a phrase is different from the literal meaning of the words used in the phrase. Damage to the right hemisphere can lead to taking figurative language literally (Schmidt, DeBuse, & Seger, 2007). For instance, a person might think the phrase "hold your horses" means to grab hold of an actual horse. Metaphors are figures of speech that compare unlike things. Damage to the right hemisphere might lead a person to think that you live with an actual farm animal when you say, "My roommate is a total pig." Perhaps because understanding humour requires a grasp of abstract language—humour often involves the use of puns and metaphors—right hemisphere damage can also disrupt the ability to understand a joke.

A role for the right hemisphere in processing information about metaphors has been demonstrated using the relatively new technique in brain science called *transcranial magnetic stimulation* or *TMS* (discussed in Part 3). Researchers can focus TMS, which delivers a strong magnetic signal, into a participant's head to temporarily inactivate a specific brain region. One such study found that TMS of the right hemisphere temporarily impaired the ability of humans to understand metaphors, and that this impairment was greatest when the metaphors were unfamiliar to the participants (Pobric et al., 2008).

If a person learns two or more languages simultaneously as a child, Broca's and Wernicke's areas are involved in the use of all languages. Interestingly, however, if an individual does not learn a second language (or third or fourth) until adulthood, the brain does not rely as heavily on Broca's and Wernicke's areas (Perani et al., 1998). Instead, it recruits other circuits to aid in the learning process. Among these are parts of the prefrontal cortex, important for working memory, and the temporal lobe, which is active in the acquisition of semantic information. The recruitment of additional brain regions not involved in language learning early in life may contribute to the greater difficulty of learning a language later in life.

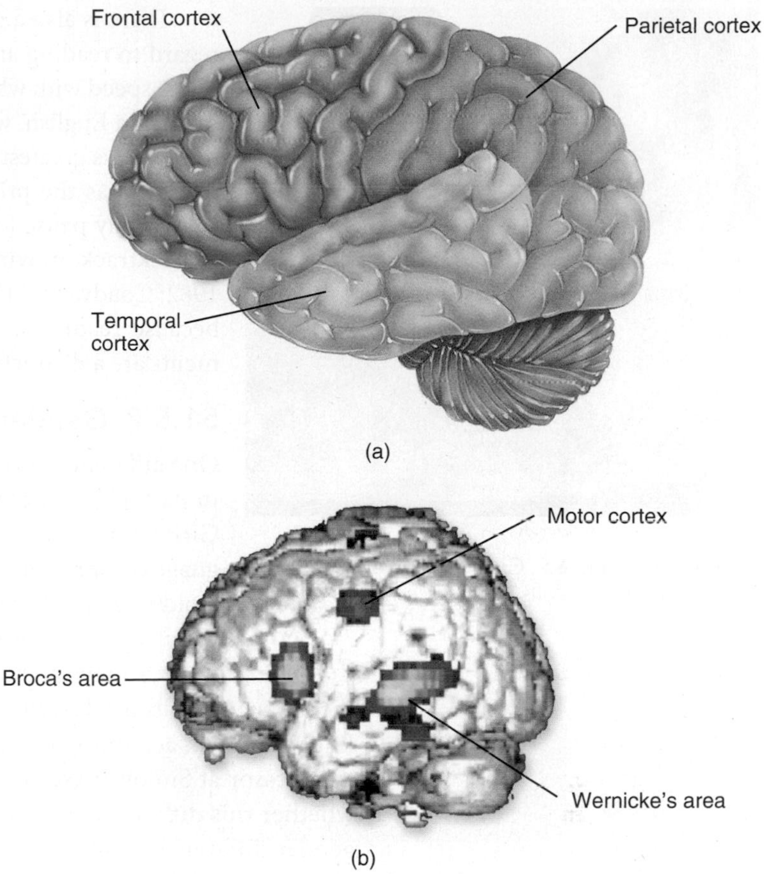

Reading also involves a wide range of brain regions. The physical actions required to read activate areas of the brain that aid in visual processing and motor functions. Since reading involves eye movements, for example, it recruits a brain region in the frontal lobe called the *frontal eye fields*. The content of what we read also affects which brain areas become more active during reading. Words of particular emotional importance, such as obscenities or disgust words, activate the amygdala. When we read words that evoke odours, such as *garlic* or *cinnamon*, the primary olfactory, or smell-related, regions of the brain become activated (González et al., 2006).

(a)

(b)

FIGURE 51-4 Scanning for language comprehension. The PET scan displays the brain activity of a person who is repeating the words of another individual. Such vocal repetitions activate (red and orange) Broca's area for speech production, Wernicke's area for language comprehension, and a motor region tied to vocalizations.

51.5 Differences in Language Acquisition

There is considerable variability among the normal population in the rate at which language is acquired and the size of vocabulary and overall verbal skills. Some evidence suggests that males and females may differ in language skills. There are even differences in the number of languages that we acquire. Although all normal people become proficient in at least one language, some people are multilingual and can become fluent in many different languages.

HOW WE DIFFER

51.5.1 Differences in Language Acquisition Among Individuals

Some of the variability in the rate of language acquisition is due to our environments. Our vocabulary size, for example, is affected by our environment, particularly early in life. For example, as described in the box earlier in the part, children in low-income households often hear fewer words and have smaller vocabularies when they start school than those from more affluent families (Lareau, 2003; Fernald, Marchman, & Weisleder, 2012).

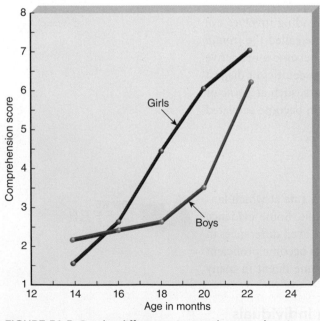

©iStockphoto.com/Chris Schmidt

Gender differences. Girls tend to outpace boys in language skills during elementary school.

There is also a great degree of variability in the normal population with regard to reading and writing skills. For instance, people differ substantially in the speed with which they can read. This skill seems to be tied to eye movements. In English, words are written on the page from left to right, and reading speed is greatest for individuals whose eyes move in the same left-to-right direction as the printed words, with no backtracking. Slower readers tend to not only pause for longer periods of time over individual words, but also to backtrack, moving their eyes back to words already passed (Lahey et al., 1982; Coady, 2013). It's not clear whether the less fluid eye movements occur because reading is more difficult, or whether the backtracking eye movements are a distraction that interferes with rapid reading.

51.5.2 Gender Differences in Language

One difference in verbal learning and overall skills that may be related, at least in part, to genetics is a notable gender difference in early language learning. Girls tend to learn to talk earlier, and on average, girls acquire speech and language comprehension at a faster rate than boys (see **Figure 51-5**) (Reznick & Goldfield, 1992; Talbot, 2010). These early differences often diminish by about age 2, however, when those boys slower to acquire language catch up.

Although boys may catch up in speaking skills, girls still seem to outpace boys in the language skills used in elementary school. As a group, girls score higher on tests of English ability, according to well-known Canadian researcher Doreen Kimura (2000), a professor at Simon Fraser University until her death in 2013. It's not clear, however, whether this difference is related to a real gender difference in language ability, or to a gender difference in some of the skills necessary to be a good student, such as paying attention, taking legible notes, and studying. By young adulthood, these differences are gone. There are no substantial male–female differences in overall critical reading or writing scores (Kimura 2000, 2004).

When considering gender differences, remember to keep in mind that even though statistical differences may exist between average scores of boys and girls or men and women, these differences do not tell us anything about individuals. Many boys acquire language skills very rapidly and become talented writers and speakers as adults.

Another important point to consider is that the gender difference in language acquisition may have an experiential component. Because boys tend to be more active than girls, and girls tend to be more social than boys, it's possible that girls are exposed to a higher degree of interactive language than boys. If young boys are constantly on the move, exploring the environment may occupy more time than language learning.

Despite the fact that there do not appear to be significant differences in overall verbal ability between adult men and women, some evidence suggests a difference in the way that women and men process language information. Neuroimaging studies have shown that, on average, women are more likely to use both hemispheres of the brain to process language information, whereas language processing in men tends to be more lateralized (Clements et al., 2006). The extent to which these differences between men and women in recruitment of neural circuitry during language processing have any functional consequence remains to be determined.

FIGURE 51-5 Gender differences in speech comprehension. Early on, there is a notable difference in language comprehension between girls and boys. Girls comprehend language at a faster rate, but this gender gap disappears by about age 2. Adapted from Reznick, J. S., and Goldfield, B. A. Rapid change in lexical development in comprehension and production. *Developmental Psychology, 28,* 406–413.

51.5.3 Learning More Than One Language

Many children grow up in multilingual homes, where two or more languages are spoken. Such children tend to learn to speak and understand language at slightly later ages than children who only need to learn a single language (Butler, 2013). The greater amount of information and decoding necessary to learn two or more languages simultaneously may explain the very slight lag.

Like first languages, multiple languages are also most readily acquired by the very young. In adulthood, the language learning process is labour intensive and often remains incomplete. By the age of 13, our language learning ability has declined substantially (see **Figure 51-6**) (Johnson & Newport, 1989; Birdsong & Milis, 2001). The difference can be seen with accents. People who learn to speak English as a second language as children speak it without an accent, whereas those who learn it as teens or adults speak English less fluidly and typically with the accent of their native tongue. A similar phenomenon exists for deaf children learning sign language. After about age 13, it becomes more difficult to learn this skill (Mayberry, 2010; Johnson & Newport, 1989).

Knowing this, many of us wish we had been exposed to multiple languages as youngsters. Those fortunate enough to have this experience can become fluent in several languages without any formal study. See "Tying It Together: Your Brain and Behaviour."

Ryerson Clark/Getty Images

Language diversity. Many Canadians speak a second language, while many acquire three or more. Canadian children may acquire English, French, Inuktitut, Salishan, Michif, or any of the many other languages spoken in Canada.

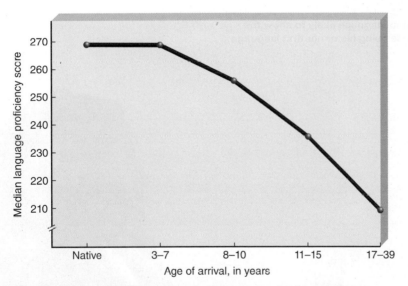

FIGURE 51-6 **The earlier we learn a new language, the more proficient we become.** Immigrants' mastery of English depends on when they begin the learning process. The proficiency of those adults who started learning their new language before age 7 is comparable to that of native speakers. However, the proficiency of those who started acquiring the language in young adulthood is much poorer. Reprinted from *Cognitive Psychology*, 21, J.S. Johnson & E.L. Newport, Critical period effects in second language learning: The influence of maturational state on the acquisition of English as a second language, pp. 60–99, Copyright 1989, with permission from Elsevier.

Tying It Together: **Your Brain and Behaviour**

Learning a Second Language

Do you speak more than one language, or are you learning a second language now? What if someone were to ask you for directions and it was clear you needed your second language to communicate with them? What parts of your brain were used when you learned a second language and what parts are being called into play as you use it to give directions? Learning a second language not only engages brain regions that are involved in language prodution and comprehension, it also activates areas important for learning semantic information, such as the hippocampus, and those important for working memory, such as the prefrontal cortex (Berwick et al., 2013). As we acquire grammatical rules and become more fluent, the regions in our brain associated with learning a first language—such as Broca's area and Wernicke's area—become primarily involved. As we activate these language production and comprehension areas more and more, we rely less and less on semantic and working memory regions.

Questions

1 How do patterns of brain activity change as we become more fluent in a second language?

2 Which part of the brain is most active when we switch from using our first language to using a second language?

3 Is a person who achieves fluency in a second language likely to show the exact same patterns of brain activation while using his or her first language versus the second language? Explain.

BECOMING FLUENT

As we become fluent in a second language, the brain becomes less active, as shown on these brain scans of someone new to a second language (intense red areas, top) versus someone with years of second language experience (lighter red areas, bottom). So, better performance means less brain activity.

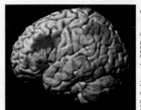

K. L. Sakai, *Science* 310 (5749):815–9, Nov. 4, 2005, figure 3.

Yapeng Wang, *Neuroimage* 35 (2):862–70, Figure 1, 2007

SWITCHING FROM ONE LANGUAGE TO THE OTHER

Once you have learned a second language, switching from your first language to the second one involves the prefrontal cortex, as shown here in this fMRI image (yellow areas). Switching from your second language back to your native tongue doesn't require the use of these brain areas, probably because it takes less effort.

Prefrontal cortex

Broca's area

Wernicke's area

Hippocampus

BEING BILINGUAL

But even when we reach the same level of proficiency in a second language as with a first language, the second language requires more brain activation, shown here (blue areas) in this fMRI image.

K. L. Sakai, *Science* 310 (5749):815–9, Nov. 4, 2005, figure 3.

Summary

Module 51: Language

LEARNING OBJECTIVE 51 Define language, describe how we learn languages, describe parts of the brain that are involved in language, and discuss differences and problems that can affect people's language skills.

- Language is a set of symbols used to communicate. Language comprehension involves understanding verbal messages, and language production involves creating them.
- The study of language can be broken into phonology (sounds), semantics (meaning), syntax (grammar), and pragmatics (practical usage).
- Most people follow a typical sequence of language acquisition that includes the ability to distinguish, but not produce, all possible phonemes at about 2 to 4 months of age, babbling at about 6 months, and speaking first words at around 1 year of age.
- The standard way we learn language suggests that we have an inborn capacity for language learning, although environment contributes as well. There appears be a sensitive or critical period before about 13 years old when it is easiest to acquire language.
- In most people, the language centres in the brain are in the left hemisphere. The main brain region important for speech production is Broca's area. The main region for language comprehension is called Wernicke's area. Several other areas of the brain are also active in language, including the frontal eye fields when we read.
- There are small average gender differences in early language learning, with girls initially learning faster. These differences disappear with time.

Key Terms

agrammatism 383
babbling 378
Broca's aphasia 383
Broca's area 383
child-directed speech 381
critical period 380
language 375
language comprehension 375

language production 375
lexical meaning 376
morpheme 376
non-verbal communication 377
overregularization 382
phoneme 376
phonology 376
pragmatics 377

semantics 376
sensitive period 380
speech 375
syntax 376
telegraphic speech 378
Wernicke's aphasia 384
Wernicke's area 384

Self-Study Questions

Multiple Choice

1. Which of the following sequences correctly orders the components of language from the smallest or most specific to the broadest?
   a) phoneme → morpheme → syntax
   b) phoneme → syntax → morpheme
   c) syntax → morpheme → phoneme
   d) syntax → phoneme → morpheme

2. By what age do most normally-developing babies begin to babble?
   a) 1 month
   b) 2 months
   c) 4 months
   d) 6 months

3. A "critical period" in language development is a period during which
   a) children are proficient in their first language.
   b) children must receive stimulation to learn language.
   c) the brain forms neural connections for language learning.
   d) the brain is receptive to language learning.

4. How does the critical period for deaf children acquiring sign language compare to the critical period for hearing children acquiring spoken language?
   a) The critical period for deaf children acquiring sign language is essentially the same as the critical period for hearing children acquiring spoken language.
   b) The critical period for deaf children acquiring sign language is longer than the critical period for hearing children acquiring spoken language.
   c) The critical period for deaf children acquiring sign language is shorter than the critical period for hearing children acquiring spoken language.
   d) There is no critical period for deaf children acquiring sign language, whereas there is a critical period for hearing children acquiring spoken language.

5. Which of the following alternatives best describes gender differences in language development from birth to about age 2?
   a) Both speech and language comprehension develop earlier in girls than in boys.
   b) Speech develops earlier in boys than in girls, but language comprehension develops earlier in girls than in boys.
   c) Speech develops earlier in girls than in boys, but language comprehension develops at the same rate in girls and in boys.
   d) There are no gender differences in language development from birth to age 2.

Fill-in-the-Blank

1. Humans make new sentences each time they speak. This refers to the concept that language is creative or _____.

2. Three-year-old Maya said, "I thinked about it." This is an example of the linguistic error called _____.

3. The term _____ refers to a deficit in either language production or language comprehension.

4. The brain region critical for speech production is _____ area, located in the motor association cortex.

Module 52: The Relationship between Language and Thought

Many of us consider our thoughts to be primarily related to language. Since we often have no trouble responding automatically with words in a conversation, it can seem that language is the natural driving force of thought. One influential psychological theory suggests that our language controls and limits our thoughts. In many cases, however, complex thoughts occur in the absence of language. So what is the relationship between thought and language? Is language simply a tool for expressing our thoughts? Or are our thoughts a consequence of the language we learn and the things we are told about the world using our native language? We will consider a few of the areas of investigation related to this question of the relationship between thought and language. You will see that the answers are not simple and not yet complete.

52.1 Thinking Without Words: Mental Imagery and Spatial Navigation

mental imagery picturing things in your mind.

During the weeks before spring break, you may enjoy picturing yourself lying in a hammock sipping a cool drink while overlooking the coast of Cuba, or skiing down the slopes of the Rocky Mountains in Banff National Park. **Mental imagery** refers to thoughts that involve conjuring internal visual representations of stored sensory input. Most of our mental imagery does not involve language (Finke, 1989; Gregory, 2010).

Another good example where language doesn't play a major role in thinking can be observed with spatial navigation thinking. Although some people use narrative to remember directions, such as, "Turn right at the second light on Main Street," in many cases, spatial thinking occurs in the form of visual imagery. You may remember the appearance of certain street corners and automatically turn right when you are triggered to do so by your visual system. Some people use dead reckoning or a "sense of direction" to navigate. This kind of directional skill—knowing that a certain direction is north, for example—is not language driven.

Our ability to use imagery to solve problems is often based closely on our spatial memories. Studies have shown that we appear to search our actual relevant memories to solve tasks requiring mental imagery. For example, if researchers give participants photos of rooms that are long and narrow with regularly spaced objects in them, and later ask the participants to describe the objects located in those rooms, the participants do so with a greater lag time between objects than if asked to carry out a similar task after looking at a photo of a smaller room (Kosslyn & Shin, 1991).

> **"**Most events are inexpressible, taking place in a realm which no word has ever entered.**"**
>
> —*Rainer Maria Rilke, German poet*

Interestingly, using mental imagery activates many of the same brain regions used for the sensory experience itself. Neuroimaging technology has allowed us to observe which

Psychology Around Us — Driving on Autopilot

For most people, spatial navigation becomes almost automatic, especially when this navigation is part of their routine. Consider as an example a daily commute to work or school. You may climb into the car, turn on the engine, and later find yourself at your destination without recalling the details of the drive. In fact, some people become so lost in their thoughts while driving that they forget if they planned to go somewhere different or unusual at the end of the day. You may arrive at your house before even realizing that you had intended to go to the store on your way home, for example.

regions of the brain become most active when people think. This type of research suggests that thinking about something can actually activate the same brain regions as sensing or doing it (Goldberg et al., 2006). There are many examples:

- When you visualize or picture in your mind an event or scene, your brain activates the visual areas that would be active if you were actually gazing at the event or scene (O'Craven & Kanwisher, 2000).
- Thinking about tastes and odours activates many of the same gustatory and olfactory brain regions involved when you really do taste or smell something (Bensafi, Sobel, & Khan, 2007).
- Thinking about fear- and anxiety-provoking subjects activates the amygdala, an area involved in anger, fear, and stress (Shin et al., 2004).

And when we do have thoughts that involve language, they activate the frontal and temporal lobes, the same areas used when we comprehend or produce spoken language (Goldberg et al., 2006).

Although some of our thinking involves mental imagery, it is obviously not sufficient for all of the complicated thoughts humans have. There are many concepts that do not have an adequate mental image. Consider thinking about love. Some symbols of love, such as a heart or Cupid with his arrow, are associated with love, but they hardly tell the whole story. Even conjuring mental images of our loved ones doesn't adequately express our thoughts about love in general. As we will discuss in the rest of the part, much of our thinking involves the use of words, often in combination with imagery.

52.2 The Influence of Language on Thought

Many psychologists believe that language greatly influences our thinking. This older theory about the relationship between thought and language is called the **linguistic relativity hypothesis**. The linguistic relativity hypothesis was advanced by Edward Sapir and Benjamin Lee Whorf (Sapir, 1921; Whorf, 1940, 1956) and suggests that the more words we have available to us related to a single concept, the more complex and detailed our thoughts are about that object or idea.

Evidence in support of the linguistic relativity hypothesis comes from cross-cultural studies that reveal large discrepancies in the number of words various languages dedicate to certain characteristics or objects. Studies have shown that extensive vocabularies for certain characteristics can lead to an ability to make finer distinctions along that dimension (Davies & Corbett, 1997). The English language, for example, has many words used to distinguish different colours. We can describe nuances of difference in shades of the colour blue, for example, by using words such as *azure, cobalt, cyan, indigo, turquoise, aquamarine*, and more. By contrast, members of the Dani tribe of Papua New Guinea have in their entire language only two words to distinguish colour, one word for light and the other for dark. Importantly, these people are not colour-blind. They can perceive differences in colour, but they do not have words to describe them (Heider, 1972). So having fewer words for things like colour does not actually limit the Danis' ability to see colour, just their ability to talk specifically about what they see.

The linguistic relativity hypothesis, as it is currently understood, suggests that because English-speaking people have words for subtle concepts or distinctions regarding colour, we are encouraged to think more about them than we would if, like the Dani, our vocabulary did not include those words. Nevertheless the number of colour words we possess does not impact our visual perception or our thoughts about the colours we can see. So the strong version of the linguistic relativity hypothesis is not

linguistic relativity hypothesis hypothesis suggesting that the vocabulary available for objects or concepts in a language influences how speakers of that language think about them.

Interfoto/Alamy

Far from colour-blind. The colourful and carefully-blended war decorations of Dani tribesmen show that these individuals from Papua New Guinea are not colour-blind, despite their limited vocabulary for colours.

supported—but are there ways in which language shapes thought? More recent research suggests that there are.

We learn about the world partly through our personal experiences. We also learn about the world by being told about it. Many of the concepts we learn as we develop have been put together and managed within the particular socio-cultural perspective of the community in which we live. If our cultural community maps a particular concept in a particular way, then that is how we will learn that concept. Therefore the difficulty children experience when acquiring concepts depends on the way the concept is structured in the local cultural community. Think about the concept of *living things*. What sorts of things are living things? In English we make several distinctions within the concept of living things (see **Figure 52-1**). English speakers first distinguish between plants and animals, but then sometimes further divide animals into human and non-human animals. The rules about when it is appropriate or insulting to refer to another person as an animal are hard to learn. For example, English-speaking children need to learn which of the following is insulting: "You are such a pig," versus "You sing like a bird." In contrast, in Indonesia living things are conceptually divided into three categories: humans, animals, and plants. With no guesswork, this structure is easier to manage and therefore Indonesian children can properly understand and master the concept of living things at an earlier age than children speaking English can (Waxman & Medin, 2006; Leddon, Waxman, & Medin 2011). The simpler language structure for the concepts makes it easier to acquire developmentally.

Another example of the way that language can shape thought starts with what the comedian Steve Martin once said, "Boy, those French have a different word for everything!" While of course that is true, as we have just seen, the linguistic relativism theory suggested that our words actually map out the world differently. The relationship between thought and language, however, goes both ways. Even if a culture has many words for snow (the linguistic relativity hypothesis), it is possible to explain the differences so that those without specific words for different types of snow can still understand the differences.

On the other hand, having a very specific word for a complex social situation suggests a clearer understanding of the situation. Howard Rheingold (2000) set out to collect words from various languages that concisely capture specific social situations. For example, the Mayan term "bol" means something like "stupid in-laws" in English, whereas the German term "treppenwitz" means something like "clever remark that comes to mind when it is too late to use it," and the Japanese term "kyoikumama" means something like "mother who pushes her child to academic achievement," and, last, our favourite, "Korinthenkacker" is a German word that literally translates to "raisin-sh%#@er" and refers to "a person overly concerned with trivial details."

So the ways that our socio-cultural communities divide up the world and our experiences lead to the emergence of new concepts, words, or phrases that are used in language to communicate our shared observations. Through those communications, we not only acquire a language, but also a way of thinking about the world.

FIGURE 52-1 **Cultural conceptions of living things.** In English we make a subordinate distinction beneath our concept of animals to distinguish humans from animals, whereas in Indonesia the distinction is simple, handled at the first basic level.

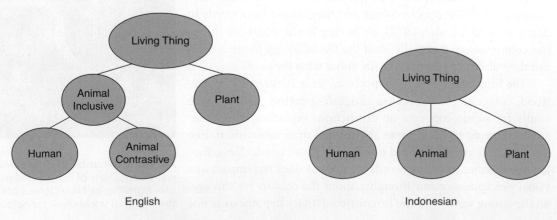

ww.wiley.com/go/comercanada

Before You Go On

What Do You Know?

1. What is mental imagery? What parts of the brain does mental imagery involve?
2. What research evidence suggests that we use mental imagery to solve problems involving our spatial memories?
3. What does the linguistic relativity hypothesis suggest about the influence of our language on our thinking and what research has been done? What are some more recent examples of this type of influence?

What Do You Think? In what ways do you believe your language influences your thoughts?

Summary

Module 52: The Relationship between Language and Thought

LEARNING OBJECTIVE 52 Describe how thought and language are related and summarize the linguistic relativity hypothesis.

- Some thoughts, including mental imagery and spatial navigation, require no words.
- The linguistic relativity hypothesis suggests that the amount of vocabulary we have available in our language for objects or concepts influences the way we think about those objects or concepts.

Key Terms

linguistic relativity hypothesis 393

mental imagery 392

Study Questions

Multiple Choice

1. If you imagine rearranging the furniture in your home and vividly picture the room, which lobe of your brain is likely to be active?
   a) frontal
   b) occipital
   c) parietal
   d) temporal
2. Which of the following statements best expresses the linguistic relativity hypothesis?
   a) Language influences thought.
   b) Language is equivalent to thought.
   c) Language is unrelated to thought.
   d) Thought determines language.

Fill-in-the-Blank

1. Mental imagery refers to thoughts that involve conjuring up _____ representations of stored sensory input.
2. Evidence supporting the linguistic relativity hypothesis comes from _____ psychology..

Module 53: Thought

LEARNING OBJECTIVE 53
Describe and summarize research on thinking processes, including problem solving, decision making, and metacognition.

We can think in many different ways. The study of cognition includes, for example, mental imagery and spatial navigation, as we have seen. Cognitive scientists also study the development of our thinking abilities, how we solve problems, how we make decisions, and even how we think about our own thoughts. We will take a look at some of their major findings in the remainder of this part. Our thinking abilities are truly impressive, but the variety and complexity of thought also means we are sometimes vulnerable to problems in our thinking. We'll also discuss two psychological disorders that are characterized primarily by disruptions in thought processes.

Different forms of thinking develop at different rates. Thoughts that involve language emerge around the time that language capabilities are forming, whereas those that involve reasoning emerge later. Michael Chandler at UBC and Jeremy Carpendale at Simon Fraser University (1998) argue that skills requiring self-awareness, such as formulating or changing long-term plans and carrying them out, require a type of thought that develops relatively late in children—not until around the time of school entrance. Changes in our thinking continue to occur throughout life. Teenagers and young adults become increasingly capable of making and carrying out long-term plans for their futures.

53.1 Thinking and Effort: Controlled and Automatic Processing

The distinction between controlled and automatic thinking is an important concept in cognitive psychology. As we discussed in Part 8 on memory, *controlled processing* is effortful and relies on a limited-capacity system, while *automatic processing* seems effortless. Automatic processing is not usually disrupted very much if we are distracted by other tasks. Experienced drivers can carry on a conversation with a passenger while driving a car, for example. However, automatic processing, such as driving, can be severely disrupted by simultaneously engaging in a task that requires more attention than speaking, such as reading or sending a text message. Controlled processing requires more attention. Most of us cannot carry on a conversation while conducting multi-digit mental arithmetic; we must direct our thoughts toward the math problem.

cognitive control the ability to direct thought in accord with one's intentions.

Cognitive control refers to the ability to direct thought and action in accord with one's intentions (Carter, Botvinick, & Cohen, 1999). Some examples of this include:

- the ability to direct attention to a specific stimulus within other competing, and perhaps stronger, stimuli, such as finding the face you are looking for within a crowd
- maintaining a new piece of information in mind against distraction, such as remembering a telephone number until you dial while on your cell phone in a crowded mall
- overcoming a compelling behaviour, such as not scratching a very itchy mosquito bite
- pursuing a complex but unfamiliar behaviour, such as learning the moves of a new sport or how to work the controls of a new videogame
- responding flexibly and productively in new situations, such as playing a complex videogame that requires anticipating future consequences

executive function the brain's ability to control and manage the mental processing of information.

dysexecutive syndrome impairments in the ability to control and direct mental activities.

The brain's ability to exert control over mental processing is referred to as **executive function**. People with damage to the frontal lobes often display a condition called **dysexecutive syndrome**, characterized by impairments in cognitive functions that depend on control, such as planning or the ability to flexibly respond in new situations.

Tom Grill/Corbis

©iStockphoto.com/Michael Krinke

Automatic processing has its limits. Even automatic processing, such as that used when driving a car, can be severely interrupted by tasks that require significant attention, such as texting. Thus, to prevent car accidents, provincial laws typically allow people to converse (a relatively non-distracting activity) on a hands-free phone while driving, but forbid them to use a hand-held cell phone. Unfortunately, hand-free cell phone use is also distracting, possibly to the same extent as hand-held use (Ishigami & Klein, 2009).

This deficit was dramatically documented in the classic case of Phineas Gage. As we discussed in Part 3, Gage was a railroad foreman who suffered damage to his prefrontal cortex when a metal spike was driven through his head in a construction accident. Before the accident, acquaintances described him as thoughtful, responsible, and of sound judgment, but following his injury, he was considered to be "capricious . . . and unable to settle on any of the plans he devised for future action" (Harlow, 1868). Changes such as these have been observed repeatedly in patients with damage to the frontal cortex.

As we age, we also develop more capacity for cognitive control. Very young children, for example, often make decisions based on impulse; if they want the cookie and it's in view, they will grab it. For this reason, problems arise with social interactions. Preschool-aged children will often fight over toys because they don't understand the concepts of waiting and fairness. As children grow, however, their decision-making process becomes more sophisticated. Usually by the time they are 6 to 8 years old, children are able to manage their impulses for the good of their interaction with their peers. During snacktime, William may save a cookie for Lydia, who is out of the room, rather than eat it himself. At an even later stage, between the ages of 9 and 12 years, children become able to make decisions with the long-term future in mind. They are more willing to make sacrifices in the immediate future to get a larger payoff later on. If given the option of getting one square of chocolate after completing a single math problem or an entire chocolate bar after a 24-hour waiting period, older children will often decide to hold out for the whole bar (Mischel, Shoda, & Rodriquez, 1989).

©iStockphoto.com/szefei

Enough for everyone. By the age of 6 to 8 years old, children have learned to better control their thoughts and actions in accord with their various intentions. Sharing everything from ice cream to toys becomes a more common occurrence.

53.2 Thinking to Solve Problems

One aspect of thinking that has received considerable attention from psychologists is that of problem solving. **Problem solving** is triggered by our desire to reach a goal. We must figure out how to get from our current state of affairs, which is in some way

problem solving determining how to reach a goal.

unsatisfactory, to our desired end state (Bourne, Dominowski, & Loftus, 1979). We use problem-solving skills in many avenues of life, from the formal mathematics problems we have all solved in school, to informal day-to-day problems, such as how to get along with a roommate.

53.2.1 Defining Our Problems

The first step in solving a problem is to figure out exactly what your problem is—to develop a representation of the problem.

> "We only think when we are confronted with problems."
>
> —*John Dewey, American psychologist*

On one end of the spectrum, we use formal problem-solving skills to solve math problems. Our goal in arithmetic is usually straightforward: to move from not knowing the correct answer to knowing it. Researchers refer to problems with easy-to-discern beginning and end states, such as arithmetic, as *well-defined problems*. We often find it fairly easy to find a strategy for solving well-defined problems because we can easily define what outcome we want from the start.

On the other end of the problem-solving spectrum are *ill-defined problems*, such as how to deal with a messy roommate. Our goal in this case might be difficult to define in precise terms. We may want to stop doing what we feel is an unfair share of housecleaning, but how will we know when we have reached that goal? As you might imagine, it's often more difficult to find solution strategies for ill-defined problems than it is for well-defined ones, because it is hard to define the desired outcome (Pretz, Naples, & Sternberg, 2003).

To define a problem, you must figure out your current state and your goal, and identify the differences between them. Consider the following problem. When driving home on a particular road, you need to make a left onto Main Street at a traffic light that is always very backed up at the time of day you travel. Your current state is frustration with the long wait at the light.

Your goal might be to find a faster way to make the turn. With this goal in mind, you could consider several ways to speed up the turn, such as altering the time of day you travel, driving faster to arrive at the intersection earlier, or merging into the line of waiting cars closer to the intersection. None of these solutions is ideal. If the problem is represented in a different way, however, a new solution may come to mind. You might, for example, change your question from, "How do I make a left onto Main Street?" to, "How can I get onto Main Street faster?"

Adopting a new goal such as this may cause you to notice that you could turn right into the parking lot of a shopping centre at the corner, then exit the lot quickly and legally onto Main Street in the direction you want to go—avoiding the left-hand turn entirely. Changing the representation of a problem doesn't guarantee you will find a solution, but it increases your chances of finding one if your new representation triggers you to consider new alternatives.

53.2.2 Strategies for Problem Solving

algorithm a problem-solving strategy that always leads to a solution.

After you have represented the problem, you must choose a strategy for finding a solution. Two major types of strategies—algorithms and heuristics—are used. An **algorithm** is a strategy that, if followed methodically, will always lead to a solution. For example, an algorithm strategy could be used to solve an arithmetic problem that includes adding up a series of 10 single-digit numbers by adding each number to the overall sum. Following this algorithm will produce a correct answer, but it can be time consuming. If you had to add up the total of 50 or 100 different numbers, you might begin to look for faster ways to solve the problem.

heuristic a shortcut thinking strategy.

To save time and effort when solving problems, we often use a set of **heuristics**, or shortcut strategies. Instead of taking the time to add together a long list of numbers, you might just estimate the total. Heuristics often help us reach a satisfactory solution, but they do not guarantee a correct answer to a problem.

You can use algorithm and heuristic strategies to solve problems in everyday life. Consider the steps you would take to find out whether or not a particular professor will be a good teacher for you before enrolling in his course. Using an algorithm method, you might question every student enrolled in the class the previous term. This method would give you the maximum amount of information and the greatest chance of reaching the correct answer. Using a heuristic strategy, you might ask a few students you know who took the course or examine the drop rate in the class for evidence of how many students decide against the course once enrolled. Heuristic methods save time and effort, but they are also riskier. Your few acquaintances might not learn as well from a teaching style that you like, for example. On the other hand they might suggest some factors you have not considered allowing you to make a better decision.

Some helpful heuristic strategies in problem solving include working backwards, forming subgoals, and searching for analogies.

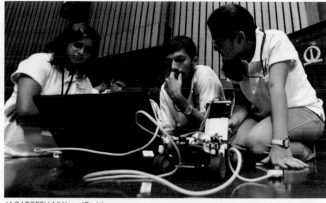

JAGADEESH NV/epa/Corbis

Two heads are better than one. For many problems, better solutions are reached when multiple persons think the problem through together. Such collaborations may increase the likelihood of gathering sufficient information and reduce the chance of falling into common problem solving traps.

- *Working backwards* is helpful for problems with well-defined goals. Starting from your goal, you think backwards, imagining a series of steps it would take you to move backwards from your goal to your current state. Once you have determined the steps between your current state and the goal, you can actually follow them in a forward order. A working backwards example is the water lily problem. Imagine that you have planted a water lily on a pond. The number of leaves the lily produces on the water's surface doubles every day. On the 30th day, the number of leaves will cover the pond and kill off all the living things in the pond. You decide to cut out the lily when it has covered half the pond. What do you need to know to work out when to cut the lily (e.g., size of the pond, size of the lily leaves, etc.)? The answer? You need to know nothing if you work backwards, as you will cut the lily on the 29th day (before its coverage doubles one more time and covers the whole pond).

- *Forming subgoals* involves dividing a larger problem into smaller ones (Catrambone, 1998). If your ultimate goal is to find out if a professor will be a good teacher for you, you may form subgoals, such as asking three former students about the professor and arranging to sit in on a lecture. Another example that is a bit more specific is called the tower of Hanoi problem. Four disks of different diameters are stacked from largest up to smallest on the leftmost of three pegs. Your task is to shift the whole stack to the peg on the far right, but only by moving one disk at a time and by never having a larger disk set on top of a smaller disk. You can see an animated solution to this problem at the following link: www.mathsisfun.com/games/towerofhanoi.html. Note that the solution involves accomplishing a series of subgoals.

- *Searching for analogies* involves recalling similar problems that you have encountered (Holyoak & Morrison, 2005). Imagine you are driving a car borrowed from a friend and it breaks down. You may not have much experience figuring out what is wrong with cars but, if you have worked on motorcycles in the past, there may be some experiences that you can draw on analogously to try to figure out what is wrong with the car. Alternatively, you might remember calling your university's information technologies help desk to get help solving a computer problem, and come up with the idea of calling a relative or friend who has expertise with car repair.

We are not always aware of using a method to solve a problem. Sometimes we seem to solve a problem quickly, without intensive effort or concentration, through a phenomenon known as *insight*. In fact, several groundbreaking scientific discoveries have been

	A	B	C	Goal
1	21	127	3	100
2	36	151	9	97
3	11	76	5	55
4	2	16	2	10
5	15	39	3	18

FIGURE 53-1 **The water jar problem.** Start at the top row (line number 1). Imagine that you have three containers (A, B, and C) that hold the number of units of water indicated across row #1. Using only those containers and no other measuring device, figure out how to end up with the goal amount of water listed in the last column of the table for that row. When you have a solution, move down to the next row and solve that problem as well. Keep moving down until you have solved all rows. Now show this problem to a friend, but have her begin with the bottom row and move up to the top row. Notice any differences? Check at the end of the module to see what the original study found by following this same procedure.

FIGURE 53-2 **The nine-dot problem.** Without lifting your pencil, draw no more than four straight lines to connect all the dots. (The solution is at the end of the module.)

mental set tendency to use problem-solving strategies that have worked in the past.

functional fixedness tendency to view objects as having only one function.

confirmation bias tendency to look for information that meets our expectations.

> **"**If the only tool you have is a hammer, it is tempting to treat everything as if it were a nail.**"**
> —*Abraham Maslow, American psychologist*

described as "eureka" moments of insight. George de Mestral took his dog for a walk in the woods and when he returned home, George noticed his pants were covered in burrs that were hard to remove. Curious, he looked at one under a microscope and saw the small hooks at the ends of the burr spines. He thought about it and, eureka, Velcro was invented (Freeman & Golden, 1997). Sometimes sudden solutions occur after an *incubation period* during which we have mentally "set aside" a problem that we've been working on. When we return to the problem after a period of time, the solution comes to mind without further conscious strategizing. Some studies suggest this type of problem solving is automatic (Novick & Bassock, 2005).

53.2.3 Problems in Problem Solving

Sometimes we fall into patterns of thinking that make it difficult to solve problems to which those patterns don't apply. One common difficulty can happen early in representing the problem. We must define the problem using relevant information and ignore any irrelevant information. When deciding what movie to go and see, you might make your decision based on the number of times you have seen trailers of a movie, rather than looking at reviews or asking friends who may have seen it already. In fact, the number of trailers released may be a function of studio concerns about the quality of the movie.

Other difficulties can occur when we get to the point of actually solving problems. Some of these are the result of heuristics. When we use the heuristic of looking for analogies, for example, we risk falling into a **mental set**, a tendency to use problem-solving strategies that have always worked in the past. If you have a certain solution in mind, you may see the problem as fitting that solution, when it does not. If you view getting onto Main Street with a mental set that sees the problem as how to make a left turn, you miss possible solutions that do not involve left turns (like making three right turns). The water jar problem shown in **Figure 53-1** and the nine-dot problem shown in **Figure 53-2** are good ways to practise overcoming mental sets.

One particular version of a mental set is referred to as **functional fixedness**, the tendency to view objects as having only one use or function. If you have ever used a coin to turn the head of a screw when you didn't have a screwdriver handy, you have overcome functional fixedness. The string problem, shown in **Figure 53-3**, is one test that psychologists have used to reveal when people are experiencing functional fixedness.

We can also hamper our ability to solve problems by adopting a **confirmation bias**, a tendency to look for information that meets our expectations when solving problems. If you have heard that all of the professors in the department in which you are thinking of taking a class are good teachers, you may only seek out opinions from students who completed the class taught by the professor whose class you are thinking of taking, rather than undertaking the more difficult task of finding people who have dropped the course. The problem with this approach is that students who stayed through the whole course would be more likely to confirm what you expect to hear, that the teacher is good, than to give you a negative, but potentially helpful, evaluation.

In one classic study, researchers revealed confirmation bias by giving participants a series of numbers: 2, 4, and 6 (Wason, 1960). They asked the participants to figure out the rule for that set by generating their own sets of numbers. Each time the participants offered a series, the experimenters told them only whether their set did or did not follow the same rule as the original set. Many participants became convinced that the rule was to increase each number by 2. They offered repeated sets of numbers, such as 8, 10, 12 or 24, 22, 20. The researchers told them that their sets conformed to the original rule, but when asked to state the original rule, these participants got it wrong. The original rule was simply that each number had to have a numerical value larger than the one before it. The numbers the participants generated

FIGURE 53-3 The string problem.
Two strings are suspended from above, and you cannot reach both of them at the same time. How can you tie them together? (The solution is at the end of the module.)

themselves conformed to the rules they created, but it didn't occur to them that other rules were possible.

The way to overcome confirmation bias is to purposely look for information that disconfirms your ideas. Participants who generated random series of numbers, such as 54, 3, 12, would have been more likely to correctly figure out the rule.

53.3 Thinking to Make Decisions

Decision making involves evaluating and choosing from among the alternatives available to us. Many of your everyday thoughts involve weighing options and making choices. First you must decide what time to wake up. A series of decisions follow, including choices about what to wear, what to eat for breakfast, with whom to spend your time, and what to do. Even when we're on a regular schedule, we don't behave like robots. We often have options to deviate from our regular course of action, and we must decide whether or not to take them.

53.3.1 Information for Decision Making

To make decisions, we need to gather or recall information relevant to each alternative. Suppose you're trying to decide which of two movies to go see. You would probably like a little information about each film to help you make your choice. You can gather information from sources outside yourself, such as movie reviews and the comments of your friends. You can also recall relevant information that you already have. You may, for example, recognize the names of some of the actors or one of the directors.

When we draw from our memories to get information, we often use heuristic shortcuts. The use of heuristics is sometimes successful, but often leads to reaching the incorrect

decision making evaluating and choosing from among options.

decision, as shown in the work of Nobel prize-winning psychologist Danny Kahneman, who developed many of his studies while working at the University of British Columbia (Stanovich, 2011; Tversky & Kahneman, 1993, 1974). These researchers describe two heuristics: the representativeness heuristic and the availability heuristic.

The **representativeness heuristic** makes the assumption that individual objects or people are members of a category if they share similar characteristics. When we use this heuristic, we draw conclusions about an object, event, or person based on a small set of specific data, often ignoring other relevant information. Suppose, for example, that one of the movies you are thinking of seeing has several characteristics that seem to identify it as a romantic comedy. You may not bother to read reviews or get other information about the movie because, based only on its presumed identity as a romantic comedy, you have a set of expectations about what the movie will be like.

Amos Tversky and Danny Kahneman (1974) nicely demonstrated people's use of the representativeness heuristic by asking research participants to read a description of an individual that included personal attributes such as, "shows no interest in political and social issues," and "spends most of his free time on . . . mathematical puzzles." After they read this paragraph, participants were also told that the individual was randomly selected from a pool that contained 70 percent lawyers and 30 percent engineers. Ignoring the strong statistical probability that the individual was more likely to be a lawyer than an engineer, most of the participants used the personal characteristics of the individual to identify him as an engineer based on a few personal characteristics.

Another approximation used to make decisions is known as the **availability heuristic**. Answer this question: are there more words in the English language that start with the letter K or that have the letter K in the third position? We will come back to this shortly. The availability heuristic refers to the likelihood that we will judge an event as more common if it is easier to think about it (Keller, Siegrist, & Gutscher, 2006; Oppenheimer, 2004; McKelvie & Drumheller, 2001). You may easily remember the one really great film made by an actor in one of the movies you are thinking about attending, but not be able to recall much about the actor's so-so work in several other films. The availability heuristic also explains why we tend to think that infrequent but highly salient and memorable events, such as plane crashes or tsunamis, are more common than they actually are. Because such events are easy to call to mind, we assume they commonly occur when, in fact, they are very rare (Foster, 2009). So what about the K question? There are actually more words in English with the letter K in the third position. However, words starting with the letter K are much more available when we try to think of them, so people usually say there are more words that start with K than have K in the third position (Tversky & Kahneman, 1974).

Another aspect of the availability heuristic that affects decision making is the fact that we tend to rely on more recently stored memories to make judgments about events. For example, patients who underwent painful medical colonoscopy procedures are more likely to remember the event as excruciatingly painful if it is over quickly and ends at a time of maximal pain, than if the procedure is extended for a longer period of time with some time at the end of diminished pain (Redelmeier, Katz, & Kahneman, 2003). Because it's easier to call more recent information to mind, we assume that it is more indicative of the overall experience.

representativeness heuristic the assumption that individuals share characteristics of the category of which they are a member.

Hans Deryk/AFP/Getty Images

Unforgettable. Because horrific scenes of airplane crashes stay in our memories, we tend to think that such crashes are more common than they actually are via the availability heuristic.

availability heuristic judging easily-recalled events as more common.

53.3.2 Rational Decision Making

After we have gathered or brought to mind information about the alternatives, how do we evaluate each one and go about picking one of them? For thousands of years, since the time of the ancient Greek philosopher Plato, philosophers have argued that it is better to rely on logical reasoning than on emotions or instinct when making decisions. And, until relatively recently, many of the theorists and researchers who studied decision making assumed that people's decisions—particularly financial decisions about what products to buy, whether to save or spend, and how to invest—were based on purely logical reasoning.

Numerous models of such rational decision-making processes exist. Many assume that we choose a set of criteria and rank each alternative on its *utility*, or its ability to satisfy each criterion (Edwards & Newman, 1986; Edwards, 1977). If you are looking for a new phone, for instance, you might evaluate its size, cost, and the number of apps that are available. Some models of rational decision making suggest that we may go even farther and give more importance or "weight" to certain criteria. If, for example, it is very important to have certain apps available on a new phone, you may weigh that criterion more highly than the phone's size and cost. According to these models, after gathering and evaluating information on each phone, you could mathematically calculate which phone is the best for you. **Table 53-1** shows a model of such a calculation. According to this model, you would choose Phone C.

For some decisions, rational models of decision making suggest that we might also take into account the *probability* that we can attain our choices. If, for example, you are choosing classes for next term, the course that ranks as your top choice may be so popular on campus that you rate your chance of getting into the class as low. In this case, you may decide to sign up for another course, instead of your top choice, as part of your rational decision-making process.

Reason-based decision-making methods such as these can help us when we have fairly few choices and evaluate them using fairly few attributes (Payne & Bettman, 2004). Sometimes we cannot use such a model until we narrow down the choices (Slovic, 1990; Tversky, 1972). You may, for example, have eliminated 15 other phones that were entirely beyond your budget before choosing only three to consider further. Sometimes the method of eliminating alternatives is the only one we need. If every phone but one is beyond your budget, you don't need to perform a complicated analysis before deciding which phone you can get.

Rational decision-making models tend to be based on assumptions that we have information available to us about all our alternatives and that we have time to ponder this information. As you may have experienced, a lot of decisions in real life don't fit these criteria (Gigerenzer & Goldstein, 1996). After you buy your phone, for example, you may want to stop in the food court at the mall for a snack. With only a few minutes to decide, you may focus on only a few of the available options—maybe the first couple of restaurants you walk by—or a few attributes of the choices—such as whether they offer a vegetarian dish. You may still think rationally about your choice, but you are

Car Culture/Corbis

"Buy one now, before they're all gone." Recognizing that emotions can interfere with careful decision making, automobile dealers typically try to create a sense of urgency and excitement when selling their products.

TABLE 53-1 Model of Rational Decision Making: Considering Both Rank and Weight (Importance)

Criterion	Weight of Criteria	Phone A		Phone B		Phone C	
		Rank	Rank × weight	Rank	Rank × weight	Rank	Rank × weight
Size	13	8	24	5	15	5	15
Cost	16	8	48	6	36	4	24
Apps	110	0	0	5	50	8	80
Total of rank × weight		**Phone A: 72**		**Phone B: 101**		**Phone C: 119**	

bounded rationality the fact that in many situations, our ability to make clear rational decisions is limited or "bounded" by things like a lack of information, time constraints, or emotions attached to aspects of the problem we are trying to solve.

using a model known as **bounded rationality** that limits the cognitive effort you need to invest (Simon, 1957). The theory of bounded rationality suggests that our ability to make decisions in a rational, logical manner is limited by incomplete information, time limits of decision making, and our own emotional feelings about one or more of the available options. All of these factors limit or "bound" our ability to behave purely rationally. Research suggests that we *successfully* use bounded rationality to make many of our decisions by doing the best we can with the cognitive resources and information that we have available at a given moment (Gigerenzer, 2004; Simon, 1990).

53.3.3 Emotions and Decision Making

Suppose you are perusing the food court for your snack and you get a craving for French fries. You might just buy some and eat them, without putting much—if any—rational thought into your decision. For a long time, decisions such as this troubled rational decision-making theorists, because such choices are not based on logical reasons. Because of the work of Danny Kahneman, however, we now know that decision making often involves irrational processes that can be driven by our emotions. In fact, people *often* rely heavily on their emotions, or "gut instinct," rather than pure reason to make decisions.

The involvement of emotions in decision making makes predicting human behaviour very difficult. There are individual differences in emotional reactions, and many of these are driven by developmental experience and temperament. Even our moods can affect our decision making. Research suggests, for example, that when we are in a positive mood, we tend to make more efficient decisions with less rational consideration of the alternatives. We also tend to be content with those choices (Schwartz et al., 2002).

Researchers have discovered a few situations in which our emotions are likely to influence decisions somewhat predictably. One of these is when we try to estimate risks in anticipating the consequences of our decisions. For example, if you buy the wrong new phone, you risk being unhappy with it or needing to take it in for lots of repairs. Research suggests that we base our decisions, at least in part, on our anticipation of how we will feel if we make a bad choice (Mellers, Schwartz, & Cooke, 1998; Mellers et al., 1997; Kahneman & Tversky, 1979), and that, in general, we try hard to avoid making decisions we will regret later (Connolly & Zeelenberg, 2002). For many of us, "bad" outweighs "good" in our anticipation, so we might make less than optimal choices just to avoid the risk of feeling bad later. Given the option to receive 10 cents of a shared (with one other person) dollar, for example, most people will opt out altogether, taking nothing instead of the 10 cents, because they would feel they had been treated unfairly by having to share the dollar. This is irrational behaviour, since 10 cents is clearly better than nothing at all.

Understanding how emotions can shift the likelihood of a purchase is of particular interest to advertisers. If the context that produces positive emotion can be identified in all situations, it can be used effectively to persuade consumers to buy. In many cases, language can play a role in producing this context by framing choices in positive or negative ways. We are more likely to buy a food that is labelled "75 percent fat-free" than one that is described as "25 percent fat," for example (Sanford et al., 2002). The first statement frames the product in terms of "fat-free," and as such is preferred to the second statement, even though the product is exactly the same in both cases.

Framing is especially effective in arousing emotions when we are estimating risks. Most university or college students would feel safer using condoms that prevent the transmission of HIV 95 percent of the time than the same condoms when they are described as failing to prevent HIV transmission 5 percent of the time (Linville, Fischer, & Fischhoff, 1993). Tversky and Kahneman (1981) provided another classic example of framing. They asked students to imagine that they were helping Health Canada select a treatment scenario for an outbreak of an expected deadly disease. Imagine that you are one of the students in their experiment. You are told that it is estimated that 600 people will contract the disease and die without treatment. You are told that Treatment Option A will save 200 of those affected, while Treatment Option B has a 1/3 probability of saving all 600 people

practically speaking | When Is It Best to Rely on Emotions for Decision Making?

Intuition, hunches, inner voice, gut, instinct—emotional decision making goes by many names, and its importance is often downplayed compared to rational thought.

Paul Thagard at the University of Waterloo suggests that emotions can play a key role in decision making (Thagard & Kroon, 2008; Thagard, 2001). He points out that emotional or intuitive decision making has some up-front advantages. It is fast—with no time needed to weigh options, the decision is immediate. It leads to decisions based on things you really care about (my family and friends are important to me so maybe going away to school is not a great idea). And finally, this approach to decision making leads directly to action.

Listing the plusses and minuses of decision options is a rational approach to decision making; however, some people find it to be a bit robot-like. Thagard offers a compromise that he calls using *informed intuition* to make decisions. This intuitive approach involves the following four steps:

1. Construct the decision problem with care. Identify the goals that will follow from your decision and the actions that will accomplish them.
2. Look at each goal and estimate its importance. This is a more intuitive or emotional process, but it will help you clearly see what you care about in the decision. Tag those goals whose importance you may have exaggerated (be honest!) or that you are emotionally over-focused upon and adjust them a bit.
3. Review how likely it is that the potential actions being considered will accomplish the goals you have in mind. How much evidence do you have for these assessments about whether the actions will accomplish the goals? If you do not have enough evidence, you probably need to change the possible actions.
4. Make your intuitive/emotional judgment about the best action to perform, while at the same time checking your emotional reaction to different options. Finally, run your decision past other people to see if it seems reasonable to them.

Let's try an example. Imagine you are trying to decide what sort of vehicle to buy to get around on for your summer job as a courier and through the term at school.

Step 1. The vehicle needs to be affordable and reliable, and so a well-researched small four-door car might be best. But

George Doyle/Getty Images

you have also been thinking that a motorcycle would be a LOT of fun.

Step 2. How important is it that your transportation be reliable, affordable, and fun? Is the fun goal maybe a bit exaggerated? Maybe it needs to be downscaled a bit.

Step 3. Would a motorcycle get you around as a courier in the summer? How about getting around town while at school in the winter? What about the car? Would a car (with a good heater) be more fun to have in the winter? What, if any, additional data would help?

Step 4. Decide to buy a car, but think about the emotional impact of making that decision. Talk to other people who have perhaps tried to keep a motorcycle running in the winter. Ask others what they think of your decision.

So, the bottom line is that decision making can (and Paul Thagard suggests should) involve an emotional or intuitive component, but one that we are aware of and use to make informed decisions.

and a 2/3 probability that none will be saved. Which option would you pick? Now what if, instead, you were offered the following two options. Treatment Option C would result in the deaths of 400 people, while with Treatment Option D there is a 1/3 probability no one will die and a 2/3 probability that all 600 will die. Which of these options would you pick? In Kahneman and Tversky's study, most people preferred Options A and D, even though options A and C are identical, as are Options B and D. The researchers explained their finding as due to differences in framing the options in terms of life or death.

The interference of emotions in making decisions is not all negative. Although it's true that being upset or anxious or feeling cheated or irrationally hopeful may impair our judgment and increase the chance that we will make an impulsive and unnecessary purchase, it is sometimes the case that emotions help us make better decisions. Research has shown that individuals often make better decisions in games with a chance element when they claim to be operating on a "hunch." Intuition is not well understood, but it is an irrational characteristic that sometimes improves decision-making capabilities. The Practically Speaking feature gives you some tips about when it can be helpful to "go with your gut."

53.4 Metacognition

metacognition thinking about one's own thoughts.

One of the most complicated forms of thought is **metacognition**, thinking about thinking. When we consider our own memories, for example, we engage in a form of metacognition. We may mull over specific facts we remember, thinking about their sources and when we learned them. We may also think about how information we have learned in the past is influencing our current interpretations of events. Metacognition involving thinking about the source of memories involves activation of the frontal cortex of the brain as well as the hippocampus, a region important for storage of information. Damage to the hippocampus can result in source amnesia, a condition that prevents accurate thinking about one's own memories (Lakhan, 2007).

Self-reflection is another form of metacognition. It involves thinking about our own identities, how we influence other people, and our relative self-worth. Self-reflection is an important human behaviour because it enables us to evaluate and modify our responses based on our past experience. We may reflect on our behaviour at a recent party, for example, and decide that we would feel better about ourselves if we were more, or perhaps less, outgoing. Then we might take steps either to overcome shyness or tone down our party persona. Self-reflection can sometimes have negative consequences if it leads to repetitive thoughts of worthlessness and anxiety. For people with specific biological tendencies, excessive self-reflection can lead to psychological disorders, such as depression and anxiety disorders (Takano & Tanno, 2009).

Frans Lanting/Corbis

Assessing metacognition in animals. Because chimps and gorillas cannot vocalize as humans do, researchers can assess their capacity for metacognition only with special strategies, such as by having them point to symbols on a keyboard or by observing their behaviour in certain learning tasks.

Another type of metacognition occurs when we infer what someone else is thinking by watching or hearing about that person's actions. This phenomenon, called *theory of mind*, is an important aspect of human thought. As we discussed in Part 4, theory of mind is an adaptive trait because it facilitates communication and peaceful living with other people. If we did not have theory of mind and instead needed explicit verbal information about the feelings and intentions of another person, social communication would be stilted.

Once we acquire this ability during development, it becomes automatic. You probably exercise your theory of mind many times a day, while assessing your roommate's mood on the basis of his actions, gauging a professor's expectations based on her demeanour, or trying to figure out what type of a person your date is from the cues you receive on the first date.

53.4.1 How Metacognition Develops

HOW WE
DEVELOP

Children gradually develop a theory of other peoples' minds, starting during the toddler years. Young children, ages 2 to 3 years, demonstrate that they lack the ability to infer the thinking of the person who is searching for them when trying to play hide-and-seek. Children this age will often "hide" by covering their eyes while remaining in a location that is not out of view. Piaget (2003) referred to this sort of preschool thinking as egocentric (see Part 4). Rather than take the point of view of the searcher, they rely on their own experience, believing that "If I can't see because my eyes are covered, no one else can see me." This lack of theory of mind disappears by about age 4 (Sabbagh et al., 2009; Aschersleben, Hofer, & Jovanovic, 2008).

Young children's developing theory of mind may contribute to jealousy and an inability to share when it makes it possible for a child to think of another child as a rival intending to take away her toys. Another behaviour that is tied to thinking about what's going on in another person's head is lying. In general, people lie for two main reasons: to prevent themselves from being punished or to make someone else feel good (Feldman, 2009; Feldman, Forrest, & Happ, 2002). Children learn very young to lie in order to avoid punishment. This behaviour seems to emerge around age 3 for most children, and by age 5 it is a fairly universal phenomenon (Talwar & Lee, 2008). If "backed into a corner" so that a child believes it's likely he will be punished, almost all 5-year-olds will lie. Theory of mind allows people to lie in hopes of preventing punishment, even if they have not explicitly been warned about the punishment (Talwar, Gordon, & Lee, 2007). Because the child is able to imagine that an adult believes the child's behaviour is wrong, she can then infer that the adult intends to punish her for the wrong behaviour.

Thinkstock/Getty

Hiding in plain sight. Young children lack the ability to infer what another person is thinking and will often "hide" by covering their eyes . . . "If I can't see you, you can't see me!"

Lying to make another person feel better, such as giving false compliments or reassurances, is another behaviour that arises during the preschool years. Unlike lying to avoid punishment, however, this type of lying seems to increase in frequency as we get older (Lind & Bowler, 2009). Have you ever complimented a friend on a new haircut or new outfit that you actually felt was less than flattering? The chances are you did not feel particularly guilty afterward, because your thoughts about how your friend feels are stronger than your desire to always tell the truth.

Although theory of mind seems to be present in very young children, other forms of metacognition are not evident until much later in development. For example, thinking about their own memories and evaluating current information in the context of the past is not a common thought process of young children. Young children often suffer from source amnesia (not remembering where they heard about certain information), which not only makes them prone to develop false memories, but also interferes with their ability to think about their memories in a meaningful way (Zola, 1998).

53.5 Problems with Thought Processes

One of the ways we can better understand how we function psychologically is to look closely at what is going on when we are not functioning well. Understanding what sorts of conditions negatively affect our thought processes can help us to better understand how those thought processes work. Many disorders include problems with thinking. In many cases, however, these conditions are primarily associated with deficits in other psychological processes; impairments in the person's thinking are not the main difficulty. Individuals with Alzheimer disease are often in a confused state, for example, but the reason they are not thinking clearly is because their memories are disrupted. In other cases, problems with thinking are tied to aberrant emotional states. Depression is often accompanied by repetitive thoughts about worthlessness and hopelessness, and cognitive therapy that targets these thoughts can often be a successful form of treatment (Rupke, Blecke, & Renfrow, 2006). Although the thought components of dementia and mood disorders are real and significant symptoms, we discuss them in other parts because these conditions are primarily associated with other psychological processes. Another two disorders, obsessive-compulsive disorder and schizophrenia, are characterized primarily by difficulties in controlling one's thoughts, so we will describe them briefly here as it is

FACING
ADVERSITY

obsessive-compulsive disorder (OCD) a mental disorder associated with abnormal anxiety-provoking thoughts that can lead to ritualistic behaviours.

worth looking at what they might suggest to us about human thought processes. They will, however, be discussed in greater detail in Part 15.

Obsessive-compulsive disorder (OCD) is defined as having uncontrollable, anxiety-provoking thoughts called *obsessions*. Many people with this disorder feel *compulsions*, or irresistible urges, to perform mental or physical ritual actions to help reduce their anxiety around their obsession (APA, 2000). People with OCD know that their obsessions are out of contact with reality, but they often find the thoughts impossible to inhibit and ignore. For example, a person might have obsessive thoughts about germs and anxiety that could lead to compulsive hand washing, or a person may have obsessive thoughts about his children being harmed that could lead to compulsively checking that the stove is not on. The impulse to engage in compulsive behaviour, such as washing one's hands over and over or repeatedly checking whether a stove has been turned off, is so strong that anxiety builds with each passing moment that the behaviour is inhibited (Magee & Teachman, 2007). OCD can range from relatively mild to extremes that render people unable to participate in normal life activities. Estimates of the prevalence of OCD are uncertain because many people with mild OCD do not receive a formal diagnosis. Conservative estimates suggest that OCD affects about 1 percent of the population (Kessler et al., 2005).

The increase in anxiety-provoking thoughts associated with OCD is a good example of the complexity of human thinking. The relationship between our thoughts and our reality is actually something that can be stretched or even broken with disorders like OCD. As we come to understand the factors underlying OCD, we may also come to understand some of the key control factors involved in non-disordered human thinking. We will examine this topic in greater detail in Part 15.

schizophrenia a mental disorder characterized by disorganized thoughts, lack of contact with reality, and sometimes auditory hallucinations.

Schizophrenia is another disorder that involves some of the most basic and most important aspects of the human thinking process. Schizophrenia is a relatively common psychotic disorder that is characterized by extreme disorganization of thinking. About 1.1 percent of people in Canada have been diagnosed with some form of schizophrenia (IMHRO, 2009). Although schizophrenia can exist in multiple forms, a common theme in the disease is a break from reality in thoughts and actions. Some people with schizophrenia experience distortions of reality, distortions in the form of *hallucinations* (usually auditory), and *delusions*, beliefs that are not based in reality (APA, 2000). They also exhibit a devastating inability to plan and control their own thoughts (Berenbaum & Barch, 1995). Furthermore, many people with this disorder suffer impaired working memory and find it impossible to keep track of information necessary to execute a simple series of actions (Piskulic et al., 2007).

Findings on the water jar problem. Did your friend find the simpler solution to the 5th row problem that you missed (Jar A plus Jar C, instead of Jar B minus Jar A minus Jar C twice)? This classic experiment by Abraham Luchins (1942) demonstrates mental set. Most people who start at the top of the list figure out a solution and then apply it to all the problems. This creates a mental set that leads them to miss the simpler two-jar solution to the last row. Those starting at the bottom of the list are much more likely to see and use the simpler solution. How did you do?

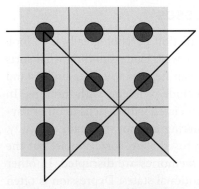

Solution to the nine-dot problem. Most people have difficulty with this problem because they see the arrangement of dots as a square and try to keep within the boundaries of the dots. This mental set limits their ability to solve the problem.

Solution to the string problem. Tie the pliers to one string and use it as a weight to swing the string closer to you. Functional fixedness can limit your ability to recognize this use for the pliers.

Schizophrenia often also includes a language component. Sometimes a person's speech and writing become entirely disorganized and out of touch with reality (Covington et al., 2005). However, in spite of the nonsensical content, many people diagnosed with schizophrenia are able to retain intact semantics and syntax in sentence construction (Covington et al., 2005). Essentially, schizophrenia attacks the parts of our thinking processes that make us rational. Understanding the effects of schizophrenia on the brain will also provide us with an understanding of higher level human thinking. Potential causes and treatments of schizophrenia will be discussed in Parts 15 and 16.

Before You Go On

www.wiley.com/go/comercanada

What Do You Know?

1. Compare and contrast controlled and automatic cognitive processing.
2. What are the two main types of strategies for solving problems? How do these two strategies differ? Give at least one example of each type.
3. What are the representativeness and availability heuristics and how do they affect decision making?
4. How can emotions affect our decision making?
5. What is metacognition? What is a theory of mind?
6. How is thinking disturbed in OCD? How are thinking and language disturbed in schizophrenia?

What Do You Think? Which of the barriers to problem solving described in this part most often seem to affect you? Which problem-solving strategies seem to work best for you?

Summary

Module 53: Thought

LEARNING OBJECTIVE 53 Describe and summarize research on thinking processes, including problem solving, decision making, and metacognition.

- We are capable of several different kinds of thought, and different types of thinking involve different brain regions, often including those related to the specific thoughts. We develop various thinking abilities gradually with age.
- Controlled processing relies on the executive function of the brain. We become increasingly able to exert cognitive control as we age.
- Problem solving is finding a way to reach a goal. Algorithms, problem-solving strategies that guarantee a solution if followed methodically, work best for well-defined problems. Shortcut strategies called heuristics may help with ill-defined problems.
- Common problem-solving heuristics include working backwards, finding analogies to other problems, and forming subgoals. Heuristics can lead to difficulties in problem solving, including mental sets, functional fixedness, and confirmation bias.
- Decision making involves evaluating and choosing from among the options available to us. We often use heuristics to recall information to make decisions, but some, including the representativeness and availability heuristics, can bias our evaluations.
- Rational models of problem solving suggest that we make elimination options and/or make weighted evaluations of the utility and probability of options. We often lack time, information, or cognitive resources for rational decision making, however, so we use a strategy of limited or bounded rationality.
- Emotions often play a role in decision making, sometimes interfering with our ability to make rational decisions, but other times helping us to make efficient choices.
- Metacognition is thinking about our own thoughts. It includes reviewing and evaluating our own memories, self-reflection, and theory of mind—inferring the intentions of other people.
- Obsessive-compulsive disorder (OCD) and schizophrenia are two mental disorders that include major thought disruptions.

Key Terms

algorithm 398

availability heuristic 402

bounded rationality 404

cognitive control 396

confirmation bias 400

decision making 401

dysexecutive syndrome 396

executive function 396

functional fixedness 400

heuristic 398

mental set 400

metacognition 406

obsessive-compulsive disorder (OCD) 408

problem solving 397

representativeness heuristic 402

schizophrenia 408

Study Questions

Multiple Choice

1. A political science professor attempts to facilitate her students' completion of a term paper assignment by requiring that they first submit a topic statement, then a list of references, then a draft of the introduction, and then, finally, the completed paper. The professor is encouraging her students to use the problem-solving strategy of _____.
   a) forming subgoals
   b) trial and error
   c) using an analogy
   d) working backwards

2. Although James worked on his chemistry homework for several hours, he still did not understand it. While taking a break to watch television, he gained insight into the processes he had studied. What term describes his "break"?
   a) critical period
   b) encoding period
   c) incubation period
   d) retrieval period

3. We tend to take evidence that is consistent with our beliefs more seriously than evidence inconsistent with our beliefs. This is known as the

a) availability heuristic.
b) confirmation bias.
c) representativeness heuristic.
d) selection bias.

Fill-in-the-Blank

1. A rule that guarantees the solution to a problem when it is correctly applied is a(n) _____.

2. When we make decisions based on how easily information comes to mind, we are using the _____ heuristic.

3. Young children are often poor eyewitnesses because they have trouble remembering where they heard about certain information, a difficulty known as _____ amnesia.

4. The ability to think about another person's intentions is linked to the _____ neurons in the frontal and parietal cortex.

PART 10

INTELLIGENCE

PART OUTLINE

©iStockphoto.com/GlobalStock

How can you tell if someone is intelligent? What sorts of behaviours should you look for? How well they did in school? How much money they earn at work? Perhaps if we had an example to work from . . . someone unmistakably intelligent. What about the character of Sheldon Cooper on TV's *The Big Bang Theory*? Is he intelligent? Well, he certainly thinks so. He sped through school, going to college at the age of 12, and he views community-college grads with disdain: ". . . you thought the opposite of stupid loser was community-college grad?" Sheldon does research in cutting-edge physics and is certain he is destined to win a Nobel Prize one day: "Although I will not have time to mention you in my Nobel speech, when I get around to writing my memoirs, I promise you a very effusive footnote, and maybe a signed copy." Indeed, Sheldon is an intelligent character who collects comics and excels in theoretical physics, and yet there are some, well, . . . issues. He is self-centred, arrogant, and socially inept, and at times in social situations he looks particularly incompetent. His friends find him extremely frustrating; after living with him for weeks at a remote North Pole research station, his friends admit that they wanted to kill him, even temporarily considering throwing his Kindle outside and locking the door when he went out to get it! He is both brilliant and seriously challenged.

Sheldon's character is built around common, if somewhat geeky, conceptions of what intelligence is. Like many other aspects of human behaviour, however, intelligence is a concept that appears simple at first glance, only to become more complicated the closer we look at it. Start with the basic question: how do you define intelligence? Most people use "smart" or "dumb" to characterize the people in their lives, and they generally have a great deal of confidence in their assessments. But answer this: when you describe a friend as a generally smart person, how are you assessing smartness? Are you thinking about how your friend performs in all situations, or are you simply impressed by how sophisticated her answers are in English class and ignoring the fact that she's just scraping by in chemistry? If you were watching Sheldon Cooper on *Big Bang*, would you be sympathetic to him despite his lack of "street smarts"? And what about Sheldon seems to be "book smart" but lacks common sense? Would Sheldon, book smarts and all, be the one you would want leading you if your plane crashes on a remote island?

So what do we mean by intelligence? Does it mean the same thing in every instance? How do we understand it, and how do we measure it? To these basic questions we must add several others:

- Can we distinguish between intelligence and talent?
- Are intelligence and wisdom the same thing?
- Are intelligence and creativity related?
- And, finally, how do we value intelligence?

Our answers to such questions will influence how we define intelligence and whether we decide that anyone is particularly high in intelligence.

Module 54: What Do We Mean by Intelligence?

LEARNING OBJECTIVE 54
Describe various ways in which intelligence has been defined and summarize the current thinking on whether intelligence is general or specific.

Although Western thinkers as far back in history as Socrates, Plato, and Aristotle have commented on intelligence, it was not until the nineteenth and early twentieth centuries that psychologists and others began to form our current notions about it. In 1921, a group of scholars attended a symposium on the subject of intelligence. In their report, they emphasized that whatever else might be involved, **intelligence** involves the ability to *learn and the ability to meet the demands of the environment effectively*. People who hope to master algebra, for example, must have the capacity to grasp mathematical principles and profit from mathematical instruction, and they must be able to apply what they learn to various problem sets and life situations. As we will see later, we need to be careful about how broadly we apply the "meeting the demands of the environment" criteria for intelligence. Sheldon, one of the main characters in the *The Big Bang Theory* television show, is certainly intelligent, and certainly well adapted to the environment of the field of physics, but he is quite inept in social situations (as evidence, consider "Sheldon's Friendship Flowchart" online, http://wordpress.morningside.edu/cdl001/friendship-algorithm, to see how he analytically manages his friendships).

intelligence the ability to learn, to meet the demands of the environment effectively, and to understand and control one's mental activities.

> **"** I know that I am intelligent, because I know that I know nothing. **"**
>
> —*Socrates, Greek philosopher*

Years later, another survey of scholars pointed to these same abilities—learning and meeting the demands of the environment—as keys to intelligence, and added a third: *the ability to understand and control one's mental activities*. This additional mental capacity was termed **metacognition** (Cornoldi, 2010). Sometimes metacognition is understood as the ability to think about one's own thinking. The ancient philosopher Socrates gave us an early example of metacognitive thinking when he proclaimed, "Know thyself." A better example might be that studying is a way of meeting the demands of the academic environment, while knowing when you have studied enough and are ready for a test is a metacognitive skill.

metacognition the ability to understand and control one's mental activities.

Defining intelligence in terms of our ability to learn, to adapt to the demands of our environment, and to reflect on and understand our own mental processes makes intuitive sense. However, this definition encompasses a wide variety of notions about what intelligence might be. To develop a more precise definition, let's begin by considering a very basic question: is intelligence just one thing, or is it a combination of many different skill sets? All current theories of intelligence consider this question in one way or another.

54.1 Is Intelligence General or Specific?

Suppose you were joining a challenging mountain-climbing expedition. Which of your team members do you think would be more likely to complete the climb successfully: a generally smart person, or a person who had mastered, one by one, a large number of important tasks associated with mountain climbing? In other words, is intelligence largely the result of a single, general factor, or does it come from a cluster of different, more focused abilities?

54.1.1 Spearman and the *g* Factor

Charles Spearman (1863–1945) was a psychologist/philosopher and British army officer who also became an influential figure in the study of intelligence. Spearman helped to develop a tool for analyzing intelligence, called **factor analysis**. Factor analysis is a statistical method for determining whether different items on a test correlate highly with one another, thus forming a unified set, or cluster, of items (Spearman, 1937, 1927, 1923, 1904). In the case of intelligence tests, for example, people who do well on vocabulary items also tend to do well on other verbal items, such as reading comprehension. Taken together, all of the test items relating to words and reading form a verbal-reasoning cluster

factor analysis a statistical method for determining whether certain items on a test correlate highly, thus forming a unified set, or cluster, of items.

Psychology Around Us — But Is He Really Smart?

In 2011, IBM supercomputer Watson played *Jeopardy!* against the two greatest human players—Brad Rutter, who has earned the most money on the program, and Ken Jennings, who holds the record for consecutive wins. In fact, the supercomputer won, and won big. Watson had a final dollar amount of $77,147 compared with Jennings' $24,000 and Rutter's $21,600.

Obviously, the challenge for Watson's programmers wasn't the issue of knowledge. Watson's hard drive included Wikipedia, encyclopedias, dictionaries, and millions of pages of additional source material. Instead, the hard part was helping Watson figure out how to respond to the puns, clever turns of phrase, and unique styling of the "answers" provided by *Jeopardy!* For example, on the second day of his appearance, Watson answered the final question, which was on American cities, with "What is Toronto?" Watson's programmers suggested that Watson did not rule out Toronto as an American city because there are several towns in the United States with

that name and also Toronto, Ontario has an American League baseball team.

In other words, whereas we think the smart part of playing *Jeopardy!* comes from knowing a lot about everything, the tricky part for Watson was learning to understand and respond to natural language—something a young child can do. Even more interesting, the hardest "answers" for Watson were often the simplest, with the fewest words. The supercomputer just didn't have the context to narrow its choices.

Watson's undertaking seemed to please most viewers in one way or another. On one hand, computer experts came away believing that the Watson prototype can form the basis for computers to become more directly responsive to natural language commands. On the other hand, everyday folks were comforted in knowing that as long as Watson thinks Toronto is a U.S. city, we don't have to get ready for our robot overlords quite yet.

---

g factor a theoretical general factor of intelligence underlying all distinct clusters of mental ability; part of Spearman's two-factor theory of intelligence.

s factor a theoretical specific factor uniquely tied to a distinct mental ability or area of functioning; part of Spearman's two-factor theory of intelligence.

that can be used to assess a person's overall verbal-reasoning skill. On Western intelligence tests, other clusters include those related to logical, spatial, and mechanical reasoning (Binder & Binder, 2011).

While Spearman granted that some people have a particular strength in one area or another, he also noticed that those who scored high on one cluster tend to score high on other clusters as well. As he put it, "A bright child tends to score higher on all aspects of an intelligence test than a dull one." Thus, he hypothesized that a general factor, the **g factor**, of intelligence, underlies all distinct clusters of mental ability. At the same time, he believed that each cluster of intelligence is further affected by a *specific factor*, an **s factor**, which is uniquely tied to that particular area of functioning (see **Figure 54-1**) (Spearman, 1937, 1927, 1923, 1904).

To illustrate this *two-factor view* of intelligence, think again about Sheldon Cooper on *The Big Bang Theory*. There is certainly some variability in some areas of Sheldon's knowledge—he cannot drive a car nor understand how to make a friend. At the same time, there are many areas where Sheldon is very knowledgeable (he is a brilliant theoretic physicist)—an assumption consistent with the existence of a general intelligence.

Over the years, many theorists have embraced Spearman's notion of a *g* factor, and researchers have repeatedly found indications that such a factor may indeed be at work (Castejon, Perez, & Gilar, 2010; Johnson et al., 2004). These theorists typically agree that the *g* factor "is not merely book learning, a narrow academic skill, or test-taking smarts. Rather, it reflects a broader and deeper capability for comprehending our surroundings—'catching on,' 'making sense' of things, or 'figuring out' what to do" (Gottfredson, 1997, p. 13).

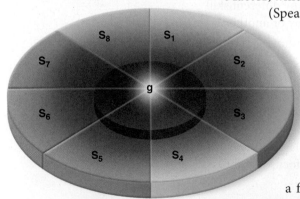

FIGURE 54-1 **Spearman's two-factor theory of intelligence.** In Spearman's model, the *g* factor of intelligence represents a broad and deep capability that underlies all other specific mental abilities, or the *s* factors.

54.1.2 Thurstone and Primary Mental Abilities

Although many theorists initially accepted and indeed continue to embrace Spearman's notion of a *g* factor of intelligence, the idea of such a general factor was controversial in Spearman's day and remains so to the present.

TABLE 54-1 Thurstone's Seven Factors of Intelligence

Factor	Examples
Verbal comprehension	Vocabulary, reading, comprehension, verbal analogies, etc.
Word fluency	The ability to quickly generate and manipulate a large number of words with specific characteristics, as in anagrams or rhyming tests
Numerical skill	The ability to quickly and accurately carry out mathematical operations
Spatial ability	Skill in spatial visualization as well as the ability to mentally transform spatial figures
Associative memory	Rote memory
Perceptual speed	Quickness in perceiving visual details, anomalies, similarities, etc.
Reasoning	Skill in a variety of inductive, deductive, and arithmetic reasoning tasks

An early critic of Spearman's ideas was Lewis L. Thurstone (1887–1955), a pioneer in psychological measurement and statistics. He argued that intelligence is made up of seven distinct mental abilities: verbal comprehension, word fluency, numerical skill, spatial ability, associative memory, perceptual speed, and reasoning (Thurstone, 1938; see **Table 54-1**). Thurstone termed these factors **primary mental abilities**.

Observing differences from person to person, Thurstone argued that each of the primary mental abilities on his list was distinct, not simply a reflection of general underlying intelligence. And, in fact, his initial work seemed to suggest that these abilities were not related. However, recognizing this theory as a direct challenge to the notion of the *g* factor, Spearman and others used factor analyses to reevaluate Thurstone's ideas. The researchers detected at least a slight tendency of those who scored high in one mental ability to score high in another (Spearman, 1939). So, Thurstone's work did not entirely dispel the notion of the *g* factor.

Despite the limitations of Thurstone's theory, the idea of distinct areas of intelligence has continued to drive theorizing about intelligence, even among those who believe that a *g* factor is at least partly involved in intellectual functioning. Let's turn next to the work of three modern theorists who have carried on Thurstone's quest to identify separate components of intelligence.

primary mental abilities seven distinct mental abilities identified by Thurstone as the basic components of intelligence.

54.2 Current Multifactor Theories of Intelligence

Most of the early theorists on intelligence agreed with Spearman that intelligence has a *g* factor at its core. Today's psychologists increasingly question the *g* factor, or at least place more emphasis on specific abilities, or *s* factors, that may affect intellectual performance. Three theorists in particular—Howard Gardner, Robert Sternberg, and Stephen Ceci—have broadened the definition of intelligence and deemphasized the *g* factor.

54.2.1 Howard Gardner's Theory of Multiple Intelligences

Are you equally successful in every academic subject? If you are like most people, you probably do better in some areas than others. If you are a good academic student, are you also

AFP/Getty Images

Who was the smartest person ever? It depends on your criteria. Although Albert Einstein's name has become synonymous with the term "brilliance," his cognitive functioning was below average in certain ways. Viewed as the ultimate absent-minded professor, he once had to call the dean's office at the Princeton Institute for Advanced Study to ask for directions to his home—located a block from campus.

Who is more intelligent? According to Howard Gardner's theory of multiple intelligences, these three extraordinary individuals each have a different kind of intelligence. For Neil Young, it's musical intelligence. For award-winning author Margaret Atwood, it's linguistic intelligence. And for physicist Stephen Hawking, it's mathematical intelligence.

Tristan Fewings/Getty Images   Phillip Chin/WireImage/Getty Images   Karwai Tang/Getty Images

theory of multiple intelligences theory that there is no single, unified intelligence, but instead several independent intelligences arising from different portions of the brain.

a good artist? Musician? Cook? Do you know someone who does not do well on academic tests, but nevertheless seems intelligent? Perhaps this person has strong leadership skills, social intuition, street smarts, or a razor-sharp sense of humour.

Psychologist Howard Gardner, influenced in part by the work of Thurstone, has advanced the **theory of multiple intelligences**, which argues that there is not a single unified intelligence (Gardner, 2011, 2008, 2004; Gardner & White, 2010). Instead, Gardner believes that there are several independent intelligences. Drawing on research from the fields of neuroscience and developmental, evolutionary, and cognitive psychology, he claims that the different intelligences come from different areas of the brain. In support of this view, he notes that damage to specific areas of the brain does not necessarily lead to a universal collapse of mental functioning. Rather, some types of functioning may be affected while others remain intact.

Gardner's research regarding people of exceptional ability has also contributed to the notion of multiple and independent intelligences. His work with individuals with *savant syndrome*, for example, seems consistent with this view. Individuals with savant syndrome often score low, sometimes extremely low, on traditional intelligence tests, yet possess startling ability in a specific area. Some have little verbal ability but are able to compute numbers with the speed of a calculator, others can draw with great skill, and still others have a keen memory for music. Stephen Wiltshire is a savant with autism who has phenomenal artistic skills. On YouTube, you can watch him draw a fully-detailed picture to scale of 4 square miles (about 6.5 km) of Rome, Italy after observing it for the first time from a helicopter for just 45 minutes (www.youtube.com/watch?v=jVqRT_kCOLI/).

Table 54-2 outlines the nine basic intelligences identified by Gardner: linguistic, logical-mathematical, musical, spatial, bodily-kinesthetic, interpersonal, intrapersonal, naturalistic, and existentialist.

Although Gardner's theory has roots in Thurstone's ideas, it is, in fact, different from Thurstone's theory in several ways. First, Thurstone held that the mental functions he identified *collectively* constitute intelligence. He did not believe, as Gardner does, that each factor is itself an "intelligence." Further, Gardner believes that the various intelligences are best measured in the contexts in which they occur. Thus, assessments conducted in real-world settings where the intelligences they are trying to tap are actually used are more useful than paper-and-pencil examinations for assessing several of the intelligences (Tirri & Nokelainen, 2008). Finally, Gardner's definition of multiple intelligences includes an important cultural component: each intelligence, he suggests, reflects "the ability to solve problems, or to create products, that are valuable within one or more cultural settings" (Gardner, 1993).

Because the various intelligences are thought to emanate from different areas, or modules, of the brain, Gardner's theory is often called a *modular model* of mental functioning (Gardner, 2000, 1993). Nevertheless, according to Gardner, the various intelligences can influence one another. For example, in addition to a well-developed musical

TABLE 54-2 Gardner's Multiple Intelligences

Type of Intelligence	Characteristics	Possible Vocations
Linguistic	Sensitivity to the sounds and meaning of words	Author, journalist, teacher
		©iStockphoto.com/ViktorCap
Logical/mathematical	Capacity for scientific analysis and logical and mathematical problem solving	Scientist, engineer, mathematician
		©iStockphoto.com/tetmc
Musical	Sensitivity to sounds and rhythm; capacity for musical expression	Musician, composer, singer
		©iStockphoto.com/Cybormama
Spatial	Ability to accurately perceive spatial relationships	Architect, navigator, sculptor, engineer
		©iStockphoto.com/baranozdemir
Bodily/kinesthetic	Ability to control body movements and manipulate objects	Athlete, dancer, surgeon
		©iStockphoto.com/hannamonika
Interpersonal	Sensitivity to the emotions and motivations of others; skillful at managing others	Manager, therapist, teacher
		©iStockphoto.com/AlexRaths
Intrapersonal	Ability to understand one's self and one's strengths and weaknesses	Leader in many fields
		©iStockphoto.com/Dean Mitchell
Naturalistic	Ability to understand patterns and processes in nature	Biologist, naturalist, ecologist, farmer
		©iStockphoto.com/StHelena
Existentialist	Ability to understand religious and spiritual ideals	Philosopher, theorist
		©iStockphoto.com/StefanBreton

Source: Based on Gardner, H. (2000). *Intelligence reframed: Multiple intelligences for the 21st century.* New York: Basic Books; Gardner, H. (1993). *Multiple intelligences: The theory in practice.* New York: Basic Books; Moran, S., Kornhaber, M., & Gardner, H. (2009). Orchestrating multiple intelligences. *Educational Leadership, 64,* (1), 22–27.

intelligence, a cellist might need a high bodily-kinesthetic intelligence to physically handle the instrument, and a high interpersonal intelligence to work in perfect harmony with other players in an orchestra.

Critics of Gardner's ideas, however, maintain that still deeper relationships exist among the various intelligences and mental functions (Gardner & Traub, 2010). There is not much data supporting the existence of the distinct intelligences that Garner suggests (Armstrong, 2009). Validating studies demonstrating that the different intelligences can be consistently and distinctly measured have yet to be accomplished (Sternberg & Grigerenko, 2004). As well, when measured, most of Gardner's intelligences correlate positively with general intelligence measures, which calls into question just how distinct Gardner's intelligences are (Visser et al., 2006). Not all human abilities have to be called intelligence.

54.2.2 Robert Sternberg's Triarchic Theory of Intelligence

triarchic theory of intelligence Sternberg's theory that intelligence is made up of three interacting components: internal, external, and experiential components.

Psychologist Robert Sternberg has proposed a **triarchic theory of intelligence** (Mandelman et al., 2010; Sternberg, 2010, 2003). Sternberg shares Gardner's view that intelligence is not a unitary mental function. According to Sternberg, however, intelligence is made up not of numerous independent intelligences, but of three interacting components, as shown in **Figure 54-2**, called internal, external, and experiential components. These are sometimes referred to as the analytic, creative, and practical components.

- *Internal (analytic)* This component of intelligence relates to the internal processing of information: acquiring information; planning, monitoring, and evaluating problems; or carrying out directions. The internal aspect of intelligence is the one most often measured by today's intelligence tests—the sort of intelligence needed for straightforward tasks and problems that we confront at school or work or in life.
- *External (creative)* Sternberg notes that some tasks are novel and so require a special way of thinking. Travelling to Cambodia for the first time, for example, requires more creative thinking than walking down a local street in your home town. Among other things, travellers would have to figure out how to get through Cambodian customs, find their way to a hotel, and order meals in restaurants—all, perhaps, without knowing the language. This component of intelligence clearly requires creativity, and it also must interact with the internal component of intelligence to bring about successful results.
- *Experiential (practical)* This type of thinking helps us adapt to or improve our environments or select new environments. Let's say you move into a new home and find that the neighbours make a lot of noise when you are trying to go to sleep.

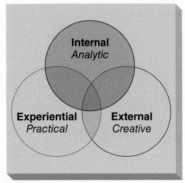

FIGURE 54-2 Sternberg's triarchic theory of intelligence. Robert Sternberg proposes that there are three components to intelligence, not multiple independent ones. In his model, intelligence is related to the successful interaction among the internal (analytic), the external (creative), and the experiential (practical) components.

At first, you might try to solve the problem by moving to another bedroom in the house (adapting to the environment). If this doesn't work, you might try installing soundproof windows or complaining to the neighbours or to the landlord (changing the environment). And, finally, if that doesn't work, you might decide to move to another house (selecting a new environment).

Sternberg suggests that practical intelligence often relies on *tacit knowledge*, "action-oriented knowledge, acquired without direct help from others, which allows individuals to achieve goals they personally value" (Sternberg et al., 1995, p. 916). A successful businessperson who earned only average grades in school has probably acquired considerable tacit knowledge, or "know-how," by working in the business environment and figuring out what is needed to get the work done. Not surprisingly, research shows that tacit knowledge is related to job success (Joia et al., 2010; Sternberg, 2003).

Sternberg argues that effective interactions among the internal, external, and experiential components are keys to achieving successful intelligence—an advantageous balance between adapting to, shaping, and selecting problems encountered within one's environment (Sternberg, 2014). Because each intellectual component in Sternberg's theory actively relates to the others, his model is considered more dynamic, or interactive, than Gardner's. There is also more research evidence in support of Sternberg's theory.

A number of studies have been able to measure and distinguish among the components of the triarchic theory of intelligence (Sternberg et al., 2000).

54.2.3 Stephen Ceci's Bioecological Theory of Intelligence

Psychologist Stephen Ceci has proposed the **bioecological model of intelligence**, which holds that intelligence is "a function of the interactions between innate potential abilities, environmental context (ecology), and internal motivation" (see **Figure 54-3**) (Barnett & Ceci, 2005; Ceci et al., 1997). According to Ceci, each person's innate abilities derive from a system of biological factors, or "resource pools." These resource pools are independent of each other, and each is responsible for different aspects of one's information-processing capabilities. Further, Ceci claims that a person's innate abilities will develop based more or less on how they interact with the individual's environmental resources, or context.

Consider, for example, a child whose biological resource pool endows her with the potential to succeed in math. Her abilities might lead to early successes in arithmetic, prompting her parents to provide environmental changes—her own computer, special enrichment opportunities in math, and so forth—that will help her to further develop her innate math potential. This encouraging environmental context will likely lead to further successes, which in turn may lead to additional environmental changes, such as enrollment in a special school.

Finally, according to the bioecological model, individuals must be internally *motivated* to fulfill their innate abilities and take advantage of their particular environments. When people feel motivated in certain areas, they tend to focus on their intellectual skills in those areas and to seek out environmental resources that are relevant. In an interesting study, Ceci found that men who were successful at race track betting and who produced complicated strategies for predicting winning horses did not demonstrate sophisticated thinking in other areas of functioning (Ceci & Liker, 1986). Clearly, such men were motivated to win serious money at the race track, and so developed complex intellectual processing and personal environmental opportunities (expertise) that might lead to that particular result (Detterman, 2014).

bioecological model of intelligence Ceci's theory that intelligence is a function of the interactions among innate potential abilities, environmental context, and internal motivation.

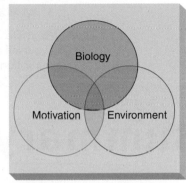

FIGURE 54-3 Ceci's bioecological model of intelligence. Stephen Ceci proposes that intelligence is the product of interaction among biological, environmental, and motivational resources, and that each resource is responsible for a different aspect of intelligence.

54.3 Where Are We Today?

Obviously, many theories on the nature of intelligence have been proposed and investigated. Is there a basic view upon which today's theorists agree? It is fair to say that the majority believe that intelligence *includes* a *g* factor—an overriding intellectual ability (Hunt, 2011; Larsen et al., 2008). However, few current theorists believe that the *g* factor is the best theory of intelligence. Most consider specific abilities (verbal, numerical, spatial skills, for example) and special factors (motivation, context, experience, and the like) to also be important in the expression of intelligence. The *g* factor is at work in every task that we confront in life, while the specific abilities and special factors come into play for some tasks but not others. This prevailing view is called a *hierarchical model* of intelligence (Castejon et al., 2010; Lubinski, 2004).

Because the *g* factor seems to play a role across all kinds of tasks, it is, of course, desirable to have a high degree of general intelligence. But the *g* factor alone will not consistently lead to outstanding performances or successes in school, work, or other areas of life. Similarly, verbal ability, high motivation, or proper environment alone rarely guarantees high intellectual achievement. Intelligence truly appears to be a complex, multifaceted phenomenon.

©iStockphoto.com/LuminaStock

Innate abilities and environmental resources. According to Ceci, a person's innate abilities develop based on how they interact with environmental resources. For example, this girl's potential to do well in math could be developed based on her access to a computer or enrollment in special math enrichment classes, and this encouraging environment would likely lead to further success in math.

> "Knowing others is intelligence; knowing yourself is true wisdom. Mastering others is strength; mastering yourself is true power."
>
> —*Tao Te Ching, Chinese philosopher*

www.wiley.com/go/comercanada

Before You Go On

What Do You Know?

1. Identify and define the two factors in Spearman's model of intelligence.
2. How does Thurstone's theory of primary mental abilities differ from Gardner's theory of multiple intelligences?
3. Name four of Gardner's intelligences. What are some of the concerns about Gardner's definition of intelligence(s)?
4. What are the three components of the triarchic theory of intelligence, and how do they contribute to mental functioning?
5. What are the main features that interact to produce intelligence in Ceci's theory?

What Do You Think? How would you define intelligence? Apply one or two of the theories to yourself and to one or two other people you know well. Do the theories fit with your general assumptions about intelligence?

Summary

Module 54: What Do We Mean by Intelligence?

LEARNING OBJECTIVE 54 Describe various ways in which intelligence has been defined and summarize the current thinking on whether intelligence is general or specific.

- Scholars early in the twentieth century defined *intelligence* as the ability to learn and to meet the demands of the environment effectively. Later, other scholars added to this definition the ability to understand and control one's mental activities, called metacognition.
- A central issue in defining intelligence is whether it is a single, general factor or a cluster of different abilities. Charles Spearman hypothesized that a general factor, or *g* factor, underlies all mental abilities, while Lewis Thurstone argued that intelligence is made up of seven distinct *primary mental abilities*.
- Although most theorists today agree that intelligence does include a *g* factor, modern theorists such as Howard Gardner, Robert Sternberg, and Stephen Ceci have tended to deemphasize the *g* factor and focus on specific abilities, or *s* factors.

Key Terms

bioecological model of intelligence 419

factor analysis 413

g factor 414

intelligence 413

metacognition 413

primary mental abilities 415

s factor 414

theory of multiple intelligences 416

triarchic theory of intelligence 418

Study Questions

Multiple Choice

1. Which of the following areas is not included in the definition of intelligence?
   a) ability to communicate
   b) ability to learn
   c) ability to meet the demands of the environment
   d) ability to understand and control our own mental activities

2. Which theory of intelligence could be described as most inclusive (meaning, considers the largest number and range of factors as part of the definition of intelligence)?

   a) Ceci's bioecological theory of intelligence
   b) Gardner's theory of multiple intelligences
   c) Spearman's two-factor theory of intelligence
   d) Sternberg's triarchic theory of intelligence

Fill-in-the-Blank

1. In a game of *Jeopardy!* against two human players, IBM's supercomputer "Watson" was weakest in terms of using and responding to _____.

Module 55: Additional Types of Intelligence

The ideas and work that we have encountered so far consider a wide range of intellectual skills. But have they captured all aspects of intelligence? A growing number of theorists are focusing on the role of intelligence in emotions, social functioning, wisdom, creativity, and personality.

LEARNING OBJECTIVE 55
Discuss several proposed types of intelligence that go beyond intellectual functioning.

55.1 Emotional Intelligence

The concept of emotional intelligence is rather new—researchers began to actively study it in the 1990s. **Emotional intelligence** refers to an individual's ability to perceive, express, and assimilate emotion, and to regulate emotion in the self and others (Cherniss, 2010; Roberts et al., 2010; Goleman, 2100). Emotionally intelligent people are thought to be self-aware, sensitive to how they feel and how their feelings change, and able to manage their emotions so that they are not overwhelmed by them. People with well-developed emotional intelligence also tend to be empathic, knowing how to comfort and encourage others. Not surprisingly, they often succeed in their careers and marriages, as parents, and as leaders (Brackett et al., 2011; Martin, 2008).

emotional intelligence an individual's ability to perceive, express, assimilate, and regulate emotion.

If we grant the existence of emotional intelligence, then the question arises: can it be measured? In fact, researchers have devised a number of ways to measure it (Roberts et al., 2010). One test is the *Multifactor Emotional Intelligence Scale* (Maul, 2011; Mayer et al., 2003; Salovey et al., 2003). This test measures 12 emotional abilities that are, in turn, grouped into four "branches of abilities"—perceiving, facilitating, understanding, and managing emotion.

Although some theorists believe that certain individuals are inherently more skilled than others in the emotional sphere, other theorists argue that emotional intelligence can be learned and they call for schools and businesses to offer systematic instruction in the understanding and management of emotions (Alegre, 2011). James Parker and his colleagues at Trent University have shown that several facets of emotional intelligence are very strong predictors of success or challenge within the university context (Parker et al., 2006, 2004). Parker has also shown that helping students to improve their skills in those areas of emotional intelligence positively impacts their academic performance and makes it more likely they will stay in university as they move from their first to second year of studies (Parker et al., 2006).

© Warner Brothers/courtesy Everett Collection/CP

Emotional intelligence and acting. Successful actors are able to perceive and regulate emotions in themselves and in others, enabling them to portray a wide range of characters. Jim Carrey, for example, has an exceptionally broad range of facial and emotional expressions he can draw on while acting.

55.2 Social Intelligence

Most people know someone who displays remarkable social savvy, a person who can walk right into a party or a meeting and just take over the room. Such people seem to know intuitively what is important to others, how to charm their way out of difficult situations, and how to gain the affection of everyone with whom they interact. Would you say these individuals are highly intelligent? Some theorists would say yes (Murphy & Hall, 2011; Goleman, 2006). Specifically, they would say that these individuals are high in *social intelligence*.

The notion of social intelligence is older than that of emotional intelligence. In fact, early in the twentieth century, the

CBC/George Stroumboulopoulos Tonight

Social intelligence for profit. People with high social intelligence seem to have a natural grasp of what is important to others and an ability to help other people "open up." *The Hour's* George Stroumboulopoulos uses his social intelligence to achieve professional success.

Katniss Everdeen is a teenage girl forced to participate in a reality show in which teenagers must hunt and kill each other to entertain the masses. Katniss is the heroine of author Suzanne Collins' dystopian young adult novel, *The Hunger Games*. Katniss is unquestionably brilliant when it comes to hunting and survival. She's a particularly deadly archer, and she is smart enough to know how to get an edge up in the competition by destroying the food supply of wealthy rivals who aren't used to going hungry.

That said, as ultracompetent as she is at surviving, she struggles with managing relationships. When her fellow tribute, Peeta, starts to show signs of interest in her, she has no idea how to respond other than to treat it as gamesmanship and strategy. Katniss is so locked in to the idea of being a survivor that she doesn't know how to form a human bond with someone else.

learning pioneer Edward Thorndike (whom you may remember from Part 7) suggested that intelligence consists of three facets: the ability to understand and manage ideas (abstract intelligence), concrete objects (mechanical intelligence), and people (social intelligence) (Thorndike, 1920). By social intelligence, Thorndike meant "the ability to understand and manage men and women, boys and girls—to act wisely in human relationships." Other theorists have described social intelligence more simply as the ability to get along with others. Either way, it is clearly an important asset, not only in interpersonal relationships, but also at school and work and in leadership roles (Furnham, 2009; Furnham, Crump, & Ritchie, 2013; Bass, 2002).

55.3 Wisdom

In myth, art, and popular culture, we often encounter characters who do not possess much formal education but who seem to have an insightful appreciation of life and the world. They are generally portrayed as experienced in the ways of the world; little about life appears to surprise them. These people are considered to possess *wisdom*, the ability to make sound judgments about important, difficult, or uncertain situations and to choose the best course of action (Karelitz, Jarvin, & Sternberg, 2010; Fowers, 2005, 2003). Are intelligence and wisdom the same thing?

Robert Sternberg (2010, 2008, 2003) believes that wisdom is a special version of intelligence, and has developed the *balance theory of wisdom* to account for this special capacity. Recall that in Sternberg's triarchic theory, intelligence consists of three aspects—analytic, creative, and practical—with practical intelligence involving the ability to effectively apply one's experiences and learning to everyday decisions. According to Sternberg, wisdom is primarily (though not entirely) the product of practical intelligence. He says that wisdom is the application of tacit knowledge—"know-how"—to solve problems in such a way that a common good is achieved and a balance maintained among the interests of the individual, the community, and society. Sternberg distinguishes wisdom from other expressions of practical intelligence by noting that wisdom involves a particular concern for the community at large and a careful balancing of interests.

More than any other dimension of intelligence, wisdom may be associated with age. When people are asked to name someone in their lives whom they consider to be wise, they are more likely to point to a grandparent, an uncle or aunt, or a parent, rather than to a teenager or young adult. Why? Because it typically takes years and repeated experiences to appreciate the needs of the community, the advantages of compromise solutions, the drawbacks of self-serving decisions, and the delicate art of balancing multiple perspectives (Ardelt, 2011; Nair, 2003). That is, it takes time and experience to acquire a high degree of wisdom. However, not all older people are wise, and some younger people are wise; although there is a strong correlation between age and wisdom, age does not *cause* wisdom (Thomas & Ute, 2013).

55.4 Creativity

Creativity is the ability to produce ideas that are both original and valuable (Kaufman & Sternberg, 2010). Like wisdom, creativity reflects collective, as well as personal, values. Societies benefit from the creativity of their members; indeed, creativity plays a key role in technological, scientific, and artistic advances. Thus, it is not surprising that different cultures define and appreciate creativity in different ways (Lubart, 2010; Runco, 2010, 2004). Creativity often requires verbal and mathematical skills in Western culture, for example, while it depends more on the ability to appreciate and interact with nature in some other cultures (Runco, 2014).

creativity the ability to produce ideas that are both original and valuable.

Psychologists who study creativity and intelligence typically believe that a high intellectual aptitude is necessary but not sufficient for creativity (Kim et al., 2010; Silvia, 2008). People who score high on intelligence tests tend to score high on tests of creativity, but beyond a certain point (that is, beyond an intelligence test score of about 120), the correlation between intelligence and creativity diminishes. Research has shown, for example, that on average, exceptionally creative architects, musicians, scientists, and engineers do not score higher on intelligence tests than do their less creative colleagues, though both groups are highly intelligent (Jauk et al., 2013). Thus, it appears that there is more to creativity than what intelligence tests measure.

Theorists and researchers have pointed to various personal qualities as being key to creativity (Cramond et al., 2010; Sternberg, 2010, 2003). At the top of the list is *intrinsic motivation*, an internal drive to create. Also cited frequently are *imagination*—an ability and willingness to reexamine problems in new ways—and a *game personality*, one that tolerates ambiguity, risk, and initial failure. Other useful qualities important to creative thought include complex thinking, broad attention, expertise in relevant fields, broad interests, high energy, independence, and self-confidence. Finally, divergent thinking is often seen as a key part of creativity. Measures of divergent thinking include seeing how many different ways people can think about simple objects or events. For example, how many different uses can you think of for a brick? The more uses you can come up with in two minutes, the higher your scores are likely to be on other measures of creativity (Runco & Acar, 2012).

Investigators have also found that creative thinking is, in fact, nurtured, inspired, and refined by creative environments (Beghetto et al., 2010; Sternberg, 2010). Creative environments share several qualities: they encourage people to be innovative; are relatively free of criticism; and provide freedom, creative role models, sufficient resources, and time to think and explore. Artist communities and schools for the performing arts aspire to be environments of this kind. Some such communities and schools succeed

Bruno Morandi/Getty Images
©iStockphoto.com/Christopher Futcher

Creativity around the world. Different cultures encourage different kinds of creativity. A woman who can decorate a customer's hand with a beautiful henna design in India (*left*) is considered highly creative and intelligent in her country, while a Canadian programmer who addresses his firm's production needs by developing a complex computer model (*right*) is considered highly creative by his colleagues.

Rene Johnston/GetStock

Creative environment? Dancers at the National Ballet of Canada are immersed in a creative environment.

in this regard, while others may become more demanding and competitive than nurturing. In addition, a creative environment need not be large or formal; it can exist in a supportive home, a positive work setting, or a comfortable class.

55.5 Personality Characteristics

Even the earliest researchers of intelligence noted a relationship between intelligence and personality, our unique patterns of experiencing and acting in the world. Although intelligence tests often seek to separate intellectual functioning from personal style, many theorists argue that the division is artificial, that personality characteristics are inherent to intellectual functioning (Feist, 2010; Mayer, 2009, 2008; Mayer, Panter, & Caruso, 2012). Indeed, David Wechsler (1961), a pioneer in intelligence testing, considered intelligence to be a manifestation of personality. He thought that emotional, motivational, and other personal characteristics (such as interest and volition) must be key components of any meaningful notion of intelligence.

Following Wechsler's lead, a number of today's theorists think of intelligence as the cognitive part of personality (Murphy & Hall, 2011; Furnham & Monsen, 2009). Others propose a complex reciprocal relationship between intelligence and personality, with intellectual, emotional, and motivational variables repeatedly affecting each other in day-to-day behaviour (Hennessey, 2010; Mayer, 2008). Consistent with such notions, studies have found that negative emotional and motivational states can impair intellectual performance to some degree, especially when the intellectual tasks demand attention or quick recall. Conversely, certain personality factors, such as self-efficacy (the belief that one can master a demanding task) and a high need to achieve, often enhance performance on intellectual tasks (Freund & Holling, 2011; Lounsbury et al., 2009, 2003).

Before You Go On
www.wiley.com/go/comercanada

What Do You Know?

1. What is emotional intelligence and how is it measured?
2. How does Robert Sternberg describe wisdom in relation to his triarchic theory of intelligence?
3. What are some factors that affect creativity?

What Do You Think? Suppose you were given the job of making up a test to assess social intelligence. What kinds of questions would you include on the test?

Summary

Module 55: Additional Types of Intelligence

LEARNING OBJECTIVE 55 Discuss several proposed types of intelligence that go beyond intellectual functioning.

- Other theorists have broadened the definition of intelligence further to include emotional intelligence, social intelligence, wisdom, creativity, and personality.

Key Terms

creativity 423

emotional intelligence 421

Study Questions

Multiple Choice

1. Emotional intelligence includes which of the following abilities?
   a) getting along with other people
   b) perceiving others' emotions and our own
   c) using emotional feedback to manage situations
   d) using emotions to solve problems

Fill-in-the-Blank

1. According to Sternberg, wisdom is most closely related to _____ intelligence.

Module 56: How Do We Measure Intelligence?

LEARNING OBJECTIVE 56
Identify important considerations in the construction of intelligence tests, discuss the history of intelligence testing, and describe some criticisms of intelligence tests.

psychometric approach an approach to defining intelligence that attempts to measure intelligence with carefully constructed psychological tests.

For better or for worse, the history of intelligence theory is completely intertwined with the history of intelligence testing. That is, both the theories psychologists propose and the tests they devise affect how they understand intelligence. It was only about a century ago that researchers and statisticians first fashioned standardized tests and statistical methods with which to assess intelligence. In the West, one of the oldest and most enduring approaches to understanding and assessing intelligence is the psychometric approach. The **psychometric approach** attempts to measure intelligence with carefully constructed psychological tests, called *intelligence tests*. The psychometric approach is also used to construct measures for other human individual difference dimensions, such as personality (Gregory, 2013).

Before examining in detail some of the ways people have measured intelligence throughout history, it's worthwhile to think about what qualities make a good intelligence test. Knowing how psychologists build and use intelligence tests will help you figure out what these tests mean. Keep in mind, though, that much of the reason we are able to think about intelligence in such a sophisticated way today is that we have benefited from the insights and mistakes of earlier theorists and researchers.

56.1 Intelligence Test Construction and Interpretation

Intelligence test constructors typically assume a comparative view of test scores; they usually measure intelligence by comparing one person's test scores with another's. However, there is no absolute or independent standard of intelligence against which to compare intelligence test scores (i.e., there is no mental dipstick to use to know someone's intelligence with absolute certainty). The use of this comparative approach gives rise to a number of cautions or limits on how we think about and use intelligence measures. First, a test must function the same in different groups of people (so that individuals do not get different scores just because they are from different ethnic groups or different parts of the country). Second, similar items on a test must relate both to one another and to the material of interest (i.e., to the things the test is supposed to predict, like school grades). To ensure that intelligence tests are grounded in sound scientific principles, psychologists design tests that adhere to three basic criteria: standardization, reliability, and validity (Bowden et al., 2011; Canivez & Watkins, 2010; Nelson, Canivez, & Watkins, 2013).

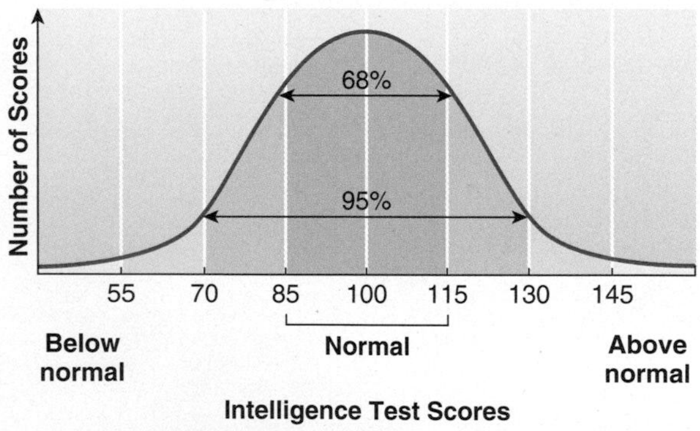

FIGURE 56-1 **The bell curve of intelligence scores.** The distribution of scores on intelligence tests follows a statistical pattern called the bell curve. Most peoples' scores fall in the middle range, with a small number scoring at the extreme ends.

standardization the use of uniform procedures in administering and scoring a test.

normal distribution a symmetrical, bell-shaped distribution in which most scores are in the middle, with smaller groups of equal size at either end.

56.1.1 Standardization

If you were the only person taking a particular intelligence test, your score would mean very little. For your score to have meaning, it must be compared with the scores of people who have already taken the same test. This group of people is referred to as a standardization or normative *sample*. If all subsequent test-takers follow the same procedures as those used by the standardization or normative sample, then each individual's test score can be compared with the scores of the sample. The process of obtaining meaningful test scores from a standardization or normative sample through the use of uniform procedures is called **standardization**.

Test results from large populations tend to follow particular patterns, called *distributions*. Scores on intelligence tests follow a **normal distribution** (or *normal curve*), a statistical pattern in which most people achieve fairly similar scores at or near the middle of the distribution, while a small number earn low scores and an equally small number earn high scores. In graph form, these results form a bell-shaped pattern, often called a *bell curve* (see **Figure 56-1**).

In a normal distribution, the scores of most people fall in the vicinity of the **median** score (that is, the middle score). The scores that are higher or lower than the median keep declining in number as the scores extend farther and farther from the median. The very lowest and the very highest scores are found at the outer edges of the bell curve. The median score is but one indicator of a population's central tendencies. Others include the **mean**, or the average score, and the **mode**, the score that occurs most frequently in the population. If a sample is properly converted into a normal distribution, the median, mean, and mode should be the same.

median the score exactly in the middle of a distribution.

mean the average score in a distribution.

mode the score that occurs most frequently in a distribution.

56.1.2 Reliability

The second criterion that is needed for a test to be of value is **reliability**. When a test is reliable, it consistently produces similar scores for the same test-takers over time. Psychologists have developed several ways to show that a test is reliable. One approach, called *test-retest reliability*, involves administering the test once and then a second time, in either the same version or a version that is slightly different. If the scores on the two administrations agree for each individual, they are said to correlate highly, and the test is considered to be reliable. Another approach, *split-half reliability*, is to divide the items on a single test into two tests, and see whether each individual's scores on the two halves of the test correlate highly. Whatever the approach used, the higher the statistical correlation between scores, the greater the reliability. Remember from Part 2 that a correlation can vary from a value of +1.00 to –1.00. To be reliable, a test must produce very similar results when administered to the same people within a short period of time (so that we can assume little has changed between testing sessions). A correlation between the first and second test administration scores that is up near +1.00 indicates that the test is stable or *reliable*.

reliability the degree to which a test produces the same scores over time.

validity the extent to which a test accurately measures or predicts what it is supposed to measure or predict.

56.1.3 Validity

A test with a high degree of reliability does not necessarily have high validity. **Validity** is the extent to which a test accurately measures or predicts what it is supposed to measure or predict. Suppose, for example, we use a broken scale to weigh the residents of a town and we weigh each resident multiple times. Assuming that, for each person, the scale repeatedly yields the same weight, the resulting weights would be said to have a high degree of reliability. The results, however, would have low validity because the weights offered by the broken scales are not accurate; that is, although everyone's weight would be uniformly reported, no one's reported weight would be correct. We would not know how much anyone actually weighs.

©iStockphoto.com/lisafx

How can we determine the validity, or accuracy, of a test? Often we can simply look at the test content. If you were to administer a test on Chinese grammar to assess students' mastery of French, the test would not demonstrate much **content validity**. By contrast, if you were taking driving lessons and your instructor tested you on your understanding of the rules of the road and other kinds of relevant information, the test would demonstrate high content validity.

Content validity. A driving test that measures the learner's understanding of the rules of the road and other relevant information has high content validity.

We can also assess the validity of tests by correlating test scores with an external criterion that we have some confidence in—a correlation called a **validity coefficient**. If, for example, we believe that intelligent people will perform better at school (because of their higher intelligence), then we expect individuals' scores on a particular intelligence test to correlate with their school grades; the higher the validity coefficient, the more valid the test is considered to be. A test need not just measure current performance. When high scores on an intelligence test continue to successfully predict high grades later in life, it is said to display high **predictive validity** (Gow et al., 2011; American Educational Research Association, 2014).

content validity the degree to which the content of a test accurately represents what the test is intended to measure.

validity coefficient a correlation coefficient that measures validity by correlating a test score with some external criterion.

predictive validity the extent to which scores on a particular test successfully predict the things it is supposed to predict.

56.2 History of Intelligence Testing

The first systematic attempts to measure intelligence were developed during the second half of the nineteenth century. The most influential approaches were those of Francis Galton in England and Alfred Binet in France. Later, in the United States, Lewis Terman and David Wechsler made important contributions.

56.2.1 Galton and "Psychophysical Performance"

Profoundly affected by the work of his half-cousin Charles Darwin, Francis Galton (1822–1911) sought to apply Darwin's ideas about evolution to the study of intelligence. He believed that by studying intellectual development, he could learn more about the evolution of the human species in general, and the inheritance of intelligence in particular (Hunt, 2010; Fancher, 2009, 2004). In particular, Galton sought to understand why some people appear to be more intelligent than others. If he could understand the evolutionary factors at work in such differences, he reasoned, steps could be taken to improve the species.

Galton, who believed in a general intelligence factor, proposed that two qualities distinguish more gifted from less gifted people: a kind of psychic energy and a heightened sensitivity to external stimuli. His theory, termed the *theory of psychophysical performance*, held that people with more energy can perform more work and, in turn, develop greater intelligence. In addition, inasmuch as people gather information from their five senses, individuals who have more highly developed senses can take in more information (Kaufman, 2000). To more accurately gauge intelligence, Galton developed tests of an individual's sensory processing, motor skills, and reaction time.

> **"**Intelligence is not to make no mistakes, but quickly to see how to make them good.**"**
>
> —*Bertholt Brecht, playwright*

Galton's work influenced many theorists. James McKean Cattell, in particular, later designed 50 psychophysical tests, expecting that the tests would support and extend Galton's ideas (Sokal, 2010; Tulsky et al., 2003). Cattell tested skills, such as how fast people can move their arm over a specified distance and how many letters in a series they can remember. Ironically, Cattell's tests eventually helped to discredit Galton's notions by supporting the idea that there is more than one general form of intelligence (Sokal, 2010; Tulsky et al., 2003).

In his doctoral dissertation, one of Cattell's students, Clark Wissler, hypothesized that people would perform consistently well or consistently poorly across the various psychophysical tests, and that those who did consistently well would display a higher level of general intelligence than those who performed poorly (Wissler, 1961). However, Wissler found that a given person's various test performances did not necessarily correlate either with each other or with academic performance. To determine whether each research participant's performances on various psychophysical tests were in fact correlated, Wissler used *correlation coefficients*—a statistical method developed by Galton. Thus, the use of Galton's own statistical tool eventually helped to challenge his theory. Although in general his psychophysical theory of intelligence was not supported, certain of his specific physical measures have been found to relate to other measures of intelligence (Sokal, 2010; Tulsky et al., 2003).

56.2.2 Alfred Binet and the Binet-Simon Intelligence Test

At the same time that Galton and his followers were developing psychophysical theories and tests, Alfred Binet (1857–1911), along with his collaborator Théodore Simon, were viewing intelligence and its measurement in a different way.

In 1904, the French government mandated compulsory education, and the Minister of Public Instruction in Paris formed a commission to devise a way to distinguish children with intellectual disabilities from those who were unsuccessful in school for other reasons, such as behavioural problems. The idea was to assign intellectually capable children to regular classes and place those with intellectual disabilities in special classes. To help determine the most appropriate type of class for each child, Binet and Simon devised the first widely applied intelligence tests (Hunt, 2010).

Bettmann/Corbis

Intelligence testing pioneers.
Alfred Binet (pictured) and Théodore Simon developed the first standardized intelligence test. The test was used to sort new arrivals into the Paris school system following the passage of mandatory school attendance laws.

Binet shared with Galton the notion of a general intelligence factor. However, regarding the psychophysical theory as "wasted time," he argued that the basis of intelligence is "judgment, otherwise called good sense, practical sense, initiative, the faculty of adapting one's self to circumstances. To judge well, to comprehend well, to reason well, these are the essential activities of intelligence." In short, Binet viewed intelligence as the "ability to demonstrate memory, judgment, reasoning, and social comprehension" (Kaufman, 2000, p. 446).

The tasks on Binet's intelligence test focused largely on language abilities, in contrast to the many non-verbal tasks devised by Galton. Binet also introduced the idea of mental age, the intellectual age at which a child is actually functioning. **Mental age** does not necessarily match chronological age. A child's mental age is indicated by the chronological age typically associated with his level of intellectual performance. Thus, the typical 11-year-old has a mental age of 11. A more intelligent 11-year-old, however, might have a mental age of 13, while a less intelligent 11-year-old might have a mental age of 9.

mental age the intellectual age at which a person is functioning, as opposed to chronological age.

Binet did not believe his intelligence test necessarily measured a child's *inborn* level of intelligence. His goal was simply to predict a student's likelihood of success in school. And, in fact, he did find a moderate correlation between performance on his test and performance in school. The test also correlated with scores on *achievement tests*—tests of knowledge about particular school subjects—although at a lower magnitude.

It is worth noting that Binet refused to use test scores to rank children. He felt that intelligence is too complex a phenomenon to draw meaningful conclusions about the *relative* intelligence among most children. He argued that it would be unfair to say that one child of average intelligence, as measured by his test, was more intelligent than another child of average intelligence. However, Binet's concerns did not stop others from extending his test in ways that he neither anticipated nor advocated.

56.2.3 Lewis Terman and the Stanford-Binet Intelligence Test

Interest in Binet's work spread throughout the world, and Stanford University professor Lewis Terman (1877–1956) adapted the Binet-Simon intelligence test for use in the United States. He realized that some of the test items, originally developed to test French children, needed to be changed to better assess the intelligence of children in the United States. The age norms, for example, did not apply to the American school children in Terman's sample. This was an important early recognition of the influence of culture in intelligence testing. Terman called his new test the Stanford-Binet Intelligence Test (Antonson, 2010; Becker, 2003; Raid & Tippin, 2009).

intelligence quotient (IQ) Terman's measure of intelligence; the ratio of a child's mental age to her chronological age, multiplied by 100.

In developing his version of Binet's test, Terman decided to state the results not simply in terms of mental age, but as a measure that would relate mental to chronological age. Thus, the famous **intelligence quotient**, or **IQ**, was devised. To arrive at this measure of intelligence, Terman calculated the ratio of mental age to chronological age and multiplied that ratio by 100 (to remove the decimal point). Thus, returning to our earlier examples, the 11-year-old with average intelligence would earn an IQ of 100 (11/11 × 100), the more intelligent child would post an IQ of 118 (13/11 × 100), and the less intelligent child's IQ would be 82 (9/11 × 100).

In addition to adapting Binet's test for use in American schools, Terman had a larger goal—a goal that today is considered reprehensible. He was an advocate of the nineteenth century *eugenics movement*, which sought to discourage people deemed as "unfit" from reproducing, while encouraging "fit" individuals to have children (Leslie, 2000). He believed that his IQ test could help determine the "fitness" of individuals to reproduce. He stated, "[T]he children of successful and cultured parents test higher than children from wretched and ignorant homes

Mark Humphrey/AP Photo

A high IQ. Michael Kearney (centre) graduated high school at 6 years of age, received his first degree (a Bachelor's degree in Anthropology) at age 10, and received his master's degree in chemistry at age 14.

As a result of eugenics research, two Canadian provinces (Alberta in 1928 and British Columbia in 1933) enacted laws requiring individuals deemed "mentally retarded" or "mentally ill" to be sterilized. Nazi practices during World War II led to public distaste for eugenics, but these laws were not repealed in Canada until 1972.

for the simple reason that their heredity is better." More generally, Terman believed that his test demonstrated that some groups of people are inherently less intelligent than others (Hegarty, 2007; Feldhusen, 2003).

Working with agencies in the United States government, Terman also administered his test to newly arrived immigrants and to almost two million World War I army recruits. His student, Arthur Otis, developed non-verbal tasks for non-English speaking individuals. Some psychologists at the time believed that the results of these alternative versions of the intelligence test proved the inferiority of people whose origins were not Anglo-Saxon. In fact, the mass testing of immigrants helped lead to a 1924 law that greatly lowered the number of people allowed to enter the United States from Southern and Eastern Europe, while increasing the number from Northern and Western Europe. This is a vivid example of how non-scientific thinking (such as prejudice and racism) can sometimes influence scientific thinking and political decision making. Despite such misuse of the early Stanford-Binet test, it remained for many years the leading intelligence testing instrument in the United States and Canada.

56.2.4 David Wechsler and the WAIS

As a young man inducted into the army during World War I, David Wechsler (1896–1981) was trained to administer and score the Stanford-Binet and other intelligence tests of the time. Over the course of his work, he came to recognize two key problems with the tests (Kaufman, 2009, 2000).

First, he realized that the distinction between mental and chronological age becomes less informative when testing adults. While it may be true that a considerable difference in intelligence may be evident between an 8-year-old and a 13-year-old, a five-year difference between adults tends to be meaningless. How much difference is there, for example, between the mental ability of a typical 30-year-old and a typical 35-year-old? Not much. Second, Wechsler, who was born in Romania and whose family immigrated to the United States when he was 6 years old, recognized the need for greater fairness when testing people who did not speak English or who spoke it poorly.

Over the course of his professional life, Wechsler devised a number of intelligence tests that took such problems into account. The first such test—the *Wechsler-Bellevue Intelligence Scale*—was published in 1939. Different versions of Wechsler's tests continue to be published by his associates to the present day (Watkins, 2010; Hartman, 2009; Tobin, 2013). The best known of these tests are the *Wechsler Adult Intelligence Scale* (*WAIS*) and the *Wechsler Intelligence Scale for Children* (*WISC*). **Figure 56-2** shows sample items from the WAIS.

Wechsler borrowed much from the Stanford-Binet and other tests; however, his tests were less dominated by tasks requiring verbal ability. There are 15 subtests on the current fourth (Canadian) edition of the WAIS (Wechsler, 2008). They are divided into four scales: Verbal Comprehension, Working Memory, Perceptual Reasoning, and Processing Speed. Figure 56-2 shows the specific scales that make up each index. Individuals who take the test receive a score on each scale. Individuals also receive an overall score that Wechsler associated with the *g* factor. In addition, Wechsler discarded the old formula for calculating an *IQ* score. Although he still called a person's overall score an *intelligence quotient*, or *IQ*, he derived the score from a normal distribution (discussed earlier in this part), rather than from a ratio. Essentially, he would compare individual scores to scores obtained over a very large sample of individuals. Using the normal distribution, Wechsler could see how much individual scores differenced from or deviated from (were higher or lower than) the general estimate of the population average. This change in IQ score generation has been adopted in most other intelligence tests.

Wechsler Adult Intelligence Scales (WAIS)–IV CDN Subtests Grouped According to Index Scores

	Subtest	Description	Example
Verbal Comprehension	Vocabulary	Test ability to define increasingly difficult words	What does repudiate mean?
	Similarities	Asks in what way certain objects or concepts are similar; measures abstract thinking	How are a calculator and a typewriter alike?
	Information	Taps a general range of information	On which continent is France?
	Comprehension	Tests understanding of social conventions and ability to evaluate past experience	Why do people need birth certificates?

Verbal IQ

	Subtest	Description	Example
Working Memory	Arithmetic	Tests arithmetic reasoning through word problems	How many hours will it take to drive 150 kilometres at 50 kilometres per hour?
	Digit Span	Tests attention and rote memory by orally presenting series of digits to be repeated forward or backward	Repeat the following numbers backward: 2 4 3 5 1 8 6
	Letter-Number Sequencing	Tests attention, concentration, mental control	For each item, repeat the numbers first in ascending order then the letters in alphabetical order (or the letters then the numbers).

Item	Trial	Correct Response	
1.	T-4-L-5-Z-2-H	2-4-5-H-L-T-Z	H-L-T-Z-2-4-5
2.	6-R-9-J-1-S-5	1-5-6-9-J-R-S	J-R-S-1-5-6-9
3.	M-1-K-5-R-2-H	1-2-5-H-K-M-R	H-K-M-R-1-2-5

Performance IQ

	Subtest	Description	Example
Perceptual Reasoning	Block Design	Tests ability to perceive and analyze patterns by presenting designs that must be copied with blocks	Assemble blocks to match this design: 
	Matrix Reasoning	Tests non-verbal abstract problem solving, inductive reasoning, and spatial reasoning	Which image goes in the empty box? 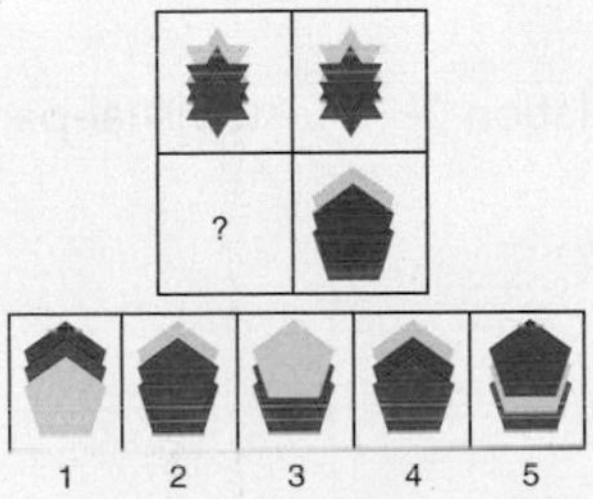

(continued)

FIGURE 56-2 **Items similar to those on the WAIS.** The widely used WAIS gives separate scores for Verbal Comprehension, Working Memory, Perceptual Reasoning, and Processing Speed, as well as an overall intelligence score.

(continued)

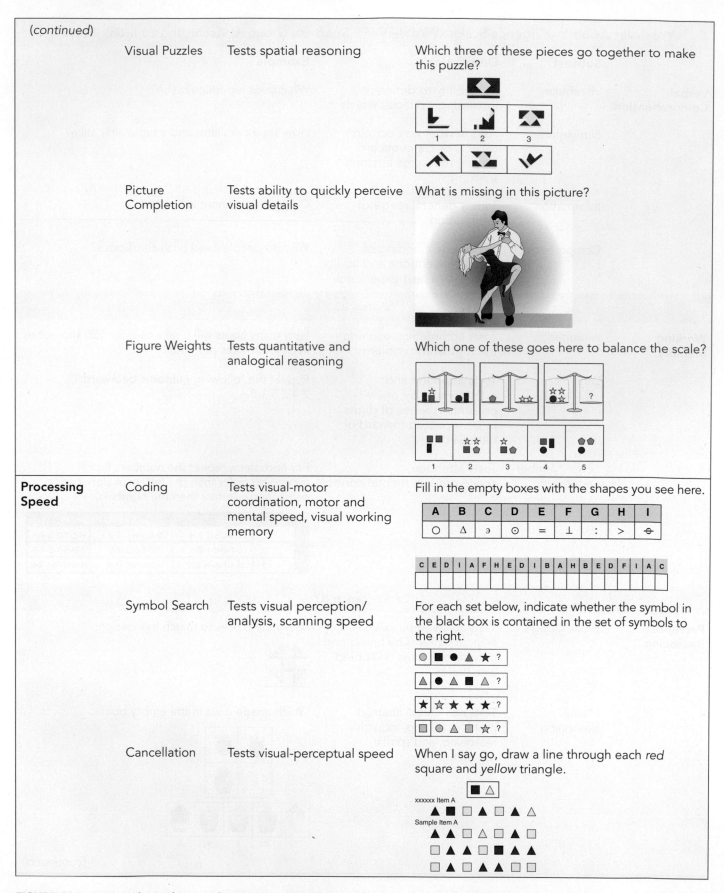

	Visual Puzzles	Tests spatial reasoning	Which three of these pieces go together to make this puzzle?
	Picture Completion	Tests ability to quickly perceive visual details	What is missing in this picture?
	Figure Weights	Tests quantitative and analogical reasoning	Which one of these goes here to balance the scale?
Processing Speed	Coding	Tests visual-motor coordination, motor and mental speed, visual working memory	Fill in the empty boxes with the shapes you see here.
	Symbol Search	Tests visual perception/analysis, scanning speed	For each set below, indicate whether the symbol in the black box is contained in the set of symbols to the right.
	Cancellation	Tests visual-perceptual speed	When I say go, draw a line through each *red* square and *yellow* triangle.

FIGURE 56-2 Items similar to those on the WAIS. (*Continued*)

Psychology Around Us | Cramming at an Early Age

To gain admission to some prestigious private schools, children as young as 4 years are required to take the Wechsler Preschool and Primary Scale of Intelligence (WPPSI). This test is a revision of the more commonly used intelligence tests for older children (WISC) and adults (WAIS). The WPPSI, now in its third edition, is intended to measure the basic components of intelligence, just as its cousins try to do with older persons.

But evidence indicates that the WPPSI is quite unreliable (unlike the WISC and WAIS). The more often preschoolers take the test, the higher they will score. It is also particularly sensitive to practice effects (when the same test is done several times). All of this calls into question the test's usefulness as an admissions test for access to exclusive private schools.

In fact, the biggest controversy surrounding the WPPSI has focused on parents' attempt to have their children practise and prepare for the test by hiring psychologists to administer the test to their young children beforehand. Many parents acquire versions of the WPPSI to train their children, some have the children attend test prep services, and others buy WPPSI flashcards from cram.com. In at least one high-profile case, a mother sued her child's preschool for $19,000, saying that the preschool had not adequately prepared her child for the WPPSI. Apparently, the preschool had merely provided a playroom where the child could interact and paint and hang out with other children. Of course, in the old days, that's what preschools were all about.

Wechsler's tests resulted from his clinical experience, not from a clear theoretical position. However, he did come to develop a broad view of what intelligence means. In particular, he believed that it is more than success on test scores. To him, intelligence is at work as individuals try to manage the day-to-day aspects of life, interact with others, and perform at work. Wechsler's broad view of intelligence has gained momentum over the years. Indeed, as we suggested earlier, it lies at the centre of most current theories of intelligence (Boake, 2002).

56.3 How Well Do Intelligence Tests Predict Performance?

The Stanford-Binet and the WAIS have very high degrees of reliability (Hunt, 2010). The correlation coefficient for retakes of each test is about +.90. Furthermore, repeated measurements of IQ across the lifespan tend to correlate very highly (Gow et al., 2011; Larsen et al., 2008). Today's leading intelligence tests are also highly correlated with school performance—a validity coefficient of about +.50 (Lynn & Meisenberg, 2010; Sternberg et al., 2001). The correlations are even higher between IQ scores and the number of years of schooling that people complete (Ceci, 1991). These findings are especially relevant considering that IQ tests were originally designed to assess for school performance.

Of course, IQ tests are meant to do more than predict school (or preschool!) performance. When we talk about IQ, though, we often think about it in terms of defining general mental ability. After all, we continue to measure IQ for adults far past school age. This is so even though most of the tasks on any IQ test relate most strongly to school performance. Although these tasks are highly relevant to the types of challenges encountered in school—math, store of knowledge, reasoning—it is unclear to what degree they measure the many other types of intelligence that we have described in this part and beyond. For example, Keith Stanovich at the University of Toronto has argued that IQ does not predict rational thinking such as that reflected in the Nobel Prize-winning work of Daniel Kahneman and Amos Tversky discussed in Part 9 (Stanovich & West, 2014).

So what does IQ mean outside the classroom? Performance on intelligence tests correlates to some degree with other areas of functioning in life, such as occupational and social achievements, income, and health-related behaviours (Hunt, 2011; Cramond et al., 2010; Lubinski, 2004). In a massive undertaking, researchers administered the same intelligence test to every 11-year-old child in Scotland in 1932 and 1947, and then followed the children's development and achievements as they

Research suggests you are just as likely to win a Nobel Prize if you have an IQ of 130 as if you have an IQ of 180 (Sulloway, 1996).

Is Intelligence an Important Part of Diagnosing Learning Disorders?

Intelligence tests have historically played a central role in defining and diagnosing learning disabilities. Children with learning disabilities or more severe learning disorders have difficulty processing certain types of information. These include, but are not limited to: language processing; phonological processing (recall Part 9); visual spatial processing; processing speed; memory and attention; and executive functions (for example, planning and decision making) (Learning Disabilities Association of Canada, 2002).

The current standard definition of learning disability that shapes education assessment, practice, and policy can be summarized by the official definition adopted by the Learning Disabilities Association of Canada (2002): "Learning disabilities refer to a number of disorders which may affect the acquisition, organization, retention, understanding or use of verbal or nonverbal information. These disorders affect learning in individuals who otherwise demonstrate at least average abilities essential for thinking and/or reasoning. As such, learning disabilities are distinct from global intellectual deficiency." This definition identifies a learning disability as reflecting a discrepancy between assessed intelligence and achievement, and viewing it as reflecting a cognitive processing disorder or condition with processing deficits (Kozey & Siegel, 2008).

Lee Gunderson and Sandra Scarr at the University of British Columbia are among many psychologists concerned about the effects associated with this discrepancy definition of learning disabilities (2001). They point out that intelligence tests play a central, sometimes provincially-mandated, role in determining if a discrepancy exists that would indicate the presence of a learning disability. The discrepancy in question is between a score on an intelligence test and either scores on an educational achievement test battery or school grades. The reasoning is that if a child is not achieving in school to the level that would be anticipated based upon their intelligence test score, then she may have a learning disability (that would be identified with a more specific learning assessment). Once the child's learning issues are identified, a specialized program of instruction or individual program plan can be created to addresses the child's challenges and draws on his strengths to assist him to achieve educationally.

Scarr and Gunderson have no concerns about this, but point out that the discrepancy approach also leads to children who are not achieving educationally but whose intelligence test scores are also low not being considered for learning disabilities. They point out that children with low reading scores and with or without low intelligence test scores benefit equally from reading disability programs (Siegel, 1992). In one study, the children with lower intelligence scores actually showed

James Shaffer/PhotoEdit

greater reading improvements in a reading program than did students without low intelligence scores (Yule, 1973). Scarr and Gunderson suggest that we focus on all students who need help with learning, rather than limiting program access to those with intelligence/achievement discrepancies.

Finally, Scarr and Gunderson warn of something called the Matthew effect. Named by sociologist Robert Merton (1968), the effect is based on a passage from the Gospel of Matthew: "For to all those who have, more will be given, and they will have an abundance; but from those who have nothing, even what they have will be taken away (Matthew 25:29)." The passage is taken to mean that the rich get richer and the poor get poorer. In terms of reading, Keith Stanovich (1986) at the University of Toronto points out that reading competence plays an increasingly important role in both school performance across all subjects and in intelligence test performance. As a consequence, children with unaddressed reading issues will have intelligence test scores that fall back further and further from those of their peers as they move through their elementary school years. If their reading issues are not picked up early, the Matthew effect will drive down their intelligence test scores over their elementary years, making it less likely that a diagnostic discrepancy will be there to be picked up. As a result, rich (good) readers get better while poor readers get poorer and are less and less likely to get the assistance they need to stop their reading (and achievement and academic self-confidence) slide.

Scarr and Gunderson conclude that we should move away from our consistent use of intelligence tests as part of the process of identifying children with learning disabilities. Instead, they suggest that we move to a more direct assessment of learning abilities so that we do not withhold support and treatment from children who would benefit from it.

moved through the lifespan (Deary et al., 2004). Performance on the IQ test at this young age was found to correlate to some degree with better health throughout life, greater independence during old age, and a longer lifespan. It would appear, then, that IQ testing does have some relevance beyond the school ages. However, it is important to recall that these relationships are correlational. We do not know that higher intelligence *caused* any of these outcomes.

56.4 Cultural Bias and Stereotypes in Intelligence Testing

Though widely used and respected, intelligence tests are subject to many criticisms, both fair and unfair. One set of concerns involves *cultural bias* (Tomes, 2010; Wicherts & Dolan, 2010; Kan et al., 2013). As mentioned earlier, different cultures may have different ideas of intelligence. For example, Western intelligence tests emphasize abilities, such as logic, mathematical skill, and verbal fluency rather than emphasizing abilities, such as getting along with others and fitting in with one's environment—abilities that are important in Chinese notions of intelligence. Such differences obviously make comparing intelligence across cultures challenging.

Furthermore, problems are not limited to comparing people from different countries, but extend to comparing members of different subcultures within a single country. For example, although Wechsler made considerable efforts to standardize the WAIS and make it as unbiased as possible, critics noted several curious oversights in earlier versions of the test. Many of its problem-solving questions reflected learning experiences and opportunities more commonly encountered in middle-class settings. For instance, the quality of the education experiences provided middle-class children is higher, and they acquire vocabularies at home and school that are more representative of the vocabulary skills assumed by intelligence test developers (Hunt, 2011; Ford, 2008; Nicpon, 2014). In addition, until the most recent revisions of the WAIS, every time a picture of a person was used for a test item, the picture was of a Caucasian person.

In part to point out the culture-specific nature of intelligence testing, sociologist Adrian Dove created the Dove Counterbalance General Intelligence Test (now called the Chitling Test; see **Table 56-1**). Dove intended the test to be at least partly a satire of the notion that

---

TABLE 56-1 Sample Items from the Chitling Test

1. A "handkerchief head" is:

(a) a cool cat, (b) a porter, (c) an Uncle Tom, (d) a hoddi, (e) a preacher.

2. Which word is most out of place here?

(a) splib, (b) blood, (c) gray, (d) spook, (e) black.

3. Cheap chitlings (not the kind you purchase at a frozen food counter) will taste rubbery unless they are cooked long enough. How soon can you quit cooking them to eat and enjoy them?

(a) 45 minutes, (b) 2 hours, (c) 24 hours, (d) 1 week (on a low flame), (e) 1 hour.

4. If you throw the dice and 7 is showing on the top, what is facing down?

(a) 7, (b) snake eyes, (c) boxcars, (d) little Joes, (e) 11.

5. "Jet" is:

(a) an East Oakland motorcycle club, (b) one of the gangs in "West Side Story," (c) a news and gossip magazine, (d) a way of life for the very rich.

6. "Bird" or "Yardbird" was the "jacket" that jazz lovers from coast to coast hung on:

(a) Lester Young, (b) Peggy Lee, (c) Benny Goodman, (d) Charlie Parker, (e) "Birdman of Alcatraz."

Find the whole test here: http://wilderdom.com/personality/intelligenceChitlingTestShort.html

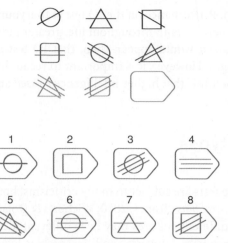

stereotype vulnerability or threat a phenomenon in which people in a particular group perform poorly because they fear that their performance will conform to a negative stereotype associated with that group.

The power of stereotype vulnerability or threat. In one study, Asian women who were encouraged to focus largely on their female identity performed poorly on a math test, while those who were led to focus on their Asian identity performed well on the math test.

a culture-free intelligence test could ever be developed. Dove's test helps us to clearly see that all intelligence tests are grounded in particular cultural (and historical) perspectives. It is likely that there will always be culture-based disagreements about intelligence tests and about what knowledge and skills are important when measuring intelligence.

Most people interested in the construction of intelligence tests have abandoned the idea of totally unbiased tests, and instead try to design tests that do not put particular cultures at an absolute disadvantage. The Progressive Matrices Test attempts to achieve this goal in part by emphasizing abstract, non-verbal skills, for example. However, there are still cultural and educational influences on scores for this measure (Owen, 1992). As such, the test is acknowledged to not be culture-free, but it is somewhat more culture fair than other intelligence tests. **Figure 56-3** shows some sample items from that test.

A related testing issue involves **stereotype vulnerability or threat**, which occurs when people in a particular group perform poorly because they fear that their performance will conform to a negative stereotype associated with their group. Several studies have found that simply suggesting to students that they will not do well on a test because of their gender or race can lower their test scores (Owens & Massey, 2011; Massey & Owens, 2014; Steele & Aronson, 2004, 1995).

In one particularly interesting study, researchers were able to use stereotype threat to manipulate the performance of Asian women on a math test (Ambady et al., 2004, 2001; Shih, Pittinsky, & Ambady, 1999). Some participants were encouraged to focus on their female identity, and they tended to perform less well on the test (in keeping with the stereotype that women are not good at math). Other participants were encouraged to focus their attention on their Asian identity, and they tended to perform better (in keeping with the stereotype that Asians are good at math). Those given no encouragement to think about their gender or racial heritage still showed the above effects, depending on whether they were tested in a room with males (implicitly drawing attention to the females' gender) or with non-Asian students (implicitly drawing attention to their racial heritage). Finally, these effects were reduced if the participants read a prepared "scientific" article which stated that the stereotypes (females bad at math and Asians good at math) were not true (Smith & White, 2002; Thoman et al., 2013).

As psychologists' awareness and ability to detect bias grows, they are becoming increasingly able to construct tests that are more sensitive and more effective. We have, for example, already noted the efforts of developers of the WAIS to make their tests less culture-specific. Overall bias can be assessed both at the general level we have discussed here and also at a more detailed level. During test construction, today's tests are also assessed for *item bias*; if individuals from a particular gender or ethnic group miss an item with high frequency, that item is considered for elimination from the test. Similarly, certain questions may become less culturally relevant even for the majority culture over time and must be exchanged for questions that better reflect current conditions. It appears that ongoing efforts to assess and challenge these sorts of bias have been somewhat successful in rendering generally non-biased testing (Ford, Moore, & Whiting, 2006; Whiting & Ford, 2006).

56.5 Is Human Intelligence Increasing?

We have observed that the median score on intelligence tests, such as the Stanford-Binet and the WAIS, is set at 100. To keep the median score at 100, the tests periodically must be *restandardized*. People taking the WAIS today, for example, are taking a version that has been reconstructed—not the version that David Wechsler designed originally.

Upon reviewing test scores over time, researchers have noticed something startling: intelligence test scores from around the industrialized world seem to be increasing, even though scores from other kinds of educational tasks and tests, such as university and college aptitude tests, are dropping (Nettelbeck & Wilson, 2004). Studies indicate that an average IQ score of 100 from 70 years ago would equate to a score of only 76 today. This puzzling phenomenon has been named the **Flynn effect**, after New Zealand researcher James Flynn (2007), who first discovered this effect in data from at least 14 nations (see **Figure 56-4**).

Researchers do not fully understand why intelligence scores have increased over time (Ceci & Kanaya, 2010; Weiss, 2010; Trahan, 2014). One possibility is that there is something wrong with the basic procedures, content, or nature of standardized intelligence tests. A more widely embraced explanation holds that intelligence is changeable and that, on average, people today exhibit higher intelligence than people did in the past. Such improvements in intelligence might be related to improvements in education around the world, better nutrition, the development of more stimulating environments, reductions in childhood disease, or evolutionary shifts in genetic inheritance (Mingroni, 2007, 2004). It is also worth noting that some theorists believe that rising intelligence test performance is due to the greater test-writing sophistication and test-taking motivation of today's students (Neisser, 1997).

Flynn effect an observed rise in average IQ scores throughout the world over time.

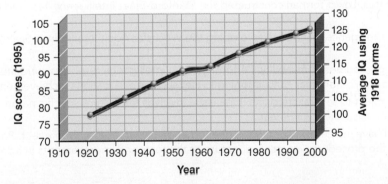

FIGURE 56-4 The Flynn effect. Flynn demonstrated that intelligence scores have increased from 1918 to 1995. The right axis of the graph shows that if the 1918 scales were used today, the average IQ score in the United States would be 125. The left axis shows that if the 1995 scales were used, the average IQ score in 1918 would equate to a score of 76 today. Source: Adapted from Weiten, W. (2007). *Psychology: Themes and variations* (7th ed.). Belmont, CA: Thomson Learning; Horgan, J. (1995). Get smart, take a test. *Scientific American*, 273(5), 1995, p. 14. Adapted with permission of Dmitry Schidlowsky Illustration.

Before You Go On

What Do You Know?

1. What three basic criteria are central to designing an intelligence test?
2. What was the original purpose of Binet's intelligence test? How did he measure intelligence?
3. How does mental age differ from chronological age?
4. How does Terman's definition of IQ differ from that of Wechsler?
5. What are the components of the WAIS and WISC intelligence tests? Give a couple of examples of what is measured on each component.
6. What are some of the ways in which intelligence tests have been shown to be culturally biased?
7. What does the concept of stereotype threat suggest about the situations in which people are tested?
8. What are some proposed causes of the Flynn effect?

What Do You Think? How would you design a culture-free intelligence test?

Summary

Module 56: How Do We Measure Intelligence?

LEARNING OBJECTIVE 56 Identify important considerations in the construction of intelligence tests, discuss the history of intelligence testing, and describe some criticisms of intelligence tests.

- The *psychometric approach* to studying intelligence attempts to measure intelligence with carefully constructed psychological tests.
- To ensure that intelligence tests are grounded in sound scientific principles, psychologists design tests that adhere to three basic criteria: *standardization*, *reliability*, and *validity*.
- Early pioneers of intelligence testing include Francis Galton, who proposed the theory of psychophysical performance, and Francis Binet, who developed a test to predict children's success in school.
- Adapting Binet's work for use in the United States, Lewis Terman constructed the Stanford-Binet Intelligence Test and devised the *intelligence quotient (IQ)*.
- David Wechsler broadened the usefulness of intelligence testing by developing the Wechsler Adult Intelligence Scale (WAIS), along with several other tests.
- Both the Stanford-Binet and the WAIS have high degrees of reliability. Performance on intelligence tests also correlates highly with school performance, and to some degree with other areas of functioning in life, such as occupational achievements.
- Although widely used, intelligence tests are subject to several criticisms. One issue involves the culture-specific nature of the tests, which may produce bias. A related problem is *stereotype threat*.
- Intelligence test scores from around the world have increased over time, a phenomenon known as the *Flynn effect*. Possible explanations include potential problems with the procedures, content, or nature of the tests and improvements in education, nutrition, health, or environments.

Key Terms

Study Questions

Multiple Choice

1. A manager at a retail store develops a test and uses it to hire new employees (only people who score high on the test will be offered the job). To examine whether people who do better on the test also perform better on the job, the manager should focus most closely on
   a) content validity.
   b) reliability.
   c) the test distribution.
   d) the validity coefficient.

2. Binet and Simon's intelligence test was created with the intention of
   a) determining which groups of people are inherently more intelligent than others.
   b) identifying gifted children for placement in advanced programs.
   c) identifying which school placement level was most appropriate for different children.
   d) using test scores to rank children according to abilities.

3. Considering the Stanford-Binet and WAIS intelligence tests, with which two sets of scores are we likely to obtain the highest correlation?
   a) a set of test scores and the same people's grades in school
   b) people taking the test at age 4 and the same people taking the test at age 40
   c) people taking the test today and the same people taking the test two weeks from now
   d) two groups of people who are unrelated to each other

Fill-in-the-Blank

1. On most intelligence tests, most people score in the middle, with a few at the very high or low ends of the scale. This pattern of scores is called a _____.

2. A child's _____ reflects the level of the child's intellectual performance, which may or may not match his chronological age.

3. A tendency called _____ occurs when individuals in particular groups know they are expected to perform poorly on a test and this expectation impairs their performance.

Module 57: Is Intelligence Governed by Genetic or Environmental Factors?

As you saw in Part 4, the nature–nurture debate centres on the question of whether particular qualities and behaviours result from genetic underpinnings or from the environment. Is a happy and healthy baby, for example, the result of robust genes, effective parental care and attention, or both? A similar question can be asked about intelligence. Do we inherit our intelligence from our parents? And if we do, does that mean that the environment has no influence, or can experiences, such as parenting, schooling, and familiarity with test taking, have an effect? Later in this module, we will examine how various psychologists answer these questions. First, though, we will consider important social questions that are raised by the search to identify the origin of intelligence.

57.1 What Are the Social Implications of the Nature–Nurture Debate?

If genes were clearly identified as the main determinant of intelligence, what might some of the social consequences be? For some, such a finding might be taken to justify claims that particular individuals or groups of people are inherently superior to others. Such people might even seek to create a social structure that assigns people to classes according to their parentage and restricts certain classes to particular social roles.

On the other hand, what if the environment were found to be more decisive in determining intelligence? Children from disadvantaged environments would be expected to lead disadvantaged lives and display, on average, lower intelligence; but then again, their environments and their intellectual level could potentially be improved. But would people who possessed environmental advantages be willing to share them with those who were deprived?

Other difficult questions involving the nature–nurture debate and intelligence have been asked with respect to gender, ethnicity, and race. Perhaps the clearest example of the serious social consequences of such questions was the Nazi claim in the early twentieth century that Aryans (Indo-Europeans who were supposedly Nordic in appearance and of German ancestry) were superior to all other groups. Although Nazi scientists failed to support this assertion, their efforts demonstrated that there will always be people who wish to use possible genetic differences in intelligence as a basis for oppressing and controlling people.

Statistically, firstborn children appear to represent a majority of Nobel Prize winners, classical music composers, and eminent psychologists. Later born appear to more likely become leaders and may, on average, be more creative (Plucker, 2003).

©iStockphoto.com/amriphoto   ©iStockphoto.com/rollover

Environmental impact. Research indicates that a stimulating environment can help facilitate the intellectual development of children, whereas a deprived environment often has a negative impact.

57.2 The Bell Curve Controversy

Consider a more recent example of the social implications of the nature–nurture debate concerning intelligence. In 1994, two researchers published a book that ignited a firestorm of controversy regarding the issue of intelligence. In *The Bell Curve*, Richard Herrnstein and Charles Murray surveyed research on the origins and nature of intelligence, and also reported their own analyses. Based on this large amount of data, the authors drew several controversial conclusions. Numerous psychologists, educators, and researchers argue that many of the authors' conclusions do not follow from the data. The conclusions offered by Herrnstein and Murray were:

1. Conventional IQ tests accurately measure intelligence.
2. IQ is an important predictor of many measures of success in life, including success at school, work, parenting, and income. Higher IQ also predicts the avoidance of welfare dependence and criminality.
3. Given such correlations, people who are high in intelligence form a cognitive elite—they reach the upper levels of society—whereas those with lower IQs fall toward the bottom.
4. Given their predictive powers, intelligence tests can and should be used as a *gating* mechanism, to allow those with high IQs access to opportunities.
5. IQ is largely heritable, passed on through the genes from one generation to the next.
6. There are clear racial and ethnic differences in intelligence.
7. It is likely, although not certain, that at least some of this difference between groups is due to genetic factors.

Herrnstein and Murray went on to argue for greater acceptance of these ideas and benign recognition of the limitations of individuals with lower IQs, making greater efforts to help them in areas of life where lower intelligence holds them back. As you might imagine, the debate over the book's conclusions and implications remains heated today. As noted above, most psychologists and researchers argue that many of the authors' conclusions do not follow from the data, and may instead reflect the authors' ideology (Nisbett, 2009; Flynn, 2008, 2000; Sternberg & Grigorenko, 2013). Furthermore, the social policies they recommend on the basis of their conclusions are unfair and racist (Richards, 2004).

A related controversy within Canadian psychology circulates around the work of Philippe Rushton (1943–2012) at University of Western Ontario. At the height of the nature–nurture debates, Rushton (2008, 1995, 1994) argued that races could be ranked in terms of a number of characteristics, including intelligence, with Asians, as a group, scoring highest, blacks the lowest, and whites in between. Rushton's work has been severely

©iStockphoto.com/Christopher Futcher

Race and intelligence controversy. In 1989, David Suzuki publicly debated Philippe Rushton at University of Western Ontario and argued strongly that Rushton's views on race and intelligence were racist, that his work was not science, and that Rushton's grants should be cancelled and he should be fired.

criticized, not just because of its harmful nature, but also because it is not based on solid scientific evidence (Nisbett, 2005). For example, intelligence is correlated with socio-economic status (parents with means can provide richer intellectual environments) and race is correlated with poverty (in North America, blacks on average have a lower standard of living than whites; Glasmeier, 2006).

Many researchers dismissed Rushton's claims and were not interested in investigating an area seen as unworthy of further work. David Suzuki, the well-known Canadian scientist and environmentalist, dedicated an episode of his CBC Radio show Quirks and Quarks to having researchers report on their work, carefully examining and refuting all of Rushton's claims (CBC Radio, 1989). Suzuki also publicly debated Rushton at University of Western Ontario (CBC Television, 1989). In that debate, Suzuki again refuted Rushton's claims and argued strongly that Rushton's views were racist, that his work was not science, and that Rushton's grants should be cancelled and he should be fired. The result was a test of university academic freedom, which states that academic researchers' university positions are protected in the event that they engage in research that is unpopular. Rushton had his teaching reduced and his access to student research pools restricted, but he kept his job and has continued to conduct research. Officials from University of Western Ontario publicly apologized for any pain caused by Rushton's views and agreed to monitor his future lectures (Helwig, 1989; Platiel & Strauss, 1989; Tenzen, 1989).

To be clear, it is important to remember three things about the sorts of claims made by Rushton. First, you should not accept them at face value, but critically search out and evaluate the scientific data related to the claims and to criticisms of those claims. Second, you should keep in mind that average race-related differences in intelligence scores have been shown to reflect differences in environmental opportunity (poverty), issues with the tests used to assess intelligence, or other issues not directly related to intelligence (Nisbett, 2005). Finally, you need to keep in mind that average differences at the population level, whether related to race and intelligence test scores or gender and spatial reasoning, tell you nothing useful when predicting the intelligence or spatial skills of individuals within those populations. Let's examine what scientists actually have learned and not learned about the nature–nurture debate on human intelligence.

57.3 Genetic Influences on Intelligence

A variety of studies suggest that genetic factors play a major role in intelligence. In particular, studies of twins and other relatives and research in molecular biology point to genes as a key contributor.

Rick Gershon/Getty Images

The heritability of intelligence. Twin studies suggest that genetics play a major role in intelligence. There is a higher correlation in IQ scores for identical twins in contrast to all other family comparisons.

57.3.1 Family Studies

Twins have received particular attention from intelligence researchers. If genetic factors are at work in intelligence, identical twins (who share all their genes) should have more similar intelligence test scores than fraternal twins (who share only about half of their genes). This expectation has been supported consistently by research (Bratko et al., 2010; Plomin & Spinath, 2004). Studies have found, on average, a correlation of +.86 between the intelligence test scores of identical twins, compared with a correlation of +.60 between the scores of fraternal twins.

Do such findings mean that intelligence is related *primarily* to genes? Not necessarily. It turns out that parents treat identical twins more similarly than fraternal twins. In fact, family studies find that identical twins are treated the most alike of all siblings, followed by same-gender fraternal twins and then different-gender twins (Felson, 2014). Perhaps, then, the more closely related intelligence scores found among identical twins are, at least in part, a reflection of more similar interactions with parents.

To help sort out the relative influence of heredity and environment, we might want to look at IQ scores for identical twins who have been raised apart from one another. If genetic factors are important determinants of intelligence, then the scores should remain closely related. Researchers have looked at the IQ scores of identical twins who were adopted at birth and placed in separate homes. The correlation between the scores of these separated identical twins is +.75 (Plomin & Spinath, 2004), an impressive statistic that seems to reflect once again the influence of genetic factors. At the same time, this correlation is not as large as the +.86 correlation for the IQ scores of identical twins who are raised together, a difference that we might attribute to those twins' shared environments.

Another approach to the heredity and intelligence question is to examine the relationships between the IQ scores of adopted children and those of their biological and adoptive parents. If heredity is more influential than environment, the IQ scores of adopted children should be more similar to those of their biological parents than to those of their adoptive parents. If environment matters more, we should find the children's IQ scores closer to their adoptive parents' scores than to the scores of their biological parents (Plomin & Spinath, 2004).

Researchers have found, on average, a correlation of +.22 between the scores of adopted children and the scores of their biological parents, and a correlation of +.19 between the children's scores and those of their adoptive parents (Plomin & Spinath, 2004). On the one hand, the children's IQ scores are somewhat related to the scores of their biological parents (correlation of +.22), indicating a possible genetic influence. On the other hand, this correlation is not especially large, nor is it significantly higher than the +.19 correlation found between the scores of the children and those of their adoptive parents. This pattern of findings indicates once again that the nature–nurture question is not a simple one to answer.

All of these family studies suggest that genes play a role in intelligence, but exactly how much of a role? Scientists have sought to answer this question by examining the specific data from many studies and arriving at an overall estimate of the heritability of intelligence. **Heritability** refers to the overall extent to which differences among people are attributable to genes. Evaluating the data from studies of twins and other relatives, researchers have determined that the heritability of intelligence is approximately 50 percent (Plomin & Spinath, 2004). It is important to note that the concept of heritability is used to explain the differences between groups of people, not to provide information about a single individual. Thus, the finding that the heritability of intelligence is around 50 percent does not mean that 50 percent of a particular individual's intelligence is inherited. Rather, it suggests that 50 percent of all differences or variabilities observed in a population's intelligence test scores are due to genetic factors.

heritability the overall extent to which differences among people are attributable to genes.

The statistical measure used to indicate the contribution of heredity to intelligence (or to any other characteristic) is the **heritability coefficient**, a number ranging from 0.00 to +1.00. A coefficient of 0.00 means that heredity has no impact on variations observed among people, whereas a coefficient of +1.00 means that heredity is the sole influence on the characteristic under investigation. For example, the heritability coefficient for Huntington's Disease, in which genetic factors are totally responsible for the emergence of the disorder, is +1.00. In contrast, as we have just observed, the heritability coefficient for intelligence is +0.50—a figure that holds in studies conducted around the world, from Canada and the United States to Russia, Japan, and India (Plomin & Spinath, 2004).

heritability coefficient a correlation coefficient used to indicate the contribution of heredity to some characteristic, such as intelligence.

57.3.2 Nature or Nurture: Which Is More Important?

It is easy to get caught up in the debate about just how much of intelligence is due to nature and how much is due to nurture. It is helpful to keep in mind a quote attributed to the well-known Canadian psychologist Donald Hebb. When asked by a journalist to specify how much of intelligence is due to nature and how much to nurture, Hebb reportedly replied,

"Which contributes more to the area of a rectangle, its length or its width?" (Meaney, 2004). Which contributes more is really the wrong question to ask. Better to try to figure out how these two general categories of factors interact and influence intelligence.

Sandra Scarr (1991) suggested that nature (heredity) may set upper and lower limits on the level of intelligence a child may develop. This range of possible outcomes is called the **reaction range**. Scarr suggested that our nature sets general limits on our intellectual achievement, but it is our nurturing environments that determine where in our reaction range we end up. The main advantage of this theory is that it focuses directly on the interaction of both nature and nurture. It helps to account for children from poor backgrounds who do well, and for children from enriched environments who do not do so well.

reaction range the upper and lower level of intelligence or other outcomes made possible by a child's genetic nature.

57.4 Environmental Influences on Intelligence

If the heritability of intelligence is 50 percent, then environmental factors are responsible for the remaining 50 percent of differences in intelligence among people. The term *environment* can have a narrow or broad meaning. It can refer to our home setting, neighbourhood, extended family, school, or socio-economic group. It even can refer to biological events and experiences that a fetus confronts in its mother's uterus. Or, it can refer to the sum of all such contexts. Four environmental influences have received particular attention in the study of intelligence: family and home, culture, occupation, and schooling.

Animal studies suggest that organisms perform better on learning and intelligence tests when they are mildly hungry (Miller, 1957).

57.4.1 Family and Home Environment

The first overtly social environment to which we are exposed in life and the one that dominates our childhood is the family and home. Our parents' childrearing methods and other characteristics, our interactions with siblings, the objects in our houses, family trips—these are all parts of our family and home environment. Do such environmental factors affect children's intelligence?

57.4.2 Cultural Influences

Most definitions of intelligence include how well people adapt to their environments. This criterion raises an important question: does the definition of intelligence change across different cultural environments? Many researchers say yes, the definition of intelligence varies from culture to culture (Smith, 2010; Georgas, 2003).

Note that this is different from asking whether people from different parts of the world (or from different racial or ethnic groups) have different levels of intelligence. That question relates more to the idea of comparing general intelligence. Instead, here we are more concerned with comparing specific skill sets that constitute intelligence in different cultures. Researchers have found that the values of a society or cultural group often have powerful effects on the intellectual skills of its members. Rice farmers in Liberia, for example, are particularly skilled at estimating quantities of rice (Cole, Gay, & Glick, 1967); and children in Botswana, with much story experience, have good memories for the details of stories (Dube, 1982). These specific skills would improve individuals' ability to survive and thrive within their cultures, and thus would be valued components of intelligence within each culture. Such principles can apply within subcultures as well; as the example at the beginning of the part demonstrates, a knowledge of theoretical physics and obscure comic hero trivia are prized abilities in some Western subcultures.

Hoang Dinh NamAFP/Getty Images

Societal needs and intelligence. An individual's particular expression of intelligence is often tied to the survival needs of his society. Rice farmers, such as these field workers during rice harvest, are often highly skilled at estimating quantities of rice and are admired for their high intelligence.

Can Parents Improve Their Children's Intelligence?

Early theories held that an individual's intellectual capacity was totally fixed at birth. The many examples presented throughout this part of how the environment can affect intelligence certainly challenge this initial assumption. In particular, we now know that interventions of various kinds can improve intellectual functioning.

Two researchers, Robert Bradley and Bettye Caldwell, have examined the impact of the home environment on intelligence and identified several parenting approaches that may help raise the IQ scores of preschoolers (Bradley, Caldwell, & Corwyn, 2003; Bradley & Caldwell, 1984). In fact, these researchers claim that such approaches are better predictors of IQ scores than factors such as socio-economic class or family structure. Current research seems to support their assertions (Sidhu et al., 2010; Mahli, Sidhu, & Bharti, 2014).

©iStockphoto.com/Feverpitched

The parent to-do list includes:

- Be emotionally and verbally responsive and involved with your child: comment on and talk about what she is looking at and noticing, draw your child's attention to things around her.
- Avoid too much restriction and punishment: within reason, allow your child to explore his environment and do things for himself.
- Organize the physical environment and the child's activity schedule: have an area of your home that is set up for the child and is child friendly.
- Provide appropriate play materials: they do not have to be expensive child play toys, just things to challenge your child and encourage activity and exploration.
- Provide a variety of forms of daily stimulation: build in some play time with your child and, when she is older, with other children. Where possible, include your child in outings to local stores or even just for walks around your neighbourhood.

Research has suggested a link between family and home environment and children's intelligence scores. A number of studies, for example, have examined the IQ scores of biological siblings and adoptive siblings. These investigations have found that when biological siblings are raised apart, the correlation between their IQ scores is +.22. In contrast, when children from different families are adopted and raised together, the correlation between their IQ scores is +.32. If family and home environment did not affect intelligence levels, we would expect a near-zero correlation between the IQ scores of adoptive siblings. Instead, they display a higher correlation than that displayed by biological siblings who are raised apart (Plomin & Spinath, 2004).

Most of the assumptions about intelligence that we have looked at so far are Western-oriented. Western views of intelligence tend to be influenced by the Western value of individualism, while some other cultures place more emphasis on the community as a whole. Moreover, Westerners tend to equate high intelligence with rapid mental processing, whereas other cultures may value depth of thinking, even if it occurs at a slower rate (Sternberg, 2007; Sternberg et al., 1981). One study found that Taiwanese-Chinese theorists typically point to five factors at the root of intelligence: (1) a general cognitive factor; (2) interpersonal intelligence (knowing about others); (3) intrapersonal intelligence (knowing about oneself); (4) intellectual self-assertion (advocating for your own intellectual achievements); and (5) intellectual self-effacement (being humble about your intellectual achievements) (Yang & Sternberg, 1997; Sternberg, 2014). While the first three qualities are similar to factors in some Western definitions of intelligence, the final two are not. Also, Westerners often believe that intelligence further involves verbal skill and the ability to solve practical problems, features absent from the Chinese list.

57.4.3 Occupational Influences

Researchers consistently have found a relationship between intelligence and job complexity. People of higher intelligence tend to work in more complex jobs (Hunt, 2011; Ganzach, 2003; Ganzach & Pazy, 2001). An obvious explanation for this relationship is that individuals of higher intelligence can handle complex jobs more readily than less intelligent people, and so are more likely to obtain and succeed in such positions.

Studies also suggest, however, that complex work may itself improve intelligence. In one study, for example, interviews with 3,000 men in various occupations seemed to indicate that more complex jobs lead to more "intellectual flexibility and independent judgment among employees" (Schooler, 2001; Kohn & Schooler, 1973). For example, a job that requires workers to organize and interpret detailed financial data, for example, may help produce more intellectual depth than one requiring workers to simply add up customer bills.

Why would more complex jobs enhance intellectual skills? Perhaps because holders of such jobs are forced to acquire a greater amount of complex information and knowledge (Kuncel et al., 2010, 2004)—the very kinds of information and knowledge that are measured on intelligence tests. The complexity factor may also help explain differences in IQ scores between urban and rural populations. A few generations ago, studies found that urban residents scored, on average, six IQ points higher than rural residents (Terman & Merrill, 1937; Seashore, Wesman, & Doppelt, 1950). One possible explanation for this difference is the greater complexity of the urban environment. More recently, this difference declined to about two points (Kaufman & Doppelt, 1976; Reynolds et al., 1987). It could be that changes in rural environments—less isolation, increased travel, mass communication, Internet access, improvements in schools, and increased use of technology on farms—have raised the level of complexity in these environments and, in turn, brought the IQ scores of rural citizens closer to those of city residents.

Lester Lefkowitz/Getty Images

Which causes which? People in complex jobs, such as this engineer working in a telecommunications control room, are often highly intelligent. Does their high intelligence qualify them for more complex work, or does the complex work increase their intelligence? Research supports both explanations.

57.4.4 School Influences

Researchers have determined that schooling is both a cause and consequence of intelligence (Shayer & Adhami, 2010; Fish, 2002; Sangwan, 2001). Children with higher intelligence test scores are more likely to be promoted from grade to grade, less likely to drop out of school, and more likely to attend college or university. In turn, schooling helps change mental abilities, including those measured on intelligence tests.

Researchers Stephen Ceci and Wendy Williams (2010, 2007, 1997) have demonstrated some interesting ties between intelligence scores and the amount of time spent in school. Students' IQ scores tend to rise during the school year and drop when schooling is discontinued or during summer vacation. Students who complete high school perform higher on intelligence tests than those who leave school early. And young children whose birthdays just make the cut-off for beginning school early earn higher intelligence scores than those of almost identical age who miss the cut-off and remain at home for an extra year.

Why might schooling help improve intelligence scores? This finding may be due in part to the fact that schools provide the opportunity both to acquire information (Who wrote *Moby Dick*? What is a square root, and how do you calculate it?) and to develop important skills such as "systematic problem-solving,

©iStockphoto.com/small_frog

Times are changing. A farmer sits out in his field while working out his agricultural needs on a laptop. Some psychologists believe that the increased use of technology on farms helps account for the recent closing of the gap between the IQ scores of urban and rural populations.

abstract thinking, categorization, sustained attention to material of little intrinsic interest, and repeated manipulation of basic symbols and operations"—skills measured on intelligence tests (Neisser, 1998, p.16).

Researchers have also shown that the *quality* of the school environment affects intellectual performance. In financially poor schools, children tend to learn less, and in turn, tend to score significantly lower on IQ tests (Johnson, 2010; Reardon, 2013).

57.5 Group Differences in IQ Scores

Recall that at the beginning of this module we discussed *The Bell Curve*, in which the authors argued that group differences in IQ may be due largely to genetic factors. We went on to discuss findings that intelligence is, indeed, heritable, but that environment plays a significant role as well. Let us now look more closely at group differences in IQ scores.

There are two trends on which most researchers of group differences in intelligence agree (Sackett & Shen, 2010; Lynn, 2008; Fish, 2002). First, racial groups do indeed differ in their average scores on intelligence tests. Second, high-scoring people (and groups) are more likely to attain high levels of education and income. In one review conducted decades ago, 52 researchers agreed that the IQ bell curve for Americans is centred around a score of 100 for white Americans and 85 for African Americans, with scores for different subgroups of Hispanic Americans falling in between (Avery et al., 1994). Similarly, a review by Wes Darou (1992) of counselling services within the former Canadian International Development Agency indicated that Aboriginal Canadians score, on average, 15 to 20 points lower on intelligence tests than their non-Aboriginal contemporaries. Likewise, researchers have noted that European New Zealanders tend to outscore native Maori New Zealanders, Israeli Jews outscore Israeli Arabs, and people with good hearing outscore the hearing impaired (Zeidner, 1990). What can we make of such trends?

Two important issues about group differences can be clarified by means of an analogy offered by geneticist Richard Lewontin (2001, 1982, 1976; Feldman & Lewontin, 2008). Suppose you start with 100 plant seeds from the same source and divide them into two groups. You plant one group of seeds in a flowerpot filled with poor soil and the other group in a flowerpot filled with fertile soil. What differences would you expect between the groups of seeds as they grow into plants? As shown in **Figure 57-1**, you should see two kinds of variation: variation between the two groups and variation within each group. When evaluating these

© Michael Austen/Alamy

Schooling and intellectual performance. Research indicates that an enriching school environment contributes to better intellectual performance.

Group 1: poor soil

Group 2: fertile soil

FIGURE 57-1 **Lewontin's plant analogy of intelligence.** If two groups of plants start out from the same source of seeds (genetics), but one group is given a better environment, the differences in height between the two groups would be mainly determined by environmental conditions. The analogy applies when evaluating group differences in IQ scores.

variations, we need to keep in mind two principles that also apply to evaluating group differences in intelligence scores:

1. *Environment contributes to variation between the groups.* The plants growing in poor soil vary from the ones growing in good soil, even though all of the plants came from the same mixture of seed. For example, the plants raised in poor soil are, on average, shorter than those raised in fertile soil. This difference is probably attributable to the environment. In short, optimal environments tend to produce optimal plants, and deficient environments tend to produce less successful plants. Similarly, on average, groups that display lower average IQ scores have been raised in worse environments than the groups with higher scores.

2. *An average variation between groups cannot be applied to individuals within each group.* In our plant example, even though on average the plants growing in poor soil are shorter than those growing in good soil, some of the poor-soil plants will be taller than others. Some will probably even be taller than the average plant in the good soil. These differences probably are attributable to normal genetic variation, since all the plants in a given pot share the same environment.

Again, this principle applies to people as well as plants. It is essential to realize that knowing someone's group membership tells you *nothing* about that person's actual intelligence. Failing to distinguish between individual performance and group norms can mislead people, produce incorrect expectations, and cause social injustices—and is prejudicial.

With this analogy in mind, let us return to the question of IQ scores and group differences. Lorenzo Cherubini and his colleagues at Brock University have looked in detail at the situation of Aboriginal education policy and practice in Ontario. They note that there is a significant gap between the levels of school success of Aboriginal and non-Aboriginal students, with Aboriginal students twice as likely to drop out and fail to complete or take much longer to complete secondary school. He argues that equal education opportunities do not just consist of attending the same schools, but require that Aboriginal children and youth work in school systems that acknowledge and celebrate Aboriginal values and heritage. This will ensure that positive identity and commitment to education and learning will be a more consistent part of the Aboriginal student experience (Cherubini et al., 2010; Cherubini, & Hodson, 2012).

Such research suggests that public policy aimed at making more equitable resources available throughout society would lead to more similar intelligence test scores across different groups (Biswas-Diener, 2011; Williams et al., 2004). Of course, this raises yet another important question: do efforts to equalize educational experiences and other environmental resources actually improve intelligence? We will consider next the effects of *environmental enrichment*—providing disadvantaged children with more stimulating environments at home and at school.

57.6 Does Environmental Enrichment Make a Difference?

Studies have indicated that young children from poor families typically receive less intellectual stimulation than do children from wealthier homes (Arnold & Doctoroff, 2003). They have, on average, far fewer books and educational toys, for example, and their parents read to them less. Only half of preschoolers from families on public assistance have alphabet books, compared with 97 percent of children from wealthy homes (Mason et al., 1990; McCormick & Mason, 1986). It appears that their early environmental limitations may place poor children at a severe disadvantage when it comes to developing intellectual and academic skills.

We can see this problem particularly clearly in institutional settings such as orphanages and in foster homes (Beckett et al., 2010; Nelson et al., 2009, 2007). During the early

1980s, psychologist J. McVicker Hunt (1982) conducted work in a poor Iranian orphanage. In an effort to improve the lives of children in the orphanage and, in turn, improve their development, he offered a program of "tutored human enrichment" (for example, basic cognitive and vocabulary instruction). He found that such early interventions did indeed help improve the cognitive functioning of the children. In other work, however, he clarified that early instruction of this kind helps to improve the intellectual capacities only of children who have been living in deprived environments, not of those who have already been living in enriched environments.

Based on findings such as Hunt's, *Project Head Start*, a United States federally-funded preschool program, was launched in 1965. The program, which has served more than 22 million disadvantaged children since its inception and now serves around one million each year, aims to enhance children's performances in school and beyond by helping to develop their cognitive and social skills as early as possible (USDHHS, 2011; Olsen & DeBoise, 2007; Ripple et al., 1999) and by reducing their involvement with child welfare (Green et al., 2014). The program continues to enjoy significant community and political support.

Jim West/PhotoEdit

Getting a head start. Two toddlers enjoy the individualized attention provided by their teacher and their ultra-stimulating classroom environment in a Head Start program in Mississippi.

Early intervention programs can extend beyond school settings. They can include going into the homes of young children; working with their parents; adding stimulating toys, books, and tools to the home; and otherwise enriching the home and community environments. It appears that such home-bound programs often help increase children's cognitive achievements. In fact, evaluation work contributed to by Mike Boyes from the University of Calgary (and one of the authors of this book) shows that earlier intervention programs, such as Healthy Families programs that identify and offer support to new, at-risk families in the form of weekly visits from a healthy family home visitor, have been successful in getting children and their families onto a better starting track toward intellectual and educational success. These programs reduce child welfare involvement and improve both child and parent functioning (Elnitsky et al., 2003). Another extensive research project has clarified that enrichment-intervention programs of various kinds achieve greater success when they (1) begin earlier in life and continue; (2) are more intensive (more hours per day and more days per year); and (3) include programs for maintaining positive attitudes and behaviours (Pungello et al., 2010; Ramey & Ramey, 2007).

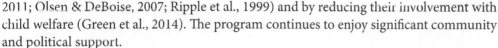

Before You Go On

www.wiley.com/go/comercanada

What Do You Know?

1. What are the main arguments of *The Bell Curve*?
2. About what percentage of intelligence is thought to be genetically determined, and what evidence supports this claim?
3. What types of environmental factors have been shown to affect intelligence?

What Do You Think? Considering the material you have read about test construction, heritability, and cultural differences, what type of learning environment would maximize the intelligence of all individuals?

Summary

Module 57: Is Intelligence Governed by Genetic or Environmental Factors?

LEARNING OBJECTIVE 57 Review the contributions of heredity and environment to intelligence, and explain how emphasizing one factor or the other can affect social policy.

- The nature–nurture debate as applied to intelligence has important social implications, exemplified by the controversial book *The Bell Curve*, whose authors argued that group differences in IQ are likely due at least in part to genetic factors.
- Family studies and research in molecular biology have indicated that heredity does play a major role in intelligence. Researchers estimate that the heritability of intelligence is about 50 percent.
- Environmental factors that affect intelligence include family and home, overall culture, occupation, and schooling.
- Group differences in IQ scores enable us only to make distinctions between groups, not to reach any conclusions about an individual within a group.
- Studies have confirmed that environmental enrichment for members of disadvantaged groups is effective in producing at least short-term cognitive gains.

Key Terms

heritability 443   heritability coefficient 443   reaction range 444

Study Questions

Multiple Choice

1. According to researchers Bradley and Caldwell, which of the following is not a suggestion for how parents can improve their children's intelligence?
   a) Avoid too much restriction and punishment.
   b) Organize the physical environment and the child's activity schedule.
   c) Provide appropriate play materials.
   d) Set high goals and reward the child for meeting them.

2. Which of the following statements about school and intellectual development is true?
   a) Children whose birthdays allow them to just make the cut-off for school attendance tend to struggle more than children who do not make the cut-off and are almost a year older when they start school.
   b) Children with very high intelligence scores tend to drop out of school because they get bored.
   c) Students' intelligence test scores tend to drop during the school year as they struggle to learn a lot of new information, and then rise during the summer when they are less stressed.
   d) When children are moved from financially poor schools to more affluent schools, their intelligence test scores tend to increase.

Fill-in-the-Blank

1. The fact that identical twins' intelligence test scores correlate more strongly than do fraternal twins' scores tells us that intelligence is at least partly _____.

2. Investigations of financially poor schools have demonstrated that the _____ of the school environment affects intellectual performance.

Module 58: The Brain and Intelligence

WHAT HAPPENS *in the* **BRAIN?**

So far in this part, we have explored several important questions concerning the nature, measurement, and sources of intelligence. We now add another question: what happens in the brain when we exhibit intelligence? Have researchers, for example, detected relationships between specific brain activities or specific brain structures and intelligence? To answer this question, let's look at four areas of investigation: brain size, brain speed, brain activity, and cortical thickness (Reynolds et al., 2008; Vernon et al., 2000).

> **LEARNING OBJECTIVE 58**
> Describe how brain size, number of neurons, processing speed, brain activity, and cortical thickness relate to intelligence.

58.1 Brain Size, Number of Neurons, and Intelligence

Researchers have been exploring correlations between brain size and intelligence since the mid-nineteenth century (Ash & Gallup, 2008; Galton, 1948, 1888). Philippe Rushton (2009) did some work here as well. Initially, limitations in technology hampered meaningful outcomes. For example, researchers could only study the brains of corpses, which certainly put a damper on testing their intelligence. Today's neuroimaging technologies, however, allow scientists to measure brain size and brain activity in living people.

Some neuroimaging findings over the past few decades have indeed suggested a possible correlation between brain size and mental functioning, but most studies of this issue fail to support this notion (Choi et al., 2008; Basten, Stelzel, & Fiebach, 2013). As we noted in Part 3, the overall size of the brain appears to be more closely related to the size of the body than to intelligence. The main exception to this is people with extremely small or extremely large brains, each of whom are more likely to exhibit intellectual disabilities than are people whose brain sizes fall within the normal range (Tramo et al., 1998).

Regardless of brain size, does the total number of neurons in a brain predict intellectual functioning? No. After all, there are, on average, 16 percent more neurons in male brains than female brains, but research has found no overall difference in IQ scores between men and women. On the other hand, intelligence may be related to the number of neurons in particular brain regions. Studies have suggested, for example, that general intelligence may be tied to the number of neurons in the brain's frontal lobes (see **Figure 58-1**) (Colom et al., 2013; Glascher et al., 2010; Tang et al., 2010). All other things being equal, people with more such neurons seem to perform better on intelligence tests.

58.2 Brain Speed and Intelligence

As discussed in Part 3, researchers often analyze the bioelectrical activity of the brain by using an *electroencephalogram (EEG)*, a device that places sensors on the outside of an individual's head and records *brain waves*. EEG research has allowed investigators to see whether intelligence is correlated with brain speed—the speed with which the brain responds successfully to various stimuli, tasks, and events (Sternberg, 2003; Deary & Stough, 1997, 1996).

One procedure, for example, involves the speed at which people process stimuli that are flashed before their eyes. In a typical study, the

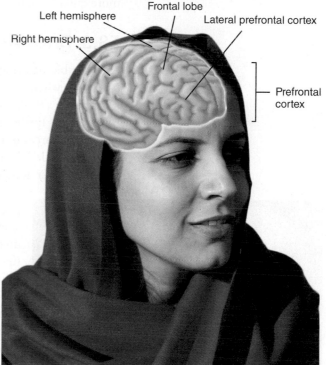

©iStockphoto.com/selimaksan

FIGURE 58-1 Brain neurons and intelligence. Studies have suggested, for example, that general intelligence may be tied to the number of neurons in the brain's frontal lobes.

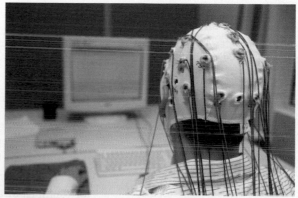

annedde/Getty Images

Speedier brains? People who score higher on intelligence tests tend to perceive correct images more quickly, as indicated by EEG readings.

experimenter briefly flashes an incomplete stimulus on one side of a screen and then quickly flashes a more complete stimulus on the other side. Viewers are asked to indicate which side the complete image appeared on. It typically takes only a fraction of a second to correctly answer this question. Still, some people are quicker than others, and those who perceive the correct image more quickly (as indicated by their EEG readings) tend to score higher on intelligence tests (especially on perceptual tasks) than those whose reactions are a bit slower. In short, more intelligent people may be physiologically wired to acquire and use information more quickly than others (Sternberg, 2003).

nerve conduction velocity (NCV) the speed with which electrical impulses are transmitted along nerve fibres and across synapses.

In a related line of research, several investigators have found significant correlations between IQ scores and **nerve conduction velocity (NCV)**, the speed with which electrical impulses are transmitted along nerve fibres and across synapses (Sternberg, 2003; Vernon et al., 2000; Reed & Jensen, 1992). Both the NCV and EEG findings fit well with studies showing that highly intelligent people are, on average, able to make decisions more quickly than less intelligent people (Demaree et al., 2010; O'Brien & Tulsky, 2008).

58.3 Brain Activity and Intelligence

Another biological approach to the study of intelligence examines how active people's brains are when solving intellectual problems. As discussed in Part 3, a *positron emission tomography (PET)* scan is a type of neuroimaging technology that can reveal where and how actively the brain is metabolizing, or breaking down, glucose at any given moment. Very active areas of the brain show up as red and orange on a PET scan's colour-coded pictures, while less active areas show up as green and blue. PET scans have generally revealed lower activity in the brains of people who are performing well on an intellectual task and higher activity in the brains of those who are performing poorly (Raichle, 2005; Haier, 2003; Posner et al., 2009, 2002). Thus, some researchers suggest that the brains of higher-performing people do not need to work as hard as the brains of lower-performing people—that is, their brains are more efficient (Grabner et al., 2003; Neubauer & Fink, 2010, 2003).

Although high intellectual performance seems to be related to an overall reduction in brain activity, PET scans have revealed that particular areas of brain activity are at work during certain types of intellectual tasks. Investigator John Duncan and his colleagues conducted a PET scan on 13 men and women while they were taking an intelligence test (Duncan, 2001; Duncan et al., 2000). They found that for each individual, the brain activity during the test was concentrated in the left lateral prefrontal cortex and the right lateral prefrontal cortex (see **Figure 58-2**)—regions located toward the front and outer sides of the brain's two hemispheres. When a test-taker was performing verbal tasks on the test, the *left* lateral prefrontal cortex was activated. (Remember from Parts 3 and 9 that language is processed predominantly in the left hemisphere of the brain.) During spatial tasks, both the left lateral prefrontal cortex and the right lateral prefrontal cortex were activated. It is worth noting that the prefrontal cortex, which sends and receives information to and from numerous other brain sites, may help people keep track of several thoughts at the same time, solve problems, produce new ideas, and filter out unimportant information.

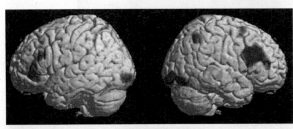
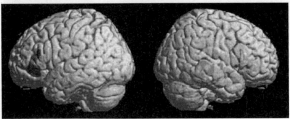

From J. Duncan, *Science*, 289 (5478): 457–460, July 21, 2000, Figures a and b.

FIGURE 58-2 The prefrontal cortex and performance on intelligence tests. The study by John Duncan and his colleagues (2000) found that the left lateral prefrontal cortex is active during the performance of a range of cognitive tasks. These PET scans from the study reveal that the left and right lateral prefrontal cortices are both active during spatial tasks (top row), while activity during verbal tasks tends to centre in the left lateral prefrontal cortex (bottom row).

While such studies are interesting, keep in mind that they do not clarify the causal relationships at work. For example, do people of higher intelligence display less brain activity overall, despite experiencing more activity in the prefrontal cortex, because they are smart, for example, or are people smart because their brain activity is more efficient? Or are both brain activity and intelligence related to yet a third causal factor that researchers have yet to discover?

58.4 Cortical Thickening and Intelligence

We have seen that various brain features, such as the number of neurons, brain speed, and brain activity, may be tied to intelligence. A related issue is whether *brain development* is related to the development of intelligence. A highly publicized study by researcher Philip Shaw and his colleagues sought to answer this question (Shaw et al., 2008, 2006).

In a longitudinal study, the Shaw team performed brain scans on 309 children and teenagers between the ages of 6 and 19 years, with each participant scanned every two years (Shaw et al. 2008, 2006; Raznahanet al., 2013). The scans revealed that throughout childhood and adolescence, individuals display changes in the thickness of the *cortex*— the folded outer layer of the brain—changes that have implications for the development of intelligence (Karama et al., 2011).

Using a neuroanatomical MRI scan, the study found that children begin with a thin cortex, which then thickens over the years and following this initial thickening then begins to thin down and continues thinning through adolescence. These changes in thickness are consistent with what is known about *neural pruning* during development. The brains of very young children produce a large number of neural synapses and neurons. As the children grow older, their brains prune the neural connections that are not being used, leaving the individuals with a much lower number of connections and, perhaps, neurons, in their teenage and adult years. It is believed that a thick cortex may reflect a higher number of neural connections and neurons, whereas a thin cortex may reflect a lower number; so as adolescence approaches and pruning occurs, the cortex becomes thinner (Karama et al., 2011).

The study further found this pattern of changes in cortical thickness to be clearest in the prefrontal regions, the brain areas closely related to intellectual activity. Thus, it appears that the development of intelligence may involve a process of synaptic and neural growth and then pruning, particularly in the prefrontal cortex—a process that is reflected by changes in cortical thickness throughout childhood and adolescence.

Beyond this general picture, Shaw and his colleagues (2008, 2006) found that the participants who were most intelligent showed a pattern of cortical thickening and thinning that was different from the pattern shown by participants with lower intelligence. That is, the highly intelligent individuals began with a rather thin cortex during early childhood, and the cortex gradually thickened until the age of 11 or 12, at which time thinning began and continued into the late teenage years. In contrast, the participants with lower intelligence began with a somewhat thicker cortex, which then further thickened until the age of 8, at which time the thinning began. Assuming that all of this reflects growth and

HOW WE
DEVELOP

Moving up the ladder. As children develop, they move toward greater intellectual independence—for example, from a child whose father reads her stories to a young woman who produces and reads her own reports. Over the same period of time, the individual's brain is undergoing synaptic pruning and other key changes.

pruning of synapses, particularly in the prefrontal cortex, it may be that the processes of growth and pruning unfold over a much longer developmental span in highly intelligent people than they do in less intelligent individuals, perhaps because more complex and sophisticated neural circuits are being constructed (Vedantam, 2006).

Are such brain changes over the course of childhood and adolescence genetically predetermined? Once again, the answer is "Not necessarily." We observed in Part 3 that the formation and pruning of neural networks are closely tied to interactions with the environment. Moreover, earlier in this part, we observed that enriching the environments of deprived young children often increases their intellectual performances. It could be that people with particularly high intelligence tend to be raised in rich social and learning environments, and that this kind of environmental stimulation contributes heavily to the pattern of cortical thickness change that such individuals displayed in the study by Shaw and his colleagues (2008, 2006).

Before You Go On

www.wiley.com/go/comercanada

What Do You Know?

1. How are brain size and number of neurons related to intelligence?
2. How do researchers measure the speed of information processing in the brain? How is this related to intelligence?
3. Is efficient processing linked to relatively lower or relatively higher activity in the brain?
4. What is the role of cortical thickness in the development of intelligence?

What Do You Think? Can you think of any other ways to explain why the brains of people who are performing better on intelligence tests are often less active than those of people who are doing poorly?

Summary

Module 58: The Brain and Intelligence

LEARNING OBJECTIVE 58 Describe how brain size, number of neurons, processing speed, brain activity, and cortical thickness relate to intelligence.

- Neuroimaging studies suggest that overall brain size is not correlated with intelligence. The number of neurons in certain brain regions, such as the frontal lobes, may be related to intellectual functioning.
- The speed with which the brain responds to stimuli, which can be measured by means of EEGs and *nerve conduction velocity* (*NCV*), also correlates with intelligence.
- PET scans, which show what areas of the brain are active at a particular moment, have generally revealed lower activity in the brains of people performing well on an intellectual task and higher activity in the brains of people performing poorly. This suggests that the brains of the higher performers may be more efficient.
- It appears that the development of intelligence involves a process of neuron growth and then neuron pruning, particularly in the prefrontal cortex—a process that is reflected by a distinct pattern of change in cortical thickness throughout childhood and adolescence.

Key Term

nerve conduction velocity (NCV) 452

Study Questions

Multiple Choice

1. Research using the electroencephalogram (EEG) and measures of nerve conduction velocity (NCV) have shown that
   a) brain processing tends to be faster in those higher in intelligence.
   b) it is impossible to determine the relationship between brain activity and intelligence.
   c) the EEG is a more sensitive measure of brain processing efficiency than the NCV method.
   d) the overall size of the brain is related to intelligence.

Fill-in-the-Blank

1. The density of neurons in the brain's _____ lobes seems to be related to intelligence.

2. Longitudinal research by Shaw suggests that changes in the thickness of the _____ have implications for the development of intelligence.

Module 59: Extremes in Intelligence

LEARNING OBJECTIVE 59
Discuss intellectual disability and giftedness.

FACING
ADVERSITY

intellectual disability term describing individuals who display general intellectual functioning that is well below average and, at the same time, poor adaptive behaviour.

Earlier in the part, we mentioned that intelligence, as measured by IQ tests, follows a normal distribution—that is, a distribution shaped like a bell curve. At either end of this curve are a small number of people who score either much lower or much higher than the people who make up the large middle. At the lower end are people who are diagnosed with intellectual disabilities, and at the higher end are those who are intellectually gifted (see **Figure 59-1**).

59.1 Intellectual Disability

Most individuals demonstrate sufficient levels of intelligence to survive on their own and to manage their daily lives. But the intellectual and adaptive functioning of some people is well below that of most other people. These individuals are said to display **intellectual disability**, a combination of general intellectual functioning that is well below average and poor adaptive behaviour (APA, 2013). That is, in addition to having an IQ score of 70 or below, many of these individuals experience great difficulty in areas such as communication, home living, self-direction, work, and safety (APA, 2013). Psychologists use the term *intellectual disability* instead of the older term of mental retardation (National Center on Birth Defects and Developmental Disabilities, 2005).

We have already observed that IQ tests and scores may be biased in various ways. It is certainly plausible that diagnoses of intellectual disability based on such tests can be subject to error (Tomes, 2010; Toth & King, 2010). Thus, to properly diagnose intellectual disability, mental health professionals must observe the functioning of an individual in his everyday environment, taking both the person's background and the community's standards into account.

The most consistent sign of intellectual disability is very slow learning (Toth & King, 2010; Hodapp & Dykens, 2003). Other areas of difficulty include attention, short-term memory, planning, and delays in language skills (Schalock et al., 2010; Edgin, Pennington, & Mervis, 2010). These difficulties vary, of course, according to the level of intellectual disability.

Because of the biases already noted in IQ assessments and scores (especially as they relate to community, linguistic, and cultural diversity), the Canadian Association of Community Living prefers to identify degrees of intellectual disability according to the level of support the person needs—intermittent, limited, extensive, or pervasive.

Markus Moellenberg/Corbis

Hayley Madden/Redferns/Getty Images

Making music. A young man with Down syndrome is the percussionist in a community orchestra (left), while a child prodigy sings opera at a school for the arts (right).

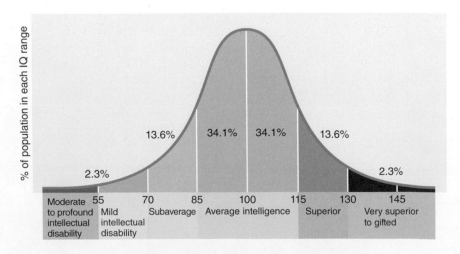

FIGURE 59-1 Extreme scores in intelligence. A small but equal number of people score at the extreme low and extreme high end of the IQ range. (Source: Anastasi & Urbina, 1997)

Around 80 to 85 percent of all people with intellectual disability fall into the category of mild disability (Dusseljee et al., 2011; Harris, 2010; APA, 2000). Mild intellectual disability is not usually recognized until children enter school. These individuals have reasonable language, social, and play skills, but they need assistance when under stress—a limitation that becomes increasingly apparent as academic and social demands increase. Often the intellectual performance of individuals with mild intellectual disability improves with age; some even stop meeting the criteria for the label after they leave school (Toth & King, 2010; Sturmey, 2008). Their jobs tend to be unskilled or semi-skilled.

Research has linked mild intellectual disability mainly to familial factors, particularly poor and unstimulating environments, inadequate parent–child interactions, and insufficient learning experiences during a child's early years (Martin 2010; Sturmey, 2008). In addition, studies suggest that a mother's moderate drinking, drug use, or malnutrition during pregnancy may lower her child's intellectual potential (Hart et al., 2010; Stein et al., 1972).

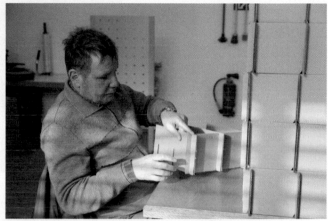
©iStockphoto.com/zudin

Intellectual disability and work. Sheltered workshops provide a broad range of vocational tasks and training opportunities for individuals with varying degrees of intellectual disability, leading, for many, to gainful employment.

Around 10 percent of persons with intellectual disability receive a label of *moderate intellectual disability*. They receive their diagnosis early in life, typically demonstrating clear deficits in language development and play during their preschool years. By middle school, significant delays in the acquisition of reading and number skills and deficits in adaptive skills become apparent. By adulthood, however, many individuals with moderate intellectual disability are able to adequately communicate and care for themselves, benefit from vocational training, and work in unskilled or semi-skilled jobs. Most of these individuals also function well in the community if they have some degree of supervision (Trembath et al., 2010; APA, 2000).

Many persons with moderate intellectual disability have **Down syndrome**, the most common of the chromosomal disorders leading to intellectual disability (Hazlett et al., 2010). Fewer than 1 of every 1,000 live births result in Down syndrome, but this rate increases greatly when the mother's age is over 35 (Centers for Disease Control, 2006). The syndrome usually is caused by the presence of extra chromosomal material on the twenty-first chromosome. The additional material disturbs normal development, resulting in characteristic features such as a small head, flat face, slanted eyes, high cheekbones, and reduced intellectual functioning (Teicher et al., 2008). More generally, they display the same range of personality characteristics as people in the general population (Fidler, 2006).

Down syndrome an inherited disorder, usually caused by the presence of extra chromosomal material on the twenty-first chromosome, that results in intellectual disability.

Approximately 3 to 4 percent of people with intellectual disability meet the criteria for *severe intellectual disability*. They typically demonstrate basic motor and communication deficits during infancy. Many have an increased vulnerability to seizure disorders. They usually require careful supervision, profit from vocational training to some degree, and can perform only basic work tasks in structured and sheltered settings. Most are able to function well in the community if they live in group homes, in community nursing homes, or with their families (Cain et al., 2010; Bebko & Weiss, 2006; APA, 2000).

Around 1 to 2 percent of people with intellectual disabilities receive a diagnosis of *profound intellectual disability*. Their limitations are very noticeable at birth or early infancy. With training, the individuals may develop or improve basic skills such as walking, may develop more expressive language, and may be able to feed themselves. They require a very structured environment, with close supervision and considerable help, including a close relationship with a caregiver, to develop adequately (Cain et al., 2010; Sturmey, 2008; APA, 2000).

59.2 Giftedness

Psychologists do not agree on how to define *giftedness* (Sternberg, Jarvin, & Grigorenko, 2011). Some researchers use IQ tests as the sole criterion, defining the top 1 or 2 percent of the tested population as gifted. For example, Lewis Terman defined gifted

Educating the gifted. A gifted 9-year-old
girl sits in her college algebra class in Nashville, Tennessee. Although getting in and out of the adult-sized desk chair can be a problem, the algebra is a snap for her.

The Tennessean, Rex Perry/AP

people as those with IQ scores above 140, and in a famous longitudinal study, he followed a group of gifted research participants over the course of their lifetime (Simonton, 2010; Leslie, 2000; Terman, 1925).

Other researchers and educators have added criteria such as school success or career achievement to IQ scores when defining giftedness. Indeed, many of the participants in Terman's study, who became known as the "Termites," achieved extraordinary success as scientists, scholars, businesspeople, and professionals (Seagoe, 1975).

Other definitions of intelligence have led to still other definitions of giftedness. Howard Gardner, whom we discussed earlier in the part, suggests that people can be gifted with high intelligence in any one of the multiple intelligences he has identified. He would consider a highly talented athlete or musician to be as gifted as a math or verbal whiz (Gardner, 1993).

Researchers have tried to look for common characteristics among gifted people (Sternberg et al., 2011; Winner, 2000). They have come up with several:

- *Environment can contribute to giftedness.* Many gifted people are raised in nurturing and stimulating environments. Terman's Termites, for example, were typically members of upper socio-economic families, and they received many years of education. It is worth noting that, contrary to stereotype, most gifted children are not pushed by demanding parents. Families do, however, tend to centre much attention on such children. Typically, the parents first recognize the budding giftedness of their children and then support it by providing high-level intellectual or artistic stimulation. Parents of highly gifted children also tend to have higher expectations of themselves, model hard work for their children, and grant the children high degrees of independence (Winner, 2000).

- *Gifted people are often intrinsically motivated.* It appears that children who are gifted at piano playing, violin playing, chess, bridge, athletics, and the like typically experience a deep, intrinsic motivation to master such domains and subject themselves to many hours of deliberate practice. Perhaps the high motivation of these children drives them and sustains their practice efforts. However, research has failed to show that gifted abilities necessarily precede extensive practice. Does this mean that a person of average intelligence and above-average motivation can readily become a concert pianist or astrophysicist? No. Other research indicates that hard work, intensive training, perseverance, and practice alone rarely lead to giftedness. In short, motivation and hard work seem to be necessary, but not sufficient, requirements for the development of giftedness (Winner, 2000).

- *Some people gifted in academic or other forms of intelligence may not be equally gifted with social and emotional intelligence.* Some psychologists have observed that gifted children often display disproportionate social and emotional difficulties, especially during adolescence. Many are socially isolated and introverted. In fact, a number of academically gifted children try to hide their giftedness in an attempt to fit in with others. Girls seem more likely than boys to do this (Winner, 2000).

Summary

Module 59: Extremes in Intelligence

LEARNING OBJECTIVE 59 Discuss intellectual disability and giftedness.

- The two extremes of intelligence, as measured by IQ tests, are represented by intellectual disability and giftedness.
- Home environmental causes of intellectual disability include poor and unstimulating environments and inadequate parent–child interactions. These causes have been associated in particular with mild intellectual disability, though they may also be at work in more severe cases.
- Other causes of intellectual disability include genetically based chromosomal abnormalities, certain prenatal conditions in the mother, complications at delivery, and injuries and infections during early childhood. These causes have been associated in particular with moderate to profound levels of intellectual disability.
- *Down Syndrome* is a genetic abnormality resulting in intellectual disability.
- Psychologists do not agree on how to define giftedness, but often identify gifted persons as having IQs at the top 1 or 2 percent of the tested population.
- Environment can contribute to giftedness, and gifted people are often highly motivated. However, academically gifted people may not be equally gifted with social and emotional intelligence.

Key Terms

Down syndrome 457

intellectual disability 456

Study Questions

Multiple Choice

1. Gifted individuals tend to have all of the following characteristics except
   a) a willingness to work hard, practise, and persevere when things get difficult.
   b) access to stimulating and nurturing environments while growing up.
   c) high levels of intrinsic motivation.
   d) IQ scores between 100 and 130.

Fill-in-the-Blank

1. An important contributor to many cases of mild intellectual disability is the _____ of the individual.

PART 11

MOTIVATION AND EMOTION

PART OUTLINE

"I don't want to die, but I accept that it can happen.**"**

motivation an internal state or condition that directs behaviour.

motive a need or desire.

The following quote refers to Buildings, Antennas, Spans, and Earth or BASE jumping. Caitlin Forsey (2009) wrote her University of British Columbia Master's thesis on the sport (in which her boyfriend participates). BASE jumping involves a parachute, but you jump from a fixed object (i.e., a building, antenna, bridge, or cliff). It differs from skydiving in other ways as well. BASE jumpers need a chute that opens much faster than a regular skydiving chute because they often jump from objects at or below 150 metres (as compared to the minimum 600 metres by very experienced skydivers). BASE jumpers do not carry a reserve chute—if their main chute does not work, well—it doesn't matter.

Sports like BASE jumping make you wonder what motivates an individual to engage in such odd behaviour. Is it an adrenalin rush? Is it an emotional high? Most certainly.

In this part we will examine the basic features of human motivation and emotion. Both terms are derived from the same Latin root word—*motare* meaning to shake or to stir or to move with purpose. Psychologists define **motivation** as a condition that directs behaviour (Reeve, 2015). This behaviour is usually directed toward a goal. For any given circumstance, your behaviour is probably the consequence of a combination of several **motives**—your needs or desires.

Beyond motivation, human action is usually accompanied by emotions. How would you define emotion? Defining an emotion is difficult, even for those who study them. There are over 500 words in the English language that refer to various aspects or forms of emotions, from *affect*, to *mood*, to *feeling*. Given this, it will not be surprising to note that researchers studying emotion have trouble agreeing on a definition (Averill, 1980; Lewis, Haviland-Jones & Barrett, 2010). Despite this lack of agreement, psychologists continue to believe that human motivation and emotions are among psychology's most important topics. We will begin with psychological theory and work related to motivation and then, later in the part, turn to theories and research related to emotion.

Module 60: Theories of Motivation

Explaining people's behaviour has always been a core part of psychologists' research interests. Over the years we have devised several theories of motivation, each of which takes a different approach to explaining what compels individuals to act as they do (**Table 60-1**). However, no single theory has yet been able to provide a complete explanation of what motivates us to engage in our many different behaviours.

LEARNING OBJECTIVE 60
Briefly explain each of the five major theories of motivation.

60.1 Instinct Theory

Instinct theory maintains that behaviours originate from a set of behavioural blueprints, or **instincts** (Fancher, 1996). Instinctive behaviours are inborn and activated by particular environmental stimuli. A good example of instinctual motivation can be observed in the migratory behaviours of birds that do not have to learn where and when to fly when the seasons change (Heinrich, 2014).

Many of our own basic motives are inborn. Some of the most critical for survival, such as eating, are present at birth (Colson, Meek, & Hawdon, 2008; Smillie, 2013). Although the range of foods considered to be rewarding changes substantially from the time we are babies until our adult lives (infants will readily eat baby food and formula, both of which adults typically consider bland and unappealing), the basic motivation to eat when hungry persists throughout life.

Humans are also naturally motivated to form social contacts. As we saw in Part 5, babies are born with a well-developed sense of smell that lets them recognize the particular scent of their mothers (Schaal & Durand, 2012). Babies are also born with reflexes that allow them to engage in primitive social behaviour. The rooting reflex, discussed in Part 4, for example, involves turning the head and using the mouth to search for a nipple. Rooting not only helps a baby to eat, but it allows the infant to seek contact with other people. Along with the ability to recognize their mothers by smell, rooting enables babies to start establishing close relationships with their mothers (Swain et al., 2007). As the baby grows, new abilities emerge, such as smiling, laughing, reaching arms out to be carried, and talking. All of these further encourage the formation of social bonds, thus increasing the chance of survival (Messinger & Fogel, 2007; Broad, Curley, & Keverne, 2006). As with eating, the nuances of this basic motivation change as we grow. For example, instead of seeking mother love, as adults we seek romantic love. In one way or another, the motivation to be socially connected remains strong throughout life.

instincts inborn behavioural tendencies, activated by stimuli in our environments.

©iStockphoto.com/temis

The grasp reflex. Infants will grasp onto a finger placed in the palm of their hand. Their grip and its strength are part of the automatic grasp reflex.

TABLE 60-1 Major Theories of Motivation	
Theory	**Approach**
Instinct	Behaviour is motivated by instincts that are inborn and that are activated by environmental stimuli
Drive reduction	Behaviour is motivated by biological needs to maintain the body in a state of balance or equilibrium
Arousal	Behaviour is motivated by the need to achieve optimum levels of arousal
Incentive	Behaviour is motivated by internal (intrinsic) or external (extrinsic) incentives or rewards
Hierarchy of needs	Behaviour is motivated by the current most basic need, when different motives compete; basic survival needs must be satisfied first before we are motivated to satisfy higher-level needs such as belonging and self-esteem

©iStockphoto.com/mayo5

Challenging a theory. This bungee jumper (like BASE jumpers) takes off from a bridge and begins a wild—and seemingly dangerous—free fall, challenging instinct theory along the way.

Although instinct theory can explain some of our behaviour and a substantial proportion of animal behaviour, instincts don't account for all behaviour, even in relatively simple creatures, such as rats (Clark, Broadbent, & Squire, 2008). In fact, studies on learning and memory would be impossible to carry out on laboratory animals if all of their behaviour was innate; the animals would never need to learn or remember anything.

Instinct theory also has trouble explaining differences among individuals (Bevins, 2001). Among humans, for example, some of us seek out experiences that others avoid or even find painful. Consider adventurers who have climbed Mount Everest, a gruelling and dangerous activity. Conversely, some individuals avoid experiences that others find rewarding and pleasurable. Some people drink alcohol while others do not, and some people exercise regularly while others do not. Clearly, these behaviours are not driven by instincts. We need other explanations for these motivations.

60.2 Drive-Reduction Theory

homeostasis a tendency of the body to maintain itself in a state of balance or equilibrium.

Drive-reduction theory is another attempt to account for motivation on the basis of internal biological factors. This theory is based on the concept of **homeostasis**, a general tendency of the body to maintain itself in a state of balance or equilibrium (**Figure 60-1**). When an external factor alters the state of balance in the organism, a motivation arises to correct that balance (Stricker & Zigmond, 1986). A simple example of this can be seen in the response of the body to heat. When the temperature rises, your body perspires and you lose water. The perspiration evaporates and cools the surface of the skin, helping to maintain the temperature balance in your body. In addition, you may feel motivated to take actions that will hasten your return to an ideal body temperature, such as shedding some layers of clothing or getting a cool drink.

FIGURE 60-1 Drive-reduction theory. When external factors alter our body's normal state of equilibrium, we are motivated to behave in ways that restore the balance.

Adapted with permission of John Wiley & Sons, Inc., from Carpenter, S., & Huffman, K. (2008). *Visualizing psychology.* Hoboken, NJ: Wiley, p. 285.

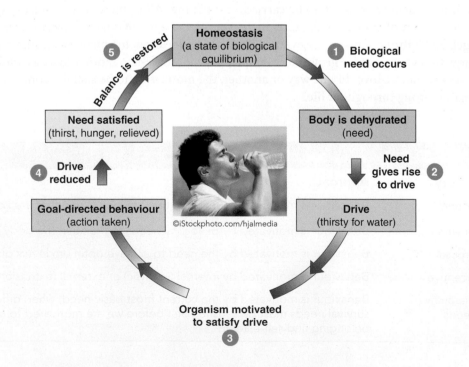

Drive-reduction theory works well to explain behaviours related to biological needs, such as cooling off when we are too hot or getting a drink of water when we are thirsty. We engage in many behaviours, however, that do not appear to be motivated by a need to keep the body in a state of equilibrium (Schneider et al., 2007). In fact, some human behaviour is designed to do just the opposite. Some people seek out adventurous situations that are designed to thrill and even terrorize for entertainment. Amusement park owners and the makers of horror films make millions of dollars every year providing an outlet for this sort of interest. It's difficult to explain the motivation to go on the West Edmonton Mall's Mindbender roller coaster or the Behemoth roller coaster at Canada's Wonderland in terms of a need to restore the body to a state of equilibrium. Instead, the main purpose is to experience excitement by throwing riders suddenly *out* of a state of emotional equilibrium. That type of thrill-seeking behaviour may be better described in terms of another theory.

Where both instinct and drive-reduction theory have problems is with the idea of voluntary decision making as part of motivation. We are capable of overriding our physiological motivational processes and doing things simply because we want to (Binswanger, 1991; Barrett et al., 2013). To address this shortfall, we need to add a few more concepts to our discussion of motivational factors.

Courtesy of Canada's Wonderland

Challenging another theory. People riding the Behemoth roller coaster at Canada's Wonderland demonstrate the limits of drive-reduction theory.

60.3 Arousal Theory

Arousal theory maintains that motivation comes from a need to achieve an appropriate level of arousal (Jones, 2003). This theory is different from drive-reduction theory in that the motivation doesn't always arise from a need to reduce arousal back to a neutral state. While some situations, such as hunger or thirst, can elevate our arousal to uncomfortable levels that we try to reduce (for example, by seeking food or drink), arousal theory states that we can also be motivated to elevate our arousal levels if they fall too low. Such under-arousal may stimulate us to seek out interesting and exciting situations (Maggini, 2000).

Arousal theory explains a number of behaviours that instinct and drive-reduction theories cannot. Consider the millions of dollars earned every year by paparazzi and the tabloids. Even though a rich knowledge in the latest celebrity gossip is unlikely to enhance your reputation, and could even cause embarrassment if your interest is discovered by co-workers or others, many of us seek out gossip because we are generally curious. Curiosity often motivates us to seek out information, even if there is no other goal involved. Arousal theory would describe the behaviour of people who follow celebrity gossip as an attempt to elevate our levels of arousal and interest.

Yerkes-Dodson law law stating that ideal performance on a task occurs when the arousal level is optimized to the difficulty level of the task.

In addition to providing motivation, our arousal levels can systematically affect our performance on tasks we undertake. The **Yerkes-Dodson law** states that ideal performance on a task occurs when our arousal level is properly matched with the difficulty of the task. Task difficulty and arousal seem to be inversely related (**Figure 60-2**). That is, our performance on difficult tasks is optimal at low to medium arousal states, while our performance on easy tasks is optimal at medium to high arousal states. This may be related to the fact that difficult tasks require more intense concentration that may be disrupted by highly arousing circumstances. Imagine, for example, that you are trying to finish writing a term paper. You may find it easier to focus on your writing if you are not highly aroused by a deadline looming only a few hours away. If, however, you are trying to read some really boring material (something other than this book, of course), you may need to periodically raise your arousal levels with snacks, stretch breaks, and the like, to help you focus on the task.

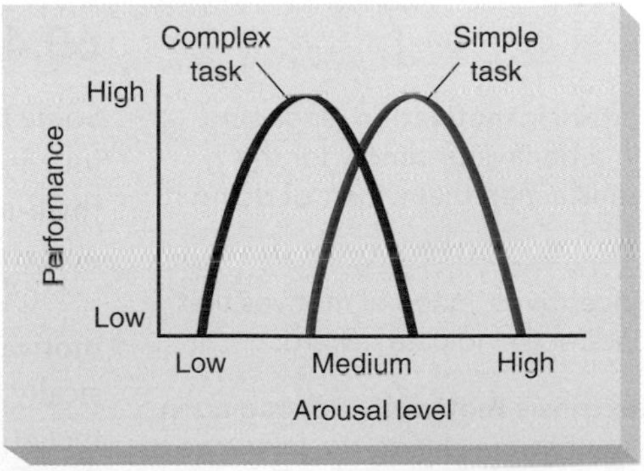

FIGURE 60-2 **The Yerkes-Dodson law.** Our optimal performance on tasks is inversely related to our arousal level. We perform difficult tasks best when our arousal level is low to medium and simple, or boring ones best when our arousal level is medium to high.

The Yerkes-Dodson law has obvious applications to sports. Athletes who fail to get sufficiently "psyched up" or aroused may never even get into the game. On the other hand, getting too "revved up" or over-aroused might lead to "choking." Ryan Gelinas and Krista Munroe-Chandler at the University of Windsor have examined how this and other psychological issues in motivation can impact the performance of hockey goaltenders (Gelinas & Munroe-Chandler, 2006; Hallman & Munroe-Chandler, 2009). They point out that each goalie (and each athlete in general) has an optimal level of arousal at which they perform their best. Some goalies need to get "psyched up" or excited to reach that optimal level, while others need to calm down so as not to become over-aroused. High levels of arousal, especially when associated with anxiety, lead to muscle tension that can slow a goalie down. It can also narrow the goalie's visual attentional field, making it less likely that the individual will take in all the information needed to properly position him or herself in the net. The aim for goaltenders is to keep them in the "zone" of optimal arousal so that they can consistently perform at their best throughout the game.

 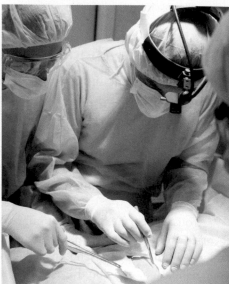

©iStockphoto.com/OJO_Images   ©iStockphoto.com/mediaphotos

The Yerkes-Dodson law in action. The baker on the left uses a knife to cut bread, while the surgeon on the right uses a sharp instrument to make an incision for surgery. According to the Yerkes-Dodson law, a high level of physical arousal will help the baker's performance but probably not the surgeon's.

60.4 Incentive Theory

intrinsic motivation engaging in a behaviour simply for the satisfaction that is part of doing it.

incentives external motives that indirectly indicate reward.

extrinsic motivation engaging in a behaviour due to the influence of factors outside ourselves.

Some behaviours are **intrinsically motivating**, which means that engaging in the behaviour is satisfying in and of itself (Schmitt & Lahroodi, 2008). For some people, taking thrill-seeking rides is intrinsically motivating. Although they may never BASE jump, they occasionally like a roller coaster ride for the pleasure they get out of doing so.

Other behaviours are driven by external motives, or **incentives**. Behaviour that is motivated by external incentives is known as **extrinsically motivated**. Rats can be extrinsically motivated: they learn their way through a maze more quickly if provided with an incentive, such as food or a way to escape something unpleasant (such as water), than they do when no incentives are involved (Komaki, 2004).

Even when our motivation to behave in a certain way involves instinct, a drive to maintain homeostasis, or a motive to achieve an optimal level of arousal, it's clear that incentives play a major role in most human behaviour. The whole purpose of the mountain of advertising around us, for example, is to present or suggest incentives for us to use particular products. *Incentive theory* highlights the influence of external stimuli in behaviour, suggesting that external rewards, such as public acclaim or financial prizes, may contribute to the motivation of some BASE jumpers. A good deal of your own behaviour as a student is probably also motivated by external factors, such as the desire to achieve high grades, graduate on time, and obtain a good job.

Incentives can be either primary or secondary, and they can be rewarding or punitive.

- *Primary incentives* are rewards or punishments that are innate; we do not have to learn to either like or dislike them. Food is a primary reward, and pain is a primary punishment, for example. Most humans instinctually find food rewarding and electric shock punishing. For that reason, these stimuli are likely to influence our behaviour. There is an adaptive, or evolutionary, component to primary rewards and punishments. Typically, stimuli that increase our chances of survival and reproduction, such as food and sex, are rewarding, while those that are potentially harmful, such as anything painful, are punishing.
- *Secondary incentives* are cues that are viewed as rewarding as a result of learning about their association with other events. For example, most people are motivated to work to earn money. Money, in and of itself, is not rewarding. It becomes motivating to us when we learn its association with the rewarding goods, such as food, that money can buy.

Although money is generally considered to be a strong motivator, its effects differ greatly from person to person. Why is this? Scientists attribute the different motivational power of certain cues to *incentive salience*, how noticeable or important a particular incentive is to us (Berridge, 2007). Incentives can become more salient and more motivating after they become associated with specific emotions (Berridge & Robinson, 2009; Robinson, Robinson, & Berridge, 2014).

Consider our motivation to work hard at a job. The first time we receive a paycheque, the things we purchase with the money may lead to happiness. This association of money with happiness may, in turn, motivate us to engage in behaviours designed to improve the chance of earning even more money, such as working harder. Alternatively, if our first work experience is a very negative one that becomes associated with boredom and unhappiness, our drive to pursue happiness through hard work is less likely to expand. We may seek to avoid work altogether, or we may be motivated to look for a better and more gratifying job. Particularly for complex behaviours, such as working at a job, there can be many incentives that motivate different individuals. Some people work to avoid punishment, such as homelessness and shame, for example, while others work to receive rewards, such as money and pride (Warr, 2011).

Motivational theories that focus on incentives often take into consideration the distinction between "liking" and "wanting" (Berridge et al., 2010). "Liking" refers to our experience of reward or pleasure that happens *at the moment* we are engaging in a particular behaviour, while "wanting" refers to the anticipation of an experience that we expect will cause us pleasure. Having a pleasurable experience in the past often leads to wanting to repeat that experience again in the future. If you really like your first live concert, you might want more like it. You might even become motivated to travel to other cities, just to attend concerts.

Neuroscientists have found that overlapping, but distinct, regions of our brains are involved in liking and wanting (Berridge & Kringelbach, 2013). Pleasure, or liking, is typically associated with systems of the brain that produce *opiates*. Opiates, such as endorphins, are naturally-occurring neurochemicals that contribute to our feelings of pleasure. Eating, drinking, and sex—biological motivations that we discuss later in this part are all associated with a release in opiates. Other experiences, such as intense physical exercise (for example, long distance running) can also stimulate the release of brain opiates, producing a phenomenon called "runner's high" (Boecker et al., 2008; Geva & Defrin, 2013).

Jorge Rios iPhoto Inc./Newscom

The big payoff. Although Canadian poker star Daniel Negreaunu has consistently won big on the world poker tour, the money he wins is not, in itself, rewarding. Rather, it is what the money can buy, the prestige attached to winning so much, and the pride the big payoff instills in him.

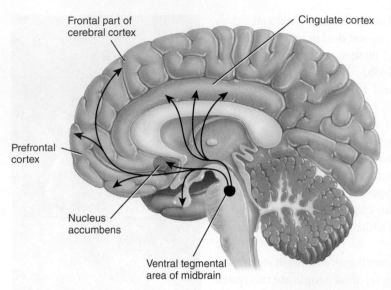

FIGURE 60-3 Reward pathways in the brain. Rewarding stimuli typically trigger dopamine neurons in the ventral tegmental area of the brain. The axons of these neurons project to the nucleus accumbens and the prefrontal cortex, activating rewarding and pleasurable feelings, while others project into the cingulated cortex.

In addition to activating the brain-opiate system, rewarding stimuli typically stimulate the release of the neurotransmitter dopamine (Berridge & Kringelbach, 2008; Arias-Carrión & Pöppel, 2007). As discussed in Part 3, dopamine is present in two major systems of the brain. One region is mostly important for movement and is affected by Parkinson's disease (Lang & Obeso, 2004), while the other is important for reinforcement learning. The latter system consists of dopamine neurons in a region of the midbrain, called the ventral tegmental area, which send their axons to two key areas in the front of the brain: the *nucleus accumbens* and the *prefrontal cortex* (**Figure 60-3**).

As we noted in Part 3, the nucleus accumbens is highly active in the experience of rewarding and pleasurable feelings (Carlezon & Thomas, 2009). The pathways of dopamine neurons from the ventral tegmental area to the nucleus accumbens and prefrontal cortex are not only activated during the reward experience, but they appear to be critical for future behaviour directed toward that reward. In other words, the dopamine system plays a critical role in "wanting."

Although incentive theory explains how our behaviour is shaped by external stimuli, not all of our behaviour is motivated by wanting a reward or avoiding a punishment. Integrating incentive theory with other motivation theories is necessary to explain the complexity of motivation.

60.5 Multiple Motivations: Hierarchy of Needs

As we have seen, a combination of factors, including innate and learned motives, interact to drive behaviour. Psychologists have also recognized that different motives can compete with one another (LaGraize et al., 2004). For instance, you might find it particularly difficult to concentrate on completing a homework assignment if you are really thirsty. The relative strength of certain motives and their ability to supersede one another led humanist psychologist Abraham Maslow to describe motives, or needs, in terms of a *hierarchy* (Maslow, 1970). **Figure 60-4** shows Maslow's hierarchy of needs.

FIGURE 60-4 Maslow's hierarchy of needs. A combination of needs, both innate and learned, drive our behaviour and sometimes are in competition. Basic survival needs at the base of the pyramid are the strongest and must be satisfied first before we are motivated to achieve our higher needs.

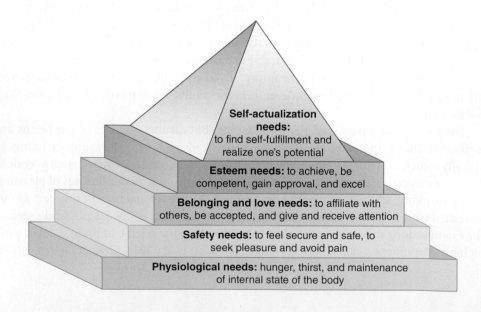

The most basic needs, such as the need to eat or drink, are at the bottom of the hierarchy pyramid. Unless these needs are satisfied, we find it difficult to generate motivation to engage in other behaviours. Above the basic needs are the safety needs: the need to feel secure and stable. It's important to realize that a balance exists between the first and second tier on the pyramid. It would not make sense for us to drink tainted water when waiting would be safer. That doesn't happen often, because water is usually not a matter of life or death in Western society. But humans, as well as other animals, will often take great risks to obtain food and water if they can't be obtained in a safer setting.

Above safety needs is the need to feel love and to belong to a social group. This need motivates us to seek companionship in the form of friends and romantic partners. It motivates the creation of families and the formation of clubs and other social organizations. Humans vary from person to person, but as a species, we are highly social and our need for human contact is often a very strong motivator of our behaviour.

Above the need to belong socially rests the need for a feeling of self-worth. This need motivates us to achieve at school, at work, and at home. Finally, at the top of the pyramid rests the need for self-actualization. As our highest need, the need for self-actualization motivates us to live up to our potential and become the best we can be. For many people, this involves engaging in selfless, altruistic behaviour, in the form of political activism or humanitarian behaviour.

According to Maslow's theory, it will be difficult to meet the need for self-actualization unless the needs below it on the pyramid have been satisfied. Even so, many people sacrifice fulfillment of some of their basic needs to meet higher needs. Physicians who are members of Doctors without Borders, for example, sacrifice their safety needs to fulfill their needs for self-actualization.

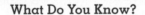

Before You Go On

www.wiley.com/go/comercanada

What Do You Know?

1. What are some examples of instinctive motivations among humans?
2. How does drive-reduction theory differ from arousal theory?
3. What is intrinsic motivation and how does it differ from extrinsic motivation?
4. Give an example of a primary incentive and a secondary incentive.
5. What are the lowest level needs in the hierarchy of needs?

What Do You Think? Consider one of your favourite leisure-time activities, such as reading novels, playing video games, or playing a sport. Whatever the activity, describe how each of the motivational theories discussed in this part would explain why you do it. Does any one theory best describe your motivation?

What can you do to improve your motivation as a student; to study more effectively, concentrate better, or set and accomplish life goals? The Learning Commons at Simon Fraser University offers a number of practical, step-by-step suggestions for how you can start, develop, and evaluate your motivational progress (www.lib.sfu.ca/slc/strategies/learning-studying/concentration-motivation).

Summary

Module 60: Theories of Motivation

LEARNING OBJECTIVE 60 Briefly explain each of the five major theories of motivation.

- Several theories offer explanations for our motivation, but no single theory can explain all our behaviour.
- Instinct theory, which suggests that environmental cues stimulate inborn behavioural instincts, best explains motivation that serves basic biological drives, such as eating, drinking, and sex.
- Drive-reduction theory suggests that internal homeostatic mechanisms produce balance within the body by reducing arousal stemming from unmet basic biological needs.
- Arousal theory explains why we sometimes seek to increase arousal levels. The Yerkes-Dodson law proposes that task performance is best if our arousal level matches that needed for a task.
- Incentive learning produces extrinsic motivation to engage in experiences that do not fulfill basic biological drives. Primary and secondary incentives may both be involved. Different incentives motivate different people. Incentive motivation involves brain systems associated with pleasure, incentive learning, and the neurochemical opiate dopamine.
- Maslow proposed that we are motivated by a hierarchy of needs, in which basic survival needs must be satisfied before higher-level needs for belonging, achievement, and self-actualization.

Key Terms

extrinsic motivation 466

homeostasis 464

incentives 466

instincts 463

intrinsic motivation 466

Yerkes-Dodson law 465

Study Questions

Multiple Choice

1. Which theory of motivation best explains the non–goal-directed behaviours associated with curiosity?
   a) Arousal
   b) Drive reduction
   c) Incentive
   d) Instinct

2. The midbrain structure that contains dopamine neurons essential for reinforcement learning is the
   a) corpus callosum.
   b) hippocampus.
   c) nucleus accumbens.
   d) ventral tegmental area.

Fill-in-the-Blank

1. Research on arousal and task performance has shown that difficult tasks are best performed under conditions of _____ arousal.

2. The _____ theory of motivation looks to internal and external rewards as motivators of behaviour.

3. Rewarding stimuli often increases levels of the neurotransmitter _____ in the brain.

Module 61: Biological Motivations: Hunger

As noted, the drive to eat is biologically ingrained or instinctual. Even newborn babies show interest in feeding soon after they are born (Smillie, 2013). The biological drive to eat remains in place throughout our lives since we need to eat to live. A person can generally last only about 40 days without food (Lieberson, 2004). Eating is not simply a matter of following an instinctive pattern of behaviour to satisfy an inborn drive, however. Instead, a number of other factors play a role in motivating how much, what, when, and even where we are motivated to eat. First, let's explore what we know about the biology of hunger.

A number of stimuli contribute to hunger signals in our brain, including how full our stomachs are, the levels of nutrients circulating in our bloodstreams, and interacting with both of those signals, the activities of key parts of our brains.

WHAT HAPPENS
in the BRAIN?

61.1 Stomach Signals

As you may have experienced, an empty stomach can trigger feelings of hunger. Physicians treating obese patients take advantage of the fact that physical signals produced by stretch receptors in the stomach are important for informing the brain to stop eating. These cues, called *satiety* signals, can be activated by surgically placing a balloon in the stomach. Since the stomach space is already partially occupied by the balloon, the stretch receptors will be activated even when the person eats a relatively small meal (Fernandes et al., 2007; Rigaud et al., 1995). Another technique that works on a similar principle is the surgical placement of a band around the stomach or physically stapling the stomach so that it is much smaller (Silberhumer et al., 2011). Many individuals who have undergone these procedures lose weight at first, but then eventually gain it back, suggesting that although signals from the stomach can influence the degree to which we are motivated to eat, these signals aren't the only mediators (Christou, Look, & Maclean, 2006).

Indeed, it turns out that satiety signals from the stomach are not even the most important hunger clues. People with no stomach at all, as a result of surgery for cancer, still experience hunger (Kamiji et al., 2009). Also, as you may have experienced, eating a small amount of food often stimulates additional hunger.

61.2 Chemical Signals

Eating occurs as a result of a complex interplay between hunger and satiety. Considerable evidence suggests that cues related to the metabolism of food can signal hunger or satiety (Erlanson-Albertsson, 2005; Wynne, Stanley, & Bloom, 2004). Some of these cues are related to levels of different chemicals produced in our blood when our bodies digest food. Two of the most well-researched of these are *glucose*, also known as blood sugar, and *lipids*, the products produced when our bodies break down fats from food. There are receptors for both glucose and lipids in the brain, which can influence hunger (Levin et al., 2004; Meister, 2000). Injections of glucose into the bloodstream, for instance, can reduce eating in experimental animals (Novin, Sanderson, & Vanderweele, 1974).

The protein **leptin** is another signal that appears to be important for regulating the amount of food eaten over long periods of time. Leptin is released from our fat cells as they grow larger. When receptors in the brain sense high levels of leptin, they in turn send signals that inhibit us from eating (Dhillon et al., 2006; Hommel et al., 2006; Schwartz, Azzara, & Heaner, 2013). Obese animals and obese humans may be insensitive to leptin. Some evidence suggests that although they have higher blood levels of leptin than normal-weight individuals, they have fewer leptin receptors in their brains, which may prevent the signal to stop eating from being generated soon enough (Bjornholm et al., 2007; Zhou & Rui, 2013).

leptin a protein produced by fat cells that is important for regulating the amount of food eaten over long periods of time.

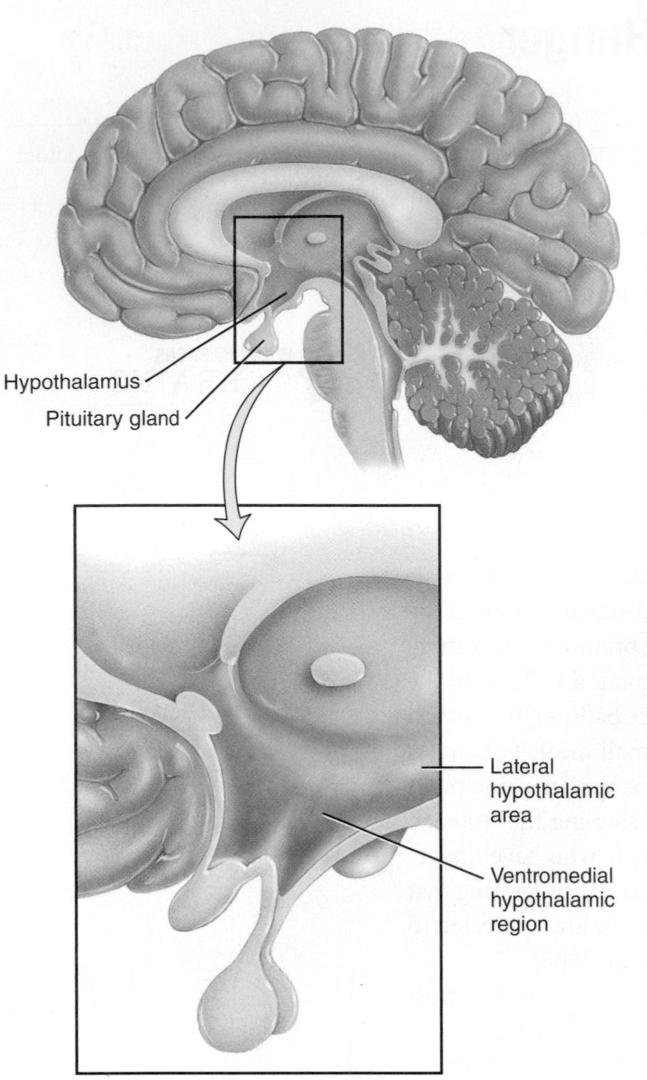

FIGURE 61-1 **How the hypothalamus affects hunger.**
This diagram shows a section of a rat's brain, locating the
ventromedial hypothalamus (VMH) and the lateral hypothalamus
(LH), which, if damaged, affects hunger.

lateral hypothalamus (LH)
a region of the hypothalamus
important in signalling thirst and
hunger.

**ventromedial region of the
hypothalamus (VMH)** a region
of the hypothalamus important in
signalling satiety.

FIGURE 61-2 **The VMH and obesity.**
The rat on the left had its ventromedial
hypothalamus destroyed, which led
to overeating and a dramatic increase
in its body weight compared to the
normal-weight rat in the picture.

Courtesy of Philip Teitelbaum

61.3 Brain Signals

Within the brain, the hypothalamus is a key mediator of eating.
As you can see in **Figure 61-1**, specific subregions in the hypothalamus have been linked to both hunger and satiety. The **lateral
hypothalamus (LH)** is important for hunger. Rodents with damage to this area dramatically under-eat; they need to be force-fed
or they will starve to death (Petrovich et al., 2002). A nearby brain
region, the **ventromedial region of the hypothalamus (VMH)**,
has been shown to play an important role in satiety. Destruction of
this region leads to overeating and obesity in rats (see **Figure 61-2**).
Humans who develop brain tumours in the VMH also increase
their food intake and become markedly heavier (Yadav et al.,
2009). A genetic condition in humans, known as Prader-Willi syndrome, is associated with an insatiable appetite leading to obesity.
This condition is believed to arise, at least in part, from dysfunction
of the hypothalamus (Hinton et al., 2006; Goldstone et al., 2012).

The identification of these two brain regions as important for
feeding behaviour led to the formation of the *dual-centre theory
of motivation*. This idea proposes that activity in one area serves
to inhibit the area that serves the opposite function. For example,
an empty stomach and low blood glucose may stimulate the LH
to motivate us to eat, while at the same time inhibiting satiety signals from the VMH. Once the stretch receptors are activated and
blood glucose reaches a certain level, the VMH would once again
become active and inhibit the LH.

Subsequent research, however, has shown that these brain
regions influence eating in a more complicated way through the
action of a hormone called *insulin* (Vogt & Bruning, 2013; Woods
et al., 2006). The VMH appears to be important for modulating the
levels of insulin in the blood. Insulin helps the body to metabolize
and use glucose. Damage to the VMH can increase insulin levels.
High insulin levels, in turn, cause our fat cells to store more glucose
and grow. Studies of animals with lesions or damage in the VMH
show that they experience increases in fat deposits, regardless of
the amount of food they eat (Yadav et al., 2009). So, it is not just a
matter of the VMH failing to provide these animals with a satiety signal; they are actually
short on blood sugar, or glucose. Because they store energy from glucose as fat more rapidly than undamaged animals, the signals of satiety, such as an increase in blood-glucose
level, don't occur. As a result, the animals continue eating.

As we have stressed throughout this
book, however, it's important to remember
that no single area of the brain acts alone,
especially in a complex behaviour such as
eating. Along with the hypothalamus, several additional brain regions participate in
eating. Our ability to taste food certainly
plays a role in eating, for example. As
described in Part 5, taste information is
processed in the regions of the prefrontal cortex. Disgust cues related to the
presentation of unpalatable food involve
the insular cortex, a region situated close
to the prefrontal cortex (Roman, Lin, &
Reilly, 2009; Roman & Reilly, 2007).

Not only are many areas of the brain involved in eating, but the brain circuitry involved in our eating behaviour is also active in a variety of motivational situations. Pathways important for general reward, punishment, and disgust under other circumstances interact with brain regions that specifically process visual, olfactory, and gustatory information to modulate eating (Rolls, 2007; De Araujo et al., 2005). For example, the same part of our brain that is active when we are enjoying the lovely scent of a flower might also be involved when we are enticed by the aroma wafting from a nearby bakery.

61.4 Hunger and Social Factors

Food is strongly associated with social interactions. Studies have shown that people eat considerably more when they are in a social setting, particularly when it is a relatively large gathering, compared to when eating alone (Lumeng & Hillman, 2007) or eating as part of a business meeting (Pliner et al., 2006).

Some researchers have also suggested that we each have an individual **body weight set point**. Researchers have long recognized that as adults, our weights tend to stabilize near a certain general level. We may fluctuate in a small range around that weight, but we typically return to the original set point, even after major deviations from it (Pasquet & Apfelbaum, 1994). This is particularly evident when people diet. A reduction in body weight is often followed by a rebound back toward the original weight, which is why so many dieters fail to achieve lasting weight loss. This isn't always the case, however. Some people do undergo dramatic weight changes in one direction or another and maintain their new weights for a considerable period of time. People who maintain a lower body weight typically make permanent changes in their eating and/or their exercise habits and persistently monitor their weight (The Look AHEAD Research Group, 2014; Dansinger et al., 2005; Warziski et al., 2008).

Other research suggests, however, that body weight set point is not the only factor at play in determining how much we eat. John Pinel at the University of British Columbia points out that set point alone is not a very powerful tool for predicting weight. He suggests that from an evolutionary point of view, our ancestors were not

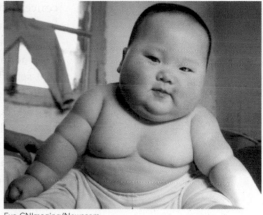

Eye-CNImaging/Newscom

Uncontrollable appetite. Prader-Willi Syndrome causes unstoppable appetite.

body weight set point a weight that individuals typically return to even after dieting or overeating.

HOW WE DIFFER

> **"**A man seldom thinks with more earnestness of anything than he does of his dinner.**"**
>
> —*Samuel Johnson, writer*

© Alex Segre/Alamy

Food and eating behaviour. The availability of food is an important additional factor in eating behaviour. Many individuals in societies such as much of North America, where food is plentiful, find their weights steadily creeping up over the years (Goryakin & Suhrcke, 2014).

concerned with overeating but with the lack of consistent food. Consequently, when food was available, our ancestors ate a lot to build up fat stores in case the next meals were some time away. Stopping eating to maintain a set point weight would not have been adaptive (Pinel, Assand, & Lehman, 2000). It is only in times of relative abundance that set point maintenance would have adaptive value. Pinel also indicates that another set point prediction, that having people consume a high-calorie drink before eating should reduce food intake, has not been shown to be effective (Lowe, 1993). Finally, the ability of learning, taste preference, and social factors (such as being offered a yummy dessert) to overwhelm set point controls on food intake also argue against the set point theory (Pinel, Assand, & Lehman, 2000). So, there is a lot more to weight maintenance than set point theory.

61.5 Hunger and Eating Disorders

We have seen that our motivation to eat is very complex, affected not only by intricate biological processes, but also by psychological, social, and cultural influences. As with any complex system, we face the potential for problems in our eating behaviour. Two of the most common problems include obesity, often related to too much eating, and eating disorders, which often involve eating too little.

61.5.1 Obesity

Obesity, a condition of extreme overweight, is determined on the basis of a weight-to-height ratio, called the **body mass index (BMI)**. Adults with a BMI of 30 or higher are considered obese, and those with BMIs between 25 and 30 are categorized as *overweight* (Health Canada, 2003). Obesity is a major health problem in North America. Twenty-five percent of the adult Canadian population is obese (Navaneelan & Janz, 2014). Being overweight or obese is associated with a variety of health problems, most notably diabetes and heart disease (Poirier et al., 2006; Huang, 2005). In addition to the physical risks they face, obese people are also more likely than those of normal weight to suffer from mood disorders, such as depression and anxiety (Friedlander et al., 2003).

Obese people are also often the victims of discrimination. A study found that people describe obese individuals as less attractive than thinner people, and ascribe a number of other unfavourable characteristics to people who are obese (Puhl & Heuer, 2010). Although overweight people are often considered as "friendly" and "happy," they are also judged more often as "lazy," "stupid," and "incompetent" than are people of normal weight (Puhl et al., 2008; Friedman et al., 2005). Obese individuals are more often turned down for jobs (NAAFA, 2009). This discrimination can even affect normal-weight individuals associated with obese people. One study looked at the hiring rate of normal-weight job applicants who happened to be sitting next to an obese person just before their interview (Hebl & Mannix, 2003). They were less likely to be hired!

Some people become obese as a result of medical conditions. Researchers estimate, however, that medical conditions cause only about 1 to 5 percent of all cases of obesity and seem to be the result of a biological abnormality unrelated to overeating (Harvey et al., 2005). In the vast majority of people, obesity is caused by overeating.

Why is overeating so common? One answer to this question may be found by considering the evolutionary perspective. Early people evolved under conditions of unpredictable food availability. At times when food was plentiful, after a successful hunt or during a time when weather conditions led to an abundance of edible plants, it was surely advantageous to overeat in preparation for subsequent food deprivation. Overeating led to fat storage that increased the chances of survival throughout periods when food was scarce. In many of today's developed cultures, especially in North America, where inexpensive high-calorie food is readily available, this built-in adaptive mechanism is being activated in a chronic and maladaptive way. Intermittent overeating followed by periods of fasting has been replaced by chronic, continuous overeating.

obesity overweight characterized as a body mass index of over 30.

body mass index (BMI) weight-to-height ratio.

Gary Salter/Corbis

Overweight and stigmatized. Relative to non-obese people, overweight individuals are stigmatized by being viewed negatively and experience lower hiring rates when applying for jobs for which they are qualified.

The problem of overeating has intensified over the past few decades, as the food and restaurant industries have increased the size of portions and prepared foods have become a mainstay of the North American diet. Consider the fact that in 1955, when McDonald's restaurants opened, a regular size adult's soft drink was 199 ml (7 ounces). In the new millennium, a child-sized serving of soft drink is 355 ml, and adults can choose from 473-, 621-, or 946-ml beverages (Young & Nestle, 2007). Burger King offers a Triple Whopper® sandwich that is 1,160 calories, more than half the recommended daily calorie allotment for an average adult male (Burger King, 2009; Department of Health and Human Services & Department of Agriculture, 2005).

Mark Peterson/Corbis

Bigger portions, bigger waists. The size and calorie count of meals and drinks at fast food restaurants have increased dramatically over the past several decades.

Consumer behaviour research strongly suggests that North Americans appreciate large-size portions because they appear to be a good value (Ledikwe, Ello-martin, & Rolls, 2005; Rolls, 2014). However, it's very difficult to regulate the amount of food you ingest when the portions are so much larger than those recommended for maintaining a healthy weight. The massive oversizing of portions so common today has, for many of us, led to an increase in energy intake, as measured in calories, without a corresponding change in energy expenditure. As a result, people gain weight.

Once people become accustomed to ingesting very large amounts of food, scaling back to sensible-sized portions can feel like deprivation. Many nutritionists often suggest that dieters eat their food from smaller plates to avoid feeling that the reduced portions are meager. This trick alone is typically not sufficient to support a substantial weight loss, however.

In fact, billions of dollars are spent every year on dieting programs and products that are designed to help overweight individuals lose weight and keep it off (Redmond, Kahan, & Cheskin, 2014). However, diet programs are often unsuccessful for long-term weight change. For this reason, many experts suggest that the best way to combat obesity is to prevent its occurrence in the first place (Bendelius, 2004; Mogan, 1984). Some approaches to obesity prevention may be suggested by identifying the risk factors for developing obesity. Why are some people more prone to obesity than others? The answer seems to involve multiple factors.

One substantial contributor to obesity is genes. Adoption and twin studies have shown that a good deal of the variation in obesity can be attributed to genetics. For example, adopted individuals tend to have the body mass indexes that more closely resemble the BMIs of their biological parents than those of their adoptive parents (Sørensen et al.,

© RGB Ventures LLC dba SuperStock/Alamy

Genes or environment? Research clearly suggests that obesity is related to genes, but there is also evidence that the eating habits of parents and other family members can play a major role in the development of this problem.

1992; Blakemore & Froguel, 2008). Moreover, identical twins separated at birth are as similar in body weight as those that were raised together (Price & Gottesman, 1991). This strongly suggests that genetics play a major role in determining obesity. Scientists do not completely understand exactly how our genes might predispose us to become obese. Some possibilities include inheriting a larger than normal number of fat cells, a lower metabolic rate (the speed at which we break down and burn the calories in food), or, as we saw earlier in the part, an abnormal leptin gene (Bjornholm et al., 2007; Farooqi et al., 2007).

Genetics alone cannot explain the rise in obesity over the past few decades in this country, however. Genes may predispose people to become overweight, but the environment must be conducive to overeating in order for them to realize this potential. As we have seen, social and cultural factors contribute to our eating behaviour. The social aspect of overeating is evident in recent findings that humans are much more likely to gain weight if they have an overweight friend, even if that person lives far away and the number of shared meals is minimal (Christakis & Fowler, 2007; Oliveira, 2013). One explanation for this correlation is that having overweight friends produces less resistance to gaining weight, perhaps because weight gain becomes associated with the positive stimulus of friendship. Obesity (especially among women) is also much more common among members of lower socio-economic groups than in higher socio-economic groups (McLaren, 2007). Researchers have suggested that this may be the result of less education about nutrition, fewer healthy food choices (the cost and availability of healthy food), and less social pressure to be thin (Monteiro et al., 2004).

Although obesity can significantly reduce quality of life, people can be overweight for decades before the negative health effects become evident. In contrast, eating disorders on the other end of the spectrum, those that involve eating too little, can lead rather abruptly to emergency situations, and even death.

61.5.2 Anorexia Nervosa and Bulimia Nervosa

anorexia nervosa eating disorder in which individuals under-eat and have a distorted body image of being overweight.

Anorexia nervosa is a condition in which individuals are preoccupied with the notion that they are fat or will become fat, and have a distorted image of being overweight (when they are not). To combat these thoughts, people with anorexia engage in extreme dieting, often eating fewer than 500 calories per day (Sadock & Sadock, 2008). The restricted eating associated with anorexia generally leads to extreme weight loss, which can be very dangerous. People who lose too much weight are at greater risk for illnesses and imbalances in their blood chemistry. In as many as 10 percent of cases, anorexic weight loss leads to death (Steinhausen, 2002).

It's important to realize that there are major differences between people who diet, even those who do so continuously, and those with anorexia. People with anorexia have a distorted body image. Even when they are dangerously thin, they still think of themselves as fat and often cannot be convinced to increase their calorie intake. They may use laxatives or exercise to burn off the small number of calories they take in. For females, this lack of nutrition can cause their periods to stop or to not start with maturity.

Anorexia can begin as early as puberty (Hudson et al., 2007). Statistics suggest that about 1 in 300 young women in Canada have anorexia (Samokhvalov et al., 2012; Government of Canada, 2006; Hoek, 2007). It is much more common in females than males, although recent years have seen an increase in the number of males diagnosed with the condition (Hudson et al., 2007).

The causes of anorexia are complex, but it is most common in cultures where food is prevalent and social pressure exists for people to be thin (Makino, Tsuboi, & Dennerstein,

2004). Similarly, many theorists have noted, with alarm, that today's media and fashion industry glamorize dangerously thin models. Anorexia often coexists with other anxiety disorders, such as obsessive-compulsive disorder (Health Canada, 2002), which we discussed in Part 9, suggesting that anorexia is just one of several possible outlets for a more general psychological disturbance.

Kristen von Ranson at the Eating Disorders Clinic in the Psychology Department at the University of Calgary studies the difficulty of treating anorexia and the importance of developing and applying evidenced-based treatment models (von Ranson, Wallace, & Stevenson, 2013). Treatment of anorexia may involve hospitalization if extreme weight loss occurs, where patients receive nutritional counselling to help restore a healthy weight. In addition, cognitive-behavioural therapy is used to attempt to help patients develop a healthier body image (Berkman et al., 2006). Adolescents with anorexia may also benefit from family therapy (Keel & Haedt, 2008).

Bulimia nervosa is a disorder in which individuals consume excessive calories and then go to extremes to prevent those calories from contributing to weight gain. People with bulimia typically rid themselves of excess food by inducing vomiting or diarrhea or by engaging in intensive exercise (Sigel, 2008). This cycle of bingeing followed by purging defines bulimia. Although people with anorexia often engage in bulimic behaviour to prevent weight gain, most people with bulimia do not appear to be underweight; some are even overweight (Probst et al., 2004). Like anorexia, bulimia is more common among females than males. Studies suggest that about 1 out of 100 young women in Canada have bulimia (Samokhvalov et al., 2012; Government of Canada, 2006; Hoek, 2007).

The causes of bulimia are difficult to pinpoint. Like anorexia, bulimia is associated with other psychological disturbances, including OCD (Godart et al., 2007; Kaye et al., 2004). A significant number of people with bulimia also engage in other damaging behaviours, such as cutting themselves (Favaro et al., 2008).

Unlike anorexia, bulimia is somewhat less likely to be fatal (Health Canada, 2002; Samokhvalov et al., 2012). However, it can produce unwanted medical and dental problems, such as constipation from overuse of laxatives and tooth decay from excessive vomiting (Cremonini et al., 2009; Arahna, de Paula Eduardo, & Cordás, 2008). The psychological effects of bulimic behaviour can be even more damaging than the physical ones. Because people with bulimia are generally ashamed of their binge–purge behaviours, they generally carry out these behaviours privately and make attempts to hide the evidence and keep their condition a secret. This secrecy, as well as the syndrome itself, often contribute to anxiety and depression (Pettersen, Rosevinge, & Ytterhus, 2008; Hayaki, Friedman, & Brownell, 2002).

Treatment of bulimia requires that patients admit that the problem exists and talk openly about it. Effective treatments for bulimia include behavioural modification, in which healthier eating behaviours are rewarded, and cognitive therapy, which attempts to help people with bulimia develop healthier views of themselves and their eating patterns (Wilson & Shafran, 2005; Bailer et al., 2004). Antidepressant drug treatments have also been found to be effective, particularly when combined with behavioural or cognitive therapy (Romano et al., 2002).

Young people with concerns about eating disorders (involving themselves or a friend or relative) can get help in several ways. First, if you or your friend or relative is a student at a college or university, the student counselling or health or wellness centre on campus will be able to arrange contact with a counsellor or therapist, or arrange for a referral to a local counselling or resource centre. A general practitioner (family doctor) will also be able to arrange a referral to someone who can talk about eating disorders and offer services. Finally, you can find out about local eating disorder resources through the Canadian National Eating Disorder Information Centre (www.nedic.ca). If you are concerned about someone in your life who you think might be struggling with an eating disorder, it is worth seeking some support and some ideas about how you can help.

bulimia nervosa eating disorder in which individuals binge and then engage in purging-type behaviour.

David Gray/Reuters

Dangerous trend. After the death of Brazilian model Ana Carolina Reston in 2006, the fashion industry has been criticized for using increasingly thin models, like this one. Reston was only 21 and weighed just 88 pounds (about 40 kg) when she died of complications from anorexia nervosa.

Before You Go On

www.wiley.com/go/comercanada

What Do You Know?

1. Describe three main categories of biological hunger signals.
2. What non-biological factors affect our eating behaviour?
3. What is obesity and what factors can contribute to it?
4. What are the characteristics of anorexia nervosa and bulimia nervosa?

What Do You Think? As a public-health effort to combat obesity, some jurisdictions are considering regulations that would require restaurants to provide calorie and other nutritional information about food on their menus. What are some potential advantages and disadvantages of providing this information to diners?

Summary

Module 61: Biological Motivations: Hunger

LEARNING OBJECTIVE 61 Summarize the factors that affect our levels of hunger and our eating behaviour.

- Hunger, our motivation to eat, is created by the interaction of signals from our stomachs, levels of food-related chemicals in our blood, and brain activity, particularly in the hypothalamus.
- Culture and individual differences interact with our basic biological need for food to determine what foods we will eat, when and with whom we like to eat, and how much we eat.
- Obesity is a major public-health problem in North America. It is usually caused by overeating, which can result from an interaction between genes and the environment.
- Anorexia nervosa is an eating disorder in which individuals believe they are fat and eat too little. Bulimia nervosa is an eating disorder in which people binge on food, then purge themselves of the food before it can add weight to their bodies.

Key Terms

anorexia nervosa 476
body mass index (BMI) 474

body weight set point 473
bulimia nervosa 477

lateral hypothalamus (LH) 472
leptin 471

obesity 474
ventromedial region of the hypothalamus (VMH) 472

Study Questions

Multiple Choice

1. What brain structure sends "hunger" signals that cause an animal to eat?
   a) Lateral hypothalamus
   b) Pons
   c) Thalamus
   d) Ventromedial hypothalamus

2. Which theory of hunger motivation proposes that activity in the lateral hypothalamus serves to inhibit the ventromedial hypothalamus, and vice versa?

a) Arousal
b) Dual-centre
c) Incentive
d) Instinct

Fill-in-the-Blank

1. One biological factor related to obesity may be an insensitivity to _____, a protein used by the brain to regulate eating.

Module 62: Biological Motivations: Sex

Another basic motivation is sex. From an evolutionary perspective, engaging in sexual behaviour is highly adaptive; the continuation of the species depends on it. However, most sexual behaviour does not occur with the goal of procreating in mind. Actually, the opposite seems to be true. Humans often engage in sexual behaviour while taking steps to avoid conception. Humans, as well as other animals, seek out and engage in sexual behaviour because it is a primary drive—it's pleasurable and rewarding.

LEARNING OBJECTIVE 62
Describe factors that affect our sexual motivation and behaviour.

62.1 Sex: Psychological and Social Factors

Although there is a basic biological instinct to engage in sexual activity, sexual motivation is strongly governed by social cues. In some species of animals, only select members of the social group reproduce. Among honeybees, for example, only the queen bee of each hive reproduces, while the other bees work to maintain the living environment (Wenseleers et al., 2004; Korb, 2010). In other groups, such as marmoset monkeys, dominant females in a social group procreate, and the other females help to raise the dominants' babies. Subordinate females must wait until a change occurs in the social order (perhaps a dominant will get old and sick and lose her rank) before they can reproduce (Barrett, Abbott, & George, 1993).

Among humans, cultural factors play an important role in determining our choice and number of sexual partners, our range of sexual practices, and the age at which sexual activity typically begins. For instance, some societies, such as certain Nigerian tribes, practise polygamy, an arrangement in which men have multiple wives. Other societies, such as the Naxi of China, practise polyandry, an arrangement in which women have multiple male sexual partners (Yan, 1986).

Societies also vary in the sexual practices that are considered taboo or unacceptable. For example, in Canada, young people have a range of protections that are in force up to their eighteenth birthday. It is not possible for anyone under 16 to provide consent for sexual activity if their partner is five years older than them (three years older if they are 12 or 13). As such, any sexual involvement with younger teens by older individuals is considered non-consensual, or what used to be referred to as statutory rape, and the older individuals are punished accordingly. The age of consent is higher (18 years of age) if exploitation (prostitution, pornography, etc.) is involved. In contrast, in some Middle Eastern countries, the earliest age of marriage (and its consummation) is 9 years old (Admon, 2009; Norman-Eady, Reinhart, & Martino, 2003).

Some sexual taboos seem to be almost universal, however, suggesting that they may be rooted in human evolution. One example of this is the incest taboo. In most cultures, incest, or having sex with close relatives, is forbidden (with rare exceptions, such as ancient Egypt, when it was deemed necessary to preserve a royal bloodline). It is also illegal for siblings to marry in most countries throughout the world. In one case in Germany, for example, a biological brother and sister who were brought up separately, then met and fell in love as young adults, were sentenced to prison after marrying (Connolly, 2007).

Why is sex between siblings so universally forbidden? From an evolutionary viewpoint, there are at least two possible reasons. First, procreation between closely related individuals increases the likelihood of passing on defective genes, particularly recessive ones. Early societies that

Jonathan Hayward/The Canadian Press

Of national concern. Winston Blackmore shares a laugh with six of his daughters and some of his grandchildren. Blackmore is the religious leader of the controversial polygamous community of Bountiful, located near Creston, B.C. and was charged with polygamy in 2014.

forbade incest may have been genetically stronger than those that did not. Second, incest taboos put pressure on societies to interact with neighbouring cultures. Historically, this meant that tribal elders would bargain about marrying their children to one another. In the process, the two tribes might increase general commerce and enhance the access to food and other forms of wealth for both groups (Leavitt, 1989; Johnson & Earle, 1987). According to these views, avoiding sex with close relatives enhances the chances for survival of a group of people. Cultural regulation of our biological drive toward sexual behaviour may also have emerged because it serves the purpose of promoting our survival as a group.

Although norms vary from culture to culture, as we have seen, all cultures do approve certain sexual practices while condemning others. Within nations, many religious, ethnic, and other subcultural groups also influence the sexual behaviour of their members. In many societies, sex is not acceptable unless the couple's relationship is considered legitimate, often as a result of marriage (Cavendish, 2010). In North America, the sexual revolution of the 1960s and 1970s loosened many social restrictions on premarital sex. Today, over 95 percent of people in the United States have sex before marriage (Finer, 2007) and about 17 percent of Canadian couples living together are unmarried (Statistics Canada, 2012). The number of young adults with multiple sexual partners has also increased. By the time most individuals reach their early 20s, they have had three to four sexual partners (Mosher, Chandra, & Jones 2005). Some sexual behaviours, such as homosexual relationships, are becoming more widely accepted. Canada has a national law allowing for marriage among same-sex couples, and increasingly strong enforcement of laws against discrimination based on sexual orientation (Larocque, 2006).

Changes in societal views of sex grew, in part, from psychology research on sexual behaviour. One of the most influential sex researchers was biologist Alfred Kinsey. Early in his career, as a junior faculty member in the United States, Kinsey was assigned to teach a course in basic sex practices along with a team of all male instructors (Moore, Davidson, & Fisher, 2010). Realizing that many of his college students were uneducated about basic sexual practices, Kinsey switched his field of study in the 1940s from insect behaviour to human sexual behaviour (Bullough, 2004). He then undertook a massive project, interviewing thousands of people to collect data on the sexual practices of ordinary Americans. Kinsey's work was widely publicized and led to the realization that many "normal" Americans engaged in sexual behaviour that was not considered to be conventional at the time, including oral sex, anal sex, and having multiple partners (Brown & Fee, 2003). Kinsey's work helped to lessen taboos about discussing these sexual practices, because people realized they were not uncommon.

62.2 Sex: Physiological and Neurological Factors

62.2.1 Sex: What Happens in the Body

During the 1950s and 1960s, researchers William Masters and Virginia Johnson brought the study of sexual behaviour into the laboratory. Masters and Johnson recorded some of the first physiological data in humans during sex. They studied the sexual responses of both men and women and described four general, and somewhat modestly described, phases of the human sexual response, as shown in **Figure 62-1** (Masters & Johnson, 1966).

- *Excitement* This is the beginning of arousal and it can last up to several hours. Heart rate quickens, though not constantly over a long period of time.
- *Plateau* At this phase, breathing and pulse rates increase. Muscles tense and a flush may appear across the chest.
- *Orgasm* Muscle tension and blood pressure reach a peak. This is quickly followed by climax, which is a series of muscle contractions (the intensity varies, particularly among women).

©iStockphoto.com/ArtistAllen

The body during sex. During sex the body goes through physiological changes and sexual responses.

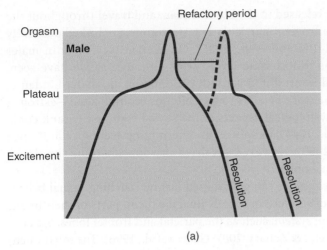

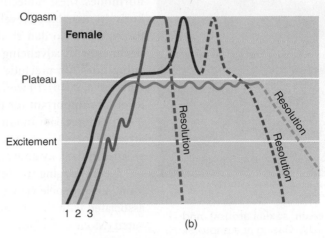

FIGURE 62-1 **Human sexual responses.** Masters and Johnson identified four phases in sexual response. Part (a) illustrates the typical pattern in males. Women experience greater variability in their sexual response. Part (b) shows three female patterns. Reprinted with permission from Masters, W. H., & Johnson V. E. (1966). *Human sexual response.* Boston: Little, Brown, p. 5. Copyright © 1966 by the Masters and Johnson Institute.

- *Resolution* Muscles relax and heart rate returns to normal. While men have a refractory period after an orgasm, during which they cannot ejaculate, women may have additional orgasms.

In the 1970s, sex therapist Helen Kaplan incorporated an additional element to the beginning of the sexual response cycle. Kaplan believed that *desire*—basically, whether or not you're "in the mood"—was a necessary condition to motivate an individual to become excited (Kaplan, 1977). The research of Masters and Johnson and those that followed, such as Kaplan, was particularly influential for North American society, because it encouraged women to enjoy sex, which was previously considered to be inappropriate (Weiss, 2000). Masters and Johnson's research also dispelled myths about aging and sexual behaviour. Prior to their research, the conventional view was that sexual behaviour was the realm of young to middle-aged adults, and that after a certain age, sexual behaviour was minimal, if not physically impossible. As a result of Masters and Johnson's research, as well as others that followed, the current view is that sexual behaviour can continue throughout old age, providing a person remains physically healthy and has a willing partner (Waite et al., 2009; DeLamater & Karraker, 2009).

Although the work of the early sex researchers was highly controversial at the time (Cochran, Mosteller, & Tukey, 1953), the publicity these researchers received had the lasting effects of increasing awareness of sexual behaviour and altering societal standards of what is considered normal (Gagnon, 1975). This early psychological research on sexuality emphasized that sexual behaviour is a wholesome and healthy activity, and that idea represented a major change in thinking compared to earlier, more restrictive attitudes. It also encouraged more extensive research into our typical physiological sexual responses, including what happens in the brain during sex, thus broadening the field of acceptable research.

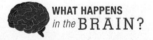

WHAT HAPPENS *in the* **BRAIN?**

62.2.2 Sex: What Happens in the Brain

Reproductive hormones are clearly important factors in modulating sexual behaviour (Raskin et al., 2009; Kudwa et al., 2006; Berman, 2005). In males, the testes and adrenal glands produce male sex hormones collectively referred to as *androgens*. In females, the ovaries produce the female sex hormones (*estrogen* and *progesterone*). Even though androgens are referred to as male sex hormones, they are produced by the adrenal glands of females too. Like all other

Shuttlecock/Dreamstime/GetStock

Sex at any age. Sexual activity can continue into old age as long as partners are willing.

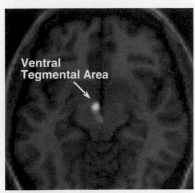

Courtesy of Lucy L. Brown, Albert Einstein College of Medicine

The brain, sexual arousal, and rewards. Gazing at a photo of one's romantic partner activates the ventral tegmental area (VTA) (shown in yellow on this fMRI image). The VTA is activated during early-stage, intense romantic love, as well as when looking at photos of loved ones for which there is no sexual interest, showing that this brain area is associated with learning about rewarding stimuli in general.

HOW WE DIFFER

hormones, these molecules are released in the blood stream and travel throughout the body. In men, blood levels of androgens, particularly testosterone, are linked positively to sex drive (Jordan et al., 2011; Simon et al., 2005). On average, sex drive in males declines with advancing age as testosterone levels drop, although as we have seen, aging does not preclude sexual interest and activity (Feldman et al., 2002; Lindau & Gavrilova, 2010). In women, the story appears to be a bit more complicated—estrogen levels are important for the physiological aspects of the sexual response (Frank et al., 2008; Lonnee-Hofffmann, et al., 2014), as well as in determining feelings about one's attractiveness (Durante et al., 2009). However, sex drive also appears to be simulated, at least in part, by androgens in women.

Neuroimaging studies show that we can get aroused just by watching sexual behaviour. When people view videos of sex acts, or merely imagine them, parts of their brains associated with the *mirror neuron system*, such as the parietal and frontal lobes, are activated (Mouras et al., 2008; Shmuelof & Zohary, 2007; Gallese et al., 1996). The mirror neuron system is made up of areas of the brain that, when we watch another person engage in a specific activity, are activated in the same way as when we actually do the same activity ourselves (Rizzolatti & Craighero, 2004). Thus, watching other people engage in sexual behaviour activates some of the same regions of the viewer's brain that would be active if the viewer were actually having sex. This activation makes viewers feel sexually aroused simply from watching.

Even if we do not consciously see an erotic picture or film, we can become aroused. In one study, researchers presented a series of photos to participants. Some of the photos were sexual, and these were rapidly shown and removed before the viewer was consciously aware of them. Even though viewers did not remember seeing anything, neuroimaging showed activation of regions of the brain associated with arousal and reward (Childress et al., 2008). Sexual behaviour is essential for survival of the species, and the rapid activation of brain regions by subtle sexual cues ensures that we are motivated to have sex.

62.2.3 Gender Differences in Sexuality

Although each person has unique preferences, beliefs, and behaviours, there do seem to be some differences between men and women when it comes to what they want in sex. Men and women differ in characteristics they perceive as attractive in a mate and in the stimuli that arouse them. Their fantasies and desired number of partners may also differ.

Evolutionary psychologists suggest that much of how heterosexual men and women interact with the opposite sex is the result of thousands of years of evolution designed to maximize our chances of survival and reproductive success. Men desire youthful, attractive mates because those attributes signal good odds for reproductive success; women are attracted to men who are dependable and strong because they will most likely be able to protect and care for children (Miller, 2000).

In addition to what makes someone attractive, men and women also differ in what arouses them. Men, on average, are aroused more quickly than women by visual stimuli (Stoléru et al., 1999; Moulier, et al., 2006). Women, on the other hand, respond more strongly than men do to physical contact and verbal expression. This may be because arousal in women is more often influenced by their relationship with a partner, as well as their own self-image, than it is in men (Peplau, 2003).

Even women's sexual fantasies are more commitment-oriented than men (Ellis & Symons, 1990), and they tend to have fewer fantasies than men (Byers, Purdon, & Clark, 1998). In one study, surveyors asked college students, "Have you had sex with over a thousand different partners in your imagination?" Males in the study were four times more likely than females to say yes (Ellis & Symons, 1990). The frequency of men's arousal and the number of their fantasies have led many psychologists to conclude that men generally have a higher sex drive. In fact, men tend to rate their own sex drives as higher than women rate theirs (Baumeister, Catanese, & Vohs, 2001).

It's important to realize that reported gender differences in sexual desire and sexual activity may reflect biases in reporting. On surveys and during interviews, women may downplay their sexual desires and behaviours because of perceived social constraints. Conversely, males may be more likely to exaggerate such feelings and behaviours to fulfill imagined expectations for men. There is no question that women and men are judged differently by society when it comes to sex. In movies, for example, women with high sex drives are often portrayed as dangerous or emotionally unstable, while men with low sex drives are often the subject of ridicule. These perceptions may influence the way that people respond to questions about their sex lives. In reality, though, women and men may be more alike than researchers once thought. Recent studies of university undergraduates are conflicted, with some finding significant differences between women and men in their desired number of partners and others not (Miller et al., 2002; Fenigstein & Preston, 2007; Schmitt et al., 2012).

©iStockphoto.com/LSOphoto

Different needs and preferences. Given gender differences regarding sexual needs, attraction, arousal, and fantasies, a couple's thoughts may be in different places at moments like this.

62.2.4 Sexual Orientation

Most people are **heterosexual**; they are sexually attracted to members of the opposite sex. The proportions of the population that identify as **homosexual** (gay or lesbian)— people who are sexually attracted to members of their own sex—vary depending on how the questions are asked. Estimates of the number of people who identify as homosexual vary. One large study (Laumann et al., 1994) suggested that about 2.8 percent of males and 1.4 percent of females primarily identify as homosexual. A more carefully designed study was conducted by Chris Bagley at the University of Calgary. Bagley argued that how you ask questions about sexual orientation and how you sample the population affects your results (for example, it is likely that there are higher proportions of gay and lesbian individuals in cities). In his study, Bagley took extra steps to make it very clear that all data gathered would carefully protect anonymity. Based on the results, Bagley suggested that the rate of homosexuality in urban settings may be as high as 10 to 15 percent (Bagley & Tremblay, 1988). Homosexuality is increasingly being recognized as a part of the diversity of life. The American Psychological Association removed homosexuality from its Diagnostic and Statistical Manual of Mental Disorders in 1973. Why are some people attracted to members of the opposite sex while others are attracted to members of the same sex? Arguments about this topic have been heated and often reflect a nature–nurture debate.

heterosexual sexual attraction to members of the opposite sex.

homosexual sexual attraction to members of one's own sex.

Alfred Kinsey believed that sexual orientation was on a continuum, with many people fitting between the two extremes of exclusively heterosexual and exclusively homosexual (Kinsey, Pomeroy, & Martin, 1948). According to this idea, each person contains a certain proportion of heterosexuality and homosexuality. It follows, then, that if a person living as a homosexual is, in fact, at least part heterosexual, intervention can cause the person to increase the heterosexual-to-homosexual ratio—that is, to emphasize heterosexual behaviours and thoughts in his or her life (Murphy, 1992; Pattison & Pattison, 1980).

Kinsey's theory is controversial, but it does suggest that sexual orientation is changeable. Based on this idea, numerous organizations have devised treatment programs to "convert" homosexuals to heterosexuality. In fact, in the late 1960s, the Masters and Johnson Institute sponsored such a program and reported conversions among the majority of participants (Masters & Johnson, 1979). These findings have not been supported, and current research strongly suggests that homosexuality is biologically based and cannot be "cured." If anything, such attempts can be damaging to the individual, since they typically produce feelings of shame and embarrassment (Cramer et al., 2008; Haldeman, 1994).

Charla Jones/Toronto Star/The Canadian Press   Tony Bock/Toronto Star/The Canadian Press

Gay marriage and the law. Former Ontario health minister, George Smitherman (left), and his partner; a couple celebrates their wedding in front of Toronto's City Hall. The relationship between the law and psychology is not always clear. Research is increasingly showing that homosexuality is a natural human phenomenon. Societal acceptance is increasing, and Canada has taken a positive step by legalizing gay marriage.

Additional evidence that homosexuality is a natural, biological phenomenon comes from repeated observations of homosexual behaviour throughout the animal kingdom. Homosexuality has been reported in both male and female birds (including one celebrated case of a homosexual penguin at the Central Park Zoo in New York City), as well as among bonobos, a type of chimpanzee (Drury, 2013; Roughgarden, 2004; Smith, 2004).

Although the exact influences leading to sexual orientation remain unknown, considerable evidence suggests that sexual orientation has a biological basis. Researchers have studied the intertwined influences of genes, hormones, and anatomical brain differences.

- *Genes* Studies suggest a strong genetic influence on sexual orientation. In other words, homosexuality tends to run in families (Bailey & Pillard, 1991; Buhrich, Bailey, & Martin, 1991). The correlation is greatest among monozygotic, or identical, twins. If one twin is homosexual, the other is also likely to have that orientation. Some evidence suggests this link exists even if the twins are raised apart (Eckert et al., 1986). As with many other traits, however, genetics do not completely determine sexual orientation; even among pairs of identical twins who share the same genes, some pairs differ in orientation (Långström et al., 2008). Researchers have therefore considered other biological factors.

- *Hormones* Some studies suggest that some homosexual males may experience different hormone levels before birth compared to heterosexual males. Studies have shown that having an older brother increases the odds of male homosexuality. With each additional older brother, the likelihood of homosexuality increases (Blanchard, 2004, 2001). In the case of younger brothers with homosexual orientations, some researchers suggest that the mother's immune system may sometimes react to male sex hormones while she is carrying a male fetus, such that in subsequent pregnancies, maternal antibodies will lessen the "masculinizing" action of hormones on the brain of the younger brother. Although this hypothesis cannot account for the majority of homosexual individuals, studies examining brain differences support the possibility that prenatal hormone exposure may be an important factor for some individuals (Rahman, 2005; Williams et al., 2000).

- *Brain anatomy* A sex difference exists in the anterior, or front, part of the hypothalamus. This region is twice as large in heterosexual men as it is in women (Orikasa, Kondo, & Sakuma, 2007). A similar size difference exists in this brain region between heterosexual men and homosexual men. The anterior hypothalamuses of homosexual men are, on average, more similar in size to those of women than to those of heterosexual men, suggesting that individual differences in masculinizing factors (most likely hormones) may contribute to changes in brain anatomy that ultimately lead to homosexual or heterosexual behaviour (LeVay, 1991).

Society is gradually becoming less discriminatory and more understanding of homosexuality. In 2006, a Statistics Canada study (2007) found that about 45,000 Canadian couples are in a same-sex relationship, one-fifth of them married. The Canadian population's view of gay marriage is split along age lines, with the majority of younger Canadians supporting it and the majority of Canadians over 60 years of age opposed to it (Angus Reid Strategies, 2009).

> **"**The State has no place in the bedrooms of the Nation.**"**
>
> —*Pierre Elliott Trudeau*

Before You Go On

www.wiley.com/go/comercanada

What Do You Know?

1. What aspects of sexual behaviour are affected by our cultural standards?
2. What are the phases of the sexual response cycle described by Masters and Johnson and what happens at each one?
3. What biological factors has research found to be related to sexual orientation?

What Do You Think? Describe the specific cultural standards for sexual behaviour that affect your peer group.

Summary

Module 62: Biological Motivations: Sex

LEARNING OBJECTIVE 62 Describe factors that affect our sexual motivation and behaviour.

- Sexual practices driven by sexual motivation vary widely as a result of cultural influences.
- Research consistently shows much variety in normal sexual behaviour throughout healthy adulthood.
- Testosterone and other hormones affect our motivation toward sexual behaviour. Many parts of our brains become active during sexual arousal and behaviour.

Key Terms

heterosexual 483

homosexual 483

Study Questions

Multiple Choice

1. Blood levels of what hormone are positively related to sex drive in men, and to a lesser extent, in women?
   a) Estrogen
   b) Insulin
   c) Progesterone
   d) Testosterone

Fill-in-the-Blank

1. Masters and Johnson found that men, but not women, have a _____ period after orgasm during which time they cannot have another orgasm.

Module 63: Psychological Motivations: Affiliation and Achievement

In the previous modules, we talked about biological motivations. Recalling Maslow's hierarchy of needs, however, you will see that we are also motivated by non-biological needs. The need to belong and the need for self-worth are *psychological* motivations that are just as important as biological needs to our health and happiness. These motivations make sense when we consider that humans live in tightly-knit social groups, and as such our connection to our social group and our sense of worth within our group is very important.

63.1 Affiliation

affiliation the need to form attachments to other people for support, guidance, and protection.

Affiliation is defined as the need to form attachments to other people for support, guidance, and protection. Going to college or university is, for many students, their first experience away from home for a prolonged period of time. Suddenly, you are on your own, without the support and comfort of your family. Those first few weeks can be quite stressful, until students become acquainted with their new surroundings and meet new people.

Being part of a social group, whether it is a family or a group of friends or an organization, helps us define who we are and allows us to feel secure about our place in the world. This need has evolved from the evolutionary advantage that groups had in being able to provide food and protection, compared to individuals living alone (Diener & Seligman, 2002).

From the moment we are born, we seek a connection with others. As we learned previously, instinct theory explains that infants automatically seek out their mother's breast, and this rooting reflex reinforces the infant's chances of survival. As we develop, relationships with friends, and later with significant others, help to raise our self-esteem. Men and women in long-term, healthy relationships have less depression and live longer (Holt-Lunstad, Birmingham, & Jones, 2008). Even elderly spouses who provide more care to each other live longer than those who are less considerate of each other (Kaplan & Kronick, 2006).

Our motivation to belong may also explain why some individuals remain in abusive relationships and join gangs. The fear of social exclusion is a powerful motivator. In fact, when people feel excluded, the anterior cingulate cortex in the frontal cortex is activated (Eisenberg, Lieberman, & Williams, 2003). Recall that this same area responds to physical pain.

Affiliation with others is an essential psychological need. When we are denied contact with other humans, we are not only unable to satisfy biological needs, but we also lose our motivation to pursue our highest level needs: self-worth and self-actualization. We are no longer driven to achieve.

Lee Mason

Trying to make gang membership less attractive. In an effort to reduce gang recruitment, the Young Warriors Network runs a number of programs aimed at strengthening community ties within Canada First Nations youth.

63.2 Achievement

The fact that you are reading this book means that you are motivated to go to school, study, and obtain a degree. You may choose to pursue additional degrees, or you may graduate and find a job. No matter what path you take, to satisfy the needs at the top of Maslow's pyramid, self-worth and self-actualization, you need to feel competent, engage with others, and possess control over your own life. **Self-determination** theory suggests that competence, relatedness, and autonomy are instinctive, and that they give purpose and meaning to life (Ryan & Deci, 2002). Not all psychologists agree with this theory, however. Other cultures, such as the Chinese, place less importance on autonomy, instead valuing collective effort.

self-determination instinctive feelings of competence, relatedness, and autonomy that give purpose to life.

As you might expect, incentives often play a role in motivating us to achieve. In school, you may be motivated intrinsically by curiosity to learn new information. In other words, the behaviour may be engaging in and of itself. Or you may be motivated extrinsically by incentives. For instance, your reason for studying hard in this course may be because you are hoping to be rewarded with an A at the end of the semester. When achievement is motivated by incentives, it is often associated with competition. People who place too much value on rewards are more likely to suffer when they fail (Sheldon et al., 2004). If they succeed, they may think that the reward, and not their motivation, was the reason for their success. In contrast, psychologists associate intrinsic motivation with the qualities of self-determination theory: competence, relatedness, and autonomy. When you strive to do well for yourself, you enjoy yourself more (Blumenfeld, Kempler, & Krajcik, 2006).

©iStockphoto.com/fatihhoca

Achievement and motivation. Achievement, marked by our own feelings of accomplishment and by recognition from others, is an important part of our motivation—even in young children.

63.2.1 Delaying Gratification

Social, or non-biological, motivations, especially those that involve incentives, are not present at birth, but are learned. In fact, incentive motivations often involve inhibiting basic biological drives to obtain the reward. Consider a restaurant server trying to earn money. If the server acted on biological instincts and ate the food off the customer's plate, then it would be difficult to keep the job and earn money.

HOW WE
DEVELOP

Delaying gratification is especially important for some of the goals you set as a student. Earning a degree takes a long period of time, during which you often set aside immediate pleasures, such as social activities, in favour of studying. This type of self-control isn't present in very small children, but instead develops over time. The ability to delay gratification requires not just an understanding of the relative worth of the rewards, but also an ability to control impulses. Impulse control also develops over time. While playing, toddlers often get into physical fights over sharing toys, whereas preschool and kindergarten-age children react this way less and less frequently. Developmental psychologists have tested the ability to delay gratification in the laboratory by offering children of varying ages the choice of getting a reward right away or waiting some amount of time to get a better reward. For example, researchers might offer a child the choice of receiving a single M&M immediately, or getting a whole bag of M&Ms if they wait 30 minutes. Studies have shown that children display

©iStockphoto.com/Blue_Cutler

Children and delaying gratification. Children have a particular amount of difficulty delaying gratification; but then, who can ignore freshly baked cookies?

a wide range of abilities to delay gratification; some are much more able to do so than others (Lemmon & Moore, 2007). Related research also suggests that the ability to delay gratification in a laboratory setting may be predictive of success in other realms, including in academic and social settings (Mischel, Shoda, & Rodriguez, 1989).

One likely explanation for the fact that very young children lack the skills necessary to work toward long-term goals and delay instant gratification along the way is that their brains are not yet developed in key areas related to these tasks. The prefrontal cortex is not yet myelinated in children, and the adult levels of synapses connecting them to other neurons are not reached until after puberty. The prefrontal cortex is not only important for mediating reward signals, but also for planning and carrying out complicated tasks that involve several steps toward the achievement of a long-term goal. This may provide some explanation for the common observation that, compared to adults, teenagers are more likely to engage in risky behaviour, jeopardizing their futures for instant gratification. You may find that as you get older, it is easier to set your sights on goals far in the future, including several years away. You realize that your actions in the here and now will contribute to your situation in the future. These are mature thought processes that cannot occur without an intact prefrontal cortex. Motivation, whether biological or psychological, is complex and inextricably linked with other cognitive processes, such as memory and emotion. In trying to understand why we do the things we do, it is important to remember that society and culture play important roles as well. Whether undertaking the challenge BASE jump or trying to ace a psychology course, our behaviours illustrate that our survival is dependent on the need for purpose. Obviously many of our activities and behaviours are also accompanied by a broad range of emotions, and it is to the nature of emotions and emotional experience that we now turn.

Before You Go On

www.wiley.com/go/comercanada

What Do You Know?

1. Why are we motivated to be socially connected?
2. What are the components of self-determination theory?
3. How do intrinsic and extrinsic motives influence achievement?
4. How does delay of gratification help us reach goals?

What Do You Think? Describe one of your long-term goals and how you might achieve that goal by dividing it into several smaller, short-term goals.

Summary

Module 63: Psychological Motivations: Affiliation and Achievement

LEARNING OBJECTIVE 63 Describe factors that influence our psychological motivations for affiliation and achievement.

- Affiliation represents our need to interact with others, not only for survival, but also for self-worth.
- Isolation puts people at risk of psychological impairments.
- Self-determination theory suggests that we need competence, relatedness, and autonomy to realize our potential.
- Achievement through intrinsic motivation does not involve incentives.
- Individuals who are able to delay gratification can focus on goals and ignore distractions.

Key Terms

affiliation 486   self-determination 486

Study Questions

Multiple Choice

1. The psychological characteristic most strongly related to the ability to delay gratification is
   a) impulse control.
   b) need for achievement.
   c) need for affiliation.
   d) predestination.

2. Which statement best describes the difference between the psychological needs for affiliation and for achievement?
   a) Achievement is defined in the same way across different societies, but affiliation is not.
   b) Affiliation is a basic psychological need, but achievement is not.

c) Affiliation is less important than achievement.
d) Brain size influences the need for affiliation, but not achievement.

Fill-in-the-Blank

1. Social exclusion leads to measurable changes in the brain, particularly in the _____ region of the frontal cortex.

2. Research has shown that _____ motivation is related to beneficial psychological characteristics such as competence and autonomy.

Module 64: What Is Emotion?

LEARNING OBJECTIVE 64
Define emotion and discuss the components, measurement, and functions of emotion.

How would you define emotion? Despite all the attention psychologists give to emotion, they have had difficulty agreeing on exactly what an emotion is. Over 500 words in the English language refer to various aspects or forms of emotions, from *affect*, to *mood*, to *feeling*. Perhaps it is not surprising that a unified definition has eluded scientists (Averill, 1980). Nevertheless, psychologists continue to believe that human emotion is among psychology's most important topics.

64.1 Components of Emotion

emotion an intrapersonal state that occurs in response to either an external or an internal event and typically involves a physiological component, a cognitive component, and a behavioural component.

Most of today's theorists define an **emotion** as an individual state that occurs in response to either an external or an internal event and that typically involves three separate but intertwined components:

1. A *physiological component*—changes in bodily arousal, such as increased heart rate, body temperature, and respiration.
2. A *cognitive component*—the subjective appraisal and interpretation of an individual's feelings and surrounding environment.
3. A *behavioural component*—the expression of emotion through verbal or non-verbal channels, such as smiling, frowning, whining, laughing, reflecting, or slouching.

Let's look more closely at each of these components. Remember, though, that when we experience an emotion, all three are at work.

64.1.1 Physiological Component

The physiological component of emotion refers to the bodily arousal we feel when experiencing a particular emotion, whether it is positive or negative. When you are nervous about giving a class presentation or going out on a first date, for example, you may notice that your heart beats faster, your hands sweat, and your mouth becomes dry. These physical manifestations of anxiety are produced by your *autonomic nervous system (ANS)*, shown in **Table 64-1**. As described in Part 3, the ANS is responsible for regulating various bodily functions and the activity of specific organs, glands, and

---

TABLE 64-1 Emotion and the Autonomic Nervous System

Sympathetic Nervous System Prepares the Body for Actions		Parasympathetic Nervous System Returns the Body to Normal State
Pupils dilate	Eyes	Pupils constrict
Salivation decreases	Mouth	Salivation increases
Perspires; goose bumps	Skin	Dries up; no goose bumps
Breathing rate increases	Lungs	Breathing rate decreases
Accelerates	Heart	Slows
Release stress hormones	Adrenal glands	Decrease release of stress hormones
Decreased motility	Digestion	Increased motility
Blood vessels constrict; blood sugar increases	Blood	Blood vessels dilate; blood sugar drops
Perspire	Palms	Dry up

Mike Kemp/Getty Images

The physiological changes we experience in emotion are controlled by the autonomic nervous system. The sympathetic branch arouses the body in situations of anxiety or danger. The parasympathetic branch returns the body to its normal state.

muscles. Other physiological changes that might occur as we experience an emotion include increased blood pressure, increased blood sugar, pupil dilation, and the inhibition of intestinal action.

Because emotions vary in intensity, some emotions may be accompanied by several physiological changes, while others may involve only a few. If, for example, you are anxious about going out with someone for the first time, you will likely experience less intense and fewer physiological reactions than if you are trying to escape from a fire in a crowded concert hall. The reason for these differences has to do with the *sympathetic nervous system*, the subdivision of the ANS that mobilizes internal resources and primes the organism to take swift action for survival—the *fight-or-flight response*. When waiting for a new date to arrive, your heart may beat faster and your palms may sweat because that is your body's way of signifying the importance of the situation to you. When you need to flee a burning building, however, more emotional arousal and energy are needed, and the body produces a more intense physiological response (Friedman & Silver, 2007). Like fear and anxiety, emotions such as happiness, excitement, and surprise also involve activation of the sympathetic nervous system. Here, too, the intensity of the physiological arousal and the number of bodily changes depend on the nature of the situation.

James Mackenzie/The Canadian Press

Emotional ingredients. Silpa Edmunds, 79, came to Inuvik, N.T., from Labrador, to tell the Truth and Reconciliation Council the story of how she survived residential school. She is showing physical signs of emotion, cognitive components (at least as reflected in what she is saying), and behavioural components.

Following an intense physiological reaction, the other component of the ANS, the *parasympathetic nervous system*, works to calm the body down and attempts to conserve energy by returning the organism to a normal state. Later, we will see how various areas of the brain and the endocrine system are involved in each of these processes.

64.1.2 Cognitive Component

The cognitive component of emotion refers to both the evaluative thoughts people have about their emotional experiences (such as "I am afraid") and the appraisal of the events that are producing the emotions. Our interpretation of an event not only helps bring about an emotional reaction, but also influences how intensely we will experience that emotion. Consider the event of coming face to face with a grizzly bear. If the grizzly bear is just a cub and is safely behind a protective barrier at the Calgary Zoo, you will probably appraise the situation as pleasant and experience an emotion such as happiness. If, however, a full-grown grizzly bear were to appear in front of you on a hiking trail in Banff National Park, you would likely appraise the situation as life-threatening and experience, among other emotions, very intense fear.

In addition to appraising the situation that gives rise to a particular emotion, people also interpret and evaluate the emotion itself, further shaping how they experience that emotion. If you love to ride roller coasters, you will most likely interpret the bodily arousal you feel while going into a big drop as excitement and thrill. If, in contrast, you dread roller coasters but are talked into riding one by friends, you will likely label that same bodily arousal as fear.

64.1.3 Behavioural Component

When you experience an emotion, you not only have particular thoughts and bodily sensations, but also express and reveal that emotion. You do so through body language, such as facial expressions, gestures, and body posture, as well as through verbal expression. For example, happiness is almost universally expressed with a smile (Leppänen & Hietanen, 2007). Conversely, someone who is frustrated may cross his arms and shrug his shoulders; someone who is angry may clench her teeth and furrow her eyebrows; and a person who is sad may frown, slump, and avoid eye contact. You can no doubt think of many more examples.

Tying It Together: **Your Brain and Behaviour**

Motivating Ourselves to Run a Marathon

Amarathon is a 42.16 km (26.2 mile) race that generally requires months of preparation. Many people follow strict regimens to help them prepare. Runners eagerly sign up for marathons all across the world, in all kinds of weather. What might motivate people to run?

When we are motivated to run for personal achievement, the reward learning pathways—the brain regions involved in basic biological reward, such as the ventral tegmental area, the nucleus accumbens, and the prefrontal cortex—are engaged. In addition, areas that are important for storing the memories of our past running experiences, such as the hippocampus and neocortex, are likely to be involved. The prefrontal cortex is also important for enabling us to attend to our goals and respond flexibly to changes in the terrain as we run. Will we beat our personal best?

Questions

1 Which region of the brain is most strongly activated by attending to goals and responding to changes in the environment?

2 What does it mean to say that exercise has beneficial effects on the brain as well as on other parts of the body?

3 In which region of the brain is increased blood flow after aerobic exercise particularly evident?

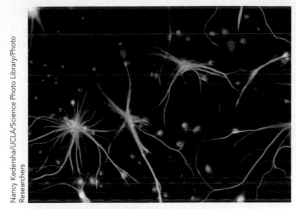

REAPING THE BENEFITS

Long-term exercise increases the number of glial cells (shown here stained with green fluorescent dyes) in the prefrontal cortex, a brain region important for reward learning and cognitive function. Glial cells assist with synaptic function and provide growth factors to sustain neurons, so an increase in their number may improve prefrontal function, potentially enhancing the rewards of running.

Nancy Kedersha/UCLA/Science Photo Library/Photo Researchers

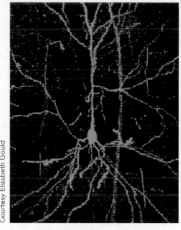

Courtesy Elizabeth Gould

GROWING NEURONS WHILE YOU BUILD MUSCLE

One of the long-term benefits of getting in shape by running is that exercise stimulates the growth of new dendrites and new synaptic connections in the neocortex (shown here in this temporal lobe pyramidal neuron stained with a fluorescent dye). More connections likely translate into greater brain function, enhancing learning and memory.

GETTING THE BLOOD FLOWING

Aerobic exercise increases our heart rate, which sends more blood throughout our body as well as to the brain. Increased blood flow in runners is particularly evident in the hippocampus, shown here in colours on this brain scan. Since the hippocampus is important for anxiety regulation, increased blood flow may contribute to the calming and mood-elevating effects often associated with exercise.

S. Small, et al., Proc Natl Acad Sci USA 104(13):5638-43, 2007

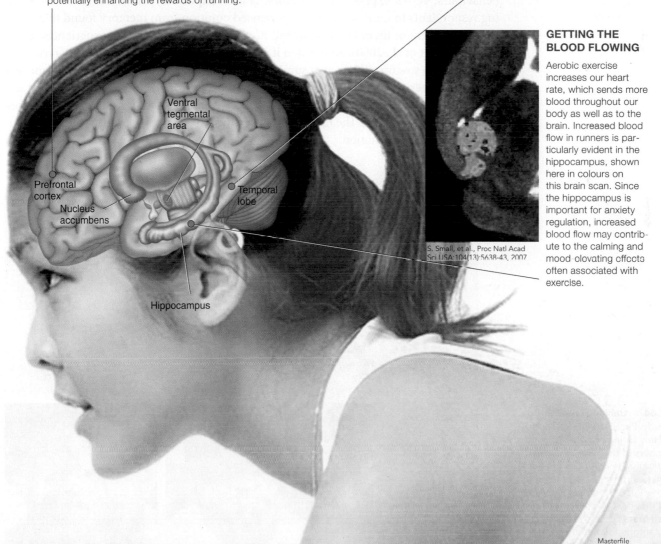

Ventral tegmental area

Prefrontal cortex

Nucleus accumbens

Temporal lobe

Hippocampus

Masterfile

If you asked people whether they preferred to feel fear or vicarious (observed in others) love, the answer would be obvious—right? Then consider this: the adjusted box office revenues of the top 25 horror films surpass those of the top 25 romances by over a billion dollars— even with *Titanic*, the highest-grossing movie of all time, included among the romances. (MPAA/Box Office Mojo, 2014)

Research suggests that most people are able to accurately identify the facial expressions associated with a number of basic emotions. Paul Ekman, a pioneer in the study of emotion and facial expressions, conducted a series of studies in which participants were asked to identify which emotion an individual was experiencing on the basis of the individual's facial cues (Cohn, Ambadar, & Ekman, 2007; Ekman, 2003; Ekman & Friesen, 1975) (see **Figure 64-1**). The television series "Lie to Me" starring Tim Roth (on Fox Broadcasting Company, 2009–2011) was based on Ekman's work. Ekman and his colleagues found that research participants can typically identify six fundamental emotions: anger, sadness, happiness, surprise, fear, and disgust. In fact, some research suggests that the ability to identify the facial expressions for these emotions is genetically programmed (Izard, 2009, 1997, 1977).

This would explain why even people from different countries and cultures seem able to recognize the same emotions depicted in photographs of facial expressions (Ekman et al., 1987; Ekman & Friesen, 1986). More recent research has suggested that the difficulty of this task varies depending on the culture of the face being read, similar to making sense of differences in language dialect from one group to another (Elfenbein, 2013).

Although less fundamental to emotional expression than non-verbal emotional behaviours, verbal expression of emotion is also important (Rimé, 2007). Studies asking respondents to recall a recently experienced emotion from memory found that more than 90 percent of them had already talked with someone about that experienced emotion (Luminet et al., 2000). And, when it comes to emotions, once people get started, it's hard for them to stop talking; after someone discloses an emotional experience to another person, that person often discusses it with yet a third person. Researchers Christophe and Rimé (2001, 1997) reported that this so-called *secondary social sharing* occurs in more than two-thirds of cases. The likelihood of sharing experiences increases with the intensity of the reported emotion.

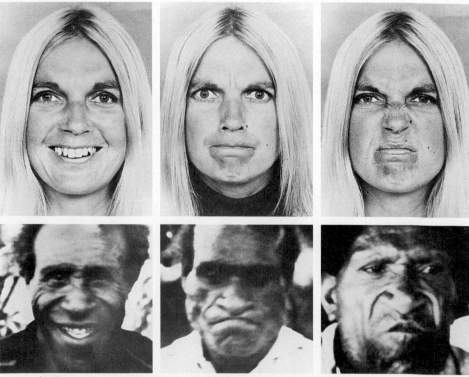

FIGURE 64-1 Universal recognition. In one study, Paul Ekman travelled to parts of New Guinea where he found that members of the Fore tribe could readily identify the emotions of happiness, anger, and disgust expressed on a Westerner's face (top row). Similarly, he found that college students in the United States easily recognized the same emotions when they were expressed on a Fore tribe member's face (lower row).

Courtesy of P. Ekman, Human Interaction Lab, University of California, San Francisco

It may be that some people have particular difficulty with the cognitive processing of emotion. Researchers have called this difficulty *alexithymia*, and have demonstrated that people with high scores on this personality-related dimension have more difficulty remembering emotion-related words (Luminet et al., 2006). Other researchers have shown that the specific areas of the brain involved in emotion processing (for example, areas of the prefrontal cortex and amygdala) are less active in individuals high on the alexithymia dimension when they are viewing emotional content (van der Velde et al., 2013).

An interesting aspect of behavioural expressions of emotion is that just by pretending to express the emotion, people may begin to experience that emotion—a phenomenon you will come across again later in this part. It is worth noting here because it suggests a strong interdependency among the three components of emotion. As we shall soon see, this complex relationship makes the development of a comprehensive theory of emotion a daunting endeavour.

64.2 Measurement of Emotions and Detecting Lies

How can you tell when someone is lying? We tend to believe that liars make less eye contact than do people telling the truth, but it turns out that is not true (Mann et al., 2012). Detecting lies has usually involved trying to detect the emotions we would expect liars to be experiencing. The problem with this approach, and the problem with polygraph machines designed to detect lies, is that many people who show emotions suggesting they might be lying are in fact telling the truth and are feeling emotions related to fear that they will not be believed. As a result, data generated through the use of classic lie detecting machines are not reliable and are not admissible in courts of law (Iacono & Lykken, 1997).

© Guy Bell/Alamy

Emotions and psychophysiological changes. Lie detectors track some of the psychophysiological changes associated with emotions.

When researchers attempt to measure emotion they typically use three kinds of information to measure an individual's emotions: (1) behavioural displays of emotion, (2) self-reports of emotion, and (3) physiological reactions.

Behavioural displays of emotion are most often observed by objective raters. These displays typically include obvious acts, such as fighting, fleeing, or making sexual advances. Behavioural displays may also include facial expressions. Researchers often observe behavioural displays in role-playing situations. The researchers attempt to evoke particular emotional responses from participants by showing them a film, giving them a small gift, or manipulating them in some other way (Isen, 2008, 2004, 1993), and then measure how well the participants perform on tasks of various kinds.

Self-ratings are the most widely-used approach to measuring a person's emotional experience. The use of such measures is based on the premise that the best way to evaluate emotional states is to simply ask individuals how they are feeling. Many questionnaires and surveys have been published that ask people to provide ratings for how happy, afraid, content, anxious, or depressed they are. However, self-reports may be inaccurate at times, as they provide only a limited picture of a person's total emotional experience and rely on a person's ability to properly identify and describe an emotional experience. For these same reasons, self-reports do not work well with children.

In recent years, researchers have developed several techniques for measuring an individual's *psychophysiological reactions* to stimuli, and have begun using such measures to assess emotional experiences (Santerre & Allen, 2007; Bradley & Lang, 2002). This approach is based on the premise that emotions vary biologically from one another, although this approach does involve some inference and assumes that there are distinct physiological patterns associated with particular emotions (Bradley & Lang, 2007, 2000). These new tools allow the measurement of emotion to go beyond questionnaire-based assessments and may provide a more thorough and accurate report of many of the processes involved in the experience of emotion (Sloan, 2004). Psychophysiological approaches include facial electromyography and assessments of heart rate, skin conductance, and the startle reflex.

- *Facial electromyography (EMG)* When a person is exposed to an emotionally-charged stimulus, such as a pleasant or unpleasant picture, certain facial muscles contract. A facial EMG measures these contractions. Studies have found that emotional reactions to unpleasant stimuli, such as pictures of mutilated bodies, are often associated with greater activity of the muscles used in frowning. That is, when we are exposed to distressing stimuli, we tend to lower and contract our eyebrows (Sloan et al., 2002; Gentsch, Grandjean, & Scherer, 2014). Conversely, when individuals are shown pleasant stimuli, such as scenic images, they display heightened activity of the facial muscles responsible for smiling.

    - *Heart rate* Reductions in heart rate have been observed when individuals are presented with unpleasant/fearful stimuli, whereas pleasant stimuli are associated with accelerations in heart rate (Löw et al., 2008; Bradley & Lang, 2000; Bradley, Cuthbert, & Lang, 1990).

    - *Skin conductance* We tend to perspire when we are emotionally aroused. One technique developed to detect and measure emotional arousal involves placing a large electrode on part of the palm of a person's hand and determining from readings of the electrode how well the skin of the hand conducts electrical activity. This technique measures what is called the galvanic skin response—or the electrical resistance of the skin—and reflects increased perspiration, so a higher conductance reading means greater arousal of emotions. Readings of skin conductance are a very useful indicator of emotional arousal (either positive or negative) and of sympathetic nervous system activity.

©iStockphoto.com/Latsalomao

Detecting facial changes. EMG measurements indicate that each emotion is accompanied by a distinct set of facial muscle contractions.

- *Startle reflex* An additional physiological indicator of emotional reactivity is the startle reflex, an involuntary movement (an eye blink, for example) that is brought on by the onset of a sudden stimulus, such as a loud burst of noise. Researchers usually measure startle reflexes by placing tiny electrodes on the muscle just below a person's eye, and assessing the magnitude of involuntary eye blinks that occur when people are startled while viewing pleasant and unpleasant pictures. Studies have revealed that eye blinks that occur while people are viewing unpleasant pictures are more pronounced than those that occur while they are viewing pleasant pictures (Bradley et al., 2007, 1990; Mallan & Lipp, 2007; Bradley, Cuthbert, & Lang, 1991). This would suggest that the underlying physiological aspects of emotion vary with type of emotional response, although this is still an inference.

- *fMRI* Recent research has demonstrated that it may be possible to reliably detect patterns of activity in the brain associated with lying (Farah et al., 2014). Thus far this approach has proved quite accurate when used at a population level (detecting a group of people asked to lie as part of a study), but lower levels of accuracy in liar detection have been shown at the individual level. As such, this technique is not yet considered admissible in court proceedings.

Although psychophysiological measures of emotion are in some respects more valid and reliable indicators of emotional states than behavioural displays and self-ratings, most investigators of emotion agree that the complexity of emotion is best measured by using multiple approaches. This also acts as a check on the possibility that we have inferred the presence of physiological reactions that may not actually be so unique. Thus, the integration of all three types of measures provides the richest picture of a person's overall emotional experience.

64.3 Functions of Emotions

Since ancient times, philosophers have often considered emotion inferior to reason, but modern researchers who study emotion have emphasized its positive effects. William James (1842–1910), perhaps the most influential emotion researcher of the last 150 years, declared that, without emotion, consciousness and cognition would be "void of human significance" (1890, p. 471). Emotions provide colour to our every experience and lie at the heart of what makes life worth living. Can you imagine riding a roller coaster without experiencing exhilaration (or fear)? How about watching your favourite movie, holding a newborn or a pet, playing your favourite sport, or spending time with your best friends without feeling some happiness or satisfaction? Without emotions, our enjoyable activities and experiences might not seem very rewarding. Clearly emotions play a large role in the meaning we take from our experiences. In this area, emotions can serve cognitive, behavioural, and social functions.

64.3.1 Cognitive Functions

One function of emotions is to help us organize our memories. As we discussed in Part 8, memories associated with emotional content are much easier to recall (Abercrombie et al., 2008). Emotions also help us to prioritize our concerns, needs, or goals in a given moment (Morris, 1992). The information we gain from noticing our emotions may help us form judgments and make decisions (Gohm & Clore, 2002). For example, a strong feeling of fear when you are preparing to withdraw money from an ATM at night in a dark and scary area of town will make it easy for you to decide to find a better location for your banking.

> "Human behaviour flows from three main sources: desire, emotion, and knowledge."
>
> —*Plato, Greek philosopher*

64.3.2 Behavioural Functions

Emotions, whether positive or negative, can not only help us perform cognitive tasks, such as remembering relevant information, prioritizing our goals, and making decisions, they can also organize our behaviour. Generally speaking, we act to minimize our experience of negative emotions and maximize our experience of positive emotions. Such actions can involve basic behaviours, including diverting our attention away from unpleasant or disgusting images in favour of more neutral or positive images, as well as more complex behaviours, such as procrastination. You have probably noticed a correlation between how terrible you believe the experience of working on a homework assignment will be and how long you delay starting that assignment. In contrast, it is very easy to find time for tasks that we find enjoyable or pleasurable, such as spending time with a partner, and these tasks are hard to delay. In this way, our emotions can help us organize our behaviours (although admittedly in ways that sometimes run counter to what is in our best interest).

Some theorists describe emotions as indicators that serve a valuable information function, telling us how to respond appropriately to events in our environments (Frijda, 2010, 2007; Parrott, 2004, 2001). Many theorists also believe that particular emotions are associated with predictable patterns of behaviour, sometimes called *action tendencies*, which help us to adapt and survive in our social and physical environments (Frijda, 2010, 2007; Gross, 1998; Lang, Bradley, & Cuthbert, 1998). Specific action tendencies associated with key emotions include the following:

- *Happiness* results when people engage in rewarding behaviours or positive interactions. Because they feel happiness and joy, they will likely continue to engage in those behaviours or interactions. Happiness and joy also signal to people that particular goals have been attained (Carver, 2004; Fredrickson, 2001).

©iStockphoto.com/Blend_Images

"Let's do this again soon." Emotions can be viewed as messengers that predict particular action tendencies. A family gathering brings this family so much joy, they are likely to repeat the activity again and again.

- *Embarrassment* often evokes forgiveness and motivates reconciliation and adherence to social norms (Parrott, 2004, 2001; Keltner & Kring, 1998). Consider, for example, that you tell one friend you are busy studying and then, when another friend asks you to go to a movie you want to see, you change your mind about studying and go to the movie. You run into the first friend at the movie. Embarrassment may not only lead you to apologize profusely, but also help to ensure that you will not do such a potentially hurtful thing again. Similarly, guilt directs people's awareness toward their transgressions and may trigger conciliatory efforts, personal change, and self-improvement.
- *Anger* signals the presence of injustice and prompts aggression, as well as other self-protective behaviours (Mayer & Salovey, 2004, 1997).
- *Anxiety* directs a person's attention toward potential threats and motivates appropriate action to avoid or cope with them (Öhman, 2000).
- *Sadness* may signal the loss of positive relationships and help people to seek needed support and assistance from others (Oatley & Jenkins, 1996; Campos, Campos, & Barrett, 1989).

Research suggests that the avoidance of negative emotion is typically a more powerful motivator than the achievement of positive emotion (Cacioppo & Berntsen, 1994).

64.3.3 Social Functions

Another important function of emotions appears to be coordination of relationships. Emotions form the foundations of relationships by helping us develop a sense that we like and trust another person. In one study, for example, viewers assigned more positive ratings of friendliness and competence to people who showed a sincere smile in their yearbook photographs than to those whose pictures had fake smiles or no smiles (Harker & Keltner, 2001).

Emotions, even when they are negative, can also improve the quality of our relationships. Research suggests, for example, that the more married couples talk about their feelings, the happier they are (Gottman & Notarius, 2002). In contrast, keeping our emotions inside may get in the way of our ability to form lasting relationships. One study found that participants who habitually kept their emotions to themselves were more likely to report problems with closeness and sharing in intimate relationships than people who talked about their emotions (Gross & John, 2003). Stéphane Côté and Ivona Hideg at the University of Toronto have shown that the ability to influence the behaviours, attitudes, and emotions of other through emotional displays is positively related to perceived workplace competence (Côté & Hideg, 2011).

Before You Go On

www.wiley.com/go/comercanada

What Do You Know?

1. What system produces the bodily arousal associated with emotions?
2. What three types of information are most commonly used by researchers to measure emotions?
3. Name four physiological indicators of emotional state.
4. What are the major functions of emotion?

What Do You Think? Think about the BASE jumping activity described in our opening example and describe what you think are the physiological, cognitive, and behavioural motivational components of those who participate in such activities.

Summary

Module 64: What Is Emotion?

LEARNING OBJECTIVE 64 Define emotion and discuss the components, measurement, and functions of emotion.

- An emotion is an intrapersonal state that occurs in response to an external or internal event and includes three components: a physiological component, a cognitive component, and a behavioural component.
- Researchers typically use three kinds of information to measure emotion: behavioural displays of emotion, self-reports of emotion, and physiological reactions.
- Emotions serve many functions. They add colour to our lives, give us information about important events in the environment, stir us to action when necessary, and help us to coordinate relationships with others.

Key Term

emotion 490

Study Questions

Multiple Choice

1. The sweaty palms and rapid heartbeat we experience as anxiety are most directly related to activation of which portion of the nervous system?
   a) Autonomic nervous system
   b) Hippocampus
   c) Occipital lobes
   d) Somatic nervous system

Fill-in-the-Blank

1. A driver who swerves to avoid a crash, then notices that his breathing and heartbeat are rapid, is experiencing the _____ component of emotion.

Module 65: Theories of Emotion

How do emotions occur? What causes them? How have they evolved in the human species? How do they develop in individuals as they move from infancy to adulthood? And what's going on in the brain while all this is happening? These are the core questions for understanding emotions, and we will turn to them next.

Since the birth of psychology, a number of theories have been proposed to explain how emotions occur and what causes them. The most prominent of these theories are: the James-Lange theory, the Cannon-Bard theory, the Schacter and Singer two-factor theory, the cognitive-mediational theory, and the facial-feedback theory. Each theory proposes a different explanation of the sequence of an emotional episode, and each emphasizes a particular component of emotion (physiological, cognitive, or behavioural). In addition, evolutionary theory has important things to say about the origins of emotion.

65.1 James-Lange Theory

As we observed earlier, William James was the earliest and one of the most influential psychologists to study emotion. James took issue with the conventional common-sense explanation of emotion, which suggested that an event triggers an emotion, which leads to physiological changes, followed by a behavioural response to the situation.

James (1884, 1890) argued that emotions actually work differently. He suggested that an emotion begins with (1) the perception of an environmental situation or event, followed by (2) the elicitation of physiological and behavioural changes, which are then (3) processed by the cortex and converted into felt emotion. James believed that our physiological response to a stimulus occurs prior to, and provides the basis for, the experience of a particular emotion.

In 1885, a Danish physiologist, Carl Lange (1834–1900), published a theory of emotion that was very similar to James's. Both theorists believed that there is no emotion to experience unless it is driven by a physiological component (Davidson, Jackson, & Kalin, 2000). Their views are collectively referred to as the **James-Lange theory of emotion**.

James-Lange theory of emotion a theory proposing that felt emotions result from physiological changes, rather than being their cause.

Although the two theories are very similar, they do have a few key differences. Whereas James believed there is a place for cognition in the context of an emotional episode, Lange viewed mental activity as having little to do with emotion. Lange (1885) postulated instead that the *vasomotor centre*, a collection of nerves and muscles that cause the blood vessels to constrict or dilate, is the root cause of all emotion: "We owe all the emotional side of our mental life, our joys and sorrows, our happy and unhappy hours, to our vasomotor system" (p. 80). **Figure 65-1** compares the James-Lange theory with the two theories that we will turn to next, the Cannon-Bard theory and the Schachter and Singer two-factor theory.

65.2 Cannon-Bard Theory

The James-Lange theory of emotion produced quite a stir in the fields of psychology and physiology, and much research was published disputing various aspects of the theory. The leading critic of the James-Lange theory was Harvard psychologist Walter Cannon (1871–1945). Central to Cannon's criticism was the James-Lange theory's notion that *visceral organs*—that is, our internal organs in which physiological arousal occurs, such as the heart—can produce complex emotional experiences. Pointing to a number of research findings, Cannon disputed the accuracy of the James-Lange theory on five different points (1927):

1. *Total separation of the visceral organs from the central nervous system does not alter emotional behaviour.* Cannon cited research on dogs and cats whose vasomotor centres had been disconnected from their central nervous systems. Even

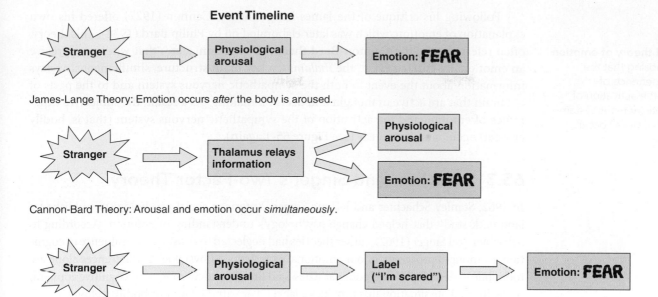

Event Timeline

James-Lange Theory: Emotion occurs *after* the body is aroused.

Cannon-Bard Theory: Arousal and emotion occur *simultaneously*.

Schachter and Singer's Two-Factor Theory: Cognition plays a role in labelling emotion.

FIGURE 65-1 Three major theories of emotion. The three major theories of emotion have different ways of accounting for how someone surprised by a stranger would react emotionally.

without the vasomotor centre that Lange believed to be of utmost importance, cats and dogs continued to display aggression and rage in the usual way (Bard, 1934). Similarly, more recent studies indicate that most human patients with spinal cord injuries continue to experience emotional excitability that is similar to their functioning prior to injury; some actually report an increase in the intensity of particular emotions (Bermond et al., 1991; Chwalisz, Diener, & Gallager, 1988).

2. *The same visceral changes often occur in different emotional states and in non-emotional states.* Recall that the arousal associated with emotions arises from the sympathetic nervous system. Cannon argued that, because the activity of the sympathetic nervous system is typically general and non-specific, several emotions probably share similar patterns of visceral activity. Cannon further noted that certain non-emotional events, such as fever, produce patterns of sympathetic nervous system activity that are similar to the patterns that accompany emotions, although they are not experienced as emotions.

3. *The viscera are rather insensitive structures.* According to Cannon, "We can feel the thumping of the heart because it presses against the chest wall, we can also feel the throbbing of the blood vessels because they pass through tissues well supplied with sensory nerves . . . [but], normally, the visceral processes are extraordinarily unde monstrative" (1927, p. 111).

4. *Visceral changes are too slow to be the source of emotional feeling.* Cannon argued that the amount of time it takes for the body's vasomotor system to communicate with the brain and send impulses back to the rest of the body is too slow "to be the occasion for the appearance of affective states" (1927, p. 112).

5. *Artificially inducing visceral changes does not produce strong emotions.* Citing research by Spanish psychologist Gregorio Marañón (1924), Cannon pointed out that the injection of adrenalin, a stimulant, into the bloodstream of research participants, which activates the sympathetic nervous system and produces visceral changes characteristic of intense emotions, does not lead to discrete and identifiable emotional reactions.

Cannon-Bard theory of emotion a theory proposing that the subjective experience of emotion and the activation of the sympathetic nervous system (that is, bodily arousal) occur simultaneously.

Following his critique of the James-Lange theory, Cannon (1927) offered his own explanation of emotion, which was later elaborated on by Philip Bard (1934). This theory, often referred to as the **Cannon-Bard theory of emotion**, states that when we perceive an emotionally-stirring event, the *thalamus*, a key brain structure, simultaneously relays information about the event to both the sympathetic nervous system and to the parts of the brain that are active in thought and decision making. As a result, the subjective experience of emotion and the activation of the sympathetic nervous system (that is, bodily arousal) occur simultaneously (see Figure 65-1 again).

65.3 Schachter and Singer's Two-Factor Theory

In 1962, Stanley Schachter and Jerome Singer, American social psychologists, published a landmark study that helped change psychology's understanding of emotion. According to Schachter and Singer (1962), earlier theories had neglected to consider the influence of cognition, or thought processes, in our emotional experiences. Physiological differences alone are too subtle to define specific emotional states, said these researchers; it is our cognitive appraisal of the immediate situation that provides a label ("I am afraid") for our bodily feelings.

Schachter and Singer's two-factor theory of emotion a theory proposing that an emotional state is a function of both physiological arousal and cognition.

According to **Schachter and Singer's two-factor theory of emotion**, "It is the cognition which determines whether the state of physiological arousal will be labeled as 'anger,' 'joy,' 'fear,' or 'whatever'" (Schachter & Singer, 1962, p. 380). Schachter and Singer suggested that, although physiological arousal is *necessary* for an emotion to occur—in fact it determines the intensity of the emotional experience—it's up to our cognitive faculties to determine our specific emotional state (see Figure 65-1).

If we were to apply Schachter and Singer's two-factor theory to the situation of a child receiving a shot, we would assume that the severity of the child's actions was determined by his level of physiological arousal. If his arousal had been mild or moderate, he might have appraised the situation differently ("This is not so bad") and might have responded in a mildly fearful or stressful way (making a face or saying "ouch"). If instead he experienced intense physiological arousal and appraised the situation in a way that led to terror ("This is going to be unbearable"), this would make him respond in ways that ultimately make the situation much more difficult.

Schachter and Singer's two-factor theory also suggests that, when the cause of our physical arousal is not immediately clear to us, we use cues from our surroundings to help us identify a cause. This can lead to mislabelling physical arousal from a non-emotional source as an emotion. Schacter and Singer (1962) conducted a well-known experiment at the University of Minnesota to test this idea (see **Figure 65-2**). They told undergraduate research participants that the study was examining the effects of a vitamin supplement (they called it *Suproxin*) on vision.

When the students arrived at the lab, they were met by an experimenter and told that they would be receiving a small injection of Suproxin and then would complete several vision tests. The participants received an injection of either epinephrine (adrenalin) or a placebo (saline solution). By producing physiological arousal, the epinephrine injections mimicked sympathetic nervous system activation. Among those who received epinephrine, one-third (the *informed group*) were told they might experience side effects, such as palpitations, trembling, and facial flushing; one-third (the *deceived group*) were told they would experience no side effects; and one-third (the *misinformed group*) were told they would experience side effects that were not in fact likely to occur, such as

© Agencja Fotograficzna Caro/Alamy

Theories of emotion. The timing of and relationships among the situations we find ourselves in, our internal physiological arousal, and our interpretations of what our circumstances mean to us are all part of the various theories of emotion. While no child likes getting shots, how intensely he or she responds can vary by age and culture.

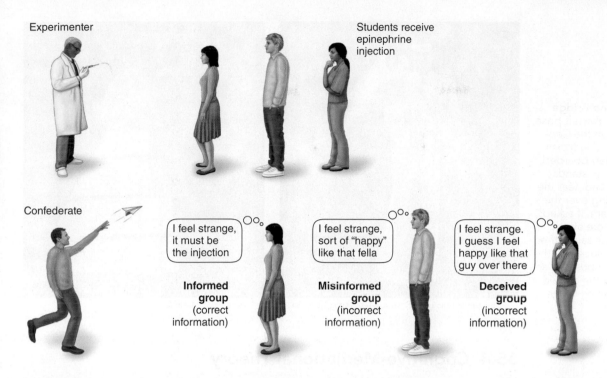

Experimenter

Students receive
epinephrine
injection

Confederate

I feel strange,
it must be
the injection

**Informed
group**
(correct
information)

I feel strange,
sort of "happy"
like that fella

**Misinformed
group**
(incorrect
information)

I feel strange.
I guess I feel
happy like that
guy over there

**Deceived
group**
(incorrect
information)

FIGURE 65-2 Testing the two-factor theory. In the absence of correct information, participants in the deceived and misinformed groups who received the epinephrine injection concluded that they were feeling happy, like the confederate who had acted euphoric.

headaches. All the participants in the placebo group were told they would have no side effects from their injections. After the participants were given the drug, a confederate of the experimenters' entered the room and acted either euphoric or angry. These manipulations allowed Schachter and Singer to create a scenario in which participants experienced bodily arousal either with or without plausible explanations for it.

As Schachter and Singer's two-factor theory had predicted, students who received an epinephrine injection but were not given a proper explanation for their bodily arousal (the deceived and misinformed groups) later reported feelings of anger or euphoria when they encountered an angry or euphoric confederate (acting that way on the instructions of the experimenter). In contrast, students in the epinephrine condition who were told to anticipate various symptoms of sympathetic nervous system activity (informed group) did not experience anger or euphoria—they were immune to any effects of the arousal manipulation. Clearly, the label of an emotion is influenced by whether or not a person has an appropriate explanation for the arousal.

Schachter and Singer's two-factor theory served to redirect the focus of emotion research toward the role of cognitive factors. Indeed, a number of studies have since provided indirect evidence for their two-factor theory. In a classic study conducted by Don Dutton of the University of British Columbia, for example, male participants were approached by an attractive female (a confederate of the researchers) and asked to complete questionnaires. Males approached by the woman while crossing the Capilano Suspension Bridge in British Columbia—a long, narrow footbridge constructed of wooden boards and wire cables suspended about 30 metres (100 feet) above a river and near very dramatic falls—later reported being more attracted to the female confederate than males who met the same woman on a wider, sturdier bridge only about 3 metres (10 feet) above the river (Dutton & Aron, 1974). The researchers concluded that the men on the shaky Capilano Bridge had experienced anxious arousal because of the height of the bridge and had misinterpreted this arousal as sexual attraction—findings consistent with Schachter and Singer's two-factor theory.

Echoes of the Capilano Bridge study. The couple on the left pose for wedding pictures on the Capilano Suspension Bridge in North Vancouver. This wooden-boarded, not-so-sturdy footbridge stands high above the water and near the sounds of water pouring over the top of the Capilano dam. If asked, they might well talk more about their strong feelings for each other rather than any fear induced by the swaying bridge and sounds of rushing water. What about the couple on the right on their much lower, less threatening bridge?

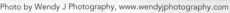

Photo by Wendy J Photography, www.wendyjphotography.com   ©iStockphoto.com/Kempter

65.4 Cognitive-Mediational Theory

One theory that built on Schachter and Singer's ideas was developed by Richard Lazarus, an influential psychologist at the University of California, Berkeley. As we shall see in Part 14, Lazarus spent much of his career investigating the role of appraisal in people's reactions to stress (Lazarus, 2007; Lazarus et al., 1965; Lazarus & Alfert, 1964). Eventually, Lazarus came to believe that appraisal must play a similar role in emotional experiences to that which it plays in stress reactions. Unlike Schachter and Singer's two-factor theory, Lazarus's theory holds that appraisal affects not only how people interpret physical arousal, but also the level of arousal itself. As such, the **cognitive-mediational theory of emotion** views cognitive interpretations of events as playing a still broader role in the experience of emotion.

In one of his early studies, for example, Lazarus and his colleagues had participants watch stressful films (featuring, for example, skin-piercing rituals among Australian tribesmen) while their autonomic nervous system activity was measured and their subjective reports of stress were recorded. Some of the viewers were told "the people in this film were not hurt or distressed by what is happening," while others were told, "many of the people you see in this film suffered severe pain and infection from these rituals." By influencing the way the participants construed what was happening in the films, Lazarus and his colleagues found they could greatly alter the participants' physiological activity and subjective stress reactions while viewing. That is, appraisal serves as a *cognitive mediator* between environmental stimuli and people's reaction to those stimuli (Lazarus, 2007, 1993).

cognitive-mediational theory of emotion a theory proposing that cognitive interpretations, particularly appraisals, of events are the keys to experiences of emotion.

65.5 Facial-Feedback Theory

We mentioned earlier, in discussing the behavioural component of emotion, that people may begin to experience an emotion just by pretending to express it. Related to this observation is the **facial-feedback theory of emotion**, which is derived from Charles Darwin's early (1872) notion that muscular activity can either strengthen or lessen the experience of emotion. According to the current facial-feedback perspective, our subjective experiences of emotion are influenced by sensory feedback we receive from the activity of our facial muscles, our **facial efference** (Izard, 2007, 1997, 1977; Tomkins, 1962). Thus, facial expressions not only express a given emotion, but also intensify the physiological experience of that emotion.

facial-feedback theory of emotion a theory proposing that subjective experiences of emotion are influenced by sensory feedback from facial muscular activity, or facial efference.

facial efference sensory feedback from facial muscular activity.

In one study, for example, participants were directed to move their facial muscles into certain positions, without directly being told which emotions they were expressing. The facial changes produced significant changes in their autonomic nervous system arousal, as indicated by increases in their heart rates, skin conductance, and finger temperatures (Ekman, Levenson, & Friesen, 1983). In a related study, research participants held pens in their mouths while rating the funniness of cartoons (Strack, Martin, & Stepper, 1988). This approach enabled the experimenters to manipulate the participants' facial expressions without calling attention to their facial activity or to the emotions normally associated with that activity. People directed to hold the pen in their teeth made a face similar to a smile, while those directed to hold the pen with their lips were unable to smile (**Figure 65-3**). Sure enough, individuals who held the pen in their teeth found the cartoons funnier than those who held the pen in their lips.

The facial-feedback theory of emotion has also been supported by studies of the *Duchenne smile*, named after French neurologist Guillaume Duchenne. Duchenne observed that smiles reflecting genuine emotion involve the activity of certain muscles near the mouth and the eyes, whereas more artificial "social smiles" involve only muscles near the mouth (see **Figure 65-4**). One experiment found that participants who displayed genuine Duchenne smiles while viewing a positive film clip displayed greater physiological arousal and experienced more positive emotion than other participants (Soussignan, 2002; Krumhuber, Likowski, & Weyers, 2014).

How might facial expressions produce physiological arousal and the subjective experience of emotion? Several explanations have been proposed. It may be that facial expressions serve as *relays* between an emotionally-stirring event and a resulting subjective experience of emotion. Indeed, psychologist Silvan Tomkins (1962) argued that emotionally-stirring stimuli activate an inborn, almost reflexive "affect program" that sends signals throughout the body by motor and circulatory pathways, bypassing the parts of the brain involved in cognition. The body reacts to these signals in forms, such as facial expressions (smiles, frowns) and other activities, which then supply sensory feedback to the brain, producing the experience of an emotion. Tomkins (1992, 1980) further argued that receptors in the face change position when people contract their facial muscles and that this sensory information is also sent to the brain, ultimately leading to a felt emotion.

> Check this out for yourself. Have several friends hold a pen in their lips for 2 minutes and then ask them to rate their level of happiness on a 1 to 10 point scale. Have another group of friends hold a pen in their teeth for 2 minutes and then rate their happiness on the same scale. Which group had the highest average happiness ratings?

Another theory is that patterns of facial muscle activity change the temperature of blood entering the brain, and by doing so affect neuron activity in the brain, eventually producing particular emotional states. In one study, researchers had research participants repeat a series of vowel sounds—*i, e, o, a, ü, ah*, and *u*—while measuring blood temperature in the participants' brains and asking them to provide a general rating of their emotional state (pleasant versus unpleasant, for example) (Zajonc, Murphy, & Inglehart,

Mark Owens/John Wiley & Sons, Inc.

Courtesy Karen Huffman

FIGURE 65-3 Testing the facial-feedback theory. When you hold a pen between your teeth, you activate facial muscles that are associated with a smile and you are more likely to report pleasant feelings than if you held the pen between your lips (Strack, Martin, & Stepper, 1988).

FIGURE 65-4 Genuine versus artificial smiles. Real or Duchenne smiles reflect genuine emotion and involve muscles near the mouth and the eyes (*left*). Social or artificial smiles involve only muscles near the mouth (*right*).

1989). The researchers hypothesized that the pronunciation of *e* and *ah* would produce muscular patterns similar to that of a smile and an expression of surprise, respectively. Similarly, the long *u* sound, *ü*, was expected to mimic aspects of facial expressions associated with negative emotions.

The results showed that facial efference of this kind did indeed produce negative and positive feelings, as well as corresponding changes in brain blood temperature. Apparently, saying the long *u* sound restricts people's ability to breathe through their noses. Breathing through the nose generally cools our blood before it reaches our brains. Because participants in the Zajonc study were breathing less through their noses, they experienced a rise in brain blood temperature and, along with that, a rise in negative emotions. In contrast, the pronunciation of *e* and *ah* increases nose breathing, allowing the cooling of blood travelling to the brain, and ultimately produces positive emotional experiences—a pattern also confirmed by participants in this study.

It is important to note that none of the theories just discussed seems to explain emotion completely. As psychologist Robert Zajonc has said, "It is unlikely that all emotions have the same etiology, are characterized by the same affective and cognitive processes, . . . or have the same underlying neuroanatomical structure and neurochemical actions" (Zajonc et al., 1989, p. 412). Thus, one emotional experience may result largely from a singular source, such as physiological arousal, cognitive appraisal, or facial expression, while others may be the product of a combination of these factors.

Masterfile

Negative emotions. Zajonc claimed that negative emotions may result from a rise in brain blood temperature.

65.6 Evolutionary Theory

Over the past 50 years, a number of theorists have suggested that emotions are innate, prewired responses that have evolved over millions of years from lower species to humans (Izard, 2007; Cosmides & Tooby, 2000; Plutchik, 1980). This perspective is based on the evolutionary theory of Charles Darwin, described in Parts 1 and 3.

In 1872, having noted the similarities in emotional expression across and within species throughout the world, Darwin published *The Expression of the Emotions in Man and Animals*. Here he argued that emotional expression in both people and animals serves a *communicative* function that is essential to survival. Emotional expressions may, for example, warn others of danger, dissuade enemies from attacking, or signal sexual receptiveness (Seyfarth & Cheney, 2003; LeDoux, 1996).

Evolutionary psychologists argue that certain emotions have been passed down through the generations because they have played an integral role in the survival of our species (Nesse & Ellsworth, 2009; Nesse, 1990). It may even be that each emotion corresponds to a particular situation that has occurred repeatedly throughout the course of evolution, and that each emotion increases an individual's ability to cope with the adaptive challenges that arise in such a situation (see **Table 65-1**). For example, organisms that experienced fear when confronted by predators most likely survived at a much higher rate than those that experienced calm during such interactions. Over time, as this situation was repeated, fear became a characteristic response to danger and, eventually, an innate, prewired, and automatic response. Such patterns of emotionality have been genetically passed on to us from generations of ancestors, making our lives much easier than if we were required to learn about every aspect of our environmental surroundings without their guidance.

TABLE 65-1 Evolutionary Links Between Emotion and Behaviour in Humans and Other Animals

Situation	Emotion	Survival Function
Threat	Fear, terror, anxiety	Fight, flight
Obstacle	Anger, rage	Biting, hitting
Potential mate	Joy, ecstasy, excitement	Courtship, mating
Loss of valued person	Sadness, grief	Crying for help
Sudden novel object	Surprise	Stopping, attending

Source: Adapted with permission of John Wiley & Sons, Inc., from Kowalski, R., & Westen, D. (2009). *Psychology* (5th ed.). Hoboken, NJ: Wiley, p. 361; data from Plutchik, R. (1980). *Emotions: A psychoevolutionary synthesis.* New York: Harper & Row.

Much of the research support for an evolutionary explanation of emotion centres on the universal and innate nature of facial expressions of emotion. As we observed earlier, Paul Ekman and his colleagues have conducted a series of studies on facial expressions of emotion (Cohn et al., 2007; Ekman, 2003; Ekman & Friesen, 1971). They found that individuals from many different cultural and language backgrounds, when presented with photographs of different facial expressions, are fairly accurate at selecting the emotions being expressed.

Based on such research on the universality of certain facial expressions and the evolution of emotion, a number of theorists have suggested that some innate, **basic emotions** are preprogrammed into all people, regardless of culture or country of origin. Tomkins (1962) has proposed that there are eight basic emotions: surprise, interest, joy, rage, fear, disgust, shame, and anguish. Other notable theorists have proposed similar lists (Frijda, 1986; Plutchik, 1980; Izard, 1977). Indeed, it appears that infants typically display the facial expressions of such fundamental emotions very early in life (Izard, 1994). Even children who are born without sight display facial expressions similar to those of sighted children of the same age (Galati et al., 2003; Goodenough, 1932).

basic emotions a group of emotions preprogrammed into all humans regardless of culture.

Before You Go On

www.wiley.com/go/comercanada

What Do You Know?
1. What is the key idea in the James-Lange theory of emotion?
2. What are Cannon's arguments disputing this idea?
3. What element did Schachter and Singer's two-factor theory add to explanations of what determines emotional experience?
4. What is facial efference?
5. What does it mean to say that emotions have been shaped by natural selection?

What Do You Think? Recall a powerful emotional experience you have had. Which of the theories of emotion detailed in this part seems to best explain your experience? Is one theory sufficient?

Summary

Module 65: Theories of Emotion

LEARNING OBJECTIVE 65 Discuss the major theories of emotion, and identify the pathways through which emotions are experienced according to each theory.

- The conventional common-sense explanation of emotion holds that an event triggers an emotion, which leads to physiological changes, followed by a response to the situation.
- In contrast, the James-Lange theory proposes that the emotion we feel results from bodily and behavioural responses to environmental stimuli, rather than causing those responses.
- According to the Cannon-Bard theory, physiological arousal by itself cannot produce complex emotional experiences. Rather, the perception of an emotionally-stirring event simultaneously sends messages to parts of the brain responsible for the subjective experience of emotion and physiological arousal.
- Schachter and Singer's two-factor theory holds that an emotional state is a function of both physiological arousal and cognition.
- Building on Schachter and Singer's two-factor theory, cognitive-mediational theory proposes that cognitive interpretations, and particularly appraisals, of events are in fact the keys to the experience of emotions.
- The facial-feedback theory of emotion, based on the ideas of Darwin, holds that facial expressions that occur in response to stimuli provide feedback to the brain that helps to shape emotional experience.
- Evolutionary theorists believe that emotions have been shaped by natural selection and that certain emotions have been passed down because of their role in the survival of our species.

Key Terms

basic emotions 507

Cannon-Bard theory of
  emotion 502

cognitive-mediational theory
  of emotion 504

facial-feedback theory of
  emotion 504

facial efference 504

James-Lange theory of
  emotion 500

Schachter and Singer's
  two-factor theory of
  emotion 502

Study Questions

Multiple Choice

1. Which theorist suggested that physiological responses to a stimulus provide the basis for experiencing an emotion?
   a) Cannon
   b) James
   c) Schachter
   d) Watson

2. According to the Cannon-Bard theory of emotion, which structure relays information about an emotionally-stirring event to the sympathetic nervous system?
   a) Anterior cingulate cortex
   b) Cerebellum
   c) Frontal cortex
   d) Thalamus

Fill-in-the-Blank

1. The finding that most people with spinal cord injuries can still experience emotional arousal is supportive of the _____ theory of emotion.

2. Facial _____ refers to the idea that smiling can lead to a happier mood.

Module 66: What About Positive Emotions?

LEARNING OBJECTIVE 66
Identify some factors that
influence whether or not a
person is happy.

After reading about the work of early emotion researchers, you may think that psychologists have a great deal to say about unpleasant or negative emotions, such as fear, anxiety, anger, and sadness, but less to say about how people experience pleasant, positive emotions, including happiness, pride, and excitement. The past decade, however, has witnessed a striking rise in research on positive emotions, particularly happiness. As you will recall from Part 1, a major new trend in the field of psychology is to focus on positive psychology (Seligman & Csikszentmihalyi, 2014; Seligman, 2007; Seligman & Steen, 2005). *Positive psychology* is the study and enhancement of positive feelings, including happiness and optimism; positive traits, such as perseverance and wisdom; positive abilities, such as interpersonal skills; and virtues that enhance the well-being of society, including altruism and tolerance. Consistent with this important new field of psychology, researchers are now conducting numerous studies on happiness. We have learned that it is indeed one of the most important and adaptive of human emotions.

In fact, regarding happiness, the news seems to be quite good. Research indicates that people's lives are, in general, more upbeat than psychologists used to think. In fact, most people around the world say they are happy—including most of those who are poor, unemployed, elderly, and disabled (**Table 66-1**) (Becchetti & Santoro, 2007; Pugno, 2007; Wallis, 2005). Of course, happiness involves different things for different people.

Consider the following results:

- Wealthy people appear only slightly happier than those of modest means (Easterbrook, 2005; Diener et al., 1993).
- Although early studies suggested only a minimal relationship between age and happiness (Myers & Diener, 1997; Inglehart, 1990), more recent studies have found that, provided they remain healthy, people over 65 actually report more happiness and less negative emotion than do younger people (Mroczek & Spiro, 2007, 2005; Mroczek, 2004).
- Over 90 percent of people with quadriplegia say they are glad to be alive, and overall, people with spinal cord injuries report feeling only slightly less happy than other people (Diener & Diener, 1996).

Men and women are equally likely to declare themselves satisfied or very happy. Overall, only one person in ten reports being "not too happy" (Myers, 2000; Myers & Diener, 1996), and only one in seven reports waking up unhappy (Wallis, 2005).

Some studies suggest that one's sense of happiness may have a genetic component (Roysamb, 2006; Lykken & Tellegen, 1996). Indeed, one of the most dominant factors in determining happiness may be temperament. Twin studies have found that identical twins' ratings of happiness are generally

©iStockphoto.com/XiXinXing

Positive psychology. According to positive psychology, positive life experiences play a role in the development of a large range of adaptive qualities such as optimism, perseverance, and wisdom.

> "For me, music making is the most joyful activity possible, the most perfect expression of any emotion."
>
> —*Luciano Pavarotti, Italian opera tenor*

A longitudinal study published in the journal *Science* found that highly optimistic people had a 55 percent reduced risk of death from any cause and a 23 percent reduced risk of heart problems, compared with highly pessimistic people (Giltay et al., 2004).

TABLE 66-1 Sample of Happiness Levels Around the World, 2010–2012

How Much People Enjoy Their Lives as a Whole, on a Scale of 0 to 10

Denmark	7.7	Belgium	7.0	South Korea	6.3
Norway	7.7	United Kingdom	6.9	Taiwan	6.2
Switzerland	7.7	Oman	6.9	Japan	6.1
Netherlands	7.5	Brazil	6.8	Slovenia	6.1
Sweden	7.5	France	6.8	Italy	6.0
Canada	**7.5**	Germany	6.7	Slovakia	6.0
Finland	7.4	Qatar	6.7	Guatemala	6.0
Austria	7.4	Chile	6.6	Angola	5.6
Iceland	7.4	Argentina	6.6	Vietnam	5.5
Australia	7.4	Singapore	6.5	Russia	5.5
Israel	7.3	Trinidad and Tobago	6.5	Indonesia	5.3
Costa Rica	7.3	Kuwait	6.5	China	5.0
New Zealand	7.2	Saudi Arabia	6.5	Mozambique	5.0
United Arab Emirates	7.1	Cyprus	6.5	Lebanon	4.9
Panama	7.1	Colombia	6.4	India	4.8
Mexico	7.1	Thailand	6.4	Iraq	4.8
United States	7.1	Uruguay	6.4	Armenia	4.3
Ireland	7.1	Spain	6.3	Niger	4.2
Luxembourg	7.1	Czech Republic	6.3	Bulgaria	4.0
Venezuela	7.0	Suriname	6.3	Togo	2.9

Source: Data from Helliwell, John; Layard, Richard; and Sachs, Jeffery (2013). *World Happiness Report 2013.* Sustainable Development Solutions Network, New York, NY. Retrieved from http://unsdsn.org/wp-content/uploads/2014/02/WorldHappinessReport2013_online.pdf

©iStockphoto.com/monkey business images

No age limit. People who are happy when younger tend to remain happy as they age. On average, older people are as likely as younger people to be happy, and perhaps more likely.

similar, and other researchers have reported that the single best predictor of future happiness is past happiness (Diener & Lucas, 1999). These findings may suggest that a temperamental predisposition to look at life optimistically is more important than an individual's life situation.

Research also indicates that happiness is linked to our personality characteristics and our typical ways of cognitively interpreting events (Farah et al, 2014; Diener et al., 2010; Stewart, Ebmeier, & Deary, 2005; Diener, 2000). Happy people are, for example, generally optimistic, outgoing, curious, and tender-minded. They also tend to possess high self-esteem, be spiritual, be goal directed, and have a sense of perseverance and of control over their lives (Peterson et al., 2007; Sahoo, Sahoo, & Harichandan, 2005; Diener & Seligman, 2002).

It appears that good relationships are related to happiness and satisfaction. Married people tend to be happier than single people (although this effect may be stronger for men than for women) (Myers, 2000; DeNeve, 1999). And in what may or may not be surprising news to you, college and university students who have close friends and significant others are happier than those who do not (Diener & Seligman, 2002).

www.wiley.com/go/comercanada

Before You Go On

What Do You Know?

1. Why do some researchers suggest that there may be a genetic component to happiness?
2. What are some of the life circumstances positively related to happiness and satisfaction?

What Do You Think? How would you advise a friend who asked you for tips on how he or she could be happier?

Summary

Module 66: What About Positive Emotions?

LEARNING OBJECTIVE 66 Identify some factors that influence whether or not a person is happy.

- Researchers have tended to focus on negative emotions, in part because of difficulties in measuring positive emotions.
- Identifying what makes people happy can be difficult. Research has shown that good relationships, employment, and good health are among the things that can make people happy. In particular, though, temperament and personality predict happiness.

PART 12
PERSONALITY

Michele Renard is a city girl, raised in the Jewish faith in Montreal. Cécile Corriveau was raised in the Catholic faith in the suburbs. Talking to them as they sit side-by-side in a room on campus, you can tell they grew up in different communities. Dark-haired Michele is dressed in the somber shades of urban chic, while Cécile sports sculpted hair, straightened teeth, and a white fur-lined jacket. Cécile has a car, while Michele does not.

The two students are at neighbouring universities in Montreal, Quebec. They share a birthday, they are exactly the same height, and they both love hip-hop.

The most important thing they share is the same Métis mother. Separated shortly after birth and given up for adoption, for most of their lives they had no idea that somewhere out there was an identical twin.

But they have many similarities in spite of growing up in different homes. They are both night people, they both love to dance, they both want to have a boy and a girl (in that order), and they both use Pantene® shampoo. They are both "B" students, even though Michele attended a top private school and Cécile went to public school. And the subject that gives them both the most trouble? Math. They look remarkably alike, but they are not exactly alike. Michele has a birthmark over her right eyebrow, and Cécile had to wear braces for five years. Plus, Michele says she's a little more outgoing than Cécile, who admits she's a very shy person.

What makes us who we are? How do we explain the striking similarities between Michele and Cécile? Are they an interesting coincidence, or do they reveal something fundamental about the nature of personality?

personality the unique characteristics that account for enduring patterns of inner experience and outward behaviour.

Personality refers to the unique characteristics that account for our enduring patterns of inner experience and outward behaviour. Personality involves a collection of stable states and characteristics and varies from one individual to another. Thus, the study of personality is much more concerned with individual differences than are other areas in psychology.

You probably do a lot of thinking about personality. Have you ever taken an online quiz to figure out which movie celebrity or superhero you most resemble? Maybe you have filled out a quiz in *Cosmopolitan* or *Cosmo* to determine how much of a pushover you are, or perhaps you have visited Queendom.com and taken some of the hundreds of tests available there. Maybe you have also spent time thinking and talking about the similarities and differences among your friends' personalities. Thinking about people's unique characteristics allows us to try to understand their behaviour and to try to predict how they might react in a given situation.

Psychological research has historically argued for a divide between explanations of nature and nurture when attempting to account for personality development. Increasingly, however, psychologists and biologists have come to acknowledge that environmental experience and biological mechanisms work together to shape personality. In this part we will first explore key historic perspectives on personality (on why people turn out the ways they do)—the *psychodynamic, humanistic, trait, situationist,* and *interactionist* perspectives.

We then look at the important role played by genetic predispositions in personality and what researchers have discovered about the contributions of *both* genetic and environmental factors. Next, we examine how personality is assessed in individuals and whether personality differs depending on gender and culture. And, finally, we describe various personality disorders.

Module 67: The Psychodynamic Perspective

As you read in Parts 1 and 6, the psychodynamic (or psychoanalytic) model emphasizes the unconscious, often dark desires that have to be held in check. Recall also from those parts that the model was formulated by the Viennese neurologist Sigmund Freud (1856–1939) at the beginning of the twentieth century. In Freud's view, the personality forms as a result of struggles between primal needs and social or moral restraints. Many other theorists who follow Freud's key principles differ from him in certain ways. However, they share his basic notion that personality and behaviour are shaped by interacting, or *dynamic*, underlying forces. Thus, all such theories, including Freud's, are referred to as *psychodynamic*.

67.1 The Structure of Personality

Central to Freud's ideas are his views of the conscious and unconscious mind. To Freud, the mind is a little like an iceberg. Only the top of the massive entity is visible to the outside world (see **Figure 67-1**). Three levels of consciousness contain the information stored in our minds, but most of that information is not available to normal awareness.

1. The topmost level is the *conscious* mind, composed of the thoughts and feelings that we are aware of at any given moment.
2. The second level, just below the surface, is the *preconscious*, which contains thoughts, memories, and ideas that can be easily brought into the conscious mind if attended to. For example, your mother's birthday or your plans for this evening remain in your preconscious until you require the information, at which point the information is transferred into your conscious awareness.
3. The deepest level, the *unconscious*, contains most of the content of our minds. We are unaware of this content and cannot become aware of it except under special circumstances. The unconscious is particularly important to the development of personality.

Freud identified three central forces in personality development: basic instinctual drives (which he called the *id*), rational thoughts (the *ego*), and moral limits (the *superego*).

The **id** is present at birth and represents basic instinctual needs and desires, such as those related to eating, sleeping, sex, and comfort. These impulses are governed by the *pleasure principle*; that is, they constantly strive for gratification. Freud believed that most of these basic impulses have sexual overtones and that sexual energy, which he called *libido*, fuels the id. Due to the simple nature of the id's needs and its urgent demand for satisfaction, the id is often described as immature and childlike. The id resides largely in the unconscious and is not readily available to consciousness.

As children grow older, they begin to learn that their id impulses cannot always be satisfied. The **ego** develops as a result of this learning. The ego works under the *reality principle*—the awareness that it is not always possible or acceptable to have all wants and desires met. Much like the id, the ego is responsible for satisfying impulses, but instead of demanding immediate and direct gratification, the ego first assesses what is realistically possible and what the social consequences of gratification might be. Freud essentially saw the ego as the rational, problem-solving force that constantly strives to keep id-based impulses from bursting forth in a destructive manner. From this description, you might conclude that the ego is largely a product of the conscious mind, but Freud believed that it works both consciously and unconsciously.

The **superego** also forms during childhood. It is in charge of determining which impulses are acceptable to express openly and which are unacceptable. The superego develops as children observe the behaviours of those in their families and their culture. As children, we *internalize*—or unconsciously adopt—the values and norms embodied in those behaviours and begin to evaluate ourselves with respect to them. The superego's standards of right and wrong comprise our moral code and remain stable over the course of our lives. Our superego might therefore be thought of as our *conscience*—an entity that

LEARNING OBJECTIVE 67
Summarize the main ideas of the psychodynamic view of personality development.

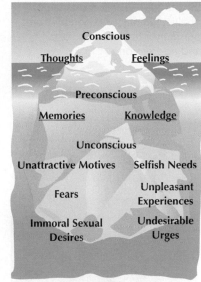

FIGURE 67-1 Freud's view of the mind. According to Freud, the mind has three levels of consciousness. The content stored in the unconscious level is especially important for personality development.

id according to psychoanalytic theory, the personality element representing basic instinctual drives, such as those related to eating, sleeping, sex, and comfort.

ego according to psychoanalytic theory, the personality element that works to help satisfy the drives of the id while complying with the constraints placed on behaviour by the environment.

superego according to psychoanalytic theory, the personality element in charge of determining which impulses are acceptable to express openly and which are unacceptable; develops as we observe and internalize the behaviours of others in our culture.

HOW WE DEVELOP

psychosexual stages according to psychoanalytic theory, stages in the development of personality; the stages—labelled oral, anal, phallic, latency, and genital—are primarily influenced by sexuality and aggression.

©iStockphoto.com/Muralinath

Oral personality in the making? Freud proposed that individuals whose nurturance needs are not adequately met during infancy may become fixated and develop an oral personality style. They may, for example, be inclined to suck their thumbs even during later childhood, chew their nails, smoke cigarettes, and show signs of dependence.

neuroses an abnormal behaviour pattern caused by unresolved conflicts between the id, ego, and superego.

leads us to feel guilt and sometimes even anxiety. Like the ego, the superego resides in both the conscious and the unconscious mind.

According to Freud, the ego acts as a mediator between the id and superego. That is, it balances the powerful desires of the id with the moral standards of the superego. Freud believed that the three forces are always in conflict to some degree. Usually, the conflict takes place at an unconscious level. What if these conflicts are not resolved? Personality problems and even psychological disorders may result if a person is not able to find acceptable compromises.

67.2 Freud's Psychosexual Stages

Freud believed that as the id, the ego, and the superego work with and against one another, children move through stages that result in the development of personality. The two drives that influence these stages most strongly are *sexuality* and *aggression*. To Freud, these drives are the most likely to cause internal conflict because they are the ones that most often fall under social and moral constraints and are most likely to be left unsatisfied. Accordingly, the stages of development are termed **psychosexual stages**. Several are named after specific *erogenous zones*, or pleasure-producing areas of the body. As shown in **Table 67-1**, Freud labelled the stages *oral, anal, phallic, latency*, and *genital*.

Freud believed that the psychosexual stages function as learning periods that can produce many individual differences in personality. Children must successfully complete, or *resolve*, the issues of each stage to form a healthy personality. As children move into a new stage, they must cope with new demands from the social environment and conflicting internal feelings. If they do not successfully resolve the conflicts that arise, they may become *fixated*, or mentally stuck at that stage of development. Freud hypothesized that a fixation may affect all subsequent development.

Freud linked fixation at different psychosexual stages to the development of distinct, sometimes abnormal, personality characteristics. For instance, Freud believed that a boy in the phallic stage focuses on his penis and a girl on her lack of a penis (so-called *penis envy*). A boy entering the phallic stage also begins to feel sexual attraction toward his mother and jealous rage toward her love interest, his father. Freud called these feelings the *Oedipus complex*, after the character in Greek mythology that inadvertently killed his father and married his mother. At the same time, the boy fears that his father will punish him for his feelings, perhaps by cutting off his source of sexual function, his penis (so-called *castration anxiety*). These feelings, of course, are unconscious, and the child's attempts to resolve the conflicts they create also occur largely at the unconscious level. If children fail to resolve such conflicts, they may suffer from **neuroses**, Freud's term for abnormal behaviour patterns characterized by anxiety, depression, and other such symptoms.

TABLE 67-1 Freud's Psychosexual Stages

Stage	Erogenous Zone	Key Conflict or Experience	Symptoms of Fixation
Oral (0–18 months)	Mouth	Weaning	Dependency on pleasures of the mouth; also general dependence on mother
Anal (18 months–3 years)	Anus	Toilet training	Excessive neatness, orderliness, stubbornness, stingy, controlling
Phallic (3–6 years)	Genitals	Attraction to opposite-sex parent	Sexual role rigidity or confusion
Latency (6 years–puberty)	None	Repression of sexual impulses; identification with same-sex parent	No fixations for this stage
Genital (puberty–adult)	Genitals	Establishing mature sexual relations and emotional intimacy	Sexual dysfunction and unsatisfactory relationships

67.3 Anxiety and Defence Mechanisms

We have seen that internal psychological conflict, often resulting in anxiety, is central to personality development in psychoanalytic theory. Because humans cannot constantly live in an unsettled state of anxiety, they must have some effective methods for handling it—methods for keeping the id forces in check. This realization forms the basis for one of Freud's major contributions to how human beings think about themselves: **defence mechanisms**. Freud described defence mechanisms as unconscious tactics employed by our egos to protect us from anxiety by dealing with id impulses. **Table 67-2** lists and describes some defence mechanisms.

Repression is the most basic defence mechanism. This strategy keeps unpleasant memories or thoughts buried deep within our unconscious minds, protecting us from the difficult and painful process of facing them. Another frequently used defence mechanism, and one that has entered into our common vocabulary, is **denial**. This occurs when a person simply refuses to recognize an existing situation. A person who gambles constantly, for example, may claim that she doesn't really gamble that much or that, even if she does, it isn't a problem and she can quit anytime. It's important to remember that, as stated above, defence mechanisms are unconscious tactics. Thus, the gambler in our example is not consciously making excuses for her behaviour when she practises denial. Examples of other defence mechanisms are described in Table 67-2.

defence mechanisms unconscious tactics employed by the ego to protect the individual from anxiety.

repression the most basic defence mechanism; the process of keeping unpleasant memories or thoughts buried deep within the unconscious mind.

denial a defence mechanism; the process of refusing to recognize an existing situation.

67.4 Evaluating Freud's Theories

The popularity of psychoanalytic theory was at its highest in the mid-twentieth century. Even today, many of Freud's ideas continue to influence the development of the field (Dumont, 2010; Solms, 2007a, 2004). However, since the mid-twentieth century, when the popularity of psychoanalytic theory was at its highest, Freud's theories have come

TABLE 67-2 Some Common Defence Mechanisms

Mechanism	Description	Example
Repression	Keeping unpleasant memories or thoughts buried in the unconscious	Forgetting the details of a tragic accident
Denial	Refusing to recognize an unpleasant reality	Refusing to admit an addiction: "I don't have a problem"
Rationalization	Creating a socially acceptable excuse to justify unacceptable behaviour	Justifying cheating on taxes because "everyone does it"
Reaction formation	Not acknowledging unacceptable impulses and over-emphasizing their opposite	Overpraising a sibling's accomplishment even though you resent his/her success
Projection	Transferring one's unacceptable qualities or impulses to others	Not trusting a co-worker but believing the co-worker does not trust you
Displacement	Diverting one's impulses to a more acceptable target	Yelling at family members after being yelled at by your boss
Sublimation	Channelling socially unacceptable impulses into acceptable activities	Redirecting aggressive behaviour by becoming a professional fighter
Regression	Reverting to immature ways of responding	Throwing a tantrum when frustrated
Identification	Enhancing self-esteem by imagining or forming alliances with others	Joining groups for their prestige value
Intellectualization	Ignoring troubling emotional aspects by focusing on abstract ideas or thoughts	Discussing various economic theories while ignoring the pain of losing your job

Psychology Around Us | Denial in Folktales

In *The Emperor's New Clothes*, two rogues come to town with a promise to weave a most beautiful cloth, so fine that it can be seen only by a very wise man. The emperor, who is very vain and especially fond of clothes, requests a suit to be made of this extraordinary material and pays the two rogues handsomely. . . . As time passes, courtiers are sent [by the emperor] to report on the weaving, and eventually the emperor himself goes to see the new suit of clothes.

[In fact] no cloth was being woven. Nevertheless, after each visit by the royal court, the beauty of the cloth was praised; that is, the non-existence of the cloth was denied. Each viewer attributed his difficulty in seeing the cloth to his own stupidity, believing that if he were smarter, he would be able to see the (non-existent) cloth. The denial is carried to an extreme when the emperor rides through the town in a grand procession, wearing the new suit. The townspeople praise the beauty of the new clothes. [Finally] a little child . . . looks at the emperor and cries aloud, "But he hasn't got anything on!" . . . The defence of denial, quite inappropriate for grown men, is exposed by a youngster. . . . (Cramer, 2006)

Monkeybusinessimages/Dreamstime/GetStock

A guilty conscience. Preschool children start to show that they feel guilt when they cause damage or harm.

under significant criticism in the scientific community. Such criticism is largely due to the fact that the key principles of psychoanalytic theory are based on observations that cannot be directly tested by scientific methods.

Freud based his theories on the cases of patients he treated in his private practice as a neurologist. When presented with puzzling symptoms, Freud pieced together clues from the patient's childhood to try to identify the cause. For example, one of his patients—a 5-year-old boy called Little Hans—had developed an intense fear of horses (Freud, 1909, 1961). Freud came to believe that the boy's anxiety was a product of his psychosexual development related to his relationship with his father. In a lengthy summary of his treatment of Hans, Freud described his procedure for helping the father and son learn to address the repressed feelings that were leading to Hans's anxiety.

Freud's case studies, such as that of Little Hans, are effective at characterizing and classifying certain types of observed behaviours. Indeed, Freud's theories can provide an explanation for almost any type of observed behaviour. For example, we might say that a man who keeps getting into fist fights is redirecting angry, unresolved feelings of aggression toward his parents onto his various acquaintances in life. At the same time, we might say that another man, who is unhappy but not hostile, is repressing those same feelings of aggression. In both cases, we have explained the man's behaviour (or non-behaviour). But recall that psychologists seek to predict as well as to describe and explain. Based only on the knowledge that a particular man has unresolved feelings of aggression toward his parents, could we predict whether or not he will be prone to hostile and fighting relationships? Probably not. This lack of predictive power is a key weakness of psychoanalytic theory.

Additionally, many of Freud's observations were based on a very small and select population of upper-class individuals from nineteenth-century Vienna. This raises questions about the theory's cross-cultural validity and highlights the fact that Freud's ideas were based on his particular—and at times narrow—views of sexuality and parenting norms, and his especially narrow views of gender roles.

At the same time, Freud's supporters argue that it is unfair to criticize psychoanalytic theory for not holding up to scientific testing when it was never intended to act as a predictive model. Rather, Freud's fundamental claim was that individuals can find meaning from looking into their past (Rieff, 1979).

On the positive side, many general aspects of Freud's theory remain relevant today, such as the idea that our relationships with our parents can influence how we form intimate emotional relationships in adulthood (Black & Schutte, 2006; Richter, 2013). In addition, some studies on defence mechanisms suggest that they are observable and can have important functions in both development and psychological disorders (Bouchard & Thériault, 2003; Perry & Bond, 2012).

©iStockphoto.com/Fertnig

Jose Luis Pelaez, Inc./Blend Images/Corbis

Setting the stage. Freud was among the first theorists to hold that parent–child relationships influence how people feel about themselves and how they handle intimacy as adults. It is obvious which of the interactions pictured here represents a healthier approach to correcting a child's mistakes, according to Freud.

Perhaps most importantly, Freud's ideas spurred the first inquiries into the functioning of the conscious and unconscious aspects of the mind and how they relate to behaviour. The study of the unconscious mind has accelerated in the last two decades. As you learned in Parts 6 and 8, numerous studies indicate that much of the information processed by the mind remains unconscious, and people rely on a variety of automatic processes to function in the world.

67.5 Other Psychodynamic Theories

Over time, some of Freud's followers split away to form their own schools of thought, becoming what are called *neo-Freudians*. Three of Freud's most notable followers were Alfred Adler, Carl G. Jung, and Karen Horney. The theories of the neo-Freudians departed from Freud's in important ways. But, as you read earlier, each held on to Freud's basic belief that human functioning is shaped by interacting, or *dynamic*, psychological forces.

67.5.1 Alfred Adler

Alfred Adler (1870–1937) believed that social needs and conscious thoughts are more important to human behaviour than sexual needs and other unconscious motivations. Adler was particularly interested in how feelings of *inferiority* motivate behaviour. In Adler's view, almost everyone has some feelings of inferiority stemming from childhood experiences of helplessness. People often make special efforts to compensate for or mask those painful feelings. Adler focused, in particular, on how feelings of inferiority are channelled into a quest for superiority. Although Adler's school of *individual psychology* has not had a major impact on personality theory, his ideas about how the need for power shapes human behaviour have gained momentum in contemporary research (Watts, 2000).

Anna Peisl/Corbis

Moving beyond inferiority. Adler proposed that a child's inevitable experiences of helplessness produce early feelings of inferiority, which can lead to a lifelong sense of inferiority or to a lifelong quest for completeness and superiority.

67.5.2 Carl Jung

Unlike Adler, Carl G. Jung (1875–1961) agreed with Freud's views on the importance of the unconscious. However, he added a new dimension: the collective unconscious. In Jung's system, the unconscious has two parts. The *personal unconscious*, formed from individual experiences, is similar to the unconscious as seen by Freud. The *collective unconscious*, however, is not a private entity like the personal unconscious. Instead, it is a cumulative storehouse of inherited memories shared by all humankind. Jung called these shared memories *archetypes*. According to Jung, archetypes are reflected in symbols

Michael Macor/San Francisco Chronicle/Corbis

The positive drives of personality. One-hundred-year-old artist Frances Dunham Catlett speaks about her work at a reception celebrating her "century of creativity." Carl Jung believed that unconscious drives toward joy and creativity are powerful forces in personality.

and images that appear in the art, literature, and religions of all cultures. The archetype of the hero, for example, can be found in the stories of almost any cultural tradition, while an archetype of mother and stepmother can be seen throughout children's fairy tales (Robertson, 1995).

Jung's *analytical psychology* also differed from psychoanalytic theory in the emphasis placed on sexuality and aggression. Jung acknowledged the importance of these forces, but argued that the unconscious also includes drives toward joy, creativity, and internal harmony (Wilde, 2011). Indeed, the search for harmony is a central theme of Jung's theory (Singer & Kimbles, 2004). He believed that each of us seeks to integrate the mind's various conscious and unconscious elements into a coherent whole, which he termed the *self*.

67.5.3 Karen Horney

Another neo-Freudian, Karen Horney (pronounced HORN-eye) (1885–1952), another neo-Freudian, accepted many of the basic principles of psychoanalysis, but went on to develop her own orientation and school of psychoanalytic training. Horney agreed with Freud that anxiety-provoking experiences in childhood can lead to lasting psychological problems, but she was particularly interested in what she called *basic anxiety*, which develops in children who experience extreme feelings of isolation and helplessness. Basic anxiety, in Horney's view, sets the stage for later neuroses.

Perhaps Horney's greatest disagreement with Freud related to the role of cultural influences on behaviour. To Freud, the basic conflicts that shape development are universal, but Horney observed distinct differences in personality structure between patients from Europe and those from the United States. She came to believe that cultural differences play a more important role in development than traditional psychoanalytic theory acknowledged. Horney rejected Freud's theories about penis envy, suggesting that what Freud was really detecting was women's envy of men's power—power that came from cultural norms, not inherent differences (Hitchcock, 2005).

---

practically Speaking Jung in the Business World

©iStockphoto.com/Images_By_Kenny

In the 1940s, a mother–daughter team, Katharine Cook Briggs and Isabel Briggs Myers, created the Myers-Briggs Type Indicator (MBTI). Today it is one of the most well-known personality tests. Employers in various job fields, employment agencies, and job counsellors administer the questionnaire to several million individuals each year, though it is not appropriate for use in hiring decisions (Wilde, 2011; Furnham, 2008). The test is popular because it describes how we interact with our environment as well as with other people. This knowledge can be extremely useful for a manager in charge of a team of employees (and for the employees themselves) from diverse backgrounds, for example. As well, it can be very helpful for individuals in organizational settings to help them figure out why their interactions with their co-workers typically go the way they do.

The MBTI is based on Carl Jung's theory of personality types, and it describes personality in terms of individual preferences for perceiving and judging the world (Kennedy & Kennedy, 2004; Montequin et al., 2013). Do you prefer a more social or solitary environment? How do you interpret the information you take in? When you make a decision, do you first think about it logically or emotionally? Are you open to several possibilities? Your answers describe your basic preferences and, theoretically, reveal a lot about the kinds of jobs you would most enjoy (Wilde, 2011; Myers et al., 1998). Knowing your preferences may also provide clues about your strengths and weaknesses at work. One thing the MBTI cannot inform you or a prospective employer about is your abilities (McCrae & Costa, 1989); it cannot tell you how well you will perform a particular job and as such it should not be used in hiring decisions.

Most psychologists warn against basing career decisions only on the MBTI (Gardner & Martinko, 1996; Abella & Dutton, 1994). Although the test may inform you that you meet the criteria of an introverted type, this does not mean

that you should avoid that sales job you were coveting. Your categorization as an introvert does not mean that you are totally lacking in extroversion qualities, nor does it mean that you cannot behave in an extroverted manner when the social/work situation calls for it. Moreover, success at the job depends on many variables beyond extroversion or other such personality traits. And finally, for most jobs, a variety of different approaches can lead to success.

Recall earlier discussions about the difference between correlation and causation. Remember that *correlation does not imply causation*; that is, simply because variables are correlated it does not mean that one of the variables *causes* the other. So even though you may have a number of characteristics that indicate you might be an introvert, this does not mean that these characteristics will cause you to succeed in one line of work over another; these characteristics simply tell us that, in general, introverts excel in certain types of jobs.

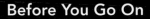

Before You Go On 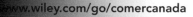 www.wiley.com/go/comercanada

What Do You Know?

1. In Freudian theory, how does a neurotic personality develop?
2. What is repression?
3. What are some common criticisms of psychoanalytic theory?
4. How did Jung's idea of the unconscious differ from Freud's?

What Do You Think? Why do you think the concept of defence mechanisms has been embraced by so many theorists (even those who are not psychodynamic) and by the public?

Summary

Module 67: The Psychodynamic Perspective

LEARNING OBJECTIVE 67 Summarize the main ideas of the psychodynamic view of personality development.

- Personality refers to the unique characteristics that account for enduring patterns of inner experience and outward behaviour.
- Sigmund Freud's psychoanalytic theory of personality depended to a large extent on his ideas about the conscious and unconscious mind. Most of the content of our minds, in Freud's view, is in the unconscious.
- Freud proposed three central forces in personality development: the id, the ego, and the superego.
- In Freud's view, personality develops as children pass through a series of psychosexual stages. Each stage is characterized by strong conflicts between the id, the ego, and the superego. Failure to resolve these conflicts can result in neuroses.
- Conflicts result in anxiety, and Freud believed that we use unconscious tactics called defence mechanisms to protect ourselves from this anxiety.
- Other psychodynamic theories include those of Alfred Adler, Carl G. Jung, and Karen Horney.

Key Terms

defence mechanisms 517

denial 517

ego 515

id 515

neuroses 516

psychosexual stages 516

repression 517

superego 515

Study Questions

Multiple Choice

1. In Freud's view, personality forms as the result of the struggle between
   a) biological drives and intellectual abilities.
   b) conscious and unconscious processes.
   c) primal needs and social or moral restraints.
   d) the individual and other people.

Fill-in-the-Blank

1. According to Freud, the _____ operates on the reality principle and the _____ operates on the pleasure principle.

2. In Freud's theory, the _____ stage of psychosexual development includes identification with the same-sex parent.

Module 68: The Humanistic Perspective

Psychodynamic theorists, particularly Freud, generally believe that personality development is driven by forces beyond our control. Humanistic psychologists offer a different view. As you first saw in Part 1, they emphasize people's potential and highlight each person's consciousness, free will, and other special human qualities. Let's consider the ideas of two key humanistic theorists: Abraham Maslow (1908–1970) and Carl Rogers (1902–1987).

68.1 Abraham Maslow

Part 1 pointed out that Abraham Maslow believed humans are basically good. In each of us, according to Maslow, is an urge to grow and fulfill our potential. Personality arises from people's striving to meet their needs (Leontiev, 2008). As you saw in Parts 1 and 11, these needs are arranged hierarchically, beginning with the need for basic physiological necessities, such as food and shelter, and becoming increasingly complex. Only after our basic needs have been met can we address more subtle needs and strive to attain more complex things. Our highest-level need is **self-actualization**—the need to fulfill our full and special potential as human beings. Maslow described self-actualization as "the full use and exploitation of talents, capacities, [and] potentialities" (1970, p. 150). He suggested that psychologists had become overly focused on biological drives and needs, overlooking the role of high-level processes and the need for more complex forms of fulfillment.

self-actualization the need of humans to fulfill their full and special potential; the highest level of need in Maslow's hierarchy of needs.

Unlike Freud, Maslow believed that more could be learned from individuals who were healthy and well-adjusted than from those who were experiencing psychological problems. In fact, he based his notion of self-actualized individuals on notable historical figures who appeared to lead rich and healthy lives: Albert Einstein and Eleanor Roosevelt, for example (Peterson & Park, 2010). The characteristics that define self-actualized people are the ability to recognize the needs and desires of others, the willingness to respond to the uniqueness of people and situations rather than responding in mechanical or fixed ways, an emotionally deep connection with a few people, spontaneity and creativity, and the ability to resist the urge to conform while still responding to reality.

Some of Maslow's ideas have been taken up by psychologist Mihaly Csikszentmihalyi (2003, 1998). Csikszentmihalyi studied *peak experiences*—moments in which people experience intense clarity of perception, feelings of joy and excitement, and a suspended

Dinodia Photos/Getty Images

©iStockphoto.com/Alexander Raths

Candidates for self-actualization. Maslow proposed that self-actualized people also recognize the needs of others and seek to address them. He believed that full self-actualization was rare. However, well-known people like Bill Gates, Bono, and Gandhi are considered to be self-actualized because of their worldwide humanitarian undertakings. However, it is important to note that many people who recognize and seek the needs of others are not self-actualized; consider the case of the volunteer hospice worker who gives selflessly of her time and energy simply to help others.

Psychology Around Us   **"In the Zone"**

When a golfer like Canadian Stephen Ames is in the zone, his mind and body are harmonized before the swing so the swing happens without any thought or effort. . . . [He] can access his peak performance throughout the round. In this zone state, golfers feel as if they are in a trance, in a heightened sense of awareness—total calm, ease and effortlessness, and mental clarity.

Other athletes also experience the zone. Ted Williams commented that when he was in the zone, he felt as if the

baseball was stopped at the plate, waiting for him to swing at it. When Michael Jordan was in the zone, making one of his spectacular leaps, he felt as if he would never come down. John Brody, the San Francisco 49ers quarterback, perceived the opposing line stopped when he was in the zone. He felt as if he had all day to throw the football downfield (King, 1997; Harmison, 2011).

---

positive psychology an area of psychology focusing on positive experiences and healthy mental functioning.

sense of time and reality. Maslow thought that such moments usually occur when a person becomes totally engrossed in an activity, such as when we hear a beautiful piece of music or experience the beauty of nature. Csikszentmihalyi's writings on peak experiences reflect psychologists' growing interest in **positive psychology**, the study of positive experiences and healthy mental functioning that we discussed in Part 11 (Baumgardner & Crothers, 2009; Seligman & Csikszentmihalyi, 2000).

68.2 Carl Rogers

self-concept a pattern of self-perception that remains consistent over time and can be used to characterize an individual.

unconditional positive regard acceptance without terms or conditions.

Carl Rogers, like Maslow, believed that human nature is fundamentally positive and that people strive for self-actualization (Rogers, 2008, 1963). However, Rogers based his theory of personality around the concept of the *self* rather than around a hierarchy of needs. For Rogers, **self-concept** is a pattern of perception that remains consistent over time and can be used to characterize an individual. Our self-concept is related both to how we see ourselves and to how others see us. Because self-concept develops in part based on how we are perceived by others, as children we need **unconditional positive regard**—acceptance without terms or conditions—from parents or other adults to develop healthy self-concepts.

The idea of unconditional positive regard became a central part of Rogers's therapeutic practice. He believed that, over the course of development, many children form *conditions of worth*, a perception that they must meet certain standards to gain the love of their parents or other important figures. These conditions of worth, often rigid or harsh in nature, can hold over into adulthood and act as a negative force that prevents a person from reaching his full potential. The implications for therapy are clear. In Rogers's *client-centred therapy*, discussed in Part 1, he worked with clients to create an atmosphere of openness, honesty, and absence of judgment, regardless of the specific type of psychological problems the persons were experiencing. He believed that only in such an atmosphere can individuals begin to put aside the conditions of worth that lie at the root of their personal maladaptive functioning (Rogers, 1995).

68.3 Evaluating Humanistic Theories

Many critics fault the humanistic theories for their overly positive focus, saying that they are simplistic and that they ignore the role of psychological dysfunction in society. In addition, it has been difficult for researchers to conduct controlled studies on such abstract concepts as self-actualization and unconditional positive regard (Wilkins, 2000). However, humanistic theories have had a pervasive influence on the field of psychology. As mentioned above, and elsewhere in the textbook, researchers in positive psychology are giving new attention to questions about how human beings can achieve their full potential for happiness. It remains to be seen how humanistic psychology will contribute to this ongoing discussion.

www.wiley.com/go/comercanada

Before You Go On

What Do You Know?

1. What is self-actualization?
2. According to Rogers, what happens if children fail to regularly receive unconditional positive regard?
3. What is a key criticism of humanistic theory?

What Do You Think? What do you think are the key qualities of a fully self-actualized person? Who might match your characterization?

Summary

Module 68: The Humanistic Perspective

LEARNING OBJECTIVE 68 Describe the humanistic theories of Abraham Maslow and Carl Rogers.

- Humanistic theorists, including Abraham Maslow and Carl Rogers, emphasized people's basic goodness and their ability to fulfill their potential.
- Maslow proposed that personality arises from people's striving to meet their needs. Human needs are arranged hierarchically, with self-actualization at the top level.
- Rogers based his theory of personality on his ideas about the importance of self-concept. He believed that children need unconditional positive regard to develop healthy self-concepts.

Key Terms

positive psychology 524
self-actualization 523

self-concept 524
unconditional positive regard 524

Study Questions

Multiple Choice

1. Maslow believed that we can learn the most about the human condition by
   a) creating an atmosphere of openness, honesty, and freedom from judgment.
   b) paying attention to the unconscious symbols in our collective ancestry.
   c) studying normal people.
   d) studying those with psychological problems.

Fill-in-the-Blank

1. Rogers claimed that in order to develop a positive self-concept, we need to accept ourselves and to receive _____ from important people in our lives.

LEARNING OBJECTIVE 69
Summarize the leading trait theories, and describe how the five-factor theory has evolved from the work of Gordon Allport and Hans Eysenck.

personality traits tendencies to behave in certain ways that remain relatively constant across situations.

Module 69: The Trait Perspective

Suppose you were asked to describe your best friend's personality. What would you say? You might use words such as *funny*, *caring*, and *outgoing*. Indeed, an early investigation revealed that there are 4,500 words to describe personality in the English language alone (Allport & Odbert, 1936). Many of these words describe personality traits. **Personality traits** are tendencies to behave in certain ways that remain relatively constant across situations. More precisely, personality traits describe our general dispositions, and those dispositions lead to our behaviours. If people are generally enthusiastic, for example, they may display their trait of enthusiasm by approaching their homework with good cheer or singing out as they walk down the street.

Many of today's personality theories are based on the premise that people's personalities are made up of collections of traits. Of course, as many theorists point out, it is often difficult to pinpoint aspects of an individual's personality that are entirely consistent across time and situations.

Human beings are natural trait theorists. It appears, though, that we are likely to explain our own behaviour in situational terms and others' behaviour in terms of personality traits. (This tendency, called the *fundamental attribution error*, is discussed further in Part 13.) For example, you didn't finish your paper because you were busy studying for two tests in your other classes, but that guy over there didn't finish his paper because he was lazy or disorganized. Thinking about others' behaviour in terms of traits helps make their behaviour predictable and gives us a sense of how our interactions with them might go.

It is also important to note that some researchers, including Hans Eysenck, use a biological explanation for the structure of personality. Although we will discuss his theory in the trait module, Eysenck's theory is also biological in nature.

It was trait theorists such as Gordon Allport (1897–1967) and Hans Eysenck (1916–1997) who first proposed that *central traits* affect a broad range of behaviour. Among researchers, it is difficult to pinpoint a standard definition for *central traits*. Generally speaking, however, trait theorists make several assumptions:

1. People have innate tendencies to respond to situations in certain ways (traits).
2. These tendencies can be linked together to form broad habits (central traits).
3. Such principles can be used to form the foundation of a scientifically testable theory.

Everyone has a number of traits. You may be cheerful, friendly, lazy, disorganized, and talkative. According to the early trait theorists, however, only a few of your traits dominate your behaviours, while others are at work less often. You may be cheerful

Psychology Around Us   Blameless, but Consistent

People may not be inclined to point to their personalities to explain their own behaviours, especially their negative behaviours. But they do seem to think that they behave consistently, even when that is not the case. Political scientist Greg Markus collected information about the political behaviours and beliefs of a large group of people in 1973 and again in 1982. Markus found that the people in his study became more conservative as they got older. But, once they changed in this way, they tended to remember themselves as having been more conservative in the past. Only a third of the people he studied were able to accurately remember their past political beliefs—their memory distortions were always in the direction of their current beliefs. For example, people who had previously been in favour of marijuana legalization, but who changed their minds, downplayed the degree to which they were ever for it in the first place. The moral of the study: most of us are probably much more inconsistent than we or others think.

in most situations (central trait)—at work, home, and school, and from taking out the garbage to playing basketball—but lazy only when it comes to cleaning your house. We will look at the ideas of Allport and Eysenck next. Then we will move on to the influential *five-factor theory* of personality.

> **"**I am what is mine. Personality is the original personal property.**"**
>
> —*Norman O. Brown, American writer and philosopher*

69.1 Gordon Allport

The influential personality theorist Gordon Allport believed that psychoanalysis "may plunge too deep, and that psychologists would do well to give full recognition to *manifest* motives before probing the unconscious" (1968, pp. 383–384). Unlike Freud, Allport did not believe that behaviour is necessarily related to unconscious tensions; rather, he argued that our behaviour can be quite healthy and organized. Over the course of his long and distinguished career, Allport emphasized the unity and uniqueness of the individual, and he believed that the present is more important than the past in understanding personality. Allport conducted detailed case studies that sought to reveal the unique collection of traits at play for each individual. Because much of his work was based on case studies, his ideas have sometimes been criticized by other trait theorists who use empirical investigations to identify the traits that run through large populations (Crandall, 1980). Nevertheless, his work on personality factors provided the starting point for many empirical studies.

69.2 Hans Eysenck and Factor Analysis

The British psychologist Hans Eysenck was a strong proponent of using reliable statistical measures to test psychological principles. To Eysenck, it was vital to develop a theory that could be scientifically tested. As a result, he strove to develop adequate measures of personality traits and, specifically, measures of their biological foundations. He hoped that eventually theorists would be able to identify clear correlations between traits and behaviours and underlying biological systems.

> *The fictional detective Sherlock Holmes was asked by his friend Dr. Watson how he had deduced that a certain man was intellectual.* **"**For answer Holmes clapped the [man's] hat upon his head. It came right over the forehead and settled upon the bridge of his nose. 'It is a question of cubic capacity,' said he; 'a man with so large a brain must have something in it.'**"**
>
> —*A. Conan Doyle,* Adventure of the Blue Carbuncle

Eysenck made particular use of *factor analysis*—which, as you may recall from Part 10, is a statistical method for analyzing correlations among variables. The use of factor analysis marked a significant turning point in the scientific study of personality theory. In the past, psychologists such as Freud and Allport had relied on case studies (one person at a time) and on their own intuition to form ideas about personality structure. Although factor analysis can also be influenced by the decisions and interpretations of a given researcher, the method provides a much more objective way of identifying relationships between variables.

Eysenck used factor analysis to identify traits that cluster together to form fundamental dimensions of personality, which he called **superfactors** (**Figure 69-1**). Eysenck eventually identified three basic superfactors: extroversion, neuroticism, and psychoticism.

superfactor a fundamental dimension of personality made up of a related cluster of personality traits.

- *Extroversion*—the degree to which a person is outgoing and enjoys interacting with others. An *extrovert* has personality traits such as impulsiveness, sociability, and assertiveness. At the other end of the spectrum, an *introvert* displays traits such as thoughtfulness, reliability, and passivity.
- *Neuroticism*—the degree to which a person tends to experience negative emotions, also known as *mental instability*.
- *Psychoticism*—the degree to which a person is vulnerable to developing the serious disorders known as *psychoses*, in which contact with reality is lost in key ways.

Superfactor

Traits

Habitual responses

Specific responses

Extroversion

Sociable · Assertive · Active · Excitement-seeking · Impulsive

FIGURE 69-1 Eysenck's model of personality. Eysenck used factor analysis to identify traits that cluster together. He described three basic trait clusters, which he called superfactors. Each superfactor, such as extroversion shown here, is made up of specific traits, and in turn each trait is made up of habitual and specific responses. Source: Adapted with permission from Eysenck, H. J. (1976). *The biological basis of personality*, p. 36. Courtesy of Charles C Thomas Publisher, Ltd., Springfield, Illinois; based on Weiten, W. (2007). *Psychology: Themes and variations* (7th ed.). Belmont, CA: Thomson Wadsworth.

Eysenck saw each of these superfactors—and the individual character traits of which each is composed—as existing on a continuum, with each person displaying a certain degree or level of each superfactor.

Although Eysenck depended on factor analysis to determine how personality traits cluster together, he needed more basic data to make factor analyses possible. To get that data, he gathered information on the traits themselves through the use of questionnaires on which people were asked to rate themselves on a number of trait-related behaviours. He administered his *Eysenck Personality Questionnaire* to people in hundreds of countries. The results indicated that his superfactors correspond to basic personality types in similar ways across many cultures (Eysenck, 2002, 1992, 1990).

Because Eysenck believed that personality traits were biologically based, he also studied the biological basis of personality traits. His belief in the biological roots of personality

Spotting the superfactors. The fundamental dimensions of personality cited in the five-factor model and other theories of personality are each on display in this photo of people passing through an airport waiting area. Can you identify examples of these key trait categories?

Baerbel Schmidt/Getty Images

has been supported by a number of studies. Several investigations of twins, for example, involved comparing the personalities of identical twins and suggested that genetics play a significant role in how individuals score on the extroversion superfactor (Pergadia et al., 2006; Heath, Cloninger, & Martin, 1994). A number of studies of hormones, blood pressure, and brain activity support the notion that biological factors are linked to the superfactors at least to some degree (Eysenck, 1990).

Eysenck's work has had an enormous influence on personality theory and research. His early emphasis on empirical research set the stage for much of the current research on personality, which relies very strongly on factor analyses. Moreover, Eysenck's personality tests have been translated into many languages, and his ideas and findings have influenced such diverse fields as education, aesthetics, politics, and psychopathology. Finally, he was one of the first psychologists to systematically investigate the possible biological basis of personality traits, an area of investigation that, as we shall see, has become a significant force in the field (Stelmack, 1997).

69.3 The Five-Factor Model

A number of factor analysis studies have derived more than three higher-order dimensions of personality, or superfactors (Poropat, 2009; Boyle, 2008; Saggino & Kline, 1996). The **five-factor theory** identifies five major trait categories, popularly known as *the Big Five* (see **Figure 69-2**): *agreeableness* (versus *disagreeableness*); *extroversion* (versus *introversion*); *neuroticism* or *emotional instability* (versus *stability*); *conscientiousness* or *dependability* (versus *irresponsibility*); and *openness to experience* or *imaginativeness* (versus *unimaginativeness*). A helpful way to memorize these five factors is with the acronym OCEAN (openness, conscientiousness, extroversion, agreeableness, and neuroticism).

If you look closely, you will notice that Eysenck's dimensions of extroversion and neuroticism are also found among the Big Five superfactors. His third dimension, *psychoticism*, however, does not appear in the five-factor model. That dimension was originally thought by Eysenck to serve as a marker of psychotic tendencies, and people with schizophrenia were indeed found to score high on this dimension. However, many people who score high on Eysenck's psychoticism dimension do not become psychotic and, in fact, they also display particular traits that are found within the Big Five superfactors of agreeableness and conscientiousness (Saggino, 2000; Scholte & De Bruyn, 2004).

Despite such differences, Eysenck would probably be happy to learn that trait theory has been reenergized in recent years, thanks largely to the popularity of the five-factor theory. Although some theorists argue that additional factors should be added to the list of five, a great many researchers believe that individual differences in personality can indeed be captured by the five broad categories of this theory (Ewen, 2010; Boyle, 2008; McCrae & Costa, 2003). Because of the theory's popularity with researchers, a significant body of relevant research has accumulated (Zuckerman, 2012, 2011; Cooper & Sheldon, 2002). This research has attempted to answer questions about both the validity and the usefulness of the five-factor approach. Most of the research discussed next thus relates directly to the five-factor theory, although some applies to trait theories in general.

five-factor theory an empirically derived trait theory that proposes five major trait categories: agreeableness/disagreeableness, extroversion/introversion, neuroticism/stability, conscientiousness/irresponsibility, and openness to experience/unimaginativeness.

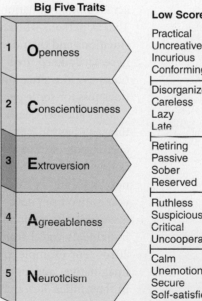

Big Five Traits	Low Scorers	High Scorers
1 **O**penness	Practical Uncreative Incurious Conforming	Imaginative Creative Curious Independent
2 **C**onscientiousness	Disorganized Careless Lazy Late	Organized Careful Disciplined Punctual
3 **E**xtroversion	Retiring Passive Sober Reserved	Sociable Active Fun-loving Affectionate
4 **A**greeableness	Ruthless Suspicious Critical Uncooperative	Soft-hearted Trusting Lenient Helpful
5 **N**euroticism	Calm Unemotional Secure Self-satisfied	Anxious Emotional Insecure Self-pitying

FIGURE 69-2 The five-factor model of personality. Studies using factor analysis have identified five broad categories of traits, known as the Big Five. Many researchers believe that individual differences in personality can be captured by these five categories.
Source: Adapted from Cattell, R. B. Personality pinned down. *Psychology Today*, July 1973, pp. 40–46

Ableimages/Getty Images

Another benefit of conscientiousness.
An elderly teacher carefully demonstrates to a student how to operate woodwork equipment both safely and productively. Studies indicate that, on average, conscientious people live longer than less responsible individuals.

69.4 Evaluating Trait Theories

A number of questions have been addressed by research into trait theories. First, do traits apply to a variety of cultures? As we mentioned, Eysenck found that his superfactors described basic types across a number of countries. In addition, there is growing evidence that people in many cultures display personality types that can be captured by at least three of the Big Five superfactors and sometimes by all five (Correa & Rogers, 2010; Nye et al., 2008; Saucier, Hampson, & Goldberg, 2000; De Raad et al., 1998).

A second question concerns the power that personality exerts over our behaviour. Consider an interesting study conducted to determine whether people are "naturally" expressive or inexpressive (DePaulo et al., 1992). To evaluate people's ability to control their expressiveness, the experimenters asked subjects to act either very expressively or very inexpressively while discussing a topic. Interestingly, even when asked to feign expressiveness, naturally inexpressive people showed less expression than did expressive people in their natural state. Similarly, when naturally expressive subjects were asked to act inexpressively, they were still more expressive than naturally inexpressive individuals. Clearly, traits are often quite powerful. Cooperative people have been shown to be more emotionally expressive than non-cooperators (Schug et al., 2010). Even when people try to behave in a manner that conflicts with a particular trait, they may have trouble doing so.

A third question is whether traits, and the behaviours they produce, remain stable across situations. The answer appears to be sometimes yes and sometimes no. In a classic investigation conducted in the early 1980s, investigators observed college students and rated their levels of *conscientiousness*, based on behaviours ranging from being punctual to completing assignments on time and tidying their rooms (Mischel & Peake, 1982; Mischel, Mendoza-Denton, & Shoda, 2002). The researchers found that levels of conscientiousness were relatively stable across *similar* situations, but not particularly consistent across very different situations. That is, persons who are punctual for class will likely be punctual for dates, because those situations and their demands are similar. However, individuals who are punctual may not necessarily keep their rooms clean. Although both of these situations require conscientiousness, the situations are quite different, leading to inconsistent displays of conscientiousness for some people.

Yet another question is whether traits, and the behaviours they dictate, are stable over time. Studies indicate that personality traits are more stable over a short period of time than over a span of years (Srivastava et al., 2003; Donnellan et al., 2015). People who conscientiously show up on time for an appointment today are likely to be punctual for appointments next week and next month. But today's punctuality is not as likely to predict punctuality a year or two from now.

Similarly, traits often show inconsistency across a person's lifespan, especially as individuals travel from childhood to adulthood (Fleeson, 2007, 2001; Edmonds et al., 2013). For example, people who score high on the *openness* superfactor (adventurous, imaginative, and untraditional) during their teenage years may display less openness in their fifties. Researchers disagree on why such lifespan changes occur. Some believe that they reflect intrinsic, biologically based maturation (McCrae, 2002), while others hold that they have more to do with changes in an individual's social environment (Srivastava et al., 2003). Either way, it is worth noting that once a person reaches adulthood, lifespan fluctuations seem to lessen, and traits become increasingly stable across the adult years (Roberts & Del Vecchio, 2000; Milojedv & Sibley, 2014; Caspi & Roberts, 1999).

The predictive value of a model is another issue of concern to researchers. Although trait theories do not necessarily claim to serve as a device for predicting what will happen in a person's life, it is tempting to apply them in this way. In fact, the idea that personality factors may be able to predict broad outcomes dates back many years. One longitudinal investigation found that the Big Five superfactor *conscientiousness* helps to predict the length of a person's life (Kern & Friedman, 2008; Friedman et al., 2014). In this study, a large number of children were followed for 70 years by several researchers. When the children were 11 years old, their parents and teachers rated them on various personality dimensions, and subsequent records were kept about these individuals and the causes of their eventual deaths. It turned out that, on average, those who had been rated as conscientious lived significantly longer than those who had not been rated as conscientious. To explain this finding, the researchers speculated that conscientiousness is related to a broad pattern of health-related behaviours, such as not smoking and not drinking—behaviours that add up over a lifetime. Similarly, research has suggested that certain personality attributes may be predictive of marital satisfaction. One study found, for example, that high agreeableness greatly increases the chances of having a happy and satisfying marriage (Botwin et al., 1997), as do conscientiousness, emotional stability, and intellectual openness.

Finally, researchers have been interested in whether traits are inherited. As suggested earlier, case studies of monozygotic, or identical, twins who have been reared apart seem to suggest that genetic factors can have a strong influence on personality. In addition, a growing number of empirical studies indicate that heredity plays a role in many dimensions of personality (Krueger et al., 2008; Plomin & Caspi, 1999). Based on such studies, the heritability of personality traits has been estimated at around 40 percent (Pervin, Cervone, & John, 2005). In short, it appears that there may be a strong genetic contribution to personality.

> **"Confidence is what you have before you understand the problem."**
>
> —*Woody Allen, screenwriter and comedy actor*

Before You Go On

www.wiley.com/go/comercanada

What Do You Know?

1. Who are Gordon Allport and Hans Eysenck, and what were their contributions to the trait perspective?
2. What is factor analysis, and how is it tied to trait theories?
3. What are the Big Five personality factors?
4. How stable are traits over time and across situations?

What Do You Think? Think of three famous people and predict how they each might score on the major trait categories of the five-factor model.

Summary

Module 69: The Trait Perspective

LEARNING OBJECTIVE 69 Summarize the leading trait theories, and describe how the five-factor theory has evolved from the work of Gordon Allport and Hans Eysenck.

- Personality traits are tendencies to behave in certain ways that remain relatively constant across situations. Trait theorists such as Gordon Allport and Hans Eysenck first proposed that central traits affect a broad range of behaviour.
- Allport conducted detailed case studies that sought to reveal the unique collection of traits at play for each individual.
- Eysenck, using factor analysis, identified three personality superfactors: extroversion, neuroticism, and psychoticism.
- Other trait theorists proposed the five-factor theory, which identified five major trait categories: agreeableness, extraversion, neuroticism, conscientiousness, and openness to experience.
- Although traits play an important role in behaviour, they can be inconsistent over time and across different situations.

Key Terms

Study Questions

Multiple Choice

1. A person who follows rules, is dependable, and checks her work carefully is probably high in which of the Big Five personality traits?
   a) Agreeableness
   b) Conscientiousness
   c) Extroversion
   d) Openness

2. All of the following statements about personality traits are true except
   a) Between three and five of the "Big Five" personality traits can be found across all cultures.
   b) Traits are not always stable across situations.

   c) Traits are powerful and difficult to disguise.
   d) Traits are stable and consistent over time and across situations.

Fill-in-the-Blank

1. A person who frequently experiences negative emotions is probably high on Eysenck's superfactor of _____.

Module 70: The Situationist and Interactionist Perspectives

Traits obviously play an important role in behaviour. As we have just seen, traits can be predictive, powerful, and consistent forces in our lives. But are traits the single key to behaviour? It seems not. As we have also just observed, traits show more consistency and are more predictive in the short run than in the long run and across similar situations than across dissimilar situations. Clearly, there is more to behaviour than traits alone. Personality theorists have wrestled with the relative importance of traits and situational factors, and as you will see, many have come to the conclusion that both are important (Reis & Holmes, 2012).

70.1 The Situationist Perspective

Over the years, as research identified the limits of trait theory and indicated the importance of situational factors, a number of personality theorists began to embrace a view called **situationism**—the notion that behaviour is governed primarily by the variables in a given situation rather than by internal traits (Mischel, 2004). These theorists acknowledged that personality factors come into play when people are making choices, reacting to events, or displaying other behaviours. Nevertheless, the theorists argued, situational "pushes" and "pulls" rule in most instances.

The behaviourist B. F. Skinner, discussed in Part 7, could be said to have viewed personality from a situationist perspective. Indeed, Skinner believed that human behaviour was completely shaped by environmental factors. What we call *personality*, Skinner saw as simply a certain consistency in what he called *response tendencies*. By that, Skinner meant that we approach life in a certain way because some of our behaviours have been rewarding to us in the past while other behaviours have not. That is, we tend to favour, or repeat, responses that have previously helped us gain a desired outcome or avoid an undesired one. Whereas a trait theorist might look at your presence in college or university as some combination of intelligence, conscientiousness, and perhaps a little neuroticism, Skinner would say that you studied because you found academic achievement to be rewarding or because studying served to keep your parents happy. Because these outcomes were sufficiently motivating, you developed a general response tendency to persist at studying, which led you to respond consistently and successfully in academic situations (Evans, 1968).

Situationism has a strong appeal. As we already mentioned, human beings appear predisposed to explain their own behaviour in situational terms, although they tend to explain others' behaviour in terms of traits. How often have you responded "it depends" when somebody has asked how you would handle a situation? Certainly, we do not like to think of ourselves as "trait machines"—robots who behave as if we were preprogrammed.

At the same time, however, we must note that there really can be no such thing as *pure* situational factors in human behaviour (Ewen, 2010). Consider, for instance, Skinner's perspective on reward. As you saw in Part 7, Skinner defined a *reinforcer* as something that leads you to engage more often in a particular behaviour. In other words, what is a reinforcer to you may not be a reinforcer to someone else. Theorists argue that even in the context of reinforcement principles, it is still *people* who choose, manipulate, interpret, and react to the situations—or reinforcements—they meet. It's hard to believe, for example, that a particular student puts off every single essay assignment until the very last minute because her reinforcers always line up in that direction. Ultimately, even as we acknowledge the power and

LEARNING OBJECTIVE 70
Describe and differentiate the situationist and interactionist views of personality.

situationism the view that behaviour is governed primarily by the variables in a given situation rather than by internal traits.

© Nightmares Fear Factory

Situationism. Situationism is a view of personality that notes that in many social situations, such as a Halloween haunted house, people respond in fairly similar ways, meaning that the situation drives their response rather than their personality.

influence of situations, we must acknowledge the power and influence of people and their personalities. Thus, it is not surprising that many situationist theorists, including Walter Mischel, the perspective's early leader, came to believe that the most appropriate models are those that try to integrate both personality variables and situational factors to explain behaviour, eventually moving to an interactionist perspective of personality.

70.2 The Interactionist Perspective

interactionism a view emphasizing the relationship between a person's underlying personality traits and the reinforcing aspects of the situations in which they choose to put themselves.

Interactionism focuses on interactions between people and situations. At the centre of the interactionist model is the idea that people influence the situations they encounter. According to this model, the choices you make, such as attending your present college or university or being enrolled in your present classes, are functions of underlying personality traits. Let's say, for example, introversion leads you to choose a school with really small classes—a choice that you suspect would make it more comfortable for you to participate in class—or a school with really large classes—a choice that you believe would make it easier for you to go unnoticed in class. Such choices are likely to result in self-fulfilling prophecies. If you choose the school with big classes, for example, the large class sizes will indeed help ensure that you can remain quiet in class and continue your introverted style. This idea that individual and situational variables interact suggests a way of moving beyond the trait-versus-situation controversy.

One of the leading interactionist theories is cognitive psychologist (and Alberta-born) Albert Bandura's *social-cognitive theory* (Bandura, 2008, 2006, 1986). Bandura is famous for introducing the concepts of modelling and self-efficacy to the study of human behaviour and personality. As you will recall, *modelling*, also known as *observational learning*, is a process by which people, especially as young children, learn to respond to particular situations by observing and imitating the behaviour of others. *Self-efficacy* refers to people's personal beliefs about their ability to achieve the goals they pursue. The higher your self-efficacy, the more likely you are to pursue a goal and, ultimately, to be reinforced by the outcome of your efforts (Maddux & Volkmann, 2010).

How do these concepts influence personality? Through a process Bandura called *reciprocal determinism*. In Bandura's way of thinking, the external environment, internal mental events (such as one's beliefs and expectations), and behaviour all interact with one another. How, for example, might your current presence in college or university be explained? Bandura might note that as a child you observed your parents or friends studying or working hard, and as a result you engaged in similar behaviour when you entered the school environment. Perhaps you were praised by teachers or your parents for good grades, which reinforced that behaviour. You may in turn have developed a confident belief that you were a good student and curious about and open to new experiences, and your high level of self-efficacy may have led you to persist in behaviours (listening, completing your homework, studying) that further led to desired reinforcements (praise, good grades, positive self-image).

The major advantage of this perspective over other theories of personality is that Bandura's theory, with its special emphasis on observable variables, such as models, behaviours, goals, and outcomes, is readily testable. There is a vast amount of data linking both modelling and self-efficacy to personality development and change across the lifespan (Hoyle, 2010; Borgen & Betz, 2008; Mroczek & Little, 2014).

With an interactionist perspective in mind, personality researchers have recently uncovered a new kind of consistency in human affairs: not trait consistency, not situation consistency, but *disposition-situation* consistency. They

©iStockphoto.com/cscredon

Bandura's theory of reciprocal determinism. In Bandura's view, personality is determined by the interaction of the external environment, internal mental events, and behaviour. For example, receiving good grades and praise for schoolwork as a child may help you believe that you are a good student and this high level of self-efficacy may further lead to behaviours (studying and doing homework) that produce further desired reinforcement—more good grades and praise.

Psychology Around Us | Influence of Movies and TV on Personality and Behaviour

©iStockphoto.com/Jason Lugo

Film and television are powerful mediums in the entertainment industry. The stories conveyed in movies and TV shows can make us laugh, cry, or even get angry. But can they fundamentally affect our personality or influence how we act? This is a subject of much debate among parents, psychologists, government organizations, and broadcasters.

Guy Paquette at Université Laval analyzed the amount of violence shown on television in Canada from 1993 to 2001. He found that despite broadcasters stating a desire to offer less violent programming, the overall number of violent acts and the number of violent acts per hour increased steadily over the period of the study. He further noted that a substantial proportion of that violence was broadcast before 7 P.M., thus increasing the likelihood that children would be exposed to it (Paquette, 2004). In another study, movie clips of violent acts were shown to university students to see whether

the brain's response to aggression changes with repeated viewing. The researchers found that a region of the brain partly responsible for regulating aggression was less active after repeated exposure to violence (Kelly et al., 2007). Such findings have appropriately raised concern among scientists and the public. At the same time, it is important to recognize that although the average North American views 200,000 dramatized acts of violence by the age of 18, most university- or college-aged individuals are far from violent (Finley, 2007). In short, as we noted in Part 7, TV and movie viewing may indeed have a potential relationship to aggressive behaviour, and perhaps to other undesirable behaviours as well, but other factors, such as parental and peer influences, may play an even more powerful role (Kim et al., 2006; Collins, 2005).

TV programs and films appear to have at least some influence on harmful and risky behaviour, but can they also affect us in a positive way? A study of the effect of the movie *Super Size Me*—a film about overeating in which the filmmaker, Morgan Spurlock, lived only on McDonald's food for one month—showed that undergraduates who viewed the film were more conscientious about their food choices afterward (Cottone & Byrd-Bredbenner, 2007). However, the study did not examine whether long-term, permanent changes in eating behaviour occurred.

Film and television are frequently blamed for negatively influencing the behaviour of children and adolescents, and such attributions may indeed have merit. At the same time, however, personality and behaviour are complex, and a variety of genetic and environmental factors interact to influence who we are. In most cases, the content of movies and TV shows probably plays only a supporting role. As well, once again, recall that *correlation does not imply causation*.

have discovered that interactive effects between dispositions (traits) and situations are common, and that disposition-situation relationships often show stability (Ewen, 2010; Mischel, 2004; Shoda & Lee Tiernan, 2002). Such stability would be reflected by the statement, "Tamara is more outgoing than her sister when she decides to go for a run, but less outgoing than her sister when visiting a museum in order to please her friends."

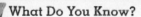

Before You Go On

www.wiley.com/go/comercanada

What Do You Know?

1. What is the situationist view of personality, and what theorists played key roles in promoting it?
2. What is the interactionist view of personality, and how does Bandura's social-cognitive theory fit into this perspective?

What Do You Think? How might Skinner and Bandura each view someone's failure to quit smoking?

Summary

Module 70: The Situationist and Interactionist Perspectives

LEARNING OBJECTIVE 70 Describe and differentiate the situationist and interactionist views of personality.

- Situationism holds that behaviour is governed primarily by the variables in a given situation rather than by internal traits. The behaviourist B. F. Skinner could be said to have viewed personality from this perspective.
- Interactionism focuses on interactions between persons and situations. Albert Bandura's social-cognitive theory is an example of interactionist theory. In Bandura's view, the environment, internal mental events, and behaviour all interact to affect behaviour through the process of reciprocal determinism.

Key Terms

interactionism 534

situationism 533

Study Questions

Multiple Choice

1. According to Skinner, what we call personality is simply consistency of what tendencies?
    a) Environmental
    b) Latent
    c) Response
    d) Situational

Fill-in-the-Blank

1. The finding that different people respond to the same reinforcer in different ways is a problem for the _____ view of personality, leading most researchers to prefer an interactionist approach.

Module 71: Personality Assessment

Go to almost any pop-culture Internet site (for example, www.queendom.com) or flip open any newspaper or popular magazine and you will likely find evidence of people's desire to understand, describe, and use personality traits. Horoscopes, personality quizzes, and even clairvoyants offer personality-based analyses and advice to thousands of people worldwide. The fact that devices such as horoscopes have been shown to be unreliable has done little to diminish their popularity.

Of course, there are also more formal tools for assessing personality, and these tools are used in a variety of important contexts. Clinicians use personality assessment tools to learn more about their clients' problems. Researchers may use them to conduct personality research or to help select participants for their studies. Employers and job counsellors often use such tools to maximize their rates of retention of the most productive employees (Li et al., 2014) or to help their work teams function more effectively (Guchait, Hamilton, & Hua, 2014). Scores on traits such as conscientiousness have, for example, been used to predict absenteeism, misconduct, and termination (Organ & Ryan, 1995). The personality tests used most frequently by these professionals are *personality inventories* and *projective tests*.

71.1 Personality Inventories

You have very likely taken a personality inventory at some time in your life. **Personality inventories** are questionnaires that require individuals to respond to a series of true–false or agree–disagree statements designed to measure various aspects of personality. These types of assessments are sometimes called self-report inventories because they depend on information that respondents supply about themselves. Today's most widely used personality inventories are the *Minnesota Multiphasic Personality Inventory 2 (MMPI-2)* and the *Revised NEO Personality Inventory (Neuroticism, Extraversion, Agreeableness, Conscientiousness, and Openness to Experience) (NEO PI-R)*. Both are considered relatively accurate and consistent. They are favoured by clinicians, employers, and other professionals largely because they are easy to administer and to score, and do not require subjective interpretations by test administrators. Each test requires individuals to respond to hundreds of statements that cover a broad range of feelings, behaviours, and inclinations (Boyle, Matthews, & Saklofske, 2008). Because of this scope, the inventories provide a summary, or *profile*, of the various traits that comprise a personality.

The *Minnesota Multiphasic Personality Inventory 2 (MMPI-2)* is one of the most widely-used personality tests (Butcher, 2011; Weiner & Greene, 2008). It is often used to assess abnormal personality characteristics and inclinations. A person's responses on this test are believed to reveal thoughts, emotions, and attitudes; personality characteristics; and possible psychological disorders. The inventory is composed of 567 items and takes approximately 60 to 90 minutes to complete.

The items were empirically derived. This means that many possible test items were administered to people with various personal styles and psychological disorders, and their responses were analyzed to determine which items had predictive value and which patterns of responses corresponded to particular personality styles and diagnostic groups. It is important to note that the test questions do not necessarily have to make intuitive sense, but are instead kept on the test if they have predictive value. For example, if most people who score high on extroversion choose "green" as their favourite colour, then the question, "What is your favourite colour?" has predictive validity and would remain on the test (even though it may not, on the face of it, have anything to do with personality).

Unlike the MMPI-2, the *Revised NEO Personality Inventory (Neuroticism, Extraversion, Agreeableness, Conscientiousness, and Openness to Experience) (NEO-PI-R)* does not

personality inventory a questionnaire designed to assess various aspects of personality.

Practically Speaking Evaluating Personality Quizzes

Image Source/Corbis

Are you dating a person with a narcissistic personality? What is your "pizza personality"? What kind of podcast are you? Personality quizzes fascinate and entertain millions of people. Magazines as varied as *Cosmopolitan* and *Chatelaine* publish personality quizzes all the time, and the Internet has numerous websites dedicated to helping you to better understand yourself.

Below are some of the pop-culture quiz types that you are most likely to come across:

- *Scenario quizzes* ask the question: When this happens, how do you react? Popular topics are love and relationships. The claim is that the answers you choose can reveal personal qualities that you may not normally attribute to yourself.
- *Preference quizzes* pose questions on a variety of topics, from your favourite colour to how you write to what time of day you like best. The claim here is that your answers illustrate enduring and broad traits such as extroversion or creativity.
- *Relational quizzes* ask you open-ended questions about how you would react to specific, imaginary events. For example, "If you saw someone being

robbed, what would you do?" The claim behind these quizzes is that your responses can tell you a lot about your values and your self-concept, or how you see yourself. But do they really do this? Consider for a moment how scientists construct tests.

Psychologists and other researchers go through a rigorous process to construct tests by relying heavily on solid test construction and knowledge of scoring, validation, and statistics. They first determine the construct; that is, what they want to measure (e.g., trait, ability, attitude, disorder, etc.). They then devise a method for testing and create the individual test items; this process is always related to a particular empirically-supported theory. Typically, once tests are constructed, researchers and specialists in the area review the test (this is formally known as a peer review process) and suggest changes. Once the test is determined to be ready to be assessed, it is administered to a sample of people. Following this, a series of statistical analyses are run on the individual item data to assess whether the test is measuring what it is intended to measure. The test is then edited and tested on a new sample of people. A final series of statistical analyses are run to see if the test represents all of the people in the population it is intended to be measuring (i.e., all age groups, socio-economic classes, gender, cultures, etc.).

A writer for a magazine, without any specialized knowledge on a given topic, is the one who typically devises the "tests" in magazines. For this reason, almost all psychologists recommend treating such pop-culture personality quizzes as entertainment at most. They may be fun, but they typically emerge from the minds of enterprising individuals or organizations, rarely undergo testing or research of any kind, and usually are without any predictive capacity. As a result, they are misleading. Always keep in mind that you should not base important decisions on the results of such quizzes, and that forming insights or views about yourself based on the results of the tests is likely to be a big mistake.

If you would like to evaluate your personality using a version of this measure, go to www.personalitytest.net/ipip/index.html.

attempt to assess maladaptive aspects of personality. It is structured to evaluate traits that comprise the five superfactors of the five-factor theory of personality.

Despite the popularity of personality inventories, some significant concerns have been raised about their use as indicators of personality. First, the tests rely on self-reports, a source of information that may not always be accurate (Feliciano & Gum, 2010; Gold & Castillo, 2010; Weiner & Green, 2008). If we are not fully aware of our own behaviour patterns, preferences, or interests, our self-reports may not reflect our actual personal style.

In one study, for example, extroverted people scored high on the extroversion scale of a personality inventory, but neurotic people did not score high on the neuroticism scale (a less socially desirable trait) of the same inventory (Spain et al., 2000). Another study, however, suggested that people are better self-judges of their neuroticism traits, while their friends are better judges of their intellectual traits (Vazire, 2010). So perhaps both social desirability and who has best access to information are both important factors in personality assessment.

Another concern is that personality tests may not always be used and applied properly. Some employers, for example, use measures of conscientiousness to predict an applicant's potential job performance. But some jobs are not well suited for conscientious people, at least not overly-conscientious people (Hogan & Hogan, 1993). As well, openness to experience (finding new ways to do things), in addition to conscientiousness, add to performance when the job is complex (Blickle et al., 2013). An individual's performance on a job that emphasizes speed or quantity of output may be hindered by extensive checking and rechecking, for example.

Still another concern is that test-takers may tailor their answers on personality inventories to try to create a good impression—a phenomenon known as **socially desirable responding** (Viswesvaran & Ones, 1999) that has been studied extensively by Delroy Paulus at the University of British Columbia (2009). The problem of socially desirable responding was, in fact, anticipated by the creators of the MMPI. They included certain questions, called *validity items*, in the questionnaire to assess the likelihood that a respondent would purposely give an answer that was socially desirable rather than accurate. Suppose, for example, that an individual keeps answering "true" to such items as "I smile at everyone I meet" and "false" to "I get angry sometimes." It is assumed that these responses, and perhaps many others as well, are instances of socially desirable responding. In such cases, test scorers may disregard or adjust the respondents' personality scores.

> **socially desirable responding** tailoring answers on personality inventories to try to create a good impression.

The use of personality tests as part of the hiring process has a long history. However, early personality tests were not demonstrated to be particularly good (reliable or valid) at predicting who the best candidate for a job would be. As a consequence, in the United States there were a number of successful lawsuits claiming that hiring decisions based on older personality tests were unfair (Rothstein & Goffin, 2006). In Canada, there was much less litigation. Currently, there are a number of better designed personality tests that do, in fact, meet legally defensible criteria for use as pre-employment selection tools (Rothstein & Goffin, 2006). The use of such tests in Canada is regulated by bodies such as human rights commissions, which limit the types of personal information employers can ask prospective employees to questions (including personality test questions) that are directly relevant to the job for which they are applying. Tests must be carefully constructed to ensure they meet these criteria and also show appropriate levels of reliability and validity (Eisenbraun, 2006).

71.2 Projective Tests

Projective tests are quite different from personality inventories (see **Figure 71-1**). These tests are commonly used by psychoanalytic clinicians and researchers and are intended to tap into a person's unconscious mind to detect personality styles and conflicts hidden beneath the surface. The most widely-used and famous projective test is the *Rorschach Inkblot Test*. During the test, participants are presented with a set of 10 inkblots and asked to explain what they see. The ambiguous shapes of the inkblots are intended to force participants to *project* structure and meaning onto the images, and the participants' responses are thought to reveal underlying psychological themes and personality issues. For example, a person who sees images of animals or weapons in the inkblots is often thought to be grappling with underlying aggressive urges.

> **projective test** a personality assessment device intended to tap a person's unconscious by presenting the person with an ambiguous stimulus and asking the person to interpret what the stimulus means.

FIGURE 71-1 Projective tests.
Clinicians often use tests that consist of vague shapes or situations to help assess personality. Shown here is an inkblot similar to those used in the Rorschach Inkblot Test and a picture similar to the ones used in the Thematic Apperception Test.

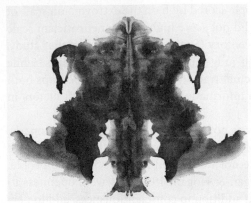

©iStockphoto.com/Zmeel Photography

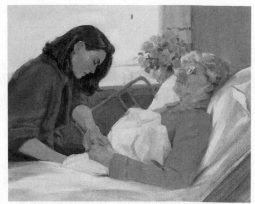

Vincent McIndoe/Stock Illustration Source/Getty Images, Inc.

Some clinicians believe that the Rorschach test provides useful suggestions that can enhance the effectiveness of therapy (Cashel, 2002). It is widely agreed in the scientific community, however, that projective tests, such as the Rorschach, display low validity, or accuracy (Bornstein, 2007; Butcher, 2010; Wood et al., 2002). Scoring of the tests depends heavily on interpretations by the test administrators—interpretations that may be affected by the assessor's professional biases or level of expertise. In addition to problems with validity, many have concerns about the reliability, or consistency, of projective tests. Studies have shown that individuals who take a Rorschach test today may offer responses that are very different from those they offered when they took the test last week, leading to different personality assessments. Look again at the sample in Figure 71-1. You can probably see why the Rorschach test might present difficulties.

An alternative and commonly-used type of projective test is the *Thematic Apperception Test (TAT)*. This tool, created in the 1930s by psychologist Henry Murray (1943), is made up of ambiguous black-and-white drawings of people in various situations. Test-takers are asked to describe and make up a story about each drawing. The uses and criticisms of the TAT are similar to those of the Rorschach. Although some systematic scoring procedures exist, most clinicians rely on their own judgments when analyzing an individual's TAT responses (Masling, 2004; Pinkerman et al., 1993). Additionally, it is difficult to know for certain that the stories created by individuals reflect how they are actually feeling; they may instead represent the individuals' projections of how they believe they should be feeling (Lilienfeld et al., 2000).

Before You Go On

www.wiley.com/go/comercanada

What Do You Know?
1. How do personality inventories differ from projective assessment techniques?
2. What is socially desirable responding and how is it addressed in the MMPI-2?
3. What are some problems with projective assessment techniques?

What Do You Think? There are so-called personality tests all over the Internet. Which ones have you come across? Why are most such tests uninformative and often misleading?

Summary

Module 71: Personality Assessment

LEARNING OBJECTIVE 71 Describe the two major types of personality tests, and give examples of each.

- Personality inventories are questionnaires that require individuals to respond to a series of true–false or agree–disagree statements designed to measure various aspects of personality.
- Two widely-used personality inventories are the *Minnesota Multiphasic Personality Inventory 2 (MMPI-2)* and the *Revised NEO Personality Inventory (Neuroticism, Extraversion, Agreeableness, Conscientiousness, and Openness to Experience) (NEO-PI-R)*. The MMPI-2 is typically used to assess abnormal personality characteristics and inclinations. The NEO-PI-R evaluates traits associated with the five-factor theory of personality.
- Projective tests are intended to tap into people's unconscious minds by having them interpret ambiguous stimuli. In the case of the Rorschach Inkblot Test, the stimuli are inkblots. In the case of the Thematic Apperception Test (TAT), they are black-and-white drawings.

Key Terms

personality inventory 537

projective test 539

socially desirable responding 539

Study Questions

Multiple Choice

1. All of the following are characteristics of projective tests except that they
   a) have a validity scale built into them that guards against socially desirable responding.
   b) have problems with reliability.
   c) include the Rorschach and the TAT.
   d) rely on clinicians' judgment for analysis.

Fill-in-the-Blank

1. Test items that are built into a personality assessment to control for social desirability responding are referred to as _____ items.

Module 72: Biological Foundations of Personality

LEARNING OBJECTIVE 72
Discuss the heritability of personality traits and some of the neural systems that may be involved in the expression of personality.

You saw earlier that the trait-versus-situation debate has moved toward an interactionist view. As we mentioned, the traditional nature–nurture debate has changed in much the same way. In recent years, many researchers have been trying to understand the *relative* contributions of genetic and environmental factors to the development of personality. Other researchers have been investigating what brain structures and other neurological factors affect personality patterns. Let's see what they have found.

HOW WE DEVELOP

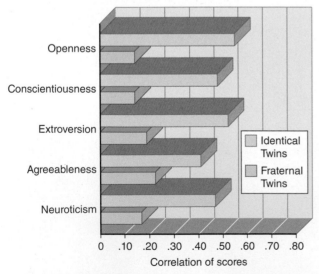

T.K. Wanstal/The Image Works

Separated at birth. Identical twins Gerald Levy and Mark Newman were separated at birth and did not meet or know of each other's existence until adulthood. In the interim, they had both become firemen and developed a range of very similar personality characteristics, mannerisms, interests, and hobbies.

FIGURE 72-1 Heritability of the Big Five traits among twins. Studies comparing identical twins (who share 100 percent of their genes) and fraternal twins reveal that the Big Five personality traits have a strong genetic component (Loehlin, 1992). Source: Adapted with permission From Weiten. *ACP Psychology: Themes and Variations, FIU EDITION, 6E. © 2004 Wadsworth, a part of Cengage Learning, Inc. Reproduced by permission. www.cengage.com/permissions

72.1 How Much Do Genetic Factors Contribute to Personality?

As we have seen throughout this book, situations in which twins are separated very early in life and raised in different families afford researchers a unique opportunity to study the separate effects of genetics, shared family and social environments, and non-shared environments. Perhaps the most famous of these twin adoption studies is the *Minnesota Study of Twins Reared Apart* (MISTRA) (Johnson et al., 2007; Segal, 2012). This investigation focused on 59 pairs of identical twins who had been raised in different families and 47 pairs of fraternal twins raised in the same household. Recall that identical twins have exactly the same genetic structure, while fraternal twins are no more genetically similar than non-twin siblings.

The twins who participated in the study spent six days taking personality and intelligence tests. The identical twins proved to be substantially more similar on every psychological dimension than the fraternal twins, even though the identical twins had been raised in separate homes and families. These results suggest that shared environments are less important than genetic factors to the development of temperament and many personality traits, although shared environments certainly do contribute (Zawadzki et al., 2001; Segal, 2012).

Some broad traits appeared to have particularly strong genetic links (see **Figure 72-1**). For example, in twin studies of personality, the superfactor *agreeableness* from the Big Five scale had an estimated heritability coefficient of .40, and the heritability coefficient (which ranges from 0 to 1.0) of the superfactor *openness* was estimated to be .55 (Bouchard, 2004). Among more specific traits, the heritability coefficient for *warmth* was estimated to be .23, while that for *excitement* was estimated to be .36 (Jang et al., 1998; Loehlin, 1992).

Some researchers have suggested that certain behavioural tendencies, which are expressions of personality, may also have an inherited component. For instance, genetic factors may contribute to an individual's tendency to watch television (Prescott et al., 1991). Even more complex behaviours, such as the tendency to get a divorce (McGue & Lykken, 1992) and to develop alcoholism (Froehlich et al., 2000; Pickens et al., 1991), have been found to be partially heritable. Of course, no single gene is at work in traits or in behaviours such as these. More likely, multiple genes interact and affect an individual's broad biological systems, and these systems contribute to the traits or behaviours in question.

The media has embraced the Minnesota Twin Study for its straightforward findings. It is easy, though, to misinterpret the meaning of heritability statistics. Based on their findings, for example, the study's authors estimated that the *heritability coefficient* of IQ is close to .70 (other studies suggest that it is closer to .50). Does this mean that IQ is 70 percent genetic and 30 percent environmental? No. As noted in Part 10, the heritability coefficient is related to the total variance in a population, not to the variance within a given individual. That is, a heritability coefficient of .70 means that 70 percent of all differences observed in the tested *population* are due to genetic factors rather than to environmental differences.

Whatever the genetic pathway, even strong proponents of a genetic model recognize that environmental experiences also play a critical role (Zuckerman, 2012, 2011). Recall that Eysenck considered personality traits to be biologically-based and proposed that the superfactor *psychoticism* served as a marker of psychotic tendencies, such as schizophrenia. Even Eysenck, however, discovered that persons who are predisposed to high levels of psychoticism will not necessarily develop schizophrenia. Their environmental experiences help determine whether they will become disabled by their genetic disposition or channel that disposition into more productive behaviours.

72.2 Personality and the Brain

Twin studies, as we have seen, suggest links between genes and personality. But these studies do not provide precise information about what biological systems affect personality patterns. The search for such systems dates back to Franz Joseph Gall (1758–1828). Gall developed the theory of **phrenology**, a method of assessing a person's mental and moral qualities by studying the shape of the skull. He believed he could pinpoint specific parts of the brain that were responsible for distinct personality qualities by feeling the bumps they raised on the skull (see **Figure 72-2**). The practice became quite widespread between 1820 and 1850 (Gall, 1833).

While Gall's techniques were later shown to be inaccurate, his ideas about the localization of brain functions and the role of the brain in personality continue to influence neurological science (Novella, 2000). Many researchers are currently attempting to uncover how brain structures, neurotransmitters, and other factors influence personality (Strelau, 2010; Joseph, 2007). Much of this research focuses on specific personality traits, but a new line of study is also examining higher-order personality variables, such as moral inclinations and self-concept (Paprzycka, 2010).

WHAT HAPPENS
in the BRAIN?

phrenology a method of assessing a person's mental and moral qualities by studying the shape of the person's skull.

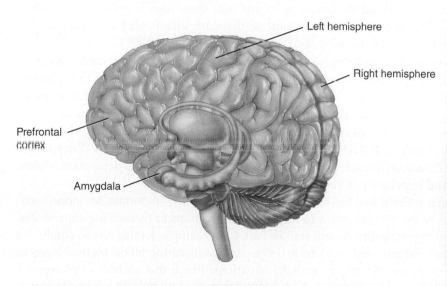

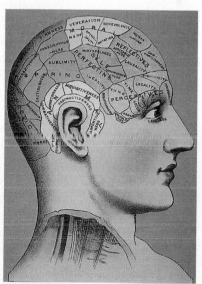

Bettmann/Corbis

FIGURE 72-2 Bumps, lumps, and personality. Franz Gall proposed that personality could be determined by measuring the bumps on a person's skull, and he diagrammed the areas associated with particular personality traits. While his assumptions were wrong, his idea that some brain functions are localized is true.

Ever wonder why you are so curious about and even fascinated by reality TV or the exploits of Justin Bieber or Miley Cyrus? According to some scientists, we may be built that way. In one study (Anderson et al., 2011), researchers showed a group of participants a set of neutral, unfamiliar faces, and then shared a piece of made-up gossip about each of the faces. The gossip could be negative, positive, or neutral. The researchers then showed the faces to the participants once again, but this time the faces were mixed in with other faces. When the faces were presented in this new manner, the researchers measured where the eye glances of the participants wandered. It turned out that their eyes focused on the faces that had nasty gossip attached to them much more than on faces that had been associated with positive or neutral gossip. All of which suggests to some observers that reality TV may be so successful partly because we are built to want to watch it.

72.2.1 Research on Neural Systems and Personality

Many studies suggest that certain *brain structures* help to regulate personality. As we have observed in previous parts, the amygdala, a structure in the limbic system, plays a key role in emotionality, motivation, and the processing of negative stimuli, especially stimuli that activate fear and avoidance responses (Haas et al., 2007; Adolphs, Russell, & Tranel, 1999). Brain imaging studies have shown that people with damage to the amygdala have difficulty becoming conditioned to fear stimuli (LeDoux, 1999). The damage may prevent the amygdala from responding to stimuli that normally excite fearful responses in people without amygdala damage. Such studies have spurred a number of psychologists to theorize that children who display an inhibited personality—characterized by shyness and fear of the unfamiliar—may have amygdalas that are *too easily* activated, causing the children to be aroused too readily by unfamiliar or stressful situations (Schwartz, Snidman, & Kagan, 1999; Lahat et al., 2014).

Cerebral hemisphere dominance may also contribute in subtle ways to personality. Some studies have hinted that people whose right hemisphere is dominant experience more negative emotions and traits while those whose left hemisphere is dominant display more positive emotions and traits (Davidson, 1998). One study found, for example, that participants who were generally sad and withdrawn displayed less activity in the left side of their prefrontal cortex—the part of the brain responsible for planned actions and thought and, in part, for emotional reactions to stress (Davidson & Fox, 1989). Moreover, the link between hemisphere dominance and personality may appear at a very early age. Psychologists have studied the brains of infants who show high levels of distress when separated from their mothers. Results indicate that such infants tend to display heightened activity in the right-side prefrontal cortex (Harman & Fox, 1997).

Neurotransmitter activity has also been linked to some personality variables. As mentioned earlier in this book, the neurotransmitter dopamine helps regulate the "pleasure pathway" (Dreher et al., 2009; Volkow & Fowler, 2000). It is central to the brain's reward systems. High dopamine activity in the reward centres, for example, has been associated with positive emotions, high energy, and lack of inhibition, while low activity of this neurotransmitter has been linked to anxiety, inhibition, and low energy levels (Zuckerman, 2007, 1995). Similarly, low serotonin activity has been associated with depression, violent behaviour, and impulsivity (Knutson et al., 1998).

Hormonal activity, too, has been tied to personality. The important hormone cortisol, secreted by the adrenal cortex to help regulate reactions to threatening experiences, has been tied to personality. As you read in Part 4, for example, Jerome Kagan conducted a famous study of inhibited children in 1994. He measured the blood cortisol levels of children as they were reacting to stressful situations. Recall that cortisol helps regulate reactions to threatening experiences. Kagan found that the children with inhibited temperaments tended to have higher cortisol stress reactions to unfamiliar situations. Recall that temperament (as discussed in Part 4) is a way to describe early-appearing stable tendencies toward particular emotional states (called reactivity) and the ability to manage these states.

72.2.2 Organizing Research Findings

Numerous studies have looked at the link between biological processes and personality, yielding findings that are complex and often confusing. One of the most compelling methods for organizing these findings has been suggested by the researchers Lee Anna Clark and David Watson, who grouped personality types into three broad categories of temperament, similar to the superfactors proposed by Eysenck and the Big Five theorists (Watson & Naragon-Gainey, 2014; Watson et al., 2008; Clark & Watson, 1999).

- *Negative emotionality* Individuals who have high levels of negative emotionality are thought to experience more negative emotions and see the world as distressing, whereas those low on this dimension are relatively peaceful and have higher levels of satisfaction.
- *Positive emotionality* Measures of positive emotionality are thought to represent a person's engagement with their environment. High scorers are social individuals who lead active lives and exhibit enthusiasm, while low scorers are shyer and have less energy and self-confidence.
- *Disinhibition versus constraint* The disinhibition/constraint dimension reflects how we regulate our various emotions. People high in disinhibition have difficulty controlling their emotional responses and tend to be impulsive, living for the moment. People high in constraint live more careful and controlled lives.

Note that negative emotionality and positive emotionality are two separate dimensions. These two types of emotionality are not necessarily at opposite ends of a spectrum. A person may score high on both, low on both, or high on one and low on the other.

Scores on the three dimensions are broadly related to particular lifestyle patterns (see **Figure 72-3**). Individuals high in negative emotionality are more likely to experience feelings such as anger, contempt, and guilt, while those high in positive emotionality tend to experience positive emotions such as joy, excitement, and pride. Some problematic lifestyle patterns may be found among individuals who score high on the disinhibition dimension. These individuals, who are high in impulsivity and do not act with long-term consequences in mind, tend to get poorer grades in school, perform more poorly in their jobs, and engage in riskier activities,

> **"**Don't you just love being with someone who's recklessly impulsive?**"**
>
> —*Homer Simpson, The Simpsons*
>
> **"**Actually, it's aged me terribly.**"**
>
> —*Marge Simpson, Homer's wife*

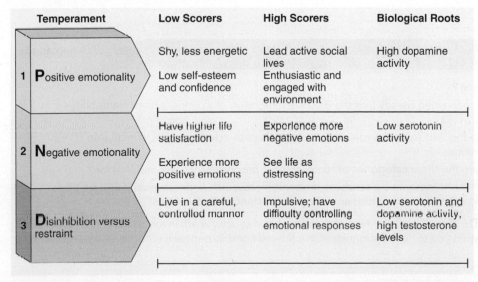

Temperament	Low Scorers	High Scorers	Biological Roots
1 **P**ositive emotionality	Shy, less energetic Low self-esteem and confidence	Lead active social lives Enthusiastic and engaged with environment	High dopamine activity
2 **N**egative emotionality	Have higher life satisfaction Experience more positive emotions	Experience more negative emotions See life as distressing	Low serotonin activity
3 **D**isinhibition versus restraint	Live in a careful, controlled manner	Impulsive; have difficulty controlling emotional responses	Low serotonin and dopamine activity, high testosterone levels

FIGURE 72-3 The biology of personality. Clark and Watson grouped the findings from personality studies into three dimensions of temperament. Research evidence suggests that biological processes are at the root of these temperament dimensions.

such as drinking and using illegal drugs (Carré et al., 2009). Interestingly, "morning people" are more likely to be high in positive emotionality, while many "night owls" are high on the disinhibition dimension (Clark & Watson, 1999).

72.2.3 Interpreting Research Findings

Although research findings suggest links between brain functioning and personality, we must, as always, take care in interpreting these findings. The links just discussed are not usually straightforward, and personality traits are never the result of a single biological process. The activity of one neurotransmitter—say, serotonin—is, at most, *partially* responsible for the regulation of a trait or emotion. Clearly, the relationships between biology and personality that have been discovered represent only a small portion of the complex neurological system.

In addition, it is important to remember that the patterns of brain activity that we have observed have not been shown to provide a causal explanation of traits. Particular biological processes associated with personality may themselves be the results of environment and experience. As you have seen, for example, studies indicate that life experiences, even very early ones, may affect both biological make-up and personality patterns, present and future. One study of rhesus monkeys found that baby monkeys who had endured high levels of abuse and rejection by their mothers displayed lower levels of serotonin activity in adulthood. Moreover, the lower their level of serotonin activity in adulthood, the more likely they were to abuse their own offspring (Maestripieri et al., 2006). Clearly, environmental factors, even at an early age, greatly affect the neurobiological system, and that impact can be enduring.

In summary, we must be very careful about the conclusions we draw from genetic and neurological personality research. First, we must keep in mind that the brain operates as a system, and personality reflects activity in a number of regions, as well as the expression of multiple genes (Bouchard, 2004). Second, we must recall that one gene may interact with other genes and affect a variety of personality dimensions (Livesley, Jang, & Vernon, 2003). Third, we need to recognize that the environment affects the operation and impact of both genetic and biological processes. Those processes in turn affect how individuals interact with their environment. Given the complex, bidirectional relationships that occur between traits, biological factors, the environment, and behaviour, the only certain conclusion that can be drawn is that much more research is needed before we can truly understand the nature and causes of personality (Maruszewski et al., 2010).

Before You Go On

www.wiley.com/go/comercanada

What Do You Know?

1. What do we mean when we say that the Big Five dimension of openness has a heritability coefficient of .55?
2. What is thought to be the role of the amygdala in the development of inhibited personalities?
3. What are the three categories of temperament proposed by Clark and Watson?
4. Why is it necessary to be careful in interpreting research findings associating particular personality traits with particular biological substances or structures?

What Do You Think? Many of the same brain structures are involved in both emotion and personality. Discuss what you think this suggests about the relationship between emotion and personality.

Summary

Module 72: Biological Foundations of Personality

LEARNING OBJECTIVE 72 Discuss the heritability of personality traits and some of the neural systems that may be involved in the expression of personality.

- Twin studies, such as the Minnesota Study of Twins Reared Apart, suggest that many personality traits have strong genetic links.
- Certain brain structures, neurotransmitters, and hormones have been associated with personality variables.
- In interpreting links between genes, physiological factors, and personality, it is important to remember that the relationships are complex and multidirectional.

Key Term

phrenology 543

Study Questions

Multiple Choice

1. The Minnesota Study of Twins Reared Apart found that
   a) both family environment and genetics predicted psychological similarity equally well.
   b) family environment was more important than genetics in predicting psychological similarity.
   c) genetics was more important than family environment in predicting psychological similarity.
   d) the interaction between genes and environment prevented the researchers from drawing firm conclusions.

2. According to research, people who score high on Clark and Watson's disinhibition dimension are more likely to
   a) be morning people.
   b) feel anger, contempt, and guilt.

c) lead active lives and exhibit enthusiasm.
d) perform more poorly at work and engage in risky activities.

Fill-in-the-Blank

1. Although research proved it to be incorrect, Gall's theory of _____ was important to our later understanding that particular brain areas have particular functions.

2. Some psychologists believe that inhibited children may have an overactive _____, a part of the brain important to the experience of negative emotion.

Module 73: Differences in Personality

So far we have focused on ideas about how personality unfolds. Let's turn now to the question of group differences in personality. Are male and female personalities inherently different? Do personalities differ among different cultures and subcultures? We will examine these questions next.

73.1 Gender Differences

The 1992 book *Men Are from Mars, Women Are from Venus* (Gray, 1992) has sold more than six million copies in North America and been translated into 40 languages. The book's premise that men and women are entirely different clearly struck a responsive chord. But how accurate is this notion?

73.1.1 Research into Gender Differences

A number of studies suggest that the widespread belief in inherent personality differences between men and women may be no more than a myth. Recent broad reviews of studies on gender differences in personality, cognitive abilities, and leadership have found that the similarities between men and women far outnumber the differences (Hyde, 2014, 2008, 2007, 2005). Differences among individuals of each gender are much larger than differences between males and females (Costa, Terracciano, & McCrae, 2001).

Michaeljung/Dreamstime/GetStock

Personality and gender differences. While some people argue that there are personality features that are more typical for one gender than the other, it is actually the case that there are more differences across individuals within each gender than there are across the genders.

Beyond all this, gender researchers have begun to note the importance of context in investigations of psychological gender differences. The situational and social context of a study—for instance, the male-to-female ratio in the experimental room—can greatly influence the nature and size of observed gender differences (Bussey & Bandura, 1999; Eagly & Wood, 1999). Many psychologists rightly stress that incorrect conclusions about certain gender differences can perpetuate stereotypes and improperly affect men and women at work, at home, and in their professional lives (Barnett & Rivers, 2004).

Nevertheless, we must be clear that some consistent sex differences have been documented. For example, women, on average, tend to be more accurate than men at assessing emotion in other people (McClure, 2000; Lambrecht, Kreifelts, & Wildgruber, 2014). The psychologist Carol Gilligan—who, along with Karen Horney, was one of the first theorists to focus on how women differ psychologically from men—argues that women and men, in fact, are most comfortable with different perspectives on the world, although she also emphasizes that one perspective is not superior to the other, and both men and women are capable of adopting the other's perspective (Gilligan, 2011, 2004). Gilligan, who was introduced in Part 4, believes that women are more attuned to interpersonal (relational) concerns when making moral decisions, while men are more likely to base such decisions on laws or abstract principles. Building on this idea, she has found that men, on average, score higher on traits that reflect individuality and autonomy, while women score higher on ones that emphasize social connectedness and empathy (Gilligan, 1982). Similarly, some investigations have indicated that women tend to display more nurturing behaviours (Feingold, 1994).

Roger Ressmeyer/Corbis

A caring life. Operating against the stereotype that females are consistently more nurturing than males, animal shelter worker Sam Wheeler has devoted much of his life to loving and caring for unfortunate dogs and cats.

After statistically comparing the results of many studies relating to gender differences in personality, psychologist Janet Hyde (2014, 2008, 2005) found only a handful of variables on which females and males differed consistently. Those that she did find, however, seem to be important. Levels of aggression—particularly physical aggression—were somewhat higher among males. In addition, males were quite different from females on measures of motor performance and sexuality, and males and females had strikingly different attitudes about sex in casual, uncommitted relationships—men were more open to sex in such instances. As we noted in Part 11, the data on gender differences in sexual attitudes may be influenced by research participants' awareness that society expects men and women to behave in certain ways sexually. Still, it is clear that, overall, differences in aggression and attitudes may lead to significant differences in the expression of personality.

73.1.2 Why Do Gender Differences in Personality Exist?

Knowing about gender differences is similar to looking at the results of a personality assessment—both provide descriptions but do little to explain *why* certain patterns exist and what those patterns may say about future behaviour. A number of theories attempt to explain the personality differences observed in men and women.

One theory explains these differences in socio-cultural terms. After all, a person's self-concept, life goals, and values all develop in a social context. According to **social role theory**, girls and boys develop different personal styles, behaviours, and skills based largely on the division of labour between the sexes and the resulting differences in gender role expectations (Koenig et al., 2011; Eagly & Koenig, 2006; Eagly, 1987). In other words, males and females develop the personality attributes that are best suited for the roles that they typically occupy. Some theorists believe that play behaviour in childhood helps teach gender roles and expectations. Young boys are expected to play competitive games, for example, and often are given aggressive-type action figures as toys. Girls, in contrast, are encouraged to play games that emphasize nurturing and interacting with peers.

Family and social relationships may also contribute to the development of personality differences between boys and girls. As children interact with their families and peers, they form ideas about gender role expectations based on how those other individuals react to their behaviours. It is particularly important that the reactions of others teach children what behaviours and ideas are not appropriate to their gender role (Henley, 1977). A little boy may, for example, face disapproval if he plays with dolls rather than action figures.

Broad cultural practices, often a reflection of religious and philosophical beliefs, are also significant in the development of male–female differences. Traditionally, men held a position of higher power than women in most societies, and this power structure had a "trickle-down" effect on smaller units of behaviour. Women, for example, often were limited to certain roles, such as child rearing, domestic work, and particular occupations (nurse, teacher, secretary). It may be that women were more likely to develop certain personality traits as a result of these constraints. Consider, for example, the superior abilities of women, on average, to read emotions and to perform in the social realm. Individuals

social role theory theory that gender differences occur because girls and boys develop different behaviours and skills based largely on differences in gender role expectations.

Psychology Around Us | Trying to Break Free of Social Roles

Efforts to break free from social roles can take a toll on individuals. Thus, even the best-intended role breakers can only go so far. Perhaps you have noticed, for example, that some men are willing to support a female friend by going to a female-oriented movie or a flower show, but the same guys are much less likely to hold a friend's purse. And on those occasions when men do go that extra mile, they are often left in an uncomfortable emotional state.

Researchers Jennifer K. Bosson and Joseph A. Vandello (2011; Bosson, Vandello, & Caswell, 2014) asked men to engage in a braiding task—half of them braided a length of rope, and half of them braided hair. Afterward, the men were given the choice of punching a bag or working a puzzle. The men who braided hair overwhelmingly opted to punch a bag. In another condition, men who were not allowed to punch a bag or engage in other aggressive behaviours reported high anxiety levels. In essence, according to Bosson and Vandello, if the men didn't get an opportunity to reassert some gender-stereotyped behaviour, their sense of manliness became threatened.

Tim Pannell/Corbis

Social roles. Social roles, such as learning how to play football with an aggressive attitude, are learned socially but become powerful influences on behaviour.

In male–female conversations, women laugh 126 percent more often than men.

who are in positions of less power or privilege may need to develop their skills at recognizing interpersonal cues and spotting the emotions of those in power to better address their own needs (Eagly & Koenig, 2006; Koenig et al., 2011; Tavris, 1991; Eagly, 1987). They can use such skills as they try to make sure their own needs are met.

A number of theorists further propose that cultural norms influence how men and women form their self-schemas. As we discussed in Part 4, *schemas* are ways we organize knowledge. A *self-schema* is an individual's cognitive framework for the knowledge he has about himself. When we need to process new information about ourselves or our interactions, we refer to these schemas for guidance. A number of studies suggest that men are more likely to have self-schemas that emphasize autonomy and independence, while women are more likely to have collectivist or relationship-based schemas (Bekker & van Assen, 2008). One team of researchers further hypothesized that an individual's self-esteem would be directly related to how well he lived up to gender-dependent schemas—a hypothesis supported by a study they conducted (Josephs, Markus, & Tarafodi, 1992). Research participants who were led to believe that they equalled or surpassed most of their peers in gender-specific skills and abilities had consistently higher levels of self-esteem.

In addition to such socio-cultural factors, biological factors may play a role in gender differences in personality. In Part 3, for example, we discussed the nature and importance of *hemispheric lateralization* in the brain. It turns out that males and females may exhibit different degrees of hemispheric lateralization. Male brains tend to be more functionally lateralized than female brains: in male brains, one hemisphere is relatively dominant for various kinds of processing, while female brains appear to be more integrated (Everhart et al., 2001; Saucier & Elias, 2001). Still other studies have found that the sex hormones, testosterone and estrogen, which are available in different amounts and often act differently in males and females, have major influences on behaviour and personal tendencies, leading many theorists to believe that they also contribute to gender differences in personality (Hines, 2004; Dabbs et al., 2001, 1997).

In summary, it is true that, on the one hand, many of our society's beliefs about male–female personality differences are incorrect or overstated. A number of psychologists worry that the Mars–Venus myth of massive gender differences serves to perpetuate harmful misconceptions. Highlighting differences between men and women, for example, may support prejudicial beliefs and discriminatory practices against women (Hyde, 2005). On the other hand, it is also true that that there is potential danger in not acknowledging the real differences that do exist between the genders. Such denial, argue a number of theorists, may serve to downplay the unique strengths and gifts of each gender. Perhaps the most appropriate response to this debate was offered by psychologist Diane Halpern, past-president of the American Psychological Association. There may be limited differences between males and females, Halpern stated, but "differences are not deficiencies" (Halpern, 2012).

73.2 Differences Among Cultural Groups

Around the world, each culture is characterized by its own values, beliefs, and to some degree, patterns of behaviour. These features help guide members of the cultural group, teaching them what they should value in life, how they should treat others in their group, and how they should view themselves in relation to society. Cultures also form their own ideas about what is important in life, and these ideas can vary widely. For example, the term *self-esteem*, so important in North American culture, is not even found in a number of languages. Clearly, people who live in a society that does not emphasize self-esteem are less likely than North Americans to spend their lives striving for it. Similarly, in North America and Western Europe, a person's goals and life path are often influenced by the culture's emphasis on autonomy and accomplishment, whereas in Asian cultures there is greater emphasis on contributing to a community and honouring one's family (Kim, Pemng, & Chiu, 2008).

Some of the most comprehensive cross-cultural research has focused on personality development in individualist and collectivist cultures. As we observed in Part 1, most collectivist cultures consider the needs of the group more important than the needs of the individual. With this orientation comes heightened emphasis on the role of individuals within their family and on social relationships in general. In turn, individuals are more likely to strive to help maintain the social order and to exhibit humility in social interactions (Triandis, 2001; Triandis et al., 1990). Collectivist values are particularly found in African, Latin American, Asian, and Middle Eastern cultures (Buda & Elsayed-Elkhouly, 1998).

> "Nurture shapes nature."
>
> —*Albert Bandura, psychologist*

In contrast, individualist cultures value individual achievement, freedom, and success. The self is seen as independent, and each individual is thought to possess a set of psychological qualities that are distinct from those of others. Unlike collectivist cultures, individualist cultures consider individual attainment more important than the needs and values of others. Indeed, competition between individuals is valued. Countries known for this type of structure are Canada, Great Britain, the United States, and Australia.

Cross-cultural psychologists have uncovered some interesting personality variations between collectivist and individualist cultures (Correa & Rogers, 2010; Oyserman et al., 2002a; Schmitt et al., 2007). One large, multi-nation study found that people in collectivist cultures tend to score higher on measures of agreeableness, for example, while people from individualist cultures score higher on measures of extroversion and openness (Hofstede & McCrae, 2004).

Happiness and success may also be defined differently from culture to culture. In collectivist societies, contentment is related to harmony in interpersonal relationships, and this emphasis affects behaviour (Kitayama, Markus, & Kurokawa, 2000). Interpersonal behaviours are tailored to the feelings and needs of others (Kashima et al., 1992). A strong sense of reciprocity and a responsibility to return favours shapes personal styles, behaviours, life goals, and measures of success. In such a culture, a sense of accomplishment comes not from individual achievements but from strong commitment to family, community, or company.

In contrast, people in more individualist cultures are less constrained by a tightly knit social network and enjoy greater personal freedom. They value their privacy and place a premium on individual human rights. Interestingly, some studies have found that people in individualist cultures report greater happiness than those in collectivist cultures (Kuppens, Realo, & Diener, 2008; Diener, Diener, & Diener, 1995). At the same time, however, individualist societies have higher rates of divorce, homicide, and stress-related disease than collectivist ones (Triandis, 2001; Popenoe, 1993; Triandis et al., 1988).

People's sense of their own personalities also differs across cultures. Individuals in collectivist cultures, for example, do not use traits to describe themselves as often as those in individualist cultures. Studies have shown that when students are asked to complete the phrase "I am . . . ," those from North America are more likely to answer using a personal trait (say, "I am friendly" or "I am honest"), while those from cultures with a collectivist orientation are more likely to describe themselves in a social manner (for example, "I am a member of the psychology department") (Cousins, 1989; Triandis, 2001, 1989). In light of such findings, some have argued that Western personality measures, such as the Big Five superfactors, are of limited usefulness in studying behaviour in collectivist cultures (Church & Katigbak, 2000).

> "Different people bring out different aspects of one's personality."
>
> —*Trevor Dunn, musician and composer*

Creasource/Corbis

Tokyo Space Club/Corbis

Different values, different personalities. The different ways in which these business meetings are being conducted in North America and Japan reflect the different values and personalities at work in individualist and collectivist cultures. Goals and personal styles in an individualist culture emphasize striving for autonomy, individual achievement, and high self-esteem. In contrast, those on display in a collectivist culture emphasize the community, cooperation, and honouring one's family.

The interplay of culture and personality is also evident when people move from one environment to another. As people become entrenched in a new cultural context, they typically absorb the norms and values of the society. Indeed, research has revealed that when individuals move from a collectivist culture to an individualist one, their personal and behavioural patterns change. One study, for example, looked at the personality traits of Chinese students who were enrolled in universities in North America (McCrae et al., 1998). Those students who had been in North America the longest, and had presumably been more exposed to Western culture, showed higher levels of extroversion and had personality profiles more similar to those of other North Americans.

Interestingly, some people who come from bicultural backgrounds seem to develop the ability to "frame switch"—that is, to change back and forth between cultural frameworks as they interpret experiences. This suggests that they may have internalized the belief systems of both cultures (Hong et al., 2000). It is not yet clear what implications frame switching has for the ties between culture and personality. This is, however, an important question as the world moves each day toward greater cultural integration.

73.3 Culture, Socio-economic Environment, and Personality

A key aspect of culture is the socio-economic environment. Even in the most prosperous nations, there are distinct differences in living conditions between those in the lowest and those in the highest income brackets. These differences have actually increased across the world in recent years (Autor, Katz, & Kearney, 2006). Although the relationship between socio-economic conditions and personality traits has received relatively little attention, investigations conducted to date suggest that it is an important topic (Caspi, 2002; Caspi, Bem, & Elder, 1989). At the very least, it appears that living conditions have a direct impact on how and whether certain personality traits translate into behaviours.

©iStockphoto.com/Syldavia

Socio-economic class, impulsivity, and behaviour. Research suggests that impulsive boys from poor neighbourhoods may be more likely to engage in delinquent behaviours than impulsive boys from wealthier communities.

For example, Annie Yessine of the National Crime Prevention Centre in Ottawa and James Bonta of Public Safety and Emergency Preparedness Canada (2009) examined the trajectories of delinquent Aboriginal youth in Manitoba. Data from the study indicated that chronically high offending youth were more likely to live in impoverished and unstable circumstances, to engage in substance use, and to experience negative peer interactions, suggesting that disorganized environments interact with individual characteristics to increase risk. Indeed, a second study directly assessed the impulsivity of a population of 13-year-old males (Lynam et al., 2000). The teens in the study came from a mixture of backgrounds, from wealthy households to poverty-stricken neighbourhoods. Their socio-economic status was found to clearly link with the outcomes of individual differences in impulsivity. Among boys who lived in poor neighbourhoods, those who displayed high levels of impulsivity were much more likely to engage in delinquent behaviours than those who displayed low levels of impulsivity. In contrast, among boys from high socio-economic status neighbourhoods, behavioural differences between those with low and high impulsivity were negligible. To explain these findings, the investigators reasoned that poor neighbourhoods produce many more triggers for delinquent acts, whereas community structures in affluent neighbourhoods may offer limited opportunities for antisocial activities. In short, particular personality characteristics will result in particular behaviours only if certain situational triggers also are in place.

Before You Go On

www.wiley.com/go/comercanada

What Do You Know?

1. What personality differences between men and women have researchers identified?
2. How does social role theory explain these differences?
3. What are some of the primary differences between the values of collectivist and individualist cultures, and how do these differences affect personality?
4. How does the socio-economic environment affect personality?

What Do You Think? Think about the personality traits of a number of people you know. Include people of different gender and different cultural or subcultural groups. Do personalities seem to differ more on a group level or on an individual level among these acquaintances? How would you explain your observation?

Summary

Module 73: Differences in Personality

LEARNING OBJECTIVE 73 Explain how gender and cultural differences can affect personality.

- Research has found many more similarities than differences between men's and women's personalities. Nevertheless, some consistent differences have been identified.
- Socio-cultural factors are thought to play an important role in gender differences in personality. According to social role theory, for example, boys and girls develop different behaviours and skills based largely on the division of labour between the sexes and the resulting differences in gender role expectations.
- Cross-cultural research into personality has focused on personality development in individualist and collectivist cultures. Some traits observed in these cultures reflect differing cultural values.
- The relationship between socio-economic conditions and personality traits has received relatively little attention. However, the investigations that have been conducted suggest that at the very least, living conditions have a direct impact on how and whether certain personality traits translate into behaviours.

Key Term

Study Questions

Multiple Choice

1. In collectivist cultures, happiness and a sense of accomplishment tend to come from
   a) harmony in interpersonal relationships.
   b) one's achievements at work.
   c) personal freedom and privacy.
   d) the amount of money one makes.

Fill-in-the-Blank

1. According to _____ theory, the gender differences typically seen in skills and behaviour are largely due to the division of labour between men and women.

Module 74: Personality Disorders

What does the description above tell us about Karen? Was she the victim of emotionally distressing circumstances? Or was her self-destructive behaviour the result of dysfunctional personal characteristics? It appears that Karen's initial positive feelings and excitement about someone new in her life were invariably followed by a turbulent phase of emotional outbursts and an eventual falling out. This pattern suggests that Karen may have a **personality disorder**, an inflexible pattern of inner experience and outward behaviour that causes distress or difficulty with daily functioning. Such patterns are enduring and differ markedly from the experiences and behaviours usually expected of people (APA, 2013).

As we suggested earlier in this part, each of us has a distinct personality and specific personality traits. Yet, for most of us, this distinct personality is also flexible. We are affected by situational factors, and we learn from our experiences. As we interact with our environment, we try out various responses to see which are more effective. This flexibility is missing in people who have a personality disorder.

Personality disorders usually become evident during adolescence or early adulthood, although some begin during childhood (APA, 2013). There is no specific data on the rate of personality disorders in Canada (Health Canada, 2002). American data suggest that the rate is somewhere between 9 and 13 percent of the general population (O'Connor, 2008; Lenzenweger et al., 2007). As in Karen's case, the effects of a personality disorder can sometimes be so subtle that they are initially unnoticeable. It may take multiple encounters over time for the maladaptive symptoms to become recognizable. In the latest edition of its diagnostic manual (DSM-5), the American Psychiatric Association (APA, 2013) states that all personality disorders share four core features:

1. rigid, extreme and distorted thinking patterns (thoughts);
2. problematic emotional response patterns (feelings);
3. impulse control problems (behaviour); and
4. significant interpersonal problems (behaviour).

Clearly, these symptoms have a significant impact on the individual's functioning in school, at work, and in social and romantic relationships (Berenson et al., 2011; Mason & Kreger, 2010).

LEARNING OBJECTIVE 74
Define personality disorders, and describe some of the key features of these disorders.

personality disorder an inflexible pattern of inner experience and outward behaviour that causes distress or difficulty with daily functioning.

Psychology Around Us | The Roommate

Karen and I met when I placed an ad in a newspaper for a new roommate. At first, I thought we were having fun living together. Then one night, about two months after she moved in, I was getting ready to go out with a friend, and Karen demanded to know where I was going. She wanted to know who I was seeing, what I was doing, and then she tried to make me feel guilty for going out. . . .

When I came home that night, it was really scary. There was a little blood on the floor, and it made a trail that led to her bedroom door. When I banged on the door to see if she was all right, she said that she'd accidentally cut herself making a sandwich, and everything was fine.

Dealing with her was starting to take a lot out of me. Then she started dating this guy, Eric, and I thought things were getting better. Karen was spending almost no time at home, and when I did see her, she would gush about how incredibly happy she was. . . .

I should have seen what was coming next, but, like an idiot, I didn't. Eric left her, and she was totally my problem again. She stayed home and cried for days at a time. She made me take care of her, telling me she was too depressed to do anything for herself. She even fantasized about the violent things she would do to Eric when she felt up to it. . . . After Eric, there was Ahmad, then James, then Stefan. Always the same story, always the same ending. And always with me in the middle. . . .

Leah Hennel/Calgary Herald, reprinted with permission of The Calgary Herald

Disregarding others. Alleged Ponzi-schemer and fraudster Milowe Brost, from Calgary, Alberta, is in custody, charged with defrauding thousands of investors of more than $300 million.

borderline personality disorder
a personality disorder characterized by severe instability in emotions and self-concept and high levels of volatility.

antisocial personality disorder
a personality disaorder characterized by extreme and callous disregard for the feelings and rights of others.

> **"**Personality disorders . . . are the only things left in psychiatry where people think you are bad.**"**
>
> —*Gary Flaxenberg, psychiatrist*

The APA committee considering changes to the previous version of the DSM (the DSM-IV TR, APA, 2000) originally proposed that personality disorders be considered more as extreme traits or dimensions rather than as discrete diagnostic categories (Pull, 2014). However, the proposed changes were voted down as being too complex to be used effectively in clinical practice. The trait approach was included as an appendix in the new edition (APA, 2013) to encourage research into its new view of personality disorders (Marely, Skodol, & Oldham, 2014).

Based on her roommate's description, Karen appears to be emotionally volatile, particularly when it comes to her relationships. Especially in the early stages of a relationship, she tends to see the men in her life as "perfect," but they inevitably fall from grace. Karen also appears to have a high sensitivity to feeling abandoned, which leads to emotional outbursts. She may even cut herself or cause some other harm as a way of dealing with that negative emotion. Her outbursts and moodiness are off-putting to the roommate and most others in her life. All these features suggest that Karen may be displaying **borderline personality disorder**. Borderline personality disorder is characterized by severe instability in mood and self-concept, which in turn contributes to a high level of instability in relationships (APA, 2000). Borderline personality disorder is often thought of as an emotion dysregulation disturbance (Sherry & Whilde, 2008; Berenbaum et al., 2003; Linehan & Dexter-Mazza, 2008) and will be discussed further in Part 15.

Individuals with **antisocial personality disorder**, most of whom are male, show an extreme and callous disregard for the feelings and rights of others. They typically exhibit impulsivity, egocentrism, and recklessness, along with a superficial charm. Dishonesty and deceit are at the root of their relationships. Indeed, they often form relationships with the intent of exploiting others for material gain or personal gratification. Many are irritable, aggressive, and quick to start fights, and a large number commit criminal acts (APA, 2000). A large study by Dan Offord (1933–2004) at McMaster University suggests that approximately 1.7 percent of the Canadian population shows signs of antisocial personality disorder at any one time (Offord et al., 1996). Another study by Rodger Bland in the department of psychiatry at the University of Alberta suggests that the incidence of this disorder is about 3.7 percent (Bland, Orn, & Newman, 1988). Moreover, cross-cultural research has shown that similar antisocial patterns of symptoms are found in both Eastern and Western cultures (Zoccolillo et al., 1999).

Many theorists have attempted to uncover the origins of personality disorders, and have highlighted factors such as the roles of biological predispositions, early experiences of abuse and neglect, and the pressures of poverty or otherwise harsh social environments (Arens et al., 2011; Bollini & Walker, 2007; Linehan & Dexter-Mazza, 2008; Millon & Grossman, 2007; Patrick, 2007). Generally, however, these disorders are not well understood.

The American Psychiatric Association's diagnostic and classification system (DSM-5) identifies 10 personality disorders, which are described briefly in **Table 74-1**. You will read more about these personality disorders in Part 15, particularly *antisocial personality disorder* and *borderline personality disorder*—the two that have received the most clinical and research attention. At that time, you will come to appreciate just how disabling and disruptive the disorders can be, in part because they are so resistant to treatment.

TABLE 74-1 The Major Personality Disorders

Marked by Odd or Eccentric Behaviour

Paranoid: Exaggerated suspicion and distrust of others; assumption that others' motives are hostile; highly guarded and emotionally withdrawn

Schizoid: Detachment from social relationships; flat emotional expression; cold or indifferent to others

Schizotypal: Behaviour that is odd or peculiar; unusual cognitive or perceptual experiences; acute discomfort with close relationships

Involve Dramatic or Emotional Behaviour

Antisocial: Extreme disregard for others; relationships are dishonest, deceitful, and exploitive; typically impulsive and reckless

Borderline: Severe instability in emotion and self-concept; impulsive and self-destructive behaviour

Histrionic: Excessive need to be noticed and be the centre of attention; emotions shallow and changeable; engagement with others superficial

Narcissistic: Characterized by high degree of self-interest and self-importance; callous attitude toward others

Characterized by High Levels of Fear and Anxiety

Avoidant: Extreme feelings of inadequacy; avoidance of social activities; inhibited personal relationships; hypersensitive to criticism

Dependent: Excessive need to be cared for by others; clinging and submissive behaviour; difficulty making decisions

Obsessive-compulsive: Preoccupied with perfectionism and control at the expense of flexibility or enjoyment; excessive devotion to work and productivity

Source: Based on American Psychiatric Association. (2013). *Diagnostic and statistical manual of mental disorders 5.* Washington, DC: APA.

Psychology Around Us — School Shootings and Videogames

On December 6, 1989, one of the deadliest shootings in Canadian history occurred at Montreal's École Polytechnique, when a young man killed 14 women students, injured 10 other women and four men, and then shot himself. The gunman claimed that feminists had ruined his life. Attempts to interpret motives for this and other shootings led researchers to focus on issues of violence against women (Mancini Billson, 2005), as well as the role of previous child abuse and its relationship to violent behaviour (Denmark et al., 2005), the role of bullying and victimization (Reid & Sullivan, 2009), the role of violence in the media, and the socio-political roles of poverty and isolation in society (O'Grady et al., 2010). The aftermath of the shootings at the École Polytechnique contributed to the passage of the Firearms Act in 1995, leading the way toward more stringent gun control laws in Canada (Rathjen & Charles, 1999). Investigators have also discovered that most school shootings are premeditated and carefully planned (Robertz, 2007).

For its part, the media has regularly tied school shootings, such as the American shootings at Columbine high school, to the playing of videogames—the two students who orchestrated the Columbine killings were, for example, avid players of Doom. But, it turns out that the behaviour of student-killers is not so easily explained. Three years after Columbine, the American Secret Service and the Department of Education published a joint report that looked at 37 school shootings over the past three decades. They concluded that only 12 percent of the school shooters had any interest in videogames (Vossekuil et al., 2002).

If videogames are not a major factor in most school shootings, what are the causes of these violent outbursts? Recent studies of the relationship between school shootings and videogames have found that family violence is more of a risk factor than fictional violence (Ferguson, 2008; Kutner & Olson, 2008). Low self-esteem, depression, and antisocial personality patterns are also factors. In addition, as we observed earlier in this book, adolescent shooters are often the victims of bullying or rejection, and some fantasize for quite a while about revenge for "perceived offenses" (Robertz, 2007).

In light of the these school shootings and other such incidents, reports (Leavitt et al., 2007) recommend increased awareness of the warning signs of potential attacks, such as a student describing plans to hurt others on a website. The hope is that identifying and addressing problems early on may prevent students with mental health problems from reaching a point where there is no turning back.

What Do You Know?
1. What is a personality disorder?
2. What do all personality disorders have in common?
3. What are the 10 personality disorders recognized by DSM-5?

What Do You Think? Personality disorders are popular subjects of fiction. Think about films or television programs that you have seen, and try to find examples of characters who may be displaying personality disorders.

Summary

Module 74: Personality Disorders

LEARNING OBJECTIVE 74 Define personality disorders, and describe some of the key features of these disorders.

- A personality disorder is an inflexible pattern of inner experience and outward behaviour that causes distress or difficulty with daily functioning.
- The American Psychiatric Association outlines 10 personality disorders in its guide for therapists.

Key Terms

antisocial personality disorder 556
borderline personality disorder 556

personality disorder 555

Study Questions

Multiple Choice

1. Personality disorder is best defined as being
   a) an inflexible pattern of inner experience and outward behaviour that causes distress or difficulty with daily functioning.
   b) characterized by a high degree of self-interest and a high, often unrealistic, degree of self-importance.
   c) characterized by extreme and callous disregard for the feelings and rights of others.
   d) characterized by severe instability in emotions and self-concept and high levels of volatility.

Fill-in-the-Blank

1. A person who is charming and manipulative and who does not feel guilty when he hurts others' feelings or takes advantage of them is likely to have _____ personality disorder.

PART 13

SOCIAL PSYCHOLOGY

PART OUTLINE

Module 75: Social Cognition: Attitudes

LEARNING OBJECTIVE 75 Explain how attitudes form and change and what role they play in behaviour.

Module 76: Social Cognition: Attributions

LEARNING OBJECTIVE 76 Discuss how people make attributions to explain their own behaviour and the behaviour of others.

Module 77: Social Forces

LEARNING OBJECTIVE 77 Describe the power of conformity and obedience in shaping people's behaviour.

Module 78: Social Relations

LEARNING OBJECTIVE 78 Review major concepts in the areas of group dynamics, helping behaviour, aggression, and interpersonal attraction.

Module 79: Social Functioning

LEARNING OBJECTIVE 79 Describe the major findings of social neuroscience about regions of the brain particularly important to our social functioning.

Dean Mitchell/Getty Images

In late June 2013, southern Alberta experienced catastrophic flooding, the worst in the history of the province. Unusually heavy rains coupled with saturated ground and a heavy snow melt from the mountains increased the size and flow of many of Alberta's rivers until Siksika First Nation reserve, Calgary, Bragg Creek, High River, Lethbridge, Medicine Hat, Exshaw, Canmore, and many other municipalities were ravaged by flooding. People lost their sense of safety and refuge as well as their homes, their belongings, their mementos, their treasures, and for five people, their lives. Damages were estimated at over $5 billion. Over 2200 Canadian Forces troops were deployed to help in the areas hardest hit.

Calgary was crippled as the Bow and Elbow Rivers spilled their banks and was one of over 32 communities in Alberta under a state of local emergency. Over 100,000 people were displaced as mandatory evacuation orders emptied 26 neighbourhoods. The downtown core closed for an unprecedented 12 days. Schools, post-secondary institutions, and businesses closed. The city ground to a halt. Many people lost all that they had. It was a disaster.

But the real story comes after the waters receded … leaving a mammoth and overwhelming cleanup effort. The indomitable spirit of Albertans and the can-do attitude of Calgarians so in evidence during the flooding surged to the forefront as residents came out in unprecedented numbers to help those in need. Virtually every person unaffected by the flooding (and many who were) donned rubber boots and work gloves and got down to the backbreaking work of cleaning up. Strangers became lifesavers and later, friends. Those too frail to help in the physical cleanup baked and cooked and laundered and watched children and pets and ran errands and supplied fresh water and cleaning supplies. Spontaneous volunteer campaigns were set up so that complete strangers could help those in need. Buses took volunteers not needed in Calgary to outlying communities.

A sign outside of a home in the residential area of Bowness said it all: "We lost some stuff, we gained a community."

The actions of people in and after such events are of particular interest to social psychologists. What moves people to give? Why do people give to absolute strangers? Social psychologists study the social forces involved in this sort of behaviour.

The British poet John Donne's famous words, "No man is an island," highlight the interconnectedness of humankind. We live in a world of approximately 7 billion people, and we influence and are influenced by others. Social psychologists devote themselves to the study of human interconnectedness. Unlike many areas of psychology that focus on individual difference, such as personality or atypical development, social psychology is based on the belief that "it is not so much the kind of person a

© STRINGER/CANADA/Reuters/Corbis

Nathan Denette/The Canadian Press

The social impact. Left, cars float in water covering a downtown street in High River, Alberta and residents and volunteers pitch in to help clean up after flooding in Calgary. Many Albertans helped each other to cope during the flood and with the aftermath.

man is, as the kind of situation in which he finds himself that determines how he will act" (Milgram, 2004, p. 101).

We might think of social psychology in a general way as the scientific study of how people are affected by other people. This informal definition covers considerable territory. Many aspects of an individual's functioning may be affected by others—thoughts, feelings, and behaviours may each reflect the influence of the social environment. Moreover, the influence of others may be direct or indirect.

Given the many ways in which people affect one another, the pioneering psychologist Gordon Allport (1954) offered a more detailed definition of social psychology that is embraced by most people in the field. That is, **social psychology** seeks to understand, explain, and predict how our thoughts, feelings, and behaviour influence and are influenced by the actual, imagined, or implied presence of others (Allport, 1985).

Which pieces of this definition should social psychologists focus on? Many social psychologists have concerned themselves with **social cognition**—how people perceive and interpret themselves and others in their social world. They have examined, for example, the attitudes people hold and the attributions that people make. Other social psychologists have paid more attention to social forces and social interactions. We will discuss each of these areas on the following pages, and examine what happens in the brain during social functioning.

social psychology an area of psychology that seeks to understand, explain, and predict how people's thoughts, feelings, and behaviours are influenced by the actual, imagined, or implied presence of others.

social cognition the way in which people perceive and interpret themselves and others in their social world.

Module 75: Social Cognition: Attitudes

LEARNING OBJECTIVE 75
Explain how attitudes form and change and what role they play in behaviour.

attitudes relatively stable and enduring evaluations of things and people.

ABC model of attitudes a model proposing that attitudes have three components: the affective component, the behavioural component, and the cognitive component.

There are few things in our world that we do not evaluate in some form or another. On some evaluations, people tend to agree. For example, most people believe that natural disasters (wildfires) are bad, that horror movies are scary, and that babies deserve love. On other topics, people are more divided—such as the proper role of government in people's lives, the best ice cream flavour, and the advisability of legalizing drugs. Psychologists refer to our relatively stable and enduring (within individuals) evaluations of things and people as **attitudes** (Petrocelli et al., 2010; Albarracin et al., 2005).

According to the **ABC model of attitudes**, attitudes have three components, as shown in **Figure 75-1** (Eagly & Chaiken, 2007; van den Berg et al., 2006):

- The *affective* component—how we feel toward an object.
- The *behavioural* component—how we behave toward an object.
- The *cognitive* component—what we believe about an object.

Before September 11, 2001, many North Americans held the attitude that their everyday world was safe from terrorism. They felt secure (affective component), went to work each day confident that terrorism would not touch their lives (behavioural component), and believed they were safe (cognitive component) (Henry et al., 2004). While many believe that the American response has generally been disproportionate to the actual level of threat (Mueller & Stewart, 2012), general surveys of Canadians indicate that 93 percent of us are satisfied with our current level of personal safety (Statistics Canada, 2009). We do not have data, but it is certainly clear that attitudes can change. We will explain how that can happen later in this module; but first, let's discuss how attitudes form in the first place.

75.1 Attitudes

Early in life, parents play a major role in shaping children's beliefs and opinions about things and people (Simpkins et al., 2012; Day et al., 2006). As we observed in Part 4, children are socialized when they acquire beliefs and behaviours considered desirable or appropriate by the family to which they belong. You are reading this textbook right now because you have been socialized in a number of ways—perhaps to believe in the value of a post-secondary education or the need for hard work to achieve your goals. This socialization may have occurred by direct transmission (your parents lecturing you about these values) or in subtler ways (Egan et al., 2007). Perhaps your mother or father praised you for your grades or punished you for not doing your homework. Over time, you might generalize these individual experiences into an overall attitude about the value of what you are doing.

As children mature, their peers, their teachers, and the media also begin to significantly influence their attitudes (Prislin & Crano, 2012; Prislin & Wood, 2005). Recall that in vicarious learning, children observe their classmates and take note of the rewards and punishments those students experience based on their behaviour. If a child sees a

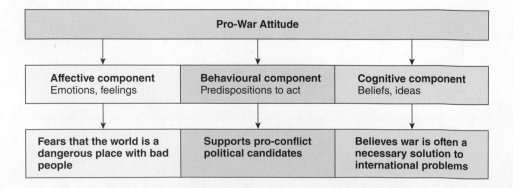

FIGURE 75-1 The ABC model of attitudes.

classmate rejected by the rest of the class for making disparaging remarks about a particular ethnic group, for example, the child may develop an attitude that such remarks are inappropriate and unacceptable. Similarly, seeing a favourite television character get whatever he wants by bullying people might foster an attitude that aggression is an acceptable way to achieve one's goals. Thus children learn attitudes in similar ways to the way they learn about other aspects of the world (Verkuyten & Thijs, 2013).

75.2 How Do Attitudes Change?

In addition to outside influences, we are also, of course, instrumental in shaping our own attitudes; that is, in addition to outside influence, the self is also a key source of attitude change. Such self-generated thought can have an important impact on our attitudes (Wood et al., 2007). Research shows that just thinking about something makes it more significant and important to a person and explains, at least in part, why attitudes tend to become more extreme over time even when there is no additional exposure to outside information. Proponents of this phenomenon have dubbed it the *mere thought effect* (Tesser, 1978). They suggest that when people have more time to think about something, they generate more attitude-consistent thoughts and these thoughts serve to polarize (i.e., make more extreme) the attitude associated with them. However, Clarkson and associates (2011) argue that polarization of an existing thought is not due simply to additional thought; instead, they argue that people become more confident in their attitudes and thoughts as they marshal more attitude-consistent thought. Can such self-generated attitudes be changed?

Jose Luis Peleaz/Blend Images/Corbis

Shaping attitudes. Many school-age children today support recycling. What influences in the media and the general culture may have helped to shape this child's attitude?

Once we have internalized a particular attitude—that is, once we have made it our own—how rigid and long lasting is that attitude? Can people experience a change of heart? In a classic social psychology experiment in the late 1950s, researchers Leon Festinger and J. Merrill Carlsmith (1959) demonstrated that when we are subtly manipulated into doing or saying something that is contrary to our private attitudes, we often change our attitudes to match the new action or statement. If, for example, you are asked to make a presentation in favour of a west coast salmon fishing ban when in fact you oppose such a ban, you may later report—and believe—that your position has shifted in the direction of support for a west coast salmon fishing ban.

In their study, Festinger and Carlsmith had research participants engage in a number of repetitive and boring tasks, such as spending an hour slowly turning square pegs on a board or adding spools to a tray and then removing them. After the tasks were done, the experimenters told the participants that the experiment was over and that they would be allowed to go home shortly—but in truth the experiment had just begun! Each participant was next told that a new group of individuals would soon arrive—individuals who would be performing the same tedious tasks but would be told ahead of time that the tasks were actually "fun" and "intriguing." The experimenter further asked each participant to help out by describing the upcoming tasks as fun and exciting to one of the new individuals. (All of the new individuals were in fact *confederates*. Confederates are people who are collaborators with the experimenters and are acting a part. In experiments where confederates play a role, participants believe the confederate to be the actual person they are pretending to be.) In spite of having found the task to have been really boring in almost all cases, the participants agreed to tell the new individuals that participating in the task was an enjoyable experience. Prior to meeting with the waiting "student" (recall this was actually a confederate), some of the participants were told they would be paid $1 (or about $8 today—a small amount of money) for helping out in this way, while others were told they would receive $20 (about $160 in today's dollars).

After presenting the positive spin on the tedious tasks to the new individuals, the participants were then asked to evaluate the experiment and to say how enjoyable they

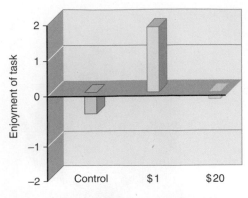

FIGURE 75-2 **Cognitive dissonance.** After describing a boring task as fun, participants in Festinger and Carlsmith's study were asked to rate their own enjoyment of the task on a scale of 25 to 15. Those paid $1 ($8 in 2012) for praising the task rated the task as more enjoyable than those paid $20 ($160 in 2012) for praising it. Source: Adapted with permission of John Wiley & Sons, Inc., from Kowalski, R., & Westen, D. (2009). Psychology (5th ed.). Hoboken, NJ: Wiley, p. 614; based on Festinger, L., & Carlsmith, J. M. (1959). Cognitive consequences of forced compliance. Journal of Abnormal and Social Psychology, 58, 203–210.

cognitive dissonance a state of emotional discomfort people experience when they hold two contradictory beliefs or hold a belief that contradicts their behaviour.

Serious dissonance. The contradiction between this doctor's professional commitment to health and his smoking behaviour may produce noxious feelings of dissonance. To reduce these feelings, he may adopt a belief such as, "Smoking helps me relieve stress and too much stress is a serious health risk."

themselves actually believed the tasks to be. This was, in fact, Festinger and Carlsmith's (1959) central area of interest. Many of the participants paid $1 for "talking up" the tasks reported the tasks to be most enjoyable, whereas those who had been paid $20 were much less likely to report the task as enjoyable (see **Figure 75-2**).

How could participants come to find the mind-numbing tasks of this study enjoyable? Why did those paid less money to convince someone else that the tasks were enjoyable find the tasks *more* enjoyable than those paid more money to do so? Theorists have offered two possible answers to these questions.

75.2.1 Cognitive Dissonance Theory

Festinger (1957) proposed that when we hold two contradictory beliefs, or when we hold a belief that contradicts our behaviour, we experience a state of *emotional discomfort*, or **cognitive dissonance**. This state is so unpleasant that we are motivated to reduce or eliminate it. One way of removing dissonance is to modify our existing beliefs (Gawronski, 2012). In Festinger and Carlsmith's (1959) study, cognitive dissonance theory would hold that the conflict between the participants' initial attitudes about the tasks (that the tasks were boring and trivial) and their later behaviour (telling someone that the tasks were enjoyable) resulted in cognitive dissonance, and this unpleasant state motivated them to change their attitudes about the tasks in positive directions (that is, to believe they actually did enjoy the task, or at least that they found it less unpleasant).

But what about the differing results for the participants in the $1 condition and those in the $20 condition? According to dissonance theory, the participants in the $20 condition experienced less dissonance because they had sufficient justification for their behaviour. Since they were well paid to say that the tasks were enjoyable, they could tell themselves, "I said the experiment was fun because I got quite a lot of money for saying it." (Remember that $20 bought quite a bit more in the late 1950s than it does today.) Thus, these participants experienced little or no discrepancy between their attitudes and their behaviour. In contrast, those who received only $1 for their positive statements had insufficient justification for their behaviour and so experienced a marked discrepancy and uncomfortable feelings of dissonance. These participants managed to reduce the uncomfortable feelings by modifying their beliefs about the tasks—that is, by later reporting (and indeed, believing) "the tasks really were kind of interesting."

Festinger's theory of cognitive dissonance has received support from hundreds of studies (McGregor, 2013; Wicklund & Brehm, 2013; Cooper, 2007, 2005, 2004) which support Fetinger's contention that dissonance creates both psychological and physiological discomfort. For example, Omid Fotuhi and colleagues from the University of Waterloo (2013) telephoned smokers from four countries (Canada, United States, United Kingdom, Australia) over three successive time periods to ask them about their smoking-related beliefs as well as to inquire about quitting behaviour. The researchers report that smokers who were not trying to quit smoking in any of the time periods as well as those who had tried to quit but relapsed had the highest levels of rationalization for their smoking behaviours (see also Borland et al., 2009 for an earlier but similar version of this research). Cognitive theory would support this finding; this theory predicts that we would ignore information that contradicts our beliefs. Kneer and colleagues (2012) argue that most smokers simply refuse to consider the health aspects of smoking.

Somewhat recent work involving fMRI assessments examined the decision phase of participants in a cognitive dissonance paradigm (Jarcho et al., 2011). Results implicated a number of brain areas (including increased activity in areas of the frontal and parietal lobes, and in subcortical structures such as the striatum, as well as decreased activity in the anterior insula—an area important for emotions and consciousness). The main finding was that the rationalization processes associated with cognitive dissonance appear to be made quickly, without extended deliberation.

75.2.2 The Self-Perception Alternative

Cognitive dissonance theory fits some instances of attitude change, but not others. In many cases, we seem to form and change attitudes in the absence of internal discomfort. You might think, for example, that you are alert, but after yawning, you might decide, "I'm tired"—not because of a need to reduce emotional tension brought about by the discrepancy between the attitude ("I'm alert") and the behaviour (a yawn), but simply because the yawn was informative. Psychologist Daryl Bem developed the **self-perception theory** of attitude change (Bem, 1972), arguing that at times we simply infer our attitudes from our behaviours. This theory minimizes the role of emotional discomfort and suggests that when we are *uncertain* of our attitudes, we simply infer what our attitudes are by observing our own behaviour, in much the same way as outsiders might observe us. According to Bem, our behaviours are often clues from which we deduce our attitudes—for example, we might decide we like roller coasters because we keep riding them, or you might decide you now like someone from high school (who you used to despise) because you are now pleasant to her at university. He argued that the students in the Festinger and Carlsmith study (1959) who were paid $1 would not have experienced tension but would have instead looked at their behaviour and concluded that they would not have lied for a dollar, so they must have enjoyed the task.

Which is correct—the cognitive dissonance or the self-perception explanation of attitude change? Historically, this has been a source of great debate in social psychology; however, research has clarified that each may be right, but one may be more relevant in particular situations than the other (Albarracín et al., 2014; Cooper et al., 2004; Petty et al., 2003). Festinger's theory of cognitive dissonance seems more applicable to situations in which we behave in ways that are strikingly out of character for us, whereas Bem's self-perception theory may be at work in situations where we behave only slightly out of character or where our attitudes are not all that clear to begin with (Olson & Stone, 2005).

self-perception theory a theory suggesting that when people are uncertain of their attitudes, they infer what the attitudes are by observing their own behaviour.

75.3 Do Attitudes Influence Behaviour?

If we know someone's attitudes, does that mean we can predict that person's behaviour? It turns out that the attitudes people express are not necessarily related to how they actually behave (McGregor, 2013; Fazio & Roskos-Ewoldsen, 2005; Cooper et al., 2004). In the 1930s, a time when many Americans held very [unacceptable] negative attitudes toward Asians, sociologist Richard LaPiere conducted a field study in which he had a Chinese couple travel across the United States and visit over 250 hotels and restaurants (LaPiere, 1934). Although managers at over 90 percent of the establishments indicated in a mailed questionnaire—received prior to the actual visit—that they would not serve Chinese guests, only one of the establishments visited by the Chinese couple actually refused them service. In fact, most of the hotels and restaurants provided above-average service, indicating that attitudes do not necessarily predict behaviour.

Of course, sometimes attitudes do predict behaviour. Research has uncovered various factors that affect the extent to which attitudes will predict behaviours (Fabrigar et al., 2006; Fazio & Roskos-Ewoldsen, 2005; Cooper et al., 2004). One of the leading factors is *attitude specificity*. The more specific an attitude, the more likely it is to predict

©IStockphoto.com/LukaTDB

"Believe what I do, not what I say." Many people who endorse healthful eating and better fitness on surveys actually consume huge quantities of junk food in their daily meals.

behaviour. If a woman specifically loves Katy Perry, for example, she is more likely to download Perry's new CD the first day it is released than someone who loves pop music more broadly. Another factor is *attitude strength*. Stronger attitudes predict behaviour more accurately than weak or vague attitudes. For example, people who feel passionately about gay rights are more likely to join a demonstration than people who are in favour of gay rights but see this as a more general issue in light of fairness and legal rights for everyone.

75.4 Are People Honest About Their Attitudes?

One reason that attitudes fail to consistently predict behaviours is that people often *misrepresent* their attitudes. In fact, analyses of most self-report questionnaires—the tools usually used by researchers to measure attitudes—cannot distinguish genuine attitudes from false ones (Carels et al., 2006; Cobb, 2002; Rosenberg, 1969). Why would people misrepresent their attitudes? There appear to be several reasons.

75.4.1 The Social Desirability Factor

Often, people state attitudes that are *socially desirable* rather than accurate. A person who privately does not trust people of a particular ethnic background, for example, may not acknowledge having this attitude for fear of being judged unfavourably by others. To eliminate the social desirability factor and measure people's genuine attitudes, some psychologists have employed the *bogus pipeline* technique (Jones & Sigall, 1971). Here, a research participant is connected to a physiological monitoring device such as a polygraph (lie-detector machine that measures physiological arousal) and is told that the device can detect deception. Participants believe the machine to be functioning and also believe that it can identify dishonesty. Therefore when individuals are connected to such a device, they are more likely to report their attitudes truthfully (Lewis & Cuppari, 2009; Nier, 2005).

For example, investigators asked students about socially sensitive issues, such as how frequently they drank, smoked, had sex, and used illicit drugs (Tourangeau et al., 1997). Participants in one group were hooked up to a device and told that it could detect inaccurate answers. The students hooked up to the machine reported performing socially sensitive behaviours relatively frequently. Control participants, who were not hooked up to the device, answered in more socially desirable ways, reporting lower frequencies of the behaviours in question. In a second bogus pipeline study, Fisher and Brunell (2014) measured gender differences in cheating behaviour. Gender differences were diminished when participants believed that their responses were being monitored by a polygraph.

> "We have all had the experience of finding that our reactions and perhaps even our deeds have denied beliefs we thought were ours."
> —*James Baldwin, writer and civil rights activist*

75.4.2 Implicit Attitudes

Another problem that researchers run into when trying to measure attitudes is that people are not always *aware* of their true attitudes (Petty et al., 2009; Bassili & Brown, 2005). In their own minds, employers may believe that applicants of all ethnicities deserve a fair interview process. But when interviewing individuals from ethnic backgrounds other than their own, the same employers may, in fact, engage in less eye contact, maintain greater physical distance, and offer less interview time than when interviewing applicants whose backgrounds are similar to their own. In such cases, the employers may have difficulty trusting people of different backgrounds, but this attitude has not reached their conscious awareness (Macan & Merritt, 2011; Baron & Banaji, 2006; Bassett et al., 2005; Greenwald et al., 2002). When attitudes such as these lie below the level of conscious awareness, they are called **implicit attitudes**.

implicit attitude an attitude of which the person is unaware.

The finding that people have implicit attitudes is reminiscent of the following observation by the famous Russian writer Fyodor Dostoyevsky:

> *Every man has reminiscences which he would not tell to everyone but only his*
> *friends. He has other matters in his mind which he would not reveal even to his*
> *friends, but only to himself, and that in secret. But there are other things which a*
> *man is afraid to tell even to himself, and every decent man has a number of such*
> *things stored away in his mind.*
>
> —*White Nights and Other Stories (1918)*

As you might imagine, measuring attitudes that the holder is not aware of presents a challenge for researchers. To get at implicit attitudes, researchers have employed one of several measures for assessing attitudes, the *Implicit Association Test (IAT)*. The IAT uses a person's reaction times to measure the strength of the implicit associations people have in their minds. The test consists of four stages.

1. First, a person is exposed to two broad categories—say, "dog" and "cat." The person is asked to categorize certain words as belonging in the "dog" category or the "cat" category—for example, fire hydrant and litter box. If the word "fire hydrant" came up and the person saw this word as more dog-related, the person would click the left button. If the word "litter box" came up and the person saw this word as more cat-related, the person would click the right button. How quickly these decisions are made is measured by reaction time, that is, how long it took to decide which button to press—the right one or the left one.

2. Next, the person is asked to complete a different task in which they must categorize words as either pleasant or unpleasant. These words are again fairly obvious, such as "poison" and "happiness." Again, a right or left button press is used and reaction time is measured.

3. Next, the categories are combined in a third task, combining, for example, dog and pleasant and cat and unpleasant. The person is asked to identify a series of words as either more dog/pleasant or more cat/unpleasant. Again, a right or left button press is used and reaction time is measured.

4. The categories are then reversed to be cat/pleasant and dog/unpleasant. Again, a right or left button press is used and reaction time is measured. The assumption is that if a person implicitly believes that dogs are more desirable than cats, the person should be quicker to identify pleasant words during the dog/pleasant combination, because the association between pleasant things and dogs is stronger. It will take this person slightly longer to make the dog/unpleasant association because it requires more effort. Similarly, cat people should respond quicker to the cat/pleasant combination.

You might find this logic convoluted and hard to accept. However, researchers have found that many Caucasian Americans who characterize themselves as not prejudiced have quicker reaction times to Caucasian American/pleasant and African American/unpleasant identifications than to Caucasian American/unpleasant and African American/pleasant ones. Such implicit attitudes appear to be stable over time, and they have been useful predictors of both subtle indicators of discomfort, such as turning one's eyes away during a conversation with someone of another race, and overt acts of racism, such as the use of slurs, physical violence, and snubbing (Rudman & Ashmore, 2007). Researchers have also used the IAT to detect bias against elderly people, overweight people (Roddy et al., 2010), women, and other groups.

If you want to see how an Implicit Association Test works, go online to www.implicit.harvard.edu and take one for yourself. You can be part of a research study with tens of thousands of participants

Bertram Gawronski and his colleagues at the University of Western Ontario have investigated different approaches to reducing both implicit and explicit components of prejudiced beliefs. They have found that diversity training and guided exposure to the groups toward which prejudiced beliefs are directed work to reduce explicit prejudiced beliefs, while fear reduction and other emotion-focused interventions work best to reduce implicit aspects of prejudice (Gawronski et al., 2008; Sritharan & Gawronski, 2010).

Gawronski's key finding is that simple, one-element efforts to reduce prejudice do not work. Instead, he argues that a multiple component effort would be more effective if it focused on several of the following options: listening to persuasive messages arguing against prejudiced views toward a particular group; having people write arguments supporting an unprejudiced perspective; and trying to reduce the affective reaction associated with a particular group by presenting information about them in neutral or non-affect associated situations. Gawronski's research has demonstrated that combinations of these sorts of approaches result in more positive changes in participants' prejudicial cognitions and emotions (Gawronski & de Houwer, 2014; Gawronski et al., 2012).

75.5 Stereotypes and Prejudice

The sadness and fear associated with the Alberta floods makes most Albertans doubly able to appreciate the events that took place during Hurricane Katrina in Louisiana in 2005. Although this event occurred when many of you were young, it remains a very important and controversial time in history. Hurricane Katrina was one of the deadliest hurricanes in the history of the United States. Almost 2,000 people died—many of them poor and many of them African American. In the wake of Hurricane Katrina, millions of people began reaching out with contributions and charity to help the people suffering. During a special charity drive, which aired on most major television networks, rap star Kanye West made the following statement about the disaster:

> *I hate the way they portray us in the media. You see a black family, it [the media] says, "they're looting." You see a white family, it says, "they're looking for food." And, you know, it's been five days [waiting for federal help] because most of the people are black. . . .*

In part, West was talking about *stereotypes*. Most of us are familiar with the notion of **stereotypes**—generalized impressions about people or groups of people based on the social category they occupy. Stereotypes can be based on age, race, and region of origin, as well as political or religious beliefs, or any other group characteristics.

Although stereotypes may be positive or negative, there is little doubt that there is a strong relationship between stereotypes and **prejudice**—negative feelings toward individuals from another group. Both stereotypes and prejudice lead to discrimination, which is a negative behaviour or action aimed at an individual or a specific group of individuals. Research by Reginald Bibby, a sociologist at the University of Lethbridge in Alberta, suggests that prejudice in the form of overt racism and sexism has decreased over time in both

stereotypes fixed overgeneralized and oversimplified belief about a person or a group of people based on assumptions about the group.

prejudice negative and unjust feelings about individuals based on their inclusion in a particular group.

Racial bias. In the aftermath of Hurricane Katrina, newspapers carried many photos of desperate and hungry people taking food from local food stores. The news caption that accompanied the photo on the left (of an African American) stated that the man had just finished "looting a grocery store," whereas the one that accompanied the photo on the right (Caucasian Americans) said that the two individuals had just finished "finding bread and soda at a local grocery store."

Dave Martin/AP

Chris Graythen/Getty Images

the United States and Canada, but has always been and continues to be lower in Canada (see **Figure 75-3**). However, despite these reductions reflecting Canada's greater acceptance of diversity, subtle biases remain (Sue et al., 2007; Dovidio et al., 2002). For example, as noted earlier, many Caucasian individuals who characterize themselves as not feeling prejudiced respond to the Implicit Association Test in a way that suggests they have some implicit negative attitudes toward African Americans and African Canadians. And, more overtly, there has been a long history in Canada of prejudice, negative attitudes, and discrimination toward our First Nations populations (Werhun & Penner, 2010; Bourassa et al., 2004).

Some psychologists believe that the human tendency to identify with a group is one of the main contributors to stereotypes and prejudice (Sherif, 1967). Evolutionary psychologists believe that as humans, we generally categorize ourselves in terms of our similarities to some people and our differences from others. Sometimes referred to as the *mere categorization effect* (Zajonc, 1968), it has come to be accepted that the mere act of categorizing individuals into groups causes them to identify themselves as "us" or "them." Understanding ourselves as members of a particular group (our *in-group*) offers us some insight into who we are. Similarly, perceiving people outside our group as members of other groups (*out-groups*) gives us information—not necessarily valid information—about who they are. This basic categorization structures our future perceptions. Denis Krebs at Simon Fraser University argues that we then use this basic categorization to identify with those we favour and with those we choose to discriminate against (Krebs et al., 1997). Since we view those in the out-group as different than ourselves or our in-group, Krebs argues that we therefore feel very little empathy for those in the out-group and thus feel justified in discriminating against them. As we will discuss in greater detail later, human beings appear to have a cognitive predisposition to see things associated with themselves as good and things not associated with themselves as less good (Fiske, 2010).

Evolutionary psychologists suggest that stereotypes and prejudice may have had some adaptive value, as our ancestors probably prized being able to quickly recognize members of their own tribe based on superficial information (Simpson & Kenrick, 2013). Early humans needed to quickly identify other figures as friends or foes, and general appearance would have been an easy way to accomplish this goal. Evolutionary psychologists also suggest that we may be prewired to think of people whom we perceive to be different from us as inferior, which may cause or justify our decisions to exclude or demean them (Durante et al., 2013; Fiske, 2000).

A view called the *realistic conflict theory* argues that competition arises between different groups because of conflict over scarce resources (Jackson, 1993). A classic study, Sherif's Robbers Cave Experiment, illustrates this theory. Remember that according to this theory, the amount of actual conflict between particular in-groups and out-groups determines the degree of prejudice or discrimination between those groups. A group of 22 11-year-old boys were taken to a camp in Robbers Cave State Park in Oklahoma. The boys were randomly divided into groups before leaving for camp. The groups were housed separately and did not know of the existence of the other group. Each group chose a name ("Rattlers" and "Eagles") and they put the name on their shirts and flags. After a week the two groups met and engaged in a series of competitions against one another. The Rattlers were the winners. The two groups began to call one another names, refused to eat in the same room, and engaged in a series of negative behaviours toward one another. Having deliberately

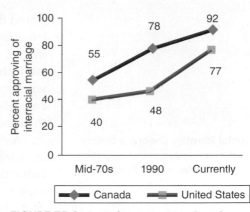

FIGURE 75-3 Prejudice over time. Canadians have expressed greater approval of interracial marriage over the last 40 years, yet studies show that subtle biases remain (Bibby, 2007).

Source: Reginald W. Bibby, "Racial Intermarriage: Canada and the U.S." Project Canada Surveys, University of Lethbridge. Release #9, 2007.

The Robbers Cave experiment. The Robbers Cave experiment is a classic study of group formation. Source: From "The Robbers Cave Experiment" by M. Sherif, O. J. Harvey, B. J. White, W. R. Hood, and C. W. Sherif, Wesleyan University Press, 1988, p. 103.

sowed the seeds of discontent, the experimenters then worked to see if the boys in the two groups could overcome their animosity. A series of problems arose that required that all of the boys work together to overcome them (contaminated drinking supply, etc.). The boys began to eat together once more and when the time came to leave, they voted to take the same bus home (Sherif, 1961). This study gave people hope that peace could flourish between former enemies if they were able to exceed the boundaries of their individual groups.

social identity theory a theory that emphasizes social cognitive factors in the onset of prejudice.

Another view, **social identity theory**, suggests that in social situations individuals often identify as a member of the group. They see themselves at times as a group member rather than as an individual (Tajfel & Turner, 2004). Social identity theory proposes that prejudice emerges through three processes:

1. *Social categorization*, in which a person affiliates with a particular group as a way of figuring out how to act and react in the world.
2. *Social identity*, in which the person forms an identity within the group.
3. *Social comparison*, in which the group member compares the group favourably with other groups, and in turn derives a sense of positive well-being from looking at himself as superior in some way.

In one of his early studies, Tajfel (1981; Jenkins, 2008) randomly assigned study participants to two groups and then had them decide how to divide a sum of money between two people identified only by their group membership and an ID number. Participants typically showed what Tajfel called an in-group bias by giving more of the money to the person in their group than the person in the other group. Even with no group interaction, the effects of social categorization, social identity, and social comparison can be seen in this result. Now think back to the in- and out-group environment that was probably evident in your high school, and see if you can identify examples of social behaviour that reflect the three central factors of social identity theory just discussed.

75.6 Attitudes and the Power of Persuasion

Earlier, we discussed how attitudes form and change. Advertisers have taken a strong interest in these processes. In fact, billions of advertising dollars are devoted each year to helping people develop particular attitudes toward products or services. If you wouldn't dream of using any computer but a MacBook Pro®, or if you much prefer Coke® over Pepsi® (or vice versa), that attitude probably has been created in part through persuasion—the

Psychology Around Us   When Prophecies Fail

Radio evangelist Harold Camping made a prediction that there would be a second coming on May 21, 2011, followed by the end of the world on October 21, 2011. Thousands of followers travelled the United States, giving up their life savings and exhorting others to repent before the world's end. As you might have guessed if you're reading this book, we are all still here.

Prophets of Armageddon and the end of the world are nothing new. What is interesting is what happens when someone makes such a prediction and it doesn't come true. In the 1950s, psychologists Leon Festinger, Henry Riecken, and Stanley Schacter (1964) infiltrated an apocalyptic cult that had been predicting the earth was going to be destroyed by a flood on December 21, 1954. The leader of the cult, Dorothy Martin, said that an alien race would stop by in their flying saucers on the appointed day and save the true believers. The psychologists watched to see what would happen to the beliefs of the followers when (if?) the flying saucers didn't come.

What they observed surprised them. After a few awkward hours of waiting, Martin reported she had received a telepathic message indicating that her followers had done such a good job spreading their message, the earth was saved—there was no need for rescue. Martin merely edited the beliefs slightly to accommodate the new information. Even more interesting, her followers became more devout than ever and more convinced that Martin had been right all along.

advertiser's best efforts to convince you that its product is far superior to anyone else's and that you must have it. Politicians running for office, interest groups looking to increase their influence, and any number of others also regularly use persuasive techniques. Indeed, most of us have had occasion to try to persuade someone else to come around to our way of thinking.

For persuasion to occur, a few elements must be present (Petty & Cacioppo, 1986). There must be, of course, a *message*, somebody to transmit the message (the *source*), and somebody to receive it (the *receiver*). In attempting to make a message persuasive, the source can use methods that follow either a central route or a peripheral route (**Figure** 75-4).

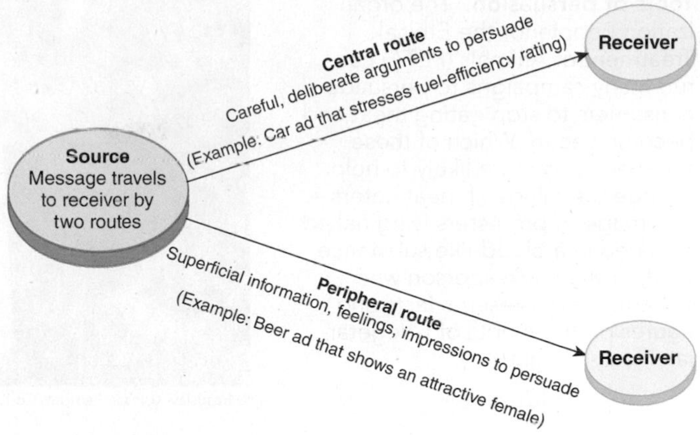

FIGURE 75-4 **Two routes to persuasion.**

75.6.1 Central Route versus Peripheral Route

The *central route* to persuasion emphasizes the content of the message, using factual information and logical arguments to persuade. This method requires a fair amount of effort on the receiver's part and is more commonly used for matters of some significance (Petty & Cacioppo, 1986). If you were trying to decide whether to buy a Mac or a PC, you might be willing to spend considerable time in careful deliberation of all the facts. After all, a computer is an expensive item and an important purchase. You might not be as interested in thinking hard about whether to buy Coke® or Pepsi®, however, or about which brand of shampoo to purchase.

The *peripheral route* relies on more superficial information. When you respond to peripheral appeals, you are responding to such factors as how attractive the spokesperson is and how amusing or engaging the message is (Petty & Cacioppo, 1986). As might be expected, decisions based on central routes to persuasion are more likely to last than decisions based on the peripheral route.

75.6.2 Aids to Persuasion

Beyond the route chosen, a number of other factors can also make a message more or less persuasive. Characteristics of the *source* are important (Petty & Cacioppo, 1986). We are more likely to be persuaded by a source who is rated as more knowledgeable or more likeable, for example. In addition, if we think of the source as more similar to us, we are more likely to be persuaded by the message. (This is part of the reason why wealthy political candidates often try to emphasize their middle-class roots by speaking in shopping malls and grocery stores.) Finally, at least in some instances, people are more likely to find a source credible and persuasive when the source presents both sides of an issue (Murphy et al., 2003).

Sometimes the key to persuasion rests on an interaction between audience characteristics and source characteristics, as shown in work by Sleey Chaiken when she was working at the University of Toronto (1980). If, for example, a source is trying to win the favour of an intelligent or highly motivated audience, an emphasis on logic and on supporting data is more likely to carry the day. If addressing a less intelligent or less interested audience, however, the source might have more success with a glossy, superficial presentation and a good haircut.

A number of *specific techniques* can further improve the chances of successfully persuading others (Chan & Au, 2011). We will mention three here. You have probably been exposed to all of these strategies (and you may have even used them).

- The *foot-in-the-door technique* involves getting someone to agree to a small request and then following up with a much larger one (Guéguen, 2002). The idea is that a bond has been forged between the requestor and the requestee, so the requestee will be inclined to grant the second request because of having granted the first one. For example, you might first ask to borrow your parents' car for an hour, and then later ask to borrow it for the evening. Scammers use this technique to bilk money from gullible lonely partners or seniors (Whitty, 2013).

Tools of persuasion. The organization People for the Ethical Treatment of Animals (PETA) has run many campaigns to persuade consumers to stop eating meat and become vegan. Which of these approaches is more likely to help change the minds of meat eaters—the image of protesters lying naked smeared in a blood-like substance (left), or the spokesperson who systematically presents facts and figures on the merits of a vegetarian lifestyle (right)?

© Rastislav Kolesar/Demotix/Corbis

Tetra Images/Getty Images

- The *door-in-the-face technique* reverses this behaviour. The technique involves making an absurd first request that will obviously be turned down, and then following it with a more moderate request (Rodafinos, Vucevic, & Sideridis, 2005). Here the idea is that if the first request is turned down, the requestee feels guilty and so is more likely to comply with a second, more reasonable, request in order to reduce the guilt. For example, a teenager might wake a parent who is napping to ask her parent to drive her to a friend's place across town. When the parent replies that it is too far, the teen then asks for a ride to the bus stop.

- *Appeals to fear* can be powerful. We frequently see these appeals in anti-smoking campaigns (Leshner et al., 2010; Halkjelsvik, 2014) and in political campaigns (Ridout & Searles, 2011). In order to work, however, an appeal to fear must have a credible source sending the message, and must make receivers truly believe that something bad will happen to them if they don't comply with the source's request. Most importantly, the appeal must provide the receiver with an explicit recommendation for change. For example, there is no sense in worrying about an asteroid hitting earth because there is nothing you can do about it. But if you use condoms when having sex you significantly reduce your chances of contracting HIV or other STDs. So advertisements urging you to use condoms are likely to be more effective than advertisements urging you to purchase protection from asteroids.

"I wish I had never started smoking."

"I was diagnosed with cancer of the larynx when I was 48. I had to have my vocal cords removed, and now I breathe through a hole in my throat." – *Leroy*

Need help to quit? 1-866-366-3667 gosmokefree.gc.ca/quit

Health Canada

© Her Majesty the Queen in Right of Canada, represented by the Minister of Health (2014).

Fear as persuasion. Anti-smoking ads commonly use fear—the fear of life-threatening illness or disgusting physical outcomes—to try to persuade smokers to quit.

Sigmund Freud's nephew, Edmund Bernays, is credited with helping to create modern advertising. Bernays applied psychoanalytic theory to link products with emotions. For example, told by psychoanalysts that women smoked less than men because cigarettes were phallic symbols of men's power, Bernays designed campaigns in the 1920s presenting smoking as a women's rights issue, calling cigarettes "torches of freedom." Smoking among women skyrocketed.

75.6.3 Barriers to Persuasion

Other strategies can interfere with persuasion. Again, we will mention only a couple.

- Forewarning an audience that you will be trying to persuade them of something will immediately raise their defenses. Although listeners in this situation may make subtle shifts toward your way of thinking, they are unlikely to change their attitudes as much as individuals who are not told that they are about to hear a persuasive speech.

- Beginning with a weak argument instead of a strong one can make subsequent arguments seem weaker. For example, a child arguing for an advance on their allowance and arguing by saying she wants the money to buy some candy might lead the parent to interpret a subsequent argument—that the child gave money to a friend at school who had no lunch—as more of an excuse than a valid argument.

Before You Go On

www.wiley.com/go/comercanada

What Do You Know?

1. What are the three components of attitudes, according to the ABC model?
2. How do cognitive dissonance theory and self-perception theory differ in their explanation of attitude change?
3. Why do people sometimes misrepresent their attitudes?
4. How does social identity theory explain prejudice?
5. What are the central and peripheral routes to persuasion?

What Do You Think? Watch a television advertisement or select a print ad and critique it according to the material in this module. For example, does the advertisement use the central or the peripheral route? Was that a good route for the advertiser to choose, considering the product being advertised?

Summary

Module 75: Social Cognition: Attitudes

LEARNING OBJECTIVE 75 Explain how attitudes form and change and what role they play in behaviour.

- *Attitudes* are relatively stable and enduring evaluations of things and people. According to the ABC model, they have affective, behavioural, and cognitive components.
- Parents play a major role in shaping children's attitudes. In older children, peers, teachers, and the media also exert an influence.
- Leon Festinger proposed that people change their attitudes when they experience cognitive dissonance—a state of emotional discomfort that arises when a person holds two contradictory beliefs or holds a belief inconsistent with his behaviour.
- The self-perception theory of attitude change minimizes the role of emotional discomfort and suggests that people simply infer what their attitudes are by observing their own behaviour.
- The attitudes people express are not necessarily related to their behaviour. In part, this is because people sometimes misrepresent their attitudes. They may wish to express socially desirable attitudes, or they may not be aware of what their *implicit attitudes* really are.
- Stereotypes and prejudice arise in part from the human tendency to identify with a group. Various explanations of prejudice come from evolutionary theories, realistic conflict theory, and social identity theory.
- People use persuasion techniques to try to influence the attitudes of others. The central route to persuasion emphasizes the content of the message, while the peripheral route depends on more superficial appeals, such as the appearance of the spokesperson.

Key Terms

ABC model of attitudes 562

attitudes 562

cognitive dissonance 564

implicit attitude 566

prejudice 568

self-perception theory 565

social identity theory 570

stereotypes 568

Study Questions

Multiple Choice

1. A woman who is participating in a march to draw attention to an issue that is important to her is demonstrating the _____ component of attitudes.
   a) affective
   b) behavioural
   c) cognitive
   d) perceptual

2. We are most likely to persuade someone to help us with a time-consuming, unappealing task if we
   a) ask the person to help with a smaller task first.
   b) begin with a weak argument, then follow up with a strong one.
   c) forewarn the person that a request is coming.
   d) make sure the person is in a bad mood.

Fill-in-the-Blank

1. Festinger's research showed that behaviour leads to attitude change only when there is no other good reason, or _____, for the behaviour.

2. Attitudes are more likely to predict behaviour when the attitudes are high in strength and/or _____.

Module 76: Social Cognition: Attributions

In many ways, we are all lay psychologists, continually trying to explain what we see in our social worlds so that we can make sense of events and predict what will happen in the future. We attempt to figure out *why* people, including ourselves, do things. Social psychologists refer to these causal explanations as **attributions**, and they are interested in what influences our attributions and how such attributions affect our subsequent decisions, feelings, and behaviours (Silvera & Laufer, 2005; Stewart, 2005).

76.1 Dispositional and Situational Attributions

Attributions may fall into one of two categories. *Dispositional*, or *internal*, attributions focus on people's traits as the cause of their behaviour (Försterling, 2013; Manusov & Spitzberg, 2008). In contrast, *situational*, or *external*, attributions focus on environmental factors as the cause of behaviour. If you fail an examination, you might make a dispositional attribution that you failed because you were not smart enough. Instead, however, you might tell yourself that the test was unfair and that your neighbour's music was so loud the night before that you couldn't get a good night's sleep—situational attributions.

What determines whether we make dispositional or situational attributions? Research suggests that when explaining *other* people's behaviour, we tend to rely more heavily on dispositional attributions. In a famous study in the 1960s, researchers had participants read a speech that expressed either support for or opposition to Cuban leader Fidel Castro. They then asked each participant to rate the extent to which the speechwriter was pro-Castro (Jones & Harris, 1967). Participants who read a speech supportive of Castro naturally rated the speechwriter as pro-Castro, and those who read a speech critical of Castro naturally rated the speechwriter as anti-Castro. These were dispositional attributions; the participants reasoned that the speeches reflected internal characteristics of the speechwriters. But then the participants were told that the speechwriters had been randomly assigned to write either a pro- or anti-Castro speech. In other words, the participants were given a reason to make a situational attribution rather than a dispositional one. Remarkably, even then, the participants rated speechwriters who had written supportive speeches as very pro-Castro and speechwriters who had written critical speeches as very anti-Castro (see **Figure 76-1**).

Social psychologist Lee Ross (2001, 1977) has referred to our reliance on dispositional attributions to explain the behaviour of other people as the **fundamental attribution error**. When we are almost hit by a speeding driver, we are likely to conclude that the driver is reckless and irresponsible, even though, in fact, she might have been racing to the hospital to see a stricken child. When we meet a woman who is not very talkative, we may conclude that she is withdrawn and arrogant, when in fact she might be a normally friendly sort who has a terrible cold. When a waiter provides unsatisfactory service, we may assume that he is disorganized, even though the fault may lie in the restaurant's kitchen or in the policies of management (Cowley, 2005).

However, we can learn not to make the fundamental attribution error—or at least to make it less often. Research conducted by a team of researchers, including Kerry Kawakami from York University, indicates that automatic stereotyping and prejudice are reduced when participants are exposed to the Situational Attributional Training Technique. The essence of this training is to get people to consider the external causes for someone's behaviour rather than to immediately jump to making an unfavourable dispositional attribution (Stewart et al., 2010).

LEARNING OBJECTIVE 76
Discuss how people make attributions to explain their own behaviour and the behaviour of others.

attributions causal explanations of behaviour.

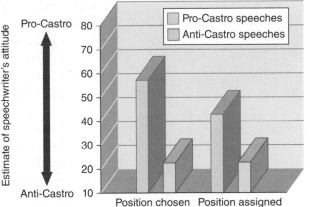

FIGURE 76-1 The fundamental attribution error. Even when told that pro-Castro or anti-Castro speechwriters had been randomly assigned their positions, research participants assumed that the speechwriters truly believed what they had written (Jones & Harris, 1967).

Source: Adapted from Myers, D. G. (2002). Social psychology (7th ed.). New York: McGraw-Hill, Figure 3-2; data from Jones, E. E., & Harris, V. A. (1967). The attribution of attitudes. Journal of Experimental Social Psychology, 3, 1–24.

fundamental attribution error the tendency to use dispositional attributions to explain the behaviour of other people.

76.2 The Actor–Observer Effect

actor–observer effect the discrepancy between how we explain other people's behaviour (dispositionally) and how we explain our own behaviour (situationally).

Social psychologists refer to the discrepancy between how we explain other people's behaviour and how we explain our own behaviour as the **actor–observer effect** (Jones & Nisbett, 1971). The idea of the actor–observer effect is that as *actors*, we tend to make situational attributions about our behaviours; and as *observers*, we tend to make dispositional attributions about the behaviour of others (**Figure 76-2**). Several explanations have been offered as to why this is so. For one thing, as actors, we have information about ourselves that observers don't have. We know from experience, for example, that we don't act the same way in every situation. For another thing, observers tend to focus on the actor, while actors need to focus more on situations. Think about a baseball game. As a fan (observer), you might watch the batter closely. But if you were the batter (actor), you'd need to pay attention to the ball, the other players, and many other aspects of your surroundings. Interestingly, if people are shown videotapes of their own behaviour—that is, if they become observers—they tend to make more dispositional attributions (i.e., make the fundamental attribution error) about the causes of their behaviour (Storms, 1973). That is, the video enables them to switch from actors to observers, and their explanations for their behaviours switch correspondingly.

As an example of the actor–observer effect, consider a class exercise developed by social psychologist Susan Fiske (2010). She tells her students, "Rate on a scale from 1 (low) to 10 (high) to what extent each of the following are reasons you chose your college [or university]."

- I had a wish to please my parents.
- I desired to get away from home.
- I wanted to go where my friends went.
- I liked the location of my college or university.
- I decided to go to a prestigious college or university.
- I was looking to find a marriage partner.
- I wanted a good social life.

After the students have completed these ratings, Fiske instructs them, "Next rate all the reasons that the *typical* student at your college [or university] picked it."

Think about how you decided to go to the college or university you are now attending by answering Fiske's questions for yourself. What sorts of factors did you consider while pondering your decision? Are you attending school close to home or away from home? Are you at a university or a college? Why this school? What do you hope to achieve? After you have considered these questions, answer the same questions in terms of why you think the typical student at your college/university picked it.

If you are like most of the students in Fiske's classes, you thought the reasons on the list described the typical student's decision better than they described yours. If that's the

FIGURE 76-2 The actor–observer effect. We tend to explain our own behaviour in terms of external factors (situational attributions), and others' behaviour in terms of their internal characteristics (dispositional attributions).

The observer

Dispositional attribution

Focuses on the personality of the actor

"He goes up to the bar a lot; he must have a drinking problem."

The actor

Situational attribution

Focuses attention on external factors

"People keep picking up my drink whenever I put it down."

©iStockphoto.com/PeopleImages

case, your ratings illustrate the actor–observer effect. Each of the reasons on the list is a dispositional attribution, relating to something internal to the person. As Fiske observes, "People see themselves as having rich, deep, and adaptive personalities, able to express almost any [behaviour] or its opposite, depending on the circumstances. *Other* people, of course, are ruled by their personalities" (Fiske, 2010, p. 116).

76.3 Exceptions to the Rule

Despite the trend just described, we do not *always* attribute other people's behaviours to their personalities. When we know that just about everyone would react the same way in a given situation, we will likely conclude that a person's behaviour in that situation is situationally caused (Malle, 2006). When most persons are robbed at gunpoint, for example, they (wisely) hand over their money. Thus, a particular robbery victim's surrender of money will usually be attributed to the powerful situational factors.

> *Researchers have found that depressed individuals sometimes have a more realistic perception of themselves and their abilities, a phenomenon known as depressive realism, or the sadder-but-wiser hypothesis (Cummins & Nistico, 2002).*

Similarly, if we are given detailed information about situational pressures, we may attribute the behaviour of other people to situational factors. Think back, once again, to the events surrounding Hurricane Katrina. Initially, most television viewers assumed that all New Orleans residents who had stayed at home rather than evacuate to another city were stubborn, or foolish, or both. However, when information later revealed that thousands of the city's residents were too poor to own a car and that all public transportation systems had shut down, most viewers shifted to a situational explanation for the residents' behaviour.

By the same token, we do not *always* attribute our own behaviour to situational factors. Let's say, for example, that you do poorly on an examination and complain that the questions were "too hard" and the grading unfair. You are, as we would expect, making a situational attribution for your poor performance. But suppose you get a good mark on the next examination. Will you explain your success by pointing out how easy the exam questions were or how generous the grading was? Not likely.

Consistent with this point, social psychologists have noted that when we explain our own behaviour, we are able, and often likely, to fluctuate between situational and dispositional attributions, depending on which puts us in a better light. In other words, we tend to attribute our successes to internal causes and our failures to external ones—a phenomenon referred to as the **self-serving bias** (Johnston & Lee, 2005; Miller & Ross, 1975). Research also has indicated that the direction of our attributions can be influenced by factors such as our moods and emotions, motives, prejudices and stereotypes, and cultural background (Forgas & Locke, 2005; Lieberman et al., 2005; Sadler et al., 2005; Sherman et al., 2005).

self-serving bias the tendency people have to attribute their successes to internal causes and their failures to external ones.

Before You Go On

www.wiley.com/go/comercanada

What Do You Know?
1. How do dispositional and situational attributions differ?
2. What is the fundamental attribution error?
3. What are some exceptions to the actor–observer effect?

What Do You Think? How do you think empathy might influence the actor–observer effect?

Summary

Module 76: Social Cognition: Attributions

LEARNING OBJECTIVE 76 Discuss how people make attributions to explain their own behaviour and the behaviour of others.

- *Attributions*, or causal explanations of behaviour, can be *dispositional* (internal) or situational (external).
- People tend to attribute their own behaviour to situational factors and the behaviour of others to dispositional factors. The reliance on dispositional factors to explain others' behaviour is the *fundamental attribution error*.
- According to the actor–observer effect, this discrepancy exists because people make situational attributions as actors and dispositional attributions as observers.
- People sometimes attribute only their failures to situational factors and attribute their successes to dispositional factors, called the self-serving bias.

Key Terms

actor–observer effect 576

attributions 575

fundamental attribution error 575

self-serving bias 577

Questions

Multiple Choice

1. The fundamental attribution error occurs when we over-estimate _____ when thinking about the causes of other people's behaviour.
   a) dispositions
   b) extenuating circumstances
   c) situations
   d) temporary factors

Fill-in-the-Blank

1. If a teacher assumes that a student is always late for class because the student is lazy and unorganized, the teacher is making a(n) _____ attribution for the student's behaviour.

Module 77: Social Forces

As bad as conditions were in the last-resort shelters after Hurricane Katrina, they were even worse in the New Orleans Convention Center. A small group of people decided to make their way to this facility, even though it had not been designated a shelter. Others followed, until the convention centre was filled with thousands of displaced souls. Those people waited for days for food and support to come. However, because the convention centre had never been formally designated a shelter, federal and state agencies did not even know anyone was there. Not until days later, when television and news reporters "found" those in the centre, were they included in the city's relief efforts.

Given the chaos and uncertainty in the aftermath of Hurricane Katrina, it is understandable that people would look for any sign of what to do or how to get help. The fact that a small group of people decisively sought shelter at the convention centre, even in the absence of any information about whether that was a good choice or not, was more than sufficient to influence many other people to seek shelter there. Even in more normal situations, *social forces* such as these exert a powerful influence on our behaviours and beliefs. Often, for example, people conform to the behaviours and opinions of others, especially when those behaviours and opinions reflect a majority position. We will discuss the social forces of conformity and obedience in this module. First, though, let's examine the related topics of *norms*, *social roles*, *conformity*, and *obedience*.

LEARNING OBJECTIVE 77
Describe the power of conformity and obedience in shaping people's behaviour.

77.1 Norms and Social Roles

Recall that, in the aftermath of Vancouver's 2011 Stanley Cup loss, many people arrived downtown after the game was over to join whatever social event was going to happen. Later, people around the country learned that a growing number of "sports fans" were

---

Psychology Around Us · More Than Tiredness

Yawning is contagious. Try it. If you have someone in the room with you right now, yawn (or fake a yawn), and see what happens (it's even more fun if you can pull it off with a group of people). Although this effect hasn't been studied specifically in humans, researchers at Emory University (Campbell et al., 2011) were able to trigger enhanced yawning in chimpanzees by showing them film footage of other chimpanzees yawning. The effect was two times larger if the chimpanzees in the movie were familiar to the chimpanzees watching the movie. Psychologists are not sure why this happens. Is it conformity? Social modelling? Peer pressure? Many social psychologists believe that contagious yawning may be a way of binding ourselves to other members of our group—that is, the sharing of an experience. More recently researchers from Liverpool (Amici et al., 2014) replicated the results of the study from Campbell et al. and were also able to show that chimpanzees were not reactive when exposed to other actions such as scratching or wiping their noses; instead, increased reactivity was limited to contagious yawning. The researchers speculate that yawning may be linked to empathy. So if you yawn and a friend or colleague yawns right along with you, don't worry—you're not boring each other; you're sharing a moment.

© Christian Hütter/imagebroker/Corbis

burning cars and breaking into stores. Such reports made most people feel very unsettled. One reason for their discomfort was that such behaviours seemed to represent a breakdown of social values and compassion. Another reason was that the behaviours defied people's social expectations. Respectable citizens are not supposed to break into stores and carry off goods, and sports fans are supposed celebrate or mourn their team's accomplishments without setting fire to vehicles. These expectations arise from the norms and roles of our society.

77.1.1 Norms

norms social rules about how members of a society are expected to act.

Society is filled with rules about how everyone is supposed to act. These conventions, referred to as **norms**, provide order and predictability. Some norms are *explicit*, or stated openly. We all know, for example, that we are supposed to stop our car when we come to a red light. Other norms are *implicit*. These norms are not openly stated, but we are still aware of them. You probably weren't taught as a child to face the front of an elevator, for instance, but when is the last time you stepped into an elevator where all the passengers had their backs to the doors?

We can also classify norms as descriptive or injunctive (Larimer et al., 2005, 2004; Larimer & Neighbors, 2003; Eagly & Karau, 2002). *Descriptive norms* are agreed-on expectations about what members of a group *do*, while *injunctive norms* are agreed-on expectations about what members of a group *ought to do*. Consider the behaviour of museum patrons, for example. The pristine appearance of the typical museum, along with signs throughout the building, regularly remind patrons not to litter in this setting. Virtually all museum goers abide by this rule, making it a descriptive norm (Kenrick & Goldstein, 2012; Kallgren et al., 2000; Cialdini et al., 1991). Other researchers have examined how norms influence behaviours and intentions. Smith and colleagues (2012) report that when injunctive and descriptive norms were in conflict, people's intentions [in this particular case] to engage in pro-environmental behaviours were weakened.

Richard T. Nowitz/Corbis

Pictorial reminder. This sign along a Newfoundland highway reminds drivers of the deadly physics of hitting a moose. It also helps remind people of the community's injunctive norm to drive responsibly. Such reminders often have a beneficial impact.

People are more likely to abide by injunctive norms if the norms are called to their attention. For example, people walking through a neighbourhood with litter cans and anti-littering signs are more likely to become aware of and follow the community's injunctive anti-littering norm. In one study of this phenomenon, researchers passed out handbills to pedestrians. Each pedestrian received a handbill promoting either the importance of not littering, the wisdom of saving electricity by turning off lights, or the responsibility of each citizen to vote (Cialdini et al., 1991). Only 10 percent of the pedestrians who had been given the anti-littering pamphlet crumpled and threw the handbill to the ground after they had finished reading it, compared with 20 percent of those who had been given the "lights out" or "voting" handbill.

77.1.2 Social Roles

social role a set of norms ascribed to a person's social position—expectations and duties associated with the individual's position in the family, at work, in the community, and in other settings.

A **social role** is a set of norms ascribed to a person's social position—expectations and duties associated with the individual's position in the family, at work, in the community, and in other settings (Glass, 2005; Alexander & Wood, 2000; Sarbin & Allen, 1968). The role of police officers, for example, is to maintain law and order. The role of parents is to nurture, rear, and teach their children and prepare them for life outside the family.

Roles often have a positive impact on people and society. Indeed, they are critical for the smooth functioning of society. They can, however, also confine people. Just as many actors complain of being "typecast" and prevented from demonstrating their versatility, people in various positions are often limited by their prescribed social roles. Many observers argue, for example, that traditional Western gender roles are oppressive for women.

When individuals in a particular group try to step out of the social roles assigned to members of that group, they may be met with negative reactions and evaluations (Morfei et al., 2004). For example, traditional Western gender roles ascribe more *communal* characteristics to women—that is, ones associated with the welfare of other people—and more *agentic* characteristics to men—that is, those associated with assertiveness, control, and confidence (Mosher & Danoff-Burg, 2008, 2005; Eagly & Koenig, 2006). In short, women in the West are expected to be caring and men to be assertive and self-assured.

Men and women are often judged harshly when they step outside their gender roles (Lindsey & Christy, 2011). For example, in heterosexual relationships, women who leave their children with the male ex-spouse following a divorce are judged more harshly than men who leave their children with their female ex-spouse (Kruk, 2010). Gender role also impacts attitudes at work. Studies find, for example, that when female managers were described to research participants as "successful," the individuals rated the woman as more hostile, selfish, quarrelsome, and subjective than successful male managers; however, in top-level positions, women are often viewed more favourably than men in similar positions (Koenig et al., 2011; Rosette & Tost, 2010; Heilman, Block, & Martell, 1995). Nevertheless, as already discussed, since only a very small proportion of women reach the upper echelons in business, the general opportunities for advancement in the business world are limited for women (Abele, 2003).

In 2006, 73.5 percent of Canadian women between 16 and 64 years of age participated in the paid workforce, compared to 82.5 percent of men (Canadian Labour Congress, 2007). As well, women are 1.6 times more likely to earn a bachelor's degree than men (Canadian Education Statistics Council, 2007). Nevertheless, on average, women occupy lower-ranking positions and earn less income than men, with women employed full-time earning an average of 73 cents for every dollar earned on average by men, though this may be partially influenced by time in position (Canadian Human Rights Commission, 2010). Women constitute only 4.4 percent of the chief executive officers (CEOs) in Fortune 500 companies, and 5 percent of CEOs in Fortune 1000 companies (Catalyst, 2014).

Males are also constrained by gender role expectations (Lowrance, 2014; Levant, 2011). For example, males are often portrayed negatively if they step outside of accepted gender role occupations (Stanley, 2012); are often viewed as occupying a marginal role in the family context (Tsai & Shumow, 2011); and are less likely to seek counselling because of the associated stigma around male control and loss of control (Vogel et al., 2014; Wester, 2010). The imbalance in opportunity and expectation needs to be addressed for both genders.

77.1.3 Roles, Gender, and Social Skills

There is a popular belief in Western society that, on average, women are more skilled socially than men, more sensitive emotionally, more expressive, and more focused on social relationships (Lindsey & Christy, 2011). For example, in a wide range of social psychology studies, it has been found that female participants tend to read non-verbal social cues more accurately than male participants (Hall et al., 2006), are more expressive with their faces and bodies during interactions and better able to read subtle emotional expressions (Hoffmann et al., 2010), and feel more empathy for the emotional experiences of others (Mestre et al., 2009). For their part, male participants tend to focus more narrowly on the tasks at hand in group activities than do female participants, emerge as leaders (as opposed to social facilitators) in group activities, and adopt more authoritarian and less participative styles when they take on leadership roles (Eagly & Koenig, 2006).

Although researchers have not fully sorted out the issue, one of the most common explanations for these differences is social roles (Kmec et al., 2014; Eagly & Wood, 2006). As we observed above, traditional Western gender roles ascribe more communal characteristics to women—including expectations that they should be friendly, unselfish, concerned about others, and emotionally expressive—and more

HOW WE
DIFFER

agentic characteristics to men—including expectations that they will be assertive, independent, and controlling. According to social role theory, people are inclined to behave in ways that are consistent with the expectations tied to their roles (Lindsey & Christy, 2011). Moreover, over the course of their lives, as people enact their social roles, their skills in the assigned realm become sharper and their corresponding attitudes more deeply ingrained.

77.1.4 Roles and Situational Demands: The Stanford Prison Experiment

As we have just discussed, social roles affect not only how others think about us, but also how we think about ourselves and how we act toward others. In 1971, Philip Zimbardo and his colleagues at Stanford University studied the power of situations and roles in a study famously known as *The Stanford Prison Experiment* (Zimbardo, 2006, 2004, 1972; Haney, Banks, & Zimbardo, 1973). At the time, Zimbardo said that it was his intention to conduct the study to show the power of the situation as a "bookend" to the Milgram study, described later in this part (Drury et al., 2012). He wanted to see what would happen to good people put into bad situations and he wanted the situation to be in a controlled experimental setting. The basement of the university's psychology department was converted into a mock prison, and 24 male students—all paid volunteers—were randomly assigned to play the roles of either prisoners or guards for what was supposed to be a period of two weeks. The situation was contrived to include elements such as coercive rules, differences in power, anonymity for guards, as well as deindividuated roles for prisoners (Zimbardo, 2007).

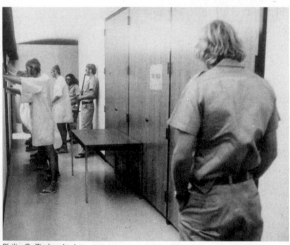

Philip G. Zimbardo, Inc.

The power of social role playing. In the famous Stanford Prison Experiment, most of the students who were assigned to play prison guards engaged in at least some abuses of power, and some guards were deemed sadistic, while those assigned to prisoner roles typically became passive, depressed, and disorganized.

The researchers wanted the experiment to mimic the experience of an actual prisoner or guard as closely as possible. "Guards" were therefore given batons, uniforms, and mirrored sunglasses, and were told that it was their responsibility to manage the prisoners and to run the prison. Guards worked eight hour shifts with breaks. "Prisoners" were arrested by police as they went about their daily lives, were fingerprinted, blindfolded, and deloused, were given prison garb (smocks without under clothing), and were forced to wear small chains around their ankles. Their belongings were taken from them and they were referred to by assigned numbers instead of by name. They were in prison 24 hours a day. On the second day, the prisoners rebelled. The rebellion was quickly quelled and the guards retaliated by stripping the prisoners naked, removing their beds from their cells, and putting the ringleader in isolation. The guards began to taunt and harass the prisoners, imposing humiliating emotional and physical punishments on them (e.g., forcing them to act out (but not actually execute) sexual acts on one another, chaining their legs together, forcing them to perform endless pushups), and denying bathroom privileges and food to prisoners who were deemed "out of line" but giving special privileges to those who were obedient (e.g., allowing smoking breaks for those they liked). The prisoners began to respond to the guards with blind obedience. Prisoners later reported that within days of beginning the simulation they felt as if they had lost their old identities. Zimbardo (2007) said that the prisoners developed "zombie like attitudes and postures, [and were] totally obedient to the escalating guard demands."

Zimbardo reported that he acted more like a warden, concerned more with the security issues facing the "prison" than by the plight of his participants. Christina Maslach, Zimbardo's girlfriend (and later his wife) forced Zimbardo to see just how extreme the situation had become. Zimbardo (2007) said, "Christina made evident . . . that human beings were suffering, not prisoners, not experimental subjects, not paid volunteers." So, after six days, the experiment was called off. The study demonstrated the situational power of roles and context in behaviour and not only explains but *predicts* real-life situations such as those at Abu Ghraib Prison where high stress environments with little surveillance by those in charge result in extreme abuses of power. Zimbardo (2007) said it best: "The situation won. Humanity lost." Each of us has to prevent situations like these from winning; each of us has to learn this lesson to keep the power of situations (and the systems in which they reside) from overriding a person's moral centre and good sense.

The Stanford Prison Experiment raised many ethical concerns in the field of psychology, primarily because the participants experienced clear psychological pain—both the prisoners, who were abused psychologically, and the guards, who were confronted with the fact that they were capable of cruelty and even sadism (Zimbardo, 2007). As you read in Part 2, there are now ethical guidelines and review procedures that all researchers must follow when conducting studies—guidelines and procedures that would make it impossible for this same study to be conducted today.

77.2 Conformity

Conformity is the tendency to yield to real or imagined group pressure. Investigators have been studying conformity for more than 60 years. Early work on this phenomenon was done by social psychologist Theodore Newcomb (1943). In a classic study, Newcomb examined the political views of students at Bennington College as they progressed through school. Although Bennington College is well known for the politically liberal leanings of many of its faculty members, during the Great Depression in the 1930s it was attended largely by children from conservative families. Newcomb found that as the students progressed through college, immersed in the Bennington culture, their political views grew more and more liberal. Moreover, these liberal views endured well into late adulthood, confirmed by interviews conducted 25 and 50 years later (Alwin, Cohen, & Newcomb, 1991; Newcomb et al., 1967). Laboratory studies tell a similar story, especially the classic work conducted by social psychologist Solomon Asch.

conformity the tendency to yield to social pressure.

77.2.1 The Asch Studies

Imagine that you agree to participate in a psychology experiment on "perceptual judgments." You and six other participants are seated around a table—you are seated second from the end—and the experimenter presents two cards to the group. The card on the left, Card A, displays a single vertical line, whereas the card on the right, Card B, displays three vertical lines of various lengths (see **Figure 77-1**). The experimenter asks each participant which of the three lines on Card B is equal in length to the line on Card A. When it is your turn, you immediately recognize that the second line on Card B matches the one on Card A. Thus, after the five participants seated ahead of you indicate that the second line on Card B is equal in length to the line on Card A, you do the same. Another set of cards is presented, and again everyone agrees. The straightforward task is moving along easily and comfortably.

Then something odd happens. On the third round, you again readily note which line on Card B matches the line on Card A—it's pretty clear that it's line 3 this time—but you are shocked to hear that the first person called upon by the experimenter answers, "line 1." You think to yourself "he needs an eye exam," but then the second person responds the same as the first. You rub your eyes, blink, and squint, but still you see that it's line 3 that matches the length of the line on Card A. After the five people ahead of you have all selected line 1, it is your turn to respond. What will you say?

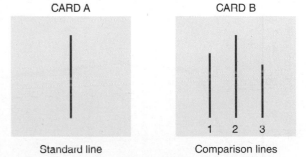

FIGURE 77-1 **The perceptual judgment task in Asch's conformity study.** Asch's participants were asked which line (1, 2, or 3) was the same length as the standard line. Despite the obvious and correct choice (line 2), when the confederates gave the wrong answer, almost 75 percent of the participants conformed and gave the wrong answer on at least one trial, too. Source: Adapted from Asch, S.E. (1955). Opinions and social pressure. *Scientific American*, 193(5), 31–35.

In fact, this classic study, conducted by social psychologist Solomon Asch (1955), was not about perceptual judgments at all, but rather was an investigation of conformity. In the study, the other "participants" were actually confederates, coached by the experimenter to give uniformly wrong answers on the third round and thereafter. Asch found that when the responses of the confederates were incorrect, almost 75 percent of the real participants conformed to the group norm and gave an incorrect response at least once.

Asch also varied the procedures in his experiment to reveal what group features might affect this "tyranny of the majority" (Martin & Hewstone, 2001), and others have followed with similar work. One key factor is group *unanimity*. The presence of even one dissenting group member dramatically reduces the likelihood that participants will conform to an incorrect group norm (Prislin & Wood, 2005). The *size* of the group also affects its influence, as does the number of choices, with fewer choices leading to an increase in conformity (Curtis & Desforges, 2013). Groups with fewer than four members, for example, do not seem to bring about a powerful conformity effect (Asch, 1955; see **Figure 77-2**). Many laboratory studies on conformity have been conducted since Asch's pioneering undertaking (Kundu & Cummins, 2013; Abrams et al., 2005, 2000). The findings of most such studies are similar to Asch's—they demonstrate the strong effects of social pressure.

77.2.2 Conformity and Culture

Conformity is viewed very differently in individualistic and collectivistic cultures (Markus & Kitayama, 1994). People in individualistic cultures often consider conformity to be a bad thing. Typically, members of this kind of culture want to stand out and be different—to have their own identity. In contrast, those in collectivistic cultures usually value fitting in with other people. They see virtue in conforming to social norms and view conformity as an indication of maturity, respect for others, and appropriate self-control. In fact, the Korean word for conformity means inner strength and maturity (Kim & Markus, 1999).

 HOW WE DIFFER

When ordering food in a restaurant, people in North America—an individualistic society—order whatever they desire (Kim & Masters, 1999). They may say, for example, "I'll have a Caesar salad, but light on the croutons and with the dressing on the side." However, in Korea, a collectivistic culture, that kind of restaurant etiquette is unthinkable. It would be seen as an inability to get along with others and as insensitive to the needs of the waiter. Thus, as you might expect, whenever Asch-like studies are conducted in collectivistic cultures, the participants show even higher rates of conformity than do participants in the North American studies (Bond & Smith, 1996). On the other hand, data from Oh (2013) suggest that this cultural difference may be more superficial than initially believed. Although collectivist cultures show a stronger tendency to comply, there was no significant difference on measures of internalization in this research.

77.3 Obedience

In the Asch studies of conformity, there were no leaders in the groups—just peers. In addition, there were no consequences for incorrect responses. No fines were imposed, nobody was hurt, and nobody had to account for or defend their decisions. But what about situations in which people are working under an authority figure, or in which they must pay a price for making an incorrect decision? Classic work by researcher Stanley Milgram offers important, and

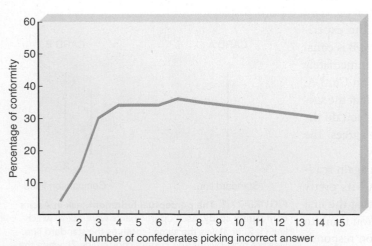

FIGURE 77-2 **Group size and conformity.** A key factor in conformity is group size. Asch found that the conformity effect is not strong when the group's size is less than four members (Asch, 1955). Source: Adapted from Asch, S. E. (1955). Opinions and social pressure. *Scientific American,* 193(5), 31–35.

unsettling, insights into situations of this kind. Milgram studied **obedience**, which occurs when people follow direct commands, usually given by an authority figure.

obedience the act of following direct commands, usually given by an authority figure.

77.3.1 Milgram's Experiment

Milgram's (1963) study is perhaps the most famous and controversial experiment in the history of psychology (Blass, 2007, 2004). Imagine that you have agreed to participate in this experiment. You arrive at the designated location and are met by a stern-looking man in a lab coat. The man introduces you to the mild-mannered "Mr. Wallace" and explains that the two of you are participating in a study of the effects of punishment on learning. One of you will be randomly assigned the role of "teacher," and the other the role of "learner." You are then given the teacher role. Although you are not aware of it, the assignment of roles has not been random at all. Mr. Wallace is a collaborator in league with the experimenter who is really only interested in your behaviour.

The experimenter takes the two of you to an adjacent room, where Mr. Wallace is prepped for his role as learner. He is told to roll up his right shirt sleeve, and the investigator attaches an electrode to his wrist. His arm is strapped down "to prevent excessive movement," and electrode paste is applied "to prevent blisters or burns." You are informed that the electrode is connected to a shock generator in the other room (**Figure** 77-3).

The two of you are told that you (as the teacher) will recite a list of word pairs. After going through the entire list, you will recite only the first word of each pair, followed by four options. Mr. Wallace will indicate which option is the correct match for the first word by pulling one of four levers. If the response is incorrect, you will administer an electric shock. Mr. Wallace mumbles something about having a heart condition, but that comment is more or less ignored by the experimenter.

You are taken to another room, unable to see Mr. Wallace, and are seated in front of a metallic, box-shaped instrument, covered with knobs and switches and labelled "Shock Generator." You notice that each switch on the shock generator's control panel is identified by a voltage—ranging from 15 volts to 450 volts—and a label—ranging from "slight shock"(15 volts) to "danger: extreme shock" (375 volts) to "XXX" (450 volts). The experimenter explains that whenever you push down a switch, Mr. Wallace will receive the corresponding shock, and this shock will stop as soon as you push the switch back up.

You are to communicate with Mr. Wallace through a microphone intercom, as the rooms are "partially soundproof." When he responds by pulling one of the four levers, one of four lights on top of the shock generator will light up. You are to administer a shock to Mr. Wallace whenever he responds incorrectly. With each successive incorrect response, you are to move up one switch on the shock generator, administering what the labels suggest are increasingly powerful—and dangerous—shocks.

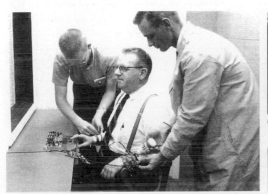

FIGURE 77-3 Milgram's obedience experiment. The photos above show the "teacher" helping the experimenter strap the "learner" into the shock apparatus and Milgram's shock generator. Most people believe that they would not administer shocks to a person crying out in protest, but Milgram's experiment found otherwise.

After Mr. Wallace offers his first incorrect response, you flick the switch identified as "15 volts." The machine springs to life, with bright red lights flashing and an ominous buzzing noise filling the air. As Mr. Wallace continues to offer incorrect responses, you are instructed to administer increasingly powerful shocks. Through the wall, you can hear Mr. Wallace moan and say things, such as "Get me out of here!" Any time you express reluctance to go on, the experimenter confidently states "Please continue" or even, "You have no choice; you must go on." After a while, Mr. Wallace stops responding to your word prompts. The experimenter tells you to treat the failure to respond as an incorrect response and administer another shock (you're up to 450 volts, or "XXX," by now). Mr. Wallace lets out an agonized scream and yells, "Let me out of here! I have heart problems!" You hear and feel Mr. Wallace banging on the adjacent wall. Then he is completely silent. There are no further responses to your word prompts or to the shocks you administer.

> **"Obedience is due only to legitimate powers."**
> —*Jean-Jacques Rousseau, Genevan philosopher and writer*

As you are reading about this study, you are probably saying to yourself that you would have refused to go on with the experiment very early on. Most people who learn about this study have that reaction. Indeed, before the study became widely known, its procedures were described to psychologists, and they predicted that only 1 percent of participants would continue with the experiment all the way through 450 volts (Milgram, 1963). Astonishingly, Milgram found that 65 percent of the participants continued with the experiment all the way through the 450 volts label, and no participant stopped before the 300-volt mark (see **Figure 77-4**). As well, more recent replications of parts of the study (as the study as a whole would not receive ethics clearance today) show that things have not changed, and under similar circumstances participants would still behave as Milgram's initial participants behaved (Burger, 2008).

77.3.2 The Milgram Controversy

It is no wonder that Milgram's study is one of psychology's most controversial. The study revealed something profoundly disturbing about human nature—namely, that we are inclined to obey authority, even if it means behaving in ways we would never predict we would behave. Milgram demonstrated that it is not just a cruel and sadistic fringe of the population that can inflict pain and suffering on innocent victims; two-thirds of the population might hurt others if ordered to do so by an authority figure. Milgram (1974) went on to explain the atrocities committed by Nazi Germany within the context of his remarkable findings, although a number of theorists have questioned the appropriateness of such a leap (Miller, 2004).

FIGURE 77-4 **The results of Milgram's obedience experiment.** Milgram found that no participant stopped administering shocks before the 300-volt mark, and that the vast majority (65 percent) continued administering shocks to the highest level (Milgram, 1963).

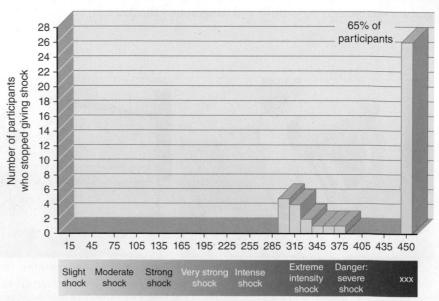

Voltage levels labelled on Milgram's shock generator

Initially, many refused to believe that Milgram's findings provided an accurate representation of people's readiness to inflict suffering. Critics attacked the experiment on various grounds. Most notably, the participants in the original study were all male. Some speculated that women might be less inclined to obey commands to inflict pain on others. Additionally, a number pointed out that the study had been conducted at Yale University. Had it been carried out at a less prestigious locale, they argued, the participants might have been less likely to obey the experimenter's commands. Finally, many questioned the ethical implications of the research.

> **"**I was just following orders.**"**
>
> *—Adolf Eichmann, high-ranking official in Nazi Germany and self-proclaimed Jewish Specialist, at his 1961 war criminal trial*

77.3.3 Follow-up Studies

Milgram spent the years following the publication of his controversial findings conducting variations of the original experiment to further clarify the nature of obedience (Milgram, 1974). To the surprise of many people, he found that female participants were no more likely to defy an experimenter's commands than the male participants in the original experiment. Milgram also set up an alternative site for his experiment, the "Research Associates of Bridgeport"—supposedly a commercial organization that was not connected with Yale. In this variation, the percentage of people who kept administering shocks through 450 volts was somewhat lower than in the original experiment, but still considerable—around 50 percent, compared with the original 65 percent.

Further to that, a meta-analysis carried out by Haslam and colleagues (2014) to evaluate factors impacting the original findings identified eight factors that predicted whether a given individual would go all the way to the 450 volt level of shock. Factors included the proximity of the experimenter to the person in the role as the teacher, as well as factors related to the connection between the teacher and the learner (e.g., three factors were related to the experimenter: how directive they were, how legitimate they were perceived to be, and how consistent they were). As well, if there was group pressure on the teacher to disobey, or proximity was indirect, the teacher's behaviour was also impacted. Finally, the behaviour of the teacher was influenced by proximity and amount of intimacy between the teacher and the learner and the distance between the experimenter and teacher.

Milgram's experiments and subsequent replications demonstrated just how ready people are to obey authority, but they also clarified that certain factors *reduce* people's willingness to obey (Lüttke, 2004).

- If a confederate served as "co-teacher" with the research participant and refused to continue, over 90 percent of the real participants followed suit and disobeyed as well.
- The *salience* of a victim's suffering—its obviousness—affected participants' obedience. Participants in Milgram's studies were, for example, less likely to obey when they could see the look on Mr. Wallace's face with each successive shock.
- A participant's *proximity* to the victim affected obedience. When Milgram's participants were seated in the room with Mr. Wallace, only about 40 percent of them continued to obey through 450 volts. Still fewer (30 percent) were obedient in a condition that had them placing Mr. Wallace's hand on a shock plate to administer the shock.

Of course, there are many occasions in life where it can be quite useful, and even advantageous, to obey commands. During military manoeuvres, surgical procedures, theatre productions, and sporting competitions, for example, a lack of obedience may result in chaos or disaster. However, Milgram's study demonstrates the dark side of obedience. In a letter to another social psychologist, Milgram wrote, "Certainly, obedience serves numerous productive functions, and you may wonder why I focus on its destructive potential. Perhaps it is because this [the holocaust] has been the most striking and disturbing expression of obedience in our time" (Blass, 2004, pg. 99).

It is important to note that Milgram's work was carried out in 1961 and 1962, prior to the advent of institutional ethics review boards. Yale University did not require informed consent from participants at that time. Instead, participants provided uninformed verbal consent and signed legal documents absolving Yale University of any liability. This type of research would not be allowed today (Haslam et al., 2014).

Before You Go On

www.wiley.com/go/comercanada

What Do You Know?
1. What are norms and what is their function in society?
2. What did Solomon Asch's experiments on conformity reveal?
3. What is the central difference between the concepts of conformity and obedience?

What Do You Think? In both Asch's and Milgram's experiments, the presence of another person who would either go against the group or refuse to obey the authority figure made it more likely that the research participant would do so as well. How would you explain this phenomenon?

Summary

Module 77: Social Forces

LEARNING OBJECTIVE 77 Describe the power of conformity and obedience in shaping people's behaviour.

- Society establishes rules, or *norms*, about how people are supposed to act. *Social roles* are sets of norms ascribed to particular social positions. Norms and roles are critical to the smooth functioning of society, but also place limits on individuals.

- Conformity is the tendency to yield to real or imagined group pressure. In a famous series of experiments, Solomon Asch found that 75 percent of research participants yielded to implicit group pressure to conform to an incorrect judgment.

- Unlike conformity, obedience involves following direct orders, usually from an authority figure. Experiments by Stanley Milgram found that 65 percent of subjects continued to follow orders to administer what they believed to be dangerous electric shocks.

Key Terms

conformity 583

norms 580

obedience 585

social role 580

Study Questions

Multiple Choice

1. A(n) _____ norm is one that is not taught directly, but that people tend to pick up on.
   a) descriptive
   b) explicit
   c) implicit
   d) injunctive

2. In Asch's original study of conformity, about what percentage of participants conformed (gave a response that they knew was incorrect) at least once?
   a) 1 percent
   b) 37 percent

   c) 66 percent
   d) 75 percent

Fill-in-the-Blank

1. Groups with fewer than _____ members do not typically show a conformity effect.

2. Milgram told his research subjects that they were participating in a study of the effects of _____ on learning.

3. In a study of cultural influences on attributions, it was found that the characteristic of _____ led Chinese participants to focus on situational causes of behaviour more than American participants did.

Module 78: Social Relations

Many social psychologists are interested in social relations. Some have studied *group dynamics*—how membership or participation in a group influences our thoughts and behaviours. Still others have attempted to determine when people choose to help others and when they will ignore others' needs. Other social psychologists have examined aggression and interpersonal attraction, trying to understand why people behave aggressively and how people come to like or love others in their social world.

LEARNING OBJECTIVE 78
Review major concepts in the areas of group dynamics, helping behaviour, aggression, and interpersonal attraction.

78.1 Group Dynamics

A **group** is an organized, stable collection of individuals in which the members are aware of and influence one another and share a common identity. Group members are thus *interdependent*—that is, the behaviour of one group member affects the behaviour of the other members. Let's consider several topics related to groups and group dynamics: *group productivity, the social facilitation effect, social loafing, group polarization,* and *groupthink.*

group an organized, stable collection of individuals in which the members are aware of and influence one another and share a common identity.

78.1.1 Group Productivity

One issue of interest to social psychologists is what makes groups productive. Not surprisingly, they have found that the optimal group size for productivity depends on the task at hand (Steiner, 1972).

- When a group is performing an *additive task*, its members must perform parallel actions. For example, to clear a property of snow after a storm, all members of a work crew must shovel snow. For such tasks, group productivity increases directly with group size.
- In contrast, when a group is faced with a *conjunctive task*, the members are only as productive as the weakest member. If, for example, group members are hiking together up a mountain, they can travel only as fast as the slowest person in the group. In this situation, a greater number of group members does not necessarily yield better performance.
- A *disjunctive task* requires a single solution. In such undertakings, the most competent person in the group is likely to provide the solution. Larger groups are typically more productive for disjunctive tasks,

©iStockphoto.com/Aldo Murillo

Group dynamics. Membership or participation in a group influences our thoughts and behaviours.

because a larger group is more likely to have a superstar member who can solve the problem at hand. Often large groups start by brainstorming for a solution to a task or problem. Asking group members to generate as many possible ideas or solutions as they can without being in any way critical of ideas proposed by others is a wonderful way to gather a broad range of possible solutions, and increases the likelihood that a useful solution will be found.
- *Divisible tasks* involve the simultaneous performance of several different activities. When groups confront such tasks, no single person works on all phases of the undertaking; thus, the different strengths of group members complement one another. For divisible tasks, larger groups tend to be more productive, provided someone or a part of the group manages or coordinates the activities of different parts of the group as they work on the components of the larger group task.

78.1.2 Social Facilitation

In many instances, our performance is enhanced when we are in the presence of others. This is one of the oldest observations in social psychology. In the late 1890s, psychologist Norman Triplett noted that cyclists tend to go faster when in the presence of other cyclists than when alone—even when they are not in competition with one another. To test his hypothesis that the presence of others can enhance individual performance, Triplett (1898) conducted an experiment in which he had children wind a fishing reel either all alone or side-by-side with other children. Triplett found that children winding side-by-side worked substantially quicker than children winding by themselves. This phenomenon was later labelled **social facilitation**. Its study was expanded to include not just physical tasks, but also mental tasks, such as solving puzzles and doing math problems (Bond & Titus, 1983).

social facilitation an effect in which the presence of others enhances performance.

As social facilitation has been studied over the years, researchers have learned that people's performance in the presence of others is more complicated than Triplett first believed. Psychologist Robert Zajonc (1965) proposed that the presence of others elevates our arousal level, which in turn facilitates performance on simple, well-learned tasks, but interferes with performance on complicated tasks. In fact, research evidence supports this suggestion. For some tasks, and for some people, performing in the presence of others can impair—rather than enhance—performance (Uziel, 2007; Strauss, 2002; Aiello & Douthitt, 2001). Zajonc's theory has received support from numerous studies and observations of both humans and animals (Bargh, 2001; Platania & Moran, 2001; Zentall & Levine, 1972).

In recent years, theorists have focused less on the mere presence of others and more on individuals' *interpretations* of and *reactions* to the presence of others (Aiello & Douthitt, 2001; Bond, 2000; Bond & Titus, 1983). If, for example, individuals do not like or trust other people in their group, their own contributions to a group project may suffer. In addition, if people believe that other group members are disregarding their ideas or efforts, their own performance in the group may decline (Fiske, 2010; Paulus et al., 2002, 1993).

Stefano Rellandini/IOPP Pool/Getty Images

Improving each other's performance. Former Canadian Olympic cyclist Clara Hughes (front right) leads the pack during the women's cycling road race at the London 2012 Olympic Games. Research indicates that cyclists tend to go faster in the presence of other cyclists than when alone—the result of social facilitation.

78.1.3 Social Loafing

Groups are often formed in hopes that an interconnected body of people can energize and motivate every individual member. However, these hopes are not always realized. When working in a group, how many times have you noticed that one or two of the group members are not pulling their weight? **Social loafing**—also known as *free riding*—refers to the phenomenon in which people exert less effort on a collective task than they would on a comparable individual task (Liden et al., 2004; Latane et al., 1979).

social loafing a phenomenon in which people exert less effort on a collective task than they would on a comparable individual task; also known as free riding.

Social loafing seems to rear its ugly head most often in large groups (Liden et al., 2004). It is most likely to occur when certain group members lack motivation to contribute, feel isolated from the group, calculate the cost of contributing as too high, or view their own contributions as unnecessary (Chidambaram & Tung, 2005; Shepperd, 1995, 1993). Research suggests that people from Western cultures are more inclined to display social loafing than people from Eastern cultures, and men are more likely to do so than women (Fiske, 2004).

Fortunately, social loafing can be minimized. When, for example, groups are highly *cohesive*—when group members all desire and value membership in the group—the social loafing phenomenon all but disappears (Hoigaard et al., 2006; Liden et al., 2004). Additionally, social loafing is reduced when group members are each explicitly reminded of their uniqueness and importance (Asmus & James, 2005), when they are given specific and challenging goals (Ling et al., 2005), when the output

©iStockphoto.com/Anthony Brown

Social loafing. Social loafers leave the work of a collective task to others in the group.

of each member is publicly identified (Williams et al., 1981), and when the members are given clear norms and comparison standards for their work (Hoigaard et al., 2006; Paulus et al., 2002). Finally, alertness tends to decrease social loafing, whereas fatigue tends to increase it (Hoeksema-van Orden, Gaillard, & Buunk, 1998).

78.1.4 Group Polarization

Have you ever begun talking about one of your favourite bands with a group of friends with similar musical tastes, and found yourself liking the band even more by the end of the conversation? When an initial tendency of individual group members is intensified following group discussion, **group polarization** occurs (Abrams et al., 2001; Isenberg, 1986). This phenomenon is not simply an example of conformity. With group polarization, the attitudes and inclinations of the individual group members are already in place, and they become more intense and more extreme as a result of the group interaction (Cooper et al., 2004).

Group polarization has been studied most often with regard to racial and ethnic bias and social and political attitudes (Prislin & Wood, 2005; Billings et al., 2000). When, for example, researchers have placed individuals with highly prejudiced attitudes in a group to discuss racial issues, the attitudes of the individuals tend to become still more prejudiced (Myers & Bishop, 1970). In similar work, it has been found that the attitudes of women with moderate leanings toward feminism become more strongly feminist following group discussions (Myers, 1975).

group polarization the intensification of an initial tendency of individual group members brought about by group discussion.

78.1.5 Groupthink

Groups often come together to solve specific problems and make decisions. We noted earlier that group cohesiveness can prevent social loafing—but sometimes, groups can become *too* cohesive and single-minded, and the group's decision making can lead to disaster. A classic example occurred in the early 1960s, when the Kennedy administration in the United States government was determined to overthrow the Communist government that Fidel Castro had instituted in Cuba. The U.S. government had trained a small group of Cuban exiles as part of a military operation to overthrow Castro. Proponents of the plan predicted that once this small militia touched down in Cuba at the Bay of Pigs, the Cuban citizens would rise up and join them. Instead, the operation collapsed, with no support from the Cuban people and no further help from the U.S. government. As a result of the failed invasion, anti-American sentiment around the globe increased, as did Castro's influence in Latin America and Cuba's ties with the Soviet Union. There is evidence that no-one within Kennedy's inner circle raised any concerns about the viability of the plan. There was a strong sense of shared certainty that the Cubans would rise up and support the small invasion force (Janis, 1972).

Psychologist Irving Janis (1972), after examining the flawed decision-making process that went into the Bay of Pigs invasion, attributed the fiasco to **groupthink**, which he defined as a form of faulty group decision making that occurs when group members strive too hard for unanimity. The goal of achieving a consensus among all group members overrides the need to realistically appraise alternative courses of action. Clearly, groupthink can have undesired consequences (Henningsen et al., 2006; Baron, 2005; Whyte, 2000).

groupthink a form of faulty group decision making that occurs when group members strive for unanimity, and this goal overrides their motivation to realistically appraise alternative courses of action.

Janis identified a number of conditions that set the stage for groupthink: (1) strong similarity in group members' backgrounds and ideologies; (2) high group cohesiveness; (3) high perceived threat; (4) elevated stress; (5) insulation from outside influence; and (6) a directive leader. Group members experience an illusion of invulnerability and have an unquestioned belief in the group's inherent morality. Typically, group members exert direct pressure against any member who expresses strong disagreement, and members protect the group from information that might shatter the shared conviction that their decisions are effective and moral (Janis, 1982).

Groupthink may have been operating within the Canadian government and across English Canada in the days leading up to the 1995 Quebec sovereignty referendum. After having the premiers of all provinces other than Quebec unite and refuse to pass amendments

NASA/Getty Images

A consequence of groupthink? In 2003, the space shuttle Columbia disintegrated during re-entry over Texas, killing all seven crew members. Just two days before the disaster, a NASA engineer had warned his supervisors of possible catastrophes on re-entry, but his message was not forwarded up the chain of command. How might groupthink have been involved in this mishandling of the warning?

to the Canadian Constitution Repatriation Act, they also ignored René Lévesque's prediction that things would not go well in the next vote on sovereignty in Quebec. Within English-speaking Canada, warnings were ignored and there was surprise when the referendum was only defeated by the narrowest of margins (49.42 percent of Quebecers voted to secede from Canada, while 50.58 percent voted to remain within Canada). Similarly, it has been suggested that some of the decisions made by the Bush administration following the 9/11 terrorist attack in New York also fit the profile of groupthink (Yetiv, 2003, 2011). Of course, without detailed information about how decisions were arrived at, it is often hard to determine whether or not groupthink played a role in the outcome.

Having identified the phenomenon of groupthink, Janis went on to propose measures that a group can take to safeguard against it. First, the leader of the group should encourage members to air objections and doubts, and should accept criticisms of the group's judgments. Additionally, various group members should be assigned the role of "devil's advocate," arguing against the group's favoured position. Finally, outside experts should be invited to group meetings and encouraged to challenge the group's core views and decisions.

Research conducted since Janis first proposed his theory suggests that groupthink is a complicated phenomenon—probably more complicated than Janis initially realized. The conditions that he believed set the stage for groupthink do not always result in unwarranted unanimity (Baron, 2005). Nor do his proposed safeguards always prevent groupthink. At the same time, research and observations clearly indicate that the phenomenon of groupthink is widespread. Not only does it often affect decision making in important policy-setting groups, as Janis recognized, but it also influences decision making in mundane and temporary groups and groups working on trivial matters (Baron, 2005; Eaton, 2001; Whyte, 2000).

78.2 Helping Behaviour

altruism self-sacrificing behaviour carried out for the benefit of others.

When people are in need, many people offer help as an expression of **altruism** (concern for or acting to help others without any expectation of compensation or reciprocation) or of another social motive. In mid-May 2011, after one-third of the town of Slave Lake in Northern Alberta was burned by a rapidly moving wildfire, offers of accommodation,

---

Psychology Around Us | Space Disasters and Groupthink

"On the morning of January 28, 1986, the space shuttle Challenger blasted off from the Kennedy Space Center in Florida. Seventy-three seconds after lift-off, the Challenger exploded, killing all seven astronauts on board . . . Following the explosion . . . information came to light about the faulty decision-making processes. . . . that [had] led to the decision to launch. Some engineers had expressed concerns about the design of the O-ring seal in the solid-fuel rocket, which could allow hot gases to leak through the joint and thereby spark an explosion. However . . . these concerns were ignored. . . .

"Unfortunately little was learned from this tragic accident because many of these same errors contributed to the loss of the Columbia space shuttle, and its seven astronauts, on February 1, 2003 [the shuttle was trying to return to earth after a 16-day mission in space]. Research now shows that prior to the Columbia disaster, some NASA engineers had grave concern about the shuttle's ability to return to earth following some tile damage it [had] experienced on lift-off. On January 28, just days before the Columbia tragedy, a landing gear specialist at NASA sent an email expressing his concerns about the tile damage. . . . However, high-level NASA administrators viewed the damage to the shuttle as minor—not a serious threat—and refused to respond. . . ." (Sanderson, 2010).

assistance, and aide poured in from across Canada. Residents of Slave Lake, while devastated by their losses, felt supported and cared for by their fellow Canadians. Other examples of altruism that have inspired others include Terry Fox's run for cancer and Rick Hansen's Man in Motion world tour in support of spinal cord research. Both of these self-less accomplishments have led to many more altruistic activities, with many people across Canada and around the world participating in Terry Fox runs.

78.2.1 Why Do We Help?

Altruism refers to self-sacrificing behaviour carried out for the benefit of others. To be altruistic, behaviour must be motivated by concern for persons in need, without concern for oneself (Post, 2005; Puka, 2004). Thus, engaging in self-sacrificing behaviour to avoid a sense of guilt or donating to charity for tax purposes would not be considered altruistic behaviour. Such acts, which are motivated by a desire to reduce one's own personal distress or to receive rewards, are sometimes called *egoistic helping behaviours* (Batson et al., 2004, 1997; Khalil, 2004).

When we engage in helping behaviour, our motives can be entirely altruistic, entirely egoistic, or some combination of the two. Surveys have revealed that in the *immediate* aftermath of the 9/11 terrorist attacks, actions such as giving blood, money, and goods and offering prayers were associated with both altruistic and egoistic motives (Piferi et al., 2006). People's motivations for giving ranged from wanting to ease the suffering of others, to hoping to reduce their own attack-induced distress and seeking to reassure themselves that other people would help them if they were in need. In contrast, *sustained* giving after the attacks—that is, giving after one or more years—may have been more consistently associated with altruistic motives (Piferi et al., 2006).

Albert Gea/Corbis

Responding to tragedy. Almost immediately after a series of terrorist bombs ripped through passenger trains in Madrid, Spain in 2004, killing 191 people and injuring 1,800 others, Spanish citizens such as these began lining up to donate blood to the victims. Altruism? Possibly. But social psychologists point out that egoistic motives may also be at work during the early reactions to tragedies of this kind.

Research further indicates that certain factors increase the likelihood of altruistic behaviour. When people empathize and identify with the individuals in need (Batson et al., 2004, 1997; Batson & Weeks, 1996), as well as when they are in close relationships (Maner & Gailliot, 2007), they are more likely to behave altruistically. Similarly, people tend to display more altruism when they take the perspective of victims (Mikulincer et al., 2005; Underwood & Moore, 1982). Not surprisingly, then, people who are generally trusting and outward-looking and who form secure attachments in their relationships are most likely to perform altruistic behaviours (Mikulincer et al., 2005; Mikulincer & Shaver, 2005). As you can see, it is often quite difficult to identify and understand the specific motives that drive people's helping behaviour, and especially to determine if their behaviour can be seen to be truly selfless and thus truly altruistic. Questions about the existence and nature of altruism have been taken up as central interests by psychologists working in the area of positive psychology (Batson et al., 2002).

Positive psychology is the scientific study of the strengths and virtues that help human beings, as individuals and families, to thrive, and communities to flourish (Peterson, 2006). Researchers in this field argue that other approaches to psychology focus on dysfunction and abnormal behaviour and, while they acknowledge the importance of remedying problems, they also argue that focusing on strength is as important as focusing on weakness. They believe that focusing on well-being is as important as focusing on suffering. Martin Seligman, widely regarded as the father of contemporary psychology, believed that the time was right for a scientifically-informed psychology about positive human functioning. Positive psychologists study empathy (Prot et al., 2014), altruism (Batson, 2014), gratitude (Tsang et al., 2014), resilience (Luthar et al., 2014), mindfulness (Kashdan & Ciarrochi, 2013), and happiness (Argyle, 2014), as well as other areas they claim make life more worth living.

78.2.2 Bystander Effect (or Bystander Apathy)

Imagine you are in a life-threatening situation and desperately need the help of others. If you could choose, would you prefer that one or two people were nearby or that a large number of people were present? If you are like most people, you probably would prefer the larger number. After all, that would mean more potential helpers. In fact, however, this may be the more dangerous choice. It turns out that, in many circumstances, the more people present in a situation where help is required, the less likely it is that any one person will give that help (Fischer et al., 2006; Garcia et al., 2002; Batson, 1991).

Consider the following story: on March 13, 1961, a woman named Kitty Genovese was stabbed to death over the course of three separate attacks spread over 30 minutes in the New York borough of Queens, while at least 38 neighbours and other onlookers failed to intervene. This rendition of a famous murder was followed by a public outcry demanding an explanation for the lack of intervention by others, including a *New York Times* article with the headline: "Thirty-Eight Who Saw Murder Didn't Call the Police" (Gansberg, 1964). Initially, many observers concluded that these 38 bystanders must have had a host of personality flaws that prevented them from helping. But were they really callous and uncaring?

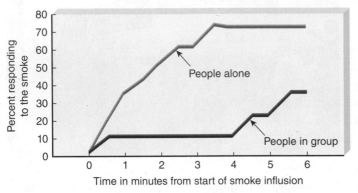

FIGURE 78-1 **Bystander intervention.** People are more likely to intervene to help when they are alone than in a group. In the presence of others, people feel less compelled to act, a phenomenon called the *bystander effect* (Darley & Latané, 1968).

Source: Adapted from Myers, D. G. (2002). *Social psychology* (7th ed.). New York: Mc-Graw Hill, Figures 3-2 and 12-4; based on Darley, J. M., & Latane, B. (1968). Bystander intervention in emergencies: Diffusion of responsibility. Journal of Personality and Social Psychology, 8, 377–383.

Social psychologists John Darley and Bibb Latané (1968) were less interested in the personality traits of these onlookers than with features of the situation that might have kept them from providing help. In a series of studies examining the impact of the presence of others on helping behaviour, Darley and Latané repeatedly demonstrated that we are, in fact, more likely to intervene when we are *alone* than when others are also present. In one of their studies, for example, participants found themselves in a situation where they smelled smoke (faked by the experimenters) while either alone or in the presence of others. When other people were present in the room, fewer than 40 percent of the participants got up to report the smoke; in contrast, 75 percent of the participants in the study reported smelling smoke when they were alone in the room (see **Figure 78-1**) (Latané & Darley, 1968). In another experiment by the two researchers, participants were placed in a situation in which they overheard a person (actually an actor) in another room having a seizure. The more people the participants believed could also hear the individual having the seizure, the less quickly they acted to help (Darley & Latané, 1968).

This phenomenon has been termed *bystander effect*. If your car is broken down in the rain at the side of the road and no-one is stopping to help, you may be experiencing firsthand the bystander effect. Researchers in addition to Darley and Latané (1968) have observed group bystander effects of this kind under a wide variety of conditions, with none, one, or more bystanders, including situations in which a person witnesses someone stealing money from another (both with and without a security camera) (van Bommel et al., 2014), graffiti was written on an elevator wall (Chekroun & Brauer, 2002), or a perpetrator is determined to be either dangerous or non-dangerous (Fischer et al., 2011).

What must occur for bystanders to intervene on someone else's behalf? Apparently, several steps are involved (Fischer et al., 2006; Darley, 2000; Latané & Darley, 1970). Bystanders must: (1) notice the event; (2) interpret the event as an emergency; (3) feel personal responsibility for acting; (4) consider what form of assistance is needed; and (5) implement action (Fischer et al., 2011).

Some theorists have focused on the third step, *feeling a sense of personal responsibility*, as the key to bystander apathy (Garcia, Garcia, & Lila, 2009). They suggest that the presence of a large number of people in an emergency situation creates a *diffusion of responsibility* (Freeman, Walker, Borden, & Latané, 1975), an effect observed in fMRI studies (Hortensius & Gelder, 2014). When others are present, we feel that we do not bear the full burden of responsibility, and thus we feel less compelled to act. We may also assume that someone else must be taking action.

Finally, research is just starting into issues of bystander reactions to violence within virtual realities, such as shared and online video games and worlds. Early work suggests that similar forces are at work shaping the behaviours of virtual bystanders as they do for bystanders in the "real" world (Rovira et al., 2009).

A newer line of research has come from Rachel Manning and her colleagues from the University of the West of England and the University of Lancaster (2007). They argue there is no evidence that all of the details of the Kitty Genovese murder are accurate. In particular, they argue that there was misinterpretation on several levels. First, there is no evidence that 38 eyewitnesses were ever involved, and that the eyewitnesses who were involved actually saw the attacks—some heard the attacks without viewing them. Indeed, there is no evidence that anyone saw the second attack (and last attack—there were never three attacks) as the final attack occurred in an inside stairwell. As well, there is evidence that the police *were* called and that at least one of the eyewitnesses discouraged the first attack by threatening the assailant from the window of his apartment. This is not to argue that the eyewitnesses could not have been more proactive and might have handled things differently and more effectively. This does, however, suggest that some aspects of the story are not supported by the evidence. Why is this important? Manning and her colleagues write:

> We suggest that, almost from its inception, the story of the 38 witnesses became a kind of modern parable—the antonym of the parable of the good Samaritan (p. 55).

Why does this matter? Although the bystander body of work is robust and standalone, we continue to view groups as detrimental to social functioning, largely based on this story of the 38 witnesses. And yet there is evidence to suggest that groups can serve a strong prosocial function and facilitate helping (Penner et al., 2005; Zimbardo, 2004). Certainly the groundswell of support seen in Calgary in the aftermath of the flooding confirmed all that we know about the positive action in groups.

Ann Cutting/Getty Images

Diffusion of responsibility. People are less likely to stop and help an apparently lost child if they are part of a large crowd than if they are walking alone on a street. Why? When many others are present, we are not as likely to feel the full burden of responsibility.

78.3 Aggression

In social psychological terms, **aggression** describes a broad category of behaviours, including physical and verbal attacks, intended to do harm to another. Aggression appears to have at least some biological underpinnings. Twin studies indicate that identical twins are more likely to share the trait of violent temper than fraternal twins, suggesting a genetic component (Baker et al., 2007; Miles & Carey, 1997; Rowe et al., 1999). High levels of the hormone testosterone have been linked with higher levels of aggression, as have low levels of the neurotransmitter serotonin. Indeed, the people most likely to be involved with violent crime are muscular young men with below-average intelligence, high levels of testosterone, and low levels of serotonin (Dabbs et al., 2001).

That said, under the right circumstances, we are all capable of aggressive acts. One major hypothesis explaining aggression in humans—the *frustration-aggression hypothesis*—holds that we become aggressive in response to frustration (Dollard et al., 1939). Any emotional stressor that impedes our progress or prevents achievement of

aggression a broad range of behaviours intended to harm others.

Digital Vision/Getty Images

Relational aggression. On average, women are more likely than men to express their anger with relational aggression (for example, ignoring the person who has angered them).

some goal elicits frustration. Aggression, then, might be a cue to push harder to achieve that goal.

The frustration-aggression hypothesis was later expanded to include the notion that any unpleasant event, ranging from experiencing a bad odour or an annoying sound to hearing bad news, leads to activation of the sympathetic nervous system (Berkowitz, 1989). As you will see in Part 14, activation of the sympathetic nervous system is associated with both anger and fear and with the fight-or-flight response. This theory suggests that if you have translated this activation to aggressive (fight) behaviour in the past, and the outcome has had a desired effect, you will continue to engage in that aggressive behaviour (Friedman & Silver, 2007).

Other factors influencing aggression probably result from both biology and environment (**Figure 78-2**). For example, as we have observed previously, men tend to be more aggressive than women—at least in some respects. Women are more likely to engage in acts of *relational aggression*, such as snubbing, gossiping, and otherwise excluding others as a means of venting frustration or anger (Archer, 2005). However, men are more likely to engage in *direct aggression*, which includes direct physical and verbal abuse. In fact, the vast majority of violent offenders are male (Demause, 2007). Because this gender disparity shows up very early in childhood, it may be at least partially attributable to biological gender differences. However, it is probably also affected by social norms within our society, where men are more permitted than women to express anger and act aggressively.

Alcohol has also been found to increase aggressive behaviour for both biological and psychological reasons (Schlauch et al., 2010; Giancola, 2002). The effects of the drug may reduce inhibitions and so make people more likely to engage in violence or verbal abuse. However, people have been shown to become more aggressive even if they only think that they have had alcohol to drink, suggesting that they are responding to social expectations about how people act when they have been drinking (Lang et al., 1975; Bushman & Cooper, 1990).

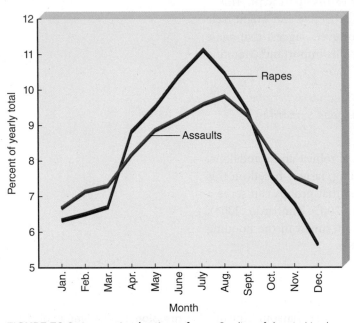

FIGURE 78-2 **Aggression by time of year.** Studies of data in North America and Europe over the last hundred years show that aggression is highest in the hottest months of the year (Anderson, 1989).

78.4 Interpersonal Attraction

Why are we attracted to some people and not others? What's the difference between liking someone and loving someone? These are questions central to the study of interpersonal attraction. Interpersonal attraction operates at three levels: *cognitively*, we think certain things about the other person; *affectively*, we experience particular feelings toward the person; and *behaviourally*, we act in certain ways toward the person (Orbuch & Sprecher, 2003; Berscheid & Walster, 1978).

78.4.1 Liking

Liking refers to fondness and affection for another person. Research has revealed five key factors that lead to liking someone.

1. *Similarity*—The more similar to us we perceive someone to be, the more likely we are to develop a fondness for that person (Lankau, Riordan, & Thomas, 2005; Bates, 2002). In addition, the more similar people are, the likelier it is that their fondness for one another will last a long time (Byrne, 1971).

2. *Proximity*—We tend to like people whom we encounter frequently more than those we do not encounter often, and we tend to like familiar people more than

unfamiliar people (Smith & Weber, 2005; Swap, 1977). How many people who you have shared two or three classes with have become friends?

3. *Self-disclosure*—We tend to initially like people who disclose personal information to us (Dindia, 2000; Taylor et al., 1981), and we tend to disclose more to people whom we initially like (Certner, 1973; Worthy et al., 1969).

4. *Situational factors*—The situations in which we encounter other people greatly affect how much we like them. It has been suggested, for example, that we like people when we experience rewards while in their presence (Lott & Lott, 1974). Furthermore, a shared humorous experience seems to be a powerful way of forging closeness with a stranger (Fraley & Aron, 2004; Lyttle, 2001). The famous playwright Oscar Wilde once said, "Laughter is not at all a bad beginning for a friendship."

5. *Physical attractiveness*—People of all ages, even babies, prefer to look at and be near attractive people (Smith & Weber, 2005; Langlois & Stephan, 1981; Dion & Berscheid, 1974). Not surprisingly, then, physical attractiveness may affect likeability.

What kinds of studies have led researchers to these conclusions? Let's examine a few of the investigations into the last factor mentioned above, physical attractiveness. In a study by social psychologist Elaine Walster and her colleagues (1966), the experimenters randomly paired participants to be dates at a dance. During a break in the dance, the participants were asked to rate how much they liked their partners. Overall, the more attractive the partner, the more likeable the partner was reported to be.

> **"**I do not believe that friends are necessarily the people you like the best. They are merely the people who got there first.**"**
>
> —*Peter Ustinov, actor*

In other studies, an attractive middle-aged person was judged to be more outgoing and more pleasant than a less attractive middle-aged individual (Adams & Huston, 1975); physically attractive college students were found to be more popular than less attractive ones among members of the same sex (Borch et al., 2011); and attractive Grade 5 students were rated as more popular by their classmates than were less attractive students (Lease et al., 2002).

Finally, one study examined the joint impact of two factors—physical attractiveness and similarity—on liking (Byrne et al., 1970). The experimenters prearranged lab dates for participants, varying both attractiveness and similarity of attitudes on certain issues. Upon their arrival, the dates were sent to a student lounge to talk for 20 minutes and then instructed to return to the lab. In the laboratory, the experimenters measured how much the date pairs liked each other by having the participants fill out a questionnaire and by observing how close together the date pair stood when they reentered the lab. It turned out that the measures of liking were indeed related to both how attractive the dates were and how similar their attitudes were.

78.4.2 Loving

Whereas liking someone involves a sense of fondness, loving is associated with a more extreme affection. When we *love* someone, we experience a strong, passionate attachment to that person. Some see loving as simply an extreme form of liking—with degree of attraction being the key distinction—whereas others see loving as a qualitatively different phenomenon (Watts & Stenner, 2005; Sternberg, 2004, 1987).

Let's first consider the question of what functions love serves. Freud viewed love as *sublimated sexual energy*—that is, a transformation of sexual desire into a more socially acceptable form (Fenchel, 2006). Evolutionary theorists emphasize love's role in propagating the species (Brumbaugh & Fraley, 2006; Wilson, 1981). According to these theorists, strong passionate attachments have ensured that over time, parents would stay together and raise their children together.

Sergio Dionisio/Getty Images

New approach, same criteria. Two people meet in a speed dating program at Bondi Beach in Australia. Speed dating is a relatively new form of social engagement in which large numbers of men and women are rotated to meet many potential partners over a series of short 3- to 8-minute "dates." What kinds of partners do speed daters choose most often? Those who are attractive and hold attitudes similar to those of the selectors.

Still other theorists argue that love's most important value is to help provide companionship, emotional support, and even protection throughout the lifespan (Seppala et al., 2013; Mikulincer et al., 2008; Mikulincer & Goodman, 2006). Loving relationships have in fact been associated with improved health (Levin, 2000). Such relationships provide us with people to confide in—and not being able to confide our troubles to someone has been associated with a host of health problems (Cornwell & Laumann, 2013; Pennebaker, 2004, 2003; Pennebaker et al., 2004). This may be one reason why recently widowed individuals are more vulnerable to disease than individuals of a similar age who have not lost a spouse (Sorrell, 2012; Troyer, 2006; Daggett, 2002).

What are the building blocks of love? Decades ago, social psychologist Zick Rubin (1970) emphasized three elements of love: attachment, caring, and intimacy. *Attachment* refers to the individual's need or desire for the physical presence and emotional support of the other person; *caring* is a feeling of concern and responsibility for the person; and *intimacy* involves the desire for close, confidential communication with the other individual.

Using this definition of love, Rubin (1973) designed a self-report scale that he hoped would be able to measure love and distinguish it from liking. The scale included *love* items, such as "If I could never be with _____, I would feel miserable" and "I feel I can confide in _____ about virtually everything," along with *like* items, such as "I think that _____ is usually well-adjusted" and "_____ is the sort of person whom I myself would like to be." In one study, Rubin had dating couples fill out this scale, alone and confidentially, focusing on their date partner in their ratings. He found that friends and lovers both scored high on the like items, but friends did not score high on the love items.

In another study, Rubin had volunteer couples come to his laboratory and sit across from each other while awaiting the start of the experiment. His assistants secretly observed the couples from behind a one-way mirror to determine which ones gazed into each other's eyes, a sign of love according to conventional wisdom. As expected, the partners who had scored high on Rubin's love scale gazed lovingly at each other more than did partners who had scored low on the scale.

Another psychologist, Robert Sternberg, whom you met back in Part 10, has proposed the **triangular theory of love**, which holds that love is composed of *intimacy*, *passion*, and *commitment* (Sternberg & Weis, 2006; Sternberg, 2004, 1986). Here, *intimacy* refers once again to feelings that promote closeness and connection, *passion* involves intense desires for union with the other person, and *commitment* refers to the decision to maintain the relationship across time. According to Sternberg, the extent and quality of each of these three components determines the nature of a particular loving relationship.

In fact, Sternberg distinguishes between eight kinds of relationship, each reflecting a particular combination of the three components (**Figure 78-3**). For example, purely *romantic* love consists of much intimacy and passion with little commitment. In contrast, couples who experience *companionate* love are high on intimacy and commitment but low on passion. Couples who experience *consummate* love are high on all three components; and those with *empty* love are high on commitment only. Sternberg also believes these relationships change over time, peaking at different points.

A number of social psychologists propose that relationships proceed through *stages* as the participants move from the fondness and affection of liking to the intimacy and commitment of loving. One theory, for example, cites four stages: exploration, bargaining, commitment, and institutionalization (Backman, 1990, 1981). In the *exploration* stage, the partners try out the

triangular theory of love a theory proposed by Robert Sternberg that love is composed of three elements: intimacy, passion, and commitment.

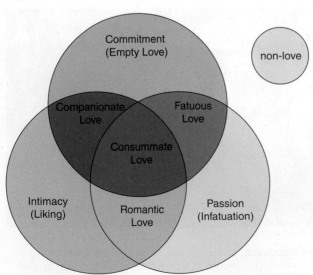

FIGURE 78-3 Sternberg's triangular theory of love. Sternberg's theory (1987) talks about the various possible combinations of intimacy, passion, and commitment and produces eight distinct types of relationship.

possible rewards and costs of a relationship. During the *bargaining* stage, they implicitly negotiate the terms of the relationship. That is, they "feel out" its ground rules—which behaviours are rewarding, which cost too much, and how the joint benefits of the relationship can be maximized. During the third stage, *commitment*, the partners grow increasingly dependent on each other. Finally, in the *institutionalization* stage, shared expectations emerge, and the relationship is recognized by the partners (and by others) as exclusive. Other theorists have proposed different specific stages, but most agree that relationships do tend to proceed step-by-step as they deepen from liking to loving, with each stop marked by changing understandings, behaviours, and feelings (Yela, 2006; Berscheid, 1983).

What determines *how* we love? Many theorists suggest that the way we express and experience love is a direct outgrowth of our early experiences with caregivers (Hazan & Shaver, 2004, 1994, 1987). For example, as we observed in Part 4, young children seem to express one of several kinds of attachment in their relationships with their parents (Ainsworth, 1979). It appears that adults display similar types of attachment in their romantic relationships. Using the attachment model, researchers Cindy Hazan and Phillip Shaver (2004) have proposed three types of lovers.

- Those with *secure* attachment styles find it relatively easy to become close to others and are comfortable depending on lovers and being depended on. They do not fear becoming too close or being abandoned.

- Those with *avoidant* attachment styles are somewhat uncomfortable being close to others and have difficulty trusting others and depending on them. In fact, they become nervous when others want to become closer to them.

- Those with *anxious-ambivalent* attachment styles worry that their lovers are less interested in closeness than they are. These insecure individuals are preoccupied with concerns that their partners do not really love them or will not stay with them. Sometimes their demands for security in relationships wind up pushing people away.

In their research, Hazan and Shaver found that approximately 53 percent of adults in relationships display a secure attachment style, 26 percent an avoidant attachment style, and 20 percent an anxious-ambivalent attachment style.

Before You Go On

www.wiley.com/go/comercanada

What Do You Know?
1. What is groupthink and under what conditions is it most likely to occur?
2. How does altruistic helping behaviour differ from egoistic helping behaviour?
3. How does the presence of other people affect the likelihood that a bystander will intervene on behalf of someone who needs help?
4. What are some of the biological underpinnings of aggressive behaviour?
5. What are the three components of Robert Sternberg's triangular theory of love and how do they interact in relationships?

What Do You Think? Think about a relationship you have had with a friend—someone you really like. Analyze the development of that relationship with reference to some of the key factors discussed in this module.

Summary

Module 78: Social Relations

LEARNING OBJECTIVE 78 Review major concepts in the areas of group dynamics, helping behaviour, aggression, and interpersonal attraction.

- The social facilitation effect occurs when the presence of others enhances a person's performance. Research shows that this effect holds for simple, well-learned tasks; but the presence of others can impair performance on more complicated tasks.
- With social loafing, people in a group exert less effort on a task than they would if performing the task alone.
- Group polarization is a phenomenon in which group discussion intensifies the already-held opinions of group members and produces a shift toward a more extreme position.
- Groups with certain characteristics—a strong similarity among members, high group cohesiveness, high perceived threat, elevated stress, insulation from outside influence, and a directive leader—may become victims of groupthink, a faulty decision-making process in which group members strive for unanimity at the expense of realistically appraising alternative courses of action.
- Helping behaviour is of two types: altruism, which is motivated by concern for others, and egoistic helping behaviour, which is motivated by a desire to reduce one's own distress or receive rewards.
- People are more likely to engage in helping behaviour when alone than when in the presence of others. Theorists propose that the presence of others may create a diffusion of responsibility, in which no single individual feels personal responsibility for acting.
- Aggression describes a broad range of behaviours intended to do harm to another. Aggression has some biological underpinnings. In addition, the frustration-aggression hypothesis proposes that aggression arises in response to frustration.
- Factors that lead to liking another person include similarity, proximity, self-disclosure, situational, and physical attractiveness.
- One description of love includes three elements: attachment, caring, and intimacy. Another, Sternberg's triangular theory of love, holds that love is composed of intimacy, passion, and commitment, which combine in varying degrees.
- Similar to young children, adults display three types of attachment in love relationships: secure attachment, avoidant attachment, and anxious-ambivalent attachment.

Key Terms

aggression 595	group polarization 591	social loafing 590
altruism 592	groupthink 591	triangular theory
group 589	social facilitation 590	of love 598

Study Questions

Multiple Choice

1. Group members who are each mowing the grass on their assigned section of a golf course are engaging in a(n) _____ task.
   a) additive
   b) conjunctive
   c) disjunctive
   d) divisible

2. The Kitty Genovese murder and subsequent research helped psychologists understand that when people fail to help others, it is usually because they
   a) are apathetic and unconcerned with other people's well-being.
   b) fail to see the benefits of helping others.
   c) get caught up in a powerful social situation.
   d) have valid reasons for failing to help.

3. According to Sternberg, a high degree of intimacy, passion, and commitment is characteristic of _____ love.
   a) consummate
   b) fatuous
   c) infatuated
   d) romantic

4. An Olympic coach is training an athlete and wants to see the athlete's time improve. You tell the coach that according to the _____ effect, he would be better off to get actual people to run against the athlete in training.
   a) groupthink
   b) social facilitation
   c) group polarization
   d) social loafing

Fill-in-the-Blank

1. Zajonc proposed that the presence of others increases our physiological _____, which then improves or impairs task performance depending on the task and the person.

2. When others are present, we may feel that we do not bear the burden of responsibility to act. This phenomenon is known as diffusion of _____.

3. Those with _____ attachment styles find it relatively easy to become close to others and are comfortable depending on lovers and being depended on.

Module 79: Social Functioning

LEARNING OBJECTIVE 79
Describe the major findings of social neuroscience about regions of the brain particularly important to our social functioning.

WHAT HAPPENS *in the* **BRAIN?**

Throughout this book, you have seen that with the help of brain-scanning procedures, researchers have tied many areas of psychological functioning, such as memory or emotions, to particular neural circuits—collections of neurons that communicate with each other. The study of social functioning is no different. Indeed, there has been so much work to uncover what happens in the brain when people are thinking and behaving socially that the field of study has been given a special title, *social neuroscience*, and the combination of brain regions that operate together when people function socially has also been given a special name in some circles, the "social brain."

One of the early clues that helped researchers to identify regions of the brain that may be at work in social cognition and behaviour came from evolutionary psychology (Adolphs, 2009, 2003). Beginning with the observation that a unique and critically important area of human functioning is social cognition—particularly the ability to infer what is going on (intentions, feelings, and thoughts) inside the minds of other people—scientists decided to pay special attention to those regions that are newer and/or bigger in human brains than in the brains of other animals. Their suspicion was that these regions may be the ones that play key roles in social functioning.

Not surprisingly, several of the brain regions that, according to brain scans, are very active during social cognition and behaviour are indeed particularly large in the human brain. For example, the *prefrontal cortex*, the part of the frontal cortex that is closest to the front of the head, is much larger in humans than in other animals (see **Figure 79-1**). As we observed in Part 3, the entire frontal cortex is somewhat larger in the human brain than in the brains of less complex animals. But the prefrontal cortex is particularly larger (Semendeferi et al., 2002).

Social cognitions and behaviours rely on many of the psychological functions that we have examined throughout this book. They require, for example, rapid identification of social stimuli and signals (for example, recognition of people), rapid retrieval of memories (to help us remember who is a friend and who is a foe), the ability to recognize the perspective of others, anticipation of others' behaviours, experiences of emotion and empathy, and moral and other evaluations of situations (to help us decide, for example, whether prosocial behaviour is in order). Thus, some of the brain regions that are highly active during social functioning turn out to be ones related to language and thought, memory, and emotion (Adolphs, 2009). To date, social neuroscientists have identified the following brain regions as among the key players in social functioning:

- *Orbitofrontal cortex*—a subregion of the prefrontal cortex, it is involved in social reasoning, reward evaluation, reading other people, and eliciting emotional states (McDonald, 2007).
- *Ventromedial prefrontal cortex*—another subregion of the prefrontal cortex, it plays a key role in the processing of rewards and punishments, interpreting nonverbal social information (such as facial expressions), making social and moral assessments and decisions, and feeling empathy (Roy et al., 2012; Koenigs et al., 2007; Shamay-Tsoory et al., 2005).
- *Insula*—a region of the cortex that is located beneath the frontal cortex, it plays a key role in empathy and in reading others. The insula is activated when we observe others in physical or emotional pain and immediately feel that pain ourselves (Harlé et al., 2012; Keysers & Gazzola, 2007).

Human

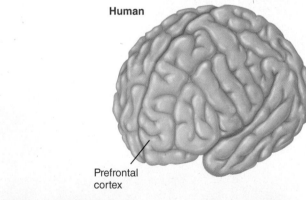

Prefrontal cortex

Rhesus monkey

Prefrontal cortex

Cat

Prefrontal cortex

FIGURE 79-1 Across the species. The prefrontal cortex of human beings is larger than that of other animals and is, at the same time, very active during social behaviour, suggesting that it plays an important role in human social functioning.

- *Amygdala*—a brain region that is located in the temporal lobe, it is, as we have seen, actively involved in the control of emotions. In social functioning, it helps us to identify the emotional facial expressions of other people and to pay particular attention to stimuli that may be unpredictable, potentially rewarding, or potentially punishing (Becker et al., 2012; Whalen et al., 2009).

We still have much to learn about how these and other regions operate together to help people function socially. Social neuroscientists are also still trying to identify the precise neural networks that enable us to so readily carry out the social cognitions and behaviours examined throughout this part.

Psychology Around Us — The Antisocial Brain: Is Revenge Sweet After All?

Is revenge a good thing? Not usually. But it may be that our brains are wired to enjoy it—at least under certain circumstances. Investigators entertained this possibility after they had research participants observe individuals taking part in a famous decision game called the Prisoner's Dilemma (Singer et al., 2006).

In the Prisoner's Dilemma game, two players are separated and accused of a crime. If one person confesses to the crime and the other doesn't, the confessor will get only one year in prison and the silent player will get five years. If both of the players remain silent, they will each be convicted of a lesser offence and get two years. If they both confess, they each get three years.

In a brain scan study, the participants were hooked up to MRIs and asked to watch confederates play the game. What the researchers found was that if one of the confederates "confessed" and the other didn't, three things happened in the brains of the observing participants: (1) the participants exhibited a strong dislike for the confessor; (2)

the participants exhibited less neural activity in pain-related areas of their brains, suggesting they had little empathy for the confessor; and (3) among the male participants, reward centres in their brains lit up when they saw the experimenters appear to be applying electric shocks to the hands of the confessor. This was taken to mean that the male participants actually got a positive charge out of seeing the confessors get what they believed was coming to them. In other words, for men, it may be that revenge, or the observation of revenge, is indeed sweet—in more than a figurative sense.

On the other hand, research from Carlsmith and colleagues (2008) indicates that revenge may not be as sweet as we might like to think. Instead, the desire for revenge prolongs reactions to the transgressor and prevents people from forgetting and therefore from healing. These authors quote Sir Francis Bacon: "A man that studieth revenge, keeps his own wounds green, which otherwise would heal, and do well" (pg. 1324). Perhaps forgiving and forgetting is the best course of medicine after all.

Before You Go On

www.wiley.com/go/comercanada

What Do You Know?

1. What is social neuroscience and what is the "social brain"?
2. Which brain regions have been identified as particularly important to our social functioning?

What Do You Think?
If you were a neuroscientist looking for parts of the brain that are important to social functioning, how would you decide where to look first?

Summary

Module 79: Social Functioning

LEARNING OBJECTIVE 79 Describe the major findings of social neuroscience about regions of the brain particularly important to our social functioning.

- Social neuroscience is the specialty of neuroscience that studies how the brain works during social functioning. Social functioning is so important and uniquely human that social neuroscientists have given the name "social brain" to the combination of brain areas that are particularly active in social functioning.
- The orbitofrontal cortex, ventromedial prefrontal cortex, insula, and amygdala all have been identified as especially important in social functioning. Researchers continue to try to pinpoint neural connections related to social functioning.

Study Questions

Multiple Choice

1. The part of the brain that is most directly related to our experience of both empathy and the ability to read others is the
   a) amygdala.
   b) hypothalamus.
   c) insula.
   d) orbitofrontal cortex.

Fill-in-the-Blank

1. Neuroscientists have found that the _____ cortex is important to social functioning and is larger in humans than in other species.

PART 14

STRESS, COPING, AND HEALTH

PART OUTLINE

Module 80: What Is Stress?

LEARNING OBJECTIVE 80 Define stress and describe the ways in which people experience stress and the kinds of situations that typically cause stress.

Module 81: Responding to Stress

LEARNING OBJECTIVE 81 Describe the physiological, emotional, and cognitive responses to stress, and explain how individual responses to stress differ.

Module 82: Coping with Stress

LEARNING OBJECTIVE 82 Discuss and evaluate several ways in which people cope with stress.

Module 83: Stress and Health

LEARNING OBJECTIVE 83 Explain how stress can cause physical illness, and discuss situations in which stress may be beneficial.

Module 84: Posttraumatic Stress Disorder

LEARNING OBJECTIVE 84 Describe the symptoms and causes of posttraumatic stress disorder, and discuss some risk factors for developing it.

©iStockphoto.com/andresrimaging

"What am I doing?" thought Ashley as she sat at her desk, unable to concentrate. "My English paper is due on Wednesday, but I'm just staring at a blank computer screen. I know I need to get started, but I can't concentrate on this paper." All sorts of thoughts are flying through Ashley's head—each one makes her chest tighten and makes her want to curl up into a ball with her eyes shut.

She has to leave for her job in less than an hour. She desperately needs the bus to be on time. Chris, her boss, has told her that if she is late again, he'll "have to find someone more reliable." And then there is the email she just got from her parents asking—once again—about her grades. She is the first child in her family to go to university, and her parents have been driving her crazy. She's glad that they are so excited, but don't they realize that asking for weekly updates only puts more pressure on her?

In fact, things aren't going so well in some of her classes. She's good at chemistry, but she finds English, especially writing, very difficult. "Just work harder," her parents tell her, as if she wasn't trying as hard as she could. Her public speaking class is a disaster: she actually had to leave in the middle of her last speech, fighting back tears.

The more trouble she has, the more she feels like just going out with her friends at night. In fact, she's gone out every night this week, always telling herself, "I'll get started on my paper tomorrow." Even though she knows she can't put her paper off any longer, she has agreed to see a movie tonight after work with some people from school.

Then there is the recent breakup with her boyfriend, Jason. She feels bad about the way their relationship ended. One night when she was late for work and in a panic, he called her and teasingly refused to let her off the phone. After a few minutes, she called him a jerk and hung up on him. It wasn't the first time she had lashed out at him, and even though she tried to apologize the next day, he said he didn't want to deal with her moods anymore.

"All right, let's try to get it together," she tells herself. "Come up with a game plan." She decides to jog to the restaurant, avoiding bus delays and getting some exercise to boot. Moreover, in the few minutes she has before she must leave for work, she forces herself to start typing. Before too long, she has two paragraphs on the screen. "Not bad," she thinks, "at least it's a start." She is finally thinking and acting constructively.

You don't need a textbook to tell you that Ashley is experiencing stress. After all, you have probably been in a similar place—too much to do, too little time, too many expectations, too little certainty about what to do next. Ashley is obviously feeling stress because she has lots of work to do and is running out of time. But she also has feelings of stress connected to something otherwise pleasant—the opportunity to socialize with friends. Things as minor as an English paper, as pleasant as the prospect of an evening out, or as awful as a life-threatening medical condition can prompt feelings of stress.

Stress affects us both physically and psychologically. Recall how you felt the last time you were stuck in a traffic jam on your way to someplace important. Chances are you had physical and psychological reactions—you may have been frustrated and angry, your stomach may have been tied up in knots, and you may even have pounded on the steering wheel or yelled. Because stress affects us this way, it can damage our health.

The effects of stress on psychological and physical health have made it a subject of major research. Some researchers are trying to clarify what makes situations stressful. Others are studying how stress affects the body. Still others are trying to figure out what responses help people to cope effectively with stress and lessen its toll. This part examines what researchers have learned about the sources and effects of stress. It also looks at ways to deal with stress, noting that certain kinds of behaviour—such as Ashley's jog to work or her decision to simply start writing her paper—can help people reduce stress or cope with it positively.

Bloom Image/Getty Images

Module 80: What Is Stress?

You probably use the word *stress* all the time. We talk about being stressed, feeling stress, or about stressful events and situations, but have you thought about what it actually means? The term has been defined in various ways, so we will begin our examination of stress with a definition. We will then discuss the ways in which people experience stress and the kinds of situations that cause stress.

LEARNING OBJECTIVE 80
Define stress and describe the ways in which people experience stress and the kinds of situations that typically cause stress.

80.1 Stress and Stressors

Stress is a state brought on by any situation that threatens or appears to threaten a person's sense of well-being, thus challenging the person's ability to cope. A situation or circumstance that triggers the stress response is called a **stressor**. Stressors can be *acute* or *chronic*. An **acute stressor** is short term and has a definite endpoint—for example, a near miss in heavy traffic. A **chronic stressor** is long term and often lacks a definite endpoint—for example, dealing with a high-pressure job or being unemployed over time.

Obviously, our definition of stress is rather broad—literally anything can cause stress. The breadth of the definition takes into account the wide range of situations that people experience as stressful, from daily pressures at work and school to more catastrophic events, such as health crises, natural disasters, and terrorist attacks. At the same time, the definition calls attention to the emotional experience of stress and how individualized stress is.

A number of psychological factors help to determine the degree to which something will cause us to experience stress. In fact, stress is actually derived more from how we *appraise* the situation than from the situation itself (Lazarus & Folkman, 1984; Folkman, 2013a, 2013b). That is, our appraisal of our ability (or inability) to cope with a situation is an important factor in how much stress we experience. For example, two people attending a party of mostly strangers may approach the party with differing levels of stress. One person may view the situation as challenging, enjoying the idea of meeting a lot of new people. Another person might instead view the same situation as highly stressful, feeling very threatened by the idea of meeting a large number of new people. In each instance, each person appraises the situation based on their perceived ability to cope. It is therefore our *perception* of threat that triggers the emotional state we connect to stress. If we do not perceive a situation as threatening, we will not feel particularly stressed. We will soon look at more psychological factors in stress, but before that, let's examine the different ways that people experience stress.

stress state brought on by any situation that threatens or appears to threaten a person's sense of well-being, thus challenging the individual's ability to cope.

stressor a situation or circumstance that triggers the stress response.

acute stressor a stressful situation or circumstance that happens in the short term and has a definite endpoint.

chronic stressor a stressful situation or circumstance that is more long term and often lacks a definite endpoint.

Brendan McDermid/Reuters/Landov

Anxious moments. A trader on the floor of the stock exchange watches the numbers on the board anxiously, waiting desperately for a favourable moment to make his move.

80.2 Ways of Experiencing Stress

By definition, people who experience stress feel threatened and challenged. But these threats and challenges come in different forms. Certainly, soldiers in combat, students whose grades are falling, and children whose parents are unhappy with them face different kinds of stress. Psychologists have in fact distinguished between four kinds of stress experience: *frustration, pressure, conflict,* and *danger* (Aldwin, 2007). These kinds of stress are not mutually exclusive.

80.2.1 Feeling Frustrated

You finally find a parking spot, and someone pulls into it just ahead of you. You try to register for a course, and it is full. You work hard, but you get a C on the test. Whenever

frustration an emotion people experience when thwarted in pursuit of a goal.

we find ourselves thwarted in the pursuit of a goal, we experience **frustration**. Life is full of frustration; it is one of our most familiar kinds of stress. Frustration can be caused by acute stressors, such as those in the situations just described, and by chronic stressors. Persons who have chronic illnesses or disabilities, for example, are likely to feel frustrated that they cannot do more. All of these experiences are bound up with the notion of trying to achieve something and having a barrier to our progress. Barriers to progress generate stress.

80.2.2 Feeling Pressured

pressure an expectation or demand that someone act in a certain way.

We all encounter a certain amount of **pressure**—the expectation that we should act in a certain way. The pride felt by Ashley's parents over their daughter's admission to university is a source of pressure, and her boss's expectation that she should arrive at work on time is another.

Pressure often comes from within. Some individuals have such high expectations of themselves that they are constantly under self-imposed stress. Think of the sources of pressure in your own life. What standards do you set for yourself academically and socially? Are you driven to achieve in athletics? How much pressure do you experience as a result of such expectations? For some, stress that comes from within is often more difficult to cope with than stress imposed by others. It may not be easy to meet the deadline for turning in a term paper, but at least when you do so, the pressure will be off. By contrast, if you set yourself a rigid standard of perfection, you may never find release from this internal pressure.

Pressure also varies along with the task and situation. One set of studies, for example, demonstrated that participants experienced greater stress when performing complex tasks in front of an audience, but that they performed significantly better without the pressure of an audience (Wan & Huon, 2005; Butler & Baumeister, 1998; Baumeister, 1984). Focusing on the specific task they are performing can also reduce perceptions of stress (Buma, Bakker, & Oudejans, 2014). Still other research has found a strong correlation between feelings of pressure and symptoms of distress, indicating that perceived discrimination is associated with increased levels of depression and an increased number of medical diagnoses (Todorova et al., 2010).

Sports and Pressure In the 1986 Western conference semi-finals between the Edmonton Oilers and the Calgary Flames, Oiler Steve Smith made a heartbreaking mistake. The game was tied 2–2 in the third period of the seventh and deciding game, and Smith was carrying the puck out from behind his own net with no-one checking him. He attempted a cross-ice clearing pass that somehow bounced off the back of his own goaltender (Grant Fuhr) and ended up in his own team's net. Calgary knocked the two-time Stanley Cup-winning Oilers out of the playoffs. Smith was devastated. It also happened to be his birthday, and he has since said that now he thinks of the goal every time he blows out his birthday candles.

What happened to Smith and to other athletes who have made mental errors in other high-pressure situations? When does pressure help athletic performance and when does it impair it? These questions have been the subject of much study. A number of explanations have been offered, but a clear understanding of the effects of pressure on athletes remains elusive (Weinberg & Gould, 2011).

We do know that performance pressure results when athletes feel strongly about the outcome of an event and believe that their own performance will have an impact on that outcome (Wallace, Baumeister, & Vohs, 2005). We also know that this pressure can result in increased physiological and psychological arousal. But researchers cannot predict the precise relationship between such arousal and performance.

For years, psychologists believed that the relationship probably follows the principle of the *Yerkes-Dodson law*. As we observed in Part 11, this psychological "law," developed in 1908 by psychologists Robert Yerkes and John Dodson, holds that performances on tasks of any kind increase along with physical or mental arousal—up to a point—but once

QMI Agency

A costly error. A dejected Steve Smith immediately after scoring on his own goal, an error that led to the Edmonton Oilers losing the Stanley Cup Western Conference semi-final game back in 1986.

an optimal, moderate level of arousal is passed, performances begin to decrease. Applying this law to athletic performances, it is generally believed that if an athlete is not aroused, his or her performance will suffer, and that if he or she is too aroused, performance will also suffer. Optimal performance is thought to occur only in the presence of a moderate level of arousal (Yerkes & Dodson, 1908).

Over the years, research has better supported an alternative version of the Yerkes-Dodson law, particularly in the realm of athletic performance. Recall from Part 12 that this alternative model holds that the level of arousal at which optimal performance occurs is a *zone* (not a single point) and varies from athlete to athlete. Some cross-country runners, for example, will perform best if they take naps right before a race, while their teammates will do best if they listen to inspiring music, visualize their opponents, and engage in intense stretching exercises before the race (Hanin, 1997).

A different line of research suggests that coaches can play a large role in helping athletes cope with performance pressure. Since anxiety tends to be lowest in athletes who believe in their performance abilities and are self-assured, research suggests that coaches can help by facilitating feelings of confidence—for example, by providing frequent, genuine encouragement and by fostering a positive environment, regardless of whether things have gone well or mistakes have occurred (Weinberg & Gould, 2003; Pineschi & Di Pietro, 2013). Here again, however, effective methods vary from athlete to athlete.

80.2.3 Feeling Conflicted

The stress Ashley feels is not simply the result of pressure from her parents. It also results in part from her desire to do two things at the same time: (1) study to earn good grades, and (2) have time to go out with her friends. In situations such as this, we experience **conflict**—discomfort brought about by two or more goals or impulses that we perceive to be incompatible. There are three basic types of conflict: *approach–approach, avoidance–avoidance,* and *approach–avoidance* (see **Figure 80-1**) (Miller, 1959; Lewin, 1935).

- As its name implies, **approach–approach conflict** occurs when we must choose between two equally desirable options. Should we have the chocolate cake or the blueberry pie? Should we buy the red backpack or the black one? In many cases, approach–approach conflicts are easy to resolve (you can't really lose with either choice), and so they are not especially stressful.
- **Avoidance–avoidance conflicts** are somewhat more stressful because here the choice is between two equally undesirable outcomes. Should you clean the garage or do the laundry? You may be tempted to do neither. If you deal with this kind of conflict by deciding to procrastinate, postpone, or avoid the choice, however, you are particularly likely to experience stress (Shafir & Tversky, 2002).

conflict discomfort brought about by two or more goals or impulses perceived to be incompatible.

approach–approach conflict conflict that occurs when a person must choose between two equally desirable options.

avoidance–avoidance conflict conflict that occurs when a person must choose between two equally undesirable options.

+ Great job offer #1
+ Great job offer #2

(a) Approach–approach conflict

- Bad job offer
- No job offer

(b) Avoidance–avoidance conflict

+ - Great job offer but have to relocate

(c) Approach–avoidance conflict

FIGURE 80-1 **Three basic types of conflict that can lead to stress.**

approach–avoidance conflict conflict that occurs when any available choice has both desirable and undesirable qualities.

- In an **approach–avoidance conflict**, any available choice has both desirable and undesirable qualities, rendering us ambivalent and indecisive. In some situations, this sort of conflict may involve only one choice with both positive and negative features. For example, if Ashley were to go out with her friends, she would enjoy herself, but she wouldn't be able to work on her paper. In other situations, more than one option may be involved. Should you buy a car that is expensive but fuel-efficient, for example, or a less expensive gas guzzler? Approach–avoidance conflicts are on display in many of our most agonizing decisions. Often people worry for some time about how to resolve them, and experience considerable stress along the way.

80.2.4 Feeling Endangered

Life-threatening situations understandably produce stress, making us feel endangered. The adrenaline rush we experience when a car in front of us suddenly stops, forcing us to swerve and slam on the brakes, is characteristic of this kind of stress. Similarly, such stress is experienced by people who face combat or are trapped in a fire. Natural disasters may also be life threatening and, in turn, stressful. Life-threatening situations created by people may also produce stress. Terrorism leaves individuals with feelings of uncertainty, sadness, and fear, making them vulnerable to the onset of stress disorders (Tracy et al., 2014; Bleich et al., 2003; Ursano et al., 2003). Indeed, terrorism may have long-term psychological effects.

80.3 Kinds of Stressors

Just as there are different ways of experiencing stress, there are different types of stressors. Indeed, stressors vary widely—from discrete life events to chronic stressors. Moreover, they can be mild, extreme, or anywhere in between. As you will see later in this part, what is stressful for one person may not be stressful for another. Still, there are several kinds of events that are likely to produce feelings of stress whenever they are experienced: daily hassles, such as traffic jams; life changes, such as the loss of a job; traumatic events, such as natural disasters; chronic negative situations, such as an enduring illness; and special socio-cultural conditions, such as racism. We will discuss each of these categories in turn, but as you know all too well, they may overlap or intersect.

Carmen Taylor/AP

Stress and terror. The aftermath of life-threatening events, like the terrorist attacks of 9/11, might lead some New Yorkers to experience a sense of intense fear at the sight of a plane in the sky, or to cringe at the sound of a bus backfiring.

daily hassles everyday annoyances that contribute to higher stress levels; also known as *micro-stressors*.

80.3.1 Daily Hassles

Probably the most familiar sources of stress are **daily hassles** (also called micro-stressors)—the everyday annoyances that leave us feeling upset and at the end of our rope. These stressors can range from minor irritations, such as lost keys or a talkative co-worker, to major problems, such as intense work pressure or conflict with a romantic partner. Some daily hassles seem to be universally upsetting, including time pressures, cash-flow problems, feelings of being cheated after making a purchase, conflicts with romantic partners, mistreatment by friends, and poor evaluations at work.

Over time, daily hassles can add up. They may become particularly stressful when they occur in combination with other stressors, leaving individuals overwhelmed (Falconier et al., 2014; Boutreyre, Maurel, & Bernaud, 2007). A hot day may not be particularly stressful by itself, but combine it with waiting in a long line to renew a driver's licence, a crying child, and a blister on your heel, and you may wind up feeling exasperated and depleted. In fact, data suggest that the accumulation of daily stressors often leads to increased health risks (Seta, Seta, & McElroy, 2002), while engaging in healthy living habits decreases the impact of university or college stress among students (Fogel & Pettijohn, 2013).

It turns out that the impact of daily hassles on health is often greater than that of a major life event (Stuart & Garrison, 2002). This is because ongoing stress may impair our immune system responses, as we shall see later. Indeed, one study found that people who face daily commutes in heavy traffic are particularly likely to miss work because of colds and flu (Novaco, Stokols, & Milanesi, 1990)—illnesses that can result from stress-induced changes in the immune system.

Researchers have developed several measures of daily hassles. Psychologist Richard Lazarus and his colleagues developed one of the first, the *Daily Hassles Scale*, in which subjects are asked to consider a list of hassles, indicate which ones they had experienced over the past month, and report how stressful each event felt (Kanner et al., 1981). Measuring the impact of daily hassles is difficult, because people vary widely in how they experience and weigh such stressors (Kohn, 1996).

Some scales have targeted the experiences of college and university students and asked about both daily hassles and major stressful events (Cardilla, 2008; D'Angelo & Wierzbicki, 2003; Kohn et al., 1990). Such scales have paid special attention to the impact of exams (Edwards & Trimble, 1992; Abella & Heslin, 1989; Folkman & Lazarus, 1985). Feelings of stress tend to be strongest just before an exam and continue (though to a lesser extent) as students wait to receive their grades and as they later try to cope with the results. See **Table 80-1** to review items on the Undergraduate Stress Questionnaire (Crandall, Preisler, & Aussprung, 1992).

TABLE 80-1 Undergraduate Stress Questionnaire

Has this stressful event happened to you at any time during the last two weeks? If it has, please check the space next to it. If it has not, please leave the space blank.

Lack of money	No sex for a while
Someone broke a promise	Someone cut ahead of you in line
Death (family member or friend)	Broke up with boyfriend/girlfriend
Dealt with incompetence at the registrar's office	Tried to decide on major
Can't concentrate	Feeling isolated
Had a lot of tests	Had roommate conflicts
Thought about unfinished work	Chequebook didn't balance
Someone did a "pet peeve" of yours	Visit from a relative and entertaining them
It's finals week	Someone you expected to call did not
Had an interview	Holiday
Had projects, research papers due	Sat through a boring class
Did badly on a test	Favourite sporting team lost
Can't finish everything you need to do	Thought about the future
Heard bad news	

Source: Undergraduate Stress Questionnaire. Crandall, C. S., Preisler, J. J., & Aussprung, J. (1992). Measuring Life Event Stress in the Lives of College Students: The Undergraduate Stress Questionnaire (USQ). *Journal of Behavioral Medicine*, 15 (6), 627–662.

These are a few of the items from this measure. If you would like to see and/or complete the whole measure, you can download it here: www.utulsa.edu/student-life/Health-and-Wellness/Counseling-and-Psychological-Services-Center.aspx (via Undergraduate Stress Questionnaire Link).

If you are concerned about how many stressful life events you have checked, you can contact your college or university counselling or wellness centre or check out some stress management resources on Health Canada's website: www.hc-sc.gc.ca/hl-vs/iyh-vsv/life-vie/stress-eng.php.

©iStockphoto.com/damircudic

Feeling stressed. The first set of midterm exams for first-year post-secondary students are often quite stressful.

life changes shifts in life circumstances that require adjustment of some kind.

80.3.2 Change

Another common source of stress is change. Those early weeks in a new school, for example, are usually quite stressful, even if they are also exciting. In the first weeks of college or university, students need to figure out what classes to take, where classrooms are located, what is expected of them, and where to buy books (as well as how to pay for them). At the same time, they are meeting many new people. Trying to find our way in new relationships can be even more complicated and challenging than finding our way to class.

Life changes—shifts in life circumstances that require adjustment of some kind—were among the first sources of stress ever studied. In 1967, investigators Thomas Holmes and Richard Rahe set out to develop a way to systematically measure how much stress people experience. They compiled a list of 43 events that were likely to change a person's life and therefore cause stress. These events ranged from the death of a spouse, to minor violations of the law, to taking a vacation (note the similarity of these items to those on the Undergraduate Stress Scale, which was adapted from the Holmes Rahe scale). Based on ratings by participants, the researchers assigned a point value to each event, ranging from 1 to 100 points, or *life-change units (LCUs)*. The point value for each event corresponded to the amount of upset and adjustment the event typically produced. The death of a spouse received a score of 100 LCUs on the scale, for example, whereas a change in responsibilities at work was 29 LCUs, and taking a vacation came in at 13 LCUs.

With this 43-item list, called the *Social Readjustment Rating Scale (SRRS)*, Holmes and Rahe set about conducting studies on the impact of stress on people's lives. First they had individuals complete the scale to determine how much stress they were under. Participants were asked to check off all those events that had occurred in their lives over a certain time period, usually the past year. Then they added up the total number of life-change units, with the sum indicating the amount of stress the person had been under. A total score of 150 LCUs or less indicated relatively little stress; 150 to 199 indicated mild stress; 200 to 299 suggested moderate stress; and over 300 LCUs pointed to major life stress. Holmes and Rahe claim that those individuals who score over 300 are more likely to experience physical illness than those who score below 150 points. The life events from the SRRS and their ratings are listed in **Table 80-2**. Notice that a life-changing event need not be an undesirable one. A number of the events on the SRRS are positive, and some can be either positive or negative. A change in living conditions, for example, may reflect a move upward or downward in life.

Think back to our part opener, where we learned that Ashley recently broke up with her boyfriend, an event that would receive a score of 65 LCUs on Holmes and Rahe's scale. In addition, she has been experiencing troubles with her boss (23 LCUs), school pressures (39 LCUs), and new social activities (18 LCUs). Since she is a relatively new student, we can assume that she changed schools (20 LCUs) and residences (19 LCUs) fairly recently. Add in her outstanding personal achievement of being the first in her family to go to university (28 LCUs), and her LCU score totals 212—a moderate level of stress over a short period of time.

We pointed out that the Social Readjustment Rating Scale includes positive as well as negative life events. Nevertheless, the scale has been criticized for looking at many more negative events than positive ones and for not including events that do not occur, like not getting a job or promotion you applied for (McLean & Link, 1994). Because of this, the scale may not give a complete picture of the effects of life change on stress levels.

Another shortcoming of the SRRS is that it does not apply equally to all populations. In developing the scale, Holmes and Rahe sampled mostly Caucasian Americans. Fewer than 5 percent of their participants were African Americans, and none were Native Americans. Subsequent research has shown this bias to be particularly problematic because

TABLE 80-2 The Social Readjustment Rating Scale

To score your susceptibility to stress on this scale, add up the life change units for the events you experienced in the last year. Scores of 150 or less indicate little stress; 150–199 mild stress; 200–299 moderate stress; and over 300 major life stress.

Life Events	Life Change Units	Life Events	Life Change Units
Death of spouse	100	Son or daughter leaving home	29
Divorce	73	Trouble with in-laws	29
Marital separation	65	Outstanding personal achievement	28
Jail term	63	Spouse begins or stops work	26
Death of a close family member	63	Begin or end school	26
Personal injury or illness	53	Change in living conditions	25
Marriage	50	Revision of personal habits	24
Fired at work	47	Trouble with boss	23
Marital reconciliation	45	Change in work hours or condition	20
Retirement	45	Change in residence	20
Change in health of family member	44	Change in schools	20
Pregnancy	40	Change in recreation	19
Sex difficulties	39	Change in church activities	19
Gain of a new family member	39	Change in social activities	18
Business readjustment	39	Mortgage or loan for lesser purchase (car, major appliance)	17
Change in financial state	38	Change in sleeping habits	16
Death of a close friend	37	Change in number of family get-togethers	15
Change to different line of work	36	Change in eating habits	15
Change in number of arguments with spouse	35	Vacation	13
Mortgage or loan for major purchase	31	Christmas	12
Foreclosure on mortgage or loan	30	Minor violations of the law	11
Change in responsibilities at work	29		

Source: Reprinted from Holmes & Rahe (1967). The Social Readjustment Rating Scale. *Journal of Psychosomatic Research,* Vol. III, 213–218. With permission from Elsevier.

Caucasian Americans and African Americans often rank life events differently. For example, although both groups rank the death of a spouse as the most stressful life event, African Americans rank personal injury or illness and major changes in work responsibilities or living conditions much higher than do Caucasian Americans (Komaroff, Masuda, & Holmes, 1989, 1986). Similarly, certain types of events, such as the death of a family member, loss of a job, credit problems, and change in residence, are generally more stressful for women than for men (Miller & Rahe, 1997). Alexandra Robinson (2013) at the University of Calgary showed that women from Canadian ethnic minorities experience more psychosocial stress during pregnancy than do non-minority group members.

Digital Vision/Getty Images

Even positive changes can be stressful. Even though they are happy events, marriages produce a high degree of stress according to research using the Social Readjustment Rating Scale.

As described by Lawrence Kirmayer of McGill University, over the past decades Canada's Aboriginal population has experienced a broad and unique array of additional stressors. These include residential schools and the "60s scoop," in which a great many Aboriginal children were removed from their communities and placed in non-Aboriginal foster homes away from family and Aboriginal culture and community. This has led to a broad range of additional stresses and challenges that are all parts of their social adjustment stress profiles. As a result, the Aboriginal population experiences increased interpersonal problems such as substance abuse, depression, and suicide, as well as increased social problems including high rates of sexual abuse, family violence, and incarceration (Kirmayer, Simpson, & Cargo, 2003; Chachamovich et al., 2013).

80.3.3 Life Change and Illness

Holmes and Rahe found that the LCU scores of sick people during the year before they became ill were considerably higher than those of healthy people (Holmes & Rahe, 1989, 1967). In fact, as stated above, if a person's life changes totalled more than 300 LCUs over the course of a year, that person was likely to develop a serious health problem.

The SRRS has been revised by researchers over the years (Hobson & Delunas, 2001; Hobson et al., 1998; Miller & Rahe, 1997). Using various scales, studies have tied a variety of life stressors to a wide range of physical problems, from upper respiratory infection to cancer (Baum, Trevino, & Dougall, 2011; Cohen, 2005; Rook, August, & Sorkin, 2011; Renzaho, 2013). Generally, the greater the amount of life stress, the higher the likelihood of medical illness. Some researchers have even found a relationship between stress and death. Widows and widowers, for example, have an elevated risk of death during their period of bereavement (Möller et al., 2011).

80.4 Lifespan Development and Stress

Although feelings of stress may be similar for both young and old people, the life changes that evoke these feelings apparently differ widely from age group to age group. As you have just seen, the most powerful stressors (in decreasing order) on the SRRS, a largely adult scale, are death of a spouse, divorce, marital separation, jail term, death of a close family member, and personal injury or illness. But how does stress affect younger age groups?

Researchers have developed special scales to measure life events and stress among traditional college and university students (Renner & Mackin, 2002; Crandall et al., 1992; Slavich & Toussaint, 2013). They have found that the most stressful life event for this population is the death of a family member or friend, much like the top life stressor for adults. Beyond this event, however, the leading life stressors for college and university students are ones that are tied to post-secondary life. They are (again in decreasing order) having to take multiple tests, enduring final exam week, applying to graduate school, being a victim of crime, having assignments in a number of different classes due on the same day, and breaking up with a romantic partner.

Moving to still younger individuals, researchers have found that the leading life stressors for children overlap to some degree with those of adults and college and university students, but, here again, they largely reflect issues unique to childhood (Sotardi, 2013; Ryan-Wenger, Sharrer, & Campbell, 2005; Neff & Dale, 1996; Coddington, 1984, 1972). Across various scales, the leading stressors for school-aged children are taking tests, having excessive homework, being made fun of or bullied, feeling left out, getting bad grades, getting in trouble, fighting with family members or friends, experiencing the death or illness of someone close, and doing something embarrassing.

Jim Young/Reuters/Landov

Early separation. This soldier consoles his young daughter prior to his departure for Afghanistan. Research suggests that family military separations of this kind often take an enormous emotional toll on the children who are left behind.

It is worth noting that the kinds of life events that produce stress tend to shift as children develop (Vasey et al., 1994). As children move from 5 years old to 12 years old, physical-type events (for example, getting sick) become less stressful, behavioural events (getting into trouble) become more stressful, and psychosocial events (fighting with friends) also become more stressful.

Finally, focus on particular life stressors seems to change from generation to generation (Ryan-Wenger et al., 2005). For example, in the 1990s, awareness about a number of different childhood events, such as experiences about being bullied and experiencing violence in school, became more recognized as stressors of childhood and therefore became prevalent items on children's life stress scales. Similarly, during the 2000s, several other powerful childhood stressors have emerged, such as cyber bullying, terrorism, and concerns over post-earthquake nuclear meltdowns.

80.4.1 Traumatic Events

Life changes are stressful because they disrupt the routines of our lives. **Traumatic events** are more extreme disruptions—unexpected events that have the power to change the way we view the world. The earthquakes and tsunamis in Japan in March 2011, the floods around Calgary in 2013, and the train disaster in Lac-Mégantic in July 2013 are examples of the stress-inducing power of single, cataclysmic events. Rape or violent assault can also be traumatizing. Such events can have profound and long-lasting effects. Victims may experience a sense of helplessness, depression, anxiety, numbness, and disorientation (Carretta & Burgess, 2013; Overmier & Murison, 2005; Carr, 2000). In some cases, the effects can last for years.

traumatic events unexpected events severe enough to create extreme disruptions.

Yasuyoshi Chiba/Stringer/Getty Images

Traumatic events. A resident walks among the rubble in the wake of the earthquake and tsunami that hit Japan in March 2011. Major disasters, such as this, can be traumatizing for survivors.

Some victims of extraordinarily traumatic events develop **posttraumatic stress disorder (PTSD)**, a condition characterized by persistent, frightening thoughts or memories of the traumatic events, along with anxiety, depression, and other symptoms. We will discuss this disorder in more detail later in this part.

Although traumatic events are usually of short duration, some can be ongoing. Suffering ongoing physical or sexual abuse or living with an alcoholic partner or parent are examples of long-lasting traumatic events. These, too, can leave victims withdrawn and experiencing recurring mental images, anxiety, and depression (Carretta & Burgess, 2013; Overmier & Murison, 2005).

posttraumatic stress disorder (PTSD) an anxiety disorder experienced in response to a major traumatic event, characterized by lingering, persistent, frightening thoughts or memories of the traumatic events, along with anxiety, depression, and other symptoms.

80.4.2 Chronic Negative Situations

A negative situation may become particularly stressful if it continues over a long, perhaps indefinite, period of time (Schmidt et al., 2009). People living in a war zone, for example, confront the fearful possibility of an attack as they go about their daily lives, attending school, shopping, or taking the bus to work. Similarly, people who live in poverty face constant concerns about meeting their basic needs and paying their debts (Freeman, 1984; Freeman & Stansfeld, 2014). An ongoing negative home environment—marked by endless arguments with a spouse or child, for example—may produce considerable stress, and so may enduring workplace problems, such as continually feeling underpaid, unappreciated, bored, or in danger of being fired (Rossi et al., 2009; Krantz, Berntsson, & Lundberg, 2005; Lundberg, 2000).

Chronic illnesses can also produce much stress over time. Such illnesses may not only cause pain, but also impose limitations and produce feelings of mortality and uncertainty in people's lives. The patients themselves are not the only ones affected by chronic illnesses; their caregivers also experience stress. Thus, parents of children with special needs—whether enduring illnesses, physical handicaps, intellectual disability, or other

©iStockphoto.com/Brendan McIlhargey

Chronic job stress. Certain jobs produce chronic stress. For example, research reveals that physicians, particularly those whose specialties deal largely with life-threatening medical problems, often experience enormous work pressure and strain.

conditions—often experience stress. So do the growing numbers of adults who must take care of aging parents or spouses. In fact, research indicates that such caregivers often suffer from depression, drink excessively, are sleep deprived, and engage in fewer healthful behaviours, such as exercise (O'Rourke et al., 2003; Yoon, 2003; Do, Cohen, & Brown, 2014).

The physical environment may also provide chronic stressors. Chronic noise, for example, often leads to tension and upset (Evans, 2001; Ferguson et al., 2013). Similarly, chronic overcrowding leads to higher bodily arousal and makes it difficult for people to relax (Fleming et al., 1987). Chronic environmental stressors may interact with each other. A noisy roommate, for example, may be both a physical and a social stressor. The roommate's loud music may bombard you and leave you with frequent headaches; at the same time, the tense relationship that develops between the two of you may produce further stress.

80.4.3 Socio-cultural Conditions

Socio-cultural conditions, such as those faced by members of ethnic minority groups who regularly confront prejudice, can be sources of stress (Liang et al., 2009). Minority-group members, including those in Canada's First Nations and Métis populations, face special challenges and stressors as they try to navigate through the dominant culture (Chachamovich et al., 2013). Foreign workers participating in Canada's temporary foreign worker program, for example, have to adjust to new ways of doing things, learn a new language, and often contend with poverty and the stress of a crowded living situation. In addition, members of minority groups often have to try to balance the demands of two cultures—their own culture and that of the dominant culture in which they live. If they are not proficient in the language or nuances of the dominant culture, they may also experience the stress of isolation and of having limited access to the main channels of communication within the dominant culture (Mino, Profit, & Pierce, 2000).

And even when minority-group members achieve success in the dominant culture, another source of stress can emerge as individuals find themselves having to assess the role that prejudice and discrimination may have played in their interactions with the dominant culture. For example, consider Jonathan, an Aboriginal Canadian man working in advertising at a large department store. Jonathan's job is to produce advertisements for special sales of fall clothing. His boss, who is Caucasian, doesn't think much of the two ideas Jonathan has proposed and tells him so. In addition to feeling disappointed and perhaps angry about the rejection of his ideas, Jonathan may experience the further stress of wondering whether his boss was reacting to his Aboriginal status or to his ideas. The suspicions, confusion, and resulting vigilance experienced by minority-group members as they interact with majority-group members, often referred to as *stereotype threat*, is a very real stressor for minority-group members, but is often invisible to those in the majority group (Schmader, Hall, & Croft, 2015; Nail, Harton, & Decker, 2003; Profit, Mino, & Pierce, 2000).

Before You Go On www.wiley.com/go/comercanada

What Do You Know?
1. What is the difference between an acute stressor and a chronic stressor?
2. What are the four types of stress experiences?
3. Define the three basic types of conflict.
4. What are daily hassles and what is their impact on health?
5. What is the Social Readjustment Rating Scale?

What Do You Think? What kinds of situations do you find especially stressful? How do they compare with what your friends find stressful? What do variations in the experience of stress tell us about stress and stressors?

Summary

Module 80: What Is Stress?

LEARNING OBJECTIVE 80 Define stress and describe the ways in which people experience stress and the kinds of situations that typically cause stress.

- Stress is a state brought on by any situation that threatens or appears to threaten a person's sense of well-being, thus challenging the person's ability to cope. A situation that triggers the stress response is a stressor. A stressor may be acute (short term) or chronic (long term).
- People may experience stress as frustration, pressure, conflict, or danger.
- Kinds of stressors include daily hassles, life changes (which can be measured by use of the Social Readjustment Rating Scale), traumatic events, chronic negative situations, and special socio-cultural conditions.

Key Terms

acute stressor 607

approach–approach
 conflict 609

approach–avoidance
 conflict 610

avoidance–avoidance
 conflict 609

chronic stressor 607

conflict 609

daily hassles 610

frustration 608

life changes 612

posttraumatic stress disorder
 (PTSD) 615

pressure 608

stress 607

stressor 607

traumatic events 615

Study Questions

Multiple Choice

1. Compared to major life events, daily hassles
   a) have a lower impact upon us
   b) can add to the effects of larger events
   c) can have greater impact than the effects of major life events
   d) are of secondary concern

2. Bob loves visiting his grandfather but hates his cooking. Bob is trying to decide whether to visit his grandfather this weekend and is experiencing an
   a) approach–approach conflict
   b) approach–avoidance conflict
   c) avoidance–avoidance conflict
   d) approach–withdraw conflict

3. Which of the following is not potentially associated with posttraumatic stress disorder?
   a) anxiety
   b) depression
   c) amnesia
   d) disorientation

4. In a study using the Social Readjustment Rating Scale, which of the following stressors was not reported as one of the top five experienced by college and university students?
   a) Applying to graduate school
   b) Death of a family member or friend
   c) Having to take multiple tests
   d) Personal injury or illness

5. Which of the following is one of the types of stress experiences identified by psychologists?
   a) Automatic
   b) Frustration
   c) Happiness
   d) Sensitization

Fill-in-the-Blank

1. If your friends were to forget to invite you to a party, it would be an example of a _____ stressor.

2. If you were to complete the Social Readjustment Rating Scale in a research project, you would be assigned a _____.

3. When a minority-group member encounters members of the majority group, they may experience _____ threat.

4. The fact that a given situation may be very stressful for one person and not at all stressful for another tells us that the _____ of threat is often more important than actual threat.

5. Emily is struggling to keep up with her classes and must choose whether to work on a paper for one class or a project for another class before heading to work. Emily is facing a(n) _____ conflict.

Module 81: Responding to Stress

We have looked at the kinds of experiences that cause stress. Let's turn next to what happens to people when they experience stress. Responses to stress fall into three general types: physiological, emotional, and cognitive. As you might expect, people vary greatly in their responses.

81.1 Physiological Responses to Stress

Although what happens in the brain is critical to the stress response, responses to stress affect both the brain and the body. Think about how you come to know that you are under stress. Typically, your breathing and heart rate quicken, you begin to sweat, your mouth gets dry, and your stomach tightens. What's happening is that your brain has perceived a challenge and is sending signals to your body to prepare to meet it. This response to stress involves a brain–body reaction. Sweating, dry mouth, and stomach tightness are some of the immediate physical effects of stress, but these effects are actually indicators of more basic physiological responses. We examine these responses next and illustrate them in **Figure 81-1**.

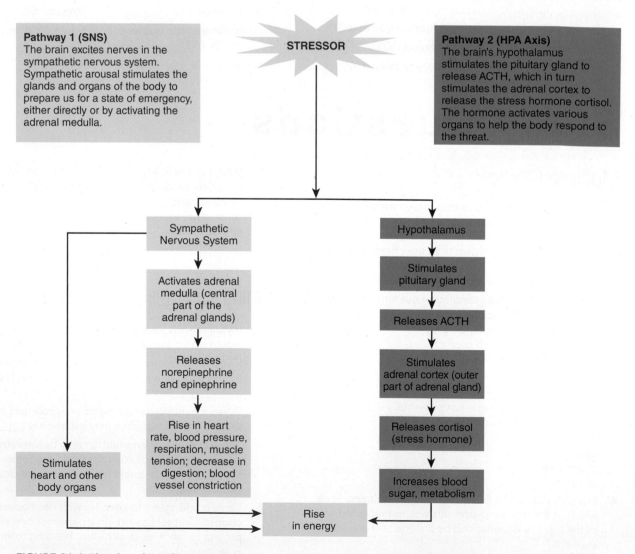

FIGURE 81-1 **The physiological response to stress.** As shown in this flow chart, the brain sends messages to the endocrine glands and bodily organs through the sympathetic nervous system (SNS) pathway and the hypothalamic-pituitary-adrenal (HPA) axis.

81.1.1 The Fight-or-Flight Response

You may remember the discussion of physiologist Walter Cannon's theory of emotion in Part 11. Cannon was the first theorist to connect the bodily arousal associated with emotional responses to the need to fight or flee. According to Cannon (1932), the fight-or-flight response is a series of physiological reactions throughout the sympathetic nervous system and the endocrine system that mobilize an organism to either fight or flee an enemy. The process begins in the brain. The brain sends messages to the endocrine glands and bodily organs along two different routes. One is through the sympathetic nervous system, which as you recall is a division of the autonomic nervous system (ANS). The other is through the hypothalamic-pituitary-adrenal (HPA) axis (Friedman & Silver, 2007).

Geoff Howe/The Canadian Press

Under fire. Riot police were in extreme danger during the riot following the Vancouver Canuck loss during the 2011 NHL playoffs.

When we confront a dangerous situation, within seconds the brain sends messages to the sympathetic nervous system, and these nerves directly stimulate organs of the body (the heart, for example). The nerves also influence organs indirectly by stimulating the adrenal glands (located at the tops of the kidneys), particularly the inner layer of those glands, an area called the *adrenal medulla*. The adrenal medulla, in turn, releases the chemicals epinephrine and norepinephrine (otherwise known as adrenaline and noradrenaline) into the bloodstream, where they are carried to various organs and muscles, further arousing the organism and enabling it to fight or flee. Normally, the biological changes associated with the fight-or-flight response subside around 15 minutes after the threatening situation eases (Friedman & Silver, 2007).

The fight-or-flight response may not entirely be about fighting or running. Recent research has shown that the release of oxytocin, when combined with estrogen in women, gives rise to affiliation motivation (Carter, 2014). This may be associated with post-partum nurturing by mothers and what is called the "tend-and-befriend" effect (Taylor, 2006), where taking care of another leads to increased feelings of affiliation and liking.

The brain also sends messages through the HPA axis (Jankord & Herman, 2009). When we are confronted by stressors, various brain regions communicate with the hypothalamus, which in turn stimulates the pituitary gland, prompting the gland to release the *adrenocorticotropic hormone (ACTH)* into the bloodstream. ACTH travels to the adrenal glands and interacts with their outer covering, an area called the *adrenal cortex*, causing the release of stress hormones called *cortisol*.

Cortisol travels to a range of body organs, where, among other activities, it helps elevate blood sugar, supply energy to the organism under stress, and protect the body from inflammation. In this way, cortisol helps prepare individuals who are under stress for their fight-or-flight response (Lupien et al., 2006; Plaford, 2013).

The HPA axis is a slower system than the sympathetic nervous system, taking minutes as opposed to seconds to have a big influence on the body. These two systems (the sympathetic nervous system and the HPA axis), activated in tandem, ensure that the organism is able to mobilize its energy to deal with a crisis, even if it takes a while. As you will see later in the part, however, problems can arise if cortisol activity remains high

Diverse Images/UIG/Getty Images

Fight-or-flight response. When faced with a dangerous or stressful situation, our brain sends messages to the sympathetic nervous system, which triggers various reactions in the body (such as the release of cortisol to supply energy) to prepare the body for the fight-or-flight response.

Some theorists argue that the fight-or-flight response may be a largely male response, and suggest that evolution may have selected a "tend-and-befriend" response to cope with stress in females. Regardless of the mechanism, in general females are more likely to have extensive and well-maintained social networks than are males (Taylor et al., 2000).

for too long. It can then become harmful, contributing in some cases to high blood pressure, inflammation, anxiety, and depression, among other problems (Kendall-Tackett, 2010; Sher, 2003; Nemeroff, 1998).

The fight-or-flight response is an early evolutionary adaptation. You can imagine how this kind of reaction might have helped early humans survive. If they suddenly came upon a grizzly bear, they were better able to either overwhelm it or escape in a hurry. But many of the stressors we face today are more subtle and more chronic—homework stress, employment pressures, relationship difficulties, and any number of other conditions. What happens when a stressor is chronic? Hans Selye considered that question in forming his theory of the general adaptation syndrome.

Psychology Around Us   A Laugh a Day Keeps the Doctor Away?

Jessica Teft/Keystone

A different approach. The real Patch Adams, physician and clown, talks here to the sister of a hospitalized child.

In a 1998 film, Robin Williams donned a white coat and a red clown nose and took a new brand of medicine to movie theatres around the world. He was playing real-life physician Patch Adams, who believes that the medical community has failed to embrace the use of laughter and humour to aid in health and healing (Marsh, 2008). While this may be a feel-good sentiment, is there actual support for the notion that laughter is the best medicine?

Research results from medicine and psychology are mixed in their support of a laughter–health link. One study found, for example, that after watching a humorous film, participants who had laughed at and enjoyed the film showed decreases in stress and improvements in their immune system activity (Bennett, 1998). On the basis of such supportive findings, psychologists have offered various explanations for how laughter might improve health (McCreaddie & Wiggins, 2008; Godfrey, 2004). Some of these explanations suggest that there is a direct link between laughter and health. One proposal, for example, holds that laughter may increase blood flow, thereby reducing blood pressure (Dolgoff-Kaspar et al., 2012). Another proposal argues that 100 laughs can provide an aerobic workout equal to 15 minutes on an exercise bike (Brickey, 2005). Still other scientists suggest that the link between laughter and health is an indirect one. One popular proposal, for example, supported by research conducted by Elsa Marsalis at the University of Toronto, suggests that humour results in greater social support, thereby aiding health, and that humour may help heal by bringing down a person's stress level (Marziali, McDonald, & Donahue, 2008).

Other research suggests that support for the humour–health link is less clear and perhaps more questionable than first thought. Some studies on this subject have failed to support the link (McCreaddie & Wiggins, 2008; Martin, 2001; Cho & Oh, 2011). Clearer verdicts on the strength of this relationship and on the theories that seek to explain it await the results of some current and future research undertakings.

In the meantime, there is nothing in the literature to suggest laughter is bad for one's health, and many health and humour experts have offered tips on how to increase one's daily quota of good humour. They suggest, for example, browsing through the humour section of a local bookstore; keeping a humour journal filled with funny newspaper headlines, bumper stickers, and notes about humorous events; and reading cartoons daily, making sure to save and post the ones that tickle your funny bone the most (Godfrey, 2004).

81.1.2 The General Adaptation Syndrome

Hans Selye was an Austrian-born endocrinologist who immigrated to Canada in 1939. He worked at McGill University and the Université de Montréal and is credited with first talking about stress in living creatures (Selye, 1993, 1956, 1936; Greenberg, Carr, & Summers, 2002). In his laboratory, Selye exposed animals to a variety of stressors. No matter what the stressor—mild shock, pain, restraint, heat, cold—he found that the animals displayed the same pattern of response: a consistent pattern that he labelled *stress* (a term he borrowed from engineers, who use it when they discuss forces that affect the structural integrity of the things they build). Selye believed we respond in much the same ways to stress, whatever its source. This insight was particularly important, because it means that, although our responses to different stressors might vary in degree, we are responding in the same basic way to all of them.

Selye also noticed that if stressors continue, the organism's body progresses through three stages of response: alarm, resistance, and finally, exhaustion. He called this three-stage response to stress the **general adaptation syndrome (GAS)** (see **Figure 81-2**).

Stage 1: When an organism is first exposed to a threat, it reacts with *alarm* and becomes aroused physically as it prepares to face the challenge by fighting or fleeing. In short, the first stage of the general adaptation syndrome corresponds to the fight-or-flight response. Because our system is focused on the stressful event or situation and mobilizing us physiologically to deal with it, our resistance to the stressful event (shown by the red line in Figure 81-2) is reduced. If the stress is too powerful, it could overwhelm us.

Stage 2: If the threat continues, the organism's body undergoes further changes in an attempt to stabilize itself—a second wave of adaptation that Selye called *resistance*. The organism's level of arousal is elevated, though slightly lower than during the initial alarm phase, as it adjusts to the stressor. If new stressors are introduced during this stage, the body is less able to marshal the energy needed to address them as it is engaged in resisting the previous stress. According to Selye, this makes the body vulnerable to *diseases of adaptation*—health problems, such as high blood pressure, asthma, and illnesses associated with impaired immune function.

Stage 3: If the organism is exposed to the stressor for still longer periods of time, its resistance gradually gives way to the third stage, *exhaustion*. In this stage, the body is depleted of energy and has little ability to resist. If the threat continues, the organism can suffer organ damage or death.

Students who have gone through final exams often have firsthand experience with Selye's general adaptation syndrome. As the exams approach, most students experience

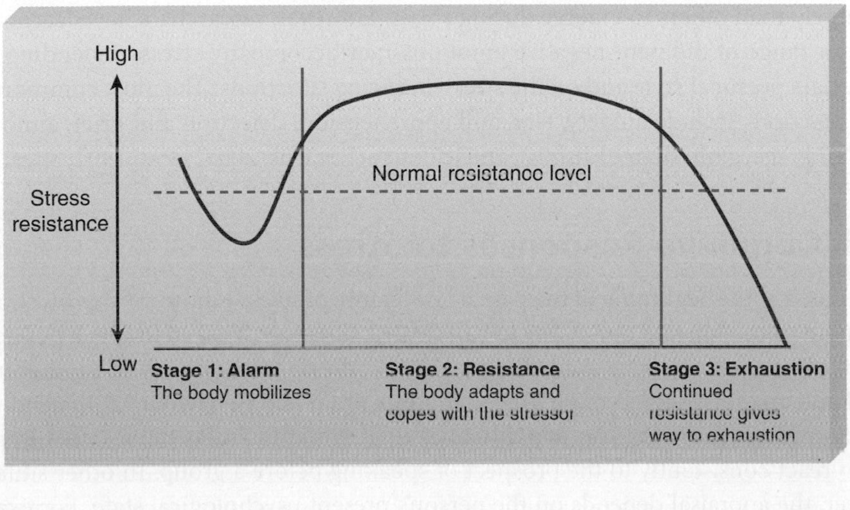

general adaptation syndrome (GAS) a three-stage response to stress identified by Hans Selye; the stages are alarm, resistance, and exhaustion.

FIGURE 81-2 **The general adaptation syndrome.** Selye proposed that the body's physiological response to prolonged stress has three stages. The red line in this figure shows the level of physiological resistance to a prolonged stressful event.

© Michael J. Kapusta

The alarm mode can save lives. As a wildfire moved closer to Slave Lake, Alberta, in 2011, residents moved into an alarm mode, fleeing the fire as quickly as possible.

alarm. When they gear up and begin patterns of late-night studying, the students are entering the resistance phase. By the end of the exam period, many students feel as if they are heading toward exhaustion, and, in fact, a number catch colds or develop other illnesses at the end of the school year. If you haven't gone through a final exam period yet, you will soon have a chance to gather your own data on this student experience.

Although the principles of Selye's theory are widely accepted today, some theorists, such as Sonia Lupien at the Université de Montréal, have questioned his claim that the stress response is the same no matter what the stressor (Lupien et al., 2007, 2006; Souza-Talarico, Marin, Sindi, & Lupien, 2011). Lupien points out that although Selye used many kinds of stressors in his experiments with animals, all were physical—pain, heat, cold, and so forth. This has led some theorists to suggest that the precursors of stress are much more specific than Selye thought, they vary depending on the type of stress, and the differences are measurable and predictable. As we shall soon see, psychological factors also play an important part in our stress experience.

81.2 Emotional Responses to Stress

Bodily arousal is only one dimension of our reaction to stressors. When people feel threatened by an event or situation, they typically experience a change in mood or emotions as well. Let's briefly revisit Ashley, the stressed-out student from the part opener. As the stressors in her life mount, Ashley feels increasingly dejected (she wants to curl up in a ball), annoyed (her inquisitive parents are "driving her crazy"), anxious (she had to leave her public speaking class in the middle of a speech), and angry (during an argument with Jason, she called him a jerk).

Note that most of Ashley's emotional responses to stress are negative. This is typical of people under stress. Researchers have found that the more stress a person experiences, the more negative her emotions (Lazarus, 2007, 1999, 1993; D'Angelo & Wierzbicki, 2003; Eberhart et al., 2011). People who generally live under severe stress tend to be more anxious, depressed, or otherwise upset than those who have relatively stress-free lives. Even within the course of a day, people feel more negative when short-term stressors emerge. Conversely, as daily stressors subside, people's moods take an upward turn (van Eck, Nicholson, & Berkhof, 1998).

It was once thought that certain negative emotions—anxiety and depression—were more likely than others to emerge during stress. However, researchers have learned that, in fact, a range of different negative emotions may accompany stress, depending on an individual's personal style and on the stress-inducing situations. The most common emotional reactions include anxiety, fear, and apprehension; dejection and grief; annoyance, anger, and rage; guilt; shame; disgust; and jealousy (Lazarus, 2007, 1993, 1991; Sher, 2003).

81.3 Cognitive Responses to Stress

As we noted at the beginning of the part, a key feature of stress is how we *appraise* both the challenging situation and our ability to handle that situation. If asked to speak publicly, for example, one person may be excited and pleased at the opportunity, while another may be fearful and anxious (see "Tying It Together: Your Brain and Behaviour" at the end of this part). Sometimes, as in the fear of public speaking, this appraisal is stable—that is, people tend to react consistently to the prospect of speaking before a group. In other situations, however, the appraisal depends on the person's present psychological state. For example,

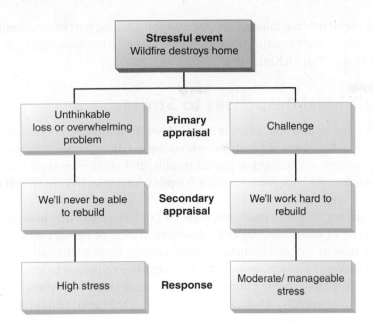

FIGURE 81-3 **The cognitive-mediational theory of stress.** Our level of stress largely depends on how we appraise a threat and evaluate our abilities to cope with it.

we may appraise a missing car key as much more stressful on the day of a final exam than on a less eventful day.

Remember Richard Lazarus and his cognitive-mediational theory of emotions, discussed in Part 11? Lazarus believed that emotion is aroused by a combination of two elements—an environmental event and personal factors such as a person's motives and beliefs. In fact, much of his early work was focused specifically on stress, and he identified two steps in how we experience stress (see **Figure 81-3**).

1. In the first step, **primary appraisal**, we examine the stressor and assess how severe it is. We may identify the stressor as a future danger (a threat), a current situation to be confronted and overcome (a challenge), or a loss or harm. The way we appraise the stressor in this first step can have important consequences for how we attempt to deal with it. Ashley, for example, appraised her term paper as a threat to be avoided rather than a challenge to be overcome.

2. In the second step, we evaluate our own resources and ability to cope with the threat, challenge, or loss. This step is called **secondary appraisal**. Perceiving ourselves as lacking the resources to deal with a problem will elevate its threat level. Conversely, by reminding ourselves of what resources we have, we can quickly decrease the threat level. Consider Ashley's more positive attitude when she musters her resources and quickly produces a few paragraphs of her paper.

One common factor in these appraisals is that the degree to which we feel in control of a situation affects how dangerous or stressful it feels. Perceptions of control (or lack of control) can greatly influence our appraisal of a stressor and, in turn, our experience of stress. Persons who believe that they can exert control over a particular stressor will experience less stress than individuals who feel no such control. A study of residents in a nursing home, for example, found that persons who were given more control over their lives (such as deciding when to attend a movie or where to receive visitors) experienced less overall stress than residents given little control. Residents with control were also twice as likely to still be alive 18 months after the study began (Langer & Rodin, 2004; Rodin & Langer, 1977; Golub & Langer, 2007).

It is important, of course, that our sense of control be realistic. People with life-threatening illnesses such as cancer or heart disease who think that they can control their disease with unproven remedies may feel less stress initially, but they are not likely to be healthier for their efforts. Patients with such illnesses can, however, experience a realistic sense of control (and a lower level of stress) by managing specific aspects of their diseases

primary appraisal appraisal of a stressor to determine how severe it is; the first stage in Richard Lazarus's description of how people experience stress.

secondary appraisal appraisal of one's personal resources and ability to cope with a stressor; the second stage in Richard Lazarus's description of how people experience stress.

(seeking out useful medical information, for example), taking part in treatment decisions, controlling some of their emotions, and seeking closer relationships with their loved ones (Thompson et al., 1993; McKinley et al., 2012).

81.4 Individual Responses to Stress

It should be clear by now that when it comes down to it, how stressed someone gets in a particular situation often depends on whom we're talking about. You probably have friends who collapse at the slightest hint of trouble, and other friends who are experts in crisis management. Perhaps you have other friends who just let trouble roll off their backs without even a suggestion of worry.

Individuals are unique in many ways. Each of us has a particular biological makeup, a preferred style of interpretation, and a favoured cluster of personality traits. In addition, we each operate within a particular social context. These individual differences profoundly influence our physical, emotional, and cognitive responses to stress. Researchers have spent considerable energy examining four areas of individuality and their relationships to stress: *autonomic reactivity*, *explanatory style*, *personality*, and *social support*.

©iStockphoto.com/MachineHeadz   Rob Marmion/Dreamstime/GetStock   ©iStockphoto.com/deeepblue

Displaying stress. Each child displays a different reaction to the first day of school: one seems overwhelmed (left), another frustrated and angry (middle), and the other unfazed (right).

81.4.1 Autonomic Reactivity and Stress

Earlier, we observed that the autonomic nervous system (ANS), particularly the sympathetic nervous system, plays a key role in stress reactions. When a person confronts a stressor, the ANS stimulates organs throughout the body, triggering feelings of physical arousal. As you might expect, people differ in how intensely the ANS responds to stressors. In some, the ANS tends to be highly reactive across various situations and springs into action, even in response to mild stressors. In others, the ANS is less reactive and so less likely to respond even to fairly significant stressors. Such basic differences in *autonomic reactivity* may cause some people to experience stress reactions more often or more intensely than other people, even in the face of identical environmental threats (Cohen & Hamrick, 2003; Spielberger, 1985, 1972, 1966).

To illustrate, let's look at cardiovascular responses to stress, which include blood pressure and heart rate. In a number of studies, researchers have measured the cardiovascular reactions of individuals confronting stressors, such as difficult cognitive or social tasks (Dhabhar, 2014; Sgoifo et al., 2003; Malkoff et al., 1993). Across a variety of situations, certain participants repeatedly display high cardiovascular reactivity, while others consistently exhibit low cardiovascular reactions.

81.4.2 Explanatory Style and Stress

The characteristic manner in which we explain events, our *explanatory style*, can make a difference in how we appraise and respond to stressors. People with generally *optimistic* explanatory styles tend to believe that, despite setbacks, things will improve (Peterson & Steen, 2009, 2002). Those with generally *pessimistic* explanatory styles have a gloomier appraisal—they believe that if things can go wrong, they usually will go wrong (Liu & Bates, 2014).

Imagine two people, each failing to make the first-string college or university soccer team. Both feel disappointed and sad. One says to herself, "I'll never make it. I'm such a dud. I should never have tried out. It was stupid of me to think I was any good at soccer." In contrast, the other individual says, "At least I tried. If I do track in the spring, I can improve my speed and make the team next year. Meanwhile, I'll talk to the coach and find out how I can improve." It is likely that the latter individual— the more optimistic one—will experience less stress than the former.

> Some two thousand years ago, the Roman poet Horace wrote, "In times of stress, be bold and valiant."

Research has supported the idea that optimistic and pessimistic explanatory styles influence stress reactions (Chang et al., 2008; Carver & Sheier, 1999). When optimistic research participants appraise stressful situations, they are more likely than pessimists to recognize positive features of the situation and to perceive the situation as manageable (Littmen-Ovadia & Nir, 2014). In turn, those with optimistic explanatory styles typically experience lower levels of stress (Chang, 2002). Similarly, it turns out that optimists are more likely to seek out social support during stressful events and to employ constructive coping techniques (Iwanaga et al., 2004). (We will discuss the importance of social support later in this module.)

Of course, few people are exclusively pessimistic or exclusively optimistic, although they may lean in one direction or other. In fact, some individuals develop an *optimistic brand of pessimism*. These individuals believe that things will go wrong but, at the same time, hope that they won't: "I probably will fail to make the soccer team, but maybe I'll get lucky. If I play my best and the others have problems, I might have a chance." Still other people are *defensive pessimists*. They anticipate negative outcomes largely to help protect themselves from disappointment (Norem & Illingworth, 2004; Norem, 2008). Deep down, they hold out hope for the best, and so manage to preserve a degree of optimism.

81.4.3 Personality and Stress

Our personalities often help set the tone for how we appraise and react to stressors (Vollrath, 2001). People who are generally timid will likely greet a stressor with more alarm than people who are generally bold. Similarly, our ongoing levels of anger, depression, curiosity, and related feelings will influence our stress reactions. Ashley's breakup, for example, appeared to be precipitated by her general tendency to react to stressors by becoming moody and critical.

One personality style that has been studied is the *hardy personality*, sometimes called the *stress-resistant personality* (Maddi, 2014; Bartone, 2003; Oulette & Di Placido, 2001). Individuals with such personalities welcome challenges and are willing to commit themselves and take control in their daily lives. Generally, they greet stressors as opportunities for growth rather than as crises, and perceive stressors as less severe than non-hardy individuals. Not surprisingly, hardy persons also seem to experience fewer and less intense feelings of stress (Beasley et al., 2003).

At the other end of the stress continuum are people with personality styles that appear to make them more prone to stress. In the late 1950s, two cardiologists, Meyer Friedman and Raymond Rosenman (1959), reported that many of their heart patients seemed to share similar personality traits: they were consistently angry, cynical, hard-driving, impatient, and time conscious. They were also competitive, ambitious, and in a hurry to do many things at once. Friedman and Rosenman claimed that individuals with this personality

Type A a personality type characterized by competitiveness, impatience, and anger and hostility.

Type B a personality type that is less aggressive, more relaxed, and less hostile than Type A.

Type C a personality type characterized by difficulty in expressing or acknowledging negative feelings.

style, which they labelled **Type A,** interact with the world in a way that produces continual stress (Jamal & Baba, 2003; Smith & Gallo, 2001; Miller, 2000; Friedman & Rosenman, 1959). In contrast, people who display **Type B** personalities are more relaxed, less aggressive, and less worried about time. People with this personality style are thought to experience lower levels of stress. In fact, most people fall between these two extremes, leaning toward one or the other but showing features of both personality patterns.

Researchers later suggested there might be a third personality pattern, **Type C.** People with this personality type are pleasant and peace loving, but have a hard time expressing or acknowledging negative feelings (Temoshok et al., 2008; Temoshok, 2003). Although their positive attitudes might be thought to protect them from stress, persons with Type C behaviour patterns are actually particularly vulnerable. When angry, Type C personalities tend to turn the anger inward. They also tend to take losses and relationship problems particularly hard. We will talk more about Type A, Type B, and Type C personality types when we discuss the relationship between stress and health later in the part.

81.4.4 Social Support and Stress

As we think back to Ashley's struggle at the beginning of the part, notice that she seems to be going through her difficulties alone, without much social support. She does not feel free to turn to family members, and she does not appear to have close friends in whom she can confide. In fact, family and social relationships seem to add to her experience of stress. Would Ashley have felt better if she could have turned to family members or friends for support? The answer is yes, according to numerous studies and observations (Taylor, 2011, 2008, 2007).

Want to find out what your personality type is? Go to http://personality-testing.info/tests/AB.php to take a short test to find out.

Social relationships can be paradoxical. On the one hand, as in Ashley's case, negative interactions with relatives and friends can be sources of significant stress (Lepore et al., 1991). On the other hand, studies have resoundingly indicated that social relationships and support help prevent or reduce stress reactions (Cohen & Janicki-Deverts, 2009; Cohen, 2004).

The positive impact of social support on stress was first revealed in animal studies. In a famous investigation, for example, twin goats were subjected to a stressful conditioning task. One goat worked in isolation and the other worked in the presence of its mother. The goat working in isolation reacted with greater anxiety and stress than did its twin (Liddell, 1950). In another study, a group of mice had to "share" a common feeding place, which created a persistent state of territorial conflict (Henry & Cassel, 1969). In one condition, the mice in the group were strangers, while in the other the mice were from the same litter. The former group showed more signs of stress than did the latter.

Studies of humans have revealed a similar role for social support in stress reactions (Taylor, 2011, 2008, 2007). It has been found, for example, that when faced with various job stressors, ranging from work overload to job conflict, workers who can rely on their supervisors, co-workers, and spouses for emotional and practical support often experience less distress than workers without such support (Beehr et al., 2003). Other studies suggest that having an intimate, confiding relationship with someone, whether a spouse, close friend, or other individual, provides the strongest kind of social support (Olpin & Hesson, 2013; Cohen & Wills, 1985).

Richard Heathcote/Getty Images

Social support can make the difference. A Korean golfer comforts her playing partner as the latter is sizing up a difficult putt on the 18th green of the Women's World Cup of Golf in 2008. The partner went on to sink the putt.

Why do people who have strong social support seem to experience less stress? Researchers are not sure. Such support may increase people's self-confidence or self-esteem as they confront stressors. It may provide individuals under stress with a greater sense of control or greater optimism that everything will turn out well. Alternatively, social feedback may change people's perspectives as they face stressors, alter their perceptions of threat, or reduce their appraisal of a stressor's importance. Finally, it may be that the reassuring presence of close friends or relatives helps to reduce the kinds of bodily arousal and negative emotions that normally feed stress reactions (Taylor, 2011, 2008, 2007).

Before You Go On

www.wiley.com/go/comercanada

What Do You Know?

1. How do the sympathetic nervous system and hypothalamic-pituitary-adrenal pathways influence our experience of stress?
2. What happens in each stage of the general adaptation syndrome?
3. What is the difference between primary appraisal and secondary appraisal?
4. How does autonomic reactivity affect how different people experience stress?
5. What are the characteristics of the hardy personality type?

What Do You Think? Can you think of any advantages to having a Type A personality? A Type C personality? Can you think of any disadvantages to having a Type B personality?

Summary

Module 81: Responding to Stress

LEARNING OBJECTIVE 81 Describe the physiological, emotional, and cognitive responses to stress, and explain how individual responses to stress differ.

- There are two main physiological pathways of stress: the sympathetic nervous system and the hypothalamic-pituitary-adrenal axis. Both lead to activation of the fight-or-flight response, which is an immediate response to a stressor.
- Hans Selye first described the effects of chronic stress, which he called the general adaptation syndrome (GAS). The syndrome has three stages: alarm, resistance, and exhaustion.
- Emotional responses to stress generally involve negative emotions. The more stress a person experiences, the more negative the emotions.
- Cognitive appraisal is an important element in responses to stress. Richard Lazarus identified two steps in this process: *primary appraisal*, in which people assess the severity of the stressor, and *secondary appraisal*, in which they evaluate how well they can cope with it.
- Individuals vary greatly in their responses to stress. Areas of difference include autonomic activity, explanatory style, personality, and availability of social support.

Key Terms

general adaptation syndrome (GAS) 621

primary appraisal 623

secondary appraisal 623

Type A 626

Type B 626

Type C 626

Study Questions

Multiple Choice

1. What does the release of cortisol during stressful experiences do for us?
   a) elevates blood sugar
   b) energizes us
   c) protects us from inflammation
   d) all of the above

2. Which of the following statements shows the correct order of the components of the physiological response to stress?
   a) hypothalamus → adrenal cortex → pituitary
   b) hypothalamus → adrenal medulla → pituitary
   c) hypothalamus → pituitary → adrenal cortex
   d) hypothalamus → pituitary → adrenal medulla

Fill-in-the-Blank

1. In the resistance phase of the general adaptation syndrome, our resistance level to the effects of stress is _____ relative to unstressed levels.

2. When faced with a stressor, the nervous system communicates with the endocrine system via the _____ axis.

3. When we are deciding what a particular situation means to us in terms of its stress potential, we are _____ the situation.

Module 82: Coping with Stress

We have seen that a number of individual differences contribute to how stressed we become. Once we feel stressed, we also differ in our efforts to manage the situation. What do you do when you feel stressed? If you feel overloaded or overburdened, do you lie in bed worrying about all that you have to do, unable to get started, or do you start making lists and timetables? If you are in a traffic jam, do you pound the steering wheel, or do you instead try to find an interesting radio station or play your favourite CD? Faced with the worrying prospect of a chemistry midterm, do you call a friend to study or light a cigarette?

Our efforts to manage, reduce, or tolerate stress are called **coping**. Although most people use this term to convey constructive efforts ("I'm coping with the situation"), a coping response may be either adaptive or maladaptive in a given situation (Kleinke, 2007; Folkman & Moskowitz, 2004). For a person faced with failing grades, for example, going out and partying or spending a lot of time video gaming are less adaptive coping responses than spending extra time studying. Each of us has preferred styles of coping that we tend to apply across various situations (Aldwin, 2007; Folkman & Moskowitz, 2004; Carver & Scheier, 2003, 1994). A person may use different coping responses in different situations, however, and some *coping-flexible* individuals are more able than others to depart from their preferred coping styles to meet the demands at hand. Let's look at some of the more common coping styles.

LEARNING OBJECTIVE 82
Discuss and evaluate several ways in which people cope with stress.

coping efforts to manage, reduce, or tolerate stress.

82.1 Lashing Out

As stressors pile up, people often say that they feel "as if they're going to explode." Thus, it is not surprising that some individuals do in fact explode—psychologically or physically. They react to stress by lashing out at other people with angry words or behaviours. Around one-quarter of adults report such reactions (Williams & Nida, 2011; Kanner, 1998).

Lashing out often occurs after a series of stressors has taken place. The particular event that triggers an aggressive outburst may seem relatively mild in itself, but for the individual under siege, it is the last straw. Recall how Ashley, the beleaguered student in our case opener, blew up at her boyfriend, Jason, during a phone conversation, calling him names and hanging up on him. Jason's crime? He had refused to let her off the phone. Ordinarily, this teasing might not have elicited such a strong reaction. But Ashley was feeling pressure from her boss, her parents, and the demands of her schoolwork. Ashley's explosive reaction isn't surprising when we consider the cumulative impact of these multiple stressors.

Everyone is capable of lashing out at others in the face of stress. For most people, it is an occasional and temporary reaction, performed before they have time to think about things and decide how to act more constructively. For some people, however, lashing out is a characteristic mode of coping. Recall that Ashley had been in the habit of lashing out at Jason. These outbursts were, in fact, a key reason that Jason decided to break up with her.

Angry outbursts, although sometimes understandable, are not typically a constructive way of dealing with stress. Such outbursts may harm relationships, produce psychological or physical damage, and lead to additional stress. Theorists and clinicians once believed that expressions of anger were cathartic, or cleansing—that is, if people expressed their anger and "got their frustrations out of their system," they would feel better and be able to move forward constructively. It turns out, however, that excessive or continuous expressions of anger usually cause further outbursts (Tavris, 2003, 1989). In one

Susana Vera/Reuters/Corbis

But does it work? In Spain, certain consulting organizations have advised clients such as these men to smash cars (or computers, TVs, or mobile phones) with sledge hammers as a way of fighting stress. The approach has caught on throughout the country, but research has not found that lashing out or venting anger are necessarily effective coping strategies.

Psychology Around Us   Cursed Response

Want a quick relief from stress? Angry outbursts may not work, but apparently shouting out your favourite curse word can help. Richard Stephens and his research group at Keele University in England had college students put their arms in a bucket of ice water for as long as they could (Stephens et al., 2009). Some of the participants were instructed to shout out curse words of their choosing while holding their arms in the water; others shouted out neutral words only. Which participants do you think were better able to keep their arms immersed in the ice water? That's right: the swearers. In fact, they kept their arms in the water almost a minute longer than the students who repeated neutral words again and again. The effect was strongest for people with lower daily swearing frequencies who do not swear very often (Stephens & Umland, 2011). Why does swearing help? The experimenters theorized that it triggers our fight-or-flight responses, which help us deal with immediate stress and negate the link between fear of pain and pain perception. But be forewarned (or relieved)—swearing has a much greater coping and pain-reduction effect for occasional swearers than for habitual swearers.

study, experimenters induced anger in participants and then directed one group of angry participants to hit a punching bag and the other group of angry individuals to sit quietly (Bushman et al., 1999). Later in the experiment, the "punching bag" participants were found to behave much more aggressively than the "sit quiet" individuals. Similarly, angry participants in another study were attracted to violent video games (Bushman & Whitaker, 2010).

In the long term, lashing out can harm or destroy a person's social support network, as in the example of Ashley and Jason. As mentioned earlier, social support is a primary defence against stress. By driving away those who could help with stress-related problems, such as anxiety and depression, a person will likely make those problems worse.

82.2 Self-Defence

In some instances, people run away from—that is, physically leave—stressors through such actions as dropping a difficult class, changing jobs, or ending a troubled relationship. More commonly, people try to make a "psychological getaway." Considering a complex detailed scholarship application may cause some students to decide not to complete the application and think "they probably don't give out very many of the awards." The student's behaviour in this story is an example of *reaction formation*—saying or doing the opposite of what one actually believes—one of Freud's defence mechanisms.

> **"**You can avoid reality, but you cannot avoid the consequences of avoiding reality.**"**
>
> —*Ayn Rand, Russian-American writer*

Recall from Part 12 that Freud explained such behaviour in psychoanalytic terms. Today, though, the notion of defence mechanisms is widely embraced, even by theorists outside the psychoanalytic model. Many psychologists believe that people often cope with stress—whether consciously or unconsciously—by engaging in defensive behaviours (Cramer, 2001; Erdelyi, 2001). These theorists also agree that the defensive behaviours often involve a high degree of self-deception (Bolger, 1990), but that this self-deception might in fact be adaptive (Taylor et al., 2003).

Although everyone reacts to stressors with defensive behaviours on occasion, some people use such behaviours regularly. In fact, some people display what theorists describe as a *repressive coping style* (Langens & Morth, 2003; Brown et al., 1996). They consistently deny negative feelings and discomfort and try to push such emotions out of awareness.

Is the use of defence mechanisms—whether occasional or continual—a helpful way to cope with stress? Sometimes, it probably is. We can all think of instances when it would be best to simply put something out of our mind, particularly if we don't have any control over the outcome (for example, waiting for our grade on a recent exam). In other instances, however, defensive coping is not constructive. After all, while we spend our time defending and avoiding, the problem typically continues (Holahan & Moos, 1990, 1985). The conflict with a roommate, the course paper that needs writing, and the medical problem that needs attention continue as stressors, and may even intensify.

It is also worth noting that defensive coping can be difficult to achieve. Research has found that people with a repressive coping style often fail to fully repress their feelings of stress (Pauls & Stemmler, 2003; Brown et al., 1996). While research participants were watching an upsetting film, for example, experimenters measured their autonomic nervous system responses. Although participants with a repressive coping style reported feeling less stress than other participants did, their autonomic responses were actually higher (for example, their heart rates and blood pressure were higher throughout the film). It may be that repressive coping behaviours *mask* stress rather than eliminate it. Or perhaps the higher autonomic activity associated with repressive coping indicates that such repression requires considerable physical effort. Either way, it is not surprising that people with this coping style have been found to experience more medical problems than people who use other coping styles do (Coy, 1998).

82.3 Self-Indulgence

Many individuals use self-indulgent coping strategies, such as overeating, smoking cigarettes, and consuming drugs and alcohol (Steptoe, 2000). Ashley went partying with her friends, for example, to deal with the stress created by her paper-writing assignment. Such strategies may help people feel better in the short term, but in most instances they fail to change the challenge at hand and so have little long-term benefit. In fact, such responses are often associated with poor adjustment and depression and anxiety (Folkman & Moskowitz, 2004; Aspinwall & Taylor, 1992).

If the problem at hand is transient and simple—recovering from a drive home in a blinding snowstorm, for example—the self-indulgence of having a bowl of ice cream or a beer may indeed help a stressed person to calm down. If, however, the problem is more complex—such as a term paper due next week—self-indulgence is unlikely to be an effective coping strategy. Eating, drinking, shopping, watching television, or surfing the Internet will not make the problem go away. In fact, it may produce still greater pressure and higher stress: while one indulges, the paper's due date keeps getting closer. Moreover, certain self-indulgent strategies, such as gambling, cigarette smoking, excessive alcohol consumption, drug use, and extreme overeating, have serious health effects (Young, 2009, 2004, 1998, 1996).

©iStockphoto.com/ThomFoto

Food and stress. Eating treats and comfort foods are less optimal ways of responding to stress.

82.4 Constructive Strategies

It is possible, of course, to cope with stress constructively rather than lashing out at others or engaging in self-defence or self-indulgence. Psychologists Richard Lazarus and Susan Folkman (1984) use the terms *problem-focused coping* and *emotion-focused coping* to distinguish between two kinds of constructive strategies. Which of these strategies we are likely to use depends in part on the nature of the problem (Stanton et al., 2009, 2002; Folkman & Moskowitz, 2004). For example, we could try to hit the highway at 4:00 a.m. as a way of dealing with morning traffic, but it is probably more practical to learn how to react calmly and philosophically to rush-hour tie-ups. Conversely, when a tornado watch is posted, figuring out how to calm down may not be as fruitful as deciding whether to leave town or head for the cellar or for higher ground.

In **problem-focused coping**, the person's efforts are aimed at dealing directly with the stressor in some way. For example, the late-to-work Ashley might ask her boss to assign her to a different work shift so that she has more time to get to work, or she might look for a new job closer to campus. She might devise a plan to buy a car so that she can save time travelling to work, or she might decide that her earlier solution of jogging to work is worth continuing. In any case, by dealing directly with the stressor, she can begin to reduce its effects.

But what about the noisy 2-year-old next door who keeps interrupting your efforts to relax in the backyard? Or the grief we experience resulting from the death of a loved one? These are not stressors that readily yield to a problem-focused approach. When we

problem-focused coping coping strategies focused on dealing directly with the stressor, such as by changing the stressor in some way.

Tying It Together: **Your Brain and Behaviour**

Stressing Out when Speaking in Public

If you are like most people, you feel stressed out when you have to give a speech in public. What is happening in the brain while you are feeling this pressure? Although you are not in physical danger, your brain is responding to the presence of an audience as if you were. Brain signals activate the sympathetic nervous system (Selye's alarm stage)—resulting in increased heart rate, sweaty palms, and a dry mouth. In the brainstem, the locus coeruleus increases arousal by changing activity in its widespread projections throughout the brain. The amygdala and cortex process sensory stimuli that in turn activate stress systems. The hypothalamus sends signals to the pituitary gland to release a hormone that stimulates the adrenal glands (located on top of your kidneys) to release cortisol, the main stress hormone. This hormone helps to mobilize energy stores so that you can cope with the stressor. Finally, the hippocampus and prefrontal cortex recognize elevated levels of cortisol and send inhibitory signals to the hypothalamus to shut down the stress response. How can you deal with this? Jeremy Jamieson has a solution called reappraisal. Jamieson and his colleagues taught stressed students how to view the physiological experience of anticipatory stress prior to public speaking in positive terms and that helped them to feel less stressed and to perform better when they stood up and spoke in public (Jamieson, 2013; Jamieson et al., 2012).

Questions

1 What is the role of the hypothalamus in responding to a stressor?

2 What does it mean to say that the effects of stress on the brain are helpful in the short term but can be harmful in the long term?

3 How does the brain response differ when a stressor is rewarding versus not rewarding?

4 Where in the brain are the stress hormone receptors that help to restore the brain to its normal state once the stressor has passed?

Masterfile

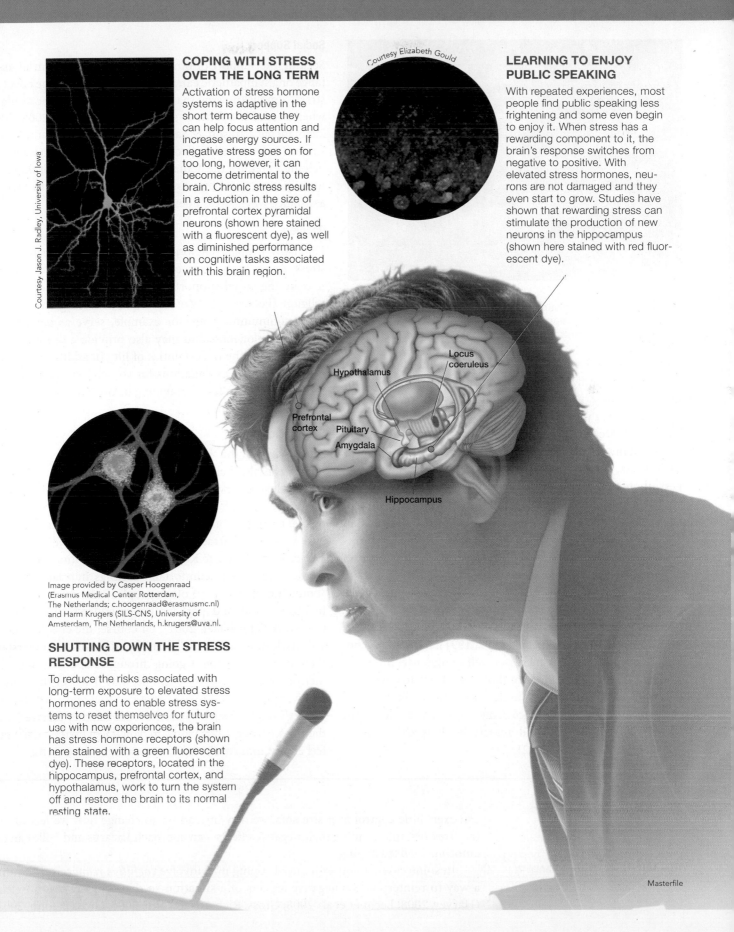

COPING WITH STRESS OVER THE LONG TERM

Activation of stress hormone systems is adaptive in the short term because they can help focus attention and increase energy sources. If negative stress goes on for too long, however, it can become detrimental to the brain. Chronic stress results in a reduction in the size of prefrontal cortex pyramidal neurons (shown here stained with a fluorescent dye), as well as diminished performance on cognitive tasks associated with this brain region.

Courtesy Jason J. Radley, University of Iowa

Courtesy Elizabeth Gould

LEARNING TO ENJOY PUBLIC SPEAKING

With repeated experiences, most people find public speaking less frightening and some even begin to enjoy it. When stress has a rewarding component to it, the brain's response switches from negative to positive. With elevated stress hormones, neurons are not damaged and they even start to grow. Studies have shown that rewarding stress can stimulate the production of new neurons in the hippocampus (shown here stained with red fluorescent dye).

Locus
coeruleus

Hypothalamus

Prefrontal
cortex

Pituitary

Amygdala

Hippocampus

Image provided by Casper Hoogenraad (Erasmus Medical Center Rotterdam, The Netherlands; c.hoogenraad@erasmusmc.nl) and Harm Krugers (SILS-CNS, University of Amsterdam, The Netherlands, h.krugers@uva.nl.

SHUTTING DOWN THE STRESS RESPONSE

To reduce the risks associated with long-term exposure to elevated stress hormones and to enable stress systems to reset themselves for future use with new experiences, the brain has stress hormone receptors (shown here stained with a green fluorescent dye). These receptors, located in the hippocampus, prefrontal cortex, and hypothalamus, work to turn the system off and restore the brain to its normal resting state.

Masterfile

Xinhua Press/Corbis

Mass relaxation. A group of 150 students in Bejing, China, receive stress relief training to help them relax during their upcoming college entrance examinations.

Stress is often unavoidable. The traffic jams, life changes, and occasional natural disasters that create stress are not going to miraculously disappear. The issue, then, is how to handle stress. Is there a way to lessen its impact so that cortisol levels, blood pressure, and the like do not soar? The answer, according to many psychologists and studies, is yes (Folkman & Moskowitz, 2004). As this part has already begun to suggest, there are quite a few things you can do the next time you anticipate or begin to feel the heart-pounding symptoms of stress.

Exercise, Meditation, and Relaxation

One of the best ways to manage physiological responses to stress is to exercise (Steptoe, 2000). In fact, it appears that people who exercise regularly reap not only physical benefits, such as lowering the activity of stress hormones (Rejeski & Thompson, 2007; Rejeski et al., 1992, 1991), but also psychological benefits, such as increased self-confidence. Similarly, research indicates that some of those who learn to quiet their thoughts and relax their muscles through meditation and relaxation training experience reductions in stress hormone activity, blood pressure, and anxiety levels (Cardoso et al., 2009; Stetter & Kupper, 2002).

Social Support

Seeking the support of others, whether in the form of assistance or a sympathetic ear, is another way to ease the effects of stress. Simply knowing that friends or family will be available when needed is a form of social support (Taylor, 2008, 2007, 2006; Pierce, Sarason, & Sarason, 1996). It appears that social support helps ease the effects of stress in at least two ways—by helping to reduce the actual number and impact of threatening situations, and by providing practical, problem-focused assistance when stress does occur.

Religion

For many people, religion is of major help in dealing with stress. As we have observed in this part, one reason for this may be the social support that the individuals derive from religion (Folkman & Moskowitz, 2004). Religion and religious communities can, for example, serve as antidotes to feelings of aloneness and may also provide a sense of order as people face the uncertainties of life. In addition, religious beliefs may offer explanations for stressful events that make those events seem less threatening or overwhelming to many people (Packer, 2000).

Self-Disclosure

Self-disclosure, the sharing of emotions and experiences with others, can also help people deal with stress. Up to a point, self-disclosure serves to release stress—consider the phrase "getting things off my chest"—but it is more than simply the venting of emotion. It helps people to channel emotions into a cohesive narrative, making stressors easier to process and deal with (Foa & Kozak, 1986). In addition, by putting fearful, angry, or uncomfortable feelings into language and "bouncing them off" of other people, individuals are forced to think about and perhaps better address those feelings (Smyth & Pennebaker, 2001). Of course, the effectiveness of self-disclosure is tied to the ability of others to understand the problems a person is going through. Rape victims or former prisoners of war, for example, may discover that certain relatives or friends simply cannot comprehend what they are going through. In such cases, the feedback they receive ("Gee, that's really rough, but I am sure you'll feel better soon") may feel empty, unhelpful, and in some cases even painful.

emotion-focused coping coping strategies focused on changing one's feelings about the stressor.

can exert little control over stressors, we may instead try to change how we feel toward the stressors, thus limiting their negative effects—an approach Lazarus and Folkman call **emotion-focused coping**.

In some cases, emotion-focused coping may involve *cognitive reappraisal*—finding a way to reinterpret the negative aspects of a situation so that they are less upsetting (Harvey, 2008; Lechner et al., 2008; Gross, Richards, & John, 2006; Gross & John, 2003).

People who are trying to come to terms with the death of a loved one or with some other catastrophic loss often look for ways to find positive meaning or purpose in their loss (Folkman & Moskowitz, 2004). Similarly, people may reinterpret threatening situations as challenges or tests, rather than catastrophes. The loss of a job, for example, might be viewed as a new beginning or new opportunity (Folkman & Moskowitz, 2000).

Changing how we think or feel about a stressor can also be a useful tactic for less traumatic stressors, such as tests and traffic jams. Rather than becoming increasingly upset over a traffic jam, for example, you may be able to shrug it off—saying, in effect, "It won't be great if I'm late, but I'll survive."

> "The greatest weapon against stress is our ability to choose one thought over another."
>
> —*William James, American psychologist and philosopher*

Before You Go On

www.wiley.com/go/comercanada

What Do You Know?

1. How can lashing out negatively affect our management of stressors?
2. What is a repressive coping style?
3. Identify and describe two forms of constructive coping.

What Do You Think? Do you tend to use constructive coping strategies, or do your responses tend to be more maladaptive? Do you adapt your coping style to the situation, or do you tend to use the same style across many different situations? How could you improve your coping style?

Summary

Module 82: Coping with Stress

LEARNING OBJECTIVE 82 Discuss and evaluate several ways in which people cope with stress.

- Coping describes efforts to manage, reduce, or tolerate stress.
- Dealing with stress by lashing out at others, using defence mechanisms such as repression, and engaging in self-indulgent behaviours such as smoking or drinking alcohol can be destructive when used in excess.
- More constructive coping strategies include directly confronting a stressor in hopes of changing the situation (*problem-focused coping*) and changing how you feel or think about the stressor to reduce its impact (*emotion-focused coping*).

Key Terms

coping 629   emotion-focused coping 634   problem-focused coping 631

Study Questions

Multiple Choice

1. The sweaty palms and rapid heartbeat we experience as anxiety are most directly related to activation of which portion of the nervous system?

a) Autonomic nervous system
b) Hippocampus
c) Occipital lobes
d) Somatic nervous system

Module 83: Stress and Health

We have seen that stress has a profound effect on bodily functioning. Thus, it should come as no surprise that researchers have found strong relationships between stress and health—or, more accurately, between stress and illness (Groer et al., 2010). Scientists' appreciation of this relationship unfolded slowly. Back in the 1930s and 1940s, researchers began to recognize that certain medical illnesses are caused by an interaction of psychological factors (particularly stress-related factors) and biological factors, rather than by biological factors alone. These special illnesses were given the label *psychosomatic* or *psychophysiological diseases*. By the 1960s, a number of medical illnesses were considered psychosomatic

Maverick/Dreamstime/GetStock

diseases. Among the most prominent were ulcers, asthma, tension and migraine headaches, and hypertension (Rice 2012; Murison, 2001; Ramadan, 2000; Sriram & Silverman, 1998). Although peptic ulcers have since been shown to be bacterial in nature (Marshall, 1994), stress is known to weaken the immune response and thereby increase vulnerability to the development of ulcers (Segerstrom, & Miller, 2004).

As the list of psychosomatic diseases grew, medical researchers began to suspect that stress might, in fact, be at work in a wide range of medical illnesses, not just in a special few. Their suspicions changed to near certainty when studies revealed that stress often contributes to coronary heart disease (the second-leading cause of death, after cancer, in Canada). Researchers continue to investigate how stress is connected to various illnesses, as well as how stress brings about its effects on body systems.

83.1 Coronary Heart Disease

Coronary heart disease involves a blocking of the coronary arteries—the blood vessels that surround the heart and are responsible for carrying oxygen to the heart muscle. The term actually refers to several problems, including blockage of the coronary arteries and *myocardial infarction* ("heart attack"). Together, such problems are the second-leading cause of death after cancer in men and women over the age of 45 in Canada, accounting for close to 50,000 deaths each year (Statistics Canada, 2007). Research has shown that most cases of coronary heart disease are related to an interaction of psychological factors, such as job stress, and physiological factors, such as high cholesterol, obesity, hypertension, smoking, and lack of exercise (Bekkouche et al., 2011; Kendall-Tackett, 2010; Statistics Canada, 2007).

Earlier, we discussed the Type A personality, which was identified by two cardiologists, Friedman and Rosenman. These doctors argued that the stress-producing behaviour of people with Type A personalities makes them more likely to develop coronary heart disease (see **Figure 83-1**). In fact, the Type A personality is also known in many circles as the *coronary-prone personality*. People with the more relaxed Type B behaviour pattern exhibit lower levels of stress and less coronary disease. In a pioneering study of more than 3,000 men, Friedman and Rosenman (1974) separated healthy men in their forties and fifties into Type A and Type B groups and then followed their health over a period of eight years. The doctors found that more than twice as many of the Type A men developed coronary heart disease. Subsequent studies found similar correlations among women (Haynes et al., 1980).

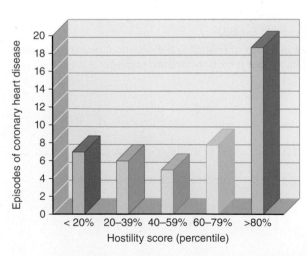

FIGURE 83-1 **Type A personality and hostility.** A key characteristic of the Type A personality is chronic hostility. People with this personality style interact with others in a way that produces continual high levels of stress and increases their risk of coronary heart disease. Source: Adapted from Niaura, R., et al. (2002). Hostility, the metabolic syndrome, and incident coronary heart disease. *Health Psychology, 21,* 588–593.

As research continued into the link between Type A behaviour and coronary heart disease, many investigators found that while a connection existed, it was weaker than that reported by Friedman and Rosenman (Gallacher et al., 2003). It now appears that only some of the Type A characteristics are strongly related to heart disease (Ben-Zur, 2002; Krantz & McCeney, 2002). In particular, research has identified the importance of negative emotions. Hostility, which includes not just feelings of anger but also enduring cognitive patterns of mistrust and cynicism, seems to be especially important (Smith & Gallo, 2001). People who score high on measures of hostility tend to experience greater stress and to have an increased risk of developing coronary heart disease, as well as other serious medical illnesses (Elovainio et al., 2011; Kendall-Tacket, 2010; Niaura et al., 2002; Miller et al., 1996).

©iStockphoto.com/undergroundw

Hostility and your heart. It is not surprising that individuals who score high on measures of hostility experience more stress and are at higher risk for heart attacks.

83.2 Stress and the Immune System

Research clearly shows that stress can result in various medical disorders. But exactly how does this effect come about? What is it about stress that makes it a threat to health? An area of study called **psychoneuroimmunology** has tried to answer this question by examining the links between stress, the immune system, and health (Kendall-Tackett, 2014; Kendall-Tackett, 2010; Kiecolt-Glaser et al., 2002).

The **immune system** is the body's system of organs, tissues, and cells that identify and destroy foreign invaders, such as bacteria and viruses, as well as cancer cells. An important group of cells in the immune system are **lymphocytes**, white blood cells that circulate through the lymphatic system and the bloodstream. When stimulated by bacterial or viral invaders, lymphocytes act to help the body fight the invaders, often by destroying body cells that have been infected by the invaders.

Researchers believe that severe stress can negatively affect the activity of lymphocytes, slowing them down and thus reducing a person's ability to fight off viral and bacterial infections (see **Figure 83-2**) (Ader et al., 2001; Dhabhar, 2011). In a pioneering study, Roger Bartrop and his colleagues (1977) in New South Wales, Australia, compared the immune systems of 26 people whose spouses had died eight weeks earlier to those of 26 similar participants whose spouses had not died. Blood samples showed that lymphocyte functioning was significantly slower in the bereaved people than in the non-bereaved individuals (Bartrop et al., 1977). Similarly, other studies have shown poor immune system functioning in persons who are exposed to long-term stressors, such as people who must provide care for relatives with Alzheimer's disease (Kiecolt-Glaser et al., 2002, 1996, 1991; Lovell, Moss, & Wetharall, 2011).

In short, during periods when healthy people confront unusual levels of stress, their immune systems slow down so that they become susceptible to illness. If stress adversely affects our very capacity to fight off illness, it is not surprising that Holmes and Rahe and other researchers have found a relationship between life stress and a wide range of illnesses. Several factors seem to influence whether and when stress will lead to immune system problems. A number of biochemical changes must occur for stress to have such an impact. Certain behavioural changes, personality styles, and social circumstances may also play a role.

83.2.1 Biochemical Activity

Remember that when stressors first appear, the sympathetic nervous system springs into action. Its activity includes an increase in the release of norepinephrine throughout the brain and body. Apparently, beyond supporting the activity of the sympathetic nervous system,

psychoneuroimmunology an area of study focusing on links between stress, the immune system, and health.

immune system the body's system of organs, tissues, and cells that identify and destroy foreign invaders, such as bacteria and viruses, as well as cancer cells.

lymphocytes white blood cells that circulate through the body and destroy foreign invaders and cancer cells; important components of the immune system.

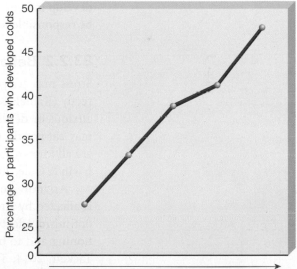

General level of psychological stress in participants' lives

FIGURE 83-2 **Stress and the common cold.** Researchers have examined the links between stress and illness. One study found that when healthy inoculation volunteers were exposed to a cold virus, those who generally reported the highest levels of stress in their lives were most likely to come down with a cold and to develop worse symptoms. Source: Based on Cohen, S., Tyrrell, D. A. J., & Smith, A. P. (1991). Psychological stress and susceptibility to the common cold. *The New England Journal of Medicine, 325, 609.*

Internal combat. This scanning electron micrograph shows a cancer cell (red) being attacked by natural killer T-cells (yellow).

Jean Claude Revy/ISM/Phototake

norepinephrine can eventually help slow the functioning of the immune system (Carlson, 2008; Groer et al., 2010; Lekander, 2002). During periods of low stress, norepinephrine travels to particular lymphocyte receptors, binds to them, and gives a message for the lymphocytes to increase activity. As stress rises and continues, however, the chemical travels to other receptors on the lymphocytes, binds to them, and gives an inhibitory message—a signal for the lymphocytes to stop their activity. Thus, the release of norepinephrine increases immune functioning at low levels of stress, but it slows down immune functioning in the face of higher and continuing stress.

Similarly, the stress hormone cortisol lowers immune system functioning during periods of extended stress. Recall that when people are under stress, their adrenal glands release cortisol. Initially, the release of this hormone stimulates body organs into action. After stress continues for 30 minutes or more, however, the stress hormone travels to particular receptor sites in the body, binds to these sites, and gives inhibitory messages meant to help calm down the stressed body (Manuck et al., 1991). Some of these receptor sites are located on the lymphocytes. When the cortisol binds to such receptors, its inhibitory messages slow down the activity of the immune system (Bellinger et al., 1994; Groer et al., 2010). Again, a chemical that initially helps people to deal with stress eventually acts to slow the immune system.

Another action of cortisol is to stimulate an increase in the production of *cytokines*—proteins that bind to receptors throughout the body and play a key role in the immune system. At early levels of stress, the cytokines help fight infection. But as stress continues, the ongoing production and spread of cytokines leads to inflammation throughout the body (Burg & Pickering, 2011; Burg et al., 2011; Kendall-Tackett, 2014; McEwen, 2002). *Inflammation* is an immune response characterized by swelling, heat, redness, and pain. Chronic inflammation of this kind may contribute to heart disease, stroke, and other illnesses.

Finally, investigators have learned that patterns of immune system responding vary from individual to individual (Finkel, et al., 2014). Certain individuals experience more profound immune system slowdowns in the face of stress than other individuals do. Moreover, these individual differences in immune system functioning tend to be consistent across stressful situations. Thus, some stressed persons are more likely than others to develop infections and other diseases. Let's look next at some individual factors that may be responsible for differences in immune system functioning.

83.2.2 Behaviour, Personality, and Social Support

Stress may trigger a series of behavioural changes that affect the immune system indirectly (Kalueff & La Porte, 2008). People under chronic stress may, for example, become anxious or depressed, perhaps even develop an anxiety or mood disorder. In turn, they may eat poorly, exercise less, have trouble sleeping, or smoke or drink. Such behaviours are all known to slow down the immune system (Brooks et al., 2011; Kibler et al., 2010; Irwin & Cole, 2005; Kiecolt-Glaser & Glaser, 2002, 1999, 1988).

An individual's personality may also help determine how much the immune system is affected by stress. Studies suggest that people who typically respond to life stress with optimism, effective coping, and resilience tend to experience better immune system functioning and to be better prepared to combat illness (Kern & Friedman, 2011; Kendall-Tackett, 2014; Taylor, 2006, 2004; Williams et al., 2011). Correspondingly, those with "hardy" or resilient personalities tend to remain healthy after stressful events, whereas those whose personal styles are less hardy are more vulnerable to illness (Bonanno et al., 2010; Ouellett & DiPlacido, 2001).

Several studies have actually noted a relationship between certain personality characteristics and cancer (Hjerl et al., 2003). People exhibiting the Type C behaviour pattern appear to be more at risk for cancer. Recall that people with the Type C personality have trouble acknowledging negative feelings and may be particularly vulnerable to stress. In addition, some studies have found that patients with certain forms of cancer who display a helpless or repressive coping style tend to have less successful recoveries than patients who express their emotions. It is important to note, however, that other studies have found no relationship between personality and cancer outcome (Jokela, et al., 2014; Urcuyo et al., 2005).

Some researchers have identified a connection between religiousness and health. Specifically, studies have found that regular attendance at a place of worship is correlated with a decreased risk of death over a particular period (Ellison et al., 2000). A few studies have also linked spirituality to better immune system functioning (Jackson & Bergeman, 2011; Folkman & Moskowitz, 2004; Koenig & Cohen, 2002). Although the relationship between attendance at a place of worship and health is not well understood, it appears to result at least in part from the social support people receive from others in their religious group.

More generally, research indicates that social support helps to protect us from the effects of stress. People who have little social support and feel lonely tend to experience poorer immune functioning when stressed than other people do (Uchino & Birmingham, 2011; Curtis et al., 2004; Cohen, 2002). Conversely, it appears that social support helps protect people from stress, poor immune system functioning, and illness and helps improve recovery from illness or surgery (Matsumoto & Juang, 2008; Cohen, 2002; Kiecolt-Glaser et al., 2002). Some studies have even suggested that patients with certain kinds of cancer who receive social support or supportive therapy often display better immune system functioning and, in turn, have more successful recoveries than patients without such social help.

The stress-reducing benefits of social support can be seen in the health of people who grow up in close-knit communities. One early study explored the low rate of stress-related illnesses among residents of the town of Roseto, Pennsylvania (Wolf, 1969). The death rate from coronary heart disease in this town was considerably lower than that in the general population, despite the fact that the residents' eating, smoking, and exercise patterns were similar to those in communities with much higher coronary death rates. Clearly, something special was responsible for the residents' good health. That something turned out to be Roseto's positive social environment. An Italian enclave, Roseto was home to extremely close, supportive, and traditional families. Relatives, friends, and local priests were always available to help out with any kind of problem. During the 1970s, Roseto's younger generation began to marry people from other backgrounds and move away. Church attendance also dropped. These social changes resulted in less social support throughout the community. Perhaps not surprisingly, the rate of heart attacks in the community increased (Greenberg, 1978).

Chris Arend/Getty Images

Healthy communities. This group of Inuit perform a "blanket toss" ceremony in which they form a ring around a blanket and use it to hurl group members into the air. Communities that share activities and remain close-knit often have lower illness rates than other communities.

83.3 The Benefits of Stress

It might be hard to believe, given the litany of problems that we have identified here, but stress can be positive. In fact, when Selye first identified stress as a concept back in 1936, he actually drew a distinction between unpleasant stressors and pleasant stressors. How can a stressor be pleasant? Think about waiting for a call from someone you met at a party last night; it can be stressful, but in an exciting way. Unpleasant stressors, according to Selye, cause **distress**—the kind of unpleasant stress on which we have generally been focusing up to now. Pleasant stressors, in contrast, cause *eustress*.

A key benefit of stress is that it helps promote positive development. Remember in Part 4 when we discussed some theorists' notion that parents can actually stunt a baby's development by meeting all the baby's needs, and that there is some optimal

distress stress caused by unpleasant situations or circumstances.

eustress the optimal level of stress needed to promote physical and psychological health.

inoculation exposing oneself to a relatively low level of stress in a controlled situation to improve later performance in a more stressful situation.

Shannon Stapleton/Reuters/Corbis

Stress inoculation? Why is this drill instructor screaming at this poor recruit? The logic behind this time-honoured training technique is that intense stressors experienced during basic training will build mental strength and resilience and make individuals more effective in actual combat.

level of frustration that facilitates development? Researchers have suggested that similar principles apply across the lifespan. That is, adverse events and the stress that they produce can force you to confront challenges, adapt to your environment, and build up strength and resilience (Tennen & Affleck, 2009, 2002; Tennen, Affleck, & Armeli, 2005; Harvey, 2008) in a manner referred to as *post-traumatic growth* (Vázquez, et al., 2014).

Today, **eustress** is defined not in terms of the stressor, but in terms of the stress level—it is the optimal level of stress that promotes physical and psychological health (Nelson & Cooper, 2005). But what exactly is an optimal level of stress? We can think about this question in a couple of ways. First, exposing yourself to a smaller level of stress in a controlled situation can improve your performance in a more stressful situation, a process called **inoculation.** If you call one friend to talk through what you want to say to another friend with whom you have been arguing, you are inoculating yourself.

As we have seen previously, another way of considering what constitutes an optimal level of stress involves looking at the relationship between stress and performance. As shown in **Figure 83-3,** researchers have found that stress can actually facilitate performance on a task, depending on the complexity of the task.

- *Performance of very easy tasks can benefit from a high level of stress.* For example, the old videogame Tetris® involves very little cognitive complexity and very low stakes, but as the computer starts dropping the pieces faster, it will get your attention and help you stay focused on the game.
- *A moderately difficult task benefits from a moderate level of stress.* Too low, and you won't get excited enough to perform your best. Too high, and you will be more likely to lose your focus or perform poorly.
- *For a complex task, low stress leads to the optimal performance.* Consider that next time you decide to make a complex dinner you have never prepared before for a few friends and don't leave quite enough time to get your house cleaned and everything prepared before they arrive. You might do better ordering out.

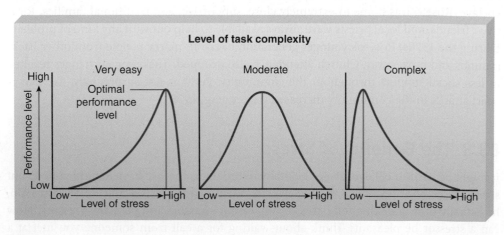

FIGURE 83-3 Stress and performance. Stress can actually benefit performance, depending on the complexity of the task. On very complex tasks, a low level of stress is optimal for performing your best; on very easy tasks, a high stress level helps you stay focused. Based on Weiten, W. (2004). *Psychology: Themes and variations* (6th ed.). Belmont, CA: Wadsworth, Figure 13.5, p. 528.

Before You Go On

What Do You Know?

1. How has stress been linked with coronary heart disease?
2. What is the connection between life changes and illness?
3. How does stress affect the immune system?
4. What factors influence whether stress will have this effect?
5. What are some beneficial effects of stress?

What Do You Think? Try to recall five events in your life or in the lives of your family members and friends that suggest a relationship between stress and illness. How might you account for those events and relationships?

Summary

Module 83: Stress and Health

LEARNING OBJECTIVE 83 Explain how stress can cause physical illness, and discuss situations in which stress may be beneficial.

- Stress can increase risk for a number of health problems. People with *Type A* personalities are prone to stress and appear to be at greater risk for coronary heart disease than the more relaxed *Type B* personalities. Using the Social Readjustment Rating Scale, researchers have found that stress-producing life changes also increase the risk of illness. *Type C* personalities are more vulnerable as they tend to internalize their anger and cope badly with relationship challenges.
- *Psychoimmunology* is an area of study that examines the links between stress, the immune system, and health.
- Severe stress may interfere with the activity of *lymphocytes*, a component of the immune system that helps the body to overcome invaders, such as bacteria and viruses.
- Stress-related biochemical changes in the body, such as changes in the activity of norepinephrine and cortisol, can eventually slow the functioning of the immune system.
- Behaviour, personality, and social support are additional factors affecting how much the immune system is slowed down by stress.
- Unlike *distress*, or negative stress, eustress offers benefits. Optimal levels of stress can promote the development of resilience and facilitate performance, especially for easy or moderately difficult tasks.

Key Terms

distress 639

eustress 640

immune system 637

inoculation 640

lymphocytes 637

psychoneuroimmunology 637

Study Questions

Multiple Choice

1. Recent research has shown that _____ is the aspect of Type A personality that is most strongly associated with coronary heart disease.
   a) competitiveness
   b) hostility
   c) impatience
   d) pessimism

2. Which type of task is best suited to moderate levels of stress?
   a) Easy
   b) Medium
   c) Difficult
   d) None of these; moderate stress is the optimal stress level for all types of tasks.

Fill-in-the-Blank

1. Although early research showed that having a Type A personality was related to the risk of coronary heart disease, recent studies have shown that the cluster of negative emotions called _____ is a better predictor of risk.

2. _____ is a neurotransmitter that tends to improve immune system functioning in times of low stress and impair it during periods of severe or prolonged stress.

Module 84: Posttraumatic Stress Disorder

As we have seen, stress, when moderate and handled constructively, can serve us well. But it can also work against us. In addition to leading to physical diseases, it can contribute to various psychological disorders, from depression to sexual dysfunctions. Moreover, it plays a central role in *posttraumatic stress disorder*, or *PTSD*, mentioned earlier in the part.

LEARNING OBJECTIVE 84
Describe the symptoms and causes of posttraumatic stress disorder, and discuss some risk factors for developing it.

In posttraumatic stress disorder, persons who have confronted an extraordinarily stressful event—combat, rape, earthquake, airplane crash, automobile accident—experience a number of severe psychological symptoms lasting for months or even years (Keane, Marx, & Sloan, 2009). They have lingering reactions of intense fear and helplessness. They may be battered by memories, dreams, or nightmares connected to the traumatic event, and may repeatedly try to avoid activities, thoughts, feelings, or conversations that remind them of the event. Many also feel detached from other people, some lose interest in activities that once brought enjoyment, and some feel dazed. A number of individuals with the disorder are easily startled, develop sleep problems, and have trouble concentrating. They may also feel extreme guilt because they survived the traumatic event while others did not (Keane et al., 2009).

While any traumatic event can trigger PTSD, certain events are particularly likely to do so. The most common causes of PTSD are combat, natural disasters, abuse, and victimization (Keane et al., 2009). As well, people who are victims of terrorism, or who live with the fear of terrorism, often experience posttraumatic stress symptoms (Tramontin & Halpern, 2007). Many people will forever remember the events of September 11, 2001, when hijacked airplanes crashed into the World Trade Center in New York City and damaged the Pentagon in Washington, D.C. One effect of these terrorist attacks is the lingering psychological effect on the people who were directly affected and their family members, as well as on millions of others who watched images of the disasters on their television sets throughout that day. Numerous studies indicate that posttraumatic stress reactions were common even in people who simply witnessed the events through the media (Marshall et al., 2007; Schlenger et al., 2002).

Wolfgang Rattay/Reuters

PTSD. Survivors mourn the dozens of teenagers and young adults killed by a lone gunman on July 22, 2011, at Utoeya, a youth camp for Norway's Labour Party.

84.1 Who Develops PTSD?

Almost 10 percent of Canadians experience posttraumatic stress disorder during their lifetimes (Burijon, 2007; Kessler et al., 2005). The disorder can occur at any age, even in childhood (Balaban, 2009). Women are at least twice as likely as men to develop PTSD (Koch & Haring, 2008).

Although anyone who experiences an unusual trauma will be affected by it, only some people develop posttraumatic stress disorder (McNally, 2001). To understand the development of this disorder more fully, researchers have looked at the same stress-related factors that we have examined throughout this part—and they have come up with promising leads.

84.1.1 Biological Factors

As we have observed, stressors trigger biochemical reactions throughout the brain and body. Apparently, in the face of extraordinarily threatening stressors, some people develop particularly strong biochemical

EPDEF/Stringer/Getty Images

Is anyone immune? Rescuers pull a survivor from the rubble of a collapsed garment factory in Bangladesh in May 2013. Most people who experience extraordinary traumatic events are capable of developing PTSD. Even rescue workers at the site of disasters often develop the disorder. Nevertheless, all things being equal, some people seem more prone to PTSD in the aftermath of traumatic events.

Chris Hondros/Getty Images

Detecting PTSD in children. The Sesame Street Muppet Rosita tells children in New York about "You Can Ask," a program that seeks to identify and deal with stress in children. The program was first formed in the aftermath of the September 11, 2001 terrorist attacks.

reactions—reactions that continue well beyond a short-term fight-or-flight period. It appears that such individuals are more likely than others to experience a posttraumatic stress disorder (Bremner & Charney, 2010; Pace & Heim, 2011; Yehuda, 2009). Consistent with this notion, researchers have found abnormal activity of the stress hormone cortisol and the neurotransmitter norepinephrine in the urine and blood of combat soldiers, rape victims, concentration camp survivors, and survivors of other traumatic events (Burijon, 2007; Delahanty et al., 2005).

Indeed, some studies suggest that people who develop PTSD have exaggerated sympathetic nervous system responses and blunted HPA axis responses to stress (Yehuda, 2001; Yehuda et al., 1998). There is also some evidence that once a posttraumatic stress disorder sets in, the individual's continuing biochemical arousal may eventually shrink the hippocampus, one of the brain areas that helps control the body's stress hormones, thus further locking in the disorder (Carlson, 2008; Mirzaei et al., 2005). At the same time, it is worth noting that, according to some research, people who are more susceptible to developing PTSD may have a smaller hippocampus to begin with (Gilbertson et al., 2002).

84.1.2 Personality

Earlier, we observed that people with certain personality styles or coping styles are particularly likely to react to threats with stress and to develop medical problems. Similarly, such styles increase the likelihood of developing a posttraumatic stress disorder (Burijon, 2007; Chung et al., 2005). It turns out, for example, that people with less resilient, or less hardy, personality styles appear more likely to develop a posttraumatic stress disorder than those with more resilient styles (Kunst, 2011; Maddi, 2007). So too are war veterans who had psychological problems before they went into combat (Dikel et al., 2005). In addition, people who typically view life's negative events as beyond their control are more likely than others to develop posttraumatic stress symptoms after criminal assaults (Taylor, 2006; Regehr et al., 1999).

84.1.3 Childhood Experience

Studies have also suggested that certain childhood experiences increase the risk of later posttraumatic stress disorders (Alter & Hen, 2009; Rapee & Bryant, 2009). People whose childhoods have been characterized by poverty appear more likely to develop this disorder when later confronting horrific events. So are people whose parents displayed psychological disorders and who experienced assault, abuse, or catastrophe at a young age (Koch & Haring, 2008; Ozer et al., 2003).

84.1.4 Social Support

Finally, the social environment may influence whether victims of traumatic events develop posttraumatic stress disorders. Earlier, we saw that inadequate social support can intensify stress reactions and slow down immune system functioning. Thus, it is not surprising that people with weak social support systems are also more likely to develop a posttraumatic stress disorder after a traumatic event (Charuvastra & Cloitre, 2008; Ozer et al., 2003). For example, rape victims who feel loved, cared for, and accepted by their friends and relatives tend to recover more successfully, as do those treated with dignity by the criminal justice system (Murphy, 2001; Sales et al., 1984).

We will look at posttraumatic stress disorder in greater detail in Part 15. In the meantime, the current discussion helps clarify once again that stress is a very powerful force. Moreover, when it is overwhelming or dealt with ineffectively, it can totally disrupt our functioning and our lives.

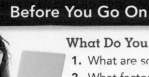

Before You Go On

www.wiley.com/go/comercanada

What Do You Know?

1. What are some symptoms of posttraumatic stress disorder?

2. What factors put a person at heightened risk for developing posttraumatic stress disorder following a traumatic event?

What Do You Think? Try to recall five events in your life or in the lives of your family members and friends that suggest a relationship between stress and illness. Having now read this part, how might you account for those events and relationships?

Summary

Module 84: Posttraumatic Stress Disorder

LEARNING OBJECTIVE 84 Describe the symptoms and causes of posttraumatic stress disorder, and discuss some risk factors for developing it.

- Posttraumatic stress disorder is characterized by persistent, frightening thoughts or memories of a traumatic event, along with anxiety, depression, and other symptoms.
- Combat, natural disasters, and abuse and victimization are among the events most likely to cause posttraumatic stress disorder.
- Not everyone affected by unusual trauma develops posttraumatic stress disorder. Factors that affect the likelihood of developing the disorder include biological factors, personality factors, childhood experiences, and the availability of social support.

PART 15

PSYCHOLOGICAL DISORDERS

Diane Markos, a 27-year-old single female, struggled with depression. Within a period of three months, she lost 7 kilograms and she felt tired all the time. She withdrew from nearly all her usual social activities and she openly acknowledged thoughts of overdosing on pills. Previous psychotherapy and treatment with antidepressant medication had produced no improvement. She was referred to a psychologist for additional treatment.

Diane's changes over the three months occurred shortly after the breakup of a relationship she had been having with a man for approximately two years. She now saw herself as fat, unattractive, and doomed to be alone. Although she had never had a wide circle of friends, the past two years had seen her social contacts become even more limited. Other than the few evenings that she spent with her boyfriend, she had gradually managed to work herself into a life of all work and no play, and she was intensely lonely.

Diane lived alone and worked full-time as a pediatric nurse while pursuing a master's degree part-time in nursing. Although she was a straight-A student, she had numerous interpersonal difficulties with fellow students and instructors. Her relations with co-workers were similarly troubled. Although she had a reputation as a good staff nurse, she had never been able to obtain a supervisory position because of her ongoing interpersonal conflicts.

Diane's early family history provided some clues to the sources of her current difficulties. As the eldest of three children, she was frequently expected to play the role of caretaker for her younger siblings. She felt that her parents' love was contingent on her playing the role of "mother's little helper." She believed that her sister and brother had been allowed to lead a much more carefree childhood.

In short, Diane saw her past and present as an unhappy life of servitude, rejection, and failure. And she could envision no other scenario for her future. She felt quite hopeless, and as a result her new therapist considered her to be a serious suicide risk (Taylor et al., 2011).

Throughout this book we have examined the nature of behaviour and mental functioning, from sensations to memory to personality. Most of our discussions have looked at "typical" functioning. And indeed, our mental life and behaviour are fascinating and complex even when they do not go astray. However, as we have repeatedly observed, functioning often does go astray. We are immediately reminded of this as we read about Diane Markos. Most who hear about Diane would likely agree that her depressed mood, isolated behaviour, and negative thinking are far from functional.

You have already come across a few of the leading psychological disorders while reading the *Facing Adversity* sections throughout this book. In this part, we will be looking even more closely at the topic of abnormal psychological functioning. First, we will see

Art and psychological disorders. Many of our greatest paintings focus on psychological dysfunction. Two of the most famous are *The Scream*, by Edvard Munch, which brings symptoms of anxiety and panic to life, and *Portrait of Dr. Gachet*, by Vincent van Gogh, about depression.

(left) Burstein Collection/Corbis/©2009 The Munch Museum/The Munch-Ellingsen Group/Artists Rights Society (ARS), NY; (right) Bettmann/Corbis

that although most people believe they know abnormal functioning when they see it, it is, in fact, a difficult concept to define. Then, we will explore the ways in which psychologists classify, assess, and explain the various kinds of abnormal functioning. In the next part, we will examine how mental health practitioners try to help the individuals whose behaviours, thoughts, or emotions are dysfunctional—individuals known as *clients* or *patients* when seen in mental health settings.

Module 85: Defining, Classifying, and Diagnosing Psychological Abnormality

abnormal psychology the scientific study of psychological disorders.

Diane Markos's emotions, behaviours, and thoughts appear to be atypical, the result of states sometimes referred to as *psychological dysfunctioning, psychopathology, psychological disorders*, or *mental disorders*. The field devoted to the scientific study of psychological disorders is usually called **abnormal psychology**.

Abnormal psychological functioning is a wide-ranging problem, as indicated in **Figure 85-1**. It has been estimated that in a given year, at least 20 percent of adults in Canada experience serious psychological disturbances (Canadian Mental Health Association, 2014b). The numbers and rates in other countries are similar (Kessler et al., 2009, 2007, 2005).

Furthermore, many people go through periods of great tension, upset, or other forms of psychological discomfort in their lives. At such times, they experience at least some of the distress found in psychological disorders.

What are your thoughts regarding the causes of mental illness? Throughout history, humans have speculated about the causes of the abnormal behaviours that seem to be a part of the human condition. In ancient times, there is evidence that "madness" was seen as a sign of demonic possession or of witch or warlock status. In many cases the "cures" were not particularly helpful to the individuals involved, given that they were intended to cast out evil spirits by burning or drowning. Many people did not survive their "cures." In more recent times, things were not much better for the mentally ill. A lack of understanding of the causes of mental illness led to a general belief that afflicted individuals were of inferior character, even less than human (Carson, Butcher, & Mineka, 2000). In the 1700s in the United Kingdom, those families that could afford it often hid their mentally ill relatives away and cared for them in isolation. Those that could not afford this had few options. Many "mad" people were left at places like Bethlehem Hospital in London, where care was minimal and the use of restraints typical. Tours through the hospital to see the mad people were a major source of revenue for the hospital (Reed, 1952).

While many argued for more humanitarian treatment for the mentally ill, reform movements did not really gain any ground until a clear connection was made between physical illness and madness. A condition called general paresis was well-known in medical circles (Beck, 2008). It usually afflicted males between 20 and 40 years of age. Initial symptoms included memory loss (short and long term), impairment of judgment, and decreases in motivation and language. Later symptoms included delusions and hallucinations, inappropriate moods and/or anger, and eventually full-blown dementia, seizures, and death. The symptoms progressed over a few months to at most one or two years, and death was inevitable. When it was discovered that general paresis was the result of a sexually transmitted infection, syphilis, two things resulted (Brown, 2008). First, it was possible to treat syphilis and avoid general paresis; second, it clearly showed that the signs of madness could be symptoms of an underlying physical illness. This gave strong support to mental health reform movements such as *moral treatment*, which led to more humane treatment for the mentally ill (Gerard, 1998).

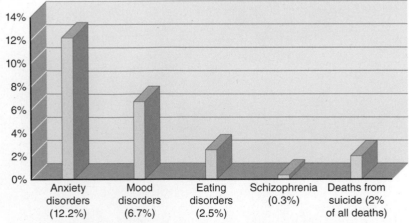

FIGURE 85-1 **How many people are diagnosed with mental disorders each year?** Nearly one-quarter of the adults in Canada each year experience symptoms that qualify for a diagnosis of at least one mental disorder.

Source: Health Canada. A Report on Mental Illnesses in Canada. Ottawa, Canada 2002 © Health Canada Editorial Board Mental Illnesses in Canada Canadian Cataloguing in Publication Data ISBN H39-643/2002E Cat. No. 0-662-32817-5.

The *medical model* approach to understanding and treating mental illness has been a major influence on our thinking and practices in assisting those struggling with mental illness over the past century. The medical model encourages a search for patterns in the symptoms people present with the goal of first identifying a syndrome—a collection of symptoms, like general paresis—that is recognized and about which one can make predictions. In the case of general paresis, the predictions made about prognosis were accurate but deadly. The next step involves a search for possible causes of the observed symptoms. Hopefully the identification of underlying causes also suggests viable treatments.

As we will see later in this part and in the next part when we look at treatment approaches, the biological basis of the medical model approach to mental illness certainly has significant research support. We will also see, however, that there are serious concerns about the limitations of the medical model. By focusing on physical/biological causes, the medical model takes focus away from the possible roles played by psychological processes and socio-cultural circumstances on mental illness and mental health (Tyrer, 2013). In the rest of this part we will provide you with a sense of these broader perspectives in mental illness and mental health.

85.1 Defining Psychological Abnormality

How do we know that someone is functioning abnormally? In other words, what is psychological abnormality? This question is not easy to answer. Although many definitions of abnormality have been proposed over the years, none is universally accepted (Pierre, 2010). Nevertheless, most of the definitions have key features in common, often called "the four Ds": deviance, distress, dysfunction, and danger.

Corbis

Early interventions. Benjamin Rush, a doctor and signatory to the American constitution, developed the tranquilizing chair shown here. It was believed to calm mental patients by reducing blood flow to the head.

- *Deviance* Behaviour, thoughts, and emotions are considered abnormal when they differ from a society's ideas about proper functioning. Judgments of deviance and abnormality vary from society to society. A society that values competition and dominance may embrace aggressive behaviour, whereas one that emphasizes cooperation may consider such behaviour unacceptable and even abnormal (Eller, 2005). Moreover, a society's values may change over time, leading to a new societal view of what is psychologically abnormal. In Western society, for example, a woman's participation in athletics, academia, or business was considered unusual and even inappropriate 100 years ago (Matsumotto, 2001). Today, people in Western cultures value that behaviour.

> **"**There is nothing either good or bad, but thinking makes it so.**"**
>
> —*William Shakespeare, Hamlet*

- *Distress* To be considered abnormal, behaviours, ideas, or emotions usually must also cause distress or unhappiness. For example, Diane Markos from the opening case feels upset and burdened most of the time by her negative feelings and thoughts and the impact they are having on her life.

- *Dysfunction* Abnormal behaviour also tends to interfere with daily functioning, as opposed to behaviour that is simply eccentric but a part of a person's life. When behaviour upsets people so that they cannot take proper care of themselves, interact well with others, or work effectively, then it is referred to as abnormal. For example, Diane's behaviours have contributed to social isolation, problems at work, and conflicts at school.

- *Danger* Some people with psychological dysfunction become dangerous to themselves or others. If, for example, individuals are consistently hostile or confused, they may put themselves, family members, or friends at risk. Recall that Diane Markos's thoughts of overdosing on pills led her therapist to consider her a serious suicide risk. It is important to note, however, that although danger is often cited as a feature of abnormal psychological functioning,

Rajesh Nirgude/AP

Does dysfunction equal abnormality? In this photo, a Tibetan man set himself on fire to protest China's occupation of Tibet. In this context, such behaviour, while self-harming, does not, by itself, indicate that he is experiencing a psychological disorder.

research indicates that it is actually the exception rather than the rule (Hiday & Burns, 2010). Despite popular views, most people who are greatly troubled or even out of touch with reality pose no immediate danger to themselves or anyone else.

As our discussion suggests, the current definition of abnormality depends heavily on social norms and values. At the same time, societies often have difficulties distinguishing between an abnormality that requires help and an eccentricity that should not be the concern of other people. We often see or hear about people who behave in ways we consider strange, such as an individual who lives alone with dozens of animals and avoids other people. The behaviour of such individuals is deviant, but unless it leads to clear distress and dysfunction, most clinicians would judge it to be eccentric rather than abnormal (Ernst, 2006).

Given such difficulties, how do psychologists determine which experiences constitute or do not constitute a psychological disorder, and how do they distinguish among various disorders? In large part, they rely upon *classification* and *diagnosis*.

Psychology Around Us   Eccentric versus Mentally Ill

Mirek Towski/FilmMagic/Getty Images

Icelandic singer Björk was once voted "most eccentric celebrity" by a BBC survey.

An eccentric is a person who deviates from common behaviour patterns or displays odd or whimsical behaviour. Eccentrics do not typically suffer from psychological disorders, and eccentricity is not an absolute but a continuum. Whereas the unusual behaviour of persons with disorders is thrust upon them and usually causes them suffering, eccentricity is chosen freely and provides pleasure. In short, "Eccentrics know they're different and glory in it" (Weeks & James, 1995, p. 14).

Many well-known people were eccentrics. Hetty Green, the richest woman in the world in the late 1800s and early 1900s, always wore the same black dress and only changed her underwear when it wore out. When her son injured his leg, she disguised herself and tried to get him into a charity hospital. Once recognized, she fled with her son, claiming she would treat him herself. He later had to have the leg amputated due to gangrene. Writer James Joyce always carried a tiny pair of lady's bloomers, which he waved in the air to show approval. Emily Dickinson always wore white, never left her room, and hid her poems in tiny boxes. Benjamin Franklin took "air baths" for his health, sitting naked in front of an open window. United States President John Quincy Adams swam nude in the Potomac River each morning. Canadian Prime Minister William Lyon Mackenzie King regularly attended séances to consult the spirits of Leonardo da Vinci, Sir Wilfrid Laurier, his mother, and several of his Irish Terrier dogs (all named Pat, with the exception of one named Bob) (Stacey, 1985). Michelangelo, who was notoriously bad-tempered, was also known for his eccentricities: he rarely ate or bathed, slept fully dressed—including his shoes—never changed his clothes, and removed his shoes so infrequently that the skin would often peel off with the shoes. Finally, Icelandic singing star Björk was once voted "most eccentric celebrity" in a large BBC survey (Brown, 2006).

Do these behaviours constitute mental illness? Most of them probably do not. Although these behaviours disregard standards for normal behaviour, they are largely benign; that is, they are not maladaptive or dysfunctional (although Hetty Green's son might disagree with this assessment!).

85.2 Classifying and Diagnosing Psychological Disorders

A symptom is a physical, behavioural, or mental feature that helps indicate a condition, illness, or disorder. Fatigue is often a symptom of depression, for example. Similarly, poor concentration can be a symptom of anxiety, and hallucinations may indicate schizophrenia (Ernst, 2006). When certain symptoms regularly occur together and follow a particular course, clinicians agree that those symptoms make up a particular mental disorder. A list of such disorders, with descriptions of the symptoms and guidelines for determining when individuals should be assigned to the categories, is known as a *classification system*.

The classification system that is used by most countries throughout the world is the **International Classification of Diseases (ICD)**, published by the World Health Organization (WHO). The ICD is now in its 10th edition (ICD-10) with the 11th edition slated for release in 2015 (Del Vecchio, 2014). The leading classification system in North America is the **Diagnostic and Statistical Manual of Mental Disorders (DSM)**, published by the American Psychiatric Association. The DSM has been revised several times since it was first published in 1952. The current version is called the DSM-5 (APA, 2013). It lists and describes the symptoms of approximately 22 major categories with more than 200 mental disorders (see **Table 85-1**). Language used in the DSM-5 reflects proposed ICD-11 naming conventions and reflects the collaborative efforts made between the WHO and DSM working groups (Reiger et al., 2013). However, the process and development of revising the DSM was one of controversy and debate, and the latest manual has not been embraced by all professionals expected to use it. For example, a number of researchers express trepidation, arguing that although conclusive knowledge about the impact of the DSM-5 will come only with time, there are flaws with the manual's content (Harkness

International Classification of Diseases (ICD) the system used by most countries to classify psychological disorders; published by the World Health Organization and currently in its 10th edition (ICD-10).

Diagnostic and Statistical Manual of Mental Disorders (DSM) the leading classification system for psychological disorders in Canada; DSM-5 is the current version.

TABLE 85-1 Disorders in DSM-5

Group	Description	Some Disorders Listed in This Group
Neurodevelopmental disorders	Disorders with their onset in the developmental period before the child enters grade school; usually involve impairments in personal, social, or academic functioning	• intellectual disability • language disorder • autism spectrum disorder • specific learning disorder
Neurocognitive disorders	Disorders where the primary clinical deficit is cognitive function. The deficit is acquired in that it reflects a decrease from a previous state of functioning, as in the case of Alzheimer's disease	• delirium • major and mild neurocognitive disorders • major or mild neurocognitive disorder due to traumatic brain injury
Substance-related and addictive disorders	Disorders that involve the activation of reward pathways and reward systems due to substance use or induced by substances; also includes gambling disorder	• alcohol use disorder • caffeine intoxication • opioid use disorder • stimulant use disorder
Schizophrenia-spectrum and other psychotic disorders	Disorders defined by abnormalities in the form of delusions, disordered thoughts or behaviours, or negative symptoms such as avolition (lack of motivation) or loss of communication ability	• delusional disorder • schizophrenia • schizoaffective disorder
Depressive disorders	The presence of sad, empty, or irritable mood that typically goes along with physical or cognitive changes	• major depressive disorder • premenstrual dysphoric disorder • disruptive mood dysregulation disorder

(continued)

TABLE 85-1 Disorders in DSM-5 (*continued*)

Group	Description	Some Disorders Listed in This Group
Bipolar and related disorders	Alternating bouts of intense positive affect that are followed or preceded by prolonged periods of sadness and other symptoms of depression; seen as a bridge between depressive disorders and disorders representing the schizophrenia spectrum	• bipolar I disorder • bipolar II disorder • cyclothymic disorder
Anxiety disorders	Disorders that share features of excessive fear or anxiety and related behavioural disturbances	• specific phobia • social anxiety disorder • generalized anxiety disorder • panic disorder
Obsessive-compulsive and related disorders	Disorders characterized by repetitive thoughts or behavioural rituals	• obsessive-compulsive disorder • body dysmorphic disorder • hoarding disorder
Trauma and stressor-related disorders	Disorders that reflect exposure to a distressing event or events	• post-traumatic stress disorder • acute stress disorder • reactive attachment disorder
Somatic symptoms and related disorders	Disorders with prominent somatic symptoms associated with impairment and distress	• somatic symptom disorder • conversion disorder • factitious disorder
Dissociative disorders	Disruption or discontinuity in the typical integration of consciousness, perception, memory, emotion, identity, or body representation	• dissociative amnesia • depersonalization/derealization disorder • dissociative identity disorder
Feeding and eating disorders	Disturbance in eating or eating-related behaviour that impairs physical health and/or psychosocial functioning	• avoidant/restrictive food intake disorder • anorexia nervosa • bulimia nervosa • binge-eating disorder
Sexual dysfunctions	Disorders with great heterogeneity that usually involve a clinically significant disturbance in the ability to respond sexually or experience sexual pleasure	• erectile disorder • female sexual interest/arousal disorder • male hypoactive sexual desire disorder
Gender dysphoria	Persistent distress due to the discrepancy between one's expressed or experienced gender versus the initially assigned gender	• gender dysphoria
Paraphilic disorders	Disorders that reflect intense and persistent sexual interest other than the stimulation found in normal physically mature and consenting human partners	• voyeuristic disorder • frotteuristic disorder • sexual sadism disorder
Sleep-wake disorders	Disorders involving dissatisfaction in the quality, timing, and/or amount of sleep	• insomnia disorder • hypersomnolence disorder • narcolepsy • central sleep apnea
Disruptive, impulse control, and conduct disorders	Under-controlled behaviours that violate the rights of others and/or bring the person into serious conflict with societal norms or authority figures	• intermittent explosive disorder • conduct disorder • kleptomania
Personality disorders	Pervasive and inflexible behavioural patterns that deviate markedly with societal expectations. These disorders often involve a lack of insight about how personal actions cause distress in others	• borderline personality disorder • narcissistic personality disorder • paranoid personality disorder • antisocial personality disorder

et al., 2014; Reiger et al., 2013; Stein et al., 2013). In particular, professionals express concerns about "fuzzy" constructs and narrowly depicted concepts in the DSM-5, as well as a lack of acknowledgement for many of the individual-level and societal-level causal mechanisms known to underlie mental disorders, such as abuse and poverty. Others contend that the psychiatric drug industry had too strong a role in the development of the latest manual (Cosgrove & Krimsky, 2012; Frances, 2010).

When clinicians decide that a person's symptoms fit the criteria for a particular disorder, they are making a **diagnosis**. Most clinicians in Canada use the DSM to help them diagnose their clients' problems. Assigning a diagnosis suggests that the client's pattern of dysfunction is basically the same as patterns displayed by many other people who show the same types of symptoms, has been researched in numerous studies, and has responded to certain kinds of treatment. It helps to ensure that clinicians are acting in a consistent manner and that they are basing their clinical and research decisions on a set of clearly articulated and shared criteria. Clinicians can then apply what is generally known about the disorder to the client with whom they are working.

As we will see later in this part, based on her pattern of symptoms, Diane Markos would probably receive a diagnosis of a mood disorder: *major depressive disorder*. A clinician might also take note of the fact that Diane has avoided people and social relationships throughout her life, largely because she fears being judged, and might further assign her a diagnosis of *avoidant personality disorder*. When people qualify for two or more diagnoses, they are said to display **comorbidity**. Comorbidity refers to the co-occurrence of two or more diagnoses in one person (Gadermann et al., 2012).

Sukree Sukplang/Reuters/Corbis

Eccentric? Bride, Kachana Ketkaew, with real scorpions on her gown kisses her groom, Bunthawee Siengwong, who has a real centipede in his mouth. She held the world record for staying in a cage with 3,400 scorpions for 32 days, he for staying with 1,000 centipedes for 28 days. Mentally disordered? Probably not.

comorbidity the condition in which a person's symptoms qualify him for two or more diagnoses.

diagnosis a clinician's determination that a person's cluster of symptoms represents a particular disorder.

Psychology Around Us — Is a Diagnosis Always Helpful?

Although mental health terms such as anxiety, depression, and schizophrenia are commonly discussed in the media, public discourse, and even daily conversations, it turns out that accurate diagnoses of these and other psychological disorders are often elusive in the clinical field. It appears that even with effective assessment techniques and carefully researched classification categories, clinicians sometimes arrive at a wrong conclusion or diagnosis (Fernbach et al., 2011).

Indeed, studies have sometimes revealed enormous errors in assessment and diagnosis, particularly in hospitals (Mitchell, 2010). In a well-known study assessing the possibility that schizophrenia was over-diagnosed and affective disorders under-diagnosed, the charts of 131 randomly selected patients from a mental hospital in New York were pulled from records and seven skilled clinicians were asked to reevaluate their diagnoses (Lipton & Simon, 1985). Whereas 89 of the patients had originally received a diagnosis of schizophrenia when they were hospitalized, only 16 received this same diagnosis on reevaluation. And while 16 patients initially had been given a diagnosis of mood disorder, 50 received that label on

reevaluation, essentially reversing the ratio of schizophrenic to affective disorder.

Furthermore, our society attaches a stigma, or negative prejudice, to mental illness (Wahlen, 2007; Brohan et al., 2010). Stereotypic beliefs about what it means to have or to have had a mental disorder can mark or stigmatize those currently or previously struggling with a mental disorder. This can make it less likely that they will seek treatment for fear of the stigmatizing consequences (Barney et al., 2006). People with such labels may find it hard to get a job, particularly one with a high level of responsibility, or to be accepted socially (Roeloffs et al., 2003). In short, such labels may stick for a long time.

Given these problems, some clinicians have argued for doing away with assessment and diagnosis. Others, however, believe that classification and diagnosis are essential to understanding and treating people with psychological difficulties. They suggest that we must simply work to increase what is known about psychological disorders and improve assessment and diagnostic techniques (Corrigan, 2007; Ben-Zeev, Young, & Corrigan, 2010).

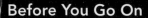

Before You Go On

www.wiley.com/go/comercanada

What Do You Know?
1. Define and explain the "four Ds" of abnormal behaviour.
2. What is the DSM-5?

What Do You Think? In this module, we talked about the stigmatizing issues associated with being diagnosed with a mental disorder. Think about people you know or people you have heard about or read about who were described as "having a mental disorder." What sorts of things did you think or assume about them simply based on this knowledge? Any negative generalizations could become part of the stigma associated with mental disorders.

Summary

Module 85: Defining, Classifying, and Diagnosing Psychological Abnormality

LEARNING OBJECTIVE 85 Identify the common features of most definitions of abnormal functioning, and describe how psychological disorders are classified and diagnosed.

- The study of psychological disorders is usually called *abnormal psychology*. Abnormal psychological functioning is a wide-ranging problem in this country.
- Definitions of psychological disorders often include the "four Ds"—deviance, distress, dysfunction, and danger.
- *The Diagnostic and Statistical Manual of Mental Disorders (DSM)* (current version DSM-5) is the leading classification system in North America.

Key Terms

abnormal psychology 650
comorbidity 655
diagnosis 655

Diagnostic and Statistical Manual of Mental Disorders (DSM) 653
International Classification of Diseases (ICD) 653

Study Questions

Multiple Choice

1. The medical model
   a) encourages a search for patterns of symptoms.
   b) is heavily dependent on social norms and values.
   c) is unconcerned with underlying etiology.
   d) disassociates physical illness and "madness."

2. Behaviour, thoughts, and emotions are considered abnormal when they differ from a society's ideas about proper functioning. Which of the following "Four D's" does this statement represent?
   a) deviance
   b) distress
   c) dysfunction
   d) danger

Fill-in-the-Blank

1. A person whose thoughts or behaviour are far outside the norm for the time and place in which he or she lives is demonstrating the _____ aspect of psychological abnormality.

2. A client who is diagnosed with both major depressive disorder and generalized anxiety disorder is said to be experiencing _____.

Module 86: Models of Abnormality

The perspectives that scientists use to explain phenomena are known as *models*, or *paradigms* (Kuhn, 1962). You can think of a model or paradigm as a big idea about how things work. So, for example, a mechanistic paradigm builds on the idea that people are like complex machines and then when something goes wrong, it is probably because something in the mechanism is broken. To understand how a clinical theorist explains disorders, we must know which model shapes the theorist's view of abnormal functioning. Thus, in this module we will examine today's most influential clinical models—the neuroscience, psychodynamic, cognitive-behavioural, humanistic-existential, socio-cultural, and developmental psychopathology models (see **Table 86-1**). In the next part, we will see how these models inform treatment.

86.1 The Neuroscience Model

Neuroscientists view abnormal behaviour as an illness brought about by a malfunctioning brain (Pliszka, 2003). As we have seen throughout the textbook, researchers have discovered connections between certain psychological or neurological disorders and problems in specific structures of the brain. Neuroscientists have also linked some mental disorders to deficient or excessive activity of different neurotransmitters. Depression, for example, seems to be related to insufficient activity of the neurotransmitters *norepinephrine* and *serotonin* (Beck & Alford, 2009). In addition to focusing on neurotransmitters, neuroscience researchers have learned that mental disorders are sometimes related to abnormal hormonal activity in the body's endocrine system. Abnormal secretions of the hormone *cortisol*, for example, also have been tied to depression (Vrshek-Schallhorn et al., 2013).

What causes these problems with brain anatomy and chemical functioning? Two factors have received particular attention from clinical theorists in recent years: *genetics* and *viral infections*.

Studies suggest that genetic inheritance plays a key role in mood disorders, schizophrenia, intellectual disability, Alzheimer's disease, and other mental disorders. It appears that in most cases, no single gene is responsible for a particular disorder (Oksenberg & Hauser, 2010). Instead, many genes combine to help produce our actions and reactions, both functional and dysfunctional. Moreover, as you have read throughout the textbook, the predispositions set up by such genes

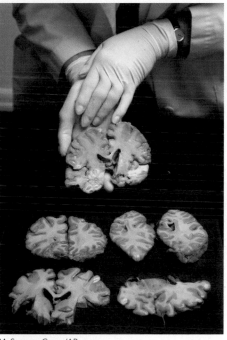

M. Spencer Green/AP

Extreme antisocial disorders and the brain. Forensic psychiatrist Helen Morrison displays slices of the brain of John Wayne Gacy, who murdered at least 33 boys and young men between 1972 and 1978. Post-mortem examinations have not revealed clear links between abnormal brain structure and the extreme antisocial patterns exhibited by Gacy and other serial killers.

TABLE 86-1 Today's Leading Models of Abnormality	
Approaches	**Causes of Abnormal Functioning**
Neuroscience Approaches	Structural or biochemical malfunctions in the brain
Psychodynamic Approaches	Unconscious conflicts often rooted in childhood
Cognitive-Behavioural Approaches	Abnormal behaviours acquired through a tightly interwoven mix of conditioning, modelling, and cognitive principles
Humanistic and Existential Approaches	Distorted views of self prevent personal growth or decision making
Socio-cultural Approaches	Societal, cultural, social, and family pressures or conflicts
Developmental Psychopathology Approach	Early risk factors combined with poor resilience throughout life stages

often will result in psychological disorders only when the individuals are also exposed to adverse environmental conditions.

Another possible source of abnormal brain structure or biochemical dysfunction appears to be viral infections. Some research suggests, for example, that schizophrenia, a disorder marked by hallucinations and other departures from reality, may be related to exposure to certain viruses before birth or during childhood (Fox, 2010). The studies suggest that a damaging virus may enter the brain of a fetus or young child and then remain quiet there until the individual reaches puberty or young adulthood. At that time, activated by hormonal changes, by another infection, or by stressful life events, the virus may set in motion the symptoms of schizophrenia. In addition to schizophrenia, research has sometimes linked viruses to mood and anxiety disorders (Fox, 2010).

Today, the neuroscience model for understanding mental dysfunction is highly regarded, and researchers are rapidly identifying valuable new information about various psychological and neurological disorders (Pliszka, 2003). As you will see in Part 16, drug treatments and biological interventions such as psychotropic medications or electroconvulsive therapy (ECT) often bring great symptomatic relief where other approaches have failed.

At the same time, some proponents of the neuroscience model seem to expect that biological factors and brain interventions alone can explain and treat all abnormal behaviours. However, to better understand mental health and mental illness we need to avoid dependency on *reductionist perspectives* that attempt to reduce complex phenomenon to a single cause. Reductionist views such as biomedical models neglect the complex interplay of biological and non-biological factors, including a person's environmental experiences. Indeed, as we have seen throughout this book, the connections in our brains unfold partly in response to the experiences that we keep having throughout our lives, beginning in the womb.

So, since we know that the mind affects the body and that the body also affects the mind, we must come to understand the complex interactions between the biological, social, psychological, and cultural variables present in the lives of all individuals. The *biopsychosocial perspective*, first identified by George Engel (1980, 1977), recognizes the links between each of these important areas of human development (Suls & Rothman, 2004). The biological component involves a focus on genetic and epigenetic factors as well as biochemical influences and differences in brain structure and function. The psychological component includes interpersonal interactions, personality variables, cognitive and learning histories and development, attitudes, and ability to cope. The social component considers socialization experiences, cultural and social interactions and variables, and life experiences. When studying mental illness, the focus is on how these variables interact to produce the behaviours being treated. However, this model can be employed for describing typical development as well.

The notion that disorders arise from an interaction of internal and external causes resulted in a model known as the *diathesis-stress model*. This model suggests that a person may inherit a genetic predisposition (a diathesis) for a disorder, but that it will remain undeveloped unless triggered by an external (stressful) life event. So, for example, you and your brother may have both inherited a predisposition for depression. However, he is in a serious car accident where two of his childhood friends are killed; he feels terrible guilt for surviving this accident, and his capacity to cope is exceeded. You experience nothing like this. Your brother develops depression and you do not. Of course, we have to also consider that individuals respond to stressful events with quite different trajectories. That is to say, you may have experienced the same adverse event as your brother, but might have responded quite differently and thereby would not have triggered a psychiatric disorder (Alloy et al., 2006).

86.2 The Cognitive-Behavioural Model

Cognitive-behavioural theorists propose that psychological disorders result largely from a combination of problematic learned behaviours and dysfunctional cognitive processes. According to this model, such behaviours and thinking processes interact with and mutually influence each other: people use their particular ways of thinking to explain their behaviours and the events in their lives, behaviours may lead to particular thoughts, various cognitions may trigger certain behaviours, and so on. Cognitive-behavioural theorists also view emotions and biological events as key variables. And, indeed, they seek to understand how these variables influence and interact with behaviours and cognitions to help bring about abnormal functioning. Both behavioural and cognitive principles lie at the centre of the model (Butler, Chapman, Forman, & Beck, 2006). Correspondingly, as you will see in Part 16, cognitive-behavioural therapists focus largely on behaviours and cognitions in their efforts to help people with psychological disorders by helping them to change their thoughts and behaviours.

To more fully understand the cognitive-behavioural model, it is useful to first examine the behavioural and cognitive components separately. In fact, at one time, the behavioural model stood alone, and behaviourists used only principles of conditioning and modelling to explain abnormal functioning. In the 1960s, however, a number of theorists began calling for a more cognitive-behavioural perspective (Beck, 1975). They argued that human beings engage in unseen *cognitive behaviours*, such as private thoughts and beliefs, and that people's cognitions greatly influence and are influenced by their behaviours.

86.2.1 The Behavioural Perspective

As we observed in Part 7, behavioural theorists use learning principles to explain human functioning. These principles focus on how the environment changes a person's behaviours. Many learned behaviours are constructive and help people to cope with daily challenges and lead satisfying lives. However, abnormal and undesirable behaviours also can be learned.

According to the behavioural perspective, abnormal behaviours are acquired by the same principles of learning as adaptive behaviours. As you saw in Part 7, for example, phobias may occur as a result of *classical conditioning* when a previously neutral object becomes paired with an unconditioned stimulus that creates fear.

Behavioural theorists also suggest that some of the many behaviours we learn through *operant conditioning* processes of reward and punishment are abnormal ones. For example, some people may learn to abuse alcohol and drugs because initially such behaviours brought feelings of calm, comfort, or pleasure. Others may develop or continue to display disordered eating patterns partly because of praise they receive for a thinner appearance or because of the comfort eating certain foods provides them (Gibson, 2012; Wilson, 2011).

Modelling, in which we learn by observing others, can also lead to abnormality. Recall from Part 7 the famous study in which children learned from a model to behave aggressively toward a Bobo doll, an inflatable clown (Bandura, Ross, & Ross, 1963). Similarly, children of psychologically dysfunctional people may develop maladaptive reactions

The Charlotte Observer, Christopher A. Record/AP

"Virtual" desensitization. Virtual reality software enables phobic clients to more vividly experience their feared objects and situations, such as flying in an airplane, during desensitization.

because of their exposure to the models presented by their parents (Rossman et al., 2013; Luyckx et al., 2011).

One of the appeals of behavioural principles is that, in contrast to psychodynamic concepts, they can be tested in the laboratory. Experimenters have used the principles of conditioning to produce clinical symptoms in research participants, suggesting that psychological disorders may in fact develop through learning (Morris et al., 2014). Moreover, as you will see in Part 16, research has indicated that behavioural interventions can be helpful to people with specific fears, compulsive behaviours, social deficits, intellectual disabilities, and a wide range of other problems (Wilson, 2011).

86.2.2 The Cognitive Perspective

According to the cognitive perspective, when people display abnormal patterns of functioning, cognitive problems are to blame. Abnormal functioning can result from several such problems, including *maladaptive beliefs* and *illogical thinking processes*.

The pioneering clinical theorists Albert Ellis (1913–2007) and Aaron Beck proposed that each of us holds broad beliefs about ourselves and our world that help to guide us through life and determine our reactions to the situations we encounter. However, some people's beliefs are unjustified and unhelpful, leading them to act and react in ways that are inappropriate and that reduce their chances of happiness (Barth, 2014; Beck & Haigh, 2014).

Such people may, for example, assume that they are failures if they are not loved or approved of by every person they know. An otherwise successful presentation in the classroom can, for example, make them sad or anxious because one listener seemed bored. Their problematic belief helps set the stage for a life hampered by tension and disappointment.

Think back to Diane Markos, whose case opened this part. She held some unjustified beliefs that may have left her particularly vulnerable to depression. Her case study further stated:

Many of her [problems] seemed to stem from underlying attitudes . . . such as: "If I care for others, they should/must care for me," or "If something good happens to me, I'll have to pay for it later with pain," or "People either love me or hate me" (Spitzer et al., 1983, p. 129).

As is discussed in Part 16, Beck also found that some people continuously think in illogical ways and keep drawing self-defeating and even pathological conclusions (Beck & Weishaar, 2011). He identified several illogical thinking processes—processes that turn out to be very common in depression and anxiety disorders. These include:

- *Selective perception*—seeing only the negative features of an event.
- *Magnification*—exaggerating the importance of undesirable events.
- *Overgeneralization*—drawing broad negative conclusions on the basis of a single insignificant event.

Diane Markos's therapist noted repeated examples of illogical thinking that helped predispose Diane to depressive reactions:

When she finally did get a B from her professor, she concluded that she had failed miserably. There was no recognition of any middle ground between total academic success and total academic failure. Moreover, she tended to magnify the importance of events like this as if they were an indictment of her as a total human being (Spitzer et al., 1983, p. 129).

The cognitive perspective has appealed to a wide range of theorists. They embrace a viewpoint that sees *thought* as a key factor in both normal and abnormal behaviour. Research supports this appeal. Investigators have found that people

©iStockphoto.com/epicurean

Cognition and psychological disorders. Social isolation and difficulties in problem solving can make it harder for people to get help with depression.

with psychological disorders do, indeed, often display the kinds of beliefs and errors in thinking described in the cognitive theories (Sharf, 2012; Ellis, 2011).

86.3 The Psychodynamic Model

The psychodynamic model has its roots in Sigmund Freud's theories. As we observed in Part 12, psychodynamic theorists believe that a person's behaviour is determined largely by underlying psychological forces of which the person is not consciously aware. Abnormal behaviours or symptoms are viewed as the consequences of conflicts between these forces or as unconscious attempts to resolve conflicts and lessen painful inner turmoil.

As we pointed out in Part 12, Freud proposed that a child's environment may prevent his id, ego, and superego from maturing properly or interacting effectively. When that happens, the child can become *fixated*, or entrapped, at an early stage of development. Such fixations affect all subsequent development and may set in motion abnormal functioning.

Freud would have suggested that the family pressures Diane Markos experienced during her early years caused an imbalance of power among her id, ego, and superego. The demands she experienced forced her to put aside many of her own id needs and to act in a mature, ego-dominated manner beyond her years. Freud would certainly have looked upon such childhood pressures and deprivations as possible roots for her adult depression.

As we also saw in Part 12, several of Freud's colleagues disagreed with key aspects of his theories. As a result, there are now a number of different psychodynamic explanations for abnormal functioning (Sharf, 2012). For example, one group of psychodynamic theorists, called *object relations* theorists, believes people are motivated primarily by a need to establish relationships with others, known as *objects*. They propose that severe problems in early relationships may result in abnormal development and psychological problems (Blum, 2010; Kernberg, 2005, 1997).

Freud and his followers helped change the way abnormal functioning is viewed (Wolitzky, 2011). Primarily because of their work, many different kinds of theorists today look for explanations outside biological processes. In addition, Freud and his followers were the first practitioners to demonstrate the value of systematically applying theory and techniques to treatment. However, as you will see in Part 16, research has often failed to support the effectiveness of psychodynamic therapies (Prochaska & Norcross, 2010).

Monalyn Gracia/Corbis

Anal personality? According to Freud, when an individual's neat and orderly personality is as extreme as this woman's (prior to storing her knickknacks, she organizes them carefully before her and enters each item on a computer file), fixation at the anal stage of development may be operating.

© iStockphoto.com/akurtz

Setting the stage. Object relations theorists believe that early relationships in life, particularly with parents, are key to adult functioning.

86.4 The Socio-Cultural Model

According to many theorists, abnormal behaviour is best understood in light of the social, cultural, and family forces brought to bear on an individual. The unique characteristics of a given society may create special stresses that heighten the likelihood of abnormal functioning in its members. Researchers have, for example, found relationships between abnormal functioning and factors such as widespread social change, socio-economic class membership, cultural background, social networks, and family systems (Cardemil et al., 2011; Tanaka-Matsumi, 2001).

Romeo Ranoco/Reuters/Landov

The economy and mental health. Thousands of Filipino job seekers line up at a 2009 job fair in Manila. Unemployment and poverty are strongly linked to psychological dysfunction.

86.4.1 Social Change

When a society undergoes major change, the mental health of its members can be greatly affected. Societies undergoing rapid urbanization, for example, usually show a rise in mental disorders (Anakwenze & Zuberi, 2013). It is not yet known which features of urbanization—overcrowding, technological change, social isolation, migration, and so forth—are most to blame. Similarly, societies in the throes of economic depression often display rises in rates of clinical depression and suicide (Miret et al., 2013).

86.4.2 Socio-Economic Class

Studies by Jitender Sareen, Brian Cox, and Murray Stein at the University of Manitoba have found that rates of psychological abnormality, especially severe abnormality, are much higher among members of the lower socio-economic classes than among members of the higher ones (Sareen et al., 2011). Perhaps the special pressures of lower-class life help explain this relationship. Poverty is linked to many stressors, including high rates of crime, unemployment, overcrowding, and even homelessness, as well as inferior medical care and limited educational opportunities. Of course, other factors may account for this relationship. People who suffer from significant mental disorders may be less effective at work, earn less money, and, as a result, drift downward to settle in a lower socio-economic class (Read, 2010; Murali & Oyebode, 2010).

86.4.3 Cultural Factors

Many theorists believe that human behaviour, including abnormal behaviour, is understood best by examining an individual's unique cultural context, including the values of that culture and the external pressures faced by members of the culture (Matsumoto & van de Vijer, 2011; Alegria et al., 2009, 2007, 2004). As we have seen throughout this book, the cultural groups that have been studied most often are ethnic and racial minority groups, along with economically disadvantaged persons, women, and homosexuals. Each of these groups faces special pressures in society that may help produce feelings of stress and, in some cases, abnormal functioning. Moreover, of course, membership in these groups often overlaps.

Researchers have learned that women are at least twice as likely as men to be diagnosed with depressive and anxiety disorders, although this may be due partially to women being more likely than men to seek treatment (Essau et al., 2010). Suicide rates in the Canadian Aboriginal population are more than twice the sex-specific rates and three times the age-specific rates of non-Aboriginal Canadians (56.3 per year per 100,000 persons for Aboriginal males and 11.8 for Aboriginal females) (McNamee & Offord, 2003). Aboriginal Canadians also display extremely high alcoholism rates (Lemstra et al., 2013). In Canada, cultural origins, immigrant status, and Aboriginal status have been linked to varying rates of mental illness and adjustment issues (Kopec et al., 2001; MacMillan et al., 2008). Racial and sexual prejudice and related problems certainly may help explain these differences (Guimón, 2010).

Steve Woods/epa/Corbis

Pressures of discrimination. In 2009, these dancers performed at an all-day anti-racism concert in Britain entitled "Love Music, Hate Racism." Multicultural research suggests that prejudice and discrimination can contribute to abnormal functioning.

A good example of the role of culture in mental health comes from the work of Michael Chandler (University of British Columbia) and Chris Lalonde (University of Victoria). They examined the youth suicide rates among a large number of First Nations Band communities in British Columbia. In addition to suicide rates, Chandler and Lalonde gathered data regarding whether each band was or had been engaged in land claim negotiations with the provincial government; whether the band had taken control of education, fire, police, and child welfare services in their community; and whether there was a physical structure in the community dedicated to their cultural heritage. Their results indicate that if all of these factors were in place, the youth suicide rate was among the lowest in Canada; if none of them were in place, the rates were among the highest in Canada (Chandler et al., 2003). These results suggest that having a strong, culturally-rich context in which to develop has a significant positive effect on individual mental health and identity development.

Another cultural factor that has received much attention from clinical researchers and therapists in recent years is religion. Researchers have studied possible links between religious faith and mental health, and have learned that the two are often correlated. Studies have found, for example, that genuinely spiritual people tend, on average, to be less lonely, pessimistic, depressed, or anxious than other people (Underwood, 2011). Moreover, as we observed in Part 14, such individuals often seem to cope better with major life stressors and appear less likely to abuse drugs or to attempt suicide. Spirituality can be a source of comfort, hope, and meaning, which may at least partially account for this spirituality effect (Koenig, 2012).

86.4.4 Social Networks and Supports

Many theorists focus on the social networks in which people operate, including their social and professional relationships. How well do they communicate with others? What kind of signals do they send to or receive from others? Researchers have often found ties between deficiencies in a person's social networks and that person's functioning (Gask et al., 2011; Vega et al., 2011; Paykel, 2006, 2003). They have observed, for example, that people who are isolated and lack social support or intimacy in their lives are more likely to become depressed when under stress and to remain depressed longer than are people with supportive spouses or warm friendships.

86.4.5 Family Systems

According to **family systems theory**, the family is a system of interacting parts—the family members—who interact with one another in consistent ways and follow rules unique to each family (Goldenberg & Goldenberg, 2011). Family systems theorists believe that the *structure* and *communication* patterns of certain families actually force individual members to react in ways that otherwise seem abnormal. If the members were to behave normally, they would severely strain the family's usual manner of operation and would actually increase their own and their family's turmoil.

Recall, for example, how Diane Markos's family was structured. She was required to be a third parent in the family, which in many ways deprived her of normal childhood experiences and emotions. In turn, she came to view her life as one of "servitude, rejection, and failure," and she experienced ongoing depression.

86.5 The Developmental Psychopathology Model

Developmental psychopathology is an area that is interested in how psychological disorders evolve, based on both genetics and early childhood experiences. Researchers interested in this area try to understand how early problematic patterns affect functioning as individuals move through later life stages (Cicchetti, 2010; Santostefano, 2010; Hinshaw, 2008). Developmental psychopathologists compare and contrast abnormal behaviour patterns with more typical ones, attempting to identify **risk factors**—biological

family systems theory a theory holding that each family has its own implicit rules, relationship structure, and communication patterns that shape the behaviour of the individual members.

developmental psychopathology the study of how problem behaviours evolve as a function of a person's genes and early experiences, and how these early issues affect the person at later life stages.

HOW WE DEVELOP

risk factors biological and environmental factors that contribute to problem outcomes.

and environmental factors that contribute to negative outcomes. In addition, they seek to identify other factors that can help children avoid or recover from such outcomes.

Like other developmental psychologists, developmental psychopathologists hold that behaviour can be analyzed in a variety of ways. A full accounting of how individuals get off-track (or stay on-track) requires looking at how genetics, early environmental influences, and their own psychological processes all collaborate to form their current pattern and functioning.

Developmental psychologists have contributed two concepts to the field of psychology: *equifinality* and *multifinality* (Fanti & Henrich, 2010; Mitchell et al., 2004). The concept of **equifinality** holds that individuals can start out from a variety of different places and yet, through their life experiences, wind up functioning (or dysfunctioning) in similar ways. **Multifinality** follows the opposite principle. It suggests that children can start from the same point and wind up in any number of different psychological places.

Let's apply these two concepts to *conduct disorder*, a disorder of childhood and adolescence characterized by repeated violations of others' rights, displays of aggression, and destructive behaviour. A child with this disorder may have been born with a difficult temperament, experienced poor parenting, or developed poor social skills (Litschge, Vaughn, & McCrea, 2010). As suggested by the notion of *equifinality*, regardless of which set of those risk factors is at play, in the beginning the outcome is the same, in this case, conduct disorder. At the same time, *multifinality* would predict that not every difficult child and not every child with ineffective parents will wind up with a conduct disorder. The vast majority will wind up with no pathology at all. So children with similar beginnings can end up in very different places.

Developmental psychopathologists are very interested in the biological, psychological, or environmental events that help buffer against or negate the impact of risk factors—events that help produce **resilience**, an ability to recover from or avoid the serious effects of negative circumstances (Dudley et al., 2011; Flouri et al., 2011; Hudziak & Bartels, 2008). In short, according to this viewpoint, it is more important to understand what goes right as it is to understand what goes wrong.

equifinality the idea that different children can start from different points and wind up at the same outcome.

multifinality the idea that children can start from the same point and wind up at any number of different outcomes.

resilience the ability to recover from or avoid the serious effects of negative circumstances.

Before You Go On

www.wiley.com/go/comercanada

What Do You Know?

1. What are the major models used by psychologists to explain abnormal functioning?
2. What major types of brain problems are linked to abnormal functioning?
3. In the view of cognitive-behavioural theorists, what kinds of problems can lead to abnormal functioning?
4. How are the humanistic and existential models similar, and how do they differ?
5. What social and cultural factors have been found to be related to abnormal functioning?

What Do You Think? How would you describe your personal model for explaining why people behave as they do?

Summary

Module 86: Models of Abnormality

LEARNING OBJECTIVE 86 Describe the major models used by psychologists to explain abnormal functioning.

- Clinicians use several major models to explain abnormal functioning, including the neuroscience, psychodynamic, cognitive-behavioural, humanistic-existential, socio-cultural, and developmental psychopathology models.
- The neuroscience model views abnormal functioning as a result of malfunctions in brain structure or chemical activity. Malfunctions can be caused by injuries or other factors, including genetics or viruses.
- Psychodynamic theorists view abnormal functioning as the result of unconscious conflicts that may have originated in our early development. Freud focused on fixations during the oral, anal, and phallic stages of development, while other theorists have focused on difficulties in ego development or our relationships with others.
- Behavioural theorists propose that abnormal behaviours develop via the same processes as more adaptive behaviours: classical conditioning, operant conditioning, and modelling. Cognitive theorists believe that abnormal functioning can result from disordered thoughts, including basic irrational assumptions, specific upsetting thoughts, and illogical thinking processes.
- Humanists suggest that people are vulnerable to psychological disorders when they develop inaccurate views of their worth or goals in life. Existentialist therapies focus on helping clients discover their personal freedom of choice and take responsibility for making choices.
- According the socio-cultural model, abnormal behaviour is best understood in light of the social, cultural, and family forces brought to bear on an individual. Important factors include social change, socio-economic class membership, cultural background, social networks, and family systems.
- Developmental psychopathology theorists are interested in how psychological disorders evolve, based on both genetics and early childhood experiences, and on how those early patterns affect people's functioning as they move through later life stages.

Key Terms

developmental psychopathology 663
equifinality 664

family systems theory 663
multifinality 664

resilience 664
risk factors 663

Study Questions

Multiple Choice

1. Which of the following statements best reflects the psycho-dynamic approach to defining abnormal behaviour?
   a) It is learned through the observation of societal norms.
   b) It is observed in other individuals we identify with.
   c) It results from maladaptive thinking patterns.
   d) It results from unconscious attempts to solve conflicts.

2. Humanistic and existential theories have in common a belief that
   a) people are naturally inclined to live constructively.
   b) people have complete freedom to give meaning to their lives or to run away from that responsibility.
   c) people must have high levels of self-awareness to live meaningful, well-adjusted lives.
   d) the therapist is an expert who can provide answers for the client.

3. Albert Ellis believed that abnormal patterns of functioning are caused primarily by
   a) faulty conditioning.
   b) imitating maladaptive models.
   c) irrational assumptions.
   d) learned helplessness.

Fill-in-the-Blank

1. The notion of modelling, first studied by _____, helps explain why people whose parents had psychological disturbances often have psychological disturbances themselves.

2. The tendency for children who start out in the same situation to end up at very different places, psychologically speaking, is called _____.

Module 87: Mood Disorders

LEARNING OBJECTIVE 87
Describe and differentiate major depressive disorder and bipolar disorder.

depression a persistent sad state in which life seems dark and its challenges overwhelming.

mania a persistent state of euphoria or frenzied energy.

major depressive disorder a disorder characterized by a depressed mood that is significantly disabling and is not caused by such factors as drugs or a general medical condition.

bipolar disorder a mood disorder in which periods of mania alternate with periods of depression.

As you saw earlier, there are more than 200 different disorders listed in DSM-5. In the rest of this part, we will look at some of the disorders that are particularly common and that have received considerable study. We begin with mood disorders. Moods are temporary, non-specific emotional states. Mood disorders are mental disorders characterized by pervasive disturbed mood as the dominant feature. There are two primary types of mood disorder: unipolar mood disorder, also called depression, and bipolar disorder, where people move between one extreme mood state to another.

Depression and mania are the key features in mood disorders. **Depression** is a low, sad state in which life seems dark and hopeless and its challenges seem overwhelming. **Mania**, the opposite of depression, is a state of breathless euphoria, or frenzied energy, in which people may have an exaggerated belief that the world is theirs for the taking. Most people with a mood disorder suffer only from depression, a pattern found in **major depressive disorder** or in a less disabling but chronic form of depression called *dysthymic disorder*. Others experience periods of mania that alternate or intermix with periods of depression, a pattern called **bipolar disorder** in its severe form and *cyclothymic disorder* in a less severe but chronic form (Frank & Michael, 2013; Beck & Alford, 2009).

87.1 Major Depressive Disorder

People more unhappy than usual often say they are "depressed." Typically, they are responding to sad events, fatigue, or unhappy thoughts. This use of the term confuses a perfectly normal mood swing with a clinical syndrome. All of us experience dejection from time to time; few of us experience major depressive disorder. This disorder brings severe and long-lasting psychological pain that may intensify as time goes by. Those who suffer from it may become unable to carry out the simplest of life's activities. Some even try to end their lives.

It is estimated that nearly 8 percent of adults in Canada are diagnosed with major depressive disorder in any given year. Another 3 percent of adults are diagnosed with mild forms of the disorder (Canadian Mental Health Association, 2014b; Health Canada, 2002). Women are at least twice as likely as men to be diagnosed with depression. It is important to note that this difference between men's and women's rates of depression could reflect a number of factors, such as women's greater tendency to seek assistance; men's tendency to deny or pay less attention to their feelings; and women's greater likelihood of carrying the stress of multiple roles as parent, spouse, and employee. These factors can lead to differential diagnosis rates, without telling us about the actual underlying rates of disorders like depression among men and women (Nolen-Hoeksema, 2001). Approximately half of people with this disorder recover within six weeks, and 90 percent recover within a year, some without treatment (Kessler, 2009). However, most of them have at least one other episode of depression later in their lives (Taube-Schiff & Lau, 2008).

The DSM-5 diagnostic criteria for a major depressive episode are listed in **Table 87-1**. Due to space limitations, we have not included the DSM diagnostic criteria for the other disorders we discuss in this part. If you are interested in reviewing the diagnostic criteria for other disorders, search online using the following terms: DSM-5 criteria for "name of disorder." This search will return many websites showing the DSM diagnostic criteria for the disorder in question. Make sure that the site you choose to view

©iStockphoto.com/PeopleImages

Mood disorders. In mood disorders, individuals experience either unipolar mood disorder (where they experience depression) or bipolar disorder (where they move from one extreme mood state to another).

Depression is the most common health-care topic searched for on the Internet each year (19 percent of searches), followed by allergies/sinuses (16 percent), bipolar disorder (14 percent), and arthritis/rheumatism (10 percent).

TABLE 87-1 The Diagnostic Criteria for a Major Depressive Episode from the DSM-5

Major Depressive Episode

A. Five (or more) of the following 9 symptoms have been present during the same two-week period and represent a change from previous functioning; at least one of the symptoms is either (1) depressed mood or (2) loss of interest or pleasure.

B. The symptoms cause clinically significant distress or impairment in social, occupational, or other important areas of functioning.

C. The episode is not attributable to the physiological effects of a substance or to another medical condition.

(1) Depressed mood most of the day, nearly every day, as indicated by either subjective report (e.g., feels sad or empty) or observation made by others (e.g., appears tearful) *Note:* In children and adolescents, can be irritable mood.

(2) Markedly diminished interest or pleasure in all, or almost all, activities most of the day, nearly every day (as indicated by either subjective account or observation made by others)

(3) Significant weight loss when not dieting or weight gain (e.g., a change of more than 5% of body weight in a month), or decrease or increase in appetite nearly every day *Note:* In children this may be a failure to make expected weight gains.

(4) Insomnia or hypersomnia nearly every day

(5) Psychomotor agitation or retardation nearly every day (observable by others)

(6) Fatigue or loss of energy nearly every day

(7) Feelings of worthlessness or excessive or inappropriate guilt nearly every day

(8) Diminished ability to think or concentrate, or indecisiveness, nearly every day

(9) Recurrent thoughts of death (not just fear of dying), recurrent suicidal ideation without a specific plan, or a suicide attempt or a specific plan for committing suicide

Source: Reprinted with permission from the *Diagnostic and Statistical Manual of Mental Disorders*, Fifth Edition. Copyright ©2013 American Psychiatric Association.

clearly states that the criteria it displays are from the DSM (the most recent version is the DSM-5) and that the site references the DSM as the source of the material. That way you can be reasonably confident that the criteria being shown are accurate.

As we saw in the case of Diane Markos, severe depression has many symptoms other than sadness, and the symptoms often feed into one another. The symptoms span five areas of functioning: emotional, motivational, behavioural, cognitive, and physical.

87.1.1 Characteristics of Depression

Most people who are depressed feel sad and dejected. They describe themselves as "miserable" and "empty." They often lose the desire to participate in their usual activities. Almost all report a lack of drive, initiative, and spontaneity. Many depressed people become uninterested in life or wish to die; others wish that they could kill themselves, and some actually try. Suicide represents the ultimate escape from life's activities and pressures. It has been estimated that between 6 and 16 percent of people who suffer from severe depression commit suicide (De Leo & San Too, 2014; Taube-Schiff & Lau, 2008).

Depressed people are usually less active and less productive than other people. They spend more time alone and may stay in bed for long periods. They may also move and even speak more slowly than others. Most hold extremely negative views of themselves. They consider themselves inadequate, undesirable, inferior, and perhaps evil. They also blame themselves for nearly every unfortunate event (Lakey et al., 2014). Another cognitive symptom of depression is pessimism. Sufferers are usually convinced that nothing will ever improve, and they feel helpless to change any aspect of their lives (Mitchell,

Digital Vision/Getty Images

Feeling blue. Feeling sad is not necessarily depression. Major depressive disorder brings severe and long-lasting psychological pain that may intensify as time goes by.

Psychology Around Us The Case of Andrea Yates

On the morning of June 20, 2001, 36-year-old Andrea Yates called police and explained that she had drowned her five children in the bathtub because "they weren't developing correctly." She recounted the order in which the children had died: first 3-year-old Paul, then 2-year-old Luke, followed by 5-year-old John, 6-month-old Mary, and 7-year-old Noah.

As many as 80 percent of mothers experience "baby blues" soon after giving birth, and between 10 and 30 percent display the clinical syndrome of *postpartum depression*. Postpartum psychosis, by contrast, is an entirely different disorder (Doucet et al., 2011; Worley, 2010).

Postpartum psychosis affects about 1 to 2 of every 1,000 mothers who have recently given birth (Posmontier, 2010). The symptoms apparently are triggered by the enormous shift in hormone levels that occur after delivery (Blackmore et al., 2009). Within days or at most a few months of childbirth, the woman develops signs of losing touch with reality, such as delusions (for example, she may become convinced that her baby is the devil); hallucinations (perhaps hearing voices); extreme anxiety, confusion, and disorientation; disturbed sleep; and illogical or chaotic thoughts (for example, thoughts about killing herself or her child).

Women with a history of bipolar disorder, schizophrenia, or major depressive disorder are particularly vulnerable to the disorder (Read & Purse, 2007). In addition, women who have previously experienced postpartum depression or postpartum psychosis have an increased likelihood of developing this disorder after subsequent births (Nonacs, 2007). Andrea Yates, for example, had developed signs of postpartum depression (and perhaps postpartum psychosis) and attempted suicide after the birth of her fourth child. At that time, however, she appeared to respond well to a combination of medications, and so she and her husband later decided to conceive a fifth child (King, 2002).

After the birth of her fifth child, the symptoms did in fact recur, along with features of psychosis. Yates again attempted suicide. Although she was hospitalized twice and treated with various medications, her condition failed to improve. Six months after giving birth to Mary, her fifth child, she drowned all five of her children.

Most clinicians who are knowledgeable about this rare disorder agree that Yates was indeed a victim of postpartum psychosis. Although only a fraction of women with the disorder actually harm their children (estimates run as high as 4 percent), the Yates case reminds us that such an outcome is indeed possible (Posmontier, 2010; Read & Purse, 2007). The case also reminds us that early detection and treatment are critical (Doucet et al., 2011).

After a second trial for murder in 2007, Yates was found *not guilty by reason of insanity* and sent to a high-security mental health facility for treatment. Some months later, she was transferred to a low-security state mental hospital where she continues to receive treatment.

2010; Joiner, 2002). Finally, people who are depressed often have physical ailments such as headaches, indigestion, constipation, dizzy spells, and general pain. They may also have disturbances in appetite and sleep (Mitchell, 2010; Neckelmann et al., 2011).

Major depressive disorders often seem to be triggered by stressful events (Brown, 2011; Hammen et al., 2009). In fact, researchers have found that depressed people experience a greater number of stressful life events during the month just before the onset of a depressive episode than do other people during the same period of time (Kendler & Gardner, 2010; Monroe & Hadjiyannakis, 2002). However, it is important to remember that stress is not just something that happens *to* us. For instance, Kate Harkness and her associates at Queen's University found evidence that higher rates of interpersonal stress generation (in a sample of adolescent girls with a history of childhood maltreatment) predicted depression (Harkness, Lumley, & Truss, 2008). Research done recently at the University of Toronto addressed whether people act in ways that keep existing stress going (i.e., stress continuation) or generate new stress. The data suggested that not only was new stress created, but stress generation was implicated in both depression and anxiety (Uliaszek et al., 2012).

Today's leading explanations for major depressive disorder point to neuroscience, psychological, or socio-cultural factors. Many theorists believe that the various explanations should be combined to more fully understand people with this disorder (Beck & Alford, 2009). We will examine them separately here so that each perspective is clear.

87.1.2 How Do Neuroscientists Explain Depression?

If people inherit a predisposition to major depressive disorder, we would expect a particularly large number of cases among the close relatives of depressed persons (Neale, 2013). Twin studies support this expectation (Richard & Lyness, 2006). One investigation, for example, looked at nearly 200 pairs of twins. When a *monozygotic* (*identical*) twin had depression, there was a 46 percent chance that the other twin would have the same disorder. In contrast, when a *dizygotic* (*fraternal*) twin had depression, the other twin had only a 20 percent chance of developing the disorder (McGuffin et al., 1996).

If genetic influences are indeed at work in unipolar depression, what biological factors might ultimately produce the disorder? Researchers have focused most often on abnormal neurotransmitter activity—namely, low activity of norepinephrine and serotonin (Goldstein et al., 2011).

In the 1950s, several pieces of evidence began to point to these neurotransmitters. First, medical researchers discovered that several medications for high blood pressure often caused depression (Ayd, 1956). As it turned out, some of these medications lowered norepinephrine activity and others lowered serotonin. A second piece of evidence was the discovery of the first truly effective antidepressant drugs. These drugs were discovered almost by accident. In 1956, Roland Kuhn, a psychiatrist working in Switzerland, was administering a new trial drug to patients with schizophrenia. The drug did not seem to work, and in fact made symptoms worse in some patients. Kuhn noticed, however, that those patients with comorbid symptoms of depression showed improvement in their depressive symptoms while on the drug. Kuhn tried the drug with patients who were only showing depressive symptoms, and many of them improved dramatically (Cahn, 2006). With these initial observations in hand, researchers soon learned that they could relieve depression by increasing either norepinephrine or serotonin activity (Bunney & Davis, 1965; Schildkraut, 1965).

An enormous number of studies over the past half-century have further supported the notion that major depressive disorder is related to low activity of norepinephrine and/or serotonin. Neuroscience research has also indicated that the body's endocrine system may play a role in depression. People with depression have been found to have high levels of cortisol, the hormone released by the adrenal glands during times of stress (Palazidou, 2012; Neumeister et al., 2005). This relationship is not all that surprising, given that stressful events often seem to trigger depression.

87.1.3 How Do Cognitive-Behavioural Theorists Explain Depression?

Cognitive-behavioural theorists believe that people with severe depression acquire distinctly negative behaviours and think in dysfunctional ways that help cause and sustain their disordered symptoms (Zuckerman, 2011). The two most influential cognitive-behavioural explanations centre on the phenomenon of learned helplessness and on the power of negative thinking.

Learned Helplessness Since the mid-1960s, psychologist Martin Seligman has been developing the *learned helplessness* theory of depression (Forgeard et al., 2011; Gillham et al., 2011; Yu & Seligman, 2002; Seligman 1992, 1975). This theory holds that people become depressed when they think (1) that they no longer have control over the rewards and punishments in their lives, and (2) that they themselves are responsible for this helpless state.

Seligman's theory first began to take shape when he was working with laboratory dogs. He found that when dogs were given inescapable shocks, they came to learn that they have no control over the unpleasant punishments (shocks) in their lives. That is, they learned that they were helpless to do anything to

Imago Source/Corbis

Breaking up is hard to do. Having your significant other break up with you can be devastating. According to the attribution-helplessness theory, if a person attributes the breakup to their own internal shortcomings rather than to more specific events, the breakup could cause depression.

Mary was 25 years old and had just begun her senior year in college. . . . Asked to recount how her life had been going recently, Mary began to weep. Sobbing, she said that for the last year or so she felt she was losing control of her life and that recent stresses (starting school again, friction with her boyfriend) had left her feeling worthless and frightened. Because of a gradual deterioration in her vision, she was now forced to wear glasses all day. "The glasses make me look terrible," she said, and "I don't look people in the eye much any more." Also, to her dismay, Mary had gained 20 pounds in the past year. She viewed herself as overweight and unattractive. At times she was convinced that with enough money to buy contact lenses and enough time to exercise she could cast off her depression; at other times she believed nothing would help. . . Mary saw her life deteriorating in other spheres, as well. She felt overwhelmed by schoolwork and, for the first time in her life, was on academic probation. . . . In addition to her dissatisfaction with her appearance and her fears about her academic future, Mary complained of a lack of friends. Her social network consisted solely of her boyfriend, with whom she was living. Although there were times she experienced this relationship as almost unbearably frustrating, she felt helpless to change it and was pessimistic about its permanence. . . .

(Spitzer et al., 1983, pp. 122–123)

change negative situations. You may recall from Part 7 that this phenomenon is called *learned helplessness*. Moreover, when later placed in a new situation where they could in fact escape shocks and control their fate, the dogs continued to act as if they were generally helpless. They would just lie in their experimental boxes and accept the shocks. Seligman noted that the effects of learned helplessness greatly resemble the symptoms of human depression, and he proposed that people become depressed after developing a general belief that they have no control over the rewards and punishments in their lives (Seligman & Maier, 1967; Seligman, 1975).

The learned helplessness explanation of depression has been revised somewhat over the past two decades. According to a newer version of the theory, the *attribution-helplessness theory*, when people view events to be beyond their control, they ask themselves why this is so (Taube-Schiff & Lau, 2008; Abramson et al., 2002, 1989, 1978). If they attribute their present lack of control to some *internal* cause (some deficiency in themselves) that is both *global* (a deficiency that is wide-ranging) and *stable* (a deficiency that will continue for a long time), they may well feel helpless to prevent future negative outcomes and they may experience depression. If they make other kinds of attributions, this depressed reaction is unlikely.

Consider a university student whose girlfriend breaks up with him. If he attributes this loss of control to an internal cause that is both global and stable—"It's my fault [internal]; I ruin everything I touch [global], and I always will [stable]"—he then has reason to expect loss of control in the future and may generally experience a sense of helplessness. According to the attribution-helplessness view, he is a prime candidate for depression. If the student instead attributes the breakup to causes that are more specific ("The way I've behaved the past couple of weeks blew this relationship"), unstable ("I don't usually act like that"), or external ("She never did know what she wanted"), he might not expect to lose control again and would probably not experience helplessness and depression.

Post-secondary students who seek and receive negative feedback from their roommates feel more depressed than students who do not receive such feedback.

Negative Thinking   Like Seligman, Aaron Beck believed that negative thinking plays a key role in depression. Beck, however, pointed to *dysfunctional attitudes*, *errors in thinking*, the *cognitive triad*, and *automatic thoughts* as the keys to the clinical syndrome (Beck & Weishaar, 2011; Beck, 2002, 1991, 1967).

Beck believes that some people develop *dysfunctional attitudes*, such as "My general worth is tied to every task I perform," and "If I fail, others will feel repelled by me." In addition, Beck believes that those same people often commit errors in their thinking, such as arbitrary inferences or magnification.

According to Beck, this steady onslaught of dysfunctional attitudes and illogical thinking eventually triggers extended rounds of negative thinking in these individuals. The thinking typically takes three forms and is therefore termed the **cognitive triad**: the individuals repeatedly interpret (1) *their experiences*, (2) *themselves*, and (3) *their futures* in negative ways that lead them to feel depressed. That is, depressed people interpret their experiences as burdens that repeatedly defeat or deprive them. They view themselves as undesirable, worthless, and inadequate. And they regularly see the future as bleak, as seen in **Figure 87-1**.

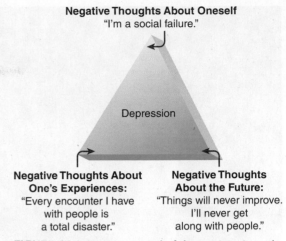

Negative Thoughts About Oneself
"I'm a social failure."

Depression

Negative Thoughts About
One's Experiences:
"Every encounter I have
with people is
a total disaster."

Negative Thoughts
About the Future:
"Things will never improve.
I'll never get
along with people."

FIGURE 87-1 **Cognitive triad of depression.** According to Aaron Beck, a regular pattern of these three types of negative thoughts increases vulnerability to depression.

Finally, depressed people experience **automatic thoughts**, a steady train of unpleasant thoughts that keep suggesting to them that they are inadequate and that their situation is hopeless. Beck labels these thoughts "automatic" because they seem to just happen, as if by reflex. In the course of only a few hours, depressed people may be visited by hundreds of such thoughts: "I'm worthless. . . . I let everyone down. . . . Everyone hates me. . . . My responsibilities are overwhelming. . . . I've failed as a parent. . . . I'm stupid. . . . Everything is difficult for me. . . . Things will never change."

cognitive triad a pattern of thinking in which individuals repeatedly interpret their experiences, themselves, and their futures in negative ways that lead them to feel depressed.

automatic thoughts specific upsetting thoughts that arise unbidden.

While it is not entirely clear whether this sort of negative thinking is a cause or a symptom of depression, Beck's explanation has received considerable research support. Several studies confirm, for example, that depressed people hold dysfunctional attitudes, and the more dysfunctional attitudes they hold, the more depressed they tend to be (Evans et al., 2005). Other research supports the theory of a cognitive triad in depressed individuals. For example, studies indicate that depressed participants recall unpleasant experiences more readily than positive ones, rate themselves lower than non-depressed subjects do, and select pessimistic statements in storytelling tests (for example, "I expect my plans will fail") (Ridout et al., 2003).

More recent research has identified an early framework for the neurobiological underpinnings for Beck's cognitive theory (Disner et al., 2011). This research suggests bottom-up activation from subcortical structures involved in emotional control that are unchecked by top-down cognitive processes from the frontal cortex. In other words, a heightened emotional response cannot be regulated. Research that integrates knowledge across various levels of analysis is helping to move the field not only toward a better understanding of etiology, but also toward a better understanding of treatment options.

87.1.4 How Do Socio-Cultural Theorists Explain Depression?

Socio-cultural theorists propose that social forces play an important role in the development of major depressive disorder. Their belief is supported by the finding, discussed earlier, that depression is often triggered by outside stressors. In addition, the unavailability of social support seems to play a significant role in the onset of depression. People who are separated or divorced display three times the depression rate of married or widowed persons, and double the rate of people who have never been married (Brown, 2010; Doss et al., 2008).

Individuals whose lives are isolated and without intimacy are particularly prone to becoming depressed during times of stress (Brown, 2010; Kendler et al., 2005). Studies conducted in England several decades ago showed that women who had three or more young children, lacked a close confidante, and had no outside employment were more likely than other women to become depressed after experiencing stressful life events (Brown, 2010; Brown et al., 2005). Studies have also found that depressed

Colin McConnell/Toronto Star via Getty Images

Bipolar disorder. Margaret Trudeau, ex-wife of former prime minister Pierre Trudeau and mother of Liberal leader Justin Trudeau, has spoken openly about her struggle with bipolar disorder and has written a book about her experiences called *Changing My Mind.* She is a fierce advocate for mental health in Canada and is engaged in fighting the stigma of mental illness.

George Frederic Handel wrote his Messiah in less than a month during a manic episode.

people who lack social support remain depressed longer than those who have a supportive spouse or warm friendships (Rao et al., 2010; Cowan et al., 2007).

87.2 Bipolar Disorder

People with a *bipolar disorder* often describe their lives as an emotional roller coaster. They shift back and forth between extreme moods, experiencing both the lows of depression and the highs of mania. Unlike people sunk in the gloom of depression, those in a state of *mania* experience dramatic and inappropriate elevation in mood. The symptoms of mania span the same areas of functioning—emotional, motivational, behavioural, cognitive, and physical—as those of depression, but mania affects these areas in an opposite way.

In mania, people have active, powerful emotions in search of an outlet. Their mood of euphoric joy or extreme agitation is out of all proportion to the actual events in the person's life. In the motivational realm, people with mania want constant excitement, involvement, and companionship. Correspondingly, they move quickly and talk rapidly and loudly. In the cognitive realm, individuals with mania usually show poor judgment and planning. Filled with optimism, they rarely listen when others try to slow them down, interrupt their buying sprees, or prevent them from investing money unwisely. They often hold an inflated opinion of themselves, and sometimes their self-esteem approaches grandiosity (for example, an exaggerated belief in their personal importance). Finally, in the physical realm, the individuals feel remarkably energetic. They typically get little sleep, yet feel and act wide awake (Anderson et al., 2012).

Surveys from around the world indicate that between 1 and 2.6 percent of all adults suffer from a bipolar disorder at any given time (Merikangas et al., 2007). According to the Canadian Mental Health Association (2014b), 1 percent of Canadians suffer from bipolar disorder. Nonetheless, bipolar is considered to be one of the most debilitating disorders globally (Magalhaes et al., 2012). According to most studies, bipolar disorders are equally common in women and men and among all socio-economic classes and ethnic groups (Anderson et al., 2012).

Throughout the first half of the twentieth century, the search for the causes of bipolar disorders made little progress. More recently, neuroscience research has produced some promising clues. There is now strong evidence that a combination of gene abnormalities plays a major role in the development of bipolar disorders (Grieco & Edwards, 2010; Schulze & McMahon, 2009). Familial, twin, and adoption studies indicate that bipolar disorder is highly heritable (heritability range: 0.85–0.89) (McGuffin et al., 2003). There is also evidence that bipolar disorder may be linked to ion dysregulation and reduced sodium pump activity (Herman et al., 2007; El-Mallakh & Huff, 2001).

The diathesis-stress model may partially account for the development of bipolar disorder. Although genes and biological factors appear to play key roles, there is growing evidence that stress and certain kinds of environmental events also must occur in order for episodes of bipolar disorder to unfold. Some studies suggest, for example, that major stress must combine with an individual's genetic predisposition for episodes of bipolar disorder to occur, particularly in early episodes (Brietzke et al., 2012; Horesch et al., 2012; Post & Miklowitz, 2010). Still other studies suggest that certain kinds of positive events (ones involving the attainment of or striving toward goals) are needed for bipolar disorders to unfold in biologically predisposed people. The idea is that individuals predisposed to develop bipolar disorder overreact to the arousal produced by goal-related events and develop the mania-related symptoms of bipolar disorder (Alloy et al., 2011; Bender & Alloy, 2011; Alloy & Abramson, 2010).

Before You Go On

What Do You Know?

1. What is learned helplessness, and what is its role in depression?
2. What is the cognitive triad?
3. How does bipolar disorder differ from major depression?

What Do You Think? Which of the explanations described in this module do you think best explains depression? Why?

Summary

Module 87: Mood Disorders

LEARNING OBJECTIVE 87 Describe and differentiate major depressive disorder and bipolar disorder.

- The key features in mood disorders are *depression*—a low, sad state—and *mania*—a state of breathless euphoria. Most people with a mood disorder suffer only from depression.
- People with *major depressive disorder* suffer a variety of symptoms, including feelings of sadness and lack of interest, low levels of activity and productivity, negative views of themselves and their lives, and physical ailments.
- Today's leading explanations for major depressive disorder point to neuroscientific, psychological, or socio-cultural factors. Many theorists believe that the various explanations should be combined.
- People with *bipolar disorder* experience not only the lows of depression, but also the highs of mania. In the manic state, they want constant excitement. They tend to show poor judgment and planning, hold inflated opinions of themselves, and show a great deal of energy.
- Although genes and biological factors appear to play key roles in the development of bipolar disorder, there is growing evidence that stress and certain kinds of environmental events also must occur in order for episodes to unfold.

Key Terms

automatic thoughts 671

bipolar disorder 666

cognitive triad 671

depression 666

major depressive disorder 666

mania 666

Study Questions

Multiple Choice

1. Beck's cognitive triad includes negative thoughts about all of the following except
   a) one's experience.
   b) oneself.
   c) others.
   d) the future.

2. People with major depressive disorder often have low levels of the neurotransmitters

a) acetylcholine and dopamine.
b) dopamine and serotonin.
c) GABA and acetylcholine.
d) norepinephrine and serotonin.

Fill-in-the-Blank

1. Dysthymic disorder is to major depressive disorder as _____ disorder is to bipolar disorder.

Module 88: Anxiety Disorders

LEARNING OBJECTIVE 88
Describe the various types of anxiety disorders, and explain some causes of these disorders.

Read through the following example of a conversation between a patient named Bob and his doctor, paying particular attention to what Bob says about his feeling of anxiety.

Bob: *It's been an awful month. I can't seem to do anything. I don't know whether I'm coming or going. I'm afraid I'm going crazy or something.*

Doctor: *What makes you think that?*

Bob: *I can't concentrate. My boss tells me to do something and I start to do it, but before I've taken five steps I don't know what I started out to do. I get dizzy and I can feel my heart beating and everything looks like it's shimmering or far away from me or something—it's unbelievable.*

Doctor: *What thoughts come to mind when you're feeling like this?*

Bob: *I just think, "Oh, Christ, my heart is really beating, my head is swimming, my ears are ringing—I'm either going to die or go crazy."*

Doctor: *What happens then?*

Bob: *Well, it doesn't last more than a few seconds, I mean that intense feeling. I come back down to earth, but then I'm worrying what's the matter with me all the time, or checking my pulse to see how fast it's going, or feeling my palms to see if they're sweating.*

Doctor: *Can others see what you're going through?*

Bob: *You know, I doubt it. I hide it. I haven't been seeing my friends. You know, they say "Let's stop for a beer" or something after work and I give them some excuse—you know, like I have to do something around the house or with my car. I'm not with them when I'm with them anyway—I'm just sitting there worrying. My friend Pat said I was frowning all the time. So, anyway, I just go home and turn on the TV or pick up the sports page, but I can't really get into that either.*

Some people suffer such disabling levels of fear and anxiety that they cannot lead a normal life. Their discomfort is too severe or too frequent; it lasts too long; or it is triggered too easily. These people are said to have an *anxiety disorder*. Anxiety disorders are collectively the most common mental disorders in Canada. In any given year, about 12 percent of the adult population suffers from one or another of the anxiety disorders identified by DSM-5 (Health Canada, 2002; Daitch, 2011; Kessler et al., 2012).

There are several kinds of anxiety disorders. Individuals with *generalized anxiety disorder* experience persistent feelings of worry and anxiety. People with *social anxiety disorder* display persistent fears of social or performance situations. People with *phobias* have a persistent and irrational fear of a specific object, activity, or situation. Individuals with *panic disorder* have recurrent attacks of terror. Those with *obsessive-compulsive disorder* feel overrun by recurrent thoughts that cause anxiety or by the need to perform repetitive actions to reduce anxiety. And those with *post-traumatic stress disorder (PTSD)* are tormented by overwhelming intrusive fears about the horrors associated with the traumatizing event—even when the event is long over and they are otherwise safe and well.

Most individuals with one anxiety disorder suffer from a second one as well (Beesdo et al., 2010). In the above example, Bob experiences the excessive worry found in generalized anxiety disorder, as well as the repeated attacks of terror that mark panic disorder.

Thinkstock/Getty Images

Feeling anxious. Anxiety is a normal part of life—everyone feels anxious sometimes. Anxiety becomes a problem when it interferes with a person's ability to participate fully in society.

Studies find that participants with generally high levels of anxiety are more likely than calmer participants to notice and remember pictures of threatening faces. Attention to happy or neutral faces is about the same in both groups.

88.1 Generalized Anxiety Disorder

People with **generalized anxiety disorder** *(GAD)* experience excessive anxiety accompanied by at least three of the following symptoms: restlessness, keyed-up behaviour, fatigue, difficulty concentrating, muscle tension, and sleep problems. These symptoms vary widely from one person to another (see **Figure 88-1**). The incessant worrying causes self-doubt, and the simplest decision represents a risky outcome; for example, worrying about whether to make spaghetti or veggie burgers for dinner.

generalized anxiety disorder (GAD) an anxiety disorder in which people feel excessive anxiety and worry under most circumstances.

Surveys suggest that as many as 4 percent of the North American population have symptoms of GAD in any given year (Kessler et al., 2010, 2005; Ritter, Blackmore, & Heimberg, 2010). Women diagnosed with the disorder outnumber men by 2 to 1. The leading explanations of generalized anxiety disorder come from the cognitive and neuroscience models.

88.1.1 How Do Cognitive Theorists Explain Generalized Anxiety Disorder?

As with depression, cognitive theorists suggest that generalized anxiety disorder is caused in part by *dysfunctional assumptions*. Aaron Beck argues that people with GAD constantly hold silent assumptions that imply they are in imminent danger—for example, "A situation or a person is unsafe until proven to be safe" or "It is always best to assume the worst" (Beck & Weishaar, 2011; Beck & Emery, 1985). Similarly, Albert Ellis (2011, 2002, 1962) claimed that people who are generally anxious hold the following "irrational" assumptions in particular:

- "It is a dire necessity for an adult human being to be loved or approved of by virtually every significant other person in his community."
- "It is awful and catastrophic when things are not the way one would very much like them to be."
- "If something is or may be dangerous or fearsome, one should be terribly concerned about it and should keep dwelling on the possibility of its occurring."
- "One should be thoroughly competent, adequate, and achieving in all possible respects if one is to consider oneself worthwhile."

(Ellis, 1962)

In recent years, some additional cognitive explanations for GAD have emerged. Sometimes called *new wave cognitive explanations*, each of these explanations builds on the notions of Ellis and Beck and their emphasis on perceived danger (Ritter et al., 2010). According to one such explanation, the *intolerance of uncertainty theory*, certain

24% worry less than a minute

38% worry 1–10 minutes

18% worry 10–60 minutes

11% worry 1–2 hours

9% worry 2 hours or more

Time devoted to worrying

FIGURE 88-1 **Some people worry more than others.** In one survey, 24 percent of post-secondary students said they spend less than 1 minute at a time worrying about something. In contrast, 9 percent worry for more than 2 hours.

Source: Adapted from Tallis, F., Davey, G., & Capuzzo, N. (1994). The phenomenology of non-pathological worry: A preliminary investigation. In G. Davey & F. Tallis (Eds.), Worrying: Perspectives on theory, assessment and treatment (pp. 61–89). Chichester, UK: John Wiley & Sons.

individuals consider it unacceptable that negative events may occur, even if the possibility of occurrence is very small. Given that life is filled with uncertain events, such individuals may come up against several "unacceptable" events each day. Worrying constantly that unacceptable events are on the verge of happening, the individuals are particularly vulnerable to the development of generalized anxiety disorder (Dugas et al., 2004).

According to this theory, people with GAD keep worrying in an effort to find "correct" solutions to situations at hand, expecting that correct solutions will restore certainty to the situations. However, because they can never really be sure that a given solution is a correct one, they are always left to grapple with intolerable levels of uncertainty, triggering new rounds of worrying and new efforts to find correct solutions.

In support of this theory, studies have found that people with GAD display greater levels of intolerance of uncertainty than people with normal degrees of anxiety (Daitch, 2011; Dugas et al., 2009, 2005, 2002). At the same time, however, recent research indicates that people with other kinds of anxiety disorders may also display high levels of intolerance of uncertainty (Nelson & Shankman, 2011).

88.1.2 How Do Neuroscientists Explain Generalized Anxiety Disorder?

WHAT HAPPENS *in the* BRAIN?

One biological explanation of generalized anxiety disorder focuses on neurotransmitter imbalances. In normal fear reactions, key neurons throughout the brain fire more rapidly, triggering the firing of still more neurons and creating a general state of excitability throughout the brain and body. This state is experienced as fear or anxiety. After neuron firing continues for a while, it apparently triggers a *feedback system*—that is, brain and body activities that reduce the level of excitability. Some neurons throughout the brain release the neurotransmitter *gamma-aminobutyric acid (GABA)*, which then binds to GABA receptors on certain neurons. GABA carries inhibitory messages. That is, when GABA is received at a neuron's receptor, it instructs those neurons to stop firing. The state of excitability is thereby halted, and the experience of fear or anxiety subsides (Atack, 2010).

Some neuroscientists now believe that a malfunction in this feedback system may cause fear or anxiety to go unchecked (Bremner & Charney, 2010; Roy-Byrne, 2005). In fact, when some investigators have reduced GABA's ability to bind to GABA receptors, they have found that animal subjects react with heightened anxiety (Lehner et al., 2010). This finding suggests that people with generalized anxiety disorder may have ongoing problems in their anxiety feedback system. Perhaps they have too few GABA receptors, or their GABA receptors do not properly capture the neurotransmitter (Lydiard, 2003). Benzodiazepines—a class of drugs that reduce anxiety (and will be discussed in greater detail in Part 16)—exert their effect by stimulating GABA.

Recent research further clarifies that the root of generalized anxiety disorder is probably more complicated than GABA alone. Other neurotransmitters, such as acetylcholine and serotonin, may also play important roles in GAD as well (Martin & Nemeroff, 2010). Moreover, emotional reactions of various kinds are tied to brain *circuits*—networks of brain structures that work together, triggering each other into action with the help of neurotransmitters and producing particular kinds of emotional reactions. It turns out that the circuit that produces anxiety reactions includes the *prefrontal cortex, anterior cingulate,* and *amygdala*. According to several studies, this circuit may function improperly in people with GAD (Schienle et al., 2011; McClure et al., 2007).

88.2 Social Anxiety Disorder

Many people worry about interacting with others or talking or performing in front of others. A number of entertainers, from singer Barbra Streisand to actor Anthony Hopkins, have described major bouts of anxiety before performing. Social fears of this kind are unpleasant and inconvenient, but usually the people who have them manage to function adequately, some at a very high level.

People with a **social anxiety disorder**, by contrast, have severe, persistent, and irrational fears of social or performance situations in which embarrassment may occur. The social anxiety may be *narrow*, such as a fear of talking in public or writing in front of others, or it may be *broad*, such as a general fear of functioning poorly in front of others. In both forms, people repeatedly judge themselves as performing less adequately than they actually do.

A social phobia can interfere greatly with one's life (Ravindran & Stein, 2011). A person who is unable to interact with others or speak in public may fail to perform important responsibilities. One who cannot eat in public may reject dinner invitations or other social opportunities. Since most people with this phobia keep their fears secret, their social reluctance is often misinterpreted as snobbery, lack of interest, or hostility.

Surveys indicate that at least 7.1 percent of people in Western countries—around three women for every two men—experience social anxiety disorder in any given year. Around 12 percent develop this problem at some point in their lives (Alfano & Beidel, 2011; Kessler et al., 2010). It often begins in late childhood or adolescence, and may continue into adulthood. Research finds that people living in poverty are 50 percent more likely than wealthier people to display a social phobia (Sareen et al., 2011). Moreover, in several studies, minority group participants scored higher than non-minority group participants on surveys of social anxiety (Stein & Williams, 2010; Schultz et al., 2008, 2006).

Lynn Alden and her colleagues at the University of British Columbia explain social anxiety as failure to meet self-determined extreme perfectionistic standards, while simultaneously viewing one's self-efficacy as too low to achieve identified standards in order to meet these high expectations (Alden et al., 2002). Similarly, Paul Hewitt from the University of British Columbia and Gordon Flett from York University and their colleagues report that socially anxious people tend to be high in perfectionistic self-presentation and cannot allow themselves to make any errors in public (Flett & Hewitt, in press; Hewitt et al., 2003).

The most influential explanations for social anxiety disorder have come from cognitive-behavioural theorists (Heimberg, Brozovich, & Rapee, 2010; Hofmann, 2007). They hold that, like people with generalized anxiety disorder, individuals with this disorder have dysfunctional cognitions that help produce and maintain their symptoms. In the case of social anxiety disorder, those cognitions all centre on the social arena. According to the cognitive-behavioural explanations, people with this disorder hold a cluster of social beliefs and expectations that work against them. These include the following (Hope et al., 2010; Koopmans et al., 1994):

- They hold unrealistically high social standards and so believe that they must perform perfectly in social situations. Given such standards, they cannot develop social goals that are reasonable and achievable.
- They view themselves as unattractive social objects.
- They view themselves as socially unskilled and inadequate.
- They believe that they are in danger of behaving incompetently in social situations.
- They believe that clumsy or inept behaviours in social situations will always lead to terrible consequences.
- They believe that they have no control over feelings of anxiety that emerge during social situations.

Cognitive-behavioural theorists contend that, as a result of this cluster of dysfunctional notions, individuals with social anxiety disorder anticipate that social disasters will occur, and so repeatedly perform "avoidance" and "safety" behaviours to help prevent or minimize such disasters (Rosenberg, Ledley, & Heimberg, 2010). Avoidance behaviours include, for example,

social anxiety disorder an anxiety disorder in which people feel severe, persistent, and irrational fears of social or performance situations in which embarrassment may occur.

Image Source/Corbis

Public performances. Most people do not enjoy standing up and presenting in front of a class or group of people. People with social anxiety disorder have particularly intense and irrational fears of not only talking or performing in front of others, but even of just being in regular social situations.

Although the poet Emily Dickinson wrote movingly about love, she was not able to interact comfortably with people. She became so reclusive that she sometimes spoke to her visitors from an adjoining room rather than talking to them face to face.

talking only to familiar persons at meetings or parties. Safety behaviours include holding on to a podium during a classroom presentation so that their hands don't tremble, or wearing makeup to cover blushing. Finally, after a social event has occurred, the individuals keep going over the details of the events in their mind. They overestimate how badly things went and what negative repercussions may unfold. These ruminations serve to keep the events alive, and also feed into the individuals' fears about future social situations (Hope et al., 2010; Rosenberg et al., 2010; Moscovitch, 2009; Hofmann, 2007).

Why do some individuals, and not others, have such dysfunctional cognitions? Researchers have identified a number of factors. These include genetic predispositions, trait tendencies, biological abnormalities, traumatic childhood experiences, and past parent–child interactions (Brozovich & Heimberg, 2011; Kuo et al., 2011; Ledley, Erwin, & Heimberg, 2008).

88.3 Phobias

phobia a persistent and unreasonable fear of a particular object, activity, or situation.

As you saw in Part 7, a **phobia** (from the Greek for "fear") is a persistent and unreasonable fear of a particular object, activity, or situation. Most phobias fall under the category *specific phobia*, an intense fear of a specific object or situation. There are five categories of specific phobia: (1) animals (dogs, cats, snakes, spiders); (2) natural environments (heights, dark, thunder); (3) situations (enclosed spaces, bridges); (4) blood and injections; and (5) other (choking, vomiting, loud noises, clowns). People can form a phobia to almost anything (red hair or bald men), but some phobias are more common than others, as shown in the box "10 Most Common Phobias." Surveys suggest that 7.7 percent of people in Canada suffer from at least one specific phobia in any given year (Kessler et al., 2010, 2009).

Fear of an animal is the most common specific phobia among women. Fear of heights is the most common specific phobia among men.

Behavioural principles provide the leading explanations for specific phobias (Gamble et al., 2010). According to behaviourists, *classical conditioning* is one way of acquiring fear reactions to objects or situations that are not really dangerous. Let's say, for example, that a frightening event, such as a lightning strike (*unconditioned stimulus*) naturally elicits a reaction of

Psychology Around Us **10 Most Common Phobias**

© Pierre Perrin/Zoko/Sygma/Corbis

spiders—arachnophobia
heights—acrophobia
public, social places—agoraphobia
social situations—social phobia
flying—aerophobia
enclosed spaces—claustrophobia
thunder—brontophobia
germs—mysophobia
cancer—carcinophobia
death—necrophobia

Sources: Van Wagner, 2007; Melville, 1978

fear (*unconditioned response*) in an individual. In such a situation, it is possible that a harmless object, such as raindrops (*conditioned stimulus*)—an object that had simply accompanied the frightening event—will come to also elicit a fear reaction (*conditioned response*) in the person. A dated but useful learning theory of phobias is Mowrer's (1950) two-factor theory of phobia learning, which suggests that the fears associated with phobic objects are learned through classical conditioning, while the avoidance behaviours associated with phobias are reinforced through operant conditioning. So, for example, a person might develop a social phobia as a result of a panic attack in a crowd (classical conditioning), and then stop going out to avoid crowds (operant conditioning).

According to behaviourists, another way of acquiring a fear reaction is through *modelling*—that is, through observation and imitation (Bandura & Rosenthal, 1966). A person may observe that others are afraid of certain objects or events and develop fears of those objects or events as well. Consider a young boy whose mother is afraid of illnesses, doctors, and hospitals. If she frequently expresses those fears, before long the boy himself may fear illnesses, doctors, and hospitals. Research has supported the theory that fears can be acquired through classical conditioning or modelling (Wilson, 2011).

88.4 Panic Disorder

Sometimes an anxiety reaction takes the form of an all-consuming, nightmarish panic. Everyone reacts with panic when a real threat occurs and they feel endangered. Some people, however, experience **panic attacks**—periodic, discrete bouts of panic or terror—in the absence of any real threat. These attacks occur suddenly, as a wave of intense fear, reach a peak within 10 minutes, and gradually pass. Individuals who experience unexpected, repeated panic attacks suffer from **panic disorder**. People who experience these attacks report that they believe they are having a heart attack or losing their mind. Panic disorder is often accompanied by **agoraphobia**, a fear of venturing into public places, especially when alone. Because of their panic attack history, some sufferers of panic disorder develop a fear of travelling to any location where escape might be difficult or help unavailable should panic symptoms develop.

Around 21 percent of people in Canada over 15 years of age have suffered from a panic attack at some point in their lives (Ramage-Morin, 2004). The rate is highest (11.8 percent) among 15- to 24-year-olds, and lowest (4.2 percent) among those over 55 years of age. Women are 1.65 times more likely than men to have experienced a panic attack in the past year (Ramage-Morin, 2004; Kessler et al., 2010, 2009, 2005).

As mentioned, neuroscientists have determined that emotional reactions are tied to brain circuits. Panic attacks appear to be produced in part by a brain circuit in the *amygdala*, *hypothalamus*, and *locus ceruleus* (Dresler et al., 2011; Elkin, 2010). Many of today's researchers believe that this brain circuit—including *norepinephrine* and other neurotransmitters—probably functions improperly, producing an excess amount of norepinephrine in people who experience panic disorder (Bremner & Charney, 2010; Burijon, 2007).

According to cognitive theorists, not only are these individuals hypersensitive to changes in arousal, but once they experience particular bodily sensations, they tend to misinterpret the sensations as signs of a medical catastrophe and fear that the symptoms are signalling that something dire is about to occur (Reinecke et al., 2011; Wenzel, 2011; Clark & Beck, 2010; Olatunji et al., 2009). As a result, affected individuals become hypervigilant, fearing the signals that indicate another attack, ceaselessly monitoring for them, and in so doing increase the likelihood they will experience another.

panic attacks periodic, short bouts of panic.

panic disorder an anxiety disorder characterized by recurrent and unpredictable panic attacks that occur without apparent provocation.

agoraphobia a phobia that makes people avoid public places or situations in which escape might be difficult or help unavailable should panic symptoms develop.

> *According to a Greek myth, Pan, the cloven-hoofed god of pastures, flocks, and shepherds, used to take naps in caves or thickets along country roads. When travellers disturbed the foul-looking god, he would let out a horrific scream. The god's appearance and scream terrified the travellers—a reaction henceforth known as panic.*

Infinityphoto/Dreamstime/GetStock

Panic attack. Many people experience difficulty "catching their breath" during a panic attack, which can lead to hyperventilation.

88.5 Obsessive-Compulsive Disorder

obsessions persistent thoughts, ideas, impulses, or images that seem to invade a person's consciousness.

compulsions irrational repetitive and rigid behaviours or mental acts that people feel compelled to perform to prevent or reduce anxiety.

obsessive-compulsive disorder (OCD) a mental disorder associated with repeated, abnormal, anxiety-provoking thoughts and/or repeated rigid behaviours.

Obsessions are persistent thoughts, ideas, impulses, or images that seem to overrun a person's consciousness. **Compulsions** are repetitive and rigid behaviours or mental acts that people feel compelled to perform to prevent or reduce anxiety. A diagnosis of **obsessive-compulsive disorder (OCD)** is made when obsessions or compulsions are severe, are viewed by the person as excessive, unreasonable, or irrational, cause great distress, consume considerable time, or interfere with daily functions.

Compulsive acts are typically responses to ward off obsessive thoughts. One study found that in most cases of OCD, compulsions represent a *yielding* to obsessive doubts, ideas, or urges. For example, a woman who has obsessive fears of contamination may yield to that fear by performing cleaning rituals. The study also found that compulsions sometimes serve to *control* obsessions. A man with obsessive images of sexual events, for example, may try to control those images by filling his mind with compulsive verbal rituals, such as repeated expressions, phrases, or chants. In all such instances, the performance of the compulsive acts reduces the anxiety produced by obsessive thoughts.

Two percent of people in Canada suffer from obsessive-compulsive disorder in a given year (Björgvinsson & Hart, 2008; Health Canada, 2002). The disorder is equally common in men and women and among people of different races and ethnic groups (Kessler et al., 2010).

Obsessions often take the form of obsessive *wishes* (for example, repeated wishes that one's spouse would die), *impulses* (repeated urges to yell out obscenities at work or at a place of worship), *images* (fleeting visions of forbidden sexual scenes), or *doubts* (concerns that one has made or will make a wrong decision). Like obsessions, compulsions take various forms but serve to reduce the anxiety brought about by the obsession. For example, *cleaning compulsions* are very common. People with these compulsions feel compelled to keep cleaning themselves, their clothing, or their homes. The cleaning may follow ritualistic rules and be repeated dozens or hundreds of times a day, making it almost impossible to have a normal life.

Paul Lapid/The Canadian Press

Obsessive-compulsive disorder. Canadian comedian, game-show host, and author of the book *Don't Touch Me*, Howie Mandel has OCD and an irrational fear of germs (*mysophobia*). He will not shake hands with anyone (including contestants on the game show he used to host, *Deal or No Deal*) because of his fear of contamination.

The experiments that led Louis Pasteur to the pasteurization process may have been driven in part by his obsession with contamination and infection. Apparently he would not shake hands, and regularly wiped his glass and plate before dining.

88.5.1 How Do Cognitive-Behavioural Theorists Explain Obsessive-Compulsive Disorder?

According to one cognitive-behavioural theory, people stumble upon their compulsions by chance. In a fearful situation, they happen just coincidentally to wash their hands, say, or dress a certain way. When the threat lifts, they link the improvement to that particular action. After repeated accidental associations, they believe that the action is bringing them good luck or actually changing the situation. As a result, they perform the same action again and again in similar situations. The act becomes a way to avoid or reduce anxiety (Frost & Steketee, 2001).

Another cognitive-behavioural theory focuses on the relationship between obsessions and compulsions and suggests that people learn to perform compulsive acts specifically because such acts reduce the anxiety aroused by their obsessions. According to this theory, some people are generally more inclined than others to experience repetitive, unwanted, and intrusive thoughts, to blame themselves for such thoughts, and to expect that the thoughts can somehow cause terrible things to happen (Clark & Beck, 2010). To avoid such negative outcomes, they learn to "neutralize" the thoughts—behave in ways meant to put matters right, make amends, and reduce their anxiety.

In support of this cognitive-behavioural explanation, studies have found that people diagnosed with obsessive-compulsive disorder do indeed experience intrusive thoughts more often than other people, resort to more neutralizing strategies, and experience reductions in anxiety after using neutralizing techniques

(Shafran, 2005; Salkovskis et al., 2003). But why do certain people experience more intrusive thoughts in the first place?

88.5.2 How Do Neuroscientists Explain Obsessive-Compulsive Disorder?

The biological explanation of this disorder features two lines of brain research. One points to abnormally low activity of the neurotransmitter serotonin, and the other to abnormal activity in key brain structures.

WHAT HAPPENS
in the BRAIN?

Some antidepressant drugs help reduce obsessive and compulsive symptoms. Since these drugs also increase serotonin activity, some researchers have concluded that the disorder may be caused by low serotonin activity (Abudy et al., 2012; Spooren et al., 2010; Stein & Fineberg, 2007). In another line of research, investigators found a link between obsessive-compulsive disorder and abnormal functioning in specific regions of the brain. Particularly important are the *orbitofrontal cortex*, a region in the prefrontal cortex, and the *caudate nuclei*, structures located within the basal ganglia. These regions are part of a brain circuit that usually converts sensory information into thoughts and actions (Craig & Chamberlain, 2010). Based on a variety of studies, many neuroscientists have come to believe that one or both of these brain regions are somewhat overactive in certain people, leading to a constant eruption of troublesome thoughts and actions (Endrass et al., 2011).

Additional parts of this brain circuit have been identified in recent years, including the *thalamus*, the *cingulate cortex*, the *striatum's caudate nucleus* and, once again, the *amygdala*. It may be that these regions also play key roles in OCD. The serotonin and brain region abnormalities may be linked. It turns out that serotonin plays a very active role in the operation of the orbitofrontal cortex, caudate nuclei, and other structures in the brain circuit. Thus, low serotonin activity might well disrupt the proper functioning of those brain structures. The hypothesis is that the cingulated cortex and hypothalamus activate the OCD impulses that are inhibited though the caudate nucleus, while the amygdala drives the fear and anxiety components of the OCD response (Shah et al., 2008).

88.6 Post-traumatic Stress Disorder (PTSD)

Stress reactions, and the sense of fear they produce, are often at play in psychological disorders. As you have seen, for example, people who experience a large number of stressful events are particularly vulnerable to the onset of depression. In addition, stress plays a more central role in *acute stress disorder* and *post-traumatic stress disorder* (PTSD).

88.6.1 Symptoms of Acute Stress Disorder and Post-traumatic Stress Disorder

Part 14 described the roles of the *autonomic nervous system (ANS)* and the *hypothalamic-pituitary-adrenal (HPA)* axis during everyday stress reactions. If people experience a threatening situation where they witness a death or there is the threat of death or injury or sexual violence, they experience levels of arousal, anxiety, and depression that are far beyond those experienced with everyday stress reactions. For example, Canadian soldiers who served in Afghanistan and residents of Slave Lake, Alberta, who had to flee from a wildfire that destroyed a substantial portion of their town, are all candidates for PTSD.

For most people, the panic reactions subside soon after the danger passes. But for others, the feelings of anxiety and depression, as well as other symptoms, persist well after the overwhelmingly distressful situation is over. These people are suffering from *acute stress disorder* or *post-traumatic stress disorder*, patterns that arise in reaction to a psychologically traumatic event with life-threatening implications, such as witnessing a murder, combat, rape, earthquake, airplane crash, or traffic accident.

If the lingering stress symptoms begin within four weeks of the traumatic event and last for less than a month, a diagnosis of **acute stress disorder** is made (APA, 2013). If the symptoms continue longer than a month, a diagnosis of **post-traumatic stress disorder (PTSD)** is

acute stress disorder an anxiety disorder in which fear and related symptoms are experienced soon after a traumatic event and last less than a month.

post-traumatic stress disorder (PTSD) an anxiety disorder in which fear and related symptoms continue to be experienced long after a traumatic event.

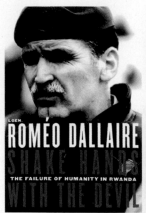

Reprinted by permission of Penguin Random House Canada; Todd Korol/Reuters/Landov

Many events can produce PTSD. Roméo Dallaire wrote about his experiences as Canada's highest ranking officer in Rwanda in his book *Shake Hands with the Devil: The Failure of Humanity in Rwanda* (left). Dallaire, a retired Canadian senator, is working to raise awareness of the atrocities of war and of PTSD. When wildfires engulfed Slave Lake, Alberta, in May 2011 (right), residents had to flee with little or no notice. Many lost their homes and all belongings in the fires. Local service providers are aware of the possibility of PTSD arising as people return to their homes and lives.

given. The symptoms of PTSD may begin either shortly after the traumatic event or months or even years afterward (Frueh, 2009). Studies indicate that as many as 80 percent of all cases of acute stress disorder develop into PTSD (Burijon, 2007). Aside from the differences in onset and duration, the symptoms of acute stress disorder and PTSD are almost identical. The individuals experience high levels of ongoing anxiety and depression. They may feel overly alert (hyper alertness), be easily startled, have trouble concentrating, and develop sleep problems (Ruzek et al., 2011; Breslau et al., 2005). They may also feel extreme guilt because they survived the traumatic event while others did not.

In addition, people with stress disorders may be besieged by recurring thoughts, memories, dreams, or nightmares connected to the traumatic event (Geraerts, 2010). They typically avoid all activities that remind them of the event and try to ignore related thoughts, feelings, or conversations. Affected individuals often also feel detached from other people or lose interest in activities that once brought enjoyment. They may feel dazed and have trouble remembering things (Marx & Sloan, 2005).

Michael Anton Van Ameringen, at McMaster University, and his colleagues conducted an incidence study looking at stress disorders in Canada. They found a lifetime PTSD prevalence of 9.2 percent in their Canadian sample, as well as a current (at the time of the survey) incidence of 2.4 percent (Peterlin et al., 2011; Taylor, 2010; Kessler et al., 2009; Van Ameringen et al., 2008). Women are at least twice as likely as men to develop stress disorders: around 20 percent of women who are exposed to a serious trauma may develop one, compared to 8 percent of men (Koch & Haring, 2008).

88.6.2 What Causes a Stress Disorder?

Clearly, extraordinary trauma can cause a stress disorder. The stressful event, however, is not the entire explanation. Certainly, anyone who experiences an unusual trauma will be affected by it, but only some people develop acute stress disorder or post-traumatic stress. To more fully explain the onset of these disorders, researchers point to individuals' biological processes, personalities, childhood experiences, social support systems, and cultural backgrounds.

- *Biological and Genetic Factors* Investigators have learned that traumatic events often trigger physical changes in the brain and body that may lead to severe stress reactions and, in some cases, to stress disorders. They have found, for example, abnormal activity of the hormone *cortisol* and the neurotransmitter *norepinephrine* in the urine, blood, and saliva of combat soldiers, rape victims, concentration camp survivors, and survivors of other severe stresses (Gerardi et al., 2010; Delahanty et al., 2005).

- Evidence from brain studies also shows that once a stress disorder begins, individuals experience further biochemical arousal, and this continuing arousal may eventually damage key brain areas, particularly the hippocampus and the *amygdala* (Bremner & Charney, 2010; Yehuda et al., 2010).

Psychology Around Us   Canadian Military and PTSD

In March 2001, in what may have been a suicide attempt, Corporal Christian McEachern drove his SUV directly into the headquarters building at CFB Edmonton. Corporal McEachern had served with Canada's peacekeeping forces in Croatia and Uganda and had been diagnosed with PTSD upon his return. He was eventually tried for this action and found guilty, but was given no jail time. His complaint about the lack of proper services for Canadian Forces personally struggling with PTSD was investigated by Canada's parliamentary ombudsman. The ombudsman found many cases of PTSD among Canada's military personal were going unidentified and untreated (Marin, 2001). A follow-up report in 2008 found that 18 of the 31 recommendations in the original report had not yet been implemented (McFadyen, 2008). There are simply not enough treatment providers to meet the needs of veterans who struggle with PTSD in Canada (Brewster, 2012).

- *Personality* Some studies suggest that people with certain personalities, attitudes, and coping styles are particularly likely to develop stress disorders (Burijon, 2007). Research has also found that people who generally view life's negative events as beyond their control tend to develop more severe stress symptoms after sexual or other criminal assaults than people who feel greater control over their lives (Taylor, 2006).

- *Childhood Experiences* Investigators have found that certain childhood experiences seem to leave some people at risk for later acute and post-traumatic stress disorders. People whose childhoods have been marked by poverty appear more likely to develop these disorders in the face of later trauma. So do people whose family members suffer from psychological disorders; who experienced assault, abuse, or catastrophe at an early age; or who were younger than 10 when their parents separated or divorced (Yehuda et al., 2010; Koch & Haring, 2008).

- *Social Support* It has been found that people whose social and family support systems are weak are also more likely to develop a stress disorder after a traumatic event. Rape victims who feel loved, cared for, valued, and accepted by their friends and relatives recover more successfully than do those without those supports (Uchino & Birmingham, 2011; Ozer, 2005). So do those treated with dignity and respect by the criminal justice system (Patterson, 2011).

Before You Go On

www.wiley.com/go/comercanada

What Do You Know?
1. What are six types of anxiety disorder?
2. How and why might generalized anxiety disorder be related to uncertainty?
3. What role do conditioning and modelling play in the development of phobias?
4. What individual factors affect who will develop post-traumatic stress disorder?

What Do You Think? The return home for many soldiers is often difficult. One of the problems they face is trying to find a way to talk about their experiences with friends and relatives; if you haven't experienced war, there's really no way to understand what soldiers go through. What sorts of things can we do to make the return home easier for Canadian soldiers?

Summary

Module 88: Anxiety Disorders

LEARNING OBJECTIVE 88 Describe the various types of anxiety disorders, and explain some causes of these disorders.

- As a group, anxiety disorders are the most common mental disorders in North America. Often, people with one type of anxiety disorder have another type as well.
- People with *generalized anxiety disorder* experience persistent feelings of worry and anxiety. Some cognitive theorists suggest that this disorder arises in people who hold certain dysfunctional or irrational assumptions, while others focus on the individual's intolerance of uncertainty. An important neuroscience explanation focuses on gamma-aminobutyric acid, a neurotransmitter involved in fear reactions.
- People with *social anxiety disorder* display severe, persistent, and irrational fears of social or performance situations. Some socio-cultural factors appear to be involved.
- People with *phobias* have a persistent and irrational fear of a specific object, activity, or situation. Behavioural principles, including classical conditioning and modelling, provide the leading explanations for specific phobias.
- People with *panic disorder* have recurrent attacks of terror. These *panic attacks* are sometimes accompanied by *agoraphobia*—a fear of venturing into public places. A neuroscience-cognitive explanation of the disorder focuses on physical sensations produced by malfunctioning brain circuitry, which are then misinterpreted.
- People with *obsessive-compulsive disorder* feel overrun by recurrent thoughts that cause anxiety (obsessions) and by the need to perform repetitive actions to reduce this anxiety (compulsions). While cognitive-behavioural theorists focus on the role of learning in these behaviours, neuroscientists focus on abnormally low levels of serotonin or abnormal functioning in specific brain regions.
- People with *post-traumatic stress disorder (PTSD)* are tormented by fear and related symptoms well after a horrifying event has ended. Although extraordinary trauma causes the disorder, not everyone who experiences such trauma develops PTSD. Differences in biological processes, personalities, childhood experiences, social support systems, and cultural backgrounds make people more or less likely to respond to trauma by developing the disorder.

Key Terms

acute stress disorder 681

agoraphobia 679

compulsions 680

generalized anxiety disorder (GAD) 675

obsessions 680

obsessive-compulsive disorder (OCD) 680

panic attacks 679

panic disorder 679

phobia 678

post-traumatic stress disorder (PTSD) 681

social anxiety disorder 677

Study Questions

Multiple Choice

1. The brain circuit that produces anxiety in a person includes all of the following brain structures except the
   a) amygdala.
   b) anterior cingulate.
   c) hippocampus.
   d) prefrontal cortex.

Fill-in-the-Blank

1. The most common category of psychological disturbance in Canada is _____ disorders.

2. Post-traumatic stress disorder and _____ disorder have similar symptoms, but those symptoms arise at different points after the traumatic event and linger for different amounts of time.

Module 89: Schizophrenia

Schizophrenia is a psychotic disorder in which people deteriorate into a world of distorted perceptions, disturbances in thoughts, emotions, behaviours, and experience motor abnormalities. People with this disorder experience **psychosis**, a loss of contact with reality. Their ability to perceive and respond to the environment becomes so disturbed that they may not be able to function at home, with friends, in school, or at work. They may have *hallucinations* (false sensory perceptions) or *delusions* (false beliefs), or they may withdraw into a private world. Psychosis is most commonly associated with schizophrenia, but a number of other disorders may feature psychotic symptoms, such as bipolar disorder or postpartum depression.

schizophrenia a mental disorder characterized by disorganized thoughts, lack of contact with reality, and sometimes hallucinations.

psychosis loss of contact with reality.

Approximately 1 of every 100 people in the world suffers from schizophrenia during his or her lifetime. Equal numbers of men and women receive this diagnosis (McGrath et al., 2008). Almost 3 percent of all those who are divorced or separated suffer from schizophrenia over the course of their lives, compared with 1 percent of married people and 2 percent of people who remain single (Miller & Mason, 2011).

According to the DSM-5, schizophrenia is diagnosed when a minimum of two symptoms appear continuously for one month and last for six months or more. The symptoms of schizophrenia can be grouped into three categories: *positive symptoms*, *negative symptoms*, and *cognitive symptoms*. *Psychomotor symptoms* are also often considered in diagnosis.

89.1 Positive Symptoms of Schizophrenia

Positive symptoms are "pathological excesses," or bizarre additions, to a person's behaviour and are not seen in people who do not have the disorder. *Delusions, disorganized thinking and speech, hallucinations,* and *inappropriate affect* are the ones most often found in schizophrenia.

Roy McMahon & Wieger Poutsma/Corbis

positive symptoms in the case of schizophrenia, symptoms that seem to represent pathological excesses in behaviour, including delusions, disorganized thinking and speech, hallucinations, and inappropriate affect.

Delusions are false beliefs that are resistant to reason or contradictory evidence, but are maintained in spite of their irrationality. *Delusions of persecution* are the most common delusions in schizophrenia (APA, 2013). People with this delusion believe they are being plotted or discriminated against, spied on, slandered, threatened, attacked, or deliberately victimized. Delusions of identity also occur; for example, the person with schizophrenia believes that he or she is Jesus Christ or Winston Churchill. People with *delusions of grandeur* often believe that they have some special talent or that they are privy

delusions blatantly false beliefs that are firmly held despite evidence to the contrary.

Psychology Around Us — Drifting into Psychosis

[Laura, a professional dancer, met her husband in Germany, and they later emigrated to the United States.] They had no children . . . [but Laura] had a dog to whom she was very devoted. The dog became sick and partially paralyzed, and veterinarians felt that there was no hope of recovery. . . . Finally [Laura's husband asked her,] "Are you going to decide to have your dog destroyed or not?" From that time on Laura became restless, agitated, and depressed. . . .

. . . Later Laura started to complain about the neighbors. A woman who lived on the floor beneath them was knocking on the wall to irritate her. According to the husband, this woman had really knocked on the wall a few times; he had heard the noises. However, Laura became more and more

concerned about it. . . . Later she . . . started to feel that the neighbors were now recording everything she said; maybe they had hidden wires in the apartment. She started to feel "funny" sensations. There were many strange things happening, which she did not know how to explain; people were looking at her in a funny way in the street. . . . She felt that people were planning to harm either her or her husband. . . . When she looked at television, it became obvious to her that the programs referred to her life. Often the people on the programs were just repeating what she had thought. They were stealing her ideas. She wanted to go to the police and report them.

(Arieti, 1974, pp. 165–168)

to secret knowledge (for example, they have the ability to fly or know that the United States is planning to infiltrate Canada).

People with schizophrenia may also exhibit *disorganized thinking and speech*. Many, for example, display **loose associations**, or **derailment**: they rapidly shift from one topic to another, believing that their incoherent statements make sense. One man with schizophrenia, asked about his itchy arms, responded:

> *The problem is insects. My brother used to collect insects. He's now a man 5 foot 10 inches. You know, 10 is my favourite number. I also like to dance, draw, and watch television.*

loose associations or **derailment** a common thought disorder of schizophrenia, characterized by rapid shifts from one topic to another.

Individuals with schizophrenia may also experience **hallucinations**, perceptions that occur in the absence of external stimuli. People who have *auditory hallucinations*, by far the most common kind in schizophrenia, hear sounds and voices that seem to come from outside their heads (APA, 2013).

Yet another positive symptom found in schizophrenia is *inappropriate affect*, emotions that are unsuited to the situation. The individuals may smile when making a serious statement or on being told terrible news, or they may become upset in situations that should make them happy. They may also undergo inappropriate shifts in mood.

hallucinations imagined sights, sounds, or other sensory events experienced as if they were real.

89.2 Negative Symptoms of Schizophrenia

Negative symptoms are those that seem to be "pathological deficits," characteristics that are lacking in an individual but that are seen in individuals without the disorder. *Poverty of speech, flat affect, loss of volition,* and *social withdrawal* are commonly found in schizophrenia.

Poverty of speech refers to a reduction in speech or speech content. Some people with this negative symptom think and say very little. Others say quite a bit but still manage to convey little meaning. In another negative symptom, *flat affect*, individuals show very little anger, sadness, joy, or other feelings. The faces of these persons are still, their eye contact poor, and their voices monotonous.

Still other persons experience *avolition*, or apathy. They feel drained of energy and interest in normal goals and are unable to start or follow through on a course of action. And, in yet another negative symptom, people with this disorder may *withdraw* from their social environment and attend only to their own ideas and fantasies. Because their ideas are illogical and confused, withdrawal helps distance them still further from reality (Behrendt & Young, 2004; Costello, 1993).

negative symptoms in the case of schizophrenia, symptoms that seem to reflect pathological deficits, including poverty of speech, flat affect, loss of volition, and social withdrawal.

Grunnitus Studio/Photo Researchers
Catatonic posturing. Some people struggling with schizophrenia demonstrate catatonic posturing, where they strike and hold bizarre positions, sometimes for hours.

catatonia extreme psychomotor symptoms of schizophrenia, including catatonic stupor, catatonic rigidity, and catatonic posturing.

89.3 Cognitive Symptoms of Schizophrenia

Cognitive impairment is a core feature of schizophrenia and affects most individuals diagnosed with the disorder. Affected cognitive functions include memory, executive function, attention, working memory, and intelligence. Undetected cognitive deficits exist and generally pre-date diagnosis of the illness (Wykes et al., 1999). Social and functional outcome is related to the degree of cognitive impairment (Green et al., 2004). Cognitive deficits are related to brain tissue changes and are consequently permanent, persisting even during symptom remission; it is therefore imperative that patients remain on their antipsychotic medications (Nuechterlein et al., 2013).

89.4 Psychomotor Symptoms of Schizophrenia

People with schizophrenia sometimes experience unusual *psychomotor symptoms*—they may move awkwardly or make odd grimaces and gestures. The gestures often seem to have a private, perhaps ritualistic, purpose. The psychomotor symptoms may take extreme forms, collectively called **catatonia**. People in a *catatonic stupor*, for example, stop responding to their environment, remaining motionless and silent for long stretches of time. Others exhibit *catatonic rigidity*, maintaining a rigid upright posture for hours and resisting efforts to be moved. Still others display *catatonic posturing*, assuming awkward, bizarre positions (a squatting position, for example) for long periods of time. They may even exhibit *waxy flexibility*, in which they maintain indefinitely postures into which they have been placed by someone else (Weinberger & Harrison, 2011).

89.5 How Do Neuroscientists Explain Schizophrenia?

Biological explanations of schizophrenia have received the most research support. This is not to say that psychological and socio-cultural factors play no role in the disorder. Rather, it has been hypothesized that a diathesis-stress relationship may account for the development of schizophrenia: perhaps people with a biological predisposition develop schizophrenia only if certain kinds of psychological events, personal stress, or societal expectations are also present.

89.5.1 Genetic Factors

Many theorists believe that people inherit a genetic predisposition to schizophrenia (Akbarian, 2010). In support of this notion, studies have found repeatedly that schizophrenia is more common among relatives of people with the disorder than among other individuals (Tamminga et al., 2008). The more closely related the relatives are to the person with schizophrenia, the greater their likelihood of developing the disorder (see **Figure 89-1**).

Researchers have been particularly interested in twins. If both members of a pair of twins have a particular trait, they are said to be *concordant* for that trait. Therefore, if genetic factors are at work in schizophrenia, identical twins (who share most genes) should have a higher concordance rate for this disorder than *fraternal twins* (who share only about 50 percent of their genes). This expectation has been supported by research (Higgins & George, 2007). Studies have found that if one identical twin develops schizophrenia, there is a 48 percent chance that the other twin will also develop schizophrenia at some point in his or her life. If the twins are fraternal, on the other hand, the second twin has approximately a 17 percent chance of developing the disorder. Considerable evidence suggests also that infection in the prenatal and perinatal environments plays an important role in the etiology of schizophrenia (Brown & Derkits, 2010).

How might genetic factors lead to the development of schizophrenia? Research has pointed to two kinds of brain abnormalities that may be inherited—*biochemical abnormalities* and *abnormal brain structures*.

89.5.2 Biochemical Abnormalities

Over the past four decades, researchers have developed the *dopamine hypothesis* to help explain schizophrenia. The first clue that high dopamine activity may contribute to schizophrenia came with the accidental discovery in the 1950s of **antipsychotic drugs**—medications that help remove the symptoms of schizophrenia (Garver, 2006; Healy, 2005). Originally used as anesthetics during surgery, the early drugs were found to also calm agitated psychotic patients. Direct tests followed, and a revolution in the treatment of schizophrenia began (Ban, 2007).

The dopamine hypothesis proposes a dysregulation or imbalance of dopamine with a hyperactive (overactive) subcortical transmission resulting in positive symptoms, and a hypoactive (underactive) cortical transmission to prefrontal cortex resulting in cognitive impairments and negative symptoms (Busatto et al., 2010; Abi-Dargham & Laruelle, 2005; McGowan et al., 2004). This hypothesis has undergone challenges and adjustments in recent years, but it is still the foundation for present biochemical explanations

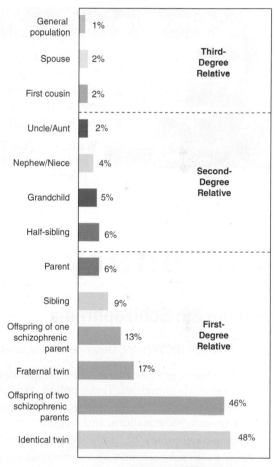

Relationship to Person with Schizophrenia

General population	1%
Spouse	2%
First cousin	2%
Uncle/Aunt	2%
Nephew/Niece	4%
Grandchild	5%
Half-sibling	6%
Parent	6%
Sibling	9%
Offspring of one schizophrenic parent	13%
Fraternal twin	17%
Offspring of two schizophrenic parents	46%
Identical twin	48%

Third-Degree Relative

Second-Degree Relative

First-Degree Relative

Percentage of Risk

FIGURE 89-1 Family connections and schizophrenia. Biological relatives of people with schizophrenia have a higher risk than the general population of developing the disorder during their lifetimes. Closer relatives (who have a more similar genetic makeup) have a greater risk than more distant relatives. Source: *Schizophrenia Genesis: The Origins of Madness*, by Irving I. Gottesman © 1991 by Irving I. Gottesman.

antipsychotic drugs medications that help remove the symptoms of schizophrenia.

of schizophrenia. Additional studies further suggest that abnormal activity of the neu-rotransmitters glutamate and serotonin may also play a role in schizophrenia (Bach, 2007).

89.5.3 Abnormal Brain Structures

During the past decade, researchers have also linked many cases of schizophrenia to ab-normalities in brain structure (Brown & Thompson, 2010; Eyler, 2008). Using brain scans, for example, they have found that many people with schizophrenia have enlarged ven-tricles (the brain cavities that contain cerebrospinal fluid), relatively small temporal lobes and frontal lobes, and abnormal blood flow in certain areas of the brain. In addition, some studies have linked schizophrenia to structural abnormalities of the hippocampus, amyg-dala, and thalamus (Leube, 2009).

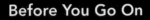

Before You Go On   www.wiley.com/go/comercanada

What Do You Know?
1. What is a psychosis?
2. What are the positive symptoms of schizophrenia? The negative symptoms? The psychomotor symptoms?
3. What biochemical abnormalities and brain structures have been associated with schizophrenia?

What Do You Think? We noted in this module that if one identical twin develops schizophrenia, there is a 48 percent chance that the other twin will do so as well. Discuss how this might support the diathesis-stress perspective.

Summary

Module 89: Schizophrenia

LEARNING OBJECTIVE 89 Describe the features of schizophrenia and some theories of what causes it.

- *Schizophrenia* is a disorder in which people deteriorate into a world of unusual perceptions, odd thoughts, disturbed emotions, and motor abnormalities. These people experience *psychosis*, a loss of contact with reality.
- Positive symptoms of schizophrenia are "pathological excesses" in behaviour. They include delusions, disorganized thinking and speech, hallucinations, and inappropriate affect.
- Negative symptoms, or "pathological deficits," include poverty of speech, flat affect, loss of volition, and social withdrawal.
- People with schizophrenia also sometimes experience unusual psychomotor symptoms, which in their most extreme form are collectively called *catatonia*.
- Many theorists believe that people inherit a genetic predisposition to schizophrenia. Two kinds of brain abnormalities might be inherited—biochemical abnormalities and abnormal brain structure.
- Although neuroscience explanations of schizophrenia have received by far the most research support, psychological and socio-cultural factors may help to bring about schizophrenia in people with a biological predisposition to develop it.

Key Terms

antipsychotic drugs 687	hallucinations 686	positive symptoms 685
catatonia 686	loose associations or derailment 686	psychosis 685
delusions 685	negative symptoms 686	schizophrenia 685

Study Questions

Multiple Choice

1. Which of the following is an example of a negative symptom of schizophrenia?
    a) being unable to show any emotion
    b) believing that others can read one's thoughts
    c) hearing voices that are not real
    d) using rapid, incoherent speech

Fill-in-the-Blank

1. In schizophrenia, _____ symptoms involve the addition of inappropriate behaviour, such as hallucinations or delusions.

2. The concordance rate for schizophrenia is much higher in _____ twins than in _____ twins, suggesting that genes play an important role in the development of the disorder.

Module 90: Other Disorders

LEARNING OBJECTIVE 90
Discuss the features and possible causes of somatic symptom and related disorders, dissociative, and personality disorders.

We have now examined three important categories of psychological disorders: mood disorders, anxiety disorders, and schizophrenia. We will conclude the part by looking briefly at three additional disorder categories: somatic symptom and related disorders, dissociative disorders, and personality disorders.

90.1 Somatic Symptom and Related Disorders

somatic symptom and related disorders excessive thought, feelings, and behaviours related to somatic symptoms.

The DSM-5 identifies **somatic** (physical) **symptom and related disorders** as defined by excessive concerns about physical health. Unlike the DSM-IV-TR, where the diagnosis required that the disorders be medically unexplained, the DSM-5 has removed this criterion. The DSM-5 includes somatic symptoms whether they can be medically explained or not. People with somatic symptom and related disorders often seek medical treatment, visiting numerous physicians and taking many different types of medications. Repeated hospitalization and surgeries are common. This behaviour is costly to the individual and to society. Frequently no medical explanation or cure is available to explain their symptoms. Typically these individuals do not consciously want or purposely produce their symptoms; they believe that their problems are genuine and experience the symptoms as completely physical (Lahmann, Henningsen, & Noll-Hussong, 2010).

There are five specific diagnoses related to somatic symptom and related disorders: somatic symptom disorder, illness anxiety disorder, conversion disorder (functional neurological symptom disorder), psychological factors affecting other medical conditions, and factitious disorder.

90.1.1 Somatic Symptom Disorder

The DSM-5 has three criteria for somatic symptom disorder (SDD): (1) the individual has one or more somatic symptoms that cause distress or significant disruption in their daily life; (2) excessive health-related anxiety and concern, as well as time and energy, are devoted to the somatic complaint; and (3) the concern has lasted for at least six months. For some, pain is of central concern.

Ailments may include pain symptoms (such as headaches and chest pain), gastrointestinal symptoms (such as nausea and diarrhea), sexual symptoms (such as erectile or menstrual difficulties), and neurological symptoms (such as double vision or paralysis). Sufferers may go from doctor to doctor in search of relief. Some may even seek multiple surgical procedures. They often describe their many symptoms in dramatic and exaggerated terms (Dimsdale & Creed, 2010; Creed, 2009).

90.1.2 Illness Anxiety Disorder

In this disorder, an individual is preoccupied with having a serious disease in spite of the lack of somatic symptoms. To meet the DSM-5 criteria, the person must engage in excessive care-seeking for at least six months and engage in excessive illness behaviours. It is important to note that a person must have minimal or no symptoms to meet this diagnosis. If symptoms are present, the person would be diagnosed with somatic symptom disorder.

90.1.3 Conversion Disorder: Functional Neurological Symptom Disorder

In *conversion disorder*, a person develops symptoms suggestive of neurological damage, such as paralysis, seizures, blindness, or loss of feeling. Symptoms may also include muscle tensing, arm or leg twitching, shaking or barking, and other odd behaviours

Sheila reported having abdominal pain since age 17, necessitating exploratory surgery that yielded no specific diagnosis. She had several pregnancies, each with severe nausea, vomiting, and abdominal pain; she ultimately had a hysterectomy for a "tipped uterus." Since age 40 she had experienced dizziness and "blackouts," which she eventually was told might be multiple sclerosis or a brain tumour. She continued to be bedridden for extended periods of time, with weakness, blurred vision, and difficulty urinating. At age 43 she was examined for a hernia because of complaints of bloating and intolerance of a variety of foods. She also had additional hospitalizations for neurological, hypertensive, and renal workups, all of which failed to reveal a definitive diagnosis. This pattern is reflective of somatic symptom disorder.

(Spitzer et al., 1981, p. 185)

(Tsuruga et al., 2008; Hong et al., 2008; Boogaarts et al., 2007). However, medical tests suggest that the bodily systems and central nervous system are healthy. The symptoms usually appear suddenly, at times of extreme stress, and last a matter of weeks. The disorders are thought to be quite rare, occurring in at most 5 of every 1,000 persons (Abbey, 2005). The affected person appears almost unconcerned by the symptoms.

Conversion disorder is difficult to distinguish from *malingering*. When people are malingering, they intentionally lie about symptoms to avoid an unwanted responsibility. This intentionality is not considered a part of conversion disorder. In general, malingers stand to benefit from their "illnesses" in some way (get out of a job or military service, receive a substantial insurance settlement, and so on) and, unlike those with conversion disorder, show an almost exaggerated interest in their symptoms.

90.1.4 Psychological Factors Affecting Other Medical Conditions

In psychological factors affecting other medical conditions, psychological factors (a) affect a documented medical condition in an adverse manner, creating unique health risks (e.g., chronic overeating creating a lack of adherence to a medical protocol for diabetes) or delaying recovery; and/or (b) exacerbate (worsen) an existing medical condition (e.g., anxiety triggering asthma attacks).

90.1.5 Factitious Disorder

In factitious disorder, people deliberately assume physical or psychological symptoms to adopt the patient role. Patients may lie about symptoms or they may actually take steps to make themselves ill, impaired, or injured—swallowing or injecting damaging drugs or substances to become genuinely ill or causing themselves bodily harm in some way. Factitious disorder can also be diagnosed in parents who fabricate illness in their children and then present them as ill, impaired, or injured. In this case the diagnosis is *factitious disorder imposed on another* (or *Munchausen by proxy*). Most cases of *factitious disorder imposed on another* involve a parent making a child ill; however, the diagnosis would hold in any instance where one person deliberately causes harm to another and then presents the other person as ill and themselves as caregiver.

90.1.6 What Causes Somatic Symptom and Related Disorders?

Although this specific categorization is relatively new, theorists have typically explained somatization disorders much as they explain anxiety disorders (Bouman, 2008; Noyes, 2008). Behaviourists, for example, believe that the fears found in the disorders are acquired through classical conditioning or modelling (Marshall et al., 2007). Cognitive theorists suggest that people with one of these types of disorders are extremely sensitive to bodily cues and come to misinterpret them (Witthoft & Hiller, 2010; Williams, 2004).

90.1.7 How Do Socio-Cultural Theorists Explain Somatic Symptom and Related Disorders?

HOW WE
DIFFER

Clinicians often use the term *somatization* when referring to the development of somatic symptoms in response to personal distress, the key feature of somatic symptom and related disorders. Somatization of any kind is considered inappropriate in Western countries (So, 2008; Escobar, 2004). Some theorists believe, however, that this position reflects a bias held by Western clinicians—a bias that sees somatic symptoms as an *inferior* (developmentally immature) way of dealing with emotions.

A worldwide view reveals that the transformation of personal distress into somatic complaints is in fact the norm in many non-Western cultures (Draguns, 2006; Kleinman, 1987). In such cultures, somatization is viewed as a socially and medically correct—and less stigmatizing—reaction to life's stressors. Studies have found very high rates of somatization in non-Western medical settings throughout the world, including China, Japan, and Arab countries (Matsumoto & Juang, 2008). Individuals in Latin countries seem to display the greatest number of somatic symptoms (Escobar, 2004, 1995; Escobar et al., 1998, 1992). Even within North America, people from Hispanic cultures display more somatic symptoms in the face of stress than do other populations. Such findings remind us once again that reactions to life's stressors are often influenced by culture. Overlooking this point can lead to knee-jerk mislabels or misdiagnoses.

90.2 Dissociative Disorders

People sometimes experience a major disruption of their memory. They may, for example, lose their ability to remember new information that they just learned or old information they once knew well. When such a change in memory lacks a physical cause, it is called a **dissociative disorder**. Part of a person's cognition or experience is no longer consciously accessible, and this aspect of memory seems to be *dissociated*, or separated, from the rest (Barlow, 2011). The DSM-5 includes three major dissociative disorders: dissociative amnesia, depersonalization/derealization disorder, and dissociative identity disorder. Although dissociative disorders are often portrayed in novels, movies, and television shows, they are in fact quite rare (Pope et al., 2007).

dissociative disorder
a psychological disorder characterized by major loss of memory without a clear physical cause; types include *dissociative amnesia, dissociative fugue,* and *dissociative identity disorder.*

90.2.1 Dissociative Amnesia

People with *dissociative amnesia* are unable to recall important information, usually of an upsetting nature, about their lives (APA, 2013). The loss of memory is much more extensive than normal forgetting and is often triggered by a traumatic event, as in wartime and natural disasters (Hunt, 2010). In most cases, the forgotten material or events eventually return, often without the help of treatment.

The memory loss generally focuses on a particular aspect of a traumatic experience rather than for an entire period of time surrounding the event. For example, a person might not be able to recall the death of a child, but would recall other events that happened during that time. Usually dissociative amnesia is characterized by sudden onset of an episode with an equally rapid disappearance.

In a type of amnesia known as *fugue*, memory loss is extensive. People not only forget their personal identities and details of their past lives, but may also flee to an entirely different location. Some individuals travel a short distance and make few social contacts in the new setting (APA, 2013). In other cases, however, the person may travel far from home, take a new name, and establish a new identity, new relationships, and even a new line of work (APA, 2013). It ought to be noted that even for those who experience exceptionally traumatizing events, fugue is rare (Speigel et al., 2012).

©iStockphoto.com/shvili

Memory loss. All of us have problems remembering something from time to time, but those with dissociative disorders have major disruptions in memory where one part of their memory seems to be dissociated from the rest.

90.2.2 Depersonalization/Derealization Disorder

In depersonalization/derealization disorder, stress alters perceptions. Memory is unaffected, but the person becomes detached from the body and/or the self. Patients report feeling as if they are observing themselves from a vantage point outside the body, or report feeling robotic or as viewing parts of their bodies as bizarre and unrelated to themselves. This disorder usually has an onset in adolescence and it can begin suddenly or gradually. Once it begins, it is chronic and can last for decades (Hunter, 2013).

Getty Images

90.2.3 Dissociative Identity Disorder

People with *dissociative identity disorder*, previously known as *multiple personality disorder*, develop two or more distinct personalities—called *subpersonalities* or *alternate personalities*—each with a unique set of memories, behaviours, thoughts, and emotions. At any given time, one of the subpersonalities takes centre stage and dominates the person's functioning (Barlow, 2011). Cases of dissociative identity disorder were first reported almost three centuries ago (Rieber, 2006, 2002). Women receive this diagnosis at least three times as often as men (APA, 2013).

90.2.4 How Do Psychodynamic Theorists Explain Dissociative Disorders?

A variety of theories have been proposed to explain dissociative disorders. Psychodynamic theorists believe that dissociative disorders are caused by *repression*, the most basic ego defence mechanism. As you read in Part 12, psychodynamic theorists believe that people fight off anxiety by unconsciously preventing painful memories, thoughts, or impulses from reaching awareness. Everyone uses repression to a degree, but people with dissociative disorders are thought to repress their memories excessively (Henderson, 2010; Fayek, 2002). In the psychodynamic view, dissociative amnesia and fugue are *single episodes* of massive repression. In each of these disorders, a person unconsciously blocks the memory of an extremely upsetting event to avoid the pain of facing it. Repression may be their only protection from overwhelming anxiety (Kikuchi et al., 2010).

In contrast, dissociative identity disorder is thought to result from a *lifetime* of excessive repression (Howell, 2011; Wang & Jiang, 2007). Psychodynamic theorists believe that continuous use of repression is motivated by traumatic childhood events, particularly abusive parenting. Children who experience such traumas may come to fear the

---

Psychology Around Us　　The Many Sides of Eric

Dazed and bruised from a beating, Eric, 29, was discovered wandering around a Daytona Beach shopping mall. . . . Transferred six weeks later to Daytona Beach's Human Resources Center, Eric began talking to doctors in two voices: the infantile rhythms of "young Eric," a dim and frightened child, and the measured tones of "older Eric," who told a tale of terror and child abuse. According to "older Eric," after his immigrant German parents died, a harsh stepfather and his mistress took Eric from his native South Carolina to a drug dealers' hideout in a Florida swamp. Eric said he was raped by several gang members and watched his stepfather murder two men.

One day . . . an alarmed counselor watched Eric's face twist into a violent snarl. Eric let loose an unearthly growl and spat out a stream of obscenities. . . . That disclosure of a new personality, who insolently demanded to be called Mark, was the first indication that [the doctors] had been dealing with . . . multiple personality.

. . . Eric gradually unfurled 27 different personalities, including three females. . . . They ranged in age from a fetus to a sordid old man who kept trying to persuade Eric to fight as a mercenary in Haiti.

(*Time*, October 25, 1982, p. 70)

dangerous world they live in and take flight from it by pretending to be another person who is looking on safely from afar. Abused children may also come to fear the impulses that they believe are the reasons for their excessive punishments. Whenever they experience "bad" thoughts or impulses, they unconsciously try to disown and deny them by assigning them to other personalities (Baker, 2010).

The psychodynamic explanation has failed to receive much research support (Meranda, 2008). Most of the support for the psychodynamic position is drawn from case histories, which report brutal childhood experiences (Ross & Ness, 2010). Yet some individuals with dissociative identity disorder do not report on abuse in their backgrounds. Moreover, child abuse is more common than dissociative identity disorder. This has left many critics asking why, if the psychodynamic explanation has merit, only a small fraction of abused children develop this disorder.

90.2.5 How Does the Neuroscience Approach Explain Dissociative Disorders?

The biological approach has nothing definitive in this area, but there have been a number of intriguing findings in recent years. For example, one study used MRI scans to examine the hippocampus and amygdala of individuals with and without dissociative disorder. Both of these brain regions were found to be significantly smaller in those with dissociative disorder. As well, these same regions have been found to be smaller in individuals with histories of childhood trauma (Vermetten et al., 2006). Other studies have shown decreased functioning in several emotional processing areas of the brains of individuals struggling with dissociative disorders (Phillips & Sierra, 2003). Finally, PET scans of the brains of individuals with and without dissociative disorders show significant differences in the level of activity in both the sensory cortex and in areas of the brain previously found to be associated with integrated body schemes (Simeon et al., 2000). This sort of understanding is the first of many steps toward a complete understanding of the etiology of dissociation.

90.3 Personality Disorders

personality disorder an inflexible pattern of inner experience and outward behaviour that causes distress or difficulty with daily functioning.

A **personality disorder** is a very rigid pattern of inner experience and outward behaviour. The pattern is seen in most of the person's interactions, continues for years, and differs markedly from the experiences and behaviours usually expected of people. Such disorders typically become recognizable in adolescence or early adulthood, although some seem to start during childhood (Westen et al., 2011). It has been estimated that as many as 9 to 15 percent of all adults may have a personality disorder (Paris, 2010; O'Connor, 2008). Personality disorders are controversial, with many researchers and clinicians arguing that having a difficult personality does not necessarily constitute a disorder. Instead, they argue that personality problems might be better conceptualized as extremes on trait scales, such as the Big Five (Trull & Durrett, 2005).

DSM-5 identifies 10 specific personality disorders that fall into three clusters: (1) odd/eccentric, (2) dramatic/erratic, and (3) anxious/inhibited. Only two of them, the *antisocial* and *borderline personality disorders*, have been studied extensively, partly because they create so many problems for other people.

90.3.1 Antisocial Personality Disorder

antisocial personality disorder a personality disorder characterized by extreme and callous disregard for the feelings and rights of others.

Sometimes described as "psychopaths" or "sociopaths," people with **antisocial personality disorder** persistently disregard and violate others' rights (APA, 2013). Aside from substance-related disorders, this is the disorder most closely linked to adult criminal behaviour. Most people with antisocial personality disorder display some patterns of misbehaviour before the age of 15, including truancy, running away, physical cruelty to animals or people, and destroying property (Holmes, Slaughter, & Kashani, 2001).

Antisocial personality disorder was referred to as "moral insanity" during the nineteenth century.

People with antisocial personality disorder lie repeatedly (Patrick, 2007). Many cannot work consistently at a job; they are frequently absent and are likely to quit their jobs altogether. They are often careless with money and frequently fail to pay their debts. They are also often impulsive, taking action without thinking of the consequences (Millon, 2011). Correspondingly, they may be irritable, aggressive, and quick to start fights.

Recklessness is another common trait: people with antisocial personality disorder have little regard for their own safety or for the safety of others, even their children. They are self-centred, and likely to have difficulty maintaining close relationships. They often have a knack for gaining personal profit at the expense of other people. The pain or damage they cause seldom concerns them; they appear to lack a moral conscience (Kantor, 2006). They think of their victims as weak and deserving of being conned or robbed.

Robert Hare of the University of British Columbia has developed a measure of psychopathy called the Psychopathy Checklist–Revised (PCL-R; Hare, 2003). Hare argues that psychopathy is a more extreme disorder than antisocial personality disorder, and argues that each should be considered separate from the other. The scale provides subscale scores on aggressive narcissism and socially deviant lifestyle. Scores on the scale correlate well with diagnoses of antisocial personality disorder, but the PCL-R is more specific. Hare's data indicate that while about 80 percent of individuals in Canadian prisons would meet the DSM criteria for antisocial personality disorder, only 20 percent would meet the PCL-R criteria for psychopathy. Further, Hare argues that the 20 percent identified by the PCL-R are responsible for 50 percent of the most serious crimes (Hare, 1993).

Beyond Robert Hare's data, there are no general Canadian data available; however, American surveys indicate that as many as 2 to 3.5 percent of people in the United States meet the criteria for antisocial personality disorder (Paris, 2010; O'Connor, 2008). It is likely that Canadian numbers are similar. The disorder is as much as four times more common among men than women.

Chris Leschinsky/Getty Images

Psychopathy and crime. Half of all serious and repeat rapists and nearly half of all murderers meet the criteria for psychopathy on Robert Hare's PCL-R scale.

What Causes Antisocial Personality Disorder?

Although the various models provide a range of explanations for antisocial personality disorder, none has managed to account for the broad range of symptoms found in the disorder. However, the behavioural and neuroscience models offer insights about particular symptoms.

According to a number of behavioural theorists, antisocial symptoms may be learned through modelling (Gaynor & Baird, 2007). As evidence, they point to the particularly high rate of antisocial personality disorder found among the parents of people with this disorder (though this could also reflect a genetic aspect of the disorder). Other behaviourists have suggested that some parents unintentionally teach antisocial behaviour by regularly rewarding a child's aggressive behaviour (Kazdin, 2005). When the child misbehaves or becomes violent in reaction to the parents' requests or orders, for example, the parents may give in to restore peace. Without meaning to, they may be teaching the child to be stubborn, and perhaps even violent.

Finally, a number of studies suggest that biological factors may play an important role in this disorder. Researchers have found, for example, that people with the disorder display lower serotonin activity than other individuals (Patrick, 2007). Among

©iStockphoto.com/Olgasea

Rewarding bad behaviour. Research suggests that some parents unintentionally teach antisocial behaviour by regularly rewarding a child's aggressive behaviour. For example, if a child defies a parent and the parent gives in to restore peace, the parent may be unintentionally teaching the child to be stubborn.

other things, low serotonin activity has been linked to both impulsivity and aggression—key features of antisocial personality disorder (Duke et al., 2013). In addition, deficient functioning has been found in the frontal lobes of persons with this disorder (Morgan & Lilienfeld, 2000). Such a deficiency could help explain the poor planning, inferior judgments, and low empathy characteristic of this disorder (Glenn et al., 2013).

Still other research reveals that people with this disorder often experience less anxiety than other people, and so may lack a key ingredient for learning (Blair et al., 2005). This would help explain why they have so much trouble learning from negative life experiences or tuning in to the emotional cues of others. Why should these individuals experience less anxiety than other people? It appears that many of them tend to respond to warnings or expectations of stress with low brain and bodily arousal (Perdeci et al., 2010; Gaynor & Baird, 2007). Perhaps because of the low arousal, the individuals easily tune out threatening or emotional situations, and so are unaffected by them.

90.3.2 Borderline Personality Disorder

borderline personality disorder
a personality disorder characterized by severe instability in emotions and self-concept and high levels of volatility.

People with **borderline personality disorder** display great instability, including major shifts in mood, an unstable self-image, and impulsivity. These characteristics combine to make their relationships very unstable as well (Mason & Kreger, 2010; APA, 2013). People diagnosed with this disorder move in and out of very depressive, anxious, and irritable states that may last anywhere from a few hours to a few days or more. Their emotions seem to be always in conflict with the world around them. They are prone to bouts of extreme anger, which may at times result in physical aggression (Leichsenring et al., 2011; Meyer, Ajchenbrenner, & Bowles, 2005; Koenigsberg et al., 2002).

Just as often, they direct their impulsive anger inward and inflict bodily harm on themselves—in the form of cutting or mutilating themselves (Whipple & Fowler, 2011). Many try to hurt themselves as a way of dealing with their chronic feelings of emptiness, boredom, and identity confusion. Suicidal threats and actions are also common. Studies suggest that 75 percent of people with this disorder attempt suicide at least once in their lives; as many as 10 percent actually do commit suicide (Gunderson, 2011; Leichsenring et al., 2011).

People with borderline personality disorder frequently form intense, conflict-ridden relationships in which their feelings are not necessarily shared by the other person. They often violate the boundaries of a relationship. Thinking in *dichotomous* (black-and-white) terms, they quickly become furious when their expectations are not met. Yet they remain very attached to the relationships, paralyzed by a fear of being left alone. Sometimes they cut themselves or carry out other self-destructive acts to prevent partners from leaving (Berenson et al., 2011).

Around 2 percent of the general population is thought to suffer from this disorder (Paris, 2010; Sherry & Whilde, 2008). Close to 75 percent of the patients who receive this diagnosis are women (Gunderson, 2011).

What Causes Borderline Personality Disorder? Borderline personality disorder is not well understood. In recent years, however, a number of theorists have developed a *biosocial* theory to explain the disorder. According to this view, the disorder actually begins during childhood. It results from a combination of internal forces (for example, difficulty identifying and controlling one's arousal levels and emotions) and external forces (for example, an environment in which a child's emotions are punished or disregarded). If children have difficulties identifying and controlling their emotions, and if their parents further teach them to ignore their intense feelings, the children may never learn how to properly recognize and regulate their emotional arousal or how to tolerate emotional distress (Arens et al., 2011; Linehan & Dexter-Mazza, 2008).

Psychology Around Us

Not Criminally Responsible on Account of Mental Disorder

How does someone get declared "not criminally responsible on account of mental disorder," and can people use this to "get away with murder"?

Is it possible for someone who was not clearly diagnosed as disordered before committing a violent act (a potential crime) to be found not responsible for the crime on account of a mental disorder? The concept of insanity, which is used in the U.S. legal system, is not a psychological one; its definition is legal. *Insanity* refers to a condition that excuses people from responsibility and protects them from punishment. From the legal point of view, a person cannot be held responsible for a crime if, at the time of the crime, the person lacked the capacity to distinguish right from wrong in order to obey the law. As Regina Schuller of York University and James Ogloff of Simon Fraser University point out, the Canadian legal outcome of "not criminally responsible on account of mental disorder" is not a diagnosis or even a psychological concept; it is simply a legal finding (Schuller & Ogloff, 2001). If a person is found "not criminally responsible by reason of mental disorder," he is neither convicted nor acquitted, and as such he is not formally sentenced. Instead, a court review board decides on the most appropriate arrangement, which could be an absolute discharge, a discharge with conditions (such as probation and/or treatment or medication), or detention in a hospital or institution.

On July 11, 2014, Bill C-14, the Not Criminally Responsible Reform Act, was passed in Canada. This legislation changed the Criminal Code of Canada regarding individuals found not criminally responsible due to a mental disorder. This bill is intended to enhance the rights of victims of violent crimes by persons found unfit to stand trial, to ensure public safety through tightened conditions for those under the authority of Review Boards, and created a new "high risk accused" category. The effort to change the legislation was driven by the parents of Tim McLean, a young man decapitated while sleeping at the back of a Greyhound bus in 2008. The man charged with the murder, Vincent Li, had been previously diagnosed with schizophrenia. He believed God told him that his own life depended on his killing McLean. Li was found not criminally responsible on account of mental disorder. Those in favour of the legislation feel that it has not gone far enough to protect the public. Conversely, 11 Canadian mental health organizations (including the Canadian Psychological Association), have expressed strong disappointment with the legislation, pointing out that it is highly stigmatizing, perpetuates fear of those with mental illness, and diminishes the rights of individuals who are mentally ill. It is important to recognize that justice is more than punishment and must be weighed against compassion and mercy.

Before You Go On

www.wiley.com/go/comercanada

What Do You Know?

1. What distinguishes a pain disorder associated with psychological factors from a conversion or somatization disorder?

2. List and describe three dissociative disorders.

3. Which disorder discussed in this module is most closely linked to adult criminal behaviour?

What Do You Think? Analyze a character from a film you have seen or a book you have read that has one of the disorders described in this module. Is the information provided in the text consistent with what you know of the character?

Summary

Module 90: Other Disorders

LEARNING OBJECTIVE 90 Discuss the features and possible causes of somatic symptom and related disorders, dissociative, and personality disorders.

- Somatic symptom and related disorders include five diagnoses: somatic symptom disorder, illness anxiety disorder, conversion disorder (functional neurological symptom disorder), psychological factors affecting other medical conditions, and factitious disorder.

- Somatic symptom and related disorders are thought to result from classical conditioning, modelling, or misinterpretation of bodily cues, similar to anxiety disorders. Cognitive theorists suggest that people with one of these types of disorders are extremely sensitive to bodily cues and come to misinterpret them.

- Changes in memory that lack a physical cause are called *dissociative disorders*. DSM-5 includes three major dissociative disorders: dissociative amnesia, depersonalization/derealization disorder, and dissociative identity disorder. In *dissociative amnesia*, people are unable to recall important information about their lives. In *depersonalization/derealization disorder*, stress alters perceptions, detaching the self from the body. In *dissociative fugue*, people not only forget their identities and their past lives, but also flee to a different location. In *dissociative identity disorder*, people develop two or more distinct personalities.

- Psychodynamic theorists believe that dissociative disorders are caused by repression, the most basic ego defence mechanism, but this view has not received strong research support.

- People with *antisocial personality disorder* persistently disregard and violate others' rights. Because of their potentially negative behaviour, such as lying, impulsiveness, and recklessness, they are frequently found in prison. According to behavioural theorists, this disorder can be learned through various means. Neuroscience explanations focus on brain factors, such as low serotonin levels, deficient frontal lobe functioning, and low arousal in response to warnings.

- People with *borderline personality disorder* display great instability, including major shifts in mood, an unstable self-image, and impulsivity. This disorder is not well understood, but a recent biosocial theory proposes that it results from a combination of internal and external forces.

Key Terms

antisocial personality disorder 694
borderline personality disorder 696

dissociative disorder 692
personality disorder 694

somatic symptom and related disorders 690

Study Questions

Multiple Choice

1. A man who forgets the details of his life and identity and sets up a new life in a different location is likely experiencing dissociative
   a) amnesia.
   b) fugue.
   c) identity disorder.
   d) somatization.

Fill-in-the-Blank

1. Research shows that people with antisocial personality disorder often have deficient functioning in the _____ lobes of the brain.

PART 16

TREATMENT OF PSYCHOLOGICAL DISORDERS

PART OUTLINE

February: *He cannot leave the house; Jefferson knows that for a fact. Home is the only place where he feels safe—safe from humiliation, danger, even ruin. If he were to go to work, his co-workers would somehow reveal their contempt for him. A pointed remark, a quizzical look— that's all it would take for him to get the message. If he were to go shopping at the store, before long everyone would be staring at him. Surely others would see his dark mood and thoughts; he wouldn't be able to hide them. He dare not even go for a walk alone in the woods—his heart would probably start racing again, bringing him to his knees and leaving him breathless, incoherent, and unable to get home. No, he's much better off staying in his room, trying to get through another evening of this curse called life. Thank goodness for the Internet. Were it not for his reading of news sites and postings to blogs and online forums, he knows he would be cut off from the world altogether.*

July: *Jefferson's life revolves around his circle of friends—Mikel and Jason from the office, where he was recently promoted to director of customer relations, and Bryant and Darnell, his weekend tennis partners. The gang meets for dinner every week at someone's house, and they chat about life, politics, and their jobs. Particularly special in Jefferson's life is Kyra. They go to movies, restaurants, and concerts together. She thinks Jefferson's just terrific, and Jefferson finds himself beaming whenever she's around. Jefferson looks forward to work each day and to his one-on-one dealings with customers. He's taking part in many activities and relationships and more fully enjoying life.*

Jefferson's thoughts, feelings, and behaviour interfered with all aspects of his life in February, yet most of his symptoms had disappeared by July. Many factors may have contributed to Jefferson's improvement—advice from friends and family members, a new job or vacation, perhaps a big change in his diet or exercise regimen. Any or all of these things may have been useful, but they could not be considered **treatment**, or **therapy**. Those terms are usually reserved for specific, systematic procedures designed to change abnormal behaviour into more normal behaviour. According to clinical theorist Jerome Frank, all forms of therapy have three essential features:

treatment or **therapy** systematic procedures designed to change abnormal behaviour into more normal behaviour.

1. A *sufferer* who seeks relief from the healer.
2. A trained, socially accepted *healer*, whose expertise is accepted by the sufferer and his social group.
3. A *series of contacts* between the healer and the sufferer, through which the healer tries to produce certain changes in the sufferer's emotional state, attitudes, and behaviour. The healing process may be brought about primarily by **psychotherapy**—in Frank's words, "by words, acts, and rituals in which sufferer, healer, and—if there is one—group participate jointly." Or it may be accomplished through **biological therapy**, consisting of "physical and chemical procedures" (Frank, 1973, pp. 2–3).

psychotherapy a treatment system in which a client and therapist use words and acts to overcome the client's psychological difficulties.

biological therapy the use of physical and chemical procedures to help people overcome psychological difficulties.

Healers are called *clinicians*, *clinical practitioners*, or *therapists*. You read about the work of *clinical researchers* in Part 15. As you saw, they systematically gather information so that they can better describe, explain, and predict psychological disorders. The knowledge that they acquire is then used by clinicians, whose role is to detect, assess, and treat people with psychological disorders.

Despite Frank's (1973) straightforward definition, clinical treatment is surrounded by conflict and confusion. In fact, Carl Rogers has been cited as saying that "therapists are not in agreement as to their goals or aims. . . . They are not in agreement as to what constitutes a successful outcome of their work. They cannot agree as to what constitutes a failure. It seems as though the field is completely chaotic and divided" (Comer, 2010).

Some clinicians view abnormality as an illness and so consider therapy a procedure that helps cure the illness. Others see abnormality as a problem in living and therapists as teachers of more

age fotostock/MaxxImages

Getting help. Therapy is a systematic procedure to help people deal with the pathology, adjustment issues, or day-to-day problems that are negatively affecting their lives.

functional behaviour and thought. Clinicians even differ on what to call the person who receives therapy. Those who see abnormality as an illness speak of the "patient," while those who view it as a problem in living refer to the "client." Because both terms are so common, this part will use them interchangeably.

Despite their differences, most clinicians do agree that large numbers of people need therapy of one kind or another. Later you will encounter evidence that therapy is indeed often helpful.

Module 91: Treatment in Today's World

LEARNING OBJECTIVE 91
Explain who receives treatment for psychological problems today, how they enter treatment, and what general features characterize different types of treatment.

A Canadian Mental Health Association (2005) survey indicates that Canadians view mental health as being as important as their physical health. Other surveys suggest that more than 20 million people—children, adolescents, and adults—in North America receive therapy for psychological problems in the course of a year (NAMI, 2011). The number and variety of problems for which treatments are available have increased during the past 110 years. When Freud and his colleagues first began conducting therapy during the late nineteenth and early twentieth centuries, most of their patients suffered from anxiety or depression. People with schizophrenia and other more severe disorders were considered poor prospects for therapy, and treatment for them was confined to custodial care in institutions (Levin, Hennessy, & Petrila, 2010).

This early view has changed since the 1950s. Anxiety and depression still dominate the therapy picture, as more than three-quarters of Canadians diagnosed with a mental illness each year suffer from one or the other of these two disorder types (Langlois et al., 2011; Health Canada, 2002). However, people with other kinds of disorders also receive therapy (NIDA, 2011; CDC, 2010; SAMHSA, 2010, 2008). People with schizophrenia and people with substance-related disorders, for example, make up a large percentage of the clients in therapy today. Moreover, large numbers of people with milder psychological problems, sometimes called "problems in living," are also in therapy. Surveys suggest that non-disordered reasons for entering therapy largely include problems with marriage, family, job, peer, school, or community relationships (Mojtabai et al., 2011).

Among other facts on its *Fast Facts about Mental Illness* page (www.cmha.ca/media/fast-facts-about-mental-illness), the Canadian Mental Health Association (2014) states the following: 20 percent of Canadians will experience a mental illness in their lifetime; 8 percent will experience a major depression; 1 percent will experience bipolar disorder; and 5 percent of households will experience mild to severe anxiety. Importantly, the Canadian Mental Health Association also states that although mental illness can be treated effectively, many people do not seek treatment because of the stigma associated with mental illness.

91.1 Who Seeks Treatment?

HOW WE DIFFER

Other characteristics of clients have also changed over the years. Until the middle of the twentieth century, therapy was primarily a privilege of the wealthy, largely because of the high fees that out-patients were required to pay. After all, Freud's fee for one session of therapy was $20 ($160 in today's dollars). The current cost of private out-patient therapy varies by service and location. Provincial psychologists' regulatory groups (e.g., the Ontario College of Psychologists) set the hourly rate for psychological therapy. The hourly rate in Canada typically ranges from $130 to $180. However, with the expansion of third-party coverage (such as Blue Cross) and the emergence of publicly-supported community mental health centres, people at all socio-economic levels now receive both out-patient and in-patient therapy.

Women used to outnumber men in therapy by four to one, partly because they were less reluctant than men to seek help. Lately, however, our society's attitudes and sex-role expectations have been changing, and men are increasingly willing to enter therapy (Vogel et al., 2007; Addis & Mahalik, 2003). In fact, more than one-third of today's therapy patients are male (NIDA, 2011; CDC, 2010). As you will see later in this part, however, members of ethnic minority groups tend to seek treatment for their psychological problems less often than members of the majority culture (Brown et al., 2014; Chen et al., 2013; Comas-Diaz, 2011, 2006).

91.2 Entering and Receiving Treatment

People enter therapy in various ways. Many decide on their own to consult a therapist. Others may do so on the advice of a friend, family member, minister, physician, or other professional with whom they have discussed their difficulties. Still others are forced into treatment. Parents, spouses, teachers, and employers may virtually order people to seek treatment if they are causing disruptions or are in obvious distress; or judges may formally pronounce people mentally disturbed and dangerous and commit them to a mental hospital for treatment.

In most cases, the decision to seek therapy is not easy. Stigma is a barrier to seeking treatment for many (Clement et al., 2014). Extensive studies indicate that most individuals are aware of their problems well before they look for help. Many wait more than two years after they first become aware that they have a problem. And it is estimated that at least half of the people with psychological disorders never seek treatment (Ndumele & Trivedi, 2011; SoRelle, 2000). Generally speaking, therapy seems to hold greater attraction for those who have a social network of "friends and supporters of therapy"—people who have themselves been clients or who express confidence in therapy as a solution to personal problems (SAMHSA, 2008, 2002; Kadushin, 1969).

The under-use of therapy has a long history. Back in the 1970s, for example, a labour union in the United States, the United Auto Workers, negotiated a contract in which management agreed to pay the entire cost of both in-patient and out-patient mental health services for a million union members. Yet, after three years, only 1 percent of eligible workers had used the benefit (Brown, 1976). Apparently they and their referral agents (shop foremen, clergy, and the like) were either unaware of the benefit, ignorant of what therapy could do for them, unlikely to think about personal problems in mental health terms, or worried about the stigma that psychological problems might bring in their social set.

Heather Stuart of Queens University (2010) has reviewed the history of efforts within Canada to reduce the stigma associated with acknowledging and obtaining treatment for mental illness. As far back as the 1950s, efforts were underway to reduce the stigma associated with mental illness and to help Canadians move toward an understanding that many mental illnesses can be treated, and that most can be treated outside of hospital settings. For example, as efforts were underway to reduce the number of mental patients treated in hospitals, there was initial resistance from the public based on unfounded fears regarding public safety if mentally ill people were treated on an out-patient basis. Since that time, there has been a significant reduction in the stigma associated with mental illness. However, perceptions of stigma continue to play a role in people's decisions about whether or not to acknowledge their mental issues and whether or not to seek treatment.

©iStockphoto.com/PeopleImages

The stigma of seeking therapy. Many people don't seek therapy because there is a social stigma associated with it. Instead, they suffer in silence. The truth is that therapy can benefit anyone, and it is not a weakness to seek help.

91.3 Conducting Treatment: Who, Where, and How

A variety of professionals conduct therapy today. Most are psychologists, psychiatrists, counsellors, and psychiatric social workers. Whatever their profession, these therapists generally see the same kinds of clients. That is, the majority of their clients are people with anxiety, depression, or relationship problems. However, although psychiatrists treat clients with depression, anxiety, and relationship issues, they see a much larger number of patients with schizophrenia, bipolar disorders, and other severe disorders than do psychologists, counsellors, or social workers. The providers of mental health services are concentrated in urban areas across Canada. As a result, there is a shortage of practitioners available to serve the needs of the many people who live in rural areas (Dyck & Hardy, 2013; Jackson et al., 2007; Smith et al., 2004). Even in the larger centres, some kinds of services are easier to access (e.g., medications through hospital psychiatric or emergency wards) than others (e.g., counselling, therapy, and support) (Kirby & Keon, 2006).

Therapy takes place in all sorts of settings, from public institutions to schools to private offices. Most clients, even those who are severely disturbed, are treated as outpatients. They live in the community and make regular visits to the therapist's office or hospital/clinic. Most of the people who receive in-patient treatment, whether in the psychiatric wards of general hospitals or in psychiatric hospitals, have severe psychological problems (Craig & Power, 2010). The Canadian health care system ensures that mental health services and necessary treatments are available to all who need them, either through hospital facilities or out-patient clinics. Therapy offered by psychologists in private practice is usually paid for by the people who seek out such mental health services; however, many workplace health insurance providers offer some coverage for psychological treatment. Nevertheless, the need to pay for services creates a significant barrier for some.

Guidelines for admitting individuals to psychiatric facilities, either voluntarily or involuntarily, are provided in the Canadian Mental Health Act. This act includes information on the conditions under which people can be admitted and detained in hospital against their will, and also outlines the rights of patients in psychiatric facilities.

Clinicians have become increasingly concerned about the negative effects of long-term institutionalization. Thus, beginning in the 1960s, they carried out a policy of *deinstitutionalization* that basically continued over the next 40 years (Davison et al., 2010). Paul Whitehead of the University of Western Ontario reported this process as being quite variable across Canada. In general terms, the number of psychiatric beds per 1,000 population went from four in 1964 to one in 1975, and the total number of psychiatric beds dropped from 54,801 in 1975 to 20,301 in 1981 (Sealy & Whitehead, 2006, 2004).

Hospitalization today usually lasts weeks instead of months or years. When people develop severe psychological disorders, therapists now try to treat them first as out-patients, usually with medications along with other forms of therapy. If this strategy proves ineffective, the patient may be admitted to a hospital for a short period (usually 24 to 72 hours) so that the condition can be monitored, diagnosed, and stabilized. As soon as hospitalization has served the purpose of stabilization, the patient is returned to the community.

In theory, this may be a reasonable treatment plan for people with severe psychological disorders. However, as you will see later, community treatment facilities have been so underfunded and understaffed over the years that they have not been able to meet the treatment needs of the majority of severely impaired people. Indeed, many people with severe psychological disorders are currently condemned to an endless cycle of hospital discharges and readmissions, and are often homeless (Sealy, 2012; Frankish, Hwang, & Quantz, 2005). According to the Canadian Institute for Health Information (2008), one-third of Canadians released from hospital following treatment for mental illness are readmitted to hospital within a year.

United Artists/Fantasy Films/The Kobal Collection

The "crazy house." For many, the perception of psychiatric care continues to be something like the treatment received by the patients portrayed in the well-known movie *One Flew Over the Cuckoo's Nest*. However, the reality is that laws and policies protect Canadians hospitalized with mental illness.

By some estimates, there are more than 400 forms of therapy in the clinical field today, each practised by clinicians who believe that their chosen methodology is highly effective (Karasu, 1992). Typically, therapists use principles and techniques that they have been trained in and that are consistent with the theories of psychological dysfunction they have been taught.

In Part 15, you read about today's leading theories for explaining psychological disorders. Proponents of those explanations have proposed corresponding treatment approaches, and clinical practitioners have put those approaches into action as they work with clients. Carl Rogers's humanistic theory, for example, identifies self-awareness and self-actualization as fundamental to good mental health. Correspondingly, therapists who follow his client-centred treatment approach listen to and empathize with clients, expecting that such techniques will help the clients become better aware of themselves and more able to actualize their special human potential.

The following modules focus on biological, psychodynamic, behavioural, cognitive-behavioural, and humanistic-existential therapies (see **Table 91-1**). Recall from our part opener, though, that all these forms of therapy have three essential features: a sufferer who seeks relief, a trained healer, and a series of contacts between the two in which the healer tries to bring about changes in the sufferer's emotional state, attitudes, and behaviour.

TABLE 91-1 Comparison of Treatments for Psychological Disorders

	Goals of Therapy	Therapy Techniques	Strengths	Weaknesses
Biological Approaches	Improve structural or biochemical functioning; relieve symptoms	Psychotropic drugs; electroconvulsive therapy (ECT); psychosurgery	• Often effective for people whose problems don't respond to other treatments	• Side effects • Not always effective • May neglect non-biological problems of clients
Psychodynamic Approaches	Discover source of conflicts and resolve them	Free association; therapist analysis of resistance, transference, and dreams; catharsis; and working through problems	• Offered first major alternative to biological treatments • Sees abnormal functioning as rooted in same processes as normal functioning • Model for many other psychological treatments	• Research does not support effectiveness of therapies
Behavioural Approaches	Learn more functional behaviours	Desensitization; aversion therapy; operant conditioning, including token economies; therapist modelling, including social-skills training	• Research often supports effectiveness of treatments	• Effects of treatment may not always last long after treatment stops • May neglect unobservable cognitive processes
Cognitive-Behavioural Approaches	Change harmful thinking patterns to more useful ones	Rational-emotive therapy; cognitive therapy; cognitive-behavioural techniques	• Considerable research support for its application to several disorders	• Dysfunctional thinking may result from, not cause, abnormal functioning
Humanistic and Existential Approaches	Provide support for honest self-appraisal, self-acceptance, and self-actualization	Client-centred and Gestalt therapy techniques; existential therapy	• Recognize positive human goals • Recognize distinctly human values and needs	• Unsupportive and limited research to test effectiveness

Before You Go On

www.wiley.com/go/comercanada

What Do You Know?
1. What trends have changed who tends to receive treatment for psychological disorders?
2. How does in-patient therapy differ from out-patient therapy?
3. What are the three key features common to all forms of therapy?

What Do You Think? Why do you suppose people tend to wait so long before seeking help for a psychological problem? If you were experiencing some sort of psychological difficulty—say, depression—how do you think you would arrive at the decision to get treatment?

Summary

Module 91: Treatment in Today's World

LEARNING OBJECTIVE 91 Explain who receives treatment for psychological problems today, how they enter treatment, and what general features characterize different types of treatment.

- More than 20 million North Americans receive therapy for psychological problems in the course of a year. Almost half suffer from anxiety and depression.
- Therapy was once primarily a privilege of the wealthy, but today people at all socio-economic levels receive treatment. Similarly, while women once outnumbered men in therapy by four to one, men today are more willing to enter therapy.
- People may enter therapy on their own or may be forced into treatment. Many never seek treatment at all.
- A variety of professionals conduct therapy, including psychologists, psychiatrists, counsellors, and psychiatric social workers.
- Most clients are treated in the community as out-patients, but some people with severe problems are treated as in-patients in private or public institutions.
- All forms of therapy have three essential features: a sufferer who seeks relief, a trained healer, and a series of contacts between the two in which the healer tries to bring about changes in the sufferer's emotional state, attitudes, and behaviour.

Study Questions

Multiple Choice

1. The most common psychological problems that lead people in Canada to seek treatment are
   a) anxiety and depression.
   b) bipolar disorder and schizophrenia.
   c) dissociative disorder and depression.
   d) schizophrenia and anxiety.

Fill-in-the-Blank

1. Most people seeking mental health services receive _____ treatment, whereby clients visit a therapist's office, but live in the community.

Module 92: Biological Treatments

Biological therapies use chemical and physical methods to help people overcome their psychological problems. The practitioners who apply such approaches are usually *psychiatrists*, therapists whose training includes medical school. The three principal kinds of brain interventions are *drug therapy*, *electroconvulsive therapy*, and *psychosurgery*. Drug therapy is by far the most common of these approaches.

92.1 Drug Therapy

Many types of biologically-caused disorders are treated with drug therapies or medical or surgical procedures that act directly on the central nervous system. We will first address the use of **psychotropic drugs**; drugs that act primarily on the brain and, in many cases, significantly reduce the symptoms of psychological disorders (Julien et al., 2011). We will then discuss other medical interventions for treating psychological disorders.

Since the 1950s, discoveries in psychopharmacology (a branch of study that focuses on the action of drugs on the mind and behaviour) have transformed the treatment of psychological disorders. Such drugs are now widely used, either as the first-line treatment for a disorder or in conjunction with psychotherapy or other interventions.

As you can see in **Table 92-1**, four major psychotropic drug groups are used in therapy: antipsychotic, antidepressant, mood stabilizers, and antianxiety drugs. **Antipsychotic drugs** help reduce the confusion, hallucinations, and delusions of *psychotic disorders*, the disorders (such as schizophrenia) marked by a loss of contact with reality, as well as the severe mood disorders accompanied by delusions. **Antidepressant drugs** help improve the mood of people who are depressed. **Mood stabilizing drugs** help level the moods of those with a bipolar disorder, the condition marked by mood swings from mania to depression. **Antianxiety drugs**, also called *minor tranquilizers* or *anxiolytics*, help reduce tension and anxiety. Let's look at each of these drug groups in turn.

LEARNING OBJECTIVE 92
Describe the major biological treatments for psychological disorders.

 **WHAT HAPPENS** *in the* **BRAIN?**

psychotropic drugs medications that act primarily on the brain.

antipsychotic drugs psychotropic drugs that help correct grossly confused or distorted thinking.

antidepressant drugs psychotropic drugs that lift the mood of depressed people.

mood stabilizing drugs psychotropic drugs that help stabilize the moods of people suffering from bipolar disorder.

antianxiety drugs psychotropic drugs that reduce tension and anxiety.

TABLE 92-1 Commonly Prescribed Psychotropic Drugs

Symptom	Type of Medication	Examples
Psychosis (loss of touch with reality)	Antipsychotics Atypical antipsychotics	chlorpromazine (Thorazine) clozapine (Clozaril) risperidone (Risperdal)
Depression	Antidepressants	trazodone (Desyrel) amitriptyline (Elavil) phenelzine (Nardil) fluoxetine (Prozac) paroxetine (Paxil) sertraline (Zoloft) venlafaxine (Effexor)
Mania	Mood stabilizers Antipsychotics	lithium (Lithonate) carbamazepine (Tegretol) valproate (Depakote) olanzapine (Zyprexa)
Anxiety	Anxiolitics Antidepressants	benzodiazepines (Valium, Xanax) fluoxetine (Prozac)

Source: Reprinted with permission of John Wiley & Sons, Inc., from Kowalski, R., & Westen, D. (2009). Psychology (5th ed.). Hoboken, NJ. Wiley, p. 574

©iStockphoto.com/skynesher

Psychopharmacology. Drugs are now widely used to treat psychological disorders, often in conjunction with other forms of therapy.

92.1.1 Antipsychotic Drugs

Beginning in about 1955, individuals suffering from schizophrenia and other disorders were frequently prescribed antipsychotic drugs. The use of these drugs and the reduction of symptoms had the effect of radically reducing the number of mentally ill involuntarily hospitalized and institutionalized patients in the decades that followed. Paul Whitehead, from the University of Western Ontario, and his colleague Patricia Sealy argued that deinstitutionalization was not implemented consistently across geographic areas, with different provinces showing variation in their timing and approaches (Sealy & Whitehead, 2004). In the years following the accidental discovery of the antipsychotic drugs, there was rapid closure of beds in psychiatric hospitals across Canada. However, there was a concomitant increase in beds in general hospitals for use by psychiatric patients. As well, because psychiatric in-patients were discharged into the community at a time when growth in community mental health services was slow across Canada, the unintended effect of releasing people incapable of caring for themselves without support, in many cases, resulted in homelessness.

The classic antipsychotic drugs include chlorpromazine (trade name: Thorazine), thioridazine (Mellaril), and haloperidol (Haldol). These drugs help patients experiencing positive symptoms such as hallucinations and paranoia. However, patients experiencing negative symptoms often get little relief from the classic antipsychotic drugs. New generation drugs, the atypical antipsychotics, such as clozapine (Clozaril), resperidone (Risperdal), and olanzapine (Zyprexa), help patients who do not respond to the typical antipsychotics, as well as some with negative symptoms such as apathy, diminished affect, and poverty of speech (Marder, 2014). These drugs have also proven to be particularly effective for schizophrenics who have persistent suicidal thoughts or who engage in self-injurious behaviours (Hor & Taylor, 2010). Studies indicate that antipsychotic drugs reduce psychotic symptoms within one and eight weeks, to lesser or greater degrees from one individual to another, about 70 percent of the time (Emsley et al., 2009).

It is thought that antipsychotic drugs work by blocking dopamine receptors, thereby blocking dopamine activity at the receptor sites (Ogino et al., 2014), although the exact nature of the relationship between the neurochemical effect and clinical outcomes is as yet unclear (Winton-Brown et al., 2014; De Manzano, 2010). It is important to note, however, that the dopamine hypothesis does not necessarily argue for more dopamine, but rather for more activity at the receptor sites. Moreover, atypical antipsychotics affect both dopamine and serotonin activity (Bradford et al., 2010), and more recent research has identified decreased glutamate activity as playing an important role (Laruelle, 2014). Therefore, a number of neurotransmitter systems have been implicated. A number of researchers have argued that the drug companies have pushed the dopamine hypothesis because they have made billions of dollars on the drugs they sell; these authors contend that this has prevented other, perhaps more productive, solutions from being pursued (Mosher et al., 2013; Healy, 2008).

Atypical antipsychotics tend to be the front line treatment for schizophrenia (Meltzer, 2013; Miyake et al., 2012). There is controversy about whether the second generation drugs are superior to the classic antipsychotic drugs, with some

©iStockphoto.com/Skyak

Mental illness and homelessness. Individuals suffering from severe mental illness are disproportionally and more seriously affected by homelessness than those without mental illness.

researchers suggesting the atypical antipsychotics are superior to the classic antipsychotic drugs (Julien et al., 2011), and other researchers suggesting no difference in effectiveness between the classic and second generation drugs (Leucht et al., 2009; Miyamoto et al., 2008). This debate aside, determining a single course of treatment for a given patient is virtually impossible. Given the multiple and complex symptoms associated with schizophrenia, the wide individual variation in the response to drugs (in terms of both efficacy and side effects), as well as the diversity of treatment options, this disorder is very difficult to treat (Massey et al., 2014). Long-term outcome is highly correlated with early diagnosis (Emsley et al., 2008), and treating negative symptoms continues to be a treatment obstacle (Gaebel et al., 2014).

Antipsychotic drugs may also cause serious side effects. The classic antipsychotic drugs can produce severe movement abnormalities, including severe shaking, bizarre-looking contractions of the face and body, and extreme restlessness (Geddes et al., 2011); can cause Parkinson-like symptoms such as tremors, posture imbalance, muscle rigidity, and so on (recall that Parkinson's is caused by too little dopamine); and in serious cases can cause a disorder called tardive dyskinesia. *Tardive dyskinesia* is a neurological disorder marked by involuntary repetitive tic-like symptoms affecting the tongue, lips, and face, as well as the trunk and extremities. Symptoms often persist well after the medication that caused the disorder has been terminated. The atypical antipsychotics do not come with these risks, but have side effects of their own. In a small percentage of cases—about 1 percent—clozapine lowers the white count in the blood cells to dangerously low numbers and the patient becomes highly susceptible to infection. As a result, those who take the drug have to take regular blood tests to monitor for this toxic reaction. The atypical antipsychotics in general are associated with obesity and diabetes (Lieberman et al., 2005). Due to the unpleasant side effects associated with the drugs, many patients discontinue their medications and relapse within a year (Tsang et al., 2009).

92.1.2 Antidepressants

Antidepressants are prescribed more than any other class of medications in North America (Olfson & Marcus, 2009). Antidepressants are primarily used for treating mood disorders, particularly depression, but some antidepressants (SSRIs, as explained below) are also useful for treating anxiety, particularly generalized anxiety disorder, OCD, and panic disorder (Baldwin et al., 2009). Antidepressants primarily target the serotonin and norepinephrine pathways (Nemeroff & Owens, 2009). Those with more severe depression tend to respond best to antidepressants, whereas those with mild to moderate depression receive little to some benefit (Fournier et al., 2010).

Prior to 1987, two classes of antidepressants were commonly prescribed: tricyclics (Elavil) and MAO inhibitors (Nardil). Tricyclics work by blocking the reuptake of serotonin and norepinephrine. The result is elevation of synaptic concentrations of these neurotransmitters in the synapse and increasing activity at both receptor sites (Nelson, 2009). Monoamine oxidase inhibitors (MAOIs) prevent the monoamine oxidase enzymes from breaking down norepinephrine, serotonin, and dopamine, thereby increasing their availability (Wimbiscus et al., 2010). Traditionally, MAOs were a last line of defence because of dietary restrictions associated with their use to prevent the spiking of blood pressure. There is now some question of whether this restriction is as necessary as once believed (Grady & Stahl, 2012).

Fluoxetine (Prozac), sertraline (Zoloft), and paroxetine (Paxil) work by blocking the reabsorption of serotonin from the synapse. For this reason, this group of drugs is called selective serotonin reuptake inhibitors (SSRIs). These drugs exert their effect by keeping serotonin

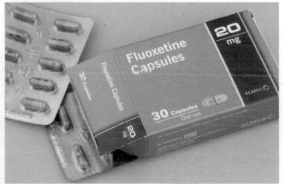

©iStockphoto.com/marcoventuriniautieri

Antidepressant drugs. The antidepressant fluoxetine (Prozac) works by blocking the reabsorption of the neurotransmitter serotonin from the synapse. By keeping serotonin in the synapse longer, the serotonin has a stronger effect.

in the synapse for longer, enabling it to exert a stronger effect (see Tying It Together: Your Brain and Behaviour). SSRIs are relatively fast acting, with approximately 60 percent of patients noting improvement after two weeks (Boland & Keller, 2009).

SNRIs or serotonin reuptake inhibitors, including drugs such as venlafaxine (Effexor) and duloxetine (Celexa), act by blocking the reabsorption of serotonin and norepinephrine from the synapse. There is some evidence that this class of drugs is somewhat more effective at treating symptoms of depression than the SSRIs (Thase & Denko, 2008). However, SNRIs have more side effects than the SSRIs, including increased risk for diabetes and cardiovascular problems (Bezchlibnyk-Butler et al., 2013).

Research shows that SSRIs are equally effective as tricyclics, but without the side effects, and their use is associated with better rates of compliance (Von Wolff et al., 2013; Boland & Keller, 2009). Since the side effects of tricyclics can include erectile dysfunction, reduced sex drive, heart arrhythmias, tremors, and confusion, SSRIs are highly desirable as a first line of treatment. In fact, the Canadian Network for Mood and Anxiety Treatments (CANMAT) partnered with the Canadian Psychiatric Association in 2001 to produce clinical guidelines for the treatment of depression. This body has approved the use of second generation antidepressants (SSRIs and SNRIs) over first generation antidepressants (tricyclics and MAOIs) as a first-line approach (Lam, 2009).

Of concern in the last 10 years or so has been the finding that antidepressants, particularly SSRIs, increase the risk for suicide especially among children, adolescents, and emerging adults (Barburi et al., 2009; Olafson et al., 2006). More recent evidence suggests that this risk is heightened within the first month or two of the patient beginning the course of treatment (Healy & Whitaker, 2003). Other studies have failed to replicate this claim for increased risk and instead argue that, after controlling for severity of depression, the risk for suicide actually goes down (Leon et al., 2011). Nevertheless, patients with serious depression need to be closely monitored when they begin treatment (Gibbons et al., 2012; Culpepper et al., 2004). Regulatory warnings from the U.S. Food and Drug Administration, as well as from Health Canada, have resulted in a black box warning for all antidepressant use in those under 18 years of age. Many are questioning the wisdom of this caution, arguing that there is no evidence for increased risk in this age group, and that untreated individuals are at greater risk than those being treated with antidepressants (Sparks & Duncan, 2013).

92.1.3 Mood Stabilizers

Mood stabilizers are used to treat intense shifts in mood from one extreme state to another, preventing both depression and mania in those with bipolar disorder. Lithium, a salt, is the most commonly prescribed drug used to maintain a stable mood and to prevent future relapse or reoccurrence of depression or mania (Chengappa & Gershon, 2013). Although lithium can be used to treat acute manic or depressive symptoms, antidepressants and antipsychotics are more commonly used (Fountoulakis, 2005). Lithium has a number of serious side effects, including thyroid and kidney disease, renal failure, loss of memory, cardiac arrhythmia, loss of bladder and bowel control, and more. As a consequence, alternatives to lithium have been identified. The most common alternative to lithium is valproate, an anticonvulsant agent. The direct mechanisms by which valproate stabilizes mood is unknown. Although patients taking valproate were more likely to continue taking their medications than those taking lithium, there is little evidence that valproate is more effective than lithium (Cipriani et al., 2013). Some patients are treated with a combination of lithium and valproate, or lithium in combination with other drugs (Post et al., 2013). In addition to other concerns, but also because of the number of unpleasant side effects associated with these drugs, patients are often unwilling to adhere to their medical protocols; men are more likely than women to be non-compliant (Murru et al., 2011).

92.1.4 Antianxiety Drugs

The most popular antianxiety drugs are in the benzodiazepine family. Common drugs are diazepam (Valium), alprazolam (Xanax), and lorazepam (Ativan). These drugs are often referred to collectively as tranquilizers. Unlike the drugs already discussed, which can take weeks to exert a full effect, antianxiety drugs immediately relieve the symptoms of anxiety (Dubovsky & Dubovsky, 2009). However, they are also fast-acting, and their effects wear off within hours.

One problem with the benzodiazepine family of drugs is that they can be abused. When a patient takes an antianxiety drug, there is an almost immediate alleviation of anxiety; patients may therefore find themselves reaching for the medication with greater and greater frequency in an effort to seek immediate relief from their unpleasant symptoms, creating psychological dependence (Fenton et al., 2010). As well, because the medication only alleviates the symptoms, the underlying causes for the anxiety are never addressed. These drugs also cause physiological dependence, and sudden cessation following heavy use is associated with withdrawal symptoms, including insomnia and increased anxiety (O'Brien, 2005).

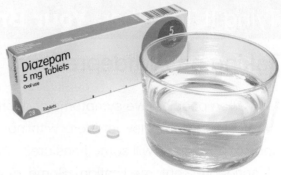

©iStockphoto.com/Gannet77

Antianxiety drugs. Antianxiety drugs, such as diazepam (Valium), provide immediate relief of anxiety symptoms; however, their effects wear off quickly, often within hours.

92.1.5 Drug Therapy Summary

Many of the medications we have discussed have radically changed the lives of many people with psychological disorders. Drugs are increasingly being prescribed for every type of mental illness. Studies have indicated that psychiatrists prescribe on average two to three prescriptions per patient (Mojtabai & Olfson, 2010), and that general practitioners provide drug therapy to the majority of patients suffering from symptoms of depression (Olfson et al., 2006). However, it is important to note that these drugs do not work for everyone and often come with potential side effects, ranging from annoying to life threatening. It is therefore important to assess whether a particular drug is effective.

In order to assess the efficacy of a particular drug, researchers must take into account how many people who are untreated get better. That is, if we do nothing, how many people will spontaneously recover? It is also important to assess whether patients are responding to a particular drug or to the *idea* of the drug. That is, it is important to assess whether patients get better because they *expect* to get better, or they get better because the medication exerts an effect. For this reason, psychologists and physicians use the technique of the double-blind procedure. In this method, some of the participants take the drug being tested and some take a placebo. (A **placebo** is an inactive substance that exerts no pharmacological effect.) Neither the patient nor the physician (or others dealing directly with the patient) know which drug the patient is taking.

Regardless of how effective a drug is, research shows that in most instances a combination of psychotherapy and drugs has a stronger effect than drugs alone (Oestergaard & Møldrup, 2011). And, as discussed throughout this book, it is also important to recall that many psychological disorders arise from the social conditions under which people live. It is therefore important that as a society we seek to redress the inequities and discrimination that underlie many of the mental illnesses people experience.

placebo an inactive substance, such as a sugar pill or distilled water, that mimics a drug but has no active ingredients.

electroconvulsive therapy (ECT) use of electric shock to trigger a brain seizure in hopes of relieving abnormal functioning.

92.2 Electroconvulsive Therapy

Another form of biological treatment is **electroconvulsive therapy** (ECT), a technique first developed in the 1930s. ECT is used primarily for people who have severe depression. ECT is administered

"If this doesn't help you don't worry, it's a placebo."

Peter C. Vey/The New Yorker/The Cartoon Bank

Tying It Together: **Your Brain and Behaviour**

Taking an Antidepressant

When people have symptoms of depression so severe that they interfere with normal functioning, physicians will sometimes prescribe the use of antidepressant medication. Some of the most commonly prescribed antidepressants are selective serotonin reuptake inhibitors (SSRIs); these drugs are known by trade names such as Celexa, Paxil, Prozac, and Zoloft. The primary action of these drugs is to increase the availability of the neurotransmitter serotonin in the brain. Neurons that make serotonin are present in the brainstem raphe nuclei. These neurons send axon projections to the cortex, hippocampus, and amygdala, among other regions. SSRIs have a multitude of effects on these brain regions, although the precise mechanisms by which the drugs alleviate symptoms of depression are not known. How might antidepressant drugs work?

Questions

1 Which area of the cerebral cortex often shows reduced activity in people who are depressed?

2 What does it mean to say that a particular drug is a "serotonin reuptake inhibitor"?

3 What is the role of the hippocampus in the recovery of someone taking antidepressent medication to relieve depression?

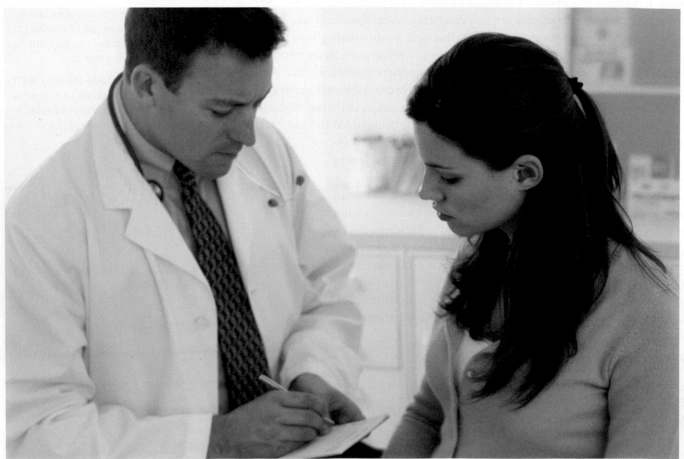

Michael A. Keller/Corbis

From Paul Keedwell, Journal of Psychopharmacology 23(7):775-88, Figure 3, 2009, Sage Publications. ©2009 British Association for Psychopharmacology.

BLOCKING SEROTONIN REUPTAKE

By blocking key receptors, SSRIs prevent the reuptake, or retention, of serotonin by presynaptic neurons (shown in this illustration), thus freeing the neurotransmitter to better activate brain regions that are targets of serotonin axons, including the hippocampus and cerebral cortex. Depression relief, however, usually does not occur until someone has taken the drug for a few weeks, suggesting that some other mechanism may also be responsible for improving mood.

Serotonin in vesicle

Presynaptic neuron

Serotonin reuptake

Serotonin reuptake blocked

SSRI

RESTORING BRAIN ACTIVITY TO NORMAL LEVELS

The prefrontal cortex of depressed individuals shows reduced activity and a lower than normal level of blood flow. Some studies suggest that antidepressants ultimately raise activity in this brain region (shown on this brain scan in yellow) and restore blood flow to levels observed in non-depressed individuals. Similar findings have been reported for the amygdala.

Amygdala

Hippocampus

Prefrontal cortex

Raphe nuclei

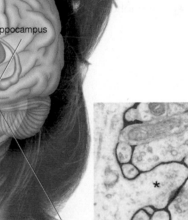

Courtesy Charles Nicholson, New York University School of Medicine

REJUVENATING THE MIND

Antidepressant use stimulates the production of synapses in the hippocampus (shown here in this electron micrograph, with the asterisk indicating a postsynaptic site). The hippocampus plays a role in cognitive function and in regulating anxiety (a feature in many cases of depression). The growth of new synapses may refresh this important brain region, enabling the formation of new connections to support a more positive outlook.

MedioImages/Photodisc/Getty Images, Inc.

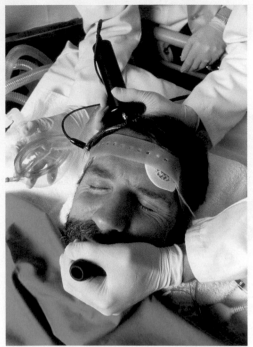

Will & Deni McIntyre/Photo Researchers, Inc.

ECT today. As we can see with this patient, today's ECT treatments are conducted with considerable medical care and many safety precautions, and include procedures that help patients sleep throughout the procedure.

in the following manner. First, a strong muscle relaxant and usually a short-acting anesthetic are administered. Next, two electrodes are attached to the patient's forehead, and 65 to 140 volts of electricity are briefly passed through the brain (Endler, 1988). The procedure produces a brain seizure that lasts up to a few minutes. After an average of seven to nine ECT sessions, spaced two or three days apart, many patients feel considerably less depressed. ECT helps approximately 70 percent of depressed patients to improve (Perugi et al., 2012).

ECT is administered less often today than it was in the past, and is typically only used in treating severe depression that has not responded to other treatments. The procedure can negatively affect short-term memory (Merkl et al., 2011). Most such memories return, but some people who have gone through ECT report ongoing memory difficulties (Freeman et al., 2013; Hanna et al., 2009; Wang, 2007). With the growing success of antidepressant medications and other forms of psychotherapy, fewer depressed patients now need this form of treatment. Nevertheless, ECT continues to be a viable treatment option when people have a severe depressive episode that does not respond to other forms of treatment or when they are suicidal. ECT is particularly effective in acute cases because it exerts a much more immediate effect than antidepressant drugs (Kobeissi et al., 2011).

Although there is evidence to indicate that ECT is an effective treatment option in some cases of severe depression, for some the use of this treatment is contentious because the mechanism by which it alters mood is not well understood. Proponents argue that the seizure reestablishes biochemical and hormonal homeostasis in the brain in systems that control mood (Medda et al., 2009; Sienaert et al., 2009).

In recent years, two other biological approaches have been developed that also directly stimulate the brain. These approaches are *vagus nerve stimulation* and *transcranial magnetic stimulation*. They appeal to many patients and clinicians because they are applied without the wide-ranging and traumatic impact of ECT.

vagus nerve stimulation
a procedure in a which an implanted device sends electrical signals to the brain through the vagus nerve; used to treat severe depression.

92.2.1 Vagus Nerve Stimulation

The vagus nerve, the longest nerve in the human body, runs from the brain stem through the neck, down the chest, and on to the abdomen. In the **vagus nerve stimulation** procedure, a surgeon implants a small pacemaker-like device called a *pulse generator* under the skin of the chest. The surgeon then guides a wire, which extends from the pulse generator, up to the neck and attaches it to the left vagus nerve (see **Figure 92-1**). Electrical signals travel periodically from the pulse generator through the wire to the vagus nerve. In turn, the stimulated vagus nerve delivers electrical signals to the brain. These signals affect the mood centres of the brain.

In 1997, Health Canada approved this procedure for treating cases of otherwise intractable epilepsy. In 2001, after noting significant increases in positive mood in epileptics receiving the treatment, it was approved as a long-term treatment for severe treatment-resistant depression (Guberman, 2004; Kennedy et al., 2009). Since this time, some research has found that the vagus nerve stimulation procedure provides significant symptomatic relief in as many as 65 percent of cases (Howland et al., 2011; Nahas et al., 2005).

Left vagus nerve

Electrodes

Pulse generator
(implanted under the skin)

FIGURE 92-1 **Vagus nerve stimulation.** In this procedure, an implanted pulse generator sends electrical signals to the left vagus nerve. That nerve then delivers electrical signals to the brain, helping to reduce depression in many people.

92.2.2 Transcranial Magnetic Stimulation

In the **transcranial magnetic stimulation (TMS)** procedure, first developed in 1985, the clinician places an electromagnetic coil on or above the patient's head. The coil sends a current into the prefrontal cortex. As you may remember from Part 15, at least some parts of the prefrontal cortex of depressed people are underactive. TMS appears to increase neuron activity in those regions, thus helping to alleviate severe depression in about 65 percent of patients after it has been administered daily for two to four weeks (Howland et al., 2011; Rosenberg et al., 2011). TMS was approved as a treatment option by Health Canada in 2001 (Kennedy et al., 2009).

transcranial magnetic stimulation (TMS) a procedure in which an electromagnetic coil placed on or above a person's head sends a current into the prefrontal cortex; used to treat severe depression.

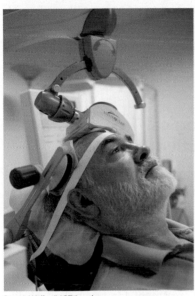

BonnieWeller/MCT/Landov

Transcranial magnetic stimulation. TMS is a non-invasive procedure used to treat depression. The electromagnetic coil is placed on the patient's head and sends a current into the prefrontal cortex.

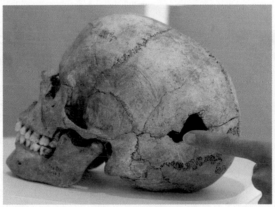

Winfried Rothermel/AP

Early roots of psychosurgery? The hole in this 5,100-year-old skull indicates that the individual underwent trephining, cutting away a circular section of the skull. Some historians believe that trephination was done to release the evil spirits that were thought to be responsible for mental dysfunction.

92.3 Psychosurgery

From time to time throughout the book, we have mentioned **psychosurgery**—brainsurgery procedures that can help some people with psychological disorders. Actually, the first use of brain surgery as a treatment for mental disorders was **trephining**, the prehistoric practice of chipping a hole in the skull to treat an injury or other disorder. Evidence indicates that trephining was used not only by prehistoric people, but also by people in classical and medieval times.

Many modern forms of psychosurgery are derived from a past technique known as a **lobotomy**. In this procedure, the surgeon cuts the connections between the brain's frontal lobes and the lower centres of the brain. Lobotomies were widely used for a few decades after the procedure was developed in the 1930s, particularly in cases of schizophrenia. By the late 1950s, however, it had become clear that lobotomies were not as effective as many psychosurgeons had been claiming. Moreover, many patients who had undergone the surgery later suffered irreversible effects, including seizures, extreme listlessness, stupor, and in some cases, death (Barahal, 1958). Thus, use of this procedure declined during the 1960s as less invasive alternative therapies became available (Valenstein, 2010).

psychosurgery brain surgery often used in hopes of relieving abnormal functioning.

trephining prehistoric practice of chipping a hole in the skull as a treatment for various brain conditions.

lobotomy surgical practice of cutting the connections between the frontal lobe and the lower centres of the brain.

deep brain stimulation
a procedure in which implanted electrodes deliver constant low stimulation to a small area of the brain; used to treat severe depression, Parkinson's disease, and epilepsy.

Psychosurgery today is much more precise than the lobotomies of the past. It has fewer negative effects, and it is apparently beneficial for some psychological and neurological disorders. One form of psychosurgery that is currently receiving considerable attention is **deep brain stimulation**—a procedure applied in cases of severe depression, Parkinson's disease, and brain seizure disorder (epilepsy). In deep brain stimulation, a surgeon drills two tiny holes into the patient's skull and implants electrodes in areas of the brain that have been implicated in the disorder. The electrodes are connected to a battery, or "pacemaker," that is implanted in the patient's chest (for men) or stomach (for women). The pacemaker powers the electrodes, sending a steady stream of low-voltage electricity to the problematic brain areas. In many cases, this repeated stimulation readjusts the person's brain activity and, over time, brings significant improvement (Blomstedt et al., 2011; Hamani et al., 2011; Mayberg et al., 2005). Although such implants have offered promising results, at present they are still considered experimental. Thus, they are used infrequently, particularly in cases of depression, and usually only after the severe disorder has continued for years without responding to other forms of treatment.

Tim Vernon, LTH NHS Trust/Photo Researchers

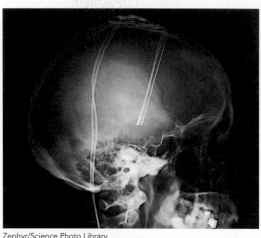
Zephyr/Science Photo Library

Deep brain stimulation. To treat severe cases of depression, Parkinson's disease, and epilepsy, electrodes are surgically implanted in the patient's brain to deliver constant low stimulation to adjust brain activity.

92.4 Biological Treatments in Perspective

Biological treatments for psychological disorders, particularly drug treatments, are very popular. They often bring great relief when other approaches have failed. However, the treatments have key limitations. As you have read, they can produce significant side effects. Moreover, more often than not, biological interventions alone are not a sufficient treatment for psychological disorders (Kosslyn & Rosenberg, 2004). Indeed, as we have seen throughout the textbook, the connections in our brains unfold partly in response to the environmental experiences that we have all through our lives, beginning in utero.

Evidence is mounting, in fact, that just as behaviour can respond to changes in our brain chemistry, so too does our brain chemistry respond to changes in behaviour. One study, for example, found that people with depression who responded to psychotherapy came to show brain responses similar to those of healthy, non-depressed individuals. In contrast, depressed individuals who did not respond to psychotherapy continued to show the abnormal brain patterns that typically accompany depression (Okamoto et al., 2006). In short, just as negative experiences can interact with brain activity to produce abnormal functioning, positive experiences can interact with the brain to make our functioning more normal.

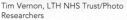

Before You Go On

www.wiley.com/go/comercanada

What Do You Know?
1. What are the three main categories of biological treatments?
2. What are some new methods of direct brain stimulation, and how are they used?

What Do You Think? Are today's clinicians and their clients too reliant on drugs as a treatment? Why or why not?

Summary

Module 92: Biological Treatments

LEARNING OBJECTIVE 92 Describe the major biological treatments for psychological disorders.

- *Drug therapy, electroconvulsive therapy (ECT)*, and *psychosurgery* are the three major categories of biological treatments.
- Psychotropic drugs, including *antianxiety, antidepressant*, and *antipsychotic drugs*, have brought relief to many, but they do not work for everyone and may have undesired side effects.
- Electroconvulsive therapy (ECT), used primarily to treat depression, is administered less often today than in the past. Two more recently developed brain stimulation treatments, *vagus nerve stimulation* and *transcranial magnetic stimulation*, have fewer wide-ranging and traumatic side effects than ECT.
- Psychosurgery today is much more precise than the lobotomies of the past, in which the connections between the frontal lobe and the lower brain centres were severed.
- Biological treatments for psychological disorders, particularly drug treatments, are highly regarded today. However, more often than not, biological interventions alone are not enough.

Key Terms

antianxiety drugs 707

antidepressant drugs 707

antipsychotic drugs 707

deep brain stimulation 716

electroconvulsive therapy (ECT) 711

lobotomy 715

mood stabilizing drugs 707

placebo 711

psychosurgery 715

psychotropic drugs 707

transcranial magnetic stimulation (TMS) 715

trephining 715

vagus nerve stimulation 714

Study Questions

Multiple Choice

1. The most commonly used brain treatment for psychological disorders is
   a) deep brain stimulation.
   b) drug therapy.
   c) electroconvulsive therapy.
   d) psychosurgery.

Fill-in-the-Blank

1. Recent research shows that electroconvulsive therapy (ECT) helps about _____ percent of depressed patients who try it.

2. One downside of _____ medications used to treat disorders such as schizophrenia is that they can cause severe shaking and contractions of the face and body.

Module 93: Psychodynamic Therapies

Following the principles of the psychodynamic model, psychodynamic therapists contend that today's emotional disorder is the result of yesterday's emotional trauma. A variety of psychodynamic therapies are now being practised, ranging from classical *Freudian psychoanalysis* to modern therapies such as *short-term psychodynamic therapy* and *relational psychoanalytic therapy*. All share the goals of helping clients to uncover past traumatic events and the inner conflicts that have resulted from them; to resolve, or settle, those conflicts; and to resume interrupted personal development. Psychodynamic therapists of different theoretical persuasions might focus on different conflicts, but they tend to use similar techniques.

93.1 Techniques of Psychodynamic Therapies

Psychodynamic therapists try to subtly guide their discussions with clients so that the clients discover their underlying problems for themselves. How do they do this? In part, they rely on such techniques as *free association*, *therapist interpretation*, *catharsis*, and *working through* (Etchegoyen, 2005).

93.1.1 Free Association

free association psychodynamic therapy technique of allowing clients to freely talk about whatever they want.

In psychodynamic therapies, the client is responsible for starting and leading each discussion. The therapist tells the individual to describe any thoughts or feelings that come to mind, even if they seem unimportant. This is the process known as **free association**. The therapist then probes the client's associations in the hope that they will eventually reveal the unconscious events that underlie the individual's problem.

93.1.2 Therapist Interpretation

resistance practice in which clients encounter a block in their free associations or change the subject to avoid a potentially painful discussion.

transference process through which clients come to act and feel toward the therapist as they did toward important figures in their childhood.

Psychodynamic therapists share their interpretations of a client's associations with the client only when they think the individual is ready to hear them. The interpretations of three phenomena—*resistance*, *transference*, and *dreams*—are thought to be of special value.

- *Resistance* Individuals demonstrate **resistance** when they encounter a block in their free associations or change the subject to avoid a potentially painful discussion. The therapist remains on the lookout for resistance, which is usually unconscious, and may point it out to the client and interpret it.

- *Transference* Psychodynamic therapists also believe that clients act and feel toward the therapist as they do toward important figures in their lives, past and present. This displacement of feelings is called **transference**. By interpreting transference behaviour, therapists may help individuals better understand how they unconsciously feel toward a parent or some other key person. In the excerpt found in the Psychology Around Us box below, a psychodynamic therapist helps a client to explore her transference.

- *Dream interpretation* Freud (1924) called dreams the "royal road to the unconscious." He believed that repression and other defence mechanisms operate ineffectively during sleep. Thus, a client's dreams can help reveal the person's unconscious instincts, needs, and wishes. Of course the dreams must be correctly interpreted. Freud distinguished a dream's *manifest content* (the consciously remembered dream) from its *latent content* (the symbolic meaning).

©iStockphoto.com/Wavebreak

Psychodynamic techniques. In order to help clients come to an appropriate understanding of their underlying problems, psychodynamic therapists interpret what the clients tell them.

93.1.3 Catharsis

Psychodynamic therapists believe that individuals must experience **catharsis** if they are to resolve internal conflicts and overcome their problems. That is, they must re-experience their past repressed feelings. Emotional catharsis must accompany intellectual insight for genuine progress to be achieved.

catharsis reliving of past repressed feelings as a means of settling internal conflicts and overcoming problems.

93.1.4 Working Through

A single session of interpretation and catharsis will not change a person. For deep and lasting insight to be gained, the client and therapist must *work through*, or examine, the same issues over and over, across many sessions, trying on the insights offered through therapy, each time with new and sharper clarity (Brenner, 1987).

93.2 Short-Term Psychodynamic Therapies

It should be clear by now that Freud's psychoanalytic therapy takes time. However, over the years the public and health care providers increased their demand for more efficient, time-limited psychotherapies. The pressure for briefer therapy is also present in Canada, though driven more by limits of coverage for therapy either though employee assistance programs or health care insurance providers. As a result, several efforts emerged to make psychodynamic therapy shorter, more efficient, and more cost-effective. In brief versions of psychodynamic therapy, called *short-term psychodynamic therapy*, clients focus on a single problem—a *dynamic focus*—such as excessive dependence on other people (Wolitzky, 2011). The therapist and client centre their discussions on this problem and work only on issues that relate to it. A relatively small number of studies have tested the effectiveness of these short-term psychodynamic therapies. Their findings, however, suggest that the approaches are sometimes quite helpful (Wolitzky, 2011; Present et al., 2008).

Iconica/Getty Images

Catharsis. Patients must re-experience past feelings in order to resolve internal conflicts and overcome their problems. Catharsis must be accompanied by intellectual insight.

93.3 Relational Psychoanalytic Therapy

Whereas Freud believed that psychodynamic therapists should take on the role of a neutral, distant expert during a treatment session, a current school of psychodynamic therapy called **relational psychoanalytic therapy** argues that therapists are key figures in the lives of clients—figures whose reactions and beliefs should be directly included in the therapy process (Luborsky et al., 2011). Thus, a key principle of relational psychoanalytic therapy

relational psychoanalytic therapy a school of psychodynamic therapy holding that therapists should work to form more equal relationships with clients.

Psychology Around Us   A Revealing Transfer

Patient: *I get so excited by what is happening here. I feel I'm being held back by needing to be nice. I'd like to blast loose sometimes, but I don't dare.*

Therapist: *Because you fear my reaction?*

Patient: *The worst thing would be that you wouldn't like me. You wouldn't speak to me friendly; you wouldn't smile; you'd feel you can't treat me and discharge me from treatment. But I know this isn't so, I know it.*

Therapist: *Where do you think these attitudes come from?*

Patient: *When I was nine years old, I read a lot about great men in history. I'd quote them and be dramatic. I'd want a sword at my side; I'd dress like an Indian.*

Mother would scold me. Don't frown, don't talk so much. Sit on your hands, over and over again. I did all kinds of things. I was a naughty child. She told me I'd be hurt. Then at fourteen I fell off a horse and broke my back. I had to be in bed. Mother told me on the day I went riding not to, that I'd get hurt because the ground was frozen. I was a stubborn, self-willed child. Then I went against her will and suffered an accident that changed my life, a fractured back. Her attitude was, "I told you so." I was put in a cast and kept in bed for months.

(Wolberg, L. R. (1967). *The technique of psychotherapy.* New York: Grune & Stratton, p. 662.)

is that therapists should also disclose things about themselves, particularly their own reactions to patients, and try to establish more equal relationships with clients as opposed to the distant analytic relationships typical of standard psychoanalysis.

93.4 Psychodynamic Therapies in Perspective

Freud and his followers have had a major impact on treatment. They were the first practitioners to demonstrate the value of systematically applying both theory and techniques to treatment. Moreover, their approaches were the first to clarify the potential of psychological, as opposed to biological, treatment. In fact their ideas have served as a starting point for many other psychological treatments.

Carefully conducted research, however, has failed to support the effectiveness of most psychodynamic therapies (Wampold et al., 2011; Neitzel et al., 2003). For the first half of the twentieth century, the value of these approaches was supported mostly by the case studies of enthusiastic clinicians and by uncontrolled research studies. Controlled investigations have been conducted only since the 1950s, and, with the exception of short-term psychodynamic therapies, only a small number of such studies have found psychodynamic therapies to be more effective than no treatment or placebo treatments (Prochaska & Norcross, 2010). Nevertheless, 15 percent of today's clinical psychologists identify themselves as psychodynamic therapists (Sharf, 2012; Prochaska & Norcross, 2010).

Before You Go On   www.wiley.com/go/comercanada

What Do You Know?
1. Contrast three types of psychodynamic therapy.
2. List and describe psychodynamic therapy techniques.

What Do You Think? Remember Jefferson, in our part opener. In treating Jefferson's psychological distress, where might a Freudian psychoanalyst start? Would this analyst be likely to achieve the results described in the time frame identified? Why or why not?

Summary

Module 93: Psychodynamic Therapies

LEARNING OBJECTIVE 93 Describe the psychodynamic treatments for psychological disorders.

- Psychodynamic therapies range from classical *Freudian psychoanalysis* to modern therapies. All share the goals of helping clients to uncover past traumatic events and the inner conflicts that have resulted from them, and to resolve those conflicts.
- Psychodynamic therapy techniques include *free association*; therapist interpretation of *resistance*, *transference*, and *dreams*; *catharsis*; and repeatedly *working through* issues.
- Recent developments in psychodynamic therapy include *short-term psychodynamic therapy* and *relational psychoanalytic therapy*.
- The psychodynamic approach has had a lasting influence on the conduct of treatment and was the first to offer an alternative to biological explanations of abnormal functioning. But the effectiveness of psychodynamic therapy is not well supported by research.

Key Terms

catharsis 719

free association 718

relational psychoanalytic therapy 719

resistance 718

transference 718

Study Questions

Multiple Choice

1. A client in therapy is asked to describe thoughts as they come to mind. What therapeutic technique does this describe?
   a) Free association
   b) Resistance
   c) Transference
   d) Working through

Fill-in-the-Blank

1. In psychodynamic therapy, dream interpretation involves examining both the _____ content (the consciously remembered details) and the _____ content (the symbolic meaning of those details).

2. Despite limited evidence of its effectiveness, the psychodynamic approach to therapy is practised by about _____ percent of clinical psychologists.

Module 94: Behavioural Therapies

Behavioural theories and treatments today are usually part of the *cognitive-behavioural model*—the perspective that combines behavioural and cognitive principles to explain and treat psychological disorders. For many years, however, behavioural treatments were applied on their own, and, even today, there are times when behavioural interventions are sufficient to treat certain problems. Thus, in this module we will look at behavioural therapies exclusively. We will then move on to cognitive-behavioural therapies in the next module.

As you may recall from Part 15, behaviourists contend that the symptoms of a psychological disorder are learned behaviours acquired through the same conditioning processes that produce normal behaviours. The goal of behavioural therapy is to identify the client's specific problem-causing behaviours and to replace them with more adaptive behaviours. The therapist's attitude toward the client is that of a teacher, rather than a healer. Behavioural techniques fall into three categories: *classical conditioning*, *operant conditioning*, and *modelling*.

94.1 Classical Conditioning Techniques

Classical conditioning treatments are intended to change clients' dysfunctional reactions to stimuli. One treatment, described in Part 7, is *systematic desensitization*. This step-by-step process is aimed at teaching people with phobias to react with calm instead of fear to the objects or situations they dread (Fishman et al., 2011; Wolpe, 1997, 1995, 1990). Clients first are trained in deep-muscle relaxation, through deep breathing, calming mental imagery, and systematic tensing and releasing of muscles. Next, they construct a *fear hierarchy* in which they list objects or situations associated with their phobia, starting with the least feared and ending with the most feared. For a client with a phobia of elevators, for example, looking at an elevator on the outside of a building a block away might be low on the fear hierarchy; watching the elevator doors close while inside the elevator might be near the top (see **Figure 94-1**). Finally, either in imagination or physically, clients confront each item on the hierarchy while they are in a state of deep relaxation, starting with the least fearful and then moving on up the list.

Research has repeatedly found that systematic desensitization and other classical conditioning techniques reduce phobic reactions more effectively than placebo treatments or no treatment at all (Olatunji et al., 2011; Kraft & Kraft, 2010). These techniques have also been helpful in treating several other kinds of problems, including sexual dysfunctions, posttraumatic stress disorder, agoraphobia, and asthma attacks (Koch & Haring, 2008). Because desensitization techniques expose individuals to the objects or situations they fear, and because this exposure seems so critical to implement, these and related approaches are often referred to as *exposure* treatments.

An opposite use of classical conditioning is known as **aversion therapy**. Here, clients *acquire* anxiety responses to stimuli that they have been finding too attractive. This approach has been used with people who want to stop excessive drinking, for example, as shown in **Figure 94-2** (Owen-Howard, 2001). In repeated sessions, the clients may be given an electric shock, a nausea-producing drug, or some other noxious stimulus whenever they reach for a drink. Aversion therapy has also been applied to help eliminate such undesirable behaviours as self-mutilation in autistic children, sexual paraphilias, and smoking (George & Weinberger, 2008; Krueger & Kaplan, 2002). However, the effects of this approach have typically been short-lived, especially for those individuals who are aware that it is the drugs and not the

FIGURE 94-1 **Fear hierarchy.** Systematic desensitization uses classical conditioning principles to reduce a person's fears. Starting with the least stressful situation on his fear hierarchy, a man with a fear of riding in an elevator is exposed to each item on the hierarchy while applying relaxation techniques. Source: Table 17-2: Reprinted with permission of John Wiley & Sons, Inc., from Kowalski, R., & Westen, D. (2009). *Psychology* (5th ed.). Hoboken, NJ: Wiley, p. 574.

Least

Looking at a building with outside elevators

Approaching a bank of elevator doors

Pressing the elevator call button

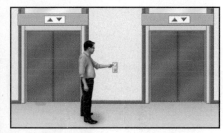

alcohol, smoking, or other behaviour that is actually causing their nausea (Lancaster et al., 2000).

94.2 Operant Conditioning Techniques

In operant conditioning treatments, therapists consistently provide rewards for appropriate behaviour and withhold rewards for inappropriate behaviour. This technique has been employed frequently, and often successfully, with hospitalized patients experiencing psychosis (Kopelowicz, Liberman, & Zarate, 2007; Paul & Lentz, 1977; Ayllon & Azrin, 1965). When such patients talk coherently and behave normally, they are rewarded with food, privileges, attention, or something else they value. Conversely, they receive no rewards when they speak bizarrely or display other psychotic behaviours.

Parents, teachers, and therapists have successfully used operant conditioning techniques to change problem behaviours in children (such as repeated tantrums) and to teach skills to individuals with autism or intellectual disabilities (Soorya et al., 2011; Spiegler & Guevremont, 2003). Rewards in such cases have included food, recreation time, social rewards, and television watching.

Operant conditioning techniques typically work best in institutions or schools, where a person's behaviour can be reinforced systematically throughout the day. Often, a whole ward or classroom is converted into an operant conditioning arena. In many such programs, desirable behaviour is reinforced with tokens that can later be exchanged for food, privileges, or other rewards (Ayllon & Azrin, 1968). Programs of this sort are called **token economy** programs.

Behavioural techniques based on operant conditioning have also been useful for depression (Lazzari et al., 2011). Recall from Part 15 that depression is often associated with a decline in pleasant activities and withdrawal. To deal with these behaviours, therapists may work with depressed individuals to identify activities the clients enjoy and then guide the individuals in adding the activities back into their lives.

Amount of anxiety

Doors open to empty elevator

Stepping onto elevator with a few other people

94.3 Modelling Techniques

Modelling therapy was first developed by the pioneering social learning theorist Albert Bandura (1977, 1969). Here, therapists demonstrate appropriate behaviours for clients. Then the clients, through a process of imitation and rehearsal, acquire the ability to perform the behaviours in their own lives. This procedure has been used to treat phobias, for example. When therapists repeatedly display calm emotions while confronting objects that are feared by phobic clients, many clients are able to

Most   In a crowded elevator as doors close

1.

| Unconditioned Stimulus: Nauseating Drug | → | Unconditioned Response: Nausea |

2.

| Conditioned Stimulus: Alcohol | + | Unconditioned Stimulus: Nauseating Drug |

3.

| Conditioned Stimulus: Alcohol | → | Conditioned Response: Nausea |

Piotr Marcinski/Shutterstock

FIGURE 94-2 Aversion therapy. Aversion therapy uses classical conditioning principles to create a negative response to a stimulus a person would like to avoid, such as alcohol. Here a woman has a drink just before the effects of a nauseating drug begin.

David Young-Wolff/PhotoEdit

We're all familiar with token economies. The token economies applied in various mental health settings operate just like the star system that most of us were exposed to in elementary school. At school, however, good work was rewarded with stars instead of tokens, and numerous stars added up to a certificate instead of privileges, treats, or other rewards.

social skills training behavioural therapy technique in which therapists serve as models and teachers to help clients acquire desired social behaviours.

overcome their phobias (Rosenthal & Bandura, 1978; Bandura, Adams, & Beyer, 1977).

Behavioural therapists have also used modelling to help people acquire or improve their social skills and assertiveness. In an approach called **social skills training**, for example, therapists point out the social deficits of clients and then role-play social situations with the clients, typically modelling more appropriate social behaviours for them. Ultimately, the clients practise the behaviours in real-life situations (Corrigan, 1991). For example, in the Psychology Around Us box, the client is a male university student who has difficulty making dates with women.

Using a combined strategy of modelling, rehearsal, feedback, and practice, therapists have successfully taught social and assertion skills to shy, passive, or socially isolated people. These techniques can help people who have a pattern of bursting out in rage or violence after building up resentment (rather than asserting themselves) over perceived social slights (Lochman et al., 2010; Fisher et al., 2004). The approach has also been used to improve the social skills of children and adults who experience depression, anxiety, or other psychological problems (Ogden, 2011; Ishikawa et al., 2010; Cooney et al., 1991).

94.4 Behavioural Therapies in Perspective

Behavioural interventions have been among the most widely researched treatment approaches in the clinical field (Wilson, 2011). Certainly, they lend themselves to research more than the psychodynamic approaches do. The removal of symptoms—the criterion of progress in behavioural therapy—is easier to observe and measure than conflict resolution—the psychodynamic criterion of improvement. Moreover, behavioural approaches have been effective for numerous problems, including specific fears, social deficits, and intellectual disabilities (Wilson, 2011, 2008).

At the same time, behavioural therapies have certain limitations. First, the improvements they bring about do not always maintain themselves without further behavioural

Psychology Around Us — Behaviour Therapy: Acquiring the Social Touch

Client: By the way, [Pause] I don't suppose you want to go out Saturday night?

Therapist: Up to actually asking for the date you were very good. However, if I were the girl, I think I might have been a bit offended when you said, "By the way." It's like you're asking her out is pretty casual. Also, the way you phrased the question, you were kind of suggesting to her that she doesn't want to go out with you. Pretend for the moment I'm you. Now, how does this sound: "There is a movie at the Varsity Theatre this Saturday that I want to see. If you don't have other plans, I'd very much like to take you."

Client: That sounded good. Like you were sure of yourself and liked the girl too.

Therapist: Why don't you try it.

Client: You know that movie at the Varsity? Well, I'd like to go, and I'd like to take you Saturday, if you don't have anything better to do.

Therapist: Well, that certainly was better. Your tone of voice was especially good. But the last line, "if you don't have anything better to do," sounds like you don't

Aspenphoto/Dreamstime/GetStock

think you have too much to offer. Why not run through it one more time.

Client: I'd like to see the show at the Varsity, Saturday, and, if you haven't made other plans, I'd like to take you.

Therapist: Much better. Excellent, in fact. You were confident, forceful, and sincere.

(Rimm, D. C., & Masters, J. C. (1979). *Behavior therapy: Techniques and empirical findings* (2nd ed.). New York: Academic Press, p. 74.)

interventions. Second, behavioural therapies, by themselves, do not appear to be particularly effective with psychological disorders that are broad or vaguely defined. Problems involving generalized anxiety, for example, are unlikely to be alleviated by step-by-step, behaviour-by-behaviour interventions (Wilson, 2011; O'Leary & Wilson, 1987). This is one of the reasons these interventions are now usually combined with cognitive approaches.

Cynthia Dopkin/Photo Researchers

Behavioural interventions. Time out is a popular behavioural technique for disciplining young children.

Before You Go On

www.wiley.com/go/comercanada

What Do You Know?

1. What are systematic desensitization and aversion therapy?
2. What principles and procedures are involved in a token economy program?
3. How does social skills training work?

What Do You Think? Does changing behaviour fully treat people's disorders?

Summary

Module 94: Behavioural Therapies

LEARNING OBJECTIVE 94 Describe the behavioural treatments for psychological disorders.

- Behavioural treatments, aimed at replacing abnormal behaviours with more functional ones, are based on learning processes. Behavioural techniques fall into three categories: *classical conditioning*, *operant conditioning*, and *modelling*.
- Systematic desensitization and *aversion therapy* rely on classical conditioning. Systematic desensitization is especially effective in treating phobias, while aversion therapy has been used to treat people who want to eliminate problem behaviours, such as drinking.
- *Token economies* follow the principles of operant conditioning and use rewards to encourage desired behaviours.
- *Social-skills training* uses modelling to help clients acquire desired social behaviours.
- Research suggests that behavioural therapies are often effective. They do not always bring lasting change outside therapy, however, and do not appear particularly effective with disorders that are broad or vaguely defined.

Key Terms

aversion therapy 722

social skills training 724

token economy 722

Study Questions

Multiple Choice

1. The behavioural therapy of systematic desensitization works primarily through the principle of
   a) extinction.
   b) negative reinforcement.
   c) positive reinforcement.
   d) punishment.

2. When therapists demonstrate appropriate behaviour to clients and then ask the clients to imitate and rehearse it, this is called

   a) a token economy.
   b) classical conditioning.
   c) modelling.
   d) social skills training.

Fill-in-the-Blank

1. Pointing out the social deficits of clients, then role playing in social situations, are approaches used in _____ training.

Module 95: Cognitive-Behavioural Therapies

Working from the assumption that dysfunctional thinking is at the centre of many psychological disorders, cognitive-behavioural therapists try to help people recognize and change their faulty thinking processes. Because different disorders involve different kinds of cognitive dysfunction, therapists may employ a range of cognitive strategies. Most such therapists also use some behavioural techniques to help clients think, behave, and feel better. Thus, their approaches are typically referred to as cognitive-behavioural. Three influential cognitive-behavioural approaches are those of Albert Ellis, Aaron Beck, and the "second-wave" cognitive-behavioural therapists (Hayes, 2004).

95.1 Ellis's Rational-Emotive Behavioural Therapy

In line with his belief that irrational assumptions give rise to abnormal functioning, Albert Ellis developed an approach called **rational-emotive behavioural therapy** (Ellis, 2011, 2005, 1962). Therapists using this approach first help clients identify the irrational assumptions that seem to govern their behavioural and emotional responses. Next, they help clients change those assumptions into constructive ways of viewing themselves and the world. One of the techniques the therapists may use is *cognitive restructuring*, in which clients learn to replace negative interpretations with more positive notions (see **Figure 95-1**).

In his own practice, Ellis would point out to clients their irrational assumptions in a blunt, confrontational, and often humorous way. Then he would model the use of alternative assumptions. After criticizing a young man's perfectionistic standards, for example, he might say, "So what if you did a lousy job on that paper? It's important to realize that one lousy paper simply means one lousy paper, and no more than that!" Ellis gave clients homework assignments requiring them to observe their assumptions at work in their everyday lives. He also required them to think of ways to test the rationality of the assumptions. And, finally, he had them rehearse new assumptions during therapy and apply them at home and work.

Silverman and colleagues (1992) reviewed research that evaluated the effectiveness of rational-emotive therapy. Their findings suggest that this form of therapy has been demonstrated to be an effective means of addressing issues for those who suffer from anxiety or assertiveness issues. For example, clients with social anxiety who are treated with this therapy improve more than socially anxious clients who receive no treatment or placebo treatments (McEvoy, 2007).

95.2 Beck's Cognitive Therapy

Aaron Beck independently developed a system of therapy that is similar to Ellis's rational-emotive behavioural therapy. Although he named his approach **cognitive therapy**, Beck has emphasized for decades that he also has clients experiment with new behaviours as a key feature of the approach.

This approach has been used most often with people who are depressed, although it also has been applied to problems ranging from panic disorder to personality disorders (Beck & Weishaar, 2011, 2008). In their work with depressed clients, Beck-like cognitive therapists help clients to identify the negative thoughts and errors in logic that pervade their thinking and help give rise to feelings of depression. The therapists also teach clients to challenge their dysfunctional thoughts, try new interpretations, and apply different ways of thinking in their daily lives. In the following excerpt, Beck guides a depressed 26-year-old graduate student to see the link between

LEARNING OBJECTIVE 95
Describe cognitive-behavioural therapies for psychological disorders.

rational-emotive behavioural therapy Ellis's therapy technique designed to help clients discover and change the irrational assumptions that govern their emotions, behaviours, and thinking.

cognitive therapy Beck's cognitive therapy technique designed to help clients recognize and change their dysfunctional thoughts and ways of thinking.

FIGURE 95-1 Cognitive restructuring. This cognitive strategy can help clients change self-defeating thinking and, in turn, open the door to new, more positive life experiences.

©iStockphoto.com/nandyphotos

Depression. Cognitive therapy is effective at identifying the negative thoughts and errors in logic that permeate the thinking of depressed individuals.

the way she interprets her experiences and the way she feels, and to begin questioning the accuracy of her interpretations.

Patient:	I get depressed when things go wrong. Like when I fail a test.
Therapist:	How can failing a test make you depressed?
Patient:	Well, if I fail I'll never get into law school.
Therapist:	So failing the test means a lot to you. . . . Did everyone who failed get depressed enough to require treatment?
Patient:	No, but it depends on how important the test was to the person.
Therapist:	Right, and who decides the importance?
Patient:	I do . . .
Therapist:	Now what did failing mean?
Patient:	(Tearful) That I couldn't get into law school.
Therapist:	And what does that mean to you?
Patient:	That I'm just not smart enough.
Therapist:	Anything else?
Patient:	That I can never be happy.
Therapist:	And how do these thoughts make you feel?
Patient:	Very unhappy.
Therapist:	So it is the meaning of failing a test that makes you very unhappy. [Moreover] you get yourself into a trap—by definition, failure to get into law school equals "I can never be happy."

(Beck, A. T., Rush, A. J., Shaw, B. F., & Emery, G. (1979). *Cognitive therapy of depression*. New York: Guilford Press, pp. 145–146.)

Around two-thirds of depressed people who are treated with Beck's cognitive approach improve. This is significantly more than those who receive no treatment and about the same as those who receive biological treatments (Beck & Weishaar, 2011; Disner et al., 2011). Research also indicates the effectiveness of Beck-like cognitive therapy in cases of panic disorder and social anxiety disorder.

95.3 Second-Wave Cognitive-Behavioural Therapies

A growing body of research suggests that the kinds of cognitive changes proposed by Ellis, Beck, and other cognitive therapists are not always possible to achieve (Sharf, 2012). Thus, a new group of cognitive-behavioural therapies, sometimes called *second-wave* cognitive-behavioural therapies, has emerged in recent years (Hollon & DiGiuseppe, 2011). These approaches help clients to *accept* many of their problematic thoughts rather than judge them, act on them, or try fruitlessly to change them. The hope is that by recognizing such thoughts for what they are—just thoughts—clients will eventually be able to let them pass through their awareness without being particularly troubled by them.

One of several disorders to which this kind of approach has been applied is generalized anxiety disorder. As you read in Part 15, this disorder is characterized by persistent and excessive feelings of anxiety and endless worrying about numerous events and activities. Second-wave cognitive-behavioural therapists guide clients with generalized anxiety disorder to recognize and then accept their dysfunctional uses of worrying (Newman et al., 2011; Ritter et al., 2010; Wells, 2010). They begin by educating the clients about the role of worrying in their disorder and have them observe their bodily arousal and cognitive responses across various life situations. Over time, the clients come to appreciate the triggers of their worrying, their misconceptions about worrying, and their misguided efforts to control their lives by worrying. As their insights grow, clients are expected to see the world as less threatening (and so less arousing), try out more constructive ways of dealing with arousal, and, perhaps most important, worry less about the fact that they worry so much. Research has begun to indicate that a concentrated focus on worrying of this kind is indeed a helpful addition to the treatment of generalized anxiety disorder (Ritter et al., 2010; Wells, 2010).

One of today's leading second-wave cognitive-behavioural approaches is *mindfulness-based cognitive therapy*, developed by psychologist Steven Hayes and his colleagues as part of their broader treatment approach called *acceptance and commitment therapy* (Antony, 2011; Treanor, 2011; Hayes et al., 2004). Here, therapists help clients to become mindful of their streams of thoughts—including their worries—at the very moments they are occurring, and to *accept* such thoughts as mere events of the mind. Once again, by accepting their thoughts rather than trying to eliminate them, the clients are expected to be less upset and affected by them.

Mindfulness-based cognitive therapy has also been applied to other psychological problems such as depression, posttraumatic stress disorder, personality disorders, and substance abuse, often with promising results (Orsillo & Roemer, 2011; Hayes et al., 2004). The approach borrows heavily from a form of meditation called *mindfulness meditation*, which teaches individuals to pay attention to the thoughts and feelings that flow through their minds during meditation and to accept such thoughts in a non-judgmental way.

95.4 Cognitive-Behavioural Therapies in Perspective

A model that sees and treats thought as the main cause of normal and abnormal behaviour offers great appeal. Accordingly, therapists from varied backgrounds have come to embrace and use cognitive-behavioural approaches. Moreover, research has supported these approaches. Cognitive-behavioural therapies have proved very effective for treating depression, social anxiety disorder, generalized anxiety disorder, panic disorder, sexual dysfunctions, and a number of other psychological disorders (Beck & Weishaar, 2011; Landon & Barlow, 2004).

But the cognitive-behavioural approaches also have their limitations. First, although disturbed cognitive functioning is found in many psychological disorders, its precise role has yet to be determined. It is not always clear that it is at the *centre* of various disorders. Correspondingly, it is not clear whether it is the behavioural or the cognitive features of the cognitive-behavioural approaches that most powerfully propel these treatments. The assumption of many therapists is that the behavioural features help bring about essential cognitive changes. But it could well be that in many cases and disorders, it is the behavioural changes that are most important. And, finally, although cognitive-behavioural therapies are certainly effective for many problems, they do not help everyone (Sharf, 2012).

Before You Go On

www.wiley.com/go/comercanada

What Do You Know?
1. What do therapists help clients to do in rational-emotive behavioural therapy?
2. What is cognitive therapy?
3. What are the goals of second-wave cognitive-behavioural therapies?

What Do You Think? We all sometimes have irrational assumptions, though they don't usually cause psychological disorders. What irrational assumptions and thoughts do you occasionally have?

Summary

Module 95: Cognitive-Behavioural Therapies

LEARNING OBJECTIVE 95 Describe cognitive-behavioural therapies for psychological disorders.

- Cognitive-behavioural therapists try to help people recognize and change their faulty thinking processes. Most such therapies use some behavioural techniques. Three influential cognitive-behavioural approaches are those of *Albert Ellis*, *Aaron Beck*, and the *"second-wave" cognitive-behavioural therapists*.
- Ellis's *rational-emotive behavioural therapy* focuses on helping clients to identify their maladaptive assumptions, test them, and change them.
- Beck's cognitive therapy guides clients to challenge their maladaptive attitudes, automatic thoughts, and illogical thinking. Research supports the effectiveness of cognitive therapy for depression and certain other disorders.
- Second-wave cognitive-behavioural therapies help clients to accept their problem behaviours rather than judge them, act on them, or try fruitlessly to change them.
- The cognitive view is quite popular today, and research suggests that cognitive treatment is often effective. It is still not clear, however, whether psychological disorders create or result from maladaptive thoughts.

Key Terms

cognitive therapy 727

rational-emotive behavioural therapy 727

Study Questions

Multiple Choice

1. Which of the following theorists would be most likely to give clients homework assignments requiring them to observe and challenge their assumptions?
   a) Beck
   b) Ellis
   c) Perls
   d) Rogers
2. Which statement about the cognitive-behavioural approach to therapy is false?
   a) It has been found to be highly effective.
   b) It is difficult to determine whether irrational thoughts are a cause or an effect of maladaptive behaviour.

   c) It is only applicable to the treatment of depression and has limited use for other conditions.
   d) Research has consistently found that there is a link between maladaptive thoughts and maladaptive behaviour.

Fill-in-the-Blank

1. Beck's approach to cognitive therapy is most commonly used to treat _____.

Module 96: Humanistic and Existential Therapies

Believing that psychological disorders are rooted in self-deceit, humanistic and existential therapists try to help clients look at themselves and their situations more accurately and acceptingly. They expect that clients will then be better able to actualize their full potential as human beings. To achieve this, humanistic and existential therapists usually emphasize present experiences rather than events from the client's past.

LEARNING OBJECTIVE 96
Describe the humanistic and existential therapies for psychological disorders.

96.1 Rogers's Client-Centred Therapy

Clinicians who practise Carl Rogers's **client-centred therapy** try to create a positive climate in which clients can look at themselves honestly and acceptingly (Raskin et al., 2011). The therapist must display three important qualities throughout the therapy:

- *Unconditional positive regard*—full and warm acceptance for the client.
- *Accurate empathy*—skillful listening, including restatements of the client's own comments.
- *Genuineness*—realness, sincere communication, no professional front or facade.

According to Rogers, clients will feel accepted by their therapists in this kind of atmosphere. They will eventually come to recognize and value their own emotions, thoughts, and behaviours once again. They will then be freed from the insecurities that have been preventing self-actualization (Rogers, 1980). The following interaction shows a therapist using the techniques Rogers advocates:

Client: In classes I feel that everyone's just waiting for a chance to jump on me. . . . When I meet somebody I wonder what he's actually thinking of me. Then later on I wonder how I match up to what he's come to think of me.

Therapist: You feel that you're pretty responsive to the opinions of other people.

Client: Yes, but it's things that shouldn't worry me.

Therapist: You feel that it's the sort of thing that shouldn't be upsetting, but they do get you pretty much worried anyway.

Client: . . . There are lots of little things that aren't true. . . . Things just seem to be piling up, piling up inside of me. . . . It's a feeling that things were crowding up and they were going to burst.

Therapist: You feel that it's a sort of oppression with some frustration and that things are just unmanageable.

Client: In a way . . . . I'm afraid I'm not very clear here but that's the way it comes.

Therapist: That's all right. You say just what you think.

(Snyder, W. V. (1947). *Casebook of non-directive counseling*. Boston: Houghton Mifflin, pp. 2–4.)

Rogers was committed to clinical research, and his commitment helped promote the systematic study of treatment. Client-centred therapy has not performed well in research, however (Sharf, 2008). Although some studies report improvements among people who receive this therapy, most controlled research finds it to be of limited effectiveness. Nevertheless, Rogers's therapy has had a very positive influence on the clinical field (Raskin et al., 2011; Kirschenbaum, 2004). As one of the first major alternatives to psychodynamic therapy, it helped open up the field to new approaches (Prochaska & Norcross, 2007).

96.2 Gestalt Therapy

Gestalt therapy, another humanistic approach, was developed in the 1950s by clinical theorist Frederick (Fritz) Perls. Gestalt therapists, like client-centred therapists, move clients toward self-recognition and self-acceptance (Yontef & Jacobs, 2011). But unlike

client-centred therapy humanistic therapy designed to help clients experience unconditional positive regard and look at themselves honestly and acceptingly.

David Woods/Corbis

An alternative source of unconditional positive regard. Based on the Rogerian principle that unconditional positive regard is highly therapeutic, pet therapy has become a widely applied intervention to help reduce the depression of people such as elderly nursing home residents. In this approach, individuals interact with various kinds of non-judgmental animals.

client-centred therapists, they often try to do this by challenging and frustrating the clients. Perls's favourite techniques included skillful frustration, role playing, and rules.

- *Skillful frustration* Gestalt therapists consistently refuse to meet their clients' expectations or demands. The aim here is to help the clients to see how often they try to manipulate others into meeting their needs.

- *Role playing* Gestalt therapists often have clients act out various roles. A person may be instructed to be another person, an object, an alternate self, or even a part of the body. Role playing can become very intense, as individuals are encouraged to fully express their feelings. They may cry out, scream, kick, or pound. Eventually they are expected to "own," or accept, feelings that previously made them uncomfortable.

- *Rules* The rules enforced by Gestalt therapists ensure that clients look at themselves closely. In certain versions of this therapy, for example, clients may be required to use "I" language instead of "it" language. They must say, "I am sad" rather than "The situation is depressing."

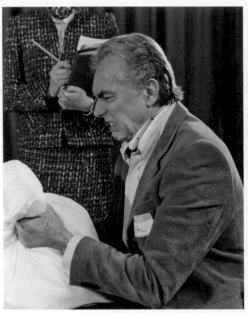 

Gestalt techniques. Gestalt therapists often guide clients, such as this man, to express their needs and feelings to an extreme through role playing and other exercises. In this session, the client moves from "strangling" a pillow (left), to banging the pillow, to hugging it (right). The pillow may represent a person about whom the client has mixed feelings.

Pascal Preti/Getty Images

Because Gestalt therapists believe that subjective experiences and self-awareness defy objective measurement, limited research has been conducted on the approach (Yontef & Jacobs, 2011; Strümpfel, 2006, 2004). Recently, Gestalt techniques have been included in a group of other treatments referred to as *emotion-focused*. These treatments emphasize attention to one's current emotional experiences as a way to reduce anxiety, depression, and other psychological difficulties (Greenberg & Goldman, 2008).

96.3 Existential Therapy

Existential therapists encourage clients to accept responsibility for their lives and their problems. They help clients to recognize their freedom so that they may choose different paths and live more meaningful lives (Yalom & Josselson, 2011; Schneider & Krug, 2010). Existential therapists also place great emphasis on the relationship between therapist and client, and try to create an atmosphere of honesty, shared learning, and growth.

Like Gestalt therapists, most existential therapists do not believe that experimental methods can properly test the effectiveness of their treatments (Yalom & Josselson, 2011). In fact, they hold that research dehumanizes individuals by reducing them to test measures. Thus, little controlled research has been done to clarify the effectiveness of this approach.

96.4 Humanistic and Existential Therapies in Perspective

By recognizing the special challenges of human existence, both humanistic and existential therapists highlight an aspect of psychological life that is typically missing from the other models (Watson et al., 2011; Cain, 2007). In addition, the factors that they say are critical to positive functioning—self-acceptance, personal values, personal meaning, and personal choice—certainly seem to be lacking in many people with psychological disorders. Such virtues aside, the broad issues of human fulfillment at the core of these approaches are hard to research. Only recently have properly controlled studies been conducted. These studies, in fact, suggest that the therapies may be beneficial in some cases (Schneider & Krug, 2010; Cain, 2007; Strümpfel, 2006). This emerging interest in research may soon lead to clearer insights about the approaches.

Before You Go On

www.wiley.com/go/comercanada

What Do You Know?
1. What are the key characteristics therapists should display in client-centred therapy?
2. What techniques are used in Gestalt therapy?
3. What are the main goals of existential therapy?

What Do You Think? What kind of clients and what kind of problems do you think would benefit most from humanistic and existential therapies?

Summary

Module 96: Humanistic and Existential Therapies

LEARNING OBJECTIVE 96 Describe the humanistic and existential therapies for psychological disorders.

- Humanistic and existential therapists try to help clients look at themselves and their situations more accurately and acceptingly.
- Therapists practising Carl Rogers's *client-centred therapy* try to provide *unconditional positive regard*, *accurate empathy*, and *genuineness*, so that clients come to value their own emotions, thoughts, and behaviours.
- Gestalt therapists use skillful frustration, role playing, and rules to help clients recognize and accept their needs and goals.
- Existentialist therapies focus on helping clients discover their personal freedom of choice and take responsibility for making choices.
- Only recently have humanistic and existential therapies begun to undergo systematic research. Early research suggests they can be beneficial for some clients.

Key Term

client-centred therapy 731

Study Questions

Multiple Choice

1. The Gestalt approach to therapy was developed by
   a) Abraham Maslow.
   b) Albert Ellis.
   c) Carl Rogers.
   d) Fritz Perls.

Fill-in-the-Blank

1. In contrast to psychodynamic therapy approaches, humanistic and existential therapies usually emphasize _____ experiences rather than conflicts from childhood.

Moduel 97: Formats of Therapy

individual therapy psychotherapy format in which the therapist sees the client alone; the oldest of the modern formats.

group therapy psychotherapy format in which a therapist sees several clients at the same time.

Thus far, our discussions of therapy have centred on treatments conducted by individual therapists with individual clients. In fact, **individual therapy** is the oldest of the modern therapy formats. Other formats, often used as alternatives to individual therapy, include *group therapy*, *family and couple therapy*, and *community treatment*. Therapists may apply their favoured techniques and principles in each of these formats, whether they be psychodynamic, behavioural, or other techniques. In addition, special strategies have been developed for use in the non-individual formats.

97.1 Group Therapy

In **group therapy**, a therapist sees several clients who are grappling with psychological problems at the same time. Group therapy became a popular format for treating people with psychological difficulties after World War II, when growing demand for psychological services forced therapists throughout North America and Europe to look for time-saving alternatives to individual therapy (Fehr, 2003). Many therapists now specialize in group therapy, and countless others conduct therapy groups as one aspect of their practice. A survey of clinical psychologists, for example, revealed that almost one-third of them practise group therapy to some degree (Norcross & Goldfried, 2005).

©iStockphoto.com/4774344sean   ©iStockphoto.com/Mark Bowden   Comstock/Getty Images

Range of formats. Individual therapy (left) used to be the only treatment format for psychological problems. Today, other formats are also used, such as group therapy (middle) and couple therapy (right).

Typically, group members meet with a therapist and discuss the problems or concerns of one or more of the members (Burlingame & Baldwin, 2011). Groups are often created with particular client populations in mind. For example, there are groups for people with alcoholism, for people who are physically handicapped, and for people who are divorced, abused, or bereaved.

On the basis of his own work and other investigations, a leading group-therapy theorist, Irvin Yalom, suggests that successful forms of group therapy share certain "curative" features (Cox, Vinogradov, & Yalom, 2008; Yalom & Leszcy, 2005):

- *Guidance* Group therapy usually provides information and advice for members.
- *Identification* Group therapy provides models of appropriate behaviour.
- *Group cohesiveness* Group therapy offers an atmosphere of solidarity in which members can learn to take risks and accept criticism.
- *Universality* Members discover that other people have similar problems.
- *Altruism* Members develop feelings of self-worth by helping others.
- *Catharsis* Members develop more understanding of themselves and of others and learn to express their feelings.
- *Skill building* Members acquire or improve social skills.

One kind of group intervention in wide use today is **self-help groups**. These groups are made up of people who have similar problems or who may be at different places in a life process (e.g., supporting a loved one with Alzheimer's) and come together to help and support one another without the direct leadership of a professional clinician (White & Madara, 2011; Mueller et al., 2007). Self-help groups have become increasingly popular over the past few decades.

Self-help groups address a wide assortment of issues. Examples include alcoholism and other forms of substance abuse, compulsive gambling, bereavement, overeating, phobias, child abuse, medical illnesses, rape victimization, unemployment, and divorce. Online self-help chat rooms and message boards are often similar to traditional self-help groups and have themselves exploded in number and popularity in recent years.

Self-help groups are popular for several reasons. Many participants have lost confidence in the ability of clinicians and social institutions to help with their particular problems. For example, Alcoholics Anonymous, the well-known network of self-help groups for people dependent on alcohol, was developed in 1934 in response to the general ineffectiveness of clinical treatments for alcoholism (Tonigan et al., 1995). Still other people are drawn to self-help groups because they find them less threatening and less stigmatizing than therapy groups.

Because groups—from conventional therapy groups to self-help groups—vary so much, it has been difficult to assess their effectiveness. Research does suggest, however, that group therapy is often of help to clients—perhaps as helpful as individual therapy (Burlingame & Baldwin, 2011; Dies, 2003). It appears that candid feedback is usually useful for group members as long as a balance is struck between positive and negative feedback.

self-help groups groups consisting of people who have similar problems and come together to help and support one another without the direct leadership of a professional clinician.

97.2 Family Therapy

Family therapy dates back to the 1950s. In this format, therapists meet with all members of a family, point out problematic behaviours and interactions between the members, and try to help the whole family change (Goldenberg & Goldenberg, 2011). Most family therapists meet with family members as a group, but some choose to see them separately. Either way, the family is viewed as the unit under treatment.

family therapy a format in which therapists meet with all members of a family to help the whole family to change.

Like group therapists, family therapists may follow the principles of any of the major theoretical models. Whatever their orientation, however, most also adhere to some of the principles of family systems theory. Family systems theory holds that each family has its own implicit rules, relationship structure, and communication patterns that shape the behaviour of the individual members, including dysfunctional behaviour. For one family member to change, the family system must change (Barker, 2007).

Family therapies are often helpful to individuals. Research has not fully clarified how helpful, however (Goldenberg & Goldenberg, 2011). Some studies have found that as many as 65 percent of individuals treated with family approaches improve, but other studies have found much lower success rates. Nor has any one type of family therapy emerged as consistently more helpful than the others (Alexander et al., 2002).

Lisa F. Young/Shutterstock

Family therapy. In family therapy, the family is treated as a unit, regardless of whether individual family members are counselled or whether the entire family is counselled together.

97.3 Couple Therapy

In **couple therapy**, also known as **marital therapy**, the therapist works with two people who are in a long-term relationship, focusing on the structure and communication patterns in their relationship (Gurman & Snyder, 2011; Baucom et al., 2010, 2009). Often

couple therapy or **marital therapy** therapy format in which a therapist works with two people who are in a long-term relationship.

this format of therapy involves a husband and wife, but the couple need not be married or even living together. Similarly, they need not be heterosexual. Indeed, some therapists specialize in working with same-sex couples.

Although some degree of discord occurs in any long-term relationship, there is growing evidence that many adults in our society experience serious marital problems. The divorce rate across North America and Europe is now close to 50 percent of the marriage rate, and has been climbing steadily in recent decades (U.S. Census Bureau, 2011). Currently, 38 percent of Canadian marriages do not survive past the thirtieth anniversary (Ambert, 2009). Many of those who live together without marrying seem to have similar levels of relationship disharmony (Harway, 2005).

Like group and family therapy, couple therapy may be conducted with any therapy orientation (Baucom et al., 2010; Shadish & Baldwin, 2005). People treated in couple therapy show greater improvements in their relationships than people who fail to receive such treatment, but no one form of couple therapy stands out as more effective than the others (Gurman & Snyder, 2011; Christensen et al., 2010). Two-thirds of treated couples display improved marital functioning. However, fewer than half of those who are treated achieve "distress-free" relationships. One-quarter of all treated couples eventually divorce.

M. Spencer Green/AP

Community mental health in action. This man with both schizophrenia and bipolar disorder is moving into his own apartment, a key step in his recovery.

community mental health treatment treatment programs that emphasize community care, including an emphasis on prevention.

97.4 Community Treatment

At one time, people with psychological disorders, especially severe disorders, had to seek help from distant facilities or institutions. Today, however, a number of **community mental health treatment** programs offer such people services from nearby agencies. Community-based treatments include community mental health centres, community day programs, and group homes and other residential services. Collectively, these agencies often play a major role in the treatment of people with severe psychological disorders, such as schizophrenia (Daly et al., 2010).

A key feature of community treatment is *prevention*. Community clinicians reach out to clients rather than wait for them, an approach that is often very successful (Conyne & Harpine, 2010; Juhnke et al., 2011). Community workers identify three types of prevention: *primary*, *secondary*, and *tertiary*.

- *Primary prevention* consists of efforts to improve community functioning and policies. The goal here is to prevent psychological disorders altogether. Community workers may lobby for better child-care facilities in the community, consult with a district school board to help develop a curriculum, offer mental health fairs or workshops on stress reduction, or provide online information and support sites.

- *Secondary prevention* consists of detecting and treating psychological disorders in the early stages, before they reach serious levels. Community workers may teach clergy, teachers, or police how to identify early signs of psychological dysfunction and how to refer people for treatment.

- *Tertiary prevention* aims to provide effective treatment immediately so that moderate or severe disorders do not become chronic problems. Unfortunately, although community agencies are able to offer tertiary care for millions of people with moderate problems, low funding often prevents them from providing care for hundreds of thousands with severe disorders (Althouse, 2010).

Psychology Around Us | In Need of Community Care

What happens to people with schizophrenia and other severe psychological disorders whose communities do not provide the mental health services they need and whose families cannot afford private treatment? Many return to their families and receive medication and support, but little else in the way of treatment (Barrowclough & Lobban, 2008). Around 8 percent receive only custodial care and medication in an alternative institution, such as a nursing home or rest home (Torrey, 2001). As many as 18 percent are placed in privately-run residences, such as boarding houses, where supervision often is provided by untrained individuals. Another 31 percent live in totally unsupervised settings, including rundown single-room-occupancy hotels or rooming houses, surviving on government disability payments and spending their days wandering through neighbourhood streets (Burns & Drake, 2011). Over 100,000 become homeless (Kooyman & Walsh, 2011), and at least 100,000 more end up in prisons because their disorders lead them to break the law (Scott, 2010).

Before You Go On

www.wiley.com/go/comercanada

What Do You Know?
1. What are self-help groups?
2. What is the main assumption of family systems therapy?
3. Describe primary, secondary, and tertiary prevention.

What Do You Think? Which therapy format appeals to you most? Least? Why? Are certain formats better suited for particular problems or client personalities?

Summary

Moduel 97: Formats of Therapy

LEARNING OBJECTIVE 97 Describe commonly used formats of therapy.

- *Individual therapy*, in which practitioners meet with one client at a time, is the oldest of the modern therapy formats.
- In *group therapy*, several clients with similar problems meet with a single therapist at the same time. *Self-help groups* are similar, but conducted without the leadership of a therapist. Both types of groups can be helpful for certain clients.
- *Family therapy* treats all members of a family, together or individually, and therapists usually consider the family as a system.
- Two people in a long-term relationship can seek *couple therapy* to help address issues in their relationship.
- *Community mental health treatment* focuses on preventing abnormal functioning through (1) primary prevention—policies that reduce psychological risk in a community; (2) secondary prevention—treating minor problems before they become serious; and (3) tertiary prevention—providing prompt treatment for moderate and severe disorders so they do not become long-term problems.

Key Terms

community mental health treatment 736
couple therapy or marital therapy 735
family therapy 735
group therapy 734
individual therapy 734
self-help groups 735

Study Questions

Multiple Choice

1. A school district launching a smoking awareness program to try to reduce the number of students who start smoking is an example of _____ prevention.
   a) educational
   b) primary
   c) secondary
   d) tertiary

Fill-in-the-Blank

1. One reason why group therapies are helpful is because they encourage group _____, or a sense of unity among group members.

Module 98: Does Therapy Work?

As we noted earlier, as many as 400 forms of therapy are currently practised in North America (Corsini & Wedding, 2011). The most important question to ask about each of them is whether the therapy really helps. **Therapy outcome studies**, which measure the effects of various treatments, typically ask one of four questions:

1. *Is therapy in general effective?* Studies reveal that therapy is often more helpful than no treatment or placebo treatments. Using a statistical technique called *meta-analysis* in which the results from a large number of studies are combined to provide a more general picture of a particular area of interest, one early review combined the results of 375 separate, controlled studies, covering a total of almost 25,000 people seen in a wide assortment of therapies (Smith, Glass, & Miller, 1980; Smith & Glass, 1977). According to this statistical analysis, shown in **Figure 98-1**, the average person who received treatment was better off than 75 percent of the untreated control clients. Other analyses have found similar relationships between treatment and improvement (Sharf, 2012; Bickman, 2005).

2. *How effective are particular therapies?* A number of studies have found that each of the major forms of therapy is of some help to clients—certainly of more help than a placebo treatment (Prochaska & Norcross, 2010; Overholser, Braden, & Fisher, 2010). Other research has compared these therapies to one another and found that no one form of therapy generally stands out over all others (Luborsky et al., 2006, 2003, 1975). If different kinds of therapy have similar overall success rates, it may be that they share common features (Sharf, 2012; Bohart & Tallman, 2010). Surveys of highly successful therapists suggest that, regardless of their particular orientations, successful therapists tend to do similar things: (1) they provide feedback to clients; (2) they help clients focus on their own thoughts and behaviour; (3) they pay careful attention to the way they and their clients interact; and (4) they try to build a sense of self-mastery in their clients (Portnoy, 2008; Korchin & Sands, 1983).

3. *Are particular therapies especially effective for certain problems?* Researchers have found that particular therapies are especially effective at treating certain disorders (Beutler, 2011; Corsini & Wedding, 2011). Behavioural therapies, for example, seem to be the most effective of all treatments for phobias (Wilson, 2011). Cognitive-behavioural therapies are particularly helpful in cases of social anxiety disorder, generalized anxiety disorder, panic disorder, and depression (Craske, 2010; Pontoski et al., 2010). And drug therapy is the single most helpful treatment for schizophrenia and bipolar disorder (Minzenberg, Yoon, & Carter, 2011). Today's clinicians may also combine two or more approaches when treating particular disorders (Cuijpers et al., 2010). Drug therapy, for example, is often combined with cognitive-behavioural therapy to treat depression or various

LEARNING OBJECTIVE 98
Summarize research on the effectiveness of therapy.

therapy outcome studies research that looks at the effects of various treatments.

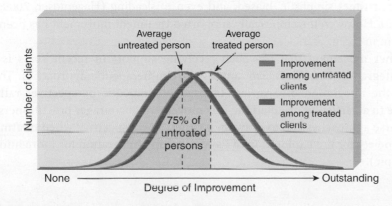

FIGURE 98-1 Is therapy generally effective?
An analysis of 375 studies of treatment effectiveness shows that the average person is better off after treatment of any kind than a similar person who does not get treatment.

anxiety disorders, although the superiority of such combinations over the individual approaches has not been supported consistently by research (Otto, McHugh, & Kantak, 2010; Pontoski & Heimberg, 2010). In fact, it is now common for clients to be seen by two therapists—one of them a *psychopharmacologist* (a psychiatrist who prescribes medications) and the other a psychologist, social worker, or other therapist who conducts psychotherapy.

4. *Is therapy equally effective across race and gender?* Studies conducted in countries across the world have found that members of ethnic and racial minority groups typically show less improvement in clinical treatment, make less use of mental health services, and stop therapy sooner than members of majority groups (Comas-Diaz, 2011, 2006; Benish et al., 2011). Given such findings, a number of clinicians have developed **culture-sensitive therapies**, which seek to address the unique issues faced by members of cultural minority groups. Clinicians using these approaches typically try to do the following (Brown, 2011; Comas-Diaz, 2011; Wyatt & Parham, 2007):

culture-sensitive therapies approaches that seek to address the unique issues faced by members of cultural minority groups.

- Be aware of the client's cultural values.
- Be aware of the stress, prejudices, and stereotypes to which minority clients are exposed.
- Be aware of the hardships faced by the children of immigrants.
- Help clients recognize the impact of both their own culture and the dominant culture on their self-views and behaviours.
- Help clients identify and express suppressed anger and pain.
- Help clients achieve a bicultural balance that feels right for them.
- Help clients raise their self-esteem—a sense of self-worth that has often been damaged by generations of negative messages.

gender-sensitive or **feminist therapies** approaches that seek to address the unique pressures of being female.

Therapies geared to the pressures of being female, called **gender-sensitive**—or **feminist—therapies**, follow similar principles (Calogero et al., 2011). In a related vein, when working with clients who are religious, many of today's therapists make a point of including spiritual issues in therapy (Aten et al., 2011; Worthington, 2011). They may, for example, encourage clients to use their spiritual resources to help them cope (Galanter, 2010).

Obviously, knowledge of how particular therapies fare with particular disorders and particular populations can help therapists and clients alike make better decisions about treatment (Beutler, 2011, 2002; Beutler et al., 2013). To help clinicians become more familiar with and apply such research findings, there is a movement in Canada, the United States, the United Kingdom, and elsewhere called the **empirically supported** or **evidence-based treatment movement** (Sharf, 2012; Pope & Wedding, 2011; Lambert, 2010). A historical review of the development of this perspective is provided by Christy Bryceland and Hank Stam (2005) at the University of Calgary. Proponents of this movement have formed task forces that seek to identify which therapies have received clear research support for particular disorders, to propose corresponding treatment guidelines, and to spread such information to clinicians. Critics of the movement worry that such efforts are at times simplistic, biased, and even misleading (Hagemoser, 2009; Westen et al., 2005). However, the empirically supported treatment movement has been gaining momentum in recent years.

empirically supported or **evidence-based treatment movement** movement to help clinicians become more familiar with and apply research findings concerning the effectiveness of particular treatments.

Another movement that has been receiving support in recent years is a move toward integration and eclecticism among psychotherapeutic approaches. This move supports the integration of a variety of psychotherapeutic perspectives rather than adherence to a particular orientation. This movement encourages practitioners to integrate diverse approaches and to draw on a variety of perspectives when treating clients (see the Society for the Exploration of Psychotherapy Integration for more information on this topic).

practically Speaking — How Do I Find and Choose a Therapist?

Selecting the right therapist is obviously a very important decision. Even if you seek assistance at the student wellness or counselling centre at your college or university (where treatment is usually free to students) or if you seek a referral to a therapist from your family doctor, a friend or relatives, or your province's College of Psychologists, you still have some choice regarding which of the available therapists you can work with.

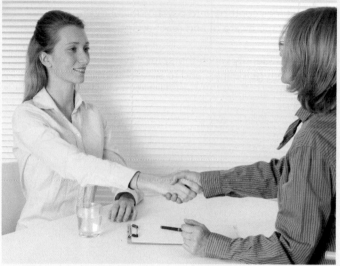

©iStockphoto.com/Lisa-Blue

Here is a list of key questions to consider when selecting a therapist. You should direct some of questions to the potential therapists themselves.

- *Where can you get names of skilled potential therapists?* Ask a professional whom you trust—a psychologist you know, such as your introductory psychology professor, someone at your local student wellness or counselling centre, a family physician, or the like— for recommendations. Many provinces or cities also provide relevant information and lists.

- *What is the professional status of the potential therapists?* Are they clinical psychologists, psychiatrists, social workers, or counsellors? Are they chartered/registered with your province's regulatory college for their profession?

- *What is the experience level of the potential therapists?* What is their overall experience in the field? What is their specific experience and success rate with your kind of problem?

- *What is the treatment orientation of the potential therapists?* Are they psychodynamic, behavioural, cognitive, humanistic, existential, or eclectic? How do they approach problems such as yours?

- *What is the success rate of their treatment orientation for problems such as yours?* Reading this part or an abnormal psychology textbook should help you with this question.

- *Do the potential therapists believe in psychotropic medication as part of therapy in certain cases?* Can they arrange for medication consults if needed?

- *How do the potential therapists match up on personal variables that are important to you?* What are their genders, ages, personalities, and the like? Although such factors do not necessarily affect a therapist's ability to help, you may personally feel that the variables could affect your comfort level or confidence in the therapy process.

- *Once you are in therapy, are you comfortable with the way things are going?* Does the therapist seem attentive, interested, and engaged? Does the therapist's approach continue to make sense to you? Do you feel you are making progress? Don't be afraid to change therapists if, after a reasonable period of time, you are not making progress. In most such instances, you are not failing at therapy. The therapy is failing you!

Before You Go On

www.wiley.com/go/comercanada

What Do You Know?

1. What does research show about whether or not therapy is generally effective?
2. What do effective therapists have in common?
3. What does research show about the effectiveness of particular therapies for certain problems?
4. Is therapy equally effective across race and gender?

What Do You Think? If a person feels that her treatment is not helping, is it likely worthwhile for that person to try to change therapists or treatment methods? Why or why not?

Summary

Module 98: Does Therapy Work?

LEARNING OBJECTIVE 98 Summarize research on the effectiveness of therapy.

- In general, receiving therapy is more likely to help people with psychological disorders than going without treatment. Research has found that each of the major forms of therapy is of some help to clients, although research also indicates that particular therapies are often best suited for certain disorders.

- Successful therapists often share similar effective elements in their approaches, regardless of their particular orientations. They provide feedback, help clients focus on their own thoughts and behaviour, pay careful attention to the way they interact with clients, and try to build a sense of self-mastery in their clients.

- Women and members of ethnic minority groups face pressures that sometimes contribute to psychological dysfunctioning. *Culture-sensitive* and *gender-sensitive therapy* approaches help clients become aware of and react adaptively to the gender-related and cultural pressures and issues they face.

- The *empirically supported* or *evidence-based treatment movement* seeks to identify which therapies have received clear research support for particular disorders, to propose corresponding treatment guidelines, and to spread such information to clinicians.

Key Terms

culture-sensitive therapies 740

empirically supported or
   evidence-based treatment movement 740

gender-sensitive or feminist therapies 740

therapy outcome studies 739

Study Questions

Multiple Choice

1. Research shows that effective therapists tend to do all of the following except
   a) encourage clients to focus on their own thoughts and behaviour.
   b) pay attention to the interactions between therapist and client.
   c) provide feedback to clients.
   d) use psychodynamic techniques such as free association and dream analysis.

Fill-in-the-Blank

1. Although all forms of therapy tend to help people, some approaches are better suited to particular problems than others. Phobias, for example, are most effectively treated with _____ therapy.

Module 99: Some Final Thoughts About the Field of Psychology

It is ironic that we end this book with parts on abnormal psychology and its treatments. Early on, we noted that many people automatically think of abnormal psychology when they hear the term *psychology*. But, as you have seen throughout this book, psychology is a broad field that studies all kinds of mental processes and behaviour. And, as you have also observed, all of those processes and behaviours—both normal and abnormal—are rather awe-inspiring. For example, disorders of memory, such as Alzheimer's disease and dissociative identity disorder, are certainly fascinating. But normal acts of memory—our very ability to encode, store, and retrieve so many experiences and pieces of information in the first place—are no less remarkable.

Psychology is a wide-ranging and complex field consisting of many sub-areas, from sensation and perception to social psychology. Each seeks to explain particular aspects of mental functioning from a particular angle. Collectively, these many sub-areas provide us with an impressive understanding of mental processes and behaviour. But it is important to recognize that this understanding is at a very early stage of development. There are many miles to go in our quest to more fully understand the subject matter of psychology.

Perhaps the most important feature of psychological study today—and one that offers enormous promise for the future—is that the sub-areas are coming together. More and more, they are being viewed as closely connected areas of study. Each helps to inform the others, and all can, collectively, provide a more integrated, complete, and accurate understanding of mental processes and behaviour. It is, for example, no longer a matter of choosing between neuroscience, cognitive psychology, and social psychology to understand how and why people behave (or don't behave) when passing by an accident scene. Rather, we seek to understand how these interacting subfields jointly account for that behaviour. In short, psychology is becoming a truly integrated field. Given this critical course correction, one can only imagine how many insights and breakthroughs regarding mental processes and behaviour lie ahead.

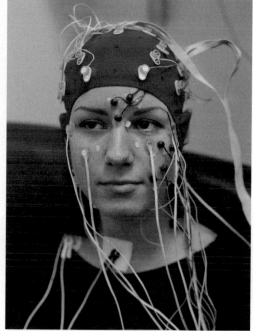

Chuck Stoody/AP

Covering all the angles. To fully understand a mental process such as "intruding thoughts," today's psychologists study the phenomenon at many levels, from measuring the brain waves of individuals while their minds wander (seen here), to determining the possible childhood roots of such thoughts.

Appendix A
Answers to Self-Study Questions

Part 1

Multiple Choice

1.1d, 1.2d, 2.1c, 2.2c, 3.1a, 3.2c, 4.1c, 4.2c, 5.1a, 5.2a

Fill-in-the-Blank

1.1. behaviour, 1.2. control, 2.1. myth, 3.1. perception, 3.2. functionalists, 4.1. punishment, 4.2. self-actualization, 4.3. evolutionary psychology, 5.1. clinical or counselling, 5.2. positive psychology

Part 2

Multiple Choice

6.1a, 6.2d, 6.3d, 7.1b, 8.1c, 8.2b, 9.1c, 9.2a, 10.1a, 10.2b

Fill-in-the-Blank

6.1. cause and effect, 6.2. theories, 7.1. biology, 7.2. eugenics, 8.1. sample, 8.2. survey, 9.1. statistics, 9.2. inferential, 10.1. institutional review board, 10.2. confidentiality

Part 3

Multiple Choice

11.1c, 11.2b, 12.1b, 13.1a, 14.1d, 15.1c, 15.2a, 15.3a, 16.1b, 17.1d

Fill-in-the-Blank

12.1. glial, 12.2. dendrites, 12.3. astroglia, 13.1. all-or-none, 13.2. differentiation, 13.3. acetylcholine (ACh), 14.1. somatic, 15.1. auditory, 15.2. medulla, 16.1. aerobic, 16.2. left

Part 4

Multiple Choice

18.1d, 19.1a, 19.2b, 20.1b, 21.1c, 21.2b, 21.3a, 21.4b, 22.1b, 23.1b

Fill-in-the-Blank

18.1. longitudinal, 19.1. qualitative, 20.1. homozygous, 21.1. pruning, 21.2. object permanence, 21.3. concrete operational, 22.1. relationships, 22.2. pituitary, 22.3. bullying, 23.1. 30s

Part 5

Multiple Choice

24.1b, 24.2d, 25.1a, 25.2a, 26.1c, 26.2a, 27.1c, 27.2d, 28.1a, 28.2b

Fill-in-the-Blank

24.1. somatosensory (touch, heat, pain), 24.2. transduction, 25.1. papillae, 25.2. hippocampus, 26.1. opposite/contralaterally, 26.2. endogenous opiates, 27.1. amplitude, 28.1. pupil, 28.2. temporal/parietal

Part 6

Multiple Choice

29.1b, 29.2d, 30.1a, 30.2d, 31.1d, 31.2b, 32.1c, 33.1c, 34.1c, 34.2d

Fill-in-the-Blank

29.1. blindsight, 30.1. implicit, 31.1. manifest, 31.2. circadian, 31.3. sleepwalking, 32.1. negative, 33.1. mindfulness, 34.1. tolerance, 34.2. dopamine, 34.3. cocaine

Part 7

Multiple Choice

35.1c, 36.1b, 36.2a, 37.1b, 38.1d, 40.1a, 40.2a, 41.1a, 42.1d, 42.2b

Fill-in-the-Blank

35.1. learning, 36.1. neutral, 37.1. primary, 37.2. shaping, 38.1. observational learning, 40.1. episodic/semantic, 40.2. process/remember, 40.3. reset/integrate, 41.1. milestones, 42.1. long-term

Part 8

Multiple Choice

43.1b, 43.2d, 44.1a, 46.1d, 47.1b, 47.2c, 48.1b, 48.2b, 49.1b, 50.1a

Fill-in-the-Blank

43.1. sensory memory, 43.2. connectionist (or PDP, or parallel distributed-processing), 44.1. rehearsal, 45.1. semantic, 46.1. cue, 47.1. proactive/retroactive, 48.1. hippocampus, 49.1. infantile, 49.2. prospective, 50.1. estrogen

Part 9

Multiple Choice

51.1a, 51.2d, 51.3b, 51.4a, 51.5a, 52.1b, 52.2a, 53.1a, 53.2c, 53.3b

Fill-in-the-Blank

51.1. generative, 51.2. overregularization, 51.3. aphasia, 51.4. Broca's, 52.1. internal, 52.2. cross-cultural, 53.1. algorithm, 53.2. availability, 53.3. source, 53.4. mirror

Part 10

Multiple Choice

54.1a, 54.2b, 55.1b, 56.1d, 56.2c, 56.3c, 57.1d, 57.2d, 58.1a, 59.1d

Fill-in-the-Blank

54.1. natural language, 55.1. practical, 56.1. bell curve, 56.2. mental age, 56.3. stereotype threat, 57.1. heritable, 57.2. quality, 58.1. frontal, 58.2. cortex, 59.1. home environment

Part 11

Multiple Choice

60.1a, 60.2d, 61.1a, 61.2b, 62.1d, 63.1a, 63.2b, 64.1a, 65.1b, 65.2d

Fill-in-the-Blank

60.1. low, 60.2. incentive, 60.3. dopamine, 61.1. leptin, 62.1. refractory, 63.1. anterior cingulate cortex, 63.2. intrinsic, 64.1. physiological, 65.1. Cannon-Bard, 65.2. efference

Part 12

Multiple Choice

67.1c, 68.1c, 69.1b, 69.2d, 70.1c, 71.1a, 72.1c, 72.2d, 73.1a, 74.1a

Fill-in-the-Blank

67.1. ego/id, 67.2. phallic, 68.1. unconditional positive regard, 69.1. neuroticism, 70.1. situationist, 71.1. validity, 72.1. phrenology, 72.2. amygdala, 73.1. social role, 74.1. antisocial

Part 13

Multiple Choice

75.1b, 75.2a, 76.1a, 77.1c, 77.2d, 78.1a, 78.2c, 78.3a, 78.4b, 79.1c

Fill-in-the-Blank

75.1. justification, 75.2. specificity, 76.1. dispositional, 77.1. four, 77.2. punishment, 77.3. collectivism, 78.1. arousal, 78.2. responsibility, 78.3. secure, 79.1. prefrontal

Part 14

Multiple Choice

80.1c, 80.2b, 80.3c, 80.4d, 80.5b, 81.1d, 81.2d, 82.1a, 83.1b, 83.2b

Fill-in-the-Blank

80.1. micro (or daily hassle), 80.2. life-change score, 80.3. stereotype, 80.4. perception, 80.5. avoidance-avoidance, 81.1. elevated, 81.2. HPA (or hypothalamic-pituitary-adrenal), 81.3. appraising, 83.1. hostility, 83.2. norepinephrine

Part 15

Multiple Choice

85.1a, 85.2a, 86.1d, 86.2c, 86.3c, 87.1c, 87.2d, 88.1c, 89.1a, 90.1b

Fill-in-the-Blank

85.1. deviance, 85.2. comorbidity, 86.1. Bandura, 86.2. multifinality, 87.1. cyclothymic, 88.1. anxiety, 88.2. acute stress, 89.1. positive, 89.2. identical/fraternal, 90.1. frontal

Part 16

Multiple Choice

91.1a, 92.1b, 93.1a, 94.1a, 94.2c, 95.1b, 95.2c, 96.1d, 97.1b, 98.1d

Fill-in-the-Blank

91.1. outpatient, 92.1. 70, 92.2. antipsychotic, 93.1. manifest/latent, 93.2. 15, 94.1. social skills, 95.1. depression, 96.1. present (or recent), 97.1. cohesiveness, 98.1. behaviour (or behavioural)

Appendix B
Statistics in Psychology

As outlined in Part 2, psychology is considered to be a science, given that it relies upon empirical observations of mental processes and behaviour in order to develop and test theories regarding the underlying laws that govern behaviour. Psychologists use statistics to help them summarize and interpret the observations (or data) that they collect in their research. Essentially there are two basic types of statistics used by psychologists: **descriptive statistics**, which include a variety of procedures used to describe and summarize the data collected, and **inferential statistics**, which are procedures that allow psychologists to draw conclusions about the data they have collected. This appendix is designed to help you better understand statistics and how psychologists use them.

descriptive statistics
statistics used to describe and summarize data.

inferential statistics
statistics used to draw conclusions about research data.

Descriptive Statistics

Statistics are commonly used in psychology to summarize data that have been collected as part of some research project or study. Such statistical summaries are referred to as descriptive statistics.

To illustrate some common descriptive techniques, consider the following data set:

46	56	50	50	59	44
61	49	50	52	32	43
67	58	51	36	58	46
51	54	53	62	50	39
42	44	51	41	53	57

Assume that the data represent scores obtained from 30 students who have taken their first test in an introductory psychology course.

If the instructor is interested in determining how well the students performed on this test, she might quickly eyeball the scores above. However, nothing may readily jump out at her in terms of things like how well the typical student is doing, what was the lowest score, what was the highest score, and so on.

One of the first things the instructor might want to do to get an idea of what's going on with student performance is to simply sort the data so that the scores are arranged from lowest to highest. Doing so produces a data set like the one in **Table B-1**. Now the instructor can look at the data set to see things like the lowest score earned by a student was 32, a fairly large number of students received scores of 50 and 51, and the highest score earned by a student was 67.

However, this still doesn't tell her a whole lot about her students' performance. To get a better idea of what's going on in this set of data, the instructor might use a number of descriptive techniques to summarize the data (this would especially be the case if there were a larger number of students in the class, such as 500). One common way to summarize such a data set is to create frequency distributions.

TABLE B-1 Thirty Exam Scores—Sorted

32	36	39	41	42	43
44	44	46	46	49	50
50	50	50	51	51	51
52	53	53	54	56	57
58	58	59	61	62	67

Frequency Distributions

ungrouped frequency distribution
a count of the number of times each specific data point or score appears in a data set.

grouped frequency distribution
a count of the number of times specific data points fall into a range of values in a data set.

There are two major types of frequency distributions: ungrouped frequency distributions and grouped frequency distributions. With an **ungrouped frequency distribution**, the number of times that each of the unique scores occurs in a data set is calculated. In our example, this would essentially be a count of how many students received a 32, how many received a 36, and so on. To create an ungrouped frequency distribution for the student exam scores, we would need to create a table with two columns—one column containing the various exam scores (sorted from smallest to largest) and another column indicating how frequently each of these scores occurred. **Table B-2** shows an example of an ungrouped frequency distribution for the 30 exam scores.

Using this ungrouped frequency distribution, the instructor can readily see that the exam scores ranged from a low of 32 (with one person receiving that score) to a high of 67 (also with one person receiving this score). In addition, she can determine that seven people earned scores of either 50 or 51.

In the current example there are 21 unique exam scores. While this is a manageable number of categories, there are many instances where there are many more unique scores. As a result, the number of categories in an ungrouped frequency distribution becomes unmanageable. In such cases (and even in the present case, as we will see), you might want to create a **grouped frequency distribution** instead.

To create a grouped frequency distribution, the instructor first creates a number of ranges, or classes of scores, to serve as the basis of the distribution. In general, there should be between five and 20 classes, and the classes need to be continuous (i.e., the classes need to encompass all of the scores from lowest to highest). **Table B-3** shows an example of a grouped frequency distribution for the 30 exam scores (each with a width of five scores). To complete the grouped frequency distribution, the instructor needs to determine how many of the 30 exam scores fall into each of the classes. For example, only one person had a score between 30 and 34 (i.e., the person who scored 32), so that class has a frequency of 1. There were two scores in the class of scores 35–39 (a 36 and a 39), so this class has a frequency of 2. The remainder of the frequencies for the classes are determined in a similar fashion.

Using this grouped frequency distribution, the instructor can identify aspects of the data set, such as there were 11 students who scored between 50 and 54, and there were only three students who scored less than 40.

Frequency distributions can be presented either in tabular format (as we have done in Tables B-2 and B-3) or, following the adage that a picture is worth a thousand words,

TABLE B-2 Ungrouped Frequency Distribution for 30 Exam Scores

Exam Score	Frequency
32	1
36	1
39	1
41	1
42	1
43	1
44	2
46	2
49	1
50	4
51	3
52	1
53	2
54	1
56	1
57	1
58	2
59	1
61	1
62	1
67	1
Total	**30**

TABLE B-3 Grouped Frequency Distribution for 30 Exam Scores

Exam Score Classes	Frequency	Midpoint
30–34	1	32
35–39	2	37
40–44	5	42
45–49	3	47
50–54	11	52
55–59	5	57
60–64	2	62
65–69	1	67
Total	**30**	

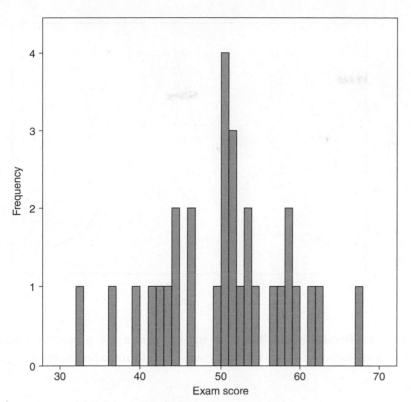

FIGURE B-1 **Histogram for 30 exam scores.**

in some type of graphic form such as a histogram or a frequency polygon. **Histograms** are commonly used to graphically represent ungrouped frequency distributions. They are similar to bar charts and are constructed using a set of two axes. One axis, the horizontal or *x*-axis, contains an ordered listing of the various values for the scores from the ungrouped frequency distribution. The other axis, the vertical or *y*-axis, provides the frequency of those scores. **Figure B-1** shows a histogram based on the ungrouped frequency distribution for the 30 exam scores.

histogram a bar chart showing the number of times specific data points fall into a range of values in a data set.

Frequency polygons are similar to histograms, but they are typically used to graphically represent grouped frequency distributions. Recall that a grouped frequency distribution summarizes the frequency of scores for each of a number of classes or ranges of scores. To create a frequency polygon from a grouped frequency distribution, you need to determine the *midpoint* (i.e., the centre) for each of the classes. In our example, the first class is from 30–34, so the midpoint of that class would be $32 \left[\dfrac{(30 + 34)}{2} \right]$, with the remaining midpoints for the classes calculated in a similar way (see Table B-3). These midpoints are then included on the horizontal axis of the frequency polygon, and the frequencies for each of the classes are included on the vertical axis. **Figure B-2** provides a frequency polygon for the grouped frequency distribution for the 30 exam scores.

frequency polygon a line graph depicting a grouped frequency distribution, which is created by connecting the midpoints of each class of data.

Measures of Central Tendency

Another common use of descriptive statistics is to summarize a collection of data with a single number that represents the entire data set. Such numbers are called **measures of central tendency**. For example, these numbers may be the most frequent number or a number that is thought to be typical of the data set. The three most common statistical measures of central tendency are the mean, median, and mode.

measures of central tendency numbers used to summarize data sets.

You most likely are already familiar with the **mean**—it is equivalent to the (arithmetic) average of the data set. As you know, to calculate an average (or the mean of a data set), total the numbers in the data set and divide by the total number of numbers. Returning to our example, to calculate the mean, total the 30 numbers and divide by 30. The total of the 30 scores is 1,505, so the mean (or average) of those scores is $\dfrac{1,505}{30} = 50.1667$.

mean the average value in a data set; the sum of all numbers in the set divided by the total number of items in the set.

FIGURE B-2 **Frequency polygon for 30 exam scores.**

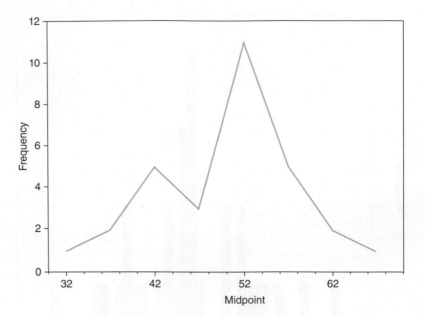

Statisticians frequently use formulas to summarize the procedures required to calculate various statistical values (like the mean). The formula for the mean is presented below:

$$\mu = \frac{\sum X}{N}$$

where: μ is the symbol for the mean,[1]
$\sum$ is summation notation and indicates the procedure of totalling the individual values in the data set,
X represents the possible values in the data set, and
N represents the number of observations.

median the data set value that represents the midpoint of an ordered set of numbers.

While the mean is the average of the set of data, the **median** represents the midpoint or middle in an ordered set of data. That is, to determine the median for a set of data, first order the set of data (from smallest to largest) and then determine the midpoint of that ordered data set. Our 30 exam scores are sorted in Table B-1. Because there is an even number of scores (or observations), the exact midpoint for the data set would be between the 15th and 16th numbers. In cases where the number of observations (or N) is even, calculate the median by taking the average of the two middle numbers in the ordered data set. In our example, the 15th highest score is 50 while the 16th highest score is 51, so for this set of data the median is $50.5 \left(\frac{50 + 51}{2} \right)$. In cases where there are an odd number of observations in the data set, the median is simply the middle number in the ordered data set.

mode the most frequent or most common value in a data set.

A third measure of central tendency that may be calculated for a set of data is the **mode**, which is the most frequently occurring score or observation. The mode can be easily determined by looking at an ungrouped frequency distribution for the set of data. As Table B-1 shows, the score of 50 was the most frequent score in our data set of 30 exam scores, with four of the 30 students earning that score. So for this set of data, the mode would be 50. In cases where there are multiple scores that each have equally high frequencies, then the data set has multiple modes (for example, if in our data set four people scored 50 and four people scored 58, then the data set would have two modes, 50 and 58).

In summary, for our example set of data we have three measures of central tendency: a mean of 50.1667, a median of 50.5, and a mode of 50. As you can see, for this set of data

---

[1] μ is the symbol for the mean of a population, whereas $\overline{X}$ is the symbol for the mean of a sample. The distinction between populations and samples is discussed later in this appendix.

the three measures of central tendency are similar to one another, and you may wonder which is the "best" measure of central tendency. We will return to this question later in the appendix.

Measures of Variability

Whereas measures of central tendency provide some idea of a typical number in a set of data, they do not tell us anything about how different the numbers in a set of data are from one another. Statistics that do this are known as **measures of variability**.

The simplest measure of variability for a set of data is the **range**, which is the difference between the largest and the smallest values in a data set. To calculate the range for our 30 exam scores, determine the largest and the smallest score and then to take the difference between them. Referring to Table B-1 the largest score is 67 while the smallest score is 32, so the range of scores is 35 (67 − 32 = 35). One advantage of the range is that it is easy to calculate, but it does have a major shortcoming: for any set of data, the range is based only on two scores and, by definition, these are extreme scores (i.e., they are the largest and smallest scores). As such, the size of the range is influenced by any extreme score, and further, the range only provides limited information about how different each of the numbers in a set of data are from one another.

To deal with the shortcomings of the range, there are a couple of related measures of variability: the variance and the standard deviation. Let's say we wanted to calculate, on average, how different each number in a set of data is from the mean. To do this we would have to calculate what is referred to as a *deviation score* for each of the observations (these are calculated by taking the difference between each score and the mean) and then calculate the average of those deviation scores (see **Table B-4**). However, when we follow this procedure a problem arises: to calculate the average of the deviation scores, we have to take the total of those scores and divide this total by the number of scores. Whenever we do this (for any set of scores), the total of the deviation scores will always be 0 (regardless of how different the scores are from one another). Thus, the average of the deviation scores is always 0 for every set of data and, as such, it is not very useful as a possible measure of variability.

Statisticians deal with this problem by calculating another measure of variability, known as the variance. The **variance** is the average of the squared deviation scores. The resulting set of scores has the property that the larger the squared deviation, the further that observation is from the mean. Thus, the larger the variance is for a set of data, the more different the scores are from one another. To calculate the variance for our 30 exam scores, take the average of the squared deviation scores, which gives a variance of 60.94 $\left(60.94 = \dfrac{1,828.167}{30}\right)$; see Table B-4).

The formula for the variance is presented below:

$$\sigma^2 = \frac{\sum(X - \mu)^2}{N}$$

where: σ^2 is the symbol for the variance,[2]
$\sum$ is summation notation and indicates the procedure of totalling the individual squared deviation scores $(X = \mu)^2$, and
N represents the number of observations.

While the variance is a useful measure of variability in that its magnitude reflects how different the numbers in a set of data are from one another, it also has a major shortcoming: the variance is not in the same metric as the original scores. For example, in calculating the variance, we determined the average of the squared deviations, so for our example the variance was approximately 61. However, that 61 is in the metric of *squared* exam scores, not the original exam scores we started with. To have a measure of variability

measures of variability indicators that tell how different the values are within a data set.

range the difference between the smallest and the largest value in a data set.

variance a calculated indicator of the degree to which values in a data set differ from the mean value of that data set; the average of squared deviations about the mean.

---

[2] σ^2 is the symbol for the variance of a population, whereas s^2 is the symbol for the variance of a sample. The distinction between populations and samples is discussed later in this appendix.

TABLE B-4 Thirty Exam Scores with the Mean, Deviation Score, and Squared Deviation Score

Exam Score (X)	Mean (μ)	Deviation Score (X − μ)	Squared Deviation Score (X − μ)²
32	50.1667	−18.17	330.029
36	50.1667	−14.17	200.695
39	50.1667	−11.17	124.695
41	50.1667	−9.17	84.028
42	50.1667	−8.17	66.695
43	50.1667	−7.17	51.362
44	50.1667	−6.17	38.028
44	50.1667	−6.17	38.028
46	50.1667	−4.17	17.361
46	50.1667	−4.17	17.361
49	50.1667	−1.17	1.361
50	50.1667	−0.17	0.028
50	50.1667	−0.17	0.028
50	50.1667	−0.17	0.028
50	50.1667	−0.17	0.028
51	50.1667	0.83	0.694
51	50.1667	0.83	0.694
51	50.1667	0.83	0.694
52	50.1667	1.83	3.361
53	50.1667	2.83	8.028
53	50.1667	2.83	8.028
54	50.1667	3.83	14.694
56	50.1667	5.83	34.027
57	50.1667	6.83	46.694
58	50.1667	7.83	61.361
58	50.1667	7.83	61.361
59	50.1667	8.83	78.027
61	50.1667	10.83	117.360
62	50.1667	11.83	140.027
67	50.1667	16.83	283.360
Totals 1,505	**1,505**	**0.00**	**1,828.167**

that is in the same metric as the original scores, we calculate the **standard deviation**—the square root of the variance. In our example of 30 exam scores, the standard deviation is 7.81 (7.81 = $\sqrt{60.94}$). The benefit of using the standard deviation as compared to the variance is that this measure of variability is in the same metric as the original scores.

Frequency Distributions—Again

If we were to obtain a very large number of measurements of one of a variety of human characteristics (e.g., physical characteristics like height or weight or psychological variables like intelligence or anxiety) and plot the frequency of the various values, we would find that the majority of scores fall near the middle of that frequency distribution. Comparatively fewer scores are associated with the more extreme values. Such distributions frequently resemble a theoretical distribution known as a **normal distribution** (sometimes, because of its shape, it may be referred to as a **bell curve**).

Normal distributions all have the same basic shape, but vary depending upon the mean and the standard deviation for the data. For example, scores on the Wechsler Adult Intelligence Scale (WAIS), discussed in Part 10, are designed to follow the normal distribution with a mean of 100 and a standard deviation of 15 (see **Figure B-3**).

Once we know that a set of scores (at least theoretically) follows a normal distribution, then we also know certain things about how those scores are distributed. First, the normal distribution is a *symmetrical distribution*—that is, the bottom half of the distribution is the same shape as the top half. Also, with the normal distribution, the three measures of central tendency, the mean, the median, and the mode, all fall in the exact same location. Based on this we know that in the case of WAIS scores that have a mean of 100, 50 percent of individuals will have scores less than 100 and similarly, 50 percent of individuals will have scores greater than 100. Further, theoretically, approximately 68 percent of people will score within plus or minus one standard deviation of the mean (i.e., between 85 and 115), and similarly about 95 percent of people will score within plus or minus two standard deviations of the mean (i.e., between 70 and 130).

Not all variables follow a normal distribution. In many instances, a large data set may have a comparatively small number of scores that are either very low or very high. For example, consider the distribution of 2010–2011 salaries for players from the Toronto Maple Leafs (Sports City, 2011). In this team, as is common in many teams in the NHL, there are a few premiere players who receive considerably higher than normal salaries, which results in a **positively skewed distribution** (sometimes referred to as a *distribution skewed to the right*). As **Figure B-4** reflects, in situations where the distribution is positively skewed, the average (or mean) for the distribution is considerably larger than the median value since the few extremely large salaries are included in the calculation of the mean. The mode also tends to be less than the median, which is also typical in positively skewed distributions.

In other instances, a distribution of scores may contain comparatively few low scores along with many more higher scores. For example, consider a nine-item true–false quiz that an instructor might

standard deviation a deviation value that is the square root of the variance; it is a statistical index of how much scores vary within a group.

normal distribution or **bell curve** a symmetrical, bell-shaped distribution in which most scores are in the middle with smaller groups of equal size at either end.

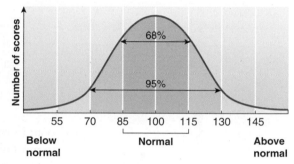

FIGURE B-3 **A normal distribution.**

positively skewed distribution a distribution where most values occur at the lower end of the scale.

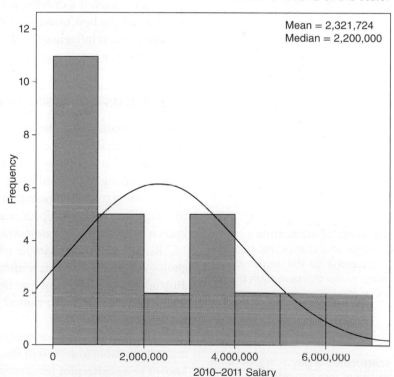

FIGURE B-4 **Example of a positively skewed distribution.**

FIGURE B-5 **Example of a negatively skewed distribution.**

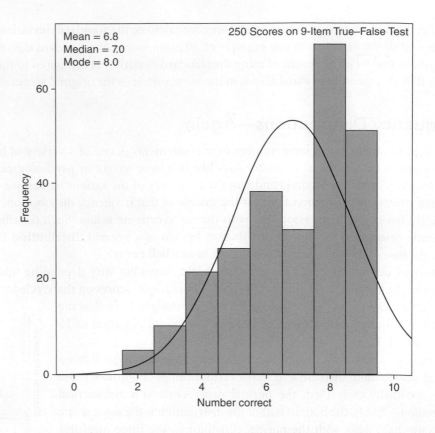

give to an introductory psychology class with 250 students. Assume that the test is quite easy, so most of the students do very well. This could result in a distribution of scores such as the one depicted in **Figure B-5**. As you can see, the mean is less than the median (again, this is because the value for the mean is influenced by the comparatively few small scores), which is also less than the mode. These types of distributions are called **negatively skewed distributions** (sometimes referred to as a *distribution skewed to the left*).

In summary, if a distribution has comparatively few small or high scores, the mean may not be the best measure of central tendency since it is the only measure of central tendency that is influenced by these types of extreme scores. In such cases, the median or mode may be a better, more representative measure of central tendency.

Measures of Association

In many situations, psychologists are interested in studying the relationship between two (or more) variables. For example, what is the relationship between exposure to televised violence and actual physical aggression? Or is there a relationship between exposure to actors smoking in the media (e.g., in movies and television) and the likelihood of a teenager deciding to start smoking? In instances such as these, we can quantify and summarize the degree of relationship or association between variables using descriptive statistics known as **measures of association**.

Recall our earlier example where we had scores from 30 students on their first psychology test (refer to this variable as *X*). Suppose that we had also asked those same 30 students the following question: "In the week before the test, how many hours did you spend playing video games?" (call this variable *Y*). **Table B-5** provides a listing of these data.

In instances where we have collected data on two variables from a group of individuals, it is possible to represent the relationship between the two variables using a display known as a **scatterplot** (or scattergram). In this display, values of one of the variables are plotted on the horizontal axis of the graph and the corresponding values of the other variable are plotted on the vertical axis. **Figure B-6** provides a scatterplot of our example data.

negatively skewed distribution
a distribution where most values occur at the upper end of the scale.

measures of association
descriptive statistics that quantify and summarize the degree of relationship or association between variables.

scatterplot a graph or plot of the values of one variable or measure associated with the values on another variable or measure.

FIGURE B-5 **Example of a negatively skewed distribution.**

TABLE B-5 Exam Scores and Hours of Video Game Playing

Student	Exam Score (X)	Hours Playing Video Games (Y)
1	32	20
2	36	10
3	39	15
4	41	10
5	42	20
6	43	14
7	44	8
8	44	12
9	46	14
10	46	14
11	49	10
12	50	12
13	50	8
14	50	10
15	50	8
16	51	6
17	51	7
18	51	4
19	52	5
20	53	0
21	53	4
22	54	5
23	56	2
24	57	5
25	58	4
26	58	2
27	59	0
28	61	1
29	62	0
30	67	3

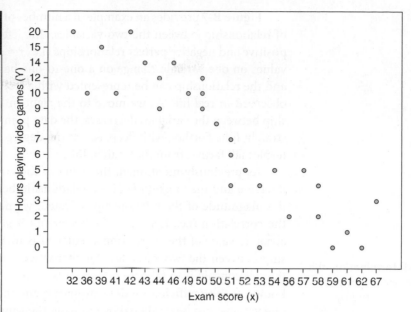

FIGURE B-6 Scatterplot showing exam scores and hours of video game playing.

On average, higher exam scores are associated with students who spent less time playing video games. Similarly, students who received the lower exam scores, on average, spent more time playing video games in the week before the exam.

While we can understand the nature of the relationship between two variables using scatterplots, we might want to have an index or number that reflects the nature of that relationship. The most commonly used measure of association between two variables is the **Pearson product-moment correlation coefficient** (often symbolized with an r and frequently referred to as simply the correlation coefficient). The correlation coefficient provides an index of the degree of (linear) relationship between two variables, with possible values of the coefficient ranging between -1 and $+1$. The value of the correlation coefficient reflects both the *magnitude* of the relationship between the two variables and the *direction* of the relationship between the two variables. Positive values of the correlation coefficient ($r > 0.00$) indicate that there is a **positive** or **direct relationship** between the variables. In instances like this, higher values on one of the variables are associated, on average, with higher values on the other variable; similarly, lower values of the one variable are associated, on average, with lower values of the other variable. In cases where the correlation coefficient is negative (i.e., $r < 0.00$), the nature of the relationship between the two variables is referred to as a **negative** or **inverse relationship**. In this case, the lower scores on one variable are, on average, associated with higher scores on the other variable and vice versa (as was the case with our example data).

Pearson product-moment correlation coefficient
a statistic indicating the degree of association or relationship between two variables or measures, ranging from -1 to $+1$.

positive or **direct relationship**
a relationship where as the value of one variable increases, so do values in another associated variable.

negative or **inverse relationship**
a relationship where as the value of one variable increases, values in another associated variable decrease.

Figure B-7 provides an example of a number of scatterplots depicting varying degrees of relationship between the two variables. The left-most scatterplots reflect instances of positive and negative perfect relationships (i.e., $r = +1$ and $r = -1$). In instances like these, values on one variable change on a one-to-one basis with changes in the other variable and the relationship can be represented with a straight line. Such relationships are rarely observed in real life. As we move to the right in Figure B-7, as the degree of relationship between the variables decreases, the data points in the scatterplot no longer fall on a straight line. Further, with decreases in the degree of relationship, the points in the scatterplot fall farther from the straight line.

As previously mentioned, the value of the correlation coefficient reflects both the *direction* and the *magnitude* of the relationship between the two variables. To interpret the magnitude of the relationship reflected, we need to consider the absolute value of the correlation (i.e., ignoring whether or not it is positive or negative). The closer the absolute value of the correlation coefficient is to 1, the stronger the degree of relationship between the two variables. An alternative way of understanding the magnitude of the relationship is to take the square of the correlation coefficient (i.e., r^2). This value is known as the **coefficient of determination** and indicates the degree to which values on one variable can be predicted by knowing the values of the other variable. For example, if the correlation between number of cigarettes smoked and life expectancy were $r = 0.80$, then we could predict with 64 percent accuracy a person's life expectancy based on how much he or she had smoked.

To calculate the Pearson product-moment correlation coefficient, take the ratio of the covariance between the two variables (which is another measure of association) and divide that by the product of the standard deviations of the two variables. The covariance between two variables (let's call them X and Y) is defined by the following formula:

coefficient of determination the degree to which values on one variable can be predicted by knowing the values of the other variable.

$$\sigma_{XY} = \frac{\sum(X - \mu_X)(Y - \mu_Y)}{N}$$

where: σ_{XY} is the symbol for the covariance,[3]

$\sum$ is summation notation and indicates the procedure of totalling the products of each pair of deviation scores $(X - \mu_X)$ and $(Y - \mu_Y)$, and

N represents the number of observations.

Table B-6 shows our example data looking at the relationship between students' exam scores (X) and hours spent playing video games (Y). The table includes the details on the initial calculations required to determine the variances for each of the variables and the covariance between the two variables.

First, consider the covariance between the two variables. The numerator for the covariance is based on the sum of the product of the individual pairs of deviation scores (i.e., $\sum(X - \mu_X)(Y - \mu_Y)$). In this example the total is negative, which reflects the inverse relationship that exists between the students' exam scores and the number of hours they spent

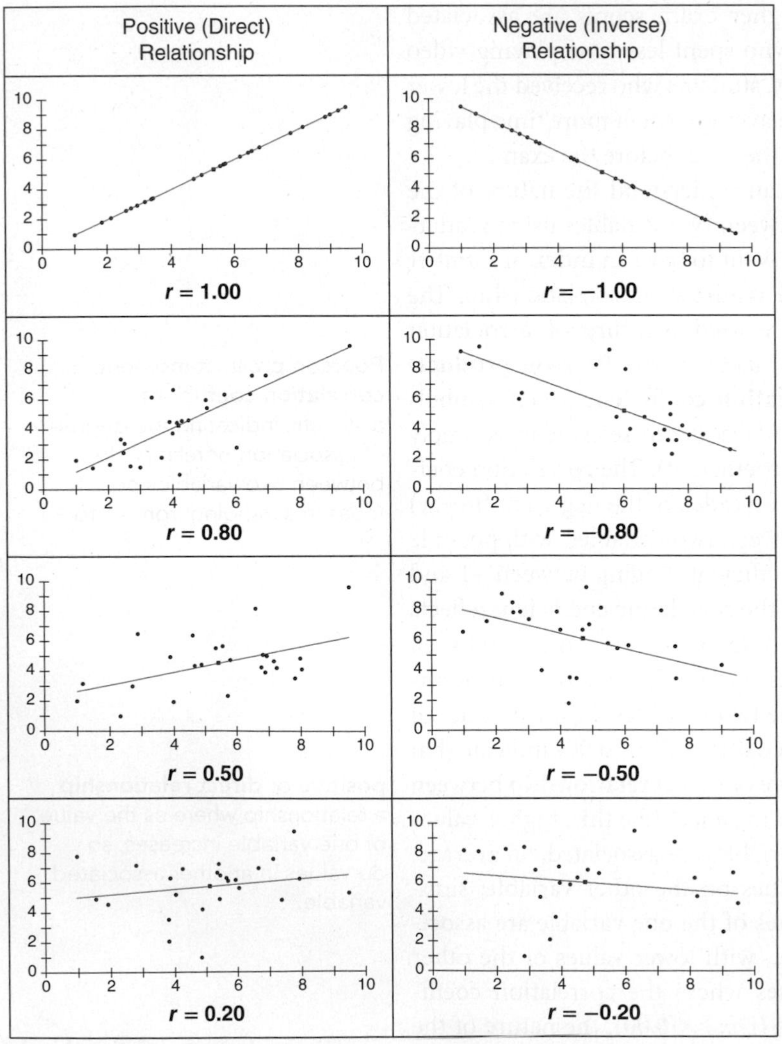

FIGURE B-7 **Scatterplots showing various degrees of relationship.**

---

[3] σ_{XY} is the symbol for the covariance of a population, whereas s_{XY} is the symbol for the covariance of a sample. The distinction between populations and samples is discussed later in this appendix.

TABLE B-6 Data Required for Calculating Pearson Correlation Coefficient

Student	Exam Score (X)	Hours Playing Video Games (Y)	X – μX	Y – μY	(X – μX)(Y – μY)	(X – μX)²	(Y – μY)²
1	32	20	−18.17	12.23	−222.24	330.03	149.65
2	36	10	−14.17	2.23	−31.64	200.69	4.99
3	39	15	−11.17	7.23	−80.77	124.69	52.32
4	41	10	−9.17	2.23	−20.47	84.03	4.99
5	42	20	−8.17	12.23	−99.91	66.69	149.65
6	43	14	−7.17	6.23	−44.67	51.36	38.85
7	44	8	−6.17	0.23	−1.44	38.03	0.05
8	44	12	−6.17	4.23	−26.11	38.03	17.92
9	46	14	−4.17	6.23	−25.97	17.36	38.85
10	46	14	−4.17	6.23	−25.97	17.36	38.85
11	49	10	−1.17	2.23	−2.61	1.36	4.99
12	50	12	−0.17	4.23	−0.71	0.03	17.92
13	50	8	−0.17	0.23	−0.04	0.03	0.05
14	50	10	−0.17	2.23	−0.37	0.03	4.99
15	50	8	−0.17	0.23	−0.04	0.03	0.05
16	51	6	0.83	−1.77	−1.47	0.69	3.12
17	51	7	0.83	−0.77	−0.64	0.69	0.59
18	51	4	0.83	−3.77	−3.14	0.69	14.19
19	52	5	1.83	−2.77	−5.07	3.36	7.65
20	53	0	2.83	−7.77	−22.01	8.03	60.32
21	53	4	2.83	−3.77	−10.67	8.03	14.19
22	54	5	3.83	−2.77	−10.61	14.69	7.65
23	56	2	5.83	−5.77	−33.64	34.03	33.25
24	57	5	6.83	−2.77	−18.91	46.69	7.65
25	58	4	7.83	−3.77	−29.51	61.36	14.19
26	58	2	7.83	−5.77	−45.17	61.36	33.25
27	59	0	8.83	−7.77	−68.61	78.03	60.32
28	61	1	10.83	−6.77	−73.31	117.36	45.79
29	62	0	11.83	−7.77	−91.91	140.03	60.32
30	67	3	16.83	−4.77	−80.24	283.36	22.72
Totals (Σ)	50.167	7.767	0.00	0.00	−1,077.83	1,828.17	909.37

playing video games. On average, the students who had higher exam scores, and who therefore also had positive deviation scores for that variable $(X - \mu_X)$, were more likely to have spent less time playing video games, and therefore had negative deviation scores for that variable $(Y - \mu_Y)$. Further, the reverse is true for students who had lower exam scores. When this happens, the covariance between the two variables will be negative and this will result in the correlation between the two variables being negative as well, since the covariance serves as the numerator for the correlation.[4] For our example data, the covariance between the two variables is:

$$\sigma_{XY} = \frac{\sum(X - \mu_X)(Y - \mu_Y)}{N} = \frac{-1,077.83}{30} = -35.93$$

The next step in calculating the correlation coefficient is to determine the standard deviation for each of the variables. Recall that the standard deviation for a variable is the square root of the variance. The variance for each of the two variables can be calculated as shown below:

$$\sigma_X^2 = \frac{\sum(X - \mu_X)^2}{N} = \frac{1,828.17}{30} = 60.94 \text{ and } \sigma_Y^2 = \frac{\sum(Y - \mu_Y)^2}{N} = \frac{909.37}{30} = 30.31$$

To obtain the standard deviations for the two variables, take the square roots of the two variances (i.e., $\sigma_X = \sqrt{60.94} = 7.81$ and $\sigma_Y = \sqrt{30.31} = 5.51$). Finally, take the covariance and divide it by the product of the two standard deviations[5]:

$$r = \frac{\rho_{XY}}{\sigma_X \sigma_Y} = \frac{-35.93}{7.81 \times 5.51} = -0.84$$

So, for our 30 students, the correlation between their exam scores and the amount of time spent playing video games is –0.84. In other words, we could predict with about 70 percent accuracy (i.e., 0.84^2) a student's exam score if we knew how many hours that person had spent playing video games. Finally, as discussed in Part 2, remember that correlations tell us nothing regarding causality. So even though there is a fairly strong negative relationship between exam scores and video game playing in our example data, we do not know whether one variable causes the other or whether there is some third variable that is responsible for the relationship. So video gaming might reduce exam scores, or low exam scores might increase video gaming, or low exam scores and high amounts of video gaming might both be due to a lack of interest in or commitment to the course in question.

Inferential Statistics

Whereas psychologists (and others) use descriptive statistics to summarize collections of data, they use *inferential statistics* to help them make informed decisions regarding the types of conclusions they can make regarding their research findings. To understand this better, let's begin with some definitions and an example.

---

[4] Note that when there is a positive relationship between the two variables, higher scores on one variable will on average be associated with higher scores on the other variables (thus the product of the corresponding deviation scores will be positive). Additionally, lower scores on one variable will on average be associated with lower scores on the other variable (and in this case, the two corresponding deviation scores will both be negative and therefore their product will be positive). In cases like this, the covariance between the two variables will be a large positive value, which will result in the correlation between the two variables being positive.

[5] This formula for the correlation coefficient is really more of a "definitional" formula and would only be used if the number of observations was small. In most instances, the correlation coefficient is calculated using one of several alternative "calculational" formulas.

Populations and Samples

In most cases, when psychologists conduct research (whether on human participants or animal subjects), what they are doing is collecting observations based on a **sample** of individuals that is drawn from a larger group or **population** (see **Figure B-8**). Consider a simple experimental study where a psychologist is interested in testing the effectiveness of a new drug to improve memory. It would be impractical (and very expensive) to test every individual who might take the drug, so the researcher obtains a sample of individuals, studies them, and then draws some type of conclusions based on the results of that study. Let's look at this procedure in more detail.

First, consider the underlying population—the group about which the psychologist ultimately wants to make conclusions—from which the psychologist is going to obtain her sample. In the case of testing a drug that supposedly improves (human) memory, we might consider the population to be all adults in North America. Since the psychologist cannot test the effect of the drug on all members of the population, she instead obtains a sample of individuals from that population. Often the ideal type of sample to obtain would be a **random sample**, in which every member of the population has an equal chance of being selected for the study. However, in many instances it is not possible to obtain a truly random sample. Instead researchers rely on sampling from a group of individuals to which they have access (e.g., first-year psychology students).

Assume that the psychologist has recruited 50 participants for her study. This study will involve two groups: the experimental group, which will receive the drug and then will have their memory tested, and a control group that will consist of participants who are treated exactly the same as the participants in the experimental group with the exception that they will not receive the drug.[6] In conducting the experiment, the researcher might randomly assign 25 participants to each of the two conditions (e.g., participants could be assigned to the experimental vs. control groups based on the results of the flip of a coin). Random assignment helps to ensure that any differences that might have existed between the two groups are evenly distributed between the groups so that the two groups are as similar as possible at the start of the study.

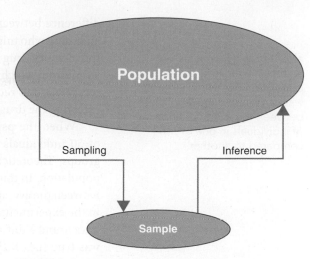

FIGURE B-8 **Relationship between population and samples.**

sample a group or set of people or items drawn from a larger population.

population the entire group of individuals about whom we hope to learn (e.g., the Canadian population consists of all Canadians).

random sample a group or set made by randomly selecting people or items from a larger population; like closing your eyes and picking any two socks from your drawer.

Hypothesis Testing

Assume that memory is assessed in this study with a standard memory test, and the researcher finds that the average score for the experimental group is 50 whereas the average score for the control group is 25. At this point, the psychologist can conclude that, on average, the experimental group had better performance on the memory test than did the control group, which she could attribute to the effect of the drug. However, the more interesting question, and the one that is at the heart of inferential statistics, is whether or not a similar finding would be obtained if the drug were given to other individuals in the population. The answer to this question comes down to the psychologist determining whether or not the difference observed between the two groups in the sample is "big enough" for her to conclude that similar differences would likely occur if the study was conducted again with a different sample of individuals.

To address this question, the psychologist can employ a technique known as **hypothesis testing**. With hypothesis testing, the psychologist sets up two hypotheses: the null hypothesis and the alternative hypothesis. Under the **null hypothesis**, the psychologist asserts that in the underlying population from which the sample was obtained, there is no

hypothesis testing testing a statement or claim about a population using a sample and, in its simplest form, looking at experimental and control group differences.

null hypothesis an assertion that in the underlying population from which the sample was obtained, there is no difference between the average performance of individuals in one group compared to another.

---

[6] In a well-designed study, the participants in the control group would not know that they were in the control group and would be administered some type of placebo (e.g., a sugar pill).

alternative hypothesis an assertion that in the underlying population from which the sample was obtained, there *is* a difference between the average performance of individuals in one group compared to another.

difference between the average performance of individuals who might receive the drug and those who might not receive the drug (in other words, this null hypothesis asserts that the memory drug is *not* effective). The **alternative hypothesis** would be that in the population from which the sample was obtained, the average performance on the memory test for individuals receiving the memory drug would be better than that for individuals not receiving the drug (in other words, asserting that the memory drug *is* effective).

When the psychologist conducts her memory drug study, she obtains her sample of 50 individuals from the underlying population and uses that sample to create two groups. Theoretically, she could have obtained many other, different samples from that population. In this particular study, the researcher finds that there is a 25-point difference between the average memory performance for participants in the control group and those in the experimental group. Now the inferential question is, how likely is it that she would have found a difference of 25 points between the two sample means *if* the null hypothesis was true (i.e., if there really was no difference in people's memory between those who receive the memory drug and those who do not)? To determine the likelihood of this finding, the psychologist needs to consider a theoretical distribution known as a **sampling distribution**. In this case, the psychologist would consider a sampling distribution for the difference between two sample means (or averages) that are taken from an underlying population in which there is no difference between the means. The characteristics of this sampling distribution are based on the variability of the sample data and the size of the samples.

sampling distribution the theoretical distribution of a sample statistic; for example, the difference between two sample means taken from a population.

In our example, assume that the standard deviation for scores on the memory test was 20 for the control group and 30 for the experimental group. If the null hypothesis was true, then we would know theoretically that all possible differences between two sample means would be normally distributed with a mean of 0 and a standard deviation of 7.21.[7] Given that we know the characteristics of the theoretical sampling distribution, we can calculate that the likelihood or probability of finding a difference of 25 points between the two sample means would be very low (in fact, it would be less than 1 chance in 1,000). In this case, the psychologist would reject the null hypothesis and could be reasonably confident in concluding that the finding she obtained in her study was not due to chance and that the drug really had some effect on memory performance.

When psychologists test hypotheses using the procedures outlined above, before analyzing their data, they determine what level of risk they would be willing to take in terms of making an incorrect conclusion. Typically psychologists set the risk of drawing an incorrect conclusion at a level of either *less than 5 in 100* times or, if they want to be more certain (and more conservative) *less than 1 in 100* times. These levels translate to what is known as the **significance level**, or the **rejection level**, for the hypothesis test, and are often reported in the literature as finding a significant difference between the groups at *p < 0.05* or *p < 0.01*. In practice, if a psychologist ends up rejecting the null hypothesis, she concludes that there is evidence to support the alternative hypothesis (e.g., that the memory drug is effective)—what she cannot say, however, is that she has "proven" the alternative hypothesis. This is because we only have information from the one sample and there is still some possibility (albeit a low one) that the sample she obtained did indeed come from a population where the drug had no effect on memory.

significance level or **rejection level** the level of risk researchers would be willing to take in terms of making an incorrect conclusion.

Effect Size

Whereas inferential statistics provide psychologists with tools to determine the likelihood of the finding in the sample being one that would also occur in the population, they do not provide information regarding the magnitude of the study's effect. For example, while a psychologist may use null hypothesis testing to find that there is a significant difference between memory performance for two groups, the hypothesis test does not tell us

---

[7] This standard deviation is known as the *standard error of the differences between means* and equals $\sqrt{\dfrac{20^2}{25} + \dfrac{30^2}{25}} = 7.21$.

about the magnitude or size of the difference—it only allows the psychologist to make a statement regarding the probability of the finding. Researchers can use another category of descriptive statistics, namely **effect size** estimates, in conjunction with hypothesis testing to help them assess the magnitude of research findings. An effect size is a standardized measure that reflects the degree of relationship or size of the difference between two or more variables. Further, since effect sizes are standardized, they can be compared across different studies (Field, 2005).

effect size a standardized measure that reflects the degree of relationship or size of the difference between two or more variables.

Two common categories of effect sizes are (1) group difference indices that estimate the magnitude of the difference between two (or more) groups; and (2) strength of association indices that estimate the degree of shared variation between two (or more) variables (Ferguson, 2009). In simple studies that involve examining the difference in average performance between two groups, Cohen's d is the most common effect size. Cohen's d is the standardized difference between two population means and can be estimated by taking the difference between the two sample means and dividing this by the standard deviation for the data. In the previous memory study example there was a 25-point difference between the two sample means; if we divide that by the standard deviation[8] of the data, then Cohen's d equals 0.98 $\left(d = \dfrac{25}{25.5} = 0.98 \right)$. In terms of interpreting effect sizes (specifically Cohen's d), a frequently used rule-of-thumb is to define effect sizes as "small, $d = .2$," "medium, $d = .5$," and "large, $d = .8$" (Cohen, 1992). Thus, for the example data, we could conclude that the memory drug has a large effect.

For non-experimental studies, a common effect size that is a measure of association is the Pearson correlation coefficient (i.e., r). In terms of interpreting r as an effect size, Cohen (1992) suggests the following: "small, $r = .1$," "medium, $r = .3$," and "large, $r = .5$." Recall that squaring the correlation coefficient provides the coefficient of determination, which tells us how much of the variability in one variable can be predicted based on scores from the other variable. With this in mind, for non-experimental research, if one could account for 1 percent of the variability, then you would have a small effect; if you could account for 9 percent of the variability, then you would have a medium effect; and if you could account for 25 percent of the variability, you would have a large effect.

Why Statistics Matter

This appendix has hopefully provided you with some insight into several of the basic statistical procedures used by psychologists as tools to summarize and interpret the data they collect as part of their research studies. Students of psychology are often surprised by the degree to which the study of psychology requires at least a basic familiarity with statistics. However, only with this type of understanding will students become better consumers of psychological research and thereby become better able to critically evaluate the claims made by psychologists. In fact, students who choose to major in psychology as undergraduates will most likely require further instruction in statistics. A survey of requirements for undergraduate degrees in psychology showed that the vast majority of universities and colleges require at least one course in statistics (Messer, Griggs, & Jackson, 1999). So if you are interested in pursuing a degree in psychology, you can expect to encounter even more statistics.

---

[8] In the case of the example study, the standard deviation of the data is obtained by using the pooled standard deviation, which can be calculated as $s^* = \sqrt{\dfrac{(n_1 - 1)s_1^2 + (n_2 - 1)s_2^2}{n_1 + n_2 - 2}} = \sqrt{\dfrac{(25 - 1)20_1^2 + (25 - 1)30_2^2}{25 + 25 - 2}} = 25.5$

Glossary

A

ABC model of attitudes a model proposing that attitudes have three components: the affective component, the behavioural component, and the cognitive component.

abnormal psychology the scientific study of psychological disorders.

absolute pitch the ability to recognize or produce any note on a musical scale.

absolute refractory period a very brief period of time after an action potential, during which a neuron is completely unable to fire again.

absolute threshold the minimal stimulus necessary for detection by an individual.

academic psychology a branch of psychology focusing on research and instruction in the various areas or fields of study in psychology.

accommodation one of two ways of acquiring knowledge, defined by Piaget as the alteration of pre-existing mental frameworks to take in new information.

action potential a sudden positive change in the electrical charge of a neuron's axon, also known as a spike or firing; action potentials are rapidly transmitted down the axon.

activation-synthesis model theory that dreams result from the brain's attempts to synthesize or organize random internally generated signals and give them meaning.

actor-observer effect the discrepancy between how we explain other people's behaviour (dispositionally) and how we explain our own behaviour (situationally).

acute stress disorder an anxiety disorder in which fear and related symptoms are experienced soon after a traumatic event and last less than a month.

acute stressor a stressful situation or circumstance that happens in the short term and has a definite endpoint.

adaptive theory of sleep theory that organisms sleep for the purposes of self-preservation, to keep away from predators that are more active at night.

addiction psychological or physical compulsion to take a drug, resulting from regular ingestion and leading to maladaptive patterns of behaviour and changes in physical response.

afferent neurons neurons that carry sensory information from the body to the central nervous system.

affiliation the need to form attachments to other people for support, guidance, and protection.

ageusia inability to taste.

aggression a broad range of behaviours intended to harm others.

agoraphobia a phobia that makes people avoid public places or situations in which escape might be difficult or help unavailable should panic symptoms develop.

agrammatism a neurological condition arising from damage to a brain region just anterior to Broca's area, where the patient is incapable of using words in grammatical sequence.

alcoholism long-term pattern of alcohol addiction.

algorithm a problem-solving strategy that always leads to a solution.

allele variation of a gene.

alternative hypothesis an assertion that in the underlying population from which the sample was obtained, there *is* a difference between the average performance of individuals in one group compared to another.

altruism self-sacrificing behaviour carried out for the benefit of others.

Alzheimer's disease most common form of dementia, usually beginning with mild memory problems, lapses of attention, and problems in language, and progressing to difficulty with even simple tasks and recall of long-held memories.

amnestic disorders organic disorders in which memory loss is the primary symptom.

amygdala brain area involved in processing information about emotions, particularly fear.

anorexia nervosa eating disorder in which individuals undereat and have a distorted body image of being overweight.

anosmia inability to smell.

anterograde amnesia ongoing inability to form new memories after an amnesia-inducing event.

antianxiety drugs psychotropic drugs that reduce tension and anxiety.

antibipolar drugs psychotropic drugs that help stabilize the moods of people suffering from bipolar disorder.

antipsychotic drugs psychotropic drugs that help correct grossly confused or distorted thinking.

antisocial personality disorder a personality disorder characterized by extreme and callous disregard for the feelings and rights of others.

applied psychology the branch of psychology applying psychological principles to practical problems in other fields, such as education, marketing, or industry.

approach–approach conflict conflict that occurs when a person must choose between two equally desirable options.

approach–avoidance conflict conflict that occurs when any available choice has both desirable and undesirable qualities.

Asperger's disorder a disorder in which persons have major social impairments yet have relatively normal intellectual, adaptive, and language skills.

assimilation one of two ways of acquiring knowledge, defined by Piaget as the inclusion of new information or experiences into pre-existing schemes.

association cortex areas of the cortex responsible for complex functions, including higher-order sensory processing, thinking, and planning—all of cortex that is neither purely sensory nor motor.

associative learning learning that involves forming associations between stimuli.

attachment a significant emotional connection to another person, such as a baby to a primary caregiver.

attitudes relatively stable and enduring evaluations of things and people.

attributions causal explanations of behaviour.

autism a severe disorder marked by extreme unresponsiveness, poor communication, and very repetitive and rigid behaviours.

automatic processing encoding of information with little conscious awareness or effort.

automatic thoughts   specific upsetting thoughts that occur unbidden.

autonomic nervous system   portion of the peripheral nervous system that comprises the sympathetic and parasympathetic nervous systems.

availability heuristic   judging easily-recalled events as more common.

aversion therapy   therapy designed to help clients to acquire anxiety responses to stimuli that the clients have been finding too attractive.

avoidance–avoidance conflict   conflict that occurs when a person must choose between two equally undesirable options.

avoidant personality disorder   a disorder involving extreme discomfort and inhibition in social relationships.

axon   the part of the neuron that carries information away from the cell body toward other neurons.

axon terminal   the end of a neuron's axon, from which neurotransmitters are released.

B

babbling   babies' production of meaningless sounds.

basic emotions   a group of emotions preprogrammed into all humans regardless of culture.

basilar membrane   structure in the cochlea where the hair cells are located.

behaviour modification   a systematic approach to change behaviour using principles of operant conditioning.

behaviour observable   activities of an organism, often in response to environmental cues.

behavioural genetics   a subfield of psychology looking at the influence of genes on human behaviour.

behaviourism   a branch of psychological thought arguing that psychology should study only directly observable behaviours rather than abstract mental processes.

biases   distorted beliefs based on a person's subjective sense of reality.

bioecological model of intelligence   Ceci's theory that intelligence is a function of the interactions among innate potential abilities, environmental context, and internal motivation.

biological therapy   the use of physical and chemical procedures to help people overcome psychological difficulties.

bipolar disorder   a mood disorder in which periods of mania alternate with periods of depression.

body mass index (BMI)   weight-to-height ratio.

body weight set point   a weight that individuals typically return to even after dieting or overeating.

borderline personality disorder   a personality disorder characterized by severe instability in emotions and self-concept and high levels of volatility.

bottom-up processing   perception that proceeds by transducing environmental stimuli into neural impulses that move onto successively more complex brain regions.

bounded rationality   the fact that in many situations, our ability to make clear rational decisions is limited or "bounded" by things like a lack of information, time constraints, or emotions attached to aspects of the problem we are trying to solve.

brainstem   the part of the brain closest to the spinal cord that serves basic functions.

Broca's aphasia   a neurological condition arising from damage to Broca's area where the patient is unable to produce coherent speech.

Broca's area   a brain region located in the frontal lobe near the motor cortex that is important for speech production.

bulimia nervosa   eating disorder in which individuals binge and then engage in purging-type behaviour.

C

Cannon-Bard theory of emotion   a theory proposing that the subjective experience of emotion and the activation of the sympathetic nervous system (that is, bodily arousal) occur simultaneously.

case study   study focusing on a single person.

catatonia   extreme psychomotor symptoms of schizophrenia, including catatonic stupor, catatonic rigidity, and catatonic posturing.

catharsis   reliving of past repressed feelings as a means of settling internal conflicts and overcoming problems.

cellular clock theory   theory suggesting that we age because our cells have built-in limits on their ability to reproduce.

cephalocaudal pattern   a pattern in which growth and development proceed from top to bottom.

cerebellum   part of the brain, near the base of the back of the head, important for motor coordination.

cerebral cortex   the largest portion of the brain, responsible for complex behaviours including language and thought.

child-directed speech   speech characterized by exaggerated emotional responses and a slower pace that is cross-culturally common among caregivers communicating with babies and young children.

chromosomes   strands of DNA; each human being has 46 chromosomes, distributed in pairs.

chronic stressor   a stressful situation or circumstance that is relatively long term and often lacks a definite endpoint.

chunking   grouping bits of information together to enhance ability to hold that information in working memory.

circadian rhythm   pattern of sleep–wake cycles that in human beings roughly corresponds to periods of daylight and night.

classical conditioning   a form of associative learning between two previously unrelated stimuli that results in a learned response.

client-centred therapy   an approach to therapy founded by Carl Rogers, based on the notion that the client is an equal and positive gains are made by mirroring clients' thoughts and feelings in an atmosphere of unconditional positive regard.

clinical and counselling psychology   the study of abnormal psychological behaviour and interventions designed to change that behaviour.

cochlea   fluid-filled structure in the inner ear; contains the hair cells.

codominance   in a heterozygous combination of alleles, both traits are expressed in the offspring.

coefficient of determination   the degree to which values on one variable can be predicted by knowing the values of the other variable.

cognition   mental processes of thinking and knowing.

cognitive control   the ability to direct thought in accord with one's intentions.

cognitive development   changes in thinking that occur over the course of time.

cognitive dissonance   a state of emotional discomfort people experience when they hold two contradictory beliefs or hold a belief that contradicts their behaviour.

cognitive-mediational theory of emotion   a theory proposing that cognitive interpretations, particularly appraisals, of events are the keys to experiences of emotion.

cognitive neuroscience   the study of mental processes and how they relate to the biological functions of the brain.

cognitive psychology   the field of psychology studying mental processes as forms of information processing, or the ways in which information is stored and operated in our minds.

cognitive therapy   Beck's cognitive therapy technique designed to help clients recognize and change their dysfunctional thoughts and ways of thinking.

cognitive triad   a pattern of thinking in which individuals repeatedly interpret their experiences, themselves, and their futures in negative ways that lead them to feel depressed.

cohort-sequential design   blended cross-sectional and longitudinal research, designed to look at how individuals from different age groups compare to one another and to follow them over time.

collectivist   a culture whose members focus more on the needs of the group and less on individual desires.

community mental health treatment   treatment programs that emphasize community care, including an emphasis on prevention.

comorbidity   condition in which a person's symptoms qualify him for two or more diagnoses.

compulsions   repetitive and rigid behaviours or mental acts that people feel they must perform to prevent or reduce anxiety.

concentration gradient   the difference in concentration of sodium ions inside and outside of the neuron.

concrete operational stage   Piagetian stage during which children are able to talk about complex relationships, such as categorization and cause and effect, but are still limited to understanding ideas in terms of real-world relationships.

conditioned response (CR)   a physical response elicited by a conditioned stimulus; it is acquired through experience and is usually the same as the unconditioned response.

conditioned stimulus (CS)   a neutral stimulus that eventually elicits the same response as an unconditioned stimulus with which it has been paired.

conditioned taste aversion   a form of classical conditioning whereby a previously neutral stimulus (often an odour or taste) elicits an aversive reaction after it's paired with illness (nausea).

conditioning   the association of events in the environment.

conduct disorder   clinical disorder in children and adolescents associated with emotional and behavioural problems, such as rule-breaking, trouble with limit-setting from authority figures, bullying and fighting with other people, and cruelty.

cones   photoreceptors responsive to colours.

confirmation bias   tendency to look for information that meets our expectations.

conflict   discomfort brought about by two or more goals or impulses perceived to be incompatible.

conformity   the tendency to yield to social pressure.

consciousness   personal awareness of ongoing mental processes, behaviours, and environmental events.

conservation   the understanding that certain properties of an object (such as volume and number) remain the same despite changes in the object's outward appearance.

content validity   the degree to which the content of a test accurately represents what the test is intended to measure.

context   the original location where you first learned a concept or idea is rich with retrieval cues that will make it more likely you will be able to recall that information later if you are in that same location or context.

continuous reinforcement   what occurs when behaviour is reinforced every time it occurs.

control group   group that has not been or will not be exposed to the independent variable.

convergence   inward movement of the eyes to view objects close to oneself.

convergent evolution   the development of similar physical characteristics or behaviours in different species that do not share a common ancestor; occurs because of exposure to similar environmental conditions for different species.

coping   efforts to manage, reduce, or tolerate stress.

corpus callosum   bundle of axons that allows communication from one side of the cortex to the other.

correlation   predictable relationship between two or more variables.

correlation coefficient   statistic expressing the strength and nature of a relationship between two variables.

couple therapy or **marital therapy**   therapy format in which a therapist works with two people who are in a long-term relationship.

creativity   the ability to produce ideas that are both original and valuable.

critical period   a window of time in development during which certain influences are necessary for the appropriate formation of the brain.

cross-cultural psychology   the study of what is generally or universally true about human beings regardless of culture.

cross-sectional design   a research approach that compares groups of different-aged people to one another.

cultural psychology   the study of how cultural practices shape psychological and behavioural tendencies and influence human behaviour.

cultural universality   behaviours and practices that occur across all cultures.

culture   a set of shared beliefs and practices that are transmitted across generations.

culture-sensitive therapies   approaches that seek to address the unique issues faced by members of cultural minority groups.

D

daily hassles   everyday annoyances that contribute to higher stress levels; also known as *micro-stressors*.

deafness   loss or lack of hearing.

debriefing   supplying full information to participants at the end of their participation in a research study.

decay theory   theory of forgetting, suggesting that memories fade over time due to neglect or failure to access over long periods of time.

decision making   evaluating and choosing from among options.

deductive reasoning   reasoning proceeding from broad basic principles applied to specific situations.

deep brain stimulation   a procedure in which implanted electrodes deliver constant low stimulation to a small area of the brain; used to treat severe depression, Parkinson's disease, and epilepsy.

defence mechanisms   unconscious tactics employed by the ego to protect the individual from anxiety.

delusions   blatantly false beliefs that are firmly held despite evidence to the contrary.

dementia   severe memory problems combined with losses in at least one other cognitive function, such as abstract thinking or language.

dendrites   the parts of neurons that receive input from other neurons.

denial   a defence mechanism; the process of refusing to recognize an existing situation.

deoxyribonucleic acid (DNA) molecules in which genetic information is enclosed.

dependent personality disorder a disorder involving a pervasive, excessive need to be taken care of and a fear of separation.

dependent variable condition or event that you expect to change as a result of variations in the independent variable.

depolarization the inside of the neuron membrane becomes *less* negative relative to the outside.

depressants class of drugs that slow the activity of the central nervous system.

depression a persistent sad state in which life seems dark and its challenges overwhelming.

descriptive research methods studies that allow researchers to demonstrate a relationship between the variables of interest, without specifying a causal relationship.

descriptive statistics statistics used to describe and summarize data.

developmental psychology the study of changes in behaviour and mental processes over time and the factors that influence the course of those constancies and changes.

diagnosis a clinician's determination that a person's cluster of symptoms represents a particular disorder.

Diagnostic and Statistical Manual of Mental Disorders (DSM) the leading classification system for psychological disorders in Canada; DSM-5 is the current version.

difference threshold or **just noticeable difference** the minimal difference between two stimuli necessary for detection of a difference between the two.

differential emotions theory a theory holding that particular emotions or sets of emotions become more prominent during specific life stages as they serve stage-related developmental processes.

discrete trait trait that results as the product of a single gene pairing.

dishabituation a form of non-associative learning whereby there is a recovery of attention to a novel stimulus following habituation.

disorder of written expression a disorder experienced as impairment in the ability to create the written word.

display rules cultural expectations that prescribe how, when, and by whom emotions should be expressed.

dissociation a splitting of consciousness into two dimensions.

dissociative amnesia psychological disorder characterized by inability to recall important information, usually of an upsetting nature, about one's life.

dissociative disorders psychological disorder characterized by major loss of memory without a clear physical cause. Types include *dissociative amnesia*, *dissociative fugue*, and *dissociative identity disorder*.

dissociative fugue psychological disorder characterized by loss of memory of personal identity and details of one's past life and flight to an entirely different location.

dissociative identity disorder psychological disorder characterized by the development of two or more distinct personalities.

distress stress caused by unpleasant situations or circumstances.

dominant trait trait that is expressed in a phenotype, no matter whether the genotype is homozygous or heterozygous for the trait.

dopamine neurotransmitter produced by neurons in the brain stem and involved in movement and reward mechanisms.

double-blind procedure study in which neither the participant nor the researcher knows what treatment or procedure the participant is receiving.

Down syndrome an inherited disorder, usually caused by the presence of extra chromosomal material on the twenty-first chromosome, that results in mental retardation.

dysexecutive syndrome impairments in the ability to control and direct mental activities.

E

effect size a standardized measure that reflects the degree of relationship or size of the difference between two or more variables.

efferent neurons neurons that carry information out from the central nervous system to the muscles and glands.

effortful processing encoding of information through careful attention and conscious effort.

ego according to psychoanalytic theory, a personality element that works to help satisfy the drives of the id while complying with the constraints placed on behaviour by the environment.

egocentrism flaws in a child's reasoning based on his or her inability to take another person's perspective.

electroconvulsive therapy (ECT) use of electric shock to trigger a brain seizure in hopes of relieving abnormal functioning.

emotion an intrapersonal state that occurs in response to either an external or an internal event and typically involves a physiological component, a cognitive component, and a behavioural component.

emotion dysregulation unhealthy attempts to regulate emotion.

emotion-focused coping coping strategies focused on changing one's feelings about the stressor.

emotional intelligence an individual's ability to perceive, express, assimilate, and regulate emotion.

emotional intensity the characteristic strength with which an individual typically experiences emotion.

empirical able to be tested in objective ways.

empirically supported or evidence-based treatment movement movement to help clinicians become more familiar with and apply research findings concerning the effectiveness of particular treatments.

encoding a basic activity of memory, involving the recording of information in our brain.

endocrine system the system that controls levels of hormones throughout the body.

endorphins naturally-occurring pain-killing chemicals (neurotransmitters) in the brain.

enkephalins naturally-occurring pain-killing chemicals (neurotransmitters) in the brain.

epigenetic changes in gene expression that are independent of the DNA sequence of the gene.

episodic memory a person's memory of personal events or episodes from his or her life.

equilibrium balance in a mental framework.

eustress the optimal level of stress needed to promote physical and psychological health.

evolution by natural selection the differential likelihood between members of a species in their ability to survive and reproduce.

evolutionary psychology field of study that examines how the process of evolution has shaped the body and brain via the interaction of our genes and the environment to produce our thoughts and behaviours.

executive function the brain's ability to control and manage the mental processing of information.

experiment controlled observation in which researchers manipulate the presence or amount of the independent variable to see what effect it has on the dependent variable.

experimental group group that is exposed to the independent variable.

explicit memory memory that a person can consciously bring to mind, such as one's date of birth.

extinction reduction of a conditioned response after repeated presentations of the conditioned stimulus alone.

extrinsic motivation engaging in a behaviour due to the influence of factors outside ourselves.

F

facial efference sensory feedback from facial muscular activity.

facial-feedback theory of emotion a theory proposing that subjective experiences of emotion are influenced by sensory feedback from facial muscular activity, or facial efference.

factor analysis a statistical method for determining whether certain items on a test correlate highly, thus forming a unified set, or cluster, of items.

family systems theory a theory holding that each family has its own implicit rules, relationship structure, and communication patterns that shape the behaviour of the individual members.

family therapy a format in which therapists meet with all members of a family to help the whole family to change.

fitness the ability of an individual to successfully grow to maturity and have offspring that perpetuate the existence of the species that the individual belongs to.

five-factor theory an empirically derived trait theory that proposes five major trait categories: agreeableness/disagreeableness, extraversion/introversion, neuroticism/stability, conscientiousness/irresponsibility, and openness to experience/unimaginativeness.

fixed interval schedule schedule of reinforcement that occurs every time a specific time period has elapsed.

fixed ratio schedule schedule of reinforcement that occurs after a specific number of responses.

flashbacks recurrence of the sensory and emotional changes after LSD has left the body.

flashbulb memory detailed and near-permanent memories of an emotionally significant event, or of the circumstances surrounding the moment we learned about the event.

Flynn effect an observed rise in average IQ scores throughout the world over time.

forgetting the inability to recall information that was previously encoded into memory.

formal operational stage Piaget's final stage of cognitive development when the child achieves hypothetical deductive reasoning and the ability to think abstractly.

fovea centre of the retina, containing only cones, where vision is most clear.

free association psychodynamic therapy technique of allowing clients to freely talk about whatever they want.

free nerve endings sensory receptors that convert physical stimuli into touch, pressure, or pain impulses.

free-radical theory theory suggesting we age because special negatively charged oxygen molecules become more prevalent in our body as we get older, destabilizing cellular structures and causing the effects of aging.

frequency polygon a line graph depicting a grouped frequency distribution, which is created by connecting the midpoints of each class of data.

frontal lobe lobe of the cortex involved in many functions, including movement and speech production.

frustration an emotion people experience when thwarted in pursuit of a goal.

functional fixedness tendency to view objects as having only one function.

functionalism a philosophical approach that considers how mental processes function to adapt to changing environments.

fundamental attribution error the tendency to use dispositional attributions to explain the behaviour of other people.

G

g factor a theoretical general factor of intelligence underlying all distinct clusters of mental ability; part of Spearman's two-factor theory of intelligence.

gate control theory of pain theory suggesting that certain patterns of neural activity can close a "gate" to keep pain information from travelling to parts of the brain where it is perceived.

gender-sensitive therapies or feminist therapies approaches that seek to address the unique pressures of being a female.

general adaptation syndrome (GAS) a three-stage response to stress identified by Hans Selye; the stages are alarm, resistance, and exhaustion.

generalized anxiety disorder an anxiety disorder in which people feel excessive anxiety and worry under most circumstances.

genes basic building blocks of our biological inheritance.

genotype a person's genetic inheritance.

Gestalt psychology the field of psychology arguing that we have inborn tendencies to structure what we see in particular ways and to structure our perceptions into broad perceptual units.

glia the cells that, in addition to neurons, make up the nervous system.

group an organized, stable collection of individuals in which the members are aware of and influence one another and share a common identity.

group polarization the intensification of an initial tendency of individual group members brought about by group discussion.

group therapy psychotherapy format in which a therapist sees several clients who have similar problems at the same time.

grouped frequency distribution a count of the number of times specific data points fall into a range of values in a data set.

groupthink a form of faulty group decision making that occurs when group members strive for unanimity and this goal overrides their motivation to realistically appraise alternative courses of action.

gustatory sense sense of taste.

H

habituation the process of habituating, in which individuals pay less attention to a stimulus after it is presented to them over and over again.

hair cells sensory receptors that convert sound waves into neural impulses.

hallucinations imagined sights, sounds, or other sensory events experienced as if they were real.

hallucinogens substances that dramatically change one's state of awareness, causing powerful changes in sensory perception.

Hawthorne effect people who are being observed in studies or at their workplace will improve or change some of their behaviour simply because they are being watched or studied, not in response to an experimental manipulation.

hemispheres two sides of the brain.

heritability the overall extent to which differences among people are attributable to genes.

heritability coefficient a correlation coefficient used to indicate the contribution of heredity to some characteristic, such as intelligence.

heterosexual sexual attraction to members of the opposite sex.

heterozygous parents contribute two different alleles to offspring.

heuristic a shortcut thinking strategy.

higher order conditioning what occurs when a previously conditioned stimulus functions as if it were an unconditioned stimulus for further conditioning.

hindbrain the part of the brain closest to the spinal cord that consists of the medulla, the pons, and the cerebellum; the reticular formation begins here and extends to the midbrain.

hippocampus brain region important for certain types of learning and memory.

histogram a bar chart showing the number of times specific data points fall into a range of values in a data set.

homeostasis a tendency of the body to maintain itself in a state of balance or equilibrium.

homosexual sexual attraction to members of one's own sex.

homozygous both parents contribute the same genetic material for a particular trait.

humanistic psychology theory of psychology that sought to give greater prominence to the special and unique features of human functioning.

hyperpolarization the inside of the neuron membrane becomes *more* negative relative to the outside.

hypnagogic state a pre-sleep period often characterized by vivid sensory phenomena.

hypnosis a seemingly altered state of consciousness during which individuals can be directed to act or experience the world in unusual ways.

hypothalamus brain structure important for motivation and control of the endocrine system.

hypothesis a general statement about the way variables relate that is objectively falsifiable.

hypothesis testing testing a statement or claim about a population using a sample and, in its simplest form, looking at experimental and control group differences.

hypothetico-deductive reasoning process of modern science where scientists begin with an educated guess about how the world works, and then set about designing small controlled observations to support or invalidate that hypothesis.

I

id according to psychoanalytic theory, the personality element representing basic instinctual drives, such as those related to eating, sleeping, sex, and comfort.

immune system the body's system of organs, tissues, and cells that identify and destroy foreign invaders, such as bacteria and viruses, as well as cancer cells.

implicit attitude an attitude of which the person is unaware.

implicit learning the acquisition of information without awareness.

implicit memory knowledge that we have stored in memory that we are not typically aware of or able to recall at will.

incentives external motives that indirectly indicate reward

independent variable condition or event that is thought to be a factor in changing another condition or event.

individual therapy psychotherapy format in which the therapist sees the client alone; the oldest of the modern formats.

individualistic a culture that places the wants or desires of the person over the needs of the group.

inductive reasoning reasoning process proceeding from small specific situations to more general truths.

inferential statistics statistics used to draw conclusions about research data.

information processing the means by which information is stored and operates internally.

information-processing model view of memory suggesting that information moves among three memory stores during encoding, storage, and retrieval.

information-processing theory a developmental theory focusing on how children learn, remember, organize, and use information from their environment.

informed consent requirement that researchers give as much information as possible about the purpose, procedures, risks, and benefits of the study so that a participant can make an informed decision about whether or not to participate.

inoculation exposing oneself to a relatively low level of stress in a controlled situation to improve later performance in a more stressful situation.

insight learning a sudden realization of a solution to a problem or leap in understanding new concepts.

insomnia sleep disorder characterized by a regular inability to fall asleep or stay asleep.

instincts inborn behavioural tendencies, activated by stimuli in our environments.

intelligence the ability to learn, to meet the demands of the environment effectively, and to understand and control one's mental activities.

intelligence quotient (IQ) Terman's measure of intelligence; the ratio of a child's mental age to his or her chronological age, multiplied by 100.

interactionism a view emphasizing the relationship between a person's underlying personality traits and the reinforcing aspects of the situations in which they choose to put themselves.

interference theory theory that forgetting is influenced by what happens to people before or after they take information in.

intermittent or partial reinforcement a schedule of reinforcement where the behaviour is only followed by reinforcement some of the time.

interneurons neurons that typically have a short axon and serve as a relay between different classes of neurons; in the spinal cord, interneurons communicate with both sensory and motor neurons.

International Classification of Diseases (ICD) the system used by most countries to classify psychological disorders; published by the World Health Organization and currently in its tenth edition (ICD-10).

intrinsic motivation engaging in a behaviour simply for the satisfaction that is part of doing it.

introspection a method of psychological study involving careful evaluation of mental processes and how simple thoughts expand into complex ideas.

ion channels pores in the cell membrane that can open and close to allow certain ions into and out of the cell.

J

James-Lange theory of emotion a theory proposing that felt emotions result from physiological changes, rather than being their cause.

L

language   a set of symbols used to communicate.

language comprehension   the process of understanding spoken, written, or signed language.

language production   the structured and conventional expression of thoughts through words.

latent learning   a form of learning that is not expressed until there is a reward or incentive.

lateral hypothalamus   a region of the hypothalamus important in signalling thirst and hunger.

law of effect   behaviours leading to rewards are more likely to occur again, while behaviours producing unpleasantness are less likely to occur again.

learned helplessness   a situation in which repeated exposure to inescapable punishment eventually produces a failure to make escape attempts.

learning   a lasting change caused by experience.

learning curve   a graph that shows change in performance on a learning task over time.

leptin   a protein produced by fat cells that is important for regulating the amount of food eaten over long periods of time.

lexical meaning   dictionary meaning of a word.

life changes   shifts in life circumstances that require adjustment of some kind.

limbic system   a group of interconnected brain structures that are associated with learning, memory, basic emotions, and drives.

linguistic relativity hypothesis   hypothesis suggesting that the vocabulary available for objects or concepts in a language influences how speakers of that language think about them.

lobotomy   surgical practice of cutting the connections between the frontal lobe and the lower centres of the brain.

long-term memory   the memory system in which we hold all of the information we have previously gathered available for retrieval and use in a new situation or task.

long-term potentiation (LTP)   phenomenon where repeated stimulation of certain nerve cells in the brain greatly increases the likelihood that the cells will respond strongly to future stimulation.

longitudinal design   a research approach that follows the same people over a period of time by administering the same tasks or questionnaires and seeing how their responses change.

loose associations or derailment   a common thought disorder of schizophrenia, characterized by rapid shifts from one topic to another.

lucid dreams   dreams in which the sleeper fully recognizes that he or she is dreaming, and occasionally actively guides the outcome of the dream.

lymphocytes   white blood cells that circulate through the body and destroy foreign invaders and cancer cells; important components of the immune system.

M

major depressive disorder   a disorder characterized by a depressed mood that is significantly disabling and is not caused by such factors as drugs or a general medical condition.

mania   a persistent state of euphoria or frenzied energy.

mathematics disorder   a deficit in mathematical ability, including the ability to do calculations, as well as the ability to understand mathematical word problems and mathematical concepts.

maturation   the unfolding of development in a particular sequence and time frame.

mean   the average value in a data set; the sum of all numbers in the set divided by the total number of items in the set.

measures of association   descriptive statistics that quantify and summarize the degree of relationship or association between variables.

measures of central tendency   numbers used to summarize data sets.

measures of variability   indicators that tell how different the values are within a dataset.

median   the data set value that represents the midpoint of an ordered set of numbers.

meditation   technique designed to turn one's consciousness away from the outer world toward one's inner cues and awareness.

medulla   part of the brain that controls basic bodily processes and regulates certain reflexes.

Meissner's corpuscles   sensory receptors that convert physical stimuli about sensory touch on the fingertips, lips, and palms.

memory   the faculty for recalling past events and past learning.

memory span   maximum number of items that can be recalled in correct order.

menopause   series of changes in hormonal function occurring in women during their 50s, which lead to the end of the menstrual cycle and reproductive capabilities.

mental age   the intellectual age at which a person is functioning, as opposed to chronological age.

mental imagery   picturing things in your mind.

mental processes   activities of our brain when engaged in thinking, observing the environment, and using language.

mental retardation   term describing individuals who display general intellectual functioning that is well below average and, at the same time, poor adaptive behaviour.

mental set   tendency to use problem-solving strategies that have worked in the past.

Merkel's discs   sensory receptors that convert information about light to moderate pressure on the skin.

metacognition   the ability to understand and control one's mental activities.

mirror neurons   neurons fired when an animal or human performs an action or when they see another animal perform the same action.

miscarriage   discharge of the fetus from the uterus before it is able to function on its own.

mnemonic devices   techniques used to enhance the meaningfulness of information, as a way of making them more memorable.

mode   the most frequent or most common value in a data set.

modelling   what occurs when an observer learns from the behaviour of another.

monocular cues   visual clues about depth and distance that can be perceived using information from only one eye.

mood stabilizing drugs   psychotropic drugs that lift the mood of depressed people.

morpheme   the smallest units of a language that convey meaning.

motivation   an internal state or condition that directs behaviour.

motive   a need or desire.

motor skills   the ability to control our bodily movements.

myelin a fatty, white substance, formed from glial cells, that insulates the axons of many neurons.

myelination development of fatty deposits on neurons that allow electric impulses to pass through neurons more efficiently.

N

narcolepsy sleep disorder marked by uncontrollable urge to fall asleep.

natural reflex an automatic involuntary response that typically occurs without learning.

naturalistic observation a study in which researchers directly observe people in a study behaving as they normally do.

negative correlation relationship in which, on average, scores on one variable increase as scores on another variable decrease.

negative punishment removal of a pleasant stimulus as a consequence of a behaviour to decrease the probability of the behaviour being repeated.

negative reinforcement removal of an unpleasant stimulus after a response to increase the probability that the behaviour will reoccur.

negative or **inverse relationship** a relationship where as the value of one variable increases, values in another associated variable decrease.

negative symptoms in the case of schizophrenia, symptoms that seem to reflect pathological deficits, including poverty of speech, flat affect, loss of volition, and social withdrawal.

negatively skewed distribution a distribution where most values occur at the upper end of the scale.

nerve conduction velocity (NCV) the speed with which electrical impulses are transmitted along nerve fibres and across synapses.

neurofibrillary tangles twisted protein fibres found within the cells of the hippocampus and certain other brain areas.

neuroimaging techniques that allow for studying brain activity and structure by obtaining visual images in awake humans.

neuroplasticity the brain's ability to create new neural pathways as a result of experience or following an injury.

neuron a nerve cell.

neuroscience the study of the brain and the nervous system.

neurosis an abnormal behaviour pattern caused by unresolved conflicts between the id, ego, and superego.

neurotransmitter receptors proteins in the membranes of neurons that bind to neurotransmitters.

neurotransmitters specialized chemicals that travel across synapses to allow communication between neurons.

non-associative learning learning that does not involve forming associations between stimuli.

non-REM sleep (NREM) Stages 1 through 4 of normal sleep pattern.

non-verbal communication body language.

norepinephrine a neurotransmitter that is important for arousal and attention.

normal distribution a symmetrical, bell-shaped distribution in which most scores are in the middle with smaller groups of equal size at either end.

norms social rules about how members of a society are expected to act.

nucleus accumbens a brain area important for motivation and reward.

null hypothesis an assertion that in the underlying population from which the sample was obtained, there is no difference between the average performance of individuals in one group compared to another.

O

obedience the act of following direct commands, usually given by an authority figure.

obesity overweight characterized as a body mass index of over 30.

object permanence an infant's realization that objects continue to exist even when they are outside one's immediate sensory awareness.

observational learning or **social learning** learning that occurs without overt training in response to watching the behaviour of others, called models.

obsessions persistent thoughts, ideas, impulses, or images that seem to invade a person's consciousness.

obsessive-compulsive disorder (OCD) a mental disorder associated with repeated, abnormal, anxiety-provoking thoughts and/or repeated rigid behaviours.

occipital lobe lobe of the cortex at the back of the skull, important for processing very visual information.

odorants airborne chemicals that are detected as odours.

olfactory bulb the first region where olfactory information reaches the brain on its way from the nose.

olfactory receptor neurons sensory receptor cells that convert chemical signals from odorants into neural impulses that travel to the brain.

olfactory sense sense of smell.

operant or **instrumental conditioning** a form of associative learning whereby behaviour is modified depending on its consequences.

operationalize to develop a working definition of a variable that allows you to test it.

operations Piagetian description of a child's ability to hold an idea in his or her mind and mentally manipulate it.

opioids class of drugs derived from the sap of the opium poppy.

optic nerve the bundle of axons of ganglion cells that carries visual information from the eye to the brain.

ossicles tiny bones in the ear called the maleus (*hammer*), incus (*anvil*), and stapes (*stirrup*).

oval window a membrane separating the ossicles and the inner ear, deflection of which causes a wave to form in the cochlea.

overregularization the process by which elementary school children over-apply newly learned grammatical rules to improperly "correct" an irregular verb (e.g., "goed" instead of "went").

P

Pacinian corpuscles sensory receptors that respond to vibrations and heavy pressure.

panic attacks periodic, short bouts of panic.

panic disorder an anxiety disorder characterized by recurrent and unpredictable panic attacks that occur without apparent provocation.

papillae bumps on the tongue that contain clumps of taste buds.

parallel distributed-processing (PDP) (or **connectionist**) **model** theory of memory suggesting that information is represented in the brain as a pattern of activation across entire neural networks.

parasympathetic nervous system the part of the autonomic nervous system active during restful times.

parietal lobe lobe of the cortex involved in processing information related to touch and complex visual information, particularly about locations.

Pearson product-moment correlation coefficient a statistic indicating the degree of association or relationship between two variables or measures, ranging from 21 to 11.

perception the conscious recognition and identification of a sensory stimulus.

perceptual constancies our top-down tendency to view objects as unchanging, despite shifts in the environmental stimuli we receive.

perceptual set readiness to interpret a certain stimulus in a certain way.

perfect correlation one in which two variables are exactly related, such that low, medium, and high scores on both variables are always exactly related.

personality the unique characteristics that account for enduring patterns of inner experience and outward behaviour.

personality disorder an inflexible pattern of inner experience and outward behaviour that causes distress or difficulty with daily functioning.

personality inventory a paper-and-pencil questionnaire designed to assess various aspects of personality.

personality traits tendencies to behave in certain ways that remain relatively constant across situations.

phenotype the observable manifestation of a person's genetic inheritance.

phobia a persistent, irrational, or obsessive fear of a specific object, activity, or situation that may arise as a result of fear conditioning.

phoneme the smallest unit of sound in a language; an individual sound such as ba, da, or ta.

phonology the study of how individual sounds or phonemes are used to produce language.

photoreceptors the sensory receptor cells for vision, located in the retina.

phrenology an unsubstantiated method of assessing a person's mental and moral qualities by studying the shape of the person's skull.

phylogeny the development of unique species over time.

pituitary gland brain structure that plays a central role in controlling the endocrine system.

placebo an inactive substance—such as a sugar pill or distilled water—that mimics a drug but has no active ingredients.

placenta nutrient-rich structure that serves to feed the developing fetus.

polygenic trait trait that manifests as the result of the contributions of multiple genes.

pons uppermost or anterior (front) part of the brainstem that includes the locus coeruleus.

population the entire group of individuals about whom we hope to learn (e.g., the Canadian population consists of all Canadians).

positive correlation relationship in which, on average, scores on two variables increase together.

positive psychology an area of psychology focusing on positive experiences and healthy mental functioning.

positive punishment presentation of an unpleasant consequence following a specific behaviour to decrease the probability of the behaviour being repeated.

positive reinforcement presentation of a pleasant consequence following a behaviour to increase the probability that the behaviour will reoccur.

positive or direct relationship as the value of one variable increases, so do values in another associated variable.

positive symptoms in the case of schizophrenia, symptoms that seem to represent pathological excesses in behaviour, including delusions, disorganized thinking and speech, hallucinations, and inappropriate affect.

positively skewed distribution a distribution where most values occur at the lower end of the scale.

postsynaptic potentials electrical events in postsynaptic neurons that occur when a neurotransmitter binds to one of its receptors.

posttraumatic stress disorder (PTSD) an anxiety disorder experienced in response to a major traumatic event, characterized by lingering, persistent, frightening thoughts or memories of the traumatic events, along with anxiety, depression, and other symptoms.

pragmatics the practical aspects of language usage, including speech pace, gesturing, and body language.

preconsciousness level of awareness in which information can become readily available to consciousness if necessary.

predictive validity the extent to which scores on a particular test successfully predict the things they are supposed to predict.

prefrontal lobe portion of the frontal cortex involved in higher-order thinking, such as memory, moral reasoning, and planning.

prejudice negative and unjust feelings about an individual based on their inclusion in a particular group.

prenatal period period of development stretching from conception to birth.

preoperational stage according to Piaget, a developmental stage during which the child begins to develop ideas of objects in the external world and the ability to work with them in his or her mind.

pressure an expectation or demand that someone act in a certain way.

primary appraisal appraisal of a stressor to determine how severe it is; the first stage in Richard Lazarus's description of how people experience stress.

primary mental abilities seven distinct mental abilities identified by Thurstone as the basic components of intelligence.

primary punisher a stimulus that is naturally aversive to an organism.

primary reinforcer a stimulus that has survival value and is therefore intrinsically rewarding.

primary sex characteristics changes in body structure that occur during puberty that have to do specifically with the reproductive system, including the growth of the testes and the ovaries.

priming activation of one piece of information, which in turns leads to activation of another piece, and ultimately to the retrieval of a specific memory.

private speech a child's self-talk, which Vygotsky believed the child uses to regulate behaviour and internal experiences.

proactive interference competing information that is learned before the forgotten material, preventing its subsequent recall.

problem solving determining how to reach a goal.

problem-focused coping coping strategies focused on dealing directly with the stressor, such as by changing the stressor in some way.

projective test a personality assessment device intended to tap a person's unconscious by presenting the person with an ambiguous stimulus and asking the person to interpret what the stimulus means.

proximodistal pattern a pattern in which growth and development proceed from the centre to the extremities.

private speech a child's self-talk, which Vygotsky believed the child uses to regulate behaviour and internal experiences.

psychoactive drugs chemicals that affect awareness, behaviour, sensation, perception, or mood.

psychoanalytic theory psychological theory that human mental processes are influenced by the competition among unconscious forces to come into awareness.

psychology the study of mental processes and behaviours.

psychometric approach an approach to defining intelligence that attempts to measure intelligence with carefully constructed psychological tests.

psychoneuroimmunology an area of study focusing on links between stress, the immune system, and health.

psychosexual stages according to psychoanalytic theory, stages in the development of personality; the stages—labelled oral, anal, phallic, latency, and genital—are primarily influenced by sexuality and aggression.

psychosis loss of contact with reality.

psychosurgery brain surgery, often used in hopes of relieving abnormal functioning.

psychotropic drugs medications that act primarily on the brain.

psychotherapy a treatment system in which a client and therapist use words and acts to overcome the client's psychological difficulties.

puberty development of full sexual maturity during adolescence.

punishment an experience that produces a decrease in a particular behaviour.

R

random sample a group or set made by randomly selecting people or items from a larger population; like closing your eyes and picking any two socks from your drawer.

random selection identifying a sample in such a way that everyone in the population of interest has an equal chance of being involved in the study.

range the difference between the smallest and the largest value in a data set.

rapid eye movement sleep (REM) stage of sleep associated with rapid and jagged brain-wave patterns, increased heart rate, rapid and irregular breathing, rapid eye movements, and dreaming.

rational-emotive behavioural therapy Ellis's therapy technique designed to help clients discover and change the irrational assumptions that govern their emotions, behaviours, and thinking.

reaction range the upper and lower level of intelligence or other outcomes made possible by a child's genetic nature.

reading disorder a deficit in reading comprehension, written spelling, and word recognition.

recall tasks memory tasks in which people are asked to produce information using no or few retrieval cues.

recessive trait trait that is only expressed if a person carries the same two genetic alleles (e.g., is homozygous for the trait).

reciprocal socialization the transactional relationship between parent and child.

recognition tasks memory tasks in which people are asked to identify whether or not they have seen a particular item before.

reflexes programmed physical reactions to certain cues that do not require any conscious thought to perform.

rehearsal conscious repetition of information in an attempt to make sure the information is encoded.

reinforcement a learning process that increases the likelihood a given response will be repeated.

reinforcer an experience that produces an increase in a certain behaviour.

relational psychoanalytic therapy a school of psychodynamic therapy holding that therapists should work to form more equal relationships with clients.

relative refractory period a brief period just after the absolute refractory period during which a neuron can only fire if it receives a stimulus stronger than its usual threshold level.

reliability the degree to which a test produces the same scores over time.

replication repeated testing of a hypothesis to ensure that the results you achieve in one experiment are not due to chance.

representativeness heuristic the assumption that individuals share characteristics of category of which they are a member.

repression the most basic defence mechanism; the process of keeping unpleasant memories or thoughts buried deep within the unconscious mind.

research ethics board (REB) research oversight group that evaluates research to protect the rights of participants in the study.

resistance practice in which clients encounter a block in their free associations or change the subject so as to avoid a potentially painful discussion.

response the way we react to stimuli.

resting potential the electrical charge of a neuron when it is at rest.

restorative theory of sleep theory that we sleep to allow the brain and body to restore certain depleted chemical resources and eliminate chemical wastes that have accumulated during the waking day.

reticular formation a complex neural network extending from the hindbrain into the midbrain that plays a central role in regulating consciousness and arousal.

retina a specialized sheet of nerve cells in the back of the eye containing the sensory receptors for vision.

retinal disparity the slight difference in images processed by the retinas of each eye.

retrieval a basic activity of memory, involving recovery of information when we need it later.

retrieval cues words, sights, or other stimuli that remind us of the information we need to retrieve from our memory.

retroactive interference learning of new information that disrupts access to previously recalled information.

retrograde amnesia inability to remember things that occurred before an organic event.

reward-deficiency syndrome theory that people might abuse drugs because their reward centre is not readily activated by usual life events.

reward learning pathway brain circuitry that is important for learning about rewarding stimuli.

rods photoreceptors most responsive to levels of light and dark.

Ruffini's end-organs sensory receptors that respond to heavy pressure and joint movement.

S

s factor a theoretical specific factor uniquely tied to a distinct mental ability or area of functioning; part of Spearman's two-factor theory of intelligence.

sample a group or set of people or items drawn from a larger population.

sampling distribution the theoretical distribution of a sample statistic; for example, the difference between two sample means taken from a population.

scaffolding developmental adjustments that adults make to give children the help that they need, but not so much that the children fail to move forward.

scatterplot a graph or plot of the values of one variable or measure associated with the values on another variable or measure.

Schachter and Singer's two-factor theory of emotion a theory proposing that an emotional state is a function of both physiological arousal and cognition.

schemas knowledge bases that we develop based on prior exposure to similar experiences or other knowledge bases.

scheme Piaget's proposed mental structures or frameworks for understanding or thinking about the world.

schizophrenia a mental disorder characterized by disorganized thoughts, lack of contact with reality, and sometimes hallucinations.

secondary appraisal appraisal of one's personal resources and ability to cope with a stressor; the second stage in Richard Lazarus's description of how people experience stress.

secondary punisher a stimulus that becomes aversive when associated with a primary punisher.

secondary reinforcer a neutral stimulus that becomes rewarding when associated with a primary reinforcer.

secondary sex characteristics changes that occur during puberty and that differ according to gender, but are not specifically related to sex.

sedative-hypnotic drugs class of drugs, the members of which produce feelings of relaxation and drowsiness.

self-actualization the need of humans to fulfill their full and special potential; the highest level of need in Maslow's hierarchy of needs.

self-concept a pattern of self-perception that remains consistent over time and can be used to characterize an individual.

self-determination instinctive feelings of competence, relatedness, and autonomy that give purpose to life.

self-help groups groups consisting of people who have similar problems and come together to help and support one another without the direct leadership of a professional clinician.

self-perception theory a theory suggesting that when people are uncertain of their attitudes, they infer what the attitudes are by observing their own behaviour.

self-serving bias the tendency people have to attribute their successes to internal causes and their failures to external ones.

semantic code cognitive representation of information or an event based on the meaning of the information.

semantic memory a person's memory of general knowledge of the world.

semantics the study of how meaning in language is constructed of individual words and sentences.

senile plaques sphere-shaped deposits of a protein known as beta-amyloid that form in the spaces between cells in the hippocampus, cerebral cortex, and certain other brain regions, as well as in some nearby blood vessels.

sensation the act of using our sensory systems to detect environmental stimuli.

sensitive period a point in development during which the brain is more susceptible to influences.

sensitization a form of non-associative learning whereby a strong stimulus results in an exaggerated response to the subsequent presentation of weaker stimuli.

sensory adaptation the process whereby repeated stimulation of a sensory cell leads to a reduced response.

sensory memory memory involving detailed, brief sensory image or sound retained for a brief period of time.

sensory receptor cells specialized cells that convert a specific form of environmental stimuli into neural impulses.

sensory transduction the process of converting a specific form of environmental stimuli into neural impulses.

serotonin neurotransmitter involved in activity levels and mood regulation.

shaping introducing new behaviour by reinforcing small approximations of the desired behaviour.

significance level or **rejection level** the level of risk researchers would be willing to take in terms of making an incorrect conclusion.

situationism the view that behaviour is governed primarily by the variables in a given situation rather than by internal traits.

sleep apnea sleep disorder characterized by repeatedly ceasing to breathe during the night, depriving the brain of oxygen and leading to frequent awakenings.

sleep spindles bursts of brain activity lasting a second or two; occur during Stage 2 sleep.

social anxiety disorder an anxiety disorder in which people may feel severe, persistent, and irrational fears of social or performance situations in which embarrassment may occur.

social cognition the way in which people perceive and interpret themselves and others in their social world.

social facilitation an effect in which the presence of others enhances performance.

social identity theory a theory that emphasizes social cognitive factors in the onset of prejudice.

social loafing a phenomenon in which people exert less effort on a collective task than they would on a comparable individual task; also known as *free riding*.

social neuroscience the study of social functioning and how it is tied to brain activity.

social phobia a disorder involving severe, persistent, and irrational fears of social situations in which embarrassment may occur.

social psychology an area of psychology that seeks to understand, explain, and predict how people's thoughts, feelings, and behaviours are influenced by the actual, imagined, or implied presence of others.

social role a set of norms ascribed to a person's social position; expectations and duties associated with the individual's position in the family, at work, in the community, and in other settings.

social role theory theory that gender differences occur because girls and boys develop different behaviours and skills based largely on the differences in gender role expectations.

social skills training behavioural therapy technique in which therapists serve as models and teachers to help clients acquire desired social behaviours.

socially desirable responding tailoring answers on personality inventories to try to create a good impression.

sociobiologists theorists who believe humans have a genetically innate concept of how social behaviour should be organized.

sodium potassium pump protein molecules in the membrane of cells that push out sodium ions and push in potassium ions.

somatic nervous system all the peripheral nerves that transmit information about body sensation and movement to and from the central nervous system.

Somatic symptom and related disorder excessive thought, feelings, and behaviours related to somatic symptoms.

somatosensory strip an area of the parietal cortex that processes tactile information coming from our body parts.

sound waves vibrations of the air in the frequency of hearing.

source misattribution remembering information, but not the source it came from; can lead to remembering information from unreliable sources as true.

spacing effect facilitated encoding of material through rehearsal situations spread out over time.

spatial navigation learning learning that involves forming associations among stimuli relevant to navigating in space.

specific learning disorder a disorder that interferes with the acquisition and use of one or more of the basic psychological processes involved in the development of academic skills: oral language, reading, written language, mathematics.

speech the expression of language through sounds.

spinal cord portion of the central nervous system that extends down the base of the brain and mediates sensory and motor information.

spontaneous recovery re-emergence of a conditioned response after extinction has occurred.

stage a distinct developmental phase in which organisms behave, think, or respond in a particular way that is qualitatively different from the way they responded before.

standard deviation statistical index of how much scores vary within a group.

standardization the use of uniform procedures in administering and scoring a test.

state-dependent memory memory retrieval facilitated by being in the same state of mind in which you encoded the memory in the first place.

stem cell undifferentiated cell that can divide to create new cells that have the potential to become any other cell type, including neurons.

stereotype threat a phenomenon in which people in a particular group perform poorly because they fear that their performance will conform to a negative stereotype associated with that group.

stereotypes fixed overgeneralized and oversimplified belief about a person or a group of people based on assumptions about the group.

stimulants substances that increase the activity of the central nervous system.

stimuli elements of the environment that trigger changes in our internal or external states.

stimulus discrimination what occurs when an organism learns to emit a specific behaviour in the presence of a conditioned stimulus, but not in the presence of stimuli similar to the conditioned stimulus.

stimulus generalization what occurs when stimuli similar to the original conditioned stimulus trigger the same conditioned response.

storage a basic activity of memory, involving retention of information for later use.

stress state brought on by any situation that threatens or appears to threaten a person's sense of well-being, thus challenging the individual's ability to cope.

stressor a situation or circumstance that triggers the stress response.

structuralism a philosophical approach that studies the structre of conscious experience.

subpersonalities alternate personalities developed in dissociative identity disorder, each with a unique set of memories, behaviours, thoughts, and emotions.

substantia nigra brain region important in fluidity of movement and inhibiting movements.

superego according to psychoanalytic theory, a personality element in charge of determining which impulses are acceptable to express openly and which are unacceptable; develops as we observe and internalize the behaviours of others in our culture.

superfactor a fundamental dimension of personality made up of a related cluster of personality traits.

suprachiasmatic nucleus (SCN) a small group of neurons in the hypothalamus responsible for coordinating the many rhythms of the body.

survey study in which researchers give participants a questionnaire or interview them.

sympathetic nervous system the part of the autonomic nervous system activated under conditions of stress.

synapses tiny spaces between the axon terminal of one neuron and the neuron through which chemical communication occurs.

synaptic pruning developmental reduction of neuronal connections, allowing stronger connections to flourish.

synaptic vesicles membrane-bound spheres in the axon terminals of neurons in which neurotransmitters are stored before their release.

syntax the system for using words (semantics) and word order to convey meaning (grammar).

systematic desensitization a process used to condition extinction of phobias through gradual exposure to the feared object or situation.

T

taste buds clusters of sensory receptor cells that convert chemical signals from food into neural impulses that travel to the brain.

telegraphic speech speech that consists of minimalistic sentences. This form of speech characterizes early toddlerhood and is the first evidence of sentence formation.

temperament biologically-based tendencies to respond to certain situations in similar ways throughout our lifetimes.

temporal lobe part of the cortex important in processing sound, in speech comprehension, and in recognizing complex visual stimuli, such as faces.

teratogens any environmental agent that causes damage during gestation.

thalamus an area of the brain that serves, in part, as a relay station for incoming sensory information.

theories ideas about laws that govern phenomena.

theory of mind an awareness of one's own mental states and the mental states of others.

theory of multiple intelligences theory that there is no single, unified intelligence, but instead several independent intelligences arising from different portions of the brain.

therapy (treatment) systematic procedures designed to change abnormal behaviour into more normal behaviour.

therapy outcome studies research that looks at the effects of various treatments.

threshold of excitation the point at which the relative influence of other neurons succeeds in causing a neuron to initiate an action potential.

token economy operant conditioning therapy program in which participants receive tokens (that can be traded for rewards) when they display desired behaviours.

tolerance mark of physical dependence on a drug, in which a person needs to take incrementally larger doses of the drug to achieve the same effect.

tonotopic map representation in the auditory cortex of different sound frequencies.

top-down processing perception processes led by cognitive processes, such as memory or expectations.

transcranial magnetic stimulation (TMS) a procedure in which an electromagnetic coil placed on or above a person's head sends a current into the prefrontal cortex; used to treat severe depression.

transduction process that involves converting stimulus energy into neural impulses that can be interpreted by the brain.

transference process through which clients come to act and feel toward the therapist as they did toward important figures in their childhood.

traumatic events unexpected events severe enough to create extreme disruptions.

trephining ancient practice of chipping a hole in the skull as a treatment for various brain conditions.

triangular theory of love a theory proposed by Robert Sternberg that love is composed of three elements: intimacy, passion, and commitment

triarchic theory of intelligence Sternberg's theory that intelligence is made up of three interacting components: internal, external, and experiential components.

tympanic membrane the ear drum.

Type A a personality type characterized by competitiveness, impatience, and anger and hostility.

Type B a personality type that is less aggressive, more relaxed, and less hostile than Type A.

Type C a personality type characterized by difficulty in expressing or acknowledging negative feelings.

U

unconditional positive regard acceptance without terms or conditions.

unconditioned response (UR) a physical response elicited by an unconditioned stimulus; it does not need to be learned.

unconditioned stimulus (US) a stimulus that on its own elicits a response.

unconscious hypothesized repository of thoughts, feelings, and sensations outside human awareness, thought in some theories to have a strong bearing on human behaviour; a state in which information is not easily accessible to conscious awareness.

unconscious state state in which information is not easily accessible to conscious awareness.

ungrouped frequency distribution a count of the number of times each specific data point or score appears in a dataset.

unipolar depression a mood disorder that includes only depression.

V

vagus nerve stimulation a procedure in a which an implanted device sends electrical signals to the brain through the vagus nerve; used to treat severe depression.

validity the extent to which a test accurately measures or predicts what it is supposed to measure or predict.

validity coefficient a correlation coefficient that measures validity by correlating a test score with some external criterion.

variable condition, event, or situation that is studied in an experiment.

variable interval schedule schedule of reinforcement that occurs after varying amounts of time.

variable ratio schedule schedule of reinforcement where the number of responses required for reinforcement is unpredictable.

variance a calculated indicator of the degree to which values in a data set differ from the mean value of that data set; the average of squared deviations about the mean.

ventromedial region of the hypothalamus a region of the hypothalamus important in signalling satiety.

vicarious learning learning that occurs when an individual observes the consequences to another's actions and then chooses to duplicate the behaviour or refrain from doing so.

violation-of-expectation an experimental approach capitalizing on infants' and toddlers' heightened reactions to an unexpected event.

voluntarism a theory in which will is regarded as the ultimate agency of human behaviour; belief that much of behaviour is motivated and that attention is focused for an explicit purpose.

W

wear-and-tear theory theory suggesting we age because use of our body wears it out.

Wernicke's aphasia a neurological condition associated with damage to Wernicke's area where a person cannot understand language.

Wernicke's area a brain region located in the temporal lobe that is important for language comprehension.

withdrawal symptoms unpleasant and sometimes dangerous side effects of reducing intake of a drug after a person has become addicted.

working memory a short-term memory store that can hold five to nine items at once.

Y

Yerkes-Dodson law law stating that ideal performance on a task occurs when the arousal level is optimized to the difficulty level.

Z

zone of proximal development the gap between what a child could accomplish alone and what the child can accomplish with help from others.

zygote a single cell resulting from successful fertilization of the egg by sperm.

References

Abbey, S. E. (2005). Somatization and somatoform disorders. In J. L. Levenson (Ed.), *The Amerian Psychiatric Publishing textbook of psychosomatic medicine* (pp. 271–296). Washington, DC: American Psychiatric Publishing.

Abele, A. E. (2003). The dynamics of masculine-agentic and feminine-communal traits: Findings from a prospective study. *Journal of Personality and Social Psychology, 85*(4), 768–776.

Abella, K., & Dutton, S. (1994). Questions and answers. *Typework, 2.*

Abella, R., & Heslin, R. (1989). Appraisal processes, coping and the regulation of stress-related emotions in a college examination. *Basic and Applied Social Psychology, 10,* 311–327.

Abercrombie, H. C., Chambers, A. S., Greischar, L., & Monticelli, R. M. (2008). Orienting, emotion, and memory: Phasic and tonic variation in heart rate predicts memory for emotional pictures in men. *Neurobiology of Learning and Memory, 90*(4), 644–650.

Abi-Dargham, A., & Laruelle, M. (2005). Mechanisms of action of second generation antipsychotic drugs in schizophrenia: insights from brain imaging studies. *European Psychiatry, 20,* 15–27.

Abosch, A., & Cosgrove, G. R. (2008). Biological basis for the surgical treatment of depression. *Neurosurgical Focus, 25*(1), E2.

Abramowitz, A. J., & O'Leary, S. G. (1990). Effectiveness of displayed punishment in an applied setting. *Behavior Therapy, 21,* 231–239.

Abrams, D., Hogg, M. A., & Marques, J. M. (2005). A social psychological framework for understanding social inclusion and exclusion. *The social pshychology of inclusion and exclusion* (pp. 1–23). New York, NY: Psychology Press.

Abrams, D., Marques, J. M., Bown, N., & Henson, M. (2000). Pro-norm and anti-norm deviance within and between groups. *Journal of Personality and Social Psychology, 78*(5), 906–912.

Abrams, D., Wetherell, M., Cochrane, S., Hogg, M. A., & Turner, J. C. (2001). Knowing what to think by knowing who you are: Self-categorization and the nature of norm formation, conformity and group polarization. In M. A. Hogg & D. Abrams (Eds.), *Intergroup relations: Essential readings* (pp. 270–288). New York, NY: Psychology Press.

Abudy, A., Juven-Wetzler, A., Sonnino, R., & Zohar, J. (2012). Serotonin and Beyond: A Neurotransmitter Perspective of OCD. In J. Zohar (Ed.), *Obsessive Compulsive Disorder: Current Science and Clinical Practice* (pp. 221–243). John Wiley & Sons.

Accolla, R., Bathellier, B., Petersen, C. C., & Carleton, A. (2007). Differential spatial representation of taste modalities in the rat gustatory cortex. *The Journal of Neuroscience, 27,* 1396–1404.

Acebo, C., Sadeh, A., Seifer, R., Tzischinsky, O., Hafer, A., & Carskadon, M. A. (2005). Sleep/wake patterns derived from activity monitoring and maternal report for healthy 1 to 5-year-old children. *Sleep, 28,* 1568–1577.

Acosta, M. C., Haller, D. L., & Schnoll, S. H. (2005). Cocaine and stimulants. In R. J. Frances, A. H. Mack, & S. I. Miller (Eds.), *Clinical textbook of addictive disorders (3rd Ed.).* New York, NY: Guilford Press.

Adams, G. R., & Huston, T. L. (1975). Social perception of middle-aged persons varying in physical attractiveness. *Developmental Psychology, 11,* 657–658.

Addis, M. E., & Mahalik, J. R. (2003). Men, masculinity, and the contexts of help seeking. *American Psychologist, 58*(1), 5–14.

Ader, R. (2003). Conditioning immunomodulation: Research needs and directions. *Brain, Behavior, and Immunity, 17*(1), S51–S57.

Ader, R., & Cohen, N. (1984). Behavior and the immune system. In W. D. Gentry (Ed.), *Handbook of behavioural medicine.* New York: Guilford.

Ader, R., Felten, D. L., & Cohen, N. (Eds.). (2001). *Psycho-neuroimmunology* (3rd Ed., Vols. 1 & 2). San Diego, CA: Academic Press.

Admon, Y. (2009). *Rising Criticism of Child Bride Marriages in Saudi Arabia.* The Middle East Media Research Institute. Retrieved from: http://memri.org /bin/articles.cgi?Page=archives&Area=ia&ID=IA50209.

Adolph, K. E., & Berger, S. E. (2006). Motor development. In D. Kuhn & R. Siegler (Eds.), *Handbook of child psychology, Vol. 2. Cognition, perception and language* (6th Ed., pp. 161–213). Hoboken, NJ: Wiley.

Adolphs, R. (2009). The social brain: Neural basis of social knowledge. *Annual Review of Psychology, 60,* 693–716.

Adolphs, R. (2003). Cognitive neuroscience of human social behaviour. *Nature Reviews Neuroscience, 4*(3), 165–178.

Adolphs, R., Russell, J., & Tranel, D. (1999). A role for the human amygdala in recognizing emotional arousal from unpleasant stimuli. *Psychological Science, 10,* 167–171.

Aftanas, L. I., & Golosheikin, S. A. (2003). Changes in cortical activity in altered states of consciousness: The study of meditation by high-resolution EEG. *Human Physiology, 29*(2), 143–151.

Aguirre, G. K. (2010). Experimental design and data analysis for fMRI. In S. H. Faro & F. B. Mohamed (Eds.), *fMRI: A guide to functional imaging for neuroscientists* (pp. 55–69). New York: Springer Science+ Business Media.

Åhs, F., Palmquist, Å. M., Pissiota, A., Appel, L., Frans, Ö., Liberzon, I., . . . & Fredrikson, M. (2011). Arousal modulation of memory and amygdala-parahippocampal connectivity: A PET-psychophysiology study in specific phobia. *Psychophysiology, 48*(11), 1463–1469.

Aiello, J. R., & Douthitt, E. A. (2001). Social facilitation from Triplett to electronic performance monitoring. *Group Dynamics: Theory, Research, and Practice, 5,* 163–180.

Ainsworth, M. D S. (1967). *Infancy in Uganda: Infant care and the growth of love.* Baltimore, MD: Johns Hopkins University Press.

Ainsworth, M. D. S. (1979). Attachment as related to mother-infant interaction. In J. S. Rosenblatt, R. A. Hinde, C. Beer, & M. Busnel (Eds.), *Advances in the study of behavior (Vol. 9).* Orlando, FL: Academic Press.

Ainsworth, M. D. S. (1985). Patterns of attachment. *Clinical Psychologist, 38*(2), 27–29.

Ainsworth, M. D. S. (1993). Attachment as related to mother-infant interaction. *Advances in Infancy Research, 8,* 1–50.

Ainsworth, M. D. S. (2010). Security and attachment. In R. Volpe (Ed.), *The secure child: Timeless lessons in parenting and childhood education* (pp. 43–53). Greenwich, CT: IAP Information Age Publishing.

Air Canada v. Canadian Transportation Agency (2008). File No. 32729. Supreme Court of Canada (Ottawa).

Akbarian, S. (2010). Epigenetics of schizophrenia. In N. R. Swerdlow (Ed.), *Behavioral neurobiology of schizophrenia and its treatment* (pp. 611–628). New York: Springer-Verlag Publishing.

Albarracín, D., Johnson, B. T., & Zanna, M. P. (Eds.) (2014). *The handbook of attitudes.* Mahwah, NJ: Erlbaum.

Albarracin, D., Zanna, M. P., Johnson, B. T., & Kumkale, G. T. (2005). Attitudes: Introduction and scope. *The handbook of attitudes* (pp. 3–19). Mahwah, NJ: Lawrence Erlbaum Associates Publishers.

Alberta Family Wellness Initiative. (2013). *AFWI's knowledge mobilization strategy: Transforming research, policy, and practice in Alberta.* Calgary, AB: Norlien Foundation.

Alden, L., Ryder, A., & Mellings, T. (2002). Perfectionism in the context of social fears: Toward a two-component model. In G. L. Flett & P. L. Hewitt (Eds.), *Perfectionism: Theory, research, and treatment* (pp. 373–391). Washington, DC: American Psychological Association. doi:10.1037/10458-015.

Aldwin, C. M. (2007). *Stress, coping, and development: An integrative perspective* (2nd Ed.). New York, NY: Guilford Press.

Aldwin, C. M., Yancura, L. A., & Boeninger, D. K. (2010). Coping across the life span. In M. E. Lamb, A. M. Freund, & R. M. Lerner (Eds.), *The handbook of life-span development,* vol 2: *Social and emotional development* (pp. 298–340). Hoboken, NJ: John Wiley & Sons.

Alegre, A. (2011). Parenting styles and children's emotional intelligence: What do we know? *The Family Journal, 19*(1), 56–62.

Alegria, A. A., Petry, N. M., Hasin, D. S., Liu, S., Grant, B. F., & Blanco, C. (2009). Disordered gambling among racial and ethnic groups in the US: Results from the national epidemiologic survey on alcohol and related conditions. *CNS Spectrums, 14*(3), 132–142.

Alegria, M., Mulvaney-Day, N., Torres, M., Polo, A., Cao, Z., & Canino, G. (2007). Prevalence of psychiatric disorders across Latino subgroups in the United States. *American Journal of Public Health, 97*(1), 68–75.

Alegria, M., Takeuchi, D., Canino, G., Duan, N., Shrout, P., Meng, X. L., et al. (2004). Considering context, place and culture: The National Latino and Asian American Study. *International Journal of Methods in Psychiatric Research, 13*(4), 208–220.

Alessio, A., Bonilha, L., Rorden, C., Kobayashi, E., Min, L. L., Damasceno, B. P., et al. (2006). Memory and language impairments and their relationships to hippocampal and perirhinal cortex damage in patients with medial temporal lobe epilepsy. *Epilepsy & Behavior, 8*(3), 593–600.

Alessio, A., Kobayashi, E., Damasceno, B. P., Lopes-Cendes, I., & Cendes, F. (2004). Evidence of memory impairment in asymptomatic individuals with hippocampal atrophy. *Epilepsy & Behavior, 5*(6), 981–987.

Alexander, J. F., Sexton, T. L., & Robbins, M. S. (2002). The developmental status of family therapy in family psychology intervention science. In H. A. Liddle, D. A. Santiseban, R. F. Levant, & J. H. Bray (Eds.), *Family psychology: Science-based interventions* (pp. 17–40). Washington, DC: American Psychological Association.

Alexander, M. G., & Wood, W. (2000). Women, men, and positive emotions: A social role interpretation. In A. H. Fischer (Ed.), *Gender and emotion: Social psychological perspectives* (pp. 189–210). New York, NY: Cambridge University Press.

Alfano, C. A., & Beidel, D. C. (Eds.). (2011). *Social anxiety in adolescents and young adults: Translating developmental science into practice.* Washington, DC: American Psychological Association.

Ali, P. A., & Naylor, P. B. (2013). Intimate partner violence: A narrative review of the feminist, social and ecological explanations for its causation. *Aggression and Violent Behavior, 18*(6), 611–619.

Allan, R.W. (1998). Operant-respondent interactions. In W. O'Donohue (Ed.), *Learning and behaviour therapy.* Boston: Allyn & Bacon.

Allen, B. (2011). The use and abuse of attachment theory in clinical practice with maltreated children. *Trauma, Violence, and Abuse, 12*, 13–22.

Allen, J. P., Chango, J., Szwedo, D. E., Schad, M. M., & Marston, E. G. (2012). Predictors of susceptibility to peer influence regarding substance use in adolescence. *Child Development, 83*(1), 337–350.

Allen, R. J., Baddeley, A. D., & Hitch, G. J. (2006). Is the binding of visual features in working memory resource-demanding? *Journal of Experimental Psychology: General, 135*(2), 298–313.

Allen, S., & Daly, K. (2007). *The effects of father involvement: An updated research summary of evidence.* Father Involvement Research Alliance, Centre for Families, Work & Well-Being, University of Guelph 2007. Retrieved from http://www.fira.ca/cms/documents/29/Effects_of_Father_Involvement.pdf.

Alloy, L. B., & Abramson, L. Y. (2010). The role of the behavioral approach system (BAS) in bipolar spectrum disorders. *Current Directions in Psychological Science, 19*(3), 189–194.

Alloy, L. B., Abramson, L. Y., Walshaw, P. D., Keyser, J., & Gerstein, R. K. (2006). A cognitive vulnerability-stress perspective on bipolar spectrum disorders in a normative adolescent brain, cognitive, and emotional development context. *Developmental Psychopathology, 18*(4), 155–1103.

Alloy, L. B., Urošević, S., Abramson, L. Y., Jager-Hyman, S., Nusslock, R., Whitehouse, W. G., & Hogan, M. (2011). Progression along the bipolar spectrum: A longitudinal study of predictors of conversion from bipolar spectrum conditions to bipolar I and II disorders. *Journal of Abnormal Psychology,* No Pages.

Allport, G. W. (1985). The historical background of social psychology. In G. Lindzey & E. Aronson (Eds.), *Handbook of Social Psychology* (Vol. 1, 3rd Ed., pp. 1–46). New York, NY: Random House.

Allport, G. W. (1968). *The Person in Psychology.* Boston, MA: Beacon Press.

Allport, G. W. (1954). *The nature of prejudice.* Oxford. England: Addison-Wesley.

Allport, G. W., & Odbert, H. S. (1936). Traitnames. A psycho-lexical study. *Psychological Monographs, 47*, 171.

Alter, M. D., & Hen, R. (2009). Serotonin, sensitive periods, and anxiety. *Stress-induced and fear circuitry disorders: Advancing the research agenda for DSM-V* (pp. 159–173). Arlington, VA: American Psychiatric Publishing, Inc.

Althouse, R. (2010). Jails are nation's largest institutions for mentally ill. *The National Psychologist, 19*(6), 1–5.

Alwin, D. F., Cohen, R. L., & Newcomb, T. M. (1991). *Political Attitudes over the Life-Span: The Bennington Women After Fifty Years.* Madison, WI: The University of Wisconsin Press.

Alzheimer Society, Ontario. (2012). A new way of looking at the impact of dementia in Canada. Retrieved from http://www.alzheimer.ca/en/on/About-dementia/Dementias/What-is-dementia/Facts-about-dementia.

Ambady, N., Paik, S. K., Steele, J., Owen-Smith, A., & Mitchell, J. P. (2004). Deflecting negative self-relevant stereotype activation: The effects of individuation. *Journal of Experimental Social Psychology, 40*(3), 401–408.

Ambady, N., Shih, M., Kim, A., & Pittinsky, T. L. (2001). Stereotype susceptibility in children: Effects of identity activation on quantitative performance. *Psychological Science, 12*(5), 385–390.

Ambert, A. M. (2009). Divorce: Facts, causes and consequences. Vanier Institute of the Family. Retrieved from http://www.vifamily.ca/node/72.

Amedi, A., Merabet, L. B., Bermpohl, F., & Pascual-Leone, A. (2005). The Occipital Cortex in the Blind: Lessons About Plasticity and Vision. *Current Directions in Physiological Science, 14*(6), 306–311.

American College of Obstetricians and Gynecologists (ACOG). (2001). Prenatal diagnosis of fetal chromosomal abnormalities. ACOG Practice Bulletin, 27.

American College of Obstetricians and Gynecologists (ACOG). (2005). *Your pregnancy and birth (4th ed.).* ACOG, Washington, DC.

American Educational Research Association. (2014). Standards for educational and psychological testing. Washington, D.C.: AERA.

American Psychiatric Association (APA). (2013). *Diagnostic and Statistical Manual of Mental Disorders, 5th edition: DSM-5.* Washington, DC: American Psychiatric Publishing.

American Psychiatric Association (APA). (2000). *Diagnostic and statistical manual of mental disorders DSM-IV-R (4th Ed.).* Washington, DC: American Psychiatric Association.

American Psychological Association. (2009). *Center for workforce studies.* Washington, DC.

Ames, E. W., & Chisholm, K. (2001). Social and emotional development in children adopted from institutions. In D. B. Bailey Jr., J. T. Bruer, F. J. Symons, & J. W. Lichtman (Eds.), *Critical thinking about critical periods.* Baltimore, MD, US: Paul H Brookes Publishing.

Amici, F., Aureli, F., & Call, J. (2014). Response facilitation in the four great apes: Is there a role for empathy? *Primates, 55*(1), 113–118.

Amsterdam, B. (1972). Mirror self-image before age two. *Developmental Psychobiology, 5*(4), 297–305.

Anakwenze, U., & Zuberi, D. (2013). Mental Health and Poverty in the Inner City. *Health & Social Work, 38*(3), 147–57.

Anastasi, A., & Urbina, S. (1997). *Psychological testing* (7th Ed.). Upper Saddle River, NJ: Prentice Hall.

Anderson, C. A. (2004). An update on the effects of playing violent video games. *Journal of Adolescence, 27*, 113–122.

Anderson, C. A. (1989). Temperature and aggression: Ubiquitous effects of heat on occurrence of human violence. *Psychological Bulletin, 106*(1), 74–96.

Anderson, C., & Platten, C. R. (2011). Sleep deprivation lowers inhibition and enhances impulsivity to negative stimuli. *Behavioural Brain Research, 217*(2), 463–466.

Anderson, E., Siejel, E. H., Bliss-Moreau, E., & Barrett, L. F. (2011). The visual impact of gossip. *Science, 332*(6036), 1446–1448.

Anderson, I. M., Haddad, P. M., & Scott, J. (2012). Bipolar disorder. *British Medical Journal, 345*, e8508.

Anderson, S. W., Bechara, A., Damasio, H., Tranel, D., & Damasio, A. R. (1999). Impairment of social and moral behavior related to early damage in human prefrontal cortex. *Nature Neuroscience, 2*(11), 103–107.

Angell, J. R. (1903). A preliminary study of the localization of sound. *Psychological Review, 10*, 1–18.

Angier, N. (2001, May 20). Bully for you. Why push comes to shove. *New York Times*, Sect. 4. p. 1.

Angus Reid Strategies. (2009). *Same Sex marriage.* Retrieved from www.visioncritical.com/public-opinion/3719/canada_more_open_to_same_sex_marriage_than_us_uk/.

Antognnini, J. F., & Carstens, E. (2003). Anesthetic effects on the reticular formation, brainstem, and central nervous system arousal. In J. F. Antognini, E. Carstens, & D. E. Raines (Eds.), *Neural Mechanisms of Anesthesia.* Totowa, NJ: Humana Press Inc.

Antonson, A. E. (2010). Stanford-Binet Intelligence Scale. In C. Clauss-Ehlers (Ed.), *Encyclopedia of Cross Cultural Psychology*, 929–930.

Antony, M. M. (2011). Recent advances in the treatment of anxiety disorders. *Canadian Psychology/Psychologie Canadienne, 52*(1), 1–9.

Apicella, C. L., Feinberg, D. R., & Marlowe, F. W. (2007). Voice pitch predicts reproductive success in male hunter-gatherers. *Biology Letters, 3*(6),682–684.

Apostolova, L. G., & Cummings, J. L. (2008). Neuropsychiatric aspects of Alzheimer's disease and other dementing illnesses. In S. C. Yudofsky & R. E. Hales (Eds.), *The American psychiatric publishing textbook of neuropsychiatry and behavioral neurosciences (5th Ed.).* Washington, DC: American Psychiatric Publishing.

Arahna, A. C. C., de Paula Eduardo, C., & Cordas, T. A. (2008). Eating disorders. Part I: Psychiatric diagnosis and dental implications. *Journal of Contemporary Dental Practice, 9*, 73–81.

Archer, J. (2005). Are women or men the more aggressive sex? In S. Fein, G. R. Goethals & M. J. Sandstrom (Eds.), *Gender and aggression: Interdisciplinary perspectives.* Mahwah, NJ: Erlbaum.

Ardelt, M. (2011). Wisdom, age, and well-being. In K. W. Schaie & S. L. Willis (Eds.), *Handbook of the psychology of aging* (7th Ed., pp. 279–291). San Diego, CA: Elsevier Academic Press.

Arens, E. A., Grabe, H., Spitzer, C., & Barnow, S. (2011). Testing the biosocial model of borderline personality disorder: Results of a prospective 5-year longitudinal study. *Personality and Mental Health, 5*(1), 29–42.

Argyle, M. (2013). *The Psychology of Happiness.* Routledge.

Arias-Carrión, Ó., & Pöppel, E. (2007). Dopamine, learning, and reward-seeking behavior. *Acta Neurobiologiae Experimentalis (Warsaw), 67*(4), 481–488.

Arieti, S. (1974). *Interpretation of schizophrenia.* New York: Basic Books.

Armel, K. C., & Ramachandran, V. S. (2003). Projecting sensations to external objects: Evidence from skin conductance response. *Proceedings From the Royal Society of London.* Series B. Biological Sciences, *270*, 1499–1506.

Armstrong, T. (2009). *Multiple intelligences in the classroom, 3rd edition.* Association for Supervision & Curriculum Development, Alexandria, Virginia.

Armstrong, V., Brunet, P. M., Chao, H., Nishimura, M., Poole, H. L., & Spector, F. J. (2006). What is so critical?: A commentary on the reexamination of critical periods. *Development and Psychobiology, 45*, 326–331.

Arnold, D. H., & Doctoroff, G. L. (2003). The early education of socio-economically disadvantaged children. *Annual Review of Psychology, 54*, 517–545.

Artero, S., Ancelin, M., Portet, F., Dupuy, A., Berr, C., Dartigues, J., Tzourio, C., Rouaud, O., Poncet, M., Pasquier, F., Auriacombe, S., Touchon, J., & Ritchie, K. (2008). Risk profiles for mild cognitive impairment and progression to dementia are gender specific. *Journal of Neurology, Neurosurgery & Psychiatry, 79*(9), 979–984.

Asch, S. E. (1955). Opinions and social pressure. *Scientific American,* 31–35.

Aschersleben, G., Hofer, T., & Jovanovic, B. (2008). The link between infant attention to goal-directed action and later theory of mind abilities. *Developmental Science, 11*(6), 862–868.

Aserinsky, E. (1996). Memories of famous neuropsychologists: The discovery of REM sleep. *Journal of the History of the Neurosciences, 5*(3), 213–227.

Ash, J., & Gallup Jr., G. G. (2008). Brain size, intelligence, and paleoclimatic variation. In G. Geher & G. Miller (Eds.), *Mating intelligence: Sex, relationships, and the mind's reproductive system* (pp. 313–335). Mahwah, NJ: Lawrence Erlbaum Associates Publishers.

Aslin, R. N., Jusczyk, P. W., & Pisoni, D. B. (2000). Speech and auditory processing during infancy: Constraints on and precursors to language. In D. Kuhn & R. S. Siegler (Eds.), *Handbook of Child Psychology, Volume 2, Cognition, Perception, and Language* (5th Ed., pp. 147–198). New York, NY: John Wiley & Sons, Inc.

Asmus, C. L., & James, K. (2005). Nominal group technique, social loafing, and group creative project quality. *Creativity Research Journal, 17*(4), 349–354.

Aspinwall, L. G., & Taylor, S. E. (1992). Modeling cognitive adaptation: A longitudinal investigation of the impact of individual differences and coping on college adjustment and performance. *Journal of Personality and Social Psychology, 63*(6), 989–1003.

Astington, J. W., & Baird, J. A. (Eds.). (2005). *Why language matters for theory of mind.* New York: Oxford University Press.

Atack, J. R. (2010). GABAA receptor subtype-selective modulators as potential nonsedating anxiolytics. In M. B. Stein & T. Steckler (Eds.), *Behavioral neurobiology of anxiety and its treatment* (pp. 331–360). New York: Springer Science + Business Media.

Aten, J. D., McMinn, M. R., & Worthington, E. L., Jr. (2011). *Spiritually oriented interventions for counseling and psychotherapy.* Washington, DC: American Psychological Association.

Atkinson, R. C., & Shiffrin, R. M. (1968). Chapter: Human memory: A proposed system and its control processes. In K. W. Spence & J. T. Spence (Eds.), *The psychology of learning and motivation* (Volume 2, pp. 89–195). New York: Academic Press.

Auld, J. M. (2007). Review of hypnosis and communication in dental practice. *Australian Journal of Clinical & Experimental Hypnosis, 35*(2), 248–250.

Autor, D., Katz, L., & Kearney, M. (2006). The polarization of the U.S. labor market. *American Economic Review, 96,* 189–194.

Averill, J. R. (1980). A constructivist view of emotion. In R. Plutchik & H. Kellerman (Eds.), *Theories of emotion* (Vol. 1, pp. 305–340). New York, NY: Academic Press.

Avery, R. D., et al. (1994, December 13). Mainstream science on intelligence. *The Wall Street Journal,* editorial page (356).

Axelrod, F. B. (2004). Familial dysautonomia. *Muscle & Nerve, 29,* 352–363.

Ayd, F. J., Jr. (1956). A clinical evaluation of Frenquel. *Journal of Nervous and Mental Disease, 124,* 507–509.

Ayllon, T., & Azrin, N. (1968). *The token economy: A motivational system for therapy and rehabilitation.* East Norwalk, CT: Appleton-Century-Crofts.

Ayllon, T., & Azrin, N. H. (1965). The measurement and reinforcement of behavior of psychotics. *Journal of the Experimental Analysis of Behavior, 8*(6), 357–383.

Azevedo, F. A., Carvalho, L. R., Grinberg, L. T., Farfel, J. M., Ferretti, R. E., Leite, R. E., Jacob Filho, W., Lent, R., & Herculano-Houzel, S. (2009). Equal numbers of neuronal and nonneuronal cells make the human brain an isometrically scaled-up primate brain. *Journal of Comparative Neurology, 513,* 532–541.

Baars, B. J. (2003). How brain reveals mind: Neuroimaging supports the central role of conscious experience. *Journal of Consciousness Studies, 10,* 100–114.

Baars, B. J. (1986). *The cognitive revolution in psychology.* New York, NY: Guilford Press.

Baars, B. J., Banks, W. P., & Newman, J. B. (Eds.). (2003). *Essential sources in the scientific study of consciousness.* Cambridge, MA: MIT Press.

Baars, B. J., & Gage, N. M. (2010). *Cognition, brain, and consciousness: Introduction to cognitive neuroscience (2nd Ed.).* San Diego, CA: Elsevier Academic Press.

Babkin, B. P. (1949). *Pavlov: A Biography.* Toronto: The University of Chicago Press.

Bach, P. A. (2007). Psychotic disorders. In D. W. Woods & J. W. Kanter (Eds.), *Understanding behavior disorders: A contemporary behavioral perspective.* Reno, NV: Context Press.

Backhaus, J., Hoeckesfeld, R., Born, J., Hohagen, F., & Junghanns, K. (2008). Immediate as well as delayed post learning sleep but not wakefulness enhances declarative memory consolidation in children. *Neurobiology of Learning & Memory, 89,* 76–80.

Backman, C. W. (1990). Attraction in interpersonal relationships. In M. Rosenberg & R. H. Turner (Eds.), *Social Psychology: Sociological Perspectives* (pp. 235–268). New Brunswick, NJ: Transaction Publishers.

Backman, C. W. (1981). Attraction in interpersonal relationships. In M. Rosenberg & R. Turner (Eds.), *Social Psychology: Sociological Perspectives.* New York, NY: Basic Books.

Bäckman, L., & Nyberg, L. (Eds.). (2010). *Memory, aging and the brain: A festschrift in honour of Lars-Göran Nilsson.* New York: Psychology Press.

Baddeley, A., Eysenck, M.W. & Anderson, M.C. (2009). *Memory.* New York, NY: Psychology Press.

Baddeley, A. D. (2010). Long-term and working memory: How do they interact? In L. Backman & L. Nyberg (Eds.), *Memory, aging and the brain: A festschrift in honour of Lars-Göran Nilsson* (pp. 7–23). New York: Psychology Press.

Baddeley, A. D. (1966). Short-term memory for word sequences as a function of acoustic, semantic and formal similarity (PDF). *Quarterly Journal of Experimental Psychology, 18*(4), 362–365.

Baddeley, A. D., & Hitch, G. (1974). *Working memory.* In G. H. Bower (Ed.), *The psychology of learning and motivation: Advances in research and theory* (Vol. 8, pp. 47–89). New York: Academic Press.

Bagley, C., & Tremblay, P. (1988) On the prevalence of homosexuality and bisexuality in a random community survey of 750 men aged 18 to 27. *Journal of Homosexuality, 36*(2), 1–18.

Bailer, U., de Zwaan, M., Leisch, F., Strnad, A., Lennkh-Wolfsberg, C., El-Giamal, N., et al. (2004). Guided self-help versus cognitive-behavioral group therapy in the treatment of bulimia nervosa. *The International Journal of Eating Disorders, 35*(4), 522–537.

Bailey, J. M., & Pillard, R. C. (1991). A genetic study of male sexual orientation. *Archives of General Psychiatry, 48*(12), 1089–1096.

Baillargeon, R. (1987). Object permanence in 3- and 4-month-old infants. *Developmental Psychology, 23,* 655–664.

Baillargeon, R. (2004). Infants' reasoning about hidden objects: Evidence for event-general and event-specific expectations. *Developmental Science, 7,* 391–424.

Baird, A. A. (2010). The terrible twelves. In P. D. Zelazo, M. Chandler, & E. Crone (Eds.), *Developmental social cognitive neuroscience* (pp. 191–207). New York: Psychology Press.

Baker, K. (2010). From "it's not me" to "it was me, after all": A case presentation of a patient diagnosed with dissociative identity disorder. *Psychoanalytic Social Work, 17*(2), 79–98.

Baker, L. A., Jacobson, K. C., Raine, A., Lozano, D. I., & Bezdjian, S. (2007). Genetic and environmental bases of childhood antisocial behavior: A multi-informant twin study. *Journal of Abnormal Psychology, 116,* 219–235.

Baker, T. B., Japuntich, S. J., Hogle, J. M., McCarthy, D. E., & Curtin, J. J. (2006). Pharmacologic and behavioral withdrawal from addictive drugs. *Current Directions in Psychological Science, 15,* 232–236.

Bakin, J. S., South, D. A., & Weinberger, N. M. (1996). Induction of receptive field plasticity in the auditory cortex of the guinea pig during instrumental avoidance conditioning. *Behavioral Neuroscience, 110,* 905–913.

Balaban, V. (2009). Assessment of children. Effective treatments for PTSD: Practice guidelines from the international society for traumatic stress studies (2nd Ed.) (pp. 62–80). New York, NY: Guilford Press.

Balaraman, S. (1962). Color vision research and the trichromatic theory: a historical review. *Psychological Bulletin, 59,* 434–448.

Baldwin, D.S., Anderson, I.M., Nutt, D.J., et al. (2009). British Association for Psychopharmacology. Evidence-based guidelines for the pharmacological treatment of anxiety disorders: recommendations from the British Association for Psychopharmacology. *Journal of Psychopharmacology, 19*(6), 567–596.

Bale, J. F. (2009). Fetal infections and brain development. *Clinical Perinatology, 36,* 639–653.

Ball, J. (2004). *Early Childhood Development Programs as Hook and Hub: Promising Practices in First Nations Communities.* University of Victoria, School of Child and Youth Care, Early Childhood Development Intercultural Partnerships Programs.

Ball, J. (2008). Promoting equity and dignity for aboriginal children in Canada. *Choices, 14*(7), 5–27.

Ball, J. (2010). Culture and Early Childhood Education. Encyclopaedia on Early Childhood Education. Retrieved from http://www.ecdip.org/docs/pdf/Politics%20of%20Comparison%20CEECD%20final%20distribute.pdf.

Ball, J., & Moselle, K. (2007). *Fathers' contributions to children's well-being.* Commissioned brief overview of research for the Public Health Agency of Canada.

Ball, J., & Simpkins, M. (2004). The community within the child. *American Indian Quarterly 28,* (3 and 4), 480–498.

Ballard, T. M., Knoflach, F., Prinssen, E., Borroni, E., Vivian, J. A., Basile, J., . . . Hernandez, M. (2009). RO4938581, a novel cognitive enhancer acting at GABAA α5 subunit-containing receptors. *Psychopharmacology, 202*(1-3), 207–223.

Ban, T. A. (2007). Fifty years chlorpromazine: a historical perspective. *Journal of Neuropsychiatric Disease and Treatment, 3*(4), 495–500.

Bandura, A. (2008). Reconstrual of "free will" from the agentic perspective of social cognitive theory. In J. Baer, J. C. Kaufman, & R. F. Baumeister (Eds.), *Are We Free? Psychology and Free Will* (pp. 86–127). New York, NY: Oxford University Press.

Bandura, A. (2006). Toward a psychology of human agency. *Perspectives on Psychological Science, 1*, 164–180.

Bandura, A. (1986). *Social foundations of thought and action: A social cognitive theory.* Englewood Cliffs, NJ: Prentice Hall.

Bandura, A. (1978). Social learning theory of aggression. *The Journal of Communication, 28*(3), 12–29.

Bandura, A. (1977). Self-efficacy: Toward a unifying theory of behavioral change. *Psychological Review, 84*(2), 191–215.

Bandura, A. (1969). *Principles of behavior modification.* Oxford, England: Holt, Rinehart, & Winston.

Bandura, A., & Rosenthal, T. (1966). Vicarious classical conditioning as a function of arousal level. *Journal of Personality and Social Psychology, 3*, 54–62.

Bandura, A., Adams, N. E., & Beyer, J. (1977). Cognitive processes mediating behavioral change. *Journal of Personality and Social Psychology, 35*(3), 125–139.

Bandura, A., Ross, D. & Ross, S. A. (1963). Imitation of film-mediated aggressive models. In R. J. Huber, C. Edwards, & D. Henning Bownton (Eds.), *Cornerstones of Psychology-Readings in the History of Psychology* (pp. 215–227). Asia: Thomson Learning Inc.

Bandura, A., Ross, D., & Ross, S. A. (1961). Transmission of aggression through imitation of aggressive models. *Journal of Abnormal and Social Psychology, 63*, 575–582.

Bandura, A., Roth, D., & Ross, S. (1963). Imitation of film-mediated aggressive models. *Journal of Abnormality and Social Psychology, 66*, 3–11.

Banich, M. T. (2009). Executive function: The search for an integrated account. *Current Directions in Psychological Science, 18*, 89–94.

Banks, M. S., & Salapatek, P. (1983). Infant Visual Perception. In M. M. Haith & J. J. Campos (Eds.), *Handbook of Psychology* (pp. 435–571). New York, NY: Wiley.

Barahal, H. S. (1958). 1000 prefrontal lobotomies: A five to ten year follow-up study. *Psychiatric Quarterly, 32*, 653–690.

Barburi, C., Esposito, E., & Cipriani, A. (2009). Selective serotonin reuptake inhibitors and risk of suicide: A systematic review of observational studies. *Canadian Medical Association Journal, 180*(30). doi: 10.1503/cmaj.081514

Bard, P. (1934). The neuro-humoral basis of emotional reactions. In C. Murchinson (Ed.), *Handbook of general experimental psychology* (pp. 264–311). Worcester, MA: Clark University Press.

Bargh, J. A. (2001). The psychology of the mere. In J. A. Bargh & D. K. Apsley (Eds.), *Unraveling the Complexities of Social Life: A Festschrift in Honor of Robert B. Zajonc* (pp. 25–37). Washington, D.C.: American Psychological Association.

Barker, P. (2007). *Basic Family Therapy* (5th Ed.). Oxford: Blackwell.

Barlow, D. H. (2002). *Anxiety and its disorders: The nature and treatment of anxiety and panic* (2nd Ed.). New York, NY: Guilford Press.

Barlow, M. R. (2011). Memory for complex emotional material in dissociative identity disorder. *Journal of Trauma & Dissociation, 12*(1), 53–66.

Barnabé-Heider, F., & Frisén, J. (2008). Stem cells for spinal cord repair. *Cell Stem Cell, 3*, 16–24.

Barnes, L. L., Wilson, R. S., Bienias, J. L., Schneider, J. A., Evans, D. A., & Bennett, D. A. (2005). Sex differences in the clinical manifestations of Alzheimer disease pathology. *Archives of General Psychiatry, 62*(6), 685–691.

Barnett, R., & Rivers, C. (2004). *Same difference: How gender myths are hurting our relationships, our children, and our jobs.* New York, NY: Basic Books.

Barnett, S. M., & Ceci, S. J. (2005). The role of transferable knowledge in intelligence. *Cognition and intelligence: Identifying the mechanisms of the mind* (pp. 208–224). New York, NY: Cambridge University Press.

Barney, L. J., Griffiths, K. M., Jorm, A. F., & Christensen, H. (2006). Stigma about depression and its impact on help-seeking intentions. *Australian and New Zealand Journal of Psychiatry, 40*(1), 51–54.

Barnier, A. J., & Council, J. R. (2010). Hypnotizability matters: The what, why, and how of measurement. In S. J. Lynn, J. W. Rhue, & I. Kirsch (Eds.), *Handbook of clinical hypnosis (2nd Ed.)* (pp. 47–77). Washington, DC: American Psychological Association.

Barnier, A. J., McConkey, K. M., & Wright, J. (2004). Posthypnotic amnesia for autobiographical episodes: Influencing memory accessibility and quality. *International Journal of Clinical and Experimental Hypnosis, 52*, 260–279.

Baron, A. S., & Banaji, M. R. (2006). The development of implicit attitudes: Evidence of race evaluations from ages 6 and 10 and adulthood. *Psychological Science, 17*(1), 53–58.

Baron, R. S. (2005). So right it's wrong: Groupthink and the ubiquitous nature of polarized group decision making. In M. P. Zanna (Ed.), *Advances in Experimental Social Psychology, Vol. 37* (pp. 219–253). San Diego, CA: Elsevier Academic Press.

Barratt, B. B. (2013). *What is psychoanalysis? 100 years after Freud's secret committee.* New York: Taylor & Francis.

Barrett, K. C., et al. (2013). *Handbook of self-regulatory processes in development: New directions and international perspectives.* New York: Psychology Press

Barrowclough, C., & Lobban, F. (2008). Family intervention. In K. T. Mueser & D. V. Jeste (Eds.), *Clinical handbook of schizophrenia* (pp. 214–225). New York: Guilford Press.

Barry, D. (1985). *Stay fit and healthy until you're dead.* New York, NY: St. Martin's Press.

Barth, F. D. (2014). Cognitive and Behavioral Models. In *Integrative Clinical Social Work Practice* (pp. 45–57). New York, NY: Springer.

Bartone, P. T. (2003). Hardiness as a resilience resource under high stress conditions. *Promoting capabilities to manage posttraumatic stress: Perspectives on resilience* (pp. 59–73). Springfield, IL: Charles C. Thomas Publisher.

Bartoshuk, L. M., Duffy, V. B., Reed, D., & Williams, A. (1996). Supertasting, earaches and head injury: genetics and pathology alter our taste worlds. *Neuroscience and Biobehavioral Reviews, 20*, 79–87.

Bartrop, R. W., Lockhurst, E., Lazarus, L., Kiloh, L. G., & Penny, R. (1977). Depressed lymphocyte function after bereavement. *Lancet, 1*, 834–836.

Bartzokis, G., Lu, P. H., Tingus, K., Mendez, M. F., Richard, A., Peters, D. G., & Mintz, J. (2010). Lifespan trajectory of myelin integrity and maximum motor speed. *Neurobiology of Aging, 31*(9), 1554–1562.

Basak, C., Boot, W. R., Voss, M. W., & Kramer, A. F. (2008). Can training in a real-time strategy video game attenuate cognitive decline in older adults? *Psychology and Aging, 23*(4), 765–777.

Bass, B. M. (2002). Cognitive, social, and emotional intelligence of transformational leaders. In R. E. Riggio, S. E. Murphy, & F. J. Pirozzolo (Eds.), *Multiple intelligences and leadership* (pp. 105–118). Mahwah, NJ: Lawrence Erlbaum Associates Publishers.

Bassett, R. L., Van Nikkelen-Kuyper, M., Johnson, D., Miller, A., Carter, A., & Grimm, J. P. (2005). Being a good neighbor: Can students come to value homosexual persons? *Journal of Psychology and Theology, 33*(1), 17–26.

Bassili, J. N., & Brown, R. D. (2005). Implicit and explicit attitudes: Research, challenges, and theory. In D. Albarracín, B. T. Johnson, & M. P. Zanna (Eds.), *The handbook of attitudes* (pp. 543–574). Mahwah, NJ: Lawrence Erlbaum Associates Publishers.

Basten, U., Stelzel, C., & Fiebach, C. J. (2013). Intelligence is differentially related to neural effort in the task-positive and the task-negative brain network. *Intelligence, 41*(5), 517–528.

Bastien, C. (2011). Insomnia: Neurophysiological and neuropsychological approaches. *Neuropsychology Review, 21*(1), 22–40.

Bastiaens, M., ter Huurne, J., Gruis, N., Bergman, W., Westendorp, R., Vermeer, B. J., & Bavinck, J. N. B. (2001). The melanocortin-1-receptor gene is the major freckle gene. *Human molecular genetics, 10*(16), 1701–1708.

Bates, J. E. (1989). Concepts and measures of temperament. In G. A. Kohnstamm, J. E. Bates, & M. K. Rothbart (Eds.), *Temperament in childhood* (pp. 3–26). Oxford, England: John Wiley & Sons, Inc.

Bates, J. E., Schermerhorn, A. C., & Goodnight, J. A. (2010). Temperament and personality through the life span. In M. E. Lamb, A. M. Freund, & R. M. Lerner (Eds.), *The handbook of life-span development*, vol. 2: *Social and emotional development* (pp. 208–253). Hoboken, NJ: John Wiley & Sons.

Bates, R. (2002). Liking and similarity as predictors of multi-source ratings. *Personnel Review, 31*(5), 540–552.

Batson, C. D. (2014). *The altruism question: Toward a social-psychological answer.* New York, NY: Psychology Press.

Batson, C. D. (1991). *The altruism question: Towards a social psychological answer.* Hillsdale, NJ: Lawrence Erlbaum Associates.

Batson, C. D., Ahmad, N., & Lishner, D. A. (2009). Empathy and Altruism. In C.R. Snyder and S.J. Lopez (Eds.), *Handbook of Positive Psychology* (pp. 417–426). New York: Oxford University Press.

Batson, C. D., Ahmad, N., & Stocks, E. L. (2004). Benefits and liabilities of empathy-induced altruism. In A. G. Miller (Ed.), *The social psychology of good and evil* (pp. 359–385). New York, NY: Guilford Press.

Batson, C. D., Ahmad, N., Lishner, D. A., & Tsang, J. (2002). Empathy and altruism. In C.R. Synder and S.J. Lopez (Eds.), *Handbook of Positive Psychology*, 485–498.

Batson, C. D., Sanger, K., Garst, E., Kang, M., Rubchinsky, K., & Dawson, K. (1997). Is empathy-induced helping due to self-other merging? *Journal of Personality and Social Psychology, 73*, 495–509.

Batson, C. D., & Weeks, J. L. (1996). Mood effects of unsuccessful helping: Another test of the empathy-altruism hypothesis. *Personality and Social Psychology Bulletin, 22*, 148–157.

Battmer, R. D., Linz, B., & Lenarz, T. (2009). A review of device failure in more than 23 years of clinical experience of a cochlear implant program with more than 3,400 implantees. *Otology & Neurotology, 30*, 455–463.

Baucom, B. R., Atkins, D. C., Simpson, L. E., & Christensen, A. (2009). Prediction of response to treatment in a randomized clinical trial of couple therapy: A 2-year follow-up. *Journal of Consulting and Clinical Psychology, 77*(1), 160–173.

Baucom, D. H., Epstein, N. B., Kirby, J. S., & LaTaillade, J. J. (2010). Cognitive-behavioral couple therapy. In K. S. Dobson (Ed.), *Handbook of cognitive-behavioral therapies* (3rd Ed., pp. 411–444). New York: Guilford Press.

Bauer, R. A. (1952). *The new man in Soviet psychology.* Cambridge, MA: Harvard University Press.

Baum, A., Trevino, L. A., & Dougall, A. L. (2011). Stress and the cancers. In R. J. Contrada & A. Baum (Eds.), *The handbook of stress science: Biology, psychology, and health* (pp. 411–423). New York: Springer Publishing Co.

Baumann, N., & Pham-Dinh, D. (2001). Biology of oligodendrocyte and myelin in the mammalian central nervous system. *Physiological Reviews, 81*(2), 871–927.

Baumeister, R. F. (1984). Choking under pressure: Self-consciousness and paradoxical effects of incentives on skillful performance. *Journal of Personality and Social Psychology, 46*(3), 610–620.

Baumeister, R. F., Catanese, K. R., & Vohs, K. D. (2001). Is there a gender difference in strength of sex drive? Theoretical views, conceptual distinctions, and a review of relevant evidence. *Personality and Social Psychology Review, 5,* 242–273.

Baumgardner, S. R., & Crothers, M. K. (2009). *Positive psychology.* Upper Saddle River, NJ: Prentice Hall/Pearson Education.

Baumrind, D. (1991). The influence of parenting style on adolescent competence and substance use. *The Journal of Early Adolescence, 11,* 56–95.

Baumrind, D., Larzelere, R. E., & Owens, E. B. (2010). Effects of preschool parents' power assertive patterns and practices on adolescent development. *Parenting: Science and Practice, 10*(3), 157–201.

Baym, C. L., & Gonsalves, B. D. (2010). Comparison of neural activity that leads to true memories, false memories, and forgetting: An fMRI study of the misinformation effect. *Cognitive, Affective, & Behavioral Neuroscience, 10*(3), 339–348.

Beach, J., & Bertrand, J. (2009). Early childhood programs and the education system. *Paediatric Child Health, 14*(10), 666–668.

Bear, M. F., Connors, B. W., & Paradiso, M. A. (2007). *Neuroscience: Exploring the Brain (3rd Ed).* Baltimore: Lippincott Williams & Wilkins.

Beasley, M., Thompson, T., & Davidson, J. (2003). Resilience in responses to life stress: The effects of coping style and cognitive hardiness. *Personality and Individual Differences, 34*(1), 77–95.

Becchetti, L., & Santoro, M. (2007). The income-unhappiness paradox: A relational goods/Baumol disease explanation. In P. L. Porta & L. Bruni (Eds.), *Handbook on the economies of happiness.* Northampton, MA: Edward Elgar Publishing.

Beck, A. T. (2002). Cognitive models of depression. In R. L. Leahy & E. T. Dowd (Eds.), *Clinical advances in cognitive psychotherapy: Theory and applications.* New York, NY: Springer.

Beck, A. T. (1991). Cognitive therapy: A 30-year retrospective. *American Psychologist, 46*(4), 368–375.

Beck, A. T. (1975). *Cognitive Therapy and the Emotional Disorders.* International Universities Press Inc.

Beck, A. T. (1967). *Depression: Clinical, experimental and theoretical aspects.* New York, NY: Harper & Row.

Beck, A. T., & Alford, B. A. (2009) *Depression: Causes and treatment.* Philadelphia, PA: University of Pennsylvania Press.

Beck, A. T., & Haigh, E. A. (2014). Advances in Cognitive Theory and Therapy: The Generic Cognitive Model. *Annual Review of Clinical Psychology, 10,* 1–24.

Beck, A. T., Rush, A. J., Shaw, B. F., & Emery, G. (1979). *Cognitive therapy of depression.* New York: Guilford Press.

Beck, A. T., & Weishaar, M. (2011). Cognitive therapy. In R. J. Corsini & D. Wedding (Eds.), *Current Psychotherapies, 9th Ed.* Florence, KY: Cengage Learning.

Beck, A. T., & Weishaar, M. E. (2008). Cognitive therapy. In R. J. Corsini & D. Wedding (Eds.), *Current psychotherapies (8th edition).* Belmont, CA: Brooks Cole.

Beck, B. J. (2008). Mental disorders due to a general medical condition. In T. A. Stern, J. F. Rosenbaum, M. Fava, J. Biederman, & S. L. Rauch (Eds.), *Massachusetts General Hospital Comprehensive Clinical Psychiatry,* 1st Ed. Philadelphia, PA: Mosby Elsevier.

Beck, H. P. (2011). Finding Little Albert: A seven-year search for psychology's lost boy. *The Psychologist, 24,* 392–395.

Beck, H. P., Levinson, S., & Irons, G. (2009). Finding little Albert: A journey to John B. Watson's infant laboratory. *American Psychologist, 64*(7), 605–614.

Becker, B., Mihov, Y., Scheele, D., Kendrick, K. M., Feinstein, J. S., Matusch, A., . . . & Hurlemann, R. (2012). Fear processing and social networking in the absence of a functional amygdala. *Biological Psychiatry, 72*(1), 70–77.

Becker, K. A. (2003). *History of the Stanford-Binet intelligence scales: Content and psychometrics.* (Stanford-Binet Intelligence Scales, Fifth Edition Assessment Service Bulletin No. 1). Itasca, IL: Riverside Publishing.

Beckett, C., Castle, J., Rutter, M., & Sonuga-Barke, E. (2010). Institutional deprivation, specific cognitive functions, and scholastic achievement: English and Romanian adoptees (ERA) study findings. *Monographs of the Society for Research in Child Development, 75*(1), 125–142.

Bedinghaus, T. (2010). Top 5 milestones in vision development. In *About.Com Guide.* Retrieved from http://vision.about.com/od/childrensvision/tp /vision_develop.htm.

Beehr, T. A., Farmer, S. J., Glazer, S., Gudanowski, D. M., & Nair, V. N. (2003). The enigma of social support and occupational stress: Source congruence and gender role effects. *Journal of Occupational Health Psychology, 8*(3), 220–231.

Beesdo, K., Pine, D. S., Lieb, R., & Wittchen, H. U. (2010). Incidence and risk patterns of anxiety and depressive disorders and categorization of generalized anxiety disorder. *Archives of General Psychiatry, 67*(1), 47–57.

Beghetto, R. A., & Kaufman, J. C. (2010). Broadening conceptions of creativity in the classroom. In R. A. Beghetto & J. C. Kaufman (Eds.), *Nurturing creativity in the classroom* (pp. 191–205). New York: Cambridge University Press.

Behrendt, R. P., & Young, C. (2004). Hallucinations in schizophrenia, sensory impairment, and brain disease: A unifying model. *Behavioral and Brain Sciences, 27,* 771–787.

Bekker, M. H. J., & van Assen, M. A. L. M. (2008). Autonomy-connectedness and gender. *Sex Roles, 59*(7–8), 532–544.

Bekkouche, N. S., Holmes, S., Whittaker, K. S., & Krantz, D. S. (2011). Stress and the heart: Psychosocial stress and coronary heart disease. In R. J. Contrada & A. Baum (Eds.), *The handbook of stress science: Biology, psychology, and health.* New York: Springer Publishing Co.

Bellinger, D. L., Madden, K. S., Felten, S.Y., & Felten, D. L. (1994). Neural and endocrine links between the brain and the immune system. In C. S. Lewis, C. O'Sullivan, & J. Barraclough (Eds.), *The psychoimmunology of cancer: Mind and body in the fight for survival.* Oxford, England: Oxford University Press.

Bem, D. J. (1972). Self-perception theory. In L. Berkowitz (Ed.), *Advances in Experimental Social Psychology, Vol. 6.* New York: Academic Press.

Benarroch, E. E. (2011). The midline and intralaminar thalamic nuclei: Anatomic and functional specificity and implications in neurologic disease (Update). *Neurology, 74.*

Benarroch, E. E. (2008). The midline and intralaminar thalamic nuclei: Anatomic and functional specificity and implications in neurologic disease. *Neurology, 71,* 944.

Bendelius, J. (2004). Prevention: the best way to help our kids avoid the obesity epidemic. *School Nurse News, 21*(3), 32–33.

Bender, R. E., & Alloy, L. B. (2011). Life stress and kindling in bipolar disorder: Review of the evidence and integration with emerging biopsychosocial theories. *Clinical Psychology Review, 31*(3), 383–398.

Benecke, M. (2002). *The dream of eternal life: Biomedicine, aging, and immortality* (trans. R. Rubenstein). New York: Columbia University Press.

Benish, S. G., Quintana, S., & Wampold, B. E. (2011). Culturally adapted psychotherapy and the legitimacy of myth: a direct-comparison meta-analysis. *Journal of Counseling Psychology, 58*(3), 279.

Benjafield, J. G., Smile, K. D., & Kingstone, A. (2010). *Cognition* (4th ed.). New York: Oxford University Press.

Benjamin Jr., L. T. (2007). *A brief history of modern psychology.* Malden, MA: Blackwell Publishing.

Benjamin Jr., L. T. (Ed.). (1997). A history of psychology: Original sources and contemporary research (2nd Ed.). New York, NY: McGraw-Hill Book Company.

Benloucif, S., Guico, M. J., Reid, K. J., Wolfe, L. F., L'hermite-Balériaux, M., & Zee, P. C. (2005). Stability of melatonin and temperature as circadian phase markers and their relation to sleep times in humans. *Journal of Biological Rhythms, 20*(2), 178–188.

Bennett, M. P. (1998). The effect of mirthful laughter on stress and natural killer cell cytotoxicity US: ProQuest Information & Learning). *Dissertation Abstracts International: Section B: The Sciences and Engineering, 58*(7), 3553.

Bensafi, M., Sobel, N., & Khan, R. M. (2007). Hedonic-specific activity in piriform cortex during odor imagery mimics that during odor perception. *Journal of Neurophysiology, 98,* 3254–3262.

Benton, A. (2000). *Exploring the History of Neuropsychology.* Oxford University Press.

Ben-Zeev, D., Young, M. A., & Corrigan, P. W. (2010). DSM-V and the stigma of mental illness. *Journal of Mental Health, 19*(4), 318–327.

Ben-Zur, H. (2002). Associations of type A behavior with the emotional traits of anger and curiosity. *Anxiety, Stress & Coping: An International Journal, 15*(1), 95–104.

Benzies, K., Magill-Evans, J., Harrison, M.J., MacPhail, S., & Kimak, C. (2008). Strengthening new fathers' skills in interaction with their 5-month-old infants: Who benefits from a brief intervention? *Public Health Nursing, 25,* 431–439.

Berenbaum, H., & Barch, D. (1995). The categorization of thought disorder. *Journal of Psycholinguist Research, 24,* 349–376.

Berenbaum, H., Raghavan, C., Huynh-Nhu, L., Vernon, L. L., & Gomez, J. J. (2003). A taxonomy of emotional disturbances. *Clinical Psychology: Science and Practice, 10,* 206–226.

Berenson, K. R., Downey, G., Rafaeli, E., Coifman, K. G., & Paquin, N. L. (2011). The rejection–rage contingency in borderline personality disorder. *Journal of Abnormal Psychology, 120*(3), 681–690.

Berger, K. T. (1988). *Zen Driving.* Ballentine Books.

Berk, L. E. (2008). *Infants, Children, and Adolescents, 6e.* Boston: Allyn & Bacon.

Berkman, N. D., Bulik, C. M., Brownley, K. A., Lohr, K. N., Sedway, J. A., Rooks, A., et al. (2006). Management of eating disorders. Evidence report/technology assessment No. 135. AHRQ Publication No. 06-E010.

Berkowitz, L. (1989). Frustration-aggression hypothesis: Examination and reformulation. *Psychological Bulletin, 106,* 59–73.

Berman, J. R. (2005). Physiology of female sexual function and dysfunction. *International Journal of Impotence Research, 17*(1), S44–51.

Bermingham-McDonogh, O., & Reh, T. A. (2011). Regulated reprogramming in the regeneration of sensory receptor cells. *Neuron, 71*(3), 389–405.

Bermond, B., Nieuwenhuyse, B., Fasotti, L., & Schuerman, J. (1991). Spinal cord lesions, peripheral feedback, and intensities of emotional feelings. *Cognition & Emotion, 5,* 201–220.

Bermudez, P., Lerch, J. P., Evans, A. C., & Zatorre, R. J. (2009). Neuroanatomical correlates of musicianship as revealed by cortical thickness and voxel-based morphometry. *Cerebral Cortex, 19,* 1583–1596.

Berr, C., Wancata, J., & Ritchie, K. (2005). Prevalence of dementia in the elderly in Europe. *European Neuropsychopharmacology, 15*(4), 463–471.

Berridge, C. W., & Waterhouse, B. D. (2003). The locus coeruleus–noradrenergic system: Modulation of behavioral state and state-dependent cognitive processes. *Brain Research Reviews, 42*(1), 33–84.

Berridge, K. C. (2007). The debate over dopamine's role in reward: The case for incentive salience. *Psychopharmacology, 191*(3), 391–431.

Berridge, K. C., & Kringelbach, M. L. (2013). Neuroscience of affect: brain mechanisms of pleasure and displeasure. *Current Opinion in Neurobiology, 23*(3), 294-303.

Berridge, K. C., & Robinson, T. E. (2009). Drug addiction as incentive sensitization. In J. Poland & G. Graham (Eds.), *Addiction and responsibility.* MIT Press, Cambridge, MA.

Berridge, K. C., Ho, C. Y., Richard, J. M., & DiFeliceantonio, A. G. (2010). The tempted brain eats: pleasure and desire circuits in obesity and eating disorders. *Brain Research, 1350,* 43-64.

Berry, J. W. (1992). *Cross-cultural psychology, research and applications.* New York, NY: Cambridge University Press.

Berry, J., Hastings, E., West, R., Lee, C., & Cavanaugh, J. C. (2010). Memory aging: Deficits, beliefs, and interventions. In J. C. Cavanaugh, C. K. Cavanaugh, J. Berry & R. West (Eds.), *Aging in America, vol 1: Psychological aspects* (pp. 255–299). Santa Barbara, CA: Praeger/ABC-CLIO.

Berscheid, E. (1983). Interpersonal attraction. In G. Lindzey & E. Aronson (Eds.), *Handbook of Social Psychology (3rd Ed.).* Reading, MA: Addison-Wesley.

Berscheid, E., & Walster, E. H. (1978). Interpersonal attraction. In G. Lindzey & E. Aronson (Eds.), *Handbook of Social Psychology* (Vol. 2, pp. 413–484). New York, NY: Random House.

Berson, D. M. (2003). Strange vision: ganglion cells as circadian photoreceptors. *Trends in Neuroscience, 26*(6), 314–320.

Bertini, M., Ferrara, M., De Gennaro, L., Moroni, F., De Gasperis, M., Babiloni, C., Rossini, P. M., Vecchio, F., & Curcio, G. (2007). Directional information flows between brain hemispheres during presleep wake and early sleep stages. *Cerebral Cortex, 17*(8), 1970–1978.

Berwick, R. C., Friederici, A. D., Chomsky, N., & Bolhuis, J. J. (2013). Evolution, brain and the nature of language. *Trends in Cognitive Sciences, 17*(2) 89–98.

Beutler, L. E. (2011). Prescriptive matching and systematic treatment selection. In J. C. Norcross, G. R. VandenBos, & D. K. Freedheim (Eds.), *History of psychotherapy: Continuity and change* (2nd Ed., pp. 402–407). Washington, DC: American Psychological Association.

Beutler, L. E. (2002). The dodo bird is extinct. *Clinical Psychology: Science and Practice, 9*(1), 30–34.

Beutler, L. E., Forrester, B., Holt, H., & Stein, M. (2013). Common, specific, and cross-cutting psychotherapy interventions. *Psychotherapy, 50*(3), 298.

Bevins, R. A. (2001). Novelty seeking and reward: Implications for the study of high-risk behaviors. *Current Directions in Psychological Science, 10*(6), 189–193.

Beyerstein. B. L. (1999). Whence cometh the myth that we only use ten percent of our brains? In S. Della Sala (Ed.), *Mind Myths: Exploring Popular Assumptions about the Mind and Brain* (pp. 1–24). Chichester, UK: John Wiley and Sons Ltd.

Bezchlibnyk-Butler, K. Z., Jeffries, J. J., Procyshyn, R. M., & Virani, A. S. (Eds.). (2013). *Clinical Handbook of Psychotropic Drugs.* Hogrefe Verlag.

Bialystok, E., & Craik, F. I. M. (2010). Structure and process in life-span cognitive development. In W. F. Overton & R. M. Lerner (Eds.), *The handbook of life-span development,* vol 1: Cognition, biology, and methods (pp. 195–225). Hoboken, NJ: John Wiley & Sons.

Bibby, R. (2007). *Racial Intermarriage: Canada and the U.S.* Project Canada Press Release #9, University of Lethbridge. Retrieved from http://www.reginaldbibby.com/images/PC_9_RACIAL_INTERMARRIAGE_AUG2907.pdf.

Bickman, L. (2005). A common factors approach to improving mental health services. *Mental Health Services Research, 7*(1), 1–4.

Billings, L. S., Vescio, T. K., & Biernat, M. (2000). Race-based social judgment by minority perceivers. *Journal of Applied Social Psychology, 30*(2), 221–240.

Bindschaedler, C., Peter-Favre, C., Maeder, P., Hirsbrunner, T., & Clarke, S. (2011). Growing up with bilateral hippocampal atrophy: From childhood to teenage. *Cortex, 47,* 931–944.

Binswanger, H. (1991). Volition as cognitive self-regulation. *Organizational Behavior and Human Decision Processes, 50*(2), 154–178.

Birdsong, D., & Milis, M. (2001). On the evidence for maturational constraints in second-language acquisition. *Journal of Memory and Language, 44*(2) 235–249.

Bisaga, A. (2008). Benzodiazepines and other sedatives and hypnotics. In H. D. Kleber & M. Galanter (Eds.), *The American Psychiatric Publishing textbook of substance abuse treatment (4th Ed.).* Arlington, VA: American Psychiatric Publishing.

Bissette, G., Seidler, F. J., Nemeroff, C. B., & Slotkin, T. A. (1996). High affinity choline transporter status in Alzheimer's disease tissue from rapid autopsy. In R. J. Wurtman, S. Corkin, J. H. Growdon, & R. M. Nitsch (Eds.), *The neurobiology of Alzheimer's disease.* New York, NY: New York Academy of Sciences.

Biswas-Diener, R. (Ed.). (2011). *Positive psychology as social change.* New York: Springer Science + Business Media.

Bitterman, M. E. (2006). Classical conditioning since Pavlov. *Review of General Psychology, 10*(4), 365–376.

Bjorgvinsson, T., & Hart, J. (2008). Obsessive-compulsive disorder. In M. Hersen & J. Rosqvist (Eds.), *Handbook of psychological assessment, case conceptualization, and treatment, Vol. 1: Adults* (pp. 237–262). Hoboken, NJ: John Wiley & Sons.

Björkman, B., Arnér, S., & Hydén, L. C. (2008). Phantom breast and other syndromes after mastectomy: Eight breast cancer patients describe their experiences over time: a 2-year follow-up study. *The Journal of Pain, 9,* 1018–1025.

Björnholm, M., Münzberg, H., Leshan, R. L., Villanueva, E. C., Bates, S. H., Louis, G. W., & Myers, Martin G., Jr. (2007). Mice lacking inhibitory leptin receptor signals are lean with normal endocrine function. *The Journal of Clinical Investigation, 117*(5), 1354–1360.

Black, K. A., & Schutte, E. D. (2006) Recollections of being loved: Implications of childhood experiences with parents for young adults' romantic relationships. *Journal of Family Issues, 27,* 1459–1480.

Blackmore, E. R., Craddock, N., Walters, J., & Jones, I. (2009). Is the perimenopause a time of increased risk of recurrence in women with a history of bipolar affective postpartum psychosis? A case series. *Archives of Women's Mental Health, 11*(1), 75–78.

Blagrove, M., Bell, E., & Wilkinson, A. (2010). Association of lucid dreaming frequency with Stroop task performance. *Dreaming, 20*(4), 280–287.

Blair, J., Mitchell, D., & Blair, K. (2005). *The psychopath: Emotion and the brain.* Malden, MA: Blackwell Publishing.

Blakemore, A. I. F., & Froguel, P. (2008). Is obesity our genetic legacy? *Journal of clinical endocrinology and metabolism, 93*(11), Supplement 1, Online publication.

Blakemore, S., Burnett, S., & Dahl, R. E. (2010). The role of puberty in the developing adolescent brain. *Human Brain Mapping, 31*(6), 926–933.

Blamey, P. J., & Sarant, J. Z. (2013). The consequences of deafness for spoken language development. *Springer Handbook of Auditory Research, 47,* 265–299.

Blanchard, R. (2004). Quantitative and theoretical analyses of the relation between older brothers and homosexuality in men. *Journal of Theoretical Biology, 230*(2), 173–187.

Blanchard, R. (2001). Fraternal birth order and the maternal immune hypothesis of male homosexuality. *Hormonal Behavior, 40*(2), 105–114.

Bland, R. C., Orn, H., & Newman, S. C. (1988). Lifetime prevalence of psychiatric disorders in Edmonton. *Acta Psychiatrica Scandinavica Supplement, 338,* 24–32.

Blass, T. (2007). Unsupported allegations about a link between Milgram and the CIA: Tortured reasoning in a question of torture. *Journal of the History of the Behavioral Sciences, 43,* 199–203.

Blass, T. (2004). *The man who shocked the world: The life and legacy of Stanley Milgram.* New York, NY: Basic Books.

Bleich, A., Gelkopf, M., & Solomon, Z. (2003). Exposure to terrorism, stress-related mental health symptoms, and coping behaviors among a nationally representative sample in Israel. *Journal of the American Medical Association, 290*(5), 612–620.

Bleske-Rechek, A., & Kelley, J. A. (2014). Birth order and personality: A within-family test using independent self-reports from both firstborn and laterborn siblings. *Personality and Individual Differences, 56,* 15–18.

Blessing, W. W. (1997). *The lower brainstem and bodily homeostasis.* New York, NY: Oxford University Press.

Blickle, G., Meurs, J. A., Wihler, A., Exen, C., Plies, A., & Gunther, S. (2013). The interactive effects of conscientiousness, openness to experience, and political skill on job performance in complex jobs: The importance of context. *Journal of Organizational Behaviour, 34*(8), 1145–1164.

Bliwise, D. L. (2010). The pit (of sleeplessness) and the pendulum (of regulation). *Sleep Medicine, 11*(1), 7–8.

Bloch, M. H., Wasylink, S., Landeros-Weisenberger, A., Panza, K. E., Billingslea, E., Leckman, J. F., . . . & Pittenger, C. (2012). Effects of ketamine in treatment-refractory obsessive-compulsive disorder. *Biological Psychiatry, 72*(11), 964–970.

Blokland, A. (1995). Acetylcholine: a neurotransmitter for learning and memory? *Brain Research Reviews, 21*(3), 285–300.

Blomstedt, P., Sandvik, U., Hariz, M. I., Fytagoridis, A., Forsgren, L., Hariz, G., & Koskinen, L. D. (2011). Influence of age, gender and severity of tremor on outcome after thalamic and subthalamic DBS for essential tremor. *Parkinsonism & Related Disorders, 17*(8), 617–620.

Blomstedt, P., Sjoberg, R. L., Hansson, M., Bodlund, O., & Hariz, M. I. (2011). Deep brain stimulation in the treatment of depression. *Acta Psychiatrica Scandinavica, 123*(1), 4–11.

Bloom, L. (1970). Language development: Form and function in emerging grammars. Cambridge, MA: MIT Press.

Blum, H. P. (2010). Object relations in clinical psychoanalysis. *The International Journal of Psychoanalysis, 91*(4), 973–976.

Blum, K., Braverman, E. R., Holder, J. M., Lubar, J. F., Monastra, V. J., Miller, D., et al. (2000). Reward deficiency syndrome: A biogenetic model for the diagnosis and treatment of impulsive, addictive, and compulsive behaviors. *Journal of Psychoactive Drugs, 32* (Suppl.), 1–68.

Blumberg, M. S., & Seelke, A. M. H. (2010). The form and function of infant sleep: From muscle to neocortex. In M. S. Blumberg, J. H. Freeman, & S. R. Robinson (Eds.), *Oxford handbook of developmental behavioral neuroscience* (pp. 391–423). New York, NY: Oxford University Press.

Blumenfeld, P., Kempler, T., & Krajcik, J. (2006). Motivation and cognitive engagement in learning environments. In R. K. Sawyer (Ed.), *The Cambridge handbook of the learning sciences* (pp. 475–488). Cambridge, MA: Cambridge University Press.

Boake, C. (2002). From the Binet–Simon to the Wechsler–Bellevue: Tracing the history of intelligence testing. *Journal of Clinical and Experimental Neuropsychology, 24*(3), 383–405.

Bock, P. (2005). Infant science: How do babies learn to talk. *Pacific Northwest: The Seattle Times Magazine,* March 6, 2005.

Boecker, H., Sprenger T., Spilker, M. E., Henriksen, G., Koppenhoefer, M., Wagner, K. J., Valet, M., Berthele, A., & Tolle, T. R. (2008). The runner's high: Opioidergic mechanisms in the human brain. *Cerebral Cortex, 18*(11), 2523–2531.

Boeree, G. C. (2006). *History of Psychology, Part One: The Ancients.* Retrieved from http://www.social-psychology.de/do/history_I.pdf.

Bohart, A. C., & Tallman, K. (2010). Clients: The neglected common factor in psychotherapy. In B. L. Duncan, S. D. Miller, B. E. Wampold, & M. A. Hubble (Eds.), *The heart and soul of change: Delivering what works in therapy* (2nd Ed., pp. 83–111). Washington, DC: American Psychological Association.

Boland, R.J., & M.B. Keller. (2009). Course and outcome of depression. In I. H. Gotlib & C. L. Hammen (Eds.), *Handbook of Depression* (2nd ed., pp. 23–43). New York: Guilford.

Boldyrev, A. A., & Johnson, P. (2007). Free radicals and cell signaling in Alzheimer's disease. *Journal of Alzheimer's Disease, 11*(2), 141.

Bolger, N. (1990). Coping as a personality process: A prospective study. *Journal of Personality and Social Psychology, 59*, 525–537.

Bollinger, T., Bollinger, A., Oster, H., & Solbach, W. (2010). Sleep, immunity, and circadian clocks: A mechanistic model. *Gerontology, 56*(6), 574–580.

Bollini, A. M., & Walker, E. F. (2007). Schizotypal personality disorder. In W. O'Donohue, K. A. Fowler, & S. O. Lilienfeld (Eds.), *Personality Disorders: Toward the DSM-V* (pp. 81–108). Thousand Oaks, CA: Sage Publications.

Bonanno, G. A., Brewin, C. R., Kaniasty, K., & La Greca, A. M. (2010). Weighing the costs of disaster: Consequences, risks, and resilience in individuals, families, and communities. *Psychological Science in the Public Interest, 11*, 1–49.

Bond, C. F. Jr. (2000). Social facilitation. In A. E. Kazdin (Ed.), *Encyclopedia of Psychology, vol. 7* (pp. 338–440). Washington, D.C.: American Psychological Association.

Bond, C. F., & Titus, L. J. (1983). Social facilitation: A meta analysis of 241 studies. *Psychological Bulletin, 94*, 265–292.

Bond, K., Ospina, M., Hooton, N., Bialy, L., Dryden, D. M., Buscemi, N., Shannahoff-Khalsa, D., Dusek, J., & Carlson, L. E. (2009). Defining a complex intervention: The development of demarcation criteria for "meditation." *Psychology of Religion and Spirituality, 1*(2), 129–137.

Bond, R., & Smith, P. B. (1996). Culture and conformity: A meta-analysis of studies using Asch's (1952b, 1956) line judgment task. *Psychological Bulletin, 119*, 111–137.

Boogaarts, H. D., Abdo, W. F., & Bloem, B. R. (2007). "Recumbent" gait: relationship to the phenotype of "astasia–abasia"? *Movement Disorders, 22*(14), 2121–2122.

Borch, C., Hyde, A., & Cillessen, A. H. N. (2011). The role of attractiveness and aggression in high school popularity. *Social Psychology of Education, 14*(1), 23–39.

Bord-Hoffman, M. A., & Donius, M. (2005). Loss in height: When is it a problem? *AAACN Viewpoint, 1*, 14–15.

Borgen, F. H., & Betz, N. E. (2008). Career self-efficacy and personality: Linking career confidence and the healthy personality. *Journal of Career Assessment, 16*(1), 22–43.

Borland, R., Yong, H. H., Balmford, J., Fong, G. T., Zanna, M. P., & Hastings, G. (2009). Do risk-minimizing beliefs about smoking inhibit quitting? Findings from the International Tobacco Control (ITC) Four-Country Survey. *Preventive Medicine, 49*(2), 219–223.

Bornstein, M. H., Tal, J., Rahn, C., Galperin, C. Z., Pecheux, M., Lamour, M., Azuma, H., Toda, S., Ogino, M., & Tamis-LeMonda, C. S. (1992). Functional analysis of the contents of maternal speech to infants of 5 and 13 months in four cultures: Argentina, France, Japan, and the United States. *Developmental Psychology, 28*, 593–603.

Bornstein, R. F. (2007). Might the Rorschach be a projective test after all? Social projection of an undesired trait alters Rorschach oral dependency scores. *Journal of Personality Assessment, 88*(3), 354–367.

Bosson, J. K., & Vandello, J. A. (2011). Precarious manhood and its links to action and aggression. *Current Directions in Psychological Science, 20*(2), 82–86.

Bosson, J. K., Vandello, J. A., & Caswell, T. A. (2014). Precarious manhood. In Ryan, M. K., & Branscombe, N. R. (Eds.), *The Sage Handbook of Gender and Psychology*. Thousand Oaks, CA: Sage.

Botwin, M. D., Buss, D. M., & Shackelford, T. K. (1997). Personality and mate preferences: Five factors in mate selection and marital satisfaction. *Journal of Personality, 65*, 107–136.

Bouchard, G., & Thériault, V. J. (2003). Defense mechanisms and coping strategies in conjugal relationships: An integration. *International Journal of Psychology, 38*(2), 79–90.

Bouchard, T., Jr. (2004). Genes, environment, and personality. *Science, 264*, 1700–1701.

Bouman, T. K. (2008). Hypochondriasis. In J. S. Abramowitz, D. McKay, & S. Taylor (Eds.), *Obsessive-compulsive disorder: Subtypes and spectrum conditions*. Oxford, UK: Elsevier.

Bourassa, C., McKay, K., & Hampton, M. (2004). Racism, sexism, and colonialism: The impact on the health of aboriginal women in Canada. *Canadian Women Studies, 24*(1), 23–29.

Bourne, L. E., Dominowski, R. L., & Loftus, W. F. (1979). *Cognitive processes.* Englewood Cliffs, NJ: Prentice Hall.

Bouteyre, E., Maurel, M., & Bernaud, J.-L. (2007). Daily hassles and depressive symptoms among first year psychology students in France: The role of coping and social support. *Stress and Health: Journal of the International Society for the Investigation of Stress, 23*, 93–99.

Bowden, S. C., Saklofske, D. H., & Weiss, L. G. (2011). Invariance of the measurement model underlying the Wechsler adult intelligence scale-IV in the United States and Canada. *Educational and Psychological Measurement, 71*(1), 186–199.

Bower, G. H. (2008). The evolution of a cognitive psychologist: A journey from simple behaviors to complex mental acts. *Annual Review of Psychology, 59*, 1–27.

Bower, G. H. (1981). Mood and memory. *American Psychologist, 36*(2), 129–148.

Bower, G. H., & Clark, M. C. (1969). Narrative stories as mediators for serial learning. *Psychonomic Science, 14*(4), 181–182.

Bowlby, J. (1999). *Attachment: Attachment and loss* (vol. 1, 2nd Ed.). New York: Basic Books.

Bowlby, J. (1969). *Attachment and loss, Vol. 1: Attachment.* New York: Basic Books.

Bowlby, J. (1958). The nature of the child's tie to his mother. *International Journal of Psycho-Analysis, XXXIX*, 1–23.

Boyd, R. (2004). Fact or fiction?: Waking a sleepwalker may kill them. *Scientific American, 1*.

Boyle, G. J. (2008). Critique of the five-factor model of personality. In G. J. Boyle, G. Matthews, & D. H. Saklofske (Eds.), *The SAGE Handbook of Personality Theory and Assessment, Vol 1: Personality Theories and Models* (pp. 295–312). Sage Publications.

Boyle, G. J., Matthews, G., & Saklofske, D. H. (2008). *The SAGE handbook of personality theory and assessment: Personality measurement and testing (Volume 2)*. Sage Publications.

Brach, J. S., FitzGerald, S., Newman, A. B., Kelsey, S., Kuller, L., VanSwearingen, J. M., & Kriska, A. M. (2003). Physical activity and functional status in community-dwelling older women. *Archives of Internal Medicine, 163*, 2565–2571.

Brackett, M. A., Rivers, S. E., & Salovey, P. (2011). Emotional intelligence: Implications for personal, social, academic, and workplace success. *Social and Personality Psychology Compass, 5*(1), 88–103.

Braddick, O. J., O'Brien, J. M. D., Wattam-Bell, J., Atkinson, J., Hartley, T., & Turner, R. (2001). Brain areas sensitive to coherent visual motion. *Perception, 30*(1), 61–72.

Bradford, A. M., Savage, K. M., Jones, D. N., & Kalinichev, M. (2010). Validation and pharmacological characterisation of MK-801-induced locomotor hyperactivity in BALB/C mice as an assay for detection of novel antipsychotics. *Psychopharmacology, 212*(2), 155–170.

Bradley, M. M., & Lang, P. J. (2007). Emotion and motivation. In J. T. Cacioppo, L. G. Tassinary, & G. G. Berntson (Eds.), *Handbook of psychophysiology (3rd Ed.)* (pp. 581–607). New York, NY: Cambridge University Press.

Bradley, M. M., & Lang, P. J. (2000). Measuring emotion: Behavior, feeling, and physiology. In R. D. Lane & L. Nadel (Eds.), *Cognitive neuroscience of emotion* (pp. 242–276). New York, NY: Oxford University Press.

Bradley, M. M., Cuthbert, B. N., & Lang, P. J. (1991). Startle and emotion: Lateral acoustic probes and the bilateral blink. *Psychophysiology, 28,* 285–295.

Bradley, M. M., Cuthbert, B. N., & Lang, P. J. (1990). Startle reflex modification: Emotion or attention? *Psychophysiology, 27,* 513–522.

Bradley, R. H., & Caldwell, B. M. (1984). The HOME inventory and family demographics. *Developmental Psychology, 20*(2), 315–320.

Bradley, R. H., Caldwell, B. M., & Corwyn, R. F. (2003). The child care HOME inventories: Assessing the quality of family child care homes. *Early Childhood Research Quarterly, 18*(3), 294–309.

Bradley, S. D., Angelini, J. R., & Lee, S. (2007). Psychophysiological and memory effects of negative political ads: Aversive, arousing, and well remembered. *Journal of Advertising, 36*(4), 115–127.

Braffman, W., & Kirsch, I. (2001). Reaction time as a predictor of imaginative suggestibility and hypnotizability. *Contemporary Hypnosis, 18*(3), 107–119.

Brandimonte, M. A., Einstein, G. O., & McDaniel, M. A. (Eds.). (2014). *Prospective memory: Theory and applications.* New York, NY: Psychology Press.

Brannon, E. M., Cabeza, R., Huettel, S. A., LaBar, K. S., Platt, M. L., & Woldorff, M. G. (2008). *Principles of cognitive neuroscience* (Vol. 83, No. 3, p. 757). Sunderland, MA: Sinauer Associates.

Bratko, D., Butkovic, A., & Chamorro-Premuzic, T. (2010). The genetics of general knowledge: A twin study from Croatia. *Personality and Individual Differences, 48*(4), 403–407.

Braun, A. R., Guillemin, A., Hosey, L., & Varga, M. (2001). The neural organization of discourse: An H215o-PET study of narrative production in English and American sign language. *Brain, 124*(10), 2028–2044.

Breedlove, S. M., & Watson, N. V. (2013). *Biological psychology: An introduction to behavioral, cognitive, and clinical neuroscience* (7th ed). Sunderland, MA: Sinauer Associates, Inc.

Breland, K., & Breland, M. (1961). The misbehavior of organisms. *American Psychologist, 16,* 681–684.

Bremner, J. D., & Charney, D. S. (2010). Neural circuits in fear and anxiety. In D. J. Stein, E. Hollander, & B. O. Rothbaum (Eds.), *Textbook of anxiety disorders* (2nd Ed., pp. 55–71). Arlington, VA: American Psychiatric Publishing.

Brenner, C. (1987) Working through: 1914–1984. *The Psychoanalytic Quarterly, 56,* 88–108.

Breslau, N., Roth, T., Burduvali, E., Kapke, A., Schults, L., & Roehrs, T. (2005). Sleep in lifetime posttraumatic stress disorder: A community-based polysomnographic study: Correction. *Archives of General Psychiatry, 62*(2), 172.

Bretherton, I. (1992). The origins of attachment theory: John Bowlby and Mary Ainsworth. *Developmental Psychology, 28,* 759–775.

Brewster, M. (2012, September 17). PTSD in Canadian military: DND doesn't have enough staff to help soldiers says Ombudsman. Canadian Press.

Brickey, M. (2005). *52 steps to grow young.* Columbus, OH: New Resources Press.

Brietzke, E., Mansur, R. B., Soczynska, J., Powell, A. M., & McIntyre, R. S. (2012). A theoretical framework informing research about the role of stress in the pathophysiology of bipolar disorder. *Progress in Neuro-Psychopharmacology and Biological Psychiatry, 39*(1), 1–8.

Broad, K. D., Curley, J. P., & Keverne, E. B. (2006). Mother-infant bonding and the evolution of mammalian social relationships. *Philosophical Transactions of the Royal Society of London, Series B, Biological sciences, 361*(1476), 2199–2214.

Broca, P. P. (1861). Loss of speech, chronic softening and partial destruction of the anterior left lobe of the brain. *Bulletin de la Société Anthropologique, 2,* 235–238.

Brodal, P. (2010). *The central nervous system: Structure and function* (4th ed.). New York, NY: Oxford University Press.

Brohan, E., Slade, M., Clement, S., & Thornicroft, G. (2010). Experiences of mental illness stigma, prejudice and discrimination: a review of measures. *BMC Health Services Research, 10*(1), 80.

Brookmeyer, R., Johnson, E., Ziegler-Graham, K., & Arrighi, H. M. (2007). Forecasting the global burden of Alzheimer's disease. *Alzheimer's and Dementia, 3*(3), 186–191.

Brooks, L., McCabe, P., & Schneiderman, N. (2011). Stress and cardiometabolic syndrome. In R. J. Contrada & A. Baum (Eds.), *The handbook of stress science: Biology, psychology, and health* (pp. 399–409). New York: Springer Publishing Co.

Brosnan, S. F., & de Waal, F. B. (2012). Fairness in animals: Where to from here? *Social Justice Research, 25,* 336-351. doi: 10.1007/s11211-012-0165-8

Brosnan, S. F., & de Waal, F. B. (2003). Monkeys reject unequal pay. *Nature, 425,* 297–299.

Brouwer, R. M., Hedman, A. M., van Haren, N. E. M., Schnack, H. G., Brans, R. G. H., Smit, D. J. A., Kahn, R. S., Boomsma, D. I., & Hulshoff Pol, H. E. (2014). In press. Heritability of brain volume change and its relation to intelligence, *NeuroImage.*

Brown, A. S. (2006). Prenatal infection as a risk factor for schizophrenia. *Schizophrenia Bulletin, 32,* 200–202.

Brown, A. S., & Derkits, E. J. (2010). Prenatal infection and schizophrenia: a review of epidemiologic and translational studies. *American Journal of Psychiatry, 167*(3), 261–280.

Brown, A. S., & Susser, E. S. (2002). In utero infection and adult schizophrenia. *Mental Retardation and Developmental Disabilities Research Reviews, 8,* 51–57.

Brown, B. S. (1976). Obstacles to treatment for blue-collar workers. *New dimensions in mental health.* Washington, DC: U.S. Department of Health, Education, and Welfare.

Brown, D. E. (1991). *Human Universals.* New York, NY: McGraw-Hill.

Brown, G. G., & Thompson, W. K. (2010). Functional brain imaging in schizophrenia: Selected results and methods. In N. R. Swerdlow (Ed.), *Behavioral neurobiology of schizophrenia and its treatment* (pp. 181–214). New York: Springer-Verlag Publishing.

Brown, G. W. (2010). Psychosocial origins of depressive and anxiety disorders. In D. Goldberg, K. S. Kendler, & P. J. Sirovatka (Eds.), *Diagnostic issues in depression and generalized anxiety disorder: Refining the research agenda for DSM-V* (pp. 303–331). Washington, DC: American Psychiatric Association.

Brown, L. F., Davis, L. W., LaRocco, V. A., & Strasburger, A. (2010). Participant perspectives on mindfulness meditation training for anxiety in schizophrenia. *American Journal of Psychiatric Rehabilitation, 13*(3), 224–242.

Brown, L. L., Tomarken, A. J., Orth, D. N., Loosen, P. T., Kalin, N. H., & Davidson, R. J. (1996). Individual differences in repressive-defensiveness predict basal salivary cortisol levels. *Journal of Personality and Social Psychology, 70*(2), 362–371.

Brown, L. S. (2011). Client diversity in psychotherapy. In J. C. Norcross, G. R. VandenBos, & D. K. Freedheim (Eds.), *History of psychotherapy: Continuity and change* (2nd Ed., pp. 475–483). Washington, DC: American Psychological Association.

Brown, R. P., Imura, M., & Mayeux, L. (2014). Honor and the stigma of mental healthcare. *Personality and Social Psychology Bulletin,* 0146167214536741.

Brown, T. A., & Rosellini, A. J. (2011). The direct and interactive effects of neuroticism and life stress on the severity and longitudinal course of depressive symptoms. *Journal of Abnormal Psychology, 120*(4), 844.

Brown, T. M., & Fee, E. (2003). Sexual behavior in the human male. *American Journal of Public Health, 93*(6).

Brown, J. (2006). Björk tops BBC list of the world's most eccentric celebrities. *The Independent.* Retrieved from www.independent.co.uk/news/media/bjoumlrk-tops-bbc-list-of-the-worlds-most-eccentric-celebrities-522245.html.

Brown, W. M., Cronk, L., Grochow, K., Jacobson, A., Liu, C. K., Popović, Z., & Trivers, R. (2005). Dance reveals symmetry especially in young men. *Nature, 438*(7071), 1148–1150.

Brozovich, F. A., & Heimberg, R. G. (2011). A treatment-refractory case of social anxiety disorder: Lessons learned from a failed course of cognitive-behavioral therapy. *Cognitive and Behavioral Practice, 18*(3), 316–325.

Brumbaugh, C. C., & Fraley, R. C. (2006). The evolution of attachment in romantic relationships. In M. Mikulincer & G. S. Goodman (Eds.), *Dynamics of romantic love: Attachment, caregiving, and sex* (pp. 71–101). New York, NY: Guilford Press.

Bruner, J. (1986). *Actual minds, possible worlds.* Cambridge, MA: Harvard University Press.

Bruner, J. (1983). *Child's talk: Learning to use language.* New York, NY: Norton.

Bryan, W. L., & Harter, N. (1897). Studies in the psychology of the telegraphic language. *Psychological Review, 4,* 27–53.

Bryceland, C., & Stam, H. J. (2005). Empirical validation and professional codes of ethics: Description or prescription? *Journal of Constructivist Psychology, 18,* 131–155.

Buchsbaum, G., & Gottschalk, A. (1983). Trichromacy, opponent colours coding and optimum colour information transmission in the retina. *Proceedings of The Royal Society of London, Series B, Containing Papers of a Biological Character, 220,* 89–113.

Buck, L. B. (1996). Information coding in the vertebrate olfactory system. *Annual Reviews in the Neurosciences, 19,* 517–544.

Buda, R., & Elsayed-Elkhouly, S. M. (1998). Cultural differences between Arabs and Americans: Individualism-collectivism revisited. *Journal of Cross-Cultural Psychology, 29,* 487–492.

Buhrich, N., Bailey, M. J., & Martin, N. G. (1991). Sexual orientation, sexual identity, and sex-dimorphic behaviors in male twins. *Behavior Genetics, 21*(1), 75–96.

Bullough, V. L. (2004). Sex will never be the same: The contributions of Alfred C. Kinsey. *Archives of Sexual Behavior, 33*(3), 277–286.

Buma, L. A., Bakker, F. C., & Oudejans, R. R. D. (2014). Exploring the thoughts and focus of attention of elite musicians under pressure. *Psychology of Music,* published first online.

Bunney, W. E., & Davis, J. M. (1965). Norepinephrine in depressive reactions: A review. *Archives of General Psychiatry, 13*(6), 483–493.

Burg, M. M., & Pickering, T. G. (2011). The cardiovascular system. In R. J. Contrada & A. Baum (Eds.), *The handbook of stress science: Biology, psychology, and health* (pp. 37–45). New York: Springer Publishing Co.

Burg, M. M., Soufer, A., Lampert, R., Collins, D., & Soufer, R. (2011). Autonomic contribution to endothelin-1 increase during laboratory anger-recall stress in patients with coronary artery disease. *Molecular Medicine (Cambridge, Mass.), 17*(5–6), 495–501.

Burgaleta, M., Head, K., Álvarez-Linera, J., Martínez, K., Escorial, S., Haier, R., & Colom, R. (2012). Sex differences in brain volume are related to specific skills, not to general intelligence. *Intelligence, 40,* 60–68.

Burger King. (2009). Burger King USA Nutritionals. Retrieved from http://www.bk.com/Nutrition/PDFs/NutritionalBrochure.pdf.

Burger, J. M. (2008). Replicating Milgram: Would people still obey today? *American Psychologist, 64*(1), 20–27.

Burgess, J. L. (2001). Phosphine exposure from a methamphetamine laboratory investigation. *Journal of Toxicology and Clinical Toxicology, 39,* 165.

Burijon, B. N. (2007). *Biological bases of clinical anxiety.* New York, NY: W. W. Norton & Company.

Burlingame, G. M., & Baldwin, S. (2011). Group therapy. In J. C. Norcross, G. R. VandenBos, & D. K. Freedheim (Eds.), *History of psychotherapy: Continuity and change* (2nd Ed., pp. 505–515). Washington, DC: American Psychological Association.

Burns, T., & Drake, B. (2011). Mental health services for patients with schizophrenia. In D. R. Weinberger & P. J. Harrison (Eds.), *Schizophrenia* (3rd Ed.). Hoboken, NJ: Blackwell-Wiley.

Busatto, G. F., Zanetti, M. V., Schaufelberger, M. S., & Crippa, J. A. S. (2010). Brain anatomical abnormalities in schizophrenia: Neurodevelopmental origins and patterns of progression over time. In W. F. Gattaz & G. Busatto (Eds.), *Advances in schizophrenia research 2009* (pp. 113–148). New York: Springer Science + Business Media.

Bushman, B. J. (2002). Does venting anger feed or extinguish the flame? Catharsis, rumination, distraction, anger, and aggressive responding. *Personality and Social Psychology Bulletin, 28,* 724–731.

Bushman, B. J.., & Whitaker, J. L. (2010). Like a magnet: Catharsis beliefs attract angry people to violent video games. *Psychological Science, 21*(6), 790–792.

Bushman, B. J., Baumeister, R. F., & Stack, A. D. (1999). Catharsis, aggression, and persuasive influence: Self-fulfilling or self-defeating prophecies? *Journal of Personality and Social Psychology, 76*(3), 367–376.

Bushman, B. J., & Cooper, H. M. (1990). Effects of alcohol on human aggression: An integrative research review. *Psychological Bulletin, 107*(3), 341–354.

Bushnik, T. (2006). Childcare in Canada. (Catalogue no. 89-599-MIE — No. 003). Retrieved from http://publications.gc.ca/Collection/Statcan/89-599-MIE/89-599-MIE2006003.pdf

Bushnik, T. (2003). Learning, earning and leaving: The relationship between working while in high school and dropping out. *Education, skills and learning - Research papers.* Statistics Canada Catalogue no. 81-595-MIE, No. 4.

Buss, D. M. (2009). The great struggles of life: Darwin and the emergence of evolutionary psychology. *American Psychologist, 64*(2), 140–148.

Buss, D. M. (Ed.). (2005). *The handbook of evolutionary psychology.* Hoboken, NJ: John Wiley & Sons.

Buss, D. M. (1999). Evolutionary psychology: The new science of the mind. Boston, MA: Allyn & Bacon.

Bussey, K., & Bandura, A. (1999). Social cognitive theory of gender development and differentiation. *Psychological Review, 106,* 676–713.

Butcher, J. N. (2011). *A beginner's guide to the MMPI-2 (3rd Ed.)* Washington, DC: American Psychological Association.

Butcher, J. N. (2010). Personality assessment from the nineteenth to the early twenty-first century: Past achievements and contemporary challenges. *Annual Review of Clinical Psychology, 6,* 1–20.

Butler, A. C., Chapman, J. E., Forman, E. M., & Beck, A. T. (2006). The empirical status of cognitive-behavioral therapy: a review of meta-analyses. *Clinical Psychological Review, 26* (1), 17–31.

Butler, C. (2011). Meditation and mindfulness may give your brain a boost. *The Washington Post, 134*(72).

Butler, J. L., & Baumeister, R. F. (1998). The trouble with friendly faces: Skilled performance with a supportive audience. *Journal of Personality and Social Psychology, 75*(5), 1213–1230.

Butler, Y. G. (2013). Bilingualism/Multilingualism and second language acquisition. In T. K. Bhatia & W. C. Ritchie (Eds.), *The Handbook of Bilingualism and Muilticulturalism.* Blackwell Handbooks in Linguistics, John Wiley and Sons.

Butterworth, B. (2010). Foundational numerical capacities and the origins of dyscalculia. *Trends in Cognitive Sciences, 14*(12), 534–541.

Butterworth, B., Varma, S., & Laurillard, D. (2011). Dyscalculia: from brain to education. *Science, 332*(6033), 1049–1053.

Byers, E. S., Purdon, C., & Clark, D. A. (1998). Sexual intrusive thoughts of college students. *Journal of Sex Research, 35,* 359–369.

Byrne, D. (1971). *The attraction paradigm.* New York, NY: Academic Press.

Byrne, D., Ervin, C., & Lamberth, J. (1970). Continuity between the experimental study of attraction and real-life computer dating. *Journal of Personality and Social Psychology, 16,* 157–165.

Cacioppo, J. T., & Berntson, G. G. (1994). Relationship between attitudes and evaluative space: A critical review, with emphasis on the separability

of positive and negative substrates. *Psychological Bulletin, 115*(3), 401–423.

Cahill, L., Prins, B., Weber, M., & McGaugh, J. L. (1994). Beta-adrenergic activation and memory for emotional events. *Nature, 371*(6499), 702–704.

Cahn, C. (2006). Obituary: Roland Kuhn, 1912–2005. *Neuropsychopharmacology, 31,* 1096.

Cain, D. J. (2007). What every therapist should know, be and do: Contributions from humanistic psychotherapies. *Journal of Contemporary Psychotherapy, 37*(1), 3–10.

Cain, N., Davidson, P., Dosen, A., Garcia-Ibañez, J., Giesow, V., Hillery, J., & Torr, J. (2010). An international perspective of mental health services for people with intellectual disability. In N. Bouras & G. Holt (Eds.), *Mental health services for adults with intellectual disability: Strategies and solutions* (pp. 37–53). New York: Psychology Press.

Calder, A. J., Beaver, J. D., Davis, M. H., van Ditzhuijzen, J., Keane, J., & Lawrence, A. D. (2007). Disgust sensitivity predicts the insula and pallidal response to pictures of disgusting foods. *The European Journal of Neuroscience, 25,* 3422–3428.

Caley, L., Syms, C., Robinson, L., Cederbaum, J., Henry, M. Shipkey, N. (2008). What human service professionals know and want to know about fetal alcohol syndrome. *Canadian Journal of Clinical Pharmacology, 15,* e117–e123.

Callaghan, B. L., Li, S., & Richardson, R. (2014). The elusive engram: what can infantile amnesia tell us about memory? *Trends in Neurosciences, 37*(1), 47–53.

Calogero, R. M., Tantleff-Dunn, S., and Thompson, J. K. (Eds.). (2011). *Self-objectification in women: Causes, consequences, and counteractions.* Washington, DC: American Psychological Association.

Cameron, H. A., & McKay, R. D. (2001). Adult neurogenesis produces a large pool of new granule cells in the dentate gyrus. *Journal of Comparative Neurology, 435,* 406–417.

Campbell, M. W., & de Waal, F. B. M. (2011). Ingroup-outgroup bias in contagious yawning by chimpanzees supports link to empathy. *PLoS ONE, 6*(4).

Campos, J. J., Campos, R. G., & Barrett, K. C. (1989). Emergent themes in the study of emotional development and emotion regulation. *Developmental Psychology, 25*(3), 394–402.

Canadian Automobile Association. (July, 2011). *Bad driving habits on the rise.* Retrieved from http://www.caa.ca/newsroom/newsroom-releases-details-e.cfm?newsItem=50&yearToShow=2011.

Canadian Council on Animal Care. (2012). *CCAC 2011 Animal Use Statistics.* Canadian Council on Animal Care, Ottawa, Ontario. Retrieved from www.ccac.ca/Documents/Publications/Statistics/CCAC_Animal_Use_Statistics_2011.pdf.

Canadian Council on Social Development. (2001). *A profile of Canadian families.* Retrieved from http://www.ccsd.ca/factsheets/family/families.pdf.

Canadian Education Statistics Council. (2007). *Education indicators in Canada: Report of the Pan-Canadian Education Indicators Program.* Catalogue no. 81-582-XPE. Retrieved from http://www.statcan.gc.ca/pub/81-582-x/81-582-x2007001-eng.htm.

Canadian Human Rights Commission. (2010). *Equal pay for work of equal value: Employers' guide.* Retrieved from http://www.chrc-ccdp.ca/publications/employers_responsibility-eng.aspx.

Canadian Institute for Health Information. (2008). *Hospital mental health services in Canada, 2005–2006.* Ottawa.

Canadian Institutes of Health Research, Natural Sciences and Engineering Research Council of Canada, Social Sciences and Humanities Research Council of Canada. (2010). *Tri-council policy statement: Ethical conduct for research involving humans.* Retrieved from http://www.pre.ethics.gc.ca/pdf/eng/tcps2/TCPS_2_FINAL_Web.pdf.

Canadian Mental Health Association. (2014a). *Youth and self-injury.* Retrieved from www.cmha.ca/.

Canadian Mental Health Association (2014b). Fast Facts about Mental Illness, accessed at www.cmha.ca/media/fast-facts-about-mental-illness.

Canadian Mental Health Association. (2005). *Physical and mental health equally important to Canadians.* Retrieved from http://www.cmha.ca/bins/content_page.asp?cid=6-20-21-386.

Canadian Psychological Association. (2000). *Canadian code of ethics for psychologists.* CPA, Ottawa.

Canadian Study of Health and Aging Working Group. (2000). The incidence of dementia in Canada. *Neurology, 55*(1), 66–73.

Canadian Wireless and Telecommunications Association. (2010). *New web site will help teach teens to practice safe texting.* Retrieved from http://cwta.ca/CWTASite/english/whatsnew_download/nov19_10.html.

Canavero, S. (2013). HEAVEN: The head anastomosis venture project outline for the first human head transplantation with spinal linkage (GEMINI). *Surgical Neurology International, 4*(2), 335–342.

Canivez, G. L., & Watkins, M. W. (2010). Exploratory and higher-order factor analyses of the Wechsler Adult Intelligence Scale-fourth edition (WAIS-IV) adolescent subsample. *School Psychology Quarterly, 25*(4), 223–235.

Cannon, W. B. (1932). *Effects of strong emotions.* Chicago: University of Chicago Press.

Cannon, W. B. (1927). The James-Lange theory of emotions: A critical examination and an alternative theory. *The American Journal of Psychology, 39*(1), 106–124.

Cappadocia, M. C., Desrocher, M., Pepler, D., & Schroeder, J. H. (2009). Contextualizing the neurobiology of conduct disorder in an emotion dysregulation framework. *Clinical Psychology Review, 29*(6), 506–518.

Cardemil, E. V., Moreno, O., & Sanchez, M. (2011). One size does not fit all: Cultural considerations in evidence-based practice for depression. In W. David, A. Rubin, & C. G. Beevers (Eds.), *Treatment of depression in adolescents and adults* (pp. 221–243). John Wiley and Sons.

Cardilla, K. (2008). Personality vulnerabilities, coping, and depression: A multimethod daily diary study of college students' coping with daily hassles. US: ProQuest Information & Learning). *Dissertation Abstracts International: Section B: The Sciences and Engineering, 69*(5), 3294.

Cardoso, R., Souza, E., & Camano, L. (2009). Meditation in health: Definition, operationalization, and technique. *Stress and quality of working life: The positive and the negative* (pp. 143–166). Charlotte, NC: Information Age Publishing.

Carels, R. A., Cacciapaglia, H. M., Rydin, S., Douglass, O. M., & Harper, J. (2006). Can social desirability interfere with success in a behavioral weight loss program? *Psychology & Health, 21*(1), 65–78.

Carey, J. C. (2003). Chromosomal disorders. In C. D. Rudolph & A. M. Rudolph (Eds.), *Rudolph's Pediatrics* (21st ed., pp. 731–741). New York: McGraw-Hill Medical Publishing Division.

Carlezon, W. A., Jr., & Thomas, M. J. (2009). Biological substrates of reward and aversion: A nucleus accumbens activity hypothesis. *Neuropharmacology, 56* (Suppl.1), 122–132.

Carlsmith, K. M., Wilson, T. D., & Gilbert, D. T. (2008). The paradoxical consequences of revenge. *Journal of Personality and Social Psychology, 95*(6), 1316.

Carlson, N. R. (2009). *Physiology of Behavior (10th Ed)*. New York: Pearson Education Inc.

Carlson, N. R. (2008). *Foundations of physiological psychology* (7th edition). Boston MA: Pearson.

Carlson, N. R. (2007). *Psychology: The science of behavior*. New Jersey, USA: Pearson Education.

Carpendale, J. I. M., & Lewis, C. (2010). The development of social understanding: A relational perspective. In W. F. Overton & R. M. Lerner (Eds.), *The handbook of life-span development*, vol. 1: *Cognition, biology, and methods* (pp. 584–627). Hoboken, NJ: John Wiley.

Carr, V. S. (2000). Stress effects of earthquakes. In G. Fink (Ed.), *Encyclopedia of stress, Vol. 2* (1–4). New York, NY: Academic Press.

Carré, J. M., Putnam, S. K., & McCormick, C. M. (2009). Testosterone responses to competition predict future aggressive behaviour at a cost to reward in men. *Psychoneuroendocrinology, 34*(4), 561–570.

Carretta, C. M., & Burgess, A. W. (2013). Symptom responses to a continuum of sexual trauma. *Violence and Victims, 28*(2), 248–258.

Carskadon, M. A. (Ed.). (2002). *Adolescent sleep patterns: Biological, social and psychological influences*. New York, NY: Cambridge University Press.

Carson, R. C., Butcher, J. N., & Mineka, S. (2000). *Abnormal psychology and modern life* (11th Edition). Boston: Allyn & Bacon.

Carter, C., & Belle-Isle, L. (2013). *Canada's new marijuana medical access program*. Canadian Drug Policy Coalition, Vancouver BC. Retrieved from http://drugpolicy.ca/2013/06/canadas-new-marijuana-medical-access-program/

Carter, C. S. (2014). Oxytocin pathways and the evolution of human behavior. *Annual Review of Psychology, 65*, 17–39.

Carter, C. S., Botvinick, M. M., & Cohen, J.D. (1999). The contribution of the anterior cingulate cortex to executive processes in cognition. *Nature Reviews Neuroscience, 10*, 49–57.

Cartwright, R. D. (2010). *The twenty-four hour mind: The role of sleep and dreaming in our emotional lives*. New York, NY: Oxford University Press.

Carver, C. S. (2004). Self-regulation of action and affect. In R. F. Baumeister & K. D. Vohs (Eds.), *Handbook of self-regulation: Research, theory, and applications* (pp. 13–39). New York, NY: Guilford Press.

Carver, C. S., & Scheier, M. (2003). Optimism. *Positive psychological assessment: A handbook of models and measures* (pp. 75–89). Washington, DC: American Psychological Association. doi:10.1037/ 10612-005.

Carver, C. S., & Scheier, M. (1999). Optimism. In C. R. Snyder (Ed.), *Coping: The psychology of what works*. New York, NY: Oxford University Press.

Carver, C. S., & Scheier, M. F. (1998). *On the self-regulation of behavior*. New York, NY: Cambridge University Press.

Carver, C. S., & Scheier, M. F. (1994). Situational coping and coping dispositions in a stressful transaction. *Journal of Personality and Social Psychology, 66*(1), 184–195.

Cashel, M. L. (2002). Child and adolescent psychological assessment: Current clinical practices and the impact of managed care. *Professional Psychology: Research and Practice, 33*(5), 446–453.

Caspi, A. (1998). Personality development across the life course. In W. Damon & N. Eisenberg (Eds.), *Handbook of child psychology: Vol. 3, Social emotional,

and personality development* (5th Ed., pp. 311–388). New York, NY: John Wiley & Sons, Inc.

Caspi, A. (2002). Social selection, social causation, and developmental pathways: Empirical strategies for better understanding how individuals and environments are linked across the life course. In L. Pulkkinen & A. Caspi (Eds.), *Paths to Successful Development: Personality in the Life Course* (pp. 281–301). Cambridge, UK: Cambridge University Press.

Caspi, A., Bem, D. J., & Elder, G. H., Jr. (1989). Continuities and consequence of interactional styles across the life course. *Journal of Personality, 57*, 375–406.

Caspi, A., & Roberts, B. W. (1999). Personality change and continuity across the life course. In L. A. Pervin & O. P. John, *Handbook of Personality Theory and Research* (Vol. 2, pp. 300–326). New York, NY: Guilford Press.

Castejon, J. L., Perez, A. M., & Gilar, R. (2010). Confirmatory factor analysis of project spectrum activities: A second-order g factor or multiple intelligences? *Intelligence, 38*(5), 481–496.

Catalyst. (2014). *Women CEOs of the Fortune 1000*. New York, NY: Catalyst.

Catrambone, R. (1998). The subgoal learning model: creating better examples so that students can solve novel problems. *Journal of Experimental Psychology: General, 127*, 355–376.

Cavallini, E., Pagnin, A., & Vecchi, T. (2003). Aging and everyday memory: The beneficial effect of memory training. *Archives of Gerontology and Geriatrics, 37*(3), 241–257.

Cavendish, M. (2010). *Sex and society*. Tarrytown, NY: Marshal Cavendish Reference.

Ceci, S. J. (1991). How much does schooling influence general intelligence and its cognitive components? A reassessment of the evidence. *Developmental Psychology, 27*(5), 703–722.

Ceci, S. J., & Kanaya, T. (2010). "Apples and oranges are both round": Furthering the discussion on the Flynn effect. *Journal of Psychoeducational Assessment, 28*(5), 441–447.

Ceci, S. J., & Liker, J. (1986). A day at the races: A study of IQ, expertise, and cognitive complexity. *Journal of Experimental Psychology, 115*, 255–266.

Ceci, S. J., & Williams, W. M. (2010). *The mathematics of sex: How biology and society conspire to limit talented women and girls*. New York: Oxford University Press.

Ceci, S. J., & Williams, W. M. (2007). Little g: Prospects and constraints. *European Journal of Personality, 21*(5), 716–718.

Ceci, S. J., & Williams, W. M. (1997). Schooling, intelligence, and income. *American Psychologist, 52*(10), 1051–1058.

Ceci, S. J., Fitneva, S. A., & Gilstrap, L. L. (2003). Memory development and eyewitness testimony. In A. Slater & G. Bremner (Eds.), *An introduction to developmental psychology* (pp. 283–310). Malden, MA: Blackwell Publishing.

Ceci, S. J., Loftus, E. F., Leichtman, M. D., & Bruck, M. (1994). The possible role of source misattributions in the creation of false beliefs among preschoolers. *International Journal of Clinical and Experimental Hypnosis, 42*(4), 304–320.

Cenci, M. A. (2007). Dopamine dysregulation of movement control in L-DOPA-induced dyskinesia. *Trends in Neurosciences, 30*, 236–243.

Centers for Disease Control and Prevention (CDC). 2010. Listeriosis (Listeria) and pregnancy. *Pregnancy*. Retrieved from http://www.cdc.gov/ncbdd/pregacy_gateway//infections-listeria.html.

Centers for Disease Control and Prevention (CDC). (2009). *Health, United States, 2008*, Table 75. Retrieved from: http://www.cdc.gov/nchs/data/hus/hus08.pdf#075.

Centers for Disease Control and Prevention (CDC). (2008). *Sexually transmitted disease surveillance, 2007*. Atlanta, GA: U.S. Department of Health and Human Services.

Centre for Addiction and Mental Health. (2004). *Canadian campus survey*. Retrieved from www.camh.net/Research/Areas_of_research/Population_Life_Course_Studies/canadian_campus0905.pdf.

Certner, B. C. (1973). Exchange of self-disclosures in same-sexed groups of strangers. *Journal of Consulting and Clinical Psychology, 40*, 292–297.

Chachamovich, E., Haggarty, J., Cargo, M., Hicks, J., Kirmayer, L. J., & Turecki, G. (2013). A psychological autopsy study of suicide among Inuit in Nunavut: methodological and ethical considerations, feasibility and acceptability. *International Journal of Circumpolar Health, 72*, 1–10.

Chadwick, M. J., Hassabis, D., Weiskopf, N., & Maguire, E. A. (2010). Decoding individual episodic memory traces in the human hippocampus. *Current Biology, 20*(6), 544–547.

Chaiken, S. (1980). Heuristic versus systematic information processing and the use of source versus message cues in persuasion. *Journal of Personality and Social Psychology, 39*, 752–756.

Chakravarthy, V. S., Joseph, D., & Bapi, R. S. (2010). What do the basal ganglia do? A modeling perspective. *Biological Cybernetics, 103*(3), 237–253.

Challis, G. B., & Stam, H. J. (1992). A longitudinal study of the development of anticipatory nausea and vomiting in cancer chemotherapy patients: The role of absorption and autonomic perception. *Health Psychology, 11*, 181–189.

Chan, A. C., & Au, T. K. (2011). Getting children to do more academic work: Foot-in-the-door versus door-in-the-face. *Teaching and Teacher Education, 27*(6), 982–985.

Chan, B. L., Witt, R., Charrow, A. P., Magee, A., Howard, R., Pasquina, P. (2007). Mirror therapy for phantom limb pain. *New England Journal of Medicine, 357*, 2206–2207.

Chan, S. M. (2010). Aggressive behavior in early elementary school children: Relations to authoritarian parenting, children's negative emotionality and coping strategies. *Early Child Development and Care, 180*(9), 1253–1269.

Chandler, M. J., & Carpendale, J. I. (1998). Inching toward a mature theory of mind. In M. D. Ferrari & R. J. Sternberg (Eds.), *Self-awareness: Its nature and development* (pp. 148–190). New York, NY: Guilford Press.

Chandler, M. J., & Lalonde, C. E. (2008). Cultural continuity as a moderator of suicide risk among Canada's first nations. In L. J. Kirmayer & G. G. Valaskakis (Eds.), *Healing traditions: The mental health of Aboriginal peoples in Canada*. Vancouver, BC: UBC Press.

Chandler, M. J., Lalonde, C. E., Sokol, B., & Hallett, D. (2003). Personal persistence, identity development, and suicide: A study of native and non-native North American adolescents. *Monographs of the Society for Research in Child Development, 68*(2), No. 273.

Chang, E. C. (2002). Optimism-pessimism and stress appraisal: Testing a cognitive interactive model of psychological adjustment in adults. *Cognitive Therapy and Research, 26*(5), 675–690.

Chang, R., Chang, E. C., Sanna, L. J., & Hatcher, R. L. (2008). Optimism and pessimism as personality variables linked to adjustment. *The SAGE handbook of personality theory and assessment, vol 1: Personality theories and models* (pp. 470–485). Thousand Oaks, CA: Sage Publications, Inc.

Changeux, J. (2011). The epigenetic variability of memory: Brain plasticity and artistic creation. In S. Nalbantian, P. M. Matthews, & J. L. McClelland (Eds.), *The memory process: Neuroscientific and humanistic perspectives* (pp. 55–72). Cambridge, MA: MIT Press.

Chansonneuve, D. (2007). Addictive behaviours among Aboriginal people in Canada. *The Aboriginal Healing Foundation*. Retrieved from http://www.ahf.ca/downloads/addictive-behaviours.pdf.

Charles, E. P., & Rivera, S. M. (2009). Object permanence and method of disappearance: Looking measures further contradict reaching measures. *Developmental Science, 12*(6), 991–1006.

Charuvastra, A., & Cloitre, M. (2008). Social bonds and posttraumatic stress disorder. In S. Fiske, D. L. Schacter, & R. Sternberg (Eds.), *Annual review of psychology (Vol. 59)*. Palo Alto, CA: Annual reviews.

Chaudhuri, A., & Bhattacharya, N. (2013). Human neural stem cell transplants in neurological disorders: Current trends and future options. In N. Bhattacharya & P. Stubblefield (Eds.), *Human Fetal Tissue Transplantation* (pp. 265–268). Springer-Verlag: London.

Chein, J. M., Moore, A. B., & Conway, A. R. A. (2011). Domain-general mechanisms of complex working memory span. *NeuroImage, 54*(1), 550–559. doi: 10.1016/j.neuroimage.2010.07.067

Chekroun, P., & Brauer, M. (2002). The bystander effect and social control behavior: The effect of the presence of others on people's reactions to norm violations. *European Journal of Social Psychology, 32*(6), 853–866.

Chelli, D., & Chanoufi, B. (2008). Fetal audition: Myth or reality? *Journal de gynecologie, obstetrique et biologie de la reproduction, 37*(6), 554–558.

Chen, X., Rubin, K. H., Cen, G., Hastings, P.D., Chen, H., and Stewart, S. (1999). In M. E. Hertzig and E.A. Farber (Eds.), *Progress in child psychiatry and child development 1999*. Taylor and Francis.

Cheng, H. L., Kwan, K. L. K., & Sevig, T. (2013). Racial and ethnic minority college students' stigma associated with seeking psychological help: Examining psychocultural correlates. *Journal of Counseling Psychology, 60*(1), 98.

Chengappa, K. R., & Gershon, S. (2013). Lithium in the Treatment of Bipolar Disorder. *Bipolar Disorder: A Clinician's Guide to Treatment Management, 139*.

Cherniss, C. (2010). Emotional intelligence: Toward clarification of a concept. *Industrial and Organizational Psychology: Perspectives on Science and Practice, 3*(2), 110–126.

Cherubini, L., & Hodson, J. (2012). Educators' perceptions of Aboriginal students' experiences: Implications of provincial policy in Ontario, Canada. *Indigenous Policy Journal, XXII*(3), 15.

Chess, S., & Thomas, A. (1996). *Temperament: Theory and practice*. New York: Brunner-Mazel.

Chessick, R. D. (2010). Returning to Freud. *Journal of the American Academy of Psychoanalysis & Dynamic Psychiatry, 38*(3), 413–440.

Cheung, A. (2007). *Education decisions of Canadian youth: A synthesis report on access to postsecondary education*. Prepared for The Higher Education Quality Council of Ontario. Retrieved from https://ospace.scholarsportal.info/bitstream/1873/9175/1/276409.pdf.

Cheung, B. Y., Chudek, M., & Heine, S. J. (2011). Evidence for a sensitive period for acculturation: Younger immigrants report acculturating at a faster rate. *Psychological Science, 22*(2), 147–152.

Chidambaram, L., & Tung, L. L. (2005). Is out of sight, out of mind? An empirical study of social loafing in technology-supported groups. *Information Systems Research, 16*(2), 149–168.

Childress, A. R., Ehrman, R. N., Wang, Z., Li, Y., Sciortino, N., Hakun, J., et al. (2008). Prelude to passion: Limbic activation by "unseen" drug and sexual cues. *PLoS ONE, 3*(1), e1506.

Chin, J. H., Ma, L., MacTavish, D., & Jhamandas, J. H. (2007). Amyloid beta protein modulates glutamate-mediated neurotransmission in the rat basal forebrain: Involvement of presynaptic neuronal nicotinic acetylcholine and metabotropic glutamate receptors. *Journal of Neuroscience, 27*(35), 9262–9269.

Chisholm, K., Carter, M. C., Ames, E. W., & Morison, S. J. (1995). Attachment security and indiscriminately friendly behavior in children adopted from Romanian orphanages. *Development and Psychopathology, 7*(2), 283–294.

Cho, E. A., & Oh, H. E. (2011). Effects of laughter therapy on depression, quality of life, resilience, and immune responses in breast cancer survivors. *Journal of Korean Academy of Nursing, 41*, 285–293.

Choi, Y. Y., Shamosh, N. A., Cho, S. H., DeYoung, C. G., Lee, M. J., Lee, J., et al. (2008). Multiple bases of human intelligence revealed by cortical thickness and neural activation. *Journal of Neuroscience, 28*(41), 10323–10329.

Choiniere, M., Dion, D., Peng, P., Banner, R., Barton, P. M., et. al. (2010). The Canadian STOP PAIN Project Part 1: Who are the patients on the waitlists of multidisciplinary pain treatment facilities? *Canadian Journal of Anesthesia, 57*(6), 539–548.

Chomsky, N. (2005). Editorial: Universals of human nature. *Psychotherapy and Psychosomatics, 74*(5), 263–268.

Chomsky, N. (1964). The development of grammar in child language: Formal discussion. *Monographs of the Society for Research in Child Development, 29*, 35–39.

Chong, L. D. (2014). Sleep Circuit. *Science, 344*(6182), 341–341.

Christakis, N. A., & Fowler, J. H. (2007). The spread of obesity in a large social network over 32 years. *New England Journal of Medicine, 357*, 370–379.

Christensen, A., Atkins, D. C., Baucom, B., & Yi, J. (2010). Marital status and satisfaction five years following a randomized clinical trial comparing traditional versus integrative behavioral couple therapy. *Journal of Consulting and Clinical Psychology, 78*(2), 225–235.

Christianson, S. A. (Ed.). (2014). *The handbook of emotion and memory: Research and theory*. New York, NY: Psychology Press.

Christman, S. D., & Propper, R. E. (2010). Episodic memory and interhemispheric interaction: Handedness and eye movements. In G. M. Davies, & D. B. Wright (Eds.), *Current issues in applied memory research* (pp. 185–205). New York: Psychology Press.

Christoff, K., Gordon, A. M., Smallwood, J., Smith, R., Schooler, J. W. (2009). Experience sampling during fMRI reveals default network and executive system contributions to mind wandering. *Proceedings of the National Academy of Sciences, 106*, 8719–8724.

Christophe, V., & Rimé, B. (2001). Exposure to the social sharing of emotion: Emotional impact, listener responses and secondary social sharing. In W. G. Parrott (Ed.), *Emotions in social psychology: Essential readings* (pp. 239–250). New York, NY: Psychology Press.

Christophe, V., & Rimé, B. (1997). Exposure to the social sharing of emotion: Emotional impact, listener responses and secondary social sharing. *European Journal of Social Psychology, 27*(1), 37–54.

Christou, N. V., Look, D., & Maclean, L. D. (2006). Weight gain after short- and long-limb gastric bypass in patients followed for longer than 10 years. *Annals of Surgery, 244*(5), 734–740.

Chudler, E. H. (2011). *Milestones in neuroscience research*. Retrieved from http://faculty.washington.edu/chudler/hist.html.

Chudley, A. E., Conry, J., Cook. J. L., Loock, C., Rosales, T., & LeBlanc, N. (2005). Fetal alcohol spectrum disorder: Canadian guidelines for diagnosis. *Canadian Medical Association Journal, 172*, S1–S21.

Chung, M. C., Dennis, I., Easthope, Y., Werrett, J., & Farmer, S. (2005). A multiple-indicator multiple-case model for posttraumatic stress reactions: Personality, coping, and maladjustment. *Psychosomatic Medicine, 67*(2), 251–259.

Church, A. T., & Katigbak, M. S. (2000). Trait psychology in the Philippines. *American Behavioral Scientist, 44*, 73–94.

Chwalisz, K., Diener, E., & Gallagher, D. (1988). Autonomic arousal feedback and emotional experience: Evidence from the spinal cord injured. *Journal of Personality and Social Psychology, 54*, 820–828.

Cialdini, R. B., Kallgren, C. A., & Reno, R. R. (1991). A focus theory of normative conduct: A theoretical refinement and reevaluation of the role of norms in human behavior. In M. P. Zanna (Ed.), *Advances in Experimental Social Psychology (Vol. 24)* (pp. 201–234). New York: Academic Press.

Cicchetti, D. (2012). Annual research review: Resilient functioning in maltreated children—past, present, and future perspectives. *Journal of Child Psychology & Psychiatry, 54*(4), 402–422.

Cicchetti, D. (2010). A developmental psychopathology perspective on bipolar disorder. In D. J. Miklowitz & D. Cicchetti (Eds.), *Understanding bipolar disorder: A developmental psychopathology perspective* (pp. 1–32). New York: Guilford Press.

Cipriani, A., Reid, K., Young, A. H., Macritchie, K., & Geddes, J. (2013). Valproate for keeping people with bipolar disorder well, after mood episodes. *Health*.

Cirelli, C., & Tononi, G. (2008). Is sleep essential? *PLOS Biology, 6*(8), e216. doi:10.1371/journal.pbio.0060216

Clark, D. A., & Beck, A. T. (2010). *Cognitive therapy of anxiety disorders: Science and practice.* New York: Guilford Press.

Clark, J. J. (2010). Life as a source of theory: Erik Erikson's contributions, boundaries, and marginalities. In T. W. Miller (Ed.), *Handbook of stressful transitions across the lifespan* (pp. 59–83). New York: Springer Science + Business Media.

Clark, L., & Watson, D. (1999). Temperament: A new paradigm for trait psychology. In L. A. Pervin & O. P. John (Eds.), *Handbook of Personality* (2nd Ed., pp. 399–423). New York, NY: Guilford Press.

Clark, R. E., Broadbent, N. J., & Squire, L. R. (2008). The hippocampus and spatial memory: Findings with a novel modification of the water maze. *Journal of Neuroscience, 27*(25), 6647–6654.

Clarkson, J. J., Tormala, Z. L., & Leone, C. (2011). A self-validation perspective on the mere thought effect. *Journal of Experimental Social Psychology, 47*, 449–454.

Clément, M-E., & Chamberland, C. (2007). Physical violence and psychological aggression towards children: Five-year trends in practices and attitudes from two population surveys. *Child Abuse and Neglect, 31*(9), 1001–1011.

Clement, S., Schauman, O., Graham, T., Maggioni, F., Evans-Lacko, S., Bezborodovs, N., . . . & Thornicroft, G. (2014). What is the impact of mental health-related stigma on help-seeking? A systematic review of quantitative and qualitative studies. *Psychological Medicine,* 1–17.

Clements, A. M., Rimrodt, S. L., Abel, J. R., Blankner, J. G., Mostofsky, S. H., Pekar, J. J., Denckla, M. B., & Cutting, L. E. (2006). Sex differences in cerebral laterality of language and visuospatial processing. *Brain Language, 98*, 150–158.

Clements, C. M., & Sawhney, D. K. (2000). Coping with domestic violence: Control attributions, dysphoria, and hopelessness. *Journal of Traumatic Stress, 13*, 219–240.

Cobb, M. D. (2002). Unobtrusively measuring racial attitudes: The consequences of social desirability effects. ProQuest Information & Learning: US. *Dissertation Abstracts International Section A: Humanities and Social Sciences, 62*(8), 2869.

Cochran, W. G., Mosteller, F., & Tukey, J. W. (1953). Some statistical problems of the Kinsey Report. *Journal of the American Statistical Association, 48*, 673–716.

Coddington, R. D. (1984). Measuring the stressfulness of a child's environment. In J. H. Humphrey (Ed.), *Stress in Childhood.* New York, NY: AMS Press.

Coddington, R. D. (1972). The significance of life events as etiologic factors in the disease of children, II: A study of a normal population. *Journal of Psychosomatic Research, 16*, 205–213.

Code, C., Hemsley, G., & Herrmann, M. (1999). The emotional impact of aphasia. *Seminars in Speech and Language, 20*(1), 19–31.

Coelho, M., & Ferreira, J. J. (2012). Late-stage Parkinson's disease. *Nature Reviews Neurology, 8*, 435–442.

Cohen, R. (1987). Suddenly, I'm the adult. *Psychology Today, 21* (May), 70–71.

Cohen, S. (2005). Psychological stress, immunity and upper respiratory infections. In G. Miller & E. Chen (Eds.), *Current directions in health psychology.* Upper Saddle River, NJ: Pearson.

Cohen, S. (2004). Social relationships and health. *American Psychologist, 59*(8), 676–684.

Cohen, S. (2002). Psychosocial stress, social networks, and susceptibility to infection. In H. G. Koenig & H. J. Cohen (Eds.), *The link between religion and health: Psychoneuroimmunology and the faith factor* (pp. 101–123). New York, NY: Oxford University Press.

Cohen, S., & Hamrick, N. (2003). Stable individual differences in physiological response to stressors: Implications for stress-elicited changes in immune related health. *Brain, Behavior, and Immunity, 17*(6), 407–414.

Cohen, S., & Janicki-Deverts, D. (2009). Can we improve our physical health by altering our social networks? *Perspectives on Psychological Science, 4*(4), 375–378.

Cohen, S., & Wills, T. A. (1985). Stress, social support, and the buffering hypothesis. *Psychological Bulletin, 98*(2), 310–357.

Cohen, S., Alper, C. M., Doyle, W. J., Adler, N., Treanor, J. J., & Turner, R. B. (2008). Objective and subjective socioeconomic status and susceptibility to the common cold. *Health Psychology, 27*(2), 268–274.

Cohen, S., Doyle, W. J., Turner, R. B., Alper, C. M., & Skoner, D. P. (2003). Emotional style and susceptibility to the common cold. *Psychosomatic Medicine, 65*, 652–657.

Cohen, S., Tyrell, D. A. J., & Smith, A. P. (1991). Psychological stress and susceptibility to the common cold. *The New England Journal of Medicine, 325*, 606–612.

Cohn, J. F., Ambadar, Z., & Ekman, P. (2007). Observer-based measurement of facial expression with the facial action coding system. In J. A. Coan & J. J. B. Allen (Eds.), *Handbook of emotion elicitation and assessment* (pp. 203–221). New York, NY: Oxford University Press.

Cole, M., Gay, J., & Glick, J. (1967). A cross-cultural study of clustering in free recall. *Psychonomic Bulletin, 1*(2), 18.

College of Ontario Psychologists. (2010). *Member search.* Retrieved from https://members.cpo.on.ca/members_search/new.

Collignon, O., Vandewalle, G., Voss, P., Albouy, G., Charbonneau, G., et al. (2011). Functional specialization for auditory-spatial processing in the occipital cortex of congenitally blind humans. *PNAS Proceedings of the National Academy of Sciences of the United States of America, 108*, 4435–4440.

Collinger, J. L., Wodlinger, B., Downey, J. E., Wang, W., Tyler-Kabara, E. C., Weber, D. J., . . . Schwartz, A. B. (2012). High-performance neuroprosthetic control by an individual with tetraplegia. *The Lancet, 381*, 557–564.

Collins, A. (2002). *In the Sleep Room: The Story of CIA Brainwashing Experiments in Canada.* Toronto: Key Porter Books.

Collins, R. L. (2005). Sex on television and its impact on American youth: Background and results from the RAND television and adolescent sexuality study. *Child and Adolescent Psychiatric Clinics of North America, 14*(3), 371–385.

Colom, R., Burgaleta, M., Román, F. J., Karama, S., Álvarez-Linera, J., Abad, F. J., Martínez, K., Quiroga, M. Á., & Haier, R. J. (2013). Neuroanatomic overlap between intelligence and cognitive factors: Morphometry methods provide support for the key role of the frontal lobes. *NeuroImage, 72*(15), 143–152.

Colson, S. D., Meek, J. H., & Hawdon, J. M. (2008). Optimal positions for the release of primitive neonatal reflexes stimulating breastfeeding. *Early Human Development, 84*(7), 441–449.

Columbo, J., & Mitchell, D. W. (2009). Infant visual habituation. *Neurobiology of Learning and Memory, 92*(2), 225–234.

Colvin, M. K., & Gazzaniga, M. S. (2007). Split-brain cases. In S. Schneider & M. Velman (Eds.), *The Blackwell companion to consciousness* (pp. 181–193). Malden, MA: Blackwell Publishing.

Comas-Diaz, L. (2011). Multicultural psychotherapies. In R. J. Corsini & D. Wedding (Eds.), *Current psychotherapies* (9th Ed.). Florence, KY: CENGAGE Learning.

Comas-Diaz, L. (2006). Cultural variation in the therapeutic relationship. In C. D. Goodheart, A. E. Kazdin, & R. J. Sternberg (Eds.), *Evidence-based psychotherapy: Where practice and research meet* (pp. 81–105). Washington, DC: American Psychological Association.

Comer, R. J. (2010). *Abnormal Psychology.* New York: Worth.

Compas, B. E. (2004). Processes of risk and resilience during adolescence: Linking contexts and individuals. In R. M. Lerner & L. Steinberg (Eds.), *Handbook of adolescent psychology (2nd Ed.)* (pp. 263–296). Hoboken, NJ: John Wiley & Sons Inc.

Compton, W. C., & Hoffman, E. (2013). *Positive psychology: The science of happiness and flourishing* (2nd ed.) Belmont: CA: Cengage Learning/Wadsworth.

Confer, J. C., Easton, J. A., Fleischman, D. S., Goetz, C. D., Lewis, D. M. G., Perilloux, C., & Buss, D. M. (2010). Evolutionary psychology: Controversies, questions, prospects, and limitations. *American Psychologist, 65*(2), 110–126.

Connolly, K. (2007). Brother and sister fight Germany's incest laws. *The Guardian,* Tuesday, February 27, 2007.

Connolly, T., & Zeelenberg, M. (2002). Regret in decision making. *Current Directions in Psychological Science, 11*, 212–216.

Connor-Greene, P. A. (2007). Observation or interpretation: Demonstrating unintentional subjectivity and interpretive variance. *Teaching of Psychology, 34*(3), 167–171.

Conrad. R., & Hull, A. J. (November 1964). Information, acoustic confusion and memory span (PDF). *British Journal of Psychology, 55*, 429–432.

Conyne, R. K., & Harpine, E. C. (2010). Prevention groups: The shape of things to come. *Group Dynamics: Theory, Research, and Practice, 14*(3), 193.

Cooney, N. L., Kadden, R. M., Litt, M. D., & Getter, H. (1991). Matching alcoholics to coping skills or interactional therapies: Two-year follow-up results. *Journal of Consulting and Clinical Psychology, 59*(4), 598–601.

Cooper, J. (2007). *Cognitive Dissonance: Fifty Years of a Classic Theory.* Thousand Oaks, CA: Sage.

Cooper, J., Kelly, K. A., & Weaver, K. (2004). Attitudes, norms, and social groups. In M. B. Brewer & M. Hewstone (Eds.), *Social Cognition* (pp. 244–267). Malden, MA: Blackwell Publishing.

Cooper, J., Mirabile, R., & Scher, S. J. (2005). Actions and attitudes: The theory of cognitive dissonance. In T. C. Brock & M. C. Green (Eds.), *Persuasion: Psychological Insights and Perspectives, 2nd Ed* (pp. 63–79). Thousand Oaks, CA: Sage Publications.

Cooper, M. L., & Sheldon, M. S. (2002). Seventy years of research on personality and close relationships: Substantive and methodological trends over time. *Journal of Personality, 70*, 783–812.

Coplan, R. J., Bowker, A., & Cooper, S. M. (2003). Parenting daily hassles, child temperament, and social adjustment in preschool. *Early Childhood Research Quarterly, 18*, 376–395.

Corballis, M. C. (1999). Are we in our right minds? In S. Della Sala (Ed.), *Mind myths: Exploring popular assumptions about the mind and brain* (pp. 25-42).

Corkin, S. (1984). Lasting consequences of bilateral medial temporal lobectomy: Clinical course and experimental findings. *Seminars in Neuroscience, 4*, 249–259.

Corbetta, M., & Shulman, G. L. (2002). Control of goal-directed and stimulus-driven attention in the brain. *Nature Reviews Neuroscience, 3*, 215–229.

Corbetta, M., Kincade, M. J., Lewis, C., Snyder, A. Z., & Sapir, A. (2005). Neural basis and recovery of spatial attentional deficits in spatial neglect. *Nature Neuroscience, 8*, 1424–1425.

Coren, S. (2010a). *Born to bark: My adventures with an irrepressible and unforgettable dog.* New York: Free Press.

Coren, S. (2010b). *Dogs all-in-one for dummies.* New Jersey: Wiley & Sons.

Coren, S. (2008a). *The Modern Dog.* New York: Free Press.

Coren, S. (2008b). *Why do dogs have wet noses?* Kids Can Press.

Coren, S. (2006a). *Why does my dog act that way? A complete guide to your dog's personality.* New York: Free Press.

Coren, S. (2006b). *The Intelligence of Dogs.* New York: Free Press.

Coren, S. (2003). *The pawprints of history: Dogs and the course of human events.* New York: Free Press.

Coren, S. (1998). *Why We Love The Dogs We Do.* New York: Free Press.

Coren, S. (1997). *What Do Dogs Know?* New York: Free Press.

Coren, S. (1996). *Sleep thieves: An eye-opening exploration into the science and mysteries of sleep.* New York: Free Press.

Coren, S. (1993). *The left-hander syndrome: The causes and consequences of left-handedness.* Vintage Books.

Coren, S., Ward, L. M., & Enns, J. T. (2004). *Sensation and perception* (6th Ed.). New Jersey: John Wiley & Sons.

Corina, D. (1998) Aphasia in users of signed languages. In P. Coppens, Y. Lebrun, & A. Basso (Eds.), *Aphasia in atypical populations.* Mahwah, NJ: Lawrence Erlbaum Associates.

Cornoldi, C. (2010). Metacognition, intelligence, and academic performance. In H. S. Waters & W. Schneider (Eds.), *Metacognition, strategy use, and instruction* (pp. 257–277). New York: Guilford Press.

Cornwell, B., & Laumann, E. O. (2013). The health benefits of network growth: New evidence from a national survey of older adults. *Social Science & Medicine, 125,* 94–106.

Correa, A. A., & Rogers, R. (2010). Cross-cultural applications of the PAI. In M. A. Blais, M. R. Baity, & C. J. Hopwood (Eds.), *Clinical applications of the personality assessment inventory* (pp. 135–148). New York: Routledge/Taylor & Francis Group.

Corrigan, P. W. (2007). How clinical diagnosis might exacerbate the stigma of mental illness. *Social Work, 52*(1), 31–39.

Corrigan, P. W. (1991). Social skills training in adult psychiatric populations: A meta-analysis. *Journal of Behavior Therapy and Experimental Psychiatry, 22*(3), 203–210.

Corsini, R. J., & Wedding, D. (Eds.). (2011). *Current psychotherapies* (9th Ed.). Florence, KY: CENGAGE Learning.

Cosgrove, L., & Krimsky, S. (2012). A comparison of DSM-IV and DSM-5 panel members' financial associations with industry: A pernicious problem persists. *PLoS Medicine, 9*(3), e1001190.

Cosmides, L., & Tooby, J. (2000). Evolutionary psychology and the emotions. In M. Lewis & J. M. Haviland-Jones (Eds.), *Handbook of Emotions, Second Edition* (pp. 91–115). New York, NY: The Guilford Press.

Costa, P. T., Jr., Terracciano, A., & McCrae, R. R. (2001). Gender differences in personality traits across cultures: Robust and surprising findings. *Journal of Personality and Social Psychology, 81,* 322–331.

Costa-Mattioli, M., Sossin, W. S., Klann, E., & Sonenberg, N. (2009). Translational control of long-lasting synaptic plasticity and memory. *Neuron, 61,* 10–26.

Costello, C. G. (1993). *Symptoms of schizophrenia.* John Wiley and Sons, Inc.

Côté, J. E., Borge, A. I., Geoffroy, M.-C., Rutter, M., & Tremblay, R. E. (2008). Nonmaternal care in infancy and emotional/behavioral difficulties at 4 years old: Moderation by family risk characteristics. *Developmental Psychology, 44,* 155–168.

Cote, S., & Hideg, I. (2011). The ability to influence others via emotion displays: A new dimension of emotional intelligence. *Organizational Psychology, 1*(1) 53–71.

Cottone, E., & Byrd-Bredbenner, C. (2007). Knowledge and Psychosocial effects of the film Super Size Me on young adults. *Journal of the American Dental Association, 107*(7), 1197–1203.

Cousins, S. D. (1989). Culture and selfhood in Japan and the U.S. *Journal of Personality and Social Psychology, 56,* 124–131.

Cousteau, J. Y., & Diole, P. (1973). *Octopus and squid: The soft intelligence.* London: Cassell.

Covington, M. A., He, C., Brown, C., Naçi, L., McClain, J. T., Fjordbak, B. S., Semple, J., & Brown, J. (2005). Schizophrenia and the Structure of language: the linguist's view. *Schizophrenia Research, 77,* 85–98.

Covino, N. A., & Pinnell, C. M. (2010). Hypnosis and medicine. In S. J. Lynn, J. W. Rhue, & I. Kirsch (Eds.), *Handbook of clinical hypnosis (2nd Ed.)* (pp. 551–573). Washington, DC: American Psychological Association.

Cowan, M. J., Freedland, K. E., Burg, M. M., Saab, P. G., Youngblood, M. E., Cornell, C. E., . . . & Czajkowski, S. M. (2007). Predictors of treatment response for depression and inadequate social support—The ENRICHD randomized clinical trial. *Psychotherapy and Psychosomatics, 77*(1), 27–37.

Cowan, N., & Chen, Z. (2009). How chunks form in long-term memory and affect short-term memory limits. In A. S. C. Thorn & M. P. A. Page (Eds.),

Interactions between short-term and long-term memory in the verbal domain (pp. 86–107). New York, NY: Psychology Press.

Cowansage, K. K., LeDoux, J. E., & Monfils, M-H. (2010). Brain derived neurotropic factor: A dynamic gatekeeper of neural plasticity. *Current Molecular Pharmacology, 3*(1), 12–29.

Cowen, P. J., & Lucki, I. (2011). Serotonin revisited. *Psychopharmacology, 213,* 167–169.

Cowley, E. (2005). Views from consumers next in line: The fundamental attribution error in a service setting. *Journal of the Academy of Marketing Science, 33*(2), 139–152.

Cox, P. D., Vinogradov, S., & Yalom, I. D. (2008). Group therapy. In R. E. Hales, S. C. Yudofsky, & G. O. Gabbard (Eds.), *The American psychiatric publishing textbook of psychiatry* (5th Ed., pp. 1329–1373). Arlington: American Psychiatric Publishing.

Coy, T. V. (1998). The effect of repressive coping style on cardiovascular reactivity and speech disturbances during stress. US: ProQuest Information & Learning. *Dissertation Abstracts International: Section B: The Sciences and Engineering, 58*(8), 4512.

Craig, K. J., & Chamberlain, S. R. (2010). The neuropsychology of anxiety disorders. In D. J. Stein, E. Hollander, & B. O. Rothbaum (Eds.), *Textbook of anxiety disorders* (2nd Ed., pp. 87–102). Arlington, VA: American Psychiatric Publishing.

Craig, L. A., Hong, N. S., & McDonald, R. J. (2011). Revisiting the cholinergic hypothesis in the development of Alzheimer's disease. *Neuroscience & Biobehavioral Reviews, 35*(6), 1397–1409.

Craig, T., & Power, P. (2010). Inpatient provision in early psychosis. In P. French, J. Smith, D. Shiers, M. Reed, & M. Rayne (Eds.), *Promoting recovery in early psychosis: A practice manual* (pp. 17–26). Hoboken, NJ: Wiley-Blackwell.

Craik, F. I. M., & Lockhart, R. S. (1972). Levels of processing: A framework for memory research. *Journal of Verbal Learning & Verbal Behavior, 11*(6), 671–684.

Craik, F. I. M., & Salthouse, T. A. (Eds.). (2011). *The Handbook of Aging and Cognition.* New York, NY: Psychology Press.

Craik, F. I. M., Routh, D. A., & Broadbent, D. E. (1983). On the transfer of information from temporary to permanent memory [and discussion]. *Philosophical Transactions of the Royal Society of London. B, Biological Sciences, 302*(1110), 341–359.

Cramer, P. (2006). *Protecting the self: Defense mechanisms in action.* New York: Guilford Press.

Cramer, P. (2001). The unconscious status of defense mechanisms. *American Psychologist, 56,* 762–763.

Cramer, R. J., Golom, F. D., LoPresto, C. T., & Kirkley, S. M. (2008). Weighing the evidence: Empirical assessment and ethical implications of conversion therapy. *Ethics & Behavior, 18*(1), 93–114.

Cramond, B., Kim, K. H., & VanTassel-Baska, J. (2010). The relationship between creativity and intelligence. In J. C. Kaufman & R. J. Sternberg (Eds.), *The Cambridge handbook of creativity* (pp. 395–412). New York: Cambridge University Press.

Crandall, C. S., Preisler, J. J., & Aussprung, J. (1992). Measuring life event stress in the lives of college students: The Undergraduate Stress Questionnaire (USQ). *Journal of Behavioral Medicine, 15,* 627–662.

Crandall, J. E. (1980). Adler's concept of social interest: Theory, measurement, and implications for adjustment. *Journal of Personality and Social Psychology, 39*(3), 481–495.

Craske, M. G. (2010). Evaluation. In *Cognitive–behavioral therapy* (pp. 115–126). Washington, DC: American Psychological Association.

Crawford, C. (2002). *Learning disabilities in Canada: Economic costs to individuals, families and society.* Ottawa: Learning Disabilities Association of Canada.

Creed, F. (2009). Somatization and pain syndromes. In E. A. Mayer & M. C. Bushnell (Eds.), *Functional pain syndromes: Presentation and pathophysiology* (pp. 227–244). Seattle, WA: IASP Press.

Cremonini, F., Camilleri, M., et al. (2009). Associations among binge eating behaviour patterns and gastrointestinal symptoms: A population-based study. *International Journal of Obesity, 33,* 342–353.

Crisp, M. (2001, April 8). Sticks and stones: "New Kid" puts comic spin on a serious situation. *Sunday News* (Lancaster, PA), p. H-1.

Crisp, S. (2010). How much sleep do children need? *NetDoctor.* London, England: Hearst Digital Network.

Crowley, S. J., Acebo, C., & Carskadon, M. A. (2007). Sleep, circadian rhythms, and delayed phase in adolescence. *Sleep Medicine, 8,* 602–612.

Csikszentmihalyi, M. (2003). *Good business: Leadership, flow, and the making of meaning.* New York, NY: Penguin Books.

Csikszentmihalyi, M. (1998). *Finding flow: The psychology of engagement with everyday life.* Basic Books.

Cuijpers, P., van Straten, A., Hollon, S. D., & Andersson, G. (2010). The contribution of active medication to combined treatments of psychotherapy and pharmacotherapy for adult depression: A metaanalysis. *Acta Psychiatrica Scandinavica, 121*(6), 415–423.

Cukan, A. (2001, March 8). *Confronting a culture of cruelty*. General feature release. United Press International.

Cummins, R. A., Nistico, H. (2002). Maintaining life satisfaction: The role of positive cognitive bias. *Journal of Happiness Studies, 3*, 37–69.

Cuninkova, L., & Brown, S. A. (2008). Peripheral circadian oscillators: Interesting mechanisms and powerful tools. *Molecular and biophysical mechanisms of arousal, alertness, and attention* (pp. 358–370). Malden, MA: Blackwell Publishing.

Cunningham, W. A., Arbuckle, N. L., Jahn, A., Mowrer, S. M., & Abduljalil, A. M. (2010). Aspects of neuroticism and the amygdala: Chronic tuning from motivational styles. *Neuropsycholgia, 48*(2010), 3399–3404.

Curcio, C. A., Sloan, K. R., Kalina, R. E., & Hendrickson, A. E. (1990). Human photoreceptor topography. *Journal of Comparative Neurology, 292*(4), 497–523.

Curtis, D. A., & Desforges, D. M. (2013). Less is More: The Level of Choice Affects Conformity. *North American Journal of Psychology, 15*(1), 89–102.

Curtis, R., Groarke, A. M., Coughlan, R., & Gsel, A. (2004). The influence of disease severity, perceived stress, social support and coping in patients with chronic illness: A 1-year follow-up. *Psychology, Health, and Medicine, 9*(4), 456–475.

Curzi-Dascalova, L., & Challamel, M. J. (2000). Neurophysiological basis of sleep development. In G. M. Loughlin, J. L. Carroll, & C. L. Marcus (Eds.), *Sleep and breathing in children: A developmental approach* (pp. 3–37). New York, NY: Marcel Dekker.

Cynkar, A. (2007, June). The changing gender composition of psychology. *Monitor on Psychology, 38*(6), 46.

Cytowic, R. E., & Eagleman, D. M. (2009). *Wednesday is Indigo Blue: Discovering the Brain of Synesthesia* (with an afterword by Dmitri Nabokov). Cambridge: MIT Press.

Czigler I., & Winkler I. (Eds.). (2010). *Unconscious memory representations in perception*. Amsterdam, Netherlands: John Benjamins Publishing Company.

D'angelo, B., & Wierzbicki, M. (2003). Relations of daily hassles with both anxious and depressed mood in students. *Psychological Reports, 92*(2), 416–418.

Dabbs Jr., J. M., Bernieri, F. J., Strong, R. K., Campo, R., & Milun, R. (2001). Going on stage: Testosterone in greetings and meetings. *Journal of Research of Personality, 35*(1), 27–40.

Dabbs, Jr., J. M., & Hargrove, M. (1997). Age, testosterone, and behavior among female prison inmates. *Psychosomatic Medicine, 59*, 477–80.

Daggett, L. M. (2002). Living with loss: Middle-aged men face spousal bereavement. *Qualitative Health Research, 12*(5), 625–639.

Daitch, C. (2011). *Anxiety disorders: The go-to guide for clients and therapists*. New York: W. W. Norton.

Dakin, R., & Montgomerie, R. (2011). In press. Peahens prefer peacocks displaying more eyespots, but rarely. *Animal Behaviour*, 1–8.

Dalton, P. (2000). Psychophysical and behavioral characteristics of olfactory adaptation. *Chemical Senses, 25*, 487–92.

Daly, A., Doherty, D. T., & Walsh, D. (2010). Reducing the revolving door phenomenon. *Irish Journal of Psychological Medicine, 27*(1), 27–34.

Daly, M., & Wilson, M. (1988). Evolutionary social psychology and family homicide. *Science, 242*, 519–524.

Damasio, A. (2010). *Self comes to mind: Constructing the conscious brain*. New York: Pantheon.

Damasio, A. R., & Geschwind, N. (1984). The neural basis of language. *Annual Review of Neuroscience, 7*, 127–147.

Damasio, H., Tranel, D., Grabowski, T., Adolphs, R., & Damasio, A. (2004). Neural systems behind word and concept retrieval. *Cognition, 92*, 179–229.

Damsa, C., Kosel, M., & Moussally, J. (2009). Current status of brain imaging in anxiety disorders. *Current Opinion in Psychiatry, 22*(1), 96–110.

Danovi, S. A. (2010). Circadian rhythms: In the heat of the night. *Nature Reviews Neuroscience, 11*(12), 788.

Dansinger, M. L., Gleason, J. A., Griffith, J. L., Selker, H. P., & Schaefer, E. J. (2005). Comparison of the Atkins, Ornish, Weight Watchers, and Zone diets for weight loss and heart disease risk reduction: A randomized trial. *Journal of the American Medical Association, 293*(1), 43–53.

Darley, J. M. (2000). Bystander phenomenon. In A. E. Kazdin (Ed.), *Encyclopedia of Psychology, vol. 1* (pp. 493–495). Washington, D.C.: American Psychological Association.

Darley, J. M., & Latane, B. (1968). Bystander intervention in emergencies: Diffusion of responsibility. *Journal of Personality and Social Psychology, 8*, 377–383.

Darwin, C. R. (1872). The Origin of the Species. *Nature* (6th ed), *5*(121), 318.

Darwin, C. R. (1859). *The Origin of the Species*. Retrieved from http://darwin-online.org.uk/pdf/1859_origin_PC_Virginia-Francis-F373.pdf.

Darwin, C. R. (1859). On the Origin of Species by Means of Natural Selection, or the Preservation of Favoured Races in the Struggle for Life. *Nature, 5*(121), 502.

Davey, G. (2011). *Introduction to applied psychology*. Hoboken, NJ: Wiley-Blackwell.

Davidson, R. J. (1998). Affective style and affective disorders: Perspectives from affective neuroscience. *Cognition and Emotion, 12*, 307–330.

Davidson, R. J., & Fox, N. A. (1989). Frontal brain asymmetry predicts infants' response to maternal separation. *Journal of Abnormal Psychology, 98*, 127–131.

Davidson, R. J., Jackson, D. C., & Kalin, N. H. (2000). Emotion, plasticity, context, and regulation: Perspectives from affective neuroscience. *Psychological Bulletin, 126*, 890–909.

Davies, I. R., & Corbett, G. G. (1997). A cross-cultural study of colour grouping: Evidence for weak linguistic relativity. *British Journal of Psychology, 88*, 493–517.

Davis, J. N. (1997). Birth order, sibship size, and status in modern Canada. *Human Nature, 8*(3), 205–230.

Davis, M. (1992). Analysis of aversive memories using the fear potentiated startle paradigm. In N. Butters & L. R. Squire (Eds.), *The neuropsychology of memory* (2nd Ed.). New York, NY: Guilford Press.

Davis, M., Ressler, K., Rothbaum, B. O., & Richardson, R. (2006). Effects of D-cycloserine on extinction: Translation from preclinical to clinical work. *Biological Psychiatry, 60*, 369–375.

Davison, G. C., Blankstein, K. R., Flett, G. L., & Neale, J. M. (2014). *Abnormal Psychology* (5th Canadian Ed.). Etobicoke, Ontario: John Wiley and Sons Canada, Ltd.

Davison, G., Blankstein, J. K., Flett, G., & Neale, J. (2010). *Abnormal Psychology* (4th Cdn. Ed.). Mississauga, ON: Wiley.

Davoli, T., Denchi, E. L., & de Lange, T. (2010). Perisitent telomere damage induces bypass of mitosis and etraploidy. *Cell, 141*, 81–93.

Day, D. M., Peterson-Badali, M., & Ruck, M. D. (2006). The relationship between maternal attitudes and young people's attitudes toward children's rights. *Journal of Adolescence, 29*(2), 193–207.

De Araujo, I. E. T., Rolls, E. T., Kringelbach, M. L., McGlone, F., & Phillips, N. (2005). Taste-olfactory convergence, and the representation of pleasantness of flavour, in the human brain. *European Journal of Neuroscience, 18*, 2059–2068.

de Haan, A. D., Prinzie, P., & Deković, M. (2010). How and why children change in aggression and delinquency from childhood to adolescence: Moderation of overreactive parenting by child personality. *Journal of Child Psychology and Psychiatry, 51*(6), 725–733.

De Leo, D., & San Too, L. (2014). Suicide and depression. *Essentials of Global Mental Health*, 367–398.

De Manzano, Ö., Cervenka, S., Karabanov, A., Farde, L., & Ullen, F. (2010). Thinking outside a less intact box: thalamic dopamine D2 receptor densities are negatively related to psychometric creativity in healthy individuals. *PLoS One, 5*(5), e10670.

De Raad, B., Perugini, M., Hrebickova, M., & Szarota, P. (1998). Lingua franca of personality: Taxonomies and structures based on the psycholexical approach. *Journal of Cross-Cultural Psychology, 29*, 212–232.

de Villers-Sidani, E., Chang, E. F., Bao, S., & Merzenich, M. M. (2007). Critical Period Window for Spectral Tuning Defined in the Primary Auditory Cortex (A1) in the Rat. *The Journal of Neuroscience, 27*, 180–189.

De Vries, R. (1969). Constancy of genetic identity in the years three to six. *Monograph of the Society for Research in Child Development, 34* (Serial No. 127).

Deary, I. J., & Stough, C. (1996). Intelligence and inspection time: Achievements, prospects, and problems. *American Psychologist, 51*(6), 599–608.

Deary, I. J., Whiteman, M. C., Starr, J. M., Fox, H. C., & Whalley, L. J. (2004). The impact of childhood intelligence on later life: Following up the Scottish mental surveys of 1932 and 1947. *Journal of Personality and Social Psychology, 86*(1), 130–147.

Debiec, J., LeDoux, J. E., & Nader, K. (2002). Cellular and systems reconsolidation in the hippocampus. *Neuron, 36*, 527–538.

DeCasper, A. J., & Spence, M. J. (1986). Prenatal maternal speech influences newborns' perception of speech sounds. *Infant Behavior and Development, 9*, 133–150.

Del Bigio, M. R. (1995). The ependyma: A protective barrier between brain and cerebrospinal fluid, *Glia, 14*(1), 1–13.

Del Giudice, M., Manera, V., & Keysers, C. (2009). Programmed to learn? The ontogeny of mirror neurons. *Developmental Science, 12*(2), 350–363.

Del Vecchio, V. (2014). Following the development of ICD-11 through World Psychiatry (and other sources). *World Psychiatry, 13*(1), 102–104.

dela Cruz, A. M. (2010). Alberta Aboriginal Head Start in urban and northern communities: longitudinal study pilot phase. *Chronic Diseases in Canada, 30*(2). Retrieved from http://www.phac-aspc.gc.ca/publicat/cdic-mcbc/30-2/ar_01-eng.php.

Delahanty, D. L., Nugent, N. R., Christopher, N. C., & Walsh, M. (2005). Initial urinary epinephrine and cortisol levels predict acute PTSD symptoms in child trauma victims. *Psychoneuroendocrinology, 30*(2), 121–128.

DeLamater, J., & Karraker, A. (2009). Sexual functioning in older adults. *Current Psychiatry Reports, 11*(1), 6–11.

Delaney, P. F., Sahakyan, L., Kelley, C. M., & Zimmerman, C. A. (2010). Remembering to forget: The amnesic effect of daydreaming. *Psychological Science, 21*(7), 1036–1042.

Demaree, H. A., Burns, K. J., & DeDonno, M. A. (2010). Intelligence, but not emotional intelligence, predicts Iowa gambling task performance. *Intelligence, 38*(2), 249–254.

Demause, L. (2007). Why males are more violent. *The Journal of Psychohistory, 35*(1), 23–33.

Dement, W. C., & Vaughan, C. (1999). *The promise of sleep: A pioneer in sleep medicine explores the vital connection between health, happiness, and a good night's sleep.* New York, NY: Dell.

Demo, D. H., Allen, K. R., & Fine, M. A. (Eds.). (2000). *Handbook of family diversity.* New York, NY: Oxford University Press.

Denes, G., & Pizzamiglio, L. (1999). *Handbook of clinical and experimental neuropsychology.* Southwick, W. Sussex, UK: The Psychology Press.

DeNeve, K. M. (1999). Happy as an extraverted clam? The role of personality for subjective well-being. *Current Directions in Psychological Science, 8*(5), 141–144.

Denmark, F. L., Krauss, H. H., Wesner, R. W., Midlarsky, E., & Gielen, U. (2005). *Violence in schools: Cross national and cross-cultural perspectives.* New York, NY: Springer Science & Business Media.

Dennis, A. B., & Pryor, T. (2014). Introduction to substance use disorders for the eating disorder specialist. In *Eating disorders, addictions and substance use disorders* (pp. 227–266). Heidelberg, Berlin: Springer.

Denver, J. Y., Lane, S. M., & Cherry, K. E. (2010). Recent versus remote: Flashbulb memory for 9/11 and self-selected events from the reminiscence bump. *The International Journal of Aging & Human Development, 70*(4), 275–297. doi: 10.2190/AG.70.4.a

Department of Health and Human Services and U.S. Department of Agriculture, 2005.

Department of Justice. (2007). *Methamphetamine report for federal-provincial-territorial ministers responsible for justice.* Retrieved from http://www.justice.gc.ca/eng/dept-min/pub/meth/sum-som.html#executive.

DePaulo, B. M., Blank, A. L., Swaim, G. W., & Hairfield, J. G. (1992). Expressiveness and expressive control. *Personality and Social Psychology Bulletin, 18,* 276–285.

Derntl, B., Schöpf, V., Kollndorfer, K., & Lanzenberger, R. (2013). Menstrual cycle phase and duration of oral contraceptive intake affect olfactory perception. *Chemical Senses, 38*(1), 67–75.

Deshpande, S. (1988). *That Long Silence.* London: Virago Press.

Detterman, D. K. (2014). Introduction to the intelligence special issue on the development of expertise: Is ability necessary? *Intelligence, 45,* 1–5.

Deutch, A. Y., & Roth, R. H. (2008). Neurotransmitters. In L. Squire, D. Berg, F. Bloom, S. Du Lac, A. Ghosh, & N. Spitzer (Eds.), *Fundamental neuroscience* (3rd ed., pp. 133–156). San Diego, CA: Elsevier.

DeValois, R. L., & DeValois, K. K. (1975). Neuronal coding of color. In E. C. Carterette & M.P. Friedman (Eds.), *Handbook of perception: Vol. V, Seeing.* New York: Academic Press.

Devenport, J. L., Kimbrough, C. D., & Cutler, B. L. (2009). Effectiveness of traditional safeguards against erroneous conviction arising from mistaken eyewitness identification. In B. L. Cutler (Ed.), *Expert testimony on the psychology of eyewitness identification* (pp. 51–68). New York, NY: Oxford University Press. doi: 10.1093/acprof: oso /9780195331974.003.003

Devi, N. P. G., Shenbagvalli, R., Ramesh, K., & Rathinam, S. N. (2009). Rapid progression of HIV infection in infancy. *Indian Pediatrics, 46,* 53–56.

Devlin, H. (2007). What is functional magnetic resonance imaging (fMRI)? *Psych Central.* Retrieved from http://psychcentral.com/lib /what-is-functional-magnetic-resonance-imaging-fmri/0001056

Dhabhar, F. S. (2014). Effects of stress on immune function: The good, the bad, and the beautiful. *Immunological Research, 58,* 193–210.

Dhabhar, F. S. (2011). Effects of stress on immune function: Implications for immunoprotection and immunopathology. In R. J. Contrada & A. Baum (Eds.), *The handbook of stress science: Biology, psychology, and health.* New York: Springer Publishing Co.

Dhillon, H., Zigman, J. M., Ye, C., Lee, C. E., McGovern, R. A., Tang, V., et al. (2006). Leptin directly activates SF1 neurons in the VMH, and this action by leptin is required for normal body-weight homeostasis. *Neuron, 49*(2), 191–203.

Di Pietro, J. (2000). Baby and the brain: Advances in child development. *Annual Review of Public Health 2000, 21,* 455–471.

Dick, A. O. (1974). Iconic memory and its relation to perceptual processing and other memory mechanisms. *Perception & Psychophysics, 16*(3), 575–596.

Diekelmann, S., & Born, J. (2010a). The memory function of sleep. *Nature Reviews Neuroscience, 11*(2), 114–126.

Diener, E. (2000). Subjective well-being: The science of happiness and a proposal for a national index. *American Psychologist, 55*(1), 34–43.

Diener, E., & Lucas, R. E. (1999). Personality and subjective well-being. In D. Kahneman, E. Diener, & N. Schwarz (Eds.), *Well-being: The foundations of hedonic psychology* (pp. 213–229). New York, NY: Russell Sage Foundation.

Diener, E., & Diener, C. (1996). Most people are happy. *Psychological Science, 7*(3), 181–185.

Diener, E., Diener, M., & Diener, C. (1995). Factors predicting the subjective well-being of nations. *Journal of Personality and Social Psychology, 69,* 851–864.

Diener, E., Ng, W., Harter, J., & Arora, R. (2010). Wealth and happiness across the world: Material prosperity predicts life evaluation, whereas psychosocial prosperity predicts positive feeling. *Journal of Personality and Social Psychology, 99*(1), 52–61.

Diener, E., Sanvik, E., Seidlitz, L., & Diener, M. (1993). The relationship between income and subjective well-being: Relative or absolute? *Social Indicators Research, 28*(3), 195–223.

Diener, E., & Seligman, M. E. P. (2002). Very happy people. *Psychological Science, 13*(1), 81–84.

Dienes, Z., Brown, E., Hutton, S., Kirsch, I., Mazzoni, G., & Wright, D. B. (2009). Hypnotic suggestibility, cognitive inhibition, and dissociation. *Consciousness and Cognition: An International Journal, 18*(4), 837–847.

Dies, R. R. (2003). Group psychotherapies. In A. S. Gurman & S. B. Messer (Eds.), *Essential psychotherapies: Theory and practice* (2nd Ed.). New York, NY: Guilford Press.

Dietrich, C., Swingley, D., & Werker, J. F. (2007). Native language governs interpretation of salient speech sound differences at 18 months. *Proceedings of the National Acadamy Sciences, USA, 104,* 27–31.

Dietrich, S., Hertrich, I., & Ackermann, H. (2010). *Visual cortex doing an auditory job: Enhanced spoken language comprehension in blind subjects.* Paper presented at the Neuroscience Conference, San Diego, CA, November.

Dijksterhuis, A. (2004). I like myself but I don't know why: Enhancing implicit self-esteem by subliminal evaluative conditioning. *Journal of Personality and Social Psychology, 86,* 345–355.

Dikel, T. N., Engdahl, B., & Eberly, R. (2005). PTSD in former prisoners of war: Prewar, wartime, and postwar factors. *Journal of Traumatic Stress, 18*(1), 69–77.

Dimsdale, J. E., & Creed, F. H. (2010). The proposed diagnosis of somatic symptom disorders in *DSM-V* to replace somatoform disorders in *DSM-IV*—A preliminary report. *Journal of Psychosomatic Research, 68*(1), 99–100.

Dindia, K. (2000). Sex differences in self-disclosure, reciprocity of self-disclosure, and self-disclosure and liking: Three meta-analyses reviewed. In S. Petronio (Ed.), *Balancing the Secrets of Private Disclosures* (pp. 21–35). Mahwah, NJ: Lawrence Erlbaum Associates Publishers.

Dion, K. K., & Berscheid, E. (1974). Physical attractiveness and peer perception among children. *Sociometry, 37,* 1–12.

Disner, S. G., Beevers, C. G., Haigh, E. A., & Beck, A. T. (2011). Neural mechanisms of the cognitive model of depression. *Nature Reviews Neuroscience, 12*(8), 467–477.

Dixon, M. J., Smilek, D., Duffy, P. L., Zanna, M. P., & Merikle, P. M. (2006). The role of meaning in grapheme-colour synesthesia. *Cortex, 42,* 243–252.

Djordjevic, J., Jones-Gotman, M., De Sousa, K., & Chertkow, H. (2008). Olfaction in patients with mild cognitive impairment and Alzheimer's disease. *Neurobiology of Aging, 29,* 693–706.

Do, E. K., Cohen, S. A., & Brown, M. J. (2014). Socioeconomic and demographic factors modify the association between informal caregiving and health in the Sandwich Generation. *BMC Public Health, 14,* 362–370.

Dobbing, J., & Sands, J. (1973). Quantitative growth and development of human brain. *Archives of Disease in Childhood, 48*(10), 757–767.

Dodgen, C. E. (2005). *Nicotine dependence: Understanding and applying the most effective treatment interventions.* Washington, DC: American Psychological Association.

Doetsch, F. (2003). The glial identity of neural stem cells. *Nature Neuroscience, 6,* 1127–1134.

Dogu, O., & Pressman, M. R. (2011). Identification of sleepwalking gene(s): Not yet, but soon? *Neurology, 76*(1), 12–13.

Doidge, N. (2007). *The Brain That Changes Itself: Stories of Personal Triumph from the frontiers of brain science.* New York: Viking.

Dolan, R. J. (2002, November 8). Emotion, cognition, and behavior. *Science, 298,* 1191–1194.

Dolgoff-Kaspar, R., Baldwin, A., Johnson, M. S., Edling, N., & Sethi, G. K. (2012). Effect of laughter yoga on mood and heart rate variability in patients awaiting organ transplantation: a pilot study. *Alternative Therapies in Health and Medicine, 18,* 61–66.

Dollard, J., Miller, N. E., Doob, L. W., Mowrer, O. H., & Sears, R. R. (1939). *Frustration and aggression.* New Haven, CT: Yale University.

Dong, G., & Ren, H. (2013). The role of age in second language acquisition— A psychological perspective. *British Journal of English Linguistics, 1*(1), 1–6.

Donnellan, M. B., Hill, P. L., & Roberts, B. W. (2015). Personality development across the life span: Current findings and future directions. In Mikulincer, M., Shaver, P. R., Cooper, M. L., & Larsen, R. J. (Eds.), *APA handbook of personality and social psychology, Volume 4: Personality processes and individual differences.* APA handbooks in psychology (pp. 107–126). Washington, DC: American Psychological Association.

Doss, B. D., Mitchell, A. E., & De la Garza-Mercer, F. (2008). Marital distress. In M. Hersen & J. Rosqvist (Eds.), *Handbook of psychological assessment, case* conceptualization, and treatment, Vol. 1: Adults (pp. 563–589). Hoboken, NJ: John Wiley & Sons.

Dossenbach, M., & Dossenbach, H.D. (1998). All about animal vision. Blackbirch Press.

Dostoyevsky, F. (1918). White nights and other stories (Vol. 10). Heinemann.

Doty, R. I. (1986). Odor-guided behavior in mammals. Experentia, 42, 257–271.

Doucet, S., Jones, I., Letourneau, N., Dennis, C., & Blackmore, E. R. (2011). Interventions for the prevention and treatment of postpartum psychosis: A systematic review. Archives of Women's Mental Health, 14(2), 89–98.

Dovidio, J. F., Gaertner, S. L., Kawakami, K., & Hodson, G. (2002). Why can't we all just get along? Interpersonal biases and interracial distrust. Cultural Diversity and Ethnic Minority Psychology, 8, 88–102.

Doweiko, H. E. (2006). Concepts of chemical dependency (6th Ed.). Belmont, CA: Thomson Brooks/Cole.

Draguns, J. G. (2006). Culture in psychopathology—psychopathology in culture: Taking a new look at an old problem. In T. G. Plante (Ed.), Mental disorders of the new millennium, Vol. 2: Public and social problems. Westport, CT: Praeger Publishers.

Drake, C. L., Roehrs, T., Richardson, G., Walsh, J. K., & Roth, T. (2004). Shift work sleep disorder: Prevalence and consequences beyond that of symptomatic day workers. SLEEP, 27(8).

Dreher, J., Kohn, P., Kolachana, B., Weinberger, D. R., & Berman, K. F. (2009). Variation in dopamine genes influences responsivity of the human reward system. PNAS Proceedings of the National Academy of Sciences of the United States of America, 106(2), 617–622.

Dresler, T., Hahn, T., Plichta, M. M., Ernst, L. H., Tupak, S. V., Ehlis, A., et al. (2011). Neural correlates of spontaneous panic attacks. Journal of Neural Transmission, 118(2), 263–269.

Drummond, M. (2011). Men's bodies throughout the life span. In C. Blazina & D. S. Shen-Miller (Eds.), An international psychology of men: Theoretical advances, case studies, and clinical innovations (pp. 159–188). New York: Routledge/Taylor & Francis Group.

Drury, J. P. (2013). Sex, gender, and evolution beyond genes. In M. Ah-King (Ed.), Challenging popular myths of sex, gender and biology. Series: Crossroads of knowledge Volume 1 (pp. 43–52). London: Springer.

Drury, S., Hutchens, S. A., Shuttlesworth, D. E., & White, C. L. (2012). Philip G. Zimbardo on his career and the Stanford Prison Experiment's 40th anniversary. History of Psychology, 15, 161–170.

Dubé, A. A., Duquette, M., Roy, M., Lepore, F., Duncan, G., & Rainville, P. (2009). Brain activity associated with the electrodermal reactivity to acute heat pain. NeuroImage, 45, 169–180.

Dube, E. F. (1982). Literacy, cultural familiarity, and "intelligence" as determinants of story recall. In U. Neisser (Ed.), Memory observed: Remembering in natural contexts (pp. 274–292). New York, NY: Freeman.

DuBois, G. E. (2010). Taste stimuli: Chemical and food. In E. B. Goldstein (Ed.), Encyclopedia of Perception, Thousand Oaks, CA: Sage.

Dubovsky, S. L., & Dubovsky, A. N. (2009). Psychopharmacology for neurologists. Seminars in Neurology, 29 (3), 200–219.

Dudai, Y. (2011). The engram revisited: On the elusive permanence of memory. In S. Nalbantian, P. M. Matthews, & J. L. McClelland (Eds.), The memory process: Neuroscientific and humanistic perspectives (pp. 29–40). Cambridge, MA: MIT Press.

Dudley, K. J., Li, X., Kobor, M. S., Kippin, T. E., & Bredy, T. W. (2011). Epigenetic mechanisms mediating vulnerability and resilience to psychiatric disorders. Neuroscience and Biobehavioral Reviews, 35(7), 1544–1551.

Dudukovic, N. M., DuBrow, S., & Wagner, A. D. (2009). Attention during memory retrieval enhances future remembering. Memory & Cognition, 37(7), 953–961.

Duesbury, E. M. (2011). The counselor's guide for facilitating the interpretation of dreams: Family and other relationship systems perspectives. New York, NY: Routledge/Taylor & Francis Group.

Dugas, M. J., Buhr, K., & Ladouceur, R. (2004). The role of intolerance of uncertainty in etiology and maintenance. In R. G. Heimberg, C. L. Turk, & D. S. Mennin (Eds.), Generalized anxiety disorder: Advances in research and practice. New York, NY: Guilford Press.

Dugas, M. J., Buhr, K., & Ladouceur, R. (2002). The role of intolerance of uncertainty in the etiology and maintenance of generalized anxiety disorder. In R. G. Heimberg, C. L. Turk, & D. S. Mennin (Eds.), Generalized anxiety disorder: Advances in research and practice. New York: Guilford Press.

Dugas, M. J., Francis, K., & Bouchard, S. (2009). Cognitive behavioural therapy and applied relaxation for generalized anxiety disorder: A time series analysis of change in worry and somatic anxiety. Cognitive Behaviour Therapy, 38(1), 29–41.

Dugas, M. J., Marchand, A., & Ladouceur, R. (2005). Further validation of a cognitive-behavioral model of generalized anxiety disorder: Diagnostic and symptom specificity. Journal of Anxiety Disorders, 19(3), 329–343.

Duke, A. A., Bègue, L., Bell, R., & Eisenlohr-Moul, T. (2013). Revisiting the serotonin–aggression relation in humans: A meta-analysis. Psychological Bulletin, 139(5), 1148–1172.

Dumont, F. (2010). A history of personality psychology: Theory, science, and research from Hellenism to the twenty-first century. New York: Cambridge University Press.

Dunbar, R. I. M. (2009). The social brain hypothesis and its implications for social evolution. Annals of Human Biology, 36(5), 562–572.

Dunbar, R. I. M., Barett, L., & Lycett, J. (2007). Evolutionay Psychology. One-World Publications: Oxford.

Dunbar, R. I. M., & Shultz, S. (2007). Evolution in the social brain. Science, 317(5843), 1344–1347.

Duncan, J. (2001). Frontal lobe function and the control of visual attention. In J. Braun, C. Koch, & J. L. Davis (Eds.), Visual attention and cortical circuits (pp. 69–88). Cambridge, MA: The MIT Press.

Duncan, S. C., Duncan, T. E., & Strycker, L. A. (2006). Alcohol use from ages 9 to 16: A cohort-sequential latent growth model. Drug and Alcohol Dependence, 81(1), 71–81.

Dupont, R. L., & Dupont, C. M. (2005). Sedatives/hypnotics and benzodiazepines. In R. J. Frances, A. H. Mack, & S. I. Miller (Eds.), Clinical textbook of addictive disorders (3rd Ed.). New York, NY: Guilford Press.

Durante, F., Fiske, S. T., Kervyn, N., Cuddy, A. J. C., Akande, A., Adetoun, B. E., . . . Storari, C. C. (2013). Nations' income inequality predicts ambivalence in stereotype content: How societies mind the gap. British Journal of Social Psychology, 52(4), 726–746.

Durante, K. M., & Li, N. P. (2009). Oestradiol level and opportunistic mating in women. Proceedings of the Royal Society of London: Biology Letters, 5(2), 19–182.

Dusseljee, J. C. E., Rijken, P. M., Cardol, M., Curfs, L. M. G., & Groenewegen, P. P. (2011). Participation in daytime activities among people with mild or moderate intellectual disability. Journal of Intellectual Disability Research, 55(1), 4–18.

Duszak, R. S. (2009). Congenital rubella syndrome—major review. Optometry, 80, 36–43.

Dutton, D. G., & Aron, A. P. (1974). Some evidence for heightened sexual attraction under conditions of high anxiety. Journal of Personality and Social Psychology, 23, 510–517.

Dworak, M., McCarley, R. W., Kim, T., Kalinchuk, A. V., & Basheer, R. (2010). Sleep and brain energy levels: ATP changes during sleep. The Journal of Neuroscience, 30(26), 9007–9016.

Dyck, K. G., & Hardy, C. (2013). Enhancing access to psychologically informed mental health services in rural and northern communities. Canadian Psychology/Psychologie canadienne, 54(1), 30.

Eagly, A. H. (1987). Sex differences in social behavior: A social-role interpretation. Hillsdale, NJ: Lawrence Erlbaum Associates.

Eagly, A. H., & Chaiken, S. (2007). The advantages of an inclusive definition of attitude. Social Cognition, 25, 582–602.

Eagly, A. H., & Karau, S. J. (2002). Role congruity theory of prejudice toward female leaders. Psychological Review, 109, 573–598.

Eagly, A. H., & Koenig, A. M. (2006). Social role theory of sex differences and similarities: Implication for prosocial behavior. In K. Dindia & D. J. Canary (Eds.), Sex differences and similarities in communication, 2nd Ed. (pp. 161–177). Mahwah, NJ: Lawrence Erlbaum Associates Publishers.

Eagly, A. H., & Wood, W. (1999). The origins of sex differences in human behavior: Evolved dispositions versus social roles. American Psychologist, 54, 408–423.

Earleywine, M. (2007). Pet politics: Marijuana and the costs of prohibition. New York, NY: Oxford University Press.

Easterbrook, G. (2005). The real truth about money. Time, 165(3), A32–A34.

Eaton, J. (2001). Management communication: The threat of group-think. Corporate Communications, 6(4), 183–192.

Eberhart, N. K., Auerbach, R. P., Bigda-Peyton, J., & Abela, J. Z. (2011). Maladaptive schemas and depression: tests of stress generation and diathesis-stress models. Journal of Social and Clinical Psychology, 30(1), 75–104.

Ebbinghaus, H. (1913). On memory: A contribution to experimental psychology. New York: Teachers College.

Eberhart-Phillips, J. E., Frederick, P. D., & Baron, R. C. (1993). Measles in pregnancy: A descriptive study of 58 cases. Obstetrics and Genecology, 26, 127–133.

Eckert, E. D., Bouchard, T. J., Bohlen, J., & Heston, L. L. (1986). Homosexuality in monozygotic twins reared apart. The British Journal of Psychiatry, 148, 421–425.

Edelstein, B. A., Stoner, S. A., & Woodhead, E. (2008). Older adults. In M. Hersen & J. Rosqvist (Eds.), Handbook of Psychological Assessment, Case Conceptualization and Treatment, Volume 1, Adults. Hoboken, NJ: John Wiley & Sons, Inc.

Edery-Halpern, G., & Nachson, I. (2004). Distinctiveness in flashbulb memory: Comparative analysis of five terrorist attacks. Memory, 12(2), 147–157.

Edgin, J. O., Pennington, B. F., & Mervis, C. B. (2010). Neuropsychological components of intellectual disability: The contributions of immediate, working, and associative memory. Journal of Intellectual Disability Research, 54(5), 406–417.

Edin, F., Macoveanu, J., Olesen, P., Tegnér, J., & Klingberg, T. (2007). Stronger synaptic connectivity as a mechanism behind development of working memory-related brain activity during childhood. *Journal of Cognitive Neuroscience, 19*(5), 750–760.

Edmonds, G. W., Goldberg, L. R., Hampson, S. E., & Barckley, M. (2013). Personality stability from childhood to midlife: Relating teachers' assessments in elementary school to observer- and self-ratings 40 years later. *Journal of Research in Personality, 47*(5), 505–513.

Edwards, J. M., & Trimble, K. (1992). Anxiety, coping, and academic performance. *Anxiety, Stress, and Coping, 5*, 337–350.

Edwards, W. (1977). How to Use Multiattribute Utility Measurement for Social Decision Making. *IEEE Transactions on Systems, Man and Cybernetics, 17*, 326–340.

Edwards, W., & Newman, J. R. (1986). Multiattribute Evaluation. In H. R. Arkes & K. R. Hammond (Eds.), *Judgment and Decision Making: An Interdisciplinary Reader* (pp. 17–34). New York, NY: Cambridge University Press.

Egan, L. C., Santos, L. R., & Bloom, P. (2007). The origins of cognitive dissonance: evidence from children and monkeys. *Psychological Science, 18*(11), 978–983.

Eggermont, J. J. (2010). Auditory system: Damage due to overstimulation. In E. B. Goldstein (Ed.), *Encyclopedia of Perception*. Thousand Oaks, CA: Sage.

Eggers, C., Fink, G. R., Möller-Hartmann, W., & Nowak, D. A. (2009). Correlation of anatomy and function in medulla oblongata infarction. *European Journal of Neurology, 16*, 201–204.

Eich, J. E. (2014). State-dependent retrieval of information in human episodic memory. *Alcohol and Human Memory*, 141–157.

Eichenwald, E., & Stark, A. (2008). Management and outcomes of very low birth weight. *New England Journal of Medicine, 358*(16), 1700–1711.

Eimas, P. D. (1975). Developmental studies in speech perception. In L. B. Cohen & P. Salapatek (Eds.), *Infant Perception: From Sensation to Cognition* (pp. 193–231). New York, NY: Academic Press.

Eimas, P. D., Siqueland, E. R., Jusczyk, P., & Vigorito, J. (1971). Speech perception in infants. *Science, 171*, 303–306.

Einstein, G. O., & McDaniel, M. A. (2010). Prospective memory and what costs do not reveal about retrieval processes: A commentary on Smith, Hunt, McVay, and McConnell (2007). *Journal of Experimental Psychology: Learning, Memory, and Cognition, 36*(4), 1082–1088. doi: 10.1037/a0019184.

Einstein, G. O., & McDaniel, M. A. (2005). Prospective memory: Multiple retrieval processes. *Current Directions in Psychological Science, 14*(6), 286–290. doi: 10.1111/j.0963-7214.2005.00382.x

Einstein, G. O., & McDaniel, M. A. (1990). Normal aging and prospective memory. *Journal of Experimental Psychology: Learning, Memory, and Cognition, 16*(4), 717–726. doi: 10.1037/0278-7393.16.4.717

Eisenberger, N. I., Lieberman, M. D., & Williams, K. D. (2003). Does rejection hurt? An FMRI study of social exclusion. *Science, 302*, 290–292.

Eisenbraun, G. A. (2006). The pros and cons of personality testing in the workplace. *LawNow*, Feb–March. Retrieved from http://findarticles.com/p/articles/mi_m0OJX/is_4_30/ai_n25001715.

Ekman, P. (2003). *Emotions revealed: Recognizing faces and feelings to improve communication and emotional life*. New York: Times Books.

Ekman, P., & Friesen, W. V. (1986). A new pan-cultural facial expression of emotion. *Motivation and Emotion, 10*, 159–168.

Ekman, P., & Friesen, W. V. (1975). *Unmasking the face: A guide to recognizing emotions from facial clues*. Oxford, England: Prentice Hall.

Ekman, P., & Friesen, W. V. (1971). Constants across cultures in the face and emotion. *Journal of Personality and Social Psychology, 17*(2), 124–129.

Ekman, P., Friesen, W. V., O'Sullivan, M., Chan, A., et al. (1987). Universals and cultural differences in the judgments of facial expressions of emotion. *Journal of Personality and Social Psychology, 53*, 712–717.

Ekman, P., Levenson, R. W., & Friesen, W. V. (1983). Autonomic nervous system activity distinguishes among emotions. *Science, 221*, 1208–1210.

El-Mallakh, R., & Huff, M. O. (2001). Mood stabilizers and ion regulation. *Harvard Review of Psychiatry, 9*(1), 23–32.

El-Sheikh, M. (Ed.). (2011). *Sleep and development: Familial and socio-cultural considerations*. New York, NY: Oxford University Press.

Elfenbein, H. A. (2013). Nonverbal dialects and accents in facial expressions of emotion. *Emotion Review, 5*(1), 90–96.

Elkin, D. (2010). *Introduction to clinical psychiatry*. McGraw-Hill Professional.

Elkind, D. (1978). Understanding the young adolescent. *Adolescence, 13*(49), 127–134.

Elkind, D. (2007). *The hurried child: Growing up too fast too soon (25th anniversary Ed.)*. Cambridge, MA: Da Capo Press.

Ellamil, M., Dobson, C., & Beeman, M. (2012). Evaluative and generative modes of thought during the creative process. *NeuroImage, 59*, 1783–1794.

Eller, J. D. (2005). *Violence and culture: A cross cultural and interdisciplinary perspective*. Thompson/Wadsworth.

Elliot, J. (2007, February 26). *Professor researches cell phone usage among college students*. Retrieved from www.physorg.com/news 91732046.html.

Ellis, A. (2011). Rational emotive behavior therapy. In R. J. Corsini & D. Wedding (Eds.), *Current psychotherapies* (9th Ed.). Florence, KY: CENGAGE Learning.

Ellis, A. (2005). Rational-emotive therapy. In R. Corsini & D. Wedding (Eds.), *Current psychotherapies* (7th Ed., pp. 166–201). Boston, MA: Thomson/Brooks-Cole.

Ellis, A. (2002). The role of irrational beliefs in perfectionism. In G. L. Flett & P. L. Hewitt (Eds.), *Perfectionism: Theory, research, and treatment* (pp. 217–229). Washington, DC: American Psychological Association.

Ellis, A. (1962). *Reason and emotion in psychotherapy*. Secaucus, NJ: Lyle Stuart.

Ellis, B. J., & Symons, D. (1990). Sex differences in sexual fantasy: An evolutionary psychological approach. *Journal of Sex Research, 27*, 527–555.

Ellison, C. G., Hummer, R. A., Cormier, S., & Rogers, R. G. (2000). Religious involvement and mortality risk among African American adults. *Research on Aging, 22*(6), 630–667.

Elovainio, M., Merjonen, P., Pulkki-Raback, L., Kivimaki, M., Jokela, M., Mattson, N., & Keltikangas-Jarvinen, L. (2011). Hostility, metabolic syndrome, inflammation and cardiac control in young adults: The young Finns study. *Biological Psychology, 87*(2), 234–240.

Elrod, S. S. (2010). Seniors Return to Retirement Jobs. *Senior Citizen Journal*, November 18.

Ely, R. (2000). Language and literacy in the school years. In J. Gleason (Ed.), *The Development of Language* (5th Ed.). Boston, MA: Allyn & Bacon.

Emerson, D. J., Weiser, B. P., Psonis, J., Liao, Z., Taratula, O., Fiamengo, A., Wang, X., Sugasawa, K., Smith, A. B. III, Eckenhoff, R. G., & Dmochowski, I. J. (2013). Direct modulation of microtubule stability contributes to anthracene general anesthesia. *Journal of the American Chemical Society, 135*(14), 5389–5398.

Empson, J. (2002). *Sleep and dreaming (3rd edition)*. Palgrave MacMillian.

Emsley, R., Chiliza, B., & Schoeman, R. (2008). Predictors of long-term outcome in schizophrenia. *Current Opinion in Psychiatry, 21*(2), 173–177.

Emsley, R., Rabinowitz, J., & Medori, R. (2006). Time course for antipsychotic treatment response in first-episode schizophrenia. *American Journal of Psychiatry, 163*(4), 743–745.

Ending Legalised Violence Against Children GLOBAL REPORT. (2013). Global Initiative to End All Corporal Punishment of Children. Retrieved from http://www.endcorporalpunishment.org/pages/pdfs/reports/GlobalReport2013.pdf.

Endler, N. S. (1988). The origins of electroconvulsive therapy. *Convulsive Therapy, 4*, 5–23.

Endrass, T., Kloft, L., Kaufmann, C., & Kathmann, N. (2011). Approach and avoidance learning in obsessive-compulsive disorder. *Depression and Anxiety, 28*(2), 166–172.

Engel, G. L. (1980). The clinical application of the biopsychosocial model. *American Journal of Psychiatry, 137*, 535–544.

Engel, G. L. (1977). The need for a new medical model: a challenge for biomedicine. *Science, 196*, 129–136.

Engel, G. S., Calhoun, T. R., Read, E. L., Ahn, T.-K., Mancal, T., Cheng, Y.-C., Blankenship, R. E., & Fleming, G. R. (2007). Evidence for wavelike energy transfer through quantum coherence in photosynthetic systems. *Nature, 446*(7137), 782–786.

Engmann, B., & Reuter, M. (2009). Spontaneous perception of melodies: hallucination or epilepsy? *Nervenheikunde* (April 28), 217–221.

Erdelyi, M. H. (2010). The ups and downs of memory. *American Psychologist, 65*(7), 623–633. doi: 10.1037/a0020440.

Erdelyi, M. H. (2001). Defense processes can be conscious or unconscious. *American Psychologist, 56*, 761–762.

Erdelyi, M. H. (1994). Hypnotic hypermnesia: The empty set of hypermnesia. *International Journal of Clinical and Experimental Hypnosis, 42*, 379–390.

Erikson, E. H. (1985). *The life cycle completed: A review*. New York, NY: W.W. Norton & Co.

Erikson, E. H. (1984). Reflections on the last stage—and the first. *Psychoanalytic Study of Children, 39*, 155–165.

Erikson, E. H. (1959). Identity and the life cycle: Selected papers. *Psychological Issues, 1*, 1–171.

Erlacher, D., & Schredl, M. (2010). Practicing a motor task in a lucid dream enhances subsequent performance: A pilot study. *The Sport Psychologist, 24*(2), 157–167.

Erlanson-Albertsson, C. (2005). Appetite regulation and energy balance. *Acta Paediatrica (Norway), Supplement, 94*(448), 40–41.

Ernst, W. (2006). *Histories of the normal and the abnormal: social and cultural histories of norms and normativity*. New York: Routledge.

Erten-Lyons, D., Woltjer, R. L., Dodge, H., Nixon, R., Vorobik, R., Calvert, J. F., . . . & Kaye, J. (2009). Factors associated with resistance to dementia despite high Alzheimer disease pathology. *Neurology, 72*(4), 354–360.

Escobar, J. I. (2004, April 15). Transcultural aspects of dissociative and somatoform disorders. *Psychiatric Times, 21*(5), 10.

Escobar, J. I. (1995). Transcultural aspects of dissociative and somatoform disorders. *Psychiatric Clinics of North America, 18*(3), 555–569.

Escobar, J. I., Canino, G., Rubio-Stipec, M., & Bravo, M. (1992). Somatic symptoms after a natural disaster: A prospective study. *American Journal of Psychiatry, 149*(7), 965–967.

Escobar, J. I., Gara, M., Silver, R. C., Waitzkin, H., Holman, A., & Compton, W. (1998). Somatisation disorder in primary care. *British Journal of Psychiatry, 173*, 262–266.

Espie, C. A. (2002). Insomnia: Conceptual issues in the development, persistence, and treatment of sleep disorders in adults. *Annual Review of Psychology, 53*, 215–243.

Essau, C. A., Lewinsohn, P. M., Seeley, J. R., & Sasagawa, S. (2010). Gender differences in the developmental course of depression. *Journal of Affective Disorders, 127*(1–3), 185–190.

Estes, W. K. (2014). *On the Descriptive and Explanatory Functions of Perspectives on Memory Research (PLE: Memory): Essays in Honor of Uppsala University's 500th Anniversary, 35.*

Etaugh, C. (2008). Women in the middle and later years. In F. L. Denmark & M. A. Paludi (Eds.), *Psychology of women: A handbook of issues and theories* (2nd Ed.). Westport, CT: Praeger Publishers/ Greenwood Publishing Group.

Etchegoyen, H. (2005). *The Fundamentals of Psychoanalytic Technique.* Karnac Books Ed., New Ed.

Eun, B. (2010). From learning to development: A sociocultural approach to instruction. *Cambridge Journal of Education, 40*(4), 401–418.

Evans, G. W. (2001). Environmental stress and health. In A. Baum, T. A. Revenson, & J. E. Singer (Eds.), *Handbook of Health Psychology* (pp. 365–385). Mahwah, NJ: Lawrence Erlbaum Associates.

Evans, J., Heron, J., Lewis, G., Araya, R., & Wolke, D. (2005). Negative self-schemas and the onset of depression in women: Longitudinal study. *British Journal of Psychiatry, 186*(4), 302–307.

Evans, R. I. (1968). *BF Skinner: The man and his ideas.* New York: Dutton.

Everhart, D. E., Shucard, J. L., Quatrin, T., & Shucard, D. W. (2001). Sex-related differences in event-related potentials, face recognition, and facial affect processing in prepubertal children. *Neuropsychology, 15*, 329–341.

Ewen, R. B. (2010). *An introduction to theories of personality* (7th Ed.). New York: Psychology Press.

Eyler, L. T. (2008). Brain imaging. In K. T. Mueser & D. V. Jeste (Eds.), *Clinical handbook of schizophrenia* (pp. 35–43). New York: Guilford Press.

Eysenck, H. J. (2002). *The dynamics of anxiety & hysteria: An experimental application of modern learning theory to psychiatry.* New Brunswick, NJ: Transaction Publishers.

Eysenck, H. J. (1992). Four ways five-factors are not basic. *Personality and Individual Differences, 13*, 667–673.

Eysenck, H. J. (1990). Biological dimensions of personality. In L. A. Pervin (Ed.), *Handbook of Personality: Theory and Research* (pp. 244–276). New York, NY: Guilford.

Eysenck, M. W., Matthews, G., Nęcka, E., Chuderski, A., Schweizer, K., & Szymura, B. (2010). Individual differences in attention: The commentaries. In A. Gruszka, G. Matthews, & B. Szymura (Eds.), *Handbook of individual differences in cognition: Attention, memory, and executive control* (pp. 283–292). New York: Springer Science + Business Media.

Faas, A. E., Spontón, E. D., Moya, P. R., & Molina, J. C. (2000). Differential responsiveness to alcohol odor in human neonates: Efects of maternal consumption during gestation. *Alcohol, 22*(1), 7–17.

Fabrigar, L. R., Petty, R. E., Smith, S. M., & Crites Jr., S. L. (2006). Understanding knowledge effects on attitude-behavior consistency: The role of relevance, complexity, and amount of knowledge. *Journal of Personality and Social Psychology, 90*(4), 556–577.

Falconier, M. K., Nussbeck, F., Bodenmann, G., Schneider, H., & Bradbury, T. (2014). Stress from daily hassles in couples: Its effects on intradyadic stress, relationship satisfaction, and physical and psychological well-being. *Journal of Marital and Family Therapy*, published first online, May 8, 2014.

Fallah, N., Mitnitski, A., Middleton, L., & Rockwood, K. (2009). Modeling the impact of sex on how exercise is associated with cognitive changes and death in older Canadians. *Neuroepidemiology, 33*, 47–54.

Faller, A., & Schuenke, M. (2004). *The human body: an introduction to structure and function.* Stuttgart, Germany: Thieme Georg Verlag.

Fancher, R. E. (2009). Scientific cousins: The relationship between Charles Darwin and Francis Galton. *American Psychologist, 64*(2), 84–92.

Fancher, R. E. (2004). The concept of race in the life and thought of Francis Galton. In A. S. Winston (Ed.), *Defining difference: Race and racism in the history of psychology* (pp. 49–75). Washington, DC: American Psychological Association.

Fancher, R. E. (1996). Mind in conflict. In *Pioneers in psychology* (pp. 393–394). New York, NY: W. W. Norton & Company, Inc.

Fanti, K. A., & Henrich, C. C. (2010). Trajectories of pure and co-occurring internalizing and externalizing problems from age 2 to age 12: Findings from the National Institute of Child Health and Human Development study of early child care. *Developmental Psychology, 46*(5), 1159–1175.

Farah, M. J., Levinson, K. L., & Klein, K. L. (1995). Face perception and within-category discrimination in prosopagnosia. *Neuropsychologia, 33*, 661–674.

Farah, M. J., Hutchinson, J. B., Phelps, E. A., & Wagner, A. D. (2014). Functional MRI-based lie detection: scientific and societal challenges. *Nature Reviews Neuroscience, 15*(2), 123-131.

Farrington, J. (2011). Seven plus or minus two. *Performance Improvement Quarterly, 23*(4), 113–116.

Farooqi, I. S., Wangensteen, T., Collins, S., Kimber, W., Matarese, G., Keogh, J. M., et al. (2007). Clinical and molecular genetic spectrum of congenital deficiency of the leptin receptor. *The New England Journal of Medicine, 356*(3), 237–247.

Farry, A., & Baxter, D. (2010). *The incidence and prevelance of spinal cord injury in Canada: Overview and extimates based on current evidence.* The Rick Hansen Institute and Urban Futures, Vancouver.

Favaro, A., Santonastaso, P., Monteleone, P., Bellodi, L., Mauri, M., Rotondo, A., et al. (2008). Self-injurious behavior and attempted suicide in purging bulimia nervosa: associations with psychiatric comorbidity. *Journal of Affective Disorders, 105*(1–3), 285–289.

Fayek, A. (2002). Analysis of a case of psychogenic amnesia: The issue of termination. *Journal of Clinical Psychoanalysis, 11*(4), 586–612.

Fazio, R. H., & Roskos-Ewoldsen, D. (2005). Acting as we feel: When and how attitudes guide behavior. In T. C. Brock & M. C. Green (Eds.), *Persuasion: Psychological Insights and Perspectives, 2nd Ed.* (pp. 41–62). Thousand Oaks, CA: Sage Publications.

Fechner, G.T. (1860). *Elemente der psychophysik* (Vol. 1). Leipzig: Breitkopf & Harterl.

Fedotchev, A. I. (2011). Modern nondrug methods of human sleep regulation. *Human Physiology, 37*(1), 113–120.

Fehr, S. S. (2003). *Group therapy: A practical guide (2nd Ed).* New York: Haworth Press.

Feinberg, D. R., Jones, B. C., Law Smith, M. J., Moore, F. R., DeBruine, L. M., Cornwell, R. E., Hillier, S. G., & Perrett, D. I. (2006). Menstrual cycle, trait estrogen level, and masculinity preferences in the human voice. *Hormonal Behavior, 49*(2), 15–22.

Feingold, A. (1994). Gender differences in personality: A meta-analysis. *Psychological Bulletin, 116*, 429–456.

Feist, G. J. (2010). The function of personality in creativity: The nature and nurture of the creative personality. In J. C. Kaufman & R. J. Sternberg (Eds.), *The Cambridge handbook of creativity* (pp. 113–130). New York: Cambridge University Press.

Feldhusen, J. F. (2003). Lewis M. Terman: A pioneer in the development of ability tests. In B. J. Zimmerman & D. H. Schunk (Eds.), *Educational psychology: A century of contributions* (pp. 155–169). Mahwah, NJ: Erlbaum.

Feldman, D. H. (2003). Cognitive development in childhood. In R. M. Lerner, M. A. Easterbrooks, & J. Mistry (Eds.), *Handbook of psychology: Developmental psychology, vol. 6* (pp. 195–210). Hoboken, NJ: John Wiley & Sons Inc.

Feldman, H. A., Longcope, C., Derby, C. A., Johannes, C. B., Araujo, A. B., Coviello, A. D., et al. (2002). Age trends in the level of serum testosterone and other hormones in middle-aged men: Longitudinal results from the Massachusetts male aging study. *Journal of Clinical Endocrinology & Metabolism, 87*(2), 589–598.

Feldman, M. W., & Lewontin, R. C. (2008). Race, ancestry, and medicine. In B. A. Koenig, S. S. Lee, & S. S. Richardson (Eds.), *Revisiting race in a genomic age* (pp. 89–101). Piscataway, NJ: Rutgers University Press.

Feldman, R. S. (2009). *The liar in your life: The way to truthful relationships.* New York: Twelve.

Feldman, R. S., Forrest, J. A., & Happ, B. R. (2002). Self-presentation and verbal deception: Do self-presenters lie more? *Basic and Applied Social Psychology, 24*, 163–170.

Feliciano, L., & Gum, A. M. (2010). Mood disorders. In D. L. Segal & M. Hersen (Eds.), *Diagnostic interviewing* (pp. 153–176). New York: Springer Publishing Co.

Felson, J. (2014). What can we learn from twin studies? A comprehensive evaluation of the equal environments assumption. *Social Science Research, 43*, 184–199.

Fenchel, G. H. (2006). *Psychoanalytic reflections on love and sexuality.* Lanham, MD: University Press of America.

Fenigstein, A., & Preston, M. (2007). The desired number of sexual partners as a function of gender, sexual risk and the meaning of "ideal." *Journal of Sex Research, 44*(1), 89–95.

Fenson, L., Dale, P. S., Reznick, J. S., Bates, E., Thal, D. J., & Pethick, S. J. (1994). Variability in early communicative development. *Monographs of the Society for Research in Child Development, 59*, 1–185.

Fenton, M. C., Keyes, K. M., Martins, S. S., & Hasin, D. S. (2010). The role of a prescription in anxiety medication use, abuse, and dependence. *American Journal of Psychiatry, 167*(10), 1247–1253.

Ferguson, C. J. (2008). The school shooting/violent video game link: Causal Relationship or moral panic? *Journal of Investigative Psychology and Offender Profiling, 5*, 25–37.

Ferguson, K. T., Cassells, R. C., MacAllister, J. W., & Evans, G. W. (2013). The physical environment and child development: An international review. *International Journal of Psychology, 48*(3) 437–468.

Fernald, A., Marchman, V. A., & Weisleder, A. (2012). SES differences in language processing skill and vocabulary are evident at 18 months. *Developmental Science, 16*(2), 234–248.

Fernandes, M., Atallah, A. N., Soares, B. G., Humberto, S., Guimarães, S., Matos, D., et al. (2007). Intragastric balloon for obesity. *Cochrane Database of Systematic Reviews (Online), 1,* CD004931.

Fernbach, P. M., Darlow, A., & Sloman, S. A. (2011). Asymmetries in predictive and diagnostic reasoning. *Journal of Experimental Psychology, 140*(2), 168–185.

Ferraro, R., Shiv, B., & Bettman, J. R. (2005). Let us eat and drink, for tomorrow we shall die: Effects of mortality salience and self-esteem on self-regulation in consumer choice. *Journal of Consumer Research, 32,* 65–75.

Festinger, L. (1957). *A Theory of Cognitive Dissonance.* Stanford, CA: Stanford University Press.

Festinger, L., & Carlsmith, J. M. (1959). Cognitive consequences of forced compliance. *Journal of Abnormal and Social Psychology, 58,* 203–210.

Field, A. P., & Nightingale, Z. C. (2009). Test of time: What if little Albert had escaped? *Clinical Child Psychology and Psychiatry, 14,* 311–319.

Figueredo, V. M., & Purushottam, B. (2013). Sudden cardiac death and alcohol. In I. Gussak & C. Antzelevitch (Eds.), *Electric diseases of the heart: Volume 2: Diagnosis and treatment* (pp. 425–440). London: Springer-Verlag.

Finckh, U. (2001). The dopamine D2 receptor gene and alcoholism: Association studies. In D. P. Agarwal & H. K. Seitz (Eds.), *Alcohol in health and disease.* New York, NY: Marcel Dekker.

Finer, L. B. (2007). Trends in premarital sex in the United States, 1954–2003. *Public Health Reports, 122,* 73–78.

Fink, B., Neave, N., Manning, J. T., & Grammer, K. (2006). Facial symmetry and judgements of attractiveness, health and personality. *Personality and Individual Differences, 41,* 491–499.

Finke, R. A. (1989). *Principles of Mental Imagery.* Cambridge, MA: MIT Press.

Finkel, D., Gerritsen, L., Reynolds, C. A., Dahl, A. K., & Pedersen, N. L. (2014). Etiology of individual differences in human health and longevity. *Annual Review of Gerontology and Geriatrics, 34*(1), 189–227.

Finley, L. L. (2007). *The Encyclopedia of Juvenile Violence.* Westport, CT: Greenwood Publishing Group.

Finnegan, L. P., & Kandall, S. R. (2008). Perinatal substance abuse. In H. D. Kleber & M. Galanter (Eds.), *The American Psychiatric Publishing textbook of substance abuse treatment (4th Ed.).* Washington, DC: American Psychiatric Publishing.

Fischer, P., Greitemeyer, T., Pollozek, F., & Frey, D. (2006). The unresponsive bystander: Are bystanders more responsive in dangerous emergencies? *European Journal of Social Psychology, 36*(2), 267–278.

Fischer, P., Krueger, J. I., Greitemeyer, T., Vogrincic, C., Kastenmüller, A., Frey, D., Heene, M., Wicher, M., & Kainbacher, M. (2011). The bystander-effect: A meta-analytic review on bystander intervention in dangerous and non-dangerous emergencies. *Psychological Bulletin, 137*(4), 517–537.

Fish, J. M. (Ed.) (2002). *Race and intelligence: Separating science from myth.* Mahwah, NJ: Lawrence Erlbaum Associates Publishers.

Fisher, L., Ames, E. W., Chisholm, K., & Savoie, L. (1997). Problems reported by parents of Romanian orphans adopted to British Columbia. *International Journal of Behavioral Development, 20*(1), 67–82.

Fisher, P. H., Masia-Warner, C., & Klein, R. G. (2004). Skills for social and academic success: A school-based intervention for social anxiety disorder in adolescents. *Clinical Child and Family Psychological Review, 7*(4), 241–249.

Fisher, T. D., & Brunell, A. B. (2014). A bogus pipeline approach to studying gender differences in cheating behavior. *Personality and Individual Differences, 61,* 91–96.

Fishman, D. B., Rego, S. A., & Muller, K. L. (2011). Behavioral theories of psychotherapy. In J. C. Norcross, G. R. VandenBos, & D. K. Freedheim (Eds.), *History of psychotherapy: Continuity and change* (2nd Ed., pp. 101–140). Washington, DC: American Psychological Association.

Fiske, S. T. (2010). *Social beings: Core motives in social psychology,* Second Edition. Hoboken, NJ: John Wiley & Sons.

Fiske, S. T. (2004). *Social beings: A core motives approach to social psychology.* Hoboken, NJ: John Wiley & Sons, Inc.

Fiske, S. (2000). Stereotyping, prejudice, and discrimination at the seam between the centuries: Evolution, culture, mind, and brain. *European Journal of Social Psychology, 30,* 299–322.

Fitch, M. T., & Silver, J. (2008). CNS injury, glial scars, and inflammation: Inhibitory extracellular matrices and regeneration failure. *Experimental Neurology, 209,* 294–301.

Fitzpatrick, E., Whittingham, J., & Durieux-Smith, A. (2014). Mild bilateral and unilateral hearing loss in childhood: A 20-year view of hearing characteristics, and audiological practices before and after newborn hearing screening. *Ear and Hearing, 35,* 10–18.

Fleeson, W. (2007). Situation-based contingencies underlying trait-content manifestation in behavior. *Journal of Personality, 75*(4), 825–862.

Fleeson, W. (2001). Towards a structure- and process-integrated view of personality: Traits as density distributions of states. *Journal of Personality and Social Psychology, 80,* 1011–1027.

Fleischman, D. A., Wilson, R. S., Gabrieli, J. D. E., Bienias, J. L., & Bennett, D. A. (2004). A longitudinal study of implicit and explicit memory in old persons. *Psychology and Aging, 19*(4), 617–625. doi: 10.1037/0882-7974.19.4.617

Fleming, I., Baum, A., Davidson, L., Rectanus, E., & McArdle, S. (1987). Chronic stress as a reactivity factor in physiologic reactivity to challenge. *Health Psychology, 11,* 221–237.

Flett, G.L., & Hewitt, P.L. (in press). Perfectionism and perfectionistic self-presentation in social anxiety: Implications for assessment and treatment. In S. Hofmann & P. DiBartolo (Eds.), *Social anxiety: Clinical, Developmental, and Social Perspectives,* 3rd ed. London: Elsevier.

Flouri, E., Hickey, J., Mavroveli, S., & Hurry, J. (2011). Adversity, emotional arousal, and problem behaviour in adolescence: The role of non-verbal cognitive ability as a resilience promoting factor. *Child and Adolescent Mental Health, 16*(1), 22–29.

Flynn, J. R. (2008). *Where have all the liberals gone? Race, class, and ideals in America.* New York: Cambridge University Press.

Flynn, J. R. (2007). *What is intelligence? Beyond the Flynn effect.* New York: Cambridge University Press.

Flynn, J. R. (2000). *How to defend humane ideals: Substitutes for objectivity.* Lincoln, NE: University of Nebraska Press.

Flynn, J. R. (1998). IQ gains over time: Toward finding the causes. In U. Neisser (Ed.), *The rising curve: Long-term gains in IQ and related measures* (p. 37). Washington, DC: American Psychological Association.

Foa, E., & Kozak, M. (1986). Emotional processing of fear: Exposure to corrective information. *Psychological Bulletin, 99,* 20–35.

Focus Adolescent Services (FAS). (2008). *Teen Violence.* online: Focusas.com.

Fodor, J. A. (2007). The revenge of the given. In B. P. McLaughlin & J. Cohen (Eds.), *Contemporary debates in philosophy of mind* (pp. 105–116). Malden, MA: Blackwell Publishing.

Fodor, J. A. (2006). Précis of the modularity of mind. In J. L. Bermúdez (Ed.), *Philosophy of psychology: Contemporary readings* (pp. 513–523). New York, NY: Routledge/Taylor & Francis Group.

Fodor, J. A. (1968). Psychological explanation: An introduction to the philosophy of psychology. New York, NY: Random House.

Fogel, G. E., & Pettijohn, T. F. (2013). Stress and health habits in college students. *Open Journal of Medical Psychology, 2*(2), 61–68.

Fogel, S. M., Smith, C. T., Higginson, C. D., & Beninger, R. J. (2011). Different types of avoidance behavior in rats produce dissociable post-training changes in sleep. *Physiology & Behavior, 102*(2), 170–174.

Foldvary, N., Nashold, B., Mascha, E., Thompson, E. A., Lee, N., McNamara, J. O., et al. (2000). Seizure outcome after temporal lobectomy for temporal lobe epilepsy: A Kaplan-Meier survival analysis. *Neurology, 54*(3), 630–634.

Fole, A., Miguens, M., Higuera-Matas, A., Alguacil, L. F., Ambrosio, E., & Del Olmo, N. (2013). Cocaine facilitates protein synthesis-dependent LTP: The role of metabotropic glutamate receptors. *European Neuropsychopharmacology, 24,* 621–629.

Folkman, S. (2013a) Stress: Appraisal and coping. *Encyclopedia of Behavioral Medicine,* 1913–1915.

Folkman, S. (2013b) Stress, coping and hope. In B. I. Carr & J. Steel (Eds.), *Psychological Aspects of Cancer.* Springer.

Folkman, S., & Lazarus, R. S. (1985). If it changes it must be a process: Study of emotion and coping during three stages of a college examination. *Journal of Personality and Social Psychology, 48,* 150–170.

Folkman, S., & Moskowitz, J. T. (2004). Coping: Pitfalls and promise. *Annual Review of Psychology, 55,* 745–774.

Folkman, S., & Moskowitz, J. T. (2000a). Stress, positive emotion, and coping. *Current Directions in Psychological Science, 9*(4), 115–118.

Folkman, S., & Moskowitz, J. T. (2000b). Positive affect and the other side of coping. *American Psychologist, 55,* 647–654.

Fontana, D. (2007). Meditation. In M. Velmans & S. Schneider (Ed.), *The Blackwell companion to consciousness.* Malden, MA: Blackwell Publishing.

Forbes, C. E., Cox, C. L., Schmader, T., & Lee, R. (2012). Negative stereotype activation alters interaction between neural correlates of arousal, inhibition and cognitive control. *Social Cognitive and Affective Neuroscience, 7,* 771–781.

Ford, D. Y. (2008). Intelligence testing and cultural diversity: The need for alternative instruments, policies, and procedures. In J. L. Van Tassel-Baska (Ed.), *Alternative assessments with gifted and talented students* (pp. 107–128). Waco, TX: Press.

Ford, D. Y., Moore, J. L., III, & Whiting, G. W. (2006). Eliminating deficit orientations: Creating classrooms and curriculums for gifted students from diverse cultural backgrounds. In M. G. Constantine & D. W. Sue (Eds.), *Addressing racism: Facilitating cultural competence in mental health and educational settings* (pp. 173–193). Hoboken, NJ: John Wiley & Sons.

Forgas, J. P. (2008). Affect, cognition, and social behavior: The effects of mood on memory, social judgments, and social interaction. In M. A. Gluck, J. R. Anderson, & S. M. Kosslyn (Eds.), *Memory and mind: A festschrift for Gordon H. Bower* (pp. 261–279). Mahwah, NJ: Lawrence Erlbaum Associates Publishers.

Forgas, J. P., & Locke, J. (2005). Affective influences on causal inferences: The effects of mood on attributions for positive and negative interpersonal episodes. *Cognition & Emotion, 19*(7), 1071–1081.

Forgeard, M. J., Haigh, E. A., Beck, A. T., Davidson, R. J., Henn, F. A., Maier, S. F., ... & Seligman, M. E. (2011). Beyond Depression: Toward a Process-Based Approach to Research, Diagnosis, and Treatment. *Clinical Psychology: Science and Practice, 18*(4), 275–299.

Forsey, C. A. (2009) *"I don't want to die but I accept that it can happen": Taking risks and doing gender among BASE jumpers*. Masters Thesis, University of British Columbia. Retrieved from https://dspace.library.ubc.ca/bitstream/handle/2429/12601/ubc_2009_fall_forsey_caitlin.pdf?sequence=1.

Försterling, F. (2013). *Attribution: An Introduction to Theories, Research and Applications*. New York, NY: Psychology Press.

Fossel, M., Blackburn, G., & Woynarowski, D. (2010). *The immortality edge: Realize the secrets of your telomeres for a longer healthier life*. Hoboken, NJ: JohnWiley and Sons.

Foster, J. D. (2009, March, 16). *Mass murder is nothing to fear*. Message posted to Psychology Today. Retrieved from www.psychology-today.com/blog/the-narcissus-in-all-us/200903/mass-murder-is-nothing-fear.

Fotuhi, O., Fong, G. T., Zanna, M. P., Borland, R., Yong, H., & Cummings, K. M. (2013). Patterns of cognitive dissonance-reducing beliefs among smokers: A longitudinal analysis from the international tobacco control (ITC) four country survey. *Tobacco Control: An International Journal, 22*(1), 52–58.

Fougnie, D. (2009). The relationship between attention and working memory. In N. B. Johansen (Ed.), *New Research on Short-term Memory*, New York: Nova Science Publishers.

Fountoulakis, K. N., Vieta, E., Sanchez-Moreno, J., Kaprinis, S. G., Goikolea, J. M., & Kaprinis, G. S. (2005). Treatment guidelines for bipolar disorder: a critical review. *Journal of Affective Disorders, 86*(1), 1–10.

Fournier, J. C., DeRubeis, R. J., Hollon, S. D., Dimidjian, S., Amsterdam, J. D., Shelton, R. C., & Fawcett, J. (2010). Antidepressant drug effects and depression severity: a patient-level meta-analysis. *Journal of American Medical Association, 303*(1), 47–53.

Fowers, B. J. (2005). *Practical wisdom as the heart of professional ethics. Virtue and psychology: Pursuing excellence in ordinary practices* (pp. 177–201). Washington, DC: American Psychological Association.

Fowers, B. J. (2003). Reason and human finitude: In praise of practical wisdom. *American Behavioral Scientist, 47*(4), 415–426.

Fowler, C. G., & Leigh-Paffenroth, E. D. (2007). Hearing. In J. E. Birren (Ed.), *Encyclopedia of gerontology* (2nd ed.). San Diego: Academic Press.

Fox, J. (2010). The insanity virus. *Discover, 31*(5), 58–64.

Fraley, B., & Aron, A. (2004). The effect of a shared humorous experience on closeness in initial encounters. *Personal Relationships, 11*, 61–78.

Frances, A. (2010). Opening Pandora's box: The 19 worst suggestions for DSM-5. *Psychiatric Times, 27*(9), 1–10.

Frank, E., & Michael, E. T. (2013). Natural history and preventative treatment of recurrent mood disorders. In S. E. Hyman (Ed.), *Depression: The Science of Mental Health*. Oxford, UK: Routledge.

Frank, J. D. (1973). *Persuasion and healing* (Rev. Ed.). Baltimore, MD: Johns Hopkins University Press.

Frank, J., Mistretta, P., & Will, J. (2008). Diagnosis and treatment of female sexual dysfunction. *American Family Physician, 77*(5), 635–642.

Frankish, C., Hwang, S., & Quantz, D. (2005). Homelessness and health in Canada: Research lessons and priorities. *Canadian Journal of Public Health, 96*(2), 23–29.

Franklin, R. J., & French-Constant, C. (2008). Remyelination in the CNS: from biology to therapy. *Nature Reviews Neuroscience, 9*, 839–855.

Fraser, D. D., Close, T. E., Rose, K. L., Ward, R., Mehl, M., Farrell, C., ... Hutchison, J. S. (2011). Severe traumatic brain injury in children elevates glial fibrillary acidic protein in cerebrospinal fluid and serum. *Pediatric Critical Care Medicine, 12*, 319–324.

Fredericks, L. E. (2001). *The use of hypnosis in surgery and anesthesiology: Psychological preparation of the surgical patient*. Springfield, IL: Charles C. Thomas Publisher.

Fredrickson, B. L. (2001). The role of positive emotions in positive psychology: The broaden-and-build theory of positive emotions. *American Psychologist, 56*(3), 218–226.

Freed, W. J. (2000). *Neural transplantation: An introduction*. Cambridge, MA: The MIT Press.

Freedman, J. L. (2002). *Media violence and its effect on aggression: Assessing the scientific evidence*. University of Toronto Press, Scholarly Publishing Division.

Freedman, V. A., Aykan, H., & Martin, L. G. (2001). Aggregate changes in severe cognitive impairment among older Americans: 1993 and 1998. *Journal of Gerontology, 56B*, S100–S111.

Freeman, A., Golden, R. (1997). *Why didn't I think of that: Bizarre origins of ingenious inventions we couldn't live without*. Wiley.

Freeman, C., Waite, J., & Easton, A. (2013). Cognitive adverse effects of ECT. *The ECT Handbook, 176*, 76.

Freeman, H. L. (1984). Housing. In H. L. Freeman (Ed.), *Mental Health and the Environment* (pp. 197–225). London: Churchill Livingston.

Freeman, H. L., & Stansfeld, S. A. (2014). Psychosocial effects of urban environments, noise, and crowding. In Ante Lundberg (Ed.), *The environment and mental health: A guide for clinicians* (pp. 147–159). New York: Routledge.

Freeman, S., Walker, M. R., Borden, R., & Latané, B. (1975). Diffusion of responsibility and restaurant tipping: cheaper by the bunch. *Personality and Social Psychology Bulletin, 1*(4), 584–587.

Frein, S. T., Jones, S. L., & Gerow, J. E. (2013). When it comes to Facebook there may be more to bad memory than just multitasking, *Computers in Human Behavior, 29*(6), 2179–2182.

Frensch, P. A., & Rünger, D. (2003). Implicit learning, current directions. *Psychological Science, 12*(1), 13–18.

Freud, S. (1961). The infantile genital organization: An interpolation into the theory of sexuality. *Standard Edition, 19*, 141–145.

Freud, S. (1924). The loss of reality in neurosis and psychosis. In *Sigmund Freud's collected papers* (Vol. 2, pp. 272–282). London: Hogarth Press.

Freud, S. (1909). Analysis of a phobia in a five-year-old boy. *Standard Edition, 10*, 5–149.

Freud, S. (1900). *The Interpretation of Dreams*.

Freund, A. M., & Lamb, M. E. (2010). Introduction: Social and emotional development across the lifespan. In R. M. Lerner, M. E. Lamb, & A. M. Freund (Eds.), *Handbook of Lifespan Developmental Psychology*. (Vol. 2, pp. 1–8). Hoboken, NJ: Wiley.

Freund, P. A., & Holling, H. (2011). Who wants to take an intelligence test? Personality and achievement motivation in the context of ability testing. *Personality and Individual Differences, 50*(5), 723–728.

Frey, K. S., Hirschstein, M. K., Snell, J. L., Edstrom, L. V., MacKenzie, E. P., & Broderick, C. J. (2005). Reducing playground bullying and supporting beliefs: An experimental trial of the Steps to Respect program. *Developmental Psychology, 41*, 479–491.

Fridlund, A. J., Beck, H. P., Goldie, W. D., & Irons, G. (2012). Little Albert: A neurologically impaired child. *History of Psychology*, doi:10.1037/a0026720

Fried, P. A., Watkinson, B., & Gray R. (2005). The neurocognitive consequences of marijuana—A comparison with pre-drug use performance. *Neurotoxicology and Teratology, 27*, 231–239.

Friedlander, S. L., Larkin, E. K., Rosen, C. L., Palermo, T. M., & Redline, S. (2003). Decreased quality of life associated with obesity in school-aged children. *Archives of Pediatrics & Adolescent Medicine, 157*(12), 1206–1211.

Friedman, H. S., Kern, M. L., Hampson, S. E., & Duckworth, A. L. (2014). A new life-span approach to conscientiousness and health: Combining the pieces of the causal puzzle. *Developmental Psychology, 50*(5), 1377–1389.

Friedman, H. S., & Silver, R. C. (Eds.) (2007). *Foundations of Health Psychology*. New York: Oxford University Press.

Friedman, K. E., Reichmann, S. K., Costanzo, P. R., Zelli, A., Ashmore, J. A., Musante, G. J., et al. (2005). Weight stigmatization and ideological beliefs: relation to psychological functioning in obese adults. *Obesity research, 13*(5), 907–916.

Friedman, M., & Rosenman, R. H. (1959). Association of a specific overt behavior pattern with increases in blood cholesterol, blood clotting time, incidence of arcus senilis and clinical coronary artery disease. *Journal of the American Medical Association, 169*, 1286–1296.

Frijda, N. H. (2010). Impulsive action and motivation. *Biological Psychology, 84*(3) 570–579.

Frijda, N. H. (2007). *The laws of emotion*. Mahwah, NJ: Lawrence Erlbaum Associates.

Frijda, N. H. (1986). *The emotions*. Cambridge, MA: Cambridge University Press.

Frith, C. (2003). The scientific study of consciousness. In M. A. Ron & T.W. Robbins (Eds.), *Disorders of brain and mind 2*. New York, NY: Cambridge University Press.

Froehlich, J. C., Zink, R. W., Li, T., & Christian, J. C. (2000). Analysis of heritability of hormonal responses to alcohol in twins: Beta-endorphin as a potential biomarker of genetic risk for alcoholism. *Alcoholism: Clinical and Experimental Research, 24*(3), 265–277.

Frost, R. O., & Steketee, G. (2001). Obsessive-compulsive disorder. In H. S. Friedman (Ed.), *Specialty articles from the encyclopedia of mental health*. San Diego: Academic Press.

Frueh, B. C. (2009). Delayed-onset post-traumatic stress disorder among war veterans in primary care clinics. *British Journal of Psychiatry, 194*(6), 515–520.

Fuchs, D., Burnside, L., & Marchenski, A. M. (2010). Children with FASD-related disabilities receiving services from child welfare agencies in Manitoba. *International Journal of Mental Health & Addiction, 8*(2), 232–244.

Fulton, J. F. (1938). *Physiology of the nervous system*. New York: Oxford University Press.

Furnham, A. (2009). The validity of a new, self-report measure of multiple intelligence. *Current Psychology: A Journal for Diverse Perspectives on Diverse Psychological Issues, 28*(4), 225–239.

Furnham, A. (2008). *Personality and intelligence at work: Exploring and explaining individual differences at work.* Hove: Psychology Press/Taylor & Francis (UK).

Furnham, A., Crump, J., & Ritchie, W. (2013). What it takes: Ability, demographic, bright and dark side trait correlates of years to promotion. *Personality and Individual Differences, 55*(8) 952–956.

Furnham, A., & Monsen, J. (2009). Personality traits and intelligence predict academic school grades. *Learning and Individual Differences, 19*(1), 28–33.

Gadermann, A. M., Alonso, J., Vilagut, G., Zaslavsky, A. M., & Kessler, R. C. (2012). Comorbidity and disease burden in the national comorbidity survey replication (NCS-R). *Depression and Anxiety, 29*(9), 797–806.

Gaebel, W., Riesbeck, M., Wölwer, W., Klimke, A., Eickhoff, M., von Wilmsdorff, M., . . . & Möller, H. J. (2014). Rates and predictors of remission in first-episode schizophrenia within 1 year of antipsychotic maintenance treatment. Results of a randomized controlled trial within the German Research Network on Schizophrenia. *Schizophrenia Research, 152*(2), 478–486.

Gagnon, J. H. (1975). Sex research and social change. *Archives of Sexual Behavior, 4*(2), 111–41.

Gahlinger, P. M. (2000). A comparison of motion sickness remedies in severe sea conditions. *Wilderness and Environmental Medicine, 11*(2), 136–167.

Gais, S., Hüllemann, P., Hallschmid, M., & Born, J. (2006). Sleep-dependent surges in growth hormone do not contribute to sleep-dependent memory consolidation. *Psychoneuroendocrinology, 31*(6), 786–791.

Galambos, N. L., Dalton, A. L., & Maggs, J. L. (2009). Losing sleep over it: Daily variation in sleep quantity and quality in Canadian students' first semester of university. *Journal of Research on Adolescence, 19*(4), 741–761.

Galanter, E. (1962). Contemporary Psychophysics. In R. Brown, E. Galanter, E. H. Hess, & G. Mander (Eds), *New Directions in Psychology.* NY: Holt, Rinehart and Winston.

Galanter, M. (2010a). Review of religion and spirituality in psychiatry. *The American Journal of Psychiatry, 167*(7), 871–872.

Galanter, M. (2010b). Spirituality in psychiatry: A biopsychosocial perspective. *Psychiatry: Interpersonal and Biological Processes, 73*(2), 145–157.

Galati, D., Sini, B., Schmidt, S., & Tinti, C. (2003). Spontaneous facial expressions in congenitally-blind and sighted children aged 8–11. *Journal of Visual Impairment and Blindness, 97*, 418–428.

Gall, F. J. (1833). The anatomy and physiology of the nervous system in general, and of the brain in particular, with observations upon the possibility of ascertaining the several intellectual and moral dispositions of man and animal, by the configuration of their heads. *The American Journal of the Medical Sciences*, Southern Society for Clinical Investigation.

Gallacher, J. E. J., Sweetnam, P. M., Yarnell, J. W G., Elwood, P. C., & Stansfeld, S. A. (2003). Is type A behavior really a trigger for coronary heart disease events? *Psychosomatic Medicine, 65*(3), 339–346.

Gallese, V., Fadiga, L., Fogassi, L., & Rizzolatti, G. (1996). Action recognition in the premotor cortex. *Brain. 119*(2), 593–609.

Gallup, G. G. (1970). Chimpanzees: Self-recognition. *Science, 167*, 86–87.

Galton, F. (1948). Co-relations and their measurement, chiefly from anthropometric data, 1888. In W. Dennis (Ed.), *Readings in the history of psychology* (pp. 336–346). East Norwalk, CT: Appleton-Century-Crofts.

Gamble, A. L., Harvey, A. G., & Rapee, R. M. (2010). Specific phobia. In D. J. Stein, E. Hollander, & B. O. Rothbaum (Eds.), *Textbook of anxiety disorders (2nd Ed.)* (pp. 525–541). Arlington, VA: American Psychiatric Publishing, Inc.

Gangestad, S. W., & Thornhill, R. (1998). Menstrual cycle variation in women's preferences for the scent of symmetrical men. *Proceedings of the Royal Society of Biological Sciences, 265*(1399), 927–933.

Gansberg, M. (1964, March 27). Thirty-eight who saw murder didn't call the police. *New York Times.*

Gantt, W. H. (1980). Review of the shaping of a behaviorism (B.F. Skinner). *The Pavlovian Journal of Biological Science, 15*, 42–44.

Ganzach, Y. (2003). Intelligence, education, and facets of job satisfaction. *Work and Occupations, 30*(1), 97–122.

Ganzach, Y., & Pazy, A. (2001). Within occupation sources of variance in incumbent perception of job complexity. *Journal of Occupational and Organizational Psychology, 74*(1), 95–108.

Garbarino, J. (2011). *The positive psychology of personal transformation: Leveraging resilience for life change.* New York: Springer Science + Business Media.

Garcia, E., García, F., & Lila, M. (2009). Public responses to intimate partner violence against women: The influence of perceived severity and personal responsibility. *The Spanish Journal of Psychology, 12*(2), 648–656.

Garcia, E., Godoy-Izquierdo, D., Godoy, J. F., Perez, M., & Lopez-Chicheri, I. (2007) Gender differences in pressure pain threshold in a repeated measures assessment. *Psychology: Health, & Medicine, 12, 567–579.*

Garcia, J., & Koelling, R. A. (1971). The use of ionizing rays as a mammalian olfactory stimulus. In H. Autrum, et al. (Eds.), *Handbook of sensory physiology: Volume 4.* New York: Springer-Verlag.

Garcia, J., Lasiter, P. S., Bermudez-Rattoni, F., & Deems, D. A. (1985). A general theory of aversion learning. *Annals of the New York Academy of Sciences, 443,* 8–21.

Garcia, S. M., Weaver, K., Moskowitz, G. B., & Darley, J. M. (2002). Crowded minds: The implicit bystander effect. *Journal of Personality and Social Psychology, 83*(4), 843–853.

García-García, F., De la Herrán-Arita, A. K., Juárez-Aguilar, E., Regalado-Santiago, C., Millán-Aldaco, D., Blanco-Centurión, C., & Drucker-Colín, R. (2011). Growth hormone improves hippocampal adult cell survival and counteracts the inhibitory effect of prolonged sleep deprivation on cell proliferation. *Brain Research Bulletin, 84*(3), 252–257.

Garcia-Rill, E., Charlesworth, A., Heister, D., Ye, M., & Hayer, A. (2008). The developmental decrease in REM sleep: The role of transmitters and electrical coupling. *Sleep: Journal of Sleep and Sleep Disorders Research, 31*(5), 673–690.

Gardner, H. (2011). Changing minds: How the application of the multiple intelligences (MI) framework could positively contribute to the theory and practice of international negotiation. In F. Aquilar & M. Galluccio (Eds.), *Psychological and political strategies for peace negotiation: A cognitive approach* (pp. 1–14). New York: Springer Science Business Media.

Gardner, H. (2008). Who owns intelligence? In M. H. Immordino-Yang (Ed.), *The Jossey-Bass reader on the brain and learning* (pp. 120–132). San Francisco, CA: Jossey-Bass.

Gardner, H. (2004). *Frames of mind: The theory of multiple intelligences.* New York: Basic Books.

Gardner, H. (2000). *Intelligence reframed: Multiple intelligences for the 21st century.* New York: Basic Books.

Gardner, H. (1993). *Multiple intelligences: The theory in practice.* New York: Basic Books.

Gardner, H., & Traub, J. (2010). A debate on "multiple intelligences." In D. Gordon (Ed.), *Cerebrum 2010: Emerging ideas in brain science* (pp. 34–61). Washington, DC: Dana Press.

Gardner, H., & White, J. (2010). Is the theory of multiple intelligences valid? In B. Slife (Ed.), *Clashing views on psychological issues* (16th Ed., pp. 198–216). New York: McGraw-Hill.

Gardner, W. L., & Martinko, M. J. (1996). Using the Myers-Briggs Type Indicator to study managers: A literature review and research agenda. *Journal of Management, 22*(1), 45–83.

Gariepy, J-L., & Blair, C. (2008). A biological window on psychological development. *Developmental Psychobiology, 50,* 1–3.

Garlow, S. J. (2002). Age, gender, and ethnicity differences in patterns of cocaine and ethanol use preceding suicide. *American Journal of Psychiatry, 159*(4), 615–619.

Garoff-Eaton, R. J., Slotnick, S. D., & Schacter, D. L. (2006). Not all false memories are created equal: The neural basis of false recognition. *Cerebral Cortex, 16,* 1645–1652.

Garry, M., & Hayne, H. (Eds.). (2013). *Do justice and let the sky fall: Elizabeth F. Loftus and her contributions to science, law, and academic freedom.* New York, NY: Psychology Press.

Garver, D. L. (2006). Evolution of antipsychotic intervention in the schizophrenic psychosis. *Current Drug Targets, 7*(9), 1205–1215.

Garvey, C. (1974). Requests and responses in children's speech. *Journal of Child Language, 2,* 41–60.

Gask, L., Aseem, S., Waquas, A., & Waheed, W. (2011). Isolation, feeling 'stuck' and loss of control: Understanding persistence of depression in British Pakistani women. *Journal of Affective Disorders, 128*(1–2), 49–55.

Gaston, K. E. (1978). Interocular transfer of a visually mediated conditioned food aversion in chicks. *Behavioral Biology, 24,* 272–278.

Gathercoal, K. A., McMinn, L., Peterson, M., & Schenk, J. (2010). Female and male psychologists in academic administration: Resource control and perceived influence. *Academic Leadership: The Online Journal, 8*(3). Retrieved from http://www.academicleadership.org/article/print/Female_and_Male_Psychologists_in_Academic_Administration_Resource_Control_and_Perceived_Influence.

Gawande, A. (2008). The itch. *The New Yorker*, June 30.

Gawronski, B. (2012). Back to the future of dissonance theory: Cognitive consistency as a core motive. *Social Cognition, 30*(6), 652–668.

Gawronski, B., & De Houwer, J. A. N. (2014). Implicit Measures in Social and Personality Psychology. In H.T. Reis and C.M. Judd (Eds.), *Handbook of Research Methods in Social and Personality Psychology* (pp. 283–310). New York: Cambridge University Press.

Gawronski, B., Deutsch, R., Mbirkou, S., Seibt, B., & Strack, F. (2008). When "just say no" is not enough: Affirmation versus negation training and the reduction of automatic stereotype activation. *Journal of Experimental Social Psychology, 44,* 370–377.

Gaynor, S. T., & Baird, S. C. (2007). Personality disorders. In D.W. Woods & J. W. Kanter (Eds.), *Understanding Behavior Disorders: A Contemporary Behavioral Perspective*. Reno, NV: Context Press.

Gazzaniga, M. S. (2010). Neuroscience and the correct level of explanation for understanding mind: An extraterrestrial roams through some neuroscience laboratories and concludes earthlings are not grasping how best to understand the mind–brain interface. *Trends in Cognitive Sciences, 14*(7), 291–292.

Gazzaniga, M. S. (2009). Two brains: My life in science. In P. Rabbitt (Ed.), *Inside Psychology* (pp. 101–116). Oxford: Oxford University Press.

Gazzaniga, M. S. (2005). Forty-five years of split-brain research and still going strong. *Nature Reviews Neuroscience, 6*, 653–659.

Gazzaniga, M. S. (1995). The visual analysis of shape and form. *The cognitive neurosciences* (pp. 339–350). Cambridge, MA: MIT Press.

Geary, D. C. (2005). *The Origin of Mind*. American Psychological Association.

Geddes, J. R., Stroup, T. S., & Lieberman, J. A. (2011). Comparative efficacy and effectiveness in the drug treatment of schizophrenia. In D. R. Weinberger & P. J. Harrison (Eds.), *Schizophrenia* (3rd Ed.). Hoboken, NJ: Blackwell-Wiley.

Gehrmann, J. (1996). Microglia: a sensor to threats in the nervous system? *Research in Virology, 147*(2–3), 79–88.

Geldard, F. A. (1972). *The human senses (2nd Ed.)*. New York: Wiley.

Gelinas, R., & Munroe-Chandler, K. (2006). Psychological skills for successful ice hockey goaltenders. *Athletic Insight: The Online Journal of Sport Psychology, 8*(2), Retrieved from http://athleticinsight.com/Vol8Iss2/Hockey PDF.pdf.

Gentsch, K., Grandjean, D., & Scherer, K. R. (2014). Coherence explored between emotion components: Evidence from event-related potentials and facial electromyography. *Biological Psychology, 98*, 7–81.

Georgas, J. (2003). Cross-cultural psychology, intelligence, and cognitive processes. In J. Georgas, L. G. Weiss, F. J. R. van de Vijver, & D. H. Saklofske (Eds.), *Culture and children's intelligence: Cross-cultural analysis of the WISC-III* (pp. 23–37). San Diego, CA: Academic Press.

George, A. (2013). Elizabeth Loftus: The false memories that pervade our lives could have therapeutic uses. *New Scientist, 219*(2931), 28–29.

George, T. P., & Weinberger, A. H. (2008). Nicotine and tobacco. In H. D. Kleber & M. Galanter (Eds.), *The American Psychiatric Publishing textbook of substance abuse treatment* (4th Ed.). Arlington, VA: American Psychiatric Publishing.

Geraerts, E. (2010). Posttraumatic memory. In G. Rosend & B. C. Frueh (Eds.), *Clinician's guide to posttraumatic stress disorder* (pp. 77–95). Hoboken, NJ: John Wiley & Sons.

Gerard, D. L. (1998). Chiarugi and Pinel considered: Soul's brain/person's mind. *Journal of the History of the Behavioral Sciences, 33*(4), 381–403.

Gerardi, M., Rothbaum, B. O., Astin, M. C., & Kelley, M. (2010). Cortisol response following exposure treatment for PTSD in rape victims. *Journal of Aggression, Maltreatment & Trauma, 19*(4), 349–356.

Gerbner, G., Gross, L., Morgan, M., & Signorielli, N. (1994). Growing up with television: The cultivation perspective. In J. Bryant & D. Zillmann (Eds.), *Media effects: Advances in theory and research* (pp. 17–41). Hillsdale, NJ: Erlbaum.

Gernsbacher, M. A., & Kaschak, M. P. (2003). Neuroimaging studies of language production and comprehension. *Annual Review of Psychology, 54*, 91–114.

Gershoff, E. T. (2002). Corporal punishment by parents and associated child behaviors and experiences: A meta-analytic and theoretical review. *Psychological Bulletin, 128*(4), 539–579.

Gershon, I. (2010). *The breakup 2.0: Disconnecting over new media*. Ithaca, NY: Cornell University Press, Sage House.

Geva, N., & Defrin, R. (2013). Enhanced pain modulation among triathletes: A possible explanation for their exceptional capabilities. *Pain, 154*(11), 2317–2323.

Gfeller, J. D., & Gorassini, D. R. (2010). Enhancing hypnotizability and treatment response. In S. J. Lynn, J. W. Rhue, & I. Kirsch (Eds.), *Handbook of clinical hypnosis (2nd Ed.)* (pp. 339–355). Washington, DC: American Psychological Association.

Giancola, P. R. (2002). Alcohol-related aggression in men and women: The influence of dispositional aggressivity. *Journal of Studies on Alcohol, 63*(6), 696–708.

Gibbons, D. E., & Lynn, S. J. (2010). Hypnotic inductions: A primer. In S. J. Lynn, J. W. Rhue, & I. Kirsch (Eds.), *Handbook of clinical hypnosis (2nd Ed.)* (pp. 267–291). Washington, DC: American Psychological Association.

Gibbons, R. D., Brown, C. H., Hur, K., Davis, J. M., & Mann, J. (2012). Suicidal thoughts and behavior with antidepressant treatment: Reanalysis of the randomized placebo-controlled studies of fluoxetine and venlafaxine. *Archives of General Psychiatry, 69*(6), 580–587.

Gibson, E. L. (2012). The psychobiology of comfort eating: implications for neuropharmacological interventions. *Behavioural Pharmacology, 23*(5 and 6), 442–460.

Giedd, J. N. (2009). Linking adolescent sleep, brain maturation and behavior. *Journal of Adolescent Health, 45*(4), 319–320.

Giedd, J. N., Blumenthal, J., Jeffries, N. O., Castellanos, F. X., Liu, H., Zijdenbos, A., . . . (1999). Brain development during childhood and adolescence: A longitudinal MRI study. *Nature Neuroscience, 2*, 861–863.

Giedd, J. N., Classen, L. S., Lenroot, R., Greenstein, D., Wallace, G. L., Ordaz, S. . . . Chrousos, G. P. (2006). Puberty-related influences on brain development. *Molecular and Cellular Endocrinology, 25*, 154–162.

Gigerenzer, G. (2004). Fast and frugal heuristics: The tools of founded rationality. In D. J. Koehler & N. Harvey (Eds.), *Blackwell handbook of judgment and decision making* (pp. 62–88). Malden, MA: Blackwell Publishing.

Gigerenzer, G., & Goldstein, D. G. (1996). Reasoning the fast and frugal way: Models of bounded rationality. *Psychological Review, 103*, 650–669.

Gilbertson, M. W., Shenton, M. E., Ciszewski, A., Kasai, K., Lasko, N. B., Orr, S. P., & Pitman, R. K. (2002). Smaller hippocampal volume predicts pathologic vulnerability to psychological trauma. *Nature Neuroscience, 5*(11), 1242–1247.

Gilchrist, A. L., & Cowan, N. (2010). Conscious and unconscious aspects of working memory. In I. Czigler & I. Winkler (Eds.), *Unconscious memory representations in perception* (pp. 1–35) Amsterdam, Netherlands: John Benjamins Publishing Company.

Gilligan, C. (2011). *Joining the resistance*. Cambridge, UK: Polity Press.

Gilligan, C. (2004). Recovering psyche: Reflections on life-history and history. *The Annual of Psychoanalysis, 32*, 131–147.

Gilligan, C. (1993). *In a different voice*. Cambridge, MA: Harvard University Press.

Gilligan, C. (1982). *In a different voice: Psychological theory and women's development*. Cambridge, MA: Harvard University Press.

Gillham, J., Adams-Deutsch, Z., Werner, J., Reivich, K., Coulter-Heindl, V., Linkins, M., & Seligman, M. E. P. (2011). Character strengths predict subjective well-being during adolescence. *The Journal of Positive Psychology, 6*(1), 31–44.

Giltay, E. J., Geleijnse, J. M., Zitman, F. G., Hoehstra, T., & Schouten, E. G. (2004). Dispositional optimism and all-cause and cardiovascular mortality in a prospective cohort of elderly Dutch men and women. *Archives of General Psychiatry, 61*, 1126–1135.

Ginandes, C. S. (2006). Six players on the inner stage: Using ego state therapy with the medically ill. *International Journal of Clinical and Experimental Hypnosis, 54*(2), 113–129.

Gingras, Y. (2002). The costs of dropping out of high school. *Pan-Canadian Education Research Agenda Symposium Report*. Retrieved from http://cesc-csce.ca/pceradocs/2000/00Gingras_e.pdf.

Gioia, G. (2007). *Expert: Millions get concussions*. Retrieved from philly.com.

Girden, E. R., & Kabacoff, R. I. (2011). *Evaluating research articles: From start to finish* (3rd Ed.). Thousand Oaks, CA: Sage Publications.

Giulio T., & Chiara, C. (2014). Sleep and the price of plasticity: From synaptic and cellular homeostasis to memory consolidation and integration. *Neuron, 81*(1), 12–34.

Gläscher, J., Rudrauf, D., Colom, R., Paul, L. K., Tranel, D., Damasio, H., & Adolphs, R. (2010). Distributed neural system for general intelligence revealed by lesion mapping. *PNAS Proceedings of the National Academy of Sciences of the United States of America, 107*(10), 4705–4709.

Glaser, V., Carlini, V. P., Gabach, L., Ghersi, M., de Barioglio, S. R., Ramirez, O. A., …Latini, A. (2010). The intra–hippocampal leucine administration impairs memory consolidation and LTP generation in rats. *Cellular and Molecular Neurobiology, 30*(7), 1067–1075. doi: 10.1007/s10571-010-9538-4

Glasmeier, A. K. (2006). *An atlas of poverty in America: One nation pulling apart*. New York: Taylor and Francis Group.

Glass, J. (2005). Sociological perspectives on work and family. In S. M. Bianchi, L. M. Casper, & B. R. King (Eds.), *Work, Family, Health, and Well-Being* (pp. 215–229). Mahwah, NJ: Lawrence Erlbaum Associates Publishers.

Glassenberg, A. N., Feinberg, D. R., Jones, B. C., Little, A. C., & Debruine, L. M. (2010). Sex-dimorphic face shape preference in heterosexual and homosexual men and women. *Archives of Sexual Behavior, 39*(4), 1289–1296.

Glenn, A. L., Johnson, A. K., & Raine, A. (2013). Antisocial Personality Disorder: A Current Review. *Current Psychiatry Reports, 15*(12), 1–8.

Godart, N. T., Perdereau, F., Rein, Z., Berthoz, S., Wallier, J., Jeammet, P., et al. (2007). Comorbidity studies of eating disorders and mood disorders. Critical review of the literature. *Journal of Affective Disorders, 97(1–3)*, 37–49.

Gödde, G. (2010). Freud and nineteenth-century philosophical sources on the unconscious. In A. Nicholls & M. Liebscher (Eds.), *Thinking the unconscious: Nineteenth-century German thought* (pp. 261–286). New York, NY: Cambridge University Press.

Godfrey, J. R. (2004). Toward optimal health: The experts discuss therapeutic humor. *Journal of Women's Health, 13*(5), 474–479.

Gogtay, N., Giedd, J. N., Lusk, L., Hayashi, K. M., Rapoport, J. L., Thompson, P. M., . . . (2004). Dynamic mapping of human cortical development during childhood through early adulthood. *Proceedings of the National Academy of Sciences, 101*, 8174–8179.

Gohm, C. L., & Clore, G. L. (2002). Four latent traits of emotional experience and their involvement in well-being, coping, and attributional style. *Cognition and Emotion, 16*, 495–518.

Gold, S. N., & Castillo, Y. (2010). Dealing with defenses and defensiveness in interviews. In D. L. Segal & M. Hersen (Eds.), *Diagnostic interviewing* (pp. 89–102). New York, NY: Springer Publishing Co.

Goldberg, A. E. (2008). Universal grammar? Or prerequisites for natural language? *Behavioral and Brain Sciences, 31*, 522–523.

Goldberg, R. F., Perfetti, C.A., & Schneider, W. (2006). Perceptual knowledge retrieval activates sensory brain regions. *Journal of Neuroscience, 26*, 4917–4921.

Goldenberg, I., & Goldenberg, H. (2011). Family therapy. In R. J. Corsini & D. Wedding (Eds.), *Current psychotherapies* (9th Ed.). Florence, KY: CENGAGE Learning.

Goldin-Meadow, S. (1999). The role of gesture in communication and thinking. *Trends in Cognitive Sciences, 3*, 419–429.

Goldstein, D. J., Potter, W. Z., Ciraulo, D. A., & Shader, R. I. (2011). Biological theories of depression and implications for current and new treatments. In D. A. Ciraulo & R. I. Shader (Eds.), *Pharmacotherapy of depression* (2nd Ed., pp. 1–32). New York: Springer Science + Business Media.

Goldstein, E. B. (2014). *Sensation and Perception* (9th ed.). Belmont, CA: Wadsworth, Cengage Learning.

Goldstein, E. B. (2010a). Constancy. In E.B. Goldstein (Ed.), *Encyclopedia of Perception*, Thousand Oaks, CA: Sage.

Goldstein, E. B. (2010b). *Sensation and Perception* (8th ed). Belmont, CA: Wadsworth, Cengage.

Goldstone, A. P., Holland, A. J., Butler, J. V., & Whittington, J. E. (2012). Appetite hormones and the transition to hyperphagia in children with Prader-Willi syndrome. *International Journal of Obesity, 36*, 1564–1570.

Goleman, D. (2011). *The brain and emotional intelligence: New insights, more than sound.* Northampton, MA: LLC.

Goleman, D. (2006). *Social intelligence: The new science of human relationships.* New York, NY: Bantam Books.

Golland, Y., Bentin, S., Gelbard, H., Benjamini, Y., Heller, R., Nir, Y., Hasson, U., & Malach, R. (2007). Extrinsic and intrinsic systems in the posterior cortex of the human brain revealed during natural sensory stimulation. *Cerebral Cortex, 17*, 766–777.

Golub, S. A., & Langer, E. J. (2007). Challenging assumptions about adult development: Implications for the health of older adults. In C. M. Aldwin, C. L. Park, & A. Spiro (Eds.), *Handbook of Health Psychology and Aging.* New York, NY: The Guilford Press.

González, J., Barros-Loscertales, A., Pulvermüller, F., Meseguer, V., Sanjuán, A., Belloch, V., & Avila C. (2006). Reading cinnamon activates olfactory brain regions. *Neuroimage, 32*, 906–912.

Gonzalez, T. (2010). Review of why kids kill: Inside the minds of school shooters. *Professional School Counseling, 13*(5), 281–282.

Goodenough, F. L. (1932). Expression of the emotions in a blind-deaf child. *Journal of Abnormal and Social Psychology, 27*, 328–333.

Goodwin, C. J. (2011). *Research in psychology: Methods and design* (6th Ed.). Hoboken, NJ: John Wiley & Sons.

Gopnik, A., & Astington, J. W. (1988). Children's understanding of representational change and its relation to the understanding of false belief and the appearance reality distinction. *Child Development, 59*, 26–37.

Gorman, T. (1996). Television: Glorious past, uncertain future. Statistics Canada, 63F0002XPB No. 6.

Goryakin, Y., & Suhrcke, M. (2014). Economic development, urbanization, technological change and overweight: What do we learn from 244 Demographic and Health Surveys? *Economics and Human Biology, 14*, 109–127.

Goto, Y., & Grace, A. A. (2008) Limbic and cortical information processing in the nucleus accumbens. *Trends in Neurosciences, 31*, 552–558.

Gottfredson, L. S. (1997). Why g matters: The complexity of everyday life. *Intelligence, 24*(1), 79–132.

Gottman, J. M., & Levenson, R. W. (1988). The social psychophysiology of marriage. In P. Noller & M. A. Fitzpatrick (Eds.), *Perspectives on marital interaction* (pp. 182–200). Clevedon: Multilingual Matters.

Gottman, J. M., & Notarius, C. I. (2002). Marital research in the 20th century and a research agenda for the 21st century. *Family Process, 41*(2), 159–197.

Goubet, N., Strasbaugh, K., & Chesney, J. (2007). Familiarity breeds content? Soothing effect of a familiar odor on full-term newborns. *Journal of Developmental and Behavioral Pediatrics, 28*, 189–194.

Gould, E. (2007). How widespread is adult neurogenesis in mammals? *Nature Reviews Neuroscience, 8*, 481–488.

Gould, S. J., & Lewontin, R. C. (1979). The sandrels of San Marco and the Panglossian paradigm: A critique of the adaptation programme. *Proceedings of the Royal Society of London, Series B, 205*, 581–598.

Gourine, A. V., Kasymov, V., Marina, N., Tang, F., Figueiredo, M., Lane, S., Teschemacher, A. G., Spyer, K. M., Deisseroth, K., & Kasparov, S. (2010). Astrocytes control breathing through pH dependent release of ATP. *Science, 329*(5991), 571–575.

Government of Canada. (2006). *The Human Face of Mental Health and Mental Illness in Canada 2006.* Accessed January 2015 at www.phac-aspc.gc.ca /publicat/human-humain06/pdf/human_face_e.pdf.

Gow, A. J., Johnson, W., Pattie, A., Brett, C. E., Roberts, B., Starr, J. M., & Deary, I. J. (2011). Stability and change in intelligence from age 11 to ages 70, 79, and 87: The Lothian birth cohorts of 1921 and 1936. *Psychology and Aging, 26*(1), 232–240. doi: 10.1037/a0021072

Grabner, R. H., Stern, E., & Neubauer, A. C. (2003). When intelligence loses its impact: Neural efficiency during reasoning in a familiar area. *International Journal of Psychophysiology, 49*(2), 89–98.

Grady, D. (1993). The vision think: Mainly in the brain. *Discover, 14*(6), 56–66.

Grady, M. M., & Stahl, S. M. (2012). Practical guide for prescribing MAOIs: debunking myths and removing barriers. *CNS Spectrums, 17*(01), 2–10.

Grainger, J., Dufau, D., Montant, M., Ziegler, J. C. & Fagot, J. (2012). Orthographic Processing in Baboons (*Papio papio*). *Science, 336*, 245–248.

Gray, J. (1992). *Men are from Mars, women are from Venus.* New York, NY: HarperCollins.

Graziano, M. S. (2006). The organization of behavioral repertoire in motor cortex. *Annual Review of Neuroscience, 29*, 105–134.

Green, B. L., Ayoub, C., Bartlett, J. D., Ende, A. V., Furrer, C., Chazan-Cohen, R., Vallotton, C., & Klevens, J. (2014). The effect of Early Head Start on child welfare system involvement: A first look at longitudinal child maltreatment outcomes. *Child and Youth Services Review, 42*, 127–135.

Green, J. P. (2010). Hypnosis and smoking cessation: Research and application. In S. J. Lynn, J. W. Rhue, & I. Kirsch (Eds.), *Handbook of clinical hypnosis* (2nd Ed.) (pp. 593–614). Washington, DC: American Psychological Association.

Greenberg, J. (1978). The Americanization of Roseto. *Science News, 113*, 378–382.

Greenberg, L., & Goldman, R. N. (2008). *Emotion-focused couples therapy.* Washington, D.C.: American Psychological Association.

Greenberg, N., Carr, J. A., & Summers, C. H. (2002). Causes and consequences of stress. *Integrative and Comparative Biology, 42*(3), 508–516.

Greene, J. (2003). From neural "is" to moral "ought:" What are the moral implications of neuroscientfic moral psychology? *Neuroscience, 4*, 847–850.

Greenwald, A. G., Banaji, M. R., Rudman, L. A., Farnham, S. D., Nosek, B. A., & Mellott, D. S. (2002). A unified theory of implicit attitudes, stereotypes, self-esteem, and self-concept. *Psychological Review, 109*(1), 3–25.

Gregory, D. (2010). Visual imagery: Visual format or visual content? *Mind and Language, 25*(4), 394–417.

Gregory, R. J. (2013). *Psychological testing: History, principles and applications* (7th ed.). Toronto, ON: Pearson.

Gregoski, M. J., Barnes, V. A., Tingen, M. S., Harshfield, G. A., & Treiber, F. A. (2011). Breathing awareness meditation and LifeSkills training programs influence upon ambulatory blood pressure and sodium excretion among African American adolescents. *Journal of Adolescent Health, 48*(1), 59–64.

Grieco, R., & Edwards, L. (2010). *The other depression: Bipolar disorder* (2nd Ed.). New York: Routledge/Taylor & Francis Group.

Groer, M., Meagher, M. W., & Kendall-Tackett, K. (2010). An overview of stress and immunity. *The psychoneuroimmunology of chronic disease: Exploring the links between inflammation, stress, and illness* (pp. 9–22). Washington, DC: American Psychological Association.

Gross, C. G. (2005). Processing the facial image: a brief history. *American Psychologist, 60*, 755–763.

Gross, J. J. (1998). The emerging field of emotion regulation: An integrative review. *Review of General Psychology, 2*, 271–299.

Gross, J. J., & John, O. P. (2003). Individual differences in two emotion regulation processes: Implications for affect, relationships, and well-being. *Journal of Personality and Social Psychology, 85*(2), 348–362.

Gross, J. J., & John, O. P. (1998). Mapping the domain of expressivity: Multimethod evidence for a hierarchical model. *Journal of Personality and Social Psychology, 74*(1), 170–191.

Gross, J. J., Richards, J. M., & John, O. P. (2006). Emotion regulation in everyday life. In D. K. Snyder, J. A. Simpson, & J. N. Hughes (Eds.), *Emotion Regulation in Families: Pathways to Dysfunction and Health* (pp. 13–25). Washington, DC: American Psychological Association.

Grossmann, K., Grossmann, K., Fremmer-Bombik, E., Kindler, H., Scheuerer-Englisch, H., & Zimmermann, P. (2002). The uniqueness of the child-father attachment relationship: Fathers' sensitive and challenging play as a pivotal variable in a 16-year longitudinal study. *Social Development, 11*(3), 301–337.

Grotenhermen, F. (2002). Review of therapeutic effects. *Cannabis and Cannabinoids: Pharmacology, Toxicology and Therapeutic Potential.* New York City: Haworth Press.

Gruneberg, M. M., & Sykes, R. N. (1993). The generalisability of confidence—accuracy studies in eyewitnessing. *Memory, 1*(3), 185–189.

Grusec, J. E., Chaparro, M. P., Johnston, M., & Sherman, A. (2013). The development of moral behavior from a socialization perspective. In M. Killen & J. G. Smetana (Eds.), *Handbook of Moral Development* (2nd ed., pp. 113–134). New York: Psychology Press.

Grusec, J. E., & Ungerer, J. (2003). Effective socialization as problem solving and the role of parenting cognitions. In L. Kuczynski (Ed.,), *Handbook of dynamics in parent–child relations* (pp. 211–228). Thousand Oaks, CA: Sage.

Guberman, A. (2004). Vagus nerve stimulation in the treatment of epilepsy. *Canadian Medical Association Journal, 171(10),* 1165–1166.

Guchait, P., Hamilton, K., & Hua, N. (2014). Personality predictors of team taskwork understanding and transactive memory systems in service management teams. *International Journal of Contemporary Hospitality Management, 26(3),* 401–425.

Guéguen, N. (2002). Foot-in-the-door technique and computer-mediated communication, *Computers in Human Behavior, 18(1),* 11–15.

Guenther, T., Lovell, N. H., & Suaning, G. J. (2012). Bionic vision: system architectures-a review. *Expert Review of Medical Devices, 9(1),* 33-48.

Guimon, J. (2010). Prejudice and realities in stigma. *International Journal of Mental Health, 39(3),* 20–43.

Gumustekin, K., Seven, B., Karabulut, N., Aktas, O., Gursan, N., Aslan, S., Keles, M., Varoglu, E., & Dane, S. (2004). Effects of sleep deprivation, nicotine, and selenium on wound healing in rats (Abstract). *International Journal of Neuroscience, 114(11),* 1433–1442.

Gunderson, J. G. (2011). Borderline personality disorder. *The New England Journal of Medicine, 364(21),* 2037–2042.

Gunderson, L., & Scarr, S. (2001). The evils of the use of IQ tests to define learning disabilities in first and second language learners. *The Reading Teacher, 55(1),* 48–55.

Gunzelmann, G., Moore, L. R., Gluck, K. A., Van Dongen, H. P. A., & Dinges, D. F. (2011). Fatigue in sustained attention: Generalizing mechanisms for time awake to time on task. In P. L. Ackerman (Ed.), *Cognitive fatigue: Multidisciplinary perspectives on current research and future applications* (pp. 83–101). Washington, DC: American Psychological Association.

Gurman, A. S., & Snyder, D. K. (2011). Couple therapy. In J. C. Norcross, G. R. VandenBos, & D. K. Freedheim (Eds.), *History of psychotherapy: Continuity and change* (2nd Ed., pp. 485–496). Washington, DC: American Psychological Association.

Gustavson, C. R., Garcia, J., Hankins, W. G., & Rusiniak, K. W. (1974). Coyote predation control by aversive conditioning. *Science, 184,* 581–583.

Gustavson, C. R., Kelly, D. J., & Sweeney, M. (1976). Prey-lithium aversions: Coyotes and wolves. *Behavioral Biology, 17,* 61–72.

Haas, B. W., Omura, K., Constable, R. T., & Canli, T. (2007). Emotional conflict and neuroticism: Personality-dependent activation in the amygdala and subgenual anterior cingulate. *Behavioral Neuroscience, 121(2),* 249–256.

Haber, S. N. (2003). The primate basal ganglia: parallel and integrative networks. *Journal of Chemical Neuroanatomy, 26(4),* 317–330.

Hackett, T. A., & Kaas, J. H. (2009). Audition. In G. G. Berntson & J. T. Cacioppo (Eds.), *Handbook of neuroscience for the behavioral sciences.* New York: NY: Wiley.

Hackney, C. M. (2010). Auditory processing: Peripheral. In E.B. Goldstein (Ed.), *Encyclopedia of Perception.* Thousand Oaks, CA: Sage.

Hagelin, J., Carlsson, H.-E., & Hau, J. (2003). An overview of surveys on how people view animal experimentation: Some factors that may influence the outcome. *Public Understanding of Science, 12(1),* 67–81.

Hagemoser, S. D. (2009). Braking the bandwagon: Scrutinizing the science and politics of empirically supported therapies. *Journal of Psychology: Interdisciplinary and Applied, 143(6),* 601–614.

Haldeman, D. C. (1994). The practice and ethics of sexual orientation conversion. *Journal of Consulting and Clinical Psychology, 62(2),* 221–227.

Halkjelsvik, T. (2014). Do disgusting and fearful anti-smoking advertisements increase or decrease support for tobacco control policies? *International Journal of Drug Policy, 25(4),* 744–747.

Hall, C. W., & Webster, R. E. (2002). Traumatic symptomatology characteristics of adult children of alcoholics. *Journal of Drug Education, 32(3),* 195–211.

Hall, J. A., Murphy, N. A., & Mast, M. S. (2006). Recall of nonverbal cues: Exploring a new definition of interpersonal sensitivity. *Journal of Nonverbal Behavior, 30(4),* 141–155.

Halladay, L. R., Zelikowsky, M. L., Blair, H. T., & Fanselow, M. S. (2012). Reinstatement of extinguished fear by an unextinguished conditional stimulus. *Frontiers in Behavioral Neuroscience, 6(2),* 18.

Halle, M. (1990). Phonology. In D. N. Osherson and H. Lasnick (Eds.), *An Invitation to Cognitive Science, Vol. 1: Language.* Cambridge MA: MIT Press.

Halliday, G. (2004). Dreamwork and nightmares with incarcerated juvenile felons. *Dreaming, 14(1),* 30–42.

Hallman, T. A., & Munroe-Chandler, K. J. (2009). An Examination of Ice Hockey Players' Imagery Use and Movement Imagery Ability. *Journal of Imagery Research in Sport and Physical Activity, 4(1).*

Halpern, D. F. (2012). *Sex differences in cognitive ability* (4th Ed.). New York, NY: Psychology Press.

Hamani, C., Diwan, M., Raymond, R., Nobrega, J. N., Macedo, C. E., Brandao, M. L., & Fletcher, P. J. (2011). Reply to: Electrical brain stimulation in depression: Which target(s)? *Biological Psychiatry, 69(4),* e7–e8.

Hamann, S. B., Ely, T. D., Hoffman, J. M., & Kilts, C. D. (2002). Ecstasy and agony: Activation of the human amygdala in positive and negative emotion. *Psychological Science, 13(2),* 135–141.

Hambree, R. (1988). Correlates, causes, effects, and treatments of test anxiety. *Review of Educational Research, 58(1),* 47–77.

Hambrick, D. Z., & Engle, R. W. (2003). The role of working memory in problem solving. In J. E. Davidson & R. J. Sternberg (Eds.), *The psychology of problem solving* (pp. 176–206). New York, NY: Cambridge University Press.

Hamel, E. (2007). Serotonin and migraine: Biology and clinical implications. *Cephalalgia, 27(11),* 1293–1300.

Hammen, C., Kim, E. Y., Eberhart, N. K., & Brennan, P. A. (2009). Chronic and acute stress and the prediction of major depression in women. *Depression and Anxiety, 26(8),* 718–723.

Hammond, D. C. (2008). Hypnosis as sole anesthesia for major surgeries: Historical & contemporary perspectives. *American Journal of Clinical Hypnosis, 51(2),* 101–121.

Han, J., Kesner, P., Metna-Laurent, M., Duan, T., Xu, L., Georges, F., . . . Zhang, X. (2012). Acute cannabinoids impair working memory through astroglial CB1 receptor modulation of hippocampal LTD. *Cell, 148,* 1039–1050.

Haney, C., Banks, C., & Zimbardo, P. (1973). Interpersonal dynamics in a simulated prison. *International Journal of Criminology & Penology, 1,* 69–97.

Haney, M. (2008). Neurobiology of stimulants. In H. D. Kleber & M. Galanter (Eds.), *The American Psychiatric Publishing textbook of substance abuse treatment (4th Ed.).* Washington, DC: American Psychiatric Publishing.

Hanin, Y. L. (1997). Emotions and athletic performance: Individual zones of optimal functioning. *European Yearbook of Sport Psychology, 1,* 29–72.

Hanna, D., Kershaw, K., & Chaplin, R. (2009). How specialist ECT consultants inform patients about memory loss. *Psychiatric Bulletin, 33(11),* 412–415.

Hardt, O., Nader, K., & Nadel, L. (2013). Decay happens: the role of active forgetting in memory. *Trends in Cognitive Sciences, 17(3),* 111–120.

Hare, R. D. (2003). *Psychopathy checklist-revised technical manual, 2nd Ed.* Toronto: Multihealth Systems, Inc.

Hare, R. D. (1993) *Without Conscience: The Disturbing World of Psychopaths Among Us.* New York, NY: Pocket Books.

Harker, L., & Keltner, D. (2001). Expressions of positive emotion in women's college yearbook pictures and their relationship to personality and life outcomes across adulthood. *Journal of Personality and Social Psychology, 80(1),* 112–124.

Harkness, A. R., Reynolds, S. M., & Lilienfeld, S. O. (2014). A review of systems for psychology and psychiatry: adaptive systems, personality psychopathology five (PSY-5), and the DSM-5. *Journal of Personality Assessment, 96(2),* 121–139.

Harkness, K. L., Lumley, M. N., & Truss, A. E. (2008). Stress generation in adolescent depression: The moderating role of child abuse and neglect. *Journal of Abnormal Child Psychology, 36(3),* 421–432.

Harlé, K. M., Chang, L. J., van 't Wout, M., & Sanfey, A. G. (2012). The neural mechanisms of affect infusion in social economic decision-making: A mediating role of the anterior insula. *NeuroImage, 61(1),* 32–40.

Harlow, H. F. (1958). The nature of love. *American Psychologist, 13(12),* 673.

Harlow, H. F., & Zimmerman, R. (1959). Affectional responses in the infant monkey. *Science, 130,* 421–432.

Harlow, J. M. (1868). Recovery from the passage of an iron bar through the head. *Publications of the Massachusetts Medical Society, 2,* 327–347.

Harlow, J. M. (1848). Passage of an iron rod through the head. *Boston Medical and Surgical Journal, 39,* 389–393. Republished in Neylan, T. C. (1999). Frontal lobe function: Mr. Phineas Gage's famous injury. *Journal of Neuropsychiatry and Clinical Neuroscience, 11,* 281–283.

Harman, C., & Fox, N. A. (1997). Frontal and attentional mechanisms regulating distress experience and expression during infancy. In N. A. Krasnegor, G. R. Lyon, & P. S. Goldman-Rakic (Eds.), *Development of the Prefrontal Cortex: Evolution, Neurobiology, and Behavior* (pp. 191–208). Baltimore, MD: Paul H Brookes Publishing.

Harmison, R. J. (2011). Peak performance in sport: Identifying ideal performance states and developing athletes' psychological skills. *Sport, Exercise, and Performance Psychology, 1(S),* 3–18.

Harper, D. (2014). *Online Etymology Dictionary.* Retrieved from http://www.etymologyonline.com.

Harrell, W. A. (1981). Verbal aggressiveness in spectators at professional hockey games: The effects of tolerance of violence and amount of exposure to hockey. *Human Relations, 34(8),* 643–655.

Harris, J. C. (2010). *Intellectual disability: A guide for families and professionals.* New York, NY: Oxford University Press.

Harrison, R. V. (2008). Noise-induced hearing loss in children: A 'less than silent' environmental danger. *Paediatric Children's Health, 13(5),* 377–382.

Harrison, Y., & Horne, J. A. (2000). The impact of sleep deprivation on decision making: A review. *Journal of Experimental Psychology: Applied, 6,* 236–249.

Hart, C., Ksir, C., & Oakley, R. (2010). *Drugs, society, and human behavior.* New York, NY: McGraw-Hill.

Hartman, D. E. (2009). Test review: Wechsler Adult Intelligence Scale IV (WAIS IV): Return of the gold standard. *Applied Neuropsychology, 16(1),* 85–87.

Harvard Medical School. (2013) *Shaq Attacks Sleep Apnea*, video. *Apnea: Understanding and Treating Obstructive Sleep Apnea.* Harvard Medical School, Division of Sleep Medicine. Retrieved from http://healthysleep.med.harvard.edu/sleep-apnea.

Harvey, J. H. (2008). Growth through loss and adversity in close relationships. *Trauma, recovery, and growth: Positive psychological perspectives on posttraumatic stress* (pp. 125–143). Hoboken, NJ: John Wiley & Sons Inc.

Harvey, N.L., Srinivasan, R. S., Dillard, M. E., Johnson, N. C., Witte, M. H., Boyd, K., et al. (2005). Lymphatic vascular defects promoted by Prox1 haploinsufficiency cause adult-onset obesity. *Nature genetics, 37*(10), 1072–1081.

Harvey, P. (2012). *An introduction to Buddhism: Teachings, history, and practices.* Cambridge, UK: Cambridge University Press.

Harway, M. (Ed.). (2005). *Handbook of couples therapy.* New York, NY: Wiley.

Hasselmo, M. E. (1999). Neuromodulation: acetylcholine and memory consolidation. *Trends in Cognitive Sciences, 3*(9), 351–359.

Hasselmo, M. E., & Wyble, B. P. (1997). Free recall and recognition in a network model of the hippocampus: simulating effects of scopolamine on human memory function. *Behavioural Brain Research, 89*(1), 1–34.

Haslam, N., Loughman, S., & Perry, G. (2014). Meta-Milgram: An empirical synthesis of the obedience experiments. *PLoS One, 9*(4), e93927.

Hassin, R. R. (2005). Nonconscious control and implicit working memory. In R. R. Hassin, J. S. Uleman, & J. A. Bargh (Eds.), *The new unconscious* (pp. 196–222). New York, NY: Oxford University Press.

Häuser, W., Urrútia, G., Tort, S., Uçeyler, N., & Walitt, B. (2013). Serotonin and noradrenaline reuptake inhibitors (SNRIs) for fibromyalgia syndrome. *Cochrane Database of Systematic Reviews,* 1.

Hawkley, L. C., Berntson, G. G., Engeland, C. G., Marucha, P.T., Masi, C. M., & Cacioppo, J. T. (2005). *Canadian Psychology/Psychologie Canadienne, 46*(3), 115–125.

Hawley, W. R., Grissom, E. M., & Dohanich, G. P. (2011). The relationships between trait anxiety, place recognition memory, and learning strategy. *Behavioural Brain Research, 216*(2), 525–530. doi: 10.1016/j.bbr.2010.08.028

Haxel, B. R., Grant, L., & Mackay-Sim, A. (2008). Olfactory dysfunction after head injury. *The Journal of Head Trauma Rehabilitation, 23,* 407–413.

Hayaki, J., Friedman, M. A., & Brownell, K. D. (2002). Shame and severity of bulimic symptoms. *Eating Behaviors, 3*(1), 73–83.

Hayatbakhsh, M. R., Najman, J. M., McGee, T. R., Bor, W., & O'Callaghan, M. J. (2009). Early pubertal maturation in the prediction of early adult substance use: A prospective study. *Addiction, 104*(1), 59–66.

Haydon, P. G., Blendy, J., Moss, S. J., & Jackson, R. F. (2009). Astrocytic control of synaptic transmission and plasticity: a target for drugs of abuse? *Neuropharmacology, 56*(1), 83–90.

Hayes, S. C. (2004). Acceptance and commitment therapy, relational frame theory, and the third wave of behavioral and cognitive therapies. *Behavior Therapy, 35*(4), 639–665.

Hayes, S. C., Follette, V. M., & Linehan, M. M. (Eds.). (2004). *Mindfulness and acceptance: Expanding the cognitive-behavioral tradition.* New York: Guilford Press.

Haynes, S. G., Feinleib, M., & Kannel, W. B. (1980). The relationship of psychosocial factors to coronary heart disease in the Framingham study: III. Eight-year incidence of coronary heart disease. *American Journal of Epidemiology, 111*(1), 37–58.

Hazan, C., & Shaver, P. R. (2004). Attachment as an organizational framework for research on close relationships. In H. T. Reis & C. E. Rusbult (Eds.), *Close relationships: Key readings* (pp. 153–174). Philadelphia, PA: Taylor & Francis.

Hazan, C., & Shaver, P. R. (1994a). Attachment as an organizational framework for research on close relationships. *Psychological Inquiry: 5*(1), 1–22.

Hazan, C., & Shaver, P. R. (1994b). Deeper into attachment theory. *Psychological Inquiry, 5*(1), 68–79.

Hazan, C., & Shaver, P. R. (1987). Romantic love conceptualized as an attachment process. *Journal of Personality and Social Psychology, 52*(3), 511–524.

Hazlett, H. C., Hammer, J., Hooper, S. R., & Kamphaus, R. W. (2010). Down syndrome. In S. Goldstein & C. R. Reynolds (Eds.), *Handbook of neurodevelopmental and genetic disorders in children* (2nd Ed., pp. 362–381). New York: Guilford Press.

Hazrati, L. N., Tartaglia, M. C., Diamandis, P., Davis, K. D., Green, R. E., Wennberg, R., . . . Tator, C. H. (2013). Absence of chronic traumatic encephalopathy in retired football players with multiple concussions and neurological symptomology. *Frontiers in Human Neuroscience, 7,* 222.

Headey, B. (2008). Life goals matter to happiness: A revision of set point theory. *Social Indicators Research, 86*(2), 213–231.

Health Canada. (2009). *Canadian Alcohol and Drug Use Monitoring Survey.* Retrieved from http://www.hc-sc.gc.ca/hc-ps/drugs-drogues/stat/_2009/summary-sommaire-eng.php.

Health Canada. (2008). *Canadian Tobacco Use Monitoring Survey.* Retrieved from http://www.hc-sc.gc.ca/hc-ps/tobac-tabac/research-recherche/stat/ctums-esutc_2008/ann-eng.php.

Health Canada. (2003a). *Canada's seniors: No. 1 – A growing population.* Ottawa, ON: Author. Retrieved from http://www.hc-sc.gc.ca/sr-sr/pubs/hpr-rpms/bull/2006-capital-social-capital/index-eng.php.

Health Canada. (2003b). *Canadian guidelines for body weight classification in adults.* Retrieved from http://www.hc-sc.gc.ca/fn-an/alt_formats/hpfb-dgpsa/pdf/nutrition/weight_book-livres_des_poids-eng.pdf.

Health Canada. (2005a). *STOP fetal alcohol syndrome/fetal alcohol effects now!* Retrieved from www.hc-sc.gc.ca/fniah-spnia/pubs/famil/_preg-gros/stop-arret-syndrome/index-eng.php.

Health Canada. (2005b). *Frequently asked questions—Medical use of marijuana.* Retrieved from http://www.hc-sc.gc.ca/dhp-mps/marihuana/about-apropos/faq-eng.php.

Health Canada. (2002). *A report on mental illness in Canada.* Retrieved from http://www.phac-aspc.gc.ca/publicat/miic-mmac/pdf/men_ill_e.pdf.

Healthwise. 2005. Miscarriage—Topic Overview. *BC Health Guide.* Retrieved from http://www.bchealthguide.org/kbase/topic/mini/hw44090/overview.htm.

Healy, A. F., Kosslyn, S. M., & Shiffrin, R. M. (Eds.) (1992). *From learning processes to cognitive processes.* Hillsdale, NJ: Lawrence Erlbaum.

Healy, D. (2008). *Psychiatric drugs explained.* Elsevier Health Sciences.

Healy, D. (2005). *Psychiatric drugs explained, 4th Ed.* Britain: Elsevier Limited.

Healy, D., & Whitaker, C. (2003). Antidepressants and suicide: risk–benefit conundrums. *Journal of Psychiatry and Neuroscience, 28*(5), 331.

Heath, A. C., Madden, P. A., Cloninger, C. R., & Martin, N. G. (1994). Genetic and environmental structure of personality. In C. R. Cloninger (Ed.), *Personality and Psychopathology.* Washington, D.C.: American Psychiatric Press.

Hebb, D. O. (2002). *The Organization of Behavior: A Neuropsychological Theory.* New York, NY: John Wiley and Sons, Inc.

Hebb, D. O. (1949). *The Organization of Behavior: A Neuropsychological Theory.* New York, NY: John Wiley and Sons, Inc.

Hebl, M. R., & Mannix, L. M. (2003). The weight of obesity in evaluating others: A mere proximity effect. *Personality and Social Psychology Bulletin, 29*(1), 28–38.

Hedden, T., & Gabrieli, J. D. E. (2004). Insights into the ageing mind: A view from cognitive neuroscience. *Nature Reviews Neuroscience, 5*(2), 87–96. doi: 10.1038/nrn1323

Hegarty, P. (2007). From genius inverts to gendered intelligence: Lewis Terman and the power of the norm. *History of Psychology, 10*(2), 132–155.

Heider, E. R. (1972). Universals in color naming and memory. *Journal of Experimental Psychology, 93*(1), 10–20.

Heilman, M. E., Block, C. J., & Martell, R. F. (1995). Sex stereotypes: Do they influence perceptions of managers? *Journal of Social Behavior and Personality, 10,* 237–252.

Heimberg, R. G., Brozovich, F. A., & Rapee, R. M. (2010). A cognitive-behavioral model of social anxiety disorder: Update and extension. In S. G. Hofmann & P. M. DiBartolo (Eds.), *Social Anxiety: Clinical, developmental, and social perspectives.* New York, NY: Academic Press.

Heinrich, B. (2014). *The homing instinct: Meaning and mystery in animal migration.* New York, NY: Houghton Mifflin Harcourt Publishing Company.

Heisz, J. J., Vakorin, V., Ross, B., Levine, B., & McIntosh, A. R. (2014). A trade-off between local and distributed information processing associated with remote episodic versus semantic memory. *Journal of Cognitive Neuroscience, 26*(1), 41–53.

Heller, A. C., Amar, A. P., Liu, C. Y., & Apuzzo, M. L. (2006). Surgery of the mind and mood: A mosaic of issues in time and evolution. *Neurosurgery, 59,* 720–733.

Helliwell, J., Layard, R., & Sachs, J. (2013). *World happiness report 2013.* Sustainable Development Solutions Network, New York, NY. Retrieved from http://unsdsn.org/wp-content/uploads/2014/02/WorldHappiness Report2013_online.pdf.

Hellman, K., Hernandez, P., Park, A., & Abel, T. (2010). Genetic evidence for a role for protein kinase A in the maintenance of sleep and thalamocortical oscillations. *Sleep: Journal of Sleep and Sleep Disorders Research, 33*(1), 19–28.

Henderson, H. A., & Wachs, T. D. (2007). Temperament theory and the study of cognitive-emotion interactions across development. *Developmental Review, 27,* 396–427.

Henderson, V. (2010). Diminishing dissociative experiences for war veterans in group therapy. In S. S. Fehr (Ed.), *101 interventions in group therapy* (rev. Ed., pp. 217–220). New York: Routledge/Taylor & Francis Group.

Henley, N. M. (1977). *Body politics: Power, sex, and nonverbal communication.* Englewood Cliffs, NJ: Prentice Hall.

Hennessey, B. A. (2010). The creativity–motivation connection. In J. C. Kaufman & R. J. Sternberg (Eds.), *The Cambridge handbook of creativity* (pp. 342–365). New York: Cambridge University Press.

Henningsen, D. D., Henningsen, M. L. M., Eden, J., & Cruz, M. G. (2006). Examining the symptoms of groupthink and retrospective sense-making. *Small Group Research, 37*(1), 36–64.

Henry, D. B., Tolan, P. H., & Gorman-Smith, D. (2004). Have there been lasting effects associated with the September 11, 2001, terrorist attacks among inner-city parents and children? *Professional Psychology: Research and Practice, 35*(5), 542.

Henry, J. P., & Cassel, J. C. (1969). Psychosocial factors in essential hypertension: Recent epidemiologic and animal experimental evidence. *American Journal of Epidemiology, 90*(3), 171–200.

Herculano-Houzel, S. (2012). The remarkable, yet not extraordinary, human brain as a scaled up primate brain and its associated cost. *Proceedings of the National Academy of Sciences of the United States of America, 109*, 10661–10668.

Herculano-Houzel, S. (2009). The human brain in numbers: A linearly scaled up primate brain. *Frontiers of Human Neuroscience, 3*, 31.

Herd, S. A., Banich, M. T., & O'Reilly, R. C. (2006). Neural mechanisms of cognitive control: An integrative model of Stroop task performance and FMRI data. *Journal of Cognitive Neuroscience, 18*, 22–32.

Herdt, G. (2010). Sex/gender, culture, and development: Issues in the emergence of puberty and attraction. In C. M. Worthman, P. M. Plotsky, D. S. Schechter, & C. A. Cummings (Eds.), *Formative experiences: The interaction of caregiving, culture, and developmental psychobiology* (pp. 356–374). New York, NY: Cambridge University Press.

Hergenhahn, B. R. (2009). *An Introduction to the History of Psychology* (6th Ed.). Belmont, CA: Thomson Wadsworth.

Hergenhahn, B. R. (2005). *An introduction to the history of psychology.* (5th Ed.). Belmont, CA: Thomson Wadsworth.

Herman, L., Hougland, T., & El-Mallakh, R. S. (2007). Mimicking human bipolar ion dysregulation models mania in rats. *Neuroscience & Biobehavioral Reviews, 31*(6), 874–881.

Herrnstein, R., & Murray, C. (1994). *The bell curve: Intelligence and class structure in American life.* The Free Press.

Herron, J. (Ed.). (2012). *Neuropsychology of left-handedness.* Toronto, ON: Elsevier.

Herry, C., Ferraguti, F., Singewald, N., Letzkus, J. J., Ehrlich, I., & Lüthi, A. (2010). Neuronal circuits of fear extinction. *European Journal of Neuroscience, 31*, 599–612.

Hertrich, I., Dietrich, S., Moos, A., Trouvain, J., Ackermann, H. (2009). Enhanced speech perception capabilities in a blind listener are associated with activation of fusiform gyrus and primary visual cortex. *Neurocase: The Neural Basis of Cognition, 15*(2), 163–170.

Hertzman, C. (2009). The state of child development in Canada: Are we moving toward, or away from, equity from the start? *Paediatric Children's Health, 14*(10), 673–676.

Herxheimer, A., & Petrie K. J. (2002). Melatonin for the prevention and treatment of jet lag (Cochrane Review). *The Cochrane Library, 2.* Oxford: Update Software.

Hewitt, P. L., Flett, G. L., Sherry, S. B., Habke, M., Parkin, M., Lam, R. W., et al. (2003). The interpersonal expression of perfection: Perfectionistic self-presentation and psychological distress. *Journal of Personality and Social Psychology, 84*, 1303–1325. doi:10.1037/0022-3514.84.6.1303.

Hiday, V. A., & Burns, P. J. (2010). Mental illness and the criminal justice system. In T. L. Scheid, & T. N. Brown (Eds.), *A handbook for the study of mental health: Social contexts, theories, and systems* (2nd Ed., pp. 478–498). New York: Cambridge University Press.

Higgins, E. S., & George, M. S. (2007). *The neuroscience of clinical psychiatry: The pathophysiology of behavior and mental illness.* Philadelphia, PA: Wolters Kluwer/Lippincott Williams & Wilkins.

Higgins, S. T., Heil, S. H., & Lussier, J. P. (2004). Clinical implications of reinforcement as a determinant of substance use disorders. *Annual Review of Psychology, 55*, 431–461.

Hilgard, E. R. (1992). Dissociation and theories of hypnosis. In E. Fromm & M.R. Nash (Eds.), *Contemporary hypnosis research.* New York, NY: Guilford Press.

Hilgard, E. R. (1991). Suggestibility and suggestions as related to hypnosis. In J. F. Schumaker (Ed.), *Human suggestibility: Advances in theory, research, and application.* Florence, KY: Taylor & Frances/ Routledge.

Hilgard, E. R. (1982). Hypnotic susceptibility and implications for measurement. *International Journal of Clinical and Experimental Hypnosis, 30*(4), 394–403.

Hillert, D. (2014). *The Nature of Language*, pp. 157–178. New York: Sprinter-Verlag.

Hilton, B. J., Assinck, P., Duncan, G. J., Lu, D., & Lo, S. (2013). Dorsolateral funiculus lesioning of the mouse cervical spinal cord at C4 not at C6 results in sustained forelimb motor deficits. *Journal of Neurotrauma, 30*, 1070–1083.

Hines, M. (2004). In A. Eagly, A. Beall, & R. Sternberg (Eds.) *The Psychology of Gender (2nd Ed.).* New York, NY: Guilford Press.

Hinshaw, S. P. (2008). Developmental psychopathology as a scientific discipline: Relevance to behavioral and emotional disorders of childhood and adolescence. In T. P. Beauchaine & S. P. Hinshaw (Eds.), *Child and adolescent psychopathology.* Hoboken, NJ: John Wiley & Sons, Inc.

Hinton, E. C., Holland, A. J., Gellatly, M. S., Soni, S., & Owen, A. M. (2006). An investigation into food preferences and the neural basis of food-related incentive motivation in Prader-Willi syndrome. *Journal of Intellectual Disability Research, 50*(9), 633–642.

Hirshfiled, S., Remien, R. H., Humberstone, M., Walavalkar, I., & Chiasson, M. A., (2004). Substance use and high-risk sex among men who have sex with men: A national online study in the USA. *AIDS Care, 16*(8), 1036–1047.

Hitchcock, S. T. (2005). *Karen Horney: Pioneer of feminine psychology.* Women in Medicine series, Chelsea House Publishers.

Hitti, M. (2004). Brain chemicals suggest marijuana's effects. *WebMD.* Retrieved from my.webmd.com/content/Article/94/102660.htm.

Hjerl, K., Andersen, E. W., Keiding, N., Mouridsen, H. T., Mortensen, P. B., & Jorgensen, T. (2003). Depression as a prognostic for breast cancer mortality. *Journal of Consultation and Liaison Psychiatry, 44*(1), 24–30.

Hobson, C. J., & Delunas, L. (2001). National norms and life-event frequencies for the revised social readjustment rating scale. *International Journal of Stress Management, 8*(4), 299–314.

Hobson, C. J., Kamen, J., Szostek, J., Nethercut, C. M., Tiedmann, J. W., & Wojnarowicz, S. (1998). Stressful life events: A revision and update of the Social Readjustment Rating Scale. *Interational Journal of Stress Management, 5*(1), 1–23.

Hobson, J. A. (2009). REM sleep and dreaming: Towards a theory of protoconsciousness. *Nature Reviews Neuroscience, 10*(11), 803–813.

Hobson, J. A. (2005). Sleep is of the brain, by the brain and for the brain. *Nature, 437*, 1254–1256.

Hobson, J. A., & McCarley, R. W. (1977). The brain as dream state generator: An activation-synthesis hypothesis of the dream process. *American Journal of Psychiatry, 134*, 1335–1348.

Hobson, J. A., Pace-Schott, E., & Stickgold, R. (2003). Dreaming and the brain: Toward a cognitive neuroscience of conscious states. In E. F. Pace-Schott, M. Solms, M. Blagrove, & S. Harnad (Eds.), *Sleep and dreaming: Scientific advances and reconsiderations* (pp. 1–50). New York, NY: Cambridge University Press.

Hobson, J. A., Sangsanguan, S., Arantes, H., & Kahn, D. (2011). Dream logic—The inferential reasoning paradigm. *Dreaming, 21*(1), 1–15.

Hobson, J. A., Stickgold, R., & Pace-Schott, E. F. (1998). The neuropsychology of REM sleep dreaming. *Neuroreport: An International Journal for the Rapid Communication of Research in Neuroscience, 9*(3), R1–R14.

Hochman, J. (2010). The eidetic: An image whose time has come? *Journal of Mental Imagery, 34*(1–2), 1–9.

Hochman, J. (2001). A basic online search on the eidetic with PsycINFO, MEDLINE and ERIC. *Journal of Mental Imagery, 25*(1–2), 99–215.

Hodapp, R. M., & Dykens, E. M. (2003). Mental retardation (intellectual disabilities). In E. J. Mash & R. A. Barkley (Eds.), *Child psychopathology* (2nd ed.). New York: Guilford Press.

Hodgkin, A. L., & Huxley, A. F. (1952). Currents carried by sodium and potassium ions through the membrane of the giant axon of Loligo. *Journal of Physiology, 116*, 449–472.

Hoeft, F., Hernandez, A., McMillon, G., Taylor-Hill, H., Martindale, J. L., Meyler, A., Keller, T. A., Siok, W. T., Deutsch, G. K., Just, M. A., Whitfield-Gabrieli, S., & Gabrieli, J. D. (2006). Neural basis of dyslexia: a comparison between dyslexic and nondyslexic children equated for reading ability. *Journal of Neuroscience, 26*, 10700–10708.

Hoek, H. W. (2007). Incidence, prevalence and mortality of anorexia and other eating disorders. *Current Opinion in Psychiatry, 19*(4), 389–394.

Hoeksema-van Orden, C. Y. D., Gaillard, A. W. K., & Buunk, B. P. (1998). Social loafing under fatigue. *Journal of Personality and Social Psychology, 75*, 1179–1190.

Hoffmann, H., Kessler, H., Eppel, T., Rukavina, S., & Traue, H. C. (2010). Expression intensity, gender and facial emotion recognition: Women recognize only subtle facial emotions better than men. *Acta Psychologica, 135*(3), 278–283.

Hoffman, L., & Thelen, M. (2010). William James and the fight for science. *Journal of Humanistic Psychology, 50*, 430–439.

Hofmann, S. G. (2007). Cognitive factors that maintain social anxiety disorder: A comprehensive model and its treatment implications. *Cognitive Behaviour Therapy, 36*(4), 193–209.

Hofmann, W., Friese, M., Schmeichel, B. J., & Baddeley, A. D. (2011). Working memory and self-regulation. In K. D. Vohs, & R. F. Baumeister (Eds.), *Handbook of self-regulation: Research, theory, and applications (2nd Ed.)* (pp. 204–225). New York, NY: Guilford Press.

Hofstede, G., & McCrae, R. R. (2004). Culture and personality revisited: Linking traits and dimensions of culture. *Cross-Cultural Research, 38*, 52–88.

Hogan, J., & Hogan, R. (1993). *The ambiguity of conscientiousness.* Paper presented at the 8th annual conference of the Society for Industrial and Organizational Psychology, San Francisco.

Hogan, Q. (2010). Labat Lecture: The primary sensory neuron: where it is, what it does, and why it matters, *Regional Anesthesia and Pain Medicine, 35*(3), 306–311.

Hoigaard, R., Säfvenbom, R., & Tonnessen, F. E. (2006). The relationship between group cohesion, group norms, and perceived social loafing in soccer teams. *Small Group Research, 37*(3), 217–232.

Holahan, C. J., & Moos, R. H. (1990). Life stressors, resistance factors, and improved psychological functioning: An extension of the stress resistance paradigm. *Journal of Personality and Social Psychology, 58*(5), 909–917.

Holahan, C. J., & Moos, R. H. (1985). Life stress and health: Personality, coping, and family support in stress resistance. *Journal of Personality and Social Psychology, 49*(3), 739–747.

Holcomb, T. F. (2010). Transitioning into retirement as a stressful life event. In T. W. Miller (Ed.), *Handbook of stressful transitions across the lifespan* (pp. 133–146). New York: Springer Science + Business Media.

Hollon, S. D, & DiGiuseppe, R. (2011). Cognitive theories of psychotherapy. In J. C. Norcross, G. R. VandenBos, & D. K. Freedheim (Eds.), *History of psychotherapy: Continuity and change* (2nd Ed.) (pp. 203–241). Washington, DC: American Psychological Association.

Holmes, A. J., Hollinshead, M. O., Bakst, L., Roffman, J. L., Smoller, J. W., & Buckner, R. L. (2012). Individual differences in amygdala-medial prefrontal anatomy link negative affect, impaired social functioning, and polygenic depression risk. *Journal of Neuroscience, 32*(50), 18087–18100.

Holmes, D. (1990). The evidence for repression: An examination of sixty years of research. In J. Springer (Ed.), *Repression and dissociation: Implications for personality, theory, psychopathology, and health* (pp. 85–102). Chicago: University of Chicago Press.

Holmes, J. (1993). *John Bowlby and attachment theory.* New York, NY: Routledge.

Holmes, S. E., Slaughter, J. R., & Kashani, J. (2001). Risk factors in childhood that lead to the development of conduct disorder and antisocial personality disorder. *Child Psychiatry & Human Development, 31*(3), 183–193.

Holmes, T. H., & Rahe, R. H. (1989). The social readjustment rating scale. In T. H. Holmes & E. M. David (Eds.), *Life change, life events, and illness: Selected papers.* New York, NY: Praeger.

Holmes, T. H., & Rahe, R. H. (1967). The social readjustment rating scale. *Journal of Psychosomatic Research, 11*, 213–218.

Holt-Lunstad, J., Birmingham, W., & Jones, B. Q. (2008). Is there something unique about marriage? The relative impact of marital status, relationship quality, and network social support on ambulatory blood pressure and mental health. *Annals of Behavioral Medicine, 35*(2), 239–244.

Holyoak, K. J., & Morrison, R. G. (2005). Analogy. In K. J. Holyoak & R. G. Morrison (Eds.), *The Cambridge Handbook of Thinking and Reasoning* (pp. 409–414). New York, NY: Cambridge University Press.

Holzman, L. (2009). *Vygotsky at work and play.* Oxford, UK: Routledge.

Hommel, J. D., Trinko, R., Sears, R. M., Georgescu, D., Liu, Z. W., Gao, X. B., Thurmon, J. J., Marinelli, M., & DiLeone, R. J. (2006). Leptin receptor signaling in midbrain dopamine neurons regulates feeding. *Neuron, 51*, 801–810.

Homstol, L. (2011). *Applications of learning theory to human-bear conflict: The efficacy of aversive conditioning and conditioned taste aversion.* Master thesis completed in partial fulfillment of the degree of Master of Science, Biological Sciences, University of Alberta.

Hong, J., Schonwald, A., & Stein, M. T. (2008). Barking vocalizations and shaking movements in a 13-year old girl. *Journal of Developmental and Behavioral Pediatrics, 29*(2), 135–137.

Hong, Y., Morris, M. W., Chiu, Y., & Benet-Martinez, V. (2000). Multicultural minds: A dynamic constructivist approach to culture and cognition. *American Psychologist, 55*, 709–717.

Hope, D. A., Burns, J. A., Hayes, S. A., Herbert, J. D., & Warner, M. D. (2010). Automatic thoughts and cognitive restructuring in cognitive behavioral group therapy for social anxiety disorder. *Cognitive Therapy and Research, 34*(1), 1–12.

Hopkin, K. (2010). Some nerve. *The Scientist, 24*(9), 52.

Hor, K., & Taylor, M. (2010). Review: Suicide and schizophrenia: a systematic review of rates and risk factors. *Journal of Psychopharmacology, 24*(4 suppl), 81–90.

Horesh, N., Apter, A., & Zalsman, G. (2011). Timing, quantity and quality of stressful life events in childhood and preceding the first episode of bipolar disorder. *Journal of Affective Disorders, 134*(1), 434–437.

Horn, M. (2005). Rude awakening: What to do with the sleepwalking defense. *Boston College Law Review, 46*, 149–182.

Horne, J. (2010). Primary insomnia: A disorder of sleep, or primarily one of wakefulness? *Sleep Medicine Reviews, 14*(1), 3–7.

Hortensius, R., & de Gelder, B. (2014). The neural basis of the bystander effect—The influence of group size on neural activity when witnessing an emergency. *NeuroImage, 93*, 53–58.

Horvath, I., Perez, I., Forrow, L., Fregni, F., & Pascual-Leone, A. (2013). Transcranial magnetic stimulation: Future prospects and ethical concerns in treatment and research. In A. Chatterjee & M. Farah (Eds.), *Neuroethics in Practice* (pp. 209–234). Oxford University Press.

Hothersall, D. (1995). *History of Psychology.* New York, NY: McGraw-Hill.

Hovakimyan, M., Haas, S. J., Schmitt, O., Gerber, B., Wree, A., & Andressen, C. (2008). Mesencephalic human neural progenitor cells transplanted into the adult hemiparkinsonian rat striatum lack dopaminergic differentiation but improve motor behavior. *Cells Tissues Organs, 188*, 373–383.

Hoveida, R., Alaei, H., Oryan, S., Parivar, K., & Reisi, P. (2011). Treadmill running improves spatial memory in an animal model of Alzheimer's disease. *Behavioural Brain Research, 216*(1), 270–274. doi: 10.1016/j.bbr.2010.08.003

Howell, E. F. (2011). *Understanding and treating dissociative identity disorder: A relational approach.* New York, NY: Routledge/Taylor & Francis Group.

Howes, C. (1999). Attachment relationships in the context of multiple caregivers. In J. Cassidy & P. R. Shaver (Eds.), *Handbook of attachment: Theory, research, and clinical applications* (pp. 671–687). New York, NY: Guilford Press.

Howland, J. G., Harrison, R. A., Hannesson, D. K., & Phillips, A. G. (2008). Ventral hippocampal involvement in temporal order, but not recognition, memory for spatial information. *Hippocampus, 18*, 251–257.

Howland, R. H., Shutt, L. S., Berman, S. R., Spotts, C. R., & Denko, T. (2011). The emerging use of technology for the treatment of depression and other neuropsychiatric disorders. *Annals of Clinical Psychiatry, 23*(1), 48–62.

Hoyk, Z., Csákvári, E., Gyenes, A., Siklós, L., Harada, N., & Párducz, Á. (2014). Aromatase and estrogen receptor beta expression in the rat olfactory bulb: Neuroestrogen action in the first relay station of the olfactory pathway? *Acta Neurobiologiae Experimentalis, 74*, 1–14.

Hoyle, R. H. (Ed.). (2010). *Handbook of personality and self-regulation.* Hoboken, NJ: Wiley-Blackwell.

Hrazdil, C., Roberts, J. I., Wiebe, S., Sauro, K., Vautour, M., et al. (2013). Patient perceptions and barriers to epilepsy surgery: Evaluation in a large health region. *Epilepsy & Behavior, 28*, 52–65.

Huang, P. L. (2005). Unraveling the links between diabetes, obesity, and cardiovascular disease. *Circulation Research, 96*, 1129–1131.

Hubel, D. H., & Wiesel, T. N. (1959). Receptive fields of single neurones in the cat's striate cortex. *The Journal of Physiology, 148*, 574–591.

Hublin, C., Kaprio, J., Partinen, M., & Koskenvuo, M. (2001). Parasomnias: Co-occurrence and genetics. *Psychiatric Genetics, 11*(2), 65–70.

Hublin, C., Kaprio, J., Partinen, M., & Koskenvuo, M. (1999). Limits of self-report in assessing sleep terrors in a population survey. *Sleep: Journal of Sleep Research & Sleep Medicine, 22*(1), 89–93.

Hudson, J. I., Hiripi, E., Pope, H. G., Jr., & Kessler, R. C. (2007). The prevalence and correlates of eating disorders in the national comorbidity survey replication. *Biological Psychiatry, 61*(3), 348–358.

Hudziak, J., & Bartels, M. (2008). Genetic and environmental influences on wellness, resilience, and psychopathology: A family-based approach for promotion, prevention, and intervention. In J. J. Hudziak (Ed.), *Developmental psychopathology and wellness: Genetic and environmental influences.* Washington, DC: American Psychiatric Publishing, Inc.

Huesmann, L. R., Moise-Titus, J., Podolski, C., & Eron, L. D. (2003). Longitudinal relations between children's exposure to TV violence and their aggressive and violent behavior in young adulthood: 1977-1992. *Developmental Psychology, 39*, 201–221.

Hughes, D. A. (2009). *Attachment-focused parenting: Effective strategies to care for children.* New York, NY: W. W. Norton.

Hughes, K. D., Lowe, G. S., & McKinnon, A. L. (1996). Public attitudes toward budget cuts in Alberta: Biting the bullet or feeling the pain? *Canadian Public Policy, 22*(3), 268–284.

Hughes, L. F., McAsey, M. E., Donathan, C. L., Smith, T., Coney, P., & Struble, R. G. (2002). Effects of hormone replacement therapy on olfactory sensitivity: Cross-sectional and longitudinal studies. *Climacteric, 5*, 140–150.

Hughes, T. F., Flatt, J. D., Fu, B., Butters, M. A., Chang, C. C. H., & Ganguli, M. (2014). Interactive video gaming compared with health education in older adults with mild cognitive impairment: a feasibility study. *International Journal of Geriatric Psychiatry.* doi:10.1002/gps.4075

Hulit, L. M., & Howard, M. R. (1997). *Born to talk: An introduction to speech and language development* (2nd Ed). Boston, MA: Annyn & Bacon.

Hunt, E. (2011). *Human intelligence.* New York, NY: Cambridge University Press.

Hunt, N. C. (2010). *Memory, war and trauma.* New York, NY: Cambridge University Press.

Hunter, E. C. (2013). Understanding and treating depersonalization disorder. In F. Kennedy, H. Kennerly, & D. Pearson (Eds.), *Cognitive Behavioural Approaches to the Understanding and Treatment of Dissociation,* 160–173.

Huttenlocher, J., Haight, W., Bryk, A., Seltzer, M., & Lyons, T. (1991). Early vocabulary growth: Relation to language input and gender. *Developmental Psychology, 27*(2), 236–248.

Hyde, J. S. (2014). Gender similarities and differences. *Annual Review of Psychology, 65*, 373–398.

Hyde, J. S. (2008, Spring). Men are from earth, women are from earth: The gender similarities hypothesis. *General Psychologist, 43*(1).

Hyde, J. S. (2007). New directions in the study of gender similarities and differences. *Current Directions in Psychological Science, 16*(5), 259–263.

Hyde, J. S. (2005). The gender similarities hypothesis. *American Psychologist, 60*, 581–592.

Hyde, M., & Power, D. (2006). Some ethical dimensions of cochlear implantation for deaf children and their families. *Journal of Deaf Studies and Deaf Education, 11*, 102–111.

Hyman Jr., I. E., & Kleinknecht, E. E. (1999). False childhood memories: Research, theory, and applications. In L. M. Williams & V. L. Banyard (Eds.), *Trauma & memory* (pp. 175–188). Thousand Oaks, CA: Sage Publications.

Hymowitz, N. (2005). Tobacco. In R. J. Frances, A. H. Mack, & S. I. Miller (Eds.), *Clinical textbook of addictive disorders (3rd Ed.)*. New York, NY: Guilford Press.

Iacoboni, M. (2009). Imitation, empathy, and mirror neurons. *Annual Review of Psychology, 60*, 653–670.

Iacono, W. G., & Lykken, D. T. (1997). The validity of the lie detector: Two surveys of scientific opinion. *Journal of Applied Psychology, 82*(3), 426–433.

Iadecola, C., & Nedergaard, M. (2007). Glial regulation of the cerebral microvasculature. *Nature Neuroscience. 10*, 1369–1376.

Iaria, G., Petrides, M., Dagher, A., Pike, B., & Bohbot, V. D. (2003). Cognitive strategies dependent on the hippocampus and caudate nucleus in human navigation: Variability and change with practice. *The Journal of Neuroscience, 23*(13), 5945–5952.

Ilik, F., & Pazarli, A. C. (2014). Reflex epilepsy triggered by smell. *Clinical EEG and Neuroscience*, doi: 10.1177/1550059414533540.

IMHRO. (2009). International Mental Health Research Organization. Retrieved from www.schizophrenia.com/szfacts.htm.

Inglehart, R. (1990). *Culture shift in advanced industrial society*. Princeton, NJ: Princeton University Press.

Ingram, D. (1986). Phonological development: Production. In P. Fletcher & M. Garman (Eds.), *Language acquisition* (2nd Ed., pp. 223–239). New York, NY: Cambridge University Press.

Inhelder, B., & Piaget, J. (1979). Procedures et structures [Procedures and structures]. *Archives de Psychologie, 47*, 165–176.

Institute of Medicine. (2011). *Relieving pain in America: A blueprint for transforming prevention, care, education and research*. Washington DC, Institute of Medicine, National Academies Press.

Irwin, M. (2001). Neuroimmunology of disordered sleep in depression and alcoholism. *Neuropsychopharmacology, 25*(5), S45–S49.

Irwin, M. R., & Cole, J. C. (2005). Depression and psychonueroimmunology. In K. Vedhara & M. Irwin (Eds.), *Human psychoneuroimmunology*. Oxford, England: Oxford University Press.

Isacson, O., & Kordower, J. H. (2008). Future of cell and gene therapies for Parkinson's disease. *Annals of Neurology, 2*, S122–S138.

Isen, A. M. (2008). Positive affect and decision processes: Some recent theoretical developments with practical implications. In C. P. Haugtvedt, P. M. Herr, & F. R. Kardes (Eds.), *Handbook of consumer psychology* (pp. 273–296). New York, NY: Taylor & Francis Group/Lawrence Erlbaum Associates.

Isen, A. M. (2004). Some perspectives on positive feelings and emotions: Positive affect facilitates thinking and problem solving. In A. Manstead, N. Frijda, & A. Fischer (Eds.), *Feelings and emotions: The Amsterdam symposium* (pp. 263–281). New York, NY: Cambridge University Press.

Isen, A. M. (1993). Positive affect and decision making. In M. Lewis & J. M. Haviland (Eds.), *Handbook of emotions* (pp. 261–277). New York, NY: Guilford Press.

Isenberg, D. J. (1986). Group polarization: A critical review and meta-analysis. *Journal of Personality and Social Psychology, 50*,1141–1151.

Ishigami, Y., & Klein, R. M. (2009). Is a hands-free phone safer than a handheld phone? *Journal of Safety Research, 40*(2), 157–164.

Ishikawa, S., Iwanaga, M., Yamashita, B., Sato, H., & Sato, S. (2010). Long-term effects of social skills training on depressive symptoms in children. *Japanese Journal of Educational Psychology, 58*(3), 372–384.

Ivanenko, A., & Johnson, K. P. (2010). Sleep disorders. In M. K. Dulcan (Ed.), *Dulcan's textbook of child and adolescent psychiatry* (pp. 449–461). Arlington, VA: American Psychiatric Publishing, Inc.

Iwanaga, M., Yokoyama, H., & Seiwa, H. (2004). Coping availability and stress reduction for optimistic and pessimistic individuals. *Personality and Individual Differences, 36*(1), 11–22.

Izard, C. E. (2009). Emotion theory and research: Highlights, unanswered questions, and emerging issues. *Emotion Theory and Research, 60*, 1–25.

Izard, C. E. (2007). Basic emotions, natural kinds, emotion schemas, and a new paradigm. *Perspectives on Psychological Science, 2*, 260–280.

Izard, C. E. (1997). Emotions and facial expressions: A perspective from differential emotions theory. In J. A. Russell & J. M. Fernandez-Dols (Eds.), *The psychology of facial expression* (pp. 57–77). New York, NY: Cambridge University Press.

Izard, C. E. (1994). Innate and universal facial expressions: Evidence from developmental and cross-cultural research. *Psychological Bulletin, 115*, 288–299.

Izard, C. E. (1977). *Human emotions*. New York, NY: Plenum Press.

Jaakkola, J. J., & Gissler, M. (2004). Maternal smoking in pregnancy, fetal development, and childhood asthma. *American Journal of Public Health, 94*, 136–140.

Jackson, B. R., & Bergeman, C. S. (2011). How does religiosity enhance well-being? The role of perceived control. *Psychology of Religion and Spirituality, 3*(2), 149–161.

Jackson, H., Judd, F., Komiti, A., Fraser, C., Murray, G., Robins, G., & Wearing, A. (2007). Mental health problems in rural contexts: What are the barriers to seeking help from professional providers? *Australian Psychologist, 42*(2), 147–160.

Jackson, J. W. (1993). Realistic group conflict theory: A review and evaluation of the theoretical and empirical literature. *The Psychological Record, 43*(3), 395–413.

Jacobs, A. K. (2008). Components of evidence-based interventions for bullying and peer victimization. In R. G. Steele, T. D. Elkin, & M. C. Roberts (Eds.), *Handbook of evidence-based therapies for children and adolescents: Bridging science and practice*. New York, NY: Spriger.

Jacobson, C. F., Wolf, J. B., & Jackson, T. A. (1935). An experimental analysis of the functions of the frontal association areas in primates. *Journal of Nervous and Mental Disease, 82*, 1–14.

Jacoby, L. L., Bishara, A. J., Hessels, S., & Toth, J. P. (2005). Aging, subjective experience, and cognitive control: Dramatic false remembering by older adults. *Journal of Experimental Psychology: General, 134*(2), 131–148.

Jaensch, E. R., & Jaensch, E. R. (2013). *Eidetic imagery and Typological Methods of Investigation: Their Importance for the Psychology of Childhood, the Theory of*. Abingdon: Routledge.

Jamal, M., & Baba, V.V. (2003). Type A behavior, components, and outcomes: A study of Canadian employees. *International Journal of Stress Management, 10*(1), 39–50.

James, W. (1890). *The principles of psychology* (Vols. 1 & 2). New York, NY: Holt.

James, W. (1884). What is emotion? *Mind, 19*, 188–205.

Jamieson, J. (2013). Public speaking and stress responses: Improving stress responses by reinterpreting the meaning of stress. *Psychology Today*. Retrieved from www.psychologytoday.com/blog/the-many-sides-stress/201306/public-speaking-and-stress-responses.

Jamieson, J., Mendea, W. B., & Nock, M. K. (2012). Improving acute stress responses: The power of reappraisal. *Current Directions in Psychological Science*, First online, 1–6.

Jang, K., McCrae, R., Angleitner, A., Riemann, R., & Livesley, W. (1998). Heritability of facet-level traits in a cross-cultural twin sample: Support for a hierarchical model of personality. *Journal of Personality and Social Psychology, 74*, 1556–1565.

Janis, I. L. (1982). *Groupthink*. Boston, MA: Houghton Mifflin.

Janis, I. (1972). *Victims of groupthink: A psychological study of foreign-policy decisions and fiascoes*. Boston, MA: Houghton Mifflin.

Jankord, R., & Herman, J. P. (2009). Limbic regulation of hypothalamo-pituitary-adrenocortical function during acute and chronic stress. *Stress, neurotransmitters, and hormones: Neuroendocrine and genetic mechanisms* (pp. 63–74). New York, NY: New York Academy of Sciences, Wiley-Blackwell.

Jankovic, J., & Aguilar, L. G. (2008). Current approaches to the treatment of Parkinson's disease. *Neuropsychiatric Disease and Treatment, 4*, 743–757.

Jansson-Fröjmark, M., Harvey, A. G., Lundh, L., Norell-Clarke, A., & Linton, S. J. (2011). Psychometric properties of an insomnia-specific measure of worry: The anxiety and preoccupation about sleep questionnaire. *Cognitive Behaviour Therapy, 40*(1), 65–76.

Jarcho, J. M., Berkman, E. T., & Lieberman, M. D. (2011). The neural basis of rationalization: Cognitive dissonance reduction during decision-making. *Social Cognitive and Affective Neuroscience, 6*, 460–467.

Jarrold, C., Tam, H., Baddeley, A. D., & Harvey, C. E. (2010). The nature and position of processing determines why forgetting occurs in working memory tasks. *Psychonomic Bulletin & Review, 17*(6), 772–777.

Jastrow, J. (1929). Review of J. B. Watson, Ways of behaviorism, psychological care of infant and child, battle of behaviorism. *Science, 69*, 455–457.

Jauk, E., Benedek, M., Dunst, B., & Neubauer, A. (2013). The relationship between intelligence and creativity: New support for the threshold hypothesis by means of empirical breakpoint detection. *Intelligence, 41*(4), 212–221.

Jaussent, I., Dauvilliers, Y., Ancelin, M., Dartigues, J., Tavernier, B., Touchon, J., . . . Besset, A. (2011). Insomnia symptoms in older adults: Associated factors and gender differences. *The American Journal of Geriatric Psychiatry, 19*(1), 88–97.

Jay, T. (1999). *Why we curse: A neuro-psycho-social theory of speech*. Philadelphia, PA: John Benjamins Publishing Co.

Jefferson, D. J. (2005). America's most dangerous drug. *Newsweek, 146*(6), 40–48.

Jefferson, T., Herbst, J. H., & McCrae, R. R. (1998). Associations between birth order and personality traits: Evidence from self-report and observer ratings. *Journal of Research in Personality, 32*, 498–502.

Jeneson, A., Kirwan, C. B., Hopkins, R. O., Wixted, J. T., & Squire, L. R. (2010). Recognition memory and the hippocampus: A test of the hippocampal contribution to recollection and familiarity. *Learning & Memory, 17*(1), 63–70. doi: 10.1101/lm.1546110

Jenkins, R. (2008). *Social identity*. Oxon, UK: Routledge.

Jensen, L. A. (Ed.). (2011). *Bridging cultural and developmental approaches to psychology: New syntheses in theory, research, and policy*. New York, NY: Oxford University Press.

Jensen, M. P. (2010). Chronic pain. In A. F. Barabasz, K. Olness, R. Boland, & S. Kahn (Eds.), *Medical hypnosis primer: Clinical and research evidence* (pp. 25–32). New York, NY: Routledge/Taylor & Francis Group.

Jenson, R. (2006). Behaviorism, latent learning and cognitive maps: Needed revisions in introductory psychology textbooks. *Behavior Analyst, 29*(2), 187–209.

Jessen, K. R., & Mirsky, R. (2005). The origin and development of glial cells in peripheral nerves. *Nature Reviews Neuroscience, 6*(9), 671–682.

Johansson, C. B., Momma, S., Clarke, D. L., Risling, M., Lendahl, U., & Frisen, J. (1999). Identification of a neural stem cell in the adult mammalian central nervous system. *Cell, 96* (1), 25–34.

Johnson, A. L. (2011). Psychoanalytic theory. In D. Capuzzi & D. R. Gross (Eds.), *Counseling and psychotherapy (5th Ed.)* (pp. 59–76). Alexandria, VA: American Counseling Association.

Johnson, A., & Earle, T. (1987). *The evolution of human societies*. Stanford, CA: Stanford University Press.

Johnson, C. H., Elliott, J., Foster, R., Honma, K. I., & Kronauer, R. (2004). Fundamental properties of circadian rhythms. In J. C. Dunlap, J. J. Loros, et al. (Eds.), *Chronobiology: Biological timekeeping*. Sunderland, MA: Sinauer Associates, Inc.

Johnson, J. G., Cohen, P., Smailes, E. M., Kasen, S., & Brook, J. S. (2002). Television viewing and aggressive behavior during adolescence and adulthood. *Science, 295*, 2468–2471.

Johnson, J. S., & Newport, E. L. (1989). Critical period effects in second language learning: The influence of maturational state on the acquisition of English as a second language. *Cognitive Psychology, 21*, 60–99.

Johnson, W. (2010). Review of intelligence and how to get it: Why schools and cultures count. *Gifted Child Quarterly, 54*(1), 72.

Johnson, W., Bouchard Jr., T. J., McGue, M., Segal, N. L., Tellegen, A., Keyes, M., et al. (2007). Genetic and environmental influences on the verbal-perceptual-image rotation (VPR) model of the structure of mental abilities in the Minnesota study of twins reared apart. *Intelligence, 35*(6), 542–562.

Johnson, W., Jung, R. E., Colom, R., & Haier, R. J. (2012). Cognitive abilities independent of IQ correlate with regional brain structure. *Intelligence, 36*(1), 18–28.

Johnston, C., & Lee, C. M. (2005). Children's attributions for their own versus others' behavior: Influence of actor versus observer differences. *Journal of Applied Developmental Psychology, 26*(3), 314–328.

Johnston, L. D., O'Malley, P. M., Bachman, J. G., & Schulenberg, J. E. (2007). *Monitoring the future national results on adolescent drug use: Overview of key findings, 2006* (NIH Publication No. 07–6202). Bethesda, MD: National Institute on Drug Abuse.

Joiner, T. E., Jr. (2002). Depression in its interpersonal context. In I. H. Gotlib & C. L. Hammen (Eds.), *Handbook of depression* (pp. 295–313). New York, NY: Guilford Press.

Jokela, M., Batty, G. D., Hintsa, T., Elovainio, M., Hakulinen, C., & Kivimäki, M. (2014). Is personality associated with cancer incidence and mortality? An individual-participant meta-analysis of 2156 incident cancer cases among 42843 men and women. *British Journal of Cancer, 110*, 1820–1824.

Jolly, J. L., Treffinger, D. J., Inman, T. F., & Smutny, J. F. (Eds.). 2011. *Parenting gifted children: The authoritative guide from the National Association for Gifted Children*. Waco, TX: Prufrock Press.

Jones, B. E. (2003). Arousal systems. *Frontiers in Bioscience, 8*, 438–451.

Jones, E. E., & Harris, V. A. (1967). The attribution of attitudes. *Journal of Experimental Social Psychology, 3*, 1–24.

Jones, E. E., & Nisbett, R. E. (1971). *The Actor and the Observer: Divergent Perceptions of the Causes of Behavior*. Morristown, NJ: General Learning Press.

Jones, E. E., & Sigall, H. (1971). The bogus pipeline: A new paradigm for measuring affect and attitude. *Psychological Bulletin, 76*, 349–364.

Jones, E. G. (2007). Neuroanatomy: Cajal and after Cajal. *Brain Research Reviews, 55*, 248–255.

Jones, P. E. (1995). Contradictions and unanswered questions in the genie case: A fresh look at the linguistic evidence. *Language and Communication, 15*, 261–280.

Jones, S. R., Fernyhough, C., & Larøi, F. (2010). A phenomenological survey of auditory verbal hallucinations in the hypnagogic and hypnopompic states. *Phenomenology and the Cognitive Sciences, 9*(2), 213–224.

Jonides, J., Lewis, R. L., Nee, D. E., Lustig, C. A., Berman, M. G., & Moore, K. S. (2008). The mind and brain of short-term memory. *Annual Review of Psychology, 59*, 193–224.

Jonides, J., Sylvester, C. C., Lacey, S. C., Wager, T. D., Nichols, T. E., & Awh, E. (2003). Modules of working memory. In R. H. Kluwe, G. Lüer, & F. Rösler (Eds.), *Principles of learning and memory* (pp. 113–134). Cambridge, MA: Birkhäuser.

Jordan, K., Fromberger, P., Stolpman, G., & Muller, J. L. (2011). The role of testosterone in sexuality and paraphilia—a neurobiological approach. Part I: Testosterone and Sexuality. *The Journal of Sexual Medicine, 8*(11), 2993–3007.

Joseph, S. V. (2007). A study of the amplitudes and latencies of the brain stem and cortical auditory evoked potentials (AEP) in relation to the personality dimension of extraversion. ProQuest Information & Learning: US. *Dissertation Abstracts International: Section B: The Sciences and Engineering, 68*(6), 4133.

Josephs, R. A., Markus, H., & Tarafodi, R. W. (1992). Gender and self-esteem. *Journal of Personality and Social, 63*, 391–402.

Josselyn, S. A., & Frankland, P. W. (2012). Infantile amnesia: a neurogenic hypothesis. *Learning & Memory, 19*(9), 423–433.

Juhnke, G. A., Granello, D. H., & Granello, P. F. (2011). *Suicide, selfinjury, and violence in the schools: Assessment, prevention, and intervention strategies*. Hoboken, NJ: John Wiley & Sons.

Julian, M. M. (2013). Age at adoption from institutional care as a window into the lasting effects of early experiences. *Clinical Child and Family Psychology Review, 16*(2), 101–145.

Julien, R. M. (2008). *A primer of drug action: A comprehensive guide to the actions, uses, and side effects of psychoactive drugs* (11th Ed.). Portland, OR: Worth Publishers.

Julien, R. M., Advokat, C. D., & Comaty, J. E. (2011). *Primer of drug action* (12th Ed.). New York, NY: Worth Publishers.

Julien, R. M., Advokat, C. D., & Comaty, J. E. (2008). *A primer of drug action: A comprehensive guide to the actions, uses, and side effects of psychoactive drugs* (11th Ed.). New York, NY: Worth Publishers.

Junco, R. (2012). Too much face and not enough books: The relationship between multiple indices of Facebook use and academic performance. *Computers in Human Behavior, 28*(1), 187–198.

Junco, R., & Cotton, S. R. (2012). The relationship between multitasking and academic performance. *Computers and Education, 59*(2), 505–514.

Just, M. A., & Carpenter, P. A. (2002). A capacity theory of comprehension: Individual differences in working memory. In T. A. Polk & C. M. Seifert (Eds.), *Cognitive modeling* (pp. 131–177). Cambridge, MA: MIT Press.

Jutras-Aswad, D., DiNieri, J. A., Harkany, T., & Hurd, Y. L. (2009). Neurobiological consequences of maternal cannabis on human fetal development and its neuropsychiatric outcome. *European Archives of Psychiatry and Clinical Neuroscience, 259*, 395–412.

Kabat-Zinn, J. (2005). *Wherever you go, there you are: Mindfulness meditation in everyday life*. New York, NY: Hyperion.

Kadushin, C. (1969). *Why people go to psychiatrists*. Oxford, UK: Atherton Press.

Kagan, J. (2011). Three lessons learned. *Psychological Science, 6*, 107–113.

Kagan, J. (2008). Behavioral inhibition as a risk factor for psychopathology. In T. P. Beauchaine & S. P. Hinshaw (Eds.), *Child and adolescent psychopathology* (pp. 157–179). Hoboken, NJ: John Wiley & Sons Inc.

Kagan, J. (2001). Biological constraint, cultural variety, and psychological structures. In A. Harrington (Ed.), *Unity of knowledge: The convergence of natural and human science* (pp. 177–190). New York, NY: New York Academy of Sciences.

Kagan, J., & Fox, N. A. (2006). Biology, culture, and temperamental biases. In E. Eisenberg (Ed.), *Handbook of child psychology: Vol. 3,. Social, emotional, and personality development* (6th ed., pp. 167–225). Hoboken, NJ: Wiley.

Kagan, J., & Snidman, N. (2004). *The long shadow of temperament*. Cambridge, MA: Harvard University Press.

Kahneman, D., & Tversky, A. (1979). Prospect theory: An analysis of decision making under risk. *Econometrica, 47*, 263–292.

Kaido, T., Otsuki, T., Kaneko, Y., Takahashi, A., Kakita, A., et al. (2010). Anterior striatum with dysmorphic neurons associated with the epileptogenesis of focal cortical dysplasia. *Seizure, 19*, 256–259.

Kakigi, R., Hoshiyama, M., Shimojo, M., Naka, D., Yamasaki, H., Watanabe, S., Xiang, J., Maeda, K., Lam, K., Itomi, K., & Nakamura, A. (2000). The somatosensory evoked magnetic fields. *Progress in Neurobiology, 61*, 495–523.

Kallgren, C. A., Reno, R. R., & Cialdini, R. B. (2000). A focus theory of normative conduct: When norms do and do not affect behavior. *Personality and Social Psychology Bulletin, 26*, 1002–1012.

Kallio, S., & Revonsuo, A. (2003). Hypnotic phenomena and altered states of consciousness: A multilevel framework of description and explanation. *Contemporary Hypnosis, 20*(3), 111–164.

Kalsbeek, A., Fliers, E., Hofman, M. A., Swaab, D. F., & Buijs, R. M. (2010). Vasopressin and the output of the hypothalamic biological clock. *Journal of Neuroendocrinology, 22*(5), 362–372.

Kalueff A. V., & La Porte, J. L. (Eds.) (2008). *Behavioral models in stress research*. Hauppauge, NY: Nova Biomedical Books.

Kamiji, M. M., Troncon, L. E., Suen, V. M., & de Oliveira, R. B. (2009). Gastrointestinal transit, appetite, and energy balance in gastrectomized patients. *The American Journal of Clinical Nutrition, 89*(1), 231–239.

Kan, K.-J., Wicherts, J. M., Dolan, C. V., & van der Mass, H. L. J. (2013). On the nature and nurture of intelligence and specific cognitive abilities: The more heritable, the more culture dependent. *Psychological Science, 24*(12), 2420–2428.

Kandel, E. R., Dudai, Y., & Mayford, M. R. (2014). The Molecular and Systems Biology of Memory. *Cell, 157*(1), 163–186.

Kane, M. J., Conway, A. R., Hambrick, D. Z., & Engle, R. W. (2007). Variation in working memory capacity as variation in executive attention and control. *Variation in Working Memory*, 21–48.

Kanner, A. D., Coyne, J. C., Schaefer, C., & Lazarus, R. S. (1981). Comparison of two modes of stress measurement: Daily hassles and uplifts versus major life events. *Journal of Behavioral Medicine, 4*, 1–39.

Kanner, B. (1998, February). Are you normal? Turning the other cheek. *American Demographics*.

Kanner, B. (1998, May). Are you normal? Creatures of habit. *American Demographics*.

Kant, I. (2003). Anthropology from a pragmatic point of view. *The history of psychology: Fundamental questions* (pp. 127–140). New York, NY: Oxford University Press.

Kantor, M. (2006). The psychopathy of everyday life. In T. G. Plante (Ed.), *Mental disorders of the new millennium, Vol. 1: Behavioral issues.* Westport, CT: Praeger Publishers.

Kaplan, H. S. (1977). Hypoactive sexual desire. *Journal of Sex & Marital Therapy, 3*(1), 3–9.

Kaplan, H., & Dove, H. (1987). Infant development among the Ache of eastern Paraguay. *Developmental Psychology, 23*(2), 190–198.

Kaplan, R. M., & Kronick, R. G. (2006). Marital status and longevity in the United States population. *Journal of Epidemiology & Community Health, 60*(9), 760–765.

Kaplan, R. M., & Pascoe, G. C. (1977). Humorous lectures and humorous examples: Some effects upon comprehension and retention. *Journal of Educational Psychology, 69*, 61–65.

Karama, S., Colom, R., Johnson, W., Deary, I. J., Haier, R., Waber, D. P., & Evans, A. C. (2011). Cortical thickness correlates of specific cognitive performance accounted for by the general factor of intelligence in healthy children aged 6 to 18. *NeuroImage, 55*(4), 1443–1453.

Karasu, T. B. (1992) *Wisdom in the practice of psychotherapy.* New York, NY: Basic Books.

Karelitz, T. M., Jarvin, L., & Sternberg, R. J. (2010). The meaning of wisdom and its development throughout life. In W. F. Overton & R. M. Lerner (Eds.), *The handbook of life-span development, vol. 1: Cognition, biology, and methods* (pp. 837–881). Hoboken, NJ: John Wiley & Sons.

Karies, C. J. (1986). *Scientists of the mind: Intellectual founders of modern psychology.* Urbana, IL: University of Illinois Press.

Karni, A., Tanne, D., Rubenstein, B. S., Askenasy, J. J. M., et al. (1994). Dependence on REM sleep of overnight improvement of a perceptual skill. *Science, 265*(5172), 679–682.

Kashdan, T. B., & Ciarrochi, J. (Eds.). (2013). *Mindfulness, acceptance, and positive psychology: The seven foundations of well-being.* New Harbinger Publications.

Kashima, Y., Siegal, M., Tanaka, K., & Kashima, E. S. (1992). Do people believe behaviours are consistent with attitudes? Towards a cultural psychology of attribution processes. *British Journal of Social Psychology, 31*, 111–124.

Kassam, A., & Patten, S. B. (2006). Canadian trends in benzodiazepine & zopiclone use. *Canadian Journal of Clinical Pharmacology, 13*(1), e121–e127.

Kauert, G., & Iwersen-Bergmann, S. (2004). Illicit drugs as cause of traffic crashes, focus on cannabis. *Sucht (German Journal of Addiction Research and Practice), 50*(5), 327–333.

Kaufman, A. S. (2000a). Intelligence tests and school psychology: Predicting the future by studying the past. *Psychology in the Schools, 37*(1), 7–16.

Kaufman, A. S. (2000b). Wechsler, David. In A. E. Kazdin (Ed.), *Encyclopedia of psychology, vol. 8* (pp. 238–239). Washington, DC: American Psychological Association.

Kaufman, A. S. (2000c). Tests of Intelligence. In R. J. Sternberg (Ed.), *Handbook of intelligence* (pp. 445–476). New York, NY: Cambridge University Press.

Kaufman, A. S., & Doppelt, J. E. (1976). Analysis of WISC-R standardization data in terms of the stratification variables. *Child Development, 47*(1), 165–171.

Kaufman J. C. (Ed.). (2009). *Intelligent testing: Integrating psychological theory and clinical practice.* New York, NY: Cambridge University Press.

Kaufman, J. C., & Sternberg, R. J. (Eds.). (2010). *The Cambridge handbook of creativity.* New York, NY: Cambridge University Press.

Kaufman, L., & Rock, I. (1989). The moon illusion thirty years later. In M. Hershenson (Ed.), *The moon illusion* (pp. 193–234). Hillsdale, NJ: Lawrence Erlbaum Assoc.

Kaye, W. H., Bulik, C. M., Thornton, L., Barbarich, N., & Masters, K. (2004). Comorbidity of anxiety disorders with anorexia and bulimia nervosa. *American Journal of Psychiatry, 161*(12), 2215–2221.

Kazdin, A. E. (2005). *Parent management training: Treatment for oppositional, aggressive, and antisocial behavior in children and adolescents.* New York, NY: Oxford University Press.

Kazdin, A. E., & Benjet, C. (2003). Spanking children: Evidence and issues. *Current Directions in Psychological Science, 12*(3), 99–103.

Kean, M.-L. (1977). The linguistic interpretation of aphasic syndromes: Agrammatism in Broca's aphasia, an example. *Cognition, 5*(1), 9–46.

Keane, M. (2008, September 29). *Texting overtakes voice in mobile phone usage.* Retrieved from www.wired.com/epicenter/2008/09/texting-overtak/.

Keane, T. M., Marx, B. P., & Sloan, D. M. (2009). Post–traumatic stress disorder: Definition, prevalence, and risk factors. *Post-traumatic stress disorder: Basic science and clinical practice* (pp. 1–19). Totowa, NJ: Humana Press.

Keates, J., & Stam, H. J. (2009). The disadvantaged psychological scene: Educational experiences of women in early Canadian psychology. *Canadian Psychology, 50*(4), 273–282.

Keel, P. K., & Haedt, A. (2008). Evidence-based psychosocial treatments for eating problems and eating disorders. *Journal of Clinical Child and Adolescent Psychology : The Official Journal for the Society of Clinical Child and Adolescent Psychology, 37*(1), 39–61.

Keller, C., Siegrist, M., & Gutscher, H. (2006). The role of the affect and availability of heuristics in risk communication. *Risk Analysis, 26*, 631–639.

Keller, F. S. (1973). *The Definition of Psychology* (2nd Ed.). Englewood Cliffs, NJ: Prentice Hall.

Kellman, P .J., & Arterberry, M. E. (2006). Infant visual perception. In D. Kuhn & R. Siegler (Eds.), *Handbook of Child Psychology: Vol 2. Cognition, Perception and Language* (6th ed., pp. 109–160). Hoboken: NJ: Wiley.

Kellman, P. J., & Arterberry, M. E. (1998). *The cradle of knowledge: Development of perception in infancy.* Cambridge, MA: MIT Press.

Kelly, C. R., Grinband, J., & Hirsch, J. (2007). Repeated exposure to media violence is associated with diminished response in an inhibitory frontolimbic network. *PLoS ONE, 2*(12), e1268.

Kelly, G. A. (1955). *The psychology of personal constructs, Vols. 1 and 2.* New York, NY: W. W. Norton.

Kelman, L. (2007). The triggers or precipitants of the acute migraine attack. *Cephalalgia, 27*, 394–402.

Keltner, D., & Kring, A. M. (1998). Emotion, social function, and psychopathology. *Review of General Psychology, 2*, 320–342.

Kendall-Tackett, K. (2014). The effects of childhgood maltreatment and of exposure to early toxic stress. In J. R. Conte (Ed.), *Child Abuse and Neglect Worldwide.* Santa Barbara, CA: Praeger.

Kendall-Tackett, K. (2010). Depression, hostility, posttraumatic stress disorder, and inflammation: The corrosive health effects of negative mental states. *The psychoneuroimmunology of chronic disease: Exploring the links between inflammation, stress, and illness* (pp. 113–131). Washington, DC: American Psychological Association.

Kendler, K. S., Myers, J., & Prescott, C. A. (2005). Sex differences in the relationship between social support and risk for major depression: A longitudinal study of opposite-sex twin pairs. *American Journal of Psychiatry, 162*(2), 250–256.

Kendler, K. S., & Schaffner, K. F. (2011). The dopamine hypothesis of schizophrenia: An historical and philosophical analysis. *Philosophy, Psychiatry, & Psychology, 18*(1), 41–63.

Kennedy, Q., Mather, M., & Carstensen, L. L. (2004). The role of motivation in the age-related positivity effect in autobiographical memory. *Psychological Science, 15*(3), 208–214.

Kennedy, R. B., & Kennedy, D. A. (2004). Using the Myers-Briggs Type Indicator in career counseling. *Journal of Employment Counseling, 41*, 38–44.

Kennedy, S. H., et al. (2009). Canadian Network for Mood and Anxiety Treatments (CANMAT) Clinical guidelines for the management of major depressive disorder in adults, IV, neurostimulation therapies. *Journal of Affective Disorders, 117*, 544–553.

Kenrick, D. T., & Goldstein, N. J. (2012). *Six degrees of social influence: Science, application, and the psychology of Robert Cialdini.* New York, NY: Oxford University Press.

Kensinger, E. A., & Corkin, S. (2003). Memory enhancement for emotional words: Are emotional words more vividly remembered than neutral words? *Memory & Cognition, 31*(8), 1169–1180.

Kensinger, E. A., Ullmann, M. T., & Corkin, S. (2001). Bilateral medial temporal lobe damage does not affect lexical or grammatical processing. Evidence from amnesic patient H.M. *Hippocampus, 11*(4), 347–360.

Keon, W. J. (2009). Early childhood education and care: Canada's challenges and next steps. *Paediatrics & Child Health, 14*(10), 660–661.

Kern, M. L., & Friedman, H. S. (2011). Personality and pathways of influence on physical health. *Social and Personality Psychology Compass, 5*(1), 76–87.

Kern, M. L., & Friedman, H. S. (2008). Do conscientious individuals live longer? A quantitative review. *Health Psychology, 27*(5), 505–512.

Kernberg, O. F. (2005). Object relations theories and technique. In E. S. Person, A. M. Cooper, & G. O. Gabbard (Eds.), *The American Psychiatric Publishing textbook of psychoanalysis* (pp. 57–75). Washington, DC: American Psychiatric Publishing.

Kernberg, O. F. (1997). Convergences and divergences in contemporary psychoanalytic technique and psychoanalytic psychotherapy. In J. K. Zeig (Ed.), *The evolution of psychotherapy: The third conference.* New York, NY: Brunner/Mazel.

Kesselring, T., & Müller, U. (2010). The concept of egocentrism in the context of Piaget's theory. *New Ideas in Psychology*. No Pages.

Kessels, R. P. C., & Postma, A. (2002). Verbal interference during encoding and maintenance of spatial information in working memory. *Current Psychology Letters: Behaviour, Brain & Cognition, 9*, 39–46.

Kessler, R. C., & Wang, P. S. (2009). Epidemiology of depression. In I. H. Gotlib and C. L. Hammen (Eds.), *Handbook of depression* (2nd ed., pp. 5 22). New York: Guilford.

Kessler, R. C., Ruscio, A. M., Shear, K., & Wittchen, H. (2009). Epidemiology of anxiety disorders. In M. B. Stein & T. Steckler (Eds.), *Behavioral neurobiology of anxiety and its treatment* (pp. 21–35). New York, NY: Springer Science + Business Media.

Kessler, R. C., Petukhova, M., Sampson, N. A., Zaslavsky, A. M., & Wittchen, H. U. (2012). Twelve-month and lifetime prevalence and lifetime morbid risk of anxiety and mood disorders in the United States. *International Journal of Methods in Psychiatric Research, 21*(3), 169-184.

Kessler, R. C., Amminger, G. P., Aguilar-Gaxiola, S., Alongo, J., & Lee, S. (2007). Age of onset of mental disorders: A review of recent literature. *Current Opinions in Psychiatry, 20*(4), 359–364.

Kessler, R. C., Berglund, P., Demler, O., Jin, R., & Walters, E. E. (2005). Lifetime prevalence and age-of-onset distributions of DSM-IV disorders in the National Comorbidity Survey Replication. *Archives of General Psychiatry, 62*, 593 602.

Kessler, R. C., Chiu, W. T., Demler, O., Merikangas, K. R., & Walters, E. E. (2005). Prevalence, severity, and comorbidity of 12-month DSM IV disorders in the National Comorbidity Survey Replication. *Archives of General Psychiatry, 62*, 617–627.

Kessler, R. C., Adler, L. A., Barkley, R., Biederman, J., Conners, C. K., Faraone, S. V., et al. (2005). Patterns and predictors of attention-deficit/hyperactivity disorder persistence into adulthood: Results from the National Comorbidity Survey Replication. *Biological Psychiatry, 57*(11), 1442–1451.

Keysers, C., & Gazzola, V. (2007). Integrating simulation and theory of mind: From self to social cognition. *Trends in Cognitive Sciences, 11*(5), 194–196.

Khalil, E. L. (2004). What is altruism? *Journal of Economic Psychology, 25*(1), 97–123.

Kibler, J. L., Joshi, K., & Hughes, E. E. (2010). Cognitive and behavioral reactions to stress among adults with PTSD: Implications for immunity and health. In K. Kendall-Tackett (Ed.), *The psychoneuroimmunology of chronic disease: Exploring the links between inflammation, stress, and illness* (pp. 133–158). Washington, DC: American Psychological Association.

Kiecolt-Glaser, J. K., Dura, J. R., Speicher, C. E., Trask, O. J., & Glaser, R. (1991). Spousal caregivers of dementia victims: Longitudinal changes in immunity and health. *Psychosomatic Medicine, 53*, 345–362.

Kiecolt-Glaser, J. K., & Glaser, R. (2002). Depression and immune function: Central pathways to morbidity and mortality. *Journal of Psychsomatic Research, 53*, 873–876.

Kiecolt-Glaser, J. K., & Glaser, R. (1999). Psychoneuroimmunology and cancer: Fact or fiction? *European Journal of Cancer, 35*, 1603–1607.

Kiecolt-Glaser, J. K., & Glaser, R. (1988). Behavioral influences on immune function: Evidence for the interplay between stress and health. In *Stress and coping across development* (pp. 189–205). Hillsdale, NJ: Erlbaum.

Kiecolt-Glaser, J. K., Glaser, R., Gravenstein, S., Malarkey, W. B., & Sheridan, J. (1996). Chronic stress alters the immune response to influenza virus vaccine in older adults. *Proceedings of the National Academy of Sciences, USA, 93*, 3043 3047.

Kiecolt-Glaser, J., McGuire, L., Robles, T. F., & Glaser, R. (2002). Psychoneuroimmunology and psychosomatic medicine: Back to the future. *Psychosomatic Medicine, 64*(1), 15–28.

Kievit, R. A., van Rooijen, H., Wicherts, J. M., Waldorp, L. J., Kan, K-J., Scholte, S., & Barsboom, D. (2012). Intelligence and the brain: A model based approach. *Cognitive Neuroscience, 3*, 89–97.

Kihlstrom, J. F. (2007). Consciousness in hypnosis. In P. D. Zelazo, M. Moscovitch, & E. Thompson (Eds.), *The Cambridge handbook of consciousness*. New York, NY: Cambridge University Press.

Kihlstrom, J. F. (2006). Repression: A unified theory of a will-o'-the-wisp. *Behavioral and Brain Sciences, 29*(5), 523.

Kihlstrom, J. F., Beer, J. S., & Klein, S. B. (2003). Self and identity as memory. In M. R. Leary & J. P. Tangney (Eds.), *Handbook of self and identity* (pp. 68–90). New York, NY: Guilford Press.

Kihlstrom, J. F., Dorfman, J., & Park, L. (2007). Implicit and explicit memory and learning. In M. Velmans & S. Schneider (Eds.), *The Blackwell companion to consciousness*. Malden, MA: Blackwell Publishing.

Kihlstrom, J. F., Mulvaney, S., Tobias, B. A., & Tobis, I. P. (2000). The emotional unconscious. In E. Eich, J. F. Kihlstrom, et al. (Eds.), *Cognition and Emotion*, London, England: Oxford University Press.

Kim, H., & Cabeza, R. (2007). Differential contributions of prefrontal, medial temporal, and sensory-perceptual regions to true and false memory formation. *Cerebral Cortex, 17*(9), 2143–2150.

Kim, H., & Markus, H. R. (1999). Deviance or uniqueness, harmony or conformity? A cultural analysis. *Journal of Personality and Social Psychology, 77*, 785–800.

Kim, J. L., Collins, R. L., Kanouse, D. E., Elliott, M. N., Berry, S. H., Hunter, S. B., Miu, A., & Kunkel, D. (2006). Sexual readiness, household policies, and other predictors of adolescents' exposure to sexual content in mainstream entertainment television. *Media Psychology, 8*(4), 449–471.

Kim, T. Y., Hon, A. H. Y., & Lee, D. R. (2010). Proactive personality and employee creativity: The effects of job creativity requirement and supervisor support for creativity. *Creativity Research Journal, 22*(1), 37–45.

Kim, Y.-H., Peng, S., & Chiu, C.-Y. (2008). Explaining self-esteem differences between Chinese and North Americans: Dialectical self (vs. Self-consistency) or lack of positive self-regard. *Self and Identity, 7*(2), 113–128.

Kimmel, S. R., & Ratliff-Schaub, K. (2007). Growth and development. In R. E. Rakel (Ed.), *Textbook of Family Medicine*, 7th Ed. Philadelphia, PA: Saunders Elsevier.

Kimura, D. (2004). Human sex differences in cognition, fact not predicament. *Sexualities, Evolution and Gender, 6*(1) 45–53.

Kimura, D. (2002). Sex differences in the brain. *Scientific American, 12*, 32–37.

Kimura, D. (2000). *Sex and cognition*. Cambridge, MA: A Bradford Book/The MIT Press.

King, J. A. (1997, January). Golf in the zone state: Attaining your peak performance. *The Club Golfer*.

King, L. (2002, March 19). Interview with Russell Yates. *Larry King Live, CNN*.

Kinnamon, S. C. (2009). Umami taste transduction mechanisms. *The American Journal of Clinical Nutrition, 90*(3), 753S–755S.

Kinsey, A. C., Pomeroy, W. B., & Martin, C. E. (1948). *Sexual behavior in the human male*. Philadelphia, PA: W. B. Saunders.

Kirby, M. J. L., & Keon, W. J. (2006). *Out of the shadows at last: Transforming mental health, mental illness and addiction services in Canada*. The Standing Senate Committee on Social Affairs, Science and Technology final report on mental health, mental illness and addiction. Retrieved from http://www.parl.gc.ca/Content/SEN/Committee/391/soci/rep/pdf/rep02may06part1-e.pdf.

Kirmayer, L., Simpson, C., & Cargo, M. (2003) Healing traditions: Culture, community and mental health promotion with Canadian Aboriginal peoples. *Australasian Psychiatry, 11*, 15–23.

Kirmayer, L. J., Tait, C. L. & Simpson, C. (2009). The mental health of Aboriginal peoples in Canada: Transformations of identity and community. In L. J. Kirmayer & G. G. Valaskakis (Eds), *Healing traditions: The mental health of Aboriginal peoples in Canada*. Vancouver, BC: UBC Press.

Kirschenbaum, H. (2004). Carl Rogers's life and work: An assessment on the 100th anniversary of his birth. *Journal of Counseling and Development, 82*(1), 116–124.

Kirschner, P. A., & Karpinski, A. C. (2010). Facebook and academic performance. *Computers in Human Behavior, 26*, 1237–1245.

Kitayama, S., Markus, H. R., & Kurokawa, M. (2000). Culture, emotion, and well-being: Good feelings in Japan and the United States. *Cognition and Emotion, 14*, 93–124.

Klaassen, E., Evers, L., De Groot, R., Veltman, D., & Jolles, J. (2012). Episodic memory encoding in middle age: effects of ageing and cognitive fatigue on brain activation.

Kleber, H. D., & Galanter, M. (Eds.). (2008). *The American Psychiatric Publishing textbook of substance abuse treatment (4th Ed.)*. Washington, DC: American Psychiatric Publishing.

Klein, G. (2004). *The power of intuition: How to use your gut feelings to make better decisions at work*. Crown Business.

Klein, J. (2011). *A vending machine for crows: An experiment in corvid learning*. Retrieved from http://www.wireless.is/projects/cros/.

Klein, N. (2007). *The shock doctrine: The rise of disaster capitalism*. New York, NY: Metropolitan Books.

Klein, R. (1999). The Hebb Legacy. *Canadian Journal of Experimental Psychology, 53*(1), 1–3.

Kleinke, C. L. (2007). What does it mean to cope? *The Praeger handbook on stress and coping (vol. 2)* (pp. 289–308). Westport, CT: Praeger Publishers/Greenwood Publishing Group.

Kleinman, A. (1987). Anthropology and psychiatry: The role of culture in cross-cultural research on illness. *British Journal of Psychiatry, 151*, 447–454.

Klonsky, E. D. (2007). The functions of deliberate self-injury: A review of the evidence. *Clinical Psychological Review, 27*, 226–239.

Klonsky, E. D., & Muehlenkamp, J. J. (2007). Self-injury: A research review for the practitioner. *Journal of Clinical Psychology, 63*(11), 1045–1056.

Klonsky, E. D., Muehlenkamp, J. J., Lewis, S. P., & Walsh, B. (2011). *Nonsuicidal self-injury*. Cambridge, MA: Hogrefe Publishing.

Kluger, J. (2007, October 29). The power of birth order. *Time*.

Klüver, H., & Bucy, P. C. (1939). Preliminary analysis of functions of the temporal lobes of monkeys. *Archives of Neurology and Psychiatry, 42*, 979–1000.

Kmec, J. A., O'Connor, L. T., & Schieman, S. (2014). Not ideal: The association between working anything but full time and perceived unfair treatment. *Work and Occupations, 41*(1), 63–85.

Kneer, J., Glock, S., & Reiger, D. (2012). Fast and not furious? Reduction of cognitive dissonance in smokers. *Social Psychology, 43*(2), 81–91.

Knopik, V. S. (2009). Maternal smoking during pregnancy and child outcomes: Real or spurious effect? *Developmental Neuropsychology, 34*(1), 1–36.

Knudson, E. I. (2004). Sensitive periods in the development of the brain and behavior. *Journal of Cognitive Neuroscience, 16*, 1412–1425.

Knutson, B., Wolkowitz, O., Cole, S., Chan, T., Moore, E., Johnson, R., et al. (1998). Selective alteration of personality and social behavior by serotonergic intervention. *American Journal of Psychiatry, 155*, 373–379.

Kobeissi, J., Aloysi, A., Tobias, K., Popeo, D., & Kellner, C. H. (2011). Resolution of severe suicidality with a single electroconvulsive therapy. *The Journal of ECT, 27*(1), 86–88.

Koch, C., & Tsuchiya, N. (2007). Attention and consciousness: Two separate processes. *Trends in Cognitive Science, 11*(1), 16–22.

Koch, W. J., & Haring, M. (2008). Posttraumatic stress disorder. In M. Hersen & J. Rosqvist (Eds.), *Handbook of psychological assessment, case conceptualization, and treatment, Vol. 1: Adults* (pp. 263–290). Hoboken, NJ: John Wiley & Sons.

Koenig, H. G. (2012). Religion, spirituality, and health: The research and clinical implications. *ISRN Psychiatry*, Volume 2012 (2012), Article ID 278730, 1–33.

Koenig, A. M., Eagly, A. H., Mitchell, A. A., & Ristikari, T. (2011). Are leader stereotypes masculine? A meta-analysis of three research paradigms. *Psychological Bulletin, 137*(4), 616–642.

Koenig, H. G., & Cohen, H. J. (2002). Psychosocial factors, immunology, and wound healing. *The link between religion and health: Psychoneuroimmunology and the faith factor* (pp. 124–138). New York, NY: Oxford University Press.

Koenigs, M., Young, L., Adolphs, R., Tranel, D., Cushman, F., Hauser, M., et al. (2007). Damage to the prefontal cortex increases utilitarian moral judgements. *Nature, 446*(7138), 908–911.

Koenigsberg, H. W., Harvey, P. D., Mitropoulou, V., et al. (2002). Characterizing affective instability in borderline personality disorder. *American Journal of Psychiatry, 159*(5), 784–788.

Koffka, K. (1935). *Principles of Gestalt psychology.* New York, NY: Harcourt, Brace, & World.

Kohlberg, L. (2008). The development of children's orientations toward a moral order: I. sequence in the development of moral thought. *Human Development, 51*(1), 8–20.

Kohlberg, L. (1994). The claim to moral adequacy of a highest stage of moral judgment. In B. Puka (Ed.), *The great justice debate: Kohlberg criticism* (pp. 2–18). New York, NY: Garland Publishing.

Kohlberg, L. (1981). *The philosophy of moral development: Moral stages and the idea of justice. Essays on moral development, Volume 16.* Harper and Row.

Kohlberg, L. (1963). The development of children's orientations toward a moral order: I. sequence in the development of moral thought. *Vita Humana, 6*(1–2), 11–33.

Kohn, M. L., & Schooler, C. (1973). Occupational experience and psychological functioning: An assessment of reciprocal effects. *American Sociological Review, 38*(1), 97–118.

Kohn, P. M. (1996). On coping adaptively with daily hassles. In M. Zeidner and N. S. Endler (Eds.), *Handbook of coping: Theory, research, applications.* New York, NY: John Wiley & Sons, Inc.

Kohn, P. M., Lafreniere, K., & Gurevitch, M. (1990). The inventory of college students' recent life experiences: A decontaminated hassle scale for a special population. *Journal of Behavioral Medicine, 13*, 619–630.

Kolb, B., & Whishaw, I. Q. (2009). *Fundamentals of human neuropsychology (6th Ed.).* New York, NY: Worth Publishers.

Komaki, J. (2004). Water can induce better spatial memory performance than food in radial maze learning by rats. *Japanese Psychological Research, 46*(1), 65–71.

Komaroff, A. L., Masuda, M., & Holmes, T. H. (1989). The Social Readjustment Rating Scale: A comparative study of Black, white, and Mexican Americans. In T. H. Holmes and E. M. David (Eds.), *Life change, life events, and illness.* New York, NY: Praeger.

Komaroff, A. L., Masuda, M., & Holmes, T. H. (1986). The Social Readjustment Rating Scale: A comparative study of Negro, white, and Mexican Americans. *Journal of Psychosomatic Research, 12*, 121–128.

Koob, G. F. (2013). Theoretical frameworks and mechanistic aspects of alcohol addiction: Alcohol addiction as a reward deficit disorder. In W.H. Sommer and R. Spanagel (Eds.), *Behavioral neurobiology of alcohol addiction* (Series title: Current topics in behavioral neuroscience (Vol. 13, pp. 3–13), Berlin: Springer-Verlag.

Koob, G. F., & LeMoal, M. (2008). Addiction and the brain antireward system. In S. Fiske, D. L. Schacter, & R. Sternberg (Eds.), *Annual review of psychology—Volume 59.* Palo Alto, CA: Annual reviews.

Koopmans, P. C., Sanderman, R., Timmerman, I., & Emmelkamp, P. M. G. (1994). The Irrational Beliefs Inventory (IBI): Development and psychometric evaluation. *European Journal of Psychological Assessment, 10*(1), 15–27.

Kooyman, I., & Walsh, E. (2011). Societal outcomes in schizophrenia. In D. R. Weinberger & P. J. Harrison (Eds.), *Schizophrenia* (3rd Ed.). Hoboken, NJ: Blackwell-Wiley.

Kopasz, M., Loessl, B., Hornyak, M., Riemann, D., Nissen, C., Pioszczyk, H., & Voderholzer, U. (2010). Sleep and memory in healthy children and adolescents—a critical review. *Sleep Medicine Reviews, 14*(3), 167–177.

Kopec, J., Williams, J. I., To, T., et al. (2001). Cross-cultural comparisons of health status in Canada using the Health Utilities Index. *Ethnicity and Health, 6*(1), 41–50.

Kopelowicz, A., Liberman, R. P., & Zarate, R. (2007). Psychosocial treatments for schizophrenia. In P. E. Nathan & J. M. Gorman (Eds.), *A guide to treatments that work* (3rd Ed., pp. 243–269). New York, NY: Oxford University Press.

Korb, J. (2010). Social insects, major evolutionary transitions and multilevel selection. In P. Kappeler (Ed.), *Animal behavior: Evolution and mechanisms* (pp. 179–211). London: Springer.

Korchin, S. J., & Sands, S. H. (1983). Principles common to all psychotherapies. In C. E. Walker (Ed.), *The handbook of clinical psychology.* Homewood, IL: Dow Jones-Irwin.

Kosslyn, S. M., & Rosenberg, R. S. (2004). *Psychology: The brain, the person, the world* (2nd Ed.). Essex, England: Pearson Education Limited.

Kosten, T. R., George, T. P., & Kleber, H. D. (2005). The neurobiology of substance dependence: Implications for treatment. In R. J. Frances, A. H. Mack, & S. I. Miller (Eds.), *Clinical textbook of addictive disorder* (3rd edition). New York, NY: Guilford Press.

Kosten, T. R., Sofuoglu, M., & Gardner, T. J. (2008). Clinical management: Cocaine. In H. D. Kleber & M. Galanter (Eds.), *The American Psychiatric Publishing textbook of substance abuse treatment* (4th edition). Washington, DC: American Psychiatric Publishing.

Kozlovskiy, S. A., Vartanov, A. V., Pyasik, M. M., & Nikonova, E. Y. (2012). Functional role of corpus callosum regions in human memory functioning. *International Journal of Psychophysiology, 85*(3), 396–397.

Kraft, D., & Kraft, T. (2010). Use of in vivo and in vitro desensitization in the treatment of mouse phobia: Review and case study. *Contemporary Hypnosis, 27*(3), 184–194.

Krantz, D. S., & McCeney, M. K. (2002). Effects of psychological and social factors on organic disease: A critical assessment of research on coronary heart disease. *Annual Review of Psychology, 53*(1), 341–369.

Krantz, G., Berntsson, L., & Lundberg, U. (2005). Total workload, work stress, and perceived symptoms in Swedish male and female white-collar employees. *European Journal of Public Health, 15*, 209–214.

Krebs, D. L. (2008). Morality: An evolutionary account. *Perspectives on Psychological Science, 3*, 149–172.

Krebs, D. L., & Denton, K. (2006). Explanatory Limitations of Cognitive-Developmental Approaches to Morality. *Psychological Review, 113*, 672–675.

Krebs, D. L., & Denton, K. (1997). Social illusions and self-deception: The evolution of biases in person perception. *Evolutionary Social Psychology, 21–48.*

Krippner, S. (1990.) *Dreamtime and Dreamwork: Decoding the Language of the Night.* Los Angeles, CA: Jeremy P. Tarcher.

Krueger, R. F., South, S., Johnson, W., & Iacono, W. (2008). The heritability of personality is not always 50%: Gene-environment interactions and correlations between personality and parenting. *Journal of Personality, 76*(6), 1485–1522.

Krueger, R. G., & Kaplan, M. S. (2002). Behavioral and psychopharmacological treatment of the paraphilic and hypersexual disorders. *Journal of Psychiatric Practices, 8*(1), 21–32.

Krüetzen, M., Mann, J., Heithaus, M. R., Connor, R. C., Bejder, L. & Sherwin, W. B. (2005). Cultural transmission of tool use in bottlenose dolphins. *Proceedings of the National Academy of Sciences USA, 102*, 8939–8943.

Kruk, E. (2010). Collateral damage: The lived experiences of divorced mothers without custody. *Journal of Divorce & Remarriage, 51*(8), 526–543.

Krumhuber, E. G., Likowski, K. U., & Weyers, P. (2014). Facial mimicry of spontaneous and deliberate Duchenne and non-Duchenne smiles. *Journal of Nonverbal Behavior, 38*, 1–11.

Ksir, C., Hart, C. L., & Oakley, R. (2008). *Drugs, society, and human behavior (12th Ed.).* Boston, MA: McGraw-Hill.

Kuboshima-Amemori, S., & Sawaguchi, T. (2007). Plasticity of the primate prefrontal cortex. *Neuroscientist, 13*, 229–240.

Kudwa, A. E., Michopoulos, V., Gatewood, J. D., & Rissman, E. F. (2006). Roles of estrogen receptors alpha and beta in differentiation of mouse sexual behavior. *Neuroscience, 138*(3), 921–928.

Kuhl, P. K. (2010). Brain mechanisms in early language acquisition. *Neuron, 67*(5), 713–727.

Kuhn, M., Popovic, A., & Pezawas, L. (2014). Neuroplasticity and memory formation in major depressive disorder: An imaging genetics perspective on serotonin and BDNF. *Restorative Neurology and Neuroscience, 32*(1), 25–49.

Kuhn, T. S. (1962). *The structure of scientific revolutions.* Chicago, IL: University of Chicago Press.

Kuncel, N. R., Hezlett, S. A., & Ones, D. S. (2004). Academic performance, career potential, creativity, and job performance: Can one construct predict them all? *Journal of Personality and Social Psychology, 86*(1), 148–161.

Kuncel, N. R., Ones, D. S., & Sackett, P. R. (2010). Individual differences as predictors of work, educational, and broad life outcomes. *Personality and Individual Differences, 49*(4), 331–336.

Kundu, P., & Cummins, D. D. (2013). Morality and conformity: The Asch paradigm applied to moral decisions. *Social Influence, 8*(4), 268–279.

Kunst, M. J. J. (2011). Affective personality type, post-traumatic stress disorder symptom severity and post-traumatic growth in victims of violence. *Stress and Health: Journal of the International Society for the Investigation of Stress, 27*(1), 42–51.

Kuo, J. R., Goldin, P. R., Werner, K., Heimberg, R. G., & Gross, J. J. (2011). Childhood trauma and current psychological functioning in adults with social anxiety disorder. *Journal of Anxiety Disorders, 25*(4), 467–473.

Kuppens, P., Realo, A., & Diener, E. (2008). The role of positive and negative emotions in life satisfaction judgment across nations. *Journal of Personality and Social Psychology, 95*(1), 66–75.

Kutner, L., & Olson, C. (2008). Grand theft childhood: The surprising truth about violent video games and what parents can do. New York, NY: Simon & Schuster.

Kwon, D. H., Kim, J. M., Oh, S. H., Jeong, H. J., Park, S. Y., Oh, E. S., . . . & Cho, Z. H. (2012). Seven-tesla magnetic resonance images of the substantia nigra in Parkinson disease. *Annals of Neurology, 71*(2), 267–277.

Labbé, E. E. (2011). *Psychology moment by moment: A guide to enhancing your clinical practice with mindfulness and meditation.* Oakland, CA: New Harbinger Publications.

Lack, L. C., & Bootzin, R. R. (2003). Circadian rhythm factors in insomnia and their treatment. In M. L. Perlis & K. L. Lichstein (Eds.), *Treating sleep disorders: Principles and practice of behavioral sleep medicine.* New York, NY: John Wiley & Sons, Inc.

Ladenson, J. H., Laterza, O., & Modur, V. (2013). U.S. Patent Application 13/929,600.

Lagercrantz, H., & Changeux, J. P. (2009). The emergence of human consciousness: from fetal to neonatal life. *Pediatric Research, 65*, 255–260.

LaGraize, S. C., Borzan, J., Rinker, M. M., Kopp, J. L., & Fuchs, P. N. (2004). Behavioral evidence for competing motivational drives of nociception and hunger. *Neuroscience Letters, 372*(1/2), 30–34.

Lahat, A., Walker, O. L., Lamm, C., Degnan, K. A., Henderson, H. A., & Fox, N. A. (2014). Cognitive conflict links behavioural inhibition and social problem solving during social exclusion in childhood. *Infant and Child Development, 23*(3), 273–282.

Lahey, B. B., Kupfer, D. L., Beggs, V. E., & Landon, D. (1982). Do learning-disabled children exhibit peripheral deficits in selective attention? An analysis of eye movements during reading. *Journal of Abnormal Child Psychology, 10*, 1–10.

Lahmann, C., Henningsen, P., & Noll-Hussong, M. (2010). Somatoforme schmerzen—Ein uberblick. [somatoform pain disorder—Overview]. *Psychiatria Danubina, 22*(3), 453–458.

Lakey, C. E., Hirsch, J. K., Nelson, L. A., & Nsamenang, S. A. (2014). Effects of contingent self-esteem on depressive symptoms and suicidal behavior. *Death Studies* (ahead-of-print), 1–8.

Lakhan, S. E. (2007). Neuropsychological generation of source amnesia: An episodic memory disorder of the frontal brain. *Journal of Medical Chemistry.* Retrieved from http://www.scientificjournals.org/journals2007/articles/1038.html.

Laland, K. N., & Galef, B. (2009). *The question of animal culture.* Cambridge, MA: Harvard University Press.

Lalasz, R. (2011). Is something wrong with the scientific method? Part 1. *Cool green science (The conservation blog of the Nature Conservancy)*, January 21.

Lam, R. W., Kennedy, S. H., Grigoriadis, S., McIntyre, R. S., Milev, R., Ramasubbu, R., . . . & Ravindran, A. V. (2009). Canadian Network for Mood and Anxiety Treatments (CANMAT) Clinical guidelines for the management of major depressive disorder in adults.: III. Pharmacotherapy. *Journal of Affective Disorders, 117*, S26–S43.

Lambert, M. J. (2010). *Prevention of treatment failure: The use of measuring, monitoring, and feedback in clinical practice.* Washington, DC: American Psychological Association.

Lambrecht, L., Kreifelts, B., & Wildgruber, D. (2014). Gender differences in emotional recognition: Impact of sensory modality and emotion category. *Cognition and Emotion, 28*(3), 452–469.

Laming, P. R., Syková, E., Reichenbach, A., Hatton, G. I., & Bauer, H. (2011). *Glial cells: Their role in behaviour.* Cambridge University Press.

Lancaster, T., Stead, L., Silagy, C., & Sowden, A. (2000). Effectiveness of interventions to help people stop smoking: findings from the Cochrane Library. *British Medical Journal, 321*, 355.

Landon, T. M., & Barlow, D. H. (2004). Cognitive-behavioral treatment for panic disorder: Current status. *Journal of Psychiatric Practices, 10*(4), 211–226.

Landsberger, H. A. (1958). *Hawthorne revisited.* Ithaca, NY: Cornell University.

Lang, A. E., & Obeso, J. A. (2004). Challenges in Parkinson's disease: restoration of the nigrostriatal dopamine system is not enough. *The Lancet Neurology, 3*(5), 309–316.

Lang, A. R., et al. (1975). Effects of alcohol on aggression in male social drinkers. *Journal of Abnormal Psychology, 84*, 508–518.

Lang, P. J., & Bradley, M. M. (2013). Appetitive and defensive motivation: Goal-directed or goal-determined? *Emotion Review, 5*, 230–234.

Lang, P. J., Bradley, M. M., & Cuthbert, B. N. (1998). Emotion, motivation, and anxiety: Brain mechanisms and psychophysiology. *Biological Psychiatry, 44*, 1248–1263.

Lange, C. G. (1885). The mechanism of the emotions. Paper originally published in 1885 and reprinted in B. Rand (Ed.), *The classical psychologists* (pp. 672–684). Boston, MA: Houghton Mifflin (1921).

Langens, T. A., & Morth, S. (2003). Repressive coping and the use of passive and active coping strategies. *Personality and Individual Differences, 35*(2), 461–473.

Langer, E. J., & Rodin, J. (2004). The effects of choice and enhanced personal responsibility for the aged: A field experiment in an institutional setting. *The interface of social and clinical psychology: Key readings* (pp. 339–348). New York, NY: Psychology Press.

Langlois, J. H., & Stephan, C. W. (1981). Beauty and the beast: The role of physical attractiveness in the development of peer relations and social behavior. In S. S. Brehm, S. M. Kassin, & F. X. Gibbons (Eds.), *Developmental social psychology.* New York, NY: Oxford University Press.

Langlois, K. A., Samokhvalov, A. V., Reh, J., Spence, S. T., Connor Gorber, S. K. (2011). Health state descriptions for Canadians: Mental illnesses. Statistics Canada, catalogue no. 82-619-MIE2005002. Ottawa: Statistics Canada.

Långström, N., Rahman, Q., Carlström, E., & Lichtenstein, P. (2008). Genetic and environmental effects on same-sex sexual behavior: A population study of twins in Sweden. *Archives of Sexual Behaviour, 39*(1), 75–80.

Lankau, M. J., Riordan, C. M., & Thomas, C. H. (2005). The effects of similarity and liking in formal relationships between mentors and protégés. *Journal of Vocational Behavior, 67*(2), 252–265.

Lanting, C. P., de Kleine, E., & van Dijk, P. (2009). Neural activity underlying tinnitus generation: results from PET and fMRI. *Hearing Research, 255*, 1–13.

LaPiere, R. (1934). Attitudes versus actions. *Social Forces, 13*, 230–237.

Lareau, A. (2003). *Unequal childhoods: Class race and family life.* University of California Press.

Larimer, M. E., Kilmer, J. R., & Lee, C. M. (2005). College student drug prevention: A review of individually-oriented prevention strategies. *Journal of Drug Issues, 35*(2), 431–456.

Larimer, M. E., & Neighbors, C. (2003). Normative misperception and the impact of descriptive and injunctive norms on college student gambling. *Psychology of Addictive Behaviors, 17*(3), 235–243.

Larimer, M. E., Turner, A. P., Mallett, K. A., & Geisner, I. M. (2004). Predicting drinking behavior and alcohol-related problems among fraternity and sorority members: Examining the role of descriptive and injunctive norms. *Psychology of Addictive Behaviors, 18*(3), 203–212.

Larocque, S. (2006). *Gay Marriage: The Story of a Canadian Social Revolution.* Toronto, ON: James Lorimer & Company.

Larry, L. L., Young Owl, M., & Kersting, M. P. (2005). *The Cambridge Dictionary of Human Biology and Evolution.* Cambridge & New York: Cambridge University Press.

Larsen, L., Hartmann, P., & Nyborg, H. (2008). The stability of general intelligence from early adulthood to middle-age. *Intelligence, 36*(1), 29–34.

Larson, E. B., Wang, L., Bowen, J. D., McCormick, W. C., Teri, L., Crane, P., & Kukull, W. (2006). Exercise is associated with reduced risk of incident dementia among persons 65 years of age and older. *Annals of Internal Medicine, 144*, 73–81.

Laruelle, M. (2014). Schizophrenia: from dopaminergic to glutamatergic interventions. *Current Opinion in Pharmacology, 14*, 97–102.

Lashley, K. S. (1948). *Brain mechanisms and intelligence, 1929.*

Lashley, K. S. (1929). *Brain mechanisms and intelligence: A quantitative study of injuries to the brain.* Chicago, IL: University of Chicago Press.

Latane, B., & Darley, J. M. (1970). *The unresponsive bystander: Why doesn't he help?* Englewood Cliffs, NJ: Prentice Hall.

Latane, B., & Darley, J. M. (1968). Group inhibition of bystander intervention in emergencies. *Journal of Personality and Social Psychology, 10*, 215–221.

Latane, B., Williams, K., & Harkins, S. G. (1979). Many hands make light the work: The cause and consequences of social loafing. *Journal of Personality and Social Psychology, 37*, 822–832.

Laumann, E. O., Gagnon, J. H., Michael, R. T., & Michaels, S. (1994). *The social organization of sexuality: sexual practices in the United States.* CSG Enterprises and Stuart Michaels.

Lavallee, C. F., Koren, S. A., & Persinger, M. A. (2011) A quantitative electroencephalographic study of meditation and binaural beat entrainment. *Journal of Alternative and Complementary Medicine, 17*(4), 351–355.

Lavie, P. (2001). Sleep-wake as a biological rhythm. *Annual Review of Psychology, 52*, 277–303.

Lawford, B. R., Young, R., Rowell, J. A., Gibson, J. N., et al. (1997). Association of the D2 dopamine receptor A1 allele with alcoholism: Medical severity alcoholism and type of controls. *Biological Psychiatry, 41*, 386–393.

Lazar, R. M., & Mohr, J. P. (2011). Revisiting the contributions of Paul Broca to the study of aphasia. *Neuropsychology Review, 21*(3), 236–239.

Lazarus, R. S. (2007). Stress and emotion: A new synthesis. In A. Monat, R. S. Lazarus, & G. Reevy (Eds.), *The Praeger handbook on stress and coping (vol. 1)* (pp. 33–51). Westport, CT: Praeger Publishers/Greenwood Publishing Group.

Lazarus, R. S. (1999). *Stress and emotion: A new synthesis*. New York, NY: Springer Publishing Co.

Lazarus, R. S. (1993a). From psychological stress to the emotions: A history of changing outlooks. *Annual Review of Psychology, 44*, 1–21.

Lazarus, R. S. (1993b). Why we should think of stress as a subset of emotion. *Handbook of stress: Theoretical and clinical aspects (2nd Ed.)* (pp. 21–39). New York, NY: Free Press.

Lazarus, R. S., & Alfert, E. (1964). The short-circuiting of threat by experimentally altering cognitive appraisal. *Journal of Abnormal and Social Psychology, 69*, 195–205.

Lazarus, R. S., & Folkman, S. (1984). *Stress, appraisal, and coping*. New York, NY: Springer.

Lazarus, R. S., Opton, E. M., Jr., Nomikos, M. S., & Rankin, N. O. (1965). The principle of short-circuiting of threat: Further evidence. *Journal of Personality, 33*, 622–635.

Lazzari, C., Egan, S. J., & Rees, C. S. (2011). Behavioral activation treatment for depression in older adults delivered via videoconferencing: A pilot study. *Cognitive and Behavioral Practice*, No Pages.

Leahey, T. H. (2005). Mind as a scientific object: A historical-philosophical exploration. In C. E. Erneling & D. M. Johnson (Eds.), *The mind as a scientific object: Between brain and culture* (pp. 35–78). New York, NY: Oxford University Press.

Leahey, T. H. (2000). *A History of Psychology* (5th Ed.). Upper Saddle River, NJ: Prentice Hall.

Learning Disabilities Association of Canada. (2002). *Official definition of learning disabilities*. Retrieved from www.ldac-acta.ca/learn-more/ld-defined/official-definition-of-learning-disabilities.

Leavitt, G. C. (1989). Disappearance of the incest taboo: A cross-cultural test of general evolutionary hypotheses. *American Anthropologist, 91*(1), 116–131.

Leavitt, M. O., Spellings, M., & Gonzales, A. R. (2007). *Report to the President on Issues Raised by the Virginia Tech Tragedy*. Washington, D.C.

Lechner, S. C., Stoelb, B. L., & Antoni, M. H. (2008). Group-based therapies for benefit finding in cancer. *Trauma, recovery, and growth: Positive psychological perspectives on posttraumatic stress* (pp. 207–231). Hoboken, NJ: John Wiley & Sons Inc.

Leddon, E. M., Waxman, S. R., & Medin, D. L. (2011). What does it mean to 'live' and 'die'? A cross-linguistic analysis of parent–child conversations in English and Indonesian. *British Journal of Developmental Psychology, 29*(3), 375–395.

Ledikwe, J. H., Ello-Martin, J. A., & Rolls, B. J. (2005). Portion sizes and the obesity epidemic. *Journal of Nutrition, 135*, 905–909.

Ledley, D. R., Erwin, B. A., & Heimberg, R. G. (2008). Social anxiety disorder. In W. E. Craighead, D. J. Miklowitz, & L. W. Craighead (Eds.), *Psychopathology: History, diagnosis, and empirical foundations* (pp. 198–233). Hoboken, NJ: John Wiley & Sons.

LeDoux, J. E. (2007). The amygdala. *Current Biology, 17*, R868–874.

LeDoux, J. E. (2003a). The emotional brain, fear, and the amygdala. *Cellular and Molecular Neurobiology, 23*(4–5), 727–738.

LeDoux, J. E. (2003b). *Synaptic self: How our brains become who we are*. Toronto, ON: Penguin.

LeDoux, J. E. (2000). Emotion circuits in the brain. *Annual Review of Neuroscience, 23*, 155–184.

LeDoux, J. E. (1999). The power of emotions. In R. Conlan (Ed.), *States of mind: new discoveries about how our brains make us who we are*. New York, NY: John Wiley & Sons, Inc.

LeDoux, J. E. (1998). Where the wild things are. *The emotional brain* (pp. 225–266). New York, NY: Simon & Schuster.

LeDoux, J. E. (1996). *The emotional brain: The mysterious underpinnings of emotional life*. New York, NY: Simon and Schuster.

LeDoux, J. E., & Doyère, V. (2011). Emotional memory processing: Synaptic connectivity. In S. Nalbantian, P. M. Matthews, & J. L. McClelland (Eds.), *The memory process: Neuroscientific and humanistic perspectives* (pp. 153–171). Cambridge, MA: MIT Press.

Lee, E., Mishna, F., & Brennenstuhl, S. (2010). How to critically evaluate case studies in social work. *Research on Social Work Practice, 20*(6), 682–689.

Lee, M. G., Hassani, O. K., & Jones, B. (2005). Discharge of identified orexin/hypocretin neurons across the sleep-waking cycle. *The Journal of Neuroscience, 25*(28), 6716–6720.

Legault, G., Delay, S., & Madore, A. (2010). Identification of a rapid eye movement sleep window for learning of the win-shift radial arm maze task for male Sprague-Dawley rats. *Journal of Sleep Research, 19*(4), 508–515.

Lehner, M., Wisłowska-Stanek, A., Taracha, E., Maciejak, P., Szyndler, J., Skórzewska, A., . . . & Płaźnik, A. (2010). The effects of midazolam and d-cycloserine on the release of glutamate and GABA in the basolateral amygdala of low and high anxiety rats during extinction trial of a conditioned fear test. *Neurobiology of Learning and Memory, 94*(4), 468–480.

Lehrer, J. (2007). *Proust was a Neuroscientist*. Houghton Mifflin Harcourt.

Leichsenring, F., Leibing, E., Kruse, J., New, A. S., & Leweke, F. (2011). Borderline personality disorder. *The Lancet, 377*(9759), 74–84.

Leitch, K. K. (2007). *Reaching for the top: A report by the advisor on healthy children & youth*. Her Majesty the Queen in Right of Canada, represented by the Minister of Health Canada, 2007. Retrieved from http://www.hc-sc.gc.ca/hl-vs/pubs/child-enfant/advisor-conseillere/index eng.php.

Lekander, M. (2002). Ecological immunology: The role of the immune system in psychology and neuroscience. *European Psychiatry, 7*(2), 98–115.

Lemmon, K., & Moore, C. (2007). The development of prudence in the face of varying future rewards. *Developmental Science, 10*(4), 502–511.

Lemstra, M. E., Nielsen, G., Rogers, M. R., Thompson, A. T., & Moraros, J. S. (2012). Risk indicators and outcomes associated with bullying in youth aged 9-15 years. *Canadian Journal of Public Health, 103*(1), 9–13.

Lemstra, M., Rogers, M., Moraros, J., & Caldbick, S. (2013). Prevalence and risk indicators of alcohol abuse and marijuana use among on-reserve First Nations youth. *Paediatrics & Child Health, 18*(1), 10–14.

Lenz, F. A., Casey, K. L., Jones, E. G., & Willis, W. (2010). *The human pain system*. Cambridge University Press.

Lenzenweger, M. F., Lane, M. C., Loranger, A. W., & Kessler, R. C. (2007). DSM-IV personality disorders in the national comorbidity survey replication. *Biological Psychiatry, 62*, 553–564.

Leon, A. C., Solomon, D. A., Li, C., Fiedorowicz, J. G., Coryell, W. H., Endicott, J., & Keller, M. B. (2011). Antidepressants and risks of suicide and suicide attempts: a 27-year observational study. *The Journal of Clinical Psychiatry, 72*(5), 580.

Leontiev, D. A. (2008). Maslow yesterday, today, and tomorrow. *Journal of Humanistic Psychology, 48*(4), 451–453.

Lepore, S. J., Evans, G. W., & Palsane, M. N. (1991). Social hassles and psychological health in the context of chronic crowding. *Journal of Health and Social Behavior, 32*(4), 357–367.

Leppänen, J. M., & Hietanen, J. K. (2007). Is there more in a happy face than just a big smile? *Visual Cognition, 15*(4), 468–490.

Leshner, G., Vultee, F., Bolls, P. D., & Moore, J. (2010). When a fear appeal isn't just a fear appeal: The effects of graphic anti-smoking tobacco messages. *Journal of Broadcasting and Electronic Media, 54*, 485–507.

Leslie, M. (2000). The vexing legacy of Lewis Terman. *Stanford Magazine,* July/August 2000, 1–21.

Leube, D. (2009). S25-04 The neural basis of disorganized symptoms in schizophrenia. *European Psychiatry, 24*(1), S141.

Leucht, S., Corves, C., Arbter, D., Engel, R. R., Li, C., & Davis, J. M. (2009). Second-generation versus first-generation antipsychotic drugs for schizophrenia: a meta-analysis. *The Lancet, 373*(9657), 31–41.

Leuner, B., Glasper, E. R., & Gould, E. (2010). Parenting and plasticity. *Trends in Neurosciences, 33*(10), 465–473.

Leuner, B., Gould, E., & Shors, T. J. (2006) Is there a link between adult neurogenesis and learning? *Hippocampus, 16*(3), 216–224.

Levant, R. F. (2011). Research in the psychology of men and masculinity using the gender role strain paradigm as a framework. *American Psychologist, 66*(8), 765.

LeVay, S. (1991). A difference in hypothalamic structure between heterosexual and homosexual men. *Science, 253*, 1034–1037.

Leventhal, E. A., Leventhal, H., Shacham, S., & Easterling, D. V. (1989). Active coping reduces reports of pain from childbirth. *Journal of Consulting and Clinical Psychology, 57*, 365–371.

Levin, B., Hennessy, K. D., & Petrila, J. (2010.) *Mental health services: a public health perspective, 3rd Ed*. New York, NY: Oxford University Press.

Levin, B. E., Routh, V. H., Kang, L., Sanders, N. M., & Dunn-Meynell, A. (2004). Neuronal glucosensing: What do we know after 50 years? *Diabetes, 53*(10), 2521–2528.

Levin, H., & Smith, D. (2013). Traumatic brain injury: Networks and neuropathology. *The Lancet Neurology, 12*(1), 15–16.

Levin, J. (2000). A prolegomenon to an epidemiology of love: Theory, measurement, and health outcomes. *Journal of Social & Clinical Psychology, 19*(1), 117–136.

Levinson, D. J. (1986). Conception of adult development. *American Psychologist, 41*(1), 3–13.

Levinson, D. J. (1984). The career is in the life structure, the life structure is in the career: An adult development perspective. In M. B. Arthur, L. Bailyn, D. J. Levinson, & H. Shepard (Eds.), *Working with careers*. New York, NY: Columbia University School of Business.

Levinson, D. J. (1977). Toward a conception of adult life course. In N. Smelser & E. H. Erikson (Eds.), *Themes of love and work in adulthood*. Cambridge, MA: Harvard University Press.

Levinson, D. J., & Levinson, J. D. (1996). *Seasons of a woman's life.* New York, NY: Alfred A. Knopf.

Lewak, R. W., Wakefield, J. A., Jr., & Briggs, P. F. (1985). Intelligence and personality in mate choice and marital satisfaction. *Personality and Individual Differences, 4,* 471–477.

Lewin, K. (1935). *A dynamic theory of personality.* New York, NY: McGraw-Hill.

Lewis, J. A., & Cuppari, M. (2009). The polygraph: The truth lies within. *Journal of Psychiatry & Law, 37*(1), 85–92.

Lewis, M. (2010). The emergence of consciousness and its role in human development. In W. F. Overton & R. M. Lerner (Eds.), *The handbook of life-span development, vol 1: Cognition, biology, and methods* (pp. 628–670). Hoboken, NJ: John Wiley & Sons Inc.

Lewis, M., & Brooks-Gunn, J. (1979). *Social cognition and the acquisition of self.* New York, NY: Plenum.

Lewis, M., Haviland-Jones, J. M., & Barrett, L. F. (Eds.). (2010). *Handbook of emotions* (3rd ed.). New York, NY: Guilford Press.

Lewis, R. L., & Gutmann, L. (2004). Snake venoms and the neuromuscular junction. *Seminars in Neurology, 24*(2), 175–179.

Lewis, T. L., & Maurer, D. (2005). Multiple sensitive periods in human visual development: evidence from visually deprived children. *Developmental Psychobiology, 46,* 163–183.

Lewis-Harter, S. (2000). Psychosocial adjustment of adult children of alcoholics. A review of the recent empirical literature. *Clinical Psychology Review, 20*(3), 311–337.

Lewontin, R. (1982). *Human diversity.* New York: Scientific American Library.

Lewontin, R. C. (2001). Gene, organism and environment. *Cycles of contingency: Developmental systems and evolution* (pp. 59-66). Cambridge, MA: The MIT Press.

Lewontin, R. C. (1976). Science and politics: An explosive mix. *PsycCRITIQUES, 21*(2), 97–98.

Li, N., Barrick, M. R., Zimmerman, R. D., & Chiaburu, D. S. (2014). Retaining the productive employee: The role of personality. *The Academy of Management Annuals, 8*(1), 347–394.

Li, Q. (2005). *Cyberbullying in schools: Nature and extent of Canadian adolescents experience.* Paper presented at the conference of the American Educational Research Association, Montreal.

Li, S. (2010). Neuromodulation of fluctuations of information processing: Computational, neural, and genetic perspectives. In P. C. M. Molenaar, & K. M. Newell (Eds.), *Individual pathways of change: Statistical models for analyzing learning and development* (pp. 23–35). Washington, DC: American Psychological Association.

Li, W., Howard, J. D., Parrish, T. B., & Gottfried, J. A. (2008). Aversive learning enhances perceptual and cortical discrimination of indiscriminable odor cues. *Science, 319,* 1842–1845.

Lian, J., Goldstein, A., Donchin, E., & He, B. (2002). Cortical potential imaging of episodic memory encoding. *Brain Topography, 15*(1), 29–36.

Liang, C. T. H., Alvarez, A. N., Juang, L. P., & Liang, M. X. (2009). The role of coping in the relationship between perceived racism and racism-related stress for Asian Americans: Gender differences. *Asian American Journal of Psychology, S*(1), 56–69.

Lichtman, J. W., Livet, J., & Sanes, J. R. (2008). A technicolour approach to the connectome. *Nature Reviews Neuroscience, 9*(6), 417–422.

Liddell, H. S. (1950). Animal origins of anxiety. *Feelings and emotions: The Mooseheart Symposium* (pp. 181–188). New York, NY: McGraw-Hill.

Liden, R. C., Wayne, S. J., Jaworski, R. A., & Bennett, N. (2004). Social loafing: A field investigation. *Journal of Management, 30*(2), 285–304.

Lieberman, A. M., Hatrak, M., & Mayberry, R. I. (2014). Learning to look for language: Development of joint attention in young deaf children. *10*(1), 19–35.

Lieberman, J. A., Stroup, T. S., McEvoy, J. P., Swartz, M. S., Rosenheck, R. A., Perkins, D. O., . . . & Hsiao, J. K. (2005). Effectiveness of antipsychotic drugs in patients with chronic schizophrenia. *New England Journal of Medicine, 353*(12), 1209–1223.

Lieberman, M. D., Jarcho, J. M., & Obayashi, J. (2005). Attributional inference across cultures: Similar automatic attributions and different controlled corrections. *Personality and Social Psychology Bulletin, 31*(7), 889–901.

Lieberson, A. D. (2004). How long can a person survive without food? *Scientific American.* Retrieved from http://www.scientificamerican.com/article.cfm?id=how-long-can-a-person-sur.

Liem, D. G., & Mennella, J. A. (2003). Heightened sour preferences during childhood. *Chemical Senses, 28,* 173–180.

Lilienfeld, S. O., & Lynn, S. J. (2003). Dissociative identity disorder: Multiple personalities, multiple controversies. In S. O. Lilienfeld, S. J. Lynn, & J. M. Lohr (Eds.), *Science and pseudoscience in clinical psychology* (pp. 109–142). New York, NY: Guilford Press.

Lilienfeld, S. O., Lynn, S., Namy, L., & Wolf, N. (2008), *Psychology: From Inquiry to Understanding.* Boston, MA: Pearson, Allyn & Bacon.

Lilienfeld, S. O., Lynn, S. J., Ruscio, J., & Beyerstein, B. L. (2010). *50 Great Myths of Popular Psychology: Shattering Widespread Misconceptions About Human Behavior.* Chichester, UK: Wiley-Blackwell.

Lilienfeld, S. O., Wood, J. M., & Garb, H. N. (2000). The scientific status of projective techniques. *Psychological Science in the Public Interest, 1,* 27–66.

Lind, S. E., & Bowler, D. M. (2009). Language and theory of mind in Autism spectrum disorder: The relationship between complement syntax and false belief task performance. *Journal of Autism and Development Disorders, 39,* 927–937.

Lindau, S. T., & Gavrilova, N. (2010). Sex, health, and years of sexually active life gained due to good health: evidence from two US population based cross sectional surveys of ageing. *The British Medical Journal,* Online First, 1–11.

Lindsay, D. S., Hagen, L., Read, J. D., Wade, K. A., & Garry, M. (2004). True photographs and false memories. *Psychological Science, 15*(3), 149–154.

Lindsey, L. L., & Christy, S. (2011). *Gender roles: A Sociological Perspective.* Pearson Prentice Hall.

Linehan, M. M., & Dexter-Mazza, E. (2008). Dialectical behavior therapy for borderline personality disorder. In D. H. Barlow (Ed.), *Clinical handbook of psychological disorders: A step-by-step treatment manual (4th Ed.)* (pp. 365–420). New York, NY: The Guilford Press.

Ling, K., Beenen, G., Ludford, P., Wang, X., Chang, K., Li, Z., Cosley D., Frankowski, D., Terveen, L., Rashid, A. M., Resnick, P., & Kraut, R. (2005). Using social psychology to motivate contributions to online communities. *Journal of Computer-mediated Communication, 10,* article 10.

Linville, P. W., Fischer, G. W., & Fischhoff, B. (1993). AIDS risk perceptions and decision biases. In J. B. Pryor & G. D. Reeder (Eds.), *The Social psychology of HIV infection.* Hillsdale, NJ: Lawrence Erlbaum Associates.

Lipton, A. A., & Simon, F. S. (1985). Psychiatric diagnosis in a state hospital: Manhattan State revisited. *Hospital and Community Psychiatry, 36*(4), 368–373.

Litschge, C. M., Vaughn, M. G., & McCrea, C. (2010). The empirical status of treatments for children and youth with conduct problems: An overview of meta-analytic studies. *Research on Social Work Practice, 20*(1), 21–35.

Little, D. M., Kraus, M. F., Joseph, B. S., Geary, E. K., Susmaras, T., Zhou, X. J., Pliskin, N., & Gorelick, P. B. (2010). Thalamic integrity underlies executive dysfunction in traumatic brain injury. *Neurology, 74*(7), 558–564.

Littmen-Ovadia, H., & Nir, D. (2014). Looking forward to tomorrow: The buffering effect of a daily optimism intervention. *The Journal of Positive Psychology, 9*(2), 122–136.

Liu, C., & Bates, T. C. (2014). The structure of attributional style: Cognitive styles and optimism-pessimism bias in the Attributional Style Questionnaire. *Personality and Individual Differences, 66,* 79–85.

Liu, H., Xu, Y., & Larson, C. R. (2009). Attenuation of vocal responses to pitch perturbations during Mandarin speech. *Journal of the Acoustical Society of America, 125*(4), 2299–2306.

Liu, Y., Grumbles, R. M., & Thomas, C. K. (2013). Electrical stimulation of embryonic neurons for 1 hour improves axon regeneration and the number of reinnervated muscles that function. *Journal of Neuropathology and Experimental Neurology, 72,* 697–707.

Livesley, W., Jang, K., & Vernon, P. (2003). Genetic Basis of Personality Structure. In I. B. Weiner (Series Ed.), T. Millon, & M. J. Lerner (Vol. Eds.), *Handbook of Psychology: Vol. 5. Personality and Social Psychology* (pp. 59–84).

Llinás, R. R., & Ribary, U. (2001). Consciousness and the brain: The thalamo-cortical dialogue in health and disease. *Annals of the New York Academy of Sciences, 929,* 166–175.

Lloyd, M., Burghardt, A., Ulrich, D. A., & Angulo-Barroso, R. (2010). Physical activity and walking onset in infants with Down syndrome. *Adapted Physical Activity Quarterly, 27*(1), 1–16.

Lochman, J. E., Barry, T., Powell, N., & Young, L. (2010). Anger and aggression. In D. W. Nangle, D. J. Hansen, C. A. Erdley, & P. J. Norton (Eds.), *Practitioner's guide to empirically based measures of social skills* (pp. 155–166). New York, NY: Springer Publishing Co.

Locke, E. A. (2007). The case for inductive theory building. *Journal of Management, 33*(6), 867–890.

Locke, J. (1689). *An essay concerning human understanding.* 38th Edition. London, England: William Tegg.

Loeffler, S. N., Myrtek, M., & Pepel, M. (2013). Mood congruent memory in daily life: Evidence from interactive ambulatory monitoring. *Biological Psychology, 93*(2), 308–315.

Loehlin, J. C. (1992). *Genes and environment in personality development.* Newbury Park, CA: Sage.

Loessl, B., Valerius, G., Kopasz, M., Hornyak, M., Riemann, D., & Voderholzer, U. (2008). Are adolescents chronically sleep-deprived? An investigation of sleep habits of adolescents in the southwest of Germany. *Child: Care, Health and Development, 34,* 549–556.

Loewi, O. (1957). On the background of the discovery of neurochemical transmission. *Journal of Mount Sinai Hospital, 24,* 1014–1016.

Loftus, E. F. (2005). Planting misinformation in the human mind: A 30-year investigation of the malleability of memory. *Learning & Memory, 12*(4), 361–366.

Loftus, E. F., & Loftus, G. R. (1980). On the permanence of stored information in the human brain. *American Psychologist, 35*(5), 409–420.

Loftus, E. F., Miller, D. G., & Burns, H. J. (1978). Semantic integration of verbal information into a visual memory. *Journal of Experimental Psychology: Human Learning and Memory, 4*(1), 19–31.

Logsdon, A. (2011). Early child development (Your baby's first six month early child development). *About.com Guide: Learning disabilities*. Retrieved from http://learningdisabilities/.about.com/od/infancyandearlychildhood.

Logue, D. M., Abiola, I. O., Rains, D., Bailey, N. W., Zuk, M., & Cade, W. H. (2010). Does signalling mitigate the cost of agonistic interactions? A test in a cricket that has lost its song. *Proceedings in Biological Science, 227*, 2571–2575.

Lomas, T., Edginton, T., Cartwright, T., & Ridge, D. (2014). Men developing emotional intelligence through meditation? Integrating narrative, cognitive and electroencephalography (EEG) evidence. *Psychology of Men & Masculinity, 15*, 213–224.

Lonnee-Hoffmann, R. A. M., Dennerstein, L., Lehert, P., & Szoeke, C. (2014). Sexual function in the late postmenopause: a decade of follow-up in a population-based cohort of Australian women. *The Journal of Sexual Medicine, 11*(8), 2029–2038.

López-Muñoz, F., Boya, J., Alamo, C. (2006). Neuron theory, the cornerstone of neuroscience, on the centenary of the Nobel Prize award to Santiago Ramón y Cajal. *Brain Research Bulletin, 70*(4–6), 391–405.

Lorenz, K. (2002). Critique of the modern ethologists' attitude. In M. H. Johnson, Y. Munakata, & R. O. Gilmore (Eds.), *Brain development and cognition: A reader* (2nd Ed.). Malden, MA: Blackwell Publishing.

Lorenz, K. (1971). *Studies in animal and human behaviour: II. trans. R. Martin* Oxford, UK: Harvard University Press.

Lorenz, K. (1970). *Studies in animal and human behaviour: I. trans. R. Martin* Oxford, UK: Harvard University Press.

Lorusso, L. (2010). Review of Aristotele e il cervello: Le teorie del piugrande biologo dell'antichita nella storia del pensiero scientifico. *Journal of the History of the Neurosciences, 19*(2), 203–206.

Lott, A. J., & Lott, B. E. (1974). The role of reward in the formation of positive interpersonal attitudes. In T. L. Huston (Ed.), *Foundation of Interpersonal attraction* (pp. 171–189). New York, NY: Academic Press.

Lounsbury, J. W., Fisher, L. A., Levy, J. J., & Welsh, D. P. (2009). An investigation of character strengths in relation to the academic success of college students. *Individual Differences Research, 7*(1), 52–69.

Lounsbury, J. W., Sundstrom, E., Loveland, J. M., & Gibson, L. W. (2003). Intelligence, "big five" personality traits, and work drive as predictors of course grade. *Personality and Individual Differences, 35*(6), 1231–1239.

Lourenç, O., & Machado, A. (1996). In defense of Piaget's theory: A reply to 10 common criticisms. *Psychological Review, 103*, 143–164.

Love, S. (2004). Post mortem sampling of the brain and other tissues in neuro-degenerative disease. *Histopathology, 44*, 309–317.

Lovell, B., Moss, M., & Wetherell, M. A. (2011). Perceived stress, common health complaints and diurnal patterns of cortisol secretion in young, otherwise healthy individuals. *Hormones and Behavior, 60*(3), 301–305.

Lövheim, H., Sandman, P., Karlsson, S., & Gustafson, Y. (2009). Sex differences in the prevalence of behavioral and psychological symptoms of dementia. *International Psychogeriatrics, 21*(3), 469–475.

Löw, A., Lang, P. J., Smith, J. C., & Bradley, M. M. (2008). Both predator and prey: Emotional arousal in threat and reward. *Psychological Science, 19*(9), 865–873.

Lowe, M. R. (1993). The effects of eating on dieting behavior: A three factor model. *Psychologial Bulletin, 114*, 100–121.

Lowrance, J. M. (2014). *The Societal Evolution of Male Stereotypes: Gender Bashing of Men in America.*

Lowry, C. A., Hale, M. W., Evans, A. K., Heerkens, J., Staub, D. R., Gasser, P. J., & Shekhar, A. (2008). Serotonergic systems, anxiety, and affective disorder: focus on the dorsomedial part of the dorsal raphe nucleus. *Annals of the New York Academy of Sciences, 1148*, 86–94.

Lu, L., & Shih, J. (1997). Personality and happiness: Is mental health a mediator? *Personality and Individual Differences, 22*, 249–256.

Lubart, T. (2010). Cross-cultural perspectives on creativity. In J. C. Kaufman & R. J. Sternberg (Eds.), *The Cambridge handbook of creativity* (pp. 265–278). New York, NY: Cambridge University Press.

Lubinski, D. (2004). Introduction to the special section on cognitive abilities: 100 years after Spearman's (1904) *General intelligence, objectively determined and measured. Journal of Personality and Social Psychology, 86*(1), 96–111.

Luborsky, E. B., O'Reilly-Landry, M., & Arlow, J. A. (2011). Psychoanalysis. In R. J. Corsini & D. Wedding (Eds.), *Current psychotherapies* (9th Ed.). Florence, KY: CENGAGE Learning.

Luborsky, L. B., Barrett, M. S., Antonuccio, D. O., Shoenberger, D., & Stricker, G. (2006). What else materially influences what is represented and published as evidence? In J. C. Norcross, L. E. Beutler, & R. F. Levant (Eds.), *Evidence-based practices in mental health: Debate and dialogue on the fundamental questions* (pp. 257–298). Washington, DC: American Psychological Association.

Luborsky, L., Rosenthal, R., Diguer, L., Andrusyna. T. P., Levitt, J. T., Seligman, D. A., . . . & Krause, E. D. (2003). Are some psychotherapies much more effective than others? *Journal of Applied and Psychoanalytic Studies, 5*(4), 455–460.

Luborsky, L., Singer, B., & Luborsky, L. (1975). Comparative studies of psychotherapies. *Archives of General Psychiatry, 32*, 995–1008.

Luchins, A. S. (1942). Mechanization in problem solving. *Psychological Monographs, 54*(248).

Luders, E., Toga, A. W., & Thompson, P. M. (2014). Why size matters: Differences in brain volume account for apparent sex differences in callosal anatomy: The sexual dimorphism of the corpus callosum. *NeuroImage, 84*, 820–824.

Luh, C. W. (1922). The conditions of retention. *Psychological Monographs, 31*.

Lumeng, J. C., & Hillman, K. H. (2007). Eating in larger groups increases food consumption. *Archives of Disease in Childhood, 92*(5), 384–387.

Luminet, O., Bouts, P., Delie, F., Manstead, A. S. R., & Rimé, B. (2000). Social sharing of emotion following exposure to a negatively valenced situation. *Cognition and Emotion 14*(5), 661–688.

Luminet, O., Vermeulen, N., Demart, C., Taylor, G. J., & Bagby, R. M. (2006). Alexithymia and levels of processing: Evidence for an overall deficit in remembering emotion words. *Journal of Research in Personality, 40*(5), 713–733.

Lundberg, U. (2000). Workplace stress. In G. Fink (Ed.), *Encyclopedia of Stress, Vol. 3* (pp. 684–692). New York, NY: Academic Press.

Lundqvist, T. (2005). Cognitive consequences of cannabis use: Comparison with abuse of stimulants and heroin with regard to attention, memory and executive functions. *Pharmacology, Biochemistry and Behavior, 81*, 330–391.

Luo, L., & Craik, F.I.M. (2008). Aging and memory: A cognitive approach. *Canadian Journal of Psychiatry, 53*(6), 346–353.

Lupien, S. J., Maheu, F., Tu, M., Fiocco, A., & Schramek, T. E. (2007). The effects of stress and stress hormones on human cognition: Implications for the field of brain and cognition. *Brain and Cognition, 65*(3), 209–237.

Lupien, S. J., Ouelle-Morin, I., Hupback, A., Walker, D., Tu, M. T., & Buss, C. (2006). Beyond the stress concept: Allostatic load—a developmental biological and cognitive perspective. In D. Cicchetti (Ed.), *Handbook Series on Developmental Psychopathology* (pp. 784–809). New York, NY: John Wiley & Sons.

Luthar, S. S., Lyman, E. L., & Crossman, E. J. (2014). Resilience and positive psychology. In *Handbook of Developmental Psychopathology* (pp. 125–140). US: Springer.

Lüttke, H. B. (2004). Experimente unter dem Milgram-paradigma. [experiments within the Milgram paradigm.]. *Gruppendynamik Und Organisationsberatung, 35*(4), 431–464.

Luyckx, K., Tildesley, E. A., Soenens, B., Andrews, J. A., Hampson, S. E., Peterson, M., & Duriez, B. (2011). Parenting and trajectories of children's maladaptive behaviors: a 12-year prospective community study. *Journal of Clininical Childhood and Adolescent Psychology, 40*(3), 468–478.

Lydiard, R. B. (2003). The role of GABA in anxiety disorders. *The Journal of Clinical Psychiatry (Supplement), 64*(3), 21–27.

Lykken, D., & Tellegen, A. (1996). Happiness is a stochastic phenomenon. *Psychological Science, 7*(3), 186–189.

Lynam, D., Caspi, A., Moffitt, T., Wikstrom, P., Loeber, R., & Novak, S. (2000). The interaction between impulsivity and neighborhood context on offending: The effects of impulsivity are stronger in poorer neighborhoods. *Journal of Abnormal Psychology, 109*, 563–574.

Lynch, G., Larson, J., Staubli, U., Ambros-Ingerson, J., & Granger, R. (1991). Long-term potentiation and memory operations in cortical networks. In R. G. Lister & H. J. Weingartner (Eds.), *Perspectives on cognitive neuroscience* (pp. 110–131). New York, NY: Oxford University Press.

Lynch, S. K., Turkheimer, E., D'Onofrio, B. M., Mendle, J., Emery, R. E., Slutske, W. S., & Martin, N. G. (2006). A genetically informed study of the association between harsh punishment and offspring behavioral problems. *Journal of Family Psychology, 20*, 190–198.

Lynn, A. B. (2008). *The EQ interview: Finding employees with high emotional intelligence*. New York, NY: AMACOM.

Lynn, R., & Meisenberg, G. (2010). National IQs calculated and validated for 108 nations. *Intelligence, 38*(4), 353–360.

Lynn, S. J., & Kirsch, I. (2006). Smoking cessation. In S. J. Lynn & I. Kirsch, *Essentials of clinical hypnosis: An evidence-based approach. Dissociation, trauma, memory, and hypnosis book series*. Washington, DC: American Psychological Association.

Lynn, S. J., Neuschatz, J., Fite, R., & Rhue, J. R. (2001). Hypnosis and memory: Implications for the courtroom and psychotherapy. In M. Eisen & G. Goodman (Eds.), *Memory, suggestion, and the forensic interview*. New York, NY: Guilford Press.

Lynn, S. J., Rhue, J. W., & Kirsch, I. (Eds.). (2010). *Handbook of clinical hypnosis (2nd Ed.)*. Washington, DC: American Psychological Association.

Lyttle, J. (2001). The effectiveness of humor in persuasion: The case of business ethics training. *Journal of General Psychology, 128*(2), 206–216.

Macan, T., & Merritt, S. (2011). Actions speak too: Uncovering possible implicit and explicit discrimination in the employment interview process. *International Review of Industrial and Organizational Psychology*, *26*, 293–337.

Mack, A., & Rock, I. (1998). *Inattentional blindness*. MIT Press/Bradford Books series in cognitive psychology. Cambridge, MA: The MIT Press.

MacLean, P. D. (1954). The limbic system and its hippocampal formation: Studies in animals and their possible application to man. *Journal of Neurosurgery, 11,* 29–44.

MacLeod, C. (2010). Hebb award winner 2010: When learning met memory. *Canadian Journal of Experimental Psychology*, *64*(4) 227–240.

Macleod, M. D., Saunders, J., & Chalmers, L. (2010). Retrieval-induced forgetting: The unintended consequences of unintended forgetting. In G. M. Davies & D. B. Wright (Eds.), *Current issues in applied memory research* (pp. 50–71). New York, NY: Psychology Press.

MacMillan, H. L., Jamieson, E., Walsh, C. A., Wong, M. Y.-Y., Faries, E. J., McCue, H.,. . . & Offord, D. R. (2008). First Nations women's mental health: Results from an Ontario survey. *Archives of Women's Mental Health, 11*(2), 109–115.

Macmillan, M. (2008). Phineas Gage—Unravelling the myth. *The Psychologist* (British Psychological Society), *21*(9), 828–831.

Macpherson, F. (2010). Impossible figures. In E.B. Goldstein (Ed.), *Encyclopedia of Perception*. Thousand Oaks, CA: Sage.

Maddi, S. R. (2014). Hardiness leads to meaningful growth through what is learned when resolving stressful circumstances. In A. Batthyany & P. Russo-Netzer (Eds.), *Meaning in Positive and Existential Psychology*. New York, NY: Springer.

Maddi, S. R. (2007). The story of hardiness: Twenty years of theorizing, research, and practice. *The Praeger handbook on stress and coping (vol. 2)* (pp. 327–340). Westport, CT: Praeger Publishers/Greenwood Publishing Group.

Maddux, J. E., & Volkmann, J. (2010). Self-efficacy. In R. H. Hoyle (Ed.), *Handbook of personality and self-regulation* (pp. 315–331). Hoboken, NJ: Wiley-Blackwell.

Maestripieri, D., Higley, J., Lindell, S., Newman, T., McCormack, K., & Sanchez, M. (2006). Early maternal rejection affects the development of monoaminergic systems and adult abusive parenting in rhesus macaques (Macaca mulatta). *Behavioral Neuroscience, 120,* 1017–1024.

Magalhaes, P. V., Kapczinski, F., Nierenberg, A. A., Deckersbach, T., Weisinger, D., Dodd, S., & Berk, M. (2012). Illness burden and medical comorbidity in the Systematic Treatment Enhancement Program for Bipolar Disorder. *Acta Psychiatrica Scandinavica, 125*(4), 303–308.

Magee, J. C., & Teachman, B. A. (2007). Why did the white bear return? Obsessive-compulsive symptoms and attributions for unsuccessful thought suppression. *Behavior Research and Therapy, 45,* 2884–2898.

Maggini, C. (2000). Psychobiology of boredom. *CNS Spectrums, 5*(8), 24–27.

Maguire, E. A., Woollett, K., & Spiers, H. J. (2006). London taxi drivers and bus drivers: A structural and neuropsychological analysis. *Hippocampus, 16*(12), 1091–1101.

Mahli, P., Sidhu, M., & Bharti, B. (2014). Early stimulation and language development of economically disadvantaged children. *Indian Journal of Pediatrics, 81*(4), 333–338.

Main, M., Hesse, E., & Kaplan, N. (2005). Predictability of attachment behavior and representational processes at 1, 6, and 19 years of age: The Berkeley longitudinal study. In K. E. Grossmann, K. Grossmann, & E. Waters (Eds.), *Attachment from infancy to adulthood: The major longitudinal studies* (pp. 245–304). New York, NY: Guilford Press.

Main, M., & Solomon, J. (1990). Discovery of a new, insecure-disorganized/disoriented attachment pattern. In T. B. Brazelton & M. Yogman (Eds.), *Affective development in infancy* (pp. 121–160). Norwood, NJ: Ablex.

Majdandžić, M., & van den Boom, D. C. (2007). Multimethod longitudinal assessment of temperament in early childhood. *Journal of Personality, 75,* 12.

Makino, M., Tsuboi, K., & Dennerstein, L. (2004). Prevalence of eating disorders: A comparison of western and non-western countries. *Medscape General Medicine, 6*(3), 49.

Malkoff, S. B., Muldoon, M. F., Zeigler, Z. R., & Manuck, S. B. (1993). Blood platelet responsivity to acute mental stress. *Psychosomatic Medicine, 55*(6), 477–482.

Mallan, K. M., & Lipp, O. V. (2007). Does emotion modulate the blink reflex in human conditioning? Startle potentiation during pleasant and unpleasant cues in the picture-picture paradigm. *Psychophysiology, 44,* 737–748.

Malle, B. F. (2006). The actor-observer asymmetry in causal attribution: A (surprising) meta-analysis. *Psychological Bulletin, 132,* 895–919.

Mancini Billson, J. (2005). After the Montreal masscre: gender and the pervasiveness of violence. In J. Mancini Billson & C. Fluehr-Lobban (Eds.), *Female well-being: toward a global theory of social change*. New York, NY: St. Martin's Press.

Mandelman, S. D., Tan, M., Kornilov, S. A., Sternberg, R. J., & Grigorenko, E. L. (2010). The metacognitive component of academic self-concept: The development of a triarchic self-scale. *Journal of Cognitive Education and Psychology, 9*(1), 73–86.

Mandler, J. M. (2004). *Foundations of the mind*. New York, NY: Oxford.

Manelis, A., Hanson, C., & Hanson, S. J. (2011). Implicit memory for object locations depends on reactivation of encoding-related brain regions. *Human Brain Mapping, 32*(1), 32–50.

Maner, J. K., & Gailliot, M. T. (2007). Altruism and egoism: Prosocial motivations for helping depend on relationship context. *European Journal of Social Psychology, 37*(2), 347–358.

Mann, A. (2014, June 10). That computer actually got an F on the Turing Test. *Wired*. Retrieved from www.wired.com/2014/06/turing-test-not-so-fast.

Mann, S., et al. (2012). Windows to the soul? Deliberate eye contact as a cue to deceit. *Journal of Nonverbal Behavior, 36*(3) 205–215.

Manning, R., Levine, M., & Collins, A. (2007). The Kitty Genovese murder and the social psychology of helping: The parable of the 38 witnesses. *American Psychologist, 62*(6), 555.

Manuck, S. B., Cohen, S., Rabin, B. S., Muldoon, M. F., & Bachen, E. A. (1991). Individual differences in cellular immune responses to stress. *Psychological Science, 2,* 1–5.

Manusov, V., & Spitzberg, B. H. (2008). Attributes of attribution theory: Finding good cause in the search for theory. In D. O. Braithwaite & L. A. Baxter (Eds.), *Engaging theories in interpersonal communication* (pp. 37–49). Thousand Oaks, CA: Sage Publications.

Mar, R. A., Tackett, J. L., & Moore, C. (2010). Exposure to media and theory-of-mind development in preschoolers. *Cognitive Development, 25*(1), 69–78.

Marañon, G. (1924). Contribution à l'etude de l'action emotive de l'adrenaline. *Rev. Franc Endocrinol, 2,* 301–325.

Maratsos, M. (2000). More overregularizations after all: New data and discussion on Marcus, Pinker, Ullman, Hollander, Rosen & Xu. *Journal of Child Language, 27,* 183–212.

Marder, S. R. (2014). Long-Term Pharmacological Management of Schizophrenia. In *Schizophrenia* (pp. 265–274). New York, NY: Springer.

Marely, L. C., Skodol, A. E., & Oldham, J. M. (2014). Clinician judgments of clinical utility: A comparison of DSM-IV-TR personality disorders and the alternative model for DSM-5 personality disorders. *Journal of Abnormal Psychology, 123*(2), 398–405.

Maren, S., Phan, K. L., & Liberzon, I. (2013). The contextual brain: implications for fear conditioning, extinction and psychopathology. *Nature Reviews Neuroscience, 14*(6), 417–428. doi:10.1038/nrn3492

Marin, A. (2001). *Report to the Minster of National Defence: Special report on the systematic treatment of CF members with PTSD*. Retrieved from http://www.ombudsman.forces.gc.ca/rep-rap/sr-rs/pts-ssp/doc/pts-ssp-eng.pdf.

Markowitsch, H. J., Welzer, H., & Emmans, D. (2010). *The development of autobiographical memory*. New York, NY: Psychology Press.

Markus, H. R., & Kitayama, S. (1994). A collective fear of the collective: Implications for selves and theories of selves. *Personality and Social Psychology Bulletin, 20,* 568–579.

Markus, H. R., Plaut, V. C., & Lachman, M. E. (2004). Well-being in America: Core features and regional patterns. In O. G. Brim, C. D. Ryff, & R. C. Kessler (Eds.), *How healthy are we? A national study of well-being at midlife* (pp. 614–650). Chicago, IL: University of Chicago Press.

Marsh, E. J. (2007). Retelling is not the same as recalling: Implications for memory. *Current Directions in Psychological Science, 16,* 16–20.

Marsh, J. (2008). Playing doctor: An interview with Patch Adams. *Greater Good Magazine, 4*(4). Retrieved from http://greatergood.berkeley.edu/greatergood/2008spring/Q_A054.html.

Marshall, B. J. (1994). Heliobacter pylori. *American Journal of Gastroenterology, 71,* 269–279.

Marshall, M. J. (2002). *Why spanking doesn't work: Stopping this bad habit and getting the upper hand on effective discipline*. Bonneville Books.

Marshall, R. D., Bryant, R. A., Amsel, L., Suh, E. J., Cook, J. M., & Neria, Y. (2007). The psychology of ongoing threat: Relative risk appraisal, the September 11 attacks, and terrorism-related fears. *American Psychologist, 62*(4), 304–316.

Martin, C. M. (2008). A meta-analytic investigation of the relationship between emotional intelligence and leadership effectiveness. ProQuest Information & Learning: US. *Dissertation Abstracts International Section A: Humanities and Social Sciences, 69*(2), 530.

Martin, E. I., & Nemeroff, C. B. (2010). The biology of generalized anxiety disorder and major depressive disorder: Commonalities and distinguishing features. In D. Goldberg, K. S. Kendler, & P. J. Sirovatka (Eds.), *Diagnostic issues in depression and generalized anxiety disorder: Refining the research agenda for DSM-V* (pp. 45–70). Washington, DC: American Psychiatric Association.

Martin, J. A. (2010). Genetic causes of mental retardation. In R. C. Dryden-Edwards & L. Combrinck-Graham (Eds.), *Developmental disabilities from childhood to adulthood: What works for psychiatrists in community and institutional settings* (pp. 127–142). Baltimore, MD: Johns Hopkins University Press.

Martin, J. H. (2003). *Neuroanatomy: Text and atlas*. McGraw-Hill.

Martin, N. (2009). The roles of semantic and phonological processing in short-term memory and learning: Evidence from aphasia. In A. S. C. Thorn

& M. P. A. Page (Eds.), *Interactions between short-term and long-term memory in the verbal domain* (pp. 220–243). New York, NY: Psychology Press.

Martin, R., & Hewstone, M. (2001). Conformity and independence in groups: Majorities and minorities. In M. A. Hogg & R. S. Tindale (Eds.), *Blackwell Handbook of Social Psychology: Group Processes* (pp. 209–234). Malden, MA: Blackwell.

Martin, R. A. (2001). Humor, laughter, and physical health: Methodological issues and research findings. *Psychological Bulletin, 127*(4), 504–519.

Maru, E., & Ura, H. (2014). GABA (A) receptor trafficking and epilepsy. *Nihon Rinsho/Japanese Journal of Clinical Medicine, 72*(5), 790–795.

Maruszewski, T., Fajkowska, M., & Eysenck, M. W. (2010). Introduction: An integrative view of personality. In T. Maruszewski, M. Fajkowska, & M. Eysenck (Eds.), *Personality from biological, cognitive, and social perspective: Warsaw lectures in personality and social psychology.* Clifton Corners, NY: Eliot Werner Publications.

Marx, B. P., & Sloan, D. M. (2005). Peritraumatic dissociation and experimental avoidance as predictors of posttraumatic stress symptomatology. *Behavioral Research and Therapy, 43*(5), 569–583.

Marziali, E., McDonald, L., & Donahue, P. (2008). The role of coping humor in the physical and mental health of older adults. *Aging and Mental Health, 12*(6), 713–718.

Masataka, N. (1998). Motherese in Japanese sign language by 6-month-old hearing infants. *Developmental Psychology, 34*, 241–246.

Mashford-Pringle, A. (2012). Early learning for Aboriginal children: Past, present and future and an exploration of the Aboriginal Head Start Urban and Northern Communities Program in Ontario. *First Peoples Child & Family Review, 7*(1), 127–140.

Mashour, G. A., Walker, E. E., & Martuza, R. L. (2005). Psychosurgery: Past, present and future. *Brain Review, 48*(3), 409–418.

Masling, J. (2004). A storied test. *PsycCRITIQUES* [np].

Maslow, A. (1970). *Motivation and personality* (rev. Ed.). New York, NY: Harper & Row.

Masnick, M. (2014). No, a 'supercomputer' did NOT pass the Turing Test for the first time and everyone should know better. *Techdirt.* Retrieved from www.techdirt.com/articles/20140609/07284327524/no-supercomputer-did-not-pass-turing-test-first-time-everyone-should-know-better.shtml.

Mason, G. F., Krystal, J. H., & Sanacora. G. (2009). Nuclear magnetic resonance imaging and spectroscopy: Basic principles and recent findings in neuropsychiatric disorders. In B. J. Sadock, V. A. Sadock, & P. Ruiz (Eds.), *Kaplan & Sadock's comprehensive textbook of psychiatry* (9th ed., Vol. 1, pp. 248–272). Philadelphia, PA: Lippincott, Williams & Wilkins.

Mason, J. M., Kerr, B. M., Sinha, S., & McCormick, C. (1990). Shared book reading in an early start program for at-risk children. *National Reading Conference Yearbook, 39*, 189–198.

Mason, P. T., & Kreger, R. (2010). *Stop walking on eggshells: Taking your life back when someone you care about has borderline personality disorder* (2nd Ed.). Oakland, CA: New Harbinger Publications.

Massey, B. W., Li, J., & Meltzer, H. Y. (2014). Pharmacogenetics in the Treatment of Schizophrenia. In *Schizophrenia* (pp. 161–173). New York, NY: Springer.

Massey, D. S., & Owens, J. (2014). Mediators of stereotype threat among black college students. *Ethnic and Racial Studies, 37*(3), 557–575.

Masters, W. H., & Johnson, V. E. (1979). *Homosexuality in perspective.* Boston, MA: Little, Brown.

Masters, W. H., & Johnson, V. E. (1966). *Human sexual response.* Oxford, England: Little, Brown.

Masuda, T. (2010). Cultural effects on visual perception. In E. B. Goldstein (Ed.), *Encyclopedia of Perception.* Thousand Oaks, CA: Sage.

Mather, M. (2009). When emotion intensifies memory interference. In B. H. Ross (Ed.), *The psychology of learning and motivation (vol 51)* (pp. 101–120). San Diego, CA: Elsevier Academic Press. doi: 10.1016/S0079-7421(09)51003-1

Mathew, R. J., Wilson, W. H., Humphreys, D., Lowe, J. V., et al. (1993). Depersonalization after marijuana smoking. *Biological Psychiatry, 33*(6), 431–441. doi: 10.1016/0006-3223(93)90171-9

Mathews, D. C., Henter, I. D., & Zarate Jr, C. A. (2012). Targeting the glutamatergic system to treat major depressive disorder. *Drugs, 72*(10), 1313–1333.

Matsumoto, D. R. (2001). *Handbook of culture and psychology.* New York, NY: Oxford University Press.

Matsumoto, D., & Juang, L. (2008). *Culture and psychology* (4th Ed.). Australia: Thomson Wadsworth.

Matsumoto, D., & van de Vijver, F. J. R. (Eds.). (2011). *Cross-cultural research methods in psychology.* New York, NY: Cambridge University Press.

Matthews, P. M. (2011). The mnemonic brain: Neuroimaging, neuropharmacology, and disorders of memory. In S. Nalbantian, P. M. Matthews, & J. L. McClelland (Eds.), *The memory process: Neuroscientific and humanistic perspectives* (pp. 99–127). Cambridge, MA: MIT Press.

Maul, A. (2011). The factor structure and cross-test convergence of the Mayer–Salovey–Caruso model of emotional intelligence. *Personality and Individual Differences, 50*(4), 457–463.

Maurer, D., & Lewis, T. L. (2014). Sensitive Periods in Visual Development. In P. Zelazo (Ed.), *Oxford Handbook of Developmental Psychology, Vol. 1* (pp. 202–236). Oxford University Press.

Maurer, D., & Lewis, T. L. (2001). Visual acuity: The role of visual input in inducing postnatal change. *Clinical Neuroscience Research, 1*, 239–247.

Mayberg, H. S., Lozano, A. M., Voon, V., McNeely, H. E., Seminowicz, D., Hamani, C., et al. (2005). Deep brain stimulation for treatment-resistant depression. *Neuron, 45*, 651–660.

Maybery, M. T., & Do, N. (2003). Relationships between facets of working memory and performance on a curriculum-based mathematics test in children. *Educational and Child Psychology, 20*(3), 77–92.

Mayberry, R. I. (2010). Early language acquisition and adult language ability: What sign language reveals about the critical period for language. In M. Marchark & P.E. Spencer (Eds.), *The Oxford Handbook of Deaf Studies, Language, and Education* (pp. 281–291). Oxford University Press.

Mayer, J. D. (2009). Personal intelligence expressed: A theoretical analysis. *Review of General Psychology, 13*(1), 46–58.

Mayer, J. D. (2008). Personal intelligence. *Imagination, Cognition and Personality, 27*(3), 209–232.

Mayer, J. D., Panter, A. T., & Caruso, D. (2012). Does personal intelligence exist? Evidence from a new ability-based measure. *Journal of Personality Assessment, 94*(2) 124–140.

Mayer, J. D., & Salovey, P. (2004). What is emotional intelligence? In P. Salovey, M. A. Brackett, & J. D. Mayer (Eds.), *Emotional intelligence: Key readings on the Mayer and Salovey model* (pp. 29–59). Port Chester, NY: Dude Publishing.

Mayer, J. D., & Salovey, P. (1997). What is emotional intelligence? In P. Salovey & D. Sluyter (Eds.), *Emotional development and emotional intelligence: Educational implications* (pp. 3–31). New York, NY: Basic Books.

Mayer, J. D., Salovey, P., Caruso, D. R., & Sitarenios, G. (2003). Measuring emotional intelligence with the MSCEIT V2.0. *Emotion, 3*(1), 97–105.

Mayer, S. J. (2005). The early evolution of Jean Piaget's clinical method. *History of Psychology, 8*, 262–382.

Mayhew, D. R., Brown, S. W., & Simpson, H. M. (2002). *The alcohol crash problem in Canada.* Traffic Injury Research Foundation of Canada for Transport Canada. Retrieved from http://www.tc.gc.ca/media/documents/roadsafety/tp11759e_2000.pdf.

Mayr, E. (2001). *What evolution is.* New York, NY: Basic Books.

Mazzoni, G., Heap, M., & Scoboria, A. (2010). Hypnosis and memory: Theory, laboratory research, and applications. In S. J. Lynn, J. W. Rhue, & I. Kirsch (Eds.), *Handbook of clinical hypnosis (2nd Ed.)* (pp. 709–741). Washington, DC: American Psychological Association.

McCabe, D. P., Roediger III, H. L., McDaniel, M. A., Balota, D. A., & Hambrick, D. Z. (2010). The relationship between working memory capacity and executive functioning: Evidence for a common executive attention construct. *Neuropsychology, 24*(2), 222–243.

McCain, M. N., & Mustard, J. F. (1999). *Reversing the real brain drain: Early Years Study.* Ontario Children's Secretariat, Toronto. Retrieved from http://www.founders.net/fn/bios.nsf/c85b89504068a23f8525673300768a53/46254872cb9d894c852568f00052b616!OpenDocument.

McCain, M. N., Mustard, J. F., & McCuaig, K. (2011). *Early Years Study 3: Making Decisions, Taking Action.* Toronto: Margaret & Wallace McCain Family Foundation.

McClelland, J. L. (2011). Memory as a constructive process: The parallel distributed processing approach. In S. Nalbantian, P. M. Matthews, & J. L. McClelland (Eds.), *The memory process: Neuroscientific and humanistic perspectives* (pp. 129–155). Cambridge, MA: MIT Press.

McClure, E. B. (2000). A meta-analytic review of sex differences in facial expression processing and their development in infants, children, and adolescents. *Psychological Bulletin, 126*, 424–453.

McClure, E. B., Monk, C. S., Nelson, E. E., Parrish, J. M., Adler, A., Blair, . . . & Pine, D. S. (2007). Abnormal attention modulation of fear circuit function in pediatric generalized anxiety disorder. *Archives of General Psychiatry, 64*(1), 97–106.

McCormick, C. E., & Mason, J. M., (1986). Intervention procedures for increasing preschool children's interest in and knowledge about reading. In W. H. Teale & E. Sulzby (Eds.), *Emergent literacy: Writing and reading* (pp. 90–115). Norwood, NJ: Ablex.

McCrae, R. R. (2002). The maturation of personality psychology: Adult personality development and psychological well-being. *Journal of Research in Personality, 36*(4), 307–317.

McCrae, R. R., & Costa, P. T. (2003). *Personality in adulthood: A five-factor theory perspective* (2nd Edition). New York, NY: Guilford.

McCrae, R. R., & Costa, P. T. (1989). Reinterpreting the Myers-Briggs Type Indicator from the perspective of the five-factor model of personality. *Journal of Personality, 57*(1), 17–40.

McCrae, R. R., Yik, M. S. M., Trapnell, P. D., Bond, M. H., & Paulhus, D. L. (1998). Interpreting personality profiles across cultures: Bilingual, acculturation and peer rating studies of Chinese undergraduates. *Journal of Personality and Social Psychology, 74*,1041–1055.

McCreaddie, M., & Wiggins, S. (2008). The purpose and function of humour in health, health care, and nursing: A narrative review. *Journal of Advanced Nursing, 61*(6), 584–595.

McCrink, K., & Wynn, K. (2004). Large-number addition and subtraction by 9-month-old infants. *Psychological Science, 15*(11), 776–781.

McDonald, R. V., & Siegel, S. (2004) The potential role of drug-onset cues in drug dependence and withdrawal. *Experimental and Clinical Psychopharmacology, 12*, 23–26.

McDonald, S. (2007). The social, emotional and cultural life of the orbitofrontal cortex. *Brain Impairment, 8*(1), 41–51.

McEvoy, P. M. (2007). Effectiveness of cognitive behavioural group therapy for social phobia in a community clinic: A benchmarking study. *Behavior Research Therapy, 45*(12), 3030–3040.

McEwen, B. S. (2002). Protective and damaging effects of stress mediators: The good and bad sides of the response to stress. *Metabolism, 51*(Suppl 1), 2–4.

McEwen, B. S., & Morrison, J. H. (2013). The brain on stress: Vulnerability and plasticity of the prefrontal cortex over the life course. *Neuron, 79*(1), 16–29.

McEwen, D. P., Jenkins, P. M., & Martens, J. R. (2008). Olfactory cilia: our direct neuronal connection to the external world. *Current Topics in Developmental Biology, 85*, 333–370.

McFadyen, M. (2008). *A long road to recovery battling operational stress injuries: Second review of the Department of National Defence and Canadian Forces action on operational stress injuries.* Retrieved from http://www.ombudsman.forces.gc.ca/rep-rap/sr-rs/osi-tso-3/doc/osi-tso-3-eng.pdf.

McGaugh, J. L. (2006). Make mild moments memorable: Add a little arousal. *Trends in Cognitive Sciences, 10*(8), 345–347. doi: 10.1016/j.tics.2006.06.001

McGaugh, J. L. (2003). *Memory and emotion: The making of lasting memories.* New York, NY: Columbia University Press.

McGaugh, J. L. (1999). The perseveration-consolidation hypothesis: Mueller and Pilzecker, 1900. *Brain Research Bulletin, 50*(5–6), 445–446.

McGowan, S., Lawrence, A. D., Sales, T., Quested, D., & Grasby P. (2004). Presynaptic dopaminergic dysfunction in schizophrenia: A positron emission tomography [18F] fluorodopa study. *Archives of General Psychiatry, 61*, 134–142.

McGrath, J., Saha, S., Chant, D., & Welham, J. (2008). Schizophrenia: a concise overview of incidence, prevalence, and mortality. *Epidemiologic Reviews, 30*(1), 67–76.

McGrath, R. E. (2011). *Quantitative models in psychology.* Washington, DC: American Psychological Association.

McGregor, R. M. (2013). Cognitive dissonance and political attitudes: The case of Canada. *The Social Science Journal, 50*(2), 168–176.

McGue, M., & Lykken, D. T. (1992). Genetic influence on risk of divorce. *Psychological Science, 3*(6), 368–373.

McGuffin, P., Katz, R., Watkins, S., & Rutherford, J. (1996). A hospital-based twin register of the heritability of DSM-IV unipolar depression. *Archives of General Psychiatry, 53*, 129–136.

McGuffin, P., Rijsdijk, F., Andrew, M., Sham, P., Katz, R., & Cardno, A. (2003). The heritability of bipolar affective disorder and the genetic relationship to unipolar depression. *Archives of General Psychiatry, 60*(5), 497–502.

McKee, A. C., Cantu, R. C., Nowinski, C. J., Hedley-Whyte, E. T., Gavett, B. E., Budson, A. E., Santini, V. E., Lee, H.-Y., Kubilus, C. A., & Stern, R. A. (2009). Chronic traumatic encephalopathy in athletes: progressive tauopathy following repetitive head injury. *Journal of Neuropathology & Experimental Neurology, 68*(7), 709–735.

McKee, A. C., Stein, T. D., Nowinski, C. J., Stern, R. A. Daneshvar, D. H., Alvarez, V. E., . . . Cantu, R. C. (2013). The spectrum of disease in chronic trauma encephalopathy. *Brain: A Journal of Neurology, 136*, 43–64.

McKelvie, S. J., & Drumheller, A. (2001). The availability heuristic with famous names: A replication. *Perceptual and Motor Skills, 92*, 507–516.

McKinley, S., Fien, M., Riegel, B., AbuRuz, M., Lennie, T. A., & Moser, D. K. (2012). Complications after acute coronary syndrome are reduced by perceived control of cardiac illness. *Journal of Advanced Nursing, 68*(10), 2320–2330.

McLaren, A. (1990) *Our Own Master Race: Eugenics in Canada, 1885–1945.* Toronto, ON: Oxford University Press.

McLaren, L. (2007). Socioeconomic status and obesity. *Epidemiologic Reviews, 29*, 29–48.

McLaughlin, C.V., & Williams, V. (2009). Normal sleep in children and adolescents. *Child and Adolescent Psychiatric Clinics of North America, 18*(4), 799–811.

McLean, D. E., & Link, B. G. (1994). Unraveling complexity: Strategies to refine concepts, measures, and research designs in the study of life events and mental health. *Stress and mental health: Contemporary issues and prospects for the future* (pp. 15–42). New York, NY: Plenum Press.

McLeod, S. A. (2009). *Jean Piaget.* Retrieved from http://www.simplypsychology.org/piaget.html.

McNally, R. J. (2001). Vulnerability to anxiety disorders in adulthood. In R. E. Ingram & J. M. Price (Eds.), *Vulnerability to psychopathology: Risk across the lifespan* (pp. 304–321). New York, NY: Guilford Press.

McNamee, J. E., & Offord, D. R. (2003). *Canadian Task Force on Preventive Health Care (2001).* Retrieved from http://www.canadiancrc.com/Canadian_Task_Force_Preventive_Health_Care_suicide.aspx.

McVicker Hunt, J. M. (1982). Toward equalizing the developmental opportunities of infants and preschool children. *Journal of Social Issues, 38*(4), 163–191.

Mech, L. D., & Boitani, L. (2003). *Wolves: behavior, ecology, and conservation.* Chicago, IL: University of Chicago Press.

Mecklinger, A., Brunnemann, N., & Kipp, K. (2011). Two processes for recognition memory in children of early school age: An event-related potential study. *Journal of Cognitive Neuroscience, 23*(2), 435–446. doi: 10.1162/jocn.2010.21455

Medda, P., Perugi, G., Zanello, S., Ciuffa, M., & Cassano, G. B. (2009). Response to ECT in bipolar I, bipolar II and unipolar depression. *Journal of Affective Disorders, 118*(1), 55–59.

Meister, B. (2000). Control of food intake via leptin receptors in the hypothalamus. *Vitamins and Hormones, 59*, 265–304.

Meldrum, B. S. (2000). Glutamate as a neurotransmitter in the brain: Review of physiology and pathology. *The Journal of Nutrition, 130*(4), 1007S–1015S.

Mellers, B. A., Schwartz, A., & Cooke, A. D. (1998). Judgment and decision making. *Annual Review of Psychology, 49*, 447–477.

Mellers, B. A., Schwartz, A., Ho, K., & Ritov, L. (1997). Decision affect theory: Emotional reactions to the outcomes of risky options. *Psychological Science, 8*, 423–429.

Mellinger, D. I. (2010). Hypnosis and the treatment of anxiety disorders. In S. J. Lynn, J. W. Rhue, & I. Kirsch (Eds.), *Handbook of clinical hypnosis (2nd Ed.)* (pp. 359–389). Washington, DC: American Psychological Association.

Meltzer, H. Y. (2013). Update on typical and atypical antipsychotic drugs. *Annual Review of Medicine, 64*, 393–406.

Meltzer, M. (2007). Leisure and innocence: The eternal appeal of the stoner movie. *Slate.*

Meltzoff, A. N., & Moore, M. K. (1977). Imitation of facial and manual gestures by human neonates, *Science, 198*, 75–78.

Melville, J. (1978). *Phobias and obsessions.* New York, NY: Penguin.

Melzack, R.(1999). From the gate to the neuromatrix. *The Journal of Pain, Suppl 6*, S121–126.

Melzack, R., & Katz, J. (2004). The gate control theory: reaching for the brain. In T. Hadjistavropoulos & K.D. Craig (Eds.), *Pain: Psychological perspectives.* Mahwah, NJ: Lawrence Erlbaum Associates, Publishers.

Melzack, R., & Wall, P.D. (1982). *The challenge of pain.* New York: NY: Basic Books.

Memmert, D. (2011). Creativity, expertise, and attention: Exploring their development and their relationships. *Journal of Sports Sciences, 29*(1), 93–102.

Menary, K., Collins, P. F., Porter, J. N., Muetzel, R., Olson, E. A., Kumer, V., Steinbach, M., Lim, K. O., & Luciana, M. (2013). Associations between cortical thickness and general intelligence in children, adolescents and young adults. *Intelligence, 41*(5), 597–606.

Mennella, J. A., Johnson, A., & Beauchamp, G. K. (1995). Garlic ingestion by pregnant women alters the odor of amniotic fluid. *Chemical Senses, 20*, 207–209.

Merenda, R. R. (2008). The posttraumatic and sociocognitive etiologies of dissociative identity disorder: A survey of clinical psychologists. *Dissertation Abstracts International: Section B: The Sciences and Engineering, 68*(8–B), 55–84.

Merikangas, K. R., Akiskal, H. S., Angst, J., Greenberg, P. E., Hirschfeld, R. M. A., Petukhova, M., et al. (2007). Lifetime and 12-month prevalence of bipolar spectrum disorder in the National Comorbidity Survey Replication. *Archives of General Psychiatry, 64*(5), 543–552.

Merkl, A., Schubert, F., Quante, A., Luborzewski, A., Brakemeier, E., Grimm, S., & Bajbouj, M. (2011). Abnormal cingulate and prefrontal cortical neurochemistry in major depression after electroconvulsive therapy. *Biological Psychiatry, 69*(8), 772–779.

Messinger, D., & Fogel, A. (2007). The interactive development of social smiling. *Advances in Child Development and Behavior, 35*, 327–366.

Mestre, M. V., Samper, P., Frías, M. D., & Tur, A. M. (2009). Are women more empathetic than men? A longitudinal study in adolescence. *The Spanish Journal of Psychology, 12*(1), 76–83.

Mesulam, M. M. (1981). A cortical network for directed attention and unilateral neglect. *Annals of Neurology, 10*, 309–325.

Meyer, A. K., Maisel, M., Hermann, A., Stirl, K., & Storch, A. (2010). Restorative approaches in Parkinson's disease: What cell type wins the race? *Journal of the Neurological Sciences, 289*, 93–103.

Meyer, B., Ajchenbrenner, M., & Bowles, D. P. (2005). Sensory sensitivity, attachment experiences, and rejection responses among adults with borderline and avoidant features. *Journal of Personality Disorders, 19*(6), 641–658.

Meyer-Luehmann, M., Spires-Jones, T., Prada, C., Garcia-Alloza, M., de Calignon, A., Rozkalne, A., Koenigsknecht-Talboo, J., Holtzman, D. M., Bacskai, B. J., & Hyman, B. T. (2008). Rapid appearance and local toxicity of amyloid-β plaques in a mouse model of Alzheimer's disease. *Nature, 451*(7179), 720–724.

Micheau, J., & Marighetto, A. (2011). Acetylcholine and memory: a long, complex and chaotic but still living relationship. *Behavioural Brain Research, 221*(2), 424–429.

Michel, G. F., & Tyler, A. N. (2005). Critical period: A history of the transition from questions of when, to what, to how. *Development and Psychobiology, 46*, 156–162.

Mikkelson, B., & Mikkelson, D. P. (2007, August 24). *Suspended animation.* Retrieved from www.snopes.com.

Mikulincer, M., & Shaver, P. R. (2005). Attachment security, compassion, and altruism. *Current Directions in Psychological Science, 14*(1), 34–38.

Mikulincer, M., Shaver, P. R., & Gillath, O. (2008). A behavioral systems perspective on compassionate love. *The science of compassionate love: Theory, research, and applications* (pp. 225–256). Wiley-Blackwell.

Mikulincer, M., Shaver, P. R., Gillath, O., & Nitzberg, R. A. (2005). Attachment, caregiving, and altruism: Boosting attachment security increases compassion and helping. *Journal of Personality and Social Psychology, 89*(5), 817–839.

Miles, D. R., & Carey, G. (1997). Genetic and environmental architecture on human aggression. *Journal of Personality and Social Psychology, 72*(1), 207–217.

Miles, S. J., & Minda, J. P. (2011). The effects of concurrent verbal and visual tasks on category learning. *Journal of Experimental Psychology: Learning, Memory, and Cognition, 37*(3), 588–607.

Milgram, S. (2004). *Obedience to authority.* New York, NY: Perennial Classics. [Original work published in 1974].

Milgram, S. (1974). *Obedience to Authority: An Experimental View.* New York, NY: Harper and Row.

Milgram, S. (1963). Behavioral study of obedience. *Journal of Abnormal and Social Psychology, 67*, 371–378.

Miller, A. G. (2004). What can the Milgram obedience experiments tell us about the holocaust? Generalizing from the social psychology laboratory. In A. G. Miller (Ed.), *The Social Psychology of Good and Evil* (pp. 193–239). New York, NY: Guilford Press.

Miller, D. B., & O'Callaghan, J. P. (2005). Aging, stress and the hippocampus. *Ageing Research Review, 4*, 123–140.

Miller, D. T., & Ross, M. (1975). Self-serving biases in the attribution of causality: Fact or fiction? *Psychological Bulletin, 82*, 213–225.

Miller, F. D., & Gauthier, A. S. (2007). Timing is everything: making neurons versus glia in the developing cortex. *Neuron, 54*, 357–369.

Miller, G., Tybur, J. M., & Jordan, B. D. (2007). Ovulatory cycle effects on tip earnings by lap dancers: Economic evidence for human estrus? *Evolution and Human Behavior, 28*, 375–381.

Miller, G. A. (1978). The acquisition of word meaning. *Child Development, 49*, 999–1004.

Miller, G. A. (1956). The magical number seven, plus or minus two: Some limits on our capacity for processing information. *Psychological Review, 63*(2), 81–97.

Miller, G. F. (2000). *The Mating Mind: How sexual choice shaped the evolution of human nature.* London, England: Heinemann.

Miller, L. C., Putcha, A., & Pederson, W. C. (2002). Men's and women's mating preferences: Distinct evolutionary mechanisms? *Current Directions in Psychological Science, 11*, 88–93.

Miller, M. A., & Rahe, R. H. (1997). Life changes scaling for the 1990s. *Journal of Psychosomatic Research, 43*(3), 279–292.

Miller, N. E. (1959). Liberalization of basic S-R concepts: Extensions to conflict behavior, motivation, and social learning. In S. Koch (Ed.), *Psychology: A study of a Science, Vol. 2.* New York, NY: McGraw-Hill.

Miller, R., & Mason, S. E. (2011). *Diagnosis: Schizophrenia—A comprehensive resource for consumers, families, and helping professionals* (2nd Ed.). New York, NY: Columbia University Press.

Miller, T. Q. (2000). Type A behavior. In G. Fink (Ed.), *Encyclopedia of Stress, Vol. 3* (pp. 623–624). New York, NY: Academic Press.

Miller, T. Q., Smith, T. W., Turner, C. W., Guijarro, M. L., & Hallet, A. J. (1996). A meta-analytic review of research on hostility and physical health. *Psychological Bulletin, 119*, 322–348.

Millington, B. (2012). Use it or lose it: Ageing and the politics of brain training. *Leisure Studies, 31*, 429–446.

Millon, T. (2011). *Disorders of personality: Introducing a DSM/ICD spectrum from normal to abnormal* (3rd Ed.). Hoboken, NJ: John Wiley & Sons.

Millon, T., & Grossman, S. (2007). *Moderating severe personality disorders: A personalized psychotherapy approach.* Hoboken, NJ: John Wiley & Sons Inc.

Milner, B., Corkin, S., & Teuber, H. L. (1968). Further analysis of the hippocampal amnesic syndrome: 14-year follow-up study of H.M. *Neuropsychologia, 6*, 215–234.

Milojedv, P., & Sibley, C. G. (2014). The stability of adult personality varies across age: Evidence from a two-year longitudinal sample of adult New Zealanders. *Journal of Research in Personality, 51*, 29–37.

Mindell, J. A., & Owens, J. A. (2003). *A clinical guide to pediatric sleep: diagnosis and management of sleep problems.* Lippincott Williams & Wilkins.

Minerd, J. (2005). Extra nerve fibers may heighten female pain perception. *Plastic and Reconstructive Surgery, 116*, 1407–1410.

Mingroni, M. A. (2007). Resolving the IQ paradox: Heterosis as a cause of the Flynn effect and other trends. *Psychological Review, 114*(3), 806–829.

Mingroni, M. A. (2004). The secular rise in IQ: Giving heterosis a closer look. *Intelligence, 32*(1), 65–83.

Minister of Justice. (2014). Marijuana for medical purposes regulations, Government of Canada, Ottawa, SOR/2013-119. Retrieved from www.laws-lois. justice.gc.ca/PDF/SOR-2013-119.pdf.

Mino, I., Profit, W. E., & Pierce, C. M., (2000). Minorities and stress. In G. Fink (Ed.), *Encyclopedia of stress, Vol. 3* (pp. 771–776). New York, NY: Academic Press.

Minzenberg, M. J., Yoon, J. H., & Carter, C. S. (2011). Schizophrenia. In R. E. Hales, S. C. Yudofsky, & G. O. Gabbard (Eds.), *Essentials of psychiatry* (3rd Ed., pp. 111–150). Arlington, VA: American Psychiatric Publishing.

Miret, M., Ayuso-Mateos, J. L., Sanchez-Moreno, J., & Vieta, E. (2013). Depressive disorders and suicide: epidemiology, risk factors, and burden. *Neuroscience & Biobehavioral Reviews, 37*(10), 2372–2374.

Mirzaei, S., Gelpi, E., Roddrigues, M., Knoll, P., & Gutierrez-Lobos, K. (2005). Progress in post-traumatic stress disorder research. In T. A. Corales (Ed.), *Focus on posttraumatic stress disorder research* (pp. 157–177). Hauppauge, NY: Nova Science Publishers.

Mischel, W. (2004). Toward an integrative science of the person. *Annual Review of Psychology, 55*, 1–22.

Mischel, W., Mendoza-Denton, R., & Shoda, Y. (2002). Situation-behavior profiles as a locus of consistency in personality. *Current Directions in Psychological Science, 11*(2) 50–54.

Mischel, W., & Peake, P. K. (1982). Beyond deja vu in the search for cross-situational consistency. *Psychological Review, 89*, 730–755.

Mischel, W., Shoda, Y., & Rodriguez, M. L. (1989). Delay of Gratification in Children. *Science, 244*(4907), 933–938.

Mitchell, A. J. (2010). Overview of depression scales and tools. In A. J. Mitchell & J. C. Coyne (Eds.), *Screening for depression in clinical practice: An evidence-based guide* (pp. 29–56). New York, NY: Oxford University Press.

Mitchell, C. M., Kaufman, C. E., Beals, J., et. al. (2004). Equifinality and multifinality as guides for prevention interventions: HIV risk/protection among American Indian young adults. *Journal of Primary Prevention, 25*(4), 491–510.

Miyake, N., Miyamoto, S., & Jarskog, L. F. (2012). New serotonin/dopamine antagonists for the treatment of schizophrenia. *Clinical Schizophrenia & Related Psychoses, 6*(3), 122–133.

Miyamoto, S., Merrill, D. B., Lieberman, J. A., Fleischhacker, W. W., & Marder, S. R. (2008). Antipsychotic drugs. *Psychiatry* (3rd. Ed., pp. 2161–2201). Hoboken, NJ: John Wiley & Sons, Inc.

Mogan, J. (1984). Obesity: prevention is the treatment. *Patient Education and Counseling, 6*(2), 73–76.

Mohr, J. P., Pessin, M. S., Finkelstein, S., Funkenstein, H. H., Duncan, G. W., & Davis, K. R. (1978). Broca aphasia: Pathologic and clinical. *Neurology, 28*(4), 311.

Mojet, J., Christ-Hazelhof, E., & Heidema, J. (2001). Taste perception with age: generic or specific losses in threshold sensitivity to the five basic tastes? *Chemical Senses, 26*(7), 845–860.

Mojtabai, R., & Olfson, M. (2010). National trends in psychotropic medication polypharmacy in office-based psychiatry. *Archives of General Psychiatry, 67*(1), 26–36.

Mojtabai, R., Olfson, M., Sampson, N. A., Jin, R., Druss, B., Wang, P. S., Wells, K. B., Pincus, H. A., & Kessler, R. C. (2011). Barriers to mental health treatment: results from the National Comorbidity Survey Replication. *Psychological Medicine, 41*(08), 1751–1761.

Moller, J., Bjorkenstam, E., Ljung, R., & Yngwe, M. A. (2011). Widowhood and the risk of psychiatric care, psychotropic medication and all-cause mortality: A cohort study of 658,022 elderly people in Sweden. *Aging & Mental Health, 15*(2), 259–266.

Monteiro, C. A., Moura, E. C., Conde, W. L., & Popkin, B. M. (2004). Public Health Reviews: Socioeconomic status and obesity in adult populations of developing countries: A review. *Bulletin of the World Health Organization, 84*(12), 940–946.

Montequin, V. R., Fernandez, J. M. M., Balsera, J. V., & Nieto, A. G. (2013). Using MBTI for the success assessment of engineering teams in project-based learning. *International Journal of Technology and Design Education, 23*(4), 1127–1146.

Moorcroft, W. H. (2003). *Understanding sleep and dreaming.* New York, NY: Springer.

Moore, B. C. J. (2010). Audition. In E.B. Goldstein (Ed.), *Encyclopedia of Perception.* Thousand Oaks, CA: Sage.

Moore, J. (2010). Philosophy of science, with special consideration given to behaviorism as the philosophy of the science of behavior. *The Psychological Record, 60*(1), 137–150.

Moore, K. L., & Persaud, T. V. N. (2008). *Before we are born* (7th ed.). Philadelphia, PA: Saunders.

Moore, N. B., Davidson, J. K., Sr., & Fisher, T. D. (Eds.). (2010). *Speaking of sexuality: Interdisciplinary readings.* New York, NY: Oxford University Press.

Moran, S., Kornhaber, M., & Gardner, H. (2009). Orchestrating multiple intelligences. *Educational Leadership, 64*(1), 22–27.

Morey, C. C., Guérard, K., & Tremblay, S. (2013). Neither separate nor equivalent: Relationships between feature representations within bound objects. *Acta Psychologica, 144*(2), 279–290.

Morfei, M. Z., Hooker, K., Carpenter, J., Mix, C., & Blakeley, E. (2004). Agentic and communal generative behavior in four areas of adult life: Implications for psychological well-being. *Journal of Adult Development, 11*(1), 55–58.

Morgan, A. B., & Lilienfeld, S. O. (2000). A meta-analytic review of the relation between antisocial behavior and neuropsychological measures of executive function. *Clinical Psychology Review, 20,* 113–136.

Morgan III, C. A., Southwick, S., Steffian, G., Hazlett, G. A., & Loftus, E. F. (2013). Misinformation can influence memory for recently experienced, highly stressful events. *International Journal of Law and Psychiatry, 36*(1), 11–17.

Morgan, M. A., Romanski, L. M., & LeDoux, J. E. (1993). Extinction of emotional learning: Contribution of medial prefrontal cortex. *Neuroscience Letters, 163,* 109–113.

Mogensen, J. (2011). Almost unlimited potentials of a limited neural plasticity: Levels of plasticity in development and reorganization of the injured brain. *Journal of Consciousness Studies, 18,* 13–45.

Morin, C. M., LeBlanc, M., Bélanger, L., Ivers, H., Mérette, C., & Savard, J. (2011). Prevalence of insomnia and its treatment in Canada. *The Canadian Journal of Psychiatry, 56*(9), 540–548.

Morison, S. J., Ames, E. W., Chisholm, K. (1995). The development of children adopted from Romanian orphanages. *Merrill-Palmer Quarterly: Journal of Developmental Psychology, 41*(4), 411–430.

Morris, S. E., Rumsey, J. M., & Cuthbert, B. N. (2014). Rethinking mental disorders: The role of learning and brain plasticity. *Restorative Neurology & Neuroscience, 32*(1), 5–23.

Morris, W. N. (1992). A functional analysis of the role of mood in affective systems. In M. S. Clark (Ed.), *Emotion* (pp. 256–293). Thousand Oaks, CA: Sage Publications, Inc.

Morton, J., & Johnson, M. H. (1991). Conspec and Conlern—A Two-Process Theory of Infant Face Recognition. *Psychological Review, 98,* 164–181.

Moscovitch, D. A. (2009). What is the core fear in social phobia? A new model to facilitate individualized case conceptualization and treatment. *Cognitive and Behavioral Practice, 16*(2), 123–134.

Moscovitch, M. (2014). *New research shows memory is a dynamic and interactive process, AAAS: EurekAlert!* Canadian Association for Neuroscience.

Mosher, C. E., & Danoff-Burg, S. (2008). Agentic and communal personality traits: Relations to disordered eating behavior, body shape concern, and depressive symptoms. *Eating Behaviors, 9*(4), 497–500.

Mosher, C. E., & Danoff-Burg, S. (2005). Agentic and communal personality traits: Relations to attitudes toward sex and sexual experiences. *Sex Roles, 52*(1–2), 121–129.

Mosher, L., Gosden, R., & Beder, S. (2013). Unbridled capitalism meets madness. *Models of Madness 2nd Edition: Psychological, Social and Biological Approaches to Psychosis, 125.*

Mosher, W. D., Chandra, A., & Jones, J. (2005). Sexual behavior and selected health measures: Men and women 15–44 years of age, United States, 2002. *Advance Data from Vital Health Statistics* (362).

Mossey, P. A., Little, J., Munger, R. G., Dixon, M. J., & Shaw, W. C. (2009). Cleft lip and palate. *Lancet, 374,* 1773–1785.

Mota-Rolim, S. A., & Araujo, J. F. (2013). Neurobiology and clinical implications of lucid dreaming. *Medical Hypotheses, 81,* 751–756.

Moulier, V. et al. (2006). Neuroanatomical correlates of penile erection evoked by photographic stimuli in human males. *NeuroImage, 33*(2) 689–699.

Moulin, D. E., Clark, A. J., Speechley, M., & Morley Forster, P. K. (2002). Chronic pain in Canada—Prevalence, treatment, impact and the role of opioid analgesia. *Pain Research & Management, 7*(4), 179–184.

Mouras, H., Stolérus, M. V., Pélégrini-Issac, M., Rouxel, R., Grandjean, B., Glutron, D., & Bittoun, J. (2008). Activation of mirror-neuron system by erotic video clips predicts degree of induced erection: an *f*MRI study. *Neuroimage, 42,* 1142–1150.

Mowrer, O. H. (1950). *Learning theory and personality dynamics: selected papers.* New York, NY: Ronald P. Co.

Mowry, M., Mosher, M., & Briner, W. (2003). Acute physiologic and chronic histologic changes in rats and mice exposed to the unique hallucinogen Salvinorin A. *Journal of Psychoactive Drugs, 35*(3), 379–382.

MPAA/Box Office Mojo. (2014). Genre index of film grosses, www2.boxofficemojo.com/genres. Accessed October 2014.

Mroczek, D. K. (2004). Positive and negative affect at midlife. In O. G. Brim, C. D. Ryff, & R. C. Kessler (Eds.), *How healthy are we? A national study of well-being at midlife* (pp. 205–226). Chicago, IL: University of Chicago Press.

Mroczek, D. K., & Little, T. D. (2014). *Handbook of Personality Development.* New York, NY: Lawrence Erlbaum Associates Ltd.

Mroczek, D. K., & Spiro III, A. (2007). Personality change influences mortality in older men. *Psychological Science, 18*(5), 371–376.

Mueller, J., & Stewart, M. G. (2012). The terrorism delusion: America's overwrought response to September 11. *International Security, 37*(1), 81–110.

Mueller, S. E., Petitjean, S., Boening, J., & Wiesbeck, G. A. (2007). The impact of self-help group attendance on relapse rates after alcohol detoxification in a controlled study. *Alcohol Alcoholism, 42*(2), 108–112.

Muise, A., Christofides, E., & Desmarais, S. (2009). More information than you ever wanted: Does Facebook bring out the green-eyed monster of jealousy? *Cyber Psychology and Behavior, 12*(4), 441–444.

Müller, U., & Racine, T. P. (2010). The development of representation and concepts. In W. F. Overton & R. M. Lerner (Eds.), *The handbook of life-span development,* vol. 1: *Cognition, biology, and methods* (pp. 346–390). Hoboken, NJ: John Wiley & Sons.

Mulvaney, M. K., & Mebert, C. J. (2007). Parental corporal punishment predicts behaviour problems in early childhood. *Journal of Family Psychology, 21,* 389–397.

Murali, V., & Oyebode, F. (2010). Poverty, social inequality and mental health. In R. Bhattacharya, S. Cross, & D. Bhugra (Eds.), *Clinical topics in cultural psychiatry* (pp. 84–99). London, England: Royal College of Psychiatrists.

Murison, R. (2001). Is there a role for psychology in ulcer disease? *Integrative Physiological and Behavioral Science, 3*(1), 75–83.

Murphy, J. G., McDevitt-Murphy, M. E., & Barnett, N. P. (2005). Drink and be merry? Gender, life satisfaction, and alcohol consumption among college students. *Psychology of Addictive Behaviors, 19,* 184–191.

Murphy, N. A., & Hall, J. A. (2011). Intelligence and interpersonal sensitivity: A meta-analysis. *Intelligence, 39*(1), 54–63.

Murphy, P. K., Long, J. F., Holleran, T. A., & Esterly, E. (2003). Persuasion online or on paper: a new take on an old issue. *Learning and Instruction, 13*(5), 511–532.

Murphy, T. (1992). Redirecting sexual orientation: Techniques and justifications. *Journal of Sex Research, 29,* 501–523.

Murphy, W. J. (2001). The Victim Advocacy and Research Group: Serving a growing need to provide rape victims with personal legal representation to protect privacy rights and to fight gender bias in the criminal justice system. *Journal of Social Distress and the Homeless, 10*(1), 123–138.

Murray, H. A. (1943). *Thematic apperception test.* Cambridge, MA: Harvard University Press.

Murru, A., Bonnin, C. M., Nivoli, A. M. A., Pacchiarotti, I., Vieta, E., & Colom, F. (2011). The unsolved problem of treatment non-adherence amongst Schizoaffective bipolar patients. *International Clinical Psychopharmacology, 26,* e39–e40.

Myers, D. G. (2000). The funds, friends, and faith of happy people. *American Psychologist, 55*(1), 56–67.

Myers, D. G. (1975). Discussion-induced attitude polarization. *Human Relations, 28*(8), 699–714.

Myers, D. G., & Bishop, G. D. (1970). Discussion effects on racial attitudes. *Science, 169,* 778–779.

Myers, D. G., & Diener, E. (1997 November). The science of happiness. *Current,* 3–7.

Myers, D G., & Diener, E. (1996). The pursuit of happiness. *Scientific American,* 70–72.

Myers, I., McCaulley, M., Quenk, N. L., & Hammer, A. L. (1998). *Manual: A guide to the development and use of the Myers-Briggs type indicator.* (3rd Ed). Palo Alto, CA: Consulting Psychologists Press.

Myrick, H., & Wright, T. (2008). Clinical management of alcohol abuse and dependence. In H. D. Kleber & M. Galanter (Eds.), *The American psychiatric publishing textbook of substance abuse treatment* (4th Ed.). Washington, DC: American Psychiatric Publishing.

Nader, K. (2003). Memory traces unbound. *Trends in Neuroscince, 26*(2), 65–72.

Nader, K., Hardt, O., & Lanius, R. (2013). Memory as a new therapeutic target. *Dialogues in clinical neuroscience, 15*(4), 475.

Nagy, T. F. (2011). *Essential ethics for psychologists: A primer for understanding and mastering core issues.* Washington, DC: American Psychological Association.

Nahas, Z., Marangell, L. B., Husain, M. M., Rush, A. J., Sackeim, H. A., Lisanby, S. H., et al. (2005). Two-year-outcome of vagus nerve stimulation (VNS) for treatment of major depressive episodes. *Journal of Clinical Psychiatry, 66*(9), 1097–1104.

Nail, P. R., Harton, H. C., & Decker, B. P. (2003). Political orientation and modern versus aversive racism: Tests of Dividio and Gaertner's (1998) integrated model. *Journal of Personality and Social Psychology, 84,* 754–770.

Nair, E. (2003). Hindsight lessons aka experiential wisdom: A review of the XXV ICAP. *Applied Psychology: An International Review, 52*(2), 165–174.

Naish, P. L. N. (2010). Hypnosis and hemispheric asymmetry. *Consciousness and Cognition: An International Journal, 19*(1), 230–234.

Nakamichi, N., Kato, E., Kojima, Y., & Itoigawa, N. (1998). Carrying and washing of grass roots by free-ranging Japanese macaques at Katsuyama. *Folia Primatologica, Basel, 69*, 35–40.

Nakano, T., Watanabe, H., Homae, F., & Taga, G. (2009). Prefrontal cortical involvement in young infants' analysis of novelty. *Cerebral Cortex, 19*, 455–463.

Nakano, T., Watanabe, H., Homae, F., Asakawa, K., and Taga, G., (2006). *Brain imaging of habituation and dishabituation in young infants.* Paper presented at the annual meeting of the XVth Biennial International Conference on Infant Studies, Westin Miyako, Kyoto, Japan.

Nakatomi, H., Kuriu, T., Okabe, S., Yamamoto, S. I., Hatano, O., Kawahara, N., … & Nakafuku, M. (2002). Regeneration of hippocampal pyramidal neurons after ischemic brain injury by recruitment of endogenous neural progenitors. *Cell, 110*(4), 429–441.

NAMI (National Alliance on Mental Illness). (2011). *Mental illness: Facts and numbers.* Arlington, VA: Author.

Nangle, D. W., Erdley, C. A., Zeff, K. R., Stanchfield, L. L., & Gold, J. A. (2004). Opposites do not attract: Social status and behavioral-style concordances among children and the peers who like or dislike them. *Journal of Abnormal Child Psychology, 32*, 425–434.

Naqvi, R., Liberman, D., Rosenberg, J., Alston, J., & Straus, S. (2013). Preventing cognitive decline in healthy older adults. *Canadian Medical Association Journal*, cmaj-121448.

Nash, J. M. (1997). Addicted. *Time*, 68–76.

National Association to Advance Fat Acceptance (NAAFA). (2009). *Weight discrimination laws.* Retrieved from www.naafaonline.com/dev2/education/laws.html.

National Center on Birth Defects and Developmental Disabilities. (2005). *Intellectual disability.* Retrieved from www.cdc.gov/ncbddd/dd/mr3.htm.

National Coalition for Visual Health. (2008). *Our vision of visual health.* Retrieved from www.visionhealth.ca/projects/documents/NCVH% 20Handout.pdf.

National Institute of Neurological Disorders and Stroke (NINDS). (2006). *Narcolepsy fact sheet.* Bethesda, MD.

Navaneelan, T. & Janz, T. (2014) *Adjusting the scales: Obesity in the Canadian population after correcting for respondent bias.* Statistics Canada, Catalougue no. 82-624-X, Health at a Glance.

Ndumele, C. D., & Trivedi, A. N. (2011). Effect of copayments on use of outpatient mental health services among elderly managed care enrollees. *Medical Care, 1.*

Neale, M. C. (2013). Genetic epidemiology of Major Depression. In S.E. Hyman (Ed.), *Depression: The Science of Mental Health.* Oxford, UK: Routledge.

Neckelmann, D., Mykletun, A., & Dahl, A. A. (2007). Chronic insomnia as a risk factor for developing anxiety and depression. *Sleep, 30*(7), 873–880.

Nee, D. E., Berman, M. G., Moore, K. S., & Jonides, J. (2008). Neuro-scientific evidence about the distinction between short- and long-term memory. *Current Directions in Psychological Science, 17*(2), 102–106.

Neff, E. J. A., & Dale, J. C. (1996). Worries of school-age children. *Journal of the Society of Pediatric Nurses, 1*, 27–32.

Neisser, U. (Ed.) (1998). *The rising curve: Long-term gains in IQ and related measures.* Washington, DC: American Psychological Association.

Neisser, U. (1967). *Cognitive psychology.* New York, NY: Applet on Century-Crofts.

Neitzel, M. T., Bernstein, D. A., Kramer, G. P. & Milich, R. (2003). *Introduction to Clinical Psychology* (6th Ed). Englewood Cliffs, NJ: Prentice-Hall.

Nelson, B. D., & Shankman, S. A. (2011). Does intolerance of uncertainty predict anticipatory startle responses to uncertain threat? *International Journal of Psychophysiology, 81*(2), 107–115.

Nelson, C. A. I., Bos, K. J., Gunnar, M. R., Sonuga-Barke, E. J. (2012). The neurobiological toll of early human deprivation. In R. McCall, M. H. Van Ijzendoorn, H. Juffer, C. J. Groark, & V. K. Groza (Eds.), *Children without permanent parental care: Research, practice, and policy* (pp. 127–146). New York, NY: Wiley-Blackwell.

Nelson, III, C. A., Furtado, E. A., Fox, N. A., & Zeanah, Jr. C. H. (2009). The deprived brain. *American Scientist, 97*(3), 222–229.

Nelson, D., & Cooper, G. (2005). Stress and health: A positive direction. *Stress and Health: Journal of the International Society for the Investigation of Stress, 21*, 73–75.

Nelson, J. (2009). Tricyclic and tetracyclic drugs. In *The American Psychiatric Publishing Textbook of Psychopharmacology*, 4th Edition. American Psychiatric Publishing, Inc.

Nelson, J. K., & Bennett, C. S. (2008). Introduction: Special issue on attachment. *Clinical Social Work Journal, 36*, 3–7.

Nelson, J. M., Canivez, G. L., & Watkins, M. W. (2013). Structural and incremental validity of the Wechsler Adult Intelligence Scale–Fourth Edition with a clinical sample. *Psychological Assessment, 25*(2), 618–630.

Nemeroff, C. B. (1998). The neurobiology of depression. *Scientific American-American Edition, 278*, 42–49.

Nemeroff, C. B., & Owens, M. J. (2009). The role of serotonin in the pathophysiology of depression: as important as ever. *Clinical Chemistry, 55*(8), 1578–1579.

Nesse, R. M. (1990). Evolutionary explanations of emotions. *Human Nature, 1*, 261–289.

Nesse, R. M., & Ellsworth, P. C. (2009). Evolution, emotions, and emotional disorders. *American Psychologist, 64*(2), 129–139.

Nestler, E. J. (2004). Molecular mechanisms of drug addiction. *Neuropharmacology, 1*, 24–32.

Neubauer, A. C., & Fink, A. (2010). Neuroscientific approaches to the study of individual differences in cognition and personality. In A. Gruszka, G. Matthews, & B. Szymura (Eds.), *Handbook of individual differences in cognition: Attention, memory, and executive control* (pp. 73–85). New York, NY: Springer Science + Business Media.

Neubauer, A. C., & Fink, A. (2003). Fluid intelligence and neural efficiency: Effects of task complexity and sex. *Personality and Individual Differences, 35*(4), 811–827.

Neuman, Y., & Nave, O. (2010). Why the brain needs language in order to be self-conscious. *New Ideas in Psychology, 28*(1), 37–48.

Neumeister, A., Charney, D. S., & Drevets, W. C. (2005). Hippocampus, VI: Depression and the hippocampus. *American Journal of Psychiatry, 162*(6), 1057.

Neuschatz, J. S., Preston, E. L., & Toglia, M. P. (2005). Comparison of the efficacy of two name-learning techniques: Expanding rehearsal and name-face imagery. *American Journal of Psychology, 118*, 79–101.

Newcomb, T. M. (1943). *Personality and social change.* New York, NY: Dryden.

Newcomb, T. M., Koening, K. E., Flacks, R., & Warwick, D. P. (1967). *Persistence and change: Bennington College and its students after 25 years.* New York, NY: John Wiley & Sons, Inc.

Newman, M. G., Castonguay, L. G., Borkovec, T. D., Fisher, A. J., Boswell, J. F., Szkodny, L. E., & Nordberg, S. S. (2011). A randomized controlled trial of cognitive-behavioral therapy for generalized anxiety disorder with integrated techniques from emotion-focused and interpersonal therapies. *Journal of Consulting and Clinical Psychology, 79*(2), 171–181.

Newport, E. L., Bavelier, D., & Neville, H. J. (2001). Critical thinking about critical periods: Perspectives on a critical period for language acquisition. *Language, brain and cognitive development: Essays in honor of Jacques Mehler, 481–502.*

Niaura, R., Todaro, J. F., Stroud, L., Spiro III, A., Ward, K. D., & Weiss, S. (2002). Hostility, the metabolic syndrome, and incident coronary heart disease. *Health Psychology, 21*(6), 588–593.

Nicholls, A. (2010). The scientific unconscious: Goethe's post-Kantian epistemology. In A. Nicholls & M. Liebscher (Eds.), *Thinking the unconscious: Nineteenth-century German thought.* New York, NY: Cambridge University Press.

Nicoll, R. A., & Roche, K. W. (2013). Long-term potentiation: Peeling the onion. *Neuropharmacology, 74*, 18–22.

Nicpon, M. F. (2014). Cognitive and psychosocial assessment. In W. Ming-Lu (Ed.), *The Oxford handbook of social class in counseling.* New York, NY: Oxford.

NIDA (National Institute on Drug Abuse). (2011). *NIDA InfoFacts: Treatment statistics.* Bethesda, MD: Author.

Niedermeyer, E., & da Silva, F. L. (2004). *Electroencephalography: Basic Principles, Clinical Applications, and Related Fields.* Lippincot Williams & Wilkins.

Nield, L. S., Mangano, L. M., & Kamat, D. M. (2008). Strabismus: A close-up look. *Consultant for Pediatricians, 7*, 17–25.

Nielsen, J. A., Zielinski, B. A., Ferguson, M. A., Lainhart, J. E., & Anderson, J. S. (2013). An evaluation of the left-brain vs. right-brain hypothesis with resting state functional connectivity magnetic resonance imaging. *PloS One, 8*(8), e71275.

Nier, J. A. (2005). How dissociated are implicit and explicit racial attitudes? A bogus pipeline approach. *Group Processes & Intergroup Relations, 8*(1), 39–52.

Nikolić, D. (2009). *Is synaesthesia actually ideaesthesia? An inquiry into the nature of the phenomenon.* Proceedings of the Third International Congress on Synaesthesia, Science and Art, Granada, Spain, April 26–29.

Nilsson, B. (1979). The occurrence of taste buds in the palate of human adults as evidenced by light microscopy. *Acta Odontologica Scandinavica, 37*, 253–258.

Nisan, M., & Kohlberg, L. (1982). Universality and variation in moral judgment: A longitudinal and cross-sectional study in Turkey. *Child Development, 53*(4), 865–876.

Nisbett, R. E. (2009). *Intelligence and how to get it: Why schools and cultures count.* New York, NY: W. W. Norton.

Nisbett, R. E. (2005) Heredity, environment, and race differences in IQ, A commentary on Rushton and Jensen (2005). *Psychology, Public Policy and Law, 11*(2), 302–310.

Nishina, A., Juvonen, J., & Witkow, M. R. (2005). Sticks and stones may break my bones, but names will make me feel sick. The psychosocial, somatic, and scholastic consequences of peer harassment. *Journal of Clinical Child and Adolescent Psychology, 34*(1), 37–48.

Nishitani, S., Miyamura, T., Tagawa, M., Sumi, M., Takase, R., Doi, H., Moriuchi, H., & Shinohara, K. (2009). The calming effect of a maternal breast milk odor on the human newborn infant. *Neuroscience Research, 63*, 66–71.

Nishiyama, R., & Ukita, J. (2013). Articulatory rehearsal is more than refreshing memory traces. *Experimental Psychology, 60*(2), 131–139.

Nixon, M. K., Cloutier, P., & Jansson, S. M. (2008). Nonsuicidal self-harm in youth: A population-based survey. *Canadian Medical Association Journal, 178*, 306–312. doi:10.1503/cmaj.061693

Nobel Prize. (2013). Nobel Media. Web. Retrieved from www.nobelprize.org/ nobel_prizes/medicine/laureates/1963/press.html.

Nolen-Hoeksema, S. (2001). Gender differences in depression. *Current Directions in Psychological Science, 10*(5), 173–176.

Nonacs, R. M. (2007). Postpartum depression. *eMedicine Clinical Reference.* Retrieved from http://www.emedicine.com/med/topic 3408.htm.

Norcross, J. C., & Goldfried, M. R. (Eds.). (2005). *Handbook of psychotherapy integration* (2nd Ed.). New York, NY: Oxford University Press.

Norem, J. K. (2008). Defensive pessimism, anxiety, and the complexity of evaluating self-regulation. *Social and Personality Psychology Compass, 2*(1), 121–134.

Norem, J. K., & Illingworth, K. S. S. (2004). Mood and performance among defensive pessimists and strategic optimists. *Journal of Research in Personality, 38*(4), 351–366.

Norgren, R., Hajnal, A., & Mungarndee, S. S. (2006). Gustatory reward and the nucleus accumbens. *Physiology & Behavior, 89*, 531–535.

Norman-Eady, S., Reinhart, C., & Martino, P. (2003). *Statutory rape laws by state.* OLR Research Report. Retrieved from http://www.cga.ct.gov/2003/ olrdata/jud/rpt/2003-R-0376.htm.

Nosek, M., Kennedy, H. P., Beyene, Y., Taylor, D., Gilliss, C., & Lee, K. (2010). The effects of perceived stress and attitudes toward menopause and aging on symptoms of menopause. *Journal of Midwifery & Women's Health, 55*(4), 328–334.

Novaco, R. W., Stokols, D., & Milanesi, L. (1990). Objective and subjective dimensions of travel impedance as determinants of commuting stress. *American Journal of Community Psychology, 18*, 231–257.

Novella, S. (2000). Phrenology: History of a pseudoscience. *The New England Journal of Skepticism.* Retrieved from http://www.theness.com/index.php/ phrenology-history-of-a-pseudoscience.

Novick, L. R., & Bassok, M. (2005). Problem solving. In K. J. Holyoak & R. G. Morrison (Eds.), *The Cambridge handbook of thinking and reasoning* (pp. 321–350). New York, NY: Cambridge University Press.

Novin, D., Sanderson, J. D., & Vanderweele, D. A. (1974). The effect of isotonic glucose on eating as a function of feeding condition and infusion site. *Physiology & Behavior, 13*(1), 4.

Noyes, R. (2008). Hypochondriasis. In M. Gelder, N. Andreasen, J. Lopez-Ibor, & J. Geddes (Eds.), *New Oxford textbook of psychiatry, vol. 2* (2nd Ed.). New York, NY: Oxford University Press.

NSDUH. (2008). *National survey on drug use.* Washington, DC: Department of Health and Human Services, Substance Abuse and Mental Health Services Administration, Office of Applied Studies.

Nuechterlein, K. H., Ventura, J., Subotnik, K. L., & Bartzokis, G. (2013). The early longitudinal course of cognitive deficits in schizophrenia. *The Journal of Clinical Psychiatry, 75*, 25–29.

Numazaki, M., & Tominaga, M. (2004). Nociception and TRP Channels. *Current Drug Targets: CNS and Neurological Disorders, 3*, 479–485.

Nunn, J. A., Gregory, L. J., Brammer, M., Williams, S. C. R., Parslow, D. M., Morgan, M. J., Morris, R. G., Bullmore, E. T., Baron-Cohen, S., & Gray, J. A. (2002). Functional magnetic resonance imaging of synesthesia: Activation of V4/V8 by spoken words. *Nature Neuroscience, 5*(4), 371–375.

Nutravite. (2006). *Most married Canadians burdened with a snoring partner.* Poll conducted by Ipsos Reid for Nutravite. Retrieved from http://www. nutravite.com/news/october.htm.

Nye, C. D., Roberts, B. W., Saucier, G., & Zhou, X. (2008). Testing the measurement equivalence of personality adjective items across cultures. *Journal of Research in Personality, 42*(6), 1524–1536.

O'Brien, A., & Tulsky, D. (2008). The history of processing speed and its relationship to intelligence. In J. DeLuca, & J. H. Kalmar, *Information processing speed in clinical populations* (pp. 1–23). New York, NY: Taylor and Francis.

O'Brien, C. P. (2008). The CAGE questionnaire for detection of alcoholism: A remarkably useful but simple tool. *Journal of the American Medical Association, 300*(17), 2054–2056.

O'Brien, C. P. (2005). Benzodiazepine use, abuse, and dependence. *Journal of Clinical Psychiatry, 66*(Suppl 2), 28–33.

O'Connor, B. P. (2008). Other personality disorders. In M. Hersen & J. Rosqvist (Eds.), *Handbook of psychological assessment, case conceptualization, and treatment, Vol 1: Adults* (pp. 438–462). Hoboken, NJ: John Wiley & Sons, Inc.

O'Connor, T., Sadleir, K. R., Maus, E., Velliquette, R. A., Zhao, J., Cole, S. L., . . . Vassar, R. (2008). Phosphorylation of the translation initiation factor eIF2alpha increases BACE1 levels and promotes amyloidogenesis. *Neuron, 60*(6), 988–1009.

O'Craven, K. M., & Kanwisher, N. (2000). Mental imagery of faces and places activates corresponding stimulus-specific brain regions. *Journal of Cognitive Neuroscience, 12*, 1013–1023.

O'Grady, W., Parnaby, P. F., & Schikschneit, J. (2010). Guns, gangs, and the underclass: A constructionist analysis of gun violence in a Toronto high school. *Canadian Journal of Criminology and Criminal Justice, 52*(1), 55–77.

O'Hara, D. (2010). Inductive reasoning comes to science. *Birth Story,* December 15, 2011.

O'Leary, K. D., & Wilson, G. T. (1987). *Behavior therapy: Application and outcome (2nd Ed.).* Englewood Cliffs, NJ: Prentice-Hall, Inc.

O'Rourke, N., Cappeliez, P., & Guindon, S. (2003). Depressive symptoms and physical health of caregivers of persons with cognitive impairment: Analysis of reciprocal effects over time. *Journal of Aging and Health, 15*(4), 688–712.

Oakley, D. A., & Halligan, P. W. (2010). Psychophysiological foundations of hypnosis and suggestion. In S. J. Lynn, J. W. Rhue, & I. Kirsch (Eds.), *Handbook of clinical hypnosis (2nd Ed.)* (pp. 79–117). Washington, DC: American Psychological Association.

Oatley, K., & Jenkins, J. M. (1996). *Understanding emotions.* Malden, MA: Blackwell Publishing.

Oberauer, K., & Kliegl, R. (2006). A formal model of capacity limits in working memory. *Journal of Memory and Language, 55*, 601–626.

Oda, A. Y. (2007). David Elkind and the crisis of adolescence: Review, critique, and applications. *Journal of Psychology and Christianity, 26*(3), 251–256.

Oestergaard, S., & Møldrup, C. (2011). Optimal duration of combined psychotherapy and pharmacotherapy for patients with moderate and severe depression: A meta-analysis. *Journal of Affective Disorders, 131*(1), 24–36.

Offord, D. R., Boyle, M. H., Campbell, D., Goering, P., Lin, E., Wong, M., & Racine, Y. A. (1996) One-year prevalence of psychiatric disorder in Ontarians 15 to 64 years of age. *Canadian Journal of Psychiatry, 41*, 559–565.

Ogawa, S., Tank, D. W., Menon, R., Ellermann, J. M., Kim, S.-G., Merkle, H., & Ugurbil, K. (1992). Intrinsic signal changes accompanying sensory stimulation: functional brain mapping with magnetic resonance imaging. *Proceedings of the National Academy of Sciences, 89*, 5951–5955.

Ogden, T. (2011). Sosial ferdighetsopplaring for barn og ungdom. [Social skills training for children and adolescents.]. *Tidsskrift for Norsk Psykologforening, 48*(1), 64–68.

Ogino, S., Miyamoto, S., Miyake, N., & Yamaguchi, N. (2014). Benefits and limits of anticholinergic use in schizophrenia: Focusing on its effect on cognitive function. *Psychiatry and Clinical Neurosciences, 68*(1), 37-49.

Oh, S. H. (2013). Do collectivists conform more than individualists? Cross-cultural differences in compliance and internalization. *Social Behavior and Personality, 41*(6), 981–994.

Öhman, A. (2000). Fear and anxiety: Evolutionary, cognitive, and clinical perspectives. In M. Lewis & J. M. Haviland-Jones (Eds.), *Handbook of emotions, 2nd Ed.* (pp. 573–593). New York, NY: Guilford Press.

Okamoto, Y., Kinoshita, A., Onoda, K., Yoshimura, S., Matsunaga, M., Takami, H., . . . & Yamawaki, S. (2006). Functional brain basis of cognition in major depression. *Japanese Journal of Psychonomic Science, 25*, 237–243.

Okie, S. (2005). Medical marijuana and the Supreme Court. *New England Journal of Medicine, 353*(7), 648–651.

Oksenberg, J. R., & Hauser, S. L. (2010). Mapping the human genome with newfound precision. *Annals of Neurology, 67*(6), A8–A10.

Olatunji, B. O., Deacon, B. J., & Abramowitz, J. S. (2009). Is hypochondriasis an anxiety disorder? *The British Journal of Psychiatry, 194*(6), 481–482.

Olatunji, B. O., Huijding, J., de Jong, P. J., & Smits, J. A. J. (2011). The relative contributions of fear and disgust reductions to improvements in spider phobia following exposure-based treatment. *Journal of Behavior Therapy and Experimental Psychiatry, 42*(1), 117–121.

Olds, J. (1958). Self-stimulation of the brain. *Science, 127*, 315–24.

Olds, J. (1956). Pleasure center in the brain. *Scientific American, 195*, 105–16.

Olds, J., & Milner, P. (1954). Positive reinforcement produced by electrical stimulation of septal area and other regions of rat brain. *Journal of Comparative and Physiological Psychology, 47*(6), 419–427.

Olfson, M., Blanco, C., Liu, L., Moreno, C., & Laje, G. (2006). National trends in the outpatient treatment of children and adolescents with antipsychotic drugs. *Archives of General Psychiatry, 63*(6), 679–685.

Olfson, M., & Marcus, S. C. (2009). National patterns in antidepressant medication treatment. *Archives of General Psychiatry, 66*(8), 848–856.

Olfson, M., Marcus, S. C., & Shaffer, D. (2006). Antidepressant drug therapy and suicide in severely depressed children and adults: a case-control study. *Archives of General Psychiatry, 63*(8), 865–872.

Oliveira, A. J., Rostila, M., de Leon, A. P., & Lopes, C. S. (2013). The influence of social relationships on obesity: Sex differences in a longitudinal study. *Obesity: A Research Journal, 21*(8), 1540–1547.

Oliveira, F. C. M. B., Fortaleza, Q. F., & Cowan, H. (2012) Haptics. *IEEE Transactions*, 2, 172–183.

Olness, K., & Kohen, D. P. (2010). Childhood problems. In A. F. Barabasz, K. Olness, R. Boland, & S. Kahn (Eds.), *Medical hypnosis primer: Clinical and research evidence* (pp. 33–39). New York, NY: Routledge/Taylor & Francis Group.

Olpin, M., & Hesson, M. (2013). *Stress management for life: A research-based experiential approach* (3rd ed.). Belmont, CA: Wadsworth, Cengage Learning.

Olsen, L., & DeBoise, T. (2007). Enhancing school readiness: The Early Head Start model. *Children and Schools, 29*, 47–50.

Olson, J. M., & Stone, J. (2005). The Influence of Behavior on Attitudes. In D. Albarracín, B. T. Johnson, & M. P. Zanna (Eds.), *The Handbook of Attitudes* (pp. 223–271). Mahwah, NJ: Lawrence Erlbaum Associates Publishers.

Ophira, E., Nassb, C., & Wagner, A. D. (2009). Cognitive control in media multitaskers. *Proceedings of the National Academy of Sciences, 106*, 15583–15587.

Oppenheimer, D. M. (2004). Spontaneous discounting of availability in frequency judgment tasks. *Psychological Science, 15*, 100–105.

Orbuch, T. L., & Sprecher, S. (2003). Attraction and interpersonal relationships. In J. Delamater (Ed.), *Handbook of social psychology* (pp. 339–362). New York, NY: Kluwer Academic/Plenum Publishers.

Organ, D., & Ryan, K. (1995). A meta-analytic review of attitudinal and dispositional predictors of organizational citizenship behavior. *Personnel Psychology, 48*, 775–802.

Orikasa, C., Kondo, Y., & Sakuma, Y. (2007). Transient transcription of the somatostatin gene at the time of estrogen-dependent organization of the sexually dimorphic nucleus of the rat preoptic area. *Endocrinology, 148*, 1144–1149.

Ormrod, J. E. (2011). *Human Learning* (6th ed). New Jersey: Prentice Hall Inc.

Orne, M. T. (1951). The mechanisms of hypnotic age regression: An experimental study. *Journal of Abnormal and Social Psychology, 46*, 213–225.

Ornstein, P. A., & Light, L. L. (2010). Memory development across the life span. In W. F. Overton & R. M. Lerner (Eds.), *The handbook of life-span development*, vol. 1: *Cognition, biology, and methods* (pp. 259–305). Hoboken, NJ: John Wiley & Sons.

Orsillo, S. M., & Roemer, L. (2011). *The mindful way through anxiety: Break free from chronic worry and reclaim your life*. New York, NY: Guilford Press.

Orzeł-Gryglewska, J. (2010). Consequences of sleep deprivation. *International Journal of Occupational Medicine and Environmental Health, 23*(1), 95–114.

Osborn, F. (1937). Development of a eugenic philosophy. *American Sociological Review, 2*(3), 389–397.

Ostrov, J. M., Gentile, D. A., & Mullins, A. D. (2013). Evaluating the effect of educational media exposure on aggression in early childhood. *Journal of Applied Developmental Psychology, 34*, 38–44. doi:10.1016/j.appdev.2012.09.005

Otto, M. W., McHugh, R. K., & Kantak, K. M. (2010). Combined pharmacotherapy and cognitive-behavioral therapy for anxiety disorders: Medication effects, glucocorticoids, and attenuated treatment outcomes. *Clinical Psychology: Science and Practice, 17*(2), 91–103.

Ouellette, S. C., & DiPlacido, J. (2001). Personality's role in the protection and enhancement of health: Where the research has been, where it is stuck, how it might move. In A. Baum, T. A. Revenson, & J. E. Singer (Eds.), *Handbook of health psychology*. Mahwah, NJ: Lawrence Erlbaum.

Ouko, L. A., Shantikumar, K., Knezovich, J., Haycock, P., Schnugh, D. J., & Ramsay, M. (2009). Effect of alcohol consumption on CpG methylated regions of H19 and IG-DMR in male gametes: Implications for fetal alcohol spectrum disorders. *Alcoholism, Clinical and Experimental Research, 33*, 1615–1627.

Overholser, J. C., Braden, A. , & Fisher, L. (2010). You've got to believe: Core beliefs that underlie effective psychotherapy. *Journal of Contemporary Psychotherapy, 40*, 185–194.

Overmier, B. J., & Murison, R. (2005). Trauma and resulting sensitization effects are modulated by psychological factors. *Psycho-neuroendocrinology, 30*, 965–973.

Overton, W. F., & Lerner, R. M. (Eds.). (2010). *The handbook of lifespan development*, vol. 1: *Cognition, biology, and methods*. Hoboken, NJ: John Wiley & Sons.

Owen-Howard, M. (2001). Pharmacological aversion treatment of alcohol dependence. I. Production and prediction of conditioned alcohol aversion. *American Journal of Drug and Alcohol Abuse, 27*(3), 561–585.

Owens, J., & Massey, D. S. (2011). Stereotype threat and college academic performance: A latent variables approach. *Social Science Research, 40*(1), 150–166.

Oyserman, D., Coon, H. M., & Kemmelmeier, M. (2002a). Rethinking individualism and collectivism: Evaluation of theoretical assumptions and meta-analyses. *Psychological Bulletin, 128*, 3–72.

Ozer, E. J. (2005). The impact of violence on urban adolescents: Longitudinal effects of perceived school connection and family support. *Journal of Adolescent Research, 20*(2), 167–192.

Ozer, E. J., Best, S. R., Lipsey, T. L., & Weiss, D. S. (2003). Predictors of posttraumatic stress disorder and symptoms in adults: A meta-analysis. *Psychology Bulletin, 129*(1), 52–73.

Öztekin, I., McElree, B., Staresina, B. P., & Davachi, L. (2009). Working memory retrieval: Contributions of the left prefrontal cortex, the left posterior parietal cortex, and the hippocampus. *Journal of Cognitive Neuroscience, 21*(3), 581–593.

Pace, T. W. W., & Heim, C. M. (2011). A short review on the psychoneuroimmunology of posttraumatic stress disorder: From risk factors to medical comorbidities. *Brain, Behavior, and Immunity, 25*(1), 6–13.

Packard, M. G., Williams, C. L., Cahill, L., & McGaugh, J. L. (2013). The anatomy of a memory modulatory system: From periphery to brain. *Neurobehavioral Plasticity: Learning, Development, and Response to Brain Insults*, 149–233.

Packer, S. (2000). Religion and stress. In G. Fink (Ed.), *Encyclopedia of Stress, Vol. 3* (pp. 348–355). New York, NY: Academic Press.

Padowski, J. M., Weaver, K. E., Richards, T. L., Laurino, M. Y., Samii, A., Aylward, E. H., & Conley, K. E. (2014). Neurochemical correlates of caudate atrophy in Huntington's disease. *Movement Disorders, 29*(3), 327–335.

Page, R. M., & Brewster, A. (2009). Depiction of food as having druglike properties in televised food advertisements directed at children: Portrayals as pleasure enhancing and addictive. *Journal of Pediatric Health Care, 23*(3), 150–158.

Paine, S., Gander, P. H., & Travier, N. (2006). The epidemiology of Morningness/ Eveningness: Influence of age, gender, ethnicity, and socioeconomic factors in adults (30–49 years). *Journal of Biological Rhythms, 21*(1), 68–76.

Palazidou, E. (2012). The neurobiology of depression. *British Medical Bulletin, 101*(1), 127–145.

Palkovitz, R., Copes, M. A., & Woolfolk, T. N. (2001). It's like . . . you discover a new sense of being: Involved fathering as an evoker of adult development. *Men & Masculinities, 4*(1), 49–69.

Palumbo, S. R. (1978). Dreaming and memory: A new information processing model. New York, NY: Basic Books.

Pantalony, D. (1997). *Prism, pendulum and chronograph-philosophers at the University of Toronto*. Retrieved from http://www.psych.utoronto.ca/museum/biblio.htm.

Paprzycka, K. (2010). Is neurobiology of personality inevitable? A philosophical perspective. In T. Maruszewski, M. Fajkowska, & M. W. Eysenck (Eds.), *Personality from biological, cognitive, and social perspectives* (pp. 13–27). Clinton Corners, NY: Eliot Werner Publications.

Paquet, L. B. (2000, September 1). Our place in space. *Legion Magazine*. Retrieved from http://www.legionmagazine.com/en/index.php/2000/09/our-place-in-space.

Paquette, G. (2004) Violence on Canadian television networks. *Canadian Child and Adolescent Psychiatric Review, 13*(1), 13–15.

Paris, J. (2010). Estimating the prevalence of personality disorders in the community. *Journal of Personality Disorders, 24*(4), 405–411.

Park, D., & Gutchess. A. (2006). The cognitive neuroscience of aging and culture. *Current Directions in Psychological Science, 15*, 105–108.

Park, D., Ramirez, G., & Beilock, S. L. (2014). The role of expressive writing in math anxiety. *Journal of Experimental Psychology: Applied, 20*(2), 103–111.

Park, D. C., Lautenschlager, G., Hedden, T., Davidson, N. S., Smith, A. D., & Smith, P. (2002). Models of visuospatial and verbal memory across the adult life span. *Psychology & Aging, 17*(2), 299–320.

Park, D. C., & Reuter-Lorenz, P. (2009). The adaptive brain: Aging and neurocognitive scaffolding. *Annual Review of Psychology, 60*, 173–196.

Parke, R. D. (1995). Fathers and families. In M. H. Bornstein (Ed.), *Handbook of parenting, vol. 3: Status and social conditions of parenting* (pp. 27–63). Mahwah, NJ: Lawrence Erlbaum Associates.

Parke, R. D., & Deur, J. L. (1972). Schedule of punishment and inhibition of aggression in children. *Developmental Psychology, 7*, 266–269.

Parker, E. S., Cahill, L., & McGaugh, J. L. (2006). A case of unusual autobiographical remembering. *Neurocase, 12*, 35–49.

Parker, J. D. A., Hogan, M. J., Eastabrook, J. M., Oke, A., & Wood, L. M. (2006). Emotional intelligence and student retention: Predicting the successful transition from high school to university. *Personality and Individual Differences, 41*, 1329–1336.

Parker, J. D. A., Summerfeldt, L. J., Hogan, M. J., & Majeski, S. A. (2004). Emotional intelligence and academic success: Examining the transition from high school to university. *Personality and Individual Differences, 36*, 163–172.

Parrott, W. G. (2004). The nature of emotion. In M. B. Brewer & M. Hewstone (Eds.), *Emotion and motivation* (pp. 5–20). Malden, MA: Blackwell Publishing.

Parrott, W. G. (2001). Implications of dysfunctional emotions for understanding how emotions function. *Review of General Psychology, 5*, 180–186.

Pasquet, P., & Apfelbaum, M. (1994). Recovery of initial body weight and composition after long-term massive overfeeding in men. *American Journal of Clininal Nutrition, 60*(6), 861–863.

Paton, C., & Beer, D. (2001). Caffeine: The forgotten variable. *International Journal of Psychiatry in Clinical Practice, 5*(4), 231–236.

Patrick, C. J. (2007). Antisocial personality disorder and psychopathy. In W. O'Donohue, K. A. Fowler, & S. O. Lilienfeld (Eds.), *Personality Disorders: Toward the DSM-V* (pp. 109–166). Thousand Oaks, CA: Sage Publications.

Patterson, D. (2011). The linkage between secondary victimization by law enforcement and rape case outcomes. *Journal of Interpersonal Violence, 26*(2), 328–347.

Patterson, D. R. (2010). *Clinical hypnosis for pain control.* Washington, DC: American Psychological Association.

Patterson, F. G. P., & Matevia, M. L. (2001). Twenty-seven years of Project Koko and Michael. In M. Biruté, F. Galdikas, N. Erickson Briggs, L. K. Sheeran, G. L. Shapiro, & J. Goodall (Eds.), *All apes great and small: African apes* (pp. 165–176). New York, NY: Springer.

Pattison, E., & Pattison, M. (1980). "Ex-gays": Religiously mediated change in homosexuals. *American Journal of Psychiatry, 137,* 1553–1562.

Paul, G. L., & Lentz, R. (1977). *Psychosocial treatment of the chronic mental patient.* Cambridge, MA: Harvard University Press.

Pauls, C. A., & Stemmler, G. (2003). Repressive and defensive coping during fear and anger. *Emotion, 3*(3), 284–302.

Paulsen, J. S. (2009). Functional imaging in Huntington's disease. *Experimental Neurology.* January 3. [Epub ahead of print].

Paulsen, O., & Sejnowski, T. J. (2000). Natural patterns of activity and long-term synaptic plasticity. *Current Opinion in Neurobiology, 10*(2), 172–179.

Paulus, D. L. (2009). Socially desirable responding: The evolution of a construct. In H. I. Barun, D. N. Jackson, & D. E. Wiley (Eds.), *The role of constructs in psychological and educational measurement.* Mahwah, NJ: Taylor & Francis and Lawrence Erlbaum Associates Ltd.

Paulus, P. B., Dugosh, K. L., Dzindolet, M. T., Coskun, H., & Putnam, V.L. (2002). Social and cognitive influences in group brainstorming: Predicting production gains and losses. In W. Stroebe & M. Hewston (Eds.), *European Review of Social Psychology* (Vol. 12, pp. 299–325). Chichester: John Wiley & Sons, Inc.

Paulus, P. B., Dzindolet, M. T., Poletes, G., & Camacho, L. M. (1993). Perception of performance in group brainstorming: The illusion of group productivity. *Personality and Social Psychology Bulletin, 19,* 78–79.

Paulussen-Hoogeboom, M. C., Stams, G. J. J. M., Hermanns, J. M. A., & Peetsma, T. T. D. (2007). Child negative emotionality and parenting from infancy to preschool: A meta-analytic review. *Developmental Psychology, 43,* 438–453.

Paus, T., Zijdenbos, A., Worsley, K., Collins, D. L., Blumenthal, J., Giedd, J. N., . . . (1999). Structural maturation of neural pathways in children and adolescents: In vivo study. *Science, 283*(5409), 1908–1911.

Paykel, E. S. (2006). Depression: major problem for public health. *Epidemiologia e Psichiatria Sociale, 15*(01), 4–10.

Paykel, E. S. (2003a). Life events and affective disorders. *Acta Psychiatrica Scandinavica, 108,* 61–66.

Paykel, E. S. (2003b). Life events: Effects and genesis. *Psychological Medicine, 33*(7), 1145–1148.

Payne, J. W., & Bettman, J. R. (2004). Walking with the scarecrow: The information-processing approach to decision research. In D. J. Koehler & N. Harvey (Eds.), *Blackwell handbook of judgment and decision making* (pp. 110–132). Malden, MA: Blackwell Publishing.

Pederson, D. R., & Moran, G. (1996). Expressions of the attachment relationship outside of the strange situation. *Child Development, 67,* 915–927.

Pederson, D. R., Moran, G., & Bento, S. (1999). *Maternal Behaviour Q-sort-Version 3.1. Professional manual.* London, ON: University of Western Ontario.

Peng, S., Zhang, Y., Zhang, J., Wang, H., & Ren, B. (2011). Glutamate receptors and signal transduction in learning and memory. *Molecular biology reports, 38*(1), 453–460.

Pennebaker, J. W. (2004). Theories, therapies, and taxpayers: On the complexities of the expressive writing paradigm. *Clinical Psychology: Science and Practice, 11*(2), 138–142.

Pennebaker, J. W. (2003). The social, linguistic and health consequences of emotional disclosure. In J. Suls & K. A. Wallston (Eds.), *Social Psychological foundations of health and illness* (pp. 288–313). Malden, MA: Blackwell Publishing.

Pennebaker, J. W., Kiecolt-Glaser, J., & Glaser, R. (2004). Disclosure of traumas and immune function: Health implications for psychotherapy. In R. M. Kowalski & M. R. Leary (Eds.), *The interface of social and clinical psychology: Key readings* (pp. 301–312). New York, NY: Psychology Press.

Penner, L. A., Dovidio, J. F., Piliavin, J. A., & Schroeder, D. A. (2005). Prosocial behavior: Multilevel perspectives. *Annual Review of Psychology, 56,* 365–392.

Penrose, R., & Hameroff, S. (2011). Consciousness in the universe: Neuroscience, quantum space-time geometry and Orch OR Theory. *Journal of Cosmology, 14.* Retrieved from http://journalofcosmology.com/Contents14.html.

Peplau, L. A. (2003). Human sexuality: how do men and women differ? *Current Directions in Psychological Science, 12,* 37–41.

Perani, D., Paulesu, E., Galles, N. S., Dupoux, E., Dehaene, S., Bettinardi, V. Cappa, S. F., Fazio, F., & Mehler, J. (1998). The bilingual brain: Proficiency and age of acquisition of the second language. *Brain, 121,* 1841–1852.

Perdeci, Z., Gulsun, M., Celik, C., Erdem, M., Ozdemir, B., Ozdag, F., & Kilic, S. (2010). Aggression and the event-related potentials in antisocial personality disorder. *Klinik Psikofarmakoloji Bülteni/Bulletin of Clinical Psychopharmacology, 20*(4), 300–306.

Pereira, A. C., Huddleston, D. E., Brickman, A. M., Sosunov, A. A., Hen, R., McKhann, G. M., Sloan, R., Gage, F. H., Brown, T. R., & Small, S. A. (2007). An in vivo correlate of exercise-induced neurogenesis in the adult dentate gyrus. *Proceedings of the National Academy of Sciences of the United States of America, 104,* 5638–5643.

Peretz, I., Cummings, S., & Dubé, M. P. (2007). The genetics of congenital amusia (tone deafness): A family-aggregation study. *American Journal of Human Genetics, 81,* 582–588.

Pergadia, M., Madden, P., Lessov, C., Todorov, A., Bucholz, K., Martin, N., & Heath, A. (2006). Genetic and environmental influences on extreme personality dispositions in adolescent female twins. *Journal of Child Psychology and Psychiatry, 47,* 902–915.

Perluigi, M., Di Domenico, F., Giorgi, A., Schinina, M. E., Coccia, R., Cini, C., & Calabrese, V. (2010). Redox proteomics in aging rat brain: Involvement of mitochondrial reduced glutathione status and mitochondrial protein oxidation in the aging process. *Journal of Neuroscience Research, 88*(16), 3498–3507.

Pernollet, J. C., Sanz, G., & Briand, L. (2006). Olfactory receptors and odour coding. *Comptes Rendus Biologies, 329,* 679–670.

Perry, C. J., & Bond, M. (2012). Change in defense mechanisms during long-term dynamic psychotherapy and five-year outcome. *The American Journal of Psychiatry, 169*(9), 916–925.

Perugi, G., Medda, P., Zanello, S., Toni, C., & Cassano, G. B. (2012). Episode length and mixed features as predictors of ECT nonresponse in patients with medication-resistant major depression. *Brain Stimulation, 5*(1), 18–24.

Pervin, L. A., Cervone, D., & John, O. P. (2005). *Personality: Theory and Research* (9th Ed.). New York, NY: John Wiley & Sons, Inc.

Peterlin, B. L., Rosso, A. L., Sheftell, F. D., Libon, D. J., Mossey, J. M., & Merikangas, K. R. (2011). Post-traumatic stress disorder, drug abuse and migraine: New findings from the national comorbidity survey replication (NCS-R). *Cephalalgia, 31*(2), 235–244.

Peterson, C. (2006). *A Primer in Positive Psychology.* New York, NY: Oxford University Press.

Peterson, C., Grant, V., & Boland, L. D. (2005). Childhood amnesia in children and adolescents: Their earliest memories. *Memory, 13*(6), 622–637.

Peterson, C., & Park, N. (2010). What happened to self-actualization? Commentary on Kenrick et al. *Perspectives on Psychological Science, 5,* 320–322.

Peterson, C., Ruch, W., Beermann, U., Park, N., & Seligman, M. E. P. (2007). Strengths of character, orientations to happiness, and life satisfaction. *Journal of Positive Psychology, 2*(3), 149–156.

Peterson, C., & Steen, T. A. (2009). Optimistic explanatory style. *Oxford handbook of positive psychology* (2nd Ed.) (pp. 313–321). New York, NY: Oxford University Press.

Peterson, C., & Steen, T. A. (2002). Optimistic explanatory style. *Handbook of positive psychology* (pp. 244–256). New York, NY: Oxford University Press.

Peterson, C., Warren, K. L., & Short, M. M. (2011). Infantile amnesia across the years: A 2-year follow-up of children's earliest memories. *Child Development, 82,* 1092–1105.

Petrescu, N. (2008). Loud music listening. *McGill Journal of Medicine, 11,* 169–176.

Petrie, K., Conaglen, J. V., Thompson, L., & Chamberlain, K. (1989). Effect of melatonin on jet lag after long haul flights. *British Medical Journal, 298,* 705–707.

Petrocelli, J. V., Clarkson, J. J., Tormala, Z. L., Hendrix, K. S. (2010). Perceiving stability as a means to attitude certainty: The role of implicit theories of attitudes. *Journal of Experimental Social Psychology, 46,* 874–883.

Petrovich, G. D., Setlow, B., Holland, P. C., & Gallagher, M. (2002). Amygdalo-hypothalamic circuit allows learned cues to override satiety and promote eating. *Journal of Comparative Physiology, 22*(19), 8748–8753.

Pettersen, G., Rosenvinge, J. H., & Ytterhus, B. (2008). The "double life" of bulimia: patients' experiences in daily life interactions. *Eating Disorders, 16*(3), 204–211.

Petty, R. E., & Cacioppo, J. T. (1986). *Communication and persuasion: central and peripheral routes to attitude change.* New York, NY: Springer-Verlag.

Petty, R. E., Fazio, R. H., & Briñol, P. (2009). The new implicit measures: An overview. In R. E. Petty, R. H. Fazio, & P. Briñol (Eds.), *Attitudes: Insights from the new implicit measures* (pp. 3–18). New York, NY: Psychology Press.

Petty, R. E., Wheeler, S. C., & Tormala, Z. L. (2003). Persuasion and attitude change. In T. Millon & M. J. Lerner (Eds.), *Handbook of psychology: Personality and social psychology, Vol. 5* (pp. 353–382). Hoboken, NJ: John Wiley & Sons Inc.

Phelps, M. E. (2006). *PET: physics, instrumentation, and scanners*. Springer.

Phillips, J. L. (1975). *The origins of intellect: Piaget's theory*. London, England: W. H. Freeman and Company.

Phillips, M. L., & Sierra, M. (2003). Depersonalization disorder: A functional neuroanatomical perspective. *Stress, 6*(3), 157–165.

Piaget, J. (2003). PART I: Cognitive development in children: Piaget: Development and learning. *Journal of Research in Science Teaching, 40*, S8–S18.

Piaget, J. (2000). *Studies in reflecting abstraction*. (R. L. Campbell, Trans). Hove: Psychology Press.

Piaget, J. (1985). *The equilibration of cognitive structures: The central problem of intellectual development* (T. Brown & K. Thampy, Trans). Chicago, IL: University of Chicago Press.

Piaget, J. (1981). *Intelligence and Affectivity*. New York, NY: Basic Books.

Piaget, J. (1972). *Essay on operative logic. (2nd Ed.)*. Dunod: 75661 Paris Cedex 14.

Piaget, J. (1965). *The moral judgment of the child*. New York, NY: Free Press.

Piaget, J., le Cozannet, R., & Samson, D. (2009). La causalité chez l'enfant (children's understanding of causality). *British Journal of Psychology, 100*, 207–224.

Pickens, R., Svikis, D., McGue, M., Lykken, D., Heston, L., & Clayton, P. (1991). Heterogeneity in the inheritance of alcoholism. *Archives of General Psychiatry, 48*, 19–28.

Pickering, G. J., Jain, A. K., & Bezawada, R. (2013). Super-tasting gastronomes? Taste phenotype characterization of foodies and wine experts. *Food Quality and Preference, 28*(1), 85–91.

Pickren, W., & Rutherford, A. (2010). *A History of Modern Psychology in Context*. Toronto, ON: University of Toronto Press.

Pierce, G. R., Sarason, I. G., & Sarason, B. R. (1996). Coping and social support. In M. Zeidner & N. S. Endler (Eds.), *Handbook of coping, theory, research, applications* (pp. 434–451). New York, NY: John Wiley & Sons, Inc.

Pierpaoli, W. (Ed.). (2005). *Reversal of aging: Resetting the pineal clock*. New York, NY: New York Academy of Sciences.

Pierre, J. M. (2010). Hallucinations in nonpsychotic disorders: Toward a differential diagnosis of "hearing voices." *Harvard Review of Psychiatry, 18*(1), 22–35.

Piferi, R. L., Jobe, R. L., & Jones, W. H. (2006). Giving to others during national tragedy: The effects of altruistic and egoistic motivations on long-term giving. *Journal of Social and Personal Relationships, 23*, 171–184.

Pinel, J. P. J. (2009). *Biopsychology*, 7th Edition. Boston, MA: Allyn & Bacon.

Pinel, J. P. J., Assanand, S., & Leman, D. R. (2000). Hunger, eating, and ill health. *American Psychologist, 55*, 1105–1116.

Pineschi, G., & Di Pietro, A. (2013). Anxiety management through psychophysiological techniques: Relaxation and psyching-up in sport. *Journal of Sport Psychology in Action, 4*(3) 181–190.

Pinker, S., & Jackendoff, R. (2005). The faculty of language: What's special about it? *Cognition, 95*, 201–236.

Pinkerman, J. E., Haynes, J. P., & Keiser, T. (1993). Characteristics of psychological practice in juvenile court clinics. *American Journal of Forensic Psychology, 11*, 3–12.

Piskulic, D., Olver, J. S., Norman, T. R., & Maruff, P. (2007). Behavioural studies of spatial working memory dysfunction in schizophrenia: A quantitative literature review. *Psychiatry Research, 150*, 111–121.

Plaford, G. R. (2013). *Fight or flight: The ultimate book for understanding and managing stress*. Gary Plaford: Xlibris LLC.

Platania, J., & Moran, G. P. (2001). Social facilitation as a function of mere presence of others. *Journal of Social Psychology, 141*(2), 190–197.

Pliner, P., Bell, R., Hirsch, E. S., & Kinchla, M. (2006). Meal duration mediates the effect of "social facilitation" on eating in humans. *Appetite, 46*(2), 189–198.

Pliszka, S. R. (2003). *Neuroscience for the mental health professional*. New York, NY: The Guilford Press.

Plomin, R., & Caspi, A. (1999). Behavioral genetics and personality. In L. A. Pervin & O. P. John (Eds.), *Handbook of personality: Theory and research*. New York, NY: Guilford Press.

Plomin, R., & Spinath, F. M. (2004). Intelligence: Genetics, genes, and genomics. *Journal of Personality and Social Psychology, 86*(1), 112–129.

Plucker, J. A. (Ed.). (2003). *Human intelligence: Historical influences, current controversies, teaching resources*. Retrieved from http://www.indiana.edu/~intell.

Plutchik, R. (1980). *Emotion: A psychoevolutionary synthesis*. New York, NY: Harper & Row.

Pobric, G., Mashal, N., Faust, M., and Lavidor, M. (2008). The role of the right cerebral hemisphere in processing novel metaphoric expressions: A transcranial magnetic stimulation study. *Journal of Cognitive Neuroscience, 20*(1), 170–181.

Poirier, P., Giles, T. D., Bray, G. A., Hong, Y., & Stern, J. S. (2006). Obesity and cardiovascular disease: Pathophysiology, evaluation, and effect of weight loss: An update of the 1997 American Heart Association Scientific Statement on Obesity and Heart Disease from the Obesity Committee of the Council on Nutrition, Physical Activity, and Metabolism. *Circulation, 113*, 898–918.

Pollak, S. D., Nelson, C. A., Schlaak, M. F., Roeber, B. J., Wewerka, S. S., Wiik, K. L., & Gunnar, M. R. (2010). Neurodevelopmental effects of early deprivation in postinstitutionalized children. *Child Development, 81*(1), 224–236.

Ponti, G., Peretto, P., Bonfanti, L., & Reh, T. A. (2008). Genesis of neuronal and glial progenitors in the cerebellar cortex of peripuberal and adult rabbits. *PLoS ONE, 3*(6), e2366.

Pontoski, K. E., & Heimberg, R. G. (2010). The myth of the superiority of concurrent combined treatments for anxiety disorders. *Clinical Psychology: Science and Practice, 17*(2), 107–111.

Pontoski, K. E., Heimberg, R. G., Turk, C. L., & Coles, M. E. (2010). Psychotherapy for social anxiety disorder. In D. J. Stein, E. Hollander, & B. O. Rothbaum (Eds.), *Textbook of anxiety disorders* (2nd Ed.) (pp. 501–521). Arlington, VA: American Psychiatric Publishing, Inc.

Pope, H. G., Jr., Poliakoff, M. B., Parker, M. P., Boynes, M., & Hudson, J. I. (2007). Is dissociative amnesia a culture-bound syndrome? findings from a survey of historical literature. *Psychological Medicine: A Journal of Research in Psychiatry and the Allied Sciences, 37*(2), 225–233.

Pope, K., & Wedding, D. (2011). Contemporary challenges and controversies. In R. J. Corsini & D. Wedding (Eds.), *Current psychotherapies* (9th Ed.). Florence, KY: CENGAGE Learning.

Popenoe, D. (1993). American family decline 1960–1990: A review and appraisal. *Journal of Marriage and the Family, 55*, 527–544.

Popper, K. (1963). *Conjectures and refutations: The growth of scientific knowledge*. London, England: Routledge & Kegan Paul.

Popper, K. R. (1959). *The logic of scientific discovery*. Oxford: Basic Books.

Porath, A., & Fried, P. A. (2005). Effects of prenatal cigarette and marijuana exposure on drug use among offspring. *Neurotoxicology and Teratology, 27*, 267–277.

Poropat, A. E. (2009). A meta-analysis of the five-factor model of personality and academic performance. *Psychological Bulletin, 135*(2), 322–338.

Porsolt, R. D. (2000). Animal models of depression: utility for transgenic research. *Reviews in the Neurosciences, 11*, 53–58.

Porter, R., & Winberg, J. (1999). Unique salience of maternal breast odors for newborn infants. *Neuroscience & Biobehavioral Reviews, 23*(3), 439–449.

Portnoy, D. (2008). Relatedness: Where existential and psychoanalytic approaches converge. In K. J. Schneider (Ed.), *Existential-integrative psychotherapy: Guideposts to the core of practice* (pp. 268–281). New York, NY: Routledge/Taylor & Francis Group.

Posmontier, B. (2010). The role of midwives in facilitating recovery in postpartum psychosis. *Journal of Midwifery & Women's Health, 55*(5), 430–437.

Posner, M. I., Petersen, S. F., Fox, P. T., & Raichle, M. E. (2009). Localization of cognitive operations in the human brain (1988). In D. J. Levitin (Ed.), *Foundations of psychological thought: A history of psychology* (pp. 279–294). Thousand Oaks, CA: Sage Publications.

Posner, M. I., Petersen, S. E., Fox, P. T., & Raichle, M. E. (2002). Localization of cognitive operations in the human brain. In D. J. Levitin (Ed.), *Foundations of cognitive psychology: Core readings* (pp. 819–830). Cambridge, MA: MIT Press.

Possehl, G. (2003). *The Indus civilization: A contemporary perspective*. AltaMira Press.

Post, R. M., Altshuler, L. L., Frye, M. A., Suppes, T., Keck Jr, P. E., McElroy, S. L.,... & Nolen, W. A. (2010). Complexity of pharmacologic treatment required for sustained improvement in outpatients with bipolar disorder. *The Journal of Clinical Psychiatry, 71*(9), 1176–86.

Post, R. M., & Miklowitz, D. J. (2010). The role of stress in the onset, course, and progression of bipolar illness and its comorbidities: Implications for therapeutics. In D. J. Miklowitz & D. Cicchetti (Eds.), *Understanding bipolar disorder: A developmental psychopathology perspective* (pp. 370–413). New York, NY: Guilford Press.

Post, S. G. (2005). Altruism, happiness, and health: It's good to be good. *International Journal of Behavioral Medicine, 12*(2), 66–77.

Postle, B. R. (2003). Context in verbal short-term memory. *Memory & Cognition, 31*(8), 1198–1207.

Power, A. E. (2004). Slow-wave sleep, acetylcholine, and memory consolidation. *Proceedings of the National Academy of Sciences of the United States of America, 101*(7), 1795–1796.

Powis, T. (1990). Paying for the past: A brainwashing victim seeks compensation. *Macleans*, March 19.

Prescott, C., Johnson, R. C., & McArdle, J. (1991). Genetic contributions to television viewing. *Psychological Science, 2*, 430–431.

Prescott, S. A., Ma, Q., & De Koninck, Y. (2014). Normal and abnormal coding of painful sensations. *Nature Neuroscience, 17*(2), 183.

Present, J., Crits-Christoph, P., Gibbons, M. B. C., Hearon, B., Ring-Kurtz, S., Worley, M., et al. (2008). Sudden gains in the treatment of generalized anxiety disorder. *Journal of Clinical Psychology, 64*(1), 119–126.

Pretz, J. E., Naples, A. J., & Sternberg, R. J. (2003). Recognizing, defining, and representing problems. In J. E. Davidson & R. J. Sternberg (Eds.), *The Psychology of Problem Solving*. Cambridge, UK: Cambridge University Press.

Price, G. R., Holloway, I., Räsänen, P., Vesterinen, M., & Ansari, D. (2007). Impaired parietal magnitude processing in developmental dyscalculia. *Current Biology, 17*, R1042–R1043.

Price, J. & Davis, B. (2008). *The woman who can't forget: The extraordinary story of living with the most remarkable memory known to science—A memoir.* New York, NY: Free Press.

Price, R. A., & Gottesman, I. I. (1991). Body fat in identical twins reared apart: Roles for genes and environment. *Behavior Genetics, 21*(1), 22903–22903.

Prinstein, M. J., & Dodge K. A. (Eds.) (2008). *Understanding peer influence in children and adolescents.* New York, NY: Guilford Press.

Prislin, R., & Crano, W. D. (2012). A history of social influence research. In A. W. Kruglanski & W. Stroebe (Eds.), *Handbook of the history of social psychology* (pp. 321–340). New York, NY: Psychology Press.

Prislin, R., & Wood, W. (2005). Social influence in attitudes and attitude change. In D. Albarracín, B. T. Johnson, & M. P. Zanna (Eds.), *The Handbook of Attitudes* (pp. 671–705). Mahwah, NJ: Lawrence Erlbaum Associates Publishers.

Probst, M., Goris, M., Vandereycken, W., Pieters, G., Vanderlinden, J., Van Coppenolle, H., et al. (2004). Body composition in bulimia nervosa patients compared to healthy females. *European Journal of Nutrition, 43*(5), 288–296.

Prochaska, J. O., & Norcross, J. C. (2010). *Systems of psychotherapy: A transtheoretical analysis* (7th Ed.). Pacific Grove, CA: Brooks/Cole.

Prochaska, J. O., & Norcross, J. C. (2007). *Systems of psychotherapy: A transtheoretical analysis* (6th Ed.). Pacific Grove, CA: Brooks/Cole.

Profit, W. E., Mino, I., & Pierce, C. M. (2000). Stress in blacks. In G. Fink (Ed.), *Encyclopedia of stress, Vol. 1* (pp. 324–330). New York, NY: Academic Press.

Prot, S., Gentile, D. A., Anderson, C. A., Suzuki, K., Swing, E., Lim, K. M., . . . & Lam, B. C. P. (2014). Long-Term Relations Among Prosocial-Media Use, Empathy, and Prosocial Behavior. *Psychological Science, 25*(2), 358–368.

Public Health Agency of Canada. (2011). *Aboriginal Head Start in urban and northern communities (AHSUNC:) AHSUNC program celebrates 15 years of success!* Retrieved from http://www.phac-aspc.gc.ca/hp-ps/dca-dea/progini/ahsunc-papacun/index-eng.php.

Public Health Agency of Canada. (2008). *Publicly funded immunization programs in Canada—Routine schedule for infants and children (including special programs and catch-up programs).* Retrieved from www.phac-aspc.gc.ca/im/ptimprog-progimpt/table-1-eng.php.

Public Health Agency of Canada. (2007). *Population Health Fund Project: Father involvement for healthy child outcomes: partners supporting knowledge development and transfer.* Retrieved from www.phac-aspc.gc.ca/.

Pugno, M. (2007). The subjective well-being paradox: A suggested solution based on relational goods. In P. L. Porta & L. Bruni (Eds.), *Handbook on the economics of happiness.* Northampton: MA: Edward Elgar Publishing.

Puhl, R. M., & Heuer, C. A. (2010). Obesity stigma: Important consideration for public health. *American Journal of Public Health, 100*(6), 1019–1028.

Puhl, R. M., Moss-Racusin, C. A., Schwartz, M. B., & Brownell, K. D. (2008). Weight stigmatization and bias reduction: perspectives of overweight and obese adults. *Health education research, 23*(2), 347–358.

Puka, B. (2004). Altruism and character. In D. K. Lapsley & D. Narvaez (Eds.), *Moral development, self, and identity* (pp. 161–187). Mahwah, NJ: Lawrence Erlbaum Associates Publishers.

Pull, C. B. (2014). Personality disorders in Diagnostic and Statistical Manual of Mental Disorders-5: Back to the past or back to the future? *Current Opinion in Psychiatry, 27*(1), 84–86.

Pungello, E. P., Kainz, K., Burchinal, M., Wasik, B. H., Sparling, J. J., Ramey, C. T., & Campbell, F. A. (2010). Early educational intervention, early cumulative risk, and the early home environment as predictors of young adult outcomes within a high-risk sample. *Child Development, 81*(1), 410–426.

Purcell, S. M., Moran, J. L., Fromer, M., Ruderfer, D., Solovieff, N., Roussos, P., ... Sklar, P. (2014). A polygenic burden of rare disruptive mutations in schizophrenia. *Nature, 506*, 185–190.

Purzycki, B.G. (2010). Cognitive architecture, humor and counterintuitiveness: Retention and recall of MCIs. *Journal of Cognition and Culture, 10*, 189–204.

Quinnell, T. G., Farooqi, I. S., Smith, I. E., & Schneerson, J. M. (2007). Screening the human prepro-orexin gene in a single-centre narcolepsy cohort. *Sleep Medicine, 8*(5), 498–502.

Quirk, G. J. (2006). Extinction: New excitement for an old phenomenon. *Biological Psychiatry, 60*, 317–318.

Quirk, G. J., Garcia, R., & González-Lima, F. (2006). Prefrontal mechanisms in extinction of conditioned fear. *Biological Psychiatry, 60*, 337–343.

Raaijmakers, J. G. W., & Shiffrin, R. M. (2002). Models of memory. In H. Pashler & D. Medin (Eds.), *Stevens handbook of experimental psychology* (3rd Ed.), *vol. 2: Memory and cognitive processes* (pp. 43–76). Hoboken, NJ: John Wiley & Sons, Inc.

Raaijmakers, J. G., & Shiffrin, R. M. (1992). Models for recall and recognition. *Annual Review of Psychology, 43*, 205–234.

Rafii, M. S., & Aisen, P. S. (2009). Recent developments in Alzheimer's disease therapeutics. *BMC Medicine, 7*, 7.

Rahman, Q. (2005). The neurodevelopment of human sexual orientation. *Neuroscience and Biobehavioral Reviews, 29*(7), 1057–1066.

Raichle, M. E. (2005). Imaging the human brain: Reflections on some emerging issues. In U. Mayr, E. Awh, & S. W. Keele (Eds.), *Developing individuality in the human brain: A tribute to Michael I. Posner* (pp. 109–123). Washington, DC: American Psychological Association.

Raid, G. H., & Tippin, S. M. (2009). Assessment of intellectual strengths and weaknesses with the Stanford-Binet Intelligence Scales—Fifth edition (SB5). In J. A. Naglieri & S. Goldstein, *Practitioner's guide to assessing intelligence and achievement* (pp. 127–152). Hoboken, NJ: John Wiley & Sons.

Raikes, H. A., Robinson, J. L., Bradley, R. H., Raikes, H. H., & Ayoub, C. C. (2007). Developmental trends in self-regulation among low-income toddlers. *Social Development, 16*, 128–149.

Rainville, P., Duncan, G. H., Price, D. D., Carrier, B., & Bushnell, M. C. (1997). Pain affect encoded in human anterior cingulate but not somatosensory cortex. *Science, 277*(5328), 968–971.

Rainville, P., Hofbauer, R. K., Bushnell, M. C., Duncan, G. H., & Price, D. D. (2002). Hypnosis modulates activity in brain structures involved in the regulation of consciousness. *Journal of Cognitive Neuroscience, 14*(6), 887–901.

Rakic, P. (2002). Adult neurogenesis in mammals: an identity crisis. *The Journal of Neuroscience, 22*(3), 614–618.

Ramachandran, V. S. (2005). Plasticity and functional recovery in neurology. *Clinical Medicine, 5*, 368–373.

Ramachandran, V. S., & Hubbard, E. M. (2001). Synaesthesia: A window into perception, thought and language. *Journal of Consciousness Studies, 8*(12), 3–34.

Ramachandran, V. S., & Rogers-Ramachandran, D. (1996). Synaesthesia in phantom limbs induced with mirrors. *Proceedings of the Royal Society of Biological Sciences, 263*(1369), 377–386.

Ramadan, N. M. (2000). Migraine. In G. Fink (Ed.), *Encyclopedia of stress* (pp. 757–770). San Diego, CA: Academic Press.

Ramage-Morin, P. L. (2004). *Panic disorder and coping, supplement to Health Reports, Volume 15.* Statistics Canada, Catalogue 82–003. Retrieved from http://www.statcan.gc.ca/pub/82-003-s/2004000/pdf/7445-eng.pdf.

Ramey, C. T., & Ramey, S. L. (2007). Early learning and school readiness: Can early intervention make a difference? In G. W. Ladd (Ed.), *Appraising the human developmental sciences: Essays in honor of Merrill-Palmer quarterly* (pp. 329–350). Detroit, MI: Wayne State University Press.

Ramponi, C., Richardson-Klavehn, A., & Gardiner, J. M. (2007). Component processes of conceptual priming and associative cued recall: The roles of preexisting representation and depth of processing. *Journal of Experimental Psychology: Learning, Memory & Cognition, 33*, 843–862.

Rao, U., Hammen, C. L., & Poland, R. E. (2010). Longitudinal course of adolescent depression: Neuroendocrine and psychosocial predictors. *Journal of the American Academy of Child & Adolescent Psychiatry, 49*(2), 141–151.

Rapee, R. M., & Bryant, R. A. (2009). Stress and psychosocial factors in onset of fear circuitry disorders. *Stress-induced and fear circuitry disorders: Advancing the research agenda for DSM-V* (pp. 195–214). Arlington, VA: American Psychiatric Publishing, Inc.

Rasch, B., & Born, J. (2013). About sleep's role in memory. *Physiological Review, 93*, 681–766.

Rash, J. A., & Prkachin, K. M. (2013). Cardiac vagal reactivity during relived sadness is predicted by affect intensity and emotional intelligence. *Biological Psychology, 92*, 106–113.

Raskin, K., de Gendt, K., Duittoz, A., Liere, P., Verhoeven, G., Tronche, F., et al. (2009). Conditional inactivation of androgen receptor gene in the nervous system: Effects on male behavioral and neuroendocrine responses. *The Journal of Neuroscience: The Official Journal of the Society for Neuroscience, 29*(14), 4461–4470.

Raskin, N. J., Rogers, C., & Witty, M. (2011). Person-centered therapy. In R. J. Corsini & D. Wedding (Eds.), *Current psychotherapies* (9th Ed.). Florence, KY: CENGAGE Learning.

Ratey, J. J. (2001). *A user's guide to the brain: Perception, attention, and the four theaters of the brain.* New York, NY: Random House.

Ratey, J. J., & Loehr, J. E. (2011). The positive impact of physical activity on cognition during adulthood: A review of underlying mechanisms, evidence and recommendations. *Reviews in the Neurosciences, 22*(2), 171–185.

Rathjen, H., & Charles, M. (1999). *From the Montreal Massacre to gun control.* Toronto, ON: McClelland & Stewart.

Rau, V., & Fanselow, M. S. (2009). Exposure to a stressor produces a long lasting enhancement of fear learning in rats. *Stress, 12*(2), 125–133.

Rauchs, G., Desgranges, B., Foret, J., & Eustache, F. (2005). The relationships between memory systems and sleep stages. *Journal of Sleep Research, 14*, 123–140.

Ravindran, L. N., & Stein, M. B. (2011). Pharmacotherapy for social anxiety disorder in adolescents and young adults. In C. A. Alfano & D. C. Beidel

(Eds.), *Social anxiety in adolescents and young adults: Translating developmental science into practice* (pp. 265–279). Washington, DC: American Psychological Association.

Rawson, R. A., & Ling, W. (2008). Clinical management: Methamphetamine. In H. D. Kleber & M. Galanter (Eds.), *The American Psychiatric Publishing textbook of substance abuse treatment (4th Ed.)*. Washington, DC: American Psychiatric Publishing.

Raznahan, A., Shaw, P. W., Lerch, J. P., Clasen, L. S., Greenstein, D., Berman, R., Pipitone, J., Chakravarty, M. M., & Giedd, J. N. (2013). Longitudinal four-dimensional mapping of subcortical anatomy in human development. *Proceedings of the National Academy of Sciences of the United States of America, 111*(4), 1592–1597.

Read, J. (2010). Can poverty drive you mad? Schizophrenia, socio-economic status and the case for primary prevention. *New Zealand Journal of Psychology, 39*(2), 7–19.

Read, J. P., Beattie, M., Chamberlain, R., & Merrill, J. E. (2008). Beyond the "binge" threshold: Heavy drinking patterns and their association with alcohol involvement indices in college students. *Addictive Behaviors, 33*(2), 225–234.

Read, K., & Purse, M. (2007, March 22). Postpartum psychosis: Linked to bipolar disorder. *About.com.* Retrieved from http://bipolar.about.com/od/relateddisorders/a/postpartumpsych.htm.

Reardon, S. F. (2013). The widening income achievement gap. *Educational Leadership, 70*(8), 10–16.

Reas, E. T. (2014). *BOLD signals of episodic memory retrieval in the hippocampus and neocortex.* San Diego, CA: University of California.

Recanzone, G. H., & Sutter, M. L. (2008). The biological basis of audition. *Annual Review of Psychology, 59*, 119–142.

Redmond, L. C., Kahan, S., & Cheskin, L. J. (2014). Commercial weight loss programs. In G. E. Mullin, L. J. Cheskin, & L. E. Matarese (Eds.), *Integrative weight management nutrition and health* (pp. 293–301). London, UK: Springer.

Reddy, L., & Kanwisher, N. (2006). Coding of visual objects in the ventral stream. *Current Opinion in Neurobiology, 16*, 408–414.

Redelmeier, D. A., Katz, J., & Kahneman, D. (2003). Memories of colonoscopy: A randomized trial. *Pain, 104*, 187–194.

Reed, R. R. Jr.(1952). *Bedlam on the Jacobean Stage.* Cambridge, MA: Harvard University Press.

Reed, T. E., & Jensen, A. R. (1992). Conduction velocity in a brain nerve pathway of normal adults correlates with intelligence level. *Intelligence, 16*(3–4), 259–272.

Reeve, J. M. (2015). *Understanding motivation and emotion* (6th Edition). New York, NY: Wiley.

Regehr, C., Cadell, S., & Jansen, K. (1999). Perceptions of control and long-term recovery from rape. *American. Journal of Orthopsychiatry, 69*(1), 110–115.

Reggia, J. A. (2013). The rise of machine consciousness: Studying consciousness with computational models. *Neural Networks, 44*, 112–131.

Reid, J. A., & Sullivan, C. J. (2009). A latent class typology of juvenile victims and exploration of risk factors and outcomes of victimization. *Criminal Justice and Behavior, 36*(10), 1001–1024.

Regier, D. A., Kuhl, E. A., & Kupfer, D. J. (2013). The DSM-5: Classification and criteria changes. *World Psychiatry, 12*(2), 92–98.

Reinecke, A., Cooper, M., Favaron, E., Massey-Chase, R., & Harmer, C. (2011). Attentional bias in untreated panic disorder. *Psychiatry Research, 185*(3), 387–393.

Reis, H. T., & Holmes, J. G. (2012). Perspectives on the Situation. In K. Deaux & M. Snyder (Eds.), *The Oxford handbook of personality and social psychology*. New York, NY: Oxford University Press.

Reissig, C. J., Strain, E. C., & Griffiths, R. R. (2009). Caffeinated energy drinks—A growing problem. *Drug and Alcohol Dependence, 99*(1–3), 1–10.

Rejeski, W. J., Gregg, E., Thompson, A., & Berry, M. (1991). The effects of varying doses of acute aerobic exercise on psychophysiological stress responses in highly trained cyclists. *Journal of Sport & Exercise Psychology, 13*(2), 188–199.

Rejeski, W. J., & Thompson, A. (2007). Historical and conceptual roots of exercise psychology. *Essential readings in sport and exercise psychology* (pp. 332–347). Champaign, IL: Human Kinetics.

Rejeski, W. J., Thompson, A., Brubaker, P. H., & Miller, H. S. (1992). Acute exercise: Buffering psychosocial stress responses in women. *Health Psychology, 11*(6), 355–362.

Rekers, G. A. (1992). Development of problems of puberty and sex roles in adolescence. In C. E. Walker & M. C. Roberts (Eds.), *Handbook of clinical child psychology, Second Edition*. Oxford, England: John Wiley & Sons, Inc.

Remler, D. K., & Van Ryzin, G. G. (2011). *Research methods in practice: Strategies for description and causation.* Thousand Oaks, CA: Sage Publications.

Renner, M. J., & Mackin, R. S. (2002). A life stress instrument for classroom use. *Handbook for teaching introductory psychology: Vol. 3: With an emphasis on assessment* (pp. 236–238). Mahwah, NJ: Lawrence Erlbaum Associates Publishers.

Renzaho, A. M. N., Houng, B., Oldroyd, J., Nicholson, J. M., D'Esposito, F., & Oldenburg, B. (2013). Stressful life events and the onset of chronic diseases among Australian adults: findings from a longitudinal survey. *European Journal of Public Health*, Advance Access, published February 8, 2013, 1–6.

Resnick, R. A. (2000). The Dynamic Representation of Scenes. *Visual Cognition, 7*, 17–42.

Resnick, R. A., O'Regan, J. K., & Clark, J. J. (1997). To see or not to see: The need for attention to perceive changes in scenes. *Psychological Science, 8*, 368–373.

Revonsuo, A. (2010). *Consciousness: The science of subjectivity.* New York, NY: Psychology Press.

Reynolds, C. R., Chastain, R. L., Kaufman, A. S., & McLean, J. E. (1987). Demographic characteristics and IQ among adults: Analysis of the WAISR standardization sample as a function of the stratification variables. *Journal of School Psychology, 25*(4), 323–342.

Reznick, J. S., & Goldfield, B. A. (1992). Rapid change in lexical development in comprehension and production. *Developmental Psychology, 28*, 406–413.

Rheingold, H. (2000). *They have a word for it: A lighthearted lexicon of untranslatable words & phrases.* Louisville, KY: Sarabande Books, Inc.

Rial, R. V., Akaârir, M., Gamundí, A., Nicolau, C., Garau, C., Aparicio, S., . . . Esteban, S. (2010). Evolution of wakefulness, sleep and hibernation: From reptiles to mammals. *Neuroscience and Biobehavioral Reviews, 34*(8), 1144–1160.

Rice, V. (2012). *Handbook of stress, coping, and health: Implications for nursing research.* Thousand Oaks, CA: Sage.

Richard, I. H., & Lyness, J. M. (2006). An overview of depression. In D. V. Jeste & J. H. Friedman (Eds.), *Psychiatry for neurologists* (pp. 33–42). Totowa, NJ: Humana Press.

Richards, G. (2004). *"It's an American thing": The "race" and intelligence controversy from a British perspective. Defining difference: Race and racism in the history of psychology* (pp. 137–169). Washington, DC: American Psychological Association.

Richardson, A. (2011). Memory and imagination in romantic fiction. In S. Nalbantian, P. M. Matthews, & J. L. McClelland (Eds.), *The memory process: Neuroscientific and humanistic perspectives* (pp. 277–296). Cambridge, MA: MIT Press.

Richardson, R. D. (2006). *William James: In the maelstrom of American modernism.* Boston, MA: Houghton Mifflin Company.

Richter, E. A. (2013). *The relationship of college students' retrospective reports of perceived parenting style and current adult attachment style with primary caregiver, romantic partner and college adjustment.* Dissertation, College of Educational and Behavioural Sciences, University of Northern Colorado.

Riddihough, G., & Zahn, L. M. (2010). What is epigenetics? *Science, 330*(6004), 611.

Ridout, N., Astell, A. J., Reid, I. C., Glen, T., & O'Carroll, R. E. (2003). Memory bias for emotional facial expressions in major depression. *Cognition and Emotion, 17*(1), 101–122.

Ridout, T. N., & Searles, K. (2011). It's my campaign I'll cry if I want to: How and when campaigns use emotional appeals. *Political Psychology, 32*(3), 439–458.

Rieber, R. W. (2006). *The bifurcation of the self: The history and theory of dissociation and its disorders.* New York, NY: Springer Science + Business Media.

Rieber, R. W. (2002). The duality of the brain and the multiplicity of minds: Can you have it both ways? *History of Psychiatry 13*(49, pt1), 3–18.

Rieff, P. (1979). *Freud: The mind of the moralist.* University of Chicago Press.

Riestra, A. R., Aguilar, J., Zambito, G., Galindo y Villa, G., Barrios, F., Garcia, C., & Heilman, K. (2011). Unilateral right anterior capsulotomy for refractory major depression with comorbid obsessive-compulsive disorder. *Neurocase: The Neural Basis of Cognition, 17*(6), 491–500.

Rigaud, D., Trostler, N., Rozen, R., Vallot, T., & Apfelbaum, M. (1995). Gastric distension, hunger, and energy intake after balloon implantation in severe obesity. *International Journal of Obesity and Related Metabolic Disorders: Journal of the International Association for the Study of Obesity, 19*(7), 489–495.

Rimé, B. (2007). The social sharing of emotion as an interface between individual and collective processes in the construction of emotional climates. *Journal of Social Issues, 63*, 307–322.

Rimm, D. C., & Masters, J. C. (1979). *Behavior therapy: Techniques and empirical findings* (2nd Ed.). New York, NY: Academic Press.

Ripple, C. H., Gilliam, W. S., Chanana, N., & Zigler, E. (1999). Will fifty cooks spoil the broth? The debate over entrusting Head Start to the states. *American Psychologist, 54*(5), 327–343.

Ritter, M. R., Blackmore, M. A., & Heimberg, R. G. (2010). Generalized anxiety disorder. In D. McKay, J. S. Abramowitz, & S. Taylor (Eds.), *Cognitive-behavioral therapy for refractory cases: Turning failure into success* (pp. 111–137). Washington, DC: American Psychological Association.

Rizzolatti, G., & Craighero, L. (2004). The mirror-neuron system. *Annual Review of Neuroscience, 27*, 169–192.

Rizzolatti, G., & Sinigaglia, C. (2008). *Mirrors in the brain: How our minds share actions and emotions.* Oxford, UK: Oxford Univerity Press.

Rizzolatti, G., Fadiga, L., Fogassi, L., & Gallese, V. (2002). From mirror neurons to imitation: Facts and speculations. In A. N. Metzoff & W. Printz (Eds.), *The imitative mind: Development, evolution, and brain bases*. Cambridge: Cambridge University Press.

Roach, K. I. (2012). Introduction: An awareness of the alarming reality of wrongful convictions in both Canada and other criminal justice systems led the Supreme Court of Canada in 2001 to overturn prior jurisprudence that. Cincinnati, OH: University of Cincinnati Law Review.

Roberts, B. W., & DelVecchio, W. F. (2000). The rank-order consistency of personality from childhood to old age: A quantitative review of longitudinal studies. *Psychological Bulletin, 126*, 3–25.

Roberts, B. W., Helson, R., & Klohnen, E. C. (2002). Personality development and growth in women across 30 years: Three perspectives. *Journal of Personality, 70*, 79–102.

Roberts, B. W., Walton, K. E., & Viechtbauer, W. (2006). Patterns of mean-level change in personality traits across the life course: A meta-analysis of longitudinal studies. *Psychology Bulletin, 132*, 1–25.

Roberts, R. D., MacCann, C., Matthews, G., & Zeidner, M. (2010). Emotional intelligence: Toward a consensus of models and measures. *Social and Personality Psychology Compass, 4*(10), 821–840.

Roberts, S. C., Little, A. C., Gosling, L. M., Jones, B. C., Perrett, D. I., Carter V., & Petrie, M. (2005). MHC assortative facial preferences in humans. *Biology Letters, 1*, 400–403.

Robertson, R. (1995). *Jungian archetypes: Jung, Goedel, and the history of archetypes*. Main, MA: Nicolas Hays.

Robertz, F. J. (2007). Deadly dreams. *Scientific American Mind, 18*(4), 52–59.

Robinson, A. (2013). *Differential effects of stress on maternal and infant health amongst Canadian ethnic minorities*. Dissertation, Division of Applied Psychology, Faculty of Education, University of Calgary. Retrieved from http://theses.ucalgary.ca/bitstream/11023/1095/2/ucalgary_2013_Robinson_Alexandra.pdf.

Robinson, M. J., Robinson, T. E., & Berridge, K. C. (2014). Incentive salience in addiction and over-consumption. *The Interdisciplinary Science of Consumption, 185–197.*

Rodafinos, A., Vucevic, A., & Sideridis, G. (2005). The effectiveness of compliance techniques: Foot in the door versus door in the face. *The Journal of Social Psychology, 145*, 237–239.

Roddy, S., Stewart, I., & Barnes-Holmes, D. (2010). Anti-fat, pro-slim, or both? Using two reaction-time based measures to assess implicit attitudes to the slim and overweight. *Journal of Health Psychology, 15*(3), 416–425.

Rodin, J., & Langer, E. J. (1977). Long-term effects of a control-relevant intervention with the institutionalized aged. *Journal of Personality and Social Psychology, 35*(12), 897–902.

Roediger III, H. L., & Craik, F. (Eds.). (2014). *Varieties of memory and consciousness: Essays in honour of Endel Tulving*. New York, NY: Psychology Press.

Roeloffs, C., Sherbourne, C., Unützer, J., Fink, A., Tang, L., & Wells, K. B. (2003). Stigma and depression among primary care patients. *General Hospital Psychiatry, 25*(5), 311–315.

Rogers, C. R. (2008). The actualizing tendency in relation to 'motives' and to consciousness. In B. E. Levitt (Ed.,), *Reflections on human potential: Bridging the person-centered approach and positive psychology* (pp. 17–32). Ross-on-Wye: PCCS Books.

Rogers, C. R. (1995). *Client centered therapy*. Constance.

Rogers, C. R. (1980). *A way of being*. Houghton Mifflin.

Rogers, C. R. (1963). Actualizing tendency in relation to "motives" and to consciousness. In M. R. Jones (Ed.), *Nebraska symposium on motivation* (pp. 1–24). Lincoln, NE: University of Nebraska Press.

Rogers, P. (2005). Caffeine and health. *Psychologist, 18*(1), 9.

Rogoff, B. (1990). *Apprenticeship in thinking: cognitive development in social context*. Oxford, UK: Oxford University Press.

Rolls, B. J. (2014). What is the role of portion control in weight management? *International Journal of Obesity, 38*, 1–8.

Rolls, E. T. (2007). Sensory processing in the brain related to the control of food intake. *The Proceedings of the Nutrition Society, 66*(1), 96–112.

Roman, C., & Reilly, S. (2007). Effects of insular cortex lesions on conditioned taste aversion and latent inhibition in the rat. *The European Journal of Neuroscience, 26*(9), 2627–2632.

Roman, C., Lin, J., & Reilly, S. (2009). Conditioned taste aversion and latent inhibition following extensive taste preexposure in rats with insular cortex lesions. *Brain Research, 1259*, 68–73.

Romanelli, P., & Esposito, V. (2004). The functional anatomy of neuropathic pain. *Neurosurgery Clinics of North America, 15*(3), 257–268.

Romano, S. J., Halmi, K. A., Sarkar, N. P., Koke, S. C., & Lee, J. S. (2002). A placebo-controlled study of fluoxetine in continued treatment of bulimia nervosa after successful acute fluoxetine treatment. *American Journal of Psychiatry, 159*, 96–102.

Rook, K. S., August, K. J., & Sorkin, D. H. (2011). Social network functions and health. In R. J. Contrada & A. Baum (Eds.), *The handbook of stress science:*

Biology, psychology, and health (pp. 123–135). New York, NY: Springer Publishing Co.

Rosenbaum, R. S., Gilboa, A., & Moscovitch, M. (2014). Case studies continue to illuminate the cognitive neuroscience of memory. *Annals of the New York Academy of Sciences, 1316*(1), 105–133.

Rosenberg, A., Ledley, D. R., & Heimberg, R. G. (2010). Social anxiety disorder. In D. McKay, J. S. Abramowitz, & S. Taylor (Eds.), *Cognitive-behavioral therapy for refractory cases: Turning failure into success* (pp. 65–88). Washington, DC: American Psychological Association.

Rosenberg, M. J. (1969). The conditions and consequences of evaluation apprehension. In R. Rosenthal & R.S. Rosnow (Eds.), *Artifact in behavioral research*. New York, NY: Academic Press.

Rosenberg, O., Isserles, M., Levkovitz, Y., Kotler, M., Zangen, A., & Dannon, P. N. (2011). Effectiveness of a second deep TMS in depression: A brief report. *Progress in Neuro-Psychopharmacology & Biological Psychiatry, 35*(4), 1041–1044.

Rosenstein, D., & Oster, H. (1988). Differential facial responses to four basic tastes in newborns. *Child Development, 59*, 1555–1568.

Rosenthal, T. L., & Bandura, A. (1978). Psychological modeling: Theory and practice. In S. L. Garfield & A. E. Bergin (Eds.), *Handbook of psychotherapy and behavior change: An empirical analysis* (2nd Ed., pp. 621–658). New York, NY: Wiley.

Rosette, A. S., & Tost, L. P. (2010). Agentic women and communal leadership: How role prescriptions confer advantage to top women leaders. *Journal of Applied Psychology, 95*(2), 221–235.

Ross, C. A., & Ness, L. (2010). Symptom patterns in dissociative identity disorder patients and the general population. *Journal of Trauma & Dissociation, 11*(4), 458–468.

Ross, L. D. (2001). Getting down to fundamentals: Lay dispositionism and the attributions of psychologists. *Psychological Inquiry, 12*, 37–40.

Ross, L. D. (1977). The intuitive psychologist and his shortcomings: Distortions in the attribution process. In L. Berkowitz (Ed.), *Advances in experimental social psychology* (Vol. 10). New York, NY: Academic Press.

Rossi, A. M., Quick, J. C., & Perrewe, P. L. (Eds.) (2009). *Stress and quality of working life: The positive and the negative*. Charlotte, NC: Information Age Publishing.

Rossman, B. R., Hughes, H. M., & Rosenberg, M. S. (2013). *Children and Interparental Violence: The Impact of Exposure*. Oxford, UK: Routledge.

Rothbart, M. K., & Bates, J. E. (2006). Temperament. In N. Eisenberg (Ed.), *Handbook of child psychology: Vol. 3. Social, emotional, and personality development* (6th ed., pp. 99–166). Hoboken, NJ: Wiley.

Rothbart, M. K., Derryberry, D., & Hershey, K. (2000). Stability of temperament in childhood: Laboratory infant assessment to parent report at seven years. In V. J. Molfese & D. L. Molfese (Eds.), *Temperament and personality development across the lifespan*. Mahwah, NJ: Lawrence Erlbaum Associates.

Rothstein, M. G., & Goffin, R. D. (2006). The use of personality measures in personnel selection: What does current research support? *Human Resource Management Review, 16*, 155–180.

Roughgarden, J. (2004). *Evolutions rainbow: Diversity, gender, and sexuality in nature and people*. Berkeley, CA: University of California Press.

Rovee-Collier, C., Hayne, H., & Columbo, M. (2001). *The development of implicit and explicit memory*. Philadelphia, PA: John Benjamins Publishing Company.

Rovira, A., Swapp, D., Spanlang, B., & Slater, M. (2009). The use of virtual reality in the study of people's responses to violent incidents. *Frontiers of Behavioral Neuroscience, 3*, 59. Retrieved from http://www.ncbi.nlm.nih.gov/pmc/articles/PMC2802544/.

Rowe, D. C., Almeida, D. M., & Jacobson, K. C. (1999). School context and genetic influences on aggression in adolescence. *Psychological Science, 10*(3), 277–280.

Roy, M., & Christenfeld, N. (2004). Do dogs resemble their owners? *Psychological Science, 15*, 361–363.

Roy, M., Shohamy, D., & Wager, T. D. (2012). Ventromedial prefrontal-subcortical systems and the generation of affective meaning. *Trends in Cognitive Sciences, 16*(3), 147–156.

Roy-Byrne, P. P. (2005). The GABA-benzodiazepine receptor complex: Structure, function, and role in anxiety. *Journal of Clinical Psychiatry, 66*(Suppl. 2), 14–20.

Roysamb, E. (2006). Personality and well-being. *Handbook of personality and health* (pp. 115–134). New York, NY: John Wiley & Sons Ltd.

Rubenzer, S. J. (2008). The standardized field sobriety tests: a review of scientific and legal issues. *Law and Human Behavior, 32*(4), 293–313.

Rubin, K. H., Cheah, C., Menzer, M. M, (2010). Peers. In M.H. Bornstein (Ed.), *Handbook of cultural developmental science*. New York, NY: Psychology Press.

Rubin, Z. (1973). *Liking and Loving*. New York, NY: Holt, Rinehart & Winston.

Rubin, Z. (1970). Measurement of romantic love. *Journal of Personality and Social Psychology, 16*, 265–273.

Rubino, G. (2011). Couples without children vs. couples with children. *eHow: Relationships & Family.* Retrieved from http://www.ehow.com/info_7904316_couples-children-vs-couples-children.html.

Rudman, L. A., & Ashmore, R. D. (2007). Discrimination and the Implicit Association Test. *Group Processes and Intergroup Relations, 10,* 359–372.

Rudy, D., & Grusec, J. E., (2001). Correlates of authoritarian parenting in individualist and collectivist cultures and implications for understanding the transmission of values. *Journal of Cross-Cultural Psychology, 32,* 202–212.

Rugg, M. D., & Vilberg, K. L. (2013). Brain networks underlying episodic memory retrieval. *Current opinion in neurobiology, 23*(2), 255–260.

Runco, M. A. (2010). Divergent thinking, creativity, and ideation. In J. C. Kaufman & R. J. Sternberg (Eds.), *The Cambridge handbook of creativity* (pp. 413–446). New York, NY: Cambridge University Press.

Runco, M. A. (2004). Creativity. *Annual Review of Psychology, 55,* 657–687.

Runco, M. A., & Acar, S. (2012). Divergent thinking as an indicator of creative potential. *Creativity Rsearch Journal, 24*(1), 66–75.

Runco, T. A. (2014). *Creativity, theories and themes: Research, development, and practice.* San Diego, CA: Academic Press.

Rupke, S. J., Blecke, D., & Renfrow, M. (2006). Cognitive therapy for depression. *American Family Physician, 73,* 83–86.

Rushton, J. P. (2009). Brain size as an explanation of national differences in IQ, longevity, and other life-history variables. *Personality and Individual Differences.* No Pages.

Rutter, M., Kumsta, R., Schlotz, W., & Sonuga-Barke, E. (2012). Longitudinal studies using a "natural experiment" design: The case of adoptees from Romanian institutions. *Journal of the American Academy of Child & Adolescent Psychiatry, 51*(8), 762–770.

Rutter, M., Sonuga-Barke, E., & Castle, J. (2010). Investigating the impact of early institutional deprivation on development: Background and research strategy of the English and Romanian adoptees (ERA) study. *Monographs of the Society for Research in Child Development, 75*(1), 1–20.

Ruzek, J. I., Schnurr, P. P., Vasterling, J. J., & Friedman, M. J. (Eds.). (2011). *Caring for veterans with deployment-related stress disorders.* Washington, DC: American Psychological Association.

Ryan, R. M., & Deci, E. L. (2002). Overview of self-determination theory: An organismic-dialectical perspective. In E. L. Deci & R. M. Ryan (Eds.), *Handbook of Self-Determination Research* (pp. 3–33). Rochester, NY: University of Rochester Press.

Ryan-Wenger, N. A., Sharrer, V. W., & Campbell, K. K. (2005, July-August). Changes in children's stressors over the past 30 years. *Pediatric Nursing, 31*(4), 282–8, 291.

Rymer, R. (1994). *Genie: A scientific tragedy.* New York, NY: Harper Paperbacks.

Sabbagh, M. A., Bowman, L. C., Evraire, L. E., & Ito, J. M. (2009). Neurodevelopmental correlates of theory of mind in preschool children. *Child Development 80*(4), 1147–1162.

Sachs, J. (2009). Communication Development in Infancy. In J. B. Gleason (Ed.), *The Development of Language* (7th Ed., pp. 40–60). Columbus, OH: Allyn & Bacon.

Sack, R. L., Auckley, D., Auger, R. R., Carskadon, M. A., Wright Jr., K. P., Vitiello, M. V., & Zhdanova, I. V. (2007). Circadian rhythm sleep disorders: Part I, basic principles, shift work and jet lag disorders: An American Academy of Sleep Medicine review. *Sleep: Journal of Sleep and Sleep Disorders Research, 30*(11), 1460–1483.

Sackett, P. R., & Shen, W. (2010). Subgroup differences on cognitive tests in contexts other than personnel selection. In J. L. Outtz (Ed.), *Adverse impact: Implications for organizational staffing and high stakes selection* (pp. 323–346). New York, NY: Routledge/Taylor & Francis Group.

Sacks, O. (1985). *The man who mistook his wife for a hat and other clinical tales.* New York, NY: Touchstone.

Sadeh, A., Mindell, J. A., Luedtke, K., & Wiegand, B. (2009). Sleep and sleep ecology in the first 3 years: A web-based study. *Journal of Sleep Research, 18*(1), 60–73.

Sadler, M. S., Lineberger, M., Correll, J., & Park, B. (2005). Emotions, attributions, and policy endorsement in response to the September 11th terrorist attacks. *Basic and Applied Social Psychology, 27*(3), 249–258.

Sadler, P., & Woody, E. (2010). Dissociation in hypnosis: Theoretical frameworks and psychotherapeutic implications. In S. J. Lynn, J. W. Rhue, & I. Kirsch (Eds.), *Handbook of clinical hypnosis (2nd Ed.)* (pp. 151–178). Washington, DC: American Psychological Association.

Sadock, B. J., & Sadock, V. A. (2008). *Kaplan & Sadock's Concise Textbook of Clinical Psychiatry.* Lippincott Williams & Wilkins.

Sadock, B. J., & Sadock, V. A. (2007). *Synopsis of psychiatry: Behavioral sciences/clinical psychiatry (10th Ed.).* Philadelphia, PA: Wolters Kluwer/Lippincott Williams & Wilkins.

Sadock, B. J., & Sadock, V. A. (2000). *Comprehensive textbook of psychiatry,* 7th ed, Vol. 2. Philadelphia, PA: Lippincott Williams and Wilkins.

Saeki, E., Baddeley, A. D., Hitch, G. J., & Saito, S. (2013). Breaking a habit: A further role of the phonological loop in action control. *Memory & Cognition, 41*(7), 1065–1078.

Saffran, J. R., Werker, J. F., & Werner, L. A. (2006). The infant's auditory world: Hearing, speech, and the beginnings of language. In D. Kuhn & R. Siegler (Eds.), *Handbook of child psychology: Vol. 2, cognition, perception and language* (6th ed). Hoboken, NJ: Wiley.

Saggino, A. (2000). The big three or the big five? A replication study. *Personality and Individual Differences, 28,* 879–886.

Saggino, A., & Kline, P. (1996). The location of the Myers-Briggs Type Indicator in personality factor space. *Personality & Individual Differences, 21,* 591–597.

Sahoo, F. M., Sahoo, K., & Harichandan, S. (2005). Five big factors of personality and human happiness. *Social Sciences International, 21*(1), 20–28.

Sahraie, A., Hibbard, P. B., Trevethan, C. T., Ritchie, K. L., & Weiskrantz, L. (2010). Consciousness of the first order in blindsight. *PNAS Proceedings of the National Academy of Sciences of the United States of America, 107*(49), 21217–21222. doi: 10.1073/pnas.1015652107

Sales, E., Baum, M., & Shore, B. (1984). Victim readjustment following assault. *Journal of Social Issues, 40*(1), 117–136.

Salkovskis, P. M., Thorpe, S. J., Wahl, K., Wroe, A. L., & Forrester, E. (2003). Neutralizing increases discomfort associated with obsessional thoughts: An experimental study with obsessional patients. *Journal of Abnormal Psychology, 112*(4), 709–715.

Salovey, P., Mayer, J. D., Caruso, D., & Lopes, P. N. (2003). Measuring emotional intelligence as a set of abilities with the Mayer-Slovey-Caruso emotional intelligence test. In S. J. Lopez & C. R. Snyder (Eds.), *Positive psychological assessment: A handbook of models and measures* (pp. 251–265). Washington, DC: American Psychological Association.

Samelson, F. (1980). J. B. Watson's Little Albert, Cyril Burt's twins, and the need for a critical science. *American Psychologist, 35,* 619–625.

SAMHSA (Substance Abuse and Mental Health Services Administration). (2010). Mental health and mental disorders. In NIMH (National Institute of Mental Health), *Healthy people 2010.* Washington, DC: Department of Health and Human Services.

SAMHSA (Substance Abuse and Mental Health Services Administration). (2008, June 16). *National survey on drug use and health.* Washington, DC: Department of Health and Human Services.

SAMHSA (Substance Abuse and Mental Health Services Administration). (2002). *National Survey on Drug Use and Health, 2002.* Washington, DC: Author.

Samokhvalov, A. V., Rehm, J., Langlois, K., Gorber, S. C., & Spence, S. (2012). *Health state descriptions for Canadians: Mental illnesses,* No. 4. Statistics Canada, Ottawa.

Sana, F., Weston, T., & Cepeda, N. J. (2013). Laptop multitasking hinders learning for both users and nearby peers. *Computers and Education, 62,* 24–31.

Sanberg, C. D., Jones, F. L., Do, V. H., Dieguez Jr., D., & Derrick, B. E. (2006). 5-HTla receptor antagonists block perforant path-dentate LTP induced in novel, but not familiar, environments. *Learning & Memory, 13*(1), 52–62.

Sanderson, C. A. (2010). *Social psychology.* Hoboken, NJ: John Wiley & Sons.

Sanford, A. J., Fay, N., Stewart, A., & Moxey, L. (2002). Perspective in statements of quantity, with implications for consumer psychology. *Psychological Science, 13,* 130–134.

Sangwan, S. (2001). Ecological factors as related to IQ of children. *Psycho-Lingua, 31*(2), 89–92.

Sankupellay, M., Wilson, S., Heussler, H. S., Parsley, C., Yuill, M., & Dakin, C. (2011). Characteristics of sleep EEG power spectra in healthy infants in the first two years of life. *Clinical Neurophysiology, 122*(2), 236–243.

Santerre, C., & Allen, J. J. B. (2007). Methods for studying the psychophysiology of emotion. In J. Rottenberg & S. L. Johnson (Eds.), *Emotion and psychopathology: Bridging affective and clinical science.* Washington, DC: American Psychological Association.

Santostefano, S. (2010). Developmental psychopathology—Self, embodiment, meaning: A holistic-systems perspective. In W. F. Overton & R. M. Lerner (Eds.), *The handbook of life-span development, vol. 1: Cognition, biology, and methods* (pp. 792–836). Hoboken, NJ: John Wiley & Sons.

Saper, C. B. (2010). A treasure trove of gene expression patterns. *Nature Neuroscience, 13,* 658–659.

Sapir, E. 1921. *Language.* New York, NY: Harcourt, Brace & Co.

Sarbin, T. R., & Allen, V. L. (1968). Role theory. In G. Lindzey & E. Aronson (Eds.), *Handbook of social psychology* (2nd Ed., Vol. 1. pp. 488–567). Reading, MA: Addison–Wesley.

Sareen, J., Afifi, T. O., McMillan, K. A., & Asmundson, G. J. G. (2011). Relationship between household income and mental disorders: Findings from a population-based longitudinal study. *Archives of General Psychiatry, 68*(4), 419–426.

Saucier, D. M., & Elias, L. J. (2001). Lateral and sex differences in manual gesture during conversation. *Laterality, 6,* 239–245.

Saucier, G., Hampson, S. E., & Goldberg, L. R. (2000). Cross-language studies of lexical personality factors. In S. E. Hampson (Ed.), *Advances in personality psychology, Vol. 1* (pp. 1–36). Hove, England: Psychology Press.

Saxvig, I. W., Lundervold, A. J., Gronli, J., Ursin, R., Bjorvatn, B., & Portas, C. M. (2007). The effect of a REM sleep deprivation procedure on different aspects of memory function in humans. *Psychophysiology, 45*(2), 309–317.

Scarr, S. (1991). Theoretical issues in investigating intellectual plasticity. In S. E. Brauth, W. S. Hall, & R. Dooling (Eds.), *Plasticity of development*. Cambridge, MA: MIT Press.

Schaal, B., & Durand, K. (2012). The role of olfaction in human multisensory development. In A. J. Bremner, D. J. Lewkowicz, & C. Spence (Eds.), *Multisensory development*. Oxford, UK: Oxford University Press.

Schachter, S., & Singer, J. (1962). Cognitive, social, and physiological determinants of emotional state. *Psychological Review, 69*, 379–399.

Schalock, R. L., Borthwick, S. A., Bradley, V. J., Buntinx, W. H. E., Coulter, D. L., Craig, E. M., Gomez, S. C., et al. (2010). *Intellectual disability: definition, classification, and systems of supports (11th Ed)*. Washington, D.C.: American Association on Intellectual and Developmental Disabilities.

Scheme, E., Lock, B., Hargrove, L., Hill, W., Kuruganti, U., & Englehart, K. (2014). Motion normalized proportional control for improved pattern recognition-based myoelectric control. *Neural Systems and Rehabilitation Engineering, IEEE Transactions, 22*(1), 149–157.

Schienle, A., Ebner, F., & Schafer, A. (2011). Localized gray matter volume abnormalities in generalized anxiety disorder. *European Archives of Psychiatry and Clinical Neuroscience, 261*(4), 303–307.

Schienle, A., Schäfer, A., & Vaitl, D. (2008). Individual differences in disgust imagery: A functional magnetic resonance imaging study. *Neuroreport, 19*, 527–530.

Schiff, W., & Foulke, E. (2010). *Tactile perception: A Source book*. New York, NY: Cambridge University Press.

Schiffman, H. R. (1996). *Sensation and perception* (4th Ed.). New York, NY: John Wiley & Sons, Inc.

Schildkraut, J. J. (1965). The catecholamine hypothesis of affective disorders: A review of supporting evidence. *American Journal of Psychiatry, 122*(5), 509–522.

Schiller, P. H., Slocum, W. M., et al. (2011). The integration of disparity, shading and motion parallax cues for depth perception in humans and monkeys. *Brain Research, 1377*, 67–77.

Schlauch, R. C., Waesche, M. C., Riccardi, C. J., Donohue, K. F., Blagg, C. O., Christensen, R. L., & Lang, A. R. (2010). A meta-analysis of the effectiveness of placebo manipulations in alcohol-challenge studies. *Psychology of Addictive Behaviors, 24*(2), 239–253.

Schlenger, W. E., Caddell, J. M., Ebert, L., Jordan, B. K., Rourke, K. M., Wilson, D., et al. (2002). Psychological reactions to terrorist attacks. *Journal of the American Medical Association, 288*(5), 581–588.

Schmader, T., Hall, W., & Croft, A. (2015). Stereotype threat in intergroup relations. In M. Mikulincer, P. R. Shaver, J. F. Dovidio, & J. A. Simpson (Eds.), *APA handbook of personality and social psychology, Volume 2: Group processes* (pp. 447–471). Washington, DC: American Psychological Association.

Schmidt, G. L., DeBuse, C. J., & Seger, C. A. (2007) Right hemisphere metaphor processing? Characterizing the lateralization of semantic processes. *Brain and Language, 100*(2), 127–141.

Schmidt, L. A., Santesso, D. L., Schulkin, J., & Segalowitz, S. J. (2007). Shyness is a necessary but not sufficient condition for high salivary cortisol in typically developing 10-year-old children. *Personality and Individual Differences, 43*, 1541–1551.

Schmidt, M. V., Sterlemann, V., & Müller, M. B. (2009). Chronic stress and individual vulnerability. *Stress, neurotransmitters, and hormones: Neuroendocrine and genetic mechanisms* (pp. 174–183). New York, NY: New York Academy of Sciences, Wiley-Blackwell.

Schmitt, D. P., Allik, J., Mccrae, R. R., & Benet-Martinez, V. (2007). The geographic distribution of big five personality traits: Patterns and profiles of human self-description across 56 nations. *Journal of Cross-Cultural Psychology, 38*(2), 173–212.

Schmitt, D. P., et al. (2012). A reexamination of sex differences in sexuality: New studies reveal old truths. *Current Directions in Psychological Science, 21*(2) 135–139.

Schmitt, F. F., & Lahroodi, R. (2008). The epistemic value of curiosity. *Educational Theory, 58*(2), 125–149.

Schmukler, M. A. (1995). Self-knowledge of body position: Integration of perceptual and action system information. In P. Rochat (Ed.), *The Self in Infancy: Theory and Research*. Elsevier.

Schnabel, J. (2010). Secrets of the shaking palsy. *Nature*, S2–S5. doi:10.1038/466S2b

Schneider, E. L., & Davidson, L. (2003). Physical health and adult well-being. In The Center for Child Well Being (Ed.), *Well-being: Positive development across the lifecourse* (pp. 407–423), Mahwah, NJ: Erlbaum.

Schneider, K. J., & Krug, O. T. (2010). *Existential–humanistic therapy*. Washington, DC: American Psychological Association.

Schneider, T. A., Butryn, T. M., Furst, D. M., & Masucd, M. A. (2007). A qualitative examination of risk among elite adventure racers. *Journal of Sport Behavior, 408*, 330–337.

Scholte, R. H. J., & De Bruyn, E. E. J. (2004). Compression of the Giant Three and Big Five in early adolescents. *Personality and Individual Differences, 36*(6) 1353–1371.

Schon, J. (2003). Dreams and dreaming: Perspectives over the century. *Psychoanalytic Psychotherapy in South Africa, 11*(2), 1–23.

Schooler, C. (2001). The intellectual effects of the demands of the work environment. In R. J. Sternberg & E. L. Grigorenko (Eds.), *Environmental effects on cognitive abilities* (pp. 363–380). Mahwah, NJ: Lawrence Erlbaum Associates Publishers.

Schooler, J. W. (2011). Introspecting in the spirit of William James: Comment on Fox, Ericsson, and Best. *Psychological Bulletin, 137*(2), 345–350.

Schredl, M., Blomeyer, D., & Gorlinger, M. (2000). Nightmares in children: Influencing factors. *Somnologie, 4*, 145–149.

Schredl, M., Ciric, P., Gotz, S., & Wittmann, L. (2004). Typical dreams: Stability and gender differences. *The Journal of Psychology, 138*(6), 485–494.

Schuel, H., Burkman, L. J., Lippes, J., Crickard, K., Mahony, M. C., Guiffrida, A., et al. (2002). Evidence that anandamide-signalling regulates human sperm functions required for fertilization. *Molecular Reproduction and Development, 63*, 376–387.

Schug, J., Matsumoto, D., Horita, Y., Yamagishi, T., & Bonet, K. (2010). Emotional expressivity as a signal of cooperation. *Evolution and Human Behavior, 31*(2) 87–94.

Schuller, R. A., & Ogloff, J. R. P. (2001). *Introduction to psychology and law: Canadian perspectives*. Toronto, ON: University of Toronto Press.

Schultz, D. P., & Schultz, S. E. (2012). *A history of modern psychology* (10th ed.). Belmont: CA: Cengage Learning/Wadsworth.

Schultz, L. T., Heimberg, R. G., & Rodebaugh, T. L. (2008). Social anxiety disorder. In M. Hersen & J. Rosqvist (Eds.), *Handbook of psychological assessment, case conceptualization, and treatment*, Vol. 1: *Adults* (pp. 204–236). Hoboken, NJ: John Wiley & Sons.

Schultz, L. T., Heimberg, R. G., Rodebaugh, T. L., Schneier, F. R., Liebowitz, M. R., & Telch, M. J. (2006). The appraisal of social concerns scale: Psychometric validation with a clinical sample of patients with social anxiety disorder. *Behavior Therapy, 37*(4), 393–405.

Schultz, W., Dayan, P., & Montague, P. R. (1997). A neural substrate of prediction and reward. *Science, 275*, 1593–1599.

Schulze, T. G., & McMahon, F. J. (2009). The genetic basis of bipolar disorder. In C. A. Zarate Jr. & H. K. Manji (Eds.), *Bipolar depression: Molecular neurobiology, clinical diagnosis and pharmacotherapy* (pp. 59–76). Cambridge, MA: Birkhauser.

Schwabe, L., Nader, K., & Pruessner, J. C. (2013). β-Adrenergic blockade during reactivation reduces the subjective feeling of remembering associated with emotional episodic memories. *Biological Psychology, 92*(2), 227–232.

Schwanenflugel, P. J., Akin, C., & Luh, W. (1992). Context availability and the recall of abstract and concrete words. *Memory & Cognition, 20*(1), 96–104.

Schwarting, R. K. W. (2003). The principle of memory consolidation and its pharmacological modulation. In R. H. Kluwe, G. Lüer, & F. Rösler (Eds.), *Principles of learning and memory* (pp. 137–153). Cambridge, MA: Birkhäuser.

Schwartz, B., Ward, A., Monterosso, J., Lyubomirsky, S., White, K., & Lehman, D. R. (2002). Maximizing versus sacrificing: Happiness is a matter of choice. *Journal of Personality and Social Psychology, 83*, 1178–1197.

Schwartz, C. E., Snidman, N., & Kagan, J. (1999). Adolescent social anxiety as an outcome of inhibited temperament in childhood. *Journal of the American Academy of Child and Adolescent Psychiatry, 38*, 1008–1015.

Schwartz, G. J., Azzara, A. V., & Heaner, M. K. (2013). Roles for central leptin receptors in the control of meal size. *Appetite, 71*(1), 466–469.

Schwartz, M. F., Saffran, E. M., & Marin, O. S. M. (1980). The problem of word order in agrammatism: Comprehension. *Brain and Language, 10*(2), 249–262.

Schwartz, S. H. (2010). *Visual perception: A clinical orientation* (4th ed). New York, NY: McGraw Hill Companies.

Scialfa, C. T., & Kline, D. W. (2007). Vision. In J.E. Birren (Ed.), *Encyclopedia of gerontology* (2nd ed.). San Diego, CA: Academic Press.

Scott, C. L. (2010). *Handbook of correctional mental health*. Arlington, VA: American Psychiatric Publishing.

Scott, W. B., & Milner, B. (1957). Loss of recent memory after bilateral hippocampal lesions. *Journal of Neurological Neurosurgery Psychiatry, 20*(1), 11–21.

Sealy, P. A. (2012). The Impact of the Process of Deinstitutionalization of Mental Health Services in Canada: An Increase in Accessing of Health Professionals for Mental Health Concerns. *Social Work in Public Health, 27*(3), 229–237.

Sealy, P., & Whitehead, P. C. (2006). The impact of deinstitutionalization of psychiatric hospitals on psychological distress of the community in Canada. *Journal of Health & Social Policy, 21*(4), 73–94.

Sealy, P., & Whitehead, P. C. (2004). Forty years of deinstitutionalization of psychiatric services in Canada: an empirical assessment. *The Canadian Journal of Psychiatry*. Retrieved from http://ww1.cpa-apc.org:8080/publications/archives/cjp/2004/april/ocaly.asp.

Seashore, H., Wesman, A., & Doppelt, J. (1950). The standardization of the Wechsler Intelligence Scale for Children. *Journal of Consulting Psychology, 14*(2), 99–110.

Segal, N. (2012). *Born together—Reared apart: The landmark Minnesota twin study*. Cambridge, MA: Harvard University Press.

Segerstrom, S. C., & Miller, G. E. (2004). Psychological stress and the human immune system: A meta-analytic study of 30 years of inquiry. *Psychological Bulletin, 130*(4), 601–630.

Seligman, M. E. P. (2007). Coaching and positive psychology. *Australian Psychologist, 42*(4), 266–267.

Seligman, M. E. P. (2002). *Authentic happiness: Using the new positive psychology to realize our potential for lasting fulfilment*. New York, NY: Free Press.

Seligman, M. E. P. (1992). Power and powerlessness: Comments on "cognates of personal control." *Applied & Preventive Psychology, 1*(2), 119–120.

Seligman, M. E. P. (1975). *Helplessness: On depression, development, and death.* San Francisco, CA: W.H. Freeman.

Seligman, M. E. P., & Csikszentmihalyi, M. (2014). Positive psychology: An introduction. In M. Csikszentmihalyi (Ed.), *Flow and the foundations of positive psychology* (pp. 279–298). London, UK: Springer.

Seligman, M. E. P., & Csikszentmihalyi, M. (2000). Positive psychology. *American Psychologist, 55*, 5–14.

Seligman, M. E. P., & Maier, S. F. (1967). Failure to escape traumatic shock. *Journal of Experimental Psychology, 74*, 1–9.

Seligman, M. E. P., Rashid, T., & Parks, A. (2006). Positive psychotherapy. *American Psychology, 61*, 774–788.

Seligman, M. E. P., & Steen, T. A. (2005). Positive psychology progress: Empirical validation of interventions. *American Psychologist, 60*(5), 410–421.

Seligman, M. E. P., Weiss, J., Weinraub, M., & Schulman, A. (1980). Coping behavior: Learned helplessness, physiological change and learned inactivity. *Behavioral Research Therapy, 18*, 459–512.

Selkoe, D. J. (2002). Alzheimer's disease is a synaptic failure. *Science, 298*(5594), 789–791.

Selkoe, D. J. (2000). The origins of Alzheimer's disease: A is for amyloid. *Journal of the American Medical Association, 283*(12), 1615–1617.

Selkoe, D. J. (1991). Amyloid protein and Alzheimer's disease. *Scientific American, 265*, 68–78.

Selye, H. (1993). History of the stress concept. *Handbook of stress: Theoretical and clinical aspects (2nd Ed.)* (pp. 7–17). New York, NY: Free Press.

Selye, H. (1956). Stress and psychobiology. *Journal of Clinical & Experimental Psychopathology, 17*, 370–375.

Selye, H. (1956). *The stress of life*. New York, NY: McGraw-Hill.

Selye, H. (1936). A syndrome produced by diverse nocuous agents. *Nature, 138*, 32.

Semendeferi, K., Lu, A., Schenker, N., & Damasio, H. (2002). Humans and great apes share a large frontal cortex. *Nature Neuroscience, 5*(3), 272–276.

Sénéchal, M., & LeFevre, J. (2014). Continuity and change in the home literacy environment as predictors of growth in vocabulary and reading. *Child Development*. doi: 10.1111/cdev.12222.

Sénéchal, M., & LeFevre, J. (2002). Parental involvement in the development of children's reading skill: A 5-year longitudinal study. *Child Development, 73*, 445–460.

Sénéchal, M., & LeFevre, J. (2001). Storybook reading and parent teaching: Links to language and literacy development. In P. R. Britto & J. Brooks-Gunn (Eds.), *The role of family literacy environments in promoting young children's emerging literacy skills: New directions for child and adolescent development* (pp. 39–52). San Francisco, CA: Jossey-Bass.

Senechal, S. (2009). *Dogs Can Sign, Too. A breakthrough method of teaching your dog to communicate to you*. Random House/Crown/TenSpeed Press.

Senior, J. (2006, July 17). Some dark thoughts on happiness [Electronic version]. *New York Magazine*.

Seppala, E., Rossomando, T., & Doty, J. R. (2013). Social connection and compassion: Important predictors of health and well-being. *Social Research: An International Quarterly, 80*(2), 411–430.

Seta, J. J., Seta, C. E., & McElroy, T. (2002). Strategies for reducing the stress of negative life experiences: An average/summation analysis. *Personality and Social Psychology Bulletin, 28*, 1574–1585.

Sewards, T. V., & Sewards, M. A. (2000). The awareness of thirst: Proposed neural correlates. *Conscious Cognition, 9*(4), 463–487.

Seyfarth, R. M., & Cheney, D. L. (2003). Meaning and emotion in animal vocalizations. In P. Ekman, J. J. Campos, J. J. Davidson, R. J. de Waal, & B. M. Frans (Eds.), *Emotions inside out: 130 years after Darwin's: The expression of the emotions in man and animals* (pp. 32–55). New York, NY: New York University Press.

Sgoifo, A., Braglia, F., Costoli, T., Musso, E., Meerlo, P., Ceresini, G., & Troisi, A. (2003). Cardiac autonomic reactivity and salivary cortisol in men and women exposed to social stressors: Relationship with individual ethological profile. *Neuroscience and Biobehavioral Reviews, 27*(1–2), 179–188.

Shackelford, T. K., & Larsen, R. J. (1997). Facial asymmetry as an indicator of psychological, emotional and physiological distress. *Journal of Personality and Social Psychology, 72*, 456–466.

Shadish, W. R., & Baldwin, S. A. (2005). Effects of behavioral marital therapy: A meta-analysis of randomized controlled trials. *Journal of Consulting and Clinical Psychology, 73*(1), 6–14.

Shafir, E., & Tversky, A. (2002). Decision making. *Foundations of cognitive psychology: Core readings* (pp. 601–620). Cambridge, MA: MIT Press.

Shafran, R. (2005). Cognitive-behavioral models of OCD. In J. S. Abramowitz & A. C. Houts (Eds.), *Concepts and controversies in obsessive-compulsive disorder*. New York, NY: Springer Science + Business Media.

Shah, D. B., Pesiridou, A., Baltuch, G. H., Malone, D. A., & O'Reardon, J. P. (2008). Functional neurosurgery in the treatment of severe obsessive compulsive disorder and major depression: Overview of disease circuits and therapeutic targeting for the clinician. *Psychiatry, 5*(9), 24–33.

Shah, N. (2007). *Obstructive sleep apnea is associated with an increased risk of coronary artery disease and death.* Presented at the International Conference of the American Thoracic Society, San Fransisco.

Shamay-Tsoory, S., Tomer, R., Berger, B. D., Goldsher, D., & Aharon-Peretz, J. (2005). Impaired "affective theory of mind" is associated with right ventromedial prefrontal damage. *Cognitive and Behavioral Neurology, 18*(1), 55–67.

Sharf, R. S. (2012). *Theories of psychotherapy & counseling: Concepts and cases* (5th Ed.). Pacific Grove, CA: Brooks/Cole.

Sharf, R. S. (2008). *Theories of psychotherapy and counseling: Concepts and cases* (4th Ed.). Belmont, NY: Thomson Brooks Cole.

Shargorodsky, J., Curhan, S. G., Curhan, G. C., & Eavey, R. (2010). Change in prevalence of hearing loss in US adolescents. *Journal of the American Medical Association, 304*(7), 772–778.

Shariff, S. (2005). Cyber-dilemmas in the new millennium: School obligations to provide student safety in a virtual school environment. *McGill Journal of Education, 40*, 467–487.

Sharma, A., Nash, A. A., & Dorman, M. (2009). Cortical development, plasticity and re-organization in children with cochlear implants. *Journal of Communication Disorders, 42*, 272–279.

Shaw, P., Greenstein, D., Lerch, J., Clasen, L., Lenroot, R., Gogtay, N., Evans, A., Rapoport, J., & Giedd, J. (2006, March 30). Intellectual ability and cortical development in children and adolescents. *Nature, 440*(7084), 619–620.

Shaw, P., Kabani, N. J., Lerch, J. P., Eckstrand, K., Lenroot, R., Gogtay, N., Greenstein, D., Clasen, L., Evans, A., Rapoport, J. L., Giedd, J. N., & Wise, S. P. (2008). Neurodevelopmental trajectories of the human cerebral cortex. *Journal of Neuroscience, 28*(14), 3586–3594.

Shayer, M., & Adhami, M. (2010). Realizing the cognitive potential of children 5–7 with a mathematics focus: Post-test and long-term effects of a 2-year intervention. *British Journal of Educational Psychology, 80*(3), 363–379.

Sheldon, K. M., Ryan, R. M., Deci, E. L., & Kasser, T. (2004). The independent effects of goal contents and motives on well-being: it's both what you pursue and why you pursue it. *Personality and Social Psychology Bulletin, 30*(4), 475–486.

Sheldon, S. A. M., & Moscovitch, M. (2010). Recollective performance advantages for implicit memory tasks. *Memory, 18*(7), 681–697.

Shenton, M. E., Hamoda, H. M., Schneiderman, J. S., Bouix, S., Pasternak, O., Rathi, Y., . . . & Zafonte, R. (2012). A review of magnetic resonance imaging and diffusion tensor imaging findings in mild traumatic brain injury. *Brain Imaging and Behavior, 6*(2), 137–192.

Shepard, T. H., & Lemire, R. J. (2004). *Catalog of teratogenic agents (11th edition)*. Baltimore, MD: Johns Hopkins University Press.

Shepperd, J. A. (1995). Remedying motivation and productivity loss in collective settings. *Current Directions in Psychological Science, 4*, 131–134.

Shepperd, J. A. (1993). Productivity loss in performance groups: A motivation analysis. *Psychological Bulletin, 113*, 67–81.

Sher, L. (2003). Daily hassles, cortisol, and depression. *Australian and New Zealand Journal of Psychiatry, 37*(3), 383–384.

Sheridan, M. A., Fox, N. A., Zeanah, C. H., McLaughlin, K. A., & Nelson, C. A. III (2012). *Variation in neural development as a result of exposure to institutionalization early in childhood.* Proceedings of the National Academy of Sciences of the United States of America, 1–6.

Sherif, M. (1967). *Group conflict and co-operation: Their social psychology*. London, UK: Routledge & Kegan Paul.

Sherif, M. (1961). *The Robbers Cave Experiment: Intergroup Conflict and Cooperation*.[Orig. Pub. as Intergroup Conflict and Group Relations]. Middletown, CT: Wesleyan University Press.

Sherman, J. W., Stroessner, S. J., Conrey, F. R., & Azam, O. A. (2005). Prejudice and stereotype maintenance processes: Attention, attribution, and individuation. *Journal of Personality and Social Psychology, 89*(4), 607–622.

Sherry, A., & Whilde, M. R. (2008). Borderline personality disorder. In M. Hersen & J. Rosqvist (Eds.), *Handbook of Psychological Assessment, Case Conceptualization, and Treatment, Vol 1: Adults* (pp. 403–437). Hoboken, NJ: John Wiley & Sons Inc.

Sherry, D. F., & Schacter, D. L. (1987). The evolution of multiple memory systems. *Psychological Review, 94*(4), 439–454.

Shih, M., Pittinsky, T. L., & Ambady, N. (1999). Stereotype susceptibility: Identity salience and shifts in quantitative performance. *Psychological Science, 10*(1), 80–83.

Shin, L. M., Orr, S. P., Carson, M. A., Rauch, S. L., Macklin, M. L., Lasko, N. B., Peters, P. M., Metzger, L. J., Dougherty, D. D., Cannistraro, P. A., Alpert, N. M., Fishman, A. J., & Pitman, R. K. (2004). Regional cerebral blood flow in the amygdala and medial prefrontal cortex during traumatic imagery in male and female Vietnam veterans with PTSD. *Archives of General Psychiatry, 61,* 168–176.

Shmuelof, L., & Zohary, E. (2007). Watching others' actions: Mirror representations in the parietal cortex. *The Neuroscientist, 13,* 667–672.

Shoda, Y., & Lee Tiernan, S. (2002). What remains invariant? Finding order within a person's thoughts, feelings, and behaviors across situations. In D. Cervone & W. Mischel, *Advances in Personality Science, 1,* 241–270.

Shonkoff, J. P., & Bales, S. N. (2011). Science does not speak for itself: Translating child development research for the public and its policy makers. *Child Development, 82,* 17–32.

Shubin, N. (2008). *Your inner fish: a journey into the 3.5-billion-year history of the human body.* Toronto, ON: Random House Books.

Shultz, D. P., & Schultz, S. E. (1987). *A history of modern psychology* (4th Ed.). Harcourt Brace Jovanovich.

Sidhu, M., Malhi, P., & Jerath, J. (2010). Intelligence of children from economically disadvantaged families: Role of parental education. *Psychological Studies, 55*(4), 358–364.

Siegel, G., Albers, R. W., Brady, S., & Price, D. (2006) *Basic neurochemistry, 7th Ed.* Elsevier.

Siegel, J. (2009). Sleep viewed as a state of adaptive inactivity. *Nature Reviews Neuroscience, 10,* 747–753.

Siegel, J. M. (2008). Do all animals sleep? *Trends in Neurosciences, 31,* 208–213. doi: 10.1016/j.tins.2008.02.001

Siegel, J. M. (2005). Clues to the functions of mammalian sleep. *Nature, 437,* 1264–1271.

Siegel, L. S. (1992). An evaluation of the discrepancy definition of dyslexia. *Journal of Learning Disabilities, 25,* 618–629.

Sienaert, P., Vansteelandt, K., Demyttenaere, K., & Peuskens, J. (2009). Randomized comparison of ultra-brief bifrontal and unilateral electroconvulsive therapy for major depression: Clinical efficacy. *Journal of Affective Disorders, 116*(1), 106–112.

Sigel, E. (2008). Eating disorders. *Adolescent Medicine: State of the Art Reviews, 19*(3), 547–72, xi.

Silberhumer, G. R., Miller, K., Pump, A., Kriwanek, S., Widhalm, K., Gyoeri, G., & Prager, G. (2011). Long-term results after laparoscopic adjustable gastric banding in adolescent patients: follow-up of the Austrian experience. *Surgical Endoscopy, 25*(9), 2993–2999.

Silvera, D. H., & Laufer, D. (2005). Recent developments in attribution research and their implications for consumer judgments and behavior. In F. R. Kardes, P. M. Herr, & J. Nantel (Eds.), *Applying social cognition to consumer-focused strategy* (pp. 53–77). Mahwah, NJ: Lawrence Erlbaum Associates Publishers.

Silverman, K., Evans, S. M., Strain, E. C., & Griffiths, R. R. (1992). Withdrawal syndrome after the double-blind cessation of caffeine consumption. *New England Journal of Medicine, 327*(16), 1109–1114.

Silverman, M. S., McCarthy, M., & McGovern, T. (1992). A review of outcome studies of rational-emotive therapy from 1982–1989. *Journal of Rational-Emotive & Cognitive Behavior Therapy, 10*(3), 111–186.

Silvia, P. J. (2008). Another look at creativity and intelligence: Exploring higher order models and probable confounds. *Personality and Individual Differences, 44*(4), 1012–1021.

Simeon, D., et al. (2000). Feeling unreal: A PET study of depersonalization disorder. *American Journal of Psychiatry, 157,* 1782–1788.

Simon, H. A. (1990). Invariants of human behavior. *Annual Review of Psychology, 41,* 1–20.

Simon, H. A. (1957). *Models of man.* New York, NY: John Wiley & Sons, Inc.

Simon, J., Braunstein, G., Nachtigall, L., Utian, W., Katz, M., Miller, S., et al. (2005). Testosterone patch increases sexual activity and desire in surgically menopausal women with hypoactive sexual desire disorder. *The Journal of Clinical Endocrinology and Metabolism, 90*(9), 5226–5233.

Simonton, D. K. (2010). Research notes: The curious case of Catharine Cox (Miles): The 1926 dissertation and her Miles–Wolfe (1936) follow-up. *History of Psychology, 13*(2), 205–206.

Simpkins, S. D., Fredricks, J. A., & Eccles, J. S. (2012). Chartering the Eccles' expectancy-value-model from mother's beliefs in childhood to youths' activities in adolescence. *Developmental Psychology, 48,* 1019–1032.

Simpson, J. A., & Kenrick, D. (Eds.). (2013). *Evolutionary Social Psychology.* New York, NY: Psychology Press.

Singer, J. L. (2003). Daydreaming, consciousness, and self-representations: Empirical approaches to theories of William James and Sigmund Freud. *Journal of Applied Psychoanalytic Studies, 5,* 461–483.

Singer, T., & Kimbles, S. L. (2004). *The cultural complex: Contemporary Jungian perspectives on psyche and society.* New York, NY: Brunner-Routledge.

Singer, T., Seymour, B., O'Doherty, J. P., Stephan, K. E., Dolan, R. J., & Frith, C. D. (2006). Empathic neural responses are modulated by the perceived fairness of others. *Nature, 439*(7075), 466–469.

Singer, T., Seymour, B., O'Doherty, J., Kaube, H., Dolan, R. J., & Frith, C. (2004). Empathy for pain involves the affective but not sensory component of pain. *Science, 303,* 1157–1162.

Singh, D. (1995). Female judgement of male attractiveness and desirability for relationships: Role of waist-to-hip ratio and financial status. *Journal of Personality and Social Psychology, 69,* 1089–1101.

Singh, D. (1994). Ideal female body shape: Role of body weight and waist-to-hip ratio. *International Journal of Eating Disorders, 16,* 283–288.

Skaret, E., Raadal, M., Kvale, G., & Berg, E. (2000) Factors relating to missed and cancelled dental appointments among adolescents in Norway. *European Journal of Oral Sciences, 108*(3), 175–183.

Skinner, B. F. (1958). Diagramming schedules of reinforcement. *Journal of the Experimental Analysis of Behavior, 1,* 67–68.

Skinner, B. F. (1957). *Verbal behavior.* New York, NY: Appleton-Century-Crofts.

Skinner, B. F., & Morse, W. H. (1958). Fixed-interval reinforcement of running in a wheel. *Journal of the Experimental Analysis of Behavior, 1,* 371–379.

Skoczenski, A. M., & Norcia, A. M. (2002). Late maturation of visual hyperacuity. *Psychological Science, 13,* 537–541.

Slater, A., Riddell, P., Quinn, P. C., Pascalis, O., Lee, K., & Kelly, D. J. (2010). Visual perception. In J. G. Bremner & T. D. Wachs (Eds.), *Wiley-Blackwell Handbook of Infant Development: Vol 1. Basic Research* (2nd ed, pp. 40–80). Chichester, UK: Wiley-Blackwell.

Slavich, G. M., & Toussaint, L. (2013). Using the stress and adversity inventory as a teaching tool leads to significant learning gains in two courses on stress and health. *Stress and Health,* First published online, doi: 10.1002/smi.2523.

Sloan, D. M. (2004). Emotion regulation in action: Emotional reactivity in experiential avoidance. *Behaviour Research and Therapy, 42,* 1257–1270.

Sloan, D. M., Bradley, M. M., Dimoulas, E., & Lang, P. J. (2002). Looking at facial expressions: Dysphoria and facial EMG. *Biological Psychology, 60*(2–3), 79–90.

Slobin, D. (1986). *The cross-linguistic study of language acquisition.* Mahwah, NJ: Earlbaum.

Slovic, P. (1990). Choice. In D. N. Osherson & E. E. Smith (Eds.), *An invitation to cognitive science: Vol. 3: Thinking.* Cambridge, MA: MIT Press.

Small, G., & Vorgan, G. (2008). Meet your iBrain. *Scientific American Mind, 19,* 42–49.

Small, G. W., Kepe, V., Siddarth, P., Ercoli, L. M., Merrill, D. A., Donoghue, N., Bookheimer, S. Y., Martinez, J., Omalu, B., Bailes, , J., & Barrio, J. R. (2013). PET scanning of brain tau in retired National Football League players: Preliminary findings. *The American Journal of Geriatric Psychiatry, 21*(2), 138–144.

Smillie, C. M. (2013). How infants learn to feed: A neurobehavioral model. In C. Watson Genna (Ed.), *Supporting sucking skill in breastfeeding infants.* Burlington, MA: Jones and Bartlett Learning.

Smith, A. M., Fried, P. A., Hogan, M. J., & Cameron, I. (2006). Effects of prenatal marijuana on visuospatial working memory: An fMRI study in young adults. *Neurotoxicology and Teratology, 28,* 286–295.

Smith, A. M., Fried, P. A., Hogan, M. J., & Cameron, I. (2004). Effects of prenatal marijuana on response inhibition: An fMRI study in young adults. *Neurotoxicology and Teratology, 26,* 533–542.

Smith, C. (2006). Symposium V—Sleep and learning: New Developments. *Brain and Cognition, 60*(3), 331–332.

Smith, C. (1996). Sleep states, memory processes and synaptic plasticity. *Behavioural Brain Research, 78*(1), 49–56.

Smith, D. (2004). Love that dare not squeak its name. *The New York Times.* Retrieved from http://www.nytimes.com/2004/02/07/arts/07GAY.html

Smith, F. G., Jones, B. C., Welling, L. L., Little, A. C., Vukovic, J., Main, J. C., & DeBruine, L. M. (2009). Waist-hip ratio predicts women's preferences for masculine male faces, but not perceptions of men's trustworthiness. *Personality and Individual Differences, 47*(5), 476–480.

Smith, J. C., Nielson, K. A., Woodard, J. L., Seidenberg, M., Durgerian, S., Antuono, P., . . . Rao, S. M. (2011). Interactive effects of physical activity and APOE-ε4 on semantic memory activation in healthy elders. *NeuroImage, 54*(1), 635–644. doi: 10.1016/j.neuroimage.2010.07.070

Smith, J. R., Louis, W. R., Terry, D. J., Greenaway, K. H., Clarke, M. R., & Cheng, X. (2012). Congruent or conflicted? the impact of injunctive and descriptive norms on environmental intentions. *Journal of Environmental Psychology, 32*(4), 353–361.

Smith, L. B. (2010). More than concepts: How multiple integrations make human intelligence. In D. Mareschal, P. C. Quinn, & S. E. G. Lea (Eds.), *The making of human concepts* (pp. 335–363). New York, NY: Oxford University Press.

Smith, L. D., Peck, P. L., & McGovern, R. J. (2004). Factors contributing to the utilization of mental health services in a rural setting. *Psychological Reports, 95*(2), 435–442.

Smith, M. L., & Glass, G. V. (1977). Meta-analysis of psychotherapy outcome studies. *American Psychologist, 32*(9), 752–760.

Smith, M. L., Glass, G. V., & Miller, T. I. (1980). *The benefits of psychotherapy.* Baltimore, MD: Johns Hopkins University Press.

Smith, R. A., & Weber, A. L. (2005). Applying social psychology in everyday life. In F. W. Schneider, J. A. Gruman, & L. M. Coutts (Eds.), *Applied Social Psychology: Understanding and Addressing Social and Practical Problems* (pp. 75–99). Sage Publications.

Smith, S. M. (1984). A comparison of two techniques for reducing context-dependent forgetting. *Memory & Cognition, 12*(5), 477–482.

Smith, T. W., & Gallo, L. C. (2001). Personality traits as risk factors for physical illness. In A. Baum, T. A. Revenson, & J. E. Singer (Eds.), *Handbook of health psychology* (pp. 139–173). Mahwah, NJ: Erlbaum.

Smyth, J. M., & Pennebaker, J. W. (2001). What are the health effects of disclosure? In A. Baum, T. A. Revenson, & J. E. Singer (Eds.), *Handbook of health psychology* (pp. 339–348). Mahwah, NJ: Erlbaum.

Snigdha, S., de Rivera, C., Milgram, N. W., & Cotman, C. W. (2014). Exercise enhances memory consolidation in the aging brain. *Frontiers in Aging Neuroscience, 6*, 3.

Snyder, W. V. (1947). *Casebook of non-directive counseling.* Boston, MA: Houghton Mifflin.

So, J. K. (2008). Somatization as cultural idiom of distress: Rethinking mind and body in a multicultural society. *Counselling Psychology Quarterly, 21*(2), 167–174.

Sokal, M. M. (2010). Scientific biography, cognitive deficits, and laboratory practice. James McKeen Cattell and early American experimental psychology, 1880–1904. *Isis, 101*(3), 531–554.

Solms, M. (2007a). Freud returns. In F. E. Bloom (Ed.), *Best of the Brain* from *Scientific American* (pp. 35–46). Washington, D.C.: Dana Press.

Solms, M. (2007b). The interpretation of dreams and the neurosciences. In L. Mayes, P. Fonagy, & M. Target (Eds.), *Developmental science and psychoanalysis: Integration and innovation. Developments in psychoanalysis.* London, England: Karnac Books.

Solms, M. (2004). Freud returns. *Scientific American, 290*(5), 82–88.

Somers, J. M., Goldner, E. M., Waraich, P., & Hsu, L. (2004). Prevalence studies of substance-related disorders: A systematic review of the literature. *Canadian Journal of Psychiatry, 49*(6).

Somerville, L. H., & Casey, B. J. (2010). Developmental neurobiology of cognitive control and motivational systems. *Current Opinion in Neurobiology, 20*, 236–241.

Song, S., Sjostrom, P. J., Reigl, M., Nelson, S., & Chklovskii , D. B. (2005). Highly nonrandom features of synaptic connectivity in local cortical circuits. *PLoS Biology, 3*(3), 1–13.

Soorya, L. V., Carpenter, L. A., & Romanczyk, R. G. (2011). Applied behavior analysis. In E. Hollander, A. Kolevzon, & J. T. Coyle (Eds.), *Textbook of autism spectrum disorders* (pp. 525–535). Arlington, VA: American Psychiatric Publishing.

SoRelle, R. (2000). Nearly half of Americans with severe mental illness do not seek treatment. *Circulation,* Electronic Pages, 101, e66. Retrieved from http://circ.ahajournals.org/content/101/5/e66.full

Sørensen, T. I., Holst, C., Stunkard, A. J., & Skovgaard, L. T. (1992). Correlations of body mass index of adult adoptees and their biological and adoptive relatives. *International Journal of Obesity and Related Metabolic Disorders: Journal of the International Association for the Study of Obesity, 16*(3), 227–236.

Sorrell, J. M. (2012). Widows and widowers in today's society. *Journal of Psychosocial Nursing and Mental Health Services, 50*(9), 14–18.

Sotardi, V. A. (2013). On everyday stress and coping strategies among elementary school children, dissertation, educational psychology. University of Arizona. Retrieved from http://arizona.openrepository.com/arizona/retrieve/568950/azu_etd_12663_sip1_m.pdf.jpg.

Soto, D., Hodsoll, J., Rotshtein, P., & Humphreys, G. W. (2008). Automatic guidance of attention from working memory. *Trends in Cognitive Sciences, 12*, 342–348.

Soussignan, R. (2002). Duchenne smile, emotional experience, and autonomic reactivity: A test of the facial–feedback hypothesis. *Emotion, 2*, 52–74.

Souza-Talarico, J. N., Marin, M.-F., Sindi, S., & Lupien, S. J. (2011). Effects of stress hormones on the brain and cognition: Evidence from normal to pathological aging. *Dementia and Neuropsychology, 5*(1), 8–16.

Spain, J., Eaton, L., & Funder, D. (2000). Perspectives on personality: The relative accuracy of self versus others in the prediction of emotion and behavior. *Journal of Personality, 68*, 837–867.

Spanos, N. P., Mondoux, T. J., & Burgess, C. A. (1995). Comparison of multi-component hypnotic and non-hypnotic treatments for smoking. *Contemporary Hypnosis, 12*(1), 12–19.

Sparks, J. A., & Duncan, B. L. (2013). Outside the black box: Re-assessing pediatric antidepressant prescription. *Journal of the Canadian Academy of Child and Adolescent Psychiatry, 22*(3), 240.

Spearman, C. (1904). "General intelligence," objectively determined and measured. *American Journal of Psychology, 15*(2), 201–293.

Spearman, C. (1923). *The nature of "intelligence" and the principles of cognition.* Oxford, UK: Macmillan.

Spearman, C. (1927). *The nature of intelligence and the principles of cognition* (2nd ed.). Oxford, UK: Macmillan.

Spearman, C. (1937). *Psychology down the ages.* Oxford, UK: Macmillan.

Spearman, C. (1939). Thurstone's work reworked. *Journal of Educational Psychology, 30*(1), 1–16.

Spencer, R. M. C., Zelaznik, H. N., Diedrichsen, J., & Ivry, R. B. (2003). Disrupted timing of discontinuous movements by cerebellar lesions. *Science, 300*, 1437–1439.

Sperling, G. (1960). The information available in brief visual presentation. *Psychological Monographs, 74*(11), 29.

Sperry, R. W. (1998). A powerful paradigm made stronger. *Neuropsychologia, 36*(10), 1063–1068.

Sperry, R. W. (1982). Some effects of disconnecting the cerebral hemispheres. *Science, 217*(4566), 1223–1226.

Spiegel, D., Lewis-Fernández, R., Lanius, R., Vermetten, E., Simeon, D., & Friedman, M. (2012). Dissociative disorders in DSM-5. *Annual Review of Clinical Psychology, 9*, 299–326.

Spiegel, H., & Spiegel, D. (2004). *Trace and treatment: clinical uses of hypnosis.* Arlington, VA: American Psychiatric Publishing.

Spiegler, M. D., & Guevremont, D. C. (2003). *Contemporary behavior therapy.* Belmont, CA: Thomson/Wadsworth.

Spielberger, C. D. (1985). Anxiety, cognition, and affect: A state-trait perspective. In A. H. Tuma & J. Maser (Eds.), *Anxiety and the anxiety disorders.* Hillsdale, NJ: Lawrence Erlbaum.

Spielberger, C. D. (1972). Anxiety as an emotional state. In C. D. Spielberger (Ed.), *Anxiety: Current trends in theory and research* (Vol. 1). New York, NY: Academic Press.

Spielberger, C. D. (1966). Theory and research on anxiety. In C. D. Spielberger (Ed.), *Anxiety and behavior.* New York, NY: Academic Press.

Spitzer, R. L., Skodol, A., Gibbon, M., & Williams, J. B. W. (1983). *Psychopathology: A case book.* New York, NY: McGraw-Hill.

Spitzer, R. L., Skodol, A., Gibbon, M., & Williams, J. B. W. (1981). *DSM-III case book* (1st Ed.). Washington, DC: American Psychiatric Press.

Spooren, W., Lesage, A., Lavreysen, H., Gasparini, F., & Steckler, T. (2010). Metabotropic glutamate receptors: Their therapeutic potential in anxiety. In M. B. Stein & T. Steckler (Eds.), *Behavioral neurobiology of anxiety and its treatment* (pp. 391–413). New York, NY: Springer Science + Business Media.

Sprenger, J. (2011). Hypothetico-deductive confirmation. *Philosophy Compass, 6*, 497–508.

Springer, S., & Deutsch, G. (1993). *Left brain, right brain.* New York, NY: Freeman.

Sprinkle, R., Hunt, S., Simonds, C., & Comadena, M. (2006). Fear in the classroom: An examination of teachers' use of fear appeals and students' learning outcomes. *Communication Education, 55*(4), 389–402.

Squire, L. R., & Schacter, D. L. (Eds.) (2002). *Neuropsychology of memory* (3rd Ed.). New York, NY: Guilford Press.

Squire, L. R., Stark, C. E., & Clark, R. E. (2004). The medial temporal lobe. *Annual Review of Neuroscience, 27*, 279–306.

Squire, P. (1988). Why the 1936 Literary Digest poll failed. *Public Opinion Quarterly, 52*(1), 125–133.

Sriram, T. G., & Silverman, J. J. (1998). The effects of stress on the respiratory system. In J. R. Hubbard & E. A. Workman (Eds.), *Handbook of stress medicine: an organ system approach.* New York, NY: CRC Press.

Sritharan, R., & Gawronski, B. (2010). Changing implicit and explicit prejudice: Insights from the associative-propositional evaluation model. *Social Psychology, 41*(3), 113–123.

Srivastava, A. S., Malhotra, R., Sharp, J., & Berggren, T. (2008). Potentials of ES cell therapy in neurodegenerative diseases. *Current Pharmaceutical Design, 14*, 3873–3879.

Srivastava, S., John, O. P., Gosling, S. D., & Potter, J. (2003). Development of personality in early and middle adulthood: Set like plaster or persistent change? *Journal of Personality and Social Psychology, 84*, 1041–1053.

Stacey, C. P. (1985). *A Very Double Life: The Private World of Mackenzie King,* Amazon.ca: C. P. Stacey: Books.

Stanley, D. (2012). Celluloid devils: a research study of male nurses in feature films. *Journal of Advanced Nursing, 68*(11), 2526–2537.

Stanovich, K. E. (2011). *Rationality and the reflective mind.* New York, NY: Oxford University Press.

Stanovich, K. E., & West, R. F. (2014). The assessment of rational thinking: IQ ≠ RT. *The Teaching of Psychology, 41*(3), 265–271.

Stanton, A. L., Parsa, A., & Austenfeld, J. L. (2002). The adaptive potential of coping through emotional approach. *Handbook of positive psychology* (pp. 148–158). New York, NY: Oxford University Press.

Stanton, A. L., Sullivan, S. J., & Austenfeld, J. L. (2009). Coping through emotional approach: Emerging evidence for the utility of processing and expressing emotions in responding to stressors. *Oxford handbook of positive psychology (2nd Ed.)* (pp. 225–235). New York, NY: Oxford University Press.

Statistics Canada. (2014a). Table 105-0501 Health indicator profile, annual estimates, by age group and sex, Canada, provinces, territories, health regions (2013 boundaries) and peer groups, occasional, CANSIM (database). Accessed: December 2014.

Statistics Canada. (2014b). Table 102-0552 Deaths and mortality rate, by selected grouped causes and sex, Canada, provinces and territories, annual, CANSIM (database). Accessed: December 2014.

Statistics Canada. (2012). 2011 Census of Population: Families, households, marital status, structural type of dwelling, collectives, *The Daily*, Wednesday September 19, 2012, www.statcan.gc.ca/daily-quotidien/120919/dq120919a-eng.pdf. Accessed October 2014.

Statistics Canada. (2011). *Family violence in Canada: A statistical profile*. Statistics Canada, Canadian Centre for Justice Statistics. Retrieved from http://www.statcan.gc.ca/pub/85-224-x/85-224-x2010000-eng.pdf.

Statistics Canada. (2010). *Canadian Internet use survey*. The Daily, Monday, May 10, 2010.

Statistics Canada. (2004). *Health reports supplement: how healthy are Canadians? Annual report. Alcohol and illicit drug dependence*. Retrieved from http://www.statcan.gc.ca/pub/82-003-s/2004000/pdf/7447-eng.pdf.

Statistics Canada. (2009). *Perceptions of personal safety and crime*. The Daily, June 25, 2015. Retrieved from http://www.statcan.gc.ca/daily-quotidien/111201/dq111201a-eng.htm.

Statistics Canada. (2007). *Family portrait: continuity and change in Canadian families and households in 2006, 2006 Census*. Retrieved from http://www.samesexmarriage.ca/docs/FamilyCensus2006.pdf.

Statistics Canada. (2006a). *Census of population*. Statistics Canada catalogue no. 97-559-XCB2006012.

Statistics Canada. (2006b). *Child care in Canada*. Catalogue no. 89-599-MIE–No. 003. Retrieved from http://www.statcan.gc.ca/pub/89-599-m/89-599-m2006003-eng.pdf .

Statistics Canada. (2005). *General Social Survey, Cycle 18 overview: Personal safety and perceptions of the criminal justice system*. Ottawa: Statistics Canada, Cat. No. 85-566-XIE. Retrieved from http://www4.hrsdc.gc.ca/.3ndic.1t.4r@-eng.jsp?iid=59.

Steele, C. M., & Aronson, J. A. (2004). Stereotype threat does not live by Steele and Aronson (1995) alone. *American Psychologist, 59*(1), 47–48.

Steele, C. M., & Aronson, J. A. (1995). Stereotype threat and the intellectual test performance of African Americans. *Journal of Personality and Social Psychology, 69*(5), 797–811.

Stein, D. J. (2008). Classifying hypersexual disorders: Compulsive, impulsive, and addictive models. *Psychiatric Clinics of North America, 31*(4), 587–591.

Stein, D. J., & Fineberg, N. A. (2007). *Obsessive-compulsive disorder*. Oxford, England: Oxford University Press.

Stein, D. J., & Williams, D. (2010). Cultural and social aspects of anxiety disorders. In D. J. Stein, E. Hollander, & B. O. Rothbaum (Eds.), *Textbook of anxiety disorders* (2nd Ed., pp. 717–729). Arlington, VA: American Psychiatric Publishing.

Stein, D. J., Lund, C., & Nesse, R. M. (2013). Classification systems in psychiatry: diagnosis and global mental health in the era of DSM-5 and ICD-11. *Current Opinion in Psychiatry, 26*(5), 493–497.

Stein, R., Gossen, E., & Jones, K. (2005). Neuronal variability: noise or part of the signal? *Nature Reviews Neuroscience, 6*(5), 389–397.

Stein, Z., Susser, M., Saenger, G., & Marolla, F. (1972). Nutrition and mental performance. *Science, 178*, 708–713.

Steinberg, D. D., Nagata, H., & Aline, D. P. (2013) *Psycholinguistics: Language, mind and world*, (2nd Ed). New York, NY: Routledge.

Steinberg, L. (2008). A social neuroscience perspective on adolescent risk-taking. *Developmental Review, 28*, 789–106.

Steiner, I. D. (1972). *Group process and productivity*. New York, NY: Academic Press.

Steinhausen, H. (2002). The outcome of anorexia nervosa in the 20th century. *American Journal of Psychiatry, 159*, 1284–1293.

Steinhausen, H. C., Blattmann, B., & Pfund, F. (2007). Developmental outcome in children with intrauterine exposure to substances. *European Addiction Research, 13*, 94–100.

Stelmack, R. M. (1997). Toward a paradigm in personality: Comment on Eysenck's (1997) view. *Journal of Personality and Social Psychology, 73*(6), 1238–1241.

Stephens, R., Atkins, J., & Kingston, A. (2009). Swearing as a response to pain. *NeuroReport: For Rapid Communication of Neuroscience Research, 20*(12), 1056–1060.

Stephens, R., & Umland, C. (2011). Swearing as a response to pain—Effect of daily swearing frequency. *The Journal of Pain, 12*(2), 1274–1281.

Stephure, R. J., Boon, S. D., MacKinnon, S. L., & Deveau, V. (2009). Internet initiated relationships: Associations between age and involvement in online dating. *Journal of Computer-Mediated Communication, 3*, 658–681.

Steptoe, A. (2000). Health behavior and stress. In G. Fink (Ed.), *Encyclopedia of Stress, Vol. 2* (pp. 322–326). New York, NY: Academic Press.

Sternberg, R. J. (2014a). The development of adaptive competence: Why cultural psychology is necessary and not just nice. *Developmental Review, 34*(3), 208–224.

Sternberg, R. J. (2014b). Teaching about the nature of intelligence. *Intelligence, 42*, 176–179.

Sternberg, R. J. (2010). Teaching for creativity. In R. A. Beghetto & J. C. Kaufman (Eds.), *Nurturing creativity in the classroom* (pp. 394–414). New York, NY: Cambridge University Press.

Sternberg, R. J. (2008). The balance theory of wisdom. In M. H. Immordino-Yang (Ed.), *The Jossey-Bass reader on the brain and learning* (pp. 133–150). San Francisco, CA: Jossey-Bass.

Sternberg, R. J. (2007a). Intelligence and culture. In S. Kitayama & D. Cohen (Eds.), *Handbook of cultural psychology* (pp. 547–568). New York, NY: Guilford Press.

Sternberg, R. J. (2007b). Who are the bright children? The cultural context of being and acting intelligent. *Educational Researcher, 36*(3), 148–155.

Sternberg, R. J. (2004). A triangular theory of love. In H. T. Reis & C. E. Rusbult (Eds.), *Close relationships: Key readings* (pp. 213–227). Philadelphia, PA: Taylor & Francis.

Sternberg, R. J. (2003a). Biological intelligence. In R. J. Sternberg & E. L. Grigorenko (Eds.), *The psychology of abilities, competencies, and expertise* (pp. 240–262). New York, NY: Cambridge University Press.

Sternberg, R. J. (2003b). A broad view of intelligence: The theory of successful intelligence. *Consulting Psychology Journal: Practice and Research, 55*(3), 139–154.

Sternberg, R. J. (2003c). *Wisdom, intelligence, and creativity synthesized*. New York, NY: Cambridge University Press.

Sternberg, R. J. (1987). Liking versus loving: A comparative evaluation of theories. *Psychological Bulletin, 102*, 331–345.

Sternberg, R. J. (1986). A triangular theory of love. *Psychological Review, 93*, 119–135.

Sternberg, R. J., Conway, B. E., Ketron, J. L., & Bernstein, M. (1981). People's conceptions of intelligence. *Journal of Personality and Social Psychology, 41*(1), 37–55.

Sternberg, R. J., & Grigorenko, E. L. (2013). *Environmental effects on cognitive abilities*. New York, NY: Lawrence Erlbaum Associates.

Sternberg, R. J., & Grigorenko, E. L. (2004). Why cultural psychology is necessary and not just nice: The example of the study of intelligence. In R. J. Sternberg and E. L. Grigorenko (Eds.), *Culture and competence* (pp. 207–223). Washington, DC: American Psychological Association.

Sternberg, R. J., & Grigorenko, E. L. (2001). Unified psychology. *American Psychologist, 56*, 1069–1079.

Sternberg, R. J., Jarvin, L., & Grigorenko, E. L. (2011). *Explorations in giftedness*. New York, NY: Cambridge University Press.

Sternberg, R. J., Wagner, R. K., Williams, W. M., Horvath, J. A., et al. (1995). Testing common sense. *American Psychologist, 50*(11), 912–927.

Sternberg, R. J., & Weis, K. (2006). *The New Psychology of Love*. New Haven, CT: Yale University.

Stetter, F., & Kupper, S. (2002). Autogenic training: A meta-analysis of clinical outcome studies. *Applied Psychophysiology and Biofeedback, 27*(1), 45–98.

Stewart, A. E. (2005). Attributions of responsibility for motor vehicle crashes. *Accident Analysis & Prevention, 37*(4), 681–688.

Stewart, C. E., Moseley, M. J., & Fielder, A. R. (2011). Amlyopia therapy: An update. *Strabismus, 19*(3), 91–98.

Stewart, M. E., Ebmeier, K. P., & Deary, I. J. (2005). Personality correlates of happiness and sadness: EQP-R and TPQ compared. *Personality and Individual Differences, 38*, 1085–1096.

Stewart, T. L., Latu, I. M., Kawakami, K., & Myers, A. C. (2010). Consider the situation: Reducing automatic stereotyping through Situational Attribution Training. *Journal of Experimental Social Psychology, 46*, 221–225.

Stickgold, R. (2011). Memory in sleep and dreams: The construction of meaning. In S. Nalbantian, P. M. Matthews, & J. L. McClelland (Eds.), *The memory process: Neuroscientific and humanistic perspectives* (pp. 73–95). Cambridge, MA: MIT Press.

Stocco, A., Lebiere, C., & Anderson, J. R. (2010). Conditional routing of information to the cortex: A model of the basal ganglia's role in cognitive coordination. *Psychological Review, 117*(2), 541.

Stoleru, S., Gregoire, M. C., Gerard, D., Decety, J., Lafarge, E., Cinotti, L., et al. (1999). Neuroanatomical correlates of visually evoked sexual arousal in human males. *Archives of Sexual Behavior, 28*, 1–21.

Stone, J. V., Hunkin, N. M., & Hornby, A. (2001). Predicting spontaneous recovery of memory. *Nature, 414*(6860), 167–168.

Storms, M. S. (1973). Videotape of the attribution process: Reversing actors' and observers' points of view. *Journal of Personality and Social Psychology, 27*, 165–175.

Stout, D., & Chaminade, T. (2012). Stone tools, language and the brain in human evolution. *Philosophical Transactions of the Royal Society B: Biological Sciences, 367*(1585), 75–87.

Strack, F., Martin, L. L., & Stepper, S. (1988). Inhibiting and facilitating conditions of the human smile: A non-obtrusive test of the facial-feedback hypothesis. *Journal of Personality and Social Psychology, 54*, 768–777.

Stranahan, A. M., Khalil, D., & Gould, E. (2007). Running induces widespread structural alterations in the hippocampus and entorhinal cortex. *Hippocampus, 17*, 1017–1022.

Stranahan, A. M., Khalil, D., & Gould, E. (2006). Social isolation delays the positive effects of running on adult neurogenesis. *Nature Neuroscience, 9*, 526–533.

Strauss, B. (2002). Social facilitation in motor tasks: A review of research and theory. *Psychology of Sport and Exercise, 3*(3), 237–256.

Strayer, R. J., & Nelson, L. S. (2008). Adverse events associated with ketamine for procedural sedation in adults [published correction appears in *American Journal of Emergency Medicine*, 27:512]. *American Journal of Emergency Medicine, 26*, 985–1028.

Streita, W. (2006). Microglial senescence: does the brain's immune system have an expiration date? *Trends in Neurosciences, 29*(9), 506–510.

Strelau, J. (2010). How far are we in searching for the biological background of personality? In T. Maruszewski, M. Fajkowska, & M. Eysenck. (Eds.), *Personality from biological, cognitive, and social perspectives: Warsaw lectures in personality and social psychology*. Clifton Corners, NY: Eliot Werner Publications.

Stricker, E. M., & Zigmond, M. J. (1986). Brain monoamines, homeostasis, and adaptive behavior handbook of physiology: Intrinsic regulatory systems of the brain (pp. 677–696). Bethesda, MD: American Physiological Society.

Strümpfel, U. (2006). *Therapie der gefühle: For-schungsbefunde zur gestalttherapie*. Cologne, Germany: Edition Huanistiche Psychologie.

Strümpfel, U. (2004). Research on gestalt therapy. *International Gestalt Journal, 27*(1), 9–54.

Struyfs, H., Molinuevo, J. L., Martin, J. J., De Deyn, P. P., & Engelborghs, S. (2014). Validation of the AD-CSF-Index in autopsy-confirmed Alzheimer's Disease patients and healthy controls. *Journal of Alzheimer's Disease.* doi: 10.3233/JAD-131085

Stuart, H. (2010) Mental disorders and social stigma: Three moments in Canadian history. In J. Cairney & D. L. Streiner (Eds.), *Mental disorder in Canada: An epidemiological perspective* (pp. 304–330). Toronto, ON: University of Toronto Press.

Stuart, T. D., & Garrison, M. E. B. (2002). The influence of daily hassles and role balance on health status: A study of mothers of grade school children. *Women & Health, 36*(3), 1–11.

Sturmey, P. (2008). Adults with intellectual disabilities. In M. Hersen & J. Rosqvist (Eds.), *Handbook of psychological assessment, case conceptualization, and treatment, Vol. 1: Adults*. Hoboken, NJ: John Wiley & Sons.

Sue, D. W., Capodilupo, C. M., Torino, G. C. (2007). Racial microaggressions in everyday life: Implications for clinical practice. *American Psychologist, 62*, 271–286.

Sugita, M. (2006). Taste perception and coding in the periphery. *Cellular and Molecular Life Sciences, 63*, 2000–2015.

Sulloway, F. J. (1996). Born to rebel: Birth order, family dynamics and creative lives. New York, NY: Pantheon.

Suls, J., & Rothman, A. (2004). Evolution of the biopsychosocial model: Prospects and challenges for health psychology. *Health Psychology, 23*(2), 119–125.

Sun, M. (Ed.). (2007). *New research in cognitive sciences.* Hauppauge, NY: Nova Science Publishers.

Super, C. M. (1976). Environmental effects on motor development: The case of African infant precocity. *Developmental Medicine & Child Neurology, 18*(5), 561–567.

Super, C. M., & Harkness, S. (2002). Culture structures the environment for development. *Human Development, 45*, 270–274.

Super, C. M., & Harkness, S. (1972). The infant's niche in rural Kenya and metropolitan America. In L. Adler (Ed.), *Issues in cross-cultural research.* New York, NY: Academic Press.

Suzuki, H., & Heath, L. (2014). Impacts of humor and relevance on the remembering of lecture details. *Humor: International Journal of Humor Research, 27*(1), 87–101.

Swain, J. E., Lorberbaum, J. P., Kose, S., & Strathearn, L. (2007). Brain basis of early parent-infant interactions: Psychology, physiology, and in vivo functional neuroimaging studies. *Journal of Child Psychology and Psychiatry, and Allied Disciplines, 48*(3–4), 262–287.

Swap, W. C. (1977). Interpersonal attraction and repeated exposure to rewarders and punishers. *Personality and Social Psychology Bulletin, 3*, 248–251.

Sweatt, J. D. (2010). *Mechanisms of memory (2nd Ed.).* San Diego, CA: Elsevier Academic Press.

Symons, D. (2004). Mental state discourse and theory of mind: Internalisation of self-other understanding within a cognitive framework. *Developmental Review, 24*, 159–188.

Synder, C. R., Lopez, S. J., & Pedrotti, J. T. (2011). *Positive psychology. The scientific and practical explorations of human strengths* (2nd ed.). Thousand Oaks: Sage.

Tachibana, M., Amato, P., Sparman, M., Gutierrez, N. M., Tippner-Hedges, R., Ma, H., . . . & Mitalipov, S. (2013). Human embryonic stem cells derived by somatic cell nuclear transfer. *Cell, 153*(6), 1228–1238.

Tager-Flusberg, H. (2001). Putting words together: morphology and syntax in the preschool years. In J. Berko Gleason (Ed.), *The development of language* (5th Ed., pp. 116–212). Boston, MA: Allyn and Bacon.

Tajfel, H. (1981). *Human groups and social categories.* Cambridge, UK: Cambridge University Press.

Tajfel, H., & Turner, J. C. (2004). The social identity theory of intergroup behavior. In J. T. Jost & J. Sidanius (Eds.), *Political psychology: Key readings in social psychology* (pp. 276–293). New York, NY: Psychology Press.

Takahashi, J., Takagi, Y., & Saiki, H. (2009). Transplantation of embryonic stem cell-derived dopaminergic neurons in MPTP-treated monkeys. *Methods in Molecular Biology, 482*, 199–212.

Takano, K., & Tanno, Y. (2009). Self-rumination, self-reflection, and depression: Self-rumination counteracts the adaptive effect of self-reflection. *Behaviour Research and Therapy, 47*, 260–264.

Talarico, J. M., & Rubin, D. C. (2009). Flashbulb memories result from ordinary memory processes and extraordinary event characteristics. In O. Luminet & A. Curci (Eds.), *Flashbulb memories: New issues and new perspectives* (pp. 79–97). New York, NY: Psychology Press.

Talarico, J. M., & Rubin, D. C. (2007). Flashbulb memories are special after all; in phenomenology, not accuracy. *Applied Cognitive Psychology, 21*(5), 557–578.

Talarico, J. M., & Rubin, D. C. (2003). Confidence, not consistency, characterizes flashbulb memories. *Psychological Science, 14*(5), 455–461.

Talbot, M. (2010). *Language and gender.* Malden, MA: Polity Press.

Talmi, D., & McGarry, L. M. (2012). Accounting for immediate emotional memory enhancement. *Journal of Memory and Language, 66*(1), 93–108.

Talmi, D., Schimmack, U., Paterson, T., & Moscovitch, M. (2007). The role of attention and relatedness in emotionally enhanced memory. *Emotion, 7*(1), 89.

Talmi, D., Ziegler, M., Hawksworth, J., Lalani, S., Herman, C. P., & Moscovitch, M. (2013). Emotional stimuli exert parallel effects on attention and memory. *Cognition & Emotion, 27*(3), 530–538.

Talwar, R., Nitz, K., & Lerner, R. M. (1991). Relations among early adolescent temperament, parent and peer demands, and adjustment: A test of the goodness of fit model. *Journal of Adolescence, 13*, 279–298.

Talwar, V., Gordon, H. M., & Lee, K. (2007). Lying in the elementary school years: verbal deception and its relation to second-order belief understanding. *Developmental Psychology, 43*(3), 804–810.

Talwar, V., & Lee, K. (2008). Social and cognitive correlates of children's lying behavior. *Child Development, 79*(4), 866–881.

Tamminga, C. A., Shad, M. U., & Ghose, S. (2008). Neuropsychiatric aspects of schizophrenia. In S. C. Yudofsky & R. E. Hales (Eds.), *The American Psychiatric Publishing textbook of neuropsychiatry and behavioral neurosciences* (5th Ed.). Washington, DC: American Psychiatric Publishing.

Tanaka-Matsumi, J. (2001). Abnormal psychology and culture. In D. Matsumoto (Ed.), *The handbook of culture and psychology* (pp. 265–286). New York, NY: Oxford University Press.

Tang, C. Y., Eaves, E. L., Ng, J. C., Carpenter, D. M., Mai, X., Schroeder, D. H., & Haier, R. J. (2010). Brain networks for working memory and factors of intelligence assessed in males and females with fMRI and DTI. *Intelligence, 38*(3), 293–303.

Tapia, J. C., & Lichtman, J. W. (2008). Synapse elimination. In L. Squire, D. Berg, F. Bloom, S. Du Lac, A. Ghosh, & N. Spitzer (Eds.), *Fundamental neuroscience* (3rd ed., pp. 469–490). San Diego, CA: Elsevier.

Tatzer, E., Schubert, M. T., Timischl, W., & Simbruner, G. (1985). Discrimination of taste and preference for sweet in premature babies. *Early Human Development, 12*(1), 23–30.

Taube-Schiff, M., & Lau, M. A. (2008). Major depressive disorder. In M. Hersen & J. Rosqvist (Eds.), *Handbook of psychological assessment, case conceptualization, and treatment, Vol. 1: Adults* (pp. 319–351). Hoboken, NJ: John Wiley & Sons.

Tavris, C. (2003). Uncivil rights—the cultural rules of anger. *Violence and society: A reader* (pp. 3–14). Upper Saddle River, NJ: Prentice Hall/Pearson Education.

Tavris, C. (1991). The mismeasure of woman: Paradoxes and perspectives in the study of gender. In J. D. Goodchilds (Ed.), *Psychological Perspectives on Human Diversity in America* (pp. 87–136). Washington, DC: American Psychological Association.

Tavris, C. (1989). *Anger: The misunderstood emotion (rev. Ed.).* New York, NY: Touchstone Books/Simon & Schuster.

Taylor, D. A., Gould, R. J., & Brounstein, P. J. (1981). Effects of personalistic self-disclosure. *Personality and Social Psychology Bulletin, 7*, 487–492.

Taylor, I., & Taylor, M. M. (1990). *Psycholinguistics: Learning and using language.* Prentice Hall.

Taylor, J., Iacono, W. G., & McGue, M. (2000). Evidence for a genetic etiology of early-onset delinquency. *Journal of Abnormal Psychology, 109*, 634–643.

Taylor, P. J., Gooding, P., Wood, A. M., & Tarrier, N. (2011). The role of defeat and entrapment in depression, anxiety, and suicide. *Psychological Bulletin, 137*(3), 391–420.

Taylor, S. E. (2011). Social support: a review. In H. S. Freidman (Ed.), *The Oxford Handbook of Health Psychology.* New York, NY: Oxford University Press.

Taylor, S. E. (2010a). Health. In S. T. Fiske, D. T. Gilbert, & G. Lindzey (Eds.), *Handbook of social psychology*, Vol. 1 (5th Ed., pp. 698–723). Hoboken, NJ: John Wiley & Sons.

Taylor, S. E. (2010b). Health psychology. In R. F. Baumeister & E. J. Finkel (Eds.), *Advanced social psychology: The state of the science* (pp. 697–731). New York, NY: Oxford University Press.

Taylor, S. E. (2008). From social psychology to neuroscience and back. *Journeys in social psychology: Looking back to inspire the future* (pp. 39–54). New York, NY: Psychology Press.

Taylor, S. E. (2007). Social support. *Foundations of health psychology* (pp. 145–171). New York, NY: Oxford University Press.

Taylor, S. E. (2006a). *Health psychology (6th Ed.)*. New York, NY: McGraw Hill.

Taylor, S. E. (2006b). Tend and befriend: Biobehavioral bases of affiliation under stress. *Current Directions in Psychological Science, 15*(6), 273–277.

Taylor, S. E. (2004). The accidental neuroscientist: Positive resources, stress responses, and course of illness. In G. G. Berntson & J. T. Cacioppo (Eds.), *Essays in social neuroscience* (pp. 133–141). Cambridge, MA: The MIT Press.

Taylor, S. E., Lerner, J. S., Sherman, D. K., Sage, R. M., & McDowell, N. K. (2003). Are self-enhancing cognitions associated with healthy or unhealthy biological profiles? *Journal of Personality and Social Psychology, 85,* 605–615.

Taylor, S. R., & Weiss, J. S. (2009) Review of insomnia pharmacotherapy options for the elderly: Implications for managed care. *Population Health Management, 12*(6) 317–323.

Teicher, M. H., Andersen, S. L., Navalta, C. P., Tomoda, A., Polcari, A., & Kim, D. (2008). Neuropsychiatric disorders of childhood and adolescence. *The American Psychiatric Publishing textbook of neuropsychiatry and behavioral neurosciences (5th Ed.)* (pp. 1045–1113). Washington, DC: American Psychiatric Publishing, Inc.

Temoshok, L. R. (2003). Congruence Matters: A Consideration of Adaptation and Appropriateness. *Advances in Mind-Body Medicine, 19,* 10–11.

Temoshok, L. R., Waldstein, S. R., Wald, R. L., Garzino-Demo, A., Synowski, S. J., Sun, L., & Wiley, J. A. (2008). Type C coping, alexithymia, and heart rate reactivity are associated independently and differentially with specific immune mechanisms linked to HIV progression. *Brain, Behavior, and Immunity, 22*(5), 781–792.

Temple, S. (2001). The development of neural stem cells. *Nature, 414,* 112–117.

Temrin, H., Buchmayer, S., & Enquist, M. (2000). Step-parents and infanticide: New data contradict evolutionary predictions. *Proceedings of the Royal Society of London B, 267,* 943–945.

Tennen, H., & Affleck, G. (2009). Assessing positive life change: In search of meticulous methods. *Medical illness and positive life change: Can crisis lead to personal transformation?* (pp. 31–49). Washington, DC: American Psychological Association.

Tennen, H., & Affleck, G. (2002). Benefit-finding and benefit-reminding. *Handbook of positive psychology* (pp. 584–597). New York, NY: Oxford University Press.

Tennen, H., Affleck, G., & Armeli, S. (2005). Personality and daily experience revisited. *Journal of Personality, 73*(6), 1465–1484.

Terman, L. M. (1925). *Genetic studies of genius: Mental and physical traits of a thousand gifted children.* Oxford, UK: Stanford University Press.

Terman, L. M., & Merrill, M. A. (1937). *Measuring intelligence: A guide to the administration of the new revised Stanford-Binet tests of intelligence.* Oxford, UK: Houghton Mifflin.

Tesser, A. (1978). Self-generated attitude change. *Advances in Experimental Social Psychology, 11,* 289–338.

Teufel, M., Biedermann, T., Rapps, N., Hausteiner, C., Henningsen, P., Enck, P., & Zipfel, S. (2007). Psychological burden of food allergy. *World Journal of Gastroenterology, 13*(25), 3456–3465.

Thagard, P. (2001). How to make decisions: Coherence, emotion, and practical inference. In E. Millgram (Ed.), *Varieties of practical inference* (pp. 355–371). Cambridge, MA: MIT Press.

Thagard, P., & Kroon, F. (2008). *Hot thought: Mechanisms and applications of emotional cognition.* MIT Press.

Thakkar, M. M., & Datta, S. (2010). The evolution of REM sleep. In P. McNamara, R. A. Barton, & C. L. Nunn (Eds.), *Evolution of sleep: Phylogenetic and functional perspectives* (pp. 197–217). New York, NY: Cambridge University Press.

Thase, M. E., & Denko, T. (2008). Pharmacotherapy of mood disorders. *Annual Review of Clinical Psychology, 4,* 53–91.

The Look AHEAD Research Group. (2014). Eight-year weight losses with an intensive lifestyle intervention: The look AHEAD study. *Obesity, 22,* 5–13.

Thelen, E. (1989). The (re)discovery of motor development: Learning new things from an old field. *Developmental Psychology, 25,* 946–949.

Thelen, E., & Smith, L. B. (2006). Dynamic systems theories. In R. M. Lerner (Ed.), *Handbook of child psychology, Vol. 1: Theoretical models of human development* (6th Ed., pp. 258–312). Hoboken, NJ: Wiley.

Theodorou, S., & Haber, P. S. (2005). The medical complications of heroin use. *Current Opinions in Psychiatry, 18*(3), 257–263.

Thoman, D. B., Smith, J. L., Brown, E. R., Chase, J., Lee, J., & Young, K. (2013) Beyond performance: A motivational experiences model of stereotype threat. *Educational Psychology Review, 25*(2), 211–243.

Thomas, A., & Chess, S. (1977). *Temperament and development.* Oxford, England: Brunner/Mazel.

Thomas, A. K., Hannula, D. E., & Loftus, E. F. (2007). How self-relevant imagination affects memory for behaviour. *Applied Cognitive Psychology, 21*(1), 69–86.

Thomas, S., & Kunzmann, U. (2013). Age differences in wisdom-related knowledge: Does the age relevance of the task matter? *The Journals of Gerontology: Series B. Psychological Science and Social Science, 69*(6), 897–905.

Thompson, R. F. (2009). Habituation: A history. *Neurobiology of Learning and Memory, 92*(2), 127–134.

Thompson, R. F. (2000). *The brain: A neuroscience primer (3rd Ed.).* New York, NY: Worth Publishers.

Thompson, S. C., Sobolew-Shubin, A., Galbraith, M. E., Schwankovsky L., & Cruzen, D. (1993). Maintaining perceptions of control: Finding perceived control in low-control circumstances. *Journal of Personality and Social Psychology, 64*(2), 293–304.

Thorndike, E. L. (1920). The reliability and significance of tests of intelligence. *Journal of Educational Psychology, 11*(5), 284–287.

Thorndike, E. L. (1933). A proof of the law of effect. *Science, 77,* 173–175.

Thurstone, L. L. (1938). *Primary mental abilities.* Chicago, IL: University of Chicago Press.

Tillmann, B., Peretz, I., & Samson, S. (2011). Neurocognitive approaches to memory in music: Music is memory. In S. Nalbantian, P. M. Matthews, & J. L. McClelland (Eds.), *The memory process: Neuroscientific and humanistic perspectives* (pp. 377–394). Cambridge, MA: MIT Press.

Tinghitella, R. M., & Zuk, M. (2009). Asymmetric mating preferences accommodated the rapid evolutionary loss of a sexual signal. *Evolution, 63,* 2087–2098.

Tirri, K., & Nokelainen, P. (2008). Identification of multiple intelligences with the multiple intelligence profiling questionnaire III. *Psychology Science, 50*(2), 206–221.

Tobin, R. (2013). An introduction to the Wechsler Intelligence Tests: Revisiting theory and practice. *Journal of Psychoeducational Assessment, 31*(2), 91–93.

Todorova, I. L., Falcon, L. M., Lincoln, A. K., & Price, L. L. (2010). Perceived discrimination, psychological distress and health. *Sociology of Health & Illness, 32*(6), 843–861.

Toga, A. W., Thompson, P. M., & Sowell, E. R. (2006). Mapping brain maturation. *Trends in Neurosciences, 29,* 148–159.

Tolman, E. C. (1948). Cognitive maps in animals and man. *Psychological Review, 55,* 189–208.

Tolman, E. C., & Honzik, C. H. (1930a). Degrees of hunger, reward and nonreward, and maze learning in rats. *University of California Publications in Psychology, 4,* 241–256.

Tolman, E. C., & Honzik, C. H. (1930b). Introduction and removal of reward, and maze performance in rats. *University of California Publications in Psychology, 4,* 257–275.

Tolman, E. C., & Gleitman, H. (1949). Studies in spatial learning; place and response learning under different degrees of motivation. *Journal Experimental Psychology, 39,* 653–659.

Tomasello, M. (2009). *The cultural origins of human cognition.* Cambridge, UK: Harvard University Press.

Tomes, Y. I. (2010). Culture and psychoeducational assessment: Cognition and achievement. In E. García-Vásquez, T. D. Crespi, & C. A. Riccio (Eds.), *Handbook of education, training, and supervision of school psychologists in school and community, vol. 1: Foundations of professional practice* (pp. 167–183). New York, NY: Routledge/Taylor & Francis Group.

Tomkins, S. S. (1992). *Affect, imagery, consciousness, vol. 4: Cognition: Duplication and transformation of information.* New York, NY: Springer Publishing Co.

Tomkins, S. S. (1980). Affect as amplification: Some modifications in theory. In R. Plutchik & H. Kellerman (Eds.), *Emotion: Theory, research and experience* (pp. 141–164). New York, NY: Academic.

Tomkins, S. S. (1962). *Affect, imagery, and consciousness.* New York, NY: Springer Publishing.

Tonigan, J. S., Toscova, R., & Miller, W. R. (1995). Meta-analysis of the literature on Alcoholics Anonymous: Sample and study characteristics moderate findings. *Journal of Studies on Alcohol, 57*(1), 65–72.

Torrente, M. P., Gelenberg, A. J., & Vrana, K. E. (2012). Boosting serotonin in the brain: Is it time to revamp the treatment of depression? *Journal of Psychopharmacology, 26*(5), 629–635.

Torrey, E. F. (2001). *Surviving schizophrenia: A manual for families, consumers, and providers* (4th Ed.). New York, NY: HarperCollins.

Toth, K., & King, B. H. (2010). Intellectual disability (mental retardation). In M. K. Dulcan (Ed.), *Dulcan's textbook of child and adolescent psychiatry* (pp. 151–171). Arlington, VA: American Psychiatric Publishing.

Tourangeau, R., Smith, T. W., & Rasinski, K. A. (1997). Motivation to report sensitive behaviors on surveys: Evidence from a bogus pipeline experiment. *Journal of Applied Social Psychology, 27,* 209–222.

Tovee, M. J. (2008). *An introduction to the visual system*. Cambridge University Press.

Townsend, F. (2000). Birth order and rebelliousness: Reconstructing the research in *Born to Rebel*. *Politics and the Life Sciences, 19*(2), 135–156.

Tracy, M., Morgenstern, H., Zivin, K., Aiello, A., & Galea, S. (2014). Traumatic event exposure and depression severity over time: Results from a prospective cohort study in an urban area. *Social Psychiatry and Psychiatric Epidemiology*, Published First Online.

Trahan, L. H., Stuebing, K. K., Fletcher, J. M., & Hiscock, M. (2014) The Flynn Effect: A meta-analysis. *Psychological Bulletin*, June 30, 2014. Advance online publication. Retrieved from http://dx.doi.org/10.1037/a0037173.

Tramo, M. J., Loftus, W. C., Stukel, T. A., Green, R. L., Weaver, J. B., & Gazzaniga, M. S. (1998). Brain size, head size, and intelligence quotient in monozygotic twins. *Neurology, 50*(5), 1246–1252.

Tramontin, M., & Halpern, J. (2007). The psychological aftermath of terrorism: The 2001 World Trade Center attack. In E. K. Carll (Ed.), *Trauma psychology: Issues in violence, disaster, health, and illness* (Vol. 1). Westport, CT: Praeger Publishers.

Trautner, P., Dietl, T., Staedtgen, M., Mecklinger, A., & Grunwald T., et al. (2004). Recognition of famous faces in the medial temporal lobe: An invasive ERP study. *Neurology, 63*, 1203–1208.

Travers, C., Martin-Khan, M., & Lie, D. (2010). Performance indicators to easure dementia risk reduction activities in primary care. *Australasian Journal on Aging, 29*, 39–42.

Trawick-Smith, J., & Dziurgot, T. (2011). "Good-fit" teacher–child play interactions and the subsequent autonomous play of preschool children. *Early Childhood Research Quarterly, 26*(1), 110–123.

Treanor, M. (2011). The potential impact of mindfulness on exposure and extinction learning in anxiety disorders. *Clinical Psychology Review, 31*(4), 617–625.

Treisman, A. M., & Kanwisher, N. G. (1998). Perceiving visually presented objects: Recognition, awareness, and modularity. *Current Opinions in Neurobiology, 8*, 218–226.

Trembath, D., Balandin, S., Stancliffe, R. J., & Togher, L. (2010). Employment and volunteering for adults with intellectual disability. *Journal of Policy and Practice in Intellectual Disabilities, 7*(4), 235–238.

Triandis, H. C. (2001). Individualism-collectivism and personality. *Journal of Personality, 69*(6), 907–924.

Triandis, H. C. (1989). Cross-cultural studies of individualism and collectivism. In J. Berman (Ed.), *Nebraska Symposium* (pp. 41–130). Lincoln, NE: University of Nebraska Press.

Triandis, H., Botempo, R., Villareal, M., Asai, M., & Lucca, N. (1988). Individualism and collectivism: Cross-cultural perspectives on self in group relationships. *Journal of Personality and Social Psychology, 54*, 332–336.

Triandis, H. C., McCusker, C., & Hui, C. H. (1990). Multimethod probes of individualism and collectivism. *Journal of Personality and Social Psychology, 59*, 1006–1020.

Triplett, N. (1898). The dynamogenic factors in pace-making and competition. *American Journal of Psychology, 9*, 507–533.

Troyer, J. M. (2006). Post-bereavement experiences of older widowers: A qualitative investigation. ProQuest Information & Learning: US. *Dissertation Abstracts International Section A: Humanities and Social Sciences, 66*(8), 3051.

Truett, K. R., Eaves, L. J., Walters, E. E., et al. (1994). A model system for analysis of family resemblance in extended kinships of twins. *Behavior Genetics, 24*(1), 35–49.

Trull, T. J., & Durrett, C. A. (2005). Categorical and dimensional models of personality disorder. *Annual Review of Clinical Psychology, 1*, 355–380.

Tsai, W. H. S., & Shumow, M. (2011). Representing fatherhood and male domesticity in American advertising. *Interdisciplinary Journal of Research in Business, 1*(8), 38–48.

Tsang, H. W., Fung, K. M., & Corrigan, P. W. (2009). Psychosocial and sociodemographic correlates of medication compliance among people with schizophrenia. *Journal of Behavior Therapy and Experimental Psychiatry, 40*(1), 3–14.

Tsang, J. A., Carpenter, T. P., Roberts, J. A., Frisch, M. B., & Carlisle, R. D. (2014). Why are materialists less happy? The role of gratitude and need satisfaction in the relationship between materialism and life satisfaction. *Personality and Individual Differences, 64*, 62–66.

Tsukiura, T., Sekiguchi, A., Yomogida, Y., Nakagawa, S., Shigemune, Y., Kambara, T., . . . Kawashima, R. (2011). Effects of aging on hippocampal and anterior temporal activations during successful retrieval of memory for face–name associations. *Journal of Cognitive Neuroscience, 23*(1), 200–213. doi: 10.1162/jocn.2010.21476.

Tsuruga, K., Kobayashi, T., Hirai, N., et al. (2008). Foreign accent syndrome in a case of dissociative (conversion) disorder. *Seishin Shinkeigaku Zasshi, 110*(2), 79–87.

Tulsky, D. S., Saklofske, D. H., & Ricker, J. H. (2003). Historical overview of intelligence and memory: Factors influencing the Wechsler scales. In D. S. Tulsky, D. H. Saklofske, G. J. Chelune, R. K. Heaton, & R. J. Ivnik

(Eds.), *Clinical interpretation of the WAIS-III and WMSIII* (pp. 7–41). San Diego, CA: Academic Press.

Tulving, E. (1974). Recall and recognition of semantically encoded words. *Journal of Experimental Psychology, 102*(5), 778–787.

Tulving, E., & Thomson, D. M. (1973). Encoding specificity and retrieval processes in episodic memory. *Psychological Review, 80*, 352–373.

Turati, C., Di Giorgio, E., Bardi, L., & Simion, F. (2010). Holistic face processing in newborns, 3-month-old infants, and adults: Evidence from the composite face effect. *Child Development, 81*(6), 1894–1905.

Turiel, E. (2010). The development of morality: Reasoning, emotions, and resistance. In W. F. Overton & R. M. Lerner (Eds.), *The handbook of lifespan development*, vol. 1: *Cognition, biology, and methods* (pp. 554–583). Hoboken, NJ: John Wiley & Sons.

Turing, A. (1950). Computing Machinery and Intelligence. *Mind, LIX*(236), 433–460.

Turkington, C., & Harris, J. R. (2009). *The Encyclopedia of the brain and brain disorders (3rd edition)*. New York, NY: Facts on File/Infobase Publishing.

Turkington, C., & Harris, J. R. (2001). *The Encyclopedia of memory and memory disorders (2nd edition)*. New York, NY: Facts on File/Infobase Publishing.

Tversky, A. (1972). Elimination by aspects: A theory of choice. *Psychological Review, 79*, 281–99.

Tversky, A., & Kahneman, D. (1993). Probabilistic reasoning. In A. I. Goldman (Ed.), *Readings in Philosophy and Cognitive Science* (pp. 43–68). Cambridge, MA: MIT Press.

Tversky, A., & Kahneman, D. (1981). The framing of decisions and the psychology of choice. *Science, 211*(4481), 453–458.

Tversky, A., & Kahneman, D. (1974). Judgment under uncertainty: Heuristics and biases. *Science, 185*, 1124–1131.

Twemlow, S. W., Fonagy, P., & Sacco, F. C. (2003). Modifying social aggression in schools. *Journal of Applied Psychoanalytical Studies, 5*(2), 211–222.

Tychsen, L. (2012). The cause of infantile strabismus lies upstairs in the cerebral cortex, not downstairs in the brainstem. *Archives of Ophthalmology, 130*(8), 1060-1061.

Tyrer, P. (2013). *Models for Mental Disorder*. Oxford, UK: John Wiley & Sons.

Uchino, B. N., & Birmingham, W. (2011). Stress and support processes. In R. J. Contrada & A. Baum (Eds.), *The handbook of stress science: Biology, psychology, and health*. New York, NY: Springer Publishing Co.

Uliaszek, A. A., Zinbarg, R. E., Mineka, S., Craske, M. G., Griffith, J. W., Sutton, J. M., . . . & Hammen, C. (2012). A longitudinal examination of stress generation in depressive and anxiety disorders. *Journal of Abnormal Psychology, 121*(1), 4–15.

Underwood, B., & Moore, B. (1982). Perspective-taking and altruism. *Psychological Bulletin, 91*, 143–173.

Underwood, L. G. (2011). The daily spiritual experience scale: overview and results. *Religions, 2*(1), 29-50.

Ungerleider, L. G., & Haxby, J. V. (1994). What and where in the human brain. *Current Opinion in Neurobiology, 4*, 157–165.

Urcuyo, K. R., Boyers, A. E., Carver, C. S., & Antoni, M. H. (2005). Finding benefit in breast cancer: Relations with personality, coping, and concurrent well-being. *Psychology of Health, 20*(2), 175–192.

Urry, H. L., Nitschke, J. B., Dolski, I., Jackson, D. C., Dalton, K. M., Mueller, C. J., Rosenkranz, M. A., Ryff, C. D., Singer, B. H., & Davidson, R. J. (2004). Making a life worth living: Neural correlates of well-being. *Psychological Science, 15*(6), 367–372.

Ursano, R. J., McCarroll, J. E., & Fullerton, C. S. (2003). Traumatic death in terrorism and disasters: The effects on posttraumatic stress and behavior. *Terrorism and disaster: Individual and community mental health interventions* (pp. 308–332). New York, NY: Cambridge University Press.

U.S. Census Bureau. (2011). The national data book. *The 2011 Statistical Abstract: International Statistics*. Retrieved from http://www.census.gov/compendia/statab/cats/international_statistics.html.

U.S. Census Bureau. (2004). *Statistics by country for narcolepsy*. US Census Bureau International Data Base. Retrieved from http://www.wrongdiagnosis.com/n/narcolepsy/stats-country.htm.

USDHHS (US Department of Health & Human Services). (2011a). *About the Office of Head Start*. Washington, DC: Author.

USDHHS (US Department of Health & Human Services). (2011b). *Head Start impact study and follow-up, 2000–2011*. Washington, DC: Author.

Uziel, L. (2007). Individual differences in the social facilitation effect: A review and meta-analysis. *Journal of Research in Personality, 41*, 579–601.

Valenstein, E. S. (2010). *Great and desperate cures: the rise and decline of psychosurgery and other radical treatments for mental illness*. Create Space.

Vallejo, M., Loyola, S., Contreras, D., Ugarte, G., Cifuente, D., Ortega, G., . . . & Agnese, M. (2014). A new semisynthetic derivative of sauroine induces LTP in hippocampal slices and improves learning performance in the Morris Water Maze. *Journal of Neurochemistry, 129*(5), 864–876.

Van Ameringen, M., Mancini, C., Patterson, B., & Boyle, M. H. (2008). Posttraumatic stress disorder in Canada. *CNS Neuroscience and Therapy, 14*(3), 171–181.

van Bommel, M., van Prooijen, J., Elffers, H., & van Lange, P. A. M. (2014). Intervene to be seen: The power of a camera in attenuating the bystander effect. *Social Psychological and Personality Science, 5*(4), 459–466.

Van Cauter, E., Leproult, R., & Plat, L. (2000). Age-related changes in slow-wave sleep and REM sleep and relationship with growth hormone and cortisol levels in healthy men. *Journal of the American Medical Association, 284,* 861–868.

Van den Akker, A., Deković, M., Prinzie, P., & Asscher, J. (2010). Toddlers' temperament profiles: Stability and relations to negative and positive parenting. *Journal of Abnormal Child Psychology, 38,* 485–495.

van den Berg, H., Manstead, A. S. R., van der Pligt, J., & Wigboldus, D. H. J. (2006). The impact of affective and cognitive focus on attitude formation. *Journal of Experimental Social Psychology, 42*(3), 373–379.

van der Velde, J., et al. (2013). Neural correlates of alexithymia: A meta-analysis of emotion processing studies. *Neuroscience and Behavioral Reviews, 37*(8), 1774–1785.

Van der Werf, Y. D., Jolles, J., Witter, M. P., & Uylings, H. B. M. (2003). Contributions of thalamic nuclei to memory functioning. *Cortex, 39,* 1047–1062.

Van der Werf, Y. D., Witter, M. P., & Groenewegen, H. J. (2002). The intralaminar and midline nuclei of the thalamus. Anatomical and functional evidence for participation in processes of arousal and awareness. *Brain Research Reviews, 39,* 107–140.

van Duijvenvoorde, A. C., Zanolie, K., Rombouts, S. A., Raijmakers, M. E., & Crone, E. A. (2008). Evaluating the negative or valuing the positive? Neural mechanisms supporting feedback-based learning across development. *Journal of Neuroscience, 28,* 9495–9503.

van Eck, M., Nicolson, N. A., & Berkhof, J. (1998). Effects of stressful daily events on mood states: Relationship to global perceived stress. *Journal of Personality and Social Psychology, 75*(6), 1572–1585.

Van Wagner, K. (2007). Phobia list: An A to Z list of phobias. *About.com.* Retrieved from http://psychology.about.com/od/.phobias/a/phobialist.htm.

Vasey, M. W., Crnic, K. A., & Carter, W. G. (1994). Worry in childhood: A developmental perspective. *Cognitive Therapy Research, 18*(6), 529–549.

Vazire, S. (2010). Who knows what about a person? The self–other knowledge asymmetry (SOKA) model. *Journal of Personality and Social Psychology, 98*(2), 281–300.

Vázquez, C., Pérez-Sales, P., & Ochoa, C. (2014). Posttraumatic growth: Challenges from a cross-cultural viewpoint. In G. A Fava & C. Ruini (Eds.), *Increasing Psychological Well-being in Clinical and Educational Settings: Interventions and Cultural Contexts, 8,* 57–74.

Vega, W. A., Ang, A., Rodriguez, M. A., & Finch, B. K. (2011). Neighborhood protective effects on depression in Latinos. *American Journal of Community Psychology, 47*(1–2), 114–126.

Verhaeghen, P. (2003). Aging and vocabulary score: A meta-analysis. *Psychology and Aging, 18*(2), 332–339. doi: 10.1037/0882-7974.18.2.332

Verheyden, S. L., Henry, J. A., & Curran, H. V. (2003). Acute, sub-acute and long-term subjective consequences of 'ecstasy' (MDMA) consumption in 430 regular users. *Human Psychopharmacology, 18*(7), 507–517.

Verheyden, S. L., Maidment, R., & Curran, H. V. (2003). Quitting ecstasy: An investigation of why people stop taking the drug and their subsequent mental health. *Journal of Psychopharmacology (Oxford), 17*(4), 371–378.

Verissimo, M., Santos, A. J., Vaughn, B. E., Torres, N., Monteiro, L., & Santos, O. (2011). Quality of attachment to father and mother and number of reciprocal friends. *Early Child Development and Care, 181*(1), 27–38.

Verkuyten, M., & Thijs, J. (2013). Multicultural education and inter-ethnic attitudes: An intergroup perspective. *European Psychologist, 18*(3), 179.

Vermetten, E., et al. (2006). Hippocampal and Amygdalar volumes in dissociative identify disorder. *American Journal of Psychiatry, 163,* 630–636.

Vernon, P. A., Wickett, J. C., Bazana, P. G., & Stelmack, R. M. (2000). The neuropsychology and psychophysiology of human intelligence. In R. J. Sternberg (Ed.), *Handbook of intelligence* (pp. 245–264). New York, NY: Cambridge University Press.

Verster, J. C., Brady, K., Galanter, M., & Conrond, P. J. (2011). *Drug abuse and addiction in mental illness: Causes, consequences and treatments.* Humana Press.

Vertes, R. P., & Eastman, K. E. (2003). The case against memory consolidation in REM sleep. In E. F. Pace-Schott, M. Solms, M. Blagrove, & S. Harnad (Eds.), *Sleep and dreaming: Scientific advances and reconsiderations.* New York, NY: Cambridge University Press.

Viggiano, D., Ruocco, L. A., Arcieri, S., & Sadile, A. G. (2004). Involvement of norepinephrine in the control of activity and attentive processes in animal models of attention deficit hyperactivity disorder. *Neural Plasticity, 11,* 133–149.

Viswesvaran, C., & Ones, D. (1999). Meta-analysis of fakability estimates: Implications for personality measurement. *Educational and Psychological Measurement, 54,* 197–210.

Vogel, D. L., Wester, S. R., Hammer, J. H., & Downing-Matibag, T. M. (2014). Referring men to seek help: The influence of gender role conflict and stigma. *Psychology of Men & Masculinity, 15*(1), 60.

Vogel, L., Brug, J., van der Ploeg, C. P. B., & Raat, H. (2007). Young people's exposure to loud music: A summary of the literature. *American Journal of Preventative Medicine, 33*(2), 124–133.

Vogt, M. C., & Bruning, J. C. (2013). CNS insulin signaling in the control of energy homeostasis and glucose metabolism—from embryo to old age. *Trends in Endocrinology & Metabolism, 24*(2), 76–84.

Volkow, N., & Fowler, J. (2000). Addiction, a disease of compulsion and drive: involvement of the orbitofrontal cortex. *Cerebral Cortex, 10,* 318–325.

Vollrath, M. (2001). Personality and stress. *Scandinavian Journal of Psychology, 42*(4), 335–347.

Volz, J. (2000). Successful aging. The second 50. *APA Monitor, 31,* 24–28.

Von Ranson, K. M., Wallace, L. M., & Stevenson, A. (2013). Psychotherapies provided for eating disorders by community clinicians: Infrequent use of evidence-based treatment. *Psychotherapy Research, 23*(3), 333–343.

Von Wolff, A., Hölzel, L. P., Westphal, A., Härter, M., & Kriston, L. (2013). Selective serotonin reuptake inhibitors and tricyclic antidepressants in the acute treatment of chronic depression and dysthymia: a systematic review and meta-analysis. *Journal of Affective Disorders, 144*(1), 7–15.

Voss, J. L. (2009). Long-term associative memory capacity in man. *Psychonomic Bulletin & Review, 16*(6), 1076–1081. doi: 10.3758/PBR.16.6.1076

Voss, U., Schermelleh-Engel, K., Windt, J., Frenzel, C., & Hobson, A. (2013). Measuring consciousness in dreams: The lucidity and consciousness in dreams scale. *Consciousness and Cognition, 22*(1), 8–21.

Vossekuil, B., Fein, R. A., Reddy, M. Borum, R., & Modzeleski, W. (2002). *The final report and findings of the Safe School Initiative: Implications for the prevention of school attacks in the United States.* Washington, D.C.

Vouloumanos, A. (2010). Three-month-olds prefer speech to other naturally occurring signals. *Language Learning and Development, 6,* 241–257.

Vouloumanos, A., & Gelfand, H. M. (2013). Infant perception of atypical speech signals. *Developmental Psychology, 49*(5), 815–824.

Vrshek-Schallhorn, S., Doane, L. D., Mineka, S., Zinbarg, R. E., Craske, M. G., & Adam, E. K. (2013). The cortisol awakening response predicts major depression: predictive stability over a 4-year follow-up and effect of depression history. *Psychological Medicine, 43*(3), 483–493.

Vygotsky, L. S. (2004). Imagination and creativity in childhood. *Journal of Russian & East European Psychology, 42*(1), 7–97.

Vygotsky, L. S. (1991). Genesis of the higher mental functions. In P. Light, S. Sheldon, & M. Woodhead (Eds.), *Learning to think.* (pp. 32–41). Florence: Taylor & Frances/Routledge.

Vygotsky, L. S. (1978). *Mind in society: Development of higher mental processes.* Cambridge, MA: Harvard University Press.

Wagner, U., Gais, S., Haider, H., Verleger, R., & Bom, J. (2004). Sleep inspires insight. *Nature, 427,* 352–355.

Wagstaff, G. F., Wheatcroft, J. M., Caddick, A. M., Kirby, L. J., & Lamont, E. (2011). Enhancing witness memory with techniques derived from hypnotic investigative interviewing: Focused meditation, eye-closure, and context reinstatement. *International Journal of Clinical and Experimental Hypnosis, 59*(2), 146–164.

Wahlen, D. (2007). *The stigma associated with mental illness.* The Canadian Mental Health Association. Retrieved from www.cmhanl.ca/pdf/Stigma.pdf.

Waite, L. J., Laumann, E. O., Das, A., & Schumm, L. P. (2009). Sexuality: measures of partnerships, practices, attitudes, and problems in the national social life, health, and aging study. *The Journals of Gerontology. Series B, Psychological Sciences and Social Sciences.* Retrieved from: http://www.ncbi.nlm.nih.gov/pubmed/19497930.

Walker, L. (1980). Cognitive and perspective taking prerequisites for moral development. *Child Development, 51,* 131–139.

Walker, L. J. (2006). Gender and morality. In M. Killen & J. G. Smetana (Eds.), *Handbook of moral development* (pp. 93–115). Mahwah, NJ: Lawrence Erlbaum Associates.

Wall, P. D. (2000). *Pain: The science of suffering.* New York, NY: Columbia University Press.

Wall, T. L., Shea, S. H., Chan, K. K., & Carr, L. G. (2001). A genetic association with the development of alcohol and other substance use behavior in Asian Americans. *Journal of Abnormal Psychology, 110*(1), 173–178.

Wallace, H. M., Baumeister, R. F., & Vohs, K. D. (2005). Audience support and choking under pressure: A home disadvantage? *Journal of Sports Sciences, 23*(4), 429–438.

Wallace, V., Menn, L., & Yoshinaga-Itano, C. (1999). Is babble the gateway to speech for all children? A longitudinal study of children who are deaf or hard of hearing. *Volta Review, 100,* 121–148.

Wallerstein, R. S. (2006). The relevance of Freud's psychoanalysis in the 21st century: Its science and its research. *Psychoanalytic Psychology, 23*(2), 302–326.

Wallis, C. (2005). The new science of happiness. *Time, 165*(3), A2–A9.

Walsh, R., & Shapiro, S. L. (2006). The meeting of meditative disciplines and western psychology: A mutually enriching dialogue. *American Psychologist, 61*(3), 227–239.

Walster, E., Aronson, E., & Abrahams, D. (1966). On increasing the persuasiveness of a low prestige communicator. *Journal of Experimental Social Psychology, 2,* 73–79.

Wampold, B. E., Hollon, S. D., & Hill, C. E. (2011). Unresolved questions and future directions in psychotherapy research. In J. C. Norcross,

G. R. VandenBos, & D. K. Freedheim (Eds.), *History of psychotherapy: Continuity and change* (2nd Ed., pp. 333–356). Washington, DC: American Psychological Association.

Wan, C. Y., & Huon, G. F. (2005). Performance degradation under pressure in music: An examination of attentional processes. *Psychology of Music, 33*, 155–172.

Wang, M., & Jiang, G-R. (2007). Psychopathological mechanisms and clinical assessment of dissociative identity disorder. *Chinese Journal of Clinical Psychology, 15*(4), 426–429.

Wang, S. S. (2007, December 4). The graying of shock therapy. *Wall Street Journal Online*. Retrieved from http://online.wsg.com/public/article_print/SB119673737406312767.html.

Wang, X. (2005). Discovering spatial working memory fields in pre-frontal cortex. *Journal of Neurophysiology, 93*(6), 3027–3028.

Warziski, M. T., Sereika, S. M., Styn, M. A., Music, E., & Burke, L. E. (2008). Changes in self-efficacy and dietary adherence: The impact on weight loss in the PREFER study. *Journal of Behavioral Medicine, 31*(1), 81–92.

Was, C. A. (2010). The persistence of content-specific memory operations: Priming effects following a 24-h delay. *Psychonomic Bulletin & Review, 17*(3), 362–368. doi: 10.3758/PBR.17.3.362

Wason, P. C. (1960). On the failure to eliminate hypotheses in a conceptual task. *Quarterly Journal of Experimental Psychology, 12*, 129–140.

Waterfield, R. (2000). *The first philosophers: The Presocratics and the Sophists*. New York, NY: Oxford University Press.

Waterhouse, J. M., & DeCoursey, P. J. (2004). The relevance of circadian rhythms for human welfare. In J. C. Dunlap, J. J. Loros, et al. (Eds.), *Chronobiology: Biological timekeeping*. Sunderland, MA: Sinauer Associates, Inc.

Watkins, M. W. (2010). Structure of the Wechsler intelligence scale for children—Fourth edition among a national sample of referred students. *Psychological Assessment, 22*(4), 782–787.

Watson, D., & Naragon-Gainey, K. (2014). Personality, emotions, and the emotional disorders. *Clinical Psychological Science, 2*(4), 422–442.

Watson, J. B. (1930). *Behaviorism* (Revised edition). Chicago, IL: University of Chicago Press.

Watson, J. B., & Raynor, R. (1920). Conditioned emotional reactions. *Journal of Experimental Psychology, 3*, 1–14.

Watt, T. T. (2002). Marital and cohabiting relationships of adult children of alcoholics: Evidence from the National Survey of Family and Households. *Journal of Family Issues, 23*(2), 246–265.

Watts, R. E. (2000). Entering the new millenium: Is individual psychology still relevant? *Journal of Individual Psychology, 56*(1), 21–30.

Watts, S., & Stenner, P. (2005). The subjective experience of partnership love: A Q methodological study. *British Journal of Social Psychology, 44*(1), 85–107.

Waxman, S. R., & Medin, D. L. (2006). Core knowledge, naming and the acquisition of the fundamental (folk)biologic concept 'alive'. In N. Miyake (Ed.), *Proceedings of the 5th International Conference on Cognitive Science* (pp. 53–55). Mahwah, NJ: Lawrence Erlbaum.

Webster, M. A. (2012). Evolving concepts of sensory adaptation. *F1000 Biology Reports, 4*, 21. doi:10.3410/B4-21

Wechsler, D. (1961). Cognitive, conative, and non-intellective intelligence. In J. J. Jenkins & D. G. Paterson (Eds.), *Studies in individual differences: The search for intelligence* (pp. 651–660). East Norwalk, CT: Appleton-Century-Crofts.

Wechsler, D. (2008). *Wechsler Adult Intelligence Scales*, Fourth Edition (WAIS-IV). Pearson Education Inc.

Wechsler, H., Lee, J. E., Kuo, M., Seibring, M., Nelson, T. F., & Lee, H. (2002). Trends in alcohol use, related problems and experience of prevention efforts among US college students 1993 to 2001: Results from the 2001 Harvard School of Public Health college alcohol study. *Journal of American College Health, 50*, 203–217.

Weekes-Shackelford, V. A., & Shackelford, T. K. (2004). Methods of filicide: Stepparents and genetic parents kill differently. *Violence Victims, 19*, 75–81.

Weeks, D., & James, J. (1995). *Eccentrics: A study of sanity and strangeness*. New York, NY: Villard.

Weinberg, R. S., & Gould, D. (2011). *Foundations of sport and exercise psychology* (5th Ed.). Champaign, IL: Human Kinetics.

Weinberg, R. S., & Gould, D. (2003). *Foundations of sport and exercise psychology*. Champaign, IL: Human Kinetics.

Weinberger, D. R., & Harrison, P. (Eds.) (2011). *Schizophrenia 3rd Ed.* Wiley-Blackwell.

Weiner, I. B., & Greene, R. L. (2008). *Handbook of personality assessment*. Hoboken, NJ: John Wiley & Sons, Inc.

Weinraub, M., Horvath, D. L., & Gringlas, M. B. (2002). Single parenthood. In M. H. Bornstein (Ed.), *Handbook of parenting: Vol. 3. Being and becoming a parent (2nd edition)*. Mahwah, NJ: Erlbaum.

Weiskrantz, L. (2009). Is blindsight just degraded normal vision? *Experimental Brain Research, 192*(3), 413–416. doi: 10.1007/s00221-008-1388-7

Weiskrantz, L. (2002). Prime-sight and blindsight. *Consciousness and Cognition: An International Journal, 11*(4), 568–581.

Weiskrantz, L. (2000). Blindsight: Implications for the conscious experience of emotion. In R. D. Lane & L. Nadel (Eds.), *Cognitive neuroscience of emotion*. London, England: Oxford University Press.

Weisleder, A., & Fernald, A. (2013). Talking to children matters: early language experience strengthens processing and builds vocabulary. *Psychological Science, 24*(11), 2143–2152.

Weiss, J. (2000). *To have and to hold: marriage, the baby boom, and social change*. Chicago, IL: University of Chicago Press.

Weiss, J. M., & Glazer, H. I. (1975). Effects of acute exposure to stressors on subsequent avoidance-escape behavior. *Psychosomatic Medicine, 37*, 499–521.

Weiss, L. G. (2010). Considerations on the Flynn effect. *Journal of Psychoeducational Assessment, 28*(5), 482–493.

Wester, S. R., Arndt, D., Sedivy, S. K., & Arndt, L. (2010). Male police officers and stigma associated with counseling: The role of anticipated risks, anticipated benefits and gender role conflict. *Psychology of Men & Masculinity, 11*(4), 286–302.

Wellman, H. M., Cross, D., & Watson, J. (2001). Meta-analysis of theory-of-mind development: The truth about false belief. *Child Development, 72*, 655–684.

Wellman, H. M., & Hickling, A. K. (1994). The mind's "I": Children's conception of the mind as an active agent. *Child Development, 65*, 1564–1580.

Wells, A. (2010). Metacognitive therapy: Application to generalized anxiety disorder. In D. Sookman & R. L. Leahy (Eds.), *Treatment resistant anxiety disorders: Resolving impasses to symptom remission* (pp. 1–29). New York, NY: Routledge/Taylor & Francis Group.

Wells, G. L., & Loftus, E. F. (2003). Eyewitness memory for people and events. In A. M. Goldstein (Ed.), *Handbook of psychology: Forensic psychology, vol. 11* (pp. 149–160). Hoboken, NJ: John Wiley & Sons, Inc.

Wender, P. H., Reimherr, F. W., Marchant, B. K., Sanford, M. E., Czajkowski, L. A., & Tomb, D. A. (2011). A one year trial of methylphenidate in the treatment of ADHD. *Journal of Attention Disorders, 15*(1), 36–45.

Wenseleers, T., Helanterä, H., Hart, A., & Ratnieks, F. L. (2004). Worker reproduction and policing in insect societies: an ESS analysis. *Journal of Evolutionary Biology, 17*(5), 1035–1047.

Wenzel, A. (2011a). Panic attacks. In *Anxiety in childbearing women: Diagnosis and treatment* (pp. 73–90). Washington, DC: American Psychological Association.

Wenzel, A. (2011b). Social anxiety. In *Anxiety in childbearing women: Diagnosis and treatment* (pp. 91–102). Washington, DC: American Psychological Association.

Werhun, C. D., & Penner, A. J. (2010). The effects of stereotyping and implicit theory on benevolent prejudice toward Aboriginal Canadians. *Journal of Applied Social Psychology, 40*(4), 899–916.

Werker, J. F. (1989). Becoming a native listener: A developmental perspective on human speech perception. *American Scientist, 77*, 54–59.

Wertz, F. J. (1998). The role of the humanistic movement in the history of psychology. *Journal of Humanistic Psychology, 38*, 42–70.

West, R. L., Bagwell, D. K., & Dark-Freudeman, A. (2008). Self-efficacy and memory aging: The impact of a memory intervention based on self-efficacy *Aging, Neuropsychology, and Cognition, 15*(3), 302–329.

Westen, D. (2002). Implications of developments in cognitive neuroscience for psychodynamic psychotherapy. *Harvard Review of Psychiatry, 10*, 369–373.

Westen, D., Betan, E., & Defife, J. A. (2011). Identity disturbance in adolescence: Associations with borderline personality disorder. *Development and Psychopathology, 23*(1), 305–313.

Westen, D., Dutra, L., & Shedler, J. (2005). Assessing adolescent personality pathology: Quantifying clinical judgment. *British Journal of Psychiatry, 186*(3), 227–238.

Wester, S. R., Arndt, D., Sedivy, S. K., & Arndt, L. (2010). Male police officers and stigma associated with counseling: The role of anticipated risks, anticipated benefits and gender role conflict. *Psychology of Men & Masculinity, 11*(4), 286.

Whalen, P. J., Davis, F. C., Oler, J. A., Kim, H., Kim, M. J., & Neta, M. (2009). Human amygdala responses to facial expressions of emotion. In P. J. Whalen & E. A. Phelps (Eds.), *The human amygdala* (pp. 265–288). New York, NY: Guilford Press.

Whipple, R., & Fowler, J. C. (2011). Affect, relationship schemas, and social cognition: Self-injuring borderline personality disorder inpatients. *Psychoanalytic Psychology, 28*(2), 183–195.

Whitaker, R. (2002). *Mad in America: Bad science, bad medicine, and the enduring mistreatment of the mentally ill*. Cambridge, MA: Perseus.

White, B. J., & Madara, E. J. (Eds.). (2011). *Self-help group sourcebook online*. Retrieved from www.mentalhelp.net/selfhelp.

White, R. J. (1999). Head transplants. *Scientific American, 10*, 24–26.

White, R. J. (1975). Hypothermia preservation and transplantation of brain. *Resuscitation, 4*, 197–210.

White, S. H., & Pillemer, D. B. (2014). Childhood amnesia and the development of a socially accessible memory system. In J. F. Kihlstrom & F. J. Evans (Eds.), *Functional Disorders of Memory (PLE: Memory)* (pp. 29–74). Hillsdale, NJ: Erlbaum.

Whitty, M. T. (2013). The Scammers Persuasive Techniques Model Development of a Stage Model to Explain the Online Dating Romance Scam. *British Journal of Criminology, 53*(4), 665–684.

Whorf, B. (1956). *Language, Thought & Reality*. Cambridge, MA: MIT Press.

Whorf, B. (1940). Science and linguistics. reprinted in *Language, Thought & Reality*. Cambridge, MA: MIT Press.

Whyte, G. (2000). Groupthink. In A. E. Kazdin (Ed.), *Encyclopedia of Psychology, Vol. 4* (pp. 35–38). Washington, D.C.: American Psychological Association.

Wicherts, J. M., & Dolan, C. V. (2010). Measurement invariance in confirmatory factor analysis: An illustration using IQ test performance of minorities. *Educational Measurement: Issues and Practice, 29*(3), 39–47.

Wickens, A. (2005). *Foundations of Biopsychology*, 2nd Edition. Harlow: Prentice Hall.

Wicklund, R. A., & Brehm, J. W. (2013). *Perspectives on Cognitive Dissonance*. New York, NY: Psychology Press.

Wickwire, E. M., Jr., Roland, M. M. S., Elkin, T. D., & Schumacher, J. A. (2008). Sleep disorders. In D. Reitman (Ed.), *Handbook of psychological assessment, case conceptualization, and treatment: Volume 2—Children and adolescents*. Hoboken, NJ: John Wiley & Sons, Inc.

Wieser, H. G. (2003). Music and the brain. Lessons from brain diseases and some reflections on the "emotional" brain. *Annals of the New York Academy of Sciences, 999,* 76–94.

Wilde, D. J. (2011). *Jung's personality theory quantified*. New York, NY: Springer-Verlag Publishing.

Wilkins, P. (2000) Unconditional positive regard reconsidered. *British Journal of Guidance & Counselling, 28*(1), 23–36.

Williams, K. D., Harkins, S. G., & Latane, B. (1981). Identifiability as a deterrent to social loafing: Two cheering experiments. *Journal of Personality and Social Psychology, 40,* 303–311.

Williams, K. D., & Nida, S. A. (2011). Ostracism: Consequences and coping. *Current Directions in Psychological Science, 20*(2), 71–75.

Williams, P. G. (2004). The psychopathology of self-assessed health: A cognitive approach to health anxiety and hypochondriasis. *Cognitive Therapy and Research, 28,* 629–644.

Williams, P. G., Smith, T. W., Gunn, H. E., & Uchino, B. N. (2011). Personality and stress: Individual differences in exposure, reactivity, recovery, and restoration. In R. J. Contrada & A. Baum (Eds.), *The handbook of stress science: Biology, psychology, and health*. New York, NY: Springer Publishing Co.

Williams, T. J., Pepitone, M. E., Christensen, S. E., Cooke, B. M., Huberman, A. D., Breedlove, N. J., et al. (2000). Finger-length ratios and sexual orientation. *Nature, 404,* 455–456.

Williams, W. M., Papierno, P. B., Makel, M. C., & Ceci, S. J. (2004). Thinking like a scientist about real-world problems: The Cornell Institute for Research on Children science education program. *Journal of Applied Developmental Psychology, 25*(1), 107–126.

Willimzig, C., Ragert, P., & Dinse, H. R. (2012). Cortical topography of intracortical inhibition influences the speed of decision making. *PNAS Proceedings of the National Academy of Sciences of the United States of America, 109,* 3107–3112.

Wilson, D. A. (2001). Receptive fields in the rat piriform cortex. *Chemical Senses, 26,* 577–584.

Wilson, G. (1981). *The Coolidge effect: An evolutionary account of human sexuality*. New York, NY: William Morrow.

Wilson, G. T. (2011). Behavior therapy. In R. J. Corsini & D. Wedding (Eds.), *Current psychotherapies* (9th Ed.). Florence, KY: CENGAGE Learning.

Wilson, G. T. (2008). Behavior therapy. In R. J. Corsini & D. Wedding (Eds.), *Current psychotherapies* (8th Ed.). Belmont, CA: Thomson Brooks/Cole.

Wilson, G. T., & Shafron, R. (2005). Eating disorders guidelines from NICE. *Lancet, 365,* 79–81.

Wilson, J. G. (2010). Repression: Psychoanalytic and Sartrean phenomenological perspectives. *Existential Analysis, 21*(2), 271–281.

Wimbiscus, M., Kostenko, O., & Malone, D. (2010). MAO inhibitors: risks, benefits, and lore. *Cleveland Clinic Journal of Medicine, 77*(12), 859–882.

Wimmer, F., Hoffmann, R. F., Bonato, R. A., & Moffitt, A. R. (1992). The effects of sleep deprivation on divergent thinking and attention processes. *Journal of Sleep Research, 1,* 223–230.

Wimmer, H., & Perner, J. (1983). Beliefs about beliefs: Representation and constraining function of wrong beliefs in young children's understanding of deception. *Cognition, 13*(1), 103–128.

Windholz, G. (1997). Ivan P. Pavlov: An overview of his life and psychological work. *American Psychologist, 52,* 941–946.

Windholz, G. (1987). Pavlov as a psychologist. A reappraisal. *Pavlov Journal of Biological Sciences, 22,* 103–112.

Winkler, J., Suhr, S. T., Gage, F. H., Thal, L. J., & Fisher, L. J. (1995). Essential role of neocortical acetylcholine in spatial memory. *Nature, 375,* 484–487.

Winningham, R. G. (2010). *Train your brain: How to maximize memory ability in older adulthood*. Amityville, NY: Baywood Publishing Co.

Winton-Brown, T. T., Fusar-Poli, P., Ungless, M. A., & Howes, O. D. (2014). Dopaminergic basis of salience dysregulation in psychosis. *Trends in Neurosciences, 37*(2), 85–94.

Wissler, C. (1961). The correlation of mental and physical tests. In J. J. Jenkins & D. G. Paterson (Eds.), *Studies in individual differences: The search for intelligence* (pp. 32–44). East Norwalk, CT: Appleton-Century-Crofts.

Witthoft, M., & Hiller, W. (2010). Psychological approaches to origins and treatments of somatoform disorders. *Annual Review of Clinical Psychology, 6,* 257–283.

Wixted, J. T. (2010). The role of retroactive interference and consolidation in everyday forgetting. In S. Della Sala (Ed.), *Forgetting* (pp. 285–312). New York, NY: Psychology Press.

Wixted, J. T. (2004). The psychology and neuroscience of forgetting. *Annual Review of Psychology, 55,* 235–269.

Wixted, J. T., & Squire, L. R. (2010). The role of the human hippocampus in familiarity-based and recollection-based recognition memory. *Behavioural Brain Research, 215*(2), 197–208. doi: 10.1016/j.bbr.2010.04.020

Woese, C., Kandler, O., & Wheelis, M. (1990). Towards a natural system of organisms: Proposal for the domains Archaea, Bacteria, and Eucarya. *Proceedings of the National Academy of Sciences USA, 87,* 4576–4579.

Wolf, S. (1969). Psychosocial factors in myocardial infarction and sudden death. *Circulation, 39,* 74–83.

Wolfson, A. R., & Richards, M. (2011). Young adolescents: Struggles with insufficient sleep. In M. El-Sheikh (Ed.), *Sleep and development: Familial and socio-cultural considerations* (pp. 265–298). New York, NY: Oxford University Press.

Wolitzky, D. L. (2011). Psychoanalytic theories of psychotherapy. In J. C. Norcross, G. R. VandenBos, & D. K. Freedheim (Eds.), *History of psychotherapy: Continuity and change* (2nd Ed., pp. 65–100). Washington, DC: American Psychological Association.

Wolman, B. (1979). *Handbook of dreams: research, theories, and applications*. Van Nostrand Reinhold.

Wolpe, J. (1997a). From psychoanalytic to behavioral methods in anxiety disorders: A continuing evolution. In J. K. Zeig (Ed.), *The evolution of psychotherapy: The third conference*. New York, NY: Brunner/Mazel.

Wolpe, J. (1997b). Thirty years of behavior therapy. *Behavior Therapy, 28*(4), 633–635.

Wolpe, J. (1995). Reciprocal inhibition: Major agent of behavioral change. In W. O'Donohue & L. Krasner (Eds.), *Theories of Behavior Therapy*. Washington, D.C.: American Psychological Association.

Wolpe, J. (1990). *The Practice of Behavioral Therapy* (4th ed). New York: Pergamon Press.

Wong, B. (2011). Color blindness. *Nature Methods, 8.6,* 441. Academic OneFile.

Wood, J. M., Garb, H. N., Lilienfeld, S. O., & Nezworski, M. T. (2002). Clinical assessment. *Annual Review of Psychology, 53*(1), 519–543.

Wood, J. V., Tesser, A., & Holmes, J. G. (Eds.). (2007). *The Self and Social Relationships*. New York, NY: Psychological Press.

Woods, S. C., Lutz, T. A., Geary, N., & Langhans, W. (2006). Pancreatic signals controlling food intake; insulin, glucagon, and amylin. *Philosophical transactions of the Royal Society of London. Series B, Biological sciences, 361*(1471), 1219–1235.

Woollett, K., & Maguire, E. A. (2011). Acquiring "the Knowledge" of London's layout drives structural brain changes. *Current Biology, 24,* 2109–2114. doi: 10.1016/j.cub.2011.11.018

Woollett, K., Spiers, H. J., & Maguire, E. A. (2009). Talent in the taxi: a model system for exploring expertise. *Philosophical Transactions of the Royal Society B, 364,* 1407–1416.

Wootton, J. (2008). Meditation and chronic pain. In J. F. Audette & A. Bailey (Eds.), *Integrative pain medicine: The science and practice of complementary and alternative medicine in pain management. Contemporary pain medicine*. Totowa, NJ: Humana Press.

Worley, L. L. M. (2010). Review of *Understanding postpartum psychosis: A temporary madness*. *Psychosomatics: Journal of Consultation Liaison Psychiatry, 51*(2), 181.

Worthington, E. L., Jr. (2011). Integration of spirituality and religion into psychotherapy. In J. C. Norcross, G. R. VandenBos, & D. K. Freedheim (Eds.), *History of psychotherapy: Continuity and change* (2nd Ed., pp. 533–543). Washington, DC: American Psychological Association.

Worthman, C. M. (2011). Developmental cultural ecology of sleep. In M. El-Sheikh (Ed.), *Sleep and development: Familial and socio-cultural considerations* (pp. 167–194). New York, NY: Oxford University Press.

Worthy, M., Gary, A. L., & Kahn, G. M. (1969). Self-disclosure as an exchange process. *Journal of Personality and Social Psychology, 13,* 59–63.

Wundt, W. M. (1883). *Philosophische studien*. Leipzig: Wilhelm Engelmann.

Wyatt, G. W., & Parham, W. D. (2007). The inclusion of culturally sensitive course materials in graduate school and training programs. *Psychotherapy: Theory, Research, Practice and Training, 22*(2, Suppl.), 461–468.

Wykes, T., Reeder, C., Corner, J., Williams, C., & Everitt, B. (1999). The effects of neurocognitive remediation on executive processing in patients with schizophrenia. *Schizophrenia Bulletin, 25*(2), 291–307.

Wynn, K. (2002). Do infants have numerical expectations or just perceptual preferences? Comment. *Developmental Science, 5*(2), 207–209.

Wynn, K. (1992). Addition and subtraction by human infants. *Nature, 358*(6389), 749–750.

Wynne, K., Stanley, S., & Bloom, S. (2004). The gut and regulation of body weight. *The Journal of Clinical Endocrinology and Metabolism, 89*(6), 2576–2582.

Yadav, R., Suri, M., Mathur, R., & Jain, S. (2009). Effect of ventromedial nucleus of hypothalamus on the feeding behavior of rats. *Journal of Clinical Biochemical Nutrition, 44(May)*, 247–252.

Yahr, P. (1977). Social subordination and scent marking in male Mongolian gerbils (Meriones unguiculatus). *Animal Behavior, 25*, 292–297.

Yalom, I. D., & Josselson, R. (2011). Existential psychotherapy. In R. J. Corsini & D. Wedding (Eds.), *Current psychotherapies* (9th Ed.). Florence, KY: CENGAGE Learning.

Yalom, I. D., & Leszcz, M. (2005). *The theory and practice of group psychotherapy* (5th Ed.). New York, NY: Basic Books.

Yan, R. (1986). Marriage, family and social progress of China's minority nationalities. In C. Chien and N. Tapp (Eds.), *Ethnicity and ethnic groups in China* (pp. 79–87). Hong Kong: New Asia Academic Bulletin.

Yang, S., & Sternberg, R. J. (1997). Conceptions of intelligence in ancient Chinese philosophy. *Journal of Theoretical and Philosophical Psychology, 17(2)*, 101–119.

Yehuda, R. (2009). Stress hormones and PTSD. *Post-traumatic stress disorder: Basic science and clinical practice* (pp. 257–275). Totowa, NJ: Humana Press.

Yehuda, R. (2001). Biology of posttraumatic stress disorder. *Journal of Clinical Psychiatry, 62*, 41–46.

Yehuda, R., Flory, J. D., Pratchett, L. C., Buxbaum, J., Ising, M., & Holsboer, F. (2010). Putative biological mechanisms for the association between early life adversity and the subsequent development of PTSD. *Psychopharmacologia, 212(3)*, 405–417.

Yehuda, R., McFarlane, A. C., & Shalev, A.Y. (1998). Predicting the development of posttraumatic stress disorder from the acute response to a traumatic event. *Biological Psychiatry, 44(12)*, 1305–1313.

Yela, C. (2006). The evaluation of love: Simplified version of the scales for Yela's tetrangular model based on Sternberg's model. *European Journal of Psychological Assessment, 22(1)*, 21–27.

Yerkes, R. M., & Dodson, J. D. (1908). The relation of strength of stimulus to rapidity of habit-formation. *Journal of Comparative Neurology and Psychology, 18*, 459–482.

Yessine, A. K., & Bonta, J. (2009). The offending trajectories of youthful Aboriginal offenders. *Canadian Journal of Criminology and Criminal Justice, 51(4)*, 435–472.

Yetiv, S. A. (2011). *Explaining foreign policy: U.S. decision-making in the Gulf Wars*. Johns Hopkins University Press.

Yetiv, S. A. (2003). Groupthink and the Gulf Crisis. *British Journal of Political Science, 33*, 419–442.

Yeung, H. H., Chen, K. H., & Werker, J. F. (2013). When does native language input affect phonetic perception? The precocious case of lexical tone. *Journal of Memory and Language, 68(2)*, 123–139.

Yontef, G., & Jacobs, L. (2011). Gestalt therapy. In R. J. Corsini & D. Wedding (Eds.), *Current psychotherapies* (9th Ed.). Florence, KY: CENGAGE Learning.

Yoon, H. (2003). Factors associated with family caregiver's burden and depression in Korea. *International Journal of Aging & Human Development, 57(4)*, 291–311.

Yoon, I. Y., Kripke, D. F., Elliott, J. A., Youngstedt, S. D., Rex, K. M., & Hauger, R. L. (2003). Age-related changes of circadian rhythms and sleep-wake cycles. *Journal of the American Geriatrics Society, 51(8)*, 1085–1091.

Yoon, T., Okada, J., Jung, M.W., and Kim, J.J. (2008). Prefrontal cortex and hippocampus subserve different components of working memory in rats. *Learning and Memory, 15*, 97–105.

Yost, W. A. (2010). Audition: Pitch perception. In E. B. Goldstein (Ed.), *Encyclopedia of Perception*. Thousand Oaks, CA: Sage.

Young, K. S. (2009). Assessment and treatment of internet addiction. *The Praeger international collection on addictions, vol 4: Behavioral addictions from concept to compulsion* (pp. 217–234). Santa Barbara, CA: Praeger/ABC-CLIO.

Young, K. S. (2004). Internet addiction: A new clinical phenomenon and its consequences. *American Behavioral Scientist, 48(4)*, 402–415.

Young, K. S. (1998). Internet addiction: The emergence of a new clinical disorder. *CyberPsychology & Behavior, 1(3)*, 237–244.

Young, K. S. (1996). Psychology of computer use: XL. addictive use of the internet: A case that breaks the stereotype. *Psychological Reports, 79(3)*, 899–902.

Young, L. R., & Nestle, M. (2007). Portion sizes and obesity: Responses of fast-food companies. *Journal of Public Health Policy, 28(2)*, 238–248.

Young, S. N., & Leyton, M. (2002). The role of serotonin in human mood and social interaction: Insight from altered tryptophan levels. *Pharmacology Biochemistry and Behavior, 71(4)*, 857–865.

Yu, D. L., & Seligman, M. E. P. (2002). Preventing depressive symptoms in Chinese children. *Prevention and Treatment, 5*, No Pages.

Yule, W. (1973). Differential prognosis of reading backwardness and specific reading retardation. *British Journal of Education Psychology, 43*, 244–248.

Zager, A., Andersen, M. L., Ruiz, F. S., Antunes, I. B., & Tufik, S. (2007). Effects of acute and chronic sleep loss on immune modulation of rats. *Regulatory, Integrative and Comparative Physiology, 293*, R504–R509.

Zahodne, L. B., Devanand, D. P., & Stern, Y. (2013). Coupled cognitive and functional change in Alzheimer's Disease and the influence of depressive symptoms. *Journal of Alzheimer's Disease, 34(4)*, 851–860.

Zajonc, R. B. (1968). Attitudinal effects of mere exposure. *Journal of Personality and Social Psychology, 9(2p2)*, 1.

Zajonc, R. B. (1965). Social facilitation. *Science, 149*, 269–274.

Zajonc, R. B., Murphy, S. T., & Inglehart, M. (1989). Feeling and facial efference: Implications of the vascular theory of emotion. *Psychological Review, 96*, 395–416.

Zatorre, R. J. (2003). Absolute pitch: a model for understanding the influence of genes and development on neural and cognitive function. *Nature Neuroscience, 6*, 692–695.

Zawadzki, B., Strelau, W., Oniszczenko, W., Roemann, R., & Angleitner, A. (2001). Genetic and environmental influences on temperament. *European Psychologist, 6*, 272–286.

Zeidner, M. (1990). Perceptions of ethnic group modal intelligence: Reflections of cultural stereotypes or intelligence test scores? *Journal of Cross-Cultural Psychology, 21(2)*, 214–231.

Zelazo, P. D. (2004). The development of conscious control in childhood. *Trends in Cognitive Sciences, 8*, 12–17.

Zelazo, P. D., & Lee, W. S. C. (2010). Brain development: An overview. In W. F. Overton & R. M. Lerner (Eds.), *The handbook of life-span development*, vol. 1: *Cognition, biology, and methods* (pp. 89–114). Hoboken, NJ: John Wiley & Sons.

Zentall, T. R. (2002). A cognitive behaviorist approach to the study of animal behavior, *Journal of General Psychology. Special Issue: Animal Behavior, 129(4)*, 328–363.

Zentall, T. R., & Levine, J. M. (1972). Observational learning and social facilitation in the rat. *Science, 178*, 1220–1221.

Zhou, P., Lowery, M. M., Englehart, K. B., Huang, H., Li, G., Hargrove, L., . . . Kuiken, T. (2007). Decoding a new neural-machine interface for control of artificial limbs. *Journal of Neurophysiology, 98*, 2974–2982.

Zhou, Y., & Rui, L. (2013). Leptin signaling and leptin resistance. *Frontiers of Medicine, 7(2)*, 207–222.

Zhu, B., Chen, C., Loftus, E. F., Lin, C., He, Q., Chen, C., . . . Dong, Q. (2010). Individual differences in false memory from misinformation: Cognitive factors. *Memory, 18(5)*, 543–555. doi: 10.1080/09658211.2010.487051.

Zimbardo, P. G. (2007). *Revisiting the Stanford prison experiment: A lesson in the power of the situation. The Lucifer Effect.* Ebury Publishing.

Zimbardo, P. G. (2006a). A situationist perspective on the psychology of evil: Understanding how good people are transformed into perpetrators. In R. Falk, I. Gendzier, & R. J. Lifton (Eds.), *Crimes of War: Iraq* (pp. 366–369). New York, NY: Nation Books.

Zimbardo, P. G. (2006b). On rethinking the psychology of tyranny: The BBC prison study. *British Journal of Social Psychology, 45(1)*, 47–53.

Zimbardo, P. G. (2004). Does psychology make a significant difference in our lives? *American Psychologist, 59(5)*, 339.

Zimbardo, P. G. (1972). Psychology of imprisonment. *Transition/Society*, 4–8.

Zimmer, C. (2001). *Evolution: The Triumph of an Idea*. New York, NY: HarperCollins Publishers.

Zimmerman, A. L., Sawchuk, M., & Hochman, S. (2012). Monoaminergic modulation of spinal viscero-sympathetic function in the neonatal mouse thoracic spinal cord. *PloS One, 7(11)*, e47213.

Zimmerman, L. K., & Stansbury, K. (2004). The influence of emotion regulation, level of shyness, and habituation on the neuroendocrine response of three-year-old children. *Psychoneuroendocrinology, 29*, 973–982.

Zoccolillo, M., Price, R., Ji, T., Hyun, C., & Hwu, H.-G. (1999). Antisocial personality disorder: Comparisons of prevalence, symptoms, and correlates in four countries. In P. Cohen, C. Slomkowski, & L. N. Robins (Eds.), *Historical and geographical influences on psychopathology* (pp. 249–277). Mahwah, NJ: Lawrence Erlbaum Associates Publishers.

Zogby, J. (2006). *Survey of teens and adults about the use of personal electronic devices and headphones*. Zogby International.

Zola, S. M. (1998). Memory, amnesia, and the issue of recovered memory: Neurobiological aspects. *Clinical Psychology Review, 18(8)*, 915–932.

Zorumski C. F., & Rubin E. H. (2011). *Psychiatry and clinical neuroscience: A primer*. New York, NY: Oxford University Press.

Zuckerman, M. (2012). Models of adult temperament. In M. Zentner & R. L. Shiner (Eds.), *Handbook of Temperament*. New York, NY: The Guilford Press.

Zuckerman, M. (2011). Trait and psychobiological approaches. In *Personality science: Three approaches and their applications to the causes and treatment of depression* (pp. 47–77). Washington, DC: American Psychological Association.

Zuckerman, M. (2007). Sensation seeking and risk. *Sensation seeking and risky behavior* (pp. 51–72). Washington, D.C.: American Psychological Association.

Zuckerman, M. (1995). Good and bad humors: biochemical bases of personality and its disorders. *Psychological Science, 6*, 325–332.

Name Index

Subject Index